# Policing

# Policing
# Key Readings

**Edited by Tim Newburn**

**WILLAN**
PUBLISHING

Published by

Willan Publishing
Culmcott House
Mill Street, Uffculme
Cullompton, Devon
EX15 3AT, UK
Tel: +44(0)1884 840337
Fax: +44(0)1884 840251
e-mail: info@willanpublishing.co.uk
website: www.willanpublishing.co.uk

Published simultaneously in the USA and Canada by

Willan Publishing
c/o ISBS, 920 NE 58th Ave, Suite 300,
Portland, Oregon 97213-3786, USA
Tel: +001(0)503 287 3093
Fax: +001(0)503 280 8832
e-mail: info@isbs.com
website: www.isbs.com

First published 2005

ISBN 1-84392-091-3 Paperback
      1-84392-092-1 Hardback

British Library Cataloguing-in-Publication Data

A catalogue record for this book is available from the British Library

Typeset by GCS, Leighton Buzzard, Bedfordshire, LU7 1AR
Project managed by Deer Park Productions, Tavistock, Devon
Printed and bound by T.J. International Ltd, Trecerus Industrial Estate, Padstow, Cornwall

# Contents

# Introduction

The study of the police has long been a staple of criminologists and, far from diminishing, appears to be growing. A number of specialist journals now exist to cater for, and facilitate, this market in ideas. The range of books on policing is increasing all the time. One of the dangers we face, however, is that the tendency to historical myopia in criminology will lead us to focus on the new at the expense of the older and established. That would be a particular shame in the field of policing for there is a hugely rich history of writing in this area. The primary aim of this reader is to bring that history to students of policing.

The basis for this volume is the view that there now exists a body of work that constitutes the core of policing studies – the *canon* if you like – that students the world over are directed to read. The volume attempts to bring such a body of work together. Now, it will be immediately obvious that there is no consensus as to what constitutes the 'core' of policing studies. Readers will have their own particular favourite pieces, articles or parts of books that they consider in some way seminal. Some of them no doubt appear here; others will not. Nevertheless, the aim of the volume is to give students of policing an indication of what many of the key arguments and developments in this field have been over the past 40 years or so. Undoubtedly there are gaps. Capacious though it is, the size of the volume means that considerable selectiveness has been applied. Furthermore, the literature included is confined to the English-speaking world; it is largely from the USA, the UK and Australia. Not only do I assume that readers will disagree with some of my selections but I actively hope they will do so. If looking at this selection prompts some readers to think of their own favourite pieces, and to wonder why they were not included (and I would genuinely like to hear if anyone is minded to write or email), then I shall feel that at least one important function has been achieved.

The volume is divided into six main sections. The first examines elements of the history of policing – primarily in the English-speaking world – and, more particularly, looks at how different models of policing have emerged over time. Part B looks at the role of the police and, more specifically, at the balance or tension between crime-fighting, order maintenance and other forms of service (and how arguments about the role of the police have developed historically). Part C looks at organization and culture, how these are theorized and understood and explores the arguments about their relationship to (the necessity of) reform of policing. Part D looks at policing models, from problem-oriented policing to community policing to zero tolerance and beyond. Part E examines some key issues such as police racism, misconduct and corruption, together with consideration of the question of ethics. The final part looks at current trends and future possibilities. With the rise of private security, increasing citizen involvement, the spectre of militarization in the face of global threats such as international terrorism, some suggest that the future of policing is bound radically to alter – or has already done so.

As ever, a large number of debts accrued during the construction of this volume. I am hugely grateful to Brian Willan and to everyone at Willan Publishing and Deer Park Productions in what, as ever, was a very efficient, thoughtful and supportive publishing process. I am very grateful also to David Kershaw for his work in copy-editing such a large volume so quickly and carefully. In selecting and planning the contents of the volume I received hugely helpful advice from a number of friends and colleagues. Needless to say, I was unable to take it all on board, but all the advice was enormously valuable whether or not it affected the final shape of the volume. My thanks in this regard to Jean-Paul Brodeur, Christopher Devery, David Dixon, Richard Ericson, Herman Goldstein, Peter Manning, Gary T. Marx, Rob C. Mawby, Peter Neyroud, Pat O'Malley, Wes Skogan and Tank Waddington.

# List of abbreviations

| | |
|---|---|
| AAPS | Aboriginal Affairs Policy Statement |
| ACPO | Association of Chief Police Officers |
| AVM | Automated Vehicle Monitoring |
| BCS | British Crime Survey |
| CAPS | Chicago Alternative Policing Strategy |
| CCC | Community Consultative Committees |
| COPE | Citizen Oriented Police Enforcement Unit |
| CSIS | Canadian Security Intelligence Service |
| CSIS/US | Center for Strategic and International Studies |
| DOD | Department of Defence |
| DOMS | Directorate of Military Support |
| EAC | Ethnic Affairs Commission |
| EAPS | Ethnic Affairs Policy Statement |
| EAS | Electronic Article Surveillance |
| ESPI | Economic Security and Proliferation Issues |
| FBI | Federal Bureau of Investigation |
| IHESI | Institute for Higher Learning in Domestic Security |
| LAPD | Los Angeles Police Department |
| NGO | Non-government organization |
| NSW | New South Wales |
| NYPD | New York Police Department |
| PCCOPS | Personal Computer Community Organization Prevention System |
| PREP | Police Recruitment Education Program |
| RCMP | Royal Canadian Mounted Police |
| ROC | Russian Organized Crime |
| SWAT | Special Weapons & Tactic Teams |
| SIRC | Security Intelligence Review Committee |
| SOB | Suppression of Burglary Unit |
| TECS | Treasury Enforcement Communication System |
| TIP | Turn in a Pusher |
| TRG | Tactical Response Group |
| US | United States |
| WMD | Weapons of Mass Destruction |

# Acknowledgements

We have made every attempt to obtain permission to reproduce material in this book. Copyright holders who we may have inadvertently failed to acknowledge should contact Willan Publishing.

We are very grateful to the following for permission to reproduce material in this volume:

**Part A**

1. John Wiley (New York) for Allan Silver, 'The demand for order in civil society', pp. 1–24, D.J. Bordua (ed.), *The Police: six sociological essays* (New York: Wiley, 1967); **2**. The author for Michael Ignatieff, 'Police and people: the birth of Mr Peel's blue locusts', *New Society*, 30 August 1979, pp. 443–445; **3**. The author and the editor, *Journal of Social History*, for Wilbur Miller, 'Cops and Bobbies 1830–1870', *Journal of Social History*, 1975, pp.81–101; **4**. The author for Mark Finnane, *Police and Government* (Oxford: OUP, 1994), pp. 3–30; **5**. The author and Oxford University Press for M. Brogden, 'The emergence of the police: the colonial dimension', in *British Journal of Criminology*, Vol. 27(1) 1987, pp. 4–14; **6**. The author and Oxford University Press for J. Styles, 'The emergence of the police', in *British Journal of Criminology*, Vol. 27 (1) 1987, pp. 15–24; **7**. The authors and the Program in Criminal Justice Policy and Management, Harvard University, for George L. Kelling and Mark H. Moore, 'The evolving strategy of policing', from *Perspectives on Policing*, November 1988 (Vol 4, pp 1–15); **8**. The authors and the Program in Criminal Justice Policy and Management, Harvard University, for Hubert Williams and Patrick V. Murphy, 'The evolving strategy of police: a minority view', from *Perspectives on Policing*, January 1990 (Vol. 13, pp. 1–15).

**Part B**

9. Taylor & Francis for Michael Banton, *The Policeman in the Community* (London: Tavistock), 1964, pp. 1–7; **10**. MIT Press for William Westley, *Violence and the Police* (Cambridge, MA: MIT Press), 1974, pp. 16–19; **11**. The author and OUP (New York) for David Bayley, *Police for the Future* (New York: OUP), 1994, pp. 29–41. **12**. Northeastern University Press for Egon Bittner, 'Florence Nightingale in Pursuit of Willie Sutton', in *Aspects of Police Work* (Boston, MA: Northeastern University Press), 1990, pp. 233–268; **13**. University of Chicago Press for William Ker Muir Jr,

*Police: streetcorner politicians* (Chicago: Chicago University Press), 1977, pp. 61–81. **14**. The author for Peter K. Manning 'The police: mandate, strategies, and appearances', in Peter K. Manning and J. Van Maanen (eds), *Policing: a view from the streets* (Santa Monica, CA: Goodyear Publishing), 1978, pp. 97–125; **15**. The author and the University of Toronto Press for Richard Ericson, 'The Police as reproducers of order', in *Reproducing Order: a study of police patrol work* (Toronto: University of Toronto Press), 1982, pp. 3–30. **16**. The authors for Joan Petersilia, P.W. Greenwood and J.M. Chaiken, 'The investigative function' in P.W. Greenwood, J.M. Chaiken and J. Petersilia (eds), *The Criminal Investigation Process* (Lexington, MA: D.C. Heath), 1977, pp. 9–13, 225–235.

## Part C

**17**. The author and Pearson Education for Jerome K. Skolnick, *Justice Without Trial* (New York: Wiley), 3rd edition, 1994, pp. 42–70; **18**. John Van Maanen for John Van Maanen, 'The asshole', in John Van Maanen and Peter Manning (eds), *Policing: a view from the streets* (New York: Random House), 1978, pp. 302–28; **19**. MIT Press for E.Reuss-Ianni and F.A.J. Ianni, 'Street cops and management cops: the two cultures of policing', in M. Punch (ed.), *Control in the Police Organization* (Cambridge, MA: MIT Press), 1983, pp. 251–74; **20**. The authors and Blackwell Publishing for Clifford Shearing and Richard Ericson, 'Culture as figurative action', *British Journal of Sociology*, Vol. 42, 4, pp. 481-506; **21**. The author and Oxford University Press for Janet Chan, 'Changing police culture', *British Journal of Criminology*, Vol. 36, no. 1, pp. 109–34; **22**. The author and Oxford University Press for P.A.J. Waddington, 'Police (canteen) sub-culture: an appreciation', *British Journal of Criminology*, Vol. 39, no. 2, pp. 287–309.

## Part D

**23**. The author and Sage Publications for Herman Goldstein, 'Improving policing: a problem-oriented approach', in *Crime and Delinquency*, Vol. 25, April 1979, pp. 236–58; **24**. The authors and Sage Publications for John E. Eck and William Spelman, 'Who ya gonna call? The police as problem-busters', in *Crime and Delinquency*, Vol. 33, January 1988, pp. 31–52; **25**. The authors and Oxford University Press (New York) for Wesley G. Skogan and Susan Hartnett, *Community Policing Chicago Style* (New York: OUP), 1998, pp. 5–12 and 237–246; **26**. Greenwood Publishing Group for Carl B. Klockars, 'The rhetoric of community policing' in J.R. Green and S.D. Mastrofski (eds), *Community Policing: rhetoric or reality* (New York: Praeger), 1988, pp. 239–258; **27**. The authors and *Atlantic Monthly* for James Q. Wilson and George Kelling, 'Broken Windows', *Atlantic Monthly*, Vol. 249, no. 3, pp. 29–38; **28**. Civitas for William Bratton, 'Crime is down: blame the police', in Norman Dennis (ed.), *Zero Tolerance: Policing a Free Society* (London: IEA), 2nd edition, 1998, pp. 29–42; **29**. The author for David Dixon, 'Beyond zero tolerance' in 'Mapping the Boundaries of Australia's criminal justice system', Proceedings of the Australian Institute of Criminology's Third National Outlook Symposium on Crime in Australia, Canberra, 22–23 March 1999; **30**. The authors and the American Society of Criminology for David Weisburd, Stephan D. Mastrofski, Ann Marie McNally, Rosann Greenspan and James J. Willis, 'Reforming to preserve: Compstat and strategic problem solving in American policing', *Criminology and Public Policy*, Vol. 2, no. 3, pp. 421–56; **31**.

The author and the American Society of Criminology, for Mark H. Moore, 'Sizing up COMPSTAT: an important administrative innovation in policing', *Criminology and Public Policy*, Vol. 2, no. 3, pp. 469–94; **32**. The authors and the University of Chicago Press for Richard V. Ericson and Kevin D. Haggerty, 'The policing of risk' in T. Baker and J. Simon (eds), *Embracing Risk* (Chicago: University of Chicago Press), 2002, pp. 238, 251–8, 262–72.

## Part E

**33**. The authors and Simon and Schuster (New York) for Jerome Skolnick and James Fyfe, *Above the Law* (New York: Free Press), 1993, pp. 1–14; **34**. The American Academy of Political and Social Science for Carl B. Klockars, 'The Dirty Harry problem', in *The Annals of the American Academy of Political and Social Science*, Vol. 452, 1980, pp. 33–47; **35**. The author and Cambridge University Press for John Kleinig, *The Ethics of Policing* (New York: Cambridge University Press), 1996, pp. 163–181 and 308–312; **36**. Macmillan Publishing for Geoffrey Marshall, 'Police accountability revisited' in D. Butler and A.H.Halsey (eds), *Policy and Politics* (London: Macmillan Press), 1978, pp. 51–65; **37**. The author and Oxford University Press for 'The legal regulation of policing' in David Dixon, *Law in Policing* (Oxford: Oxford University Press), 1997, pp. 280–318.

## Part F

**38**. The author and Blackwell Publishing for Robert Reiner, 'Policing a postmodern society', *Modern Law Review*, Vol. 55, no. 6, pp. 761–81; **39**. The author and Sage Publications for Pat O'Malley, 'Policing, politics and post-modernity', *Social and Legal Studies: an international journal*, Vol. 6, 1997, no. 3, pp. 363–81; **40**. The authors and Blackwell Publishing for David H. Bayley and Clifford D. Shearing, 'The future of policing', *Law and Society Review*, Vol. 30, no. 3, pp. 585–606; **41**. The authors and Oxford University Press for Trevor Jones and Tim Newburn, 'The transformation of policing? Understanding current trends in policing systems', *British Journal of Criminology*, Vol. 42, no. 1, 2002, pp. 129–146. **42**. The author and Oxford University Press for Frances Heidensohn, *Women in Control? The role of women in law enforcement* (Oxford: Oxford University Press), 1992, pp. 237–249; **43**. The author and the University of California Press for Gary T. Marx, 'The new surveillance', from Gary T. Marx, *Undercover: Police surveillance in America* (Berkeley: University of California Press), 1988, pp. 206–33; **44**. Northeastern University Press for Col. Charles J. Dunlap Jr, 'The thick green line: the growing involvement of military forces in domestic law enforcement', in P.B. Kraska (ed.), *Militarizing the American Criminal Justice System* (Boston, MA: Northeastern University Press), 2001, pp. 29–42; **45**. The author and Taylor & Francis (http://www.tandf.co.uk/journals) for Jean-Paul Brodeur, for 'Cops and Spooks: the uneasy partnership', *Police Practice and Research: an international journal*, Vol. 1, no. 3, 1999, pp. 1–25.

# The emergence and development of the police

## Introduction

None of what we understand by the police, or by policing, today makes much sense without some comprehension of whence it came. In fact, formal policing – a body of constables or officers employed by the state – is a relatively new phenomenon and, moreover, many of the emerging patterns of provision we are now witnessing are arguably more resonant of the eighteenth century than the twentieth. All students of policing should have some knowledge of the history of the emergence of state-based policing and of the gradual transformation of police legitimacy and of policing styles. This first part of the volume examines the emergence of formal policing forms in the USA, UK and Australia, whilst also briefly touching on debates concerning colonial policing and the export of Anglo-American models. Why the police emerged when they did, and in the form they did, are the central concerns here.

Allan Silver (1, 7) writes of the rise of fear of the 'dangerous classes' of the eighteenth and nineteenth centuries brought about by the proximity of the rapidly expanding urban poor in emergent industrial nations such as France, England and the USA. By the mid-nineteenth century, however, he suggests England was experiencing some relief from the widespread fear of riot and rebellion and, rather, was subject once again to a more diffuse concern with general criminality. In the USA, by contrast, the dangerous classes remained an ongoing preoccupation much later in the century. Though the focus of public concern was framed somewhat differently in these nations, it was a general context of rising expectations about the level of public peace that the public police bureaucracy emerged. Their role, as Silver puts it, was as a sophisticated and convenient form of garrison force against an internal enemy. Thinking of the police in such terms requires, as Ignatieff says, 'a certain mental struggle against one's sense of their social necessity'. Focusing on the London Metropolitan Police he looks back to the early nineteenth century when their introduction was greeted by far from unanimous public approbation. The resistance to the arrival of the 'blue locusts' was initially associated in part with radical politics, but had a broader and deeper link with concerns about the growing power of the state and with the dangerous potential of 'standing armies'. Though Whiggish and functionalist accounts have it that the police were simply a rational response to growing (fear) of crime and disorderliness, for the poor the coming of professional policing brought huge new intrusions into most aspects of daily life. Arguably, therefore, the greatest achievement of the new police was to challenge existing popular conceptions of criminality and impose a new code whilst simultaneously challenging the deep-rooted assumption that redress was essentially a private rather than a public or official matter.

Yet, predictably of course, policing developed in different forms in different places. Wilbur Miller (**3**, 80) compares the contexts in which the London and New York forces emerged and, in particular, the more contentious and conflictual political circumstances in London in the early eighteenth century. The emergent impersonal authority characteristic of British policing was, Miller suggests, a deliberate policy adopted by the first Commissioners, Rowan and Mayne, to steer a course between the maintenance of order under difficult circumstances, and the need to quell fears of police oppression. By contrast, the New York policeman's authority 'was personal, resting on closeness to the citizens and their informal expectations of his power instead of formal bureaucratic or legal standards' and in its early years was controlled by locally elected officials and officers recruited from the district they patrolled. Miller repeats a lovely quotation from Harriet Martineau, writing in 1838, in which she describes English police as 'agents of a representative government, appointed by responsible rulers for the public good', and the American police as 'servants of a self-governing people, chosen by those among whom their work lies'. According to Miller, perhaps the most crucial distinction in the working practices of the two sets of officers was the generally more constrained autonomy of the London 'Bobby' compared with his New York counterpart. Most particularly, the New York officers' use of force was less obviously constrained than the London officers' – hence the truncheon rather than the pistol.

According to Brogden (**5**, 69), 'ethnocentricity, inadequate comparative knowledge of policing, and a-historicism are the hallmarks of the Anglo-American sociology of the police' and, following the early chapters on the introduction of the new police, we reproduce three chapters on 'colonial policing'. As Mark Finnane (**4**, 48) describes, the early European settlers in Australia in the late eighteenth century brought with them some consciousness of the role of the constable, but no model police force. In due course in the mid-nineteenth century, ideas about formalized policing gained force, influenced by English and Irish models, but inflected in important ways by the political realities of colonial government and by circumstances less riven by political and social conflict than was the case in Britain. The new police came to Australia at approximately the moment they became established in England. Centralized police forces, controlled via state capitals, and eventually through an individual commissioner, were a defining feature. Convictivism and the resistance of indigenous peoples profoundly shaped Australian policing not least by reinforcing centralized policing solutions to local conflicts – and antagonistic relations between indigenous peoples and police in Australia are even now far from insignificant.

As Finnane's analysis of the birth of Australian policing demonstrates, and Brogden in his typically polemical style outlines, the history of policing requires some appreciation of 'colonial conquest and of imperial legitimation to institutional development in Victorian England'. Shedding the ethnocentric blinkers reveals a series of potential policing models other than the Metropolitan model favoured by Peel. These included, Brogden argues, the preventative 'high' police associated originally with the regime of Louis XIV, policing as the administration of the affairs of the state, commercial police work and, crucially, colonial police work. In the colonies for the large part (Australia may have been something of an exception) a policy of 'policing strangers by strangers' was adopted, with further distance guaranteed by an officer class drawn often from officers that had originally served in the Metropolitan Police or the Royal Irish Constabulary. Though colonial policing mirrored many of the characteristics of the policing of Victorian society it also had some distinctive features including, Brogden suggests, being directly controlled by the civil power and their close proximity (both in terms of location and ties) to the military.

John Styles (**6**, 80), in a response to Brogden's analysis, takes issue with a number of elements of his historical analysis. Critically, he suggests that the adjectives applied by Brogden to the 'new police' – salaried, professional, organized, state-appointed, preventive and uniformed –are not that helpful in separating them from the preceding forms of policing provision. Thus, salaried constables were widespread in the eighteenth century and many of the paid local watches were quite highly organized. Moreover, the alleged *preventive* character of the new police, he argues, probably underestimates the extent to which reformers such as Fielding and Chadwick prioritized prevention as well as overestimating the extent to which the Metropolitan Police were actually proactive in approach. Though uniformed, and therefore more obviously distinctive than their predecessors, Styles argues that the development of paid policing and police forces was happening long before the establishment of the Metropolitan Police in 1829. A similar approach, he suggests, can be taken to our comparative understanding of policing: whilst there are important parallels and links between British and colonial policing in the nineteenth century, 'there are not two watertight historical models of British policing, one English and one colonial'. Styles reminds us that by the mid-eighteenth century there existed police forces (loosely termed) in Italy, France and in the City of London. It was only later in the century that questions of social order in England and Ireland came increasingly to revolve around the idea of formalizing a system of policing.

How, then, has policing developed? Looking back from the vantage point of the late 1980s, George Kelling and Mark Moore (**7**, 88) explore the evolution of policing strategies and styles in the USA. They identify three different eras, each characterized by a particular strategy of policing. The 'political era' ran from the introduction of the police into municipalities around the 1840s through to the early 1900s. This was followed by the 'reform era' which was established in the 1930s and reached its high point in the 1950s, being replaced, gradually, since the 1970s with the 'community problem-solving era'. The 'political era' is so-called because of the close ties between police departments and local municipalities and political leaders. Indeed, Kelling and Moore argue that something of a symbiotic relationship existed between local politicians and local police departments. Like their British counterparts, functionally they delivered a broad range of services. By contrast, though a centralized, quasi-military organization, they were perhaps more decentralized, with close political ties at the ward level. Foot patrol was the central tactic, and detective work had yet to develop its more elite and prestigious connotations.

Predictably, the close relationship between policing and politics in the USA in the nineteenth and early twentieth centuries resulted in a largely continuous struggle for control over the organization. Though reform attempts punctuated the eighteen hundreds it was not until the 1930s that significant reshaping of the police organization took place. Associated initially with August Vollmer and later with O.W. Wilson and J. Edgar Hoover, the period from the 1930s to 1970s saw a reorientation of the relationship between police and local politics, and significant changes to the police organization and police 'technologies'. In parallel with Hoover's reform of the previously corrupt and inefficient Federal Bureau of Investigation (FBI), police reformers sought to professionalize the police and to reinforce its authority. In part, this was done by severing what were perceived to be the overly close ties with local politics – partly through reform of recruitment; some chiefs became civil servants rather than appointees, and in many jurisdictions officers ceased to be recruited from, and live within, the areas they policed. In theory, policing 'became a legal and technical matter left to the discretion of professional police executives under the guidance of law'. In consequence, the police function narrowed and became more obviously focused on crime control and the catching of criminals – other social service functions being downgraded and often derided. Much work became standardized, with special problems increasingly being dealt with by specialist units. The main tactics were preventive patrol – now by car – and rapid response to calls for service (both reinforced over time by the spread of telephones and radios). Professionalization also led to the progressive redefining of citizens merely as relatively passive recipients of services: as Kelling and Moore put it, 'the metaphor of the thin blue line reinforced [the police's] need to create isolated independence and autonomy in terms that were acceptable to the public'.

For a combination of reasons the reform strategy faced considerable problems from the 1960s onward. Not least, this was because of the rapid rise in crime and the apparent inability of reformed police departments to stem it. Fear of crime and of disorder also rose, in part fuelling, and in part fuelled by, the rapid transformation of the nature and demographics of many major American cities. Though problematic relations between police and public were evident quite widely, police–minority relationships were very obviously increasingly strained in this period and the civil rights and anti-war movements posed considerable challenges to the police. Moreover, financial constraints increasingly hit police departments, especially many large urban metropolitan departments, and competition from a growing and vibrant private sector did little for the confidence of the public sector. Kelling and Moore's conclusion is that the reform strategy was largely successful in the 1940s and 1950s (with a continuing caveat about the degree to which rank-and-file officers were marching in tune with their reform executives) but came under increasing strain in the 1960s and 1970s. They go on to suggest that 'all was not negative for police' in this period with some notable successes emerging. Most generally, they suggest that there was increasing realization that information was the key factor in aiding police in dealing with crime. Over time there emerged a new era organized around the theme of 'community problem-solving' .

Community problem-solving involves a broadening of the police function to include conflict resolution and problem-solving through the organization and provision of services. Where the reform strategy had attempted to control crime through preventive patrol, the new era 'emphasised crime control and prevention as an indirect result of, or an equal partner to, the other activities'. This involved some decentralization of management and decision-making, a reorientation of relationships between police and citizenry, greater emphasis on the management of demand, and a much more central focus on information as a key policing technology. Kelling and Moore's identification of these ideal-typical or paradigmatic models of stages through which policing has developed is helpful not only in making sense of some of the key transformations within the USA – the focus of their attention – but also on policing elsewhere. For whilst British, continental European and Australian policing, for example, may not be characterized in quite the same way, or have changed at quite the same points in time, their model is a useful starting point for the identification of commonalities and differences. That said, given the broad nature of such 'modelling', there are also questions that might be raised as to the accuracy of their portrayal of the history and development of policing in the USA. The most trenchant critique is made by Hubert Williams and Patrick Murphy who suggest that Kelling and Moore pay scant regard to the ways in which slavery, segregation, discrimination and racism have been major determinants of the development of, and the experience of, policing within minority communities in the USA.

Williams and Murphy (**8**, 109) argue that Kelling and Moore's history invests too much significance in the influence of police executives and too little in broader social and political forces, most notably racism. Thus, in connection with the political era they draw attention to the 'slave patrols', established in the eighteenth century, as a more realistic starting point for a history of US policing and, consequently, suggest that insufficient attention is paid to the social unrest associated with immigration, population growth and industrialization/migration in the establishment of the new system of policing. Though police authority is alleged to have been drawn primarily from the law and from local political leaders in this period, Williams and Murphy argue that:

> with neither political power nor legal standing, blacks could hardly be expected to share in the spoils of the political era of policing. There were virtually no black police officers until well into the twentieth century. Thus, police attention to, and protection for, areas populated primarily by racial minorities was rare during this era.

Similarly, they argue that the changes associated with the 'reform era' are likely to have been of little significance to the majority of black Americans. The shift from an era in which local politics was key, to an era in which the law became much more significant, was of little obvious benefit to those that lacked either political power or the support of the law. What then of community problem-solving? According to Williams and Murphy, 'to organized, empowered communities, this strategy … offered extraordinary opportunities to participate in structuring the nature of police services delivered … Those without such resources – and those most in need of police services – often found themselves in a long queue'.

As Williams and Murphy's critique rightly demonstrates, the histories of policing cannot easily be separated from the histories of particular societies 'as a whole'. Whether the focus is on the emergence of 'new' policing in Australia in the mid-nineteenth, the Metropolitan Police in London some decades earlier, or formal police departments in the USA, the experience of minorities and indigenous peoples, and the control and disciplining of minorities and 'lower orders' more generally, are absolutely central not simply to the shape and nature of the police organizations themselves but go to the heart of the rationale for their very introduction.

# 1. The demand for order in civil society: a review of some themes in the history of urban crime, police, and riot

*Allan Silver*

**Criminals and the 'dangerous classes'**

Crime and violence in the life of city dwellers have long evoked complaints which have a quite contemporary tone. Peaceful and propertied people in eighteenth-century London, for example, confronted a level of daily danger to which they and their spokesmen reacted indignantly. It was in such terms that Daniel Defoe dedicated a pamphlet on crime to the Lord Mayor of London:

> The Whole City, My Lord, is alarm'd and uneasy; Wickedness has got such a Head, and the Robbers and Insolence of the Night are such, that the Citizens are no longer secure within their own Walls, or safe even in passing their Streets, but are robbed, insulted and abused, even at their own Doors … The Citizens … are oppressed by Rapin and Violence; Hell seems to have let loose Troops of human D—— ls upon them; and such Mischiefs are done within the Bounds of your Government as never were practised here before (at least not to such a degree) and which, if suffered to go on, will call for Armies, not Magistrates, to suppress.[1]

In the body of his pamphlet, Defoe describes a situation of pervasive insecurity, stressing the mounting and unprecedented extent of criminal attack. The idea of crime wave is already quite explicit:

> Violence and Plunder is no longer confin'd to the Highways … The Streets of the City are now the Places of Danger; men are knock'd down and robb'd, nay, sometimes murther'd at their own Doors, and in passing and repassing but from House to House, or from Shop to Shop. Stagecoaches are robb'd in High-Holbourn, White-Chappel, Pall-Mall, Soho and at almost all the Avenues of the City. Hackney-Coaches and Gentlemen's Coaches are stopt in Cheapside, St. Paul's Church-yard, the Strand, and other the most crowded streets, and that even while the People in Throngs are passing and repassing … 'Tis hard that in a well-govern'd City … it should be said that her Inhabitants are not now safe …[2]

We may note in passing that equally contemporary themes richly abound in magazines that urban Americans read six decades ago. To cite but two examples:

> Individual crimes have increased in number and malignity. In addition to this … a wave of general criminality has spread over the whole nation … The times are far from hard, and prosperity for several years has been wide-spread in all classes. Large sums are in unaccustomed hands, bar-rooms are swarming, pool-rooms, policy shops and gambling houses are full, the, races are played, licentiousness increases, the classes who 'roll in wealth' set intoxicating examples of luxury and recklessness, and crime has become rampant.[3]

In that period, it was, of course, commonplace also to ascribe the fundamental causes of mass criminality to large-scale immigration:

> In the poorer quarters of our great cities may be found huddled together the Italian bandit and the bloodthirsty Spaniard, the bad man from Sicily, the Hungarian, the Croatian and the Pole, the Chinaman and the Negro, the cockney Englishman, the Russian and the Jew, with all the centuries of hereditary hate back of them. They continually cross each others' path. It is no wonder that altercations occur and blood is shed … We claim to be a rich and prosperous city and yet we cannot afford to employ enough policemen to keep thieves and burglars out of our houses and thugs and robbers from knocking us on the head as we walk along our own streets … The bald, bare, horrible fact is that the conditions existing in Chicago today are the most criminal and damnable of any large city on the face of the earth.[4]

Thus the current rhetoric of concern about crime and violence draws on established motifs of both older and newer vintage: an indignant sense of pervasive insecurity; a mounting current of crime and violence as a result of both unaccustomed prosperity and prolonged poverty; the bad example of the self-indulgent wealthy; the violent proclivities of immigrants and other newcomers; and the ironic contrast between the greatness of the metropolis and the continued spread of crime.

But at times there was a somewhat different attitude toward urban crime and violence. In the London and Paris of the late eighteenth and the early nineteenth centuries, people often saw themselves as threatened by agglomerations of the criminal, vicious, and violent – the rapidly multiplying poor of cities whose size had no precedent in Western history. It was much more than a question of annoyance, indignation, or personal insecurity; the social order itself was threatened by an entity whose characteristic name reflects the fears of the time – the 'dangerous classes'. The phrase occurs repeatedly. Thus, an anonymous essayist of 1844 writes of the situation in urban England, where (destitution, profligacy, sensuality and crime, advance with unheard-of-rapidity in the manufacturing districts, and the dangerous classes there massed together combine every three or four years in some general strike or alarming insurrection which, while it lasts, excites universal terrors …'.[5] But even where the term is not explicitly invoked, the image persists – one of an unmanageable, volatile, and convulsively criminal class at the base of society.[6]

8

This imagery is only in part the product of class antagonisms in early industrial society; rather, the working classes were included in an older and continuing concern with criminality.[7] Urban administrators regarded the swelling numbers of the poor as unmanageable. Indeed, the image of the 'dangerous classes', as distinct from that of pervasive criminality, seems to have flourished especially during periods of very rapid population growth, reflecting the migration of the numerous poor, without employment skills or a history of urban life. During this period, the labor force of the metropolis was still not primarily industrial.[8] Thus, the events and antagonisms of early industrialism inflamed but did not create the image of the 'dangerous classes'. It referred primarily to the unattached and unemployed. An advocate of police reform in London, writing in 1821, defined the problem in these terms:

> The most superficial observer of the external and visible appearance of this town, must soon be convinced, that there is a large mass of unproductive population living upon it, without occupation or ostensible means of subsistence; and, it is notorious that hundreds and thousands go forth from day to day trusting alone to charity or rapine; and differing little from the barbarous hordes which traverse an uncivilized land ... The principle of [their] action is the same; their life is predatory; it is equally a war against society, and the object is alike to gratify desire by stratagem or force.[9]

As class tensions involving the threat of riot and revolutionary violence subsided in London, the older concern with diffuse criminality rather than the 'dangerous classes' reemerged. Thus, Henry Mayhew's immense reportage on London's criminals, vagabonds, and casually employed, published in 1861, was suffused variously by moralism, indignation, pity, compassion, horror, and mere curiosity – but not by the sense of dread that had earlier afflicted those confronted by the dangerous classes.[10] Indeed, contemporary writing in midcentury London exhibits a sense of relief and victory over the forces of mass violence. Contrasting the present with the past, a writer in 1856 observed that 'the only quarter in which any formidable riot could take place would be eastward, in the neighborhood of the docks, where there are at least twelve thousand sailors in the river or on shore, ready for a spree, fearless and powerful, and acting with an undoubted esprit de corps. These, if associated with the seven or eight thousand dock labourers and lightermen, would certainly produce a force difficult to cope with'.[11] Such a prospect clearly was judged as a great improvement.

To judge from contemporary accounts, New York did not experience a comparable sense of relief or improvement. Indeed, it appears that by 1872 New York was already being compared unfavorably to London with respect to crime and violence:

> ... If the vice and pauperism of New York are not so steeped in the blood of the populace [as in London and other European cities] they are even more dangerous ... They rob a bank, when English thieves pick pockets; they murder, where European prolétaires cudgel or fight with fists; in a riot they begin what seems about to be the sacking of a city, where English rioters merely batter policemen or smash lamps ...[12]

For this observer, whose book is largely concerned with relief and other remedial programs among New York's poor, the dangerous classes are very much a part of the city – which, after all, had only a decade earlier suffered the great Draft Riot of 1863:

> There are thousands upon thousands in New York who have no assignable home, and 'flit' from attic to attic, and cellar to cellar; there are other thousands more or less connected with criminal enterprises; and still other tens of thousands, poor, hard-pressed ... Let but Law lift its hand from them for a season, or let the civilizing influences of American life fail to reach them, and, if the opportunity afforded, we should see an explosion from this class which might leave the city in ashes and blood.[13]

Such rhetoric is not, as we have seen, an inevitable expression of concern with criminality, riot, and violence – even when these were of an order unthinkable in daily urban life today.[14]

What are some of the factors that underlie relationships between urban criminality and disorder and the significance ascribed to them by the peaceful and propertied classes? An adequate answer to this question would need to consider important aspects of economic, political, and urban history, the labor movement, and demography. For our purposes, however, we will focus on two aspects of the situation that until recently have been neglected: the significance of the police and the culture of riotous protest.

## The policed society

Some modern nations have been police states; all, however, are policed societies. Practical men have never underestimated, though they have often distorted, the importance of the police. Sociological theory in the 'social control' tradition, however, has usually slighted the police in favor of normative or voluntary processes.[15] The significance of the police, for our purposes, can best be understood as they appeared to a generation for whom modern police were an unprecedented innovation – Englishmen in the middle third of the nineteenth century.

The London police, created in 1829, were from the beginning a bureaucratic organization of professionals.[16] One of their tasks was to prevent crime by regularly patrolling beats, operating under strict rules which permitted individual discretion. The police also had a mission against the 'dangerous classes' and political agitation in the form of mobs or riots. On all fronts they were *so* successful that initial and strong objections to them rapidly diminished; from being a considerable novelty, they quickly became a part of 'British tradition'.

The policed society is unique in that central power exercises potentially violent supervision over the population by bureaucratic means widely diffused throughout civil society in small and discretionary operations that are capable of rapid concentration. All of these characteristics struck contemporary observers as remarkable. Fear of mob or riot diminished when early police showed that fluid organization can overcome numbers:

There seems to be no fear a London mob will ever prove a serious thing in the face of our present corps of policemen. A repetition of the Lord George Gordon riots would be an impossibility. Those who shudder at the idea of an outbreak in the metropolis containing two millions and a half of people and at least fifty thousand of the 'dangerous classes' forget that the capital is so wide that its different sections are totally unknown to each other. A mob in London is wholly without cohesion, and the individuals composing it have but few feelings, thoughts or pursuits in common. They would immediately break up before the determined attack of a band of well-trained men who know and have confidence in each other.[17]

Another writer put the same point in more impersonal terms:

As each police constable being alone might easily be over-powered, and as the men of each section, or even division, might be inferior in numbers to some aggregation of roughs or criminals collected in a given spot, it is arranged that ... reserves of force can be gathered ... and concentrated upon the disquieted area, and as the commissioners command the whole district, and the force is organized and united, while roughs act in small areas, and have diverse and selfish interests, the peace of London may be held secure against violence.[18]

The peaceful and propertied classes appreciated two other advantages of the modern police: they relieved ordinary respectable citizens of the obligation or necessity to discharge police functions, especially during emergencies; and they also made less likely a resort to the military for the purposes of internal peace-keeping. Both involved changes in the relationship of these classes to the criminal or disorderly.

In unpoliced society, police functions were often carried out – if at all – by citizens rotating in local offices (sheriffs, constables, magistrates) or acting as members of militia, posses, Yeomanry corps, or watch and ward committees.[19] Not only was this system inefficient but it also directly exposed the propertied classes to attack. Agrarian men of property were frequently willing to undertake these tasks. Thus the Yeomanry, a cavalry force whose characteristic tactic was the sabre charge, was largely composed of small landowners[20] who were especially zealous in police duty against mobs and riots and especially disliked by working people.[21] For these reasons, the Yeomanry were particularly popular among the landowning classes as a means of defense. Praising them in the course of a parliamentary debate in 1817, for example, a member observed that 'the people would in many instances be debarred from violence by seeing those arrayed against them to whom they were accustomed to look up to as their masters'.[22]

But this machinery exposed the Yeomanry, once an emergency had passed, to direct attack in the course of daily life.[23] It also enabled private persons sometimes to modify police missions to suit their own proclivities and convenience. Thus, during the extensive agricultural uprisings of 1830 in southern England, fifty men of the village of Holt enrolled as special constables and 'declared their willingness to turn out to protect all property except threshing machines; they did not wish to show disrespect to their poorer neighbors'.[24] Yet threshing machines were the very form of property then under attack.

The urban and industrial propertied classes, however, were much less eager to take up the tasks of self-defense as volunteer or co-opted police. Landowning military officers attempting to encourage self-defense among commercial or industrial capitalists met with much reluctance. Replying in 1819 to advice from Wellington, the army commander in the newly industrializing north of England replied in exasperated terms:

> I have always fought against the dispersal of my force in trivial detachments; it is quite impossible to defeat the disaffected if they rise, and at the same time to protect any town from plunder; that resistance should be made by the inhabitants ... But I am sorry to say the general remark from the manufacturers is that government is bound to protect them and their property.[25]

We are dealing here not merely with the classic confrontation of an agrarian military tradition and a pacific commercial and industrial one; what also emerges is a specific demand for the bureaucratization of police functions. Not only did the manufacturing classes wish to avoid personal danger and inconvenience while protecting their property, but they also saw that – contrary to the social rationale underlying the yeomanry – the use of social and economic superiors as police exacerbated rather than mollified class violence.[26] This emerges clearly in the testimony of one Thomas Ashton, 'the owner of considerable property in manufactures, and the employer of about 1500 persons', before the Royal Commission of 1839 concerned with extending the professional police from London to the provinces.[27] Among other reforms, Ashton favored the use of personnel from outside a locality affected by violence and for a reason other than the reluctance of local personnel to act against their neighbors:

> On such urgent occasions, I think it extremely desirable that a stipendiary magistrate should be sent into the district and entrusted with the administration of the law. A great majority of the more serious disturbances originate in disputes between master and servant. The local magistracy is chiefly composed of the resident landowners and manufacturers, and the irritation of the workmen against their employers is greatly increased when they find the person, with whom the disputes have arisen openly supported by, and giving directions to, the military, and subsequently punishing them for breaches of the peace, which would never have been committed unless such disputes had occurred. Ought the employer to be placed in such a situation? Is it likely that animosities would be allayed or peace maintained by it? What safety has the proprietor of machinery?

This reasoning was accepted by the commissioners in their report, which was largely written by the Benthamite reformer Edwin Chadwick:

In several instances where there was an effective resistance given to the rioters, we have been informed that the animosities created or increased, and rendered permanent by arming master against servant, neighbour against neighbour, by triumph on one side and failure on the other: were even more deplorable than the outrages actually committed ... The necessity for such painful and demoralizing conflicts between connected persons should be avoided by providing a trained and independent force for action in such emergencies ... The constitutional authority of the supreme executive is then emphatically asserted. In reply to recent inquiries made of local authorities in the manufacturing districts, why they took no steps for the repression of riotous or alleged treasonable proceedings within their districts, why so long a career of criminal incitements was permitted, the prevelant answer has been, that such proceedings were understood to be exclusively within the province of government.[28]

Thus, at a time when the agrarian rich often sought to multiply and, reconstruct the traditional means of self-defense against violent uprising and attack, those who sprang from the newer sources of wealth turned toward a bureaucratic police system that insulated them from popular violence, drew attack and animosity upon itself, and seemed to separate the assertion of 'constitutional' authority from that of social and economic dominance.[29]

Other means than a bureaucratic police – especially the army itself – were available for this purpose. But although the army played a crucial role during crises or situations with revolutionary potential, it was ill-equipped to meet the enduring needs of a policed society.[30] It was largely officered by an agrarian class which sometimes did not distinguish itself for zeal in protecting the property of manufacturers.[31] More fundamentally, however, it was difficult for the army to act continuously in small dispersed units in civilian society, although it might do so on an emergency basis. More characteristic of the army was an alternation between no intervention and the most drastic procedures – the latter representing a declaration of internal war with lingering consequences of hate and resentment.[32] The police were designed to penetrate civil society in a way impossible for military formations and by doing so to prevent crime and violence and to detect and apprehend criminals.[33] Early descriptions by contemporaries describe both sorts of police action, taken today as routine, as novel and startling.[34]

The police penetration of civil society, however, lay not only in its narrow application to crime and violence. In a broader sense, it represented the penetration and continual presence of central political authority throughout daily life. In an important defense of characteristically modern social arrangements, Edward Shils has argued that close integration of the social and geographic periphery is a unique achievement of 'mass society'. In his view

mass society is not the most peaceful or 'orderly' society that has ever existed; but it is the most consensual. The maintenance of public peace through apathy and coercion in a structure of extremely discontinuous interaction is a rather different thing from its maintenance through consensus in a structure of more continuous interaction between center and periphery ...[35]

But in Shils' account the integration of the periphery emerges entirely as a moral or normative process:

> The mass of the population is no longer merely an object which the elite takes into account as a reservoir of military and labor power or as a possible or actual source of public disorder ... Most of the population ... stand in closer moral affinity and in a more frequent, even though mediated, interaction with the center than has ever been the case ... The greater proximity to the center – to the institutions which constitute it and the views which are embodied in it. There is, accordingly, a greater feeling within the mass of being a part of the same substance of which one is oneself formed.

That the modern nation represents an unprecedented extension of the organizational and moral community is undoubted. But the wholly normative language in which this account is cast risks eliding the simultaneous extension of the police throughout the 'periphery' both as the agent of legitimate coercion and as a personification of the values of the 'center'. Far from being a latter-day consequence of organizing the police for purely coercive tasks, this was explicit in early police doctrine and much remarked upon by early observers. Their accounts stress the capacity of bureaucratic organization to make the values of the 'center' palpable in daily life by means of detached persons operating on organizationally defined missions.

> Amid the bustle of Piccadilly or the roar of Oxford Street, P.C.X. 59 stalks along, an institution rather than a man. We seem to have no more hold of his personality than we could possibly get of his coat buttoned up to the throttling-point. Go, however, to the section-house ... and you no longer see policemen, but men ... They are positively laughing with each other![36]

And they also stress the power of the police over mass disorder, which stems not only from superior organization and the rational application of force but also from its presence as the official representative of the moral order in daily life:

> The baton may be a very ineffective weapon of offence, but it is backed by the combined power of the Crown, the Government, and the Constituencies. Armed with it alone, the constable will usually be found ready, in obedience to orders, to face any mob, or brave any danger. The mob quails before the simple baton of the police officer, and flies before it, well knowing the moral as well as physical force of the Nation whose will, as embodied in law, it represents. And take any man from that mob, place a baton in his hand and a blue coat on his back, put him forward as the representative of the law, and he too will be found equally ready to face the mob from which he was taken, and exhibit the same steadfastness and courage in defense of constituted order.[37]

In this setting, early police doctrine and observers agreed from the beginning that it was necessary to rely on the moral assent of the general population; even the earliest policemen were elaborately instructed in the demeanor and behavior required to evoke, establish, and sustain that assent.[38] This was more than a mere technical convenience. The replacement of intermittent military intervention in a largely unpoliced society by continuous professional bureaucratic policing meant that the benefits of police organization – continual pervasive moral display and lower long-term costs of official coercion for the state and propertied classes – absolutely required the moral cooperation of civil society.

Thus, the extension of moral consensus and of the police as an instrument of legitimate coercion go hand in hand. Along with other ramifying bureaucratic agencies of the center, the police link daily life to central authority. The police, however, rely not only on a technique of graduated, discretionary, and ubiquitous coercion but also on a new and unprecedentedly extensive form of moral consensus. The center is able to supervise daily life more closely and continuously than ever before; but police organization also requires pervasive moral assent if it is to achieve the goals peculiar to its technique. In earlier times, as we have seen, voluntaristic and nonbureaucratic police permitted the sabotage of official coercion by allowing participating classes to make their services conditional. In a policed society (as distinct from a police state), a hostage is also given to fortune: the fundamental assent, not of the classes who comprise volunteer or nonprofessional quasi-police, but of the general population. Without at least a minimal level of such assent, coercive functions become costly in exactly the ways that those who created the policed society in England sought to avoid. In this sense, then, the extension of the moral community and of the police are aspects of the same historical development.

## Cultures of riotous protest

The themes of mass criminality and of political riot and mob protest have long been intertwined. In a notable and recent contribution George Rudé has been especially concerned to refute the classic view – associated with such nineteenth-century conservatives as Burke, Taine, and Le Bon – that political crowds, mobs, and riots are essentially criminal in character.[39] According to Rudé's analysis, demonstrating crowds and mobs in the latter half of the eighteenth and the first half of the nineteenth century were characteristically composed not of pauperized, unemployed and disorganized 'rabble' but of locally resident, respectable, and employed people.[40] It is not surprising that privileged classes attempt to define popular protest criminal – that is, fundamentally and unconditionally illegitimate. But this rhetoric and the very real fears of privileged and propertied people facing recurrent popular agitation in an un-policed age, must not lead us to overlook the evidence for another aspect of this older relationship between elite and agitational population: riots and mobs, however much they were feared and detested, were also often means of protest that articulately communicated the desires of the population to a responsive, if not sympathetic, elite.[41]

This is a major feature of Eric Hobsbawm's analysis of the pre-industrial 'city mob'.[42] While stressing that such mobs were a 'pre-political phenomenon' and often reacted directly to fluctuations in wages and food prices, Hobsbawm also emphasizes, in effect, the normative character of such riots:

> ... There was the claim to be considered. The classical mob did not merely riot as a protest, but because it expected to achieve something by its riot. It assumed that the authorities would be sensitive to its movements, and probably also, that they would make some immediate concession; for the 'mob' was not simply a casual collection of people united for some *ad hoc* purpose, but in a recognized sense, a permanent entity, even though rarely permanently organized as such.[43]

Insisting with Rudé on the essentially noncriminal character of such riotous protests, Hobsbawm summarizes the system as a whole:

> Provided that the ruler did his duty, the populace was prepared to defend him with enthusiasm. But if he did not, it rioted until he did. This mechanism was perfectly understood by both sides, and caused no political problems beyond a little occasional destruction of property ... The threat of perennial rioting kept rulers ready to control prices and distribute work or largesses, or indeed to listen to their faithful commons on other matters. Since the riots were not directed against the social system, public order could remain surprisingly lax by modern standards.[44]

We will briefly illustrate the system as described by Hobsbawm and Rudé with an example from rather late in this period – London in 1831.[45] 'Illuminations' were occasions on which those favoring a given cause or person placed lights in their windows; and it often happened that demonstrating crowds went from house to house demanding that those within 'illuminate' and smashing their windows or sacking their houses if they did not. The residences thus besieged were usually selected with precision – the ruling class in eighteenth- and early nineteenth-century cities was not anonymous, physically inaccessible, or effectively insulated by a professional and preventive police force. Such a crowd, pressing for electoral reform of the Commons, gathered in April 1831. The following is a contemporary account of its doings, clearly written from an unfriendly point of view:

> ... The reformers of London endeavoured to get up an illumination on Monday, the 25th; but that having been a failure, they prevailed on the Lord Mayor to announce another for the evening of Wednesday the 27th. On that evening, the illumination was pretty general ... The mobs did a great deal of mischief. A numerous rabble proceeded along the Strand, destroying all windows that were not lighted ... In St. James' Square they broke the windows in the houses of the Bishop of London, the Marquis of Cleveland and Lord Grantham. The Bishop of Winchester and Mr. W.W. Wynn, seeing the mob approach, placed candles in their windows, which thus escaped. The mob then proceeded to St. James' street

where they broke the windows of Crockford's, Jordan's, the Guards, and other Club houses. They next went to the Duke of Wellington's residence in Piccadilly, and discharged a shower of stones which broke several windows. The Duke's servants fired out of the windows over their heads to frighten them, but without effect. The policemen then informed the mob that the corpse of the Duchess of Wellington was on the premises, which arrested further violence against Apsley House ...[46]

After the action just described the mob marched off to attack other residences, including that of Robert Peel, the political founder of the police. At every point the normative character of the mob is clear. In this case their cause was generally popular, and they had the support of the Lord Mayor and many other worthies favoring reform, whereas many mob actions, of course, lacked such sanctions. But 'antagonistic cooperation' between the mob and parts of the elite had a long history.[47] Indeed, even prereform electoral politics sometimes required parts of the elite not only to compete for the favor of the people but to expose themselves to rough treatment by electors and nonelectors alike. Thus, a French observer of 1819, watching the customary postelection procession of successful parliamentary candidates, described a scene which Halevy calls 'one long familiar to the English public':

[They] were immediately pelted with filth, greeted with a shower of black mud ... I saw Lord Nugent with one side all black ... Lord John Russell attempted with difficulty to wipe off the stinking patches of dirt which continually bespattered his cheeks ... Some had their windows broken and their furniture damaged. The houses of Lord Castlereagh and several others met with the same fate. The constables were insufficient to restore order, and the troops had to be called out.[48]

The English elite, then, sometimes lived on rather casual terms with popular volatility so long as the latter did not – as for a time the 'dangerous classes' and early working class movements seemed to – challenge the fundamentals of the current system. They did not do so willingly, to be sure, but in a kind of symbiosis in which 'consideration' was exchanged for 'support'. Thus, to see everyday, nonrevolutionary violence or unruliness solely or even largely as an impediment to the emergence of stable democracy is to blur important dis-tinctions between kinds of popular violence and ways in which it may be integrated into a political system. Popular violence which forms part of an articulate system of demands and responses, in which needs and obligations are reasonably clear to each party, may not be at all necessarily 'irrational', 'criminal', or 'pointless' – to use words often applied to riotous protest in contemporary democracies. Indeed, the English case suggests that – granted the many other conditions that lie outside our present scope – such a system may well conduce to the establishment of stable democracy. For although Hobsbawm calls the system 'pre-political', it is one in which ordinary people express their will and elites have learned to listen.[49] The existence of the normative culture of mob and riot in many places other than England is enough to show – if the disclaimer need be made at all – that the mere existence of normative riot and violence is not a sufficient condition for the

17

emergence of institutionalized democracy.[50] Yet in an age when institutions did not organize, represent, or press the claims of ordinary people, and in which the streets were therefore a political arena, it is important to distinguish between kinds of popular violence, rather than consider it wholly as an anachronism.

## The demand for order in contemporary democracy

Such a protodemocratic system of riotous demand and elite response, however, is confined to unpoliced, hierarchical, pre-industrial society. It is not found where entrepreneurs or managers, career bureaucrats, or professional politicians have displaced former ruling groups; where popular volatility may disrupt tightly woven political and market ecologies; and where the state makes its presence felt ubiquitously in the form of police. In the latter situation, the demand for 'law and order' becomes what it was not before – a constitutional imperative stemming from an unprecedentedly pervasive consensus and personified and enforced by police. Simultaneously, the standards of daily decorum increasingly restrict occasions for normative violence; thus Georg Sorel observed at the start of [the last] century how marked had been the decline of daily and casual violence during the last, and how crucial a role these new standards played in the emerging policy of the liberal democratic state toward both the working and dangerous classes.[51]

With rising standards of public order has come an increasing intolerance of criminality, violence, and riotous protest. Daniel Bell has suggested that a breakdown of spatial barriers between the daily round of urban propertied classes and the criminal or unruly poor has made the former more aware of violence in daily life.[52] We may perhaps envisage three stages in such a sequence: one in which the prosperous or respectable often lived in unimagineable closeness to crime and the threat of riot or mob; a second in which these groups succeeded in insulating themselves – spatially, by regroupment in and outside the centers of cities and organizationally, by the police;[53] and a third in which penetrations of these barriers evoke a response which would be considered exorbitant by the standards of earlier years.

The character of the police as a public bureaucracy may also raise expectations about the level of public peace it is possible to attain. As the instrument of public policy they are easily seen in terms of a naive social instrumentalism – as technicians applying efficient means that are in principle capable of fully realizing their ends. Have not public bureaucracies eliminated plague, solved the enduring problems of urban sanitation, and prevented gross impurities in purchased foods? Why cannot the police similarly 'clean up' crime and control violence?[54] In short, the historic and strategic success of the police raises expectations and exposes them to pressures engendered by the idea of a uniformly peaceful civil society.[55]

Not only are expectations of public order higher than before, but the arena to which these expectations refer has expanded. It has done so not only because of the continuing, though obviously very incomplete, extension of a single moral order throughout the national community – a process which takes territoriality rather than the divisions of class, locality, or group as its ideal boundaries. The arena of expectation widens as smaller formations – regions, states, local communities – find it harder to control or influence the moral climate in which they live. The 'nationalization' of civil rights, federal involvement in municipal programs like housing, the erosion of the power of localities to control the content of mass media, pressure from judiciaries on informal and quasilegal police practices – all mean that smaller formations come to see themselves as less able to control or influence their moral destiny.[56] Thinking themselves more vulnerable to incursion from the larger society, they extend moral demand and expectations to a wider environment than in the past was thought relevant to daily life.

These trends mesh with others. The imagery of the 'dangerous classes' is being reborn in contemporary America. The nascent demand for a pervasively benign environment arises as the urban poor, disorganized, and unemployed – especially Negroes – bear more heavily upon the awareness and daily life of an urban society in which proportionately more people are 'respectable' than ever before.[57] Violence, criminality, and riot become defined not only as undesirable but as threatening the very fabric of social life. Police forces come to be seen as they were in the time of their creation a sophisticated and convenient form of garrison force against an internal enemy.[58] Lacking a strong tradition of urban violence as a form of articulate protest, it is all the easier to define such events as merely criminal.[59] Such definitions work not only on the respectable but also on the riotous poor. Like American society as a whole, the American poor lack a traditional past: on neither side of the boundaries of class and race do the conditions for 'articulate riot' exist in generous measure. 'Criminal' acts like looting and violent assault are likely to dominate riotous protest, rather than explicitly political gestures. Similarly, the propertied and respectable are ill-prepared to react in terms other than a confrontation with uncontained and shapeless criminality. Articulate riot, however, requires that both rioters and their target or audience jointly define the meaning of riotous acts. The frequency with which recent riots by Negroes in American cities are interpreted officially as 'meaningless'[60] contrasts with the ability of the English elite, especially before it was severely threatened from the late eighteenth century on, to interpret the meaning of riotous behavior.

Current concern over violence and riot, then, involves a problem of the political language in which these events are described and interpreted. The problem is likely to sharpen as the official stance, relying in part upon the rhetoric of diagnostic sociology, becomes strained by the urgent pressure of events. The gap between the official diagnostic style and a cultural response that makes little provision for 'normative riot' is likely to widen as the urban situation grows even more aggravated. It therefore remains to be seen whether American elites – creative, professional, and political – can or will sustain a diagnostic posture that seeks and interprets the meaning of these events.

It is not to idealize even the optimal 'traditional' political society – that of England – with its brutalities, squalidness, and hardness of soul, to point out that it often provided the unorganized poor with a language by which, in the absence of representative institutions or the ability to participate in them, they might articulately address the propertied classes through riot and disorder. And it is not to derogate the American adventure in modernity to suggest that, however richly endowed with representative and responsive institutions, it has not provided such a language or those in its cities who have long been outside their compass – a language whose grammar is shared by speaker and listener, rioter and pillaged, violent and frightened.

*From Allan Silver, 'The demand for order in civil society' in D.J. Bordua (ed.)* The Police: Six Sociological Essays *(New York: Wiley), 1967, pp 1–24.*

## Notes

1  *An effectual Scheme for the Immediate Prevention of Street Robberies and Suppressing of all other Disorders of the night; with a Brief History of the Night-houses and an Appendix Relating to those Sons of Hell call'd Incendiaries* (London, 1730).
2  *Ibid.*, pp. 10–11.
3  James M. Buckley, 'The Present Epidemic of Crime', *The Century Magazine*, (November 1903), p. 150.
4  James Edgar Brown, 'The Increase of Crime in the United States', *The Independent* (April 11, 1907), pp. 832–3.
5  'Causes of the Increase of Crime', *Blackwood's Magazine* (July 1844), p. 2. The phrase appears in another work published four years later, *The Communist Manifesto* – where, however, it is instantly interpreted in terms of the 'lumpen-proletariat' idea.
6  Honoré Antoine Frégier, *Les Classes Dangereuses de la Population dans les Grandes Villes* (Paris, 1840) is a work often cited by contemporaries. A relevant modern work on Paris is Louis Chevalier's *Classes Laborieuses et Classes Dangereuses à Paris pendant la Première Moitié du XIX Siècle* (Paris, 1958). In the Paris of that time, he writes, 'le proliferation des classes dangereuses était ... l'un des faits majeurs de l'existence quotienne de la capitale, l'un des grands problèmes de l'administration urbaine, l'une des principales préoccupations des tous, l'un des formes les plus incontestables de l'angoisse sociale'. The city was one 'où le crime a une importance et une signification que nous ne comprenons guère ...' (pp. iii–iv).
7  Influential books expressing this concern were Henry Fielding's *Enquiry into the Causes of the Late Increase of Robbers* (1751) and Patrick Colquhoun's *Treatise on the Police of the Metropolis* (1796). According to Chevalier (*op. cit.*, pp. 451–68), the Parisian bourgeoisie made little distinction between the 'industrious' and the 'dangerous' poor.
8  According to the census, the population of London tripled in the first half of the nineteenth century. On its occupational composition, see the *Census of Great Britain in 1851* (London, 1845), p. 182, *passim*.
9  George Mainwaring, *Observations on the Present State of the Police of the Metropolis* (London, 1821), pp. 4–5. The anonymous essayist of 1844, quoted above on the connection between the dangerous classes and the 'manufacturing districts', went on to write: 'In examining the classes of society from which the greater part of the crime comes, it will be found that at least three-fourths, probably nine-tenths, comes from the very lowest and most destitute ... If we examine who it is that compose this dismal substratum, this hideous *black band of society*, we shall find that it is not made up of any one class more than another – not of factory workers more than labourers, carters or miners – but it is formed by an aggregate of the most unfortunate or improvident of *all classes* ...' *Blackwood's Magazine* (July 1844), p. 12 (italics in original).
10  This was the fourth and final volume of *London Labour and the London Poor*, separately titled *Those That Will Not Work*.
11  *London Quarterly Review* (July 1856), p. 94. Many observers, though still concerned with criminality, acknowledge a change for the better at this time. Remarking that accounts of the earlier situation in London 'seem like tales of another country', a writer in 1852 went on to detail improvements: 'No member of Parliament would now venture to say that it was dangerous to walk in the streets of London by day or night ... Bad as the dens of infamy in London still are, they are not to be compared with those older places of hideous profligacy ... In the most disorderly part of the town, such as St. Giles, Covent Garden, and Holborn, the streets every Sunday morning exhibited the most outrageous scenes of fighting, drunkenness and depravity ... Crimes too, are greatly diminished in atrocity. The large gangs of desperate robbers, thirteen or fourteen in number, now no longer exist ...' *Edinburgh Review* (July 1858), p. 12–13.

12  Charles L. Brace, *The Dangerous Classes of New York* (New York, 1872), p. 26.
13  *Ibid.*, p. 29.
14  Thus, Defoe saw the intolerable conditions of his time as a result of the arrogance and bad influence of a rapidly increasing group of prostitutes and their 'bullies'; and his solution was to disperse them by raids (*op. cit.*, pp. 26–32).
15  In the book which more than six decades ago named and founded this tradition, E.A. Ross was crisply aware of the expanding role of police: 'In the field of physical coercion, there is an increase in the number of lictors, bailiffs, police, and soldiers told off to catch, prod, beat, and hold fast recalcitrants, and they are brought under a stricter discipline. They are more specialized for their work, and an *esprit de corps* is carefully cultivated among them' *Social Control* (New York, 1901), pp. 398–9. Furthermore, Ross was quite tough-minded about the cause of this development: 'All this does not happen by simple fiat of the social will. Certain groups of persons – the executive, cabinet, the central government, the party machine, the higher clergy, the educational hierarchy, "authorities" of every kind in short – are always striving for more power. When the need of a more stringent control makes itself felt, they find the barriers to their self-aggrandizement unexpectedly giving way before them. Formerly they were held in check, while now they find encroachment strangely easy' (*Ibid.*). Neither kind of emphasis survived the subsequent failure of works in social control to treat the characteristics of the policed society in a comprehensive way or to see organized and legitimate coercion as intrinsic to social control. (Representative treatises are L.L. Bernard, *Social Control*, New York, 1939, and Richard T. LaPiere, *A Theory of Social Control*, New York, 1954.) Ross himself distinguished between the normative processes of 'public opinion' – uniquely flexible, preventive, and ubiquitous – and the coercive effects of 'law' – which were clumsy, retrospective, and remote (*op. cit.*, pp. 89–105). Important and influential as this distinction is, it tends to obscure – as we shall see – some of the distinctive features of policed society. Recent attempts to incorporate civil violence in the framework of social theory are included in *Internal War*, Harry Eckstein, ed. (New York, 1964), especially the essays by Eckstein, Parsons, and Feldman.
16  Useful accounts of British police history are the writings of Charles Reith, especially *The Police Idea* (1938), *British Police and the Democratic Ideal* (1943), *The Blind Eye of History* (1952), and *A New Study of Police History* (1956). See also F.C. Mather, *Public Order in the Age of the Chartists* (Manchester, 1959). Like most contributors to the English literature on 'public order', these writers – especially Reith – work from palpably conservative assumptions.
17  'The Police and the Thieves', *London Quarterly Review* (July 1856), p. 93.
18  'The Metropolitan Police System', *Westminster Review* (January 1873), p. 16. An early historian of the New York Draft Riot of 1863 was similarly impressed by the decisive contribution of the telegraphic system in linking police stations within the city to each other and to those in Brooklyn. He devoted considerable space to the mob's attacks on the telegraphic system, citing the defense of its equipment and personnel as a key phase in the struggle for control of the streets. See J.T. Headley, *The Great Riots of New York*, 1873).
19  A good summary is in F.C. Mather, *Public Order in the Age of the Chartists*, pp. 75–95.
20  John Fortesque, *A History of the British Army* (London, 1923) Vol. XI, p. 43). Since the yeomanry were required to supply their own horses and equipment, their status as agrarian men of property was largely assured. See K. Chorley, *Armies and the Art of Revolution* (London, 1943), p. 167.
21  J.L. and B. Hammond, *The Town Labourer* (London, 1928), p. 89. Also, F.C. Mather, *op. cit.*, p. 148. Yeomanry, for example, precipitated the 'Peterloo' massacre.
22  Quoted in Reith, *The Police Idea*, p. 191.
23  For example, many resigned when they received threatening letters after Peterloo. See Ione Leigh, *Castlereagh* (London, 1951), p. 127.
24  J.R.M. Butler, *The Passing of the Great Reform Bill* (London, 1941), p. 132.
25  Despatch of General Byng quoted in Reith, *The Police Idea*, p. 202.
26  'Respectable tradesmen cannot, without detriment to themselves, be so engaged as constables ...' (George Mainwaring, *Observations on the Police ...*, p. 46).
27  *First Report of the Commissioners Appointed as to the Best Means of Establishing an Efficient Constabulary Force in the Counties of England and Wales* (London, 1839), pp. 158–9.
28  *Ibid.*, p. 205.
29  'I hope to get up a troop of Yeomanry at Cheltenham', wrote Lord Ellenborough during the critical year of 1832, 'but this requires delicate management ... Yeomanry however we must have, or we shall be beaten.' A. Aspinall, *Three Early Nineteenth Century Diaries* (London, 1952), p. 275.
30  See the accounts in F.C. Mather, *Public Order in the Age of the Chartists*, pp. 153–81, and Joseph Hamburger, *James Mill and the Art of Revolution* (New Haven, 1963), pp. 203–14.

31  See, for example, Frank Darvell, *Popular Disturbances and Public Order in Regency England* (Oxford, 1934), pp. 80–1, 267–8.

32  All these points of superiority of police over army were explicit among those who advocated or created the early professional police. See for example, the *First Report of The Commissioners ...* , *op. cit.*, pp. 159–61; George Mainwaring, *Observations on the Present State of the Police ...*, p. 69; Charles Reith, *British Police and the Democratic Ideal*, pp. 9–30; and *Edinburgh Review* (July 1852), p. 6.

33  Great stress was initially laid on the 'preventive principle', at the time a new principle in internal peace-keeping. See Reith, *ibid.*, pp. 18–23, and the same author's *A New Study of Police History*, pp. 221–4. For the view of a contemporary advocate of police, see Mainwaring, *op. cit.*, pp. 9–10.

34  Note, for example, the obvious astonishment that underlies an account of the tracing of a burglar, who had robbed a house in central London, to an obscure hiding place in the East End ('The Police System of London', *Edinburgh Review*, July 1852, pp. 8–10).

35  'The Theory of Mass Society', *Diogenes* (1962) pp. 53–4 (for this and succeeding quotations).

36  'The Police and the Thieves', *London Quarterly Review* (July 1856), p. 93.

37  'The Police of London', *London Quarterly Review* (July 1870), p. 48.

38  Charles Reith, *A New Study of Police History*, pp. 140–2.

39  *The Crowd in History, 1730–1848* (New York, 1964), pp. 7–8, 199–204.

40  *Ibid.*, p. 47–65.

41  Expressions of this fear are vivid and aboundingly frequent. 'At this time,' wrote the Tory poet Southey in 1812, 'nothing but the Army preserves us from the most dreadful of all calamities, an insurrection of the poor against the rich, and how long the Army may be depended upon is a question which I scarcely dare ask myself' (Elie Halevy, *A History of the English People*, New York, 1912, Vol. I. p. 292). Seven years later a peer discussing the political situation observed: 'We are daily assailed with undisguised menace, and are little removed from the expectation of open violence ...' (*Substance of the Speech of the Rt. Hon. Lord Grenville in the House of Lords, November 19, 1820*, London, p. 23). A year later in a memorandum to Liverpool, Wellington, then Prime Minister – urging the creation of a police force – wrote: 'I feel the greatest anxiety respecting the state of the military in London ... Very recently strong symptoms of discontent appeared in one battalion of the guards ... There are reports without number in circulation respecting all the Guards ... Thus, in one of the most critical moments that ever occurred in this country, we and the public have reason to doubt the fidelity of the troops, the only security we have, not only against revolution but for the lives and property of every individual in this country who has anything to lose ...' (quoted in Reith, *The Police Idea*, p. 213). Robert Peel, fearing for his family's safety at their country estate, left London during the crisis of 1831 and asked a friend to send weapons. 'I have this day got you fourteen carbines, bayonets, and accoutrements,' the friend replied. 'How will you have them sent to you? I have only desired a cask of ball cartridges to be put in the case' (Tresham Lever, *The Life and Times of Sir Robert Peel*, New York, 1942, p. 144). A general description of the situation is given in Reith, *Police Principles and the Problem of War*, pp. 46–8. In his revisionist account, *James Mill and the Art of Revolution*, Joseph Hamburger maintains that this standard portrait of elite mentality is exaggerated and that it does not apply to the Whig reformers in the period before 1832, who were more concerned with long-range than with imminent crises (see pp. 33–47).

42  *Primitive Rebels: Studies in Archaic Forms of Social Movements* (Manchester, 1959).

43  *Ibid.*, p. 111.

44  *Ibid.*, p. 116.

45  See the summary of this theme in *The Crowd in History*, pp. 254–7. See also the interesting article by R.B. Rose, 'Eighteenth Century Price Riots and Public Policy in England', *International Review of Social History* (1961), pp. 277–92, and more general remarks in this connection by Joseph Hamburger, *op. cit.*, pp. 199–202.

46  *Annual Register*, 1831, p. 68. Quoted by Reith in *British Police and the Democratic Ideal*, pp. 90–1. Hamburger places this incident squarely in the 'tradition of riot' (see *James Mill ...*, pp. 139–42).

47  It is Hamburger's thesis that in the case of the Reform Crisis of 1830–1832, proreform leaders manipulated the threat of the mob, rather than wielding a substantial revolutionary threat. But this sort of manipulation was itself a tradition – for a case that succeeded before the mob ever took to the streets, see Thomas Perry, *Public Opinion, Propaganda and Politics in Eighteenth Century England: a Study of the Jew Bill of 1753* (Cambridge, Massachusetts, 1962). So strong was this tradition that Lady Holland, the wife of the great Whig aristocrat prominent in the struggle for reform, could remark disapprovingly on Wellington's reaction to the prospect of mob attack on his house: 'Is it not strange that the Duke of Wellington has boarded with very thick planks *all* his windows upstairs to Piccadilly and the Park? ... The work of *darkness* began on Coronation Day and is now completed. He says, I hear, that it is to protect his plate glass windows from the mob, who will assail him on the Reform Bill! As it cannot be for thrift, it

looks like defiance; and the mob will be irritated when they discover his intentions' Earl of Ilchester, ed., *Elizabeth, Lady Holland to Her Son* (London, 1946), p. 118. (italics in original.)

48 Halevy, *op. cit.*, p. 118.

49 It is suggestive to compare Hobsbawm's perceptive comment on the situation in parts of Europe which did not experience a comparably gradual development of democratic institutions. Speaking of popular riot and enthusiasm in support of the *status quo*, he remarks: 'Legitimate monarchs or institutions like churches may not welcome this. The Emperor Francis I of Austria took a poor view of the revolutionary legitism of his people, observing correctly: "Now they are patriots for me; but one day they may be patriots against me!" From the point of view of the genuinely conservative institution, the ideal is obedience, not enthusiasm, whatever the nature of the enthusiasm. Not for nothing was "Ruhe ist die Erste Bürgerpflicht" (Tranquility is the first duty of every citizen) the slogan of every German princeling' (*Primitive Rebels ...*, p. 119).

50 See Hobsbawm, *passim*. See also the comprehensive discussion by Charles Tilly, 'Reflections on the Revolution of Paris', *Social Problems* (Summer 1964), pp. 99–121, which, among other matters, deals with the literature on these themes in the case of France.

51 See Chapter 6 of *Reflections on Violence*. On the special sensitivity of modern society to public disorder, see Karl Polyani, *The Great Transformation* (New York, 1944), pp. 186–7: 'The market system was more allergic to rioting than any other economic system we know ... In the nineteenth century breaches of the peace, if committed by armed crowds, were deemed an incipient rebellion and an acute danger to the state; stocks collapsed and there was no bottom to prices. A shooting affray in the streets of the metropolis might destroy a substantial part of the nominal national capital.'

52 'The Myth of Crime Waves: The Actual Decline of Crime in the United States', in *The End of Ideology* (New York, 1962), pp. 151–74.

53 'The beats vary considerably in size; in those parts of the town which are open and inhabited by the wealthier classes, an occasional visit from a policeman is sufficient, and he traverses a wide district. But the limits of the beat are diminished, and of course the frequency of the visits increased in proportion to the character and the density of the population, the throng and pressure of traffic, and concentration of property, and the intricacy of the streets ... Nor must it be supposed that this system places the wealthier localities at a disadvantage, for it is an axiom in police that you guard St. James' by watching St. Giles' ('The Police System of London', *Edinburgh Review*, July 1852, p. 5). St. Giles was one of the most notorious of London's 'rookeries'.

54 It is more than accidental that Edwin Chadwick [...] was also a prime mover in the reform of urban sanitation. See his report, *Sanitary Conditions of the Labouring Population in England, 1842* (London, 1843).

55 See Bell, *op. cit.*, p. 152 on the relationship between better policing and a 'higher' crime rate. The artifactual character of this relationship, sometimes hard for contemporaries for whom the police are taken for granted to grasp, was obvious to an observer witnessing the transition to a policed society. See 'Causes of the Increase of Crime', *Blackwood's Magazine* (July 1844), p. 5.

56 Attempting to account for respectable people's greater awareness of violence in daily life, Bell has also suggested that the emergence of heterogeneous audiences for the mass media, which include groups previously less exposed to violent themes, has heightened awareness of violence even as its occurrence in daily life has declined (*ibid.*, pp. 170–4). Simultaneously, local communities and states are losing their formal powers to control such materials and are relying more often on informal control. (See Richard Randall, *Some Political Theories in Motion Picture Censorship Decisions: Prior Restraint Reconsidered*. Paper delivered at the Midwest Conference of Political Science, Bloomington, Indiana, April 1965.)

57 Here we follow Shils' argument, *op. cit.*, p. 56.

58 For the American police this situation may render a chronic problem acute. At the time when the police are more urgently charged than ever before to do society's 'dirty work' but also are more stringently supervised by the public, various interest groups and the judiciary, their morale and operating problems are further exacerbated by their failure to embody moral consensus in the eyes of the general community, their 'clientele', and themselves as thoroughly as do the British police. For detailed observations about some of these matters, especially the last, see Michael Banton, *The Policeman in the Community* (London, 1964), a comparative account of Scottish and American police forces.

59 Obviously, the rural South would require special treatment. See W.J. Cash, *The Mind of the South* (New York, 1941), *passim*, and H.C. Brearly, 'The Pattern of Violence', in W.T. Couch, ed., *Culture in the South* (Chapel Hill, 1934). Our focus, however, is on urban situations. Thus, for example, there is a suggestion in that the few food riots of nineteenth-century New York, in 1837 and 1857, were carried out largely by foreign-born, rather than native, poor. See the chapters on these episodes in J.F. Headley, *The Great Riots of New York* (New York, 1873).

60   I am indebted to Robert Fogelson's analysis (as yet unpublished) of these riots and of the official responses to them – notably the McCone Commission's report on the Watts riot of August 1965.

# 2. Police and people: the birth of Mr Peel's 'blue locusts'

*Michael Ignatieff*

Thinking about the history of the police requires a certain mental struggle against one's sense of their social necessity. Over the past 150 years, the London police have inserted themselves into our social subconscious as facts of life. Whether we trust them or not, we cannot imagine the city doing without them. It takes a small but appreciable stretch of the historical imagination to put oneself back into the time when there were no professional police on the streets, and when the idea of such a force seemed pregnant with danger for the 'liberties of Englishmen'.

The first patrols of the Metropolitan police set out on their beats on 29 September 1829, dressed in top hats, blue swallowtail coats, heavy serge trousers and boots, and equipped with a wooden rattle and a truncheon. To us, their coming has the weight of historical inevitability, but this was not so the Londoners of 1829. So pervasive was the resistance to their arrival that we need to ask ourselves, as we approach their 150th anniversary, how such a decisive enlargement of the powers of the state became possible at all.

The crowds who surged across Blackfriars Bridge on a November night in 1830, after listening to orator Hunt at the Rotunda, chanted, 'Reform! No Wellington! No Peel! No New Police!' Next day, when the King stepped from his carriage in St James Palace Yard after opening parliament, the crowds surged against the line of blue serge protecting him and called out, 'Down with the Raw Lobsters! No Martial Law! No Standing Armies!' At nightfall, abusive crowds eddied accusingly around constables who were patrolling in the West End.

The agitation against the new police was stubborn and protracted, continuing in the pages of the radical press and in meetings of parish vestries, and then bursting out into the streets again in 1833 when police used the flats of their sabres to disperse a radical meeting in Coldbath Fields. A coroner's jury, outraged by the brutality of the force, handed in a verdict of justifiable manslaughter on the body of a policeman killed in the affray. The jurymen were heroes of British fair play. Pewter mugs with their portraits were on the mantelpiece of many a radical parlour.

In London, opposition to the police passed out of the vocabulary of radical politics sometime after 1848, but a brooding residue of collective hostility remained among the London poor. This was especially so among costermongers whom, as Mayhew reported in 1851, continued to regard 'serving out a copper' as a matter of honour, well worth the inevitable prison sentence. Outside

London, the introduction of the 'blue locusts' brought angry crowds into the streets of many northern industrial towns during the 1840s.

There was something weightier than prejudice in the momentum of this resistance. In the cry, 'No Standing Armies,' there resonated an echo of the 18th century commonwealth and country party comparison between 'continental despotism' (meaning standing armies, police spies, *lettres de cachet* and Bastilles) and 'English liberty' (meaning rule of law, balanced constitution, unpaid constables and local justices of the peace). It was this robust constitutionalism which damned Pitt's Police Bill of 1785 as 'a new engine of power and authority, so enormous and extensive as to threaten a species of despotism'. These arguments held the field until 1829.

The idea of a bureaucratic central force also offended against a tradition which held that social control should be a private, local and voluntary matter, best left to the master of the household, the parish beadle, and the JP. A 'paid police', no longer responsible to the community, would set servant spying on master and master denouncing servant. In this rhetoric, there is resistance to something we now take for granted – the right of the state to intervene in the disputes of the household.

From our vantage point today, this localism may seem an obvious anachronism in the London of the 1820s. But it was not so for many Londoners, for whom the parish still seemed a genuine boundary of administration and community. While discernibly swollen by new population, the London of the 1820s had not been ravaged by industrialism. The myth of the 'dangerous classes' was not yet a waking nightmare of the propertied. The social chasm between East End and West End had still to be dug. The geographic separation of classes in the city had not yet replaced the 18th century jumble. A Londoner like the Bow Street Runner, Townshend, could still discern the lineaments of the London of his youth in the city of his old age. He could plausibly assert that the London of the Gordon riots, the criminal 'Alsatias' and the twisting corpses atop Temple Bar, was at least as turbulent and unruly as the London of the 1820s.

Certainly there were many philanthropists, police magistrates and MPs who had concluded by 1820 that the growth of the city made policing inevitable. Yet their views did not command the consensus of the powerful and the propertied. Looking back ourselves, we tend to view the London of the 1820s through the bifocals of alarmists (from Fielding through Colquhoun to Chadwick). We fail to notice that they were contending unequally against a deeply entrenched constitutionalist libertarianism as well as a more subconscious and reflexive sense of social continuity. As late as 1822, the alarmists were having the worst of the argument. The county gentlemen and urban professional men on the 1822 police committee concluded that a professional police could not be reconciled with the liberties of Englishmen.

To interpret the coming of the new police, therefore, as a 'response' to crime and disorder, 'caused' by urban growth – to see the force as the work of a bourgeois consensus brought together by social fear – is to rewrite history in the language of a retrospective fatalism.

The most that can be said is that Wellington convinced Peel he should set up a civilian force specialising in crowd control after witnessing the embarrassingly inept performance of the soldiery called out to control rioting after Queen

Caroline's trial. This may have been the motivation of the Police Bill of 1829; but it doesn't explain how, within three generations, the force had managed to insert itself into popular awareness as a legitimate fact of London life.

The social history of the police's insertion into the warrens, courts and alleyways of St Giles, Spitalfields and Bethnal Green is usually told as a straightforward Whiggish progress from suspicion to cooperation. Yet how rapidly or easily was this progress to legitimacy achieved? Obviously, some of the skilled or regularly employed working class benefited immediately from the new police. To the extent that the washing on their lines or the tools in their boxes were now marginally more secure from theft, and they could use the police courts to secure a stay of eviction or to recover a small debt, they had some reason to believe the rhetoric proclaiming the police as 'servants' of the community.

## The submerged tenth

But among the 'submerged tenth' who struggled to survive in the catch-as-catch-can labour market of the docks and the sweated trades, the rhetoric encountered rougher sailing. To the casual poor, the coming of the new police only meant a greater chance of being arrested for 'drunkenness', 'loitering', 'common assault', 'vagrancy' or whatever else the duty sergeant decided to write in his big book. The hackney coachmen and the street sellers, for their part, knew the police as their licensers, as the ones with whom they waged a bickering, bantering struggle for control of a 'pitch' or a profitable position on the street. For the destitute, the police were the prying inspectors of common lodging houses, the inquisitors at the entrance to the workhouse and the cloaked figures who trained the sharp light of the bulls-eye lantern on your face as you lay awake at night in the 'coffins' of the night refuge.

In all these guises, the poor of London experienced the coming of the new police as a massive intensification of outside supervision over their ways of living and surviving – an intrusion which broke the casual, callous contract of disregard between rich and poor in the 18th century. A new contract between rich and poor, between police and people, had to be made.

The Police Commissioners' speeches about the necessity of securing the 'cooperation' of the public were more than hollow pieties. Without poor people willing to come forward as witnesses and as prosecutors, or simply to point a breathless constable in the direction of the running figure who had just vanished down an alley, the police would have been powerless over all but the most transparent street illegal behaviour.

The history of the emerging inter-dependence between police and people has not yet been written, but we know what questions to ask. When would a fight in the street or a stairway be handled by bystanders or neighbours, and when would a child be sent running for 'the constable' When a publican or shopkeeper found his till empty, when would he go to the police, and when would he pay a visit himself to the shopboy's mother, or to a fence?

For the working poor, it must be remembered, going to the police was usually the last in a range of responses to crisis – a range which included dealing directly with the families of suspected persons, or engaging the services of the underworld network of fences, informers, enforcers, loan-sharks and debt collectors. The success of the police in securing the cooperation of the public depended less on keeping a rosy image of impartiality than on securing a near-monopoly over the market in violence and redress.

We still do not understand which range of 'official' crimes were also accepted as 'crimes' within different working class communities, and which were not. There were at least two, often three or four, overlapping definitions of crime competing for the allegiances of the community. The success of the police, both ideologically and practically, depended on convincing people to accept the official code of illegal behaviour, and turn to 'official' channels for redress.

To win this cooperation, the police manipulated their powers of discretion. They often chose not to take their authority to the letter of the law, preferring not to 'press their luck' in return for tacit compliance from the community. In each neighbourhood, and sometimes street by street, the police negotiated a complex, shifting, largely unspoken 'contract'. They defined the activities they would turn a blind eye to, and those which they would suppress, harass or control. This 'tacit contract' between normal neighbourhood activities and police objectives, was sometimes oiled by corruption, but more often sealed by favours and friendships. This was the microscopic basis of police legitimacy, and it was a fragile basis at best. A violent or unfair eviction by the police, for example, could bring a whole watching street together in a hostility to be visited on policeman afterwards, in the frozen silence which would descend when he stepped into the 'local'.

The bargain might also be overturned by events outside the community. The memory of the Trafalgar Square police charges in 1886 must have cast a pall over policemen's beats in Poplar, Stepney and Bethnal Green.

### Fair play?

In this social history, there is no clear passage in popular behaviour from suspicion to cooperation. Support for the police, then as now, was inherently unstable. This was because of the inevitable conflict between their image as impartial embodiments of British fair play, and their social role as defenders of property against the propertied.

Given this conflict, such acceptance as they could secure depended less on rhetoric and myth, than on imperceptibly slipping into the realm of necessary and inevitable facts of British life. To argue that their legitimacy rested on a massive popular consensus in the 19th century is to ignore the depth of the opposition to their coming, the highly sectorial character of their appeal, and the fragility of the contract they negotiated with the urban neighbourhood.

It is worth emphasising the fragile character of public support for the police in the last century, because our deepening economic and social crisis is fostering a plaintive nostalgia for a simpler, happier past. It is widely believed that there used to be a time, 'before this crisis', 'when Macmillan was Prime Minister', 'before the war', when policemen were 'respected', and police work could count on unstinting popular support. For those of us whose memories were formed by television, this undertow of feeling carries us back to the mythic figure of Dixon of Dock Green, on smiling patrol down a leafy, eternally sunlit suburban lane.

This longing to return to a past when 'authority' was 'respected' only takes us one small step closer to the 'law and order' state. Against this use of the past, the historically minded can plausibly object.

*From Michael Ignatieff, 'Police and people: the birth of Mr. Peel's blue locusts,* New Society, 30 August 1979 (Vol. 49), pp 443–5.*

# 3. Cops and Bobbies, 1830–1870

*Wilbur R. Miller*

Policemen are a familiar feature of modern urban life, the most conspicuous representatives of the political and social order. However, until American society seemed to be falling apart in the mid-1960s, social historians on this side of the Atlantic gave only a passing nod to the cop on the beat.[1] Like other institutions which people have taken for granted, the police are products of distinct historical circumstances, the complex process of social discipline and resistance fostered by the industrial revolution. As Allan Silver points out, the police represented an unprecedented extension of the government into the lives of ordinary citizens.[2] Some people welcomed and others resented this extension, while at the same time its nature and degree varied in different societies. A comparison of the mid-nineteenth-century London police – the first modern full-time patrol force created in 1829 – and the New York City police – the second such force outside of the British Empire, created in 1845 – reveals how different political and social developments influenced the principles and practices of police authority.

## I

The statutes which established London and New York's police forces provided only a skeleton around which a definition of authority and a public image of the police could develop. Consequently London's Metropolitan Police owed much to Charles Rowan and Richard Mayne, the army officer and lawyer whom Sir Robert Peel appointed to head his new force, while the New York police were formed and reformed by a succession of elected and appointed officials throughout the mid-nineteenth century.[3] However much individuals may be credited or blamed for various aspects of the police, they worked within a social context which encouraged some responses and discouraged others. To understand the nature of police authority one must examine the societies which produced the forces.

Although the British metropolis was a much larger city than the 'metropolis of the New World', both were heterogeneous cities marked by gulfs between wealth and poverty and recurrent social conflict. Michael Banton, to whom I am indebted for much of the con-ceptualization later in this article, argues that police authority reflects the degree of heterogeneity in modern societies. He finds that the stability of Scottish police authority reflects a culturally homogeneous society with widely shared expectations, while the instability of American police authority reflects a culturally heterogeneous society with few shared expectations.[4] However, it is difficult to maintain that nineteenth-century London was more homogeneous than contem-porary New York. Disraeli spoke of England's 'two nations, the rich and the poor' despite their ethnic homogeneity, and social conflict in London had more serious political implications than ethnic squabbles in New York. An examination of the *quality* of conflict in the two cities seems more promising for understanding the nature of police authority than an effort to measure their relative degrees of heterogeneity.

Formed in response to political violence and ordinary crimes against property,[5] the London force took to the streets amidst England's constitutional crisis over parliamentary representation for disenfranchised middle-class citizens. The politically-dominant landed aristocracy met the challenge from the industrial and commercial middle classes, backed by a reserve of working-class anger and violent protest, by tying them to the existing order through the electoral reform of 1832. The next challenge, fended off rather than co-opted, arose from various working class groups dissatisfied with selecting one or two wealthy men to carry out the schemes of 'one or two wealthy associations', the political parties under the new system of representation.[6] Culminating in Chartism, which included demands for universal suffrage, annually elected Parliaments and abolition of the property qualifications for M.P.s among its demands, working-class protest was defeated largely by the middle-class commitment to the social order. After a lull during the prosperous fifties and early sixties, working-class groups again demanded the franchise. Reflecting the increased economic power of workers organized into trade unions, the reform of 1867, another co-optive measure, gave urban workers the vote without altering the balance of social and economic power.[7]

Recurrent political crises were of profound importance to the police force charged with upholding the social order and controlling a turbulent population in the national capital, to which people looked with hope or apprehension in difficult times. Since disenfranchised protestors could have impact on Parliament only 'out of doors' – demonstrations in the streets – policemen inevitably collided with them. Would these confrontations feed the fire of social conflict? Would the police be identified as the cutting edge of the ruling minority's oppression? Since their role was fundamentally political amidst challenges to the legitimacy of the government, the conmmanders of the force had to devise a strategy for containing conflict if they expected the new police to survive the Tory government which created them.

The New York police worked within a different context to their London brethren. New York was not a metropolis in the European sense, the seat of national government as well as center of culture and commerce. Except in the spectacular draft riots of 1863, Americans did not look to New York for the nation's political fate as Englishmen looked to London.[8]

New York did have its own local disorder, the ethnic conflicts which punctuated the era. While not as portentious as London's political disturbances, they did have consequences for the nature of police authority. The presence of large groups of immigrants in American cities gave a distinct tone to class conflict. Antagonism between skilled and unskilled urban workers increased with the filling of the unskilled ranks by immigrants, especially Irish, in the mid-nineteenth century. Native-born workers, concerned about the degradation of their trades by industrialization, regarded the unskilled Irishman, willing to work for longer hours and lower wages, as an economic and social threat. This rivalry between elements of the working class undercut their sense of common interest against the employers. In fact, the native-born skilled workers who dominated American trade unions accepted the existing political system of representative democracy, believing that it gave all men an equal chance to rise in the world. The rowdy Irishman threatened to disrupt cherished institutions. Organized labor joined the propertied classes in denouncing the Irish draft rioters. While George T. Strong 'would like to see war made on Irish scum as in 1688', the leading labor newspaper pictured them as 'thieving rascals ... who have never done a day's work in their lives'.[9] The paper remarked, 'The people have too much at stake to tolerate any action beyond the pale of the law ... No improvement can be made by popular outbursts upon the great superstructure created by the wisdom of our fathers'.[10] In England such rhetoric was rarely embraced by workingmen; America's propertied and working classes alike saw a political order they valued threatened by irresponsible foreigners who did not appreciate democracy.

Since the New York police upheld the political institutions of representative democracy which most Americans valued, there was little pressure for them to transcend social conflict to ensure their own survival. Instead of supporting the rule of a small elite which was challenged by the majority of London's population, the police supported a political order threatened by an alien minority. Thus to a great extent the police were free to treat a large group of the community as outsiders with little fear for the consequences as long as their actions coincided with most people's expectations.

What sort of police authority emerged from the different social circumstances of London and New York? In both cities pure repression was unacceptable, in London because of past failures and tendency to promote more violence, and in New York because it was unacceptable to American democracy.[11] In societies with representative governments, whether aristocratic like England or democratic like America, the police ultimately depend on the voluntary compliance of most citizens with their authority. As Edwin Chadwick said, 'A police force ... must owe its real efficiency to the sympathies and concurrent action of the great body of the people'.[12] The commanders of the two forces had to define the institution to win this public support.

London's Police Commissioners, Rowan and Mayne, had an especially difficult task: they had to develop a force sufficiently strong to maintain order but also restrained enough to soothe widespread fears of police oppression. The combination of strength and restraint became the foundation of the London Bobby's public image. To achieve acceptance the Commissioners sought to identify the police force with the legal system, which embodied the strength of national sovereignty and the restraint of procedural regularity and guarantees of civil liberties. While the laws of England were hardly a pure realm of justice above contemporary social inequality, they were the broadest available source of external legitimation for the police.

Definition of the force as agents of the legal system made their authority *impersonal*, derived from legal powers and restraints instead of from the local community's informal expectations or the directives of the dominant political party.[13] Amid social conflict the Commissioners, in their own words, 'endeavoured to prevent the slightest practical feeling or bias, being shewn or felt by the police'.[14] With varying levels of success during their long terms of office Rowan and Mayne determined that 'the force should not only be, in fact, but be believed to be impartial in action, and should act on principle'.[15]

Behind this commitment to impersonal authority was the strength the police gained from being an independent agency of the national government. The Metropolitan Police, created by Act of Parliament, had no links with London's local government, and the Commissioners, appointed for life, were responsible to the Home Secretary who exercised only a broad authority over them. As a national institution the police could draw upon a reservoir of symbolic as well as physical power. 'Power derived from Parliament,' said a contemporary observer, '... carries with it a weight and energy that can never be infused by parish legislation; and in respect of an establishment for general security, it is doubly advantageous, by striking terror into the depredator, and arming the officer with augmented confidence and authority'.[16] Similarly, 'the mob quails before the simple baton of the police officer, and flies before it, well knowing the moral as well as physical force of the Nation, whose will, as embodied in law, it represents'.[17] Although both the strength and moral authority of the police required several years to develop, impersonal authority proved to be a secure foundation of police legitimacy.

Rowan and Mayne's notion of impersonality extended into many aspects of their force's structure and practice. They made the police into a tightly-disciplined body of professionals divorced from the localities they served. The men were kept out of partisan politics (Bobbies could not vote until 1885) and were often recruited from outside of London. They wore a blue uniform which further separated them from ordinary citizens. The Commissioners inculcated loyalty and obedience, enforced by quick dismissal for infractions, expecting the men to be models of good conduct by subordinating their impulses to the requirements of discipline and the legal system they represented. An observer of the 1850s vividly captured the police image: 'P.C. X59 stalks along, an *institution* rather than a man. We seem to have no more hold of his personality than we could possibly get of his coat buttoned up to the throttling point'.[18]

The New York policeman was less thoroughly molded than his London brother, but he did embody a distinct image which reflected conscious efforts as well as circumstantial results. His authority was *personal*, resting on closeness to the citizens and their informal expecta-tions of his power instead of formal bureaucratic or legal standards.[19] Instead of having to rise above social conflict by identification with the legal system, New York officials created a force which conformed to pre-existing, widely accepted patterns of democratic government. Survival of the new police depended originally on its ability to incorporate ideals of democracy in which authority was not only supposed to serve the people but also be the people. Until 1857, when the state government took over the force, it was directly controlled by popularly-elected local officials and policemen were recruited from the population of the district they patrolled. They did not wear a distinguishing blue uniform until 1853. As representatives of municipal instead of national government, the New York policeman did not have the symbolic authority his London colleague could invoke. Nor did he have the same reserve of physical force to back up his power: he was much more alone on the streets than his London colleague (New York always had fewer patrolmen in proportion to the citizens than London) and his effectiveness depended more on his personal strength than on broader institutional authority.[20]

New Yorkers rejected many important features of the London police as too authoritarian for democratic America. In the late fifties, the *Times* and Mayor Fernando Wood agreed that New York policemen were not as disciplined and efficient as their London brethren, but this was a necessary price of America's healthy social mobility and its citizens' independent spirit.[21] The New York patrolman was more a man than an institution because democracy suspected formal institutional power and profesional public officials.[22] Paradoxically, lack of institutional power also meant lack of institutional restraints, and the personal New York policeman often ended up with more awesome power than his impersonal London counterpart.

## II

The most important element of the distinction between the impersonal and personal approach is the amount of discretionary authority the patrolman exercised. Every policeman has to exercise personal discretion in his duties – decisions about when and how to act, whom to suspect and whom to arrest. Such choices are the most important part of his work, distinguishing the policeman from the soldier who does not act without direct orders.[23] Nevertheless, the commanders of the force and the judiciary set wide or narrow boundaries to discretion, and various public reactions to the police often center around the degree of discretion people think patrolmen should exercise. Consistent with his image of impersonal authority derived from the powers and restraints of the legal system, the London Bobby's personal discretion was more regulated than that of his New York colleague. Not as closely bound by the legal system, the New York patrolman often acted in the context of official and public toleration of unchecked discretionary power. The London policeman upholding an artistocratic, hierarchical society had more limits on his personal power than the democratic New York policeman.

The patrolman's most formidable discretionary power is his ability to use force to maintain his authority. The commanders of both the London and New York police warned their men to use lethal violence only for self-defense and prescribed punishments for violators of this essential principle.[24] In practice, however, the New York policeman's use of force was much less carefully monitored than in London.

As is well known, the London Commissioners carefully supervised Bobbies' use of force. They inculcated coolness and restraint, restricting the police arsenal to the truncheon. Except in unusually dangerous circumstances, London patrolmen never carried firearms. The Peelers could rely on muscle and blunt weapons partly because their antagonists were not usually more formidably armed, although revolvers seemed to be spreading in the underworld in the late sixties. There was some escalation of weaponry and incidents of unwarranted police violence did occur, but the Commissioners punished men who flouted their rule that restraint was the best way to win public acceptance of the force.[25]

New York's locally-controlled Municipal Police carried only clubs, but when the state government took over the force in 1857 – prompted by a mixture of reform and partisan motives – many New Yorkers violently expressed their hostility to the new Metropolitan force and the police replied in kind. Individual Captains encouraged their men to carry revolvers for self-protection against a heavily-armed under-world.[26] By the end of the 1860s, revolvers were standard equipment, although they were never formally authorized.[27] Guns seemed to be popping throughout the city, the civilians uncontrolled by effective legislation and the police unchecked by their superiors. The New York *Times* complained that shooting was becoming a substitute for arrest and described the patrolman as 'an absolute monarch, within his beat, with complete power of life and death over all within his range … without the forms of trial or legal inquiry of any kind'.[28] Amidst a vicious cycle of criminal and police violence, the patrolman was free to exercise much greater physical force than his London colleague.

Whether he made his arrest violently or quietly the New York patrolman consistently exercised broader personal discretion than the London Bobby. In both cities policemen had wide power to arrest people on suspicion of criminal intent, from stopping and searching people in the street to taking them to a magistrate for examination. Such arrests were more carefully scrutinized by police and judicial officials in London than in New York.

The London Commissioners reduced (although they did not eliminate) complaints of arbitrary arrest by warning their men to be extremely careful about whom they detained, directing that they pay attention to external indicators of social class as a guide to their suspicions.[29] These guidelines did not lift police scrutiny from workers in middle- and upper-class neighborhoods and Parliament endorsed this use of police authority and later expanded stop-and-search and arrest powers.[30] However, the judiciary contributed to control of police discretion by carefully checking patrolmen's grounds for arrest, and higher courts directed that people could be detained without formal trial and charges for only five days in normal circumstances or a maximum of two weeks in unusual cases.[31] Generally magistrates' committals of suspects for jury trial did not keep pace with London's population growth during the 1830–70 period, possibly reflecting declining crime or the shift of many petty offenses to a Justice of the Peace's summary jurisdiction from 1847 to 1861.[32] However, since the conviction rate in higher courts in proportion to magistrates' committals *increased* during the period, and higher court convictions in proportion to policemen's arrests also increased, it is quite likely that policemen were arresting and magistrates committing people on grounds that were increasingly firm over the years.[33]

Contemporary American observers testified to London's cautious use of arrest on suspicion when they mistakenly reported that Bobbies could arrest only for overt acts.[34] George W. Walling, who joined the New York force in 1848, said that 'A New York police officer knows he has been sworn in to "keep the peace", and he keeps it. There's no "shilly-shallying" with him; he doesn't consider himself half-patrolman and half Supreme Court judge'. He did not hesitate to arrest on suspicion even if it were 'often a case of "giving a dog a bad name and then hanging him", – men being arrested merely because they are known to have been lawbreakers or persons of bad character'.[35] Moreover, the Police Justices (elected Justices of the Peace) did not check this aggressiveness. Judges in over-crowded courts did not take time to investigate police charges, tacitly encouraging hasty or arbitrary arrests on suspicion by accepting police testimony without oath or corroboration, refusing prisoners the opportunity of defending themselves, and failing to inform them of their rights or frightening them into confessions.[36] People arrested on suspicion were usually held in the Tombs, but the magistrates also allowed the police to confine them in the station-house while they 'worked up a case' against them.[37] There was no time limit for detention on suspicion until a reforming judge instituted the English practice in the early 1850s. This seems to have satisfied the New York Prison Association, which had led a public outcry against abuses of detention on suspicion, but it did not attempt to change other practices.[38]

Discretion played an important part in arrests for overt acts as well as on suspicion. Checks could help prevent arbitrary arrests because sometimes both London and New York patrolmen charged people with disorderly conduct when their offense was merely unruliness or disrespect for the officer's authority.[39]

Rowan and Mayne warned Bobbies that 'No Constable is justified in depriving any one of his liberty for words only and language however violent towards the P.C. himself is not to be noticed ... a Constable who allows himself to be irritated by any language whatsoever shows that he has not a command of his temper which is absolutely necessary in an officer invested with such extensive powers by the law'.[40] They put teeth into the warning by forbidding desk officers to discharge people arrested for disorderly conduct who promised to behave in the future. Thus they prevented policemen from using the disorderly conduct charge to scare people into respecting them without having to bring a weak case before the magistrate. The only grounds for station-house discharge was false arrest, which had to be reported immediately to Scotland Yard.[41] Although they never eliminated arbitrary disorderly conduct arrests (an epidemic of them broke out in the sixties), the Commissioners kept them in check.[42]

The commanders of the New York force also expected their men to be calm under provocation, and a high official said that disorderly conduct arrests were covered by 'a good many rules'.[43] However, there is little to suggest that such arrests were limited in practice. A journalist contended that they usually depended 'exclusively upon the fancy of the policeman', who had 'a discretionary power that few use discreetly'.[44] New York patrolmen made many more disorderly conduct arrests than their London brethren. In 1851 they made one for each 109 people; London officers made one for each 380 people. In 1868–69, New York's absolute number of disorderly conduct arrests was greater than London's: 14,935 compared to only 2,616 in the much larger British metropolis.[45] Although there is plenty of evidence that New York was more rowdy than London,[46] the great discrepancy probably reflects London's discouragement of disorderly conduct charges. The heads of the New York force left disposition of patrolmen's charges, without any special checks on disorderly conduct arrests, up to station-house desk officers.[47]

New York patrolmen's free hand for disorderly conduct arrest may illustrate the use of personal action to compensate for lack of institutional authority. Patrolmen could not arrest for assault without a warrant unless they had seen the attack or the victim was visibly wounded. London policemen labored under a similar restriction until they were granted full powers in 1839. In New York, arrests for disorderly conduct may have compensated for limitations of arrest for assault.[48]

After arrest and lock-up came police interrogation and evidence-gathering. Earlier discussions of arrest on suspicion revealed that in New York there was little regulation of these practices. Judges readily accepted police evidence with little concern about how they obtained it. Moreover, the police had no scruples about obtaining confessions by entrapment or 'strategem'.[49]

In London all levels of the criminal justice system scrutinized interrogation and evidence-collection. With judges and high officials looking over their shoulders, the Commissioners reiterated warnings against false incrimination or distortion of evidence in the courtroom.[50] Repetition of such warnings suggests that policemen engaged in improper practices, but the men at the top were determined to keep them in line.

Until the 1850s, English courts were extremely sensitive about police interrogation, especially inducement of prisoners' confessions by promises or threats. Their concern may have been a carry-over from the days of a harsh penal code when confession of even minor crimes brought death or transportation for life.[51] The Commissioners' directives to their men reflected this sensitivity.[52] Sometimes Bobbies took such cautiousness too much to heart, preventing voluntary confessions because they feared criticism from judges and defense counsel.[53] Following a Court of Queen's Bench decision in 1852, judges began to relax their restrictions on confessions, increasingly accepting prisoners' statements as evidence against them. Nevertheless the Attorney General of England and the Police Commissioners were concerned that patrolmen not carry this too far by presenting all incriminating statements as confessions.[54] The courts seem to have returned to earlier strict interpretations in a case of 1865, and the police fell into line.[55]

Official concern was important because of the power of the police within the criminal justice system of England – they served as public prosecutors, taking charge of serious cases in the higher courts with jury trial as well as petty cases before magistrates. In New York, serious cases left police hands after arrest and became the popularly-elected District Attorney's responsibility. He decided whom to prosecute and how to conduct the case. Critics charged that he was lenient towards his constituents and abused 'plea bargaining', which allowed criminals to escape deserved punishment by pleading guilty to lesser offenses.[56] New York policemen, with greater leeway in arrest and interrogation practices than their London brethren, had less power over the outcome of serious cases. Because of the police role in the courtroom, the London Commissioners realized that suspicion of deceit or prosecutorial bias would undermine public acceptance of the force. Watchfulness at all levels of the criminal justice system satisfied a Parliamentary inquiry that England did not need a public prosecutor like the American District Attorney.[57]

The trial is the last stage of police participation in the administration of criminal justice. Police–judicial relations are important for understanding patrolmen's attitudes toward discretionary power and procedural regularity. From their viewpoint, their most significant relationship with judges is how many arrests are rewarded with convictions. A vital element of the policeman's psychology, convictions make the officer feel that his job is worthwhile, giving meaning to his work by validating his judgment to arrest a person. Having made a quick decision, he finds it hard to admit error.[58] Low convictions in proportion to arrests can make policemen into frustrated antagonists of the judiciary, ready to substitute street-corner justice for procedural regularity.

London Bobbies often criticized judicial decisions, but the Com-missioners insisted that they keep their comments to themselves and required strict decorum and impartiality in the courtroom.[59] Perhaps more significant, convictions for all crimes in the higher and lower courts increased relative to arrests during the mid-nineteenth century. Averaging about 45 percent of arrests during the 1830s and 1840s, convictions rose to around 55 percent of arrests during the 1860s.[60] Bad in the early years of the force, police–judicial relations improved after 1839, with settlement of a jurisdictional dispute between the Commissioners and magistrates.[61] Increasing convictions suggest that police and judicial standards of proper procedure were moving toward each other.

Although judges in New York made few procedural demands on policemen, from the early days of the force and increasingly after state takeover of the police in 1857 police officials complained of bad relations with the judiciary and charged judges with leniency toward major and minor offenders alike.[62] Lacking statistics comparable to those of London, it is difficult to evaluate these accusations. Available information indicates high conviction rates for drunkenness and vagrancy, slightly fewer convictions for petty larceny compared to arrests than in London, very few assault and battery convictions and in more serious crimes during the 1860s about one conviction for every three arrests.[63] Judges seem to have been more lenient toward serious than petty offenders, whereas in London conviction rates were generally higher for serious crimes.[64] Paradoxically, judges seemed to have overlooked arbitrary arrest practices but let many offenders off. This may have been a last-minute effort to regulate the police – Police Justice Michael Connolly was a crusader against brutality[65] – but the absence of clear guidelines for the police made patrolmen and judges into adversaries.[66] They never moved toward a single standard of conduct.

## III

Looking back over the survey of police practices, we have seen the London patrolman's impersonal authority resting on control of discretionary power through the legal system and the directives of the judiciary and heads of the force. In contrast, the New York policeman's authority rested on unregulated discretion and less concern for working within legal restraints. The two forces did not develop their images in isolation. As part of the societies which created them, public perceptions of crime and the role of the police were important underpinnings of their authority.

Recognizing that various classes or groups would react differentially to the police, the London Commissioners hoped that the new force had 'conciliated' the populace and obtained the goodwill of all respectable persons'.[67] On the whole they achieved this goal, although antagonism to the force remained in 1870.

'Respectable persons' were not always middle class, but the Victorian middle classes did see themselves as custodians of respectability. Although hardly united in interest and outlook, the groups composing the middle classes would have shared suspicion of a police too closely linked to the landed aristocracy. They accepted aristocratic domination of politics as long as it was not oppressive. They were always ready to criticize arbitrary policemen, but as their own political influence consolidated over the years, they came to see Bobbies mainly as useful servants for coping with the various unpleasantries of urban life. Rowan and Mayne noticed that predominantly middle-class complaints against the police shifted from oppressiveness to inefficiency during the 1830s. They had to remind complainants that policemen lacked legal power to do many of the things that were expected of them.[68]

The middle classes came to depend for protection and peace and quiet upon an institution which fostered social stability by the restrained exercise of power. Karl Polanyi's argument that the fragility of the industrial and commercial economy tied to the stock market made riotous disorder intolerable in the nineteenth century applies to repressive violence as well. 'A shooting affray in the streets of the metropolis might destroy a substantial part of the nominal national capital … stocks collapsed and there was no bottom in prices'.[69] In England the military, not the mob, had done the shooting in the past. A police force which contained disorder with a minimum of violence increased people's sense of security and contributed to economic stability. Generally, London's propertied classes believed that public order was steadily improving in the metropolis. Commentators recognized that police restraint as well as power contributed to this orderliness.[70] In the Sunday trading riots of 1855 in Hyde Park, when policemen got out of hand and brutalized innocent spectators as well as participants, the London *Times* joined radical working-class papers in condemning police excesses. The lesson was clear: respectable citizens as well as the populace expected restraint.[71] The middle classes, seeing themselves as the repository of such virtues, usually took pride in a police force with a reputation for respectability and 'habitual discretion and moderation of conduct'.[72]

During the sixties, a period of economic uncertainty and working-class unrest, 'respectable' fear of crime and disorder mounted. The garotting or mugging scare of 1862, the reform riot of 1866 and increasingly violent robberies along with hunger riots in the winters of the late sixties made Londoners question police efficiency. Significantly complaints focused on lack of manpower and the declining quality of recruits, poor administrative methods and excessive bureaucratization and militarization, instead of demands for arming the police or allowing them broader discretion than the law defined.[73] Parliament's response was tougher laws for the police to enforce rather than a redefinition of the force's impersonal authority. Alan Harding is right in calling some of the harsher provisions of the Habitual Criminals Act of 1869 (aimed at the paroled convicts whom most people blamed for the crime wave) 'positively medieval', but the act was a precise administrative control which judges interpreted strictly, continuing to monitor police discretionary power.[74] The new law expanded authority but also defined its limits. The police themselves recruited more men, reformed administrative procedures and after Mayne's death in 1868, expanded the detective division which he had always distrusted.[75] They did not resort to violence or unregulated discretionary power. Although strained by a crime wave, impersonal authority was still viable.

Having obtained and retained the 'good will' of at least most 'respectable persons', could the police achieve the more formidable goal of conciliating 'the populace'? Although working-class reaction to the police was as varied as the often conflicting and competing groups which made up the proletariat, generally a working man or woman was more likely to see the police (whom they preferred to call 'crushers' instead of 'Bobbies') as masters instead of servants. Subordination of the force to the legal systems simply meant that it was part of the apparatus which upheld 'one law for the rich, another law for the poor'. This view that the scales of justice were weighted in favor of the rich and powerful, and only slightly less so toward the middle classes, was the most common theme of working-class social criticism.[76] The Commissioners' concern for the rights of 'respectable' Londoners meant that social class was often the basis of police treatment of citizens. Although the Bobby was expected to be polite to 'all people of every rank and class', a writer friendly to the police could say, 'although well-dressed people always meet with civility … it is possible that the ragged and the outcaste may occasionally meet with the hasty word or unnecessary force from the constable, who is for them the despot of the streets'.[77] The other side of the coin is that some workers felt that the police were ignoring their neighborhoods, allowing disorder they would not tolerate in 'respectable' areas.[78] This partly reflected the dangerousness of some rookeries and dockland slums, but also the Commissioners' policy of 'watching St. James's while watching St. Giles's' – patrolling slum areas not to protect the inhabitants from each other, but to keep them from infiltrating nearby prosperous neighborhoods.[79] Workers could complain of both too much and too little police power. Their feelings came out in the popular music-hall songs of the sixties, such as 'The Model Peeler', an off-color account of police oppression and dereliction. 'Oh, I'm the chap to make a hit,/No matter where I goes it,' runs the chorus; 'I'm quite a credit to the force,/And jolly well they knows it./I take folks up, knock others down,/None do the thing genteeler,/I'm number 14 double X,/And called the Model Peeler'.[80] Impersonal authority, like so much else in Victorian England, seemed reserved for 'respectable' people.

Nevertheless, the force does seem to have worked toward conciliating 'the populace'. Except among persistently antagonistic groups like the coster-mongers,[81] the police did achieve at least a grumbling working-class acquiescence to their authority. By the 1860s, there was more violence against them in the music halls than on the streets.[82] Partly this acquiescence reflected the clearly-established power of the, force – 'People feel that resistance is useless', Mayne declared. However, the police also made some effort to reduce working-class antagonism. Their concern for restraint in handling political demonstrations was one (imperfectly achieved) aspect. They also deliberately stayed as much as possible away from the enforcement of Sunday blue laws, which working-class Londoners bitterly resented as middle-class dictation of their life style. This was not a case of failure to enforce existing laws, for that would undermine police subordination to the legal system, but of successfully lobbying in Parliament against new measures which evangelical Sabbatarians sought in the Victorian era.[83] Upholding a hierarchical social order, the police never won the 'good will' of the working classes, but because they rejected pure repression the Commissioners achieved at least acquiescence to police authority. The force had authority, not mere power.

Across the Atlantic the reactions of both middle- and working-class New Yorkers to the police were more ambivalent than in London. By limiting the force's institutional power but tolerating broad personal discretion, New York's officials revealed a distrust of institutions but great trust in men: Alexis de Tocqueville argued that democratic Americans empowered their officials with broad discretion because they elected them, being able to remove them if they were dissastisfied. In aristocracies like England, on the other hand, appointed officials independent of both rulers and ruled had to have more formal checks on their discretion to prevent oppression.[84] Although New York policemen were never themselves elected, they were at first directly and after 1853 indirectly accountable to elected officials and the broad directives of public opinion remained their guidelines instead of formal limitations of their personal power.

Turning from theory to public reactions to the police, Tocqueville's notion is complicated by the institutional rivalry of the police and judiciary. 'Respectable' New Yorkers, although they criticized democracy's immersion of the force in partisan politics and sought to move it closer to London's independent professionalism,[85] usually sided with the police in their controversy with the judiciary, which often owed its position to local, in many cases working-class Irish, constituencies. This taking of sides was most pronounced after state (Republican) take-over of the police in 1857, while the Police Justices remained in the unclean (Democratic) hands of local politicians who courted the votes of ignorant and impoverished immigrants. Thus, to a great extent, the propertied classes formed the constituency of the police force, while the propertyless made up the support of the lower levels of the judiciary, the Police Justices. Recurrent quarrels between police officials and judges were contests, to some extent before but especially after 1857, between representatives of different class and ethnic constituencies. Such battle lines had been occasionally drawn in the early years of the London force, but rarely later on.

Since respectable citizens did not expect justice from the courts, they turned to policemen, tolerating their broad personal authority in the war against crime. Although one's view of the police often depended on one's politics, this toleration frequently transcended partisanship. 'If to put down crime,' said the Democratic *Herald* in 1856, 'it were necessary for us to have a Turk as Chief of Police, we, for our own parts, would go for the Turk, turban, Koran and all.'[86]

A later journalist remarked of John A. Kennedy, the tough Republican General Superintendent of the Metropolitan Police, that although called 'king Kennedy' among 'the masses', respectable citizens regarded him more highly. 'He has often exceeded his power, and has committed acts that smack strongly of petty tyranny; but there can be no doubt of the fact that he has earnestly and faithfully labored for the cause of law and order.'[87] A little petty tyranny was acceptable in the interests of law and order, especially in light of 'a general, and perfectly natural feeling in the community, that it is a positive godsend to get rid of one of the many scoundrels who infest our streets, by any means and through any agency possible' when people lacked faith in 'the capacity or common honesty of our legal tribunals'.[88] New York was a violent city, whose disorder seemed to be steadily outstripping a police force plagued with manpower shortages and disciplinary problems. Citizens worried about the well-armed politically influential lumpenproletarian 'volcano under the city'.[89] Violence and distrust of the courts placed a premium on physical force and personal authority instead of London's restrained impersonal authority. Democratic ideology and disorder combined to create a policeman who often seemed more authoritarian than aristocratic England's London policeman.

How did New York's largely Irish immigrant 'masses' view the police? James Richardson suggests that they had fewer grievances against the locally-controlled Municipal Police than the state-controlled Metropolitan Police. Nevertheless, the large number of Irish patrolmen in Irish wards, because of the Municipal force's local residency requirement, did not guarantee smooth relations with the working class Irish public. Irish officers often arrested their countrymen for petty offenses, and complaints of violence or improper arrest, averaging some 29 a year between 1846 and 1854, were not much fewer when Irish officers confronted their countrymen than when WASP policemen dealt with Irish citizens.[90] Common ethnicity may not have been sufficient to overcome class antagonism – policemen seem to have been recruited from skilled workers while the people they arrested were pre-dominantly unskilled laborers.[91] Relations worsened under the state-controlled Metropolitan Police, despite a proportion of Irish patrolmen similar to the levels of the old force.[92] Hatred of the new force, often politically motivated underlay much of the draft rioters' ferocity, to which Irish policemen replied, in kind earning the gratitude of respectable New Yorkers.[93] Irish Democrats' antagonism to the Republican state force, roused by judicial and journalistic champions, resembled London radicals' hatred of the police in the 1830s. The anger was as much against whom the police represented as what they did.

The Metropolitan Police do not seem to have made efforts to reduce Irish working-class hostility. Their enforcement of Sunday laws, as bitterly resented by immigrants in New York as by London workers, increased hostility to the force. The old Municipal Police had ignored blue laws except under sporadic Sabbatarian pressures; the Metropolitans, responding to sustained Sabbatarian influence, enforced strict new measures which roused the opposition and evasion of normally peaceful Germans as well as the volatile Irish. The police could not claim impartiality when they enforced laws passed by one group against another's customs and amusements. Eventually enforcement of the blue laws broke down, becoming a convenient tool for Boss Tweed to keep saloon keepers in line and a lucrative source of pay-offs for all levels of the police force. Such corruption seems only to have increased 'respectable' criticism without significantly improving relations with the working classes.[94]

## IV

Although she wrote before the creation of New York's force, Harriet Martineau captured the difference between London and New York's police. She identified the English police as 'agents of a representative government, appointed by responsible rulers for the public good', and the American police as 'servants of a self-governing people, chosen by those among whom their work lies'.[95] The London policeman represented the 'public good' as defined by the governing classes' concern to maintain an unequal social order with a minimum of violence and oppression. The result was impersonal authority. The New York policeman represented 'self-governing people' as a product of that self-government's conceptions of power and the ethnic conflicts which divided that people. The result was personal authority.

*From William Miller 'Cops and Bobbies 1830–1870',* Journal of Social History, *1975 (Vol. IX), pp 73–88.*

## Notes

1   Notable exceptions are Selden D. Bacon's unpublished Ph.D. dissertation (Yale, 1939), 'The Early Development of American Municipal Police', and James F. Richardson's dissertation (New York University, 1961), 'The History of Police Protection in New York City, 1800–1870', which was not published until 1970 as part of his book *The New York Police: Colonial Times to 1901* (New York, 1970).
2   Allan Silver, 'The Demand for Order in Civil Society: A Review of Some Themes in the History of Urban Crime, Police and Riot', in David J. Bordua, ed., *The Police: Six Sociological Essays* (New York, c. 1967), 12–14.
3   For Rowan and Mayne, see Charles Reith, A *New Study of Police History* (Edinburgh, 1956) and Belton Cobb, *The First Detectives and the Early Career of Richard Mayne, Commissioner of Police* (London, 1957), both *passim*. Rowan served 20 years (1829–50), Mayne almost 40 years (1829–68). For the administrative history of the New York Police, see Richardson, *N.Y. Police,* chs. 2–7.
4   Michael Banton, *The Policeman in the Community* (New York, 1964), esp. ch. 8.
5   For background on the London police, see Charles Reith, *The Police Idea: Its History and Evolution in England in the Eighteenth Century and After* (London, 1938), and Leon Radzinowicz, *A History of English Criminal Law and Its Administration from 1750,* 4 vols. (London, 1948–68), vol. IV.
6   Walter Bagehot, *The English Constitution* (New York, n.d., first pub. 1868), 14 (quotation).
7   For English political history see e.g., Asa Briggs, *The Making of Modern England, 1784–1867: The Age of Improvement* (New York, 1965), chs. 5–10.
8   For the significance of America's federal system in violence and its control, see David J. Bordua 'Police', in David L. Sills, ed., *International Encyclopedia of the Social Sciences,* 17 vols. (New York c. 1968), XI, 175–6; Richard Hofstadter, 'Reflections on Violence in the United States', in Hofstadter and Michael Wallace, eds, *American Violence* (New York, 1971), 10.
9   George Templeton Strong, *Diary,* quoted by Richardson, *N.Y. Police,* 141–42; *Fincher's Trades Review,* July 25, 1863, quoted by David Montgomery, *Beyond Equality: Labor and the Radical Republicans 1862–1872* (New York, 1967), 106–7.
10   *Fincher's Trades Review, loc. cit.*
11   F.C. Mather, *Public Order in the Age of the Chartists* (Manchester, c. 1959), chs. I, III; Richardson, *N.Y. Police,* ch. 2.
12   Edwin Chadwick, 'On the Consolidation of the Police Force, and the Prevention of Crime', *Fraser's Magazine* 67 (Jan., 1868), 16. Full discussion of the consensual basis of police power is in Silver, 'Demand for Order', 6–15.
13   My contrast between impersonal and personal authority (discussed below) is my distillation of several writers' ideas, importantly from Banton, *Policeman in the Community.* See also James Q.

Wilson, *Varieties of Police Behavior: The Management of Law and Order in Eight Communities* (Cambridge, Mass., 1968), chs. 4–6, and Jerome Skolnick, *Justice without Trial: Law Enforcement in Democratic Society* (New York, c. 1966), 42–70. The impersonal and personal models are meant to be a rough guide, not, precise definitions.

14   Commissioners to J. Scanlon, March 2, 1842, Metropolitan Police Records, Public Record Office 1/41, letter 88301 (hereafter cited as Mepol).

15   Parliamentary Papers 1839, XIX, First Report, Constabulary Force Commissioners (hereafter cited as PP), 324. Rowan was one of the authors.

16   Anon., 'Principles of Police, and Their Application to the Metropolis', *Fraser's Magazine* 16 (Aug. 1837), 170.

17   Anon., 'The Police of London', *London Quarterly Review* (July 1870), 48, quoted by Silver, 'Demand for Order', 14.

18   A. Wynter, 'The Police and the Thieves', *Quarterly Review* 99 (June 1856), 171 also quoted by Silver, 'Demand for Order', 13–14. The writer goes on to say that off-duty, one sees the men as human beings: their public and private roles are separated. For the various features of the London police mentioned in this paragraph, see. e.g., Reith, *New Study*, chs. X–XIII.

19   See note 13 above.

20   In 1856, New York had one policeman per 812 citizens, London one per 351 (N.Y. City Board of Aldermen Documents, 1856, XXIII no. 10, Mayor's Annual Message, 35) (hereafter cited as BAD). For later complaints of shortages, see N.Y. State Assembly Documents, 1859, II no. 63, Metro Police Annual Report 1858 6–7 (hereafter cited as AD), and Edward Crapsey, *The Netherside of New York: Or, the Vice, Crime, and Poverty of the Great Metropolis* (New York, 1872), 12. For the features of the police mentioned in this paragraph, see Richardson, *N.Y. Police*, chs. 3–5.

21   N.Y. *Times*, Dec. 9, 1857 4; BAD–1856, XXIII no. 10, Mayor's Annual Message 33–4.

22   For the general mid-nineteenth-century suspicion of expertise, see Daniel Calhoun, *Professional Lives in America: Structure and Aspiration 1750–1850* (Cambridge, Mass. 1965), 4–15, 193–4; also Andrew Jackson's famous fears that professional officials would lose touch with the people and threaten the democracy in which 'the duties of public officers are, or at least admit of being made, so plain and simple that men of intelligence may readily qualify themselves for their performance' (James D. Richardson, comp., *A Compilation of the Messages and Papers of the Presidents*, 22 vols. [New York, c. 1897, ed. of 1915], III, 1012).

23   Among the most important discussions of police discretion are Banton, *Policeman*, 127–46; Skolnick, *Justice*, ch. 4; Wayne R. LaFave, *Arrest: the Decision to Take a Suspect into Custody* (Boston, 1965), *passim*: and Joseph Goldstein, 'Police Discretion not to Invoke the Legal Process: Low Visibility Decisions in the Administration of Justice', *Yale Law Journal* 69 (1960), 543–94.

24   Wynter, 'Poice and Thieves', 170; Police Orders (London) Sept. 6, 1832 (hereafter cited as PO), Mepol 7/2, folio 93; Aug. 21, 1830, Mepol 7/1, ff. 95–96. For New York, *Rules and Regulations for Day and Night Police of the City of New York; with Instructions as to the Legal Powers and Duties of Policemen* (New York, 1846), 6; *Ibid.*, 1851, 6–7; *Manual for the Government of the Police Force of the Metropolitan Police District of the State of New York* (in AD 1860, II no. 88), 90.

25   Charles Reith, *British Police and the Democratic Ideal* (London, 1943), 36; PP 1834, XVI, Metro. Police, test. Rowan, 12, q. 180; Kellow Chesney, *The Victorian Underworld* (London, 1970), 111, 119; [Thomas Wontner], *Old Bailey Experience* (London, 1833), 338; *Lloyd's Weekly Newspaper*, May 10, 1868, 6.

26   Richardson, 'History of Police Protection', 305–08; N.Y. *Herald*, July 14, 1857, 1; July 15, 1857, 1. Apparently some Municipal Policemen had carried pistols on dangerous assignments. William Bell, ms. *Journal* 1850–51 (New York Historical Society) describes an all-out battle with some rescuers of his prisoner. He intimidated them with his pistol, but in the ensuing affray the gun miraculously never went off. In 1857 one Captain told a reporter that George W. Matsell, Chief of the Municipal Police, had 'made it a standing rule to look upon every man as a coward and unfit to be put a second time on duty, where he had descended to the use of a pistol' (*Herald*, July 15, 1857, 1).

27   James D. MacCabe, *The Secrets of the Great City: A Work Descriptive of the Virtues and the Vices, the Mysteries, Miseries and Crimes of New York City* (Philadelphia, 1868), 72.

28   *Times*, May 10, 1867, 4; Nov. 18, 1858, 4 (quotation).

29   PO March 8, 1830, Mepol 7/1, f. 243; April 9, 1831, *Ibid.*, f. 193; Aug. 4, 1831, Mepol 7/2, f.20; PP 1837, Third Report, Criminal Law Commissioners, App. I, test. Mayne, 20.

30   In the Metropolitan Police Act of 1839, and the Habitual Criminals Act of 1869. There were enough fears of police power, however, that the 1839 Act's stop-and-search provisions were not adopted outside of London. See Delmar Karlen, Geoffrey Sawer, Edward M. Wise, *Anglo-American Criminal Justice* (New York, 1967), 116.

31    PO March 1, 1843, Mepol 7/8, f. 259; PP 1871, XXVIII, Metro. Police Annual Report 1870, 8; N.Y. State Senate Documents, 1856, II no. 97, Police Investigation (hereafter cited as SD) test. J.W. Edmonds, 166.

32    J.J. Tobias, *Crime and Industrial Society in the 19th Century* (London, 1967), 227–8. Contemporaries often used declining committals to verify their belief in declining crime, but modern students agree with Edwin Chadwick that committals reflect the reporting and prosecution of crime more than its actual occurrence. Chadwick, 'Preventive Police', *London Review* 1 (Feb. 1829), 260–2.

33    The basis of this conclusion is the committal and conviction figures in the Parliamentary *Returns of Criminal Offenders* before 1855 and the *Judicial Statistics,* 1856 on. See also sources cited in note 60 below.

34    M.H. Smith, *Sunshine and Shadow in New York* (Hartford, 1868), 180–1; George W. Walling, *Recollections of a New York Chief of Police* (New York, 1887), 196.

35    Walling, *loc. cit.*

36    SD 1856, II no. 97, Police Investigation Report, 3; test. Abraham Beal, General Agent New York Prison Association, 103–4; test. Police Justice Daniel Clark, 43; AD 1849, VI no. 243, Annual Report, N.Y. Prison Association 1848, 59 (hereafter cited as NYPA); AD 1850, VIII no. 198, NYPA 1849, 25–6.

37    SD 1856, II no. 97, Police Investigation, test. Police Justice G.W. Pearcey, 15, 23–4; test. Capt. G.W. Walling, 91–2; text. ex-Police Justice W.J. Roome, 34; SD 1861, II no. 71, test. Metro. Police Supt. J.A. Kennedy, 6–9.

38    For criticisms see AD 1849, VI no. 243, NYPA 1848, 44; AD 1850, VIII no. 198, NYPA 1849, 25–6. The NYPA dropped its attacks after the early fifties.

39    'Necessity is the mother of invention', *Punch* quipped, 'so when you find it necessary to make a charge against somebody you have locked up, invent one'. *Punch's Almanack for 1854,* 4, in *Punch's 20 Almanacks 1842–1861* (London, 1862?). Paul Chevigny, *Police Power: Police Abuses in New York City* (New York, c. 1969), ch. 8, discusses 'cover charges' like disorderly conduct in the modern context.

40    PO June 3, 1930, Mepol 7/1, ff. 63–4.

41    PO July 13, 1833, Mepol 7/2, f. 152.

42    See PO Jan 4, 1863, Mepol 7/24, 12; Sept. 30, 1865, Mepol 7/26, 275; Sept. 12, 1866, Mepol 7/27, 287.

43    *Rules and Regulations,* 1851, 38; *Manual,* 1860, 90; SD 1861, II no. 71, Police Investigation, test. Metro. Comm. T.C. Acton, 29 (quotation).

44    Crapsey, *Netherside,* 27; SD 1861, II no. 71, Police Investigation, test. Police Justice J.H. Welch, 14.

45    1851 figures: PP 1852–53, LXXXI, Arrest Statistics, 290; BAD 1856, XIII no. 16, Chief's Semi-Annual Report, 12–13. I computed the ratios from London's estimated population, 1851, in the above source and New York's 1851 population in Joseph Shannon, comp. *Manual of the Corporation of the City of New York* 1868 (New York, 1869), 215. London 1869 figures are in PP 1870, XXXVI, Metro. Police Annual Report 1869, table 5, 18 (listing 'disorderly characters' which I have assumed to be the same as disorderly conduct). N.Y. figures are in AD 1870, II no. 16, Metro. Police Annual Report 1869, 74. The disparity of these latter figures is all the more impressive considering that London was over twice as populous as New York.

46    See below, note 89.

47    SD 1861, II no. 71, Police Investigation, test. Comm. T.C. Acton, 25.

48    The policy is set forth in *Rules and Regulations,* 1846, 39; and *Ibid.,* 1851, 55. The phrasing is verbatim from London's PO June 25, 1833, Mepol 7/2, f. 14. The *Manual,* 1860 is silent on assault powers.

49    SD 1856, II no. 97, Police Investigation test. Capt. J. Dowling, 149; Walling, *Recollections,* 38–9.

50    PO July 26, 1851, Mepol 7/15, f. 290; Feb 26, 1869, Mepol 7/31, 58; Memo of 1854 by Mayne, Mepol 2/28, loose.

51    For judicial sensitivity, see the case of *Regina v. Furley,* Central Criminal Court 1844, in *1 Cox's Criminal Law Cases* 76. The court constructed the policeman's traditional warning to suspects that what they say may be held against them as a threat or inducement to confession. For possible impact of old harsh, see PP 1845, XIV, Eighth Report, Criminal Law Commissioners, App A, letter of H.W. Woolrych, 281.

52    PO Nov. 3, 1837, Mepol 7/5, f. 284.

53    PO May 15, 1844, Mepol 7/9, f. 245; PP 1845, XIV, Eighth Report, Criminal Law Commissioners, App. A, letter of Lord Chief Justice Denman, 211; William Forsyth, 'Criminal Procedure in Scotland and England' (1851) in *Essays Critical and Narrative* (London, 1874), 41–42.

54  The case if *Regina's v. Baldry*, Court of Queen's Bench 1852, in 2 *Dennison's Crown Cases Reserved* 430. See also James Fitzjames Stephen, *A History of the Criminal Law of England*, 3 vols. (London, 1883), I, 447. For Commissioners' views, Mayne's 1854 memo, Mepol 2/28; the views of Attorney General A.J.A. Cockburn are in PP 1854–55, XII. Public Prosecutors, 186, q. 2396.

55  PO Sept. 22, 1865, Mepol 7/26, 268; Jan. 2, 1866, Mepol 7/27, 13.

56  AD 1866, III no. 50, NYPA 1865, 128, 134, 150; AD 1865, III no. 62, NYPA 1864, 222; Alexander Callow, *The Tweed Ring* (New York, c. 1965), 148.

57  See PP 1854–55, XII, Public Prosecutors, report and testimony.

58  William A. Westley, *Violence and the Police: A Sociological Study of Law, Custom, and Morality* (Cambridge, Mass., c. 1970), 81–82; Albert J. Reiss, Jr., *The Police and the Public* (New Haven, 1971), 134–8.

59  PP 1837–38, XV, Police Offices, test. Rowan, 101, q. 1078; PO Nov 29, 1829, Mepol 7/1, f. 241; Nov. 5, 1830, Mepol 7/1, f. 130; July 9, 1834, Mepol 7/3, f. 45; Sept 27, 1837, Mepol 7/5, f. 279; July 26, 1851, Mepol 7/15, f. 290; Memo of 1854, Mepol 2/28, loose; PO May 13, 1865, Mepol 7/26, 138.

60  I have computed these approximate percentages from statistics in Anon., 'The Police System of London', *Edinburgh Review* 96 (July 1852), 22 (1831–41); Joseph Fletcher, 'Statistical Account of the Police of the Metropolis', *Journal of the Statistical Society* 13 (1850), 258 (1842–48); PP 1871, XXVIII, Metro. Police Ann. Report 1870, 21 (1850–70).

61  See Reith, *New Study*, 150–1; Radzinowicz, *English Criminal Law*, IV, 172ff.

62  BAD 1852, XIX pt 1 no. 7, Chief's Semi-Annual Report, 107; SD 1856, II no. 97, test. Capt. J.W. Hartt, 101; Capt. J. Dowling, 157; AD 1861, I no. 27, Metro. Police Ann. Report 1860, 6; AD 1867, VII no. 220, Metro. Police Ann. Report 1866, 11–12.

63  Tenth Precinct Blotter, May 25–Aug. 27, 1855; July 27–Aug. 26, 1856, Ms. N.Y. City Municipal Archives; SD 1861, II no. 71, Police Investigation, test. Comm. T.C. Acton, 27; J.W. Edmonds, 163–64. Arrest figures for assault and battery and petty larceny are found in the police annual reports. They can be compared with convictions for these offenses in the Court of Special Sessions published in Shannon, comp., *Manual* 1868, 178. Convictions for 'simple larceny' in London were 54 percent of arrests in 1868; for petty larceny in New York 29 percent of arrests in 1868–69. Convictions for 'common assault' in London in 1869 were 55 percent of arrests compared to New York's 8 percent for assault and battery in 1868–69. (See AD 1870, II no. 17, Metro. Police Ann. Report 1869, 24 [arrests]; AD 1870, VI no. 108, Ann. Report of the Secretary of State on Criminal Statistics 1869. 144–6 [convictions]; PP 1870, XXXVI, Metro. Police Annual Report 1869, table 5, 18). Comparison of N.Y. felony arrests and convictions is in AD 1867, VII no. 20, Metro. Police Annual Report, 1866, 11–12.

64  This is based on a comparison of the proportion of convictions in indictable offenses and offenses summarily tried by a magistrate in the Parliamentary *Judicial Statistics*, 1856–70.

65  See N.Y. *Times*, April 14, 1867. 5; N.Y. *World*, Feb. 11, 1867, 4.

66  For this remark I am indebted to a letter from James Richardson, commenting on an earlier draft of this paper.

67  PO Oct. 15, 1831, Mepol 7/2, f. 41.

68  See statement (of which I could not locate the original) quoted in Reith, *British Police*, 183, and Comms. to Home Office Jan 6, 1835, Mepol 1/17, letter 27751. By 1835 complaints in the Mepol letter books are overwhelmingly of alleged neglect of duty. Later Mayne wrote to H. Fitzroy, Sept. 29, 1853: 'The public now expect to see a constable at all places at every moment that he may be required' (Mepol 1/46, n.p.).

69  Karl Polanyi, *The Great Transformation* (New York, 1944), 186–7, phrase order rearranged.

70  Some contemporary comment on orderliness in the 1850s includes Charles Dickens, 'The Sunday Screw', *Household Words* 1 (June 22, 1850), 291–2; *Illustrated London News* 18 (May 31, 1851), 501 and June 28, 1851, 606, on working-class orderliness at the Great Exhibition; Wynter, 'Police and Thieves', 173. On the police role, see Frederic Hill, *Crime: Its Amount, Causes, and Remedies* (London, 1853), 6–7; Anon., *The Great Metropolis*, 2 vols., 2nd ed. (London, 1837), I, 11; PP 1837–8, XV, Police Offices, test. Rowan and Mayne, 183–5, qq. 2091, 2094, 2102; PP 1854–5, X, Sale of Beer, test. Mayne, 86, q. 1138. See also Silver, 'Demand for Order', 5.

71  London *Times*, July 3, 1855, 8; *Reynold's Newspaper*, July 29, 1855, 8; *Lloyd's Weekly Newspaper*, July 8, 1855, 6. According to the *Times*, July 16, 1855, 12, overt antagonism to the police was short-lived. The riots are discussed by Brian Harrison, 'The Sunday Trading Riots of 1855', *Historical Journal* 7 (1965), 219–45.

72  Anon, 'The Metropolitan Police and What Is Paid Them', *Chambers's Magazine* 41 (July 2, 1864), 424.

73  Good accounts of complaints and the state of the force are in the *Times*, Dec. 29. 1868, and in 'Custos', *The Police Force of the Metropolis in 1868* (London, 1868).

74  Alan Harding, *A Social History of English Law* (Baltimore, 1966), 366; W.L. Burn, *The Age of Equipoise: A Study of the Mid-Victorian Generation* (New York, c. 1965), 176–94.

75 J.F. Moylan, *Scotland Yard and the Metropolitan Police* (London, 1929) 150–7. For Mayne's distrust of detectives, see, e.g., Memo to Superintendents, Jan. 23, 1854, Mepol 2/28, loose. Mayne did turn more to detection in the sixties than earlier, but his successor as Commissioner, Col. E.Y.W. Henderson, considerably expanded the detective force. See PP 1870, XXXVI, Metro. Police Ann. Report 1869, 3–4.

76 For expressions of this grievance, see *Illustrated London News* 3 (Dec. 23, 1843), 406; see also *Reynold's Newspaper*, May 2, 1852, 8; July 25, 1858, 9; Aug. 17, 1862, 4; April 5, 1863, 4; Feb. 9, 1868, 4; *Lloyd's Weekly Newspaper*, July 5, 1863, 1; Thomas Wright, *Our New Masters* (London, 1969, first pub. 1873), 155–6.

77 PP 1830, XXIII, Instructions to Metro. Police, 11; Anon., 'Metropolitan Police', 426. Cf. Mrs J.C. Byrne, *Undercurrents Overlooked*, 2 vols. (London, 1860), I, 51, 54–5.

78 *East London Observer*, June 6, 1868, 5; July 4, 1868, 4; Dec. 5, 1868, 4.

79 For danger, Chesney, *Victorian Underworld*, 92–3; Byrne, *Undercurrents*, I, 78–9; James Greenwood, *The Wilds of London* (London, 1874), 1, 56. For police policy, PP 1834, XVI, Metro. Police, test. Rowan, 11, qq. 165–7; *Hansard's Parliamentary Debates* 1830, n.s. vol. 25, col. 358; and Anon., 'Police System of London', (1852), 9. Study of the distribution of the London police reveals the most policemen usually in neighbourhoods where poverty rubbed shoulders with wealth.

80 'The Model Peeler' by C.P. Cove, *Diprose's Music-Hall Song-Book* (London, 1862), 50. Cf. the number Mrs. Byrne heard in 1860 in *Undercurrents*, I, 256–7.

81 For the costermongers, see Henry Mayhew, *London Labour and the London Poor*, 4 vols. (2nd ed., 1862–64), I, 22.

82 For workers as leaders of the early opposition, see *Hansard's Parliamentary Debates 1833*, 3rd. ser. vol. 16, col. 1139; PP 1833, Cold Bath Fields Meeting, test. Supt. Baker, C Division, 159, qq. 3914, 3917; J. Grant, *Sketches in London* (London, 1838), 391.

83 Mayne states his outlook on this problem succinctly in PP 1867–8, XIV, Sunday Closing, 8, qq. 127–8.

84 Alexis de Tocqueville in Francis Bowen, ed., *Democracy in America*, 2 vols. (2nd ed., Cambridge, Mass., 1863; first pub. in U.S. 1835–40), I, 265–8.

85 See Richardson, *N.Y. Police*, chs. 3–5, 7.

86 *N.Y. Herald*, March 25, 1856, 4.

87 MacCabe, *Secrets*, 70–1. The *Herald*, however, did not like the Republican Superintendent, calling him 'Mr. Fouche' Kennedy' (Dec. 22, 1860, 6).

88 *Times*, Nov. 18, 1858, 4, editorializing on the first killing of an offender by a patrolman.

89 William O. Stoddard's *The Volcano under the City* (New York, 1887) is an account of the draft riots which reminds its readers that the volcano is still simmering. For similar imagery see Samuel B. Halliday, *The Lost and Found: Or, Life among the Poor* (New York, 1860), 332; and Junius Henri Bowen, *The Great Metropolis: A Mirror of New York* (Hartford, 1869), 74. On New York's violence, see Richardson, 'History', 393ff.; *Times*, May 10, 1855, 4; AD 1859, II no. 63, Metro. Police Ann. Report 1858, 14; AD 1865, II no. 35, Metro. Police Ann. Report 1864, 11–13; Crapsey, *Netherside*, 29–30; and especially Charles Loring Brace, *The Dangerous Classes of New York, and Twenty Years' Work among Them* (New York, 1872), arguing that New York could claim 'elements of the population even more dangerous than the worst of London' (p. 25).

90 The figures are rough calculations based on the surnames of officers and complainants in the Complaints against Policemen, 1846–1854, City Clerk Papers, N.Y.C. Municipal Archives.

91 This conclusion rests on fragmentary records, the Applications for Positions as Policemen 1855, Boxes 3209–10, City Clerk Papers, N.Y.C. Municipal Archives. Of 43 successful applicants, only 3 were unskilled laborers and 7 drivers or other transport workers. Twenty-two were various sorts of skilled workers, one a mechanic, five shopkeepers, five clerks or other white-collar workers. The arrest statistics in the police reports reveal the overwhelming preponderance of unskilled offenders.

92 For the increase of Irish officers in the Metropolitan Police after a decline in 1857–58, I counted Irish surnames in the lists in D.T. Valentine, comp., *Manual of the Corporation of the City of New York* (New York, 1848–68), for 1856 (last year of the old force), 1858 and 1861 (the last year policemen's names are listed).

93 See AD 1864, III no. 28, Metro. Police Ann. Report 1863, 13. Joel Tyler Headley, *The Great Riots of New York 1712–1873* (New York, 1873), 305–6, MacCabe, *Secrets*, 70–1, praise the Irish policemen.

94 See Richardson, *N.Y. Police*, 52, 57, 110, 154–6, 182–5.

95 Harriet Martineau, *Morals and Manners*, (Philadelphia, 1838), 192. Here 'police' refers to the old constabulary and night watch system which preceded modern forces in America.

# 4. A 'new police' in Australia

*Mark Finnane*

In contrast to police in England, America or Canada, most police in Australia are characterised by their organisation on a State-wide jurisdiction.[1] Like the Irish constabulary, which provided many of the early personnel and some of the organisational principles of police in Australia, the colonial police were, in general, administered from the capitals of the colonies. This important fact defined the conditions under which policing in Australia has operated only weakly as a community resource rather than a state imposition.

What were the factors which produced in Australia a centralised, bureaucratically organised police substantially autonomous of political control? The early developments were dominated by the colonial condition of settlement in Australia. Social conditions, anxieties about the new societies as well as the prevailing forms of government were all intimately involved. The inter-relation of these factors was played out differently in the various colonies. For most of the colonies, however, the crucial developments were at mid-century during the attainment of colonial self-government. To understand the colonial formation of Australian policing we must understand above all what occurred in the mid-nineteenth century.

## The idea of the police

Histories of police provide two quite different accounts of the formation of modern police. The first says that crime is a perennial problem, that it has been accelerated by the conditions of modern life, especially by industrialism and urbanisation and that police forces were created as a response to rising crime. In this view policing is essentially a good thing, and police forces represent the successful achievement by the modern state of a means of social control in the absence of the norms and social bonds of traditional community life.

The second account suggests that modern police forces are marked by the conditions of their emergence in societies socially divided, above all by class. Police forces are not socially neutral instruments of a general social will for order, but the creation of specific interests seeking to maintain their conditions of privilege in an unequal society. Hence, police inevitably function to protect the interests of the dominant class in society.[2]

In Australia, the former position was taken by the author of the first substantial work on police. In *The Australian Police Forces*, published in 1960, a Victorian police public relations officer, G.M. O'Brien, reviewed briefly the formation and subsequent history of each of the State police forces. For O'Brien, the 'police force is, in the democratic communities of the British Commonwealth, society's shield and safeguard', a bulwark against anarchy as he put it.[3] More recently, the historian of the Victoria Police, Robert Haldane, has presented a view of that force which, while not seeking to hide many unsavoury elements of its history, presents it primarily as the police which the people deserved.[4] In its rhetorical context such a claim is perhaps unexceptional. Yet its view of 'the people' is too generalised and unhistorical in its presumption of the capacity of the general will to influence decisively the shape and functions of institutions like the police. Such accounts also adopt a teleology of police development whereby all that has happened in the past may always be explained by the history of progress. When a police historian writes that in 1853 'the nexus between Justices and local Constables was severed, thereby bringing Western Australia's police organisation into the nineteenth century',[5] the meaning of police history is reduced to a positive progression from antiquity to modernity.

By contrast, radical critics of the police in Australia, while rarely devoting extended treatment to the history of the police, have viewed the police as inevitably, and usually wilfully, the agents of an oppressive state. Thus it was one of the greatest signs of the treacherous nature of the convicts, according to Humphrey McQueen, that some so willingly played the role of policeman. In their structuralist account of Australian history, Connell and Irving see the police as a state apparatus which played a central role in organising the development of Australian capitalism and the consent of the working classes. In the view of Andrew Moore, historian of the 'secret armies' which were a feature of inter-war political history, there is 'a special relationship which exists between police forces and the capitalist class', intensified at times of crisis.[6] The history of policing in Australia as in other societies suggests much to confirm such views of the importance of the police to the interests of the powerful within government and outside it.

Nevertheless, in their attention primarily to the functions of police (expression of the social will to order or protection of class interests), neither of these views is sufficient to understand the conditions under which police developed in Australia. Since Australian police forces were formed in precisely that period which helped define what the modern idea of police should be, we need to attend to the development of that idea and the contexts of its generation.

When the first European settlers arrived at Botany Bay in 1788, they did not bring with them the rudiments of a police force. What did arrive was some consciousness of the role of 'the constable'.[7] The security of the settlement was primarily the responsibility of the military, sent with the First Fleet. But within a short period of time there was already a proposal, from within convict ranks even, for the appointment of a constable who would assist in the prevention of theft and assault in the settlement of Sydney. The proposal arose in a context which would have been conscious of the demands for reform of the police which had been emerging since the middle of the eighteenth century.

These demands arose in the major urban centres of the British Isles. In the largest, London, the magistrates John and Henry Fielding had initiated the major English police experiment of the eighteenth century – the Bow Street Runners. In the second largest, Dublin, the first town or city police Act of Britain or Ireland had created the Dublin Metropolitan Police in 1786. In spite of the later preoccupation of historians of police with a distinction between the 'civilian' style policing of London and the paramilitary style of Irish policing (allegedly highly influential in colonial contexts), the impetus to police reform in the late eighteenth and early nineteenth centuries was strongly urban, preventive and 'civil'.[8]

What characterised the demands for police reform from this time was above all the suggestion for a paid and permanent police. Insofar as there existed a police before this time, it was voluntaristic, and locally-organised. The much vaunted 'English constable' was an ancient office, subject to the direction of local magistrates or justices of the peace. By the late eighteenth century, the effectiveness of the office was being attacked.[9]

The idea of police reform, as it developed in early nineteenth-century England, was diverse in objective. When some spoke of a new police they conceived of an agency which would bring about order not just through increasing the certainty of apprehension, but by extending the regulation of social life. Hence Patrick Colquhoun advocated in 1803 a police for London which would encompass a wide range of duties. An organised police would make possible a better society because it would bring under notice an extraordinary range of irregularities which characterised the unwieldy metropolis of London.

In these ideas Colquhoun was evoking a concept of police which was more familiar on the continent of Europe. There, especially in Germany, the articulation of a method of statecraft had included a general theory of the administration of society by a centralised 'police'. In this context 'police' was something more than its institutional embodiment: it summed up the possibility of a government of social life for the well-being of the whole population.[10] In the social reform England of the 1830s, the generalised potential of police received a powerful push from the ambitions of the social reformer and bureaucratic architect, Edwin Chadwick, who extended the concept of regulation of urban life in ways which suggested the continuing importance of a broad-ranging concept of police.[11] In later police histories this broader notion of police was suppressed, in spite of the significant number of non-crime functions of police which continued in the nineteenth century and later.[12]

While such an all-encompassing notion of the idea of 'police' takes us some distance from the particular development of police in Britain, Ireland or Australia, its significance lies in it marking one end of a spectrum of possibilities for the scope of policing. Indeed, we will see that in the sometimes peculiar circumstances of colonial settlement, police took on functions which have all the marks of being part of the exercise of government broadly conceived.

To this idea of police – one which stressed the contributions which a well administered constabulary might make to the general welfare of society – another and more familiar one was added. This stressed the role of police in the control of public disorder. In England, and especially in Ireland, social protest and dissent in the early nineteenth century prompted numerous proposals for a permanent police which could maintain the peace. In the former, local resistance to the demands of central government limited the speedy adoption of a permanent police to London (1829), only slowly spreading to other cities, towns and boroughs in the following three decades. In Ireland, with a weaker local government base, the central government based in Dublin Castle framed initiatives for the establishment of a regular constabulary, from 1814 on, with a view to enforcing a minimum standard of order in the heavily populated and unruly countryside. The formation of the Irish constabulary as a nationwide permanent police in 1836 represented a determination to establish conditions of order in a society which was already, in the words of one of its historians, a 'social laboratory'.[13]

Disorder itself was not a unified subject of concern. The violence of early nineteenth-century Ireland, with agrarian crimes sharing a sometimes invisible boundary with political protest, was disorder of quite a different kind to that of urban crime which preoccupied many of the theories of English policing. The functions of the peace preservation forces in Ireland, which preceded the Irish constabulary, were reactive: the outbreak of trouble in a disturbed district would lead to the dispatch of a unit of armed police to quell the trouble. Much was hoped, however, of the urban police in terms of their preventive function – regular patrolling would limit the incidence of crime. As time went on these two principles converged. The Irish constabulary, with its rural barracks and patrols which went out from them, was comparable in many respects to the urban police whose early days were marked by a good deal of hostility in various centres in the British Isles.[14]

In the context which most influenced Australian policing, the idea of police thus emerges as one which is complex in composition. It encompassed ideas of good government at one extreme, justifying non-crime functions which police have often had to assume even if under protest. In the form more familiar to us today the police would act as a more effective means of controlling crime through detection of criminals and prevention of criminal acts. At the other end of the spectrum, the police would act as the ultimate guarantors of social and political order through the control of dissent and protest.

How influential were these ideas of policing in the early colonial period in Australia? And what were the institutional means of their transmission? That is, to what extent were the ideas which found embodiment in the new police in Britain and Ireland reproduced or transformed in the colonial context? We know (potentially at least) a good deal about ideas of policing in the colonial period because they were important matters of political debate. Moreover, the specifically British and Irish dominance of colonial culture, regenerated by migration in every decade of the nineteenth century, meant that colonial ideas about police and criminal justice shared an immediacy with those being considered in the United Kingdom.

Hence, in considering the police arrangements in New South Wales in 1856, the Board appointed by the colonial secretary favoured 'a general system of trained Police', one which was explicitly modelled on the new police forces in the

British Isles. The model, it is fair to say, was somewhat fuzzy in its definition, but the mid-century appreciation of the innovative character of police developments in Britain and Ireland is evident in the Board's summary of the rationale for the police:

> The principle involved in the system on which the Irish, the London Metropolitan, and the various bodies of the new Rural Police in the counties of Great Britain have been formed, which is now partially in existence here …we understand to consist in this: – That the Executive Police should be subject to an uniformity of discipline and ultimate direction throughout large tracts of country and, to a certain extent, throughout an entire territory.[15]

While favouring a separation of 'judicial and executive functions,' the Board reserved its opinion on the relation between the magistracy and police, a subject of considerable contention in these decades. A matter of interest in the Board's statement of the principle of the new police, is the clear equation of the Irish and various British police forces, by contrast with the tendency of later commentators to distinguish between these two forces. The core of the police, in the Board's view, was its uniform discipline and direction under a governing authority.

Hence the pattern, familiar to Australian historians, of deference to ideas from 'Home' is repeated in policing matters. Yet it was evident to these colonial politicians that colonial circumstances required colonial solutions. A failing of the existing police Act was, said the Board, 'the machinery established therein not having been suitable for adapting a general system of trained Police to the peculiar circumstances of this Colony'.[16] Thus deference to imperial example did not mean indifference to local contexts. The shape of policing organisation was an outcome, not just of ideas, but of state formation and social conditions in the settlements.

## The colonial state

Australian police forces are today distinguished by a particular relation to government which can be traced in its legal form to statutes of the mid-nineteenth century. The colonial Acts creating police forces specified that the police were to be headed by a single responsible officer, variously titled commissioner, chief commissioner or inspector-general, who was to administer the police subject to the direction of the colonial secretary or other responsible minister.

These colonial legislaters required that the police were to be controlled from the centre of political power, rather than by local authorities. Correlatively, the police in each colony was to be a single, unified body. Policing was a function for which the state, rather than local communities, took responsibility. The control of all police by a single officer made for hierarchical, and increasingly bureaucratic organisations. The police statutes reflected political choices perhaps appropriate to early colonial society but not for ever after. In these, as in many other matters of government in Australia, however, the institutional frameworks determined at an early stage proved remarkably resilient.

Such choices about administration of the police also imply exclusions. A decision to vest authority in a single commissioner subject to the direction of the colonial secretary excluded for the most part the magistracy and judiciary from an overview of policing practices. It excluded too the participation or supervisory role of locally elected or representative officials. In consequence, the commissioner became the most important figure in policing, since few ministers would be in a position to know or be capable of knowing the intricacies of a police organisation.

Yet the tendency to a uniform and centralised pattern of organisation in Australian police forces was not immediately consolidated. The process of centralisation of colonial police in Australia involved the attrition of at least three important institutional arrangements of the earliest periods of colonial policing in Australia. First, the early system of magistrate control of police was passed over in favour of control by executive government through the police commissioner. Second, local forces, and thereby the possibility of local control, were eliminated. Third, the process required a suppression of specialised police, those who had previously operated under a strictly limited remit. In sum, the story was one of the substantial accretion of state executive power in Australia in the matter of policing.

Who should control the police? The matter was, at one level, scarcely a subject for contention. The police were established at the instance of the governing authorities. In New South Wales, the governors from Captain Phillip on were authorised to appoint constables and in 1810 Macquarie appointed a permanent police for Sydney under a superintendent and 'Police Magistrate', D'Arcy Wentworth. There began a mode of organisation of policing which was strongly determined by government direction. Victoria and Queensland, as off-shoots of this jurisdiction, shared with it a police directed by government.

In South Australia, policing was again organised at the instance of the governor from the earliest stages of settlement. Reluctance of free settlers (indeed the 'greatest repugnance' in the governor's words) to assume the office of constable led to Governor Hindmarsh requesting Colonial Office approval for establishing a police force.[17] When South Australia some decades later assumed responsibility for the Northern Territory, its policing responsibilities were carried out through a sub-inspector answerable (in theory) to the commissioner in Adelaide.[18] In Western Australia, the responsibility for policing was immediately assumed by the Lieutenant Governor, Captain James Stirling, who appointed justices who were to be responsible for constables appointed on a part-time basis. The role of initially strong state control is confirmed by the case of Tasmania, which was at first governed by a network of police magistrates responsible directly to Governor Arthur. Only later did decentralisation mark Tasmania off briefly from the rest of the country.[19]

For all of the Australian colonies, therefore, the control of police was from the earliest moment vested in the governor. Yet the path from the governor's prerogative in the appointment of constables or police forces under single police heads with substantial authority was not inevitable. It was fought out in often contentious circumstances.

This was so because governors did not retain absolute authority in colonies which were growing at a sometimes furious pace. Most obviously was this the case in the 1850s. But the changing mix of population in a place like New South Wales produced social conflict between old and new settlers and between emancipated convicts and free settlers in particular. The justices of the peace, originally appointed by governors as a means of securing order in the infant colonies, sought power in their own right and in some places opposed the pretensions and power of the government-directed police magistrates. Colonial politics consisted for much of the period before self-government in struggles between what was often seen as the autocratic power of governors and the aspirations of civilian justices to a power of their own.

This politics impacted on the history of policing through the issue of control of the police. The appointment of police constables subject to the direction of magistrates was a common feature of early police organisation. The distinction between policing and judicial functions as separate offices was blurred at this time. Hence, the superintendence of police was frequently in the hands of government-appointed police magistrates whose tasks were also those of adjudicating in the summary courts.[20]

It was this arrangement which was fundamentally altered by the re-organisation of policing at mid-century and later. The establishment of administrative control by an officer such as a commissioner rather than by a local magistrate was a clear direction of government to separate judicial and policing functions. Vestiges of the former role of magistrates were retained to a limited degree in disciplinary proceedings in Victoria, for example, the *Police Act* of 1853 empowered local magistrates to 'discipline' police in their locality by hearing summary cases of complaints against the police.[21] In Queensland, the legislation went somewhat further than this, at least for the first six years, when police magistrates were given responsibility as inspectors of police for their districts, in spite of the primary control being exercised by the commissioner in Brisbane. The result was profound administrative confusion, with evidence that magistrates were responsible for the policing of their districts, but not able to control the movement of police in and out of them, at the behest of the commissioner in Brisbane. In spite of support from Darling Downs squatters and their political friends for the role of the magistrates in policing, the appointment of police magistrates as inspectors was brought to an end in 1870. Thereafter the magistrates' role contracted to that of hearing charges against police in disciplinary matters.[22]

The matter of judicial versus bureaucratic control of the police was linked in some ways to the issue of local control through municipal government of police. As we have seen, police in Australia were not some outgrowth of community innovation – they were a state-authorised imposition. Nevertheless, the expansion of police was often a response to local demands for security, whether against Aborigines, or against bushrangers, gold robbers and stock thieves as well as disorder in rural towns. Prior to the consolidation of police at mid-century, the mechanism of response to such requests for local protection was extension of the *Towns Police Act* to particular locales. Under such an arrangement in New South Wales, police constables were appointed by and responsible to local magistrates. The development of a structure of local government in the 1840s provided an opportunity for true local political control of policing arrangements. As Palmer explains, the attempts of Governor Gipps in 1842 to establish district councils entailed a shift from central to at least part local funding of police. But even where this ambition succeeded in winning local support, as in the incorporation of Melbourne, the difficulty of raising local rates proved an enormous stumbling block. Moreover, the political elite in the legislative council rebuffed Gipps' attempt to require half the cost of police to be raised by local government.[23]

Outside New South Wales (and perforce Victoria and Queensland before separation), other attempts to establish local responsibility for police were exerted by the governing authorities. In South Australia, this extended to an adaptation of English country police legislation of 1840 requiring a contribution to police costs for foot patrols in local police districts. The continuation of this legislation in South Australia was motivated by desires both of government to exercise economy in police expenditure, and of police administrators to secure a buffer against constant demands for retrenchment as the colony faced difficult financial circumstances.[24] The arrangement was of a kind with that which later developed in Canada, with some local governments (at city and provincial level) contracting with the Royal Canadian Mounted Police for the provision of police services. But it fell short of that to the degree that it was only a partial recuperation of costs incurred in gazetted police districts, and the costs of commissioned officers were by statute excluded from the process, being solely the responsibility of the colonial government. And it was well short of the potential for local control embodied in English police affairs in the later nineteenth century: the governing statute in South Australia was concerned only with means of recuperating the cost of foot constables in any police district, and provided no provision by which local government might direct or influence local police activities. The commissioner's authority was preserved intact in such arrangements. Local funding remained in place until the relevant rating provisions were repealed in 1938. By this stage local contribution had contracted to just over eleven per cent of the police budget.[25]

Only in Tasmania was there a sustained attempt to localise police administration in ways which went beyond financial considerations. Indeed the mid-century movement from local to central control which we have been tracing was reversed in Tasmania. There it was that from 1856 to 1898 policing was organised on a municipal basis. The degree to which this arrangement was intended as a means of exhorting local responsibility for police affairs was evident at the outset in a royal commission on the public service. This transfer from central to local responsibility was evidently a response in part to the distaste for the previous system of government controlled police magistrates, associated with Tasmania's convict regime.[26] The decentralisation of police, initiated by legislation of 1858 (for Hobart and Launceston) and 1865 (extended to other municipalities), was endorsed by the royal commission of 1857 as a means of inducing a 'habit of general action for a collective good among a people who, hitherto, have looked to the Government to take action even in matters more immediately affecting local interests.[27]

The experiment with municipal policing lasted four decades. Central direction, however, was far from absent. The appointment of an inspector-general provided a means of monitoring police forces in the different localities, establishing general rules for the guidance of police, but adapting them as necessary to the particular circumstances of a municipality. That office was from 1867 also responsible for the Territorial Police, appointed in non-municipal districts. In municipalities, appointment and maintenance of police services was mandatory, but also from 1867 it was possible for a municipality to surrender control of its police to the government. For reasons which do not appear ever to have been satisfactorily explored, the system of municipal police began to break down in the following decade. Attempts in 1877 by the colonial secretary to move towards centralisation were stemmed by municipal oppposition, but a Parliamentary committee of 1886 strongly endorsed the arguments in its favour, in spite of some significant minority support from witnesses for the virtues of municipal control. 'Divided authority' between police of the territorial and municipal regimes was regarded as impeding the efficient pursuit of offenders. Even so, the desire for retention of some degree of local control was evident in the 1886 Parliamentary recommendations. Yet when centralisation came, in 1899, there was no statutory remnant of the old system, and Tasmania conformed to the Australian model of single administration police forces in a State jurisdiction.[28] A royal commission reviewing the new arrangements in 1906 found no reason to comment on the loss of municipal control, noting among other matters that about 5,000 pounds had been saved by centralisation, with a substantial reduction in the number of senior police as compared to the old local system,[29] of a territorial and 21 municipal police forces.

A final consequence of the reorganisation of policing in the colonial period was the amalgamation of specialised police forces. This was closely related to the process describe above, with a presumption that unified and central control must mean the elimination of specialist units. Such a development did not entail a constraint on the previous tasks of specialised forces. In New South Wales, the haphazard expansion of the colony's policing resources in the period after Macquarie saw no less than 'six separate forces independently controlled' by the 1840s: the Sydney police, the mounted police, the Sydney water police, a rural constabulary controlled by the rural magistracy, a border police responsible to the commissioners of crown lands, and the native police.[30] What appeared to later observers as the chaotic nature of police administration implied by these multiple forces is confirmed by the difficulties in securing a general responsibility for police located in one office. Thus the Bigge Commission in 1820 had recommended an 'appointment of an officer to take charge of the police of the colony as a whole'.[31] Yet the first appointee to such a position, Captain F.N. Rossi as 'Principal Superintendent of Police at New South Wales', was, according to the historian of the police in New South Wales at this period, never more than head of the Sydney police, since he also had to perform duties on the magistrates' bench.[32] The emergence of the Sydney police as a distinct administrative entity was eventually confirmed by statute in 1833, in a measure which prescribed the responsibility of police for a broad range of municipal governing duties.

The complex history of the various police forces in New South Wales up to the 1850s has been told in a number of places. The point at issue here is the effect of centralisation in 1862. This was not only a matter of administrative nicety, but marked the consolidation of settlement. Only a few years before, the New South Wales Parliament had felt it necessary to endorse the continuance of the native police on the grounds that the process of settlement at the colony's extremes still required something other than a regular police force. The implication, scarcely disguised in this and other official mandates for the work of the native police, was that its duties were somewhat outside the bounds of legally accountable policing. As the 1856 Board of Inquiry had it:

> It would be probably impracticable to maintain a police force of a more regular kind, adequate to the maintenance of proper relations with the indigenous tribes.

The nature of this police force in fact precluded 'amalgamation with the other police, and so do its uses'.[33] In the event, however, New South Wales was saved the trouble of amalgamation of the native police as by this time they were serving the 'Northern Districts', and were transferred to Queensland jurisdiction after separation of the northern colony in 1859. The exceptional nature of the native police was confirmed by the lengthy period which it survived as a separate entity in Queensland till the end of the century.

With the exception of the native police, then, centralisation meant the incorporation of other policing entities within the administration of the head of the police department in each colony. Henceforth, specialised police duties such as gold escort, or control of bushranging, would be carried out by the colonial police, with the rewards and ignominy that came with success or failure in such activity becoming a part of the political context of policing, affecting among other matters, the relations between governments, ministers and police department heads.

How significant were police as an arm of public administration in the colonial state in Australia? The varying ratios of police to population, or the comparison of police with other public service employment, suggests the changing priorities of government over time. The long term trends in police to population ratios are summarised in Table [4.1]. In spite of different starting points in terms of chronology and relative police strength, it is worth noting the similarity of the trends between colonies/States. South Australia, Australia's most concentric region, dominated by the role of Adelaide and its hinterland, is the exception of the u-shaped curve of these trends. Its ratios were already low in the 1860s and only increased notably after the 1940s, along with those of other States.

This data suggests something about linear trends in police employ-ment. But how important was policing as a government function in the colonial context and after? An answer to this question has already been implied by the suggestion that policing was one of the earliest functions of the colonial state. The enormous variety of administrative functions which police assumed in the course of the refinement of the colonial apparatus of government was another indicator of their significance. More concrete measures might include the importance of police expenditure in colonial budgets and their relative significance as employers of labour.

**Table 4.1** Police to population ratios: Australia, 1861–1981

| Year | NSW | Vic | Old | SA | WA | Tas |
|------|------|------|------|------|------|------|
| 1861 | 265.8 | 247.9 | 516.3 | 120.6 | na | na |
| 1871 | 166.8 | 137.6 | 358.0 | 102.4 | na | na |
| 1881 | 160.3 | 124.0 | 309.6 | 131.3 | 399.1 | na |
| 1891 | 148.2 | 134.1 | 239.8 | 120.7 | 433.3 | na |
| 1901 | 158.9 | 122.8 | 173.6 | 99.5 | 271.0 | 148.5 |
| 1911 | 153.5 | 124.3 | 152.9 | 116.1 | 165.4 | 123.0 |
| 1921 | 131.4 | 113.0 | 140.9 | 119.3 | 151.2 | 112.7 |
| 1931 | 142.7 | 117.1 | 140.5 | 128.9 | 131.4 | 115.6 |
| 1941 | 133.0 | 120.4 | 152.6 | 146.4 | 126.8 | 127.7 |
| 1951 | 133.9 | 126.5 | 190.4 | 147.0 | 150.3 | 146.1 |
| 1961 | 138.0 | 137.5 | 172.7 | 150.9 | 155.9 | 164.7 |
| 1971 | 160.6 | 144.6 | 169.9 | 174.1 | 161.6 | 210.1 |
| 1981 | 182.0 | 208.0 | 179.5 | 247.8 | 205.4 | 231.4 |

*Source*: S.K. Mukherjee *et al*, *Source Book of Australian Criminal and Social Statistics, 1804–1988*, AIC, Canberra, 1988.

In the 1890s for example, comparison of numbers of police with numbers of state school teachers suggests a varying commitment from colony to colony to the two major functions of policing and education. Interpreting that commitment, however, is complicated by the different stages of settlement which each colony had reached. [ … The] older colonies had a proportionately greater commitment to education compared to those regions which still had a substantial frontier element in their policing administration. This is confirmed by the above comparison of police to population ratios for the different colonies in the nineteenth century. As settlement consolidated and the heavy personnel requirements of the frontier diminished, policing gave way to other government services in importance. By 1900, vital state services such as education provided very substantial employment for teachers.

The relative importance of police as an area of public service employment, however, was to remain stable or increase after this. The three big employee cohorts in New South Wales at the beginning of the twentieth century, for example, were education, railways and police. Railways, of central importance to the maintenance of the colonial economy and of colonial revenue, employed 3,446 staff in 1905 in New South Wales, at a time when there were already 2,310 police in the State. Teachers continued to dominate government employment, with 5,577 personnel.[34]

Over the twentieth century the number of police employees per capita has increased markedly. The general decline in per capita employment of police [ … ] lasted to the Second World War. Indeed, the low point of police employment in Australia was in the period after World War One. The reason was a combination of low labour supply together with government economies. A consequence may have been reduced attention to reported crime and preventive patrolling, leading in turn to low rates of prosecution in the 1920s, a phenomenon of the period.[35]

From the 1940s however, and especially from the 1970s, there has been a substantial increase in the proportion of police to population in Australia. Haldane has observed that one reason for the post-war increase was a change in police working hours.[36] The reduction in the average working week in 1948 was accompanied by an expansion in police numbers in Victoria to compensate for the reduced availability of police. In other States, post-war conditions limited the availability of recruits, restricting the introduction of a forty-hour week in Queensland.[37] Other changes in awards and conditions over the course of the twentieth century meant a convergence of police working conditions with those of other Australian workers, including substantial improvements in leave. A proper appreciation of changing police personnel provision over long periods of time has to take careful account of this context. Increasing the numbers of police employed has not always meant a simple increase in numbers of police available on the streets or for crime investigation.

## Settlement and policing in Australia

Australian historians have been inclined to attribute great significance to the convict origins of settlement in a number of the States in accounting for the later formation of social attitudes and behaviour towards police. Without addressing the generality of the *convict* influence, we can be confident of at least one thing: namely, that the conditions of early colonial settlement were very significantly related to the prominence of the question of policing in debates over government and authority during the first part of the nineteenth century.[38]

In this respect, the Australian colonies were scarcely unique. The establishment of authoritative police forces in other parts of the Empire was closely related to the main forms of social conflict and ideas about the state of political order. Two striking examples of this are to be found in quite different places, Ireland and Canada. The former example has been discussed earlier. In Canada, the foundation of the north-west mounted police provided a striking contrast to Australian examples. Indeed, it has been argued by a historian of the Prairies, Gerald Friesen, that 'the force is central to an understanding of western Canada and, by extension, of Canada as a whole'.[39]

The peculiar role of the Mounties, a *national* force of a kind which was never contemplated in the quite different conditions of Australian settlement, was in fact forged in circumstances somewhat similar to those affecting the Australian and New Zealand police. That is, the issue of the colonial and imperial response to the status of the indigenous peoples of these colonies was central. But the Mounties appeared as a national force in this context, to make possible the orderly extension of the Canadian federation. While some of the Australasian forces were created similarly to deal with the threat of indigenous resistance, for example in New Zealand and to some extent in South Australia, other colonial police were formed in contexts which were more generally related to the concerns of good order, peace-keeping and government, within the boundaries of settlement. While Australian colonies had their own Mounties, their frontier police, their native troopers, there is little in Australia of the extraordinary positive image and connection to national well-being, which the heritage of the Mounties delivers in Canada.[40]

Reviewing the development of the new police in New South Wales compared to England and North America, Michael Sturma has argued that the urban conditions which have been seen as so significant for the emergence of police in the latter two cases were far from dominant in the colonies.[41] A range of settlement conditions obtained in Australia. These include the phenomena of convict society in New South Wales, Tasmania and Western Australia; the significant resistance to settlement which prompted the formation of the native police in some colonies; the urban disorder of the 1840s during a period of economic contraction and political conflict; and the impact of the goldrushes in Victoria and New South Wales.

Convictism played its role in the early development of police forces in Australasia. But its significance cannot be exaggerated. New Zealand and South Australasia had no convicts to speak of, while Victoria's convict inhabitants were of limited importance in the colony's development. After the 1840s, only Western Australia received convicts. In Tasmania and New South Wales (which lost its northern settlements in the separation of Queensland in 1859), convictism was central to the early history of policing. Yet other factors in colonial settlement quickly took over from convictism in shaping colonial institutions. Moreover, as recent historical debates about the nature of convict society demonstrate, there is only limited agreement about what convictism means as a determining element in Australian colonial institutions.[42]

Little significance should be attached to the fact that many of the early police were themselves convicts or ex-convicts. Given the subsequent history of policing as a career in Australia, the historical judgements which link public attitudes to police in Australia to the convict personnel of the force are highly speculative, and fail to acknowledge the evidence of later consent to policing.[43] What is more relevant is that the perceived need of government to control movements of convicts and ex-convicts of 'doubtful character' early contributed to the state appointment of police magistrates and constables, notably in Tasmania and New South Wales. Where conditions were not conducive to settlement, then the colonial authorities themselves directed special police forces, such as the mounted or border police in New South Wales, to keep order beyond the reach of the magistrates.[44]

Convictism extended its influence beyond the convict colonies to the degree that the non-convict colonies, such as New Zealand and South Australia, early sought protection from escaped convicts and immigrant ex-convicts through establishing police to capture them or impede their entry.[45] A degree of social protectionism developed as respective colonies aspired to construct a society which was free of the taint of convict origins and immune to the potential harms arising from the free movement of those identified as criminals in other colonies. At the close of the century began a rush of legislative assertion of this fear of the contaminating influence of the criminal classes as a number of States enacted an Influx of Criminal Prevention Acts.[46]

The resistance of the original inhabitants of Australia and New Zealand was at least as influential as convictism in the development of policing in the colonies. The history of policing in these years is in part the history of a search for the means by which the Aborigines or Maoris could be accommodated through service in policing. Police work was one of the first means by which indigenous people would become agents of their own dispossession. In some places this service was especially bloody, in others less so. [While the history of the native police in Australia is explored later in this book], some comments are necessary here to assess the role of Aboriginal–settler relations in the organisation of colonial policing.

Indigenous resistance stimulated a number of important developments in the colonial police. First, it impelled a centralised police solution to the problem of conflict at the borders of settlement. Conflict between Aborigines and settlers early determined that the policing of those areas which were beyond the pale of settlement should be a matter of colonial government responsibility. This was the case for two reasons.

On the one hand, the governors and the incipient legislative councils faced pressure from settlers to protect them from raids by Aboriginal groups. On the other, government in the colonies, under some pressure from London, was in theory duty-bound to protect indigenous inhabitants from the adverse effects of settlement. The border police and then the native police were expedients developed to adjudicate these conflicting demands. From the beginning this confusing responsibility rendered the policing solution ineffective on the second count and sometimes on the first as well. Notoriously in some districts the native police became themselves the cause and origin of further law and order problems.

Regardless of the failure of the native policing policies, however, their significance can be addressed from other directions. Perhaps most importantly they signified the status of Australia and New Zealand as colonies – places of occupation by European settlers with limited regard for the rights or desires of the occupying inhabitants. From this aspect, the centralising tendencies of native policing policy signify the impossibility of a localised police, with a police controlled and directed by the community of settlers in a limited space. This was an option in Australia, as we have seen, and one which left traces even after the gold rushes in some places. Is it significant that the one place where a localised police survived the centralising tendencies of the mid-century, Tasmania, was the colony in which settlement had by the 1830s almost destroyed the Aboriginal population? Thereafter the Tasmanians were left only to ponder their convict taunt.[47]

But otherwise the particular history of Australian settlement was one in which indigenous resistance perennially posed the question of the responsibility of colonial governments to regulate the conditions of settlement. Magistrates were suspect vehicles of colonial policy towards Aborigines if only because they tended so often to be settlers themselves and therefore burdened with a conflict of interest. Initially they were suspect in any case since they did not possess those semi-military skills requisite for the task of forcible dispossession. Later they were bypassed as native policing was increasingly brought under the more regulated and hierarchical direction of the various government-appointed officers and then by the colonial commissioners of police. By the 1880s, the tasks of native policing were largely those of north and central Australia. The perils of leaving the responsibility too much in local hands was evident in the 1880s in the Kimberleys. There, close relations between squatters and police played a critical role in perpetuating conflict with Aborigines, at a time when in Queensland the tide of policy was beginning to turn, to favour means of mediation, paternalistic as these might be on later reflection.[48]

In such colonial origins was epitomised the antagonistic relation of Australian policing of Aborigines until late in the twentieth century. Law enforcers could envisage the employment of the indigenous population, but always on terms which addressed primarily the security and concerns of the occupying settlers. The fact that some of the indigenous population might obtain advantage from service in the cause of colonial policing helps to explain the meaning it had for them.[49] But it does nothing to disguise the thoroughly subordinated place which was occupied by native troopers and later trackers in the first century of Australian policing – a sign of the more generally subordinated place of Aborigines in Australian society.

Urban contexts have been regarded as a critical element in the formation of police forces in many countries. Australian colonisation was a product of urban development in Britain. The Australian colonies developed and thrived on the export of pastoral production and mineral extraction, feeding the demand from British factories and urban centres. Yet from early in the nineteenth century large sections of the Australian population congregated in the cities and towns of the coastal fringe. Especially they were concentrated in Sydney and Melbourne, other colonial capitals waiting until the 1880s for significant growth. Cities of the nineteenth century were the focus of experiments in government and of discourses about the fabric of social order. These affected profoundly the history of policing, though in colonial Australia not exclusively so, as we have already seen.

Urban order and disorder were implicated in some important police initiatives of the mid-century. The enactment of legislation governing the policing of Sydney metropolis was the origin of urban policing in many of its most important respects in Australia. Not only were the formal structures of police organisation signalled, but of particular note was the specification of police powers relating to the preservation of public order and municipal regulation. Such powers were transmitted to police as they formed in the other towns of the colonies, being adopted for Melbourne for example in 1838.[50]

When historians speak of the development of policing in the early nineteenth century, it is often in reference to the perceived problems of urban disorder.[51] While there is reason for questioning the *determining* role of this factor in Australian policing, it was far from absent in the years leading up to the mid-century reorganisation of policing. Notably, in Sydney it was a New Year's Day riot in 1850 which led directly to the establishment of a Legislative Council Select Committee which in turn prompted moves towards a centralised New South Wales police, with a sounder administrative structure than had been the case to then. The anxiety over the riot followed a decade in which the condition of

Sydney had been a matter of concern for the political elite, with disturbances related to economic conditions and to attempts to reintroduce transportation to the colony. The inefficiency and even mismanagement of the Sydney police in these circumstances prompted demands for police reform which were addressed in the following decade.

The centripetal development of South Australia perhaps ensured that urban concerns were always going to be of particular concern in the development of police there.[52] Urban order was again a matter for attention, though always to be set beside the need to attend to Aboriginal–settler conflict and the problems of bushrangers and intrusive ex-convicts from the other colonies. The importance of a well-disciplined police became evident in 1848 when a riot between police and sailors in Port Adelaide led to the death of a man injured by a police bayonet. Commissioner Dashwood considered the action a failure of police discipline.[53] It was a rare instance of a fatality at police hands in the control of urban disorder in nineteenth-century Australia.

Separating the influence of urban factors from the powerful impact of the gold rushes on the formation of the colonial police is difficult. The colonial police have been tainted in popular memory by a number of seemingly deplorable episodes. The most notorious is their alleged responsibility for provoking the agitation among gold miners leading to the Eureka rebellion. The events of that period, however, do not exhaust the historical meaning of the gold rushes for the history of policing in the Australian colonies.

In two colonies, Victoria and New South Wales, the gold rushes were centrally involved in determining the political decision to establish a centralised police. In others, especially New Zealand (1860s), Queensland (1870s), and Western Australia (1890s), the responsibility for managing and regulating the gold fields and the associated bullion trade was an important responsibility of the colonial police. South Australia was principally affected insofar as the gold rushes created personnel and administrative problems for the police – problems shared with the other colonies.

Gold discoveries changed colonies irreversibly. Politically and socially they could not be the same after the enormous influxes of population swamped the steadily growing pastoral economies of eastern Australia. Similar effects awaited Western Australia in the 1890s. Police on the goldfields were responsible for managing some of the most difficult and volatile sections of the Australian colonial population in the nineteenth century. The problems of instability and mobility, fanned by rumours of new discoveries, added to the difficulties of regulating a population without social roots in their place of settlement.

Gold was an additional impetus for strong centralised policy. Local regulation would have meant little for a population likely to shift locale at a moment's notice. Labour shortages and heavy flows of goods in and out of each colony provided further perceptions of a need for greater government intervention. From this context flowed the ambition to create a police force which would be capable of exercising substantial authority in the colony. In spite of Eureka, the development in Victoria in the 1850s of a police force with a centralised administrative structure and a set of regulations to sustain its efficiency, was a substantial contribution to the capacity of colonial government to rule in unstable times. It was the Victorian police rules which tended to become the model for the other Australasian police forces. Further, when similar social demands emerged in New Zealand, it was to Victoria that New Zealand authorities turned in their search for commanders and personnel.[54]

Goldfields were the site of other social problems which were implicated in the development of the New South Wales police. At Lambing Flat in 1860, European miners rioted and assaulted Chinese diggers.[55] The event epitomised the racism of the period. It also prompted the New South Wales Premier to move quickly to address the evident incapacity of the goldfields police to act to protect the victims. Hence, the New South Wales police emerged in a new and divided society.

Yet gold was not the only catalyst for the reorganisation of the New South Wales police. As John Hirst has argued, their early history was marked even more critically by the flurry of bushranging which characterised the aftermath of the gold rushes. On Hirst's account, the failure of the police curb the outbreak of bushranging in the 1860s brought the whole institution of police to a point of disbandment. The problems lay in the inappropriate training and staffing of the New South Wales police. Rather than depend on colonial born bushmen for the policing task, the policy driving the formation of the New South Wales police was to staff it with gentlemen officers from a military or British/Irish policing background, with a constabulary of the same country of origin. Bushranging, the armed robbery of travellers, coaches and rural townships by young bush horsemen, was a social phenomenon for which police from such backgrounds were ill-equipped to deal.

So poorly in fact did the police deal with it that they became the laughing stock of many in the colonial populace empathising with the superior bush skills of the bushrangers. The phenomenon was not restricted to New South Wales. In Victoria, it reached its apogee in the Kelly outbreak in the late 1870s. The repercussions of the police failure to deal effectively with the Kelly gang were felt in Victoria well into the following decade, leading to a reorganised police administration and detective force. Something of the same images of police incompetence confronting mythical rural heroes characterised responses to the stock thieves, the Kenniff brothers, in southern Queensland in the early 1900s.[56]

It is with good reason then that Hirst concludes that the alleged poor reputation of police in Australia, perhaps especially in New South Wales, derives not from their convict origins but from the disastrous performance of police in the bushranging era. The personnel of the colonial police of the later nineteenth century in any case did not have convict origins. And the circumstances under which most forces were consolidated from the 1850s multiplied the social forces which shaped and were affected by police.

## Conclusion

The new police came to Australia in the 1850s and 1860s at the same time as their consolidation in England, and two decades after their establishment in Ireland. It can be seen from the review of the historical conditions which both constructed and constrained them in Australia that this was nevertheless a distinctive process. There was not a simple transmission of a new institution of government from the metropolis to the periphery of the Empire.

Thus the often-noted influence of the colonial state in Australian settlement evaluated in a policing organisation which was itself highly centralised. Not only in most colonies were all the various police establishments brought together in the one administration, but this administration was then made subject to the powerful authority of a single commissioner, subject *de jure* to the direction of a responsible minister. In Australia, with the temporary exception of Tasmania, the possibility of a significant level of local control of policing was early waived in favour of metropolitan control in each colony. This was the most important long-term consequence of the particular formation of police in the colonies.

While the new police in England and Ireland were conceived and born in circumstances of great social and political conflict and controversy, one could argue that this was much less so in these colonies. The judgment is perhaps a matter of degree. But in the various social contexts which have been outlined above, the traces of later patterns might be seen. The tendency of colonial elites to view with fear or suspicion any sign of lower order resistance produced an expectation of policing as primarily a reactive and, if necessary, repressive force.

The fateful decisions to found the native police in New South Wales and Port Phillip originated a peculiar relation between police in New South Wales and was to endure and be transformed in every generation thereafter. If the police force was an archetypal institution of modern government, then the policing of Aborigines was to become an emblem of all that such government might imply: the bureaucratic transformation of social relations under the ultimate threat of force.

Finally, the mix of contexts described here was brought to its head in conflict over the role of police in the service of government in the 1850s. The gold rushes brought on political and social change of enormous importance to later colonial development. By stimulating policing reform and consolidation in Victoria, they had a major impact on the organisation of policing in other colonies in Australasia. And in so doing, they played a critical role in the colonial state.

*From Mark Finnane,* Police and Government *(Oxford: Oxford University Press) 1994, pp 9–30.*

## Notes

1   For a recent overview of the comparative organisation of police forces in the English-speaking countries see D.H. Bayley, 'Comparative Organization of the Police in English-speaking Countries', in *Modern Policing*, M. Tonry and N. Morris (eds), Chicago and London: The University of Chicago Press, 1992.

2   For critical reviews of the history of policing see especially R. Reiner, *The Politics of the Police*, Wheatsheaf Books, Sussex, 1985; C. Emsley, *The English Police: A Political and Social History*, Harvester Wheatsheaf, Hemel Hempstead, 1991; and, for Australia, M. Sturma, 'Policing the Criminal Frontier in Mid-nineteenth Century Australia, Britain and America' in *Policing in Australia: Historical Perspectives*, M. Finnane (ed.), NSW University Press, Kensington, 1987; M. Finnane and S. Garton, 'The Work of Policing: Social Relations and the Criminal Justice System in Queensland, Part 1', *Labour History*, 62, 1992, pp. 52–70 and D. Moore, 'Origins of the Police Mandate: The Australian Case Reconsidered', *Police Studies*, 14, 1991, pp. 107–20.

3   G.M. O'Brien, *The Australian Police Forces*, Oxford University Press, Melbourne, 1960, p. 2.

4   R. Haldane, *The People's Force: A History of the Victoria Police*, Melbourne University Press, Carlton, 1986.

5   V. Doherty, 'Western Australia', in *Police Source Book 2*, B. Swanton, et al., (eds), Australian Institute of Criminology, Canberra, 1985, p. 428.

6   See H. McQueen, *A New Britannia*, Penguin, Ringwood, 1970; R.W. Connell and T.H. Irving, *Class Structure in Australian History: Documents, Narrative and Argument*, Longman Cheshire, Melbourne, 1980; A. Moore, 'Policing Enemies of the State: The New South Wales Police and the New Guard, 1931–32,' in *Policing in Australia*, M. Finnane (ed.).

7   On the police in early New South Wales, see D. Neal, *The Rule of Law in a Penal Colony*, Cambridge University Press, Melbourne, 1991, ch. 6; H. King, 'Some Aspects of Police Administration in New South Wales 1825–1851', *Journal of the Royal Australian Historical Society*, 42, 5, 1956, pp. 205–30.

8   S.H. Palmer, *Police and Protest in England and Ireland 1780–1850*, Cambridge University Press, Cambridge, 1988; D. Philips, ' "A New Engine of Power and Authority": The Institutionalization of Law-Enforcement in England, 1780–1830' in *Crime and Law: The Social History of Crime in Western Europe Since 1500*, V.A.C. Gatrell, B. Lenman, and G. Parker (eds), Europa Publications, London, 1980; and for a sceptical view of the 'influential' Irish model, see R. Hawkins, 'The "Irish Model" and the Empire: A Case for Reassessment,' in *Policing the Empire: Government, Authority and Control, 1830–1940*, D.M. Anderson and D. Killingray (eds), Manchester University Press, Manchester, 1991.

9   See Emsley, *English Police*, pp. 15–40; Philips, 'A New Engine', in *Crime and the Law*, Gatrell et al., (eds).

10  See e.g. P. Pasquino, 'Theatricum Politicum: The Genealogy of Capital–Police and the State of Prosperity', in *The Foucault Effect: Studies in Governmentality*, G. Burchell, C. Gordon and P. Miller (eds), The University of Chicago Press, Chicago, 1991.

11  See O. MacDonagh, *Early Victorian Government*, Weidenfeld and Nicholson, London, 1977, p. 167ff; Philips, 'A New Engine ...', in *Crime and the Law*, Gatrell et al., (eds).

12  For the implications of the broader notion of police see e.g. Emsley, *English Police*, introduction: L. Johnston, *The Rebirth of Private Policing*, Routledge, London, 1992, pp. 4–6; E. Monkonnen, 'History of Urban Police', in *Modern Policing*, M. Tonry and N. Morris (eds), The University of Chicago Press, Chicago and London, 1992.

13  W.L. Burn, cited in O. MacDonagh, *Ireland: The Union and its Aftermath*, George Allen and Unwin, London, 1977, p. 34; see also MacDonagh, *Early Victorian Government*, ch. 10.

14  Cf Palmer, *Police and Protest*; Hawkins, 'The "Irish Model" ' in *Policing the Empire*, Anderson and Killingray (eds); R. Storch, 'The Plague of the Blue Locusts: Police Reform and Popular Resistance in Northern England, 1840–1857', *International Review of Social History*, 20, 1975, pp. 61–90; R. Storch 'The Policeman as Domestic Missionary: Urban Discipline and Popular Culture in Northern England, 1850–1880', *Journal of Social History*, 9, 1976, pp. 481–509; W.G. Carson, 'Policing the Periphery, 1798–1900', *Australian and New Zealand Journal of Criminology*, 17, 4, 1984, pp. 207–32.

15  Report of the Board of Inquiry, 26 July, 1856, *NSW Legislative Assembly Votes and Proceedings, 1856–7*, vol. I, pp. 1149–50.

16  Ibid., p. 1149.

17  R. Clyne, *Colonial Blue: A History of the South Australian Police Force 1836–1916*, Wakefield Press, Netley, 1987, pp. 7–8.

18  G. Reid, *A Picnic with the Natives: Aboriginal–European Relations in the Northern Territory to 1910*, Melbourne University Press, Melbourne, 1990, ch. 6.

19  O'Brien, *Australian Police Forces*, pp. 42–3, for Western Australia; R. Wettenhall, 'Government and the Police', *Current Affairs Bulletin*, 53, 10, 1977, p. 22.

20  H. Golder, *High and Responsible Office: A History of the NSW Magistracy*, Oxford University Press, Melbourne, 1991.

21  D. Palmer, 'The Making of the Victorian Colonial Police: From Colonisation to the New Police', MA (Criminological Studies) thesis, La Trobe University, 1990, p. 74 (16 Vic no. 24, s.xii).

22  Rules for the General Government and Discipline of Members of the Police Force of Queensland, 1869, Queensland, Legislative Council, *Papers*, 1869; W.R. Johnston, *The Long Blue Line: A History of the Queensland Police*, Boolarong Press, Brisbane, 1992, pp. 12–15.

23  Palmer, 'Making of the Victorian Colonial Police', pp. 96–100.

24  Clyne, *Colonial Blue*, p. 148.

25  The provision was eventually repealed by the *Police Act Amendment Act* (South Australia) 1938, s.3, South Australian Report of the Commissioner of Police, 1935, p. 33, *Proceedings of the Parliament of South Australia, 1935*, vol. 2, for amounts recuperated from corporations in the 1930s.

26  Wettenhall, 'Government and the Police' p. 22; H. Reynolds, 'That Hated Stain: The Aftermath of Transportation in Tasmania', *Historical Studies*, 53, 1969, pp. 19–31.

27  State of the Public Service, Report of the Commission, p. 7, Tasmania *Parliamentary Papers* (hereafter *PP*) 1857 and Wettenhall, 'Government and the Police', p. 22.

28  R. Wettenhall, *A Guide to Tasmanian Government Administration*, Platypus Publications, Hobart, 1968, pp. 251–2; O'Brien, *Australian Police Forces*, pp. 32–7; Select Committee on Centralisation of Police, 1886, Tasmania, *PP*.

29  Royal Commission on the Organisation and Administration of the Police Force, p. 2, Tasmania *PP*, 1906.

30  King, 'Some Aspects of Police Administration,' p. 214; in Victoria on the eve of consolidation in 1853, there were seven autonomous forces: Haldane, *People's Force*, pp. 27–8.

31  King, 'Some Aspects,' p. 216.

32  Ibid.

33  Board of Inquiry, 1856, p. 1151 (see above, note 14).

34  See NSW Public Service List, NSW *PP*, 1905.

35  See J. Allen, *Sex and Secrets: Crimes Involving Australian Women*, Oxford University Press, Melbourne, 1990.

36  Haldane, *People's Force*, pp. 234–5.

37  Board of Inquiry into Police Conditions, p. 5, Tasmania *PP*, vol. 141, 1949.

38  See, e.g. M. Sturma, *Vice in a Vicious Society*, UQP, St Lucia, 1983; Neal, *Rule of Law*; R. Walker, 'Bushranging in Fact and Legend', *Historical Studies*, 11, 1964, pp. 206–21; Golder, *High and Responsible Office*; A. Davidson, *The Invisible State*, Cambridge University Press, Melbourne, 1990, pp. 110–18; P.J. Byrne, *Criminal Law and Colonial Subject*, Cambridge University Press, 1993.

39  G. Friesen, *The Canadian Prairies*, University of Toronto Press, Toronto, 1984, p. 163.

40  See, on Canada, Friesen, *Canadian Prairies*; on new Zealand, R. Hill, *Policing the Colonial Frontier: The Theory and Practice of Coercive Social and Racial Control in New Zealand, 1767–1867*, Govt Printer, Wellington, 1984; on South Australia, Clyne, *Colonial Blue*; on colonial policing generally, see M. Brogden, 'An Act to Colonise the Internal Lands of the Island: Empire and the Origins of the Professional Police', *International Journal of the Sociology of Law*, 15, 1987, pp. 179–208 and Anderson and Killingray (eds), *Policing the Empire*.

41  Sturma, 'Policing the Criminal Frontier'.

42  See, e.g., debate between D. Neal, 'Free Society, Penal Colony, Slave society, Prison?', *Historical Studies*, 89, 1987, p. 497, and J. Hirst, 'Or None of the Above', *Historical Studies*, 89, 1987, p. 519.

43  See, e.g., R. Ward, *The Australian Legend*, Oxford University Press, Melbourne, 1957, and following him, McQueen, *New Britannia*, and A. McCoy, *Drug Traffic, Narcotics and Organised Crime in Australia*, Harper and Row, Sydney, 1980; on consent to policing in the later nineteenth-century Australia see S. Wilson, 'Police Work: The Role of the Police in the Kalgoorlie Community, 1897–1898', *Journal of Australian Studies*, 11, 1982, pp. 9–20, and R. Walker, 'Violence in Industrial Conflicts in New South Wales in the Late Nineteenth Century', *Historical Studies*, 86, 1986, pp. 54–70.

44  Neal, *Rule of Law*, ch. 6.

45  Clyne, *Colonial Blue*, pp. 22–7; Hill, *Policing the Colonial Frontier*, Part 2, pp. 544–94.

46  NSW, 1903; Queensland, 1905; Tasmania, 1909.

47  Reynolds, ' "That Hated Stain" '; L. Ryan, *The Aboriginal Tasmanians*, University of Queensland Press, St. Lucia, 1981.

48  Cf N. Loos, *Invasion and Resistance: Aboriginal–European Relations on the North Queensland Frontier 1861–1897*, ANU Press, Canberra, 1982, and Johnston, *Long Blue Line*, for Queensland; and A. Gill, 'Aborigines, Settlers and Police in the Kimberleys, 1887–1905', *Studies in Western Australian History*, 1, 1977.

49  M.H. Fels, *Good Men and True: The Aboriginal Police of the Port Phillip District, 1837–1853*, Melbourne University Press, Melbourne, 1988.

50  See Palmer, 'Making of the Victorian Colonial Police', pp. 109–11, on the significance of the Act's extension to Melbourne; also Haldane, *People's Force*, p. 15.

51  Cf Palmer, *Police and Protest*; Storch, 'The Plague of the Blue Locusts' and 'The Policemen as Domestic Missionary'; Sturma, 'Policing the Criminal Frontier'.

52  Cf J. Hirst, *Adelaide and the Country, 1870–1917*, Melbourne University Press, Carlton, 1973, on the later significance of Adelaide's dominance of the State.

53  Clyne, *Colonial Blue*, pp. 102–3.

54  Hill, *Policing the Colonial Frontier*, Part 2, ch. 7, for the influence of Victorian police in Otago.

55  C. Connolly, 'Explaining the "Lambing Flat" Riots of 1861', in *Who Are Our Enemies? Racism and the Working Class in Australia*, A. Curthoys and A. Markus (eds), Hale and Iremonger, Sydney, 1978.

56  J. Hirst, *The Strange Birth of Colonial Democracy*, Allen and Unwin, Sydney, 1988, pp. 218–241; J. McQuilton, 'Police in Rural Victoria', in *Policing in Australia*, Finnane (ed.); Johnston, *Long Blue Line*, p. 151.

# 5. The emergence of the police – the colonial dimension

*Mike Brogden*

Modern police history begins not in Britain itself but in Ireland, with the passing of the Irish Peace Preservation Force Act in 1814, when Peel was Irish Secretary (Jeffries, 1952, p. 53).

## Introduction

The Irish legislation is as arbitrary a debut of the professional police as the normative references to the Metropolitan Police Act 1829. Other organised forces had been in existence for many years prior to that date. Salaried state-appointed policing was hardly an invention of the Anglo-Saxon race. Ethnocentricity, inadequate comparative knowledge of policing, and a-historicism are the hallmarks of the Anglo-American sociology of the police. Chauvinism still prevails, among today's Reithians (Pike, 1985), as well as the Bunyanesque camp-followers (Scraton, 1985). The failure to consider the wider contours of the emergence of the professional police has been near-total.

In the radical case, there is a particular irony. In one recent British public order incident, the type of police tactics used were described as '… imported direct from Hong Kong' (*The Listener* 31.10.1985). The Hong Kong practices in turn derived initially from the same medley of experimentation that gave rise to both the Metropolitan Police and to the Royal Irish Constabulary (successor to the Peace Preservation Force and the ancestor of the Royal Ulster Constabulary). In Manchester, in March, 1985, with the visit of the then Home Secretary, the wheel had turned full circle.

The tunnel vision of students of British policing has frustrated an adequate account of police origins and functions. Explanations have been bound by context and by an insular historiography. One gap in that literature can be plugged. The imperial circumstances of professional policing in Britain need to be explored. Before entering that field, there are, however, two preliminaries.

There are rival versions of the emergence of Anglo-American policing. Each of these interpretations has been subject to considerable individual criticism. However, they suffer from a common defect. They contain the *idée fixe* that salaried policework was, like the spinning jenny, a British invention. In fact, there are *competing* models of professional policework, in terms of practices – whatever duties were eventually assumed – and designated functions – whatever those who paid the law enforcement bills actually wanted. There is no inexorable law that made the British style and organisation of policework (as conventionally portrayed) the norm from which to assess critically the functions of the professional police in Western societies.

An appreciation of the imperial context permits a fresh appraisal. More sense can be made of the police public order role in present society by inserting the material omitted from most police histories – the centrality of colonial conquest and of imperial legitimation to institutional development in Victorian England. 'The history of England is also the history of our colonies ...' (Sumner, 1982, p. 8).

*Orthodox explanations and critique of police emergence*

There are several conventional explanations of the origins of professional policing in Britain in the 1820s and 1830s. The early histories emphasised the importance of the 'mob'. Alternatively, crime fears were viewed as the catalyst. Thirdly, accounts of the development of policing in the United States have centred upon the more complex features of the urbanisation and migration process. Fourthly, a law of inexorable administrative proliferation has been detailed. Finally, there have been more radical commentaries, with debts variously to Foucault and to more materialist histories, and relating the rise of professional policing to the conjunctural crisis of early capitalism.

Critchley, for example, assumed that riots were the precipitating factor in the formation of the New Police. More recently, several American studies have followed Silver (1967) in elaborating on the riot theme (for example, Walker, 1977). Tolerance of public disorder waned, as its manifestations were transformed from symbolic protest to material destruction. Urban property owners called increasingly for organised protection. As the social protests of the slum dwellers spilt over the boundaries, the traditional form of lower class political articulation collided with the new bourgeois standards of the industrialising city. This clash brought forth a reaction in the form of the professional police, as one element in the new disciplinary order.

The criticisms of the 'riot' explanation are well established. Several writers have argued (Monkkonen, 1981; Field, 1981; Emsley, 1983) that there were few such precipitating riots, and often a long interval between those conflicts and police formation. It is a mistake to over-emphasise the cause and effect relationship between mob violence and the creation of the New Police. In any case, violent street disorder continued to be a prominent feature of Anglo-American city life long after the arrival of professional policing.

Rising crime levels featured in many of the earlier accounts. A concern with crime dominated the original Parliamentary debate (Stead, 1977). Chadwick's (selective) production of witnesses to the 1839 Royal Commission emphasised the fear of crime. Many of the Reithian historians have taken it for granted that the creation of police was due to criminal threats to persons and to property, and was a natural concomitant of urban growth. More recent studies (e.g. Johnson, 1979) have explained police modernisation in the nineteenth century in terms of rising crime. They assumed that the traditional watch/constable system could not handle the rising wave of crime, which was produced by urban population growth.

Dismissal of the 'crime explanation' has several components. It is doubtful whether crime was actually rising in London prior to the development of the Metropolitan Police (Phillips, 1980) or in United States cities before they established police forces (Monkkonen, 1981). For Harring (1983), social deviance was a product of the changes imposed upon the working class of the period, rather than a cause of police reform. Crime control was one way in which the new institutions of industrial capitalism could be legitimised. There was no necessity for a rising crime rate to be responded to by a uniformed and preventative police when, traditionally, other methods had been the conventional response: temperance campaigns for those who blamed the demon drink, educational reform where crime was blamed on illiteracy (Johnson, 1979), or variations in penal measures (Monkkonen, 1981).

Crime and the mob have latterly been merged in the accounts of writers in the social disorganisation tradition; linking together the processes of immigration and of urbanisation (Lane, 1967; Richardson, 1970). Police departments were not established to reduce crime or control riots. They were organised on behalf of urban elites to supervise the migrant poor, who were increasingly seen as a potentially 'dangerous class' (embodied in the United States in the tramping phenomenon of the early Industrial Revolution: Levett, 1975). People control rather than crime or riot control was the primary cause. Until the lower orders could be socialised by the institutions of education and democracy into the practices of industrialism, they had to be regulated.

There are evident problems here. Like the previous explanations, they contain a causal flaw. They confuse what the police ended up actually doing with the reason for their coming into existence. Police duties are conflated with intended police functions, the latter being deduced from documentation of the former. As Monkkonen (1981) phrases it sardonically, it is equally plausible to argue that the police were created to look for lost children because that was what they ended up doing.

Other writers have developed ideas associated with the Weberian tradition. The older accounts (Radzinowicz, 1955) suggest that New Police arose as part of the general administrative 'tidying-up' of the disorderly edges of society. The same model of organisation that apparently served well in times of external conflict, with its apparent predictability, impartiality, and efficiency, could similarly be utilised as the major agency for 'ordering' and regulating the city. Local elites considered that a '… regular force of patrolmen answering to a central office and on duty round the clock was a conveniently flexible instrument of administration' (Lane, 1980, p. 8). As an instrument of city government, the new police were the most convenient municipal agency.

The most forcible representative of this thesis is Monkkonen (1981) American cities adopted uniformed police as part of the shift from class-based politics to liberal pluralistic and professional urban administration, based on formal social control bureaucracies. When urban elites abandoned positions of power, and class-based political representation was replaced by ethnic representation, the administration of city business could no longer work on a particularistic basis, and the modern bureaucratic notion of rule-based, universalistic standards became the urban goal. Ideas of policing and policing organisation were 'contagiously diffused' from large cities to small as a gradual form of innovation.

The critical factors in police reform were demography and city size. Police organisation developed when a critical limit was reached.

This account suffers from epistemological and empirical defects. As Monkkonen himself argued in relation to earlier explanations, it imputes a remarkable causal awareness to city officers prior to the event. City elites are attributed a more far-sighted view of their own interests than nineteenth century history suggests. Further, as Harring argues (1983), there was no inevitable innovation process. Some United States cities reduced force establishments after the first few years. Others emphasised alternative forms of city regulation, from the appointment of municipal garbagemen in Chicago to technological innovations (such as the telegraph), instead of increasing police manpower.

Finally, more critical writers have located professional police emergence within the conjunctural crisis of the onset of industrial capitalism. The nascent working-class had to be disciplined by new forms of coercion and legitimation. A New Police, combining both those elements, was to be a major weapon in that victory (Harring, 1979), ensuring the stability of the social relations of production. As private policing increased in cost to the new manufacturers, property owners and merchants, the police institution was socialised and its cost transferred from the private to the public sector (Spitzer and Scull, 1977). Professional policing was one of several forms of social organisation that emerged to maintain and strengthen the position of the new city ruling classes, and hence to regulate the nascent class struggle.

All these accounts are insufficient. In the first place, they assume that because the professional police in Anglo-American societies developed in the form that they did, such development was inevitable. This deterministic history denies any contingent social contribution to that change (Emsley, 1983). Secondly, many explanations of the *origins* of the professional police are based on the duties assumed after their formation. There is a confusion between what the police actually did and the causes that brought them about. The fact that they 'may' have been effective against social disorder, crime, migrant workers, and working-class people does not, of itself, prove that was why they were created. Nor does the diffusion model tell us why a particular form of policework arose in London at the outset.

## The emergence of alternative forms of policework

The major reason for the inadequacy of the orthodox explanations is their ethnocentricity. They commence from the domain assumption of the early Metropolitan model of professional police work. It is presupposed that the London Metropolitan model, as conventionally portrayed, was the only possible prototype. None of the above explanations disputes the authenticity and inevitability of that particular form or organisation. Anglo-American police history fails to recognise alternative formulations of policework. A wider reading offers many possibilities.

The first is a *preventative police,* a model whose midwives were the Ministers of Louis XIV (Brodeur, 1983). 'High policing' (police concern with the affairs of state) from Louis XIV, through the times of Fouché, to the present Sureté, has a history of its own. From this perspective, policing in relation to the 'low crime' of the streets may be perceived of as an aberration from the primary police commitment to the defence of the realm. In this view of the police function, the Prevention of Terrorism Act 1974, would be the proper descendant of professional policing, and community policing merely a peculiar deviation. In high policing, the police function as the early-warning system of the despotic or corporate state.

A second model is the traditional European practice which regarded policing as the *administration* of the affairs of state. Donzelot notes that Enlightenment thought saw the '... science of policing (as) regulating everything that relates to the present condition of society, in strengthening and improving it, in seeing that all things contribute to the welfare of the members that compose it' (Donzelot, 1979, p. 7). Similarly in France by the eighteenth century, the term police had come to mean the administration of a city and the social order which that administration was meant to bring (Emsley, 1983). In the Victorian city, police work was shorthand for a form of local administration. It often had minimal connection with the preventative Rowan-and-Mayne model. (We, only have to recall Charles Reith's reference to agricultural fertiliser as 'police-manure' to appreciate some of those functions.)

Thirdly, there is the neglected influence of *commercial policework* on police development. Apart from Spitzer and Scull (1977), some older references to Colquhoun's experiments with the River Thames Police, and critical assessments of the hue-and-cry and thief-taking (Klockars, 1985), the history of private policing as a profit-making activity is usually by-passed, and its influence on the functions of the public police ignored. However, recent accounts have suggested the value of considering the private sector. In England, private bodies such as the Associations for the Prosecution of Felons survived long into the nineteenth century (Phillips, 1977). In public police detective departments, private rewards remained common (Klockars, 1985). More importantly, in the United States, private policing actually expanded commensurately with state policing. For example, until the founding of the F.B.I. in 1924, public police forces were confined to city and state territories with only the private agencies able to ship presumed offenders across jurisdictional boundaries (Kakalik and Wildhorn, 1977). Private policing, despite its complementarity to the state sector (Shearing and Stenning, 1983), is notable only by its absence in the literature.

An ethnocentric explanation of police emergence and functions also ignores those various *democratic* types of policework and of police organisation that have dotted a more authoritarian plain. There are latter-day examples such as Bittner's (1975) account of a 'team-based' and decentralised model of police organisation in the context of advanced capitalism. One historical experiment rarely receives as much as a foot-note (Emsley, 1983). In the French Revolutionary context of 1848, a transient police agency guarded the streets of Paris under Minister Caussidiere. That body of '*montagnards*' elected its own officers, and recruited and promoted members on the basis of their political commitment to the new revolutionary state. Police priorities were directed against those who committed crimes against property or persons, not against public disorder. Critically their function was to conciliate on the street, not to repress on behalf of the state. Brady has described a contemporary version of such a policing system in Cuba (Brady, 1982).

Finally, taking nineteenth century history seriously entails paying some attention to the *colonial police work* that originated in response to the same manifest imperatives of riot, crime, social disorganisation, ordering, and class control. Colonial policing functioned to legitimate central rule from Westminster. Colonial policework, and perhaps in turn British police work, was pre-eminently missionary work to legitimise external governance.

Principally the traditional histories miss one major salient feature of the policing of early nineteenth century Britain: its growing importance as an imperial power. Orthodox accounts of police emergence have resulted in the treatment of other forms of policing as simply aberrations from the English: a kind of academic imperialism. But there is another kind of imperial tradition in the study of police origins and functions.

There are in reality only marginal differences between the colonial police and nineteenth century British policing; not the sharp polarities often depicted in the orthodox comparisons between the Metropolitan Police and the Royal Irish Constabulary (Tobias, 1972). Conventional representations of the Royal Irish Constabulary as the direct ancestor of the colonial police ignore the areas of congruence between the former and the Metropolitan, and the specific contribution of the Westminster model to the colonies.

## The relevance of colonial policework

In a major overview of the sociology of policing, Cain (1979) pointed to the lack of consideration of the colonial police. Davis (1985) noted the failure of those studies which have grasped the comparative dimension to recognise the centrality of colonial conquest and incorporation in the development of the British police. (George Orwell's first encounter with the British style of policing was as an Inspector in the Burmese colonial police.)

This lacuna, the failure to acknowledge the imperial commitment, has been acknowledged in one study of Victorian institutional development. Johnson (1982), in an original account of the professionalisation of medicine, argued that the search for 'professional' standards of conduct, and for controls over occupational membership, was inextricably linked to the growth of the imperial state. One way that British rule was imposed or legitimised in the colonies was through the imposition of occupational standards and criteria derived from the British national context. Throughout the Empire, local particularistic rules over the practice of medicine and over the qualities of the practitioners were used to eliminate local competition and, more importantly, to incorporate the colonial territory within the imperial institutional domain. Local medicine was either incorporated as a subsidiary version of the imperial constructions, or delegitimated. Indigenous definitions of medical need and supply were displaced by imperial professional formulations. This thesis on the medical profession gives a major clue to understanding the use of law in the Empire.

Jeffries (1952) documented one problem of the early rulers of the colonial territories. Faced with the quandary of ruling by coercion or consent, they achieved a compromise in a system of law that incorporated some local practices while delegitimising others. The police forces were of the people, but insulated from them and not governed by them. Legal discourse was reconstructed in imperial terms. The continuing dilemma was to persuade the indigenous population that it was not sufficiently advanced to sustain its own judicial practices and law enforcement procedures until it had absorbed the colonial legal construction.

Several authors have acknowledged the critical links between the origins of the English police system and the development of colonial institutions. Bayley (1969) recounted the influence of the British police system in Asia, Africa, and the Middle East. Others made an indirect connection, by comparing the original Irish and Metropolitan forces (Tobias, 1972).

In sum, there is evidence of an immediate link between British policing and colonial practices. British institutions, from medicine to law enforcement, were transplanted to the Empire: to delegitimise indigenous customs; to impose centralised social control; and to incorporate local society as a branch of imperial society.

## Colonising through law

The central predicament of the early imperial state, both in relation to the mainland provinces, and to the new colonies of Africa, Asia, and the West Indies, was to legitimise its authority not only externally but also internally. The rule of London was spread by a variety of devices. Cultural imperialism succeeded coercion (taking, as G.B. Shaw has described it, the territory as a grateful gift from God). This ranged from the imposition of imperial measures of time, the official language of imperial rule, official criteria for professional practice in medicine, and accounting (central to the affairs of the colonial trading companies), and principally through images of law.

In the colonial policing literature, there is ample evidence of imperial arrogance in relation to indigenous law and legal practices, as they imposed British criteria. In the Sind, Sir Charles Napier denied any legitimacy to native institutions (Jeffries, 1952, p. 31). In Hong Kong, the first British governors regarded local law enforcement as non-existent (Crisswell and Watson, 1982, p. 8) no matter how coherent some contemporary civil servants might regard those social norms (Falconer in Ceylon, quoted in Griffiths, 1971).

According to a study of the early Royal Canadian Mounted Police, this delegitimation process together with the installation of imperial rule by the colonial police served varied economic, social and political functions (Morrison, 1975). In the Yukon, the entry of the Mounties to the settlements of gold-diggers disrupted the evolving democratic communal decision-making process, and established a particular capitalist notion of social order in determining that rules were based on property rights. Law was a weapon to ensure imperial rule.

## Policing the provinces, policing the colonies

In several ways, early colonial policing paralleled and reflected less-noted features of Metropolitan policing. In the use of alien rank-and-file, the recruitment of officers, the provision of task forces for outside excursions, the style of policing, the commitment to a preventative function, and even in the stated rationale for formation, the colonial police had a filial relation not just to the Royal Irish Constabulary, but to the practices and organisation of the London Metropolitan Police. Diffusion of ideas between British and colonial policing encompassed the period from Colquhoun (Edwardes, 1923) to the Palestine mandate (Bowden, 1975). Underpinning all these relations was the assumption that colonial police officers drew on the same body of common law powers as did the Metropolitan police (no matter how alien they were to the native tradition).

The original London recruitment of 'alien' patrol officers is acknowledged, if given inadequate emphasis (Miller, 1977, pp. 26–7). This imperial policy of 'policing strangers by strangers' was conducted throughout the colonial domains: in India (Cox, n.d., p. 147), in Ceylon (Dep, 1979), in Hong Kong (Jeffries, 1955), throughout the African colonies (Cramm, 1969; Jeffries, 1952; Foran, 1962), and in the West Indies (Cramm, 1969; Jeffries, 1952). Further insulation from the local populace was guaranteed at command level. In England and Wales, the officer ranks were predominantly filled at the outset by ex-soldiers who had already been alienated from the local habitat (Miller, 1977; Steedman, 1985). Throughout the colonies, the officers were predominantly of British stock (Jeffries, 1952; Bowden, 1978). Policing practices were diffused by officers who started their careers in the Metropolitan Police or the Royal Irish Constabulary before being promoted to the supervision of a colonial force (Jeffries, 1952), even taking the original training manual with them (Foran, 1962).

Colonial police forces had a major reserve function: available in emergency to be rushed to squash distant disorder. In the United Kingdom, the big city forces provided manpower reserves for troubled provinces (Critchley, 1978; Brogden, 1982). That facility was not as pronounced as in Ireland and in the colonies, where police officers commonly lived in barracks, in the form of a gendarmerie, to respond to external emergencies. But the differences were ones of degree rather than absolutes; although some colonial police forces adopted a punitive, para-military function as in the case of the British South African Police (Godly, 1935).

The relationship between the 'home' police and the colonies ranged from the trivial (the Columbo force was at one time clad in Metropolitan uniform: Cox, n.d.) to more serious policing practices. The summary justice that characterised the policing of the lower classes in Victorian England was commonly followed in the colonies. Prostitutes were herded into the ghetto areas, and suspicious characters requested to leave town (in the Yukon – Morrison, 1975; In Bombay – Edwardes, 1923; and in Nairobi – Foran, 1962). Notions of preventative policing (supposedly a unique feature of the mainland British style) justified the creation of colonial forces long before the Metropolitan Police Act 1829. A preventative patrol police was introduced into Columbo as early as 1806 (Pippet, 1938) and at slightly later dates in Bombay (Edwardes, 1923), Jamaica and in British Guiana (Cramm, 1969).

Similar rationales paved the way for a paid police in colonies and in Victorian England. Riot was a common justification. In Jamaica, the emancipation of the slaves created a proletariat deemed threatening by their 'betters' (Jeffries, 1952). In Madras, the first police were developed after a mutiny (riot) and intended to 'keep vigilant observation over the community and to prevent secret plots' (Griffiths, 1971). In Bombay, levels of crime and the incursion of rural migrants were the primary catalysts (Edwardes, 1923).

But most commonly, professional policing was directly linked to the commercial interests of an expanding capitalism in search of new markets and resources. Colonial police history is essentially the history of that socialisation of police work. The British South Africa Company, the Royal Nigeria Company, and the Imperial British East Africa Company amongst others, established policing systems. The East Indian Company spread its police tentacles as far as Singapore. The primary justifications for the new police were the exigencies of trade and company profit (Jeffries, 1952; Foran, 1962).

Most of the future British colonies commenced their imperial connection as the private domains of limited companies based in London. Colonial ventures were profit-motivated. Like the Liverpool merchants and shopkeepers (Brogden, 1983) committed to the cheap reproduction of labour and to distraints on competitors, the colonial governments saw the economic imperative as foremost in establishing a professional police.

In several ways therefore, colonial policing replicated the policing of Victorian society. There were differences of degree rather than in intent and organisation. This is not to deny that there were certain distinctions between the policing of Britain and the policing of the colonies, rather to suggest that the two types of policing are not separate categories but ranged on a continuum, in which some features are more heavily weighted towards the extremes than are others.

## The unique features of colonial policing

There remain some discontinuities, situations in which the model for the colonies was clearly and absolutely the Royal Irish Constabulary, with few obligations to Rowan and Mayne. Principal amongst these similarities (and leaving the question of armaments aside) were the form of control; the physical location of the police, and their link with the military (Bayley, 1969).

In Ireland, the Royal Irish Constabulary was a national force controlled from Dublin Castle (Tobias, 1972). Similarly, in Hong Kong and the Indian provinces, the police were under the control of a civil official who was normally subordinate to the Governor. The colonial police were directly at the service of the civil power, not maintained at some distance as with the mediating common law powers of the English police. However, not too much should be made of this difference. In the first place, the relationship between the local police commanders and civil authorities in England and Wales arguably was less clear-cut than the common law view suggests (Brogden, 1982). Secondly, as colonial policing evolved, in many colonies a similar structure of law enforcement developed as in the imperial state; with the separation of the enforcement arm from the judicial function (Jeffries, 1952).

The second key difference between Westminster-model forces and the colonial police lies in their physical location and their close proximity to the military. Like some Continental forces today (for example, the *Guarda Civil*, the *Gendarmerie Nationale*, and the *Bereitschaftspolizei*), the colonial police were often accommodated in barracks separate from the civil population. The Hong Kong Police in particular followed the Royal Irish Constabulary directly in this practice, as in the carrying of armaments, and in the form of control. The British South African Police had the clearest link with the military. In the African colonies generally, in emergencies (such as during World War I), the colonial police forces were conscripted as an arm of the military (Foran, 1962). But not all colonial forces had such a relationship: the important Indian Police Act 1861 attempted to distinguish between policing and military functions in that country.

### Incorporation and delegitimation

Internal colonisation, like external colonisation, is faced with a strategic problem in relation to its legitimacy (Brogden, 1987). The imperial state can impose its own arbitrary institutions. Alternatively, it can seek to incorporate existing features of the society within a larger construction defined in terms of imperial interests, practices which are re-shaped while maintaining their traditional connection with the indigenous society.

In British society, the second strategy developed, principally through a re-construction of the 'citizen-in-uniform' and 'original powers' theme. Police officers could justify their practices by reference to the 'reconstructed' images of the pre-industrial tythingman and parish constable (Hall *et al.*, 1978). Internal police colonialism drew heavily on this connection between provincial working-class cultures and the new dominant ideology of industrial capitalism. In many of the Asian colonies, a similar structure was pursued (Griffiths, 1971, p. 56; Jeffries, 1952).

However, in colonies that had been acquired by conquest, from the Sind to Rhodesia, the indigenous legal system was ignored and a new imperial system imposed from above. In Hong Kong, in most of the African colonies and in the West Indies, local institutions, including the legal system and its appendages, were largely delegitimised. Local law enforcement practices were invalidated and imperial structures imposed.

The exploration of facets of colonial policing, such as the processes of incorporation and the delegitimisation of existing legal structures, permits a fresh consideration of policing in mainland Britain. Robert Storch's domestic missionaries (Storch, 1970) were in fact just that: apostles of the Westminster law enforcement gospel in provincial England (despite their coercive exaggeration in some radical citations of that author's work).

*From M. Brogen, The emergence of the police: The Colonial dimension, British Journal of Criminology, Vol. 27, (1) 1987, pp 4–14.*

### References

Bayley, D.H. (1969). *The Police and Political Development In India*. London: Sage.

Bittner, E. (1974). 'Florence Nightingale in Pursuit of Willie Sutton: A Theory of the Police', in Jacob, H. (ed.) *The Potential for Reform in Criminal Justice*. Beverly Hills: Sage. 17–44.

Bowden, T. (1976). *Men in the Middle – The UK Police*. London: Institute for the Study of Conflict.

Bowden, T. (1978). *Beyond the Limits of the Law*. Harmondsworth, Middlesex: Penguin.

Brady, J. (1982). 'Law in Revolutionary Context'. In C. Sumner (ed.) *Crime, Justice and Underdevelopment*. London: Heinemann.

Brodeur, J.P. (1983). 'High Policing and Low Policing: Remarks about the Policing of Political Activities', *Social Problems*, 30: 5, pp. 507–20, June.

Brogden, M.E. (1983). 'Policing a Mercantile Economy', *4th European Conference on Critical Legal Studies*, University of Kent.

Brogden, M.E., (1987). 'An Act to Colonize the Interior Lands of the Island', *International Journal of the Sociology of Law*.

Cain, M.E. (1979). 'Trends in the Sociology of Policework', *International Journal of the Sociology of Law*, 7.2, 143–67.

Cox, E.C. (n.d.). *Police and Crime in India*. London: Stanley Parks and Co.

Cramm, J. (1969). *The World's Police*. London: Cassell.

Crisswell, C. and Watson, M. (1982). *The Royal Hong Kong Police*. Hong Kong: Mannela.

Critchley, T.A. (1978). *A History of Police in England and Wales* (2nd. ed.). London, Constable [1st ed.: 1967].

Critchley, T.A. (1970). *The Conquest of Violence*. London: Batsford.

Davis, J. (1985). 'Review of Emsley: Policing and its Context', *International Journal of the Sociology of Law*, 13, 3.

Dep, M. (1979). *A History of the Ceylon Police*, Vol. II. Columbo: n.p.

Donzelot, J. (1979). *The Policing of Families*. New York: Pantheon Books.

Edwardes, S.M. (1923). *The Bombay City Police 1672–1916*. London: Oxford University Press.

Emsley, C. (1983). *Policing and its Context 1750–1870*. London: Macmillan.

Field, J. (1981). 'Police, Power, and Community in a Provincial English Town, 1815–75', in V. Bailey (ed.) *Policing and Punishment in 19th century Britain*. London: Croom Helm. 42–64.

Foran, W.R. (1962). *The Kenya Police 1877–1960*. London: Robert Hale.

Godley, R.S. (1935). *Khaki and Blue*. London: Dickson and Thompson.

Griffiths, P. (1979). *To Guard My People – The History of the Indian Police*. London: Ernest Benn.

Hall, S., Critcher, C., Jefferson, T., Clarke, J. Roberts, B. (1978). *Policing the Crisis*. London: Macmillan.

Harring, S.L. (1979). 'Class Conflict and the Suppression of Tramps in Buffalo, 1892–1894', in Messinger, S.I. and Bittner, E. (eds.) *Criminology Review Yearbook*. Beverly Hills: Sage.

Harring, S.L. (1983). *Policing a Class Society*. New Brunswick: Rutgers U.P.

Jeffries, C. (1952). *The Colonial Police*. London: Max Parrish.

Johnson, D.R. (1979). *Policing the Urban Underworld*. Philadelphia: Temple U.P.

Johnson, T. (1982). 'The State and the Professions', in A. Giddens and G. Mackenzie (eds) *Social Class and the Division of Labour*. Cambridge: Cambridge U.P. 186–209.

Kakalik, J.S. and Wildhorn, S. (1977). *The Private Police*. New York: Crane Russak.

Klockars, C.B. (1985). *The Idea of Police*. London: Sage.

Lane, R. (1967). *Policing the City*. Cambridge, Mass: Harvard U.P.

Lane, R. (1980). 'Urban Police and Crime in Nineteenth Century America', in N. Morris and M. Tonry (eds) *Crime and Justice: An Annual Review Research*. Chicago: Chicago University Press. 1–44.

Levett, A.E. (1975). *Centralisation of City Police in the Nineteenth Century United States*. Ph.d. dissertation, Ann Arbor: University of Michigan.

Miller, W.R. (1977). *Cops and Bobbies*. Chicago: University of Chicago Press.

Monkkonen, E.H. (1981). *Police in Urban America, 1860–1920*. London: Cambridge U.P.

Morrison, W. (1975). 'The North West Mounted Police and the Klondike Gold Rush', in G. Mosse (ed.) *Police Forces in History*. London: Sage. 263–76.

Phillips, D. (1980). 'A New Engine of Power and Authority: The Institutionalisation of Law Enforcement in England 1780–1830', in V. Gatrell, B. Lenman and G. Parker (eds) *Crime and the Law*. London: Europa. 155–89.

Pippet, K. (1938). *A History of the Ceylon Police*, Vol. I. Columbo: n.p.

Radzinowicz, L. (1955). *A History of English Criminal Law and its Administration*, Vol. III, London: Stevens.

Richardson, J.F. (1970). *The New York Police: Colonial Times to 1901*. New York: Oxford University Press.

Scraton, P. (1985). *The State of the Police*. London: Pluto.

Shearing, C. and Stenning, P. (1983). Private security: Implications for social control, *Social Problems*, 30, 5, 493–506, June.

Silver, A. (1967). 'The Demand for Order in Civil Society', in D. Bordua (ed.) *The Police*. New York: Wiley. 1–24.

Spitzer, S. and Scull, A. (1977). 'Social Control in Historical Perspective', in D. Greenberg (ed.) *Corrections and Punishment*. Beverly Hills: Sage. 265–86.

Stead, P.J. (1977) 'The New Police', in D.H. Bayley (ed.) *Police and Society*. London: Sage. 73–84.

Steadman (1984) *Policing the Victorian Community*. London: Routledge.

Storch, R. (1976) 'The Policeman as Domestic Missionary', *J. Soc. Hist.*, IX: 4, Summer, 481–509.

Sumner, C. (1982). *Crime, Justice, and Underdevelopment*. London: Heinemann.

Tobias, J.J. (1972). 'Police and the Public in the U.K.', *Journal of Contemporary History*. 7: 1, 201–20.

Walker, S. (1977). *A Critical History of Police Reform*. Lexington: D.C. Heath.

# 6. The emergence of the police – explaining police reform in eighteenth and nineteenth century England

*John Styles*

In his chapter 'The Emergence of the Police – The Colonial Dimension', Mike Brogden challenges what he sees as the hallmarks of the Anglo-American sociology of the police: ethnocentricity, inadequate comparative knowledge of policing, and a-historicism. As a corrective, he argues that explanations of the character and emergence of the English police must take into account the wider context of British colonial policing in the nineteenth and twentieth centuries. There is a good deal here with which current historians of the English police will wholeheartedly agree. They too are anxious to contest the tendency in some sociological work to conflate intentions with outcomes: to equate, for example, the rationales for new forms of policing offered by eighteenth and nineteenth century police reformers with the kind of policing that emerged from the reform process. Like Brogden, they are conscious of the necessity for a comparative dimension. Police historians have long acknowledged the importance that French policing played in the debates that surrounded late eighteenth and early nineteenth century police reform in England. They are aware that to evaluate changes in English policing it is essential to establish a much wider sense of what policing was like in other places and periods (Emsley, 1983).

That said, there remain aspects of Brogden's essay with which I and many other historians will take issue, in particular his understanding of the terms police and policing, and his handling of the linkages (both historical and analytical) between the history of policing in England and elsewhere. These areas of disagreement oblige us to confront key issues concerning the emergence and character of the English police; issues that are currently at the forefront of research and debate among historians.

Brogden places great emphasis on colonial policing, but he invokes colonial and other models of policing primarily in order to oblige us to re-evaluate the emergence and character during the early nineteenth century of the 'new' police. Like most sociologists and historians who have considered the emergence of the English police, Brogden's chronological focus is the period between the 1820s and the 1850s, which saw the establishment, eventually on a nation-wide basis, of the 'new' police in England. In contrast to many accounts of police emergence, his rightly emphasises that there were a variety of policing strategies available in early nineteenth century England, that there was no inevitability about the eventual outcome of police reform, and that many of the characteristics of the early Metropolitan police and the provincial forces modelled upon it were neither new in 1829, nor uniquely English.

These propositions raise a number of important and unsettling questions for Brogden's own analysis. In particular, why does Brogden conduct his discussion of English police emergence (both with regard to what constitutes police and to the timing of police emergence) by reference to the early Metropolitan force? The answer appears to be that Brogden is not concerned, first and foremost, with the historian's task of explaining the *processes* that brought about changes in policing in the eighteenth and nineteenth centuries. Rather, his primary concern is to identify historical *models* of policing other than the early Metropolitan one, so that 'more sense can be made of the police public order role in present society, by inserting the material omitted from most police histories'. In other words, Brogden is anxious to use the history of British colonial policing to challenge the way that the early Metropolitan model (as conventionally represented) has been employed in modern debates about British policing. This challenge entails a critical juxtaposition of the colonial and Metropolitan models, not a fundamental re-appraisal of the historical processes by which policing was re-constituted in either the colonial or the English settings (it should also be pointed out that it involves a characterisation of the chronology and, to a lesser extent, the practice of policing in the British colonies which is excessively monolithic and lacks a sense of context).

Although historians are not and should not be unaware of the relationships between their own work and modern debates, they are usually acutely conscious of the need to avoid anachronism; to avoid explanations for eighteenth or nineteenth century innovations and priorities simply in terms of modern concerns. If Brogden's undoubted insights are to contribute to a historical explanation of changes in policing that is not anachronistic, two issues require much more careful evaluation – the definition and the chronology of police emergence. These are important because so many attempts to explain changes in policing propose a causal link between some aspect of the socio-economic context (crime, industrialisation, urbanisation, the 'needs' of capital) and particular institutional innovations, yet fail to specify with sufficient precision the timing of the particular innovation and its extent (as well as the precise nature of the socio-economic influences). Such conceptual woolliness blocks critical examination of the causal *mechanisms* being proposed.

This is not the place to embark on a general discussion of the historical utility and meaning of the terms police and policing. However, some of the *problems* of definition and their implications can be illustrated simply by considering the adjectives Brogden uses in his essay to distinguish the 'new' police of the second quarter of the nineteenth century. They are described variously as salaried, professional, organised, state-appointed, preventative, uniformed, or simply new. The multiplicity of adjectives should immediately alert us to the problems of definition involved. A cursory examination of the history of policing quickly demonstrates that the 'new' police forces cannot be easily distinguished from their predecessors by most of these epithets.

*Salaried* constables and watchmen were already widespread in England in the eighteenth century and became increasingly so in the early nineteenth century. Whether it is appropriate to describe such officials as *professional*, a word which carries overtones of career, training and uniform standards of performance, is questionable. But then it is also questionable whether the 'new' police forces, often initially recruited from among pre-existing watchmen and characterised by high staff turnovers in their early years, should be so described. Many of the paid local watches of the late eighteenth and early nineteenth centuries were *organised*, in the sense that they were forces subject to some degree of internal co-ordination and discipline. The product of piecemeal local legislation or initiative, these watch forces did not amount to an organised, national police system, but it is not at all clear that the 'new' police, at least before the last quarter of the nineteenth century, represented an organised national system, given the continuing diversity of local practice. It was only between the 1870s and the end of the nineteenth century that a new bureaucratic uniformity, imposed by the Home Office, began to emerge (Steedman, 1984; Gatrell, 1987). This lack of uniformity was partly because, with the well-known and significant exception of the Metropolitan force, the 'new' police were not *state-appointed*, in the sense of being subject to formal direct control by a central government minister or department. Like borough watch forces and parish constables before them, most of the 'new' police were subject to appointment by local notables holding local office, although in the counties the coming of the 'new' police involved a shift in the level of control within the local state apparatus, away from the notables who dominated parish society (mainly farmers and the better-off tradesmen) to the county magistrates (predominantly gentry).

Of course, the adjective that was and is most often used to distinguish the 'new' police is *preventative*. Edwin Chadwick, perhaps the foremost advocate of police reform in the first half of the nineteenth century, and the early leaders of the Metropolitan force constantly emphasised that the 'new' police were to be pro-active rather than re-active. They were to prevent crime, mainly through a system of surveillance by patrol, rather than to undertake detective work after the event. In practice, the currency enjoyed by this narrow and purist definition of prevention was shortlived. Earlier police reformers, like Sir John Fielding in the third quarter of the eighteenth century, had seen prevention as being a matter *both* of pro-active surveillance *and* deterrence through effective detection. By the third quarter of the nineteenth century the Metropolitan police were in effect adopting a similar approach. Moreover, it is doubtful whether the sort of preventative patrolling adopted by the Metropolitan force in its early years was different in kind from that undertaken by pre-existing watch forces, although this is an area that requires more research.

In what sense then, if any, were the 'new' police new? To some extent, the fact that they were *uniformed* distinguished them visually from most pre-existing watchmen and constables, who had generally only carried staves or badges, or worn a great coat: The type of uniform adopted in 1829 publicly identified the 'new' police as a disciplined, integrated unit with semi-military associations, although the choice of blue uniform rather than red emphasised their difference from the army. This emphasis on public identification is no coincidence, because in many ways the most striking distinguishing feature of the 'new' police is that they were presented and perceived as something *new*. Although they were far from homogeneous and in most respects drew on existing practice, the fact that, in London and the counties, highly identifiable and self-consciously innovatory forces were superimposed, at a stroke, on a variety of local policing practices represented a significant and very visible change.

That said, it should be clear from the preceding discussion that there are considerable problems with any typology which traces police emergence to the establishment of the 'new' police alone. The development of paid policing and police forces in England was happening long before the setting up of the Metropolitan force in 1829, while professionalisation, central direction and national standardisation remained weak long after that date. In other words, if we take police emergence loosely to refer to the development of paid police forces (as a rough and ready way of avoiding that teleology which reduces historical inquiry to tracing the origins of a modern phenomenon), then the process of police emergence in England was a protracted and uneven one, in which the Metropolitan police was only one, albeit crucial element.

Having thus established some sense of the extended chronology of police innovation in England, we are now in a better position to consider the relationship between developments in England and those elsewhere. A striking feature of that relationship is that it is most unlikely that policing in Britain's extra-European colonies had a significant influence during the major part of the protracted period of police emergence in England. Most of the colonial forces were established in the second half of the nineteenth century, the period that saw the most dramatic expansion of formal empire. There may well have been important colonial influences on English policing during this later period, perhaps through the transfer of senior personnel, or perhaps through central government as it came to exercise an increasingly dirigiste influence over English forces and set professional priorities that may have reflected colonial imperatives. It is hard to see, however, given the chronology, that these would represent sufficiently important influences on the character of English policing to oblige us, in Brogden's words, 'to recognise the centrality of colonial conquest and incorporation to the development of the British police'.

Of course, comparative history is not simply a matter of tracing the direct influences that practices in one setting had on innovation in another. Comparison also provides us with a sense of the variety of possible police responses to similar perceived problems, of the diverse uses to which similar institutions can be put in different settings and of the diverse meanings they can acquire. Hence Brogden is right to alert us to the fact that there are many parallels between policing in nineteenth century England and colonial policing, particularly with regard to preventative patrolling and local autonomy in day-to-day policing, and to ask us to consider the implications of those parallels. There are not two watertight historical models of British policing, one English and one colonial. However, it is important to point out that many of the same parallels can be identified between nineteenth century English police practice and policing in eighteenth century France or nineteenth century Ireland. The problem that Brogden's comparative exercise has identified here is not one that is peculiar to English and colonial policing, but is inherent in the crude compartmentalisation of police styles that pervades police rhetoric, the older police histories and much sociological writing on the police. Successful comparative history requires extreme care in the specification of what is to be compared and why.

Although comparison can provide a vital analytical perspective on institutional change, historical explanation of such change must ultimately be anchored in the specific historical context in which the particular change at issue took place. I shall conclude by considering some of the implications of the issues of definition and comparison raised by Brogden's essay for the ways recent historians have tried to explain the emergence of the police *in England*.

As Brogden illustrates, most of what he calls the orthodox accounts of the establishment of the 'new' police in England in the 1820s and 1830s have been couched in terms of problem-response models. The introduction of the 'new' police is explained as the response of the governing classes to perceived problems of riot, crime, social disorganisation, working class indiscipline, or some combination of these and other problems. At their worst, such accounts have crudely juxtaposed some very generally specified problem: increased levels of 'antisocial' behaviour, or accentuated class conflict resulting from industrialisation and urbanisation, and a response: the 'new' police, which is presented as the inevitable and the wholly appropriate outcome (for example, Reith, 1938; Critchley, 1967). In recent (and continuing) work, the same explanatory models have been used with much more historical sensitivity. Such work displays an awareness of the extended chronology of police emergence, of the changing and diverse ways problems were perceived, and of the variety of possible responses. In this work outcomes were not predetermined, economic and social circumstance were conditioning and constraining rather than determining, and policy debate was an important independent influence (for example, Phillips, 1980; Jones, 1983; Reiner, 1985).

This kind of pluralistic, open-ended approach is not without its problems, however. It avoids the pitfalls of teleology and vulgar functionalism, but its inherent particularism runs the risk either of obscuring general issues altogether, or of simply perpetuating, in a more nuanced guise, the types of general explanation found in earlier work. What is missing here is an effort to explore the wider administrative and policy-forming context within which decisions were made. Attempts to explain police reform need to consider much more seriously how institutional innovation in late eighteenth and early nineteenth century England was facilitated or limited by the structure and organisation of the British state, and by the fundamental assumptions which prevailed among those who shaped policy about the *capacity* of the state to influence social life. Both state structures and prevailing assumptions about state capacity have their own independent histories, which cannot simply be reduced to problems of crime or disorder, to class interest, or to 'industrialisation'.

A comparative perspective can be particularly helpful in grappling with this kind of issue. Take, for example, the question of how the terms of policy debate and innovation were set. How were broad understandings of what constituted appropriate and feasible responses to perceived threats to order constructed? How, in particular, did notions of police as a *system*, in which forces of paid patrolling officers would play a key role, establish themselves on the agenda of debate in England?

In considering these questions, it is important to bear in mind that, in the mid-eighteenth century, various kinds of what can loosely be termed police forces were already familiar in continental Europe – the primarily detective *Sbirri* in parts of Italy, the more preventative urban police forces and *Marechaussée* in France (Hughes, 1983; Williams, 1979; Cameron, 1981). At the same period, moreover, the City of London itself had a force of over seven hundred paid watchmen. In other words, the idea of a force of men paid to uphold aspects of the internal security of parts of the country was neither entirely new in England, nor without well-developed continental parallels. It was only from the later eighteenth century, however, that discussion in Britain of problems of crime, riot and disorder came to be conducted predominantly in terms of the desirability or otherwise of some *system* of police, in which such a force would have a decisive role. The threats to social order in England posed by crime or riot, or more loosely associated with industrialisation or urbanisation or radical politics, cannot, of themselves, satisfactorily explain this shift in discourse. After all, later eighteenth century problems of riot, crime, and urbanisation were far from being unprecedented. Morever, a similar shift in the terms of debate was associated from the 1780s onward with the threat to order posed by popular agrarian movements in *rural* Ireland (Boyle, 1973; Broeker, 1970). Irrespective of the source and precise nature of the perceived threat, from the later eighteenth century, discussion in British governing circles of problems of order (broadly defined) increasingly came to revolve around the creation of a system of police.

One of the important elements in the shift in debate was a growing dissatisfaction with the existing apparatus of law enforcement: a dissatisfaction which reflected not so much some inherent, essential weakness in that apparatus, but rather changing assessments of what it should be expected to deliver. Again a comparative perspective can be of assistance in refining our analysis of this change.

French policing institutions owed much to two characteristics of the seventeenth and eighteenth century French state. First, and more importantly, to the state's efforts to establish centralised institutions of administration to challenge the entrenched and highly particularistic power of local elites. Second, to its policy of financing the wars resulting from its ambitions on the international stage through the creation of a multiplicity of venal (including police) offices. Neither of these considerations were influential in England. Perhaps the greatest achievement of the Medieval English state was the establishment of an exceptionally centralised and uniform system of law and administration, in which central authority was exercised through local elites who were themselves represented at the centre in parliament (a point that casts considerable doubt on Brogden's argument that the nineteenth-century English police had to perform the *same* task as colonial forces in establishing the legitimacy of central institutions in the English provinces). England, moreover, fought few wars in the sixteenth and seventeenth centuries, and the financing of its many expensive and successful eighteenth-century wars was organised through an efficient tax bureaucracy, not through the creation and sale of jobs in the state apparatus.

The absence of a French-style system of police in eighteenth century England did not, therefore, simply represent a perverse tolerance for administrative inefficiency and a wilful predisposition to ignore, in the name of English liberty, superior continental models of policing; a predisposition which persisted until, towards the end of the century, problems of disorder became so pressing as to necessitate reform. The lack of police in England needs to be thought about in terms of the absence there of the administrative and fiscal imperatives that shaped the eighteenth century French system of policing.

The situation in eighteenth century England was not, however, a static one. One important change concerned the way in which local administration and, in particular, the magistracy were perceived. Increasingly, the performance of magistrates came to be judged in terms of a notion of disinterested public service, rather than in terms of the individual justice's personal authority in his locality, as had previously been the case (Landau, 1984). A public service model of the magistracy brought in its train more demanding and uniform standards of magisterial performance. If magistrates failed to match up to these new criteria when faced with a variety of threats to order, including those which figure so prominently in the orthodox police histories (and often they did fail to do so), then alternatives to the magistracy as then constituted were likely to be canvassed. Insofar as the new criteria extolled impersonal public service and disinterested administrative efficiency, some sort of bureaucratic police system, incorporating a stipendiary magistracy and a paid police force to sustain the authority of that magistracy, was likely to be prominent among the alternatives. Particulars of the French policing apparatus became increasingly well known during the eighteenth century (Mildmay, 1763). The success in England of the Excise service, a highly effective and non-venal tax bureaucracy, increased confidence that a salaried government service could be made to fulfil the administrative goals set for it, although huge doubts persisted about the political dangers posed by such organisations (Torrance, 1978).

Exactly why standards of magisterial performance came to change is a matter of complex political, intellectual and administrative shifts during the late seventeenth and eighteenth centuries; shifts that are not yet fully understood (Landau, 1984). What *is* clear is that these changes in standards cannot be explained merely by reference to problems of crime, public order and social transformation at the end of the eighteenth century and the beginning of the nineteenth. It should also be evident that this is a problem of explanation to which comparative history of the kind Brogden proposes can make a valuable contribution.

This essay has criticised some of Michael Brogden's specific suggestions regarding comparative police history. The purpose has been to clarify the ways comparative history might be used in explaining the emergence of the police, not to dismiss the desirability of such a history. Brogden's call for more comparative historical work, and his concern, as a sociologist working primarily on aspects of modern policing, to explore the historical dimension are admirable. Both deserve enthusiastic support from historians of police.

*From J. Styles, The emergence of the police, British Journal of Criminology, Vol. 27 (1) 1987, pp 15–22.*

## References

Bittner, E. (1975). 'Florence Nightingale in Pursuit of Willie Sutton: A Theory of the Police', in Jacob, H. (ed.) *The Potential for Reform in Criminal Justice*. Beverly Hills: Sage. 17–44.

Bowden, T. (1975). *Men in the Middle – The UK Police*. London: Institute for the Study of Conflict.

Boyle, K. (1973). 'Police in Ireland before the Union: II', *The Irish Jurist*, 8.

Broeker, G. (1970). *The Police: Autonomy and Consent*. London: Academic Press.

Cameron, I.A. (1981). *Crime and Repression in the Auvergne and the Guyenne, 1720–1790*. Cambridge: Cambridge University Press.

Edwardes, S.M. (1923). *The Bombay City Police 1672–1916*. London: Oxford University Press.

Gattrell, V.A.C. (1987). 'Crime, Authority and the Policeman-State, 1750–1950', in Thompson, F.M.L. (ed.) *The Cambridge Social History of Britain, 1750–1950*. Cambridge: Cambridge University Press.

Hughes, S. (1983). 'Fear and Loathing in Bologna and Rome: The Papal Police in Perspective' (paper presented to the Past and Present Society Colloquium on Police and Policing, Oxford, July 1983).

Jones, D.J.V. (1983). 'The New Police, Crime and People in England and Wales, 1829–1888', *Transactions of the Royal Historical Society*. Fifth Series, 33.

Landau, N. (1984). *The Justices of the Peace, 1679–1760*. Berkeley: University of California Press.

Mildmay, Sir W. (1763). *The Police of France*. London.

Phillips, D. (1980). 'A New Engine of Power and Authority: The Institutionalisation of Law Enforcement in England 1780–1830', in V. Gatrell, B. Lenman and G. Parker (eds) *Crime and the Law*. London: Europa. 155–89.

Steedman, C. (1984). *Policing the Victorian Community*. London: Routledge.

Williams, A. (1979). *The Police of Paris 1718–1789*. Baton Rouge: Louisiana State University Press.

# 7. The evolving strategy of policing

*George L. Kelling and Mark H. Moore*

Policing, like all professions, learns from experience. It follows, then, that as modern police executives search for more effective strategies of policing, they will be guided by the lessons of police history. The difficulty is that police history is incoherent, its lessons hard to read. After all, that history was produced by thousands of local departments pursuing their own visions and responding to local conditions. Al-though that varied experience is potentially a rich source of lessons, departments have left few records that reveal the trends shaping modern policing. Interpretation is necessary.

## Methodology

This essay presents an interpretation of police history that may help police executives considering alternative future strategies of policing. Our reading of police history has led us to adopt a particular point of view. We find that a dominant trend guiding today's police executives – a trend that encourages the pursuit of independent, professional autonomy for police departments – is carrying the police away from achieving their maximum potential, especially in effective crime fighting. We are also convinced that this trend in policing is weakening *public* policing relative to *private* security as the primary institution providing security to society. We believe that this has dangerous long-term implications not only for police departments but also for society. We think that this trend is shrinking rather than enlarging police capacity to help creative civil communities. Our judgment is that this trend can be reversed only by refocusing police attention from the pursuit of professional autonomy to the establishment of effective problem-solving partnerships with the communities they police.

Delving into police history made it apparent that some assumptions that now operate as axioms in the field of policing (for example that effectiveness in policing depends on distancing police departments from politics; or that the highest priority of police departments is to deal with street crime; or that the best way to deal with street crime is through directed patrol, rapid response to calls for service, and skilled retrospective investigations) are not timeless truths, but rather choices made by former police leaders and strategists. To be sure, the choices were often wise and far-seeing as well as appropriate to their times. But the historical perspective shows them to be choices nonetheless, and therefore open to reconsideration in the light of later professional experience and changing environmental circumstances.

We are interpreting the results of our historical study through a framework based on the concept of 'corporate strategy'.[1] Using this framework, we can describe police organizations in terms of seven interrelated categories:

- The sources from which the police construct the legitimacy and continuing power to act on society.
- The definition of the police function or role in society.
- The organizational design of police departments.
- The relationships the police create with the external environment.
- The nature of police efforts to market or manage the demand for their services.
- The principal activities, programs, and tactics on which police agencies rely to fulfil their mission or achieve operational success.
- The concrete measures the police use to define operational success or failure.

Using this analytic framework, we have found it useful to divide the history of policing into three different eras. These eras are distinguished from one another by the apparent dominance of a particular strategy of policing. The political era, so named because of the close ties between police and politics, dated from the introduction of police into muni-cipalities during the 1840s, continued through the Progressive period, and ended during the early 1900's. The reform era developed in reaction to the political. It took hold during the 1930's, thrived during the 1950's and 1960's, began to erode during the late 1970's. The reform era now seems to be giving way to an era emphasizing community problem-solving.

By dividing policing into these three eras dominated by a particular strategy of policing, we do not mean to imply that there were clear boundaries between the eras. Nor do we mean that in those eras everyone policed in the same way. Obviously, the real history is far more complex than that. Nonetheless, we believe that there is a certain professional ethos that defines standards of competence, pro-fessionalism, and excellence in policing; that at any given time, one set of concepts is more powerful, more widely shared, and better understood than others; and that this ethos changes over time. Sometimes, this professional ethos has been explicitly articulated, and those who have articulated the concepts have been recognized as the leaders of their profession. O.W. Wilson, for example, was a brilliant expositor of the central elements of the reform strategy of policing. Other times, the ethos is implicit – accepted by all as the tacit assumptions that define the business of policing and the proper form for a police department to take. Our task is to help the profession look to the future by representing its past in these terms and trying to understand what the past portends for the future.

**The political era**

Historians have described the characteristics of early policing in the United

States, especially the struggles between various interest groups to govern the police.[2] Elsewhere, the authors of this paper analyzed a portion of American police history in terms of its organizational strategy.[3] The following discussion of elements of the police organizational strategy during the political era expands on that effort.

### Legitimacy and authorization

Early American police were authorized by local municipalities. Unlike their English counterparts, American police departments lacked the powerful, central authority of the crown to establish a legitimate, unifying mandate for their enterprise. Instead, American police derived both their authorization and resources from local political leaders, often ward politicians. They were, of course, guided by the law as to what tasks to undertake and what powers to utilize. But their link to neighbourhoods and local politicians was so tight that both Jordan[4] and Fogelson[5] refer to the early police as adjuncts to local political machines. The relationship was often reciprocal: political machines recruited and maintained police in office and on the beat, while police helped ward political leaders maintain their political offices by encouraging citizens to vote for certain candidates, discouraging them from voting for others, and, at times, by assisting in rigging elections.

### The police function

Partly because of their close connection to politicians, police during the political era provided a wide array of services to citizens. Inevitably police departments were involved in crime prevention and control and order maintenance, but they also provided a wide variety of social services. In the late 19th century, municipal police departments ran soup lines; provided temporary lodging for newly arrived immigrant workers in station houses;[6] and assisted ward leaders in finding work for immigrants, both in police and other forms of work.

### Organizational design

Although ostensibly organized as a centralized, quasi-military organization with a unified chain of command, police departments of the political era were nevertheless decentralized. Cities were divided into precincts, and precinct-level managers often, in concert with the ward leaders, ran precincts as small-scale departments – hiring, firing, managing, and assigning personnel as they deemed appropriate. In addition, decentralization combined with the primitive communica-tions and transportation to give police officers substantial discretion in handling their individual beats. At best, officer contact with central command was maintained through the call box.

### External relationships

During the political era, police departments were intimately connected to the social and political world of the ward. Police officers often were recruited from the same ethnic stock as the dominant political groups in the localities, and continued to live in the neighbourhoods they patrolled. Precinct commanders consulted often with local political representatives about police priorities and progress.

*Demand management*

Demand for police services came primarily from two sources: ward politicians making demands on the organization and citizens making demands directly on beat officers. Decentralization and political authorization encouraged the first; foot patrol, lack of other means of transportation, and poor communications produced the latter. Basically, the demand for police services was received, interpreted, and responded to at the precinct and street levels.

*Principal programs and technologies*

The primary tactic of police during the political era was foot patrol. Most police officers walked beats and dealt with crime, disorder, and other problems as they arose, or as they were guided by citizens and precinct superiors. The technological tools available to police were limited. However, when call boxes became available, police administra-tors used them for supervisory and managerial purposes; and, when early automobiles became available, police used them to transport officers from one beat to another.[7] The new technology thereby increased the range, but did not change the mode, of patrol officers.

Detective divisions existed but without their current prestige. Operating from a caseload of 'persons' rather than offenses, detectives relied on their caseload to inform on other criminals.[8] The 'third degree' was a common means of interviewing criminals to solve crimes. Detectives were often especially valuable to local politicians for gathering information on individuals for political or personal, rather than offense-related, purposes.

*Measured outcomes*

The expected outcomes of police work included crime and riot control, maintenance of order, and relief from many of the other problems of an industrializing society (hunger and temporary homelessness, for example). Consistent with their political mandate, police emphasized maintaining citizen and political satisfaction with police services as an important goal of police departments.

In sum, the organizational strategy of the political era of policing included the following elements:

- Authorization – primarily political.
- Function – crime patrol, order maintenance, broad social services.
- Organizational design – decentralized and geographical.
- Relationship to environment – close and personal.
- Demand – managed through links between politicians and precinct commanders, and face-to-face contacts between citizens and foot patrol officers.
- Tactics and technology – foot patrol and rudimentary investigations.
- Outcome – political and citizen satisfaction with social order.

The political strategy of early American policing had strengths. First, police were integrated into neighborhoods and enjoyed the support of citizens – at least the support of the dominant and political interests of an area. Second, and probably as a result of the first, the strategy provided useful services to communities. There is evidence that it helped contain riots. Many citizens believed that police prevented crimes or solved crimes when they occurred.[9] And the police assisted immigrants in establishing themselves in communities and finding jobs.

The political strategy also had weaknesses. First, intimacy with community, closeness to political leaders, and a decentralized organiza-tional structure, with its inability to provide supervision of officers, gave rise to police corruption. Officers were often required to enforce unpopular laws foisted on immigrant ethnic neighbourhoods by crusading reformers (primarily of English and Dutch background) who objected to ethnic values.[10] Because of their intimacy with the community, the officers were vulnerable to being bribed in return for nonenforcement or lax enforcement of laws. Moreover, police closeness to politicians created such forms of political corruption as patronage and police interference in elections.[11] Even those few departments that managed to avoid serious financial or political corruption during the late 19th and early 20th centuries, Boston for example, succumbed to large-scale corruption during and after Prohibition.[12]

Second, close identification of police with neighbourhoods and neighbourhood norms often resulted in discrimination against strangers and others who violated these norms, especially minority ethnic and racial groups. Often ruling their beats with the 'ends of their nightsticks', police regularly targeted outsiders and strangers for rousting and 'curbstone justice'.[13]

Finally, the lack of organizational control over officers resulting from both decentralization and the political nature of many appointments to police positions caused inefficiencies and disorganization. The image of Keystone Cops – police as clumsy bunglers – was widespread and often descriptive of realities in American policing.


## The reform era

Control over police by local politicians, conflict between urban reformers and local ward leaders over the enforcement of laws regulating the morality of urban migrants, and abuses (corruption, for example) that resulted from the intimacy between police and political leaders and citizens produced a continuous struggle for control over police during the late 19th and early 20th centuries.[14] Nineteenth-century attempts by civilians to reform police organizations by applying external pressure largely failed; 20th-century attempts at reform, originating from both internal and external forces, shaped con-temporary policing as we knew it through the 1970's.[15]

Berkeley's police chief, August Vollmer, first rallied police executives around the idea of reform during the 1920's and early 1930's. Vollmer's vision of policing was the trumpet call: police in the post-flapper generation were to remind American citizens and other institutions of the moral vision that had made America great and of their responsibilities to maintain that vision.[16] It was Vollmer's protégé, O.W. Wilson, however, who taking guidance from J. Edgar

Hoover's shrewd transformation of the corrupt and discredited Bureau of Investigation into the honest and prestigious Federal Bureau of Investigation (FBI), became the principal administrative architect of the police reform organizational strategy.[17]

Hoover wanted the FBI to represent a new force for law and order, and saw that such an organization could capture a permanent constituency that wanted an agency to take a stand against lawlessness, immorality, and crime. By raising eligibility standards and changing patterns of recruitment and training, Hoover gave the FBI agents stature as upstanding moral crusaders. By committing the organization to attacks on crimes such as kidnapping, bank robbery, and espionage – crimes that attracted wide publicity and required technical sophistication, doggedness, and a national jurisdiction to solve – Hoover established the organization's reputation for professional competence and power. By establishing tight central control over his agents, limiting their use of controversial investigation procedures (such as undercover operations), and keeping them out of narcotics enforcement, Hoover was also able to maintain an unparalleled record of integrity. That, too, fitted the image of a dogged, incorruptible crime-fighting organization. Finally, lest anyone fail to notice the important developments within the Bureau, Hoover developed impressive public relations programs that presented the FBI and its agents in the most favourable light. (For those of us who remember the 1940s, for example, of the most popular radio phrases was, 'The FBI in peace and war' – the introductory line in a radio program that portrayed a vigilant FBI protecting us from foreign enemies as well as villains on the '10 Most Wanted' list, another Hoover,/FBI invention.)

Struggling as they were with reputations for corruption, brutality, unfairness, and downright incompetence, municipal police reformers found Hoover's path a compelling one. Instructed by O.W. Wilson's texts on police administration, they began to shape an organizational strategy for urban police analogous to the one pursued by the FBI.

### Legitimacy and authorization

Reformers rejected politics as the basis of police legitimacy. In their view, politics and political involvement was the *problem* in American policing. Police reformers therefore allied themselves with Progressives. They moved to end the close ties between local political leaders and police. In some states, control over police was usurped by state government. Civil service eliminated patronage and ward influences in hiring and firing police officers. In some cities (Los Angeles and Cincinnati, for example), even the position of chief of police became a civil service position to be attained through examination. In others (such as Milwaukee), chiefs were given lifetime tenure by a police commission, to be removed from office only for cause. In yet others (Boston, for example), contracts for chiefs were staggered so as not to coincide with the mayor's tenure. Concern for separation of police from politics did not focus only on chiefs, however. In some cities, such as Philadelphia, it became illegal for patrol officers to live in the beats they patrolled. The purpose of all these changes was to isolate police as completely as possible from political influences.

Law, especially criminal law, and police professionalism were established as the principal bases of police legitimacy. When police were asked why they performed as they did, the most common answer was that they enforced the law. When they chose not to enforce the law – for instance, in a riot when police isolated an area rather than arrested looters – police justification for such action was found in their claim to professional knowledge, skills, and values which uniquely qualified them to make such tactical decisions. Even in riot situations, police rejected the idea that political leaders should make tactical decisions; that was a police responsibility.[18]

So persuasive was the argument of reformers to remove political influences from policing, that police departments became one of the most autonomous public organizations in urban government.[19] Under such circumstances, policing a city became a legal and technical matter left to the discretion of professional police executives under the guidance of law. Political influence of any kind on a police department came to be seen as not merely a failure of police leadership but as corruption in policing.

### The police function

Using the focus on criminal law as a basic source of police legitimacy, police in the reform era moved to narrow their functioning to crime control and criminal apprehension. Police agencies became *law enforcement* agencies. Their goal was to control crime. Their principal means was the use of criminal law to apprehend and deter offenders. Activities that drew the police into solving other kinds of community problems and relied on other kinds of responses were identified as 'social work', and became the object of derision. A common line in police circles during the 1950s and 1960s was, 'If only we didn't have to do social work, we could really do something about crime'. Police retreated from providing emergency medical services as well – ambulance and emergency medical services were transferred to medical, private, or firefighting organizations.[20] The 1967 President's Commission of Law Enforcement and Administration of Justice ratified this orientation: heretofore, police had been conceptualized as an agency of urban government; the President's Commission reconceptualized them as part of the criminal justice system.

### Organizational design

The organization form adopted by police reformers generally reflected the *scientific* or *classical* theory of administration advocated by Frederick W. Taylor during the early 20th century. At least two assumptions attended classical theory. First, workers are inherently uninterested in work and, if left to their own devices, are prone to avoid it. Second, since workers have little or no interest in the substance of their work, the sole common interest between workers and management is found in economic incentives for workers. Thus, both workers and management benefit economically when management arranges work in ways that increase workers' productivity and link productivity to economic rewards.

Two central principles followed from these assumptions: division of labor and unity of control. The former posited that if tasks can be broken into components, workers can become highly skilled in particular components and thus more efficient in carrying out their tasks. The latter posited that the workers' activities are best managed by a *pyramid of control*, with all authority finally resting in one central office.

Using this classical theory, police leaders moved to routinize and standardize police work, especially patrol work. Police work became a form of crimefighting in which police enforced the law and arrested criminals if the opportunity presented itself. Attempts were made to limit discretion in patrol work: a generation of police officers was raised with the idea that they merely enforced the law.

If special problems arose, the typical response was to create special units (e.g., vice, juvenile, drugs, tactical) rather than to assign them to patrol. The creation of these special units, under central rather than precinct command, served to further centralize command and control and weaken precinct commanders.[21]

Moreover, police organizations emphasized control over workers through bureaucratic means of control: supervision, limited span of control, flow of instructions downward and information upward in the organization, establishment of elaborate record-keeping systems requiring additional layers of middle managers, and coordination of activities between various production units (e.g., patrol and detectives), which also required additional middle managers.

### External relationships

Police leaders in the reform era redefined the nature of a proper relationship between police officers and citizens. Heretofore, police had been intimately linked to citizens. During the era of reform policing, the new model demanded an impartial law enforcer who related to citizens in professionally neutral and distant terms. No better characterization of this model can be found than television's Sergeant Friday, whose response, 'Just the facts, ma'am', typified the idea: impersonal and oriented toward crime solving rather than responsive to the emotional crisis of a victim.

The professional model also shaped the police view of the role of citizens in crime control. Police redefined the citizen role during an era when there was heady confidence about the ability of professionals to manage physical and social problems. Physicians would care for health problems, dentists for dental problems, teachers for educational problems, social workers for social adjustment problems, and police for crime problems. The proper role of citizens in crime control was to be relatively passive recipients of professional crime control services. Citizens' actions on their own behalf to defend themselves or their communities came to be seen as inappropriate, smacking of vigilantism. Citizens met their responsibilities when a crime occurred by calling police, deferring to police actions, and being good witnesses if called upon to give evidence. The metaphor that expressed this orientation to the community was that of the police as the 'thin blue line'. It connotes the existence of dangerous external threats to communities, portrays police as standing between that danger and good citizens, and implies both police heroism and loneliness.

*Demand management*

Learning from Hoover, police reformers vigorously set out to sell their brand of urban policing.[22] They, too, performed on radio talk shows, consulted with media representatives about how to present police, engaged in public relations campaigns, and in other ways presented this image of police as crime fighters. In a sense, they began with an organizational capacity – anticrime police tactics – and intensively promoted it. This approach was more like selling than marketing. Marketing refers to the process of carefully identifying consumer needs and then developing goods and services that meet those needs. Selling refers to having a stock of products or goods on hand irrespective of need and selling them. The reform strategy had as its starting point a set of police tactics (services) that police promulgated as much for the purpose of establishing internal control of police officers and enhancing the status of urban police as for responding to community needs or market demands.[23] The community 'need' for rapid response to calls for service, for instance, was largely the consequence of police selling the service as efficacious in crime control rather than a direct demand from citizens.

Consistent with this attempt to sell particular tactics, police worked to shape and control demand for police services. Foot patrol, when demanded by citizens, was rejected as an outmoded, expensive frill. Social and emergency services were terminated or given to other agencies. Receipt of demand for police services was centralized. No longer were citizens encouraged to go to 'their' neighbourhood police; all calls went to a central communications facility. When 911 systems were installed, police aggressively sold 911 and rapid response to calls for service as effective police service. If citizens continued to use district, or precinct, telephone numbers, some police departments disconnected those telephones or got new telephone numbers.[24]

*Principal programs and technologies*

The principal programs and tactics of the reform strategy were preventive patrol by automobile and rapid response to calls for service. Foot patrol, characterized as outmoded and inefficient, was abandoned as rapidly as police administrators could obtain cars.[25] The initial tactical reasons for putting police in cars had been to increase the size of the areas police officers could patrol and to take advantage away from criminals who began to use automobiles. Under reform policing, a new theory about how to make the best tactical use of automobiles appeared.

O.W.Wilson developed the theory of preventive patrol by automobile as an anticrime tactic.[26] He theorized that if police drove conspicuously marked cars randomly through city streets and gave special attention to certain 'hazards' (bars and schools, for example), a feeling of police omnipresence would be developed. In turn, that sense of omnipresence would both deter criminals and reassure good citizens. Moreover, it was hypothesized that vigilant patrol officers moving rapidly through city streets would happen upon criminals in action and be able to apprehend them.

As telephones and radios became ubiquitous, the availability of cruising police came to be seen as even more valuable: if citizens could be encouraged to call the police via telephone as soon as problems developed, police could respond rapidly to calls and establish control over situations, identify wrong-doers, and make arrests. To this end, 911 systems and computer-aided dispatch were developed throughout the country. Detective units continued, although with some modifications. The 'person' approach ended and was replaced by the case approach. In addition, forensic techniques were upgraded and began to replace the old 'third degree' or reliance on informants for the solution of crimes. Like other special units, most investigative units were controlled by central headquarters.

### Measured outcomes

The primary desired outcomes of the reform strategy were crime control and criminal apprehension.[27] To measure achievement of these outcomes, August Vollmer, working through the newly vitalized Inter-national Association of Chiefs of Police, developed and implemented a uniform system of crime classification and reporting. Later, the system was taken over and administered by the FBI and the *Uniform Crime Reports* became the primary standard by which police organizations measured their effectiveness. Additionally, individual officers' effectiveness in dealing with crime was judged by the number of arrests they made; other measures of police effectiveness included response time (the time it takes for a police car to arrive at the location of a call for service) and 'number of passings' (the number of times a police car passes a given point on a city street). Regardless of all other indicators, however, the primary measure of police effectiveness was the crime rate as measured by the *Uniform Crime Reports*.

In sum, the reform organizational strategy contained the following elements:

- Authorization – law and professionalism.
- Function – crime control.
- Organizational design – centralized, classical.
- Relationship to environment – professionally remote.
- Demand – channeled through central dispatching activities.
- Tactics and technology – preventive patrol and rapid response to calls for service.
- Outcome – crime control.

In retrospect, the reform strategy was impressive. It successfully integrated its strategic elements into a coherent paradigm that was internally consistent and logically appealing. Narrowing police functions to crime fighting made sense. If police could concentrate their efforts on prevention of crime and apprehension of criminals, it followed that they could be more effective than if they dissipated their efforts on other problems. The model of police as impartial, professional law enforcers was attractive because it minimized the discretionary excesses which developed during the political era. Preventive patrol and rapid response to calls for service were intuitively appealing tactics, as well as means to control officers and shape and control citizen demands for service. Further, the strategy provided a comprehensive, yet simple, vision of policing around which police leaders could rally.

The metaphor of the thin blue line reinforced their need to create isolated independence and autonomy in terms that were acceptable to the public. The patrol car became the symbol of policing during the 1930s and 1940s; when equipped with a radio, it was at the limits of technology. It represented mobility, power, conspicuous presence, control of officers, and professional distance from citizens.

During the late 1960s and 1970s, however, the reform strategy ran into difficulty. First, regardless of how police effectiveness in dealing with crime was measured, police failed to substantially improve their record. During the 1960s, crime began to rise. Despite large increases in the size of police departments and in expenditures for a new forms of equipment (911 systems, computer-aided dispatch, etc.), police failed to meet their own or public expectations about their capacity to control crime or prevent its increase. Moreover, research conducted during the 1970s on preventive patrol and rapid response to calls for service suggested that neither was an effective crime control or apprehension tactic.[28]

Second, fear rose rapidly during this era. The consequences of this fear were dramatic for cities. Citizens abandoned parks, public transportation, neighbourhood shopping centres, churches, as well as entire neighbourhoods. What puzzled police and researchers was that levels of fear and crime did not always correspond: crime levels were low in some areas, but fear high. Conversely, in other areas levels of crime were high, but fear low. Not until the early 1980s did researchers discover that fear is more closely correlated with disorder than with crime.[29] Ironically, order maintenance was one of those functions that police had been downplaying over the years. They collected no data on it, provided no training to officers in order maintenance activities, and did not reward officers for successfully conducting order maintenance tasks.

Third, despite attempts by police departments to create equitable police allocation systems and to provide impartial policing to all citizens, many minority citizens, especially blacks during the 1960s and 1970s, did not perceive their treatment as equitable or adequate. They protested not only police mistreatment, but lack of treatment – inadequate or insufficient services – as well.

Fourth, the civil rights and antiwar movements challenged police. This challenge took several forms. The legitimacy of police was questioned: students resisted police, minorities rioted against them, and the public, observing police via live television for the first time, questioned their tactics. Moreover, despite police attempts to upgrade personnel through improved recruitment, training, and supervision, minorities and then women insisted that they had to be adequately represented in policing if police were to be legitimate.

Fifth, some of the myths that undergirded the reform strategy – police officers use little or no discretion and the primary activity of police is law enforcement – simply proved to be too far from reality to be sustained. Over and over again research showed that use of discretion characterized policing at all levels and that law enforcement comprised but a small portion of police officers' activities.[30]

Sixth, although the reform ideology could rally police chiefs and executives, it failed to rally line police officers. During the reform era, police executives had moved to professionalize their ranks. Line officers, however, were managed in ways that were antithetical to professionalization. Despite pious testimony from police executives that 'patrol is the backbone of policing', police executives behaved in ways that were consistent with classical organizational theory – patrol officers continued to have low status; their work was treated as if it were routinized and standardized; and petty rules governed issues such as hair length and off-duty behavior. Meanwhile, line officers received little guidance in use of discretion and were given few, if any, opportunities to make suggestions about their work. Under such circumstances, the increasing 'grumpiness' of officers in many cities is not surprising, nor is the rise of militant unionism.

Seventh, police lost a significant portion of their financial support, which had been increasing or at least constant over the years, as cities found themselves in fiscal difficulties. In city after city, police departments were reduced in size. In some cities, New York for example, financial cutbacks resulted in losses of up to one-third of departmental personnel. Some, noting that crime did not increase more rapidly or arrests decrease during the cutbacks, suggested that New York City had been overpoliced when at maximum strength. For those concerned about levels of disorder and fear in New York City, not to mention other problems, that came as a dismaying conclusion. Yet it emphasizes the erosion of confidence that citizens, politicians, and academicians had in urban police – an erosion that was translated into lack of political and financial support.

Finally, urban police departments began to acquire competition: private security and the community crime control movement. Despite the inherent value of these developments, the fact that businesses, industries, and private citizens began to search for alternative means of protecting their property and persons suggests a decreasing confidence in either the capability or the intent of the police to provide the services that citizens want.

In retrospect, the police reform strategy has characteristics similar to those that Miles and Snow[31] ascribe to a defensive strategy in the private sector. Some of the characteristics of an organization with a defensive strategy are (with specific characteristics of reform policing added in parentheses):

- Its market is stable and narrow (crime victims).
- Its success is dependent on maintaining dominance in a narrow, chosen market (crime control).
- It tends to ignore developments outside its domain (isolation).
- It tends to establish a single core technology (patrol).
- New technology is used to improve its current product or service rather than to expand its product or service line (use of computers to enhance patrol).
- Its management is centralized (command and control).
- Promotions generally are from within (with the exception of chiefs, virtually all promotions are from within).
- There is a tendency toward a functional structure with high degrees of specialization and formalization.

A defensive strategy is successful for an organization when market conditions remain stable and few competitors enter the field. Such strategies are vulnerable, however, in unstable market conditions and when competitors are aggressive.

The reform strategy was a successful strategy for police during the relatively stable period of the 1940s and 1950s. Police were able to sell a relatively narrow service line and maintain dominance in the crime control market. The social changes of the 1960s and 1970s, however, created unstable conditions. Some of the more significant changes included: the civil rights movement; migration of minorities into cities; the changing age of the population (more youths and teenagers); increases in crime and fear; increased overview of police actions by courts; and the decriminalization and deinstitutionalization move-ments. Whether or not the private sector defensive strategy properly applies to police, it is clear that the reform strategy was unable to adjust to the changing social circumstances of the 1960s and 1970s.

## The community problem-solving era

All was not negative for police during the late 1970s and early 1980s, however. Police began to score victories which they barely noticed. Foot patrol remained popular, and in many cities citizen and political demands for it intensified. In New Jersey, the state funded the Safe and Clean Neighborhoods Program, which funded foot patrol in cities, often over the opposition of local chiefs of police.[32] In Boston, foot patrol was so popular with citizens that when neighborhoods were selected for foot patrol, politicians often made the announcements, especially during election years. Flint, Michigan, became the first city in memory to return to foot patrol on a citywide basis. It proved so popular there that citizens twice voted to increase their taxes to fund foot patrol – most recently by a two-thirds majority. Political and citizen demands for foot patrol continued to expand in cities throughout the United States. Research into foot patrol suggested it was more than just politically popular, it contributed to city life: it reduced fear, increased citizen satisfaction with police, improved police attitudes toward citizens, and increased the morale and job satisfaction of police.[33]

Additionally, research conducted during the 1970s suggested that one factor could help police improve their record in dealing with crime: information. If information about crimes and criminals could be obtained from citizens by police, primarily patrol officers, and could be properly managed by police departments, investigative and other units could significantly increase their effect on crime.[34]

Moreover, research into foot patrol suggested that at least part of the fear reduction potential was linked to the order maintenance activities of foot patrol officers.[35] Subsequent work in Houston and Newark indicated that tactics other than foot patrol that, like foot patrol, emphasized increasing the quantity and improving the quality of police–citizen interactions had outcomes similar to those of foot patrol (fear reduction, etc.).[36] Meanwhile, many other cities were developing programs, though not evaluated, similar to those in the foot patrol, Flint, and fear reduction experiments.[37]

The findings of foot patrol and fear reduction experiments, when coupled with the research on the relationship between fear and dis-order, created new opportunities for police to understand the increasing concerns of citizens' groups about disorder (gangs, prostitutes, etc.) and to work with citizens to do something about it. Police discovered that when they asked citizens about their priorities, citizens appreciated the inquiry and also provided useful information – often about problems that beat officers might have been aware of, but about which departments had little or no official data (e.g., disorder). Moreover, given the ambiguities that surround both the definitions of disorder and the authority of police to do something about it, police learned that they had to seek authorization from local citizens to intervene in disorderly situations.[38]

Simultaneously, Goldstein's problem-oriented approach to policing[39] was being tested in several communities: Madison, Wisconsin; Baltimore County, Maryland; and Newport News, Virginia. Problem-oriented policing rejects the fragmented approach in which police deal with each incident, whether citizen- or police-initiated, as an isolated event with neither history nor future. Pierce's findings about calls for service illustrate Goldstein's point: 60 percent of the calls for service in any given year in Boston originated from 10 percent of the households calling the police.[40] Furthermore, Goldstein and his colleagues in Madison, Newport News, and Baltimore County discovered the following: police officers enjoy operating with a holistic approach to their work; they have the capacity to do it successfully; they can work with citizens and other agencies to solve problems; and citizens seem to appreciate working with police – findings similar to those of the foot patrol experiments (Newark and Flint)[41] and the fear reduction experiments (Houston and Newark).[42]

The problem confronting police, policymakers, and academicians is that these trends and findings seem to contradict many of the tenets that dominated police thinking for a generation. Foot patrol creates new intimacy between citizens and police. Problem-solving is hardly the routinized and standardized patrol modality that reformers thought was necessary to maintain control of police and limit their discretion. Indeed, use of discretion is the *sine qua non* of problem-solving policing. Relying on citizen endorsement of order maintenance activities to justify police action acknowledges a continued or new reliance on political authorization for police work in general. And, accepting the quality of urban life as an outcome of good police service emphasizes a wider definition of the police function and the desired effects of police work.

These changes in policing are not merely new police tactics, however. Rather, they represent a new organizational approach, properly called a community strategy. The elements of that strategy are:

### Legitimacy and authorization

There is renewed emphasis on community, or political, authorization for many police tasks, along with law and professionalism. Law continues to be the major legitimating basis of the police function. It defines basic police powers, but it does not fully direct police activities in efforts to maintain order, negotiate conflicts, or solve community problems. It becomes one tool among many others. Neighborhood, or community, support and involvement are required to accomplish those tasks. Professional and bureaucratic authority, especially that which tends to isolate police and insulate them from neighborhood influences, is lessened as citizens contribute more to definitions of problems and identification of solutions. Although in some respects similar to the authorization of policing's political era, community authorization exists in a different political context. The civil service movement, the political centralization that grew out of the Progressive era, and the bureaucratization, professionalization, and unionization of police stand as counterbalances to the possible recurrence of the corrupting influences of ward politics that existed prior to the reform movement.

### The police function

As indicated above, the definition of police function broadens in the community strategy. It includes order maintenance, conflict resolution, problem solving through the organization, and provision of services, as well as other activities. Crime control remains an important function, with an important difference, however. The reform strategy attempts to control crime directly through preventive patrol and rapid response to calls for service. The community strategy emphasizes crime control *and prevention* as an indirect result of, or an equal partner to, the other activities.

### Organizational design

Community policing operates from organizational assumptions different from those of reform policing. The idea that workers have no legitimate, substantive interest in their work is untenable when programs such as those in Flint, Houston, Los Angeles, New York City, Baltimore County, Newport News, and others are examined.

Consulting with community groups, problem-solving, maintaining order, and other such activities are antithetical to the reform ideal of eliminating officer discretion through routinization and standardization of police activities. Moreover, organizational decentralization is inherent in community policing: the involvement of police officers in diagnosing and responding to neighborhood and community problems necessarily pushes operational and tactical decisionmaking to the lower levels of the organization. The creation of neighborhood police stations (storefronts, for example), reopening of precinct stations, and establishment of beat offices (in schools, churches, etc.) are concrete examples of such decentralization.

Decentralization of tactical decisionmaking to precinct or beat level does not imply abdication of executive obligations and functions, however. Developing, articulating, and monitoring organizational strategy remain the responsibility of management. Within this strategy, operational and tactical decisionmaking is decentralized. This implies what may at first appear to be a paradox: while the number of managerial levels may decrease, the number of managers may increase. Sergeants in a decentralized regime, for example, have managerial responsibilities that exceed those they would have in a centralized organization.

At least two other elements attend this decentralization: increased participative management and increased involvement of top police executives in planning and implementation. Chiefs have discovered that programs are easier to conceive and implement if officers themselves are involved in their development through task forces, temporary matrix-like organizational units, and other organizational innovations that tap the wisdom and experience of sergeants and patrol officers. Additionally, police executives have learned that good ideas do not translate themselves into successful programs without extensive involvement of the chief executive and his close agents in every stage of planning and implementation, a lesson learned in the private sector as well.[43]

One consequence of decentralized decisionmaking, participative planning and management, and executive involvement in planning is that fewer levels of authority are required to administer police organizations. Some police organizations, including the London Metropolitan Police (Scotland Yard), have begun to reduce the number of middle-management layers, while others are contemplating doing so. Moreover, as in the private sector, as computerized information gathering systems reach their potential in police departments, the need for middle managers whose primary function is data collection will be further reduced.

### External relationships

Community policing relies on an intimate relationship between police and citizens. This is accomplished in a variety of ways: relatively long-term assignment of officers to beats, programs that emphasize familiarity between citizens and police (police knocking on doors, con-sultations, crime control meetings for police and citizens, assignment to officers of 'caseloads' of households with ongoing problems, problem-solving, etc.), revitalization or development of Police Athletic League programs, educational programs in grad and high schools, and other programs. Moreover, police are encouraged to respond to the feelings and fears of citizens that result from a variety of social problems or from victimization.

Further, the police are restructuring their relationship with neighborhood groups and institutions. Earlier, during the reform era, police had claimed a monopolistic responsibility for crime control in cities, communities, and neighborhoods; now they recognize serious competitors in the 'industry' of crime control, especially private security and the community crime control movement. Whereas in the past police had dismissed these sources of competition or, as in the case of community crime control, had attempted to coopt the movement for their own purposes,[44] now police in many cities (Boston, New York, Houston, and Los Angeles, to name a few) are moving to structure working relationships or strategic alliances with neighborhood and community crime control groups. Although there is less evidence of attempts to develop alliances with the private security industry, a recent proposal to the National Institute of Justice envisioned an experimental alliance between the Fort Lauderdale, Florida, Police Department and the Wackenhut Corporation in which the two organizations would share responses to calls for service.

### Demand management

In the community problem-solving strategy, a major portion of demand is decentralized, with citizens encouraged to bring problems directly to beat officers or precinct offices. Use of 911 is discouraged, except for dire emergencies. Whether tactics include aggressive foot patrol as in Flint or problem solving as in Newport News, the emphasis is on police officers' interacting with citizens to determine the types of problems they are confronting and to devise solutions to those problems. In contrast to reform policing with its selling orientation, this approach is more like marketing: customer preferences are sought, and satisfying customer needs and wants, rather than selling a previously packaged product or service, is emphasized. In the case of police, they gather information about citizens' wants, diagnose the nature of the problem, devise possible solutions, and then determine which segments of the community they can best serve and which can be best served by other agencies and institutions that provide services, including crime control.

Additionally, many cities are involved in the development of demarketing programs.[45] The most noteworthy example of de-marketing is in the area of rapid response to calls for service. Whether through the development of alternatives to calls for service, educational programs designed to discourage citizens from using the 911 system, or, as in a few cities, simply not responding to many calls for service, police actively attempt to demarket a program that had been actively sold earlier. Often demarketing 911 is thought of as a negative process. It need not be so, however. It is an attempt by police to change social, political, and fiscal circumstances to bring consumers' wants in line with police resources and to accumulate evidence about the value of particular police tactics.

### Tactics and technology

Community policing tactics include foot patrol, problem-solving information gathering, victim counselling and services, community organizing and consultation, education, walk-and-ride and knock-on-door programs, as well as regular patrol, specialized forms of patrol, and rapid response to emergency calls for service. Emphasis is placed on information sharing between patrol and detectives to increase the possibility of crime solution and clearance.

### Measured outcomes

The measures of success in the community strategy are broad: quality of life in neighborhoods, problem solution, reduction of fear, increased order, citizen satisfaction with police services, as well as crime control. In sum, the elements of the community strategy include:

- Authorization – community support (political), law, professionalism.
- Function – crime control, crime prevention, problem-solving.
- Organizational design – decentralized, task forces, matrices.
- Relationship to environment – consultative, police defend values of law and professionalism, but listen to community concerns.

- Demand – channeled through analysis of underlying problems.
- Tactics and technology – foot patrol, problem-solving, etc.
- Outcomes – quality of life and citizen satisfaction.

## Conclusion

We have argued that there were two stages of policing in the past, political and reform, and that we are now moving into a third, the community era. To carefully examine the dimensions of policing during each of these eras, we have used the concept of organizational strategy. We believe that this concept can be used not only to describe the different styles of policing in the past and the present, but also to sharpen the understanding of police policymakers of the future.

For example, the concept helps explain policing's perplexing experience with team policing during the 1960s and 1970s. Despite the popularity of team policing with officers involved in it and with citizens, it generally did not remain in police departments for very long. It was usually planned and implemented with enthusiasm and main-tained for several years. Then, with little fanfare, it would vanish – with everyone associated with it saying regretfully that for some reason it just did not work as a police tactic. However, a close examination of team policing reveals that it was a strategy that innovators mistakenly approached as a tactic. It had implications for authorization (police turned to neighbourhoods for support), organizational design (tactical decisions were made at lower levels of the organization), definition of function (police broadened their service role), relationship to environ-ment (permanent team members responded to the needs of small geographical areas), demand (wants and needs came to team members directly from citizens), tactics (consultation with citizens, etc.), and outcomes (citizen satisfaction, etc.). What becomes clear, though, is that team policing was a completing strategy with different assumptions about every element of police business. It was no wonder that it expired under such circumstances. Team and reform policing were strategically incompatible – one did not fit into the other. A police department could have a small team policing unit or conduct a team policing experiment, but business as usual was reform policing.

Likewise, although foot patrol symbolizes the new strategy for many citizens, it is a mistake to equate the two. Foot patrol is a tactic, a way of delivering police services. In Flint its inauguration has been accom-panied by implementation of most of the elements of a community strategy, which has become business as usual. In most places, foot patrol is not accompanied by the other elements. It is outside the mainstream of 'real' policing and often provided only as a sop to citizens and politicians who are demanding the development of different policing styles. This certainly was the case in New Jersey when foot patrol was evaluated by the Police Foundation.[46] Another example is in Milwaukee, where two police budgets are passed: the first is the police budget; the second, a supplementary budget for modest levels of foot patrol. In both cases, foot patrol is outside the mainstream of police activities and conducted primarily as a result of external pressures placed on departments.

It is also a mistake to equate problem solving or increased order maintenance activities with the new strategy. Both are tactics. They can be implemented either as part of a new organizational strategy, as foot patrol was in Flint, or as an 'add-on', as foot patrol was in most of the cities in New Jersey. Drawing a distinction between organizational add-ons and a change in strategy is not an academic quibble; it gets to the heart of the current situation in policing. We are arguing that policing is in a period of transition from a reform strategy to what we call a community strategy. The change involves more than making tactical or organizational adjustments and accommodations. Just as policing went through a basic change when it moved from the political to the reform strategy, it is going through a similar change now. If elements of the emerging organizational strategy are identified and the policing institution is guided through the change rather than left blindly thrashing about, we expect that the public will be better served, policymakers and police administrators more effective, and the profession of policing revitalized.

A final point: the classical theory of organization that continues to dominate police administration in most American cities is alien to most of the elements of the new strategy. The new strategy will not accom-modate to the classical theory: the latter denies too much of the real nature of police work, promulgates unsustainable myths about the nature and quality of police supervision and creates too much cynicism in officers attempting to do creative problem-solving. Its assumptions about workers are simply wrong.

Organizational theory has developed well beyond the stage it was at during the early 1900s, and policing does have organizational options that are consistent with the newly developing organizational strategy. Arguably, policing, which was moribund during the 1970s, is beginning a resurgence. It is overthrowing a strategy that was re-markable in its time, but which could not adjust to the changes of recent decades. Risks attend the new strategy and its implementation. The risks, however, for the community and the profession of policing, are not as great as attempting to maintain a strategy that faltered on its own terms during the 1960s and 1970s.

*From George Kelling and Mark H. Moore, 'The evolving strategy of policing',* Perspectives on Policing, *November 1988 (Vol. 4), pp 1–15.*

## Notes

1 Kenneth R. Andrews, *The Concept of Corporate Strategy*, Homewood, Illinois, Richard D. Irwin, Inc., 1980.
2 Robert M. Fogelson, *Big-City Police*, Cambridge, Harvard University Press, 1977; Samuel Walker, *A Critical History of Police Reform: The Emergence of Professionalism*, Lexington, Massachusetts, Lexington Books, 1977.
3 Mark H. Moore and George L. Kelling, 'To Serve and Protect: Learning from Police History', *The Public Interest*, 7, Winter 1983.
4 K.E. Jordan, *Ideology and the Coming of Professionalism: American Urban Police in the 1920's and 1930's*, Dissertation, Rutgers University, 1972.
5 Fogelson, *Big-City Police*.
6 Eric H. Monkkonen, *Police in Urban America, 1860–1920*, Cambridge, Cambridge University Press, 1981.

7   *The Newark Foot Patrol Experiment*, Washington, D.C., Police Foundation, 1981.
8   John Eck, *Solving Crimes: The Investigation of Burglary and Robbery*, Washington, D.C., Police Executive Research Forum, 1984.
9   Thomas A. Reppetto, *The Blue Parade*, New York, The Free Press, 1978.
10  Fogelson, *Big-City Police*.
11  Ibid.
12  George L. Kelling, 'Reforming the Reforms: The Boston Police Department', Occasional Paper, Joint Center for Urban Studies of M.I.T. and Harvard, Cambridge, 1983.
13  George L. Kelling, 'Juveniles and Police: The End of the Nightstick', in *From Children to Citizens; Vol. II: The Role of the Juvenile Court*, ed. Francis X. Hartmann, New York, Springer-Verlag, 1987.
14  Walker, *A Critical History of Police Reform: The Emergence of Professionalism*.
15  Fogelson, *Big-City Police*.
16  Kelling, 'Juveniles and Police: The End of the Nightstick'.
17  Orlando W. Wilson, *Police Adminstration*, New York: McGraw-Hill, 1950.
18  'Police Guidelines', John F. Kennedy School of Government Case Program #C14–75–24, 1975.
19  Herman Goldstein, *Policing a Free Society*, Cambridge, Massachusetts, Ballinger, 1977.
20  Kelling, 'Reforming The Reforms: The Boston Police Department'.
21  Fogelson, *Big-City Police*.
22  William H. Parker, 'The Police Challenge in Our Great Cities', *The Annals* 29 (January 1954): 5–13.
23  For a detailed discussion of the differences between selling and marketing, see John L. Crompton and Charles W. Lamb, *Marketing Government and Social Services*, New York, John Wiley and Sons, 1986.
24  Commissioner Francis 'Mickey' Roache of Boston has said that when the 911 system was instituted there, citizens persisted in calling 'their' police – the district station. To circumvent this preference, district telephone numbers were changed so that citizens would be inconvenienced if they dialled the old number.
25  *The Newark Foot Patrol Experiment*.
26  O.W. Wilson, *Police Administration*.
27  A.E. Leonard, 'Crime Reporting as a Police Management Tool', *The Annals* 29 (January 1954).
28  George L. Kelling et al., *The Kansas City Preventive Patrol Experiment: A Summary Report*, Washington, D.C., Police Foundation, 1974; William Spelman and Dale K. Brown, *Calling the Police*, Washington, D.C., Police Executive Research Forum, 1982.
29  *The Newark Foot Patrol Experiment*; Wesley G. Skogan and Michael G. Maxfield, *Coping With Crime*, Beverly Hills, California, Sage, 1981; Robert Trojanowicz, *An Evaluation of the Neighborhood Foot Patrol Program in Flint, Michigan*, East Lansing, Michigan State University, 1982.
30  Mary Ann Wycoff, *The Role of Municipal Police Research as a Prelude to Changing It*, Washington, D.C., Police Foundation, 1982; Goldstein, *Policing a Free Society*.
31  Raymond E. Miles and Charles C. Snow, *Organizational Strategy, Structure and Process*, New York, McGraw-Hill, 1978.
32  *The Newark Foot Patrol Experiment*.
33  *The Newark Foot Patrol Experiment*; Trojanowicz, *An Evaluation of the Neighborhood Foot Patrol Program in Flint, Michigan*.
34  Tony Pate et al., *Three Approaches to Criminal Apprehension in Kansas City: An Evaluation Report*, Washington, D.C., Police Foundation, 1976; Eck, *Solving Crimes: The Investigation of Burglary and Robbery*.
35  James Q. Wilson and George L. Kelling, 'Police and Neighborhood Safety: Broken Windows', *Atlantic Monthly*, March 1982: 29–38.
36  Tony Pate et al., *Reducing Fear of Crime in Houston and Newark: A Summary Report*, Washington, D.C., Police Foundation, 1986.
37  Jerome H. Skolnick and David H. Bayley, *The New Blue Line: Police Innovation in Six American Cities*, New York, The Free Press, 1986; Albert J. Reiss, Jr., *Policing a City's Central District. The Oakland Story*, Washington, D.C., National Institute of Justice March 1985.
38  Wilson and Kelling, 'Police and Neighborhood Safety: Broken Windows'.
39  Herman Goldstein, 'Improving Policing: A Problem-Oriented Approach', *Crime and Delinquency*, April 1979, 236–58.
40  Glenn Pierce et al., 'Evaluation of an Experiment in Proactive Police Intervention in the Field of Domestic Violence Using Repeat Call Analysis', Boston, Massachusetts, The Boston Fenway Project, Inc., May 13, 1987.
41  *The Newark Foot Patrol Experiment*; Trojanowicz, *An Evaluation of the Neighborhood Foot Patrol Program in Flint, Michigan*.
42  Pate et al., *Reducing Fear of Crime in Houston and Newark: A Summary Report*.

43    James R. Gardner, Robert Rachlin, and H.W. Allen Sweeny, eds, *Handbook of Strategic Planning*, New York, John Wiley and Sons, 1986.
44    Kelling, 'Juveniles and Police: The End of the Nightstick'.
45    Crompton and Lamb, *Marketing Government and Social Services*.
46    *The Newark Foot Patrol Experiment*.

# 8. The evolving strategy of police: a minority view

*Hubert Williams and Patrick V. Murphy*

... there is an underside to every age about which history does not often speak, because history is written from records left by the privileged. We learn about politics from the political leaders, about economics from the entrepreneurs, about slavery from the plantation owners, about the thinking of an age from its intellectual elite.

– Howard Zinn[1]

## Introduction

Kelling and Moore, in their recent interpretation of the strategic history of American policing, succinctly summarize that history as falling generally into three eras: (1) political, (2) reform, and (3) community.[2] This attempt to create paradigms, as with all such attempts, should be seen metaphorically, providing us with ways to crystallize the complexities of history in simplified terms. Seen in this way, their analysis provides useful insights and a clearer interpretation of the changing role of police in American society – at least with respect to the majority in that society. Despite its utility, we find their analysis disturbingly incomplete. It fails to take account of how slavery, segregation, discrimination, and racism have affected the development of American police departments – and how these factors have affected the quality of policing in the Nation's minority communities. Furthermore, we find Kelling and Moore to be silent on the important role that minorities have played in the past, and will play in the future, in affecting and improving the quality of policing in America. These omissions seriously diminish the accuracy and objectivity of their analysis and make it less useful than it otherwise could be in understanding the past and predicting the future of American policing.

This chapter addresses these omissions by adding a 'minority perspective'. Ours represents a 'minority perspective' in two different senses. First, our understanding of what factors have shaped the evolution of policing was shared by only a minority of those participating in the discussions of the Harvard Executive Session on Community Policing. Whereas Kelling and Moore (and many others) attempted to explain the evolution of policing in terms of strategic choices made by police executives who were developing a professional ideology, we see policing as powerfully conditioned by broad social forces and attitudes – including a long history of racism. They see police departments as largely autonomous; we see them as barometers of the society in which they operate.

Second, our view is particularly attuned to how institutions, norms, and attitudes have dealt with racial minorities and how those dealings affected the role of police during each of the eras described by Kelling and Moore. More optimistically, we believe that improvements have occurred in the last several years and that further improvements are possible, although not assured, in the future. We are particularly aware of the implications for African-American minorities, but we believe that the patterns set in these relations have importantly affected relations with other racially distinctive minorities such as Hispanics, Asians, Native Americans, and other people of color.

In this chapter, we contend that the strategies of police in dealing with minorities have been different from those in dealing with others, that the changes in police strategies in minority communities have been more problematic, and that, therefore, the beneficial consequences of those changes for minorities have been less noticeable. Specifically, we argue that:

- The fact that the legal order not only countenanced but sustained slavery, segregation, and discrimination for most of our Nation's history – and the fact that the police were bound to uphold that order – set a pattern for police behaviour and attitudes toward minority communities that has persisted until the present day. That pattern includes the idea that minorities have fewer civil rights, that the task of the police is to keep them under control, and that the police have little responsibility for protecting them from crime within their communities.
- The existence of this pattern of police behaviour and attitudes toward minority communities meant that, while important changes were occurring in policing during our Nation's history, members of minority groups benefited less than others from these changes – certainly less than it might have seemed from the vantage point of the white community and the police executives who were bringing about those changes.
- The Kelling and Moore discussion of the 'political era' of policing, a period generally defined by them as extending from after Reconstruction through the first decade of the twentieth century, neglects the early role of the first varieties and functions of police in this country – as well as the legal and political powerlessness of minority communities in both the North and the South. This omission means that their analysis fails to recognize that members of those minority communities received virtually none of the benefits of policing that were directed to those with more political clout.
- Many of the most notable advances in policing brought about by the advent of the 'reform era' proved to be elusive, if not counter-productive, for minorities. Several of the hiring and promotional standards, although implemented as antidotes to the rampant nepotism and political favoritism that had characterized policing during the 'political era' proved to be detrimental to blacks – just at the time when, to a limited extent, because of their increasing

political power, they were beginning to acquire the credentials that would have allowed them to qualify by the old standards.

- The potential of 'professional policing' during the reform era was not fully realized – either for minorities or for whites – until the civil rights revolution of the late 1960s and the coming to power of progressive mayors, both black and white, and the police executives appointed by them who were capable of bringing about changes relevant to blacks and other minorities. It was that movement, led primarily by black Americans, and that political empowerment that finally began to produce the putative benefits of professional policing: a fairer distribution of police services, less use of deadly force, greater respect for individual rights, and equal opportunity for minorities within the Nation's police departments. Without that movement, the promise of professional policing would have remained hollow.
- The minority community also played a key role in initiating the era of community policing. It was the riots of the late 1960s – and the election of many black and white progressive mayors, who appointed likeminded police chiefs – that stimulated broad social investments in police agencies, therefore putting the issue of police–community relations inescapably on the minds of police executives and the mayors who appointed them. The fact that police actions triggered many of the riots and then could not control them revealed to everyone the price of having a police department backed only by the power of the law, but not by the consent, much less active support, of those being policed.
- The era of community policing holds potential benefits and hazards for the quality of American policing. The potential benefits lie in the fundamental tenet of community policing: the empowerment of communities to participate in problem solving and decisions about delivery of services based on the needs of individual neighborhoods. The hazards lie in the possibility of excluding those communities that have been the least powerful and least well organized and thus repeating the historical patterns of race relations in the United States. If, however, the more recent trends towards inclusion of African-Americans and other minorities in policing and in the broader society are continued, then community policing might finally realize a vision of police departments as organizations that protect the lives, property, and rights of all citizens in a fair and effective way.

### The political era: policing the powerless

Kelling and Moore argue that during the political era, from the introduction of the 'new police' in the 1840s until the early 1900s, American police derived both their authority and resources from local political leaders. We maintain that their account is based largely on an analysis of policing in the cities of the northeastern United States, mostly following the Civil War and Reconstruction, and omitting the im-portance of racial and social conflicts in the origination of American police departments. As such, their analysis omits several crucial parts of the story of policing in America: the role of 'slave patrols' and other police instruments of racial oppression; the role of the police in imposing racially biased laws; and the importance of racial and social turmoil in the creation of the first versions of America's 'new police'.

Most analyses of early American history reflect an understandable, white, twentieth-century bias toward northern, urban, white conditions. While the literature is replete with studies of the growth of law enforcement in northern urban areas in general[3] and northern cities such as Boston,[4] Chicago,[5] Detroit,[6] and New York City,[7] in particular, little attention has been paid to police development outside the urban North. Kelling and Moore reflect a similar bias. Since the vast majority of blacks in the early years of America lived in the South, and about 80 percent of those lived outside of cities, this perspective creates a significant distortion.

Prominent police historian Samuel Walker has noted the difficulty of establishing dates marking the origins of American modern-style policing, that is, a system of law enforcement involving a permanent agency employing full-time officers who engage in continuous patrol of fixed beats to prevent crime. The traditional analyses, based on urban evidence, have suggested that such policing evolved from older systems of militias, sheriffs, constables, and night watches, and culminated in the 'new police' of Boston in 1838, New York City in 1845, Chicago in 1851, New Orleans and Cincinnati in 1852, Philadelphia in 1854, St. Louis in 1855, Newark and Baltimore in 1857, and Detroit in 1865.[8]

As Richardson points out, however, these analyses neglect that:

> [many other cities with] elaborate police arrangements were those with large slave populations where white masters lived in dread of possible black uprisings. Charleston, Savannah, and Richmond provided for combined foot and mounted patrols to prevent slaves from congregating and to repress any attacks upon the racial and social status quo. In Charleston, for example, police costs constituted the largest item in the municipal budget.[9]

Indeed, as both Walker[10] and Reichel[11] contend, there is a strong argument to be made that the first American modern-style policing occurred in the 'slave patrols', developed by the white slave owners as a means of dealing with runaways. Believing that their militia was not capable of dealing with the perceived threat, the colonial State governments of the South enacted slave patrol legislation during the 1740s, e.g., in South Carolina:

> Foreasmuch [sic] as many late horrible and barbarous massacres have been actually committed and many more designed, on the white inhabitants of this Province, by negro slaves, who are generally prone to such cruel practices, which makes it highly necessary that constant patrols should be established.[12]

Neighboring Georgians were also concerned with maintaining order among their slaves. The preamble to their 1757 law establishing and regulating slave patrols contends:

... it is absolutely necessary for the Security of his Majesty's Subjects in this Province, that Patrols should be established under proper Regulations in the settled parts thereof, for the better keeping of Negroes and other Slaves in Order and prevention of any Cabals, Insurrections or other Irregularities amongst them.[13]

Such statutes were eventually enacted in all southern States. Although specific provisions differed from States to State,[14] most of these laws responded to complaints that militia duty was being shirked and demands that a more regular system of surveillance be established.

In Georgia, all urban white men aged sixteen to sixty, with the exception of ministers of religion, were to conduct such patrol 'on every night throughout the year'. In the countryside, such patrols were to 'visit every Plantation within their respective Districts once in every Month' and whenever they thought it necessary, 'to search and examine all Negro-Houses for offensive weapons and Ammunition'. They were also authorized to enter any 'disorderly tipling-House, or other Houses suspected of harbouring, trafficking or dealing with Negroes' and could inflict corporal punishment on any slave found to have left his owner's property without permission.[15]

Foner points out that 'slave patrols' had full power and authority to enter any plantation and break open Negro houses or other places when slaves were suspected of keeping arms; to punish runaways or slaves found outside their plantations without a pass; to whip any slave who should affront or abuse them in the execution of their duties; and to apprehend and take any slave suspected of stealing or other criminal offense, and bring him to the nearest magistrate.[16] Understandably, the actions of such patrols established an indelible impression on both the whites who implemented this system and the blacks who were the brunt of it.

Reflecting the northern, urban perspective, Kelling and Moore begin their consideration of American policing only after the earliest 'new police' were established in the 1840s and 1850s. Even so, their analysis neglects to point out the importance of the role played by social discord in general, and the minority community in particular, in the creation of these departments. Phenomenal increases in immigration, rapid population growth, and major changes in industrialization led to more and more people, many of whom were from an impoverished, rural background, settling in an alien urban environment. Conflicts between black freedmen and members of the white urban working class significantly contributed to social unrest.

In 1830 Alexis de Tocqueville toured the United States to study prison reform. Unfamiliar with American norms, he was surprised to discover that there was more overt hostility and hatred toward blacks in the North, where slavery did not exist, than in the South, where it did. Those who challenged the status quo by demanding the abolition of slavery suffered verbal and physical abuse in northern cities.[17] This tension was reflected in a number of race riots in the mid-1830s in America's major cities. New York City had so many racial disorders in 1834 that it was long remembered as the 'year of the riots'. Boston suffered three major riots in the years 1834 to 1837, all of which focused on the issues of anti-abolitionism or anti-Catholicism. Philadelphia, the 'City of Brotherly Love', experienced severe anti-Negro riots in 1838 and 1842; overall, the city had eleven major riots between 1834 and 1849. Baltimore experienced a total of nine riots, largely race-related, between 1834 and the creation of its new police in 1857. In a desperate attempt to cope with the social disorder brought about by this conflict, America's major cities resorted to the creation of police departments. Clearly, this was a case of the political system responding to incendiary conflict within the society at large by demanding that the police be reorganized to deal with those conflicts.

In their discussion of the political era, Kelling and Moore observe that the police found their legitimacy either in politics or in law. For blacks, both before and several generations after the Civil War, neither of these bases of legitimacy provided much, if any, opportunity to shape policing to their benefit. As the authors point out, local political machines often recruited and maintained police in their positions, from foot officer to police chief. In return, the police encouraged voters to support certain candidates and provided services designed to enhance that support. Departments were organized in a decentralized manner, giving officers a great deal of discretion in carrying out their responsi-bilities. Police officers were closely linked to the neighborhoods in which they patrolled, often living there and usually of the same ethnic stock as the residents.

For those with political influence, this era provided close proximity to power. Good jobs could be had. Special favors could be obtained. The police could be expected to be extremely sensitive to community concerns – or lose their jobs if they were not.

For those with no access to political power, however, the situation was very different. Before slavery was abolished, the issue of black political power in the South was moot. The Constitution itself provides a sardonic reflection on the state of political power assigned to slaves. The group of white delegates assembled in Philadelphia never even considered slave representation, slave votes, or slave power. The only issue was whether a *slave owner* would enjoy a three-fifths increment of representation for every slave he owned.

During the debate, William Paterson stated bluntly that slaves were 'no free agents, have no personal liberty, no faculty of acquiring property, but on the contrary, are themselves property' and hence like other property 'entirely at the will of the masses'. To make certain there was no mistake, the Constitution explicitly prohibited Congress from abolishing the international slave trade to the United States before 1808.

Early American law enforcement officials in slave States were empowered – and expected – to enforce statutes carrying out the most extreme forms of racism, not restricted solely to enforcing slavery. In 1822, for example, Charleston, South Carolina, experienced a slave insurrection panic, caused by a supposed plot of slaves and free blacks to seize the city. In response, the State legislature passed the Negro Seamen's Act, requiring free black seamen to remain on board their vessels while in Carolina harbors. If they dared to leave their ships, the police were instructed to arrest them and sell them into slavery unless they were redeemed by the ship's master. The other coastal slave States soon enacted similar legislation.

Berlin presents this brief synopsis of Southern justice:

> Southern law presumed all Negroes to be slaves, and whites systematically barred free Negroes from any of the rights and symbols they equated with freedom. Whites legally prohibited Negro freemen from moving freely, participating in politics, testifying against whites, keeping guns, or lifting a hand to strike a white person … In addition they burdened free Negroes with special imposts, barred them from certain trades, and often tried and punished them like slaves. To enforce their proscriptive codes and constantly remind free Negroes of their lowly status, almost every State forced free Negroes to register and carry freedom papers, which had to be renewed periodically and might be inspected by any suspicious white.[18]

Police supervision further strengthened the registration system. City officials periodically ordered police to check the papers of all newly arrived free Negroes or investigate freedmen who failed to register or lacked visible means of support.[19]

Outside the slave States, the rights of blacks were only somewhat less restricted. Although Henry David Thoreau and William Lloyd Garrison exaggerated when they called Massachusetts a slave State, their harsh denunciation is a reminder that a black person could be a slave there or in any of the other 'free' States because of the protection afforded by the Federal and State constitutions for masters' rights in fugitive and sojourning slaves. It fell to agents of law enforcement, constables and members of the day and night watches, to carry out these laws. By 1800, some 36,505 northern Negroes still remained in bondage, most of them in New York and New Jersey.[20]

Several northern States enacted gradual emancipation statutes after the Revolution. Because such statutes freed only children born after a specified date, however, many slaves remained unaffected, and the freed children were held in apprenticeship until some time in their adult years. The State of New Jersey was typical. In 1804, the legislature freed the children born to slave mothers after July 4 of that year; the child so freed would be 'apprenticed' to its mother's owner, men until age 25, women until 21. Only in 1844 did it remove all barriers to the freeing of slaves. Again, these laws were also enforced by the local constable.

Even after the northern States took action to free slaves – ranging from constitutional provisions in Vermont in 1777 to gradual-abolition acts in New Jersey in 1804 and New York in 1817, the legal and political rights of blacks were quite circumscribed. Every new State admitted to the Union after 1819 restricted voting to whites. Only five States – Massachusetts, Rhode Island, Maine, New Hampshire, and Vermont – provided equal voting rights for black and white males. Illinois, Ohio, Indiana, Iowa, and California prohibited black testimony in court if whites were a party to the proceeding, and Oregon forbade Negroes to hold real estate, make contracts, or maintain lawsuits. Massachusetts banned intermarriage of whites with blacks and enforced segregation in hotels, restaurants, theaters, and transportation. Berlin describes a raid in 1853 in which St. Louis police raided well-known hangouts of freedom, whipped those who were unregistered, and shipped them out of town. Such raids continued for almost a year.[21]

Litwack describes the situation of northern blacks this way:

In virtually every phase of existence, Negroes found themselves systematically separated from whites. They were either excluded from railway cars, omnibuses, stagecoaches, and steamboats or assigned to special 'Jim Crow' sections; they sat, when permitted, in secluded and remote corners of theaters and lecture halls; could not enter most hotels, restaurants, and resorts, except as servants; they prayed in 'Negro pews' in the white churches, and if partaking of the sacrament of the Lord's Supper, they waited until the whites had been served the bread and wine. Moreover, they were often educated in segregated schools, punished in segregated prisons, nursed in segregated hospitals, and buried in segregated cemeteries.[22]

Indeed, as pointed out by C. Vann Woodward, an eminent historian of the South, 'One of the strangest things about Jim Crow [the laws and practices separating the races] was that the system was born in the North and reached an advanced age before moving South in force'.[23]

With neither political power nor legal standing, blacks could hardly be expected to share in the spoils of the political era of policing. There were virtually no black police officers until well into the twentieth century. Thus, police attention to, and protection for, areas populated primarily by racial minorities was rare during this era.

## The reform era: policing by the law for those unprotected by it

According to Kelling and Moore's interpretation, the basic police strategy began to change during the early 1900s. By the 1930s, they argue, the reform era of policing was in fully sway. Strikingly, their discussion completely overlooks the momentous events of the Civil War and Reconstruction, a time of great change in the legal and political status of minorities.

In the earliest days of the Civil War, President Lincoln and other northern politicians insisted that the issue of slavery had little to do with the conflict. In fact, in July 1861, when Congress assembled in special session, one of its first acts was to pass, almost unanimously, the Crittenden Resolution, affirming that the 'established institutions' of the seceding States were not to be a military target. To a large extent, this position was dictated by political forces – to keep the border States in the Union, generate support among the broadest constituency in the North, and weaken the Confederacy by holding out the possibility that they could return to the Union with their property, including their slaves, intact.[24]

Eventually, however, as the Confederacy put slaves to work as military laborers and the presence of Union troops precipitated large-scale desertion of plantation slaves, this policy was overcome by events. On January 1, 1863, Lincoln signed the Emancipation Proclamation. Bowing to political reality, however, he excluded from its purview the 450,000 slaves in Delaware, Kentucky, Maryland, and Missouri; 275,000 in Union-occupied Tennessee; and tens of thousands in occupied portions of Virginia and Louisiana.

By 1864, the Senate approved the 13th amendment, abolishing slavery throughout the Union, but it failed to receive the necessary two-thirds majority in the House. Eventually, in January 1865, this amendment narrowly won House approval and was sent to the States for ratification. Although several Southern legislatures were reluctant to lend their support, this amendment was ratified by the end of the year. To some, this not only ended one of America's most shameful institutions but offered the hope of the beginning of a Nation where North and South, black and white, were ruled by one law impartial over all. As we know with historical hindsight, such an interpretation was far too optimistic.

Even at the time, questions were raised about the practical implications of the amendment. James A. Garfield asked 'What is freedom? Is it the bare privilege of not being chained? ... If this is all, then freedom is a bitter mockery, a cruel delusion'. More to the point, Frederick Douglass maintained, 'Slavery is not abolished until the black man has the ballot'.[25]

In fact, a political vacuum developed between 1865 and 1867 in which the opponents of the extension of full citizenship to blacks were able to exercise great influence. President Andrew Johnson, with hopes of receiving the support of his fellow Southerners in the election in 1868, left the definition of black rights to the individual States. They accepted the opportunity with a vengeance. In addition to prohibiting black suffrage, the provisional legislatures passed the Black Codes, a series of State laws intended to define the freedmen's new rights and responsibilities.

Mississippi and South Carolina enacted the first and most severe Black Codes toward the end of 1865. Mississippi required all blacks to possess, each January, written evidence of employment for the coming year. Laborers leaving their jobs before the contract expired would forfeit wages already earned and, as under slavery, be subject to arrest by any white citizen. A person offering work to a labourer already under contract risked imprisonment or a fine. Blacks were forbidden to rent land in urban areas. Vagrants – under whose definition fell the idle, disorderly, and those who 'misspend what they earn' – could be punished by fines or involuntary plantation labor; other criminal offenses included 'insulting' gestures or language, 'malicious mischief', and preaching the Gospel without a license. In case anything had been overlooked, the legislature declared all existing penal codes defining crimes by slaves and free blacks 'in full force' unless specifically altered by law. South Carolina's Code barred blacks from any occupation other than farmer or servant except by paying an annual tax ranging from $10 to $100.[26]

Virtually all of the former Confederate States enacted such laws. Blacks protested most bitterly, however, against apprenticeship laws, which seized upon the consequences of slavery – the separation of families and the freedmen's poverty – to provide planters with the unpaid labor of black minors. Generally, these laws allowed judges to bind to white employers black orphans and those whose parents were deemed unable to support them. The former slave owner usually had first preference, the consent of the parents was not required, and the law permitted 'moderate corporal chastisement'.[27]

This entire complex of Black Codes was enforced:

> ... by a police apparatus and judicial system in which blacks enjoyed virtually no voice whatever. Whites staffed urban police forces as well as State militias, intended, as a Mississippi white put it in 1865, to 'keep good order and discipline amongst the negro population'.[28]

Sheriffs, justices of the peace, and other local officials proved extremely reluctant to prosecute whites accused of crimes against blacks. In those rare cases in which they did prosecute, convictions were infrequent and sentences were far more lenient than blacks received for the same crimes. For example, Texas courts indicted some 500 white men for the murder of blacks in 1865 and 1866, but not one was convicted.[29]

Largely in response to the Black Codes, Congress passed, over President Johnson's veto, the Civil Rights Act of 1866. This act defined all persons born in the United States (except Indians) as national citizens and spelled out rights they were to enjoy equally without regard to race – making contracts, bringing lawsuits, and enjoying 'full and equal benefit of all laws and proceedings for the security of person and property'. No State law or custom could deprive any citizen of these rights. Furthermore, Federal officials were authorized to bring suit against violations and made all persons, including local officials, who deprived a citizen of a civil right liable to fine or imprisonment.

To institutionalize the legal implications of the Civil War beyond the reach of shifting political majorities and presidential vetoes, Congress, after a long struggle, passed the 14th amendment, providing, among other things, that equal protection under the law be afforded to every citizen. Although it implicitly acknowledged the right of States to limit voting because of race, they could do so only at the expense of losing a significant portion of their congressional representation.

The 1866 congressional election essentially became a referendum on the 14th amendment – Republicans in favor, President Johnson and the Democrats opposed. The Republicans won an overwhelming victory, large enough to give them well over the two-thirds majority required to override a veto. In contrast, all Southern legislatures except Tennessee repudiated the amendment by enormous majorities.

Frustrated, and sensing its political strength, the Congress passed, again over Johnson's veto, the Reconstruction Act of 1867. This act divided the eleven Confederate States, except Tennessee, into five military districts and stipulated the process by which new State governments could be created and recognized. This process required the ratification of the 14th amendment, writing of new constitutions providing for manhood suffrage, and approval of these constitutions by a majority of registered voters.

After two years of 'Presidential Reconstruction', characterized by a lack of commitment to the extension of full rights to blacks, the era of 'Radical Reconstruction' began. Given the right to vote, many blacks participated in – and won – election to the new State legislatures. To allay any concerns that the issue had not been addressed completely, Congress passed the 15th amendment, providing the right to vote to all persons, regardless of 'race, color, or previous state of servitude', and prohibited the abridgement of that right by Federal and State governments. The Civil Rights Act of 1875 outlawed the exclusion of blacks from hotels, theaters, railroads, and other public accommodations.

The results of black suffrage on policing were not long in coming. Blacks appeared in several southern police departments soon after Radical Reconstruction began, especially where Republicans were in office and where blacks constituted a large percentage of the population. Black police appeared in Selma, Alabama, in 1867; Houston, Texas, in 1870; and Jackson, Mississippi, in 1871.[30] In New Orleans, a majority of whose population was black, a police board composed of three black members out of five appointed a police force that included 177 blacks by 1870.[31]

Such change was not always easy, however. In July 1868, in Raleigh, North Carolina, under the headline 'The Mongrel Regime!! Negro Police!!' the Conservative *Daily Sentinel* announced the appointment of four black police officers and concluded that 'this is the beginning of the end'.[32] Race riots occurred in Jackson and Meridian, Mississippi, because black police attempted to use their police authority over whites.[33]

In 1872, a Republican mayor in Chicago appointed the first black policeman in the North, where black suffrage was not required by Congress. Three years later, a mayor belonging to the People's Party replaced that officer with another black. In 1880, the Republicans won the mayor's office again, resulting in the appointment of four more black policemen. These officers all worked in plain clothes – in part not to offend the sensibilities of racist whites – and were assigned to black neighborhoods, practices adopted in most departments that hired blacks at that time. By 1894 there were 23 black policemen in Chicago.[34] Blacks were appointed in other cities in the North soon after those in Chicago: in Washington, D.C., in 1874; in Indianapolis in 1876; in Cleveland in 1881; in Boston in 1885.[35]

Lane provides one of the most thorough and fascinating analyses of the political complexities involved in appointing the first black police officers.[36] The approximately 7,000 blacks in Philadelphia's Seventh Ward had become a consistent Republican constituency, accounting for more than 10 percent of the party's vote. During the 1880 mayoral campaign, however, the black vote became a target of both parties' attention. Although the Seventh Ward voted overwhelmingly for the Republican candidate, the winner was Samuel King, a reform Democrat. Mayor King then appointed Alexander Davis and three other black men to the police department.

The selection criteria applied in appointing these Philadelphia officers reflect a common pattern in the choice of the earliest black officers. As Lane points out:

> In an era before any sort of civil service, when many officers were semiliterate at best, the four blacks chosen, although currently trapped in unskilled jobs, were characteristically overqualified.[37]

Davis, although born a slave, had graduated from Lincoln University, worked as a schoolteacher, and founded a newspaper. Only one of the other blacks appointed at that time had no experience beyond 'laboring work'.

Despite their qualifications, the appointment of the first black police officers in Philadelphia produced the same responses as were seen in many other cities. Several officers quit the force in protest. The new men were assigned to beats in or near black neighborhoods and immediately attracted crowds of spectators, saying such things as 'Ain't he sweet' or 'Is the thing alive?'

As in Philadelphia, most departments, to appease the racial attitudes of whites, did not allow black officers to arrest whites or to work with white officers. Even as late as 1961, a study reported by the President's Commission on Law Enforcement and Administration of Justice found that 31 percent of the departments surveyed restricted the right of blacks to make felony arrests; the power of black officers to make misdemeanour arrests was even more limited.[38]

Miami established a different designation for the two races: blacks were 'patrolmen' and whites were 'policemen'. In Chicago, blacks were largely confined to the Southside districts; in St. Louis, the 'black beats' ranged from the central downtown area to the Northside. Los Angeles established a special 'black watch' for the predominantly black Newton Station district.

After the initial dramatic changes brought about by the effects of Radical Reconstruction, the situation for blacks – and policing – began to revert to the *status quo ante*. As early as 1867, black suffrage went down to defeat in referendums in Minnesota, Ohio, and Kansas. Moderates within the Republican party began to back away from 'extreme radical measures' such as egalitarianism. The Ku Klux Klan, founded in 1866 in Tennessee as a social club, launched a reign of terror against Republican leaders, black and white. In some parts of the South, armed whites blocked blacks from voting. Violence spread, especially in Georgia and Louisiana where, unable to hold meetings, Republicans abandoned their presidential campaign. By 1868, Republicans, the stalwart supporters of black rights, began to lose some of their strength in the South.[39]

By 1872, the presidential election focused on southern policy, the Democrats emphasizing the evils of Reconstruction and the need to restore local self-government. Although the Republicans won, a significant number of former Radicals supported the Democratic ticket, indicating that their campaign themes were more powerful than the returns would indicate.

While political support for Radical Reconstruction waned, debate about whether the 14th amendment applied only to States raged throughout the Nation – and has continued to do so even in the last decade. Presidents Grant and Hayes retreated from strict enforcement of the so-called 'Reconstruction amendments'. The Supreme Court began to shift away from the strict interpretation of the 13th amendment to the narrower 14th and 15th. This shift, in turn, encouraged legislators to narrow their concerns as well.

In 1874, a long-awaited compilation of the United States laws, known as the *Revised Statutes*, was produced. This document rearranged the Nation's laws into supposedly relevant, logical categories. Inexplicably, however, this rearrangement failed to list the Civil Rights Act of 1866 either in the published text or in the 'historical' documentation. Instead, various parts of the 1866 law were scattered throughout the document, under various chapter headings. Civil rights as an independent subject worthy of the attention of lawyers, judges, law professors, and an entire generation of law students was neither easily researched nor, by implication, important. One by one, case by case, the legal rights of blacks were ruled away.

Against this already ominous backdrop came the Compromise of 1877, by which the Federal Government agreed to end Reconstruction, withdraw military forces from the South, and cease enforcing civil rights laws. In exchange, the election of the Republican candidate for president, Rutherford B. Hayes, was assured. The dyke that had laboriously been constructed against racist retaliation was suddenly broken. The stage was set for a massive reversal of the gains made in the previous 20 years.

In 1883, the Supreme Court, in deciding five litigations joined as the *Civil Rights Cases*, declared the Civil Rights Act of 1875 unconstitutional. Reflecting the earlier debates over the Reconstruction amendments, the ruling was based on the premise that those amendments prohibited only States, not individuals, from infringing on the equal protection and due process guaranteed to individuals by the Constitution.

Moreover, in 1896, the Supreme Court, in the landmark decision of *Plessy* v. *Ferguson*, found State laws that required segregation of the races in public accommodations to be constitutional, thereby endorsing the proposition that public facilities could be 'separate but equal'. This decision virtually completed the quarter-century-long process of standing the law established by the Reconstruction amendments on its head. The effects were quickly seen in police departments. In depart-ment after department, blacks lost their jobs, either by dismissal or by being forced to resign. The disappearance of blacks from the New Orleans police department serves as the most dramatic example of this trend. From a high of 177 black officers in 1870, the number dropped to 27 in 1880. By 1900, only five black officers remained; by 1910 there were none. The city did not appoint another black to the police force until 1950.

It is in this context that the Kelling and Moore discussion of the reform era must be interpreted. They argue that police reformers, led by August Vollmer and O.W. Wilson, changed the basic orientation of American policing in response to the excesses of the political era. The paradigm thus adopted, they contend, rejected politics as the source of authority for the police, replacing it with law and professionalism.

In an effort to curtail the close relationship between local political leaders and police, civil service replaced patronage and influence in the selection, assignment, and retention of police officers. Individual police officers were expected to avoid becoming closely associated with, and therefore contaminated by, the areas in which they patrolled. In some cases, they were prohibited from living in their beats. To further eliminate local political influence, functional control was centralized. By the time this era had reached its peak, during the 1950s and 1960s, police departments had become largely autonomous agencies, led by professionals guided by law, immune from political influence.

As dramatic as this change must have appeared to the white middle class inhabitants of America's major cities, the transition to the reform era was barely noticeable to blacks and other minorities. Relying on law, rather than politics, as the source of police authority had many desirable aspects for those provided full protection by the law. Once again, however, for those who lacked both political power and equal protection under the law, such a transformation could have little significance.

Even the particular mechanisms implemented to bring about reform proved to be of little avail to blacks and other minorities. Civil service examinations, for example, designed to avoid the influence of patronage and nepotism, provided slight consolation for those who had been denied access to quality education. These examinations, which accord-ing to some experts, reveal less about the qualifications of the applicants than about the cultural biases of the examiners, winnowed out a far higher proportion of blacks than whites. In Boston, for example, the examiners failed 75 per cent of the blacks as opposed to 35 per cent of the whites in 1970. In Atlanta, in the same year, 72 per cent of the blacks and only 24 per cent of the whites failed. In New York, in 1968, 65 per cent of the blacks as opposed to 31 per cent of the whites failed. Mexicans and Puerto Ricans fared even worse, perhaps because the tests were given in English.[40]

Background investigations, which blacks and other minorities are more likely to fail than whites, also served as a barrier to inclusion. Fogelson reports evidence indicating that investigators rejected 41 per cent of black applicants as opposed to 29 per cent of whites in St. Louis in 1966; 68 per cent of the blacks, as opposed to 56 per cent of the whites, were rejected in Cleveland in 1966; and 58 per cent of the blacks, as opposed to 32 per cent of the whites, in Philadelphia in 1968.[41] He concludes that these disparities were a function of two things, notwithstanding racial prejudice. First, many departments were unwilling to accept any applicant who had been arrested or convicted for any criminal offense, no matter how trivial – the President's Crime Commission showed that blacks were more likely to have a criminal record than whites.[42] Second, most departments were reluctant to hire anyone who was truant from school, changed jobs too often, associated with known criminals, or had broken military regulations, all of which are more prevalent among blacks and other minorities than among whites.[43] Regardless of the merits of these criteria, their effect was the same – the exclusion of minorities.

Centralization of control also provided little help for minorities, inasmuch as it meant that already strained relations with the police officer on the beat translated into even more strained relations with a distant government downtown. Reduced contacts with local officers meant that limited opportunities to bridge the racial barrier became even more limited.

In their efforts to attract qualified recruits, the reformers not only raised salaries, increased benefits, and improved working conditions, they also extended their recruitment efforts. One method of expanding the pool of applicants was to abolish residency requirements. This reform, although defended by reformers on professional grounds, handicapped the blacks, Hispanics, and other minorities by slowing down the ethnic turnover in police departments. Without such a change, as whites fled from the inner cities, the increasing percentage of minorities remaining could have been expected to have been more readily reflected in the ranks of the police. Furthermore, despite heavy immigration of minorities to the Nation's urban centers, the competitive edge that had been experienced earlier by the Irish and other white ethnic minorities no longer held sway.

Despite its limitations, the reform era provided, for members of the majority, a marked improvement in the delivery of professional police services. For members of minority groups, however, the change from the political era, in which they lacked political power, to the reform era, in which they lacked the support of the law, meant, for the most part, more of the same. In only 7 of the 26 cities for which the Kerner Commission collected data was the percentage of nonwhite police officers equal to as much as one-third of the percentage of nonwhites in the city.[44]

## The community era: policing disintegrating communities

By the late 1970s and early 1980s, according to Kelling and Moore, we had entered the era of community policing. Although law remained a source of authority, the police began once again to recognize that, ultimately, they are dependent on neighborhood, or community, support to achieve their goals. Turning to the citizens they serve for consultation, the police realized that more was expected of them than simply enforcing the law. Looking at people as clients of their services, the police found that they were also being judged on their ability to maintain order, resolve conflict, protect rights, and provide other services. In order to be able to remain responsible to community concerns, organizational decentralization was necessary. To remain even more flexible, officers were given authority and discretion to develop responses appropriate to local needs.

To organized, empowered communities, this strategy of policing offered extraordinary opportunities to participate in structuring the nature of police services delivered. As a result of community demands, for example, programs such as foot patrol were revived, long before they were found to be effective in reducing fear and, in some cases, crime. Despite the popularity of such initiatives, a closer examination of the areas in which such foot beats were created reveals one of the serious problems with this approach. In the State of New Jersey, for example, where foot patrol was funded by the Safe and Clean Neighborhoods Program, most foot beats were instituted in areas with strong community or business organizations – or both – with strong support from and access to political leaders. Those without such resources – and those most in need of police services – often found themselves in a long queue.

Although the 1954 Supreme Court decision in *Brown* v. *Board of Education Topeka* began to provide blacks and other minorities with their just share of legal rights and remedies, that provision came only with 'all deliberate speed' . As this glacially slow process continued, something more virulent occurred in minority communities, especially in the inner cities. Those who could afford to do so moved into less crowded, more comfortable, neighborhoods, leaving behind vacant houses – and those who could not afford an alternative. Businesses closed. Tax bases eroded. Among those who remained, unemployment, especially among minority youths, grew markedly higher than among whites. The incomes of employed minorities was significantly lower than those of whites. The quality of education deteriorated. School dropout rates rose precipitously. Infant mortality rates reached alarming levels. Decent, affordable housing became scarce. More and more children were born to unwed mothers. Drug and alcohol use became endemic. Crime and the fear of crime soared out of control.

The convergence of these factors produced a vicious circle. The police, regardless of the era or the strategic paradigm, must, along with families and other community institutions, concern themselves with crime and the fear of crime. The inner cities, where families, schools, jobs, and other community institutions were disintegrating at a rapid pace, presented the police with the most serious crime problems of all. But the police, because of a gross underrepresentation of minorities among their ranks, a lack of sensitivity and understanding of minority concerns and culture, and, therefore, a lack of community support, were least able to deal effectively in the inner cities – precisely where they were needed most.

Frustrated and angry, many blacks came to see the police as symbolizing the entire 'system' – those institutions and resources that had been so unresponsive to their needs. Tensions rose, culminating in the series of riots in America's inner cities during the middle and late 1960s. Many Americans had their first glimpse of ghettos as they burned through the night. Reflecting the nature and extent of the underlying problems, Senator Robert Kennedy observed, after visiting the scene of the Watts riot, 'There is no point in telling Negroes to observe the law ... It has almost always been used against them'. Despite the tragic destructiveness of those riots, they did concentrate the minds of the Nation's leaders wonderfully. In 1967, President Johnson appointed the National Advisory Commission on Civil Disorders (the Kerner Commission) to investigate the causes of the disorder and to recommend solutions. In a trenchant analysis, the commission report concluded that 'Our Nation is moving toward two societies, one black, one white – separate and unequal'.[45] Essentially, they said what lay behind the riots was a long historical pattern of racism on the part of whites in America. In one of the most forceful passages of their report, the commissioners observed:

> What white Americans have never fully understood – but what a Negro can never forget – is that white society is deeply implicated in the ghetto. White institutions created it, white institutions maintain it, and white society condones it.[46]

Specifically, the Kerner Commission found that many of the riots had been precipitated by police actions, often cases of insensitivity, sometimes incidents of outright brutality. They saw an atmosphere of hostility and cynicism reinforced by a widespread belief among many blacks in a 'double standard' of justice and protection. More generally, they concluded that:

In many ways the policeman only symbolizes much deeper problems. The policeman in the ghetto is a symbol not only of law, but of the entire system of law enforcement and criminal justice.[47]

The report offered five basic suggestions to address this situation:

- Change operations in the inner city to ensure proper officer conduct and to eliminate abrasive practices.
- Provide adequate police protection to inner city residents to eliminate the high level of fear of crime.
- Create mechanisms through which citizens can obtain effective responses to their grievances.
- Produce policy guidelines to assist police in avoiding behaviors that would create tension with inner city residents.
- Develop community support for law enforcement.

Fearful that new conflagrations would occur otherwise, and responding in many cases to newly elected black and progressive white mayors, many departments followed the commission's recommendations. As a result, a number of improvements have occurred that have reduced the barriers between the police and the inner city. Many more blacks and other minorities are now patrolling our streets. Strict rules against the unnecessary use of weapons, brutality, harassment, verbal abuse, and discourtesy have been promulgated and enforced. The use of aggressive patrol techniques has been curtailed, restricted to those situations in which it is justified. Steps have been taken to ensure adequate patrol coverage and rapid response to calls for service from inner city areas. Open, impartial, and prompt grievance mechanisms have been established. Policy guidelines have been implemented to direct officers' discretion in potentially tense situations. New approaches – storefront offices, adopting (or even organizing) neighborhood groups, addressing the causes of fear – have been put into effect to improve relations with the community.

Because of these changes, the relationship between the police and citizens has improved considerably in the last several years – to a large extent in white middle-class neighborhoods, to a lesser extent in the inner city. Any transition to an era of community policing will be both a cause and an effect of these improvements. But such a transition is far from complete in the inner city. A recent assessment by the Commission on the Cities found that, despite a brief period of improvement, the conditions that produced the dissolution of ghetto communities are actually getting worse. 'Quiet riots', the report concludes, are occurring in America's central cities: unemployment, poverty, social disorganization, segregation, housing and school deterioration, and crime are worse now than ever before.[48] These 'quiet riots', although not as alarming or as noticeable to outsiders as those of the 1960s, are even more destructive of human life. Under such conditions, it is unreasonable to expect that the residents of the inner city will have the characteristics – whether social, economic, or political – that are required to sustain the partnership required of the community policing approach.

Furthermore, although the police are better prepared to deal with residents of the inner city than they were 20 years ago, they are far from having totally bridged the chasm that has separated them from minorities – especially blacks – for over 200 years. There are still too few black officers, at all levels. Racism still persists within contemporary police departments. Regardless of rules and guidelines, inappropriate behavior on the streets still occurs. Complaints about different treatment, patrol coverage, and response time persist. And empirical studies have shown that community-oriented approaches that are effective in most neighbourhoods work less well, or not at all, in areas inhabited by low-income blacks and other minority groups.

We welcome the prospect of entering the community era of policing. In a dramatic way, this represents a return to the first principles of policing as established in London in 1829. As Critchley so aptly put it, 'From the start, the police was to be ... in tune with the people, understanding the people, belong to the people, and drawing its strength from the people'.[49] Once community policing becomes a pervasive reality, we will have finally approximated the attainment of that goal. We have begun to bring such fundamental changes about in many of our Nation's police departments. But because of the devastation afflicting our inner cities and the inability of our police to relate to those neighborhoods, the areas that most require a transition to the community era will unfortunately be the last to experience such a change.

## Summary

Kelling and Moore have contributed a valuable addition to our repertoire of concepts for understanding the strategic history of American policing. Their interpretation of the shifts in policing from a political to a reform to a community era provides useful insights. It is our contention, however, that the applicability of this interpretation is confined largely to the white majority communities of our Nation. For blacks, and to a lesser extent other minority groups, the utility of this analysis is quite limited.

During the political era, for example, blacks were completely powerless, leaving them unable to exert the influence necessary to affect police strategy. According to the paradigm Kelling and Moore posit to have prevailed in the reform era, police strategy was determined largely on the basis of law, which left blacks almost completely unprotected. Finally, the community era requires an empowered, cohesive com-munity to be able to deal with a sensitive, responsive police agency; neither precondition prevails in many contemporary minority neighborhoods.

Significant progress has been made, however. Large numbers of blacks and other minorities have joined – and in many cases have become leaders of – our major departments. The use of violence by police against minorities has declined dramatically in the last decade. Special efforts have been made to provide training to make our police officers sensitive to the needs and concerns of minority communities. Enlightened, better educated police leadership has opened the profession to new approaches and ideas. The rising popularity of community-oriented policing will undoubtedly further improve the relationship between the police and minorities.

We think it is a particularly hopeful sign in this regard that many of the most articulate proponents of community policing are themselves African-American police executives. Their unswerving emphasis, in their statements of values, on the protection of constitutional rights and the protection of all citizens, gives us reason to be optimistic about the future of policing.

Nevertheless, the history of American police strategies cannot be separated from the history of the Nation as a whole. Unfortunately, our police, and all of our other institutions, must contend with many bitter legacies from that larger history. No paradigm – and no society – can be judged satisfactory until those legacies have been confronted directly.

*From Hubert Williams and Patrick V. Murphy, 'The evolving strategy of police: a minority view', in* Perspectives on Policing, *January 1990 (Vol. 13), pp 1–15.*

## Notes

1 Howard Zinn, *The Politics of History*. Boston, Beacon Press, 1970: 102.
2 George L. Kelling and Mark H. Moore, 'The Evolving Strategy of Policing', *Perspectives on Policing*, No. 4. Washington, D.C., National Institute of Justice and Harvard University, November 1988.
3 Robert M. Fogelson, *Big-City Police*. Cambridge, Harvard University Press, 1977. J.F. Richardson, *Urban Police in the United States*. Port Washington, New York, National University Publications, 1974.
4 Roger Lane, *Policing the City: Boston, 1822–1885*. Cambridge, Harvard University Press, 1967. E.A. Savage, *A Chronological History of the Boston Watch and Police, from 1631–1865*. Available on Library of American Civilization fiche 13523, 1865.
5 J. Flinn, *History of the Chicago Police from the Settlement of the Community to the Present Time*. Montclair, New Jersey, Patterson Smith, 1975.
6 J. Schneider, *Detroit and the Problem of Order, 1830–1880: A Geography of Crime, Riot, and Policing*. Lincoln, University of Nebraska, 1980.
7 J.F. Richardson, *The New York Police: Colonial Times to 1901*. New York, Oxford University Press, 1970.
8 Samuel Walker, *A Critical History of Police Reform: The Emergence of Professionalism*. Lexington, Massachusetts, Lexington Books, 1977: 4–6.
9 Richardson, *Urban Police*, n. 3 above: 19.
10 Walker, *A Critical History*, n. 8 above.
11 P.L. Reichel, 'Southern Slave Patrols as a Transitional Police type', *American Journal of Policing*, 7, 2: 51–77.
12 T. Cooper, ed., *Statutes at Large of South Carolina*, v. 3, part 2, Columbia, South Carolina, A.S. Johnston, 1838: 568.
13 A. Candler, ed., *The Colonial Records of the State of Georgia*, v. 18, Atlanta, Chas. P. Byrd, State Printer, 1910: 225.
14 Alabama: W.L. Rose, ed., *A Documentary History of Slavery in North America*, New York, Oxford University Press, 1976. Arkansas: O.W. Taylor, *Negro Slavery in Arkansas*, Durham, North Carolina, Duke University, 1958. Georgia: R.B. Flanders, *Plantation Slavery in Georgia*, Cos Cob, Connecticut, John E. Edwards, 1967; B. Wood, *Slavery in Colonial Georgia*, Athens, University of Georgia Press, 1984. Kentucky: J.W. Coleman, Jr., *Slavery Times in Kentucky*, New York, Johnson Reprint Company, 1940; I.E. McDougle, *Slavery in Kentucky 1792–1865*, Westport, Connecticut, Negro Universities Press, 1970. Louisiana: S. Bacon, *The Early Development of American Municipal Police: A Study of the Evolution of Formal Controls in a Changing Society*, unpublished dissertation, Yale University, University Microfilms No. 66-06844, 1939; J.G. Taylor, *Negro Slavery in Louisiana*, New York, Negro Universities Press, 1963; E.R. Williams, Jr., 'Slave Patrol Ordinances of St. Tammany Parish, Louisiana, 1835–1838', *Louisiana History*, v. 13 (1972): 399–411. Mississippi: C.S. Sydnor, *Slavery in Mississippi*, New York, Appleton Century Co., 1933.

Missouri: H.A. Trexler, 'Slavery in Missouri: 1804–1865', in H. Trexler, *Slavery in the States: Selected Essays*, New York, Negro Universities Press, 1969. North Carolina: G.G. Johnson, *Antebellum North Carolina: A Social History*, Chapel Hill, University of North Carolina, 1937. Tennessee: C.P. Patterson, *The Negro in Tennessee, 1790–1865*, New York, Negro Universities Press, 1968; C.C. Mooney, *Slavery in Tennessee*, Westport, Connecticut, Negro Universities Press, 1971. Virginia: J. Ballagh, Jr., *A History of Slavery in Virginia*, New York, Johnson Reprint Co., 1968; A Stewart, 'Colonel Alexander's Slaves Resist the Patrol', in W.L. Rose, ed., *A Documentary History of Slavery in North America*, New York, Oxford University Press, 1976.

15 B. Wood, *Slavery in Colonial Georgia*, n. 14 above: 123–4.

16 P.S.Foner, *History of Black Americans: From Africa to the Emergence of the Cotton Kingdom*, Westport, Connecticut, Greenwood, 1975; 206.

17 Richardson, *Urban Police*, n. 3 above: 21.

18 I. Berlin, *Slaves Without Masters: The Free Negro in the Antebellum South*, New York, Pantheon Books, 1974: 316–17.

19 Berlin, above: 319.

20 L.F. Litwack, *North of Slavery: The Negro in the Free States, 1790–1860*. Chicago, University of Chicago Press, 1961: 3.

21 Berlin, n. 18 above: 330.

22 Litwack, *North of Slavery*, n. 20 above: 97.

23 C.V. Woodward, *The Strange Career of Jim Crow*, New York, Oxford University Press, 1966: 17.

24 E.F. Foner, *Reconstruction: America's Unfinished Revolution, 1863–1877*. New York, Harper and Row, 1988: 4–5.

25 Foner, above: 66–7.

26 Foner: 199–200.

27 Foner: 201.

28 Foner: 203.

29 Foner: 204.

30 M. Delaney, 'Colored brigades, "negro specials" and colored policemen: a history of blacks in American police departments', unpublished manuscript, no date: 12.

31 J.W. Blassingame, *Black New Orleans, 1860–1880*. Chicago, University of Chicago Press, 1973: 244.

32 H.N. Rabinowitz, *Race Relations in the Urban South, 1865–1890*, Urbana, University of Illinois Press, 1980: 41.

33 V.L. Wharton, *The Negro in Mississippi, 1865–1890*. New York, Harper and Row, 1965: 167.

34 Walker, *A Critical History*, n. 8 above: 10.

35 Delaney, 'Colored brigades', n. 30 above: 20.

36 R. Lane, *Roots of Violence in Black Philadelphia: 1860–1900*. Cambridge, Harvard University Press, 1986: 60–7.

37 Lane, above: 64–5.

38 President's Commission on Law Enforcement and Administration of Justice, *Task Force Report: The Police*. Washington, D.C., U.S. Government Printing Office, 1967: 170.

39 Foner, *Reconstruction*, n. 24 above: 342.

40 Fogelson, *Big-City Police*, n. 3 above: 250.

41 Fogelson, above: 251.

42 President's Commission on Law Enforcement and Administration of Justice, *Task Force Report: Science and Technology*, Washington, D.C., U.S. Government Printing Office, 1967: 216–28.

43 Fogelson, n. 3 above: 251.

44 *Report of the National Advisory Commission on Civil Disorders*, Washington, D.C., U.S. Government Printing Office, 1968: 321.

45 *Report*: 1.

46 *Report*: 2.

47 *Report*: 299.

48 F.R. Harris and R. Wilkins, *Quiet Riots: Race and Poverty in the United States*, New York, Pantheon Books, 1988.

49 T.A. Critchley, *A History of Police in England and Wales, 1900–1966*, London, Constable and Company, Ltd., 1967: 46.

# The role and function of the police

## Introduction

Much, if not all, of what follows in this section of the volume, and many of the others derives from and builds on the work of Michael Banton (**9**, 132). The very first sentence of his book, for example – 'A cardinal principle for the understanding of police organization and activity is that the police are only one among many agencies of social control' – contains an admonition that all scholars working in this area would do well to remind themselves of. In the extract reproduced here, Banton goes further to suggest, in fact, that the police are relatively unimportant in the enforcement of law. Rather, in many respects, they are 'peace officers', whose contacts with citizens centre more upon assistance than on dealing with offences. In parallel with Banton, as one of the earliest scholars of policing, William Westley (**10**, 137) begins with an exploration of the police role. He reproduces a long passage from August Vollmer in which the great police administrator adumbrates a huge list of police tasks. He notes, however, that it is incomplete, saying 'nothing of the amount of time the police act as a public information bureau, of their attempts to settle family disputes, of the extensive guard duty that they perform in the nightly checking of doors and windows and the inspection of homes of people away on vacation'. Each jurisdiction, he says, will have additions to Vollmer's list, 'for each city finds in the police a group who can be assigned that which no other groups can perform'.

David Bayley (**11**, 141), the leading scholar of the comparative study of policing, asks the apparently simple question, 'what do the police do?' His answer is that much policing around the world is strikingly similar in approach, focusing primarily on two tasks, what he calls 'authoritative intervention' (*pace* Bittner) and 'symbolic justice'. Against the common conception, relatively little police time is spent dealing with crime and, such time as is spent on such activities, tends to be focused on crimes that have already been committed. In shaping police work, the public are crucial: 'almost all [the police] do is undertaken at the request of some member of the public. If the public stopped calling the police, the police would have to reinvent their job.' After patrol – which accounts for between two fifths (Japan) and two thirds (USA) of police work – the next major task is criminal investigation, accounting for between one eighth (Canada) and one fifth (Japan) of police personnel. Again, however, such work Bayley notes is largely reactive. Patrol and criminal investigation are followed by traffic – another major consumer of policing time. Though there are of course variations in policing, it is the commonalities that are most striking. Indeed, so striking are they that Bayley indicates it is potentially plausible to suggest 'that police forces are organised to do the same sorts of work regardless of the social circumstances they confront'.

Of all the scholars who have sought to shine light on what is special or different about what the police do, or how they do it, it is perhaps the work of Egon Bittner (**12**, 150) that has been most influential. His argument is that 'police are empowered and required to impose or, as the case may be, coerce a provisional solution upon emergent problems without having to brook or defer to opposition of any kind, and that further, their competence to intervene extends to every kind of emergency, without any exceptions whatever.' Policing should not, and cannot, be reduced to law enforcement, it is about bringing a particular form of authority to bear, he argues, on events containing 'something-that-ought-not-to-be-happening-and-about-which-somebody-had-better-do-something-now'. It is not that this infuses everything police officers do, merely what distinguishes it.

Patrol and beat work continue to constitute an important core of policing. As police scholars have long noted, the majority of such work is focused on the poorest sections of any community being policed, and William Ker Muir Jr (**13**, 173) explores officers' experiences of this form of 'dirty work' – a series of ways of working in part outside the law. He describes the physicality, the violence – what he calls the use of 'lawless force'. Violence was useful on Skid Row, he says, both instrumentally and symbolically, but this had to be maintained at all times: 'Once terror had been made the means of domination, there was no turning back.' He also describes a different model, however; a 'professional' response, involving the use of strategies within the law, with developed relationships with local citizenry and heightened local confidence. At the heart of this – and we return to it later in the volume in connection with 'community policing' – was communication; 'mankind's passion for talking to and about one another'.

One of the joys of working and studying within the general territory of policing is that there are a number of scholars whose style of writing ranks among the finest in social science. Peter Manning (**14**, 191) is one of these and his summary of the argument he makes in the article reproduced here bears repeating in some detail. 'The police have trouble', he says:

> They have been assigned the task of crime prevention, crime detection and the apprehension of criminals ... have staked out a mandate that claims to include the efficient, apolitical, and professional enforcement of the law ... The police have staked out a vast and unmanageable social domain. And what has happened as a result of their inability to accomplish their self-proclaimed mandate is that the police have resorted to the manipulation of *appearances*.

The consequence, he argues, is that law enforcement becomes self-justifying, more concerned with working towards its own ends than in understanding and responding to community concerns and needs. The cloak beneath which police actions and dilemmas are masked is 'professionalism'.

However impossible a mandate, crime control is fairly firmly fixed in the public mind as the essence of police work. Not only an impossible mandate, but also a very misleading picture of police activity for, as Richard Ericson (**15**, 215) argues, 'the police, especially the patrol police, actually spend only a tiny fraction of their time dealing with crime or something that could potentially be made into a crime'. Rather, and following Banton, Bittner, Manning and others, Ericson argues that the police mandate is to use their powers to 'transform troublesome, fragile situations back into a normal or efficient state'; not to produce a new order, but to maintain and reinforce the existing one. In one of the earliest sightings of the influence of Michel Foucault in this arena, Ericson suggests that the work of the police may be understood as one of classification, recording and management of populations and phenomena, and that understanding the relationship between the reproduction of order within the police organization and the reproduction of social order is a central task in the sociology of policing.

A huge amount of police scholarship has focused on the visible patrol work undertaken by the police – and this is reflected in many of the extracts reproduced in this volume. Of course, as has been repeatedly noted, the police undertake a very broad range of functions in addition to patrol, not the least of which is criminal investigation. One of the earliest, and most comprehensive, studies of police investigation was undertaken by Greenwood, Chaiken and Petersilia (16, 247). They begin by exploring both stereotypes of the detective function and early critical accounts of this policing 'elite'. Much of what they have to say echoes some of the key lessons from other areas of police work: many if not most minor matters are simply not investigated, officers are frequently diverted into activities that lead them away from core tasks, and that the vast majority of clear-ups are the result of patrol work rather than investigative activities.

# 9. The police as peace officers

*Michael Banton*

A cardinal principle for the understanding of police organization and activity is that the police are only one among many agencies of social control. This is generally appreciated by police administrators, even though their public statements sometimes fail to recognize it. One American police chief, for example, writes:

> A condition precedent to the establishment of efficient, professional law enforcement in a community is a desire and a demand on the part of the residents for that type of service. In this respect, law enforcement does not differ greatly from private industry. The one factor which predetermines the success of any business is the market ... A second lesson the police administrator can draw from industry is that markets are created ... The vital elements of civilized life, including our most sacred institutions, at one time or another have been laboriously *sold* to the people (Parker, 1954, p. 6).

One of his captains echoes him:

> ... not only do we have a product to sell (law enforcement) which often meets with strong sales resistance ... (Gourley, 1954, p. 136).

And another police chief declares in similar vein:

> We have a pretty good product to sell in the protection of life and property and with 300 officers selling police efficiency 24 hours a day ... (Carolina City Police Department, Information Bulletin No. 1).

Though the police are concerned to a very important extent with law enforcement it is not a product, nor is it to be attributed to the police. Indeed the police are relatively unimportant in the enforcement of law.

Consider, for example, some of the variations in criminality. In the average United States city of 500,000 people there were, in 1962, thirty-six cases of murder and non-negligent manslaughter, and sixty of forcible rape; whereas in Edinburgh in the same year there were two of murder, two of culpable homicide, and eight of rape. The Edinburgh figures are lower not because the police are more efficient or meet less 'sales resistance' but because the community is more orderly. Social control – as Homans demonstrated so well in *The Human Group* (1950) – a property of states of social relations, not something imposed from outside. The level of control, be it high or low, is determined by the kinds of social relationship that exist among the individuals who make up the society, and their effectiveness in getting people to follow prescribed patterns of behaviour. The number of people who obey the law and follow such patterns without ever a thought for police efficiency is striking testimony to the power of social norms and humanity's methods of training children to observe them: most people grow up so well conditioned that they cannot feel happy if they infringe the more important norms. Thus control is maintained by the rewards and punishments which are built into every relationship, and which are evident in the conferring and withholding of esteem, the sanctions of gossip, and the institutional, economic, and moral pressures that underlie behavioural patterns. Law and law-enforcement agencies, important though they are, appear puny compared with the extensiveness and intricacy of these other modes of regulating behaviour.

The communities with the highest level of social control are small, homogeneous, and stable like small tribal societies in out-of-the-way regions, or the more remote villages in industrial nations. In such communities social order is maintained to a very large extent by informal controls of public opinion, and there is little resort to formal controls such as legislation or the full-time appointment of people to law-enforcement duties. Most tribal societies have no police forces, prisons, or mental hospitals: they are small enough to be able to look after their own deviants. The small society with a simple technology can afford to have its 'village idiot'; the large and complex one cannot, for many people would not recognize him and he might easily injure himself or create havoc in the affairs of others. Village societies are usually tightly knit communities because everyone is so dependent upon everyone else. If there is only one shop, everyone has to go there at some time or other, and the shopkeeper has to keep on reasonably friendly terms with all the local inhabitants. If there are two grocers, people may feel obliged to patronize the one who attends the same church as they do. Residents cannot disregard the opinion of their neighbours because there may come a situation in which they will need their cooperation. In these circumstances the job of the policeman is to oil the machinery of society, not to provide the motive power of law enforcement.

The orderliness of the small homogeneous society is not simply a matter of economics and social organization; as in any other kind of society it has moral qualities. In the village society, the rich are under greater obligation than their city counterparts to recognize responsibilities to the unfortunate; village people are involved in one another's affairs at work and in leisure whereas, in urban districts, social contacts and the sense of mutual commitment are more restricted. In homogeneous societies girls and boys grow up attuned to the social order, accepting their place in it and believing the distribution of rewards to be reasonably just. People who live together like this are agreed in what they consider right and wrong, so it can be said that the highly integrated society is characterized by a high level of consensus, or agreement on fundamental values. These moral judgments pervade social life and do not stop short when business relations are in question. The policeman obtains public cooperation, and enjoys public esteem, because he enforces standards accepted by the community. This gives his role considerable moral authority and sets him apart from the crowd socially, much as does the role of minister of religion.

Life in a small highly integrated society has many attractions, but most people find the rewards of economic progress even more attractive, and the two sets of values do not go well together. In the traditional kind of society the various social institutions are so interrelated that an alteration in one affects all the others and it is difficult to introduce changes. In an economically developing society, however, people and resources have to be moved around. Individuals have to pursue their private benefit and to fight the community controls that put a brake on change. Some people receive great rewards, greater than their moral deserts; others, who are scarcely less worthy, are much less fortunate. In a developing economy rewards are distributed according to economic criteria: the successful businessman is honoured because he has been successful – money comes itself to have a moral value. At many points economic values clash with community values and frequently break them. For instance, a man may have had an exemplary career for the first forty-five or fifty years of his life and hold an honoured if not particularly distinguished position in the community; then suddenly technological discoveries affect the industry in which he works. His skills become obsolete, the plant is reorganized, and he has to begin again. He may have to take a lower-paid job or to work under people who were previously his juniors, and this inevitably undermines his position in the community. In numerous sectors of industrial society, people appear to take many of their criteria for community ranking from the economic order and the occupational hierarchy. In one way and another industry is continually imposing on the community its own criteria of economic rewards.

Another example which makes the same point in a different way can be drawn from the effect of the introduction of the automobile upon the social structure of the Southern States of America. These were communities in which Negroes were expected to defer to Whites and to allow them precedence. When Negroes acquired automobiles the question arose whether precedence should be determined by the rule-of-the-road or by local custom. For a time the answer depended on the speed of the vehicle: below 25 mph the white driver, especially if it was a woman, expected the Negro driver to give way; above that speed no one took risks (Myrdal *et al.*, 1944, p. 1368). Nowadays there is hardly any of this. Driving rules cannot be based upon particularistic criteria of skin colour: they must be the same for every driver, otherwise the confusion would be interminable. Thus new technical developments impose their own logic and upset community values of deference to older persons, to women, and, in some situations, to persons of superior social class or race.

Community life cannot be organized upon purely economic or technological principles because many important factors, like mother-love, neighbourliness, sympathy, and so on, cannot be valued in a market. They have a different logic. Industrial life can take place only within the larger context of society which creates the demand for various kinds of product, and if, in seeking to maximize its own goal of productivity, industry overturns these social values, it can destroy the context within which it seeks to operate. Major strikes – especially in towns dominated by a particular industry – sometimes illustrate how people can feel when deep-set community values are disturbed and notions of justice wounded. Perhaps the most extreme example of what happens when economic ends are unregulated is the gold-mining or prospecting camp, in which everything is subordinated to individual greed for gold, and community life is at its most tenuous. Yet even in the residential suburbs of Europe and North America the effect of increasing industrialization upon community values can be observed. People move house or employment as opportunity offers, and they seek less the rewards of community approval; their goals are the financial rewards of occupational success and they know that social approval will follow when these have been attained. In these circumstances there is less feeling that the social order is a just one, and less agreement upon moral standards. The majority, however, seem to feel that the lower sense of community is more than offset by the rewards of economic advance.

No social changes are without their costs, and one of the principal costs of making the social structure more flexible is the decline in social integration. An index of this is the crime rate. In 1962 the number of crimes known to the police in England and Wales rose by 11 per cent over the previous year, and in Scotland by 8 per cent. Between 1938 and 1960 the incidence of larceny, breaking and entering, receiving, fraud and false pretences, sexual offences, violence against the person, and a small residue of other offences increased by 225 per cent. In the United States the crime rate for 1962 was 5 per cent above that for the previous year and 19 per cent above that for 1958, after adjustment for population growth.

As the problem of maintaining order becomes more severe, societies increasingly adopt formal controls, summarized by an anthropologist as 'courts, codes, constables, and central authority'. In the early days the parish constable was simply a citizen on duty. All able-bodied men were expected to give their services in turn, being elected for a year and serving without payment. By the eighteenth century this system had broken down completely in London and, after serious disorders, a permanent constabulary was created in 1829. But the authority that the new police exercised was still that of the citizen constable. Under English law every citizen is still technically bound to arrest anyone who commits a felony in his presence; this is his civic duty and he can be punished if he fails to perform it, though admittedly there is no record of anyone's being prosecuted for such a failure in recent times. Under both English and Scottish law a citizen must go to the assistance of a constable if called upon to do so. The policeman does have certain common law powers as acknowledged by judicial authorities, and he has since been given others by express direction of Acts of Parliament, but the core of his authority stems from his responsibilities as a citizen and the representative of citizens. Judicial decisions of both English and Scottish courts make it clear that the constable is not the employee of the local authority: he exercises his powers and discharges his duties as the independent holder of a public office. If he wrongly arrests and detains someone, then he is personally liable for his actions should the aggrieved party open civil proceedings against him. Nor would it be completely correct to regard the constable as a servant of the Crown: he does not have the immunities of the Crown servant and he cannot shelter behind the orders of a superior – as, for example, a soldier sometimes can. In this sense the constable is a professional citizen: he is paid to discharge obligations which fall upon all citizens, and his obligations are to the community as a whole.

With the changes in police methods necessitated by the increase in crime this conception of the police officer is becoming somewhat anachronistic though it retains a sentimental appeal. Some years ago a Home Secretary observed: 'The British policeman is a civilian discharging civilian duties and merely put into uniform so that those who need his help know exactly where to look for assistance.' Today, especially in connection with the traffic laws, this description is not accurate: the policeman is increasingly seen as an official exercising authority and power over citizens. A division is becoming apparent between specialist departments within police forces (detectives, traffic officers, vice and fraud squads, etc.) and the ordinary patrolman. The former are 'law officers' whose contacts with the public tend be of a punitive or inquisitory character, whereas the patrolmen [...] are principally 'peace officers' operating within the moral consensus of the community. Whereas the former have occasion to speak chiefly to offenders or to persons who can supply information about an offence, the patrolmen interact with all sorts of people and more of their contacts centre upon assisting citizens than upon offences.

In contrasting village society with the big industrial nation it is difficult not to convey a false impression. Even in the small-scale stable society consensus is never perfect; it is only relatively high. An even greater mistake would be to imply that consensus is absent under urban conditions. Certainly in some urban situations the moral controls are weak and the formal organization has to impose strict penalties, but there are many basic issues – such as ideas of duty to kinsfolk, work-mates, and neighbours – where popular morality remains powerful. In many urban residential neighbourhoods there is a very real sense of community even if informal social controls are less extensive than in the village. Policemen, being subconsciously aware of their dependence upon these other mechanisms of control, prefer to work as peace officers and to see their role in these terms. There is in Britain a current of opposition to specialization in police work and to the employment of civilian auxiliaries, which cannot easily be explained but which seems to rest upon this ideal of the policeman as a peace officer.

*From Michael Banton,* The Policeman in the Community, *(London: Tavistock) 1964, pp 1–7.*

## References

Gourley, G. Douglas (1954). Police–public relations. *Annals of the American Academy of Political and Social Science*, 291.

Homans, George C. (1950). *The human group*. New York: Harcourt Brace.

Myrdal, Gunnar *et al.* (1944). *An American dilemma*. New York: Harper.

Parker, William H. (1954). The police challenge in our great cities. *Annals of the American Academy of Political and Social Science*, 291.

# 10. Responsibilities of the police

*William Westley*

The exact function of the police within a city is difficult to delineate, ranging as it does from the formal assignment of duties and responsibilities with respect to law enforcement and the maintenance of order to its frequent informal control of the illegal structure of the town, and its adjudication of the differences between section and class moralities. This not only differs from department to department depending on the city in which they are located, but also changes with the perspective in which it is described. Thus, Whyte (1943, p. 138) has described the police of *Street Corner Society* as exercising a careful control over the illegal gambling operations in the town by supporting certain groups and 'cracking down' on others; and again he has stated that the police function as buffer between the values of the middle class and the values of the slum. Lohman has pointed out that the police function to support and enforce the interests of the dominant political, social, and economic interest of the town, and only incidentally to enforce the law.[1] Subsequently, we shall demonstrate that the value structure of the police strongly supports this viewpoint [ ... ]. However, even in the formal duties of the police one can obtain considerable understanding of their position and function in society. These formal duties are an intrinsic part of their everyday routine, and without them society would be seriously incapacitated.

### Police duties in general

August Vollmer (1936), a leading police administrator, states that in addition to their better known responsibilities with respect to the prevention of major crimes and the control of vice and traffic, the duties of the police include:

> ... the enforcement of federal law violations that may come to the attention of the municipal police; all state laws, felonies and misdemeanors that are not included under the classification of major crimes; and the multitudinous city ordinances that cover  every variety of subject imaginable; search for missing persons and the restoration to their families of children found or of adults who have wandered away from their homes, the search for lost property or animals, and the delivery of these to the rightful owners.

Besides the foregoing duties, the police are required to take possession of dead bodies found, and to conduct inquiries to ascertain the cause of death. Investigations of this kind must be conducted with extreme care because what appears to be a natural death may later prove to be a murder. Sick and injured persons receive first aid from trained policemen and in many cities these persons are conveyed either to their homes or to hospitals in police ambulances. The police are also responsible for collecting information to be presented at coroners' inquests in suicide cases, and for caring for persons who have attempted without success to end their lives. Handling the insane and feeble minded, and providing for their immediate care or ultimate commitment to an institution, is another form of general police service to which the public, gives little thought, but which consumes much of the police officers' time ... they must take care of riots incident to strikes, subversive activities, or racial disagreements. They must inspect business places which are required to be licensed and investigate conditions incident to the health of the community.

However, even this list is incomplete, for it says nothing of the amount of time the police act as public information bureau, of their attempts to settle family disputes, of the extensive guard duty that they perform in the nightly checking of doors and windows and the inspection of the homes of people away on vacation. Each city will have its additions to Vollmer's list, for each city finds in the police a group who can be assigned that which no other groups can perform.

### Duties, Department X

To substantiate Vollmer's material, we quote at length from the Police Handbook given to all policemen in our City X. In this book, a quotation from the law of the state appears as follows:

Section 48–6110. DUTIES OF POLICE FORCE. It is hereby made the duty of such police force, and the members thereof are specially empowered at all times, within such city, to preserve peace; prevent crime; detect and arrest offenders; suppress riots, mobs and insurrections; disperse unlawful and dangerous assemblages, and assemblages which obstruct the free passage of public streets, sidewalks, parks and places; protect the rights of persons and property; guard the public health; preserve order at elections and meetings; direct the movement of teams and vehicles in streets, alleys or public places; remove all nuisances in public streets, parks or highways; arrest all street beggars and vagrants; provide proper police assistance at fires; assist, advise and protect strangers and travelers in public streets or at railroad stations; carefully observe and inspect all places of business under license, or required to have the same, all houses of ill fame or prostitution and houses where common prostitutes resort or reside, all lottery or policy shops, all gambling-houses, cockpits, dance houses and resorts; and to suppress and restrain all unlawful or disorderly conduct or practices and enforce and prevent the violation of all ordinances and laws in effect in such city. The chief of police and each captain, in his precinct, shall possess the power of supervision and inspection over all pawnbrokers, vendors, junkshop keepers, cartmen, expressmen, dealers in second-hand merchandise, intelligence offices and auctions; and any members of such force may be authorized, in writing by the chief, to exercise the same powers. Such chief or captain may, by written authority, empower any member of such police force, when in search of stolen property, of evidence, or of suspected offenders, to examine the books, business or premises of any of the persons named in this section and to examine property in whosesoever possession the same shall be. (Acts 1905, ch. 129, No. 164, p. 219.)

It can be seen from these accounts of the duties of the police that the service functions of the police constitute an important part of their responsibility and the major part of their time. This is not in accordance with the popular conception of the police as a crime prevention and criminal apprehension unit. Such activities are in large measure the job of the detective bureau, as will be delineated later, and form only a relatively small portion of the patrolman's activities. This is in itself a characterization of the police function, for by any measure the patrol and traffic divisions include the bulk of the personnel in any police department. In Department X the detective bureau contains about 30 men, while the patrol and traffic bureaus contain approximately 160 men.

### The 'dirty work'

Second, the listings reveal that much of the policeman's job consists of 'dirty work'. It consists of dealing with drunks, with the insane, with the dead, with the vice-ridden, with the ill. It is a necessary function in any modern community, but an exceedingly unpleasant and in some sense degrading one.

The police, then, can be said to have, in addition to their obvious responsibilities with respect to law enforcement, a tremendous number of service duties, which in themselves constitute an important and essential part of their function in the ongoing life of the community. In an emergency of almost any type – of human relations, of health, of nature – the police are among the first to be called in, and generally people expect them to do something about it. In one sense they can be said to fill in the lacunae between the existent formal control embodied in the law and the agencies of the community and the rapidly breaking down formal controls related to change and transition in society.

*From William Westley,* Violence and the Police, *(Cambridge, MA: MIT Press) 1970, pp 16–19.*

### Notes

1   Lohman, personal conversations.
2   Based on the annual school census taken in that city.

## References

Vollmer, August, *The Police and Modern Society*. Berkeley, Calif: University of California Press, 1936.
Whyte, William S. *Street Corner Society*. Chicago: University Press 1943.

# 11. What do the police do?

*David H. Bayley*

## Introduction

The research findings described here are based on four years, from 1989 to 1993, of intensive research with 28 police forces in five countries – 7 in Australia, 3 in England and Wales, 6 in Canada, 3 in Japan and 9 the United States. The countries were chosen because they are similar politically and economically and are accessible for research on the police. Each police force studied provided information on their performance from existing records and files and it is a reflection of what police managers themselves have at hand when they make decisions about police activities. I made a special point of visiting commands where something explicitly new or experimental was taking place. Within each police force I collected information about the activities of a cross section of police stations selected from urban, suburban and rural locations. Information on police performance was collected from 12 front-line stations in Australia, 8 in England and Wales, 3 in Canada, 12 in Japan and 11 in the United States. In addition, I observed police operations in the field and interviewed police managers and supervisors at all levels.

## Patrolling

Patrolling is by far the biggest assignment in policing. In the United States 65 per cent of police officers are assigned to patrol work, 64 per cent in Canada, 56 per cent in England and Wales, 54 per cent in Australia, and 40 per cent in Japan. These officers work round the clock every day of the year, in uniform, usually in marked radio patrol cars.

Patrol work is determined almost entirely by what the public ask the police to do. Contrary to what most people think, the police do not enforce their own conception of order on an unwilling populace. Almost all they do is undertaken at the request of some member of the public. If the public stopped calling the police, the police would have to re-invent their job.

Driving slowly around their assigned beats, patrol officers wait for radio dispatchers to relay calls that have come over the well-publicised emergency telephone numbers. In cities, over 90 per cent of the work of patrol officers is generated by dispatch. Self-initiated, or proactive work in police jargon, occurs more frequently in less developed or rural areas.[1]

Stopping motor vehicles that have violated traffic law accounts for the largest proportion of self-generated work, at least, in Australia, Canada and the United States. Patrol officers spend the rest of their time discouraging behaviour that they view as disruptive or unseemly, such as drunks sleeping in front of doorways, teenage boys hanging around on street corners, prostitutes soliciting, or men urinating against a wall around the corner from a busy bar.

Very little of the work patrol officers do has to do with crime. British and U.S. studies have consistently shown that not more than 25 per cent of all the calls to the police are about crime, more often the figure is 15–20 per cent.[2] Moreover, what is initially reported by the public as a crime is often found not to be a crime by the police who respond.[3] For example, lonely elderly people may report burglaries in progress so that police will come and talk to them for a while. Thus, the real proportion of requests to the police that involve crime may be more like 7–10 per cent.

Most of the genuine crime the police are called upon to handle is minor. In the United States, using the categories provided by the Uniform Crime Reports, one finds that from 1984 to 1990 violent crime (homicide, forcible rape, aggravated assault, robbery) averaged 13 per cent of all reported serious crime (violent crime plus burglary, larceny theft and auto theft). In Australia violent crime accounts for about 2 per cent of reported serious crime. The ratio of reported violent to serious crime tends to be higher in large cities, but violent crime still represents only 25 per cent of the total of reported crime in New York city, 12 per cent in Houston, 26 per cent in Los Angeles, 16 per cent in Montreal and 17 per cent in Toronto.

If one compares violent crime to all crime no matter how trivial, such as minor shoplifting, disturbing the peace, vandalism, minor property theft, and so on, the proportion is much lower. In 1990 violent crimes accounted for around 1 per cent of all reported crime in Australia, 9 per cent in Canada, 5 per cent in England and Wales, and 1 per cent in Japan.

Not only *is* crime a minor part of patrol work and often not especially serious, the trail is almost always cold by the time the police arrive, with the culprit having been gone for hours and often days. This is typical of crimes against property, the largest category of serious crimes.

If the majority of police officers are not directly fighting crime, what are they doing? The answer is they are restoring order and providing general assistance. In the apt words of Egon Bittner[4] the key function of the police is to stop 'something that ought not to be happening and about which someone had better do something now'. Police interrupt and pacify situations of potential or ongoing conflict. Typical instances are young men drinking beer on a street corner and making rude remarks, tenants refusing to leave an apartment from which they have been evicted, a dog barking persistently late at night, a truculent and inconsiderate neighbour obstructing a driveway with his car. Most of the time the police do not use the criminal law to restore calm and order. They rarely make arrests, though the threat of doing so always exists.

When officers are called to actual or potential conflicts they try to 'sort out', as the British say, what has been going on and to produce a truce that will last until the officer gets away. Is there an offence? Who is the victim? This searching for the truth is often very difficult. People lie brazenly, which explains in large part why the police become cynical and hard to convince. Or people tell self-serving, partially true stories. The police 'sort out' situations by listening patiently to endless stories about fancied slights, old grievances, new insults, mismatched expectations, infidelity, dishonesty and abuse. They hear all about the petty, mundane, tedious, hapless, sordid details of individual lives. Patient listening and gentle counselling are undoubtedly what patrol officers do most of the time.

The most common, as well as the most difficult, conflict situations the police handle are disputes within families. Officers round the world claim that such disturbances are more common on days when public assistance cheques are delivered, because then people have the money to drink.

Research into the handling of domestic disputes in the United States shows that the police routinely pursue eight different courses of action.[5] Most commonly, they simply leave after listening, without doing anything at all (24 per cent). Next, they give friendly advice about how to avoid a repetition of the incident (16 per cent). Arrest is the next most commonly used action, occurring in 14 per cent of incidents. British police also make arrests in domestic disputes about 23 per cent of the time, they only 'advise' 50 per cent of the time.[6] Police also pointedly warn people what will happen if they are called back; promise future help if it is needed; give explicit advice to one or the other about what they should do to extricate themselves from the conflict; make sure one party leaves the scene; or suggest referral to third parties, professional or otherwise.[7]

The infrequency of arrests is not just true of police responses to disputes. In general, patrol officers, who are responsible for most contacts with the general population, rarely make arrests. In the United States in 1990, police officers made an average of 19 arrests a year.[8] That is less than one arrest per officer every 15 working days. In Canada, police officers make one criminal arrest a month and encounter a recordable criminal offence only once a week.[9]

Although police rarely enforce the law in their manifold encounters with the public, it would be wrong to suggest that the power to arrest is not important. The threat is potent, whatever the outcome of particular encounters. The power to arrest is what makes their intervention authoritative. Police *can* forcibly stop people from doing what they are doing; they *can* push people into bare cells with wet concrete floors and slam shut the heavy barred door behind them. As US police officers sometimes say 'Maybe I can't give 'em a rap (a conviction), but I sure can give them the ride'.

Disputes are not the only situations in which the police are called upon to intervene authoritatively. People come to the police with all sorts of urgent problems hoping they are able to help. These requests, which vastly outnumber disturbances, are as varied as the needs of the public. Such calls require service, not force or law enforcement. In the United States requests of this kind are referred to as 'cats-in-a-tree' situations and in Australia as 'frogs-in-the-drain' cases.

Most patrol work is boring, whether it involves restoring order or providing services. Most of the incidents to which patrol officers respond are routine and undramatic. Los Angeles police estimate that not more than 7 per cent of their dispatched calls require an emergency response. Police in Edmonton, Canada, say 18 per cent, in Seattle 13 per cent, and in Kent, England, 4 per cent. Actually, officers soon learn that often what seems like an emergency probably isn't, so they often dawdle in situations that would seem to require a fast response. Patrol , officers spend a lot of time simply waiting for something to happen. They spend most of the time driving methodically around, guided by their extensive knowledge of where incidents are likely to occur. Like tour guides in the museum of human frailty, they can point to houses where they are repeatedly called to mediate family disputes, up-market apartment complexes where young swingers frequently hold noisy parties, troublesome 'biker' bars where drugs are sold, business premises patrolled by a vicious dog, street corners where drug dealers collect, car parks often hit by thieves, warehouses with poor alarm systems and places where police officers have been shot and wounded.

By and large, the people police deal with are life's refugees. Uneducated, poor, often unemployed, they are both victims and victimisers. Hapless, befuddled, beaten by circumstances, people like these turn to the police for the help they can't give themselves. There is little the police can do for them except listen, shrug and move on. The police try to distinguish the few who are genuinely vicious from the majority who are not and treat them differently. Although patrol work is mostly trivial and non-criminal, it is nonetheless fraught with uncertainty. Officers can never forget that at any moment the boredom of a long shift cap be shattered by a call that can be harrowing, traumatic, dangerous or life-threatening. The dilemma for patrol officers is that they must prepare for war even though they are rarely called upon to fight. To relax invites risk; to be constantly on guard invites over-reaction.

## Criminal investigation

The next biggest job in policing after patrolling is criminal investigation. It accounts for 14 per cent of police personnel in Canada, 15 per cent in England and Wales and the United States, 16 per cent in Australia and 20 per cent in Japan. Criminal investigation is done by detectives, who do not usually work in uniform and have more flexible hours than patrol officers. Detectives in small police departments or those assigned to field stations tend to be generalists, investigating whatever crime occurs. The rest, usually working out of headquarters, are assigned to speciality units, such as homicide, robbery, vice, narcotics, auto theft and burglary. In recent years some forces have added new specialities such as bias crime, child abuse, sexual assault and computer crime.

Like patrol, criminal investigation is overwhelmingly reactive. Whatever preventive effect detectives have comes primarily through deterrence – that is, by removing particular offenders from the streets or by demonstrating to would-be offenders that crime does not pay. Detectives rarely anticipate crime and prevent it from happening. They occasionally 'stake-out' the sites of likely criminal activity or clandestinely watch known criminals in order to catch them in the act. Both tactics have been shown to be costly relative to the amount of criminal activity discovered. Undercover penetration of criminal conspiracies, featured so often in films and television, is rare. A common tactic, especially during the 1980s, was for detectives to pose as people willing to do something illegal, such as buying drugs or receiving stolen property.[10]

What do the vast majority of detectives who investigate crime do? Basically, they talk to people – victims, suspects, witnesses – in order to find out exactly what happened in particular situations and whether there is enough evidence to arrest and prosecute suspects with a reasonable likelihood of conviction. In most cases detectives make very quick judgements about whether an investigation should be undertaken. It depends on two factors: first, whether a credible perpetrator has been fairly clearly identified and, second, whether the crime is especially serious or repugnant – the sort that attracts public attention. Except when forced to do so by public pressure, police do not invest resources in cases in which they have no idea who the criminal might be. Such cases are almost always burglaries and most robberies.

Detectives, quickly formulate a theory about who committed the crime and then set about collecting the evidence that will support arrest and prosecution. They know if perpetrators cannot be identified by people on the scene the police are not likely to find the criminals on their own. Nor is physical evidence especially important in determining whether a case is pursued, it is used as confirmation – to support testimony that identifies suspects. The absence of physical evidence might mean a case cannot be made; it may also disconfirm a theory. But it hardly ever leads to the identification of persons not already suspected by the police. In short, criminal investigations begin with the identification, then collect evidence; they rarely collect evidence and then make an identification.

Like doctors in a war zone, criminal investigators employ a triage strategy. If a crime cannot be solved more or less on the spot, the case will probably be closed and the detectives will move on to more promising cases.

Because most crime suspects cannot be identified readily, most crimes go unsolved. Japan is the exception among developed democratic countries. There the police solve about 58 per cent of all crime reported to them. The United States has one of the worst records: only 22 per cent of even the most serious crimes are solved; in England and Wales 35 per cent, in Canada 45 per cent and in Australia 30 per cent. The likelihood of solving a crime varies with the nature of the offence, with higher rates for confrontational crimes and lower rates for property crimes. In the United States police solve 46 per cent of violent crimes against people and 18 per cent of property crimes. Amongst serious crimes, homicide is the most likely to be solved, 67 per cent, and motor vehicle theft the least likely, 15 per cent.[11]

Detectives spend most of their time talking to people strongly suspected of being involved in crimes in an attempt to get them to confess. Interrogations are generally fairly low key and straightforward. Detectives simply confront a suspect with the evidence they have. They do not have to be very clever because most of the time suspects do confess. Sometimes they make threats which have much more to do with the ability of the police to persist than with physical force. Sometimes they bluff and sometimes they cajole.

Detectives also work hard to get 'secondary clearances', that is, when a person who is prosecuted – or sometimes convicted – for one crime confesses to other crimes. Many burglaries are cleared-up in this way. Studies in Britain and the United States indicate that the only sure way for a police force to increase a low clear-up rate is to give more attention to obtaining secondary clearances.[12]

Perhaps the most demanding part of a detective's job is developing expertise in the legal requirements for collecting and reporting evidence. Few have formal legal training, yet they need to understand how prosecutors will use their evidence and the challenges it will face in court. Detectives complain that paperwork is becoming increasingly more intricate and burdensome as a result of changes in court rulings and legislation. Research shows that for every hour detectives talk to people and search for evidence they spend half an hour on paperwork.

Although criminal investigation is regarded as the epitome of policing, it is not at all clear that it requires skills that are peculiar to the police. Many detectives admit off the record that investigation can be done by anyone who is intelligent, poised and willing to learn the intricacies of the criminal law. As one experienced detective chief inspector in England said, 'criminal investigation work is the sort of work any good Prudential Insurance man could do'.[13]

## Traffic

The third big job the police undertake is the regulation of motor vehicle traffic. In Japan 17 per cent of police officers are assigned to traffic units, 10 per cent in Australia, 7 per cent in England and Wales and the United States and 6 per cent in Canada. Traffic regulation is important for two reasons; first, the number of people killed or injured in traffic accidents and the monetary value of damage to property are substantially higher than result from crime; second, a larger cross section of the populace comes into contact with the police through the enforcement of traffic laws than in any other way.

Traffic officers generally work in marked cars patrolling major roads for the purpose of preventing motor vehicle accidents. They do this by enforcing laws against dangerous driving as well as against defective vehicles and by controlling traffic flow in potentially hazardous circumstances, such as those associated with accidents, spillage of toxic substances, parades, sporting events and construction sites. Their work is more self-initiated than that of patrol officers or detectives. They go where the problems are.

Traffic officers tend to be zealous, convinced that what they are doing is very important. They also feel beleaguered, unappreciated and understaffed. Their reaction may have to do with the view among police officers that traffic regulation is peripheral to 'crime fighting'.

Enforcement of traffic laws is a means to an end – maintaining order and safety – not an end in itself. Traffic officers, like patrol officers, use the law as a tool for obtaining compliance. Traffic policing is highly discretionary, requiring officers to make a lot of decisions on the spot whether the law should be enforced. Traffic officers can almost always find an excuse to stop a vehicle, if not for speeding or driving mistakes then for mechanical vehicle defects.

When traffic officers stop a car for a driving violation, their options are not simply whether or not to impose a punishment. They can either apply an official penalty with or without a stern lecture, warn the driver, arrest the driver for being intoxicated or for another crime, or take no action. In England and Wales an official penalty is applied in only 25 per cent of traffic stops.[14]

## Other work

Patrol, criminal investigation and traffic regulation are the largest areas of modern operational policing occupying about 85 per cent of all police personnel. Most of the rest is accounted for by administration: 11 per cent in Japan, 10 per cent in Canada, 9 per cent in the United States, 7 per cent in England and Wales and 6 per cent in Australia. Administration includes recruitment, training, public relations and all the housekeepmg functions of purchasing, paying, supervising and so forth.

All the other operational units are very small, designed to support patrol, criminal investigation and traffic regulation in specialised ways. The most well known special units are probably the dog squad and the special weapons and tactics team (or SWAT) – these units are used in incidents such as hostage takings or barricaded suspects or rescue operations.

Large police forces may also have permanent formations of riot police – the *Kidotai* in Japan, the Mobile Reserves in England and Wales and the Task Force in New York City. Police forces in cities that are political centres, for example, Tokyo, London and New York are called upon to protect important persons.

The people who must give explicit attention to anticipating and preventing crime, apart from routine uniform patrolling and the undercover work of a few investigators, barely show up on most organisational charts. Specialised crime prevention units account for 6 per cent of personnel in Japan – by far the largest among the police forces studied. In Australia the figure is 4 per cent, in large United States forces 3 per cent, in Canada 1 per cent, and in England and Wales less than 1 per cent. These 'crime prevention' units are relatively new, dating generally from the 1980s.

Some police forces are also responsible for a number of other activities including inspection and licensing of firearms, bars, liquor stores and gaming parlours; serving of warrants and summonses; dealing with lost and found property; background checks on government employees; transporting emergency medical supplies. In short, police often perform a host of ancillary tasks given them by government, largely for reasons of convenience.

The point is that although the police are expected to prevent crime, people expect them to do many other things – things that are not noticed until they are not available.

## Variations in police work

Policing is strikingly similar from place to place, at least as indicated by organisational assignments. Among the forces studied about 60 per cent of police personnel patrol and respond to requests for service, 15 per cent investigate crime, 9 per cent regulate traffic and 9 per cent administer. Within countries the proportion of officers assigned to different specialities varies considerably among forces – less in Japan and England and Wales, more in Australia and the United States.

These differences are not systematic, that is, related to features of social context, such as crime rates of population densities. Two factors are indicative. First, the proportions of officers on the major assignments differ very little among urban, suburban and rural police stations. Second, the proportion of officers assigned to different sorts of work has not changed significantly among the forces surveyed during the last 20 years. [...]

Although these data do not constitute a definitive test, they suggest that police forces are organised to do the same sorts of work regardless of the social circumstances they confront. Crime and social conditions certainly vary amongst urban, suburban and rural police jurisdictions but police organisations are staffed in almost exactly the same way everywhere. Although social conditions, particularly crime, changed between 1970 and 1990 in the five countries studied, police organisations did not. What the police are prepared to do does not change with what needs doing.

There are several reasons for this. The first is bureaucratic politics. Existing organisational units fight hard to maintain their share of resources. A second reason is that police forces are sometimes compelled to adhere to national standards for staffing. In England and Wales Her Majesty's Inspectorate of Constabulary, a central government agency, monitors force staffing patterns and recommends adjustments to fit the preferred model. In Japan the National Police Agency has the same functions. In the United States so-far voluntary processes of accreditation exert the same homogenizing effect.

Finally, police officers are part of an international professional culture, reinforced by conferences, seminars and workshops, exchanges of personnel and trade publications. They continually look over their shoulders to determine whether their forces follow what the profession considers 'efficient, modern and progressive'. In short, they copy one another, especially a few 'flagship' forces such as Los Angeles and New York City, the London Metropolitan Police and the Royal Canadian Mounted Police.

For all these reasons, police organisations do not adapt to the work they must do. Rather the work they must do is adapted to the police organisation.

*From David Bayley*, Police for the Future *(New York: Oxford University Press), 1994, pp 29–41.*

## References

1 Bayley, D.H. (1985) *Patterns of Policing*. New Brunswick, NJ: Rutgers University Press.
2 Whitaker, G. *et al.*,. (1981) *Measuring Police Agency Performance*. Washington, DC: Law Enforcement Assistance Agency. Mimeo. Morris, P. and Heal, K. (1981) *Crime Control and the Police: A Review of Research*. Home Office Research Study No. 67. London: HMSO. Thames Valley Police (1991) *Annual Report of the Chief Constable*.

3  Gilsinian, J.F. (1989) They is clowning tough: 911 and the social construction of reality. *Criminology*, 27, pp. 329–44. Reiss, A.J. (1971) *The Politics of the Police*. New Haven: Yale University Press.

4  Bittner, E. (1970) *The Functions of the Police in Modern Society: A Review of Background Factors, Current Practices and Possible Role Models*. Chevy Chase, MD: National Institute of Mental Health.

5  Bayley, D.H. (1986) The tactical choice of police patrol officers. *Journal of Criminal Justice*, 14, pp. 32–48.

6  Shapland, J. and Hobbs, D. (1989) Policing priorities on the ground. In Morgan, R. and Smith, D.H. (eds) *Coming to Terms with Policing*. London: Routledge.

7  McIver, J.P. and Parks, R.B. (1981) Evaluating police performance. In Bennett, R. (ed) *Police at Work: Policy Issues and Analysis*. Beverly Hills, CA: Sage Publications.

8  Bureau of Justice Statistics (1988, 1990, 1991) *Sourcebook of Criminal Justice Statistics*. Washington, DC: Government Printing Office.

9  Ericson, R.V. and Shearing, C.D. (1986) The scientification of police work. In Bohme, G. and Stehr, N. (eds) *The Knowledge Society*. Dordrecht: D. Reidel Publishing Company.

10 Marx, G.T. (1988) *Undercover Police Work: The Paradoxes and Problems of a Necessary Evil*. Berkeley, CA: University of California Press.

11 Bureau of Justice Statistics (1988, 1990, 1991) *Sourcebook of Criminal Justice Statistics*. Washington, DC: Government Printing Office.

12 Eck, J.E. (1982) *Problem Solving: The Investigation of Residential Burglary and Robbery*. Washington, DC: Police Executive Research Forum.
Burrows, J. (1986) *Investigating Burglary: The Measurement of Police Performance*. Home Office Research Study No. 88. London: HMSO.

13 McClure, J. (1980) *Spike Island: Portrait of a British Police Division*. New York: Pantheon Books.

14 Skogan, W.C. (1990) *Police and the Public in England and Wales: A British Crime Survey Report*. Home Office Research Study No. 117. London: HMSO.

# 12. Florence Nightingale in pursuit of Willie Sutton: a theory of the police

*Egon Bittner*

Among the institutions of modern government the police occupies a position of special interest: it is at once the best known and the least understood. Best known, because even minimally competent members of society are aware of its existence, are able to invoke the services it provides with remarkable competence, and know how to conduct themselves in its presence. How and how well the police is known, and the ways it matters in the lives of people, vary considerably over the spectrum of social inequality. But to imagine people who are not at all touched by the police one must conjure images of virtually complete isolation or of enormous wealth and power. Least understood, because when people are called upon to explain on what terms and to what ends police service is furnished they are unable to go beyond the most superficial and misleading commonplace which, moreover, is totally unrelated to the interactional skill that manifestly informs their dealings with policemen. What is true of people generally is true of the police as well. Policemen have not succeeded in formulating a justification of their existence that would recognizably relate to what they actually do (not counting those activities the doing of which they disavow or condemn). The situation is not unlike that of a person who, asked to explain how he speaks, offers an account which, while itself linguistically in perfect order, does not even come close to doing justice to the skill involved in producing the utterance.

In this chapter I propose to explain the function of the police by drawing attention to what their existence makes available in society that, all things being equal, would not be otherwise available, and by showing how all that policemen are called upon to do falls into place when considered in relationship to it. My thesis is that police are empowered and required to impose or, as the case may be, coerce a provisional solution upon emergent problems without having to brook or defer to opposition of any kind, and that further, their competence to intervene extends to every kind of emergency, without any exceptions whatever. This and this alone is what the existence of the police uniquely provides, and it is on this basis that they may be required to do the work of thief-catchers and of nurses, depending on the occasion. And while the *chances* that a policeman will recognize any problem as properly his business depend on some external regulation, on certain structured social interest, and on historically established patterns of responsiveness and responsibility, every stricture arising out of these factors is defeasible in every *specific case* of police work. This means that the appropriateness of police action is primarily determined with regard to the particular and actual nature of the case at hand, and only secondarily by general norms. The assessment whether the service the police are uniquely competent to provide is on balance desirable or not, in terms of, let us say, the aspirations of a democratic polity, is beyond the scope of the argument. But in reviewing practice and organization I will weigh what is against what ought to be, by certain criteria internal to the enterprise.

The chapter is frankly argumentative and intended to furnish grist to the mills of debate. Hence, I shall not attempt to view all questions from all sides, and I will especially avoid giving consideration to mere administrative expediency or yielding to those demands of reasonableness that are connected with taking a live-and-let-live attitude. All this counts, to be sure, but I will try not to let it count in what I have to say; and in arguing as strongly as I know how, I do not aim to dismiss polemic opponents but to pay tribute to them. My plan is to begin with a cursory review of some preliminaries – dealing mainly with the police idea – in ways I consider indispensable for what will follow. Next I shall sketch a rather ordinary and common event in police work, and use it to explain what a policeman is required to do in this situation, in such situations, and by extension, in any situation whatever. Finally, I will attempt to characterize the problems that appear to summon police intervention and to define the role force plays in these interventions. In wrapping things up I will comment about the practical significance of police work in society and about the skills that come into play, or should come into play, in this regard.

## The official basis of law enforcement mandates

While we use the term police to refer to specific corps of public officials, it bears mentioning that original usage embraced the entire field of internal government, as distinct from the conduct of foreign affairs. Sir Francis Bacon, for example, asserted that in being 'civil or policied' a nation acquired the right to subdue others that were 'altogether unable or indign to govern' (Bacon, 1859, 29). In time this usage gave way to one restricted to the exercise of proscriptive control in matters affecting the public interest. Blackstone stated that 'public police and economy … mean the due regulation and domestic order of the Kingdom, whereby the individuals of the state, like members of a well governed family, are bound to conform their general behavior to the rules of propriety, good neighborhood and good manners, and to be decent, industrious and inoffensive in their respective stations' (Blackstone n.d., 161). This definition is located in the volume dealing with public wrongs, in relation to a specific class of delicts, called offenses against the public police and economy. By the end of the nineteenth century this class of delicts is treated by Sir James Fitzjames Stephen as lying outside of the scope of criminal law, but is, nevertheless, explicitly related to the existence of the then existing police forces in England (Stephen, 1833, 246). Though both Blackstone and Stephen treat the category of police offenses cursorily, they do furnish *legal authority* for each item discussed. The intent at scrupulous legalization of proscriptive control also inheres in the 'idiom of apologetics which belongs to the vocabulary of constitutional law' (Hamilton and Rodee, 1937, 192), commonly invoked to justify abridgements of civil liberties in the interest of 'public health, morals, and safety' (Mugler *v.* Kansas, 1887). Indeed, in keeping with American concepts of legality, Mr. Justice Harlan, speaking for the majority in Mugler, reserved the right of judicial review of statutes enacted in the exercise of police power.

Most of the offenses against the public police mentioned by Blackstone are no longer regarded as culpable. But the domain of legally sanctioned proscriptive control he discussed has expanded enormously since the commentaries appeared, as have the provisions of criminal law. There are scarcely any human activities, any interpersonal relations, any social arrangements left that do not stand under some form of governmental regulation, to the violation of which penalties are attached. To say that modern life is thus controlled does not mean saying that it is more controlled than earlier life. Tribesmen, peasants, or citizens of colonial townships most assuredly did not live in a paradise of freedom. In fact, the most widely accepted explanation of the proliferation of formal control, which associates it with the growth of a market-oriented, industrial, and urban order, implies primarily a shift from reliance on informal mechanisms of traditional authority to reliance on legal rational means (Weber, 1947, 324).

Urbanism brought with it the need for explicitly formal regulations because the lives of the people living in cities are replete with opportunities of infringing upon one another and virtually devoid of incentives to avoid it. The former is due to the sheer congestion of very large numbers of people, the latter to the social distance between them. More importantly, perhaps, urban strangers cannot entrust their fate to the hope of somehow muddling through because of the manner in which they attend to the business of making a living, and because of the permanent significance of this interest in their lives.

Two conditions must be met to satisfy the need for formal governmental control that would bind effectively the behavior of individuals to rules of propriety. The first, already recognized in the treatment Blackstone accorded to the matter, is that all controls rest on specific authorization set forth in highly specific legal norms. The second, explicitly acknowledged by Stephen, is that the implementation of the authorizing norm must be entrusted to impersonal enforcement bureaucracies. In sum, 'the due regulation and domestic order' in our times is the task of a host of law enforcement bureaucracies, each using procedures legitimized by, and incidental to, the attainment of explicitly formulated legal objectives.

Naturally, the actual interests and practices of enforcement officials are rarely as specific or explicit as the verbal formulations of their respective mandates. Hence, for example, while the formal authorization of the work of a health inspector may be clear and specific, things are apt to become a bit sticky when he undertakes to match factual realities with provisions of statutes. The amount of discretionary freedom it takes to fill the interstices of the legal formulation of law enforcement competence probably varies from one bureaucracy to the next. Agents concerned with weights and measures are probably less free than building inspectors. On the whole, however, it is safe to assume that none will busy himself, nor be permitted to busy himself, outside of the sphere of his mandate. More importantly, there is no mystery about the proper business of such law enforcement agents, and citizens are generally quite able to hold them to their limits. For example, though a truant officer's enforcement activities could be rich and varied, especially if he happens to be dedicated to his tasks, he can claim legitimate interest in the child's health, the conditions of his home, or some such matter, only insofar as they can be linked with school attendance. In practice it can be debated whether the connection he sees is defensible or not, but there is not debate about the terms on which the question must be decided. Because it is known what a truant officer is supposed to do, therefore he can be held to account for doing more or doing less than his mandate authorizes or requires him to do, and by the same token, the officer can reject demands he deems *ultra vires*.

It would seem reasonable to expect that the proper business of the police – that is, of the corps of officials who inherited the name once used to refer to the entire domain of internal, proscriptive regulation – should be determined in the manner in which the business of all other law enforcement bureaucracies is determined. That is, one would expect that their service and powers be derivative from some substantive authorizing norm. And, indeed, it is commonly assumed that the penal code contains this authorization, in addition to which the police are required to enforce other laws, in particular laws regulating vehicular traffic, and beyond that may have some responsibilities concerning such matters as the licensing of the possession of firearms or the operation of certain business enterprises, which vary greatly from place to place. All in all, however, activities relating to crime control are generally considered basic to the mandate of the police by both citizens and police officials, at least in the sense that its needs are regarded as having priority over other needs (Gorman et al., 1973; Leonard and More, 1971).[1] Though I will argue that this presumption is misguided and misleading, and that one could not possibly understand or control what policemen actually do by assuming it, it must be said that it is not without some carefully laid foundations, the import of which is difficult to overcome.

The following considerations appear to justify the presumption that the police are a law enforcement agency whose mandate is basically derivative of the provisions of penal codes. First, the police, together with many others, cultivate and propagate the image of the policeman as the vanguard fighter in the war on crime. Americans from the members of congress to readers of tabloids are convinced that what the police do about crime is the main part of the struggle against it and that, therefore, doing something about it is the policeman's main care. Second the formal bureaucratic organization of police work stringently reinforces the view that the police are primarily dedicated to criminal law enforcement. Police training, such as it is, heavily emphasizes criminalistics, criminal law, and related matters; the internal administrative differentiation of departments tends to reflect primarily formal criminal enforcement specializations and units are designated by names of species of offenses; and police recordkeeping is almost wholly dedicated to the recording of law enforcement activity as a result of which crime control is the only documentable output of police work. Most importantly, perhaps, career advancement in departments is heavily determined by an officer's show of initiative and ability in criminal law enforcement or, at least, an officer who has some so-called good pinches to his credit can always count that this will weigh more heavily in his favor when it comes to assessing his overall performance than any other factor. Third, the criminal process is virtually always set into motion by the police, and prosecutors, judges, and correctional personnel are heavily dependent on the police to remain occupied. Moreover, the part the police play in the administration of justice is very specific and indispensable. They are charged with the responsibility of conducting investigations leading to the identification of suspects and with securing the evidence required for successful prosecution. And they are obliged to apprehend and detain identified suspects, in the course of which they are empowered to use force if force is necessary. Fourth, the work of a certain number of policemen – the number is probably not very large but large enough to be significant – is in fact quite plainly determined by the provisions of the penal code in more or less the same manner in which the work of building inspectors is determined by building codes. These are officers assigned to various detective bureaus, whose daily routines consist of investigating crimes, arresting offenders, and of otherwise being engaged with matters related to efforts to obtain convictions.

In sum, the exercise of internal, proscriptive control by modern governments has been highly legalized, at least since the end of the eighteenth century. The exercise of this control is assigned to specifically authorized bureaucracies, each of which has a substantively limited field of enforcement competence. Even though it is allowed that officials retain a measure of discretionary freedom, the terms on which substantive decisions can be made are not in dispute. In accordance with this view the police often are viewed as one of several enforcement bureaucracies whose domain of competence is determined by penal codes and certain other statutory delegations.

## The police and criminal law enforcement

With all this admitted as true, why can the police mandate not be conceived as embodying the law enforcement mandate inhering in criminal law enforcement? The answer is quite simple. Regardless of how strenuously criminal law enforcement is emphasized in the image of the policeman and in police administration, and regardless of how important police work might actually be for keeping the administration of criminal justice in business, the activity of criminal law enforcement is not at all characteristic of day-to-day, ordinary occupational practices of the vastly preponderant majority of policemen. In other words, when one looks at what policemen actually do, one finds that criminal law enforcement is something that most of them do with the frequency located somewhere between virtually never and very rarely.

Later in this chapter I will address this paradox directly and try to assign to criminal law enforcement its proper place within police work. Before moving on to this, however, I must touch on some matters connected with manpower allocation, opportunity for crime control, and routine work orientation. Unfortunately the data base on which the first two observations rely is poor, partly because the information available on these matters is not as good as it could be, but in larger measure because the actuarial ratios and frequencies I shall mention are drawn from data produced to meet requirements of accounability rather than strictly factual reporting. A word of caution is in order here; it is all too easy to fall into an attitude of supercilious critique concerning the poverty of data. The fact is that neither the police nor functionaries in other practical endeavors should be expected to keep records that would make it convenient for scholars to study them. Indeed, they usually have good reasons for keeping what in the scholar's view appear to be poor records (Garfinkel and Bittner, 1967, 186–207).

According to a survey of municipal police departments of cities in the 300,000 to 1,000,000 population range which is, alas, neither exhaustive nor complete, 86.5 percent of all police line personnel – that is, excluding officers occupying supervisory positions from sergeant up – are assigned to uniformed patrol (Kansas City Police Department, 1971; Wilson, 1963, 293).[2] Though this figure excludes persons holding the civil service rank of patrolman while assigned to detectives' bureaus, it probably overestimates the relative size of the force of patrol men actually working on the streets. But it would certainly seem safe to assume that four out of five members of the line personnel do the work of patrolmen, especially since patrol sergeants, whose work is essentially of the same nature as the work of those they supervise, are not included in the 86.5 per cent. But the importance of the uniformed patrol in the police is not altogether derivative from the preponderance of their number. They represent, in even greater measure than their numbers indicate, the police presence in society. In fact, I will argue that all the other members of the police – in particular, the various special plainclothes details – represent special refinements of police-patrol work that are best understood as derivative of the mandate of the patrol, even though their activities sometimes take on forms that are quite unlike the activities of the patrol. But I should like to make clear now that in subordinating the work of the detectives to the work of the patrol *conceptually*, I do not intend to cast doubts on the special importance the work of the former has for the prosecutors and judges. Indeed, I hope to make clear by dint of what circumstance prosecutors and judges come to be the beneficiaries of a service they ordinarily take for granted but for which – in rather rare moments of candor – they profess to lack understanding.

For the reasons I indicated, and because of reasons I hope to add as I go along, the following remarks will concern primarily the work of the uniformed patrol. But I do intend to make references to other parts of the police wherever such references are called for. In fact, the first observation about criminal law enforcement pertains equally to the work of detectives and patrolmen.

It is well known that the penal codes the police are presumed to enforce contain thousands of titles. While many of these titles are obscure, unknown, or irrelevant to existing conditions, and the administration of criminal justice is concentrated around a relatively small fraction of all proscribed acts, the police select only some, even from that sample, for enforcement. Relying mainly on my observations, I believe the police tend to avoid involvement with offenses in which it is assumed that the accused or suspected culprits will not try to evade the criminal process by flight. Characteristically, for example, they refer citizens who complain about being defrauded by businesses or landlords directly to the prosecutor. The response is also often given in cases involving other types of allegations of property crimes involving persons, real or fictional, who own substantial property. To be sure, in some of these instances it is possible that the wrong is of a civil rather than a criminal nature, and it also should be taken into account that a principle of economy is at work here, and that the police disavow responsibility for some delicts simply because of lack of resources to deal with them. It is at least reasonable to suggest, however, that police interest in criminal law enforcement is limited to those offenses in which the perpetrator needs to be *caught* and where catching him *may* involve the use of physical force. The point in all this is not that the police are simply ignorant of, and uninterested in, the majority of the provisions of the penal code, but that their selectivity follows a specific principle, namely, that they feel called upon to act only when *their* special competence is required, and that special competence is related to the possibility that force *may* have to be used to secure the appearance of a defendant in court. This restriction is certainly not impermeable, and it happens often enough that policemen are for a variety of circumstantial reasons required to proceed in cases in which the voluntary appearance of a defendant in court is not in doubt. Interestingly, however, in many of these cases the police are likely to put on a symbolic show of force by gratuitously handcuffing the arrested person.

It has become commonplace to say that patrolmen do not invoke the law often. But this is not a very good way of putting things because it could also be said that neurosurgeons do not operate often, at least not when compared with the frequency with which taxi drivers transport their fares. So it might pay to try to be a bit more specific about it. According to estimates issued by the research division of the International Association of Chiefs of Police, 'the percentage of the police effort devoted to the traditional criminal law matters probably does not exceed ten percent' (Niederhoffer, 1969, 75). Reiss, who studied the practices of the patrol in a number of American metropolitan centers, in trying to characterize a typical day's work, stated that it defies all efforts of typification 'except in the sense that *the modal tour of duty does not involve an arrest* of any person' (Reiss 1971, 19). Observations about arrest frequency are, of course, not a very good source of information about law enforcement concerns. Yet, while they must be viewed skeptically, they deserve mention. According to the Uniform Crime Reports, 97,000 detectives and patrolmen made 2,597,000 arrests, including 548,000 for Index Crimes.[3] This means that the average member of the line staff makes twenty-six arrests annually, of which slightly more than five involve serious crimes. Though it is admittedly no more than a rough guess, it would seem reasonable to say, allowing for the fact that detectives presumably do nothing else, that patrolmen make about one arrest per man per month, and certainly no more than three Index Crime arrests per man per year. In any case, these figures are of the same order of magnitude as reported in the draft of a report on police productivity, where it was said that patrolmen assigned to New York City's Anti-Crime Squad average about fifteen felony arrests per man per year, while a 'typical uniformed patrolman makes only about three felony arrests per year'. In Detroit members of the Special Crime Attack Team make ten felony arrests per man per year, 'considerably more than the average patrolman' (National Commission on Productivity, 1973, 39f.). And the figures are also in good accord with estimates reported by the President's Commission on Law Enforcement and Administration of Justice, where it was calculated on the basis of data drawn from the operations of the Los Angeles Police Department that 'an individual patrol officer can expect an opportunity to detect a burglary no more than once every three months and a robbery no more than once every fourteen years' (Institute for Defense Analysis, 1967, 12).

It could be said, and should be considered, that the mere frequency of arrest does not reflect police work in the area of criminal law enforcement adequately. Two points deserve attention in this regard: first, that clearing crimes and locating suspects takes time; and second, that policemen frequently do not invoke the law where the law could be invoked and thus *are* involved in law enforcement, albeit in an unauthorized way.

In regard to the first point, it is certainly true that there are some cases that are subject to dogged and protracted investigation. It is even not unheard of that uniformed patrolmen work on some crime for long periods while attending to other duties. This, however, is not characteristic of the work of either detectives or patrolmen generally. For instance, in the majority of reported burglaries, a patrolman or a team of patrolmen are dispatched to survey the scene; this is followed by investigations done by detectives, who, after writing up a report of their investigation, in the majority of cases simply move on to the next case (Conklin and Bittner, 1973, 206–23).[4] Along these lines, Conklin reports that criminal *investigations* of robberies produce clearances only in one out of fifty cases (Conklin, 1972, 148f.). And even if it were to be assumed that detectives engage in five investigations for every one they conclude successfully – no doubt a gross exaggeration – it would still remain that in the run-of-the-mill crime the kind of investigation common lore associates with detective work is not characteristic of the police, and could not be, if only because the press of new business pushes old cases into the dead file. I must add that the whole matter of crime investigation is complicated, involving activities that I did not mention. But I only intended to show that the spacing of arrests is not due to the fact that the policemen need time to work out a solution. All this means is that cases are solved, when they are solved, either at the time the offense takes place or shortly thereafter or, by and large, not at all. The information required for such solution must be mobilizable in short order, or the quest will be abandoned. In other words, either a detective knows quite clearly in the case where to turn or he will not try to pursue the matter. That he often knows where to turn is part of his craft (Bittner, 1970: 65ff.).[5]

The other point, that ,policemen make law enforcement decisions of 'low visibility', is the topic of a fairly substantial body of literature.[6] According to the prevailing view expressed in this literature, patrolmen usurp the rights of judges in a host of minor offenses and, by not invoking the law, exculpate the offender. While most authors find such practices reasonable and for the most part desirable, they also recommend that the exercise of such discretion should be placed under administrative, if not statutory, regulation (Davis, 1971). They urge that, though it appears to make good sense that policemen do not enforce statutes pertaining to gambling literally and in every applicable case, it is not right that the decision when to proceed and when to desist should be left entirely to the lights of the individual officers. Provided with more detailed instructions officers would be, presumably, on firmer grounds and, hopefully, less arbitrary. Unfortunately, underlying the approach is a presumption that begs the principal question; namely, whether in making the arrests they make, and not making the arrests they do not make, policemen are acting as the *functionaries of the law* they invoke or fail to invoke, as the case may be. All available information about the practices of patrolmen place this presumption in grave doubt, especially in regard to laws pertaining to minor offenses. I am not aware of any descriptions of police work on the streets that support the view that patrolmen walk around, respond to service demands, or intervene in situations, with the provisions of the penal code in mind, matching what they see with some title or another, and deciding whether any particular apparent infraction is serious enough to warrant being referred for further process. While it does happen occasionally that patrolmen arrest some person merely because they have probable cause to believe that he has committed crimes, this is not the way all but a small fraction of arrests come about. In the typical case the formal charge *justifies* the arrest a patrolman makes but is *not* the *reason* for it. The actual reason is located in a domain of considerations to which Professor Wilson referred as the need 'to handle the situation',[7] and invoking the law is merely a device whereby this is sometimes accomplished. Since the persons who are arrested at a backyard game of craps are not arrested because they are gambling but because of a complex of situational factors of which no mention is made in the formally filed charge, it would seem specious to try to refine the law pertaining to the charge, since any policeman worth his salt is virtually always in a position to find a *bona fide* charge of some kind when he believes the situation calls for an arrest. If criminal law enforcement means acting on the basis of, and in accordance with, the law's provisions, then this is something policemen do occasionally, but in their routine work they merely avail themselves of the provisions as a means for attaining other objectives.

In sum, the vastly preponderant number of policemen are assigned to activities in which they have virtually no opportunities for criminal law enforcement, and the available data indicate that they are engaged in it with a frequency that surely casts doubts upon the belief that this is the substance, or even the core, of their mandate. Moreover, criminal law enforcement by the police is limited to those offenses in which it is assumed that force may have to be used to bring the offender to justice. Finally, in the majority of cases in which the law is invoked, the decision to invoke it is not based on considerations of legality. Instead, policemen use the provisions of the law as a resource for handling problems of all sorts, of which *no mention* is made in the formal charge.

## The elements of routine police practice

To explain by what conception of duty policemen feel summoned into action, and what objectives they seek to attain, I should like to use an example of ordinary practice. One of the most common experiences of urban life is the sight of a patrolman directing traffic at a busy street intersection. This service is quite expensive and the assignment is generally disliked among policemen. Nevertheless it is provided on a regular basis. The reason for this is not too difficult to divine. Aside from the private interests of citizens in maintaining safe and otherwise suitable conditions for the use of their automobiles, there is the consideration that the viability of urban life as we know it depends heavily on the mobility of vehicular traffic. No one knows, of course, how helpful police traffic control is in general, much less in the special case of a single patrolman directing traffic at a particular place and time. However uncertain the value of traffic control, the uncertainty is resolved in favor of having it simply because of the anticipated gravity of the consequences its absence might engender. In sum, traffic control is a matter of utmost seriousness. Despite its seriousness and presumed necessity, despite the fact that assignments are planned ahead and specifically funded, no assignment to a traffic control post is ever presumed to be absolutely fixed. The assigned officer is expected to be there, all things being equal, but he is also expected to have an independent grasp of the necessity of his presence. The point is not that this opens the possibility of a somewhat more casual attitude toward traffic control than the police care to admit, but rather that there exists a tacit understanding that no matter how important the post might be, it is always possible for something else to come up that can distract the patrolman's attention from it and cause him to suspend attending to the assigned task.

This understanding is not confined to traffic control assignments, but functions in all prior assigned tasks without any exceptions whatever, regardless whether the assignment involves investigating a heinous crime or feeding ice cream to a lost child, and regardless whether the prior assignment derives from the most solemn dictates of the law or whether it is based on mundane commands of immediate superiors. I am saying more than merely that patrolmen, like everybody else, will suspend the performance of an assigned task to turn to some extraordinary exigency. While everybody might respond to the call of an emergency, the policeman's vocational ear is *permanently and specifically attuned* to such calls, and his work attitude throughout is permeated by preparedness to respond to it, whatever he might happen to be doing. In the case at hand, it is virtually certain that any normally competent patrolman would abandon the traffic post to which he was assigned without a moment's hesitation and without regard for the state of the traffic he was supposed to monitor, if it came to his attention that a crime was being committed somewhere at a distance not too far for him to reach in time either to arrest the crime in its course, or to arrest the perpetrator. And it is virtually certain that all patrolmen would abandon their posts even when the probability of arresting the crime or its perpetrator was not very high and even when the crime was of the sort which when reported to the police in the ordinary manner – that is, some time after it happened – would receive only the most cursory attention and would tend to remain unsolved in nine out of every ten reported cases. Finally, there is no doubt that the patrolman who would not respond in this manner, would thereby expose himself to the risk of an official reprimand, and to expressions of scorn from his co-workers, and from the public.

Yet there exists no law, no regulation, no formal requirement of any kind that determines that practice. Quite the contrary, it is commonly accepted that crime control cannot be total, must be selective, and that policemen cannot be expected to rush to the scene of every crime and arrest every offender. Why then should all concerned, inside and outside the police, consider it entirely proper and desirable that a patrolman abandon his post, exposing many people to serious inconvenience and the whole city to grave hazards, to pursue the dubious quest of catching a two-bit thief?

At the level of reason the patrolman himself might advance, the action merely follows the impulse to drop everything and catch a crook. And it seems perfectly reasonable that policemen should follow this impulse more readily than others, since they presumably are being paid for it. Thus considered, the action draws its justification from the public sentiment that a crime must not be allowed to pass without at least an attempt to oppose it and from the policeman's special obligation in this regard. This sentiment is certainly a very important aspect of the policeman's frame of mind; it directs his interests, establishes priorities, furnishes justification for action, governs the expectations of reward and honor, and ultimately supplies the rhetoric with which his ready aggressiveness is explained.

But I have argued earlier that, the strength of this sentiment notwithstanding, criminal law enforcement could not possibly be the fulcrum on which the police mandate rests. How then do I explain the alacrity of the patrolman's response? Let me begin with an aside which is in its own way important but not central to the argument. For the patrolman, rushing to the scene of a crime is an opportunity to do something remarkable that will bring him to the attention of his superiors in a way that might advance his career. This aspect of his vocational interest is not rooted in the work he does but in the administrative setting within which it is done. Skolnick (1966, 231) has furnished extensive documentation for the importance of this factor in police work. Still, however important the explanation is, it fails in explaining police routines generally.

When I stated in the vignette that the patrolman will abandon his assignment to rush to the scene of a crime, I assumed without saying that the crime would be something like an act of vandalism, an assault, or a burglary. But if the crime that came to the attention of the officer had been something like a conspiracy by a board of directors of a commercial concern to issue stock with the intention of defrauding investors, or a landlord criminally extorting payments from a tenant, or a used-car dealer culpably turning back an odometer on an automobile he was preparing for sale, the patrolman would scarcely lift his gaze, let alone move into action. The real reason why the patrolman moved was not the fact that what was taking place was a crime in general terms, but because the particular crime was a member of a class of problems *the treatment* of *which will not abide*. In fact, the patrolman who unhesitatingly left his post to pursue an assailant would have left his post with just a little hesitation to pull a drowning person out of the water, to prevent someone from jumping off the roof of a building, to protect a severely disoriented person from harm, to save people in a burning structure, to disperse a crowd hampering the rescue mission of an ambulance, to take steps to prevent a possible disaster that might result from broken gas lines or water mains, and so on almost endlessly, and entirely without regard to the substantive nature of the problem, as long as it could be said that it involved *something-that-ought-not-to-be-happening-and-about-which-someone-had-better-do-something-now!* These extraordinary events, and the directly intuited needs for control that issue from them, are what the vocational interests of patrolmen are attuned to. And in the circumstances of such events citizens feel entitled and obliged to summon the help of the police. Naturally, in retrospect it is always possible to question whether this or that problem should or should not have become the target of police attention, but most people will agree that urban life is replete with situations in which the need for such service is not in doubt, and in which, accordingly, the service of the police is indispensable.

It is scarcely possible not to notice that the definition of the police mandate escaped Ockham's Rasor. It cannot be helped; I have seen policemen helping a tenant in arrears gain access to medication which a landlord held together with other possessions in apparently legal bailment, I have seen policemen settling disputes between parents as to whether an ill child should receive medical treatment, I have seen a patrolman adjudicating a quarrel between a priest and an organist concerning the latter's access to the church. All this suggests more than the obvious point that the duties of patrolmen are of a mind-boggling variety, it compels the stronger inference that no human problem exists, or is imaginable, about which it could be said with finality that this certainly could not become the proper business of the police.

It is fair to say that this is well known even though police work is not thought of in these terms. It must be assumed to be well known because in almost all instances the police service is a response to citizen demands, which must be taken as reflecting public knowledge of what is expected of the police. But evidently it is not thought of in these terms when it comes to writing books about the police, to making up budgets for the police, and to training policemen, administering departments, and rewarding performance. And even though the fact that policemen are 'good' at helping people in trouble and dealing with troublesome people has received some measure of public recognition recently,[8] the plaudits are stated in ways reminiscent of 'human interest stories' one finds in the back pages of the daily papers. More importantly, when it is asked on what terms this police service is made available in every conceivable kind of emergency, the usual answer is that it happens by default because policemen are the only functionaries, professionals, officials – call them what you will – who are available around the clock and who can be counted on to make house calls. Further, it is often said that it would be altogether better if policemen were not so often called upon to do chores lying within the spheres of vocational competence of physicians, nurses and social workers, and did not have to be all things to all men. I believe that these views are based on a profound misconception of what policemen do, and I propose to show that no matter how much police activity seems like what physicians and social workers might do, and even though what they actually have to do often could be done by physicians and social workers, the service they perform involves the exercise of a unique competence they do not share with anyone else in society. Even if physicans and social workers were to work around the clock and make house calls, the need for the police service in their areas would remain substantial, though it certainly would decline in volume. Though policemen often do what psychologists, physicians, or social workers might be expected to do, their involvement in cases is never that of surrogate psychologists, physicians, or social workers. They are in all these cases, from the beginning, throughout, and in the last analysis, policemen, and their interest and objectives are of a radically distinct nature. Hence, saying that policemen are 'good at' dealing with people in trouble and troublesome people does not mean that they are good at playing the role of other specialists. Indeed, only by assuming a distinct kind of police competence can one understand why psychologists, physicians, and social workers run into problems in *their* work for which they seek police assistance. In other words, when a social worker 'calls the cops' to help him with his work, he mobilizes the kind of intervention that is characteristic of police work even when it looks like social work.

To make clear what the special and unique competence of the police consists of I should like to characterize the events containing 'something-that-ought-not-to-be-happening-and-about-which-somebody-had-better-do-something-now', and the ways police respond to them. A word of caution: I do not intend to imply that everything policemen attend to can be thus characterized. That is, the special and unique police competence comes into play about as often as practicing medicine, doing engineering, or teaching – in the narrow meanings of these terms  come into play in what physicians, engineers, and teachers do.

First, and foremost, *the need to do something* is assessed with regard for actually existing combinations of circumstances. Even though circumstances of need do become stereotyped, so that some problems appear to importune greater urgency than others, the rule *it depends* takes precedence over typification, and attention is directed to what is singular and particular to the here-and-now. Policemen often say that their work is almost entirely unpredictable; it might be more correct to say that anything unpredictable that cannot be dismissed or assimilated to the usual is *pro tanto* a proper target of police attention. That experience plays an important part in the decision making goes without saying, but it is not the kind of experience that lends itself easily to the systemization one associates with a body of technical knowledge. Most often the knowledge upon which patrolmen draw is the acquaintance with particular persons, places, and past events. Patrolmen appear to have amazingly prodigious memories and are able to specify names, addresses, and other factual details of past experiences with remarkable precision. Indeed, it is sometimes difficult to believe that all this information could be correct. However this may be, the fact that they report their activities in this manner, and that they appear to think in such terms, may be taken as indicative of the type of knowledge they depend on in their work. It could be said that while anything at all could become properly the business of the police, the patrolman can only decide whether anything in particular is properly his business after he 'gets there' and examines it.

Second, the question whether some situational need justifiably requires police attention is very often answered by persons who solicit the service. Citizen demand is a factor of extraordinary importance for the distribution of police service, and the fact that someone did 'call the cops' is, in and of itself, cause for concern. To be sure, there are some false alarms in almost every tour of duty, and one reason why police departments insist on employing seasoned policemen as dispatchers is because they presumably are skilled in detecting calls which lack merit. Generally, however, the determination that some development has reached a critical stage, ripe for police interest, is related to the attitudes of persons involved, and depends on common sense reasoning. For example, in a case involving a complaint about excessive noise, it is not the volume of the noise that creates hazards for life, limb, property, and the public order, but that the people involved say and otherwise show that the problem has reached a critical stage in which something-had-better-be-done-about-it. Closely connected with the feature of critical emergency is the expectation that policemen will handle the problem 'then-and-there'. Though it may seem obvious, it deserves stressing that police work involves no continuances and no appointments, but that its temporal structure is throughout of the 'as soon as I can get to it' norm, and that its scheduling derives from the natural fall of events, and not from any externally imposed order, as is the case for almost all other kinds of occupations. Firemen too are permanently on call, but the things they are called upon to do are limited to a few technical services. A policeman is always poised to move on any contingency whatever, not knowing what it might be, but knowing that far more often than not he will be expected to *do something*. The expectation to do something is projected upon the scene, the patrolman's diagnostic instinct is heavily colored by it, and he literally sees things in the light of the expectation that he somehow *has* to handle the situation. The quick-witted and decisive activism of the police is connected with the fact that they are attuned to dealing with emergencies; and in many instances the response-readiness of the policeman rounds out the emergency character of the need to which the response was directed.

Third, though police departments are highly bureaucratized and patrolmen are enmeshed in a scheme of strict internal regulation, they are, paradoxically, quite alone and independent in their dealings with citizens. Accordingly, the obligation to do something when a patrolman confronts problems – that is, when he does police work – is something he does not share with anyone. He may call for help when there is a risk that he might be overwhelmed, and will receive it; short of such risks, however, he is on his own. He receives very little guidance and almost no supervision; he gets advice when he asks for it, but since policemen do not share information, asking for and giving advice is not built into their relations; his decisions are reviewed only when there are special reasons for review, and records are kept of what he does only when he makes arrests. Thus, in most cases, problems and needs are seen in relationship to the response capacity of an individual patrolman or teams of two patrolmen, and not of the police as an organized enterprise. Connected with the expectation that he will do what needs to be done by himself is the expectation that he will limit himself to imposing provisional solutions upon problems. Though they often express frustration at never solving anything – especially when they arrest persons and find them quickly back on the street – they do what they do with an abandon characteristic of all specialists who disregard the side effects of their activities. As they see it, it is none of their concern that many provisional solutions have lasting consequences. In fact, it would be quite well put to say that they are totally absorbed with making arrests, in the literal sense of the term. That is, they are always trying to snatch things from the brink of disaster, to nip untoward development in the bud, and generally to arrest whatever must not be permitted to continue; and to accomplish this they sometimes arrest persons, if circumstances appear to demand it.

Fourth and finally, like everybody else, patrolmen want to succeed in what they undertake. But unlike everybody else, they never retreat. Once a policeman has defined a situation as properly his business and undertakes to do something about it, he will not desist till he prevails. That policemen are uniquely empowered and required to carry out their decisions in the 'then-and-there' of emergent problems is the structurally central feature of police work. There can be no doubt that the decisive and unremitting character of police intervention is uppermost in the minds of people who solicit it, and that persons against whom the police proceed are mindful of this feature and conduct themselves accordingly. The police duty not to retreat in the face of resistance is matched by the duty of citizens not to oppose them. While under common law citizens had the right to resist illegal police action, at least in principle, the recommendations contained in the Uniform Arrest Act, the adoption of which is either complete or pending before most state legislatures, provides that they must submit. To be sure, the act pertains only to arrest powers, but it takes little imagination to see that this is sufficient to back up any coercive option a policeman might elect.[9]

The observation that policemen prevail in what they undertake must be understood as a *capacity* but not a necessarily invariant practice. When, for example, a citizen is ordered to move or to refrain from what he is doing, he may actually succeed in persuading the policeman to reverse himself. But contrary to judges, policemen are not required to entertain motions, nor are they required to stay their orders while the motion receives reasoned consideration. Indeed, *even* if the citizen's objection should receive favorable consideration in *subsequent* review, it would still be said that 'under the circumstances' he should have obeyed. And even if it could be proved that the policeman's action was injudicious or in violation of civil liberties, he would be held to account only if it could also be proved that he acted with malice or with wanton frivolity.[10]

In sum, what policemen do appears to consist of rushing to the scene of any crisis whatever, judging its needs in accordance with canons of common sense reasoning, and imposing solutions upon it without regard to resistance or opposition. In all this they act largely as individual practitioners of a craft.

## The specific nature of police competence

The foregoing considerations suggest the conclusion that what the existence of the police makes available in society is a unique and powerful capacity to cope with all kinds of emergencies: unique, because they are far more than anyone else permanently poised to deal with matters brooking no delay; powerful, because their capacity for dealing with them appears to be wholly unimpeded. But the notion of emergency brings a certain circularity into the definition of the mandate. This is so because, as I have indicated, the discernment of the facts of emergency relies on common sense criteria of judgment, and this makes it altogether too easy to move from saying that the police deal with emergencies, to saying that anything the police deal with is, *ipso facto*, an emergency. And so, while invoking the notion of emergency was useful to bring up certain observations, it now can be dispensed with entirely.

Situations like those involving a criminal on the lam, a person trapped in a burning building, a child in desperate need of medical care, a broken gas line, and so on, made it convenient to show why policemen move decisively in imposing constraints upon them. Having exploited this approach as far as it can take us, I now wish to suggest that the specific competence of the police is wholly contained in their capacity for decisive action. More specifically, that the feature of decisiveness derives from the authority to overpower opposition in the 'then-and-there' of the situation of action. *The policeman, and the policeman alone, is equipped, entitled, and required to deal with every exigency in which force may have to be used, to meet it.* Moreover, the authorization to use force is conferred upon the policeman with the mere proviso that force will be used in amounts measured not to exceed the necessary minimum, as determined by an intuitive grasp of the situation. And only the use of deadly force is regulated somewhat more stringently.[11]

Three points must be added in explanation of the foregoing. First, I am *not* saying the police work consists of using force to solve problems, but only that police work consists of coping with problems in which force *may have to be used*. This is a distinction of extraordinary importance. Second, it could not possibly be maintained that everything policemen are actually required to do reflects this feature. For a variety of reasons – especially because of the ways in which police departments are administered – officers are often ordered to do chores that have nothing to do with police work. Interestingly, however, the fact that a policeman is quite at the beck and call of his superior and can be called upon to do menial work does not attenuate his powers *vis-à-vis* citizens in the least. Third, the proposed definition of police competence *fully embraces* those forms of criminal law enforcement policemen engage in. I have mentioned earlier that the special role the police play in the administration of criminal justice has to do with the circumstance that 'criminals' – as distinct from respectable and propertied persons who violate the provisions of penal codes in the course of doing business –can be counted on to try to evade or oppose arrest. Because this is so, and to enable the police to deal effectively with criminals, they are said to be empowered to use force. They also engage in criminal investigations whenever such investigations might be reasonably expected to be instrumental in making arrests. But the conception of the police role in all this is upside down. It is *not* that policemen are entitled to use force because they must deal with nasty criminals. Instead, the duty of handling nasty criminals devolves on them *because* they have the more general authority to use force *as needed* to bring about desired objectives. It is, after all, no more than a matter of simple expediency that it should be so; and that it is so becomes readily apparent upon consideration that policemen show little or no interest in all those kinds of offenders about whom it is not assumed that they need to be caught, and that force may have to be used to bring them to the bar of justice.

## Conclusions

There is a threefold paradox in the awesome power of the policeman to make citizens obey his command, both legitimately and effectively. First, how come such a power exists at all? Second, why has the existence of this power not received the consideration it deserves? Third, why is the exercise of this power entrusted to persons recruited from a cohort from which all those with talent and ambitions must be assumed to have gone on to college and then to other occupations? I shall attempt to answer these questions in the stated order.

The hallmark of the period of history comprising the past century and a half is a succession of vast outbreaks of internal and international violence, *incongruously combined* with an unprecedently sustained aspiration to install peace as a stable condition of social life.[12] There can be no doubt that during this period the awareness of the moral and practical necessity of peace took hold of the minds of almost all the people of our world, and while the advocacy of warfare and of violent revolution has not disappeared, it has grown progressively less frank and arguments in their favor seem to be losing ground to arguments condemning violence. The sentiments in favor of peace draw in part on humane motives, but they derive more basically from a profound shift of values, away from virtues associated with masculine prowess and combativeness, and toward virtues associated with assiduous enterprise and material progress. There is still some glamor left in being an adventurer or warrior, but true success belongs to the businessman and to the professional.[13] Resorting to violence – outside of its restricted occasions, notably warfare and recreation – is seen as a sign of immaturity or lower-class culture (Miller, 1958, 5–19; Adorno *et al.* 1950). The banishment of violence from the domain of private life – as compared, for instance, with its deliberate cultivation in medieval chivalry – the lesser part of the story. More important is the shift in the methods of government to an almost complete civil and pacific form of administration. Physical force has either vanished or is carefully concealed in the administration of criminal justice, and the use of armed retainers to collect taxes and to recruit into the military are forgotten. Paper, not the sword, is the instrument of coercion of our day. But no matter how faithfully and how methodically the dictates of this civil culture and of the rule of law are followed, and no matter how penetrating and far-reaching the system of peaceful control and regulation might be, there must remain some mechanism for dealing with problems on a catch-as-catch-can basis. In fact, it would seem that the only practical way for banishing the use of force from life generally is to assign its residual exercise – where according to circumstances it appears unavoidable – to a specially deputized corps of officials, that is, to the police as we know it. Very simply, as long as there will be fools who can insist that their comfort and pleasure take precedence over the needs of firemen for space in fighting a fire, and who will not move to make room, so long will there be a need for policemen.

I must leave out one possible explanation for the neglect of the capacity to use force as the basis of the police mandate; namely, that I am wrong in my assessment of its fundamental importance. I have no idea why the authors of many superb studies of various aspects of police work have not reached this conclusion. Perhaps they were either too close to, or too far from, what they were researching. But I believe I know why this feature of police work has escaped general notice. Until recently the people against whom the police had cause to proceed, especially to proceed forcefully, came almost exclusively from among the blacks, the poor, the young, the Spanish-speaking, and the rest of the urban proletariat, and they still come preponderantly from these segments of society: This is well known, much talked about, and I have nothing to add to what has already been said about expressions of class and race bias. Instead, I should like to draw attention to a peculiar consequence of this concentration. The lives of the people I mentioned are often considered the locus of problems in which force may have to be used. Not only do most of the criminals with whom the police deal hail from among them, but they, more often than other members of society, get into all sorts of troubles, and they are less resourceful in handling their problems. And so it could be said that the police merely follow troubles into trouble's native habitat and that no further inferences can be drawn from it, except, perhaps, that policemen are somewhat too quick in resorting to force and too often resort to it for what seem to be inadequate reasons, at least in retrospect. Of course, the rise of the counterculture, the penetration of drug use into the middle classes, the civil rights movements of the 1960s, and the student movement have proven that the police do not hesitate to act coercively against members of the rest of society. But that too has been mainly the target of critique, rather than efforts to interpret it. And the expressions of indignation we hear have approximately the effect 'Gesundheit' has on whatever causes a person to sneeze. The police are naturally baffled by the response; as far as they can see they did what they always did whenever they were called upon to intervene. In point of fact policemen did, *mutatis mutandis*, what physicians do under similar circumstances. Physicians are supposed to cure the sick through the practice of medicine, as everyone knows. But when they are consulted about some problem of an ambiguous nature, they define it as an illness and try to cure it. And teachers do not hesitate in treating everything as an educational problem. It is certainly possible to say that physicians and teachers are just as likely to go overboard as policemen. This does not mean, however, that one cannot find in these instances the true nature of their respective bags of tricks more clearly revealed than in the instances of more standard practice. In the case of the police, it merely obscures matters to say that they resort to force only against powerless people, either because it is more often necessary or because it is easier – even though these *are* important factors in determining frequency – for in fact, they define every summons to action as containing the possibility of the use of force.

The reasons why immense powers over the lives of citizens are assigned to men recruited with a view that they will be engaged in a low-grade occupation are extraordinarily complicated, and I can only touch on some of them briefly.

Perhaps the most important factor is that the police were created as a mechanism for coping with the so-called dangerous classes (Silver, 1967, 1–24). In the struggle to contain the internal enemy and in the efforts to control violence, depredation, and evil, police work took on some of the features of its targets and became a tainted occupation. Though it may seem perverse, it is not beyond comprehension that in a society which seeks to banish the use of force, those who take it upon themselves to exercise its remaining indispensable residue should be deprecated. Moreover, in the United States the police were used blatantly as an instrument of urban machine-politics, which magnified opportunities for corrupt practices enormously. Thus, the American urban policeman came to be generally perceived as the dumb, brutal, and crooked cop. This image was laced by occasional human interest stories in which effective and humane police work was portrayed as the exception to the rule. The efforts of some reformers to purge the police of brutality and corruption have inadvertently strengthened the view that police work consists of doing what one is told and keeping one's nose clean. To gain the upper hand over sloth, indolence, brutality, and corruption, officials like the late Chief William Parker of Los Angeles militarized the departments under their command. But the development of stringent internal regulation only obscured the true nature of police work. The new image of the policeman as a snappy, low-level, soldier-bureaucrat created no inducement for people who thought they could do better to elect police work as their vocation. Furthermore, the definition of police work remained associated with the least task that could be assigned to an officer. Finally, the most recent attempts to upgrade the selection of policemen have been resisted and produced disappointing results. The resistance is in large measure due to the employee interests of present personnel. It seems quite understandable that the chiefs, captains, and even veteran patrolmen would not be happy with the prospect of having to work with recruits who outrank them educationally. Furthermore, few people who have worked for college degrees would want to elect an occupation that calls only for a high school diploma. And those few will most likely be the least competent among the graduates, thereby showing that higher education is more likely to be harmful than helpful. And it is true, of course, that nothing one learns in college is particularly helpful for police work. In fact, because most college graduates come from middle-class backgrounds, while most of police work is directed toward members of the lower classes, there is a risk of a cultural gap between those who do the policing and the policed.

But if it is correct to say that the police are here to stay, at least for the foreseeable future, and that the mandate of policemen consists of dealing with all those problems in which force may have to be used, and if we further recognize that meeting this task in a socially useful way calls for the most consummate skill, then it would seem reasonable that only the most gifted, the most aspiring, and the most equipoised among us are eligible for it. It takes only three short steps to arrive at this realization. First, when policemen do those things only policemen can do, they invariably deal with matters of absolutely critical importance, at least to the people with whom they deal. True, these are generally not the people whose welfare is carefully considered. But even if democratic ideals cannot be trusted to ensure that they will be treated with the same consideration accorded to the powerful, practicality should advise that those who never had a voice in the past now have spoken and succeeded in being heard. In sum, police work, at its core, involves matters of extraordinary seriousness, importance, and necessity. Second, while lawyers, physicians, teachers, social workers, and clergymen also deal with critical problems, they have bodies of technical knowledge or elaborate schemes of norms to guide them in their respective tasks. But in police work there exists little more than an inchoate lore, and most of what a policeman needs to know to do his work he has to learn on his own. Thus, what ultimately gets done depends primarily on the individual officer's perspicacity, judiciousness, and initiative. Third, the mandate to deal with problems in which force may have to be used implies the special trust that force will be used only *in extremis*. The skill involved in police work, therefore, consists of retaining recourse to force while seeking to avoid its use, and using it only in minimal amounts.

It is almost unnecessary to mention that the three points are not realized in police work. Far too many policemen are contemptuous toward the people with whom they deal and oblivious to the seriousness of their tasks. Few policemen possess the perspicacity and judiciousness their work calls for. And force is not only used often where it need not be used, but gratuitous rudeness and bullying is a widely prevalent vice in policing. While all this is true, I did not arrive at those points by speculating about what police work could be. Instead I have heard about it from policemen, and I saw it in police work. I say this not to make the obvious point that there exist, in many departments, officers whose work already embodies the ideals I mentioned. More important is that there are officers who know what police work calls for far better than I can say, and from whom I have learned what I said. As far as I could see they are practical men who have learned to do police work because they had to. No doubt they were motivated by respect for human dignity, but their foremost concern was effectiveness and craftsmanship. Perhaps I can best describe them by saying that they have in their own practices placed police work on a fully reasoned basis, moving from case to case as individual practitioners of a highly complex vocation.

Though I cannot be sure of it, I believe I have written as a spokesman of these officers because I believe one must look to them to make police work what it should be. But the chances that they will prevail are not very good. The principal obstacle to their success is the presently existing organization of police departments. I cannot go into details to show how the way police work is administratively regulated constitutes a positive impediment in the path of a responsible policeman, quite aside from the fact that most of his work is unrecognized and unrewarded.[14] But I would like to conclude by saying that, far from providing adequate disciplinary control over patent misconduct, the existing organizational structures encourage bad police work. Behind this is the ordinary dose of venality and vanity, and the inertia of the way things are. But the principal cause is an illusion. Believing that the real ground for his existence is the perennial pursuit of the likes of Willie Sutton – for which he lacks both opportunity and resources – the policeman feels compelled to minimize the significance of those instances of his performance in which he seems to follow the footsteps of Florence Nightingale. Fearing the role of the nurse or, worse yet, the role of the social worker, the policeman combines resentment against what he has to do day in, day out with the necessity of doing it. And in the course of it he misses his true vocation.

One more point remains to be touched upon. I began with a statement concerning the exercise of proscriptive control by government, commonly referred to as law enforcement. In all instances, except for the police, law enforcement is entrusted to special bureaucracies whose competence is limited by specific substantive authorization. There exists an understandable tendency to interpret the mandate of the police in accordance with this model. The search for a proper authorizing norm for the police led to the assumption that the criminal code provided it. I have argued that this was a mistake. Criminal law enforcement is merely an incidental and derivative part of police work. They do it simply because it falls within the scope of their larger duties – that is, it becomes part of police work exactly to the same extent as anything else in which force may have to be used, and only to that extent. Whether the police should still be considered a law enforcement agency is a purely taxonomic question of slight interest. All I intended to argue is that their mandate cannot be interpreted as resting on the substantive authorizations contained in the penal codes or any other codes. I realize that putting things this way must raise all sorts of questions in the minds of people beholden to the ideal of the Rule of Law. And I also realize that the rule of law has always drawn part of its strength from pretense; but I don't think pretense is entitled to immunity.

*From Egon Bittner, 'Florence Nightingale in pursuit of Willie Sutton', in* Aspects of Police Work *(Boston, MA: Northeastern University Press) 1990, pp 233–68.*

## Notes

Florence Nightingale is the heroic protagonist of modern nursing; Willie Sutton, for those who are too young to remember, was in his day a notorious thief.

1 Most textbooks on the police emphasize this point and enumerate the additional law enforcement obligations; see, for example, A.C. Gorman, F.D. Jay and R.R.J. Gallati (1973); V.A. Leonard and H.W. More (1971).
2 Kansas City Police Department (1971). The survey contains information on 41 cities of 300,000 to 1,000,000 population. But the percentage cited in the text was computed only for Atlanta, Boston, Buffalo, Dallas, Denver, El Paso, Fort Worth, Honolulu, Kansas City, Memphis, Minneapolis, Oklahoma City, Pittsburgh, Portland, OR, St. Paul, and San Antonio, because the data for the other cities were not detailed enough. The estimate that detectives make up 13.5 percent of line personnel comports with the estimate of O.W. Wilson (1963, 293), who stated that they make up approximately 10 percent of 'sworn personnel'.
3 Federal Bureau of Investigations, Uniform Crime Reports (1971). The data are for 57 cities of over 250,000 population, to make the figures correspond, at least roughly, to the data about manpower drawn from sources cited in n. 2, above. I might add that the average arrest rate in all the remaining cities is approximately of the same order as the figures I use in the argument. The so-called Index Crimes comprise homicide, forcible rape, robbery, aggravated assault, burglary, larceny, and auto theft. It should also be mentioned that arrests on Index Crime charges are not tantamount to conviction and it is far from unusual for a person to be charged, e.g., with aggravated assault, to induce him to plead guilty to simple assault, quite aside from failure to prosecute, dismissal, or exculpation by trial.
4 I have accompanied patrolmen and detectives investigating burglaries in two cities and should like to add on the basis of my observation and on the basis of interviews with officers that, in almost all of these cases, there is virtually no promise of clearance, that in most of them the cost of even a routine follow-up investigation would exceed the loss many times over, and that, in

any case, the detectives always have a backlog of reported burglaries for which the reporting victims expect prompt consideration. I might also add that it seemed to me that this largely fruitless busywork demoralizes detectives and causes them to do less work than I thought possible. See J.E. Conklin and E. Bittner (1973).

5    I have reference to the ramified information systems individual detectives cultivate, involving informants and informers, which they do not share with one another. I have touched on this topic in E. Bittner (1970).

6    The work that brought this observation into prominence is J. Goldstein (1960); a comprehensive review of the problem is contained in W. LaFave (1965).

7    J.Q. Wilson (1968, 31, chap. 2). The observation that policemen make misdemeanor arrests most often on practical rather than legal considerations has been reported by many authors; cf., for example J.D. Lohman and G.E. Misner (1966, 1968ff.). I have discussed this matter extensively in E. Bittner (1967a). Wistfully illuminating discussions of the topic are to be found, among others, in J. Hall (1953); J.V. Henry (1966); C.D. Robinson (1965).

8    The first expression of recognition is contained in E. Cumming,  I. Cumming and L. Edell (1965); cf. also E. Bittner (1967b).

9    S.B. Warner (1942); *Corpus Juris Secundum* (vol. 6, 613ff.); M. Hochnagel and H.W. Stege (1966).

10   There exists legal doctrine supporting the contention that resisting or opposing the police in an emergency situation is unlawful, see H. Kelsen (1961, 278ff.), and H.L.A. Hart (1961, 20ff.). I cite these references to show that the police are legally authorized to do whatever is necessary, according to the nature of the circumstances.

11   'Several modern cases have imposed [a] standard of strict liability ... upon the officer by conditioning justification of deadly force on the victim's actually having committed a felony, and a number of states have enacted statutes which appear to adopt this strict liability. However, many jurisdictions, such as California, have homicide statutes which permit the police officer to use deadly force for the arrest of a person "charged" with a felony. It has been suggested that this requirement only indicates the necessity for reasonable belief by the officer that the victim has committed a felony' (Note, *Stanford Law Review* [1961, 566–609]).

12   The aspiration has received a brilliant formulation in one of the most influential documents of modern political philosophy, Immanual Kant (1913); a review of the growth of the ideal of peace is contained in P. Reiwald (1944).

13   Literary glorification of violence has never disappeared entirely, as the works of authors like Nietzche and Sorel attest. In the most recent past, these views have again received eloquent expression in connection with revolutionary movements in Third World nations. The most remarkable statement along these lines is contained in the works of Franz Fanon.

14   But I have given this matter extensive consideration in E. Bittner (1970).

## References

Adorno, T.W. *et al. The Authoritarian Personality*. New York: Harper and Row, 1950.

Bacon, F. 'An Advertizement Touching an Holy War,' Vol. 7 of *Collected Works*. London: Spottiswood, 1859.

Bittner, E. 'Police on Skid Row: A Study of Peacekeeping.' *American Sociological Review*, 32 (1967a): 600–715.

Bittner, E. 'Police Discretion in Emergency Apprehension of Mentally Ill Persons.' *Social Problems* 14 (1967b): 278–992.

Bittner, E. *The Functions of the Police in Modern Society*. Washington, D.C.: U.S. Government Printing Office, 1970.

Blackstone, W. *Commentaries on the Laws of England*. Vol. 4. Oxford, England: Clarendon, n.d.

Conklin, J.E. *Robbery and the Criminal Justice System*. Philadelphia: J.B. Lippincott, 1972.

Conklin, J.E. and E. Bittner. 'Burglary in a Suburb.' *Criminology* 11 (1973): 206–32.

*Corpus Juris Secundum*. 'Arrest.' Vol. 6.

Cumming, E., I. Cumming and L. Edell. 'Policemen as Philosopher, Guide and Friend.' *Social Problems* 12 (1965): 276–86.

Davis, K.C. *Discretionary Justice: A Preliminary Inquiry*. Urbana, Ill.: University of Illinois Press, 1971.

Federal Bureau of Investigations. *Uniform Crime Reports*. Washington, D.C.: U.S. Government Printing Office, 1971.

Garfinkel, H. and E. Bittner. 'Good Organizational Reasons for "Bad" Clinic Records.' In H. Garfinkel, *Studies* in *Ethnomethodology* 180–207. Englewood Cliffs, N.J.: Prentice-Hall, 1967.

Goldstein, J. 'Police Discretion Not to Invoke the Criminal Process.' *Yale Law Journal* 69 (1960): 543–94.

Gorman, A.C., F.D. Jay and R.R.J. Gallati. *Introduction to Law Enforcement and Criminal Justice.* Rev. ed. Springfield, Ill.: C.C. Thomas, 1973.

Hall, J. 'Police and the Law in a Democratic Society.' *Indiana Law Journal* 23: 133–77, 1953.

Hamilton, W.H. and C.C. Rodee. 'Police Power'. In *Encyclopedia of the Social Sciences.* Vol. 12. New York: Macmillan Co., 1937.

Hart, H.L.A. *The Concept of* Law. Oxford, England: Clarendon Press, 1961.

Henry, J.V. 'Breach of Peace and Disorderly Conduct Laws: Void for Vagueness?' *Howard Law Journal* 12 (1966): 318–31.

Hochnagel, M. and H.W. Stege. 'The Right to Resist Unlawful Arrest: An Outdated Concept?' *Tulsa Law Journal* 3 (1966): 40–46.

Institute for Defense Analysis. President's Commission on Law Enforcement and Administration of Justice. *Task Force Report: Science and Technology.* Washington, D.C.: U.S. Government Printing Office, 1967.

Kansas City Police Department. *Survey of Municipal Police Departments.* Kansas City Mo., 1971.

Kant, I. [1795]. 'Zum Ewigen Frieden: Ein Philosophischer Entwurf.' In *Kleinere Schriften zur Geschichtsphilosophie, Ethik and Politik.* Leipzig: Felix Meiner, 1913.

Kelsen, H. *General Theory of Law and State.* New York: Russel and Russel, 1961.

LaFave, W. *Arrest: The Decision to Take a Suspect into Custody.* Boston: Little, Brown and Co., 1965.

Leonard, V.A. and H.W. More. *Police Organization and Management.* 3d ed. Mineola, N.Y.: Foundation Press, 1971.

Lohman, J.D. and G.E. Misner. *The Police and the Community.* Report prepared for the President's Commission on Law Enforcement and Administration of Justice. Vol. 2. Washington, D.C.: U.S. Government Printing Office, 1967.

Miller, W.B. 'Lower-class Culture as a Generating Milieu of Gang Delinquency.' *Journal of Social Issues* 14 (1958). 5–19.

National Commission on Productivity. 'Report of the Task Force to Study Police Productivity.' Mimeo. Draft. 1973.

Niederhoffer, A. *Behind the Shield: The Police in Urban Society.* Garden City; N.Y.: Anchor Books, 1969.

Note. 'Justification for the Use of Force in Criminal Law.' *Stanford Law Review* 13 (1961): 566–609.

Reiss, A.J., Jr. *The Police and the Public.* New Haven: Yale University Press, 1971.

Reiwald, P. *Eroberung des Friedens.* Zürich: Europa Verlag, 1944.

Robinson, C.D. 'Alternatives to Arrest of Lesser Offenders.' *Crime and Delinquency* 11 (1965) 8–11.

Silver, A. 'The Demand for Order in Civil Society: A Review of Some Themes in the History of Urban Crime, Police, and Riot.' In *The Police: Six Sociological Essays*, ed. D.J. Bordua, 1–24. New York: John Wiley and Sons, 1967.

Skolnick, J.H. *Justice without Trial: Law Enforcement in a Democratic Society.* New York: John Wiley and Sons, 1966.

Stephen, J.F. *A History of Criminal Law in England.* Vol. 3. London: Macmillan and Co., 1883.

Warner, S.B. 'Uniform Arrest Act.' *Vanderbilt Law Review* 28 (1942): 315–47.

Weber, M. *The Theory of Social and Economic Organization.* Translation edited by T. Parsons. Glencoe, Ill.: Free Press, 1947.

Wilson, J.Q. *Varieties of Police Behavior: The Management of Law and Order in Eight Communities.* Cambridge, Mass.: Harvard University Press, 1968.

Wilson, O.W. *Police Administration.* 2d ed. New York: McGraw-Hill, 1963.

# 13. The paradox of dispossession: skid row at night

*William Ker Muir Jr*

In the United States where the poor rule, the rich have always something to fear from the abuse of their power. This natural anxiety of the rich may produce a secret dissatisfaction; but society is not disturbed by it, for the same reason that withholds the confidence of the rich from the legislative authority makes them obey its mandates: their wealth, which prevents them from making the law, prevents them from withstanding it. Among civilized nations, only those who have nothing to lose ever revolt; ...Alexis de Tocqueville, *Democracy in America* (1835)

> Up in the hills there are some very important, very influential and very rich people, whom you don't treat the same as people in other areas. You don't run a car check on a guy who lives on Lookout Peak. There may be a few who don't pay their tickets, but most do. Ed Andros, *Laconia Police Department* (1972)

## I

In 1835 Tocqueville wrote that the rich inevitably were timid and hence presented little threat to democracy. Because they had so much to lose from an attempted revolt against political authority, they would endure their frustrations and submit. They were the victims of the paradox of dispossession: 'The less one has, the less one has to lose.' They had too much to lose.

In 1972, Ed Andros, a Laconia policeman, made a similar observation: because the wealthy 'up in the hills' would suffer so many subtle injuries if hauled before a traffic judge for nonpayment of traffic violations, it was a practical certainty they were not scofflaws. They would have paid for their past violations of the laws despite their dissatisfaction with them. It was usually only the poor who would flout the law, not pay their tickets, and be fearless enough to rebel.[1]

The very poorest citizenry in Laconia inhabited skid row. In the daytime, in the commercial area near skid row, Laconians exchanged goods and services and lived up to moral standards of conduct, sensing that they were going to benefit from an unbroken system of mutual obligations. They hardly noticed the inhabitants of skid row, who slunk and got drunk and looked on at a world which had no commerce with them.

At night, things changed. Laconia's dispossessed became more obvious and more ominous. The center of their activity was at Michigan and Commerce, the hub of a dozen bars which hardly closed except for five hours in the early morning. Nearby business establishments also remained open throughout the night – cheap movie houses and hotels. In the recessed entryways of these dark buildings, prostitutes, pimps, and their clientele bung out, along with drug traffickers, winos, thieves, and robbers. While they might appear to the uninitiated to be transients, each of these individuals inhabited a limited territory. The stranger stood out, and the news quickly spread through the community grapevine about who he was and what his business was. Every citizen in nighttime skid row had a business of sorts.

In civilized terms, however, the people whose ways of life took them to Michigan and Commerce each night were 'judgment-proof'. They had no money, no family, no job, no property, no respectability, no health, no skills, and no hope. Without denying the significance of loss of liberty, the humiliations of jail, and the dangers of prison life, we can fairly say that in jail they would eat better, sleep more warmly, be cleaner, and have safer companionship. A few of them were probably due to go to jail eventually anyway; warrants were out for their arrest for some previous infraction from which they had fled. They were life's losers; they possessed nothing except their links to a free world in which they were misfits.

They characteristically lacked something more – a moral compulsion to comply with the constituted authorities. Breaking the law pricked few consciences on skid row. A sense of mutual obligation between skid row denizens and the world which shunned them was nonexistent.

Skid row was so close to anarchy at night that the Laconia Police Department assigned foot patrolmen to it. By 1970 the walking beat had disappeared from most city streets, and for good reasons: increased police responsibilities, intensified reliance on technology, the diminished density of the modern city, and the high costs of police labor made greater efficiency mandatory, and so policemen were assigned to patrol in cars.

In densely populated parts of the city where the crime rate was high, however, the foot patrolman retained an advantage over his motorized counterparts. The department felt that his presence more effectively suppressed the extensive purse-snatching and mugging and vice than a passing patrol car.

The foot patrolmen in Laconia were almost invariably veteran police officers; selection for such duty was regarded as an honor. They were likely to be big men (over 74 inches and 200 pounds). They worked in teams of two. They usually visited each bar three times a night to see if things were orderly and whether the owner still had affairs under control. The last nightly visit was to close the bar and to protect the owner from being robbed of his night's receipts. In passing from bar to bar, the pair of officers dealt with trouble as they saw it. They also could respond to radio calls dispatched over the small portable transceivers they carried on their belts.

Some time during the night, there would be trouble. A veteran walking patrolman described this typically dangerous incident: 'It was Michigan and

Commerce. This colored prostitute was chasing three whites with a knife around a car. Naturally five colored men came in to help her, and suddenly about fifty or sixty colored people in a crowd were all around. We arrested her, and she was hollering prejudice and that she was being arrested because she was black.' The lawful goals of the policemen in the short run were to disarm the woman, find out what had caused the problem between her and the 'three whites', settle it one way or another, and pacify the crowd. In the long run their goals could probably be defined in terms of diminishing violence and injury on the beat: what means would best reach this general objective was a subject of disagreement.

The goals of the men and women of skid row often were unknown to the policemen. At a minimum, the woman wished to retain her knife and coerce the white threesome to satisfy their obligation to her. The latter wanted to save their skins and escape arrest and notoriety for their misdeeds: For reasons of loyalty, money, revenge, or excitement, the prostitute's five assistants wanted to stop the policemen from arresting her. Some in the crowd, carried away by the solidarity of the moment or the hope of anonymity, might have wanted to hurt the two policemen or, at least, hoped to frighten them enough to hamper them in performing their appointed duties in the future.

In short, the objectives of the policemen and of skid row were in-compatible. Whose goals would obtain, those of the authorities or their antagonists? Which side would control the encounter and the human behavior in it? What means could cops use to govern the situation and to defend themselves?

## II

At Michigan and Commerce, the policeman was the man of property. He had a job and if he kept it for twenty-five years, he would have a generous pension coming. He had a family which depended on him. He had many possessions, and he .had been taught from childhood the value of owning things (and indeed the importance of his job of protecting the property of others would be diminished if he believed otherwise).

Jim Longstreet was typical. He had been on the department for four years. Son of a railroad man, a breezy-talking, well-muscled, somewhat undisciplined athlete, Longstreet had only a high school diploma and lacked confidence that he could ever amount to much in a world where knowledge and cleverness were crucial: 'I don't have the education.' He enjoyed physical challenges, and in police work he had enjoyed mixing it with the citizenry – going 'into some of the bad places' which trafficked in dope and stolen goods 'and jacking them up'. 'As far as I'm concerned, what I like is the worst beat with a little leeway. That's when I'm happiest.'

But Longstreet did not get leeway. While his job was technically protected by civil service, any citizen could complain to Internal Affairs that Longstreet had violated a law or regulation or had acted without good judgment. Internal Affairs could recommend that he be fired or reprimanded. To be sure, a police officer had some protection by virtue of the procedures of the department. The complaint had to be in writing; the complaint could be challenged by the policeman. An officer could appeal an adverse decision of Internal Affairs to the

Civil Service Board and to the courts thereafter. Moreover, to make the complaint in the first place, a citizen had to have some faith that his effort to follow through would be worthwhile – a faith which many self-proclaimed victims did not have (erroneously, in light of the severity of Internal Affairs in Laconia). Nevertheless, the sanctuary of civil service was by no means invulnerable. Policemen had been discharged for alleged misconduct sufficiently frequently to be ominous, and a suspension or even a reprimand could adversely affect chances for assignments to good details, departmental respect, and promotions. Longstreet himself had been before Internal Affairs several times and had had to shave the truth in disconcerting ways when he found that the administration was out of step with his police philosophy and would not back him up. He had received written reprimands. He had undergone an extensive FBI investigation for alleged violations of the civil rights of another and was being sued for $25,000.

What was more, he was married, had a child, and owned a house in the suburbs. He had begun to work part-time as a security officer in a department store to keep ahead of his debts. With a stake in the future, he found himself no longer 'going the route' with citizens who revolted against his authority. Worried about sticking his neck out, he found himself doing 'nothing' for a week, making just enough arrests to keep the sergeant off his back, and taking a walk when a guy said, 'Screw you'. 'I'm not without worry about the repercussions,' he said at one point. 'My rule is no ticket is worth it if he's going after my job, and I'll let him have his way. It's sickening; you shouldn't have to do it. But I'm paranoid about this stuff,' he blurted at another point.

> A guy worries about the repercussions if you did get into a hot situation …
> I'm lucky. I've just bought a new house. I got a family. If I got fired, I don't
> know what I'd do. I could get a job. I'm still young, but when I get older and
> get fired, What could I do. The salary, it's good, and you live right up to it.
> Two or three hundred dollars less, and I'd be in a real bind. I earn fifteen
> thousand dollars but I've got no savings account. If I were to make less
> money, I'd have to make a lot of changes. I worry about security. I think of it
> more and more. My house, my daughter, more and more security. So when
> you see a job that looks like it might blow up, you sometimes want to say,
> 'So what?' and move on.

Moving on, however, was easier to talk about than to accomplish. Avoiding hot situations required certain conditions.

First, unless a policeman who practiced the avoidance response was working his beat alone, he had to be in collusion with others; an eager partner could compel him to get involved. It was true that policemen had some choice of partners, and a sergeant was usually glad to defer to their desires to work with personalities that meshed. Sergeants usually tried to alleviate the natural tensions which built up between two large men, cooped up in a car for eight hours, breathing the same air, never out of each other's sight, interdependent for every decision. In this free-selection condition, practitioners of avoidance were likely to find inactive soul mates for partners.

The collusion, however, had to extend beyond the partnership to be foolproof. Since squad members from different beats covered one another, a norm had to exist within the squad not to punish or highlight or talk pejoratively about the noninvolvement of fellow officers. Officers had to agree on a kind of social *laissez-faire*: Live and let live. On the other hand, if it was proper for one squad member publicly to upbraid the 'laziness' or the 'cowardice' of another, then any attempt to take a walk would be made public. Each officer and each recruit to a squad had to be indoctrinated with the avoidance philosophy lest he rock the boat.

The supervisor of the squad, its sergeant, would have to countenance noninvolvement by his men. Inaction was significantly more difficult to detect than active misconduct like brutality. In order to perceive nonevents, persons had to have a perspective, a sense of 'something missing'. The sergeant had a chance to see that his men were taking a walk, for he, alone of all the supervisors, monitored the radio, checked the policemen's logs, and supervised a small enough group of men to individuate them in his mind.

A second condition was that the victims of police noninvolvement had to lack the motivation, perspective, and capability to complain about it. The naturally indignant, the rich, and the aware – the somebodies, in short – were worrisome because they could and did make complaints about policemen who paid them no heed. However, the submissive, the poor, the undereducated – it was highly unlikely that they would ever cast public light on police neglect.

Of course, third persons might act on behalf of the public. Observers accompanying the policeman, curious newspaper reporters, public officials, and political leaders could publicize police shortcomings in meeting their responsibilities. If policemen were to get away with avoidance, these public spokesmen had to be silenced: the police department had to be made a closed organization: city politics had to be kept low-key; and newspaper reporters had to be seduced or intimidated into indifference.

Only if there existed these three conditions – collusion, selective nonenforcement, and suppression – could the avoidance response happen widely. Yet it was possible, and when policemen did take a walk when the situation got hot, what happened as a result?

There were two sets of consequences, one for the community and one for the policeman himself.

On the beat there would inevitably be a number of the dispossessed who would recognize that the beat policeman was not around when the going got tough. They were persons who stood to profit from the policeman's absence – the strong-arm, the bully, the vicious. The grapevine would carry the news to their like-minded associates. When might made right, when the rebels against authority knew they were in control, skid row went to hell in a hand basket.

So did the community surrounding skid row. On the edge of skid row lived good people – old folks, sick folks, hardworking poor, recent immigrants to the city, minorities, small businessmen – struggling to maintain the margin of survival. They improved their daily lot; they raised children; they grew gardens; they cleaned and painted. They depended on police for protection from the predators. When they found that they did not enjoy police protection, they ceased to expose themselves and their possessions. They no longer went out in the evening. They refused to open their doors to strangers. They could not open their windows at night for ventilation. They stopped working in their gardens or maintaining the exteriors of their houses. They shut down their businesses. They turned in on themselves, dispossessing themselves of those very amenities which attracted the vicious to them. They learned to retaliate: they purchased guns and used them. They might even put themselves under the protection of a patron; stores employed private security police; and, as happened in a number of American cities, a community might assemble a vigilante patrol.[2]

In the communities where police permitted the dispossessed to rule by force, freedom became the freedom to prey on others. There was no equality between the brute and the benign. Those who were left in command were civilization's scoundrels. Creativity and civilization disappeared. The pleasure of the moment predominated. Matters that took time to develop had to be forgotten: a business, a garden, even a family would be destroyed before they survived their term or would be seized for ransom as they became more valuable. The long term had to be sacrificed in the name of survival. There was no hope.

As for the policeman who chose to 'move on', dependent as he was on other policemen's covering up for him, he stopped speaking out in criticism of his fellow officers. A conspiracy of silence overtook him, requiring him to cover up not only his own avoidance behavior but also that of others – and any more egregious misconduct, including brutality or venality. The cop who avoided difficulty had to cope with feelings of cowardice, of having betrayed those motives to help which emanated from his religion and upbringing – his deepest self. He derived less gratification from his job because he could no longer hold his whole life up to his previous standards of conduct. These feelings of cowardice and inadequacy led to intense frustration, often resulting in brutality whenever conditions would shield him from repercussion. One old officer recalled with the deepest revulsion a fellow officer who was a habitual avoider:

> I remember walking with him, and an old wino began badmouthing him. Just an old wino in his cups, perfectly harmless, and this guy charges toward him to slam him. I got in his way, and said, 'What are you doing with this old man?' His answer was, 'He's not that old'. I told him, this was not the time when you get tough. 'How come you didn't get tough with that big black guy back at Digby's Diner?' I asked; 'you didn't get tough with him.' 'Well, this guy isn't going to talk to me like that,' he says. He was going to slam this old man against the wall. 'Why didn't you knock that big black guy over?' I said, and I wouldn't let him past me, but he was going to make that old man toe the line … I knew that he was a coward. He'd use that uniform as a form of bravado. He was always lying, and he was guilty of police brutality.

## III

If the citizen was so dispossessed that he was without even respectability, hope, or freedom, things which policemen might legitimately take as hostages, it was possible for a policeman to threaten things which the law forbade him to threaten. He could defend himself by implacably escalating the stakes; he could begin to take illegal hostages. Even the dispossessed possessed something – their physical integrity. Society, however, conventionally gave sanctuary against bodily assaults. Some policemen violated that sanctuary; in doing so, they became lawless.

The sanctuary for human life consisted in part of departmental regulations: 'The policy of this Department is that members shall exhaust every other means before resorting to the use of firearms.'

There were also laws against battery and homicide that applied to policemen who used more force than reasonable to subdue a citizen. In part, the sanctuary was provided by the force of moral obligations. Moreover, this moral aversion to injuring or killing another was reinforced by the practical consequences for a policeman of shooting someone: an extensive shooting board inquiry conducted by the department into the discharge of any police weapon, the increased likelihood of a riot, the intensification of community resentment.

Despite these considerable safeguards which civilization created for individual life, some policemen dared the wrath of the gods and recurrently desecrated the sanctuary.

Bee Heywood was 'an old-time policeman', as he liked to describe himself. He was a brawny, red-haired Irishman who first joined the department because he loved motorcycles. As a member of the department motorcycle team (which he had organized), he had become national hill climbing champion. Born out of state, he had come to Laconia in his adolescence at a lime when his parents had been divorced and his mother had remarried. 'Laconia then was a tough town, especially along lower Wichita Avenue. Besides I had a temper, and I couldn't stand anyone to hit me in the face. I'd always fight if they hit me in the face. I remember one old fella who told me that the big fellas on my paper route always knew I'd fight them, that I ought to turn and walk away. He said, 'They just egg you on, and your temper gets you all that stuff'.

As Bee Heywood grew up and became a policeman, he stayed the same, only more so. He retained his temper, and he found that it was prized in the police department of the 1950s, which had believed in the efficacy of selective harassment. He had 'gone to Knuckletown' with a great many residents of skid row.

That was half the story. The other half was that Heywood was a tremendously likable, open, thoughtful, natural, and confident man. He had begun our interview by warning me that he was a 'naturally suspicious' person, particularly of 'pantywaists' from a university, and that he was likely to refuse to answer many of my questions. Then he proceeded to talk nonstop on every subject conceivable for four and a half hours. He was a convert to Mormonism, a member of the John Birch Society, deeply sentimental, heroically stubborn, and had an uncanny memory for detail. At bottom, however, he was a physical man who learned about and sensed the world through his body. A motorcyclist, a stunt flyer, a man who 'raced boats, raced cars, waterskied, rode horses, broke a horse of my own when I was 14', fisherman, hunter, boxer, football player, he had survived an on-the-job broken back and was in his twenty-sixth year on the department, still working despite his eligibility for retirement. Bee Heywood had never accepted the old man's admonition to 'turn and walk away'.

Being one who used violence against the dispossessed, living according to the law of the jungle instead of the laws of civilization, was a wearying, fearful, soul-searching job. Heywood's own eloquent testament summed up a dozen years of skid row patrol:

Sometimes it's real unpleasant; it's a real tough job. I don't enjoy it like I used to. As you get older, you don't want bitter fights, quarrels, enemies. As you get older, you want a little more peace, friends; you want to get away from all the strife. You just men-tioned about hippies and narcotics addicts. When I transferred out of motorcycles after I broke my back, I couldn't take this downtown beat – the pimps and the hypes and the hoods and the crims. It really got me down, but as time passed, I think I just got used to the habit of staying downtown. It was not appalling to me, you might say, after a time. I used to work construction before coming here, and I found that often at first I didn't like a job, but by making myself stay with it, by giving it a probation, often I grew to like it. Well, if I didn't like police work, I would quit. I came to ask myself for some reasons why I was put down here. When I was in the Air Force during World War II a chaplain came up to me and said I should remember three questions. Well, I didn't think much about it at the time, but since those three questions, I've really begun to think more and more of them: Where did you come from? What are you going to do here? Where are you going after? So I kept asking myself that question about my work. And the answer I finally came to was, I was down here to protect life and property from the animals, the strong-arm thugs. I was here to protect the pensioners and the old women, and the young servicemen from the thugs, the prostitutes who'd entice a guy into a room and when she got him there, she'd say, 'Pardon me, let me see if my husband is around' and she'd open the door and in would walk two dudes who'd look real mean and send that serviceman running, feeling lucky he got away with his pants. I figured the old people really needed help; they really had to get shielded. So I began to feel I was really doing a job that needed to be done.

In providing the shield, Heywood did not always act lawlessly. If he had the self-restraint or the time to delay, he would investigate exhaustively until he got something on one of the dispossessed which would justify putting 'the animal' behind bars. He was a tenacious adversary.

I remember one fella. I made an FC report on the man [that is, he asked the citizen to identify himself]. He started mouthing off, 'You silly cops, you can't put me in jail', and acting smart. After that I went through our active vagrancy file, and there was nothing on him. But I take a certain pride in my work, and I finally got him into jail. I had to do it on my own time, but I finally busted him for a burglary of the Rivers Liquor Store. I caught him busting out with a carton of liquor. I had a hunch he would hit Rivers. So each night I'd put on my plain clothes, and I'd wait in the dark, watching the place in the cold. The night I caught him I was about to leave. Boy, it was cold, when sure enough, he comes walking up the driveway with a couple of guys, carrying pry bars, and then they break the lock, and as they're coming out with the liquor, I get a gun on them and say, 'Don't run fellas. If you do, I'll kill you. Just don't tempt me, or I'll have to shoot.' After, I told him his mistake was calling me names. 'You shouldn't' talk to a policeman like that.'

But often things were otherwise; he lacked the time and the patience to fulfill his responsibility of cleaning up downtown with the opportunities the law limited him to. So he handled the punks – physically.

I remember once I hit one guy with a club. He had a steel plate in his head, and he went to the hospital. I really sweated that one out. I was in the right, but you really think about it, having a life on your hands. You don't sleep at night. Since then, I haven't used my club. I use my fists

He did use his fists. He also used his tongue to taunt and to egg on the resistance which made it right to use his fists. He beat up the punks and held his adversaries at bay by threat of brutality.

To be able to act violently required a stringent set of conditions. Obviously a policeman like Heywood, who frequently resorted to the enforcement response, had to have the capability – the strength and the cunning to win fights, to suppress by brute force.

When the adversary was one of a crowd, he had not only to fight with savagery but also to appear to be a savage in order to prevent the crowd from acting in concert. Most crucial to having sufficient capability was having another policeman with like habits and capacities as a partner. One man could barely handle a single adversary. Two men patrolling together and willing to respond viciously could take the measure of a crowd.

Second, there had to be collusive backup. The sanctuaries that safeguarded human safety were located in a separation of powers. The legislature created them and the judiciary supervised the administration of these sanctuaries. The policeman lacked control over these independent powers. An officer who practiced the enforcement response against the dispossessed therefore had to cover up his lawlessness. He had to be backed up by his fellow officers, his supervisors, and his chief administrators; and backing him up meant lying, falsification of reports, secrecy, and suppression of witnesses. Violence was far more difficult to hide than inaction, because the victims of the brutality knew what policemen to blame. A victim of the enforcement response had to be perpetually cowed into silence, compounding the need for continuing oppression.

If these difficult conditions could be satisfied, what were the effects on the beat of such police action?

Using lawless force unquestionably escalated the conflicts on skid row. Police violations of the taboo against physical threats licensed the unscrupulous citizen to violate it too. The simplicity and symmetry of the *lex talionis*, an eye for an eye and a tooth for a tooth, had a great attraction on skid row, as if in the absence of the artificial restraints of religion and law, this simple form of retribution would naturally flourish. The ethic of individual equality saturated skid row thought, and violation of principle by one side justified reciprocal violation by the other. In short, one consequence of police brutality was that lawlessness and the taste for vindication spread epidemically.

Moreover, the usefulness of violence was increased by keeping its memory alive within skid row. The recollection of the brutal example reminded the citizenry of the policeman's terrifying capability. If the community forgot it, it had to be repeated. To refrain from the enforcement response would undermine the effects of the policeman's reign of terror. Forgiveness had the effect of unleashing the hatred of skid row, previously suppressed by fear. In the adversary context which brutality created, steps to reconcile differences appeared to be appeasement, cowardice, and an invitation to retaliate. Once terror had been made the means of domination, there was no turning back.[3]

Another consequence was that the community of the dispossessed were motivated to remain so. A community oppressed by threats would be worse off the more it developed a stake in the world. As badly off as the dispossessed were under the threat of bodily violence, they would be even more vulnerable to police lawlessness if they got a dog, made a friend, planted a flower bed, tried to become respectable, painted a room, or had hope, for these would become hostages at the mercy of any cop who resorted to brutality. Ever mindful that they had to mistrust the policeman, they felt they were better off low profile and unpropertied, as little vulnerable to police injury or scorn as possible. The policeman's atrocious reputation made a garrison state of his beat.

The personal effects of his atrocity were severe. The nightly work of officers like Heywood became 'terrifying'. They were preoccupied with the tasks of self-defense. They knew they would get no help 'from those bastards ... when you get in trouble'. They were frightened of ambush and reprisal. They were frightened that their methods would be discovered and prosecuted. As one young officer observed, 'Hot dogs have much more to worry about; they're always on edge'.

Then, too, an officer like Heywood tended to obtain little information about the community. No one except finks and flatterers, hoping for leniency, told him anything, and what information he did get put him on his guard or misled him into lowering it. The news he was given contained nothing insightful about the community, nothing about whom to help and how.

Also, a policeman who ignored the taboo against hurting citizens ran the risk of destroying the very sanctuaries to which he and his fellow policemen entrusted their own lives. Other policemen were aware of the effects of a fellow officer's barbarity and resented it and the counter-violence it begot.

In addition, an officer who was guilty of enforcement responses found himself forced to take responsibility for the abuses perpetrated by his fellow officers. Bound by a conspiracy to cover up each other's brutal acts, Heywood and his colleagues were mutually implicated. Heywood could disclose no horror of any magnitude, lest his own illegalities unraveled in the disclosure. Solidarity alone guaranteed self-preservation. Complicity with his fellow officers complicated matters; it forced Heywood to disregard the difference between countenancing the 'necessary' abuses he perpetrated and the 'sadistic' abuses of his fellow conspirators.

One final effect must be noted. Men like Heywood, distressed by the undesirable implications of the lawless means to which they resorted, urgently looked for good deeds to perform. Heywood sought out people to rescue, and his acts of goodwill were meaningful – vital to him. 'The most satisfying feeling is the feeling you are needed, that you are helping.' To accomplish these good deeds, he gave inordinate time.[4] He needed to be kind. It was like an urgent search for expiation after having contracted with the devil. Men like Heywood needed opportunities to restore their souls, and his compulsion to alleviate the troubles of his fellow man served as a reminder of the complexity and the redeemability of the human soul.

## IV

Captain Hook was not a Laconia police officer. He was a businessman. His business was providing security services to other businessmen. He sold private police protection to merchants, theater managers, barkeepers, grocers, and landlords. He employed a half-dozen beefy roughnecks like himself to assist him in handling the numerous jobs he had contracted. The Laconia Police Department licensed him and his employees to carry concealed revolvers while acting as security guards. In addition, the captain's men carried blackjacks and steel knuckles, and the captain fondled a menacing spiked nightstick.

Captain Hook did not wear a uniform. In the daytime he strutted around in a dirty T-shirt which stretched over his belly. Two American flags tattooed into his upper arms augmented the impressiveness of his biceps. On the roof of his twenty-year-old Chevrolet was a yellow rotating blinker light, and he had installed a bullhorn system in the front of the car. A bullet hole, prominent and unrepaired, was in the center of the car's rear window, testimony to the violence in the captain's wake.

The captain was tough, unscrupulous, and remorseless. Officer Longstreet said he was 'three bricks short of a load', a phrase suggesting the disproportion between muscles and brain. He had served as a bouncer at numerous Laconia bars, and the punishments he had inflicted on uncooperative or nonpaying bar patrons were legendary in the police department. When he capitalized on his brutal talents to enter the security policing business, he continued to apply his barroom techniques and found new markets for them. For example, the captain was hired by one landlord who owned a notorious apartment house nicknamed the Taj Mahal. The landlord wanted to get rid of some tenants he deemed undesirable and asked the captain to help. The captain's method allegedly was to go door to door, displaying his spiked baton and ordering the tenants to leave in a day and a half, or else. One day, in front of a half-dozen policemen, without shame or fear, the captain and the landlord congratulated themselves on the fact that 'the homos were no longer there'. Each policeman had a good idea of the illegal extortion the captain had practiced on the tenants. None of the officers, however, was ready to denounce the captain or cite him for his strong-arm practices.

In fact, a kind of partnership existed between some of the squads and Captain Hook. The deal was that the captain patrolled skid row and the enterprises which served it. He cowed skid row with his bullying tactics. At the same time, he protected the businessmen, who were pleased by his high-handed but effective unofficial procedures.

The key to the deal between the captain, the police, and the businessmen was official leniency. The policemen bent the law, looking the other way from the captain's daily violations of it. By failing to halt him, they unleashed him. As a result of his exemption from legal restrictions, the captain could provide his customers with a unique and brutal service, one for which he could ask a monopolist's premium. It was a good deal for all. Policemen delegated part of the dirty business of keeping the peace on skid row to a nonofficial vigilante. His salary in turn was paid by the merchants and businessmen who profited most from the captain's activity. The police were not obviously implicated; it was just a matter of their never having sufficient evidence to charge the captain and his cronies with the assaults and batteries they committed.[5]

Leniency, studied ignorance, inaction – these were the patronage a policeman could dispense. Absolute secrecy became more important as the size of the favor grew. At one extreme, the minuscule patronage of transporting six juveniles to their weekly jazz band rehearsals in a police car was openly tolerated by the area supervisor because in exchange the kids passed on information about burglaries and muggings in the neighborhood. This patronage was so minimal that few precautions had to be taken to keep the public unaware of it. Other minor forms of leniency which policemen regularly dispensed were permitting kids to congregate in large groups in the parks, overlooking parking violations, countenancing a little dice game behind a fence, and allowing a bar to stay open a few minutes past the lawful closing time. As a *quid pro quo*, the peace was preserved and everyone involved was discreetly silent about the arrangements. As the degree of leniency increased, however, the deals became more vulnerable to public criticism, demanding greater efforts at secrecy. Permitting Captain Hook's vigilantes to range unhampered was a serious business. Revealing the arrangement would have been devastating to all parties.[6]

The point is that any police department, even one as free from graft as Laconia's, had a great deal of potential illegal patronage to dispense, giving it the power to purchase cooperation and social repression. Such a patronage system required complicity because it was outside the law. In Laconia the system was not so extreme that the department had to close itself off from all public scrutiny. It was a system that applied only to part of skid row activities. However, this corruption of authority was extremely subtle, and it imperceptibly grew. Its utility was so obvious and its initial cost so modest that even the most scrupulous of policemen found it difficult to speak out against it.

The most serious effect of this delegation of power to a vigilante was that he ruled part of skid row outside the rule of law. He had no training in self-restraint, few incentives to practice it, and considerable immunity from legal, political, and police criticism. His unspoken contract with the police placed few real constraints on his conduct; at most, he was to be discreet in choosing victims who would not complain and he was to use some intelligence in hiring employees. Undermining the policemen's efforts to keep the captain in line was their recognition that his effect on skid row would be enhanced by the extortionate advantages resulting from his bizarre behavior, his cruel reputation, and his lawlessnes – he acted in ways that official policemen could not. By allowing him to do away with legal principles governing proper standards of police conduct, however, policemen found it increasingly difficult to discern the line between actions which were necessary and excesses which were sadistic. The result was that few policemen ever blew the whistle on the captain, and he knew that his license was, for practical purposes, extremely broad.

Inequality was officially countenanced on the beat. Captain Hook, the guy who did the policemen's dirty work, got away with illegal activity, while men less useful but also less cruel could not. Whether it set a cynical example, whether it encouraged disrespect for the law's supposed evenhandedness, was unknown. What was certain, however, was that policemen on skid row had difficulty asserting that the police did not play favorites.

The problem with vigilantism was that the deal between official and nonofficial peace-keepers fell outside the law and social acceptance. Being outlaws, the participants had exchanged hostages; each could be prosecuted if the deal was exposed. The policeman who delegated his job to an outlaw like the captain had escaped the clutches of the dispossessed, but by means which placed him in the captain's clutches. Thus, while skid row may have become more secure, the policeman who resorted to this kind of reciprocity response was less safe. He had to hide the captain's record of misconduct, because the whole arrangement would unravel if that record came to light.

Covering up a delegation of power to vigilantes on any larger scale than was practiced in Laconia would have meant closing the beat and the department to all outside scrutiny. Without the presence of outsiders, the police chief would have been less informed, or at least less certain that he was informed, about the street conduct of his men. If outsiders were forbidden to observe and inquire about department practice, the opportunities for fruitful dialogue and innovation would have materially diminished.

Because a 'contract' between vigilantes and official police involved the 'participants' putting themselves in a mutually extortionate situation, it tended to be worse for the party who had more to lose from exposure. Unquestionably, the policeman was the more vulnerable. Since Captain Hook was both the less vulnerable and the more active partner in the deal, he set the pace. It was Captain Hook who determined the scope of obligation of his passive partners, the police. As he widened the scope of his dreadful activities, the policemen found that they were increasingly required to ignore the calls for assistance from the captain's victims. The moral problems this increasing avoidance presented to policemen who wanted to help the oppressed was extremely great.

## V

Each of the three means of dealing with the dispossessed which has been described thus far required secrecy and complicity between partners, on the squad, throughout the department, and with the community. Each response was lawless or unrespectable. The difficulty of coping with the dispossessed was so great that law-abiding policemen – or, rather, policemen who wanted to perform services within the law – were forced outside the law merely to cope.

The professional response, however, was a way of effectively working within the rule of law. Some policemen developed their beat; they established relationships with their citizenry. They did not pay for it by surrendering their authority, nor did they develop a schedule of inducements and penalties outside the law.

Mike Marshall was a walking patrolman, a rangy ex-basketball player who had played professionally for eleven years before putting on a police uniform. His education was acquired through nineteen years of experience in Laconia streets. It was a minimal education, adequate only because he had specialized in patrolling skid row. As he argued so simply, 'In this world, you pick out what you can do, what you think you'd be good at, and do it'.

He neither understood nor tolerated hippies, demonstrators, and people who spoke out against America, but he never met one on his beat. He knew human nature in skid row, where it was 'more down to earth'. He liked his 'bums'.

> I think I know everybody on my beat. Maybe 5,000 persons. And I try to learn all their first names and their faces … I prefer to have them call me 'Mike', and they prefer to have me call them that way. A wino comes up, and by calling you by your first name he gets a feeling of equality. By giving them a feeling of equality, you are making a friend of them. Even though I put a lot of them in jail, they are friends, so-called friends. A lot will get drunk for a week; then they'll want you to put them in jail a week or so. They know when they've had enough. Otherwise, they'll die. An awful lot ask to go to jail.

He was not afraid of them because he knew which ones had weapons and which ones did not.[7]

Furthermore, he was respected and trusted because he had worked his beat. He had performed countless good works on skid row, for numerous people, and with equitable regularity. The gravest widespread need of the community of bums was financial. Bums needed money for wine whenever they were caught short. Their problem was Marshall's opportunity. He helped them in their time of necessity and merited their friendship. The citizens of skid row:

> knew that if they were short a few cents for the price of a bottle of wine, they could come to us. Every night they are into me for a couple of dollars. I'd bet I have three or four hundred dollars loaned out. Once in a while , one will pay you back. Probably one in five. There are fifteen or twenty of them that always pay you back. The day the welfare check comes out, they pay you the twenty-five cents or dollar they borrowed. How did it get started? I think I probably offered the first few times. I saw them looking at their hand in front of the liquor store, looking for the dime or quarter they did not have. So I'd hand it to them, and you'd see them smile, and you made friends for life. Actually they're not bad people. Whether they pay you or not, they'll come by and tell you they will. You don't really expect it. You

know what it's going for, but you know you're not going to cure them of their drinking.

Marshall enjoyed what Tocqueville referred to as 'that respectable power which men willingly grant to the remembrance of a life spent in doing good before their eyes'.[8] The bums trusted him, placing confidence in the humanitarian system of checks and balances which they saw as forestalling any abuse of power. In developing his beat, Marshall neutralized the fear, the distrust, the antagonism which citizens naturally experienced in the presence of unmeasured authority.

Thus, when Marshall and his partner of twelve years, disarmed the knife-wielding prostitute and she began 'hollering prejudice' no confrontation materialized. 'But the citizens knew that was not the reason. And they were on our side. That really helped us. Had they not known us, we would, have been in a great deal of trouble. In skid row they were "good citizens". They're the winos, the bums, the pimps around the area, and other prostitutes. They knew we were not out to arrest them.

Marshall's development of skid row had transformed the dispossessed of that community into 'good citizens', into people who had something to lose and therefore something to protect – a line of credit, a decent friendship, a good public servant, whatever it was that Marshall had come to represent through 'a life spent in doing good before their eyes'.

The conditions which made this professional response possible were very different from the circumstances required by the avoidance, the enforcement, and the reciprocal responses. For one thing, the professional response depended on mankind's passion for talking to and about one another, not on its capacity to keep a secret. Developing a beat required a grapevine to spread the news of good works far and wide: Doing good without a communication system to advertise it would not have been effective. If only a handful of citizens knew of Marshall's value to the community, or if men did not understand that their own affection for Marshall was widely shared throughout the community, then the sense of solidarity necessary to stand up for him would have been missing. No one man was strong enough to help Marshall against the prostitute and her five assistants. Only action in concert was sufficient to suppress them. Each citizen had to know that his defense of Marshall would be immediately supported by his fellow citizens.

The condition of open deeds openly advertised limited what Marshall could do by way of public service. He had to do the kind of good works which were equally available to all. He had to anticipate that his kindness to one person would excite everyone else to demand equivalent treatment. His good deeds created a principle of responsibility which no one had felt before. If Marshall fell short of that standard of responsibility thereafter, he was blameworthy, undepend-able, and unrespectable.

Marshall could and did handle this raising of public expectations by mastering important democratic skills. For one thing, he became eloquent. He mastered the knack of talking with his citizenry and establishing principles of distributive justice. He gave money after expressing the principle of 'to each according to his need', a standard which permitted him to justify denying requests for large sums of money or necessities other than food or drink.

He economized. The service he provided was inexpensive. He gave out nickels and dimes, the kind of support which he could afford when universalized. He did not dispense five dollars at a time, lest he have to discriminate between the favored few and the needy multitude.[9]

He became empathetic and in touch with his citizenry. He found out what they really desired. What he donated to them had to be something they valued, not something he thought would be good for them. Gratitude did not flow from buying a wino a cup of coffee.

Finally, he knew the law so that he could prudently stay within it. An illegal favor, witting or unwitting, would require secrecy. If he had tried to develop his beat by bending the law, Marshall would have been compromised. He would have been in constant jeopardy that someone would call him to account and require him to undo the good works he had done. Only by acting within the law could he have gained the necessary independence from outside intrusion. Of course, he had to have the legal leeway to dispense favors within the law. Marshall could not have developed his beat by nickel-and-diming his winos' necessities in a time of prohibition or under an officious set of departmental regulations prohibiting such loans.

One consequence of this professional response was that the community tended to develop confidence in the beat patrolman. It became more open, had a greater sense of security, and enjoyed a number of little productive happinesses. For the officer himself, one result was that he developed a feeling of safety, a more informed understanding of his beat, and considerable moral gratification from doing the job well. Not all the possible consequences were desirable, of course. A policeman who had developed his beat well often felt a twinge of hostility toward newcomers coming into the area and other sources of social change. He became conservative. To this tendency was added a proprietary feeling about 'my' beat. A policeman good at the professional response often became so involved with his beat that he failed to see the bigger city-wide picture. If a chief were not aware of this possibility for his most skilled policemen, misunderstandings could arise which caused the chief to be angry with their arrogance and them to be frustrated by the imperception of their chief. Finally, community support had a tendency to give those men who could develop their beats a false sense of well-being; they tended to let down a little or to cut corners. They were flattered, and sometimes they confused admiration for their office with admiration for themselves personally. Overconfidence and a tendency to take some unmerited pleasure in oneself, however, are not problems unique to policemen.

*From William Ker Muir Jr,* Police: Streetcorner Politicians *(Chicago, IL: University of Chicago Press), 1977, pp 61–81.*

## Notes

1   The reader might first interpret Officer Andros's statement as an illustration of a dual system of justice – leniency for the rich and severity for the poor. In fact, however, Officer Andros was not talking about whether he would ticket a wrongdoer 'in the hills': he would and did. Andros

was discussing the question whether he would *also* run a 'car check' on the 'very rich' driver. A 'car check' was a procedure which took up to five minutes and involved a call to a central computer to discover whether there were any outstanding warrants for the driver's arrest. Andros was saying that the probabilities that a rich man would ignore a warrant for his arrest were so low that it was not worth further delaying the ticketed 'guy who lives on Lookout Peak' to run a fruitless car check on him.

2   See Samuel Lubell, *The Hidden Crisis in American Politics* (New York: Norton, 1970), chap. 4.

3   Parenthetically, some threats did not create perpetual hatred. When the objective of these threats was the welfare of the person being threatened and he ultimately realized it, the threats received a justification which cut the vicious cycle of power and reprisal. An atrocity, such as Heywood's use of force on skid row punks, however, was self-interested; its purpose was inevitably seen to be the policeman's own gain, not the good of the citizens against whom it was used.

4   For example: 'The best case to tell is about Joey Lewis. He lived out in Westfield Village. He was a big kid; he'd been kicked out of school a lot. He had a bad temper he was a bully, so to speak. I remember seeing him first; he was making a lot of noise in the Boston Diner. He had his feet up on the table. Well, there's one thing I can't stand is to have a kid talk back to an officer. I came into the Boston Diner, and I said, "Son, why are your feet on the table? This is not a pigpen". He began to mouth back that it was none of my business. I told him, "This is my business. Get your feet off the table". I jerked him off the chair, and I kicked him flat. He was a big kid then, but he was young and not coordinated at that time. I told him, "Look, you're too big for me to fool with. I'm going to treat you like a man. Now you get back in my police car over there, and if you don't you're going to find yourself in the hospital, and don't be too long about it". He was real sullen and complained about his rights. "You've lost all your rights, fooling around with these schoolgirls. I'm going to lock you up on a vagrancy offense. Why aren't you in school?" Well, it turned out that the wagon was tied up; so I decided to take the bull by the horns. I asked permission to take the boy home. So I make out the juvenile citation on him and took him to his house. I knocked on the door, and I said, "Mrs. Lewis? I've arrested this boy of yours. Is his father home?" "He'll be home in about five minutes." Well, it was a beautiful home, the kind of home you could eat off the floor of. She says to me, "What did he do now?" I said, "Can't you handle this big monster of yours?" And she says, "No, Joey's too big for me; he pretty much goes as he pleases." I said, "For pete's sake, what do you think the police department is for? This boy is going to prison if we don't get him off the wrong track. He's nothing but a bully; he's surly; he won't talk with people." Well, it was a beautiful home, and the people were well spoken. "We are your police department," I said, 'I'm in a hurry now, but we've got to get organized. This boy of yours: he's idle. He's not doing anything. He's been kicked out of school, and he's been beaten up enough for today. I'm leaving him in your custody, and I don't want him to leave this house. You understand, Joey? Meantime, I'll be back Monday on my day off and I'm going to help you out." "Can I go to the show Sunday?" Joey asks. And I say, "Okay, but don't bully anyone." The kid weighs about 215 pounds. I went to juvenile because I wanted to handle the matter myself. Juvenile had a good talk with the mother. Meanwhile, I got some paint wholesale, and I said to Joey, "You gotta learn something. Here's a paintbrush." He started on the back of his house so if he botched up; it wouldn't show so much. We had a talk before we got started. "We have to have a boss," I said; "I'll be the boss and you go along with it, or I'll thrash the daylights out of you. You've been a terrible trial to your parents, but I'm not going to wait a minute to fight you. We don't have the fight if you accept me as a boss. There'll be no hard feelings. I'll be a real fair boss. In the meantime I'll get you a job." I went down to a local bar I knew to see if there was a job available for after hours. "Is he trustworthy?" I said I didn't know, "but he's good at lugging heavy crates." So he got the job, and I got him some more painting jobs, cheap jobs. And when he got better, I went to a painting contractor. I told him the kid was good and he's not afraid to work. Well, after a while, the contractor came to me and said the kid was damn good. He became an apprentice painter. He was going to Edgehill High School meantime, and. he finished his school and they wanted him in the draft. Well, they drafted him, and for three years, I didn't hear from him. Then one day I was walking up Michigan and an officer came by and said, "Say, Bee, a couple of big colored marines were looking for you. One's a big son-of-a-bitch." I went along, and I saw two guys standing at the Michigan Theater. Both are sergeants, and I hear one say to the other (it was Joey Lewis), "This is the man I've been telling you about." The other guy is as black as the ace of spades and he says, "He thinks you're God." So I say, "Let's go down to Johnson's. I'd like to find out what you're doing." Both are sergeants and they're tough. But Joe is six foot five inches, and he must weigh 235 pounds, and he's got a real physique. He was making a career out of the Marines. I had really straightened him out. "Of all the guys I've met on this job," I told Joey, "this one instance with you makes it all worthwhile. Are you going to go to college

now?" "No," he said, "I'm going to make a career out of the Marines." He had a nice wife and a couple of children. I was never sure he'd really make it. Belligerent – man, I have never seen such belligerence. I'd say, "Why have you got the chip on your shoulder? I came to help you," I said, "and I'm going to make you do what nobody else could. I know you dislike me. Let's get it out on the table. You think I dislike you. Well, you're mistaken." Later he confessed to me what was bothering him. "I didn't know myself what it was," said Joey. "It was hard; I hated white people. I didn't realize I was hiding it all inside me." I said, "I can understand," and we'd talk about things, and we bridged the gap.'

5  Masao Maruyama provides an intriguing glimpse of the influence in pre-World War II Japanese politics of the *ronin*, those adventurers and soldiers of fortune who bartered their cunning, courage, and readiness to break the law for wealth and influence. Masao Maruyama *Thought and Behavior in Modern Japanese Politics* (New York: Oxford University Press, 1969), pp. 128–30.

6  At the extreme to which leniency might go, one could imagine cities where a group was permitted to monopolize the traffic in illegal drugs in exchange for suppressing the crimes of others. Such an extreme corruption of authority did not take place in Laconia, but it would have required utmost conspiratorial silence if it did.

7  For instance, he talked of the effects of the Supreme Court's legal restraints on searches and seizures: 'there are many pushers on skid row but rarely will a pusher carry a gun because if he does, we can pat him down and find what's in his pockets. They don't want us going into their pockets.'

8  Alexis de Tocqueville, *Democracy in America*, trans. Henry Reeve (New York: Vintage, 1945), 1: 51.

9  In working-class areas, a policeman could give advice on repossession, insurance matters, getting gypped at the store, and how to get help for a child with school problems. Advice was cheap to the knowledgeable policeman. It did require some mental capital, investments in learning the law and mastering the procedures of bureaucracies.

# 14. The police: mandate, strategies, and appearances

*Peter K. Manning*

All societies have their share of persistent, chronic problems – problems of life, of death, problems of property and security, problems of man's relationship to what he consecrates. And because societies have their quota of troubles, they have developed ways in which to distribute responsibility for dealing with them. The division of labor that results is not only an allocation of functions and rewards, it is a moral division as well. In exchange for money, goods, or services, these groups – such as lawyers or barbers or clergymen or pharmacists – have a *licence* to carry out certain activities that others may not. This license is a legally defined right, and no other group or groups may encroach upon it.[1]

The right to perform an occupation may entail the permission to pick up garbage or to cut open human bodies and transfer organs from one to another. What it always involves, however, is a series of tasks and associated attitudes and values that set apart a specialized occupational group from all the others. Further, the licensed right to perform an occupation may include a claim to the right to define the proper conduct of others toward matters concerned with the work. The claim, if granted, is the occupation's *mandate*. The mandate may vary from a right to live dangerously to the right to define the conditions of work and functions of related personnel.

The professional mandate is not easily won, of course, for clients are often unwilling to accept the professional definition of their problem. Professions claim a body of theory and practice to justify their right to discover, define, and deal with problems. The medical profession, for example, is usually considered the model of a vocation with a secure license and mandate. Yet even in medicine the client may refuse to accept the diagnosis; he may change physicians or fail to follow doctor's orders or insist upon defining his troubles as the product of a malady best cured by hot lemonade or prayer. The contraction and expansion of an occupation's *mandate* reflects the concerns society has with the services it provides, with its organization, and with its effectiveness. In times of crisis, it is the professions that are questioned first.[2]

Some occupations are not as fortunate as others in their ability to delimit a societal 'trouble' and deal with it systematically. The more power and authority a profession has, the better able it is to gain and maintain control over the symbolic meanings with which it is associated in the public's mind. As we have become less concerned with devils and witches as causes of mental illness, clergymen have lost ground to psychiatrists who have laid claim to a secular cure for madness; in this sense, mental illness is a product of the definitions supplied by psychiatry. A profession, therefore, must not only compete with its clientele's definitions, it must also defend itself against the definitions of competing groups. Is a backache better treated by a Christian Scientist, an osteopath, a chiropractor, a masseuse, or an M.D.? Professional groups whose tools are less well-developed, whose theory is jerry-built or unproved, and who are unable to produce results in our consumer-oriented society will be beset with public doubt, concern, and agitation. In other words, these are the groups that have been unable to define their mandate for solving social 'troubles' in such a way that it can be accomplished with ease and to the satisfaction of those they intend to serve.

The police have trouble. Among the many occupations now in crisis, they best symbolize the shifts and strains in our changing socio-political order. They have been assigned the task of crime prevention, crime detection and the apprehension of criminals. Based on their legal monopoly of violence, they have staked out a mandate that claims to include the efficient, apolitical, and professional enforcement of the law. It is the contention of this article that the police have staked out a vast and unmanageable social domain. And what has happened as a result of their inability to accomplish their self-proclaimed mandate is that the police have resorted to the manipulation of *appearances*.

We shall attempt to outline the nature of the police mandate, or their definition of social trouble, their methods of coping with this trouble, and the consequences of their efforts. After developing a sociological analysis of the paradoxes of police work and discussing the heroic attempts – *strategies* – by police to untangle these paradoxes, we shall also consider the recommendations of the President's crime commission[3] and assess their value as a means of altering and improving the practical art of managing public order.

To turn for the moment to 'practical matters' the same matters to which we shall return before concluding, the troubles of the police, the problems and paradoxes of their mandate in modern society, have become more and more intense. Police today may be more efficient in handling their problems than were the first Bobbies who began to patrol London in 1829. Or they may not be. There may or may not be more crime. Individual rights may or may not be greatly threatened by crime or crime-fighters, and the enforcement of law in view of recent Supreme Court decisions may or may not be a critical issue in crime control. The police may or may not have enough resources to do their job, and they may or may not be allocating them properly. Peace-keeping rather than law enforcement may or may not be the prime need in black communities, and the police may or may not need greater discretionary powers in making an arrest. But however these troubles are regarded, they exist. They are rooted deeply in the mandate of the police.

## Some sociological assumptions

This chapter makes several assumptions about occupations, about people as they execute occupational roles, about organizations as loci or structures for occupational activities and about the nature of society. Not all activity taking place 'on the job' can be construed as 'work'; goldbricking is not unknown in American society and some professionals have even been known to use their places of work to conduct business somewhat outside the mandate of their organization. An individual's 'organizational' behavior varies with what the organization is said to require or permit, with his particular place in the organizational hierarchy, and with the degree of congruence between the individual's personal definition of his role and the organization's definition of his role. In a given situation, then, organizational rules and regulations may be important sources of meanings ('He's working hard'), or other criteria may provide more relevant meanings of behavior ('He can't be expected to work. His wife just had a baby'). The ways in which people explain or account for their own organizational activities and those of others are problematic. How do people refer to their organizational roles and activities? How do they construct their moral obligations to the organization? What do they think they owe the organization? How does this sense of obligation and commitment pattern or constrain them in another role – the role of golfer or father or politician?

People as they perform their roles are actors. They are alert to the small cues that indicate meaning and intention – the wink, the scowl, the raised eyebrow. Those who attend to these behavioral clues are the audience. All actors try to maximize the positive impression they make on others, and both experience and socialization provide them with a repertoire of devices to manage their appearance.

People as actors in roles must also make assumptions about their audience. The politician, for example, must make certain assumptions about his constituency, the lawyer certain assumptions about clients. Assumptions are an important part of urban life. Some actors with white faces, for instance, may make certain assumptions about others with black faces, that they will be ill-mannered or badly educated and that any request for directions is a prelude to a holdup. Assumptions are not simply individual in nature; they are shared, patterned, and passed on from one social group to the next.

One of the most important aspects of assumptions, however, is that they are the basis for strategies.[4] Strategies arise from the need of organizations and individuals to cope with persistent social problems about which assumptions have been made. Strategies are often a means of survival in a competitive environment; they can be inferred from the allocation of resources or from the behavior and pronouncements of an organization. In short, strategies assist any organization within the society in managing its appearance and in controlling the behavior of its audience.

All organizations and individuals, we assume, are bent on maximizing their impressions in order to gain control over an audience.[5] The audience for the police is diverse; it should be considered to be many audiences. For the police must convince the politicians that they have used their allocated resources efficiently; they must persuade the criminals that they are effective crimefighters; they must assure the broader public that they are controlling crime. Rather than a single rhetoric – the 'use of words to form attitudes or induce actions in other human agents'[6] – directed toward convincing one audience, the police must develop many rhetorics. Linguistic strategies to control audience are only one of many ploys used by the police organization to manage its impression. Not all the results of the use of rhetorics are intended; the consequence of the rhetorical 'war on crime' in Detroit in the fall of 1969, to cite one example, was a continued advance in the city's downtown crime rate. Moreover, rhetoric can take on different meanings even within the organizational hierarchy. To patrolmen, the term 'professionalism' means control over hours and salary and protection from arbitrary punishment from 'upstairs'; to the chief and the higher administrators, it relates to the public-administration notions of efficiency, technological expertise, and standards of excellence in recruitment and training.

*Tactics* are the means by which a strategy is implemented. If the strategy is to mount a war on crime, then one tactic might be to flood the downtown area with scooter-mounted patrolmen. Tactics, in other words, are the ways in which one group of people deals with others in face-to-face encounters. How does the policeman handle a family quarrel in which the wife has the butcher knife and the husband already knows how sharp it is? Strategies pertain to general forms of action or rhetoric while tactics refer to the specific action or the specific words used to best meet a specific, problematic situation.[7] The tactic of flattery may be far more effective – and safer – in wresting the butcher knife than a leap over the kitchen table.

All occupations possess strategies and tactics, by means of which they attempt to control their most significant audiences. However, our analysis must do more than describe the existence of such means of creating impressions. So far as the police are concerned, impression management, or the construction of appearances, cannot substitute for significant control of crime. To maintain the dramaturgic metaphor, we suggest that there are significant flaws and contradictions in the performance of the police that cast a serious doubt on the credibility of their occupational mandate.

The mandate of the police is fraught with difficulties, many of them, we shall argue, self-created. They have defined their task in such a way that they cannot, because of the nature of American social organization, hope to honor it to the satisfaction the public. We will argue that the appearances that the police create – that they control crime and that they attain a high level of efficiency – are transparent on close examination, that they may, in fact, be created as a sop to satisfy the public's impossible expectations for police performance. By utilizing the rhetoric of crime control, the police claim the responsibility for the social processes that beget the illegal acts. They cannot control these social processes that are embedded in American values, norms, and cultural traditions. Creating, the appearance of controlling them is only a temporizing policy; it is not the basis for a sound, honorable mandate.

The police mandate and the problems it creates in American society are our central concern. We will rely on the concepts of actor, organization, and audience, of mandate, and of strategy and appearances. We will show that the police mandate, as presently defined, is full of contradictions. We will further demonstrate that the strategies and tactics of the American police are failing in a serious way to meet the need of controlling crime.

## The occupational culture of the police

Before beginning an analysis of the police mandate, a brief comment is necessary about the occupational culture of our law enforcers. The American police act in accord with their assumptions about the nature of social life, and their most important assumptions originate with their need to maintain control over both their mandate and their self-esteem. The policeman's self is an amalgam of evaluations made by the many audiences before whom he, as social actor must perform: his peers, his family, his immediate superiors and the higher administrators, his friends on and off duty. His most meaningful standards of performance are the ideals of his *occupational culture*. The policeman judges himself against the ideal policeman as described in police occupational lore and imagery. What a 'good policeman' does is an omnipresent standard. The occupational culture, however, contains more than the definition of a good policeman. It contains the typical values, norms, attitudes, and material paraphernalia of an occupational group.

An occupational culture also prompts the assumptions about everyday life that become the basis for organizational strategies and tactics. Recent studies of the occupational culture of the police allow the formulation of the following postulates or assumptions, all of which are the basis for police strategies to be discussed later:

1  People cannot be trusted; they are dangerous.
2  Experience is better than abstract rules.
3  You must make people respect you.
4  Everyone hates a cop.
5  The legal system is untrustworthy; policemen make the best decisions about guilt or innocence.
6  People who are not controlled will break laws.
7  Policemen must appear respectable and be efficient.
8  Policemen can most accurately identify crime and criminals.
9  The major jobs of the policeman are to prevent crime and to enforce laws.
10  Stronger punishment will deter criminals from repeating their errors.[8]

Some qualifications about these postulates are in order. They apply primarily to the American noncollege-educated patrolman. They are less applicable to administrators of urban police departments and to members of minority groups within these departments. Nor do they apply accurately to nonurban, state, and federal policemen.

We shall now describe the paradoxes of the police mandate, the strategies of the police in dealing with their troubles, and some of the findings and recommendations of the President's crime commission as they bear on the current attempt by the police to make a running adjustment to their problems.

## The 'impossible' mandate

The police in modern society are in agreement with their audiences – which include their professional interpreters, the American family, criminals and politicians – in at least one respect: they have an 'impossible' task. Certainly, all professionals have impossible tasks insofar as they try to surmount the problems of collective life that resist easy solutions. The most 'successful' occupations, however, have managed to construct a mandate in terms of their own vision of the world. The policeman's mandate, on the other hand, is defined largely by his publics – not, at least at the formal level, in his own terms.

Several rather serious consequences result from the public's image of the police. The public is aware of the dramatic nature of a small portion of police work, but it ascribes the element of excitement to all police activities. To much of the public, the police are seen as alertly ready to respond to citizen demands, as crime-fighters, as an efficient, bureaucratic, highly organized force that keeps society from falling into chaos. The policeman himself considers the essence of his role to be the dangerous and heroic enterprise of crook-catching and the watchful prevention of crimes.[9] The system of positive and negative sanctions from the public and within the department encourages this heroic conception. The public wants crime prevented and controlled; that is, it wants criminals caught. Headlines herald the accomplishments of G-Men and FBI agents who often do catch dangerous men, and the reputation of these federal authorities not infrequently rubs off on local policemen who are much less adept at catching criminals.

In an effort to gain the public's confidence in their ability; and to insure thereby the solidity of their mandate, the police have encouraged the public to continue thinking of them and their work in idealized terms, terms, that is, which grossly exaggerate the actual work done by police. They do engage in chases, in gunfights, in careful sleuthing. But these are rare events. Most police work resembles any other kind of work: it is boring, tiresome, sometimes dirty, sometimes technically demanding, but it is rarely dangerous. Yet the occasional chase, the occasional shootout, the occasional triumph of some extraordinary detective work have to been seized upon by the police and played up to the public. The public's response has been to demand even more dramatic crook-catching and crime prevention, and this demand for arrests has been converted into an index for measuring how well the police accomplish their mandate. The public's definitions have been converted by the police organization into distorted criteria for promotion, success, and security. Most police departments promote men from patrol to detective work, a generally more desirable duty, for 'good pinches' – arrests that are most likely to result in convictions.[10] The protection of the public welfare, however, including, personal and property safety, the prevention of crime, and the preservation of individual civil rights, is hardly achieved by a high pinch rate. On the contrary, it might well be argued that protection of the public welfare could best be indexed by a low arrest rate. Because their mandate automatically entails mutually contradictory ends – protecting both public order and individual rights – the police resort to managing their public image and the indexes of their accomplishment. And the ways in which the police manage their appearance are consistent with the assumptions of their occupational culture, with the public's view of the police as a social-control agency, and with the ambiguous nature of our criminal law.

### The problematic nature of law and order

The criminal law is one among many instrumentalities of social control. It is an explicit set of rules created by political authority; it contains provisions for punishment by officials designated with the responsibility to interpret and enforce the rules which 'should be uniformly applied to all persons within a politically defined territory'.[11] This section discusses the relationships between the laws and the mores of a society, the effect of the growth of civilized society on law enforcement, and the problematic nature of crime in an advanced society. The differential nature of enforcement will be considered as an aspect of peace-keeping, and will lead to the discussion of the police in the larger political system.

A society's laws, it is often said, reflect its customs; it can also be said that the growth of the criminal law is proportionate to the decline in the consistency and binding nature of these mores. In simpler societies, where the codes and rules of behavior were well known and homogeneous, sanctions were enforced with much greater uniformity and predictability. Social control was isomorphic with one's obligations to family, clan, and age group, and the political system of the tribe. In a modern, differentiated society, a minimal number of values and norms are shared. And because the fundamental, taken-for-granted consensus on what is proper and respectable has been blurred or shattered, or, indeed, never existed, criminal law becomes a basis of social control. As Quinney writes, 'Where correct conduct cannot be agreed upon, the criminal law serves to control the behavior of all persons within a political jurisdiction'.[12]

Social control through the criminal law predominates in a society only when other means of control have failed. When it does predominate, it no longer reflects the mores of the society. It more accurately reflects the interests of shifting power groups within the society. As a result, the police, as the designated enforcers of a system of criminal laws, are undercut by circumstances that accentuate the growing differences between the moral order and the legal order.

One of these complicating circumstances is simply the matter of social changes, which further stretch the bond between the moral and the legal. The law frequently lags behind the changes in what society deems acceptable and unacceptable practice. At other times, it induces changes, such as those pertaining to civil rights, thereby anticipating acceptable practice. The definition of crime, then, is a product of the relationship between social structure and the law. Crime, to put it another way, is not a homogeneous entity.

The perspective of the patrolman as he goes about his daily rounds is a legalistic one. The law and the administrative actions of his department provide him with a frame of reference for exercising the mandate of the police. The citizen, on the other hand, does not live his life in accordance with a legalistic framework; he defines his acts in accordance with a moral or ethical code provided him by his family, his religion, his social class. For the most part, he sees law enforcement as an intervention in his private affairs.

No matter what the basis for actions of private citizens may be, however, the patrolman's job is one of practical decision-making within a legalistic pattern. His decisions are expected to include an understanding of the law as a system of formal rules, the enforcement practices emphasized by his department, and a knowledge of the specific facts of an allegedly illegal situation. The law includes little formal recognition of the variation in the private arrangement of lives. Even so, the policeman is expected to take these into account also. No policeman can ever be provided with a handbook that could tell him, at a moment's notice, just what standards to apply in enforcing the law and in maintaining order. Wilson summarizes the difficulty inherent in law enforcement as follows:

> Most criminal laws define *acts* (murder, rape, speeding, possessing narcotics), which are held to be illegal; people may disagree as to whether the act should be illegal, as they do with respect to narcotics, for example, but there is little disagreement as to what the behaviour in question consists of. Laws regarding disorderly conduct and the like assert, usually by implication, that there is a condition ('public order') that can be diminished by various actions. The difficulty, of course, is that public order is nowhere defined and can never be defined unambiguously because what constitutes order is a matter of opinion and convention, not a state of nature. (An unmurdered person, an unraped woman, and an unpossessed narcotic can be defined so as to be recognizable to any reasonable person.) An additional difficulty, a corollary of the first, is the impossibility of specifying, except in the extreme case, what degree of disorder is intolerable and who is to be held culpable for that degree. A suburban street is quiet and pleasant; a big city street is noisy and (to some) offensive; what degree of noise and offense, and produced by whom, constitutes disorderly conduct?[13]

The complexity of law enforcement stems from both the problem of police 'discretion' and the inherent tensions between the maintenance of order and individual rights. The law contains rules on how to maintain order; it contains substantive definitions of crime, penalties for violations, and the conditions under which the commission of a crime is said to have been intended.[14] Further, the law contains procedures for the administration of justice and for the protection of the individual. The complexities of law enforcement notwithstanding, however, the modern policeman is frequently faced with the instant problem of defining an action as either legal or illegal, of deciding, in other words, whether to intervene and, if so, what tactic to use. He moves in a dense web of social action and social meanings, burdened by a problematic, complex array of ever-changing laws. Sometimes the policeman must quickly decide very abstract matters. Though a practitioner of the legal arts, his tools at hand are largely obscure, ill-developed, and crude. With little formal training, the rookie must learn his role by absorbing the theories, traditions, and personal whims of experienced patrolmen.

*Police work as peace-keeping*[15]

The thesis of two recent major works on the police, Wilson's *The Varieties of Police*

*Behavior* and Skolnick's *Justice without Trial*, can be paraphrased as follows: the policeman must exercise discretion in matters involving life and death, honor and dishonor, and he must do so in an environment that he perceives as threatening, dangerous, hostile, and volatile. He sees his efficiency constrained by the law and by the police organization. Yet, he must effectively manage 'disorder' in a variety of unspecified ways, through methods usually learned and practiced on the job. As a result of these conditions; the policeman, in enforcing his conception of order, often violates the rights of citizens.

Many observers of police work regard the primary function of a policeman as that of a *peace-keeper*, not a *law enforcer*. According to this view; police spend most of their time attending to order-maintaining functions, such as finding lost children, substituting as ambulance drivers or interceding in quarrels of one sort or another. To these observers, the police spend as little as 10 to 15 percent of their time on law enforcement – responding to burglary calls or trying to find stolen cars. The large-scale riots and disorders of recent years accounted for few police man-hours. Wilson illustrates the peace-keeping (order maintenance) and law-enforcement distinction this way:

> The difference between order maintenance and law enforcement is not simply the difference between 'little stuff' and 'real crime' or between misdemeanors and felonies. The distinction is fundamental to the police role, for the two functions involve quite dissimilar police actions and judgments. Older maintenance arises out of a dispute among citizens who accuse each other of being at fault; law enforcement arises out of the victimization of an innocent party by a person whose guilt must be proved. Handling a disorderly situation requires the officer to make a judgment about what constitutes an appropriate standard of behavior; law enforcement requires him only to compare a person's behavior with a clear legal standard. Murder or theft is defined; unambiguously, by statutes; public peace is not. Order maintenance rarely leads to an arrest; law enforcement (if the suspect can be found) typically does. Citizens quarreling usually want the officer to 'do something', but they rarely want him to make an arrest (after all, the disputants are usually known or related to each other). Furthermore, whatever law is broken in a quarrel is usually a misdemeanor, and in most states, an officer cannot make a misdemeanor arrest unless one party or the other will swear out a formal complaint (which is even rarer).[16]

The complexity of the law and the difficulty in obtaining a complainant combine to tend to make the policeman underenforce the law – to overlook, ignore, dismiss, or otherwise erase the existence of many enforceable breaches of the law.

Some researchers and legalists have begun to piece together, a pattern of the conditions under which policemen have a tendency not to enforce the law. From a study of police in three Midwestern states, LaFave has concluded that two considerations characterize a decision not to arrest. The first is that the crime is unlikely to reach public attention – for example, that it is of a private nature or of low visibility – and the second is that underenforcement is unlikely to be detected or challenged.[12] Generally, the conditions under which policemen are less likely to enforce the law are those in which they perceive little public consensus on the law, or in which the law is ambiguous. LaFave found that policemen are not apt to enforce rigorously laws that are viewed by the public as dated, or that are used on the rare occasions when the public order is being threatened.

There is a certain Benthamic calculus involved in all arrests, a calculus that is based on pragmatic considerations such as those enumerated by LaFave. Sex, age, class, and race might also enter into the calculus of whether the law should be enforced. In a case study of the policeman assigned to skid row, Bittner illustrates the great degree of discretion exercised by the policeman. Yet the law, often reified by the policeman, is rarely a clear guide to action – despite the number of routine actions that might be termed 'typical situations that policemen perceive as *demand conditions* for action without arrest'.[18]

In the exercise of discretion, in the decision to enforce the law or to underenforce, the protection of individual rights is often at stake. But individual rights are frequently in opposition to the preservation of order, as a totalitarian state exemplifies in the extreme. The police try to manage these two contradictory demands by emphasizing their peace-keeping functions. This emphasis succeeds only when a consensus exists on the nature of the order (peace) to be preserved. The greater the difference in viewpoint between the police and the public on the degree and kind of order to be preserved, the greater will be antagonism between the two; the inevitable result of this hostility will be 'law breaking'.

The resolution of the contradictions and complexities inherent in the police mandate, including the problems of police discretion, of individual rights, of law enforcement and peace-keeping, is not helped, however, by the involvement of police in politics. Politics only further complicates the police mandate. The law itself is a political phenomenon, and at the practical level of enforcing it, the local political system is yet another source of confusion.

### The police in the political system

In theory, the American police are apolitical. Their own political values and political aims are supposed to be secondary to the institutional objective of law enforcement. In practice, however, police organizations function in a political context; they operate in a public political arena and their mandate is defined politically. They may develop strategies to create and maintain the appearance of being apolitical in order to protect their organizational autonomy, but they are nonetheless a component of American political machinery. There are three reasons why the police are inextricably involved in the political system, the first and most obvious being that the vast majority of the police in this nation are locally controlled [...] Responsibility for maintaining public order in America is decentralized, and law-enforcement officers are largely under the immediate control of local political authorities.

The second reason why the police are an integral part of the political system is this: law is a political entity, and the administration of criminal law unavoidably encompasses political values and political ends. The police are directly related to a political system that develops and defines the law, itself a product of interpretations of what is right and proper from the perspective of different politically powerful segments within the community.

The third reason why the police are tied to the political system emanates from the second; the police must administer the law. Many factors pattern this enforcement, but they all reflect the political organization of society. The distribution of power and authority, for example, rather than the striving for justice, or equal treatment under the law, can have a direct bearing on enforcement.

Because law enforcement is for the most part locally controlled, sensitivity to local political trends remains an important element in police practice. Since the police are legally prohibited from being publicly political, they often appeal to different community groups, and participate *sub rosa* in others, in order to influence the determination of public policy. Community policy, whether made by the town council or the mayor or the city manager, affects pay scales, operating budgets, personnel, administrative decisions, and, to some extent, organizational structure. The police administrator must, therefore, be responsive to these controls, and he must deal with them in an understanding way. He must be sensitive to the demands of the local politicians – even while maintaining the loyalty of the lower ranks through a defense of their interests.

There are several direct effects of the political nature of the police mandate. One is that many policemen become alienated; they lose interest in their role as enforcers and in the law as a believable criterion. The pressures of politics also erode loyalty to the police organization and not infrequently lead to collusion with criminals and organized crime.

The policeman's exposure to danger, his social background, low pay, low morale, his vulnerability in a repressive bureaucracy all conspire to make him susceptible to the lures of the underhanded and the appeals of the political. Studies summarized by Skolnick[19] reveal a political profile of the policeman as a conservative, perhaps reactionary, person of lower-class or lower-middle-class origin, often a supporter of radical right causes, often prejudiced and repressive, often extremely ambivalent about the rights of others. The postulates, or assumptions of the police culture, the suspiciousness, fear, low self-esteem, and distrust of others are almost diametrically opposed to the usual conception of the desirable democratic man.

Thus, the enforcement of some laws is personally distasteful. Civil rights legislation, for example, can be anathema. Or truculence can be the reaction to an order relaxing controls in ghettos during the summer months. It is the ambivalence of policemen toward certain laws and toward certain local policies that fragments loyalty within a department and causes alienation.

There is another consequence of the political nature of the police mandate: the police are tempted. They are tempted not to enforce the law by organized crime, by the operators of illegal businesses such as prostitution, and by fine 'law-abiding', illegally parked citizens. All too frequently, the police submit to temptations, becoming in the process exemplars of the corruption typical of modern society, where the demand for 'criminal services' goes on at the station house.

Police and politics within the community are tightly interlocked. The sensitivity of the police to their political audiences, their operation within the political system of criminal justice, and their own personal political attitudes undermine their efforts to fulfill their contradictory mandate and to appear politically neutral.

### The efficient symptom-oriented organization

The Wickersham report, the Hoover administration's report on crime and law enforcement in the United States, was published in 1931. This precursor of the Johnson administration's *The Challenge of Crime in a Free Society* became a rallying point for advocates of police reform. One of its central themes was the lack of 'professionalism' among the police of the time – their lack of special training, their corruption, their brutality, and their use of illegal procedures in law enforcement. And one of its results was that the police, partly in order to demonstrate their concern with scientific data gathering on crime and partly to indicate their capacity to 'control' crime itself, began to stress crime statistics as a major component of professional police work.

Crime statistics, therefore – and let this point be emphasized – became a police construction. The actual amount of crime committed in a society is unknown – and probably unknowable, given the private nature of most crime. The *crime rate*, consequently, is simply a construction of police activities. That is, the crime rate pertains only to 'crimes known to the police', crimes that have been reported to or observed by the police and for which adequate grounds exist for assuming that a violation of the law has, in fact, taken place. (The difference between the *actual* and *known crimes* is often called the 'dark figure of crime'.) Of course, the construction of a crime rate placed the police in a logically weak position in which they still find themselves. If the crime rate is rising, they argue that more police support is needed to fight the war against crime; if the crime rate is stable or declining, they argue that they have successfully combated the crime menace – a heads-I-win-tails-you-lose proposition.

In spite of their inability to control the commission of illegal acts (roughly, the actual rate), since they do not know about all crime, the police have claimed responsibility for crime control, using the crime rate as an index of their success. This use of the crime rate to measure success is somewhat analogous to their use of a patrolman's arrest rate as an indication of his personal success in law enforcement. Questions about the actual amount of crime and the degree of control exercised are thus bypassed in favor of an index that offers great potential for organizational or bureaucratic control. Instead of grappling with the difficult issue of defining the ends of police work and an operational means for accomplishing them, the police have opted for 'efficient' law-enforcement defined in terms of fluctuations of the crime rate. They transformed concern with undefined ends into concern with available means. Their inability to cope with the causes of crime – which might offer them a basis for defining their ends – shifts their 'organizational focus' into symptomatic concerns, that is, into a preoccupation with the rate of crime, not its reasons.

This preoccupation with the symptoms of a problem rather than with the problem itself is typical of all bureaucracies. For one characteristic of a bureaucracy is goal-displacement. Bureaucratic organizations tend to lose track of their goals and engage in ritual behavior, substituting means for ends. As a whole, bureaucracies become so engrossed in pursuing, defending, reacting to, and, even, in creating immediate problems that their objective is forgotten. This tendency to displace goals is accelerated by the one value dear to all bureaucracies – efficiency. Efficiency is the be-all and end-all of bureaucratic organizations. Thus, they can expend great effort without any genuine accomplishment.

The police are burdened with the 'efficiency problem'. They claim to be an efficient bureaucratic organization, but they are unable to define for themselves and others precisely what it is they are being efficient about. In this respect, they do not differ from other paper-shuffling organizations. The police's problem is that the nature of their work is uncertain and negatively defined. It is uncertain in the absence of a consensus not only between the police and the public but also among themselves as to what the goals of a police department should be. It is defined in the negative because the organization punishes its members – patrolmen – for violating departmental procedures but offers no specifications on what they should do or how they should do it.

What do the police do about the problematic nature of law, about the problems arising from their involvement with politics, about their preoccupation with the symptoms of crime rather than the causes? Do they selectively adopt some strategies at the expense of others? Do they vacillate? Are the roles of the organization's members blurred? Before answering these questions, let us examine how the police, through various strategies, manage their appearance before the public. The questions will then be easier to answer.

## Major strategies of the police

The responsibilities of the police lead them to pursue contradictory and unattainable ends. They share with all organizations and occupations, however, the ability to avoid solving their problems. Instead, they concentrate on managing them through strategies. Rather than resolving their dilemmas, the police have manipulated them with a professional eye on just how well the public accepts their dexterity. Thus, law enforcement becomes a self-justifying system. It becomes more responsive to its own needs, goals, and procedures than to serving society. In this section, we will show the ways in which the police have followed the course of most other bureaucratic institutions in society, responding to their problems by merely giving the appearance of facing them while simultaneously promoting the trained incapacity to do otherwise.

The two primary aims of most bureaucracies, the police included, are the maintenance of their organizational autonomy and the security of their members. To accomplish these aims, they adopt a pattern of institutional action that can best be described as 'professionalism'. This word, with its many connotations and definitions, cloaks all the many kinds of actions carried out by the police.

The guise of professionalism embodied in a bureaucratic organization is the most important strategy employed by the police to defend their mandate and thereby to build self-esteem, organizational autonomy, and occupational solidarity or cohesiveness. The professionalization drives of the police are no more suspect than the campaigns of other striving, upwardly mobile occupational groups. However, since the police have a monopoly on legal violence, since they are the active enforcers of the public will, serving theoretically in the best interests of the public, the consequences of their yearnings for prestige and power are imbued with far greater social ramifications than the relatively harmless attempts of florists, funeral directors, and accountants to attain public stature. Disinterested law enforcement through bureaucratic means is an essential in our society and in any democracy, and the American police are certainly closer to attaining this ideal than they were in 1931 at the time of the Wickersham report. Professionalism *qua* professionalism is unquestionably desirable in the police. But if in striving for the heights of prestige they fail to serve the altruistic values of professionalism, if their professionalism means that a faulty portrait of the social reality of crime is being painted, if their professionalism conceals more than it reveals about the true nature of their operations, then a close analysis of police professionalism is in order.

Police professionalism cannot be easily separated in practice from the bureaucratic ideal epitomized in modern police practice. The bureaucratic ideal is established as a means of obtaining a commitment from personnel to organizational and occupational norms. This bureaucratic commitment is designed to supersede commitments to competing norms, such as obligations to friends or kin or members of the same racial or ethnic group. Unlike medicine and law, professions that developed outside the context of bureaucracies, policing has always been carried out, if done on a full-time basis, as a bureaucratic function.

Modern police bureaucracy and modern police professionalism are highly articulated, although they contain some inherent stresses that are not our present concern. The strategies employed by the police to manage their public appearance develop from their adaptation of the bureaucratic ideal. These strategies incorporate the utilization of *technology* and *official statistics* in law enforcement, of *styles of patrol* that attempt to accommodate the community's desire for public order with the police department's preoccupation with bureaucratic procedures, of *secrecy* as a means of controlling the public's response to their operations, of *collaboration* with criminal elements to foster the appearance of a smoothly run, law-abiding community, and of a *symbiotic relationship* with the criminal justice system that minimizes public knowledge of the flaws within this largely privately operated system.

## The effectiveness of police strategies

The police have developed and utilized the strategies outlined above for the purpose of creating, as we have said, the appearance of managing their troublesome mandate. To a large extent, they are facilitated in the use of these strategies, in being able to project a favorable impression, by a public that has always been apathetic about police activity. Moreover, what activity the public does observe is filtered through the media with its own special devices for creating a version of reality. The public's meaning of police action is rarely gathered from first-hand experience, but from the constructed imagery of the media – which, in turn, rely upon official police sources for their presentation of the news. The police for their part, understandably, manipulate public appearances as much as they possibly can in order to gain and maintain public support.

The specific strategies used by the police to create a publicly suitable image […] described [earlier were]: the guise of professionalism; the implementation of the bureaucratic ideal of organization; the use of technology, official statistics, and various styles of patrol; secrecy; collaboration with corrupt elements; and the establishment of a symbiotic relationship with the courts. This section will present evidence by which to evaluate these strategies. The term 'effectiveness' is used only in the context of how well these devices accomplish the ends which the public and the police themselves publicly espouse; the recommendations and evaluations of the President's crime commission will be central in making judgments of police effectiveness. This appraisal of how well the police manipulate their appearance will also be a guideline for evaluating the recommendations of the commission's task force report on the police.

*Professionalism and the bureaucratic ideal*

The assumptions of professionalism and of a bureaucratic organization include a devotion to rational principles and ends that may then be translated into specific work routines having predictable outcomes. The police are organized in a military command fashion, with rigid rules and a hierarchy governing operations. However, the patrolman, the lowest man in the hierarchy – and usually the least well-trained and educated – is in the key position of exercising the greatest amount of discretion on criminal or possibly criminal activities. Especially in his peace-keeping role and in dealing with minor infractions (misdemeanors), the patrolman has wide discretionary power concerning if, when, why, and how to intervene in private affairs.

Police work must both rely on discretion and control it. Excessive inattention and excessive attention to infractions of the law are equally damaging to a community. However, the complexity of the law, its dynamic and changing properties, the extensiveness of police department regulations, policies, and procedures, and the equivocal, relativistic nature of crime in regard to certain situations, settings, persons, and groups make it impossible to create a job description that would eliminate the almost boundless uncertainty in police patrol.

Neither professionals nor bureaucrats, however, have yet found an effective means of controlling discretion. If an organization cannot control those of its members with the greatest opportunity to exercise discretion, it flounders in its attempts to accomplish its stated purposes. Two general principles suggest why the police have not been able to control discretion. The first has to do with the general problem of control and the second with the specific nature of police work.

Men are unwilling to submit completely to the will of their organizational superiors. Men will always attempt to define and control their own work. Control means the right to set the pace, to define mistakes, to develop standards of 'good' production and efficiency. But as surely as superiors seek to control the quality and the extent of work performed by their subordinates in a hierarchy, just as surely will they meet with attempts to reshape and subvert these controls.

In the specific instance of police bureaucracies, the patrolman conceives of himself as a man able to make on-the-spot decisions of guilt or innocence. He does not think of himself as a bureaucratic functionary nor as a professional. Further, since the police organization itself has become far more interested in efficiency than in purpose, since it is unable to specify its overall objectives, the patrolman finds it difficult, if not impossible, to demonstrate that necessary devotion to rational ends required of professionalism and bureaucratic organizations. Until police departments are able to control the amount and kind of discretion exercised by their members, and until the police are able, with the help of lawyers and other citizens, to develop positive means of motivation and reward in line with clear, overall policy directives, the failure of what we have called the professionalism–bureaucracy strategy is an absolute certainty.

### Technology, statistics, and the crime rate

This section will evaluate the strategy of technology in the control and prevention of crime, the use of statistics, and the significance of the so- called crime rate. Given the sociological nature of crime, let it be said immediately that present technology deals with unimportant crime and, that the FBI index of crimes, by which we base judgments of police effectiveness, is biased and an unrealistic reflection of the actual crime rate.

One of the striking aspects of the President's crime commission report is the thoroughly sociological nature of the document. The discussion of the causes of crime [earlier in this book] points to the growth of the urbanism, anonymity, the breakdown in social control, and the increasing numbers of frustrated and dissatisfied youth who have always constituted the majority of known lawbreakers. There are no labels such as 'evil people', 'emotionally disturbed', 'mentally ill', or 'criminally insane'. The first set of recommendations under prevention in the summary pages of the report are 'sociological': strengthen the family, improve slum schools, provide employment, reduce segregation, construct housing. All these matters are patently and by definition out of the control of the police.

There is every evidence that the police themselves subscribe to a thoroughly social, if not sociological, definition of the causes of crime – that is, that crime is the manifestation of long-established social patterns and structures which ensnare and implicate the police and the criminals as well as the general public. And they are doubtless correct.

Surveys done by the President's crime commission revealed that there are always contingencies in the information police receive about a crime even before they are able to investigate it. These contingencies involve such matters as the nature of the relationship between the victim and the offender and whether or not the victim believes the police are competent to investigate and solve the crime. Computer technology depends on informational 'input'. On that point, the police seem both unable to define what sort of information would be useful and unable to obtain, and probably never can obtain in a democratic society, information that would make them better able to enforce the law.

The facts in the problem of 'crime prevention' overwhelmingly doom the present professionally based notion that the application of science and technology will begin to ease the distress the police feel as they face the escalating demands of their audiences. Also, it would be easier to assess the value of the technology strategy if we were able to define exactly to what end the technology would be applied and in what ways it could be expected to work.

### Styles of patrol

Police strategy is subject to many contingencies. It is a basic principle of public administration that policy made at the higher echelons of an organization will be effective only if each successively lower level of the organization complies with that policy and is capable of carrying it out. It is also a truism that participants at the lowest level in the hierarchy are the most 'difficult' to mobilize and integrate into the organization. A style of patrol is basically the manner in which an administrative police policy is executed. The policy may prescribe that the patrolman overlook certain types of illegal acts; it may order that he minimally enforce particular laws or be sensitive to and strictly enforce others. If the administrative order setting a patrol style does not win the cooperation of the patrolman it is certain to fail. Thus, the success of any high-echelon policy that involves the performance of the patrolman is contingent upon his compliance with that policy. If the administrator's orders are not binding on the patrolman, no distinctive style of patrol will result; all that will be demonstrated will be the responses of the patrolman to other aspects of his social environment, especially, how his fellow patrolmen perform.

The success of this strategy is dependent upon the capacity of the administrator to create loyalty to his internal policies. With the rise of police unions, the discontent of the black patrolman, low pay, and relatively less security for the policeman, organizational control is a major problem in all the large police departments [...]

The effectiveness of the watchman, legalistic, and service styles of patrol will also depend on the degree of political consensus among the community groups patrolled, the clarity of the boundaries of community groups neighborhoods, competition between the police and self-help or vigilante groups, and the relative importance of nonoccupational norms in enforcement practice – that is, the importance of racial or ethnic similarities between the patrolman and the people in his neighborhood. If a clear social consensus on the meaning of the law and what is expected of the police can be established within a community, a well-directed policy of control over police patrol is the most logical and rational approach to police work. In some communities, largely suburban and middleclass, the police can carry out what their public demands and a degree of harmony exists. This consensus is absent in our inner cities.

*Secrecy and collaboration*

The use of secrecy by the police is, as we have pointed out, a strategy employed not only to assist them in maintaining the appearance of political neutrality but to protect themselves against public complaints. Secrecy also helps to forestall public efforts to achieve better police service and to secure political accountability for police policy. Police collaboration with criminal elements – corruption, in other words – has much the same effect since it decreases the pressure to enforce 'unenforceable' laws against certain segments of the police's clientele.

These two strategies were among the major concerns of the President's crime commission task force on police. The task force's report devoted major attention to the fact that political forces influence police actions and policies. The report affirmed the political nature of police work; what concerned the writers of the report was the nature and type of political influence on police actions. Their recommendations, furthermore, were based on their recognition of the fact that the police have been fairly successful in managing the appearance of being apolitical.

There are several reasons why the police strategies of secrecy and collaboration will continue in force: (1) as long as the client – the public – is seen as the enemy, the police will treasure their secrecy and use it to engineer public consent to their policies and practices; (2) as long as a new political consensus is not formed on the nature and type of police control necessary in society as a whole, the organized, self-serving survival aims of police organizations will emerge victorious. Any well-organized consensual, secretive organization can resist the efforts of an unorganized public, managed by rhetoric and appearances, to reform it; (3) as long as there remains a lack of consensus on the enforcement of our 'moralistic' laws, police corruption and selective law enforcement will continue. Collaboration to reduce adversary relationships with the criminal segment of society will always be an effective strategy – providing a sudden upsurge in public morality doesn't temporarily subject the police to a full-scale 'housecleaning'. Replacements would, of course, be subject to the same pressures and would, in all likelihood, eventually take the same line of least resistance.

One solution to corruption is said to be better educated, more professional policemen. By recruiting better educated men, the more professionalized police departments also seek to diminish the expression of political attitudes on the job and the tendency of policemen to form political power groups based on their occupation. These are also assumptions made by the crime commission's task force on police. There is, however, no evidence that college-educated or better-paid policemen are 'better policemen'; nor is there any evidence that 'better men' alone will solve the essentially structural problems of the occupation.

We can tentatively conclude from this review that corruption will remain with us as long as laws remain which stipulate punishments for actions on which a low public consensus exists. It will remain when there is likely to be a low visibility of police performance, and it will remain while there is a high public demand for illegal services – gambling, prostitution, abortion – and the concomitant need of the police for information on these services from the practitioners themselves.

### Symbiosis and justice

Although the police have the principal discretion in the field with reference to the detection, surveillance, and appraisal of alleged offenders, the final disposition of a criminal case must be made in the courts. The police are thus dependent on the courts in a very special way for their successes. The ideal model of the criminal justice system makes the police essentially the fact gatherers and apprehenders, while the courts are to be the decision-makers.

The police attempt to appear efficient has led them as we have noted before to seek the good pinch, the arrest that will stand up in court. With victimless crimes, such as those involving gambling or drugs or prostitution, the police control the situation since they alone decide whether an offense has been committed and whether they have a legal case against the offender. To control the success rate in these cases, the police create a gaggle of informants, many of whom are compelled to give the police evidence in order to stay free of a potential charge against themselves for a violation similar to the one they are providing information about. In the case of more serious crimes, the problems are more complex; in these cases the police must rely on other informants, and their discretion on arrests and charges are more often exercised by administrators and prosecuting attorneys.

In the prosecution stage, the bureaucratic demands of the court system are paramount. Abraham Blumberg describes these demands and the tension between efficiency and 'due process':

> The dilemma is frequently resolved through bureaucratically ordained shortcuts, deviations and outright rule violations by the members of the courts, from judges to stenographers, in order to meet production norms. Because they fear criticism on ethical as well as legal grounds, all the significant participants in the court's social structure are bound into an organized system of complicity. Patterned, covert, informal breaches, and evasions of 'due process' are accepted as routine – they are institutionalized – but are nevertheless denied to exist.[20]

The net effect of this strain within the court system is to produce a higher rate of convictions by means of encouraging a plea of guilty to a lesser charge. As far as the police are concerned, then, the strategy of symbiosis is sound.

There are several undesirable effects of this symbiosis. First, it encourages corruption by permitting the police to make decisions about the freedom of their informants; it gives them an illegal hold and power over them, and thus it undercuts the rule of law. Second, many offenders with long criminal records are either granted their freedom as informants or allowed to plead guilty to lesser charges in return for the dismissal of a more serious charge. Skolnick calls this the 'reversal of the hierarchy of penalties', because the more serious crimes of habitual criminals are prosecuted less zealously than the minor violations of first offenders. Third, it helps blur the distinction between the apprehension and prosecution aspects of our criminal-justice system.

## Conclusions and proposed reforms

The allocation of rewards in a society represents both its division of labor and its configuration of problems. Ironically, the allocation of rewards is also the allocation of societal trouble. Societal trouble in a differentiated society is occupational trouble. The ebb and flow of rewards emanating from the division of labor becomes structured into persistent patterns that are sustained by continuous transactions among organizations and occupational groups. Occupational structures reflect societal structures, but they reflect them in ways that have been negotiated over time. The negotiation is based upon the universal human proclivity to differentiate roles, organizations, and occupations. The more dependent an organization is upon its environment for rewards, the more likely it is to rely on the management and presentation of strategies to establish the appearance of autonomy.

Organizations without a high degree of autonomy in the environments in which they operate are greatly constrained by the internal pressure of competing aims and roles of members. The agreement on problems, goals, values, and self-concepts that emerges from occupational socialization and functioning is a strong basis for influencing organizational direction. The occupational standards in this case subvert the rule of law as a system of norms outside the informal norms of the occupation. The policeman's view of his role and his occupational culture are very influential in determining the nature of policing. The basic source of police trouble is the inability of the police to define a mandate that will minimize the inconsistent nature of their self-expectations and the expectations, of those they serve.

The problems derived from a contradictory mandate remain unaffected by the efforts of the institution to solve them; they do, however, take the shape into which they have been cast by institutional functionaries. Cooley long ago discussed the process of institutional ossification, the process by which institutions stray from serving the needs of their members and their publics, thereby losing the loyalty of those within and the support of those without. The consequences of institutional ossification as related to the police are twofold. First, the police begin to search for a so-called higher order of legitimacy; they, make appeals to morality, to patriotism, to 'Americanism', and to 'law and order' to shore up eroded institutional charters and to accelerate their attempts to control and manipulate their members and clients. Second, the police, as they develop a far greater potential for controlling those they serve through their presentational strategies, come to serve themselves better than ever before.

The problem of the police is essentially, the problem of the democratic society, and until the central values and social structures of our society are modified (and I think we are seeing such a modification), there can be no real change in the operation of social control. The needed changes are, by and large, not those dealt with in the crime commission report. And this is telling. For an eminently sociological document, it did not focus on the heart of the problem: our anachronistic, moralistic laws, with which the police are burdened, and our dated political system, which is unable to bring political units into a state of civil accountability. The focus of the report and recommendations was predictably on symptoms of crime, not on causes of crime. The 'managerial focus' of the report, or its public-administration bias, outlined needed reforms, but not ways in which to implement them, and the problem of efficiency was never really faced.

Not surprisingly for a political document having a variety of public functions, the report has little to say about the nature of the present criminal laws. It dwells, like the police themselves, on means, not ends. As Isidore Silver points out in a critique of the report, more than one-half of the crimes committed do not harm anyone: more than one-third are for drunkenness, and a small but important portion are for other 'crimes without victims'. Most crimes are committed by juveniles who inexplicably 'grow out' of their criminality. In 1965, 50 percent of the known burglaries and larcenies were committed by youths under 18.[21] The report does note what was a central point of our discussion of the political nature of crime, that police corruption is, in almost every instance, a consequence of trying to enforce admittedly unenforceable laws. The demand for services provided by homosexuals, by gamblers [and] prostitutes [...] is high, and the supply is legally made unavailable to anyone who wants to remain in the so-called 'law-abiding' category. The laws, in effect, create the crime and the criminals.

Changes in laws to reduce their absolutistic element and to free people who deviate with little harm to others from the onus of criminalization cannot be accomplished without a parallel change in the nature of police accountability. As we have seen, the strategies of secrecy and rhetoric used by the police play on the fears of society and provide a basis for police control. The managerial reforms contained in the task force report – more public debate on and greater internal and external control over police actions – are needed. Even more urgently required are specific ways in which the cities can control the police and make them strictly accountable for their actions – methods, that is, which go a good deal further than merely disposing of the chief or convening a judicial review board. To give city governments this kind of control over the police, however, entails the reorganization of police departments themselves so that their goals are clear and defined and so that the occupational rewards within the police organization are aligned with public goals.

Three interrelated organizational changes must be made to ensure that police attend to the job of maintaining public order. One is to reorganize police departments along functional lines aimed at peace-keeping rather than law enforcement; the second is to allocate rewards for keeping the peace rather than for enforcing the law; the third is to decentralize police functions to reflect community control without the diffusion of responsibility and accountability to a central headquarters.

Present police departments are organized in a military fashion, orders move down the line from the chief to departmental sections assigned law-enforcement functions. These sections usually include such divisions as traffic, patrol, records, detective, juvenile, intelligence, crime-lab, and communications. The principal basis for the assignment of functions, however, is law enforcement;[22] what is needed is a new set of organizational premises so that the basis for the assignment of functions is not law enforcement but the maintenance of order. As Wilson explains:

If order were the central mission of the department, there might be a 'family disturbance squad', a 'drunk and derelict squad', a 'riot control squad', and a 'juvenile squad'; law enforcement matters would be left to a 'felony squad'. Instead, there is a detective division organized, in the larger departments, into units specializing in homicide, burglary, auto theft, narcotics, vice, robbery, and the like. The undifferentiated patrol division gets everything else. Only juveniles tend to be treated by specialized units under both schemes, partly because the law requires or encourages such specialization. The law enforcement orientation of most departments means that new specialized units are created for every offense about which the public expresses concern or for which some special technology is required.[23]

What is called for, then, is a new organizational pattern that will provide a domestic unit (as is now being tried in New York City), a juvenile unit, and a drunk unit with a detoxification center, all with a peace-keeping orientation and peace-keeping functions. Only a felony squad and perhaps a riot squad should be used to enforce the law.

One of the obvious ways in which to improve the morale of the patrolman is to let him do a greater amount of investigative work and to take on the responsibility for 'solving' some of the crimes originating with his patrol. Rewards could then be allocated in accord with the more limited ends of peace-keeping – for instance, in rewarding a patrolman for a decline in the number of drunks who reappear in court. Since no comprehensive policy can be imagined to guide order maintenance, limited ends for various departments must be developed and subjected to public review. The key is to allow the policeman to develop judgment about the motives and future intentions of people with whom he comes in contact, and to reward him for peace-keeping, not 'good pinches' alone.

This reappraisal of the allocation of rewards means, of course, that there must be greater coordination of police and other agencies within the criminal justice system in order to increase the benefits to the client (the offender or the criminal) and break down the isolation of the police.[24] To allow the policeman to assume greater peace-keeping responsibilities would allow him to play a functional role parallel to that of the better general practitioner of medicine: the referral specialist, the coordinator of family health, the source of records and information, and the family friend and counselor. Such an organizational change in the policemen's function would, naturally enough, make community control of the police a greater possibility. It would begin to bridge the chasm between the police and many hostile segments within the public, a process that could be facilitated by the creation of a community-relations division within police departments.

The third needed modification of the present structure of police work is the development of decentralized operations. One of the major trends of the last ten years has been the increase in the lack of attachment people have for their major institutions. Police today suffer from a crisis of legitimacy, and this crisis is heightened by their failure to promote a sense of commitment to their operations by the citizens they serve. One way in which to introduce commitment and a sense of control over the police by members of a community is to make the police more accessible. St. Louis, for example, has experimented with 'storefront' police stations, staffed by a few men who are available as advisers, counselors, protectors, and friends of the people in the immediate neighborhood. If the police should begin to differentiate the role of the patrolman to include the functions of a peace-keeping community agent, the control of these agents should reside in the community. Thus public participation in the decision-making processes of the police would begin at the precinct or neighborhood level; it would not be simply in the form of a punitive civilian review board or a token citizen board at headquarters.

We began with the notion of trouble, police trouble, the troublesome mandate of the policeman. There will be little succor for him as long as our social structure remains fraught with contradictory value premises, with fragmented political power and the consequent inadequate control of the police, with the transformation of public trusts into institutional rights. There will be little succor for him as long as our political agencies resist moving to de-moralize our criminal laws. As it is, we can expect that the management of crime through police strategies and appearances will continue to be a disruptive element in American society.

*From Peter K. Manning,* Policing: A view from the street *(Santa Monica, CA: Goodyear Publishing), 1978, pp 97–125.*

## Notes

1  See Everett C. Hughes, *Men and Their Work* (New York: The Free Press, 1958), chap. 6; *idem,* 'The Study of Occupations', in *Sociology Today,* ed. R.K. Merton, Leonard Broom, and L.S. Cottrell (New York: Basic Books, 1959), 442–58.
2  Hughes, *op. cit.*
3  The President's Commission on Law Enforcement and Administration of Justice (hereafter cited as President's Commission). *The Challenge of Crime in a Free Society* (Washington, D.C.: U.S. Government Printing Office, 1967); and *idem. Task Force Report: The Police* (Washington, D.C.: US Government Printing Office, 1967).
4  The important, sociological notions of 'strategy' and 'tactics' come from military theory and game theory. See, for example, Erving Goffman, *The Presentation of Self in Everyday Life* (Garden City, NY: Doubleday, 1959).
5  *Ibid.*
6  Kenneth Burke, *A Grammar of Motives and a Rhetoric of Motives* (New York: Meridian Books, 1962), 565.
7  D.W. Ball makes this distinction between rhetoric and what he terms 'situated vocabularies' in 'The Problematics of Respectability', in Jack D. Douglas, ed., *Deviance and Respectability* (New York: Basic Books, 1970).
8  These postulates have been drawn from the work of Michael Banton, *The Policeman in the Community* (New York: Basic Books, 1965); the articles in *The Police: Six Sociological Essays,* ed. David Bordua (New York: John Wiley and Sons, 1967), esp. those by Albert J. Reiss and David Bordua, and John H. McNamara; Arthur Niederhoffer, *Behind the Shield* (Garden City, NY: Doubleday, 1967); Jerome Skolnick, *Justice without Trial* (New York: John Wiley and Sons, 1966); and William A. Westley, 'Violence and the Police', *American Journal of Sociology,* 59 (July 1953), 34–41; *idem,* 'Secrecy and the Police', *Social Forces,* 34 (March 1956), 254–57; *idem,* 'The Police: Law; Custom and Morality', in Peter I. Rose, ed. *The Study of Society* (New York: Random

House, 1967). See also James Q. Wilson, *Varieties of Police Behavior: The Management of Law and Order in Eight Communities* (Cambridge, MA: Harvard University Press 1968), *idem*, 'The Police and their Problems: A Theory', *Public Policy*, 12 (1963), 189–216; *idem*, 'Generational and Ethnic Differences among Police Officers', *American Journal of Sociology*, 69 (March 1964), 522–8.

9 Although the imagery of the police and their own self-definition coincide on the dangers of being a policeman, at least one study has found that many other occupations are more dangerous. Policemen kill six times as many people as policemen are killed in the line of duty. In 1955, Robin found that the rate of police fatalities on duty, including accidents, was 33 per 100,000, less than the rate for mining (94), agriculture (55), construction (76), and transportation (44). Between 1950 and 1960, an average of 240 persons were killed each year by policemen – approximately six times the number of policemen killed by criminals. Gerald D. Robin, 'Justifiable Homicide by Police Officers', *Journal of Criminal Law, Criminology and Police Science*, 54 (1963), 225–31.

10 Niederhoffer, *Behind the Shield*, 221.

11 See Richard Quinney, 'Is Criminal Behavior Deviant Behavior?' *British Journal of Criminology*, 5 (April 1965), 133. The material in this section draws heavily from Quinney. See also R.C. Fuller, 'Morals and the Criminal Law', *Journal of Criminal Law, Criminology and Police Science*, 32 (March–April 1942), 624–30.

12 Quinney, *op. cit.*, 133.

13 Wilson, *op. cit.*, 21–2.

14 Skolnick, *op. cit.*, 7–8, 9.

15 This perspective on police work is emphasized by Wilson *op. cit.*; Banton, *op. cit.*; and Skolnick, *op. cit.* In addition, see the more legalistically oriented work of Wayne R. LaFave, *Arrest*, ed. F.J. Remington (Boston: Little, Brown, 1965); Joseph Goldstein, 'Police Discretion not to Invoke the Legal Process: Low-Visibility Decisions in the Administration of Justice', *Yale Law Journal*, 69 (1960), 543–94; and Herman Goldstein, 'Police Discretion: The Ideal Versus the Real', *Public Administration Review*, 23 (September 1963), 140–48.

16 James Q. Wilson, 'What Makes a Better Policeman?' *Atlantic*, 223 (March 1969), 131.

17 LaFave, *op. cit.*

18 Egon Bittner, 'The Police on Skid-Row: A Study of Peace-Keeping', *American Sociological Review*, 32 (October 1967), 699–715.

19 Jerome Skolnick, ed., *The Politics of Protest* (New York: Simon and Schuster, 1969), 252–3.

20 Abraham Blumberg, *Criminal Justice* (Chicago: Quadrangle Press, 1967), 69.

21 Isidore Silver, Introduction to *The Challenge of Crime in a Free Society* (New York: Avon Books, 1968), 25. The President's Commission, *Task Force Report: The Courts*, discusses substantive criminal law, however, and does make some suggestions for legal change.

22 President's Commission, *Task Force Report: The Police*, charts on 46–7.

23 Wilson, *op. cit.*, 69.

24 See John P. Clark, 'The Isolation of the Police: A Comparison of the British and American Situations', in John Scanzoni ed., *Readings in Social Problems* (Boston: Allyn & Bacon, 1967), 384–410. See also David Bordua, 'Comments on Police–Community Relations', mimeographed (Urbana: University of Illinois, n.d.).

# 15. The police as reproducers of order

*Richard V. Ericson*

## Policing: expansive and expensive

Police forces funded by government are a fact of life. The acceleration of their growth and the dispersal of their activities are now so widespread we tend to forget that the modern policing system has been in existence only 150 years. Before that, policing and crime control were mainly in the hands of the 'private' sector (cf Beattie, 1981).

The new police system was not introduced and accepted overnight. At least in Britain, the new police had to work constantly at establishing their legitimacy. There was a general cultural resistance to plainclothes detectives of any type (Moylan, 1929; Miller, 1979; Ericson, 1981: chapter 1), and uniformed officers only gained acceptance via 'tacit contracts' with local populations whereby they used their discretion in law enforcement in exchange for the co-operation of citizens in matters that served the interests of the police and the state (Cohen, 1979; Ignatieff, 1979). As front-line agents in the 'reproduction of social order,' the police eventually gained acceptance and established systematic patterns of operation on this micro-level of everyday transactions with the citizenry. Indeed, they set out to do this from the beginning, after repeated governmental failures in using military force to handle disorder (Silver, 1967).

The legitimacy of modern policing, and its success at keeping intact the glass menagerie of social order, continue to rely first and foremost on this micro-level. However, as policing has evolved it has also entered into other arenas of 'legitimation work'. In keeping with the general trend in modern organizations, police forces have been made professional and bureaucratic. Criteria of efficiency and effectiveness have evolved, particularly in 'crime' work, and these criteria are used in 'selling' the organization to the community.

As we will consider in more detail, the police have been assigned, and have taken on, an impossible responsibility for controlling crime as the key indicator of their success at reproducing order (Manning, 1971, 1977). Regardless of their success in other respects, they have been successful in using their crime work to increase their resources and the dispersal of their activities. Their 'product' of crime control is conveniently elastic, carries a virtuous ring, and cannot be easily assailed: who can deny a people's desire for peace and security, or at least for a *feeling* of security?

There can be no doubt that recent decades have witnessed a major transformation in police organizations in terms of size and resources. In the past three decades in Ontario, for example, the trend has been toward fewer, but larger, more bureaucratic, and more centrally controlled, police forces. In the Toronto area each municipality previously had a separate police force, but these were amalgamated to form the Metropolitan Toronto Police Force in 1957. In the 1970s, several regional municipalities were formed in Ontario, and with them came the amalgamation of many small municipal forces into large, bureaucratic regional forces. Furthermore, many small rural municipalities disbanded their own police forces in favour of using the large, centralized Ontario Provincial Police force. In Ontario in 1962 there were 278 municipal police forces. By 1975 there were only 128.

This trend has been duplicated in other Canadian provinces, and in Britain. Always the argument is that bigger is better (and maybe cheaper). Moreover, whenever a small municipality clings to at least the feeling of autonomy that comes with maintaining its own police force, it is subject to continuing and various pressures to conform with the trend to larger units (Murphy, 1981). If police officers in these small forces are caught by allegations of wrongdoing, the central authorities argue that such things are almost inevitable in forces of this type and that the obvious cure is to take them over as part of a larger regional or provincial policing unit (e.g. 'Tillsonburg Police Probe Ordered,' *Toronto Star*, September 30, 1980). The authorities apparently do not stop to think about the fact that large regional, metropolitan, and national police forces have also experienced continuing, sometimes systematic, wrongdoings by their officers.[1]

At the same time that police forces have expanded through amalgamation, they have also multiplied their manpower and technological resources. Spending on the police in Canada increased at a level far outstripping the rate of inflation (Solicitor General of Canada, 1979). This increase is greater than that in other segments of the system of crime control, and the recent rate of growth is also greater than in other areas of government 'welfare' spending (Chan and Ericson, 1981). Between 1962 and 1977 the number of police personnel per 1,000 population increased 65 per cent from 1.7 to 2.8 (Statistics Canada, *Police Administration Statistics*, 1962 to 1977). While this enormous expansion has been accompanied by greater degrees of specialization in police services, most of this growth has been in patrol policing.[2]

Given this expansion of the police, one would expect to find some basic research on obvious questions: How do the police spend their time? What do they concentrate on and what do they ignore? How do they accomplish their results in dealings with the public? Whose interests are served by these outcomes? What does all of this tell us about the role of the police? What wider functions of the police can be theorized from this?

There is an evolving research tradition that focuses upon these general questions. However, this research is largely American, with a few British studies and virtually no Canadian studies. This [extract], and the research upon which it is based, are aimed at addressing these questions in the Canadian context. The main vehicle for doing this is the use of data collected on the basis of systematic observation in a large Canadian municipal police force. These data are compared with the existing research literature on the police, and related to wider theoretical issues of concern to 'socio-legal' scholars. Before outlining the research design and presenting the results, I shall raise the theoretical issues and define the concepts which inform them.

## The police, crime, and reproducing order

Conventional wisdom–fuelled by the police themselves along with the media, some academics, and other instruments of social reproduction – equates police work with crime work. In television 'cop shows,' in news reports on individual criminal cases, in police annual reports listing levels of crime and clearance rates, and in the research literature dealing with the effectiveness of police as crime fighters, the image is constantly reinforced that crime is, after all, almost everything the police are about.[3] Of course there is talk about the police as a social-service agency – usually including the well-worn assertion that the police are the only 24-hour-a-day 7-days-a-week social-service agency – but in the minds of police officers, in keeping with the thinking of the public, real police work is crime work.

This view has remarkable currency, given that the police, especially the patrol police, actually spend only a tiny fraction of their time dealing with crime or something that could potentially be made into crime, For example, research by the British Home Office included a survey of 12 urban policing areas and found that on average only 6 per cent of a patrol policeman's time was spent on incidents finally defined as 'criminal' (cited by McCabe and Sutcliffe, 1978). Similarly, Reiss (1971: 96) employs data from the Chicago police department to document 'the low productivity of preventive patrol for criminal matters alone, since only about two-tenths of 1 per cent of the time spent on preventive patrol is occupied in handling criminal matters. What is more, only 3 percent of all time spent on patrol involves handling what is officially regarded as a criminal matter'. Various ethnographic studies also document the fact that most patrol-officer contacts with the public do not involve criminal matters (e.g. Cumming et al, 1970; Punch and Naylor, 1973; Cain, 1973; Payne, 1973; Comrie and Kings, 1975; Punch, 1979). Reiss (1971: 73) reports from his Chicago study that 58 per cent of complaints were regarded by the complainants as criminal matters, but only 17 per cent of patrol dispatches to complainants resulted in official processing as criminal incidents.

It is clear that the patrol police do not often have the occasion to designate something as a criminal matter. Indeed, the vast majority of their time is spent alone in their patrol cars without any direct contact with citizens. For example, Pepinsky (1975: 4) reports that more than 85 per cent of police patrol time is spent *not* dealing with citizens.

If, in light of this evidence, one is still committed to a view of the patrol police as crime fighters, one could argue that by their visible presence on the street the patrol police are preventing crime. However, this argument is difficult to sustain. In the Kansas City study by Kelling and associates (1974), it was found that increasing preventive patrol by a factor of two or more over a one-year period had no significant impact upon the incidence of crime (for reviews of this type of research, see Clarke and Heal, 1979; Kelling et al, 1979). Even the most optimistic researchers (Wilson and Boland, 1979) produce results which question the advantage of flooding the streets with large numbers of patrol officers, and of aggressive proactive – i.e. police-initiated – patrol. In their survey of 35 American cities, Wilson and Boland present data to argue that police resources (patrol units on the street), and on-the-street-activity,[4] independently affect the robbery rate after controlling various socio-economic factors. However, the same analysis demonstrates no similar effect for rates of burglary and auto theft.

Furthermore, there is no apparent value in having more patrol cars available for quick response (Pate et al, 1976), except perhaps in a tiny minority of incidents with elements of violence, and as a means of reassuring the citizen with a *feeling* of security. In a recent critique of their own research, Kelling et al (1979) conclude that the introduction and subsequent technological 'refinements' of mobile patrol operations have had no appreciable effect on the incidence of crime (for similar critiques of the role of police technology, see Skolnick, 1966; Rubinstein, 1973; Manning, 1977).

Another factor to consider in deciding whether flooding the streets with patrol officers can stem the tide of crime waves is police recording practices. Given the propensity of bureaucratic police forces to measure the productivity of officers, increasing manpower may increase recording, especially of minor matters (McDonald, 1969, 1976; Chan and Ericson, 1981).

Of course, the primary function of the uniformed police has always been to patrol the petty. Thus in the 1830s, following the establishment of the new police in London, 85 per cent of arrests were for non-indictable offences such as public drunkenness and disturbing the peace (Ignatieff, 1978). Apparently, the more police one has the more petty matters will be pursued, especially if organizational procedures are in place to measure and reward that pursuit.

Evidence from these various sources leads one to conclude that patrol police work is not primarily or essentially about crime prevention or law enforcement. It leads one to question what is the place of the criminal law in the work of patrol officers, and to ask what else is going on as they go about their work. Several researchers on the police, along with other 'socio-legal' scholars and social theorists, have provided some answers to these questions. We shall summarize their views – an apparently shared understanding that the patrol police are essentially a vehicle in the 'reproduction of order'.

'Order' is a multi-faceted word that has at least seven meanings pertinent to our concerns (*Oxford Paperback Dictionary*, 1979: 445): 'a condition in which every part or unit is in its right place or in a normal or efficient state, *in good working order: out of order*; the condition brought about by good and firm government and obedience to the laws, law and order; a system of rules or procedure; a command, an instruction given with authority; a written direction ... giving authority to do something; a rank or class in society, the lower orders; a kind or sort or quality, *showed courage of the highest order.*'

The mandate of police patrol officers is to employ a system of rules and authoritative commands to transform troublesome, fragile situations back into a normal or efficient state whereby the ranks in society are preserved. This is to be done according to means which appear to be of the highest quality and is directed at the appearance of good and firm government.

Of course, it is not the mandate of the police to produce a new order. On the contrary, their everyday actions are directed at reproducing the existing order (the 'normal or efficient state') and the order (system of rules) by which this is accomplished. They are one tool of 'policing' in the wider sense of all governmental efforts aimed at disciplining, refining, and improving the population. As such, most of what they do is part of the social machinery of verifying and reproducing what is routinely assumed to be the case (cf Berger and Luckmann, 1966: chapter 2). Their sense of order and the order they seek to reproduce are that of the *status quo*.[5]

The order arising out of their action is a reproduction because it is made with reference to the existing order and designed to keep it in its original form. However, the 'seed of change' is contained in every 'interactional sequence' (Giddens, 1976) and the outcome may not quite duplicate what was there before the interaction. Moreover, the term 'reproduction' implies that order is not simply transmitted in an unproblematic manner but is worked at through processes of conflict, negotiation, and subjection.

The police are the most visible front-line agents for ordering the population. They represent the extreme end of the 'carceral continuum' (Foucault, 1977), serving as a model of judicial-legal ideology. To the extent that they are successful in portraying their work as professional according to the principles of formal legal rationality (cf Balbus, 1973) and bureaucratic rationality, the police accomplish legitimacy as agents of the state. They can convince the citizenry that they are being policed as legal subjects instead of 'class' subjects (cf Cohen, 1979: 129–30).

The police have always had an ideological function as well as a repressive function. They have been repeatedly employed as an 'advance guard' of municipal reform, especially for altered uses of social space and time (public order), and protection of property, to ensure free circulation of commodities (including labour power) (*ibid*: 120). Yet part of their success has been to present their problems as technical, related to the control of crime, rather than as ideological: they have difficulty controlling crime because the laws are inadequate; they do not have the communications system necessary to reduce response time; they do not have sufficient manpower to have a deterrent effect, and so on.

The police actively campaign to have the community believe that things will be more orderly if the police are supplied with better cars, better crime laboratories, better-trained police officers, more enabling laws, and so on. The effort is reflected in extensive public relations, including follow-up interviews with victims of crime to make it appear that something is being done (Greenwood *et al* 1975; Sanders, 1977; Ericson, 1981), displays at shopping plazas, lectures to students and to other selected groups in the community, and using press officers who generate contacts with the media and 'feed' them (cf Fishman, 1978, 1980). In these efforts the police are concerned not with the dangerous 'symbolic assailant' as conceived by Skolnick (1966), but rather with the symbolic support of 'respectable' citizens who encourage police efforts directed at anyone but themselves.

In addition to reproducing legal and bureaucratic ideology, the police also impose social discipline in the name of public propriety (Cohen, 1979). They are responsible for establishing a fixed presence in the community for systematic surveillance. They patrol with a suspicious eye for the wrong people in the wrong places at the wrong times, reproducing a 'social penalty of time and place' (Foucault, 1977). Far from being unsystematic and arbitrary, this work is based on established rules and produces regular results. The patrol officer is more likely to watch closely and stop on suspicion a young man in his 'shagwagon'[6] than a granny in her stationwagon, because the former is more likely to have contraband and is deemed more in need of being kept in his proper place.

The police have a sense of the order they are there to reproduce. This is reflected in the activities they are taught to pursue, in the techniques they are taught to use in pursuit, and in their own identification with the values of middle-class respectability. In keeping with the entire reproductive apparatus of the state, they are there to ensure that everyone possible appears to be the middle Canadian in theory and the working Canadian in practice. Their sense of order is reflexive: they think that they are doing what the powerful and respectable want at the same time as they see this as something they themselves support, but in a way that sustains their own sense of autonomy and purpose.

As Bittner (e.g. 1967, 1967a, 1970) and Manning (e.g. 1977, 1979, 1980) have argued, this sense of order frames the resources needed to maintain it. That is, in dealing with any particular situation the patrol officer decides what, if anything, is out of order and then employs the various tools at his disposal to reconstruct order. If he is seeking compliance from a citizen, he can rely upon the aura of the general authority of his office; his procedural legal powers to detain, search, and use physical force; his substantive legal powers to charge; and various manipulative strategies that form art of the 'recipe' knowledge of his craft. In short, he 'negotiates order', variously employing strategies of coercion, manipulation, and negotiation (Strauss, 1978).[7] This work is always carried out with respect to rules, including legal rules, administrative rules, and 'recipe' rules of the occupational culture of line officers. In other words, it is the work of producing and controlling deviance, of using social rules in the construction of social order (cf Douglas, 1971).

This view of how order is constituted is neither 'high sociology' (Rock, 1979) nor empiricist sociology of the 'phenomenological' variety. Rather, it is a 'search ... for a joining of social structural and social interactional considerations but with [an] antideterministic stance still intact' (Strauss, 1978: 16; see also Ranson et al., 1980). Attention is focused upon the strategies of coercion, manipulation, and negotiation, and the patterns these indicate, which allow particular parties to secure their interests and sustain advantages over others. These strategies are conceived as deriving from social structure, and their use in interaction serves to reproduce dialectically social structure. The task of the sociologist using this model is primarily empirical: to examine at close hand the strategic interaction as it is used by one's subjects in the reproduction of social order.[8]

Within this 'transactional' view, the police are conceived as 'enacting' their environment as well as reacting to it (Weick, 1969: 63–4; Manning, 1979: 29). While they are responsive to the community and operate within particular elements of social organization (Black, 1968), they also carve out part of their mandate based on properties of their own organization. On the macro-level, this interplay is indicated by such things as public-relations campaigns, setting up special units (e.g. community-relations officer units; ethnic-relations units), and 'selling' the organization in terms of the community's 'crime problem'. On the micro-level the mutual influences of the community organization and police organization are seen in the level and nature of reactive (citizen-initiated) mobilization and proactive (police-initiated) mobilization and in the specific approach taken by police officers and citizens in various types of troubles they come together to deal with.

In studying the reciprocal influences between community forces and police forces, there is no point in trying to weigh up the forces on each side and making a final decision as to who controls. Apart from the inevitable looseness of any such measurement, by the time such an exercise was completed new forces would have come into play requiring remeasurement or, more probably, a new system of measurement. However, one thing is clear. In the past few decades the police, along with other forms of governmental policing, have become a force to be reckoned with. As Banton (1964: 6) has observed, the police have changed their role from being 'professional citizens' who carry out 'obligations which fall on all citizens', to 'an official exercising authority and power over citizens'. Much of this authority and power comes from within the bureaucratic organization of policing rather than from the law or other community sources.

Something not so clear is the complex ways the police, and political powers in the community, maintain their legitimacy while going about their everyday work. People do not like to be interfered with, lectured, badgered, and harassed, yet the patrol officer must do these things every day. Perhaps they are able to do this routinely because of the macro-level 'selling job' done by the administration, associations of chiefs of police, police associations, politicians, and the media. 'The more resources allocated to increasing the efficiency of repressive policing, the more manpower has to be poured into "community relations" to restabilize the public image of the force' (Cohen, 1979: 133).

As stated earlier, a major part of this 'image work' is carried out in terms of the police mandate to control crime. A lot of work is done via the media, and official statistics of crime rates and clearance rates, to support the view that the police are struggling to keep the lid on the massive amounts of deviance in the community. The police are held responsible for crime control, even though the causes of crime (social, economic, cultural, and political) are clearly beyond their control (cf Manning, 1971, 1977, 1980).

This situation is ripe for contradiction. The police have to show that they can keep the lid on crime and generally keep the streets clean, yet not so successfully as to suggest that they do not need more resources to fight crime and other filthy activity. Thus there has to be a lot of the disorder they are selling themselves as being able to reduce in order to justify more resources. More generally, the police are agents of the *status quo*, of consensus, yet each incident they deal with belies the consensus they symbolize. Some researchers (e.g. Wilson, 1968) have observed that in more heterogeneous communities where conflict is great there is likely to be a trend toward policing that is oriented to law enforcement. The irony is that the less the consensus the more the police are used as symbols to produce the appearance that there is consensus.

The very existence of crime control in a community indicates that other means of control have failed and is testimony to the degree of conflict in the community. Moreover, high levels of crime control mean that the symbolic aspects of the wider institutions of law itself are failing. The more repressive the reaction becomes, the more visible are the main contours of conflict and contradiction. In these circumstances the police are most able to increase their own power, even to the point of having some effect on the legislative process itself (Chambliss and Seidman, 1971: especially 68; see also Hall et al, 1978; Cohen, 1979; Taylor, 1980).

This process has the characteristics of 'deviance amplification' as discussed by 'labelling' theorists (Wilkins, 1964; Schur, 1971; Ericson, 1975; Ditton, 1979). The typical reaction to *indicators* of conflict such as crime is to expand the apparatus of control. This occurs not only in more visible forms such as increased resources for the police, but also in expansion of the welfare state (Chan and Ericson, 1981). One effect is an amplifying spiral of official reactions, including an increased rate of officially designated crime (McDonald, 1976: especially chapter 6).

All of this leads one to suspect that the police and other agencies in the reproductive apparatus are not out to eradicate the phenomena they deal with, but to classify, record, contain, and use them in perpetuity (Foucault, 1977). One must suspect that their mandate to constitute and deal with crime distorts more fundamental processes and that the popular conception of the police as crime fighters must itself be treated as creating a problem for both the police and the community. Crime control is an impossible task for the police alone. They are expected to handle a phenomenon caused by social, political, economic, and cultural forces beyond their control and have to give the *appearance* that things are (more or less) under control. Thus there is bound to be a gulf between the structured rhetoric about the police and crime and the everyday reality of policing. One part of the order the police reproduce is the mystical one of crime control, of 'lawandorder,' but their everyday work is of a different order.[9]

The empirical focus of the research reported [here] is the everyday work of the patrol police and the structures reproduced by their work. These structures have systems of rules which control, guide, and justify their actions. We now turn to a discussion of those rules as they relate to the more general question of police powers (discretion) and how these powers are used in the reproduction of order.

## Police discretion and uses of rules

Discretion is the power to decide which rules apply to a given situation and whether or not to apply them. Legal scholars traditionally view discretion in terms of what *official* rules can be held to govern the actions of policemen. These rules include laws and administrative instructions. For example, Pound (1960) sees discretion as an authority conferred by law to make considered judgments under specified conditions; it belongs 'to the twilight zone between law and morals' where the official has the autonomy to make judgments within a framework provided by the law.

Some lawyers and sociologists have defined discretion in terms of whether decisions are, or can be, reviewed according to official rules. Thus Goldstein (1960) is concerned with decisions of 'low visibility' in which the police officer takes no official action – he does not write an official report and does not invoke the criminal process via arrest and charge. Goldstein sees these actions as discretionary because there is no routine opportunity for administrative or judicial review. This is similar to Reiss's (1974: 67) definition of discretionary justice existing 'whenever decisions made in criminal cases are not legally or practically open to re-examination'.

'Low visibility' is just one resource available to police officers to maintain control over their decisions. Moreover, while a specific decision may not be reviewed, or may not even be practically reviewable, legal and administrative rules are nevertheless taken into account in making the decision. These rules remain 'invisible', but they do have an effect.[10]

The question of effects brings us to the essential aspects of the concept of discretion. Davis (1969:4) refers to discretion as existing 'whenever the *effective* limits on [the official's] power leave him free to make a choice among possible courses of action or inaction' (emphasis added). The limits are not only the formal expectations of the criminal law and administrative rules, but also expectations from other sources such as the occupational culture of police officers and specific groups in the community. Black (1968: 25) provides a complementary definition of police discretion 'as the autonomy of decision-making that an officer has'.

Obviously the definition of discretion in terms of effective limits and autonomy incorporates a conception of *power*. Power involves the probability that one party in an encounter can effect a course of action and outcome he desires in spite of the contrary wishes and/or actions of the other parties. As such power is a *potential* element in any interaction but it is not necessarily exercised. It is therefore difficult to gauge power empirically, except via an analysis of the power resources of the parties being studied, and through observing instances and rates of compliance. As a potential element power mediates between actors' intentions and the realization of outcomes. In use, power involves the mobilization of resources to effect outcomes which serve particular interests.

Another way of formulating the definitions of discretion provided by Davis and by Black is to say that in situations where others do not have the power to circumscribe the person's action, he himself has power because he can choose a course of action and effect an outcome that reflects that choice. Any analysis of decisions made during a sequence of interactions must take into account the relative power advantages of the participants. Who has the advantage is heavily dependent upon access to and control over resources that can be mobilized to influence others to one's own advantage (Turk, 1976). Thus, a focal point for the analysis of power is the resources available to effect it. 'The use of power in interaction can be understood in terms of resources or facilities which participants bring to and mobilize as elements of its production, thus directing its course' (Giddens, 1976: 112).

One group's acquisition of autonomy may involve another group's loss of autonomy, In what area does a group have the ability to coerce, manipulate, or negotiate the establishment of its own rules which others conform to? Those who have control over the law-making process, other agencies of crime control, police supervisors, and various groups of citizens are all able to use rules limiting the choices of patrol officers, while these officers can in turn use rules from these sources and their own 'recipe' ruled to control their working environment.

The use of rules in organizational contexts has been a key topic of enquiry among sociologists studying police work. Part of this enquiry has focused on the discovery of the framework of rules used by police officers to constitute their 'sense of order'.[11] This is necessarily an empirical task. For the sociologist, as for the actors he studies, 'to know a rule is not to be able to provide an abstract formulation of it, but to know how to apply it to novel circumstances, which includes knowing about the context of its application' (Giddens, 1976: 124). Rules as stated formally have a fictional character; this can only be understood, and the operating rules gleaned, by examining rules in action (Chambliss and Seidman, 1971). As Manning (1977a: 44) emphasizes, 'since the context of rules, not the rules themselves, nor the rules about the rules (so characteristic of formal organizations), determine the consequential (i.e., actionable) meanings of acts, situated interactions, accounts and shared understandings should be examined'.

Rules serve as tools of power and as justifiers of actions taken. In the case of criminal-law rules, the police have an enabling resource to control what and whom are proceeded against and to legitimate actions taken. The law provides 'cover' in two senses. It provides 'blanket' cover through the wide range of substantive offences available to handle any troublesome situation the officer is likely to confront (Bittner, 1967, 1967a, 1970; Chatterton, 1976). Also, the legal procedures for police actions are so enabling that there are very few instances when what the officer wishes to do cannot be legitimated legally (McBarnet, 1979, 1981).

Beyond this, the police officer has control over the production of 'facts' about a case, and this control of knowledge becomes a very potent form of power. The rules are not only taken into account, but they also form part of the account to legitimate the action taken (Kadish and Kadish, 1973; Sanders, 1977; Ericson, 1981, 1981a). In sum, the normative order of rules made applicable and the meanings applied to a situation are closely related (Giddens, 1976: 109, 110). The powerful nature of rules is not to be gleaned from 'perceptible determination of behaviour', but rather in how rules 'constrain people to *account* for their rule-invocations, rule violations, and rule applications' (Carlen, 1976, referring to Durkheim, 1964).

The motive for patrol officers' actions comes from particular interests defined within their occupational culture. This includes an array of 'recipe' rules which guide him on how to get the job done in ways that will appear acceptable to the organization, which persons in what situations should be dealt with in particular ways (e.g. who should be 'targeted' for stops on suspicion, who should be charged for specific offence-types, etc.), how to avoid supervisors and various organizational control checks, when it is necessary to produce 'paper' regarding an incident or complaint, and so on. No matter what interests provide the motive, the law can provide the *opportunity* to achieve an outcome reflecting those interests (McBarnet, 1976, 1979, 1981).

The criminal law becomes a 'residual resource' used when other methods of resolving a situation are unavailable or have been tried and are unsuccessful. Similar to the way citizens use the police (cf Black, 1968; Reiss, 1971), police use the law according to what other forms of social control are available and can be used effectively. For the patrol police, this is particularly the case in interpersonal disputes and problems of public order and decorum. When all else fails or is deemed likely to fail, the officer decides he must remove one party in the conflict from the situation, and consequently he arrests someone. A specific infraction with a clearly applicable law does not determine the arrest, but rather the law is used to make the arrest to handle the situation. As Chatterton (1973, 1976) found, charges are sometimes used 'as the legal vehicle for conveying someone to the police station and ... the grounds for the *decision to use it* [are] to be found elsewhere than in the reasons provided to justify its use to the courts'.[12]

The patrol officer's concern for the law as an 'all purpose control device' (Bittner, 1970: 108) bears on how he can make it applicable across a range of situations. From his viewpoint, the broader the applicability the better the law, which may explain why the police resist legal changes which decrease their repertoire (cf Goldstein, 1970: 152). When the law is changed, other laws have to be used to serve the same purpose. For example, Ramsay (1972: 65) refers to liquor-law changes in Saskatchewan which prevented police officers from continuing to charge for intoxication in public places; RCMP members continued to arrest and charge persons intoxicated in public places, substituting the 'causing a disturbance' provision of the Criminal Code.

The procedural criminal law is also enabling for the patrol police.[13] As McBarnet (1976, 1979, 1981) has argued, Packer's (1968) dichotomy between a due-process model of procedural protections for the accused and a crime control model of expedient law enforcement turns out to be not a dichotomy at all, especially in countries such as England, Scotland, and Canada where the suspect and accused do not have entrenched rights. In the law as written, and the law in action, 'due process if *for* crime control'. That is, the rules of procedure as written and used explicitly serve the expedient ends of law enforcement. Even in the United States, where rights are entrenched, there is frequently no empirical referent in law for ideals such as the rule of law or due process (Black, 1972). Furthermore, empirical studies on the implementation of due-process rules such as *Miranda* v *Arizona* (1966) 384 US 436 US Sup Ct indicate that the rules are routinely sidestepped or incorporated into existing police practices (e.g. Wald *et al*, 1967; Medalie *et al*, 1968; Ayres, 1970). As Thurman Arnold (1962), cited by Carlen (1976: 95), states, 'When a great government treats the lowliest of criminals as an equal antagonist ... we have a gesture of recognition to the dignity of the individual which has an extraordinary dramatic appeal. Its claim is to our emotions, rather than on our common sense.' As pragmatic actors whose 'recipe' rules for practice are based on common sense, the police can use the procedural law to achieve the outcomes they deem appropriate.

Criminal-law rules, along with administrative rules and rules within the occupational culture, are also useful to patrol officers in formulating accounts that will justify their actions. Thus, rules are used prospectively in taking action, and retrospectively in showing to interested others (especially supervisory officers and the courts) that the action taken was justifiable and appropriate. Prospectively, one rule of the occupational culture is 'Unless you have a good story, don't do it' (Chatterton, 1979: 94). Justice becomes a matter of justifications, as patrol officers set out to do what they believe is necessary to put things in order. They seek the 'cover' of legitimate justifications and take their decisions with a view to 'covering their ass' *vis à vis* any possible source of objection. Indeed, this is the only form of 'under-cover' work patrol officers routinely undertake! In addition to other forms of patrol work, they patrol the facts of 'what happened', transforming a conflict with a colourful kaleidoscope of complexities into a black-and-white 'still' of factual-legal discourse.

Manuals provide instruction on how to write reports to impress favourably other actors in the crime-control network (e.g. Inbau and Reid, 1967: 129). Socio-legal research also informs us about techniques of this nature. Sanders (1977) examines the process of report construction, showing how the same facts can be used to legitimate a range of offence types, or no offence at all. Wald and associates (1967: 1554) suggest that the police often take statements from accused persons simply as a basis for convincing the prosecutor that a case exists at all. Skolnick (1966: 133) notes how the rules of criminal discovery in the jurisdiction he studied require the prosecutor to allow the defence lawyer to examine arrest reports, producing a situation where 'the police do not report as the significant events leading to arrest what an unbiased observer viewing the situation would report. Instead they compose a description that satisfies legal requirements without interfering with their own organizational requirements.

In saying the police officer is able to construct the facts of the case, we are not saying that it is a fabrication, although there are many accounts of police fabrication and perjury (see Buckner, 1970: especially 99–100; Morand, 1976; Morris, 1978). Our point is that the rules become embedded in the formulations used to make the case, so that it is difficult to distinguish between the generation of fact, its provision to senior officers and the court, and the use of rules for its accomplishment (see Sanders, 1977: especially 98–99; and generally, Ditton, 1979). Thus, the way in which factual accounts and rules are intertwined makes it difficult to establish what is a fabrication and what is not.

In summary, rules are a power resource of the patrol officer in accomplishing whatever seems appropriate to the situation. Discretion takes rules into account; it is not necessarily a deviation from or outside legal rules. As we shall see in the next section, these rules have many sources and can serve varied functions. Ours is not a government of law; it is a government of men who *use* law. [14]

## The organizational forums of police work

Patrol officers go about their work sensitive to expectations from the organizations within which they operate, including the community, the law and court organizations, and the police organization. The literature on the police deals with influences from each of these sources, but individual studies tend to emphasize one source to the virtual, and sometimes complete, exclusion of others.

One tradition of enquiry explores the influence of the community. These studies consider the influence on police decisions of citizens dealing with the police (informant, victim, complainant, suspect, accused) and of the circumstances in which they encounter the police (who mobilizes the police, where the encounter takes place, the nature of the matter in dispute). These studies are similar to the multiple-factor approaches used in asking why people commit crimes, but here the question has shifted to why a policeman charges people, records an occurrence, and so on.

Patrol officers typically have little information besides the appearance of an individual and of a situation. They can perhaps learn more from accounts and from documents shown them (e.g. driver's licence), and the CPIC (Canadian Police Information Centre) system. Many encounters involve 'negotiation of status claims' (Hudson, 1970: 190) – officers look for and employ status 'cues' to determine what action they should take; in this sense, 'police activity is as much directed to who a person is as to what he does' (Bittner, 1970: 10).[15] The more that other types of information are lacking, the more the officer is likely to forge a stereotypical response based on a 'second code' (MacNaughton-Smith, 1968) of these criteria, which may ultimately be used to define the situation as a legal problem.

The studies of this type are centred upon two central variables of American sociological inquiry, race and socio-economic standing, as these are influenced by and influence other variables, especially demeanour, the nature of the incident (seriousness, evidence available, dispute type), and whether the person is 'out of place'. Some researchers have argued that variables of citizen input make spurious simple relationships between status and role characteristics and police decision-making; to the extent members of racial minorities and those of low socio-economic standing tend to be 'unstable', less deferential, and to request particular forms of police action, police activity towards them is different from that towards other types of citizens.

Black (1968) demonstrates that in reactively mobilized encounters, the most important determinants (in addition to seriousness of the alleged offence and evidence questions) of police action to record an occurrence or arrest are the preference of 'the complainant, the social distance between complainant and suspect, and the degree of deference shown by both complainant and suspect. When the complainant's preference for action is unclear the degree of deference shown by the suspect becomes a significant influence. In these situations, blacks tend to be more disrespectful towards the police, thereby increasing the probability of arrest (Black, 1971: 1101). 'Negroes, it is clear, have a disproportionate vulnerability to arrest mainly because they are disproportionately disrespectful toward police officers' (Black, 1968: 231).

Sykes and Clark (1975) attempt to show that it is because lower-status people have less ability to express deference that they more often end up being officially processed. They confirm Black's findings concerning non-white lower-status citizens, who are more likely to be unilaterally disrespectful to the police than whites and those of higher status. They show also that the police are reciprocally more disrespectful to young, male suspects in order-maintenance situations and least likely to be disrespectful in service calls involving women, senior citizens, and the middle class.

Several other researchers, using a variety of methods, have considered the influence of the offender's deference and demeanour on police action. Sullivan and Siegel (1974: 253), in a decision-game study, found that the 'attitude of the offender' was the most important item selected by police-officer subjects in reaching a final decision about whether or not to arrest. Research on police handling of juvenile offenders has also emphasized this aspect (Werthman and Piliavin, 1967; Chan and Doob, 1977). Similarly, it has been shown that traffic-law offenders are more likely to be ticketed if they are 'offensive' than if they are 'respectful' (Gardiner, 1969: 151; Pepinsky, 1975: 41).

There is no consensus among researchers on all facets of police response to citizens' preference and suspects' deference. In the research by Reiss and Black, in 14 per cent of reactive encounters the complainant requested unofficial handling of a felony or misdemeanour, and the police invariably complied (Reiss, 1971: 83). Moreover, Black (1968: 216–17) concludes that 'the police are more likely to arrest a misdemeanor suspect who is disrespectful toward them than a felony suspect who is civil'. In their research, Clark and Sykes (1974: 483n) found that the police almost invariably record, and arrest where possible, in felonies regardless of complainant preference or suspect deference.

Other explanations claim that the poor and blacks are particularly vulnerable when 'out of place', i.e. in social or geographical contexts in which they do not normally participate (Bayley and Mendelsohn, 1969:93; Werthman and Piliavin, 1967:78; Rubinstein, 1973: part II). Others have attempted to demonstrate that the important influences are the occupational and domestic stability of the suspect. For example, Skolnick (1966: 84–5) argues that blacks are more likely to be arrested by warrant officers because they are less likely 'to possess the middle-class virtues of occupational and residential stability' that would lead the officers to believe that fine payments could be met. Green (1970) presents data to demonstrate that blacks are more likely to possess such lower-class characteristics as residential mobility and working at marginal jobs or being unemployed, and that these characteristics rather than race *per se* account for higher arrest rates. Werthman and Piliavin (1967: 84) point out that citizens with these characteristics are aware of how the police assess them and manipulate their appearances accordingly. For example, some of their subjects who were unmarried wore wedding rings 'in order to bolster their moral status in the eyes of the police'.

The influence of personal characteristics, especially socio-economic status, has also been shown to vary by how the police are mobilized and the nature of the matter in dispute. Black (1968) and Reiss (1971) introduced the distinction between proactive (police-initiated) and reactive (citizen-initiated) mobilizations. Proactive policing is directed at lower-status citizens who present problems of public order, or who are out of place. As John Stuart Mill remarked, one of the benchmarks of civilization is the extent to which the unpleasant or uncivilized aspects of existence are kept away from those who most enjoy the benefits of civilization. Patrol officers have a mandate to reproduce civilization in this form, maintaining the boundaries of deviant ghettos and keeping the streets clean of those who are, at the most, offensive rather than offenders (Scull, 1977; Cohen, 1979).

Proactive policing also occurs in traffic regulation, and here higher-status people have frequent contact with the police. Proactive traffic work has been identified as a major area of conflict between the police and the public, e.g. Royal Commission on the Police, 1962: 114; Willett, 1964; Black, 1968: 14. Higher-status citizens view the police largely as reactive agents responding to their complaints, not as proactive pursuers of minor technical violations (Cressey, 1974: 219). Furthermore, they know patrol officers frequently do not charge for traffic offences. Several writers (*ibid*: 227; LaFave, 1965: 131–2; Grosman, 1975: 2) have stressed that when the police are known to ignore violations systematically this becomes a public expectation; a hostile reaction can occur when someone is selected out and issued a summons. Enforcement of traffic laws is the one area where technically based full enforcement of observed violations is possible, and yet discretion is very frequently used there. Order is reproduced through *selective* use of the law.

According to Reiss and Black, the vast majority of patrol police mobilizations are reactive (87 per cent in their study). They use this finding in support of their argument that the patrol police are dependent on citizens and operate mainly as servants responsive to public demands.

Citizens mobilize the police ('the law') as a power resource to assist in handling their own troubles and conflicts: 'The empirical reality of law is that it is a set of resources for which people contend and with which they are better able to promote their own ideas and interests against others' (Turk, 1976: abstract of article). Mobilizing the police as the first step in using the law is usually done 'less for a sense of civic duty than from an expectation of personal gain' (Reiss, 1971: 173). The 'middle orders' do not typically initiate direct contact with the police except when they are victims of property crime (Black, 1968: 185). The 'lower orders' frequently use the police for this purpose and also mobilize them to handle interpersonal conflicts because other forms of social control have failed, are unavailable, or are absent. There may be conflict over the rules of a relationship, with at least one party trying to establish order by the threat of using the external formal rules which the police have at their disposal (*ibid*: 108, 181). Research shows that this type of demand is especially frequent at particular times and in particular places (Cumming *et al*, 1970: 187) and among the 'lower orders' (Black, 1971, 1972, 1976; Meyer, 1974: 81–2; Bottomley, 1973: 45).

Obviously mobilization, type of dispute, citizen characteristics, and citizen input influence decision-making by patrol officers […] However, we must also consider the internal dynamics of the police organization and the legal organization within which the police operate. There are major limitations in studies which concentrate on characteristics of the community. These studies, following the work of Reiss and Black, tend to overemphasize the reactive role of the police and their apparent dependence on the public. Reiss and Black's findings on reactive policing probably reflect their sampling methods [...] and their model is generally one of 'stimulus-response'. Many encounters, however, are long-lasting and complex, with both sides trying to coerce, manipulate, and/or negotiate an outcome that serves particular interests.

'Crime is, above all, a function of the resources available to know it' (Manning, 1972: 234). The citizen can choose not to inform the police about a particular instance of trouble. If he reports it, he can formulate the trouble in ways he believes will influence police actions in the direction he himself wants. He also has choices about giving police access to information (e.g. school, employment, credit records); the police are dependent upon 'those socially structured features of everyday life which render persons findable' (Bittner, 1967a: 706). He can also influence the patrol officer by appealing police actions through the citizen complaint bureau of the police department or through legal action.[16]

The police officer in turn has several resources at his disposal. These include the law, the 'low visibility' of his actions, and the general aura of his office. Manning (1979: 24–6) suggests the significance of calls for service has been exaggerated in previous research. The officer has discretionary power outside the control of his supervisors to transform the encounter. He can use his organizational resources to convince the citizen that the action he is taking is the most appropriate and legitimate one (for examples, see Ericson, 1981: chapter 5). The officer's efforts are eased by the public-relations work of the force as a whole. 'One of the first explanations for police investment in provision of services only peripherally related to law enforcement is that this gives them knowledge and control in situations that have been previously associated with disruption of law and order' (Clark and Sykes, 1974: 462). If the force in general, or a specific policy, is sold properly it can help to further citizen co-operation in providing information and can ultimately generate more crime and other products for the police to commit to their records.[17]

In sum, the more appropriate model is a transactional one of stimulus-interpretation-response. General patterns may be revealed in quantifying status-role and dispute characteristics, but one must also examine how these patterns, and indeed the decisions themselves, are produced. A blend of quantitative and qualitative analysis is called for, and this is the approach we have taken.

A qualitative analysis allows for a better account of the role of legal and police organizational elements. For example, even a cursory examination of the law reveals that many citizen characteristics treated by researchers as 'extra-legal' are an integral part of the written law. This is clearly the case in police handling of juveniles; showing that charging and cautioning are significantly related to status, stability, and respectability should therefore come as no surprise (e.g. Chan and Doob, 1977). Similarly, specific statutes, such as the Bail Reform Act in Canada, for handling adult offenders, rely explicitly on criteria of stability and respectability such as place of residence and previous criminal record. Furthermore, what happens inside a police organization influences the initiation of encounters with citizens and what happens during those encounters. Available manpower, organizational priorities, production expectations, 'recipe' rules for 'targeting' segments of the population, and many other elements influence transactions and the production of case outcomes. In sum, the patrol officer's sense of order in the community is inextricably bound up with his sense of legal order and police organizational order, and these must be taken into consideration in a full account of police work.

Another aspect of legal organization which patrol officers incorporate into their actions is the organization of the court system, including the roles and rules used by judges, justices of the peace, defence lawyers, and crown attorneys. While the historic constitutional position of the constable is that he is answerable to the law alone, in practice he must justify his actions to other actors whose job it is to use the law. He must establish relationships with the various actors in court and respond to their expectations and rules (some of which may have the force of law), in order to achieve outcomes that serve organizational interests.

The constitutional position of the police has meant that the judiciary has not generally interfered with police discretion to investigate or to invoke the criminal process. For example, in the well-known *Blackburn* cases in Britain – *R. v Metropolitan Police Commissioner ex parte Blackburn* (1968) 1 All ER 763; *R. v Metropolitan Police Commissioner ex parte Blackburn* (1973) 1 All ER 324 – the court of appeals stated the opinion that the courts will only intercede regarding a chief officer's discretion where there is an abdication of responsibility for law enforcement in a particular area of criminal law. For example, if a police force had a policy not to charge for housebreaking or theft where the loss was relatively small, the courts would step in; but there would be no intervention in individual cases, or where the policy covers types of crime such as statutory rape involving couples close in age. In everyday law enforcement it is up to the police themselves to decide what action to take.

In spite of this general distance, there are obviously many ways in which judges can and do influence police actions. They can alter the administrative organization of the court in a way that leads to a change in police practice. For example, Gardiner (1969: 132) describes a situation where night-shift police officers were reluctant to issue traffic summonses because they would have to work irregular hours by appearing in court on the next day shift; a traffic-court judge began to allow deferred appearances in court, and the night-shift officers began to write more traffic tickets. Judges also have considerable control *within* some areas of the law. The law of confessions in Canada is made by judges, and decision-making on the admissibility of confessions in each individual case is largely subjective (Kaufman, 1974).

Judicial practices in sentencing can influence police practices in charging. Some researchers (e.g. Grosman, 1969; Klein, 1976) have pointed out that the tendency of Canadian judges to give concurrent sentences for multiple convictions gives the police less bargaining power in laying multiple charges with the intention of later withdrawing some in exchange for a guilty plea. British research indicates that in jurisdictions where police are reluctant to caution rather than charge people for minor offences, the courts tend to give a relatively large number of nominal sentences such as discharges; conversely, where police cautioning rates are high nominal sentencing rates are low (Bottomley, 1973: 72; Steer, 1970: 20). The unwillingness of the courts to grant sentences other than discharges for certain types of offences and offenders may encourage the police to handle them without charge. The court can support the local police in the way it deals with certain types of charges that arise out of conflicts between police and citizens, such as 'assault police' or 'causing a disturbance' (see Williams, 1974: 186–7). The degree to which the court upholds these charges, which usually rely solely on police testimony, may affect the degree to which the police will use formal charges in these situations as opposed to more summary actions.

Similar to their use of rules coming from other sources, police officers incorporate the rules of judicial practice into their own practices. They are very successful at doing this, in some cases continuing or even strengthening their existing practices while managing a show of conformity with the new rules. Of course, this is a typical result of attempts to introduce new rules in any organizational setting.[18]

The police are able to sustain control over the criminal process because of their 'positional advantage' (Cook, 1977) *vis à vis* the other agents of criminal control. The police have 'low visibility' to these other agents and produce the information required by these others. The latter are thus heavily dependent and must act on trust without any routine independent checks on how the police have made their case.

The research literature abounds with examples of these relationships and speculation on their effects. Blumberg (1970: especially 281) describes how the police develop exchange relationships with prosecutors and defense counsel, who are co-opted as 'agent mediators' to encourage the accused to enter guilty pleas. Prosecutors are heavily dependent on the police for evidence and they reciprocate by accepting police recommendations and practices in a way that allows the police to influence the decision-making authority of the prosecutor (Skolnick, 1966: especially 179, 191; Ericson, 1981: chapter 6). Applications for warrants from justices are routinely granted, usually without question (LaFave, 1965:34; Ericson 1981: chapter 6). Similarly, police information and recommendations are crucial in decisions to grant release from custody and bail conditions (Bottomley, 1973: especially 101–3).

Undoubtedly, the police officer must keep in mind the rules of these others as he goes about preparing his case, operating with a set of 'prefigured justifications' (Dalton, 1959) in the event his actions are challenged. However, because of his skill at doing this and because of the organizational arrangements in court, he is rarely challenged. In the vast majority of cases the accused pleads guilty, and the judge knows little if anything as to why that decision was made, including police influences on it. While there is a formal judicial power to enquire into whether or not the plea of guilty was in order – *Adgey* v *The Queen* (1973) 23 CRNS 278 – this is rarely done (cf Grosman, 1969: 30). In this sense most criminal cases result in a determination of guilt without judicial review and control, and the process takes on many of the features of an inquisitorial system (Heydebrand, 1977). Only those cases going to trial have a public adversarial nature,[19] and this includes *possible* counter-accusations that call police judgments into question. In the small minority of cases that go to trial, the trial can be viewed as an appeal from police decisions about an individual (cf Law Reform Commission of Canada, 1973: 9–10).

Typically, when the police officer decides to invoke the criminal process, he 'not only satisfies probable cause but also concludes after his careful evaluation that *the suspect is guilty and an arrest is therefore just*' (Reiss, 1971: 135; see also Wilson, 1968: 52). In proceeding to court, he is primarily seeking routine confirmation of what he assumes to be the case. If this confirmation is not routinely forthcoming, he may see that the other agents are calling into question his judgmental processes, his legitimacy, and their trust. It may be seen as an attack on his competence and, by implication, on police competence. The possible effects are many, ranging from rethinking the desirability of charging in similar situations to an alteration in strategies of presentation in court while otherwise continuing to do the same thing. As Newman (1966: 196) states, 'Efforts at control are resisted by the police, who do not rethink the propriety of the enforcement program but rather adopt alternative methods of achieving their objectives.'

Overall, the legal organization within the court structure is enabling for the police. 'Social order depends upon the co-operative acts of men in sustaining a particular version of the truth' (Silverman, 1970: 134). The ordering of the criminal process is very much under the influence of the police because their versions of the truth are routinely accepted by the other criminal-control agents, who usually have neither the time nor the resources to consider competing truths. In the vast majority of cases, the effective decision is made by the police, with the co-operation of the prosecutor, free from direct judicial constraint. The message from the literature seems to be that when additional formal rules and opportunities for judicial review are created, the police are still able to construct truth in a way that allows their version and their desired outcome to be accepted. This has led one commentator to conclude that a system of judicial control of the police is not practically possible. 'The absence of sufficient information is one reason why it would be unrealistic to expect the courts to investigate and control the discretionary powers of the police in law enforcement, especially those concerned with prosecutions, through the familiar process of judicial review of administrative action' (Williams, 1974: 164).

One must look *within* the police organization to see how legal rules are placed in the context of other organizational rules. Additionally, it is necessary to examine dynamics within the police organization because most police decisions are not directly related to criminal law anyway. As we saw earlier, very little of the patrol officer's time is spent doing criminal-law investigation or enforcement. Most of the time is spent waiting or looking for trouble. When trouble is reported or discovered, the possibility of defining the matter as criminal may be taken into account, but this is only one among a range of justifiable choices. A host of decisions about mobilizations and information-gathering form the bulk of all decisions by patrol officers, and they are subject to few if any formal rules from outside the police organization. In sum, a full view of police decision-making requires a look inside the police organization to see how internal expectations articulate with those from the outside.

The research record suggests that increasing bureaucratization and professionalization have brought the police organization increased autonomy from the community (Reith, 1943; Silver, 1967; Bordua, 1968; Fogelson, 1977;

Miller, 1977; Ignatieff, 1979). Studies of attempts at organized community control of the police and of dealings between police administrations and police commissions show that the police are able to co-opt community efforts at control to serve their own organizational interests (e.g. Norris, 1973; Evans, 1974; Washnis, 1976; Brogden, 1977). In Britain, several researchers are arguing that the police have become a fundamental force in shaping community structure, using the media and other sources of power (e.g. Bunyan, 1976; Hall *et al*, 1978; Cohen, 1979; Taylor, 1980).

At the level of the individual patrol officer, bureaucratization has meant distancing from the community. Encounters between citizens and officers involve *a* policeman, not *the* policeman, with less personalized contact and the displacement of responsibility to a more anonymous entity. Bureaucratization and professionalization also foster a greater orientation to law enforcement (Wilson, 1968; Murphy, 1981).

In addition to insulating the patrol officer from the community, bureaucratization and professionalization can militate against internal control of the line officer while giving the appearance of greater control. In an ironic and contradictory fashion, bureaucratization and professionalization can have a strong debureaucratizing effect, shifting power into the hands of line officers as a collective force (Clark and Sykes, 1974: 473). As the size and degree of specialization within the police organization increase, the line officers come to rely on their immediate colleagues, rather than distant superiors, for co-operation (Cain, 1973: 222). Moreover, expansion and specialization lead to increased conflict, with sub-units establishing their own interests, often in direct conflict with those of other sub-units (Banton, 1964: especially 263; Skolnick, 1966). Various means are used to create and perpetuate internal power resources, such as not communicating, or selectively communicating, essential information (Bittner, 1970: 65).

The police organization differs from most other organizations in the extent to which essential decisions and the input of knowledge occur among the lowest-ranking members and filter upwards. In most industrial concerns policies are set by the board and senior executives and are then passed on to managers who oversee their implementation by those working on the line. The line member's task is to carry out what has been delegated to him, although he can of course object that the demands are too stringent or develop other ways of accomplishing the task. In the police organization, the administration can establish general production guidelines, but it is much more heavily dependent on the decisions taken and information produced by line members.

Wilson (1968: 7) points out, 'The police department has the special property ... that within it discretion increases as one moves *down* the hierarchy'. This is owing to both the 'low visibility' of these decisions and their 'situated' nature. As Wilson (p. 66) goes on to state, due to the fact the administrator 'cannot in advance predict what the circumstances are likely to be or what courses of action are most appropriate –because, in short, cannot be there himself – he cannot in advance formulate a policy that will "guide" the patrolman's discretion by, in effect, eliminating it' (see also Bittner, 1974; Punch, 1979). Given the variety of human beings and troubles the patrol officer deals with, it is unlikely that rules could be written short of a compendium on the manners of society (Laurie, 1970: 111).

The police officer's rules for action are the 'recipe' rules learned on the job. Of course, these rules take into account rules from other sources – the community, the criminal law, and the police administration – especially as they are useful in the formulation of accounts for justifying actions taken. However, these 'recipe' rules also cover a range of circumstances and practices not directly addressed within other rule systems. They 'are not the administrative rules, which derive substantially from the criminal code or municipal regulations, but are those "rules of thumb" that mediate between the departmental regulations, legal codes, and the actual events he witnesses on the street' (Manning, 1977: 162–3). They cover a wide range of matters, such as whom to stop on suspicion in what circumstances; when official paper is necessary as opposed to a notebook record or nothing at all; how to prepare official paper; when and how to charge, including charging-up and multiple-charge possibilities; how to deal with lawyers and crown attorneys in the construction of case outcomes; and so on.

Many of the 'recipe' rules are known only among line officers. The rules of the 'law in action' are fully known and thus predictable only to them, and not to police administrators, other criminal-control agents, and the public. Patrol officers control the creation of these rules, their use, and knowledge about them in ways that fundamentally secure their power within the organizational 'order of things'.

The administration attempts to compensate for lack of control by emphasizing bureaucratic and professional standards. As mentioned earlier, this accomplishes the appearance of control, but also strengthens tendencies it was designed to oppose, especially 'occupational individualism and defensive fraternal solidarity' (Bittner, 1970: 67). Administrative control systems provide cover for the control systems within the occupational environment of patrol officers. They '(a) protect against the claim that something was not done; (b) punish persons after the fact; (c) maintain the appearance of evaluation, if not evaluational capacity; (d) maintain autonomy among and between units within the system by leaving the principal integrative bases tacit and unspecified' (Manning, 1979: 26; see also Manning, 1977: chapter 6).

The police administration's efforts at control are multifaceted and include a disciplinary code, direct supervision, measurement of production, and a division of labour in terms of resources.

The appearance of a disciplined and cohesive unit, the embodiment of consensus, is created through the use of military-style dress and procedures. This gives a police patrol operation *some* of the characteristics of 'total institutions' as described by Goffman (1961). Definitions of reality constructed within the organization are intended to exclude conflicting meanings and thereby solidify particular orientations to the range of problems the patrol officer has to deal with. This is accomplished by techniques such as 'identity stripping' in the initial training and socialization phase for new members of the organization, and by an appearances code that includes such things as military-style uniforms and 'parades' before each shift. The result is an image of strict control over symbolically important matters even if they have little to do with the essential work of patrol officers. Unlike in total institutions, however, members are not cut off from routine contact with those outside. On the contrary, the central task of patrol officers is to confront outsiders and to engage directly in conflicts over competing definitions of reality.

The disciplinary code provides an enabling framework for the administration in its efforts to create an appearance of organizational order (for an analysis, see Ericson, 1981a). As Rubinstein (1973: 41) observes, 'The Duty Manual offers almost unlimited opportunities to bring charges against a man'. The rules, subsumed under provincial police acts (e.g. Ontario Police Act RSO 1970) and departmental orders, are written in such broad and general form that they resemble rules for maintaining 'good order and discipline' within prisons (Ericson, 1981a). Every police officer violates them. Some have even noted that rules are contradictory, so that following one necessarily entails violation of others (Ramsay, 1972). The rules place the patrol officer in a state of 'dependent uncertainty' (Cain, 1973: especially 181), because he knows the administration can always 'get' him if he falls from official grace in other matters of importance. Just as patrol officers use enabling criminal-law rules to deal selectively with troublesome citizens, the police administration is able to use Police Act and departmental rules to deal selectively with troublesome officers.

The appearances code has another control function for the administration: to the extent that petty complaints regarding dress, coffee breaks, cheap meals at restaurants, etc, become the focal point of occupational grievances, the administration can play out concessions in these areas and deflect the more fundamental labour-management problems which characterize any bureaucratic working environment. Concerted effort at control from line-officers even in the apparently strong police-union movement in the United States (Juris and Feuille, 1973; Halpern, 1974) is deflected into these areas of petty grievance, deflating the opposition of line officers and ultimately co-opting them.

The administration also employs line supervisors (patrol sergeants) to patrol and enforce its conception of internal order (see especially Rubinstein, 1973: chapter 2; Muir, 1977). These supervisors develop procedures covering a variety of matters, from office routine to handling prisoners. They give daily briefings which include directions about what areas of enforcement to concentrate on or ease up on. They spend considerable time patrolling in a platoon area. Their ability to listen in on messages from dispatchers to patrol officers means they can respond to any dispatched call, and this possibility is constantly kept in mind by patrol officers. The patrol sergeant and other higher-ranking officers review any official written reports submitted by patrol officers, and this is also kept in mind in deciding whether and how to construct reports (Reiss, 1971: 124–5).

Part of the 'recipe' knowledge the patrol officer learns is directed at controlling supervisors. This takes the form of an exchange, whereby the officer follows the appearances code and formulates official reports in the appropriate bureaucratic framework in return for leniency in areas which ease the humdrum nature of patrol work. A lot of time and energy is spent on 'easing' work (Cain, 1973; Chatterton, 1979), but the first requirement is to gain the co-operation of the patrol sergeant. This is relatively easy given the importance of the appearances code within large bureaucratic police forces.[20]

Productive appearances are of considerable significance. Measures of productivity serve to inform supervisors what a patrol officer is up to, and they also provide data with which the organization as a whole can 'sell' itself. One obvious form of control is the development of quota requirements for enforcement activity. For example, researchers have documented how patrol-officer involvement in traffic-law enforcement can be influenced by a quota system. Wilson (1968: 97) reports that in Oakland a quota of 2 tickets per traffic division officer per hour was met with an actual rate of 1.97 tickets per traffic division officer per hour over a six-week period selected at random (see also Gardiner, 1969).

Another form of influence is the establishment of policy and attendant rules concerning charging. Senior administrators have attempted to articulate criteria concerning the decision to charge or caution. The rate of cautioning has been shown to be significantly influenced by the preferences, ideological or otherwise, of particular police chiefs (Steer, 1970: 17).

Research has shown that adoption of production criteria fundamentally affects decision-making about arrest and charging. One consequence of measurement in any organization is overproduction in the areas that can be measured and underproduction in the areas more difficult to measure (Etzioni, 1961). For example, detectives concentrate on cases that can be cleared rather than on those which require considerable investigative attention and are unlikely to result in a measureable payoff (Greenwood, 1975; Ericson, 1981). Similarly, patrol officers are more likely to concentrate on measureable areas of proactive enforcement, such as traffic, liquor, and narcotics, rather than on more abstract areas of reproducing order, if they are explicitly rewarded for doing so (cf Fisk, 1974: 25).

The emphasis upon 'clearances' of all sorts rather than just charges can lead to a number of other practices. In his research, Steer (1970: especially 21, 38) found that when adults are formally cautioned, the caution is typically employed as an alternative to no formal action, because of a lack of evidence, rather than as an alternative to prosecution. Indeed, Steer found that many cautions are given for activities that do not legally constitute a crime and could be more suitably written off as unfounded. Cautioning procedures thus help to swell clearance rates and make suspects arrested and investigated with no substantial grounds believe that there were grounds but that the police are exercising leniency.

Police officers with a high volume of cases to work on and perceiving administrative expectations to clear as many as possible may try to obtain a greater number of clearances for each arrest and reduce the overall number of investigations and arrests (Chaiken, 1975: chapter 9). This is frequently accomplished by having the suspect admit to a large number of offences on the promise that he will not be charged for them. Lambent (1970) reports that in a sample of 2,000 recorded property offences in Birmingham, 43 per cent of those cleared were done so by this method. LaFave (1965: 374) records that in Detroit, when talking with an accused, 'the interrogating detectives stress the fact that any additional offences admitted are "free offences" in that there will be no prosecution for them'. Skolnick (1966: 78) cites the case of two accused persons who received lenient sentences in exchange for admitting to over 500 burglaries.

Where police officers perceive extreme organizational pressure for production they may turn to more extreme methods, including excessive use of physical force (cf Whitaker, 1964). However, the research literature shows that such measures are relatively rare because they are not necessary (cf Skolnick, 1966: especially 174; Reiss, 1968: 12; Wald *et al.*, 1967: 1549). The other tactics enumerated above provide enough resources to allow the line officer to proceed by way of the carrot rather than the stick. These procedures become bureaucratically accepted and routinized, allowing predictability and control in a way that other approaches, such as excessive physical force, cannot accomplish.

These practices have important ramifications for the productive efforts of police organizations as a whole. They lead to the production of crime rates in a way that seriously affects their validity as measures of crime control, although they serve the organization's 'crime-fighting' image. Several writers have pointed out that similar processes operate in other organizational contexts (see generally, Ditton, 1977, 1979). For example, Bensman and Gerver's (1963) study of an airplane factory revealed that line workers used an illegal tool that caused long-term hazards to airplane safety. They did so because it helped to meet production quotas; moreover, its use was condoned *sub rosa* by superiors. There are also many similarities in the work of bailiffs (McMullan, 1980). In sum, members of occupational cultures, in response to bureaucratic demands, can be adaptive and creative in producing their own rules to achieve their own needs. Those in the police organization can circumvent expectations from the wider organization of crime control and indeed alter the nature of both organizations.

Administrative influence affects resource allocation and the division of labour. For example, various types of dispatch systems regarding calls for service have control implications for patrol officers (Cordner, 1979; Manning, 1979; Jorgensen, 1979). In most police organizations, dispatched calls are tape-recorded and also recorded on a card system by the communications officer and dispatch officer. The officer is required to report back to the dispatcher on what happened, although if he is not filing official paper this may be only a brief coded message. Pepinsky (1975, 1976) found that in dispatches where the dispatcher named an offence, especially other than traffic, sex, or assault, the officer filed an official report on the offence as dispatched subject only to routine collaboration by the complainant (see also Jorgensen, 1979). Some police forces have attempted to control further through the instalment of vehicle-locator systems. Moreover, some forces may circumvent collusion among dispatchers and patrol officers by having civilian dispatchers, who do not have the experience of, and affinity with, the occupational culture of patrol officers.

While there appears to be substantial control via the dispatch system, ethnographers (e.g. Rubinstein, 1973; Manning, 1977, 1979) have documented the many means by which patrol officers collectively resist this form of control. Those who book off on a call can remain booked off while they go about their personal business after handling the call. Dispatchers can 'cover' for patrol officers who are 'missing' and the subject of inquiry from supervisors. The majority of calls do not result in official paper, and these can be accounted for in ways the dispatcher is unable to check. Even when official paper is submitted, there is usually no systematic linking of the paper with the original dispatch; moreover, most supervisors know that events become transformed and there is no meaning in a correlation between dispatcher labels and the officer's final accounting. There are strategies for circumventing vehicle-locator systems, e.g. finding spots where the signals are distorted.

Specialized division of labour characterizes urban police forces. An obvious division is between uniformed patrol officers and detectives. For example, in the Metropolitan Toronto Police Department there is an administrative regulation stipulating that uniformed personnel must turn over all arrested suspects to the detective branch for further investigation and charging, except in provincial-statute cases and areas of the Criminal Code dealing with driving and public order (Johnson, 1978). This type of bureaucratic ordering significantly influences what the respective units work at (see Ericson, 1981: especially chapter 3).

Obviously, it is essential to examine the internal order of police organizations because it is there that the sense of order from community and legal organizations is translated into action. A fully social account of patrol-officer discretion must inquire into the sense of order derived from each of the organizational forums within which he operates, and ascertain how this sense of order frames what he does on the job. In this way we shall learn something about the reproduction of order within organizations (cf Ranson *et al.*, 1980) and how this articulates with the reproduction of social order.

*From Richard V. Ericson, 'The police as reproducers of order' in* Reproducing Order: a study of Police patrol work *(Toronto: University of Toronto Press), 1982, pp 3–30.*

## Notes

1 For example, allegations of brutality and other wrongdoings by members of the Waterloo Regional Police Force (Ontario Police Commission, 1978) and by members of the Metropolitan Toronto Police Force (Morand, 1976), and allegations of various illegalities and wrongdoings by members of the Royal Canadian Mounted Police (Mann and Lee, 1979; McDonald Commission, 1981).

2 The figures on police personnel per 1,000 population include full-time employees other than sworn police officers. Police-officer strength in 1977 was 2.3 per 1,000 population. The vast majority are uniformed patrol officers. In the police force we studied as part of the research [...], less than 20 per cent of police-officer personnel were assigned to detective units (Ericson, 1981). In a survey of American municipal and county police departments, Chaiken (1975: vii) discovered that on average 17.3 per cent of police-officer personnel are assigned to detective units.

3 This view is the dominant one in criminology and contributes more than anything else to making that subject less than respectable academically. As Hay (1975: 24n) notes, 'Historians have accepted the assumptions of reformers, which are also those of modern criminology: that the criminal law and the police are no more and no less than a set of instruments to manage, something called crime. Effective detection, certain prosecution and enlightened rehabilitation will accomplish this practical task. Criminology has been disinfested of grand theory and class purpose. Much of it has thereby become ideology.'

4 Wilson and Boland categorized 'police activity' as 'aggressive' if a city had a high volume of traffic citations, on the assumption that those highly proactive in this area are also highly aggressive in making proactive stops on suspicion. This assumption may be correct to the extent that traffic stops are also used to check out suspicions about the vehicle's occupants [...]. However, the assumption requires confirmation from first-hand observation rather than solely from police records as employed by Wilson and Boland. A higher proactive-stop rate may be characteristic of police forces that have a lack of better things to do, including a lack of serious crime, which may be explained by factors independent of the police operation. For a critique of the work by Wilson and Boland, see Jacob and Rich (1980).

5 Of course, changing the *status quo* will not change the structural position of the police. As E.P. Thompson (1979: 325) remarks: 'The police, as defenders of "law and order", have a vested interest in the status quo, whether the *status* be capitalist or communist, and whether the *quo* be that of Somoza's Nicaragua or Rokosi's Hungary: that is, the occupation is one which is supportive of statist and authoritarian ideologies. And, more simply, in whatever kind of society, the police will always have good reasons for pressing for more resources, more powers, and more pay. There is nothing sinister about this, in an alert and democratic society, since, once these things are understood, proper measures will be taken to ensure that the police have adequate resources for their legitimate functions, and to curtail in the strictest way those functions which are not. This is not a new problem. It is a problem we have lived with ... for centuries.'

6 'Shagwagon' is a slang term for a van or truck that has been customized with a finished interior and is used for driving adventures as well as amorous adventures. It was a term in currency among patrol officers and youths at the time the research for this book was undertaken.

7 This perspective is within the 'social action' tradition in sociology. 'Social action' theorists emphasize the 'situated', 'negotiated', 'tenuous', 'shifting' nature of social order: 'Order is something at which members of any social, any organization, must work. For the shared agreements, the binding contracts – what constitute the grounds for an expectable, non-surprising, taken-for-granted, even ruled orderliness – are not binding and shared for all time ... In short, the bases of concerted action (social order) must be reconstituted continually' (Strauss *et al.*, 1963: 129).

8 Mennell (1974: 116–17) counsels: 'Social order is the result of some people being able to coerce others into obedience; or it rests on general agreement among the members of society; or it stems from their striking bargains with each other which are to everyone's individual advantage as well as the collective advantage. But it is unhelpful to see these viewpoints as mutually exclusive. For the sociologist, social order must be a matter for empirical investigation.'

9 Friedenberg (1975: 90–1) suggests in a different context why social problems such as crime are perpetuated through mystification instead of being potentially subject to eradication: 'Public figures in quest of power have always found it useful to exploit prevailing myths, for it is the nature of myths both to dramatize conflict – psychic and social – and to conceal that conflict's real dynamism, thus ensuring that policies based on myth will not actually remedy the situation they dramatize. The day the boulder stays at the top of the hill, Sisyphus is out of office ... The very fact that politicians must accept and promote a formulation of social problems that so distorts the underlying dynamics as to make any real assessment of it impossible simply means that the popular conception itself becomes the problem, and usually a more serious problem than the one to which it refers.'

10 As Bittner (1970: 24) observes on the effect of established court rules upon police decision-making: 'The norms observable in open court reach down and govern even the process of its evasion. In the criminal process, like in chess, the game is rarely played to the end, but it is the rare chess player who concedes defeat merely to save time. Instead, he concedes because he knows or can reasonably guess what would happen if he persisted to play to the end. And thus the rules of the end-game are valid determinants of chess-playing even though they are relatively rarely seen in action.'

11 Manning (1977, 1977a, 1980) is the leading student of this link between rules and the sense of order used by the officer to place police work in context: 'The sense of order that emerges from and is displayed in organizationally bounded encounters is in part dependent upon the rules that are called upon or invoked by participants to order the interaction. Rules, although tacitly understood, make salient the set of assigned features of events that interactants take into account as members-in-role. Rules are thus resources to be used tacitly by participants, and by doing so participants negotiate the limits upon organizationally sanctionable activities' (1977a: 57).

12 This point has been repeatedly stressed by Bittner (1967, 1967a, 1970). Based on his observations of patrol policing in a skid row area, Bittner (1967a: 710) concludes: 'Patrolmen do not really enforce the law, even when they do invoke it, but merely use it as a resource to solve certain pressing practical problems in keeping the peace ... The problem patrolmen confront is not which drunks, beggars or disturbers of the peace should be arrested and which can be let go as exceptions to the rule. Rather, the problem is whether, when someone "needs" to be arrested, he should be charged with drunkenness, begging, or disturbing the peace.'

As Bittner (1970: 109) states elsewhere, the substantive law in these circumstances is simply employed as a convenient tool without regard to abstract principles such as legality: 'In discretionary law enforcement involving minor offences, policemen use existing law largely as a pretext for making arrests ... Because persons who in the judgment of the police should be detained must be charged with something the law recognizes as valid grounds for detention, many arrests have the outward aspects of adhering to principles of legality. In point of fact, however, the real reasons for invoking the law are wholly independent of the law that is being invoked. The point to be emphasized is not that this procedure is illegal, though it often enough is, but that it has nothing to do with considerations of illegality.'

13 For a detailed analysis of the procedural criminal law in Scotland and England as it supports police practices, see McBarnet (1976, 1979, 1981). For a similar analysis in the Canadian context see Freedman and Stenning (1977) and Ericson (1981a). See also Ratushny (1979) [...].

14 The ideal of full enforcement and the rule of law has been particularly emphasized by some American legal scholars (e.g. Goldstein, 1960; Packer, 1968). Goldstein states that it is the duty of the police to carry out the dictates of the law by investigating every situation in which a criminal-law violation is suspected, to attempt to ascertain who violated the law, and to present the relevant information to the prosecutor for his further action. He documents that many American police acts specifically state this duty of full enforcement. The related ideal of the rule of law or principle of legality means that the police as agents of the criminal law should be restricted in their power to judge and punish by explicit rules which provide a justificatory framework for action or inaction. The aim is to reduce arbitrariness in police action, allowing assessment in review of the 'justice' of their action.

As stated earlier, in Canada there are no entrenched rights which might curtail a procedural law that is enabling for the police. Moreover, there is no provincial or federal statute explicitly imposing the duty of full enforcement, and the police officer's broad duties and responsibility for following directives from both police and political superiors are emphasized (Cameron, 1974: 40). There is some contradiction between the constable's constitutional position as having an original authority in law, and his organizational position as a subordinate who must follow orders on penalty of possible legal proceedings under the Police Act, but this has apparently caused little conflict (see Williams, 1974; Gillance and Khan, 1975; Oliver, 1975; Ericson, 1981a). In Canada, there is a recognition that ours is a government of both laws and men.

15 Reviews of this literature are provided by Box (1971) and Hagan (1979). Of course, the police are only one of many occupational groups employing moral judgments about status claims as a means of assessing what actions to take. For example, the medical profession makes moral judgments in discriminating among clients seeking the use of hospital emergency services (Roth, 1972).

16 The empirical record indicates that while citizens have these resources of resistance, manipulation, and coercion, they do not often use them. Citizens routinely turn over documents to the police and provide other information without question (Ericson, 1981), and the channel of formal complaint is not often used, especially by the 'lower orders', who have recurrent dealings with the police (Russell, 1976). This is particularly important regarding the previously mentioned 'low visibility' of the police. The patrol officer operates with 'high visibility' to those with whom he has regular contact, but these people typically have relatively little power. They therefore have no recourse or, except in an isolated and sporadic manner, cannot mobilize resources to take action if they do have recourse.

17 For example, Steer (1970: 10) reports that the development of juvenile liaison schemes in the United Kingdom resulted in more people reporting offences to the police because they believed the police would not prosecute and might even assist the offender. The net result was an overall increase in the number of offences known to the police. Skolnick and Woodworth (1967) report on differential enforcement of statutory rape by two police forces in California; the force which gained routine access to sources in welfare agencies for family support had a dramatically higher enforcement rate than the force which did not.

18 In the case of the police, this has been particularly well documented with respect to the law of confessions and the accused's right to silence (e.g. Wald et al, 1967; Medalie et al, 1968; Chambliss and Seidman, 1971; Greenawalt, 1974; Zander, 1978). It has also been shown to happen in relation to policies and attendant rules emanating from the police administration (e.g. Chatterton, 1979; James, 1979). Examples from other organizational settings include the way in which prison guards have dealt with apparent due-process protections for inmates (Harvard Center for Criminal Justice, 1972), and the way in which school principals have circumvented attempts to control their disciplinary actions against troublesome students (Gaylin et al., 1978: 136ff).

19 The argument can be made that while not publicly visible in the courtroom, pre-trial 'plea bargaining' sessions between counsel for the defence, police, and prosecutor take on an adversarial character (e.g. Utz, 1978). [...]

20 Bittner (1970: 55) summarizes the matter: 'Because the real work of the policeman is not set forth in the regulations, it does not furnish his superior a basis for judging him. At the same time, there are no strongly compelling reasons for the policeman to do well in ways that do not count in terms of official occupational criteria of value. The greater the weight placed on compliance with internal departmental regulations, the less free is the superior in censoring unregulated work practices he disapproves of, and in rewarding those he admires, for fear that he might

jeopardize the loyalty of officers who do well on all scores that officially count – that is, those who present a neat appearance, who conform punctually to bureaucratic routine, who are visibly on the place of their assignment, and so on. In short, those who make life easier for the superior, who in turn is restricted to supervising just those things. In fact, the practical economy of supervisory control requires that the proliferation of intradepartmental restriction be accompanied by increases in license in areas of behaviour in unregulated areas. Thus, one who is judged to be a good officer in terms of internal, military-bureaucratic codes will not even be questioned about his conduct outside of it.'

## References

Arnold, T. 1962 *The symbols of government*. New York: Harcourt, Brace and World.

Ayres, R. 1970 'Confessions and the Court' in A. Niederhoffer and A. Blumberg, eds *The Ambivalent Force*. Waltham, Mass.: Ginn, pp 274–8.

Banton, M. 1964 *The Policeman in the Community*. London: Tavistock.

Bayley, D. and Mendelsohn, H. 1969 *Minorities and the Police: Confrontation in America*. New York: Free Press.

Beattie, J. 1981 'Administering Justice without Police: Criminal Trial Procedure in Eighteenth Century England,' in *Proceedings of A Symposium on the Maintenance of Order in Society*. Ottawa: Canadian Police College.

Bensman, J. and Gerver, I. 1963 'Crime and Punishment in the Factory: The Function of Deviancy in Maintaining the Social System,' *American Sociological Review* 28: 588–98.

Berger, P. and Luckmann, T. 1966 *The Social Construction of Reality: A Treatise in the Sociology of Knowledge*. Harmondsworth: Penguin.

Bittner, E. 1967 'Police Discretion in Emergency Apprehension of Mentally Ill Persons,' *Social Problems* 14: 278–92.

Bittner, E. 1967a 'The Police on Skid Row: A Study of Peace Keeping,' *American Sociological Review* 32: 699–715.

Bittner, E. 1970 *The Functions of the Police in Modern Society*. Rockville, Md.: NIMH.

Bittner, E. 1974 'A Theory of the Police,' in H. Jacob ed. *The Potential for Reform of Criminal Justice*. London: Sage, pp 17–44.

Black, D. 1968 'Police Encounters and Social Organizations: An Observation Study,' PhD dissertation, University of Michigan.

Black, D. 1970 'Production of Crime Rates,' *American Sociological Review* 35: 733–48.

Black, D. 1971 'The Social Organization of Arrest,' *Stanford Law Review* 23: 1087–111.

Black, D. 1972 'The Boundaries of Legal Sociology,' *Yale Law Journal* 81 (6): 1086–110.

Blumberg, A. 1970 'The Practice of Law as a Confidence Game: Organizational Cooptation as a Profession,' in A. Niederhoffer and A. Blumberg, eds *The Ambivalent Force*. Waltham, Mass.: Ginn, pp 279–92.

Bordua, D. 1968 'The Police,' in D. Sills ed. *International Encyclopedia of Social Science*. New York: Free Press, pp 174–81.

Bottomley, A. 1973 *Decisions in the Penal Process*. Oxford: Martin Robertson.

Box. S. 1971 *Deviance, Reality and Society*. New York: Holt, Rinehart and Winston.

Brogden, M. 1977 'A Police Authority – the Denial of Conflict,' *Sociological Review* 25: 325–49.

Buckner, H. 1970 'Transformations of Reality in the Legal Process,' *Social Research* 37: 88–101.

Bunyan, T. 1976 *The Political Police in Britain*. London: Julian Friedman.

Cain, M. 1973 *Society and the Policeman's Role*. London: Routledge and Kegan Paul.

Cameron, N. 1974 'The Control of Police Discretion,' Draft manuscript, Centre of Criminology, University of Toronto.

Carlen, P. 1976 *Magistrates' Justice*. Oxford: Martin Robertson.

Chaiken, J. 1975 *The Criminal Investigation Process. Vol. II: Survey of Municipal and County Police Departments*. Santa Monica: Rand Corp.

Chambliss, W. and Seidman, R. 1971 *Law, Order and Power*. Reading, Mass.: Addison-Wesley.

Chan, J. and Doob, A. 1977 *The Exercise of Discretion with Juveniles*. Toronto: Centre of Criminology, University of Toronto.

Chan, J. and Ericson, R. 1981 *Decarceration and the Economy of Penal Reform*. Toronto: Centre of Criminology, University of Toronto.

Chatterton, M. 1973 'A Working Paper on the Use of Resources – Charges and Practical Decision-Making in Peace-Keeping.' Paper presented to seminar on the sociology of police, Bristol University.

Chatterton, M. 1976 'Police in Social Control,' in *Control without Custody*. Cropwood Papers, Institute of Criminology, University of Cambridge.

Chatterton, M. 1979 'The Supervision of Patrol Work under the Fixed Points System,' in S. Holdaway (ed.) *The British Police*. London: Edward Arnold.

Clark, J. and Sykes, R. 1974 'Some Determinants of Police Organization and Practice in Modern Industrial Democracy,' in D. Glaster *Handbook of Criminology*. Chicago: Rand-McNally, pp 455–94.

Clarke, R. and Heal, K. 1979 'Police Effectiveness in Dealing with Crime: Some Current British Research,' *The Police Journal* 52 (1): 24–41.

Cohen, P. 1979 'Policing the Working-Class City,' in B. Fine *et al.*, *Capitalism and the Rule of Law*. London: Hutchinson.

Cohen, S. 1979 'Guilt, Justice and Tolerance: Some Old Concepts for a New Criminology,' in D. Downes and P. Rock eds *Deviant Interpretations*. Oxford: Martin Robertson.

Comrie, M.D. and Kings, E.J. 1975 'Study of Urban Workloads: Final Report.' Home Office Police Research Services Unit (unpublished).

Cook, K. 1977 'Exchange and Power of Networks of Interorganizational Relations,' *The Sociological Quarterly* 18: 62–82.

Cordner, G. 1979 'Police Patrol Work Load Studies: A Review and Critique.' Unpublished paper, Michigan State University.

Cressey, D. 1974 'Law, Order and the Motorist,' in R. Hood ed. *Crime, Criminology and Public Policy*. London: Heinemann, pp. 213–34.

Cumming, E. *et al.*, 1970 'Policeman as Philosopher, Guide and Friend,' in A. Niederhoffer and A. Blumberg eds *The Ambivalent Force*. Waltham, Mass.: Ginn, pp. 184–92.

Dalton, M. 1959 *Men who Manage*. New York: Wiley.

Davis, K. 1969 *Discretionary Justice*. Baton Rouge: Louisiana State University Press.

Ditton, J. 1977 *Part-Time Crime*. London: Macmillan.

Ditton, J. 1971 *American Social Order*. New York: Free Press.

Douglas, J. 1971 *American Social Order*. New York: Free Press.

Durkheim, E. 1964 *Rules of Sociological Method*. Trans. S.A. Solovay and J.H. Mueller. New York: Free Press.

Ericson, R. 1974 'Psychiatrists in Prison: On Admitting Professional Tinkers into a Tinkers' Paradise,' *Chitty's Law Journal* 22 (1): 29–33.

Ericson, R. 1975 *Criminal Reactions: The Labelling Perspective*. Farnborough: Saxon House.

Ericson, R. 1981 *Making Crime: A Study of Detective Work*. Toronto: Butterworths.

Ericson, R. 1981a 'Rules for Police Deviance,' in C. Shearing ed. *Organizational Police Deviance*. Toronto: Butterworths.

Etzioni, A. 1961 *A Comparative Analysis of Complex Organizations*. New York: Free Press.

Evans, P. 1974 *The Police Revolution*. London: Allen and Unwin.

Fishman, M. 1978 'Crime Waves as Ideology,' *Social Problems* 25: 531–43.

Fishman, M. 1980 *Manufacturing the News*. Austin: University of Texas Press.

Fisk, J. 1974 *The Police Officer's Exercise of Discretion in the Decision to Arrest: Relationship to Organizational Goals and Societal Values*. Los Angeles: UCLA Institute of Government and Public Affairs.

Fogelson, R. 1977 *Big-City Police*. Cambridge, Mass.: Harvard University Press.

Foucault, M. 1977 *Discipline and Punish: The Birth of the Prison*. Trans. Alan Sheridan. New York: Pantheon.

Freedman, D. and Stenning, P. 1977 *Private Security, Police and the Law in Canada*. Toronto: Centre of Criminology, University of Toronto.

Friedenberg, E. 1975 *The Disposal of Liberty and other Industrial Wastes*. New York: Doubleday.

Gardiner, J. 1969 *Traffic and the Police: Variations in Law Enforcement Policy*. Cambridge, Mass.: Harvard University Press.

Gaylin, W. *et al.*, 1978 *Doing Good: The Limits of Benevolence*. New York: Pantheon.

Giddens, A. 1976 *New Rules of Sociological Method*. London: Hutchinson.

Gilliance, K. and Khan, A. 1975 'The Constitutional Independence of a Police Constable in the Exercise of the Powers of his Office,' *Police Journal* 48 (1): 55–62.

Goffman, E. 1961 *Asylums*. New York: Doubleday.

Goldstein, H. 1970 'Police Discretion: The Ideal versus the Real,' in A. Niederhoffer and A. Blumberg, eds *The Ambivalent Force*. Waltham, Mass.: Ginn, pp 148–56.

Goldstein, J. 1960 'Police Discretion not to Invoke the Criminal Process: Low Visibility Decisions in the Administration of Justice,' *Yale Law Journal* 69: 543–94.

Green, B. 1970 'Race, Social Status and Criminal Arrest,' *American Sociological Review* 35: 476–90.

Greenawalt, K. 1974 'Perspectives on the Right to Silence,' in R. Hood ed. *Crime, Criminology and Public Policy*. London: Heinemann.

Greenwood, P. *et al.*, 1975 *The Criminal Investigation Process. Volume III: Observations and Analysis.* Santa Monica: Rand Corp.

Grosman, B. 1969 *The Prosecutor.* Toronto: University of Toronto Press.

Grosman, B. 1975 *Police Command: Decisions and Discretion.* Toronto: MacMillan.

Hagan, J. 1979 'The Police Response to Delinquency: Some Observations on a Labelling Process,' in E. Vaz and A. Lodhi eds *Crime and Delinquency in Canada.* Scarborough: Prentice-Hall.

Hall, S. *et al.*, 1968 *Policing the Crisis.* London: Macmillan.

Halpern, S. 1974 *Police Association and Department Leaders: The Politics of Cooptation.* Lexington, Mass.: Lexington Books.

Harvard Center for Criminal Justice 1972 'Judicial Intervention in Prison Discipline,' *Journal of Criminal Law and Criminology* 63: 200–28.

Hay, D. 1975 'Property, Authority and the Criminal Law,' in D. Hay *et al.*, *Albion's Fatal Tree.* Harmondsworth: Penguin.

Hydebrand, W. 1977 'Organizational Contradictions in public Bureaucracies: Toward a Marxian Theory of Organizations,' Sociological *Quarterly* 18: 83–107.

Hudson, J. 1970 'Police–Citizen Encounters that Lead to Citizen Complaints,' *Social Problems* 18: 179–93.

Ignatieff, M. 1978 *A Just Measure of Pain.* London: Macmillan.

Ignatieff, M. 1979 'Police and People: The Birth of Mr. Peel's "Blue Locusts,"' *New Society* (30 August): 443–5.

Inbau, F. and Reid, J. 1967 *Criminal Interrogation and Confessions.* Baltimore: Williams and Wilkins.

Jacob, H. and Rich, M. 1980 'The Effects of the Police on Crime: A Second Look', *Law and Society Review* 15: 109–22.

James, D. 1979 'Police–Black Relations: The Professional Solution,' in S. Holdaway ed. *The British Police.* London: Edward Arnold, pp. 66–82.

Johnson, C. 1978 'Police Discretion as Rule Governed Action.' MA dissertation, Centre of Criminology, University of Toronto.

Jorgensen, B. 1979 *Transferring Trouble: The Initiation of Reactive Policing.* Unpublished research report, Centre of Criminology, University of Toronto.

Juris, H. and Feuille, P. 1973 *Police Unionism.* Lexington, Mass.: Lexington Books.

Kadish, M. and Kadish, S. 1973 *Discretion to Disobey: A Study of Lawful Departures from Legal Rules.* Stanford: Stanford University Press.

Kaufman, F. 1974 *The Admissibility of Confessions.* Toronto: Carswell.

Kelling, G. *et al.*, 1974 *The Kansas City Preventive Patrol Experiment.* Washington, DC: Police Foundation.

Klein, J. 1976 *Let's Make a Deal.* Lexington, Mass.: Lexington Books.

LaFave, W. 1965 *Arrest: The Decision to Take a Suspect into Custody.* Boston: Little, Brown.

Lambert, J. 1970 *Crime, Police and Race Relations.* London: Oxford University Press.

Laurie, P. 1970 *Scotland Yard.* London: The Bodley Head.

Law Reform Commission of Canada. 1973 *Evidence: Compellability of the Accused and the Admissibility of His Statements.* Study Paper.

McBarnet, D. 1976 'Pre-Trial Procedures and the Construction of Conviction,' in P. Carlen ed. *The Sociology of Law.* Keele: Department of Sociology, University of Keele.

McBarnet, D. 1979 'Arrest: The Legal Context of Policing,' in S. Holdaway ed. *The British Police.* London: Edward Arnold.

McBarnet, D. 1981 *Conviction: Law, the State and the Construction of Justice.* London: Macmillan.

McCabe, S. and Sutcliffe, F. 1978 *Defining Crime: A Study of Police Decisions.* Oxford: Basil Blackwell.

McDonald Commission, 1981 *Final Report.* Ottawa: Ministry of Supply and Services.

McDonald, L. 1969 'Crime and Punishment in Canada: A Statistical Test of the "Conventional Wisdom",' *Canadian Review of Sociology and anthropology* 6 212–36.

McDonald, L. 1976 *The Sociology of Law and Order.* London: Faber and Faber.

McMullan, J. 1980 'Maudit Voleurs: Racketeering and the Collection of Private Debts in Montreal,' *Canadian Journal of Sociology* 5: 121–43.

MacNaughton-Smith, P. 1968 'The Second Code: Toward (or away from) an Empire Theory of Crime and Delinquency,' *Journal of Research in Crime and Delinquency* 5: 189–97.

Mann, E. and Lee, J. 1979 *R.C.M.P.* vs. *The People.* Don Mills: General Publishing.

Manning, P. 1971 'The Police: Mandate, Strategy and Appearances' in J. Douglas ed. *Crime and Justice in American Society.* Indianapolis: Bobbs-Merrill, pp 149–94.

Manning, P. 1972 'Observing the Police: Deviants, Respectables and the Law,' in J. Douglas ed. *Research on Deviance.* New York: Random House, pp. 213–68.

Manning, P. 1977 *Police Work.* Cambridge, Mass.: MIT Press.

Manning, P. 1977a 'Rules in Organizational Context: Narcotics Law Enforcement in Two Settings,' *Sociological Quarterly* 18: 44–61.

Manning, P. 1979 'Organization and Environment: Influences on Police Work.' Paper presented to the Cambridge Conference on Police Effectiveness, Cambridge, England, 11–13 July.

Manning, P. 1980 *The Narcs' Game: Organizational and Informational Limits on Drug Law Enforcement.* Cambridge, Mass.: MIT Press.

Medalie, R. et al., 1968 'Custodial Police Interrogation in Our Nation's Capital: The Attempt to Implement Miranda,' *Michigan Law Review* 66: 1347–422.

Mennell, S. 1974 *Sociological Theory.* New York: Praeger.

Meyer, J. 1974 'Patterns of Reporting Non-Criminal Incidents to the Police,' *Criminology* 12: 70–83.

Miller, W. 1977 *Cops and Bobbies.* Chicago: University of Chicago Press.

Miller, W. 1979 'London's Police Tradition in a Changing Society,' in S. Holdaway ed. *The British Police.* London: Edward Arnold.

Morand, Mr Justice. 1976 *Royal Commission into Metropolitan Toronto Police Practices.* Toronto: Queen's Printer.

Morris, P. 1978 'Police Interrogation in England and Wales.' A critical review of the literature prepared for the UK Royal Commission on Criminal Procedure.

Moylan, J.F. 1929 *Scotland Yard.* London: Putnam.

Muir, W. 1977 *Police: Street Corner Politicians.* Chicago: University of Chicago Press.

Murphy, C. 1981 'Community and Organizational Influences on Small Town Policing.' PhD dissertation, Department of Sociology, University of Toronto.

Newman, D. 1966 *Conviction: The Determination of Guilt or Innocence without Trial.* Boston: Little, Brown.

Norris, D. 1973 *Police Community Relations.* Lexington, Mass.: Lexington Books.

Oliver, I. 1975 'The Office of Constable – 1975,' *Criminal Law Review* 313–22.

Ontario Police Commission. 1978 *Inquiry into Police Practices in the Waterloo Regional Police Force.* Toronto: Ontario Police Commission.

Packer, H. 1968 *The Limits of the Criminal Sanction.* London: Oxford University Press.

Pate, T. et al., 1976 *Police Response Time: Its Determinants and Effects.* Washington, DC: Police Foundation.

Payne, C. 1973 'A Study of Rural Beats,' *Police Research Services Bulletin* 12: 23–9.

Pepinsky, H. 1975 'Police Decision-Making,' in D. Gottfredson ed. *Decision-Making in the Criminal Justice System: Reviews and Essays.* Rockville, Md.: NIMH, pp 21–52.

Pepinsky, H. 1976 'Police Patrolmen's Offense-Reporting Behavior,' *Journal of Research in Crime and Delinquency* 13 (1): 33–47.

Pound, R. 1960 'Discretion, Dispensation and Mitigation: The Problem of the Individual Special Case,' *New York University Law Review* 35: 925.

Punch, M. 1979 *Policing the Inner City.* London: Macmillan.

Punch, M. and Naylor, T. 1973 'The Police: A Social Service,' *New Society* 24 (554): 358–61.

Ramsay, J. 1972 'My Case against the R.C.M.P.,' *MacLean's* (July): 19.

Ranson, S. et al., 1980 'The Structuring of Organizational Structures.' *Administrative Science Quarterly* 25: 1–17.

Ratushny, E. 1979 *Self-Incrimination in the Criminal Process.* Toronto: Carswell.

Reiss, A. 1968 'Police Brutality – Answers to Key Questions,' *Trans-Action* (July–August): 10–19.

Reiss, A. 1971 *The Police and the Public.* New Haven: Yale University Press.

Reiss, A. 1974 'Discretionary Justice,' in D. Glaser ed. *Handbook of Criminology*, Chicago: Rand McNally, pp. 679–99.

Reith, C. 1943 *The Police and the Democratic Ideal.* London: Oxford University Press.

Rock, P. 1979 'The Sociology of Crime, Symbolic Interactionism and Some Problematic Qualities of Radical Criminology,' in D. Downes and P. Rock eds *Deviant Interpretations.* Oxford: Martin Robertson, pp. 52–84.

Roth, J. 1972 'Some Contingencies of the Moral Evaluation and Control of Clientele: The Case of the Hospital Emergency Service,' *American Journal of Sociology* 77: 839–56.

Royal Commission on the Police (United Kingdom). 1962 *Final Report.* London: HMSO.

Rubinstein, J. 1973 *City Police.* New York: Farrer, Strauss and Giroux.

Russell, K. 1976 *Complaints against the Police: A Sociological View.* Leicester, UK: Milltak Ltd.

Sanders, W. 1977 *Detective Work.* New York: Free Press.

Schur, E. 1971 *Labeling Deviant Behavior.* New York: Harper and Row.

Scull, A. 1977 *Decarceration.* Englewood Cliffs, NJ: Prentice-Hall.

Silver, A. 1967 'The Demand for Order in Civil Society: A Review of Some Themes in the History of Urban Crime, Police, and Riot,' in D. Bordua ed. *The Police: Six Sociological Essays.* New York: Wiley, pp. 1–24.

Silverman, D. 1970 *The Theory of Organizations.* London: Heinemann.

Skolnick, J. 1966 *Justice without Trial.* New York: Wiley.

Skolnick, J. and Woodworth, J. 1967 'Bureaucracy, Information and Social Control: A Study of a Morals Detail,' in D. Bordua ed. *The Police: Six Sociological Essays*. New York: Wiley, pp. 99–136.

Solicitor General of Canada. 1979 *Selected Trends in Canadian Criminal Justice*. Ottawa: Communication Division, Ministry of the Solicitor General of Canada.

Steer, D. 1970 *Police Cautions – A Study in the Exercise of Police Discretion*. Oxford: Basil Blackwell.

Strauss, A. 1978 *Negotiations*. San Francisco: Jossey-Bass.

Strauss, A. *et al.*, 1963 'The Hospital and its Negotiated Order,' in E. Friedson ed. *The Hospital in Modern Society*. New York: Free Press.

Sullivan, D. and Siegel, L. 1974 'How Police Use Information to Make Decisions,' *Crime and Delinquency* 18: 253–62.

Sykes, R. and Clark, J. 1975 'A Theory of Deference Exchange in Police Civilian Encounters,' *American Journal of Sociology* 81 (3): 584–600.

Taylor, I. 1980 'The Law and Order Issue in the British and Canadian General Elections of 1979: Crime, Populism and State,' *Canadian Journal of Sociology* 5: 285–311.

Thompson, E.P. 1979 'On the New Issue of Postal Stamps,' *New Society* 50: 324–6.

Turk, A. 1976 'Law as a Weapon in Social Conflict,' *Social Problems* 23: 276–92.

Utz, P. 1978 *Settling the Facts: Discretion and Negotiation in the Criminal Courts*. Lexington, Mass.: Lexington Books.

Wald, M. *et al.*, 1967 'Interrogation in New Haven: The Impact of Miranda,' *Yale Law Journal* 76: 1521–648.

Washnis, G. 1976 *Citizen Involvement in Crime Prevention*. Lexington, Mass.: Lexington Books.

Weick, K. 1969 *The Social Psychology of Organizing*. Reading, Mass.: Addison-Wesley.

Werthman, C. and Piliavin, I. 1967 'Gang Members and the Police,' in D. Bordua ed. *The Police: Six Sociological Essays*. New York: Wiley, pp. 56–98.

Whitaker, B. 1964 *The Police*. Harmondsworth: Penguin.

Wilkins, L. 1964 *Social Deviance*. London: Tavistock.

Willett, T. 1964 *Criminal on the Road*. London: Tavistock.

Williams, D. 1974 'Prosecution, Discretion and the Accountability of the Police,', in R. Hood ed. *Crime, Criminology and Public Policy*. London: Heinemann, pp. 161–95.

Wilson, J. 1968 *Varieties of Police Behavior*. Cambridge, Mass.: Harvard University Press.

Wilson, J. and Boland, B. 1979 'The Effect of the Police on Crime,' *Law and Society Review* 12: 367–90.

Zander, M. 1978 'The Right of Silence in the Police Station and the Caution,' in P. Glazebrook ed. *Reshaping the Criminal Law*. London; Stevens, pp. 108–19.

# 16. The investigative function

*P. Greenwood, J.M. Chaiken and J. Petersilia*

## Stereotypes of the investigator's role

Three common stereotypes influence the public's perception of investigative effectiveness. First is the media image, which some detectives would claim for themselves while others would deplore it – the resourceful, streetwise cop, who always gets his man. Next is the historical stereotype, the image that old-timers on the force have of the detective's contribution to law and order. Finally, the critical stereotype – which recent objective studies have tended to develop. Some combination of these alternative stereotypes provides the basis for current investigative policies in most police departments today.

The media image of the working detective, particularly pervasive in widely viewed television series, is that of a clever, imaginative, perseverant, streetwise cop who consorts with glamorous women and duels with crafty criminals. He and his partners roam the entire city for days or weeks trying to break a single case, which is ultimately solved by means of the investigator's deductive powers. This image is the one that some investigators prefer – perhaps with a degree of sanitizing. They would concede that criminals are rarely as crafty or diabolical as depicted in the media, but might not quarrel with the media characterization of their own capabilities.

Some current investigative practices appear mainly as a means to preserve a media-like image or to give a victim the kind of services he expects largely because of that image. That is, fingerprint dusting, mug shot showing, or questioning witnesses are often done without any hope of developing leads, but simply for public relations.

The stereotyped images held by older police administrators are influenced by the special status that detectives once held in earlier times.[1] Not too many years ago various forms of illicit activity such as vice, gambling, prostitution, and speakeasies were much more openly tolerated by city governments than they are today. The existence of these illegal, but accepted, enterprises created problems for the city police. How could they keep such institutions under control without driving them completely out of business? The police dealings with these institutions were frequently carried on by detectives. The detectives ensured that the businesses were run in a somewhat orderly fashion and that 'undesirables' who attempted to take part were driven out. By this delicate handling of a troublesome situation the detectives often won the favor of the business leaders and politicians connected with these activities. Such political connections made the detective a man of respect and influence.

Allowing these illegal enterprises to continue had special investigation benefits for the police. When serious crimes did occur or when public pressure was brought to bear on the police to deal with a particular problem, these illegal activities provided a valuable source of information to which the detectives could turn. Not surprisingly, thieves and con men would often be customers of the vice and gambling operations, or have close contacts with people engaged in such business. If the police really wanted information on a particular criminal activity, the detectives could turn to their contacts within the illicit activities and either solicit information as, a favor or extort it by threatening the safety of the illegal operation. Thus the 'effectiveness' of detective operations frequently depended on maintaining close contacts with a select group of potential informers.

Another role detectives played in addition to that of policing illicit activities was that of dispensing street-corner justice. A good cop was expected to maintain order without resorting to the courts. He did this by persuasion, and by threats, and by actual physical force, if necessary. Only in those instances where it was clear that his presence alone would not deter crime did he bring in a suspect for criminal proceedings.

Detectives played a prominent role in the exercise of this discretionary justice because they were less visible than a uniformed patrolman when it came to breaking down doors or pummeling offenders on the street. Because of their experience they were expected to be more diplomatic in handling these incidents – part of the detective's basic working knowledge included which individuals could be treated roughly without getting the department into trouble. The detectives who could handle or clear up delicate situations without causing a commotion were highly valued by police and city administrators.

Another method formerly available to help a detective close cases was the third-degree or the extended interrogation. *Miranda*,[2] increased enforcement of civil liberties, and the rise of community review boards put a limitation on this type of activity. It is no longer acceptable for detectives to arrest a suspect and keep him in custody simply for investigative purposes. The use of physical or psychological                                                     force in an attempt to extort a confession or to get information about other suspects in a case is no longer permissible, under current due process requirements.

We have no empirical evidence concerning the results produced by these various techniques; therefore any comparisons between the effectiveness of historical and current approaches is purely speculative. However, it is obvious that investigators once possessed a number of investigative tactics that are no longer permissible.

A more critical stereotype of investigative effectiveness can be gleaned from a number of studies which attempt to analyze how detectives go about their work.

The earliest critic was probably Raymond Fosdick (1921). After visiting police departments in all of the major cities of the United States, he criticized detectives for:

- Lack of civil service standards in selection.

- Lack of training.

- Poor coordination with patrol operation.

- Lack of effective supervision.

- Lack of ordinary 'business systems' for handling their administrative work.

In many departments, these criticisms are equally appropriate today. More recent analysts have argued that:

- Police agencies do not routinely collect and summarize data that can be used to determine the effectiveness of investigation activities. Clearance and arrest statistics in particular are unsuitable because they fail to distinguish outputs of investigative efforts from those of other units in the department. Clearance data alone are also extremely unreliable indicators of police performance because of their subjective nature.
- The solution rate of crimes assigned to detectives appears insensitive to the number assigned, implying that detectives can accurately predict which cases can be solved and work on only those, or that the cases solve themselves.

- A high proportion of cases are closed when a patrol unit makes an arrest at the scene of the crime.

- Investigators make scant use of indirect evidence such as fingerprints, toolmarks, etc.

Uncomplimentary views are also being espoused by a number of progressive chiefs who have seen reforms and new initiatives take hold in every other area of policing, but find their detectives the last bastion of the *status quo*. In their departments, an appointment to the detective bureau is no longer viewed as the best path to promotion. In some departments (Los Angeles Police Department, for instance) an independent detective bureau no longer exists. Investigators are now assigned directly to a local operations commander.

Many of these chiefs are quite candidly critical of the old freewheeling detective style of operation. They see their detectives as simply trying to preserve the freedom and prerequisities of their jobs without making any efforts to adapt to the rapidly shifting community and legal climate in which they must work.

# [...]

In many ways our work has confirmed the findings of previous researchers, either by repeating their results in different cities or by producing information that helps explain why the earlier findings were correct. We have attempted to assure that our results have national applicability by collecting survey data from

153 departments, by conducting interviews in 29 departments located in various regions of the country, and by reviewing our conclusions with the members of our advisory board and working investigators [...] Nonetheless, many of the studies were conducted in a single department or a small number of departments, so that undoubtedly exceptions exist.

## Arrest and clearance rates

*Department-wide arrest and clearance rates are unreliable measures of the effectiveness of investigative operations. The vast majority of clearances are produced by activities of patrol officers, by the availability of identification of the perpetrator at the scene of the crime, or by routine police procedures.*

The fact that clearance rates can be manipulated by administrative practices was previously established by Greenwood (1970), Greenberg *et al.*, (1972), and Skolnick (1966). Our cross-sectional analysis of FBI Uniform Crime Reporting data for 1972 is consistent with this observation, since we showed that the number of clearances claimed for each arrest for a Part I crime ranged from a low of 0.38 to a high of 4.04, a factor of over 10. The ratio from high to low was even larger for each individual crime type, such as robbery or auto theft. Some departments claim a clearance for an auto theft whenever the vehicle is recovered, while others will not claim a clearance unless the perpetrator is arrested and charged for the instant offense. Clearance statistics are also affected by the amount of effort devoted to classifying reported crimes as 'unfounded' (i.e., the police find there is no evidence that a crime was actually committed). This practice reduces reported crime rates as well as increasing reported clearance rates.

With administrative discretion playing such a large role in determining a department's clearance rates, any attempt to compare effectiveness among departments using clearance rates is evidently meaningless. Even comparisons over time within a single department are unreliable unless steps are taken to assure that no change occurs in administrative practices concerning clearances and classification of crimes. Arrest rates are also unreliable measures of effectiveness since arrests can be made without resulting in any clearance.[3] The frequency of such events can be judged from the fact that in half of all departments the number of arrests for Part I crimes exceeds the number of clearances.[4]

Quite apart from the unreliability of arrest and clearance rates is the fact that they reflect activities of patrol officers and members of the public more than they reflect activities of investigators. Isaacs (1967), Conklin (1972), and our analysis of case samples [...] showed that approximately 30 percent of all clearances are produced by pickup arrests by patrol officers who respond to the scene of the crime. After the completion of our study, Bloch and Bell (1976) published findings in Rochester which, although intended for another purpose, permit calculating the fraction of clearances by arrest that were produced by on-scene arrest, most of which are presumably by patrol officers. Their data showed that, for burglary, 31.7 percent of clearances by arrest arose from on-scene arrests, with the analogous figure for robbery being 31.1 percent and for larceny 28.7 percent.

In roughly another 50 percent of cleared crimes (less for homicide and auto theft), the perpetrator is known when the crime report is first taken, and the main jobs for the investigator are to locate the perpetrator, take him or her into custody, and assemble the facts needed to present charges in court. This finding is also consistent with the work of other researchers. Isaacs (1967) studied 1,905 crimes reported to the Los Angeles Police Department and found that of 336 crimes cleared by arrest, 203 (or 60 percent) had a named suspect in the initial crime report, and of 1,556 crimes without a named suspect, 133 (or 8.6 percent) were cleared by arrest. Conklin (1972) studied 259 robberies reported to the Boston Police Department in 1968 and found that in 74 percent of cleared robberies the suspect was known by arrest at the scene or by victim identification. Smith,[5] in a study of 59 cleared robberies in Oakland in 1969, found that a victim or witness was responsible for case solution in 61 percent and that the suspect was known at the time the crime report was filed in 80 percent of cleared robberies. Recent studies by Greenberg et al., (1975) and Bloch and Bell (1976), while not specifically addressing the exact topic of this finding, provide adequate information for the reader to deduce that the same pattern prevails for the times and locations studied.

Hence, with around 30 percent of clearances produced by on-scene arrest and another 50 percent (approximately) by initial identification, around 20 percent of cleared crimes could possibly be attributed to investigative work, but we found [...] that most of these were also solved by patrol officers, members of the public who spontaneously provide further information, or routine investigative practices that could also have been followed by clerical personnel.

In fact, for Kansas City we estimated that at most 2.7 percent of all Part I crime clearances could be attributed to special techniques used by investigators. [...] The results for individual crime types in five other departments were not significantly different from those in Kansas City. Therefore, somewhere around 97 percent of cleared crimes will be cleared no matter what the investigators do, as long as the obvious routine follow-up steps are taken. Of course, included in the 2.7 percent are the most interesting and publicly visible crimes reported to the department, especially homicides and commercial burglaries. But the thrust of our analysis is that all the time spent by investigators on difficult cases where the perpetrator is unknown results in only 2.7 percent of the clearances.

This finding has now been established for a sufficiently large number of departments that there can be little doubt of its general correctness, with some variation, in all departments. By establishing a restricted interpretation of what constitutes 'routine processing', a department might find that investigative skill or 'special action' contributes to as much as 10 percent of all its clearances. Even so, the basic conclusion remains the same. Only in cases of homicide, robbery, and commercial theft did we find that the quality of investigative efforts could affect the clearance rate to any substantial extent. Conversely, the contribution of victims, witnesses, and patrol officers is most important to the identification and apprehension of criminal offenders.

*Department-wide arrest and clearance statistics vary primarily according to the size of the department, the region of the country in which it is located, and its crime workload (number of reported crimes per police officer). Variations with investigative training, staffing, procedures, and organization are small and do not provide much guidance for policy decisions.*

Once the nature of investigators' contributions to arrest and clearance rates is understood, it must be anticipated that variations in these rates among departments are explained primarily by characteristics that have nothing to do with the organization and deployment of investigators. This is in fact what we found from our national survey data. The three most important determinants of a department's arrest and clearance rates are its size, the region of the country it is located in, and its crime workload.

Large departments (measured by number of employees, budget, or population of the jurisdiction) claim more clearances per arrest in all crime categories than do smaller departments. However, the arrest rates of large departments do not differ from those in small departments.

Departments in the South Central states claim higher clearance rates than those in other regions, which follow in the order North Central, South Atlantic, Northeast, and West. However, arrest rates vary in almost exactly the reverse order. Evidently these differences reflect administrative practices or patterns of crime commission rather than differences in effectiveness.

In regard to crime workload, we found that departments having a large number of reported crimes per police officer have lower arrest rates than other departments. This relationship arises in the following way. The number of arrests per police officer in a year was found to rise nearly (but not quite) in direct proportion to the number of reported crimes per police officer until a certain threshold was reached. Beyond this threshold, increasing workload is associated with very small increases in the number of arrests per police officer. The thresholds are at approximately 35 Part I crimes per police officer per year and 3.5 crimes against persons per police officer per year. These thresholds are fairly high, as only about 20 percent of departments have greater workload levels.

These findings are consistent with the assumption that a city can increase its number of arrests or decrease the number of crimes (or both) by increasing the size of its police force, but the effect of added resources would be greatest for cities above the threshold.

In regard to clearance rates, the data showed that departments with high crime workload tend to claim more clearances per arrest than cities with low crime workload. As a result, clearance rates are less sensitive to workload than arrest rates. Although clearance rates for every crime type were found to decrease with increasing workload, the decreases were not significant for some types of crimes.

These workload relationships apply to all police officers, not just investigators. Although investigators are known to make more arrests per year than patrol officers, and our data confirmed this, the effect was not large enough that we could find a significant variation according to the fraction of the force in investigative units. In other words, if the total number of officers in a department is kept fixed, switching some of them into or out of investigative units is not likely to have a substantial effect on arrest or clearance rates.

Aside from the effects of size, region of the country, and workload on clearance and arrest rates, we did find a few smaller effects of possible interest.

Departments that assign a major investigative role to patrolmen have lower clearance rates, but not arrest rates, than other departments. This appears to reflect the fact that patrolmen cannot carry files around with them and therefore do not clear old crimes with new arrests. Departments with specialized units (concentrating on a single crime such as robbery) were found to have lower arrest rates, but not clearance rates, for the types of crimes in which they specialize, as compared with departments having generalist investigators. Departments in which investigators work in pairs had lower numbers of arrests per officer than those in which they work singly. Since we did not collect data permitting a comparison of the quality of arrests produced by solo and paired investigators, this finding must be interpreted with caution. The practice of pairing investigators, which is common only in the Northeast, is nonetheless brought into sufficient question that further research appears warranted.

Most other characteristics of investigators were found to be unrelated to arrest and clearance rates. These include the nature and extent of training for investigators, their civil service rank or rate of pay, and the nature of their interactions with prosecutors. However, this absence of correlations probably indictates more about the inadequacies of arrest and clearance rates as measures of effectiveness than about the inherent value of training and other characteristics.

## How investigators' time is spent

*While serious crimes are invariably investigated, many reported felonies receive no more than superficial attention from investigators. Most minor crimes are not investigated.*

From an analysis of the computer-readable case assignment file maintained by the Kansas City Police Department, [...], and observations during site visits, it was determined that although a large proportion of reported crimes are assigned to an investigator, many of these receive no more attention than the reading of the initial crime incident report; that is, many cases are suspended at once. The data show that homicide, rape, and suicide invariably resulted in investigative activity; while other serious types of cases received significant attention (i.e., at least a half-hour of a detective's time) in at least 60 percent of the instances. Overall, however, less than half of all reported crimes receive any serious attention by an investigator, and the great majority of cases that are actively investigated receive less than one day's attention. The data [...] imply that for homicides, rape, other felony sex crimes, kidnapping, aggravated assault, robbery, burglary, auto theft, and larceny *together*, 64.8 percent did not receive as much as a half-hour's attention from an investigator.

The net result is that the average detective does not actually work on a large number of cases each month, even though he may have a backlog of hundreds or thousands of cases that were assigned to him at some time in the past and are still theoretically his responsibility. [The data] showed that in Kansas City the number of worked-on cases per detective was generally under one per day, with the exception of the Missing Persons Unit.

*An investigator's time spent on casework is preponderantly consumed in reviewing reports, documenting files, and attempting to locate and interview victims. For cases that are solved (i.e., a suspect has been identified), an investigator's average time in post-clearance processing is longer than the time spent in identifying the perpetrator. A substantial fraction of time is spent on noncasework activities.*

In Kansas City, the breakdown of investigators' time was as follows. About 45 percent was spent on activities not attributable to individual cases. This includes administrative assignments, speeches, travel, reading teletypes, general surveillance of junkyards, pawnshops, gathering spots for juveniles, and the like, as well as slack time (for example, in a unit that is on duty at night to respond to robberies and homicides). The remaining 55 percent of the time is spent on casework. Of this, 40 percent (or 22 percent of the total) is spent investigating crimes that are never solved, just over 12 percent (or 7 percent of the total) is spent investigating crimes that are eventually solved, and nearly 48 percent (or 26 percent of the total) is spent on cleared cases after they have been solved. While these figures apply only to Kansas City, we have reviewed them, as well as more detailed tabulations, with investigators from other cities and compared them with our observational notes. We concluded they are approximately correct for other cities, with variations primarily in the areas of slack time (if investigators are not on duty at night) and time spent in conference with prosecutors.

Thus, investigators spend about 93 percent of their time on activities that do not lead directly to solving previously reported crimes. How are they to be judged on the quality of these activities? The time they spend on cases after they have been cleared serves the important purpose of preparing cases for court (this activity will be discussed below). The time they spend on noncasework activities serves a general support function for casework activities and therefore may be useful in ways that are difficult to quantify. The time they spend on crimes that are never solved can only be judged in terms of its public relations value and a possible deterrent value, because most of these crimes can be easily recognized at the start. (They are primarily the ones for which there is no positive identification of the perpetrator available at the scene of the crime.) Police administrators must ask themselves whether the efforts devoted to investigating crimes that are initially unsolved are justified by either the small number of case solutions produced by these activities or the associated public relations benefits.

## Collecting and processing physical evidence

*Many police departments collect more physical evidence than can be productively processed. Allocating more resources to increasing the processing capabilities of the department is likely to lead to more identifications than some other investigative actions.*

The ability of a police agency to collect and process the physical evidence at crime scenes is thought to be an important component of the criminal investigation process. However, in our study we focused on the role of physical evidence in contributing to the *solution* of crimes, as distinguished from its value in proving guilt once the crime is solved.

Earlier studies by Parker and Peterson (1972) and the President's Commission on Crime in the District of Columbia (1966) showed that in only a small number of felony offenses were evidence technicians requested to process the crime scene, and even when the crime scene was processed a significant portion of the available evidence might not be retrieved. Police administrators, aware of these deficiencies, have begun to experiment with a variety of organizational changes designed to increase the number of crime sites processed for physical evidence.

Our analysis of the physical evidence collection and processing activities of six police departments which employ different procedures [...] confirmed that a department can assure a relatively high recovery rate of latent prints from crime scenes by a sufficient investment in evidence technicians and by routinely dispatching technicians to the scene of felonies. The latent print recovery rate is also increased by processing the crime scene immediately following the report of the incident rather than at a later time.

However, the rate at which fingerprints were used to identify the perpeptrator of a burglary was essentially unrelated to the print recovery rate. In fact, [...] 1 to 2 percent of the burglary cases in each of three departments were cleared by identification from a latent print, despite substantial differences in operating procedures. In Richmond, evidence technicians are dispatched to nearly 90 percent of the reported burglaries and recover prints from 70 percent of the scenes they process, but the fraction of burglaries solved by fingerprints is about the same as in Long Beach or Berkeley, where evidence technicians are dispatched to the scene less frequently and lift prints less often.

The most plausible explanation as to why lifting more prints does not actually result in a higher rate of identifications appears to be that the fingerprint file searching capabilities of police departments are severely limited. If a suspect is known, there is little difficulty in comparing his prints with latent prints that have been collected. Thus, latent prints may help to confirm suspect identifications obtained in other ways. But in the absence of an effective means to perform 'cold searches' (where the suspect is unknown), the availability of a latent print cannot help to solve the crime.

From a comparison of the fingerprint identification sections in Washington, D.C., Los Angeles, Miami, and Richmond, we determined that 4 to 9 percent of all retrieved prints are eventually matched with those of a suspect in each of the departments. However, the number of 'cold-search' matches produced per man-year differed substantially among departments, according to the size of their inked print files and the attention devoted to this activity. In some departments, technicians performing cold searches produced far more case solutions per man- year than investigators.

The inference we reached was that an improved fingerprint *identification* capability will be more productive of identifications than a more intensive print *collection* effort. Although some techniques and equipment currently available to police departments were found to enhance identification capability, the technology needed to match single latent prints to inked prints is not fully developed and appears to us to be a high-priority item for research.

## Preparing the case for prosecution

*In many large departments, investigators do not consistently and thoroughly document the key evidentiary facts that reasonably assure that the prosecutor can obtain a conviction on the most serious applicable charges.*

Police investigation, whether or not it can be regarded as contributing significantly to the *identification* of perpetrators, is a necessary police function because it is the principal means by which all relevant evidence is gathered and presented to the court so that a criminal prosecution can be made. Thus, police investigators can be viewed as serving a support function for prosecutors.

Prosecutors have frequently contended that a high rate of case dismissals, excessive plea bargaining, and overly lenient sentences are common consequences of inadequate police investigations. The police, in response, often claim that even when they conduct thorough investigations, case dispositions are not significantly affected. We undertook the study [...] to illuminate the issues surrounding the controversy between police and prosecutor about responsibilities for prosecutorial failures.

A data form containing 39 questions that a prosecutor might want the police to address in conducting a robbery investigation was developed on the basis of discussions with prosecutors, detectives, and police supervisors. When this form was used to analyze the completeness of robbery investigations in two California prosecutors' offices, chosen to reflect contrasting prosecutorial practices concerning felony case screening, but similar workload and case characteristics, it was found that the department confronted by a stringent prosecutorial filing policy (Jurisdiction A) was significantly more thorough in reporting follow-on investigative work than the department whose cases were more permissively filed (Jurisdiction B). Yet, even the former department fell short of supplying the prosecutor with all of the information he desired; the data show that each of 39 evidentiary questions considered by a prosecutor to be necessary for effective case presentation were, on the average, covered in 45 percent of the cases in Jurisdiction A, while 26 percent were addressed by the department in Jurisdiction B.

We then determined whether the degree of thorough documentation of the police investigation was related to the disposition of cases, specifically to the rate of dismissals, the heaviness of plea bargaining, and the type of sentence imposed. Our analysis showed differences between the two jurisdictions. For example, none of the sampled cases was dismissed in Jurisdiction A; furthermore, 60 percent of the defendants pled guilty to the charges as filed. By comparison, in Jurisdiction B about one-quarter of the sampled cases were dismissed after filing, and only one-third of the defendants pled guilty to the charges as filed.

A comparison between the two offices concerning the heaviness of plea bargaining was shown [earlier]. Although plea bargaining appears lighter in Jurisdiction A, this may simply reflect that the gravity of criminal conduct in the A cases was less than in the B cases, i.e., special allegations were considerably more frequent to begin with in B. One cannot conclude that only the quality of documentation of the police investigation accounted for the difference.

A similar conclusion was reached with respect to sentence imposed. That is, differences in sentencing were found, but in light of variations in other case characteristics these differences might not necessarily be related to thoroughness of documentation. This analysis leads us to suggest that police failure to document a case investigation thoroughly *may* have contributed to a higher case dismissal rate and a weakening of the prosecutor's plea bargaining position.

## Relations between victims and police

*Crime victims in general strongly desire to be notified officially as to whether or not the police have solved their case, and what progress has been made toward convicting the suspect after his arrest.*

How much information to give the victim and when it is appropriate to convey it were the questions behind a telephone survey taken of robbery and burglary victims […]. This study must be regarded as exploratory; the survey was conducted simply as an initial attempt to explore how victims feel about receiving information feedback regarding their specific case, and which types of information they feel are most important.

Responses to questions about the victim's desire to know the progress of his or her case showed a large majority in favor of such information. Responses on whether or not the victim desired to be told of a police decision to suspend or drop investigative effort on his or her case, if such a decision were made, suggested a consistent preference for knowledge about this police decision, but with an observable tendency in cleared robbery cases (a relatively small segment of the underlying population) to the contrary.

Responses that the victims made when asked what their reactions would be if they had been told that no further investigation was intended on their cases revealed that approximately one-third of our sample would react negatively to unfavorable feedback (and the proportion would be higher if the data were weighted to reflect the relative numbers of each crime type).

To the extent that our survey results may reach beyond the confines of our small sample, they broadly underscore the belief that there exists a strong market for information feedback to victims from the police. But they also tend to confirm the view that giving unfavorable information to victims creates undesirable reactions in attitude toward the police in some of these victims. Finally our results suggest that other repercussions from information feedback, of which the police are sometimes apprehensive, are of slight significance. Few victims, no matter how much distressed by information coming to them from the police, indicated they would act inimically to police interests.

## Proactive investigation methods

*Investigative strike forces have a significant potential to increase arrest rates for a few difficult target offenses, provided they remain concentrated on activities for which they are uniquely qualified; in practice, however, they are frequently diverted elsewhere.*

In contrast to the typically reactive mode of most investigators assigned to Part I crimes, some police departments have shifted a small number of their investigators to more proactive investigation tactics. These units are usually established to deal with a particular type of offender such as known burglars, robbery teams, or active fences.

The proactive team members often work quite closely with other investigators, but unlike regular investigators they are not assigned a caseload of reported crimes. Instead they are expected to generate other sources of information to identify serious offenders. These other sources may include informants they have developed, intelligence data from surveillance activities, or undercover fencing operations which the police operate themselves.

The primary objective in establishing these units is to reduce the incidence of the target crime. The reduction is supposed to result from the containment effect of successfully arresting and prosecuting offenders and the deterrent effect which the publicity given these programs is expected to have on others. Therefore, the arrest productivity of these units is typically used as a measure of their primary effect. Changes in the incidence rate for the target crime type is also cited for this purpose. The chief problem in using these two measures is the difficulties in isolating the unique effects of the proactive units from either other activities of the police department or external factors affecting crime or arrest rates.

In the course of our study we looked at several such units by either examining evaluation reports or direct observation. In general, they all seemed to result in a much higher number of arrests for the officers assigned than other types of patrol or investigative activities. Consistent effects on targeted crime rates could not be identified.

In order to determine which activities of these units actually resulted in arrests, we examined a sample of cases from two of them in considerable detail. These units were the Miami STOP Robbery Unit and the Long Beach (California) Suppression of Burglary (SOB) Unit.

By examining a sample of robbery cases in Miami, we determined that although the STOP officers averaged 4 arrests per man-month, half of which were for robbery, in 10 out of 11 of these arrests the STOP officer was simply executing a warrant obtained by some other unit or accompanying another officer to make the arrest.

In Long Beach, the Suppression of Burglary officers averaged 2.4 arrests per man-month, half of which were for burglary or receiving stolen property. An analysis of 27 of their arrests disclosed that just half (13) resulted from their own work, with the remainder representing referral arrests or routine investigation which any other unit could have handled.

Our general conclusion from these observations was that proactive techniques can be productive in making arrests, particularly for burglary and fencing To be effective, such units must be staffed with highly motivated and innovative personnel. Their efforts must also be carefully monitored to ensure that they do not become diverted to making arrests for other units and that their tactics do not become overly aggressive so as to infringe on individual liberties.

*From Joan Petersilia, 'The investigative function' in P.W. Greenwood, J.M. Chaiken and J. Petersilia (eds.)* The Criminal Investigation Process *(Lexington, MA: D.C. Heath), 1977, pp 9–13, 225–35.*

## Notes

1  This brief historical account was compiled from information presented by Smith (1960), Fosdick (1921), and Franklin (1970).
2  The rights enumerated in *Miranda* v. *Arizona*, 384 U.S. 436 (1966).
3  In some jurisdictions, persons may be arrested 'for investigation' without a crime being charged. In all jurisdictions persons are occasionally arrested by error and are subsequently released by a prosecutor or magistrate without any clearance being claimed by the police.
4  Instances in which several perpetrators are arrested for a single crime may also explain an arrest/clearance ratio over 1.
5  William Smith, 'Robbery: Getting Caught', Chapter 2 in Volume 4 of Feeney (1973).

## References

Bloch, Peter, and Bel, James *Managing Investigations: The Rochester System*. The Urban Institute, Police Foundation, 1976.

Conklin, John. *Robbery and the Criminal Justice System*. J.B. Lippincott Co., Philadelphia, 1972.

Feeney, Floyd *et al.*, *The Prevention and Control of Robbery, Volume I: The robbery Setting, the Actors and some Issues; Volume II: The Handling of Robbery Arrestees: some Issues of Fact and Policy; Volume III: The Geography of Robbery; Volume IV: The Response of the Police and other Agencies to Robbery; Volume V: The History and Concept of Robbery*. The Center on Administration of Criminal Justice, University of California at Davis, 1973.

Fosdick, Raymond. *American Police Systems*. The Century Company, New York, 1921.

Franklin, Charles (Frank Hugh Usher). *The Third Degree*. Robert Hale, London, 1970.

Greenberg, Bernard, *et al.*, *Enhancement of the Investigative Function, Volume I: Analysis and Conclusions; Volume III; Investigative Procedures – Selected Task Evaluation; Volume IV: Burglary Investigative Checklist and Handbook*. Stanford Research Institute, Menlo Park, California, 1972. (Volume II not available.)

Greenberg, Bernard, *et al. Felony Investigation Decision Model – an Analysis of Investigative Elements of Information*. Stanford Research Institute, Menlo Park, California, December, 1975.

Greenwood, Peter W. *An Analysis of the Apprehension Activities of the New York City Police Department*. The New York City – Rand Institute, R-529-NYC, September, 1970.

Isaacs, Herbert H. 'A Study of Communications, Crimes, and Arrests in a Metropolitan Police Department', Appendix B of Institute for Defense Analyses, *Task Force Report: Science and Technology, a Report to the President's Commission on Law Enforcement and Administration of Justice*. U.S. Government Printing Office, Washington, D.C., 1967.

Parker, Brian, and Peterson, Joseph. *Physical Evidence Utilization in the Administration of Criminal Justice*. School of Criminology, University of California at Berkeley, 1972.

President's Commission on Crime in the District of Columbia. *Report of the President's Commission on Crime in the District of Columbia*. U.S. Government Printing Office, Washington, D.C., 1966.

Skolnick, Jerome. *Justice without Trial: Law Enforcement in a Democratic Society*. John Wiley and Sons, Inc., New York, 1966.

# Police culture

## Introduction

How are we to understand the police organisation and the outlook of police officers? In the opening chapter in this section Jerome Skolnick (**17**, 264) provides a sketch of what he calls the policeman's 'working personality', defined by three central elements: the potential of 'danger', linked to 'authority', set within a context in which efficiency is demanded. Danger makes the officer especially attentive to signs of potential violence and lawbreaking. The requirement on the officer to enforce laws provides authority but, together with the element of danger, produces and reinforces police solidarity and social isolation. Moreover, he says, police officers tend to be emotionally and politically conservative: 'If the element of danger in the policeman's working role tends to make the policeman suspicious, and therefore emotionally attached to the status quo, a similar consequence may be attributed to the element of authority. The fact that a man is engaged in enforcing a set of rules implies that he also becomes implicated in *affirming* them.'

Part of the police officer's 'working personality' (according to Skolnick) is suspiciousness. Such suspiciousness leads to the identification and grouping of citizens into various classifications according to John Van Maanen (**18**, 280), one of which is 'Assholes'. Van Maanen's analysis of the nature and role of this figure leads to what is undoubtedly the finest opening sentence in all policing literature: 'The asshole – creep, bigmouth, bastard, animal, mope, rough, jerkoff, clown, scumbag, wiseguy, phony, idiot, shithead, bum, fool, or any of a number of anatomical, oral, or incestuous terms – is part of every policeman's world.' Whereas 'suspicious persons' are known by their appearance, and 'know nothings' are only generally known by the police because they have made some request for assistance, 'assholes' are a stigmatized group 'and treated harshly on the basis of their failure to meet police expectations arising from the interaction situation itself' The stigmatization process, he says, has three stages: 'affront', 'clarification' and 'remedy'. Affront involves some challenge to the officer's authority; clarification is the process by which the officer determines what this affront 'means'; and remedy is the course of action taken in response to the clarification of the nature of the affront. The importance of this, Van Maanen argues, is that the process is close to the heart of the patrol officer's definition of his task providing, among many other things, a practical and moral justification for his existence.

Studying police precincts in New York City, Elizabeth Reuss-Ianni and Francis Ianni (**19**, 297) identified what they referred to as 'two cultures' of policing. Prior to the Knapp Commission on corruption in the 1970s it appears officers felt that relationships within the police organization were 'organic' with a shared, rather undifferentiated culture or ethos. Although the 'street cop culture' continued to exist after this time it was joined by a competing ethos at the management level of operations. This ethos embodied not the traditions of the job but the 'theories and practice of scientific management and public administration'. The Iannis argue that both cultures in policing share the same general goals – identified by them as combating crime and ensuring public safety – but differ in the ways in which they define these goals and, perhaps even more importantly, in the methods they identify as the most appropriate means of achieving these goals. They draw a number of other contrasts. Street cops focus on the local and decision-making takes place on a personal and largely immediate level. For management cops, crime problems are broader, are more concerned with future planning and with the political contexts of decisions. Of course the similarities and differences between the two cultures are more nuanced than this in practice but the general distinction is useful, the Iannis argue, as a means of understanding the ways in which police organizations respond to change, of analysing conflict within the organization and, more speculatively, how new sentiments within the organization might be stimulated.

Clifford Shearing and Richard Ericson (**20**, 315) take a critical look at extant work on police culture and, in particular, the assumption that 'rules' guide action. 'Faced with a choice between an elegant but deterministic and tautological model that requires the invention of implicit rules that are forced on people, and one that is sensitive to the experience of agents but has an ephemeral and cloud-like quality to it, sociologists have,' they argue, 'by and large, chosen flawed elegance.' Attempting to shift away from a reified conception of culture they seek to focus on culture as 'figurative action'. At the heart of this approach they take officers' 'stories' as instructions for seeing the world and acting in it. In such a conception culture, rather than a rulebook, is a storybook. Stories are largely open-ended, providing guidance for action rather than rules that dictate action: 'culture should be conceived of as a poetic system that enables action through a trope and precedent based logic.' This, they argue, both reduces the tendency in much of the sociology of the police to treat officers as cultural dopes and enables a more subtle understanding of change, discontinuity and ambiguity.

The theme of changing police culture is picked up by Janet Chan (**21**, 338). She is critical of the tendency – albeit something of an unintended one – for writing about police culture to treat it as undifferentiated or monolithic. She suggests that what is often being described is the Iannis' 'street cop culture' rather than 'management cop culture' or, indeed, any other ethos that may exist. She is also critical of a number of other features she identifies in extant work in this area, namely, the implicit passivity of police officers in such work, the implicit isolation of the police organization from broader political and cultural factors, and the implied lack of scope for change. In seeking to reorient our thinking in this area she builds on work by Shearing and Ericson (see above) and, more particularly, Pierre Bourdieu. She borrows Bourdieu's terms 'field' and 'habitus' to distinguish between the structural conditions of police work (the field) and the cultural knowledge deployed by officers (habitus). These exist in a dynamic relationship and form the basis for her analysis of organizational change within the New South Wales Police Force. In this view, it is crucial that police culture (or cultures) is understood in relation to the conditions of policing and, therefore, that 'it is unproductive to debate whether rule-tightening or changing culture [are] more important' in seeking to bring about reform.

Though it will not have been especially evident in the preceding readings, there is a focus in much writing on police culture on aspects that are negative or in some way problematic (and, indeed, Part E of this volume looks in greater at issues of racism and corruption, for example). In the final reading in this part, Peter Waddington (**22**, 364) returns to the literature on police culture, and in particular the idea of a 'canteen sub-culture', and argues that there is an important distinction to be drawn between canteen talk and public action. Building on Shearing and Ericson's focus on story-telling, Waddington seeks an appreciative understanding of the role that expressive behaviour within the private world of the police station (the 'canteen') plays in sustaining occupational esteem through performance: 'Essentially, therefore, police sub-culture operates mainly as a palliative, rather than as a guide to future action,' he argues. Policing is exceptional – indeed, a form of 'dirty work' – in which actors seek both to normalize it and glorify it. We should not, therefore, he argues, interpret canteen war stories as a simple reflection of, and guide to, the ways in which officers act on the street. Rather, 'if we wish to explain (and not just condemn) police behaviour on the streets, then we should look not in the remote recesses of what officers say in the canteen or privately to researchers, but in the circumstances in which they act'.

# 17. A sketch of the policeman's 'working personality'

*Jerome Skolnick*

A recurrent theme of the sociology of occupations is the effect of a man's work on his outlook on the world.[1] Doctors, janitors, lawyers, and industrial workers develop distinctive ways of perceiving and responding to their environment. Here we shall concentrate on analyzing certain outstanding elements in the police milieu, danger, authority, and efficiency, as they combine to generate distinctive cognitive and behavioral responses in police: a 'working personality'. Such an analysis does not suggest that all police are alike in 'working personality', but that there are distinctive cognitive tendencies in police as an occupational grouping. Some of these may be found in other occupations sharing similar problems. So far as exposure to danger is concerned, the policeman may be likened to the soldier. His problems as an authority bear a certain similarity to those of the schoolteacher, and the pressures he feels to prove himself efficient are not unlike those felt by the industrial worker. The combination of these elements, however, is unique to the policeman. Thus, the police, as a result of combined features of their social situation, tend to develop ways of looking at the world distinctive to themselves, cognitive lenses through which to see situations and events. The strength of the lenses may be weaker or stronger depending on certain conditions, but they are ground on a similar axis.

The policeman's 'working personality' is most highly developed in his constabulary role of the man on the beat. For analytical purposes that role is sometimes regarded as an enforcement speciality, but in this general discussion of policemen as they comport themselves while working, the uniformed 'cop' is seen as the foundation for the policeman's working personality. There is a sound organizational basis for making this assumption. The police, unlike the military, draw no caste distinction in socialization, even though their order of ranked titles approximates the military's. Thus, one cannot join a local police department as, for instance, a lieutenant, as a West Point graduate joins the army. Every officer of rank must serve an apprenticeship as a patrolman. This feature of police organization means that the constabulary role is the primary one for all police officers, and that whatever the special requirements of roles in enforcement specialties, they are carried out with a common background of constabulary experience.

The process by which this 'personality' is developed may be summarized: the policeman's role contains two principal variables, danger and authority, which should be interpreted in the light of a 'constant' pressure to appear efficient.[2] The element of danger seems to make the policeman especially attentive to signs indicating a potential for violence and lawbreaking. As a result, the policeman is generally a 'suspicious' person. Furthermore, the character of the policeman's work makes him less desirable as a friend, since norms of friendship implicate others in his work. Accordingly, the element of danger isolates the policeman socially from that segment of the citizenry which he regards as symbolically dangerous and also from the conventional citizenry with whom he identifies.

The element of authority reinforces the element of danger in isolating the policeman. Typically, the policeman is required to enforce laws representing puritanical morality, such as those prohibiting drunkenness, and also laws regulating the flow of public activity, such as traffic laws. In these situations the policeman directs the citizenry, whose typical response denies recognition of his authority, and stresses his obligation to respond to danger. The kind of man who responds well to danger, however, does not normally subscribe to codes of puritanical morality. As a result, the policeman is unusually liable to the charge of hypocrisy. That the whole civilian world is an audience for the policeman further promotes police isolation and, in consequence, solidarity. Finally, danger undermines the judicious use of authority. Where danger, as in Britain, is relatively less, the judicious application of authority is facilitated. Hence, British police may appear to be somewhat more attached to the rule of law, when, in fact, they may appear so because they face less danger, and they are as a rule better skilled than American police in creating the appearance of conformity to procedural regulations.

## The symbolic assailant and police culture

In attempting to understand the policeman's view of the world, it is useful to raise a more general question: What are the conditions under which police, as authorities, may be threatened?[3] To answer this, we must look to the situation of the policeman in the community. One attribute of many characterizing the policeman's role stands out: the policeman is required to respond to assaults against persons and property. When a radio call reports an armed robbery and gives a description of the man involved, every policeman, regardless of assignment, is responsible for the criminal's apprehension. The *raison d'être* of the policeman and the criminal law, the underlying collectively held moral sentiments which justify penal sanctions, arises ultimately and most clearly from the threat of violence and the possibility of danger to the community. Police who 'lobby' for severe narcotics laws, for instance, justify their position on grounds that the addict is a harbinger of danger since, it is maintained, he requires one hundred dollars a day to support his habit, and he must steal to get it. Even though the addict is not typically a violent criminal, criminal penalties for addiction are supported on grounds that he may become one.

The policeman, because his work requires him to be occupied continually with potential violence, develops a perceptual shorthand to identify certain kinds of people as symbolic assailants, that is, as persons who use gesture, language, and attire that the policeman has come to recognize as a prelude to violence. This does not mean that violence by the symbolic assailant is necessarily predictable. On the contrary, the policeman responds to the vague indication of danger suggested by appearance. Like the animals of the experimental psychologist, the policeman finds the threat of random damage more compelling than a predetermined and inevitable punishment.

Nor, to qualify for the status of symbolic assailant, need an individual ever have used violence. A man backing out of a jewelry store with a gun in one hand and jewelry in the other would qualify even if the gun were a toy and he had never in his life fired a real pistol. To the policeman in the situation, the man's personal history is momentarily immaterial. There is only one relevant sign: a gun signifying danger. Similarly, a young man may suggest the threat of violence to the policeman by his manner of walking or 'strutting', the insolence in the demeanor being registered by the policeman as a possible preamble to later attack.[4] Signs vary from area to area, but a youth dressed in a black leather jacket and motorcycle boots is sure to draw at least a suspicious glance from a policeman.

Policemen themselves do not necessarily emphasize the peril associated with their work when questioned directly, and may even have well-developed strategies of denial. The element of danger is so integral to the policeman's work that explicit recognition might induce emotional barriers to work performance. Thus, one patrol officer observed that more police have been killed and injured in automobile accidents in the past ten years than from gunfire. Although his assertion is true, he neglected to mention that the police are the only peacetime occupational group with a systematic record of death and injury from gunfire and other weaponry. Along these lines, it is interesting that of the two hundred and twenty-four working Westville policemen (not including the sixteen juvenile policemen) responding to a question about which assignment they would like most to have in the police department,[5] 50 per cent selected the job of detective, an assignment combining elements of apparent danger and initiative. The next category was adult street work, that is, patrol and traffic (37 per cent). Eight per cent selected the juvenile squad,[6] and only 4 per cent selected administrative work. Not a single policeman chose the job of jail guard. Although these findings do not control for such factors as prestige, they suggest that confining and routine jobs are rated low on the hierarchy of police preferences, even though such jobs are least dangerous. Thus, the policeman may well, as a personality, enjoy the possibility of danger, especially its associated excitement, even though he may at the same time be fearful of it. Such 'inconsistency' is easily understood. Freud has by now made it an axiom of personality theory that logical and emotional consistency are by no means the same phenomenon.

However complex the motives aroused by the element of danger, its consequences for sustaining police culture are unambiguous. This element requires him, like the combat soldier, the European Jew, the South African (white or black), to live in a world straining toward duality, and suggesting danger when 'they' are perceived. Consequently, it is in the nature of the policeman's situation that his conception of order emphasize regularity and predictability. It is, therefore, a conception shaped by persistent *suspicion*. The English 'copper', often portrayed as a courteous, easy-going, rather jolly sort of chap, on the one hand, or as a devil-may-care adventurer, on the other, is differently described by Colin MacInnes:

> The true copper's dominant characteristic, if the truth be known, is neither those daring nor vicious qualities that are sometimes attributed to him by friend or enemy, but an ingrained conservatism, and almost desperate love of the conventional. It is untidiness, disorder, the unusual, that a copper disapproves of most of all: far more, even than of crime which is merely a professional matter. Hence his profound dislike of people loitering in streets, dressing extravagantly, speaking with exotic accents, being strange, weak, eccentric, or simply any rare minority – of their doing, in fact, anything that cannot be safely predicted.[7]

Policemen are indeed specifically *trained* to be suspicious, to perceive events or changes in the physical surroundings that indicate the occurrence or probability of disorder. A former student who worked as a patrolman in a suburban New York police department describes this aspect of the policeman's assessment of the unusual.

> The time spent cruising one's sector or walking one's beat is not wasted time, though it can become quite routine. During this time, the most important thing for the officer to do is notice the *normal*. He must come to know the people in his area, their habits, their automobiles and their friends. He must learn what time the various shops close, how much money is kept on hand on different nights, what lights are usually left on, which houses are vacant … only then can he decide what persons or cars under what circumstances warrant the appellation 'suspicious'.[8]

The individual policeman's 'suspiciousness' does not hang on whether he has personally undergone an experience that could objectively be described as hazardous. Personal experience of this sort is not the key to the psychological importance of exceptionality. Each, as he routinely carries out his work, will experience situations that threaten to become dangerous. Like the American Jew who contributes to 'defense' organizations such as the Anti-Defamation League in response to Nazi brutalities he has never experienced personally, the policeman identifies with his fellow cop who has been beaten, perhaps fatally, by a gang of young thugs.

## Social isolation

The patrolman in Westville, and probably in most communities, has come to identify the black man with danger. James Baldwin vividly expresses the isolation of the ghetto policeman:

… The only way to police a ghetto is to be oppressive. None of the Police Commissioner's men, even with the best will in the world, have any way of understanding the lives led by the people they swagger about in twos and threes controlling. Their very presence is an insult, and it would be, even if they spent their entire day feeding gumdrops to children. They represent the force of the white world, and that world's criminal profit and ease, to keep the black man corraled up here, in his place. The badge, the gun in the holster, and the swinging club make vivid what will happen should his rebellion become overt …

It is hard, on the other hand, to blame the policeman, blank, good-natured, thoughtless, and insuperably innocent, for being such a perfect representative of the people he serves. He, too, believes in good intentions and is astounded and offended when they are not taken for the deed. He has never, himself, done anything for which to be hated – which of us has? And yet he is facing, daily and nightly, people who would gladly see him dead, and he knows it. There is no way for him not to know it: there are few things under heaven more unnerving than the silent, accumulating contempt and hatred of a people. He moves through Harlem, therefore, like an occupying soldier in a bitterly hostile country; which is precisely what, and where he is, and is the reason he walks in twos and threes.[9]

While Baldwin's observations on police–Negro relations cannot be disputed seriously, there is greater social distance between police and 'civilians' in general regardless of their color than Baldwin considers. Thus, Colin MacInnes has his English hero, Mr. Justice, explaining:

… The story is all coppers are just civilians like anyone else, living among them not in barracks like on the Continent, but you and I know that's just a legend for mugs. We *are* cut off: we're *not* like everyone else. Some civilians fear us and play up to us, some dislike us and keep out of our way but no one – well, very few indeed – accepts us as just ordinary like them. In one sense, dear, we're just like hostile troops occupying an enemy country. And say what you like, at times that makes us lonely.[10]

MacInnes' observation suggests that by not introducing a white control group, Baldwin has failed to see that the policeman may not get on well with anybody regardless (to use the hackneyed phrase) of race, creed, or national origin. Policemen whom one knows well often express their sense of isolation from the public as a whole, not just from those who fail to share their colour. Westville police were asked, for example, to rank the most serious problems police have. The category most frequently selected was not racial problems, but some form of public relations: lack of respect for the police, lack of cooperation in enforcement of law, lack of understanding of the requirements of police work. One respondent answered:

As a policeman my most serious problem is impressing on the general public just how difficult and necessary police service is to all. There seems to be an attitude of 'law is important, but it applies to my neighbor – not to me'.

Of the two hundred and eighty-two Westville policemen who rated the prestige police work receives from others, 70 per cent ranked it as only fair or poor, while less than 2 per cent ranked it as 'excellent' and another 29 per cent as 'good'. Similarly, in Britain, two thirds of a sample of policemen interviewed by a Royal Commission stated difficulties in making friends outside the force; of those interviewed 58 per cent thought members of the public to be reserved, suspicious, and constrained in conversation; and 12 per cent attributed such difficulties to the requirement that policemen be selective in associations and behave circumspectly.[11]

A Westville policeman related the following incident:

> Several months after I joined the force, my wife and I used to be socially active with a crowd of young people, mostly married, who gave a lot of parties where there was drinking and dancing, and we enjoyed it. I've never forgotten, though, an incident that happened on one Fourth of July party. Everybody had been drinking, there was a lot of talking, people were feeling boisterous, and some kid there – he must have been twenty or twenty-two – threw a firecracker that hit my wife in the leg and burned her. I didn't know exactly what to do – punch the guy in the nose, bawl him out, just forget it. Anyway, I couldn't let it pass, so I walked over to him and told him he ought to be careful. He began to rise up at me, and when he did, somebody yelled, 'Better watch out, he's a cop'. I saw everybody standing there, and I could feel they were all against me and for the kid, even though he had thrown the firecracker at my wife. I went over to the host and said it was probably better if my wife and I left because a fight would put a damper on the party. Actually, I'd hoped he would ask the kid to leave, since the kid had thrown the firecracker. But he didn't so we left. After that incident, my wife and I stopped going around with that crowd, and decided that it we were going to go to parties where there was to be drinking and boisterousness, we weren't going to be the only police people there.

Another reported that he seeks to overcome his feelings of isolation by concealing his police identity:

> I try not to bring my work home with me, and that includes my social life. I like the men I work with, but I think it's better that my family doesn't become a police family. I try to put my police work into the background, and try not to let people know I'm a policeman. Once you do, you can't have normal relations with them.[12]

Although the policeman serves a people who are, as Baldwin says, the established society, the white society, these people do not make him feel accepted. As a result, he develops resources within his own world to combat social rejection.

## Police solidarity

All occupational groups share a measure of inclusiveness and identification. People are brought together simply by doing the same work and having similar career and salary problems. As several writers have noted, however, police show an unusually high degree of occupational solidarity.[13] It is true that the police have a common employer and wear a uniform at work, but so do doctors, milk-men, and bus drivers. Yet it is doubtful that these workers have so close knit an occupation or so similar an outlook on the world as do police. Set apart from the conventional world, the policeman experiences an exceptionally strong tendency to find his social identity within his occupational milieu.

Compare the police with another skilled craft. In a study of the International Typographical Union, the authors asked printers the first names and jobs of their three closest friends. Of the 1,236 friends named by the 412 men in their sample, 35 per cent were printers.[14] Similarly, among the Westville police, of 700 friends listed by 250 respondents, 35 per cent were policemen. The policemen, however, were far more active than printers in occupational social activities. Of the printers, more than half (54 per cent) had never participated in any union clubs, benefit societies, teams, or organizations composed mostly of printers, or attended any printers' social affairs in the past 5 years. Of the Westville police, only 16 per cent had failed to attend a single police banquet or dinner in the past *year* (as contrasted with the printers' *5 years*); and of the 234 men answering this question, 54 per cent had attended 3 or more such affairs *during the past year*.

These findings are striking in light of the interpretation made of the data on printers. Lipset, Trow, and Coleman do not, as a result of their findings, see printers as an unintegrated occupational group. On the contrary, they ascribe the democratic character of the union in good part to the active social and political participation of the membership. The point is not to question their interpretation, since it is doubtlessly correct when printers are held up against other manual workers. However, when seen in comparison to police, printers appear a mini-mally participating group; put positively, police emerge as an exceptionally socially active occupational group.

## Police solidarity and danger

There is still a question, however, as to the process through which danger and authority influence police solidarity. The effect of danger on police solidarity is revealed when we examine a chief complaint of police: lack of public support and public apathy. The complaint may have several referents including police pay, police prestige, and support from the legislature. But the repeatedly voiced broader meaning of the complaint is resentment at being taken for granted. The policeman does not believe that his status as civil servant should relieve the public of responsibility for law enforcement. He feels, however, that payment out of public coffers somehow obscures his humanity and, therefore, his need for help.[15] As one put it:

Jerry, a cop, can get into a fight with three or four tough kids, and there will be citizens passing by, and maybe they'll look, but they'll never lend a hand. It's their country too, but you'd never know it the way some of them act. They forget that we're made of flesh and blood too. They don't care what happens to the cop so long as they don't get a little dirty.

Although the policeman sees himself as a specialist in dealing with violence, he does not want to fight alone. He does not believe that his specialization relieves the general public of citizenship duties. Indeed, if possible, he would prefer to be the foreman rather than the workingman in the battle against criminals.

The general public, of course, does withdraw from the workaday world of the policeman. The policeman's responsibility for controlling dangerous and sometimes violent persons alienates the average citizen perhaps as much as does his authority over the average citizen. If the policeman's job is to ensure that public order is maintained, the citizen's inclination is to shrink from the dangers of maintaining it. The citizen prefers to see the policeman as an automaton, because once the policeman's humanity is recognized, the citizen necessarily becomes implicated in the policeman's work, which is, after all, sometimes dirty and dangerous. What the policeman typically fails to realize is the extent he becomes tainted by the character of the work he performs. The dangers of their work not only draws policemen together as a group but separates them from the rest of the population. Banton, for instance, comments:

> ... patrolmen may support their fellows over what they regard as minor infractions in order to demonstrate to them that they will be loyal in situations that make the greatest demands upon their fidelity ...
>
> In the American departments I visited it seemed as if the supervisors shared many of the patrolmen's sentiments about solidarity. They too wanted their colleagues to back them up in an emergency, and they shared similar frustrations with the public.[16]

Thus, the element of danger contains seeds of isolation which may grow in two directions. In one, a stereotyping perceptual shorthand is formed through which the police come to see certain signs as symbols of potential violence. The police probably differ in this respect from the general middle-class white population only in degree. This difference, however, may take on enormous significance in practice. Thus, the policeman works at identifying and possibly apprehending the symbolic assailant; the ordinary citizen does not. As a result, the ordinary citizen does not assume the responsibility to implicate himself in the policeman's required response to danger. The element of danger in the policeman's role alienates him not only from populations with a potential for crime but also from the conventionally respectable (white) citizenry, in short, from that segment of the population from which friends would ordinarily be drawn. As Janowitz has noted in a paragraph suggesting similarities between the police and the military,

> '... any profession which is continually preoccupied with the threat of danger requires a strong sense of solidarity if it is to operate effectively.

Detailed regulation of the military style of life is expected to enhance group cohesion, professional loyalty, and maintain the martial spirit'.[17]

## Social isolation and authority

The element of authority also helps to account for the policeman's social isolation. Policemen themselves are aware of their isolation from the community, and are apt to weight authority heavily as a causal factor. When considering how authority influences rejection, the policeman typically singles out his responsibility for enforcement of traffic violations.[18] Resentment, even hostility, is generated in those receiving citations, in part because such contact is often the only one citizens have with police, and in part because municipal administrations and courts have been known to utilize police authority primarily to meet budgetary requirements, rather than those of public order. Thus, when a municipality engages in 'speed trapping' by changing limits so quickly that drivers cannot realistically slow down to the prescribed speed or, while keeping the limits reasonable, charging high fines primarily to generate revenue, the policeman carries the brunt of public resentment.

That the policeman dislikes writing traffic tickets is suggested by the quota system police departments typically employ. In Westville, each traffic policeman has what is euphemistically described as a working 'norm'. A motorcyclist is supposed to write two tickets an hour for moving violations. It is doubtful that 'norms' are needed because policemen are lazy. Rather, employment of quotas most likely springs from the reluctance of policemen to expose themselves to what they know to be public hostility. As a result, as one traffic policeman said:

> You learn to sniff out the places where you can catch violators when you're running behind. Of course, the department gets to know that you hang around one place, and they sometimes try to repair the situation there. But a lot of the time it would be too expensive to fix up the engineering fault, so we keep making our norm.

When meeting 'production' pressures, the policeman inadvertently gives a false impression of patrolling ability to the average citizen. The traffic cyclist waits in hiding for moving violators near a tricky intersection, and is reasonably sure that such violations will occur with regularity. The violator believes he has observed a policeman displaying exceptional detection capacities and may have two thoughts, each apt to generate hostility toward the policeman: 'I have been trapped,' or 'They can catch me; why can't they catch crooks as easily?' The answer, of course, lies in the different behavior patterns of motorists and 'crooks'. The latter do not act with either the frequency or predictability of motorists at poorly engineered intersections.

While traffic patrol plays a major role in separating the policemen from the respectable community, other of his tasks also have this consequence. Traffic patrol is only the most obvious illustration of the policeman's general responsibility for maintaining public order, which also includes keeping order at public accidents, sporting events, and political rallies. These activities share one feature: the policeman is called upon to *direct* ordinary citizens, and therefore to restrain their freedom of action. Resenting the restraint, the average citizen in such a situation typically thinks something along the lines of 'He is supposed to catch crooks; why is he bothering me?' Thus, the citizen stresses the 'dangerous' portion of the policeman's role while belittling his authority.

Closely related to the policeman's authority-based problems as *director* of the citizenry are difficulties associated with his injunction to *regulate public morality*. For instance, the policeman is obliged to investigate 'lovers' lanes', and to enforce laws pertaining to gambling, prostitution, and drunkenness. His responsibility in these matters allows him much administrative discretion since he may not actually enforce the law by making an arrest, but instead merely interfere with continuation of the objectionable activity.[19] Thus, he may put the drunk in a taxi, tell the lovers to remove themselves from the back seat, and advise a man soliciting a prostitute to leave the area.

Such admonitions are in the interest of maintaining the proprieties of public order. At the same time, the policeman invites the hostility of the citizen so directed in two respects: he is likely to encourage the sort of response mentioned earlier (that is, an antagonistic reformulation of the policeman's role) and the policeman is apt to cause resentment because of the suspicion that policemen do not themselves strictly conform to the moral norms they are enforcing. Thus, the policeman, faced with enforcing a law against fornication, drunkenness, or gambling, is easily liable to a charge of hypocrisy. Even when the policeman is called on to enforce the laws relating to overt homosexuality, a form of sexual activity for which police are not especially noted, he may encounter the charge of hypocrisy on grounds that he does not adhere strictly to prescribed heterosexual codes. The policeman's difficulty in this respect is shared by all authorities responsible for maintenance of disciplined activity, including industrial foremen, political leaders, elementary schoolteachers, and college professors. All are expected to conform rigidly to the entire range of norms they espouse.[20] The policeman, however, as a result of the unique combination of the elements of danger and authority, experiences a special predicament. It is difficult to develop qualities enabling him to stand up to danger, and to conform to standards of puritanical morality. The element of danger demands that the policeman be able to carry out efforts that are in their nature overtly masculine. Police work, like soldiering, requires an exceptional calibre of physical fitness, agility, toughness, and the like. The man who ranks high on these masculine characteristics is, again like the soldier, not usually disposed to be puritanical about sex, drinking, and gambling.

On the basis of observations, policemen do not subscribe to moralistic standards for conduct. For example, the morals squad of the police department, when questioned, was unanimously against the statutory rape age limit, on grounds that as late teenagers they themselves might not have refused an attractive offer from a seventeen-year-old girl.[21] Neither, from observations, are policemen by any means total abstainers from the use of alcoholic beverages. The policeman who is arresting a drunk has probably been drunk himself; he knows it and the drunk knows it.

More than that, a portion of the social isolation of the policeman can be attributed to the discrepancy between moral regulation and the norms and behavior of policemen in these areas. We have presented data indicating that police engage in a comparatively active occupational social life. One interpretation might attribute this attendance to a basic interest in such affairs; another might explain the policeman's occupational social activity as a measure of restraint in publicly violating norms he enforces. The interest in attending police affairs may grow as much out of security in 'letting oneself go' in the presence of police, and a corresponding feeling of insecurity with civilians, as an authentic preference for police social affairs. Much alcohol is usually consumed at police banquets with all the melancholy and boisterousness accompanying such occasions. As Horace Cayton reports on his experience as a policeman:

> Deputy sherriffs and policemen don't know much about organized recreation; all they usually do when celebrating is get drunk and pound each other on the back, exchanging loud insults which under ordinary circumstances would result in a fight.[22]

To some degree the reason for the behavior exhibited on these occasions is the company, since the policeman would feel uncomfortable exhibiting insobriety before civilians. The policeman may be likened to other authorities who prefer to violate moralistic norms away from onlookers for whom they are routinely supposed to appear as normative models. College professors, for instance, also get drunk on occasions, but prefer to do so where students are not present. Unfortunately for the policeman, such settings are harder for him to come by than they are for the college professor. The whole civilian world watches the policeman. As a result, he tends to be limited to the company of other policemen for whom his police identity is not a stimulus to carping normative criticism.

## Correlates of social isolation

The element of authority, like the element of danger, is thus seen to contribute to the solidarity of policemen. To the extent that policemen share the experience of receiving hostility from the public, they are also drawn together and become dependent upon one another. Trends in the degree to which police may exercise authority are also important considerations in understanding the dynamics of the relation between authority and solidarity. It is not simply a question of how much absolute authority police are given, but how much authority they have relative to what they had, or think they had, before. If, as Westley concludes, police violence is frequently a response to a challenge to the policeman's authority, so too may a perceived reduction in authority result in greater solidarity. Whitaker comments on the British police as follows:

> As they feel their authority decline, internal solidarity has become increasingly important to the police. Despite the individual responsibility of each police officer to pursue justice, there is sometimes a tendency to close ranks and to form a square when they themselves are concerned.[23]

These inclinations may have positive consequences for the effectiveness of police work, since notions of professional courtesy or colleagueship seem unusually high among police.[24] When the nature of the policing enterprise requires much joint activity, as in robbery and narcotics enforcement, the impression is received that cooperation is high and genuine. Policemen do not appear to cooperate with one another merely because such is the policy of the chief, but because they sincerely attach a high value to teamwork. For instance, there is a norm among detectives that two who work together will protect each other when a dangerous situation arises. During one investigation, a detective stepped out of a car to question a suspect who became belligerent. The second detective, who had remained overly long in the back seat of the police car, apologized indirectly to his partner by explaining how wrong it had been of him to permit his partner to encounter a suspect alone on the street. He later repeated this explanation privately, in genuine consternation at having committed the breach (and possibly at having been culpable in the presence of an observer). Strong feelings of empathy and cooperation, indeed almost of 'clannishness', a term several policemen themselves used to describe the attitude of police toward one another, may be seen in the daily activities of police. Analytically, these feelings can be traced to the elements of danger and shared experiences of hostility in the policeman's role.

Finally, to round out the sketch, policemen are notably conservative, emotionally and politically. If the element of danger in the policeman's role tends to make the policeman suspicious, and therefore emotionally attached to the status quo, a similar consequence may be attributed to the element of authority. The fact that a man is engaged in enforcing a set of rules implies that he also becomes implicated in *affirming* them. Labor disputes provide the commonest example of conditions inclining the policeman to support the status quo. In these situations, the police are necessarily pushed on the side of the defense of property. Their responsibilities thus lead them to see the striking and sometimes angry workers as their enemy and, therefore, to be cool, if not antagonistic, toward the whole conception of labor militancy.[25] If a policeman did not believe in the system of laws he was responsible for enforcing, he would have to go on living in a state of conflicting cognitions, a condition which a number of social psychologists agree is painful.[26]

## Conclusion

The combination of *danger* and *authority* found in the task of the policeman unavoidably combine to frustrate procedural regularity. If it were possible to structure social roles with specific qualities, it would be wise to propose that these two should never, for the sake of the rule of law, be permitted to coexist. Danger typically yields self-defensive conduct, conduct that must strain to be impulsive because danger arouses fear and anxiety so easily. Authority under such conditions becomes a resource to reduce perceived threats rather than a series of reflective judgments arrived at calmly. The ability to be discreet, in the sense discussed above, is also affected. As a result, procedural requirements take on a 'frilly' character, or at least tend to be reduced to a secondary position in the face of circumstances seen as threatening.

If this analysis is correct, it suggests a related explanation drawn from the realm of social environment to account for the apparent paradox that the elements of danger and authority are universally to be found in the policeman's role, yet at the same time fail to yield the same behavior regarding the rule of law. If the element of danger faced by the British policeman is less than that faced by his American counterpart, its ability to undermine the element of authority is proportionately weakened. Bluntly put, the American policeman may have a more difficult job because he is exposed to greater danger. Therefore, we would expect him to be less judicious, indeed less discreet, in the exercise of his authority. Similarly, such an explanation would predict that if the element of actual danger or even the perception of such in the British policeman's job were to increase, complaints regarding the illegal use of his authority would also rise.

Recently there have been spectacular cases supporting this proposition. One of these, resulting in a government inquiry which suspended two top police officers, took place at Sheffield on March 14, 1963. Several detectives brutally assaulted four men in five successive and separate relays with a truncheon, fists, and a rhinoceros whip. The report of the Inquiry concludes that the police were undoubtedly guilty of 'maliciously inflicting grievous bodily harm of a serious nature on two prisoners'.[27] The assaults were described as 'deliberate, un-provoked, brutal and sustained … for the purpose of inducing confessions of crime'. The detectives had been formed into a 'Crime Squad' which felt it had the authority to use 'tough methods to deal with tough criminals and take risks to achieve speedy results'. The leading offender told the Inquiry 'that criminals are treated far too softly by the Courts, that because criminals break rules, police may and must do so to be a jump ahead, that force is justified as a last resort as a method of detection when normal methods fail, and that a beating is the only answer to turn a hardened criminal from a life of crime'.[28]

Perhaps the most interesting feature of the report are the mitigating factors the Inquiry took into account. They found that the detectives were overworked (in a city where crime was on the rise); that the detectives were, and felt, under pressure to obtain results; that the use of violence had been encouraged by hints beforehand by senior officers; that senior officers instituted, witnessed, and joined in the violence and were wholly inadequately dealt with by the chief constable; and that the detectives were told to give a false account in court by a senior officer, who concocted it. The entire report suggests that the detectives who engaged in the beatings were not unusual men. There was no evidence of mental instability on their part, neither of psychosis, psychopathy, nor neurosis. Not one man on the force reported the incident, although several had learned of it. The report gives the feeling that while the event itself was exceptional, the conditions leading to it, such as overwork, pressure to produce, and encourage-ment by superiors, were ordinary. Although the report does not use the language of social science, it strongly suggests that the structural and cultural conditions in the police force supported this sort of response.

Also interesting is the evident racial bias of the Sheffield police. One of them testified he carried his rhinoceros whip to deal with 'coloured informants'. The racial issue appears increasingly significant for the British police as a whole. The *New York Times* reported on May 3, 1965 that although the London police force is six thousand men short of full strength, not one colored applicant has been accepted, even though fifteen West Indians, six Pakistanis and six Indians tried to join the force in the preceding three years. The official reason given is that the applicants did not meet the qualifications. Apart from three part-time constables in the Midlands, however, there was, at the time of the report, not one colored policeman in Britain, even though Pakistanis, Indians, and West Indians, all officially classified as colored by the British, account for nearly 2 per cent of the population.

Suggestions have been made to enlist colored policemen for colored neighborhoods, or to bring in trained colored policemen from the Commonwealth. Others have asked for the introduction of colored policemen in white neighbourhoods, especially in London. The *New York Times* story closes with a suggestion by one critic, Anthony Lester, that British police chiefs take a trip to New York to see how Negro policemen fit in. 'Policemen have a different status here than in the States', he is reported to have said. 'They are more a father figure, a symbol of authority with their tall helmets and slow walk. It's difficult to get people to accept colored men in this job. They have had no Negro officers in the Army, no way of getting used to taking orders from colored men.'

To complete the analogy of similarity of police action with similarity of social conditions, problems of police behavior also appear to be correlated with the restriction of marihuana use, a recent police phenomenon in England. Colin MacInnes argues, in a letter published in the fall of 1963, that when the London police began vigorously enforcing the marihuana law:

> … it looks as if the hallowed myth that English coppers never use violence, perjury, framing of suspects – let alone participate in crimes – is at last being shattered in the public mind. Now, what has been foolish about this legend is not that coppers *do* do these things – as all police forces do and must – but that national vanity led many to suppose that our coppers were far nicer men than any others.[29]

Although MacInnes' statement may be overly strong, it does suggest that those who too clearly contrast American and British police in favor of British are probably generally wrong. Of course, there are always individual as well as group differences in police behavior. However, even if conduct varies more than MacInnes indicates, and conduct will vary with relations of the police organization to the community, the character of the substantive criminal law being enforced, and the social conditions of the community, it is nevertheless likely that the variables of danger and authority in the policeman's role, combined with a constant pressure to produce, result in tendencies general enough and similar enough to identify a distinctive 'working personality' among police. The question becomes one of understanding what the police do with it […].

*From Jerome Skolnick*, Justice without Trial, *(New York: Wiley), 3rd edition, 1994, pp 42–70.*

## Notes

1 For previous contributions in this area, see the following: Ely Chinoy, *Automobile Workers and the American Dream* (Garden City: Doubleday and Company, Inc., 1955); Charles R. Walker and Robert H. Guest, *The Man on the Assembly Line* (Cambridge: Harvard University Press, 1952); Everett C. Hughes, 'Work and the Self', in his *Men and their Work* (Glencoe, Illinois: The Free Press, 1958), pp. 42–55; Harold L. Wilensky, *Intellectuals in Labor Unions: Organizational Pressures on Professional Roles* (Glencoe, Illinois: The Free Press, 1956); Wilensky, 'Varieties of Work Experience', in Henry Borow (ed.), *Man in a World at Work* (Boston: Houghton Mifflin Company, 1964), pp. 125–54; Louis Kriesberg, 'The Retail Furrier: Concepts of Security and Success', *American Journal of Sociology*, **57** (March, 1952), 478–85; Waldo Burchard, 'Role Conflicts of Military Chaplains', *American Sociological Review*, **19** (October, 1954), 528–35; Howard S. Becker and Blanche Geer, 'The Fate of Idealism in Medical School', *American Sociological Review*, **23** (1958), 50–6; and Howard S. Becker and Anselm L. Strauss, 'Careers, Personality, and Adult Socialization', *American Journal of Sociology*, **62** (November, 1956), 253–63.

2 By no means does such an analysis suggest there are no individual or group differences among police. On the contrary, most of this study emphasizes differences, endeavoring to relate these to occupational specialities in police departments. This chapter, however, explores similarities rather than differences, attempting to account for the policeman's general disposition and to behave in certain ways.

3 William Westley was the first to raise such questions about the police, when he inquired into the conditions under which police are violent. Whatever merit this analysis has, it owes much to his prior insights, as all subsequent sociological studies of the police must. See his 'Violence and the Police', *American Journal of Sociology*, **59** (July, 1953), 34–41; also his unpublished Ph.D. dissertation *The Police: A Sociological Study of Law, Custom, and Morality*, University of Chicago, Department of Sociology, 1951.

4 See Irving Piliavin and Scott Briar, 'Police Encounters with Juveniles', *American Journal of Sociology*, **70** (September, 1964), 206–14.

5 A questionnaire was given to all policemen in operating divisions of the police force: patrol, traffic, vice control, and all detectives. The questionnaire as administered at police line-ups over a period of three days, mainly by the author but also by some of the police personnel themselves. Before the questionnaire was administered, it was circulated to and approved by the policemen's welfare association.

6 Indeed, the journalist Paul Jacobs, who has ridden with the Westville juvenile police as part of his own work on poverty, observed in a personal communication that juvenile police appear curiously drawn to seek out dangerous situations, as if juvenile work without danger is degrading.

7 Colin McInnes, *Mr. Love and Justice* (London: New English Library, 1962), p. 74.

8 Peter J. Connell, 'Handling of Complaints by Police', unpublished paper for course in Criminal Procedure, Yale Law School, Fall, 1961.

9 James Baldwin, *Nobody Knows my Name* (New York: Dell Publishing Company, 1962), pp. 65–7.

10 McInnes, *op. cit.*, p. 20.

11 Royal Commission on the Police, 1962, Appendix IV to *Minutes of Evidence*, cited in Michael Banton, *The Policeman in the Community* (London: Tavistock Publications, 1964), p. 198.

12 Similarly, Banton found Scottish police officers attempting to conceal their occupation when on holiday. He quotes one as saying: 'If someone asks my wife 'What does your husband do', I've told her to say, "He's a clerk," and that's the way it went because she found that being a policeman's wife – well, it wasn't quite a stigma, she didn't feel cut off, but that a sort of invisible wall was up for conversation purposes when a policeman was there' (p. 198).

13 In addition to Banton, William Westley and James Q. Wilson have noted this characteristic of police. See Westley, *op. cit.*, p. 294; Wilson, 'The Police and their Problems: A Theory', *Public Policy*, **12**, (1963), 189–216.

14 S.M. Lipset, Martin H. Trow, and James S. Coleman, *Union Democracy* (New York: Anchor Books, 1962), p. 123.

15 On this issue there was no variation. The statement 'the policeman feels' means that there was no instance of a negative opinion expressed by the police studied.

16 Banton, *op. cit.*, p. 114.

17 Morris Janowitz, *The Professional Soldier: A Social and Political Portrait* (New York: The Free Press of Glencoe, 1964).

18 O.W. Wilson, for example, mentions this factor as a primary source of antagonism toward police. See his 'Police Authority in a Free Society', *Journal of Criminal Law, Criminology and Police Science*, **54** (June, 1964), 175–7. In the current study, in addition to the police themselves, other

people interviewed, such as attorneys in the system, also attribute the isolation of police to their authority. Similarly, Arthur L. Stinchcombe, in an as yet unpublished manuscript, 'The Control of Citizen Resentment in Police Work', provides a stimulating analysis, to which I am indebted, of the ways police authority generates resentment.

19  See Wayne R. La Fave, 'The Police and Nonenforcement of the Law', *Wisconsin Law Review* (1962), 104–37, 179–239.

20  For a theoretical discussion of the problems of leadership, see George Homans, *The Human Group* (New York: Harcourt, Brace and Company, 1950), especially the chapter on 'The Job of the Leader', pp. 415–40.

21  The work of the Westville morals squad is analyzed in detail in an unpublished master's thesis by J. Richard Woodworth. *The Administration of Statutory Rape Complaints: A Sociological Study* (Berkeley: University of California, 1964).

22  Horace R. Cayton, *Long Old Road* (New York: Trident Press, 1965), p. 154.

23  Ben Whitaker, *The Police* (Middlesex, England: Penguin Books, 1964), p. 137.

24  It would be difficult to compare this factor across occupations, since the indicators could hardly be controlled. Nevertheless, I felt that the sense of responsibility to policemen in other departments was on the whole quite strong.

25  In light of this, the most carefully drawn lesson plan in the 'professionalized' Westville police department, according to the officer in charge of training, is the one dealing with the policeman's demeanor in labor disputes. A comparable concern is now being evidenced in teaching policemen appropriate demeanor in civil rights demonstrations. See, e.g., Juby E. Towler, *The Police Role in Racial Conflicts* (Springfield: Charles C. Thomas, 1964).

26  Indeed, one school of social psychology asserts that there is a basic 'drive', a fundamental tendency of human nature, to reduce the degree of discrepancy between conflicting cognitions. For the policeman, this tenet implies that he would have to do something to reduce the discrepancy between his beliefs and his behavior. He would have to modify his behavior, his beliefs, or introduce some outside factor to justify the discrepancy. If he were to modify his behavior, so as not to enforce the law in which he disbelieves, he would not hold his position for long. Practically, then, his alternatives are to introduce some outside factor, or to modify his beliefs. However, the outside factor would have to be compelling in order to reduce the pain resulting from the dissonance between his cognitions. For example, he would have to be able to convince himself that the only way he could possibly make a living was by being a policeman. Or he would have to modify his beliefs. See Leon Festinger, *A Theory of Cognitive Dissonance* (Evanston, Ill.: Row-Peterson, 1957). A brief explanation of Festinger's theory is reprinted in Edward E. Sampson (ed.), *Approaches, Contexts, and Problems of Social Psychology* (Englewood Cliffs, N.J.: Prentice-Hall, 1964), pp. 9–15.

27  Sheffield Police Appeal Inquiry, Cmnd. 2176, November, 1963.

28  *Ibid.*, p. 5.

29  'The Silly Season', *Partisan Review*, **30** (Fall, 1963), 430, 432.

# 18. The asshole

*John Van Maanen*

I guess what our job really boils down to is not letting the assholes take over the city. Now I'm not talking about your regular crooks ... they're bound to wind up in the joint anyway. What I'm talking about are those shitheads out to prove they can push everybody around. Those are the assholes we gotta deal with and take care of on patrol ... They're the ones that make it tough on the decent people out there. You take the majority of what we do and its nothing more than asshole control (a veteran patrolman).[1]

## Police typifications

The asshole – creep, bigmouth, bastard, animal, mope, rough, jerkoff, clown, scumbag, wiseguy, phony, idiot, shithead, bum, fool, or any of a number of anatomical, oral, or incestuous terms – a part of every policeman's world.[2] Yet the grounds upon which such a figure stands have never been examined systematically. The purpose of this chapter is to display the interactional origins and consequences of the label asshole as it is used by policemen, in particular, patrolmen, going about their everyday tasks. I will argue that assholes represent a distinct but familiar type of person to the police and represent, therefore, a part of their commonsense wisdom as to the kinds of people that populate their working environment. From this standpoint, assholes are analytic types with whom the police regularly deal. More importantly, however, I will also argue that the label arises from a set of situated conditions largely unrelated to the; institutional mandate of the police (i.e., to protect life and property, arrest law violators, preserve the peace, *etc.*) but arises in response to some occupational and personal concerns shared by virtually all policemen.

According to most knowledgeable observers, nothing characterizes policing in America more than the widespread belief on the part of the police themselves that they are primarily law enforcers – perpetually engaged in a struggle with those who would disobey, disrupt, do harm, agitate, or otherwise upset the just order of the regime. And, that as policemen, they and they alone are the most capable of sensing right from wrong; determining who is and who is not respectable; and, most critically deciding what is to be done about it (if anything). Such heroic self-perceptions reflecting moral superiority have been noted by numerous social scientists concerned with the study of the police. Indeed, several detailed, insightful, and thoroughly accurate mappings of the police, perspective exist.[3] For instance, learned discussions denote the various 'outgroups' perceived by the police (e.g., Harris 1973; Bayley and Mendelsohn, 1969); or the 'symbolic assailants' which threaten the personal security of the police (e.g., Skolnick, 1966; Neiderhoffer, 1967; Rubenstein, 1973); or the 'suspicious characters' recognized by the police via incongruous (nonordinary) appearances (e.g., Sacks; 1972; Black, 1968). These reports provide the background against which the pervasive police tropism to order the world into the 'for us' and 'against us' camps can most clearly be seen.

Yet these studies have glossed over certain unique but together common-sensical properties of the police situation with the attendant consequence of reifying the police position that the world is in fact divided into two camps. Other than noting the great disdain and disgust held by many police officers toward certain predefined segments of the population they presumably are to serve, these studies fail to fully describe and explain the range and meaning attached to the various labels used by the police themselves to affix individual responsibility for particular actions occurring within their normal workaday world. Furthermore, previous studies do not provide much analytic aid when determining how the various typifications carried by the police are recognized as relevant and hence utilized as guides for action by a police officer in a particular situation. In short, if police typifications are seen to have origins as well as consequences, the popular distinction between 'suspicious' or 'threatening' and the almost mythologized 'normal' or 'respectable' is much too simple. It ignores not only the immediate context in which street interactions take place, but it also disregards the critical signs read by the police within the interaction itself which signify to them both the moral integrity of the person with whom they are dealing and the appropriate recipe they should follow as the interaction proceeds.[4] Therefore, any distinction of the 'types' of people with whom the police deal must include an explicit consideration of the ways in which the various 'types' are both immediately and conditionally identified by the police. Only in this fashion is it possible to accurately depict the labels the police construct to define, explain, and take action when going about their routine and nonroutine tasks.

To begin this analysis, consider the following typology which suggests that the police tend to view their occupational world as comprised exhaustively of three types of citizens (Van Maanen, 1974). These ideal types are: (1) 'suspicious persons' – those whom the police have reason to believe may have committed a serious offense; (2) 'assholes' – those who do not accept the police definition of the situation; and (3) 'know nothings' – those who are not either of the first two categories but are not police and therefore, according to the police, cannot know what the police are about.

This everyday typification scheme provides a clue to the expectations, thoughts, feelings, and behaviors of the police. For example, 'suspicious persons' are recognized on the basis of their appearance in public surroundings. Such an appearance is seen as a furtive, nonroutine, *de trop*, or, to use Sacks's (1972) nicely turned phrase, 'dramatically torturous'. Crucially, such persons, when they provide the police reason to stop and interrogate them, are treated normally in a brisk, though thoroughly professional, manner. It is not their moral worth or identity which is at issue, but rather it is a possible illegal action in their immediate or not-so-immediate past which is in question. From the patrolman's point of view, he is most interested in insuring that formal procedural issues are observed. Hence the personal production of a professional police performance is called for and is presented – at least initially.[5] On the other end of the continuum reside the 'know nothings', the 'average' citizens, who most generally come under police scrutiny only via their request for service. The 'know nothing' may be the injured or wronged party or the seeker of banal information and as such is treated with a certain amount of deference and due respect by the patrolman. 'Assholes', by way of contrast, are stigmatized by the police and treated harshly on the basis of their failure to meet police expectations arising from the *interaction situation itself*. Of course, street interaction may quickly transform suspicious persons into know nothings and know nothings into assholes, or any, combination thereof. But it is the asshole category which is most imbued with moral meaning for the patrolman – establishing for him a stained or flawed identity to attribute to the citizen upon which he can justify his sometimes malevolent acts. Consequently, the asshole may well be the recipient of what the police call 'street justice' – a physical attack designed to rectify what police take as personal insult. Assholes are most vulnerable to street justice, since they, as their title implies, are not granted status as worthy human beings. Their actions are viewed by the police as stupid or senseless and their feelings as incomprehensible (if they can even be said to have feelings). Indeed, as I will show, the police consistently deny an asshole a rationale or ideology to support their actions, insisting that the behavior of an asshole is understandable only as a sudden or lifelong character aberration. On the other hand, suspicious persons are less likely candidates for street justice because, in the majority of cases, their guilt may still be in question, or, if their guilt has been in fact established, their actions are likely to seem at least comprehensible and purposeful to the police (i.e., a, man steals because he needs money; a man shoots his wife because she 'two-timed' him; *etc.*). Also, there are incentives for the suspicious person to cooperate (at least nominally) when subject to police attention. The suspicious person may well be the most co-operative of all the people with whom the police deal on a face-to-face basis. This is, in part, because he is most desirous of presenting a normal appearance (unafraid, unruffled, and with nothing to hide), and, in part, because if he is in fact caught he does not want to add further difficulty to his already difficult position. Finally, know nothings are the least likely candidates for street justice since they represent the so-called client system and are therefore those persons whom the police are most interested in impressing through a polished, efficient, and courteous performance.

At this point, I should note that the above ideal types are anything but precise and absolute. One purpose of this chapter is to make at least one of these categories more explicit. But since I am dealing primarily with interior, subjective meanings negotiated in public with those whom the police interact, such typifications will always be subject to severe situational, temporal, and individually idiosyncratic restriction. Hence, an asshole in one context may be a know nothing in another, and vice versa. In other words, I am not arguing in this chapter that a general moral order is shared by all policemen as their personalized but homomorphic view of the world. Indeed, the moral order subscribed to by police is complex, multiple, and continually shifts back and forth between that which is individual and that which is collective. What I will argue, however, is that particular situational conditions (i.e., provocations) predispose most policemen toward certain perceptions of people which lead to the application of what can be shown to be rule-governed police actions. My objective, then, is simply to begin teasing out the underlying structure of police thought and to denote the features of what might be called the secondary reality of police work. The remainder of this chapter is divided into four sections. The next section, 'Patrol work', describes very briefly certain understandings shared by street-level patrolmen as to what is involved in their work. In a sense, these understandings are akin to behavioral rules that can be seen to mobilize police action; hence they represent the grounds upon which the figure of the asshole is recognized. The following section, 'Street justice', deals with the characteristic processes involved in discovering, distinguishing, and treating the asshole. Some conclusions revolving around the relationship between the police and the asshole are suggested in the next section. And, finally, a few of the broad implications that flow from this analysis are outlined in the last section.

## Patrol work

Policing city streets entails what Hughes (1958) refers to as a 'bundle of tasks'. Some of these tasks are mundane; many of them are routine; and a few of them are dangerous. Indeed, patrol work defies a general job description since it includes an almost infinite set of activities – dogcatching, first-aid, assisting elderly citizens, breaking up family fights, finding lost children, pursuing a fleeing felon, directing traffic, and so forth. Yet, as in other lines of endeavor, patrolmen develop certain insider notions about their work that may or may not reflect what outsiders believe their work to be. Such notions are of course attached firmly to the various experientially based meanings the police learn to regularly ascribe to persons, places, and things – the validity of which is established, sustained, and continually reaffirmed through everyday activity. Because these meanings are, to some degree, shared by patrolmen going about similar tasks, their collective representation can be detailed and linked to certain typical practices engaged in on the street by the police. Thus, to understand the police perspective on, and treatment of, the asshole, it is necessary also to understand the manner in which the policeman conceives of his work. Below is a very short summary of certain interrelated assumptions and beliefs that patrolmen tend to develop regarding the nature of their job.

### Real police work

Many observers have noted the pervasive police tendency to narrowly constrict their perceived task to be primarily – and to the exclusion of other alternatives – law enforcement. As Skolnick and Woodworth (1967: 129) suggest evocatively, 'when a policeman can engage in real police work – act out the symbolic rites of search, chase and capture – his self-image is affirmed and morale enhanced'. Yet, ironically, opportunities to enact this sequence are few and far between. In fact, estimates of the time police spend actually in real police work while on patrol vary from 0 percent (as in the case of the quiet country policeman for whom a street encounter with a *bona fide* 'criminal' would be a spectacular exception to his daily tour of duty) to about 10 or 15 percent (as in the case of the busy urban patrolman who works a seamy cityside district in which the presence of pimps, dealers, cons, and burglars, among others, is the everyday rule). Nonetheless, most of the policeman's time is spent performing rather dry, monotonous, and relatively mundane activities of a service nature – the proverbial clerk in a patrol car routinely cruising his district and awaiting dispatched calls (see Cain, 1971; Reiss, 1971; Webster, 1970; and Cummings, Cummings and Edell, 1965, for further discussion on how the police, spend their time).

Within these boundaries, notions of real police work develop to provide at least a modicum of satisfaction to the police. To a patrolman, *real police work* involves the use of skills and special abilities he believes he possesses by virtue of his unique experience and training. Furthermore, such a perspective results in minimizing the importance of other activities he is often asked regularly to perform. In fact, an ethos of 'stay-low-and-avoid-trouble-unless-real-police-work-is-called-for' permeates police organizations (Van Maanen, 1973, 1974, 1975). Only tasks involving criminal apprehension are attributed symbolic, importance. For the most part, other tasks, if they cannot be avoided, are performed (barring interruption) with ceremonial dispatch and disinterest.

### Territoriality

A central feature of policing at the street level is the striking autonomy maintained (and guarded jealously) by patrolmen working the beat. All patrol work is conducted by solo officers or partnerships (within a squad to whom they are linked) responsible for a given plot of territory. Over time, they come to know, in the most familiar and penetrating manner, virtually every passageway – whether alley, street, or seldom-used path – located in their sector. From such knowledge of this social stage come the corresponding evaluations of what particular conditions are to be considered good or bad, safe or unsafe, troubled or calm, usual or unusual, and so on. Of course, these evaluations are also linked to temporal properties associated with the public use of a patrolman's area of responsibility. As Rubenstein (1973) suggests, the territorial perspective carried by patrolmen establishes the basic normative standard for the proper use of place. And those perceived by patrolmen to be beyond the pale regarding their activities in space and time are very likely to warrant police attention.

### Maintaining the edge

Charged with enforcing ambiguous generalized statutes, and operating from an autonomous, largely isolated position within the city, it is not surprising that police have internalized a standard of conduct which dictates that they must control and regulate all situations in which they find themselves. At one level, police feel they have the right to initiate, terminate, or otherwise direct all encounters with members of the public. Yet such perceptions penetrate more broadly into the social scheme of things, for police feel furthermore that the public order is a product of their ability to exercise control. The absence of trouble on their beat becomes, therefore a personalized objective providing intimate feedback as to one's worth as a patrolman. Activity which may threaten the perceived order becomes intolerable, for it signifies to the patrolman that his advantage over the conduct of others (his 'edge') is in question. It is a source of embarrassment in front of a public audience, and sometimes it is considered a disgrace to the police uniform if it is viewed by one's peers or departmental superiors. Clearly, such activity cannot be allowed to persist, for it may indicate both to a patrolman's colleagues and to his superiors that the officer no longer cares for his job and has, consequently, lost the all-important respect of those he polices (endangering, it is thought, other policemen who might work the same district). Hence, to 'maintain one's edge' is a key concept *vis-à-vis* the 'how to' of police work. And, as all policemen know, to let down the facade (for they do recognize the contrived nature of the front) is to invite disrespect, chaos, and crime.

### The moral mandate

In light of the above three features of the police frame, it should be clear that police are both representatives of the moral order and a part of it. They are thus committed ('because it is right') to maintaining their collective face as protectorates of the right and respectable against the wrong and the not-so-respectable. Situations in which this face is challenged – regardless of origin – are likely to be responded to in unequivocal terms. For example, Cain (1971) writes that when the authority of an officer is questioned by a member of the non police public, the officer has three broad responses available to him. He may (1) physically attack the offender; (2) swallow his pride and ignore the offender; or (3) manufacture a false excuse for the arrest of the offender. What this suggests is a highly personalized view on the part of the police as to their moral position and responsibility, one in which an attempt on the part of the citizen to disregard the wishes of a policeman may be viewed by the police as a profaning of the social and legal system itself. Such an act can also be seen to provoke moral and private indignation on the part of the officer as an individual, thus providing him with another *de rigeur* excuse to locate an appropriate remedy. Since the police personally believe that they are capable of making correct decisions regarding the culpability of an involved party, justice is likely, in the case of an offense to the moral sensibilities of a police officer, to be enacted quickly, parsimoniously, and self-righteously – whether it be the relatively trivial swift kick in the pants or the penultimate tragedy involved in the taking of a life. Thus, the moral mandate felt by the police to be their just right at the societal level is translated and transformed into occupational and personal terms and provides both the justification and legitimation for specific acts of street justice.

This truncated picture of the occupational frame involved in the doing of police work provides the rubric upon which we now can examine the making of an asshole. As one would expect, assholes are not afforded the protection of the more structured relationships police maintain with other of their categories of persons – the suspicious and the know nothings. Rather, they fall outside this fragile shelter, for their actions are seen as 'senseless', so 'aimless' and 'irrational' that recognizable and acceptable human motives are difficult for the police to discover (i.e., from the patrolmen's perspective, there are not legitimate reasons to distrust, disagree with, make trouble for, or certainly hate the police). In this sense, it is precisely the 'pointlessness' of an individual's behavior that makes him an asshole and subjects him to the police version of street justice.

## Street justice

Policeman to motorist stopped for speeding: 'May I see your driver's license, please?'
Motorist: 'Why the hell are you picking on me and not somewhere else looking for some real criminals?'
Policeman: 'Cause you're an asshole, that's why ... but I didn't know that until you opened your mouth.'

The above story represents the peculiar reality with which patrolmen believe they must contend. The world is in part (and, to policemen, a large part) populated by individuals to whom an explanation for police behaviour cannot be made, for, as the police say, 'assholes don't listen to reason'. The purpose of this section is to explore the commonplace and commonsense manner in which the tag asshole arises, sticks, and guides police action during a street encounter. This stigmatization process is divided into three stages which, while analytically distinct, are highly interactive and apt to occur in the real world of policing almost simultaneously. For convenience only, then, these phases are labeled *affront*, *clarification*, and *remedy*.

Throughout this discussion it should be remembered that the asshole is not necessarily a suspected law violator – although the two often overlap, thus providing double trouble, so to speak, for the labeled. Importantly the police view of the asshole as deviant is a product of the immediate transaction between the two and not a product of an act preceding the transaction. This is not to say, however, that certain classes in society – for example, the young, the black, the militant, the homosexual – are not 'fixed' by the police as a sort of permanent asshole grouping. Indeed, they are. Yet such bounded *a priori* categories can do policemen little good – except perhaps when dealing with the racial or bohemian obvious – for such stereotypes are frequently misleading and dysfunctional (e.g., the 'hippie' who is a detective's prized informant; the black dressed in a purple jumpsuit, who happens to be a mayor's top aide; the sign carrying protestor who is an undercover FBI agent). And, even in cases in which *a priori character* judgments are a part of the decision to stop an individual, the asshole label, if it is to play a determining role in the encounter, must arise anew. That is to say, if the asshole distinction is to have a *concrete* as opposed to *abstract* meaning, it must in some manner be tied fundamentally and irresolutely to observable social action occurring in the presence of the labeling officer.

Certainly, a policeman's past experience with an individual or with a recognizable group will influence his street behavior. For example, a rookie soon discovers (as a direct consequence of his initiation into a department) that blacks, students, Mexicans, reporters, lawyers, welfare workers, researchers, prostitutes, and gang members are not to be trusted, are unpredictable, and are usually 'out-to-get-the-police'. He may even sort these 'outsiders' into various categories indicative of the risk he believes they present to him or the implied contrast they have with his own life-style and beliefs. Yet, without question, these categories will never be exhaustive – although the absolute size of what patrolmen call their 'shit lists' may grow over the years. Consequently, to understand the police interpretation and meaning of the term 'asshole' we must look directly into the field situations in which it originates.

### Affront: challenge

When a police officer approaches a civilian to issue a traffic citation or to inquire as to the whys and wherefores of one's presence or simply to pass the time of day, he directly brings the power of the state to bear on the situation and hence makes vulnerable to disgrace, embarrassment, and insult that power. Since the officer at the street level symbolizes the presence of the Leviathan in the everyday lives of the citizenry, such interactions take on dramatic properties far different from ordinary citizen-to-citizen transactions (Manning, 1974a; Silver, 1967). In a very real sense, the patrolman-to-citizen exchanges are moral contests in which the authority of the state is either confirmed, denied, or left in doubt. To the patrolman, such contests are not to be taken lightly, for the authority of the state is also his personal authority, and is, of necessity, a matter of some concern to him. To deny or raise doubt about his legitimacy is to shake the very ground upon which his self-image and corresponding views are built.

An affront, as it is used here, is a challenge to the policeman's authority, control, and definition of the immediate situation. As seen by the police, an affront is simply a response on the part of the other which indicates to them that their position and authority in the interaction are not being taken seriously. It may occur with or without intent. Whether it is the vocal student who claims to 'know his rights', the stumbling drunk who says he has had 'only two beers', or the lady of the evening who believes she is being questioned only because she is wearing 'sexy clothes', the police will respond in particular ways to those who challenge or question their motive or right to intervene in situations that they believe demand police intervention. Clearly, overt and covert challenges to police authority will not go unnoticed. In fact, they can be seen to push the encounter to a new level wherein any further slight to an officer, however subtle, provides sufficient evidence to a patrolman that he may indeed be dealing with a certifiable asshole and that the situation is in need of rapid clarification. From this standpoint, an affront can be seen, therefore, as disrupting the smooth flow of the police performance. The argumentative motorist, the pugnacious drunk, the sometimes ludicrous behavior of combatants in a 'family beef' all interfere [with], and hence make more difficult, the police task. Of course, some officers relish such encounters. In this sense, ironically, the asshole gives status to the police rather than takes it away. However, since the label is itself a moral charge (and it need not be made salient or verbally expressed), it is open theoretically for rebuttal and evidence may or may not be forthcoming which will substantiate or contradict the charge. Such evidence is gathered in the next analytic stage.

## Clarification: confrontation

Based upon a perceived affront, the patrolman must then attempt to determine precisely the kind of person with whom he is engaged. It is no longer an idle matter to him in which his private conceptions of people can be kept private as he goes about his business. But the patrolman is now in a position wherein he may discover that his taken-for-granted authority on the street is not exactly taken for granted by another. Two commonsensical issues are critical at this point in an encounter. *First*; the officer must determine whether or not the individual under question could have, under the present circumstances, acted in an alternative fashion. To wit, did the perceived affront occur by coercion or accident through no fault of the person? Did the person even know he was dealing with a police officer? Was he acting with a gun at his head? And so on. *Second*, and equally important, given that the person could have acted differently, the officer must determine whether or not the individual was aware of the consequences that might follow his action. In other words, was the action frivolous, naive, unserious, and not meant to offend? Did the person know that his actions were likely to be interpreted offensively by the police? The answers to these two questions, provide patrolmen with material (or lack of it) to construct and sustain an asshole definition. Let us examine in some depth these questions, for they raise the very issue of personal responsibility which is at the nexus of the asshole definition.[6]

McHugh (1969) argues persuasively that the social construction of deviant categories is a matter of elimination which proceeds logically through a series of negotiated offers and responses designed to fix responsibility for a perceived deviant act (i.e., a deviant act requires a charge before it can be said to have happened). Police follow a similar paradigm when filling, emptying, or otherwise attending to their person categories. Again, the first item to be determined in this process is the issue of whether or not the person had alternative means available to him of which he could reasonably be expected to be aware. For example, the speeding motorist who, when pulled to the side of the road, could be excused for his abusive language if it were discovered by the officer that the motorist's wife was at the same time in the back seat giving birth to a child. Similarly, juveniles 'hanging out' on a public street corner at certain times of the day may be sometimes overlooked if the police feel that 'those kids don't have anyplace to go'. On the other hand, if it can be determined that there is no unavoidable reason behind the affronting action, the individual risks being labeled an asshole. The drunken and remorseless driver, the wife who harangues the police officer for mistreating her husband after she herself requested police service to break up a family fight, or the often-warned teenager who makes a nuisance of himself by flagrantly parading in public after curfew are all persons whom the police believe could have and should have acted differently. Their acts were not inevitable, and it could be expected that they had available to them conventional alternatives.

Given that there are no compelling deterministic accounts readily available to the patrolman to excuse a particular affront, the officer must still make a judgment about the offender's motive. In other words, as the second issue listed above suggests, the policeman must decide whether or not the person knows what he is doing. Could the person be expected to know of the consequences which follow an affront to an officer of the law? Indeed, does the person even realize that what he is doing is likely to provoke police action? Could this particular person be expected to knowbetter? All are questions related to the establishment of a motive for action. For example, the stylized and ceremonial upright third finger when attached to the hand of a thirty-year-old man is taken by the police very differently from the same gesture attached to the hand of a four-year-old child. Loud and raucous behavior in some parts of a city may be ignored if the police feel 'the people there don't know any better'. Or the claim that one is Jesus Christ resurrected and is out to do battle with the wages of sin may indicate to the police that they are either in the presence of a 'dope-crazed radical hippie freak' or a 'soft-brained harmless mental case', depending, perhaps, on the offender's age. If the person is young, for instance, responsibility is likely to be individualized – 'it is his fault'; however, if the person is old, responsibility is likely to be institutionalized – 'he can't help it, he's a nut'.

Summarily, the police have available to them two principles of clarification. One concerns the means available to a person guilty of anaffront, and the other concerns the purposes behind the affront itself. If the affront is viewed as unavoidable or unintended, the person is unlikely to be subjected to shabby or harsh treatment at the hands of the police. The asshole, however, is one who is viewed as culpable and blameworthy for his affronting action, and, as the next section details, he will be dealt with by the police in ways they feel appropriate.

### Remedy: solution

The above portrait of the clarification principles utilized by police in labeling assholes suggests that certain typical police responses can be displayed by a simple fourfold typology. Figure 18.1 depicts the relationship between the police officer's assessment of responsibility for the affront and denotes, within each cell, the typical police response given the various possible assessments.

Cell A represents the subject case of this essay since it involves a flagrant (inexcusable) disregard for the sentiments of the police. To the police, those falling into this category are unmistakably assholes and are therefore prominent candidates to be the recipients of street justice – the aim of which is to punish or castigate the individual for a moral transgression. Persons placed in this category are also the most likely to be placed under questionable arrest. This is not so because of the original intent of the encounter (which often, by itself, is trivial) but rather because of the serious extralegal means utilized by the police to

|  | Does the person know what he is doing? | | |
|---|---|---|---|
|  |  | Yes | No |
| Could the person act differently under the circumstances? | Yes | A Castigate | B Teach |
|  | No | C Ignore | D Isolate |

**Figure 18.1**

enforce their particular view of the situation upon the recalcitrant asshole – 'hamming-up' or 'thumping' (beating).[7] And, as Reiss (1971) suggests, the use of force is not a philosophical question to the police but rather one of who, where, when, and how much.

The use of such means requires of course that the officer manufacture *post facto* a legally defensible account of his action in order to, in the vernacular of the day, 'cover his ass'.[8] Such accounts in legalese most often take the form of 'disorderly conduct', 'assaulting a police officer', 'the use of loud and abusive language in the presence of women and children', 'disturbing the peace', or the almost legendary – due to its frequent use – 'resisting arrest'. The asshole from this position is subject to a police enactment of double jeopardy – justice without trial in the streets and justice, perhaps with trial, in the courts. And regardless of the outcome in the latter case, there is usually only one loser. I should emphasize, however, that I am not saying the behavior of the asshole may not be brutish, nasty, and itself thoroughly vicious. I am simply suggesting that behavior violating extralegal moral codes used by police to order their interactions – whether it be inconsiderate, barbarous, or otherwise – will be responded to in what police believe to be appropriate ways.

Cell B of Figure 18.1 also represents a serious, affront to, police integrity, and it too may be an affront which calls for an extra-legal response. An illustration provided by the remarks of a patrolman is useful in this context:

> Those goddamn kids got to learn sooner or later that we won't take a lot of shit around Cardoza (a local college campus). Next time I see one of those punks waving a Viet Cong flag I'm gonna negotiate the little bastard back into an alley and kick his rosy red ass so hard he ain't gonna carry nothing for awhile. Those kids gotta be made to see that they can't get away with this type of thing.

Whether or not such a prediction was actually carried, out does not matter, for the quotation itself indicates that 'teaching' occupies a particularly prominent position in the police repertoire of possible responses. Thus, the uncooperative and surly motorist finds his sobriety rudely questioned, or the smug and haughty college student discovers himself stretched over the hood of a patrol car and the target of a mortifying and brusque body search. The object of such degradation ceremonies is simply to reassert police control and demonstrate to the citizen that his behavior is considered inappropriate. Teaching techniques are numerous, with threat, ridicule, and harassment among the more widely practiced. Other examples are readily available, such as the morally-toned lectures meted out to those who would attempt to bribe, lie, or otherwise worm their way out of what a policeman sees to be a legitimate traffic citation, the traditional – but vanishing – 'kick in the ass' administered to a youngster caught stealing an apple or cutting school. The intent in all these cases is clear. The person must be taught a lesson. And whether the teaching occurs in public or in the back of an alley, the person must be shown the error of his ways. He has acted perhaps out of ignorance, but nevertheless the police feel they must demonstrate that they will not casually overlook the action. However, I should note that the person in this category will remain an asshole in the eyes of the police until he has apparently learned his lesson to the satisfaction of the officers on the scene. Here a display of remorse is no doubt crucial to the police.[9]

Cell C represents the case in which the police are likely to excuse the affront due to the extenuating circumstances surrounding the affront. When it is clear to the police that there are indeed mitigating conditions, their response is to ignore the error – pretend, as it were, that such an affront never happened. For example, it is understandable to the police that the victim of a mugging may be somewhat abusive toward them when they interrogate him just after the crime (although there is a fine line to be drawn here). Similarly, if a teenage male vigorously defends the chaste and virtuous intentions of him and his girlfriend while questioned by the police in a concealed and cozy corner of a public park, it is understood by the police, that the boy has few other acceptable alternative lines available. The police response is typically to adopt a somewhat bemused tolerance policy toward actions which under different circumstances might have produced the orb and scepter.

Finally, cell D in Figure 18.1 concerns the case of an affront which police take to lie beyond the responsibility of the actor. While such action cannot normally be allowed to continue, the moral indignation felt by police is tempered by the understanding that the person is not aware nor could be easily made aware of the rule-breaking nature of his actions. The police response is to isolate the offender, not to punish him. Thus, the 'mental case' is shipped to the county hospital for observation and treatment; the 'foul-mouthed child' is returned to those responsible for his behavior; the out-of-state tourist prowling an area close to his hotel but frequented by prostitutes is informed of his 'oversight' and told in unmistakable terms to vacate the territory. It is important to note that police feel justified in using only enough force or coercive power to seal off the offender from public (and, by implication, their own) view. To use more force would be considered unreasonable.

It has been my purpose here to suggest that much of what the general public might see as capricious, random, or unnecessary behavior on the part of the police is, in fact, governed by certain, rather pervasive interpretive rules which lie close enough to the surface such that they can be made invisible. Certain police actions, following the model presented above, can be seen, then, to be at least logical if not legal. Furthermore, much of the power of these rules stems from their tacit or taken-for-granted basis. Indeed, were the rules to be questioned, the game could not continue. However, while these rules are applied in a like fashion by all police in a given interactional episode, the specific situated behavior of a citizen that is taken as a sign which leads to isolating, ignoring, teaching, or castigating a given individual is no doubt quite different across patrolmen. Here, the police game continues as it does because, in part, the asshole label swallows up and hides whatever individual differences exist across patrolmen. Thus, language neatly solves the problem of misunderstanding that would arise among the police were the rules to be articulated and standards sought as to how they should be a applied.

## Some conclusions

It is possible, of course, to see the preceding ritualized sequence as an isolated and rarely indulged propensity of the police. However, in this section, I will argue that indeed such a sequence and the corresponding identification and treatment of the asshole is intimately related to the police production and represents an aspect of, policing that is near the core of the patrolman's definition of his task. In essence, the existence of an asshole demonstrates and confirms the police view of the importance and worth of themselves both as individuals and as members of a necessary occupation. However, several other, somewhat more practical and everyday features of police work insure the ominous presence of the asshole in the police world.

First, the labeling of individuals as assholes can be seen as a technique (although invisible to most) useful to patrolmen in providing distance between themselves and their segmented audiences – to be liked by the people in the street is, in the defensive rhetoric of patrolmen, a sign of a bad cop. By profaning and degrading the actions of another, social distance can be established and maintained – a guarantee, so to speak, that the other will not come uncomfortably close. Thus, the asshole simplifies and orders the policeman's world and continually verifies his classification scheme regarding those who are 'like him' and those who are 'unlike him'. Relatedly the labeling serves also as an immediate call to action denoting a consensually approved (by the police culture) means for remedying 'out-of-kilter' situations.

Second, the label not only describes and prescribes, but also explains and makes meaningful, the statements and actions of others. In fact, an entire set of action expectations (i.e. 'they are out to. make the police look bad') can be ascribed as motives to the asshole. In this sense, the police function in street interaction is not unlike that of a psychiatrist diagnosing a patient. Both explain perceived deviancy in terms of a characterological genesis. Hence, the label implies that a different, inappropriate and strange motivational scheme is used by the 'type of person' known as an asshole. In this manner, an act is made understandable by stripping away whatever meaning might be attributed to it by the actor. Thus, to make sense of the act is to assume that it does not make sense – that it is stupid, irrational, wrong, deranged, or dangerous. Any other assumption would be too threatening.

Third, the labeling process must be viewed as serving an occupational purpose. I suggested previously that the urban policeman is primarily a keeper of the peace yet he defines his job in terms of law enforcement. Furthermore, as others have noted, many patrolmen try to convert peacekeeping situations to those of law enforcement (e.g., Bittner, 1967, 1970; Wilson, 1969; Piliavin and Briar, 1964). Since real police work is seldom available, marginally legitimate arrests of assholes provide a patrolman excitement and the opportunity to engage one's valued skills. Perhaps the police cliché, 'a good beat is full of deadbeats', reflects structural support for the asshole labeling phenomena.

Fourth, the discovery and subsequent action taken when the police encounter the asshole provides an expressive outlet – almost ceremonial in its predictability – for much of the frustration policing engenders. To the patrolman, one particular asshole symbolizes all those that remain 'out there' untouched, untaught, and unpunished. Such emotional outbursts provide, therefore, a reaffirmation of the moral repugnance of the asshole. Whether the officer responds by placing the handcuffs on the person's wrists such that they cut off circulation (and not incidentally cause intense, almost excruciating pain) or pushes a destitute soul through a shop window, these actions release some of the pent-up energies stored up over a period in which small but cumulative indignities are suffered by the police at the hands of the community elites, the courts, the politicians, the uncaught crooks, the Press, and numerous others. The asshole stands, then, as a ready ersatz for those whom the police will never – short of a miracle – be in a position to directly encounter and confront.

Finally, the asshole can be seen as a sort of reified other, representing all those persons who would question, limit, or, otherwise attempt to control the police. From this standpoint, knowing that there are assholes at large serves perhaps to rally and solidify police organizations around at least one common function. Thus, the police are, to a limited degree, unified by their disdain of those who would question their activities. Perhaps one could say that the police represent what Simmel (1950) referred to as an 'invisible church' in which the faithful are fused together through their common relation to an outside phenomenon.

Consequently, assholes are not simply obscure and fanciful figments of the bedeviled imagination of the police. On the contrary, they define to a surprising degree what the police are about. And while the internal satisfactions and rewards involved in 'slamming around' an asshole may seem esoteric if not loathsome to the outsider, to the patrolman who makes his living on the city streets they are not.

## Postscript

The foregoing description and explanation of an overlooked aspect of urban policing highlights the fact that the police officer is anything but a Weberian bureaucrat whose discretion and authority are checked rigidly. The collective myth surrounding the rulebound 'policeman-as-public-servant' has no doubt never been very accurate. By virtue of their independence from superiors, their carefully guarded autonomy in the field, their deeply felt notions about real police work and those who would interfere with it, and their increasing isolation from the public they serve (as a result of mobile patrol, rotating shifts, greater specialization of the police, and the growing segmentation of the society at large with its own specialized and emerging subcultures), police–community 'problems' will not disappear. And, since the police view their critics as threatening and as persons who generally should be taught or castigated, one could argue that the explosive potential of citizen–police encounters will grow.

Additionally, if the police become more sensitive to public chastisement, it could be expected that something of a self-fulfilling prophecy might well become a more important factor in the street than it is presently. That is to say, if the police increasingly view their public audience as foes – whose views are incomprehensible if not degenerate or subversive – it is likely that they will also magnify clues which will sustain the stereotype of citizen-as-enemy escalating therefore the percentage of street interactions which result in improper arrest and verbal or physical attack. Thus, the fantasy may well become the reality as stereotypes are transformed into actualities. In fact, the future may make prophetic Brendan Behan's half-jesting remark that he had never seen a situation so bad that a policeman couldn't make it worse.

To conclude, this chapter has implied that there is a virtual – if unintended – license in this society granted to police. In particular, when it comes to the asshole, police actions are not governed at all, given the present policies of allowing the watchers to watch themselves. It would seem that something is amiss, and, if the practical morality in urban areas is not exactly inverted, it is at least tilted. If the asshole is indeed a critical aspect of policing, then there is serious risk, involved in the movement to 'professionalize' the police. As other observers have remarked, successful occupational professionalization inevitably leads to increased autonomy and ultimately increased power for members of the occupation (Becker, 1962; Hughes, 1965). Professionalism may well widen the police mandate in society and therefore amplify the potential of the police to act as moral entrepreneurs. From this perspective, what is required at present is not professional police but accountable police.

*From John Van Maanen, 'The asshole', in John Van Maanan and Peter Manning (eds),* Policing: a view from the streets *(New York: Random House), 1978, pp 302–28.*

## Notes

1    All police quotes are taken from field notes I compiled of conversations and observations taking place during a year of participant observation in what I have referred to anonymously in my writings as the Union City Police Department (a large, metropolitan force employing over 1,500 uniformed officers). The quotes are as accurate as my ear, memory, and notes allow) [...] I should note also, that in this essay I use the terms 'police', police officers', 'patrolman', and 'policemen' somewhat interchangeably. However, unless I indicate otherwise, my comments are directed solely toward the street level officer – the cop on the beat – and not toward his superiors, administrators, or colleagues in the more prestigeful detective bureaus.

2    I chose the term 'asshole' for the title of this essay simply because it is a favorite of working policemen (at least in Union City). The interested reader might check my assumption by a casual glance at what several others have to say about this linguistic matter. Most useful in this regard are the firsthand accounts police have themselves provided and can be found, for example, in Terkel (1968, 1974); Drodge, (1973); Mass (1972); Olsen (1974); Whittemore (1973); Walker (1969). I should note as well that such labeling proceeds not only because of its functional use to the police but also because it helps officers to capture perceptual distinctions (i.e., labels are 'good to think'). Thus assholes are conceptually part of the ordered world of police – the statuses, the rules, the norms, and the contrasts that constitute their social system.

3    See, for example: Rubenstein's (1973) report on the Philadelphia police; Westley's (1970) study of a midwestern police department in the late 1940s; Wilson's (1968) global accounting of the police perspective; Reiss's (1971) research into police–community interactions; LaFave's (1965) treatment of the police decision to arrest; Cain's (1973) and Banton's (1964) observations on the British police; and Berkeley's (1969) cross-cultural view of policing in democratic societies. What comes out of these excellent works is, tantamount to a reaffirmation of Trotsky's famous dictum, 'There is but one international and that is the police'.

4    For example, Skolnick's (1966) idea that policemen are 'afraid' of certain categories of persons distorts the nature of the occupational perspective. More to the point, policemen are disgusted by certain people, envious of others, and ambivalent toward most. At times they may even vaguely admire certain criminals – those that the British police call 'good villains' (Cain, 1971). Fear must of course be given its due, but the occasion of fear hangs more upon unforeseen situational contingencies (the proverbial dark alley, desolate city park, or underlife tavern) than upon certain individuals.

5   Certainly this may not always be the case. For example, some 'suspected persons', due to the nature of their alleged crime (e.g., child molestation, drug dealing, indecent exposure, political sabotage, assault [or worse] upon a police officer, *etc.*) are likely to provide a strong sense of moral indignation on the part of the arresting (or stopping) officers. In such cases, once identity has been established to the satisfaction of the police (and it should be noted that errors are not unknown – particularly in these volatile cases), the person suspected is transformed immediately into an asshole and is subject to a predictably harsh treatment., Thus, in effect the label arises from an offense which occurred outside the immediate presence of the officers. However, since the spoiled identity must be reestablished anew in the immediate surroundings, the properties of the 'affront' correspond analytically to the more familiar case outlines in the text. And while the distinction has theoretical value regarding the norms of the police culture (i.e., that it is not the denounced *per se* that is important, but rather it is the denouncer that matters – 'says who?'), its practical implications are questionable because patrolmen rarely encounter such situations.

6   In most regards, the asshole is a classic case of the deviant – although not trans-situationally so. See Matza (1969), Becker (1963), and Cohen (1965) for a systematic elaboration of the ideas which underpin this analysis.

7   By the term 'extralegal' I am merely implying that the formal police mandate excludes such moral considerations from actions inducing decisions made by officers on the street. The notion of professional policing makes this explicit when it is suggested that patrolmen (must act impersonally without regard to individual prejudice.

8   The 'cover-your-ass' phenomena associated with urban policing is described in more depth in Van Maanen (1974). See also Manning (1974b) for a theoretical view of the more general construct, the police lie; and Chevigny (1968) for a presentation of numerous disturbing case studies.

9   Arrests are, of course, sometimes used to teach someone a lesson. However, police believe that in many cases the asshole will arrange his release before the patrolman will have completed the paperwork necessitated by the arrest. And since the affront was moral, the legal justification to 'make the case' in court may be lacking. Thus, the classroom more often than not is in the street. Given the opportunity to teach the asshole either by 'turning him in' or 'doing him in', most police would choose latter.

## References

Banton, Michael (1964). *The Policeman in the Community*. New York: Basic Books.

Bayley, D.H., and Mendelsohn, H. (1969). *Minorities and the Police: Confrontation in America*. New York: Free Press.

Becker, Howard S. (1962). The nature of a profession. In *Education for the Professions*, 61st Yearbook of the Society for the Study of Education, Part 2. Chicago: University of Chicago Press.

Becker, Howard S. (1963). *Outsiders*. New York: Free Press.

Berkeley, George E. (1969). *The Democratic Policeman*. Boston: Beacon Press.

Bittner, Egon (1970). *The Functions of the Police in Modern Society*. Washington, DC: United States Government Printing Office.

Bittner, Egon (1967). The police on skid row. *American Sociological Review*, 32: 699–715.

Black, Donald (1968). Police Encounters and Social Organization: An Observational Study. Unpublished Ph.D. Dissertation, University of Michigan.

Cain, Maureen (1971). On the beat: interactions and relations in rural and urban police forces. In Cohen, S. (ed.). *Images of Deviance*. Middlesex, England: Penguin Books.

Cain, Maureen (1973). *Society and the Policeman's Role*. London: Kegan Paul.

Chevigny, Paul (1968). *Police Power: Police Abuses in New York*. New York: Pantheon.

Cohen, Albert K. (1965). The sociology of the deviant act. *American Sociological Review*, 30: 5–14.

Cumming, E., Cumming, I., and Edell, L. (1965). The policeman as philosopher, guide and friend. *Social Problems*, 12: 276–86.

Drodge, Edward F. (1973). *The Patrolman: A Cop's Story*. New York: New American Library.

Harris, Richard N. (1973). *The Police Academy: An Inside View*. New York: John Wiley and Sons.

Hughes, Everett C. (1958). *Men and their Work*. Glencoe, IL: Free Press.

Hughes, Everett C. (1965). Professions. In K.S. Lynn (ed.). *Professions in America*. Boston: Beacon Press.

LaFave, W.R. (1965). *Arrest: The Decision to Take a Suspect into Custody*. Boston: Little, Brown and Company.

Manning, Peter K. (1971). The police: mandate, strategies and appearances. In J. Douglas (ed.). *Crime and Justice in America*. Indianapolis: Bobbs-Merrill.

Manning, Peter K. (1974a). Dramatic aspects of policing: selected propositions. *Sociology and Social Research*, 59 (October).

Manning, Peter K. (1974b). Police lying. *Urban Life*, 3 (October).

Maas, Peter (1973). *Serpico*. New York: The Viking Press.

Matza, David (1969). *Becoming Deviant*. Englewood Cliffs, NJ: Prentice-Hall.

McHugh, Peter (1969). A common-sense perception of deviancy. In J. Douglas (ed.). *Deviance and Respectability*. New York: Basic Books.

Neiderhoffer, Arthur (1969). *Behind the Shield*. Garden City, NY: Doubleday.

Olsen, Jack (1974). *Sweet Street*. New York: Simon and Schuster.

Piliavin, I., and Briar, S. (1964). Police encounters with juveniles. *American Journal of Sociology*, 70: 206–14.

Reiss, Albert J. (1971). *The Police and the Public*. New Haven: Yale University Press.

Rubinstein, Jonathan (1973). *City Police*. New York: Farrar, Straus and Giroux.

Sacks, Harvey (1972). Notes on police assessment of moral character. In D. Sudnow (ed.). *Studies in Social Interaction*. New York: The Free Press.

Silver, Allen (1967). The demand for order in civil society. In D. Bordua (ed.). *The Police: Six Sociological Essays*. New York: John Wiley & Sons.

Simmel, Georg (1950). The *Sociology of Georg Simmel*. Translated, edited, and with an introduction by Kurt H. Wolff. New York: The Free Press.

Skolnick, Jerome (1966). *Justice without Trial*. New York: John Wiley and Sons.

Skolnick, Jerome, and Woodworth, J.R. (1967). Bureaucracy, information and social control. In D. Bordua (ed.). *The Police: Six Sociological Essays*. New York: John Wiley and Sons.

Terkel, Studs (1968). *Division Street: America*. New York: Random House.

Terkel, Studs (1974). *Working*. New York: Pantheon.

Van Maanen, John (1972). Pledging the Police: A Study of Selected Aspects of Recruit Socialization in a Large Police Department. Unpublished Ph.D. Dissertation, University of California, Irvine.

Van Maanen, John (1973). Observations on the making of policemen. *Human Organizations*, 32: 407–18.

Van Maanen, John (1974). Working the streets: a developmental view of police behavior. In H. Jacobs (ed.). *Reality and Reform: The Criminal Justice System*. Beverly Hills: Sage Publications.

Van Maanen, John (1975). Police socialization. *Administrative Science Quarterly*, 20: 207–28.

Walker, T. Mike. (1969). *Voices from the Bottom of the World: A Policeman's Journal*. New York: Grove Press.

Webster, J.A. (1970). Police task and time study. *Journal of Criminal Law, Criminology and Police Science*, **61**: 94–100.

Westley, William (1970). *Violence and the Police*. Cambridge: MIT Press (originally a Ph.D. Dissertation, University of Chicago, 1951).

Whittemore, L.H. (1973). *The Super Cops*. New York: Stein and Day.

Wilson, James Q. (1967). Police morale, reform and citizen respect: the Chicago case. In D. Bordua (ed.). *The Police: Six Sociological Essays*. New York: John Wiley and Sons.

Wilson, James Q. (1968). *Varieties of Police Behavior*. Cambridge: Harvard University Press.

# 19. Street cops and management cops: the two cultures of policing

*Elizabeth Reuss-Ianni and Francis A.J. Ianni*

One of the most common findings of the last few decades of organizational research is that it is the immediate work or peer group and not the larger organization that motivates and controls the individual's behavior. Similarly, several major studies by social scientists have documented the significance of the informal social and behavioral systems in determining police practice.[1] Case studies of various policing units or subunits point to the importance of the social, behavioral; and administrative structures at these lower levels of organization in understanding how policing is conducted in a community. Understanding how the police precinct operates as a working social/administrative/operations unit is critical to understanding the forces affecting the management and practice of police work. It is equally important as a framework for examining how the police organization resembles or differs from similar organizations in other sectors of society and consequently which schemes for management and organizational growth and development are appropriate.

Despite these findings, organizational theory and practice in police work continues to develop from and reinforce a concern with administration and decision-making at the central headquarters level. Police administrators follow the advice of management consultants who simply translate productivity programs designed for business or industry into programs similarly intended to make the 'business' of policing more productive or efficient. Nationally, as police departments increase in size and scope, more time and money is spent designing programs to make particular departments more efficient, effective, and responsive. The results have been disappointing. Change strategies or techniques have more often resulted in moving lines or boxes on some organizational chart. Not surprisingly, police administrators frequently hold conferences on problems of internal communication, hoping to understand how and why their power and authority gets lost, dissipated, or diverted as it moves down through the chain of command toward implementation. The problem of management and control becomes even more complex and critical as police administrators attempt to reconcile the demand for improved employee relations and working conditions with the demand for greater productivity, efficiency, and responsiveness to the community.

While social scientists have studied and documented the realities of policing, organizational specialists who provide the police managerial ideology seem determined to ignore them. Consequently, planners and decision-makers pay little attention to actual police practice, designing new programs and procedures based on seemingly rational and logical grounds while ignoring street-level practices that have more impact on day-to-day operation and, therefore, the actual outcome of any intended program or plan.

Police precincts have generally been viewed as a subset of the formal organization of a police department, as an administrative unit deliberately designed and constructed to achieve specified goals defined by the organization as a whole. As such, the precinct is seen as responsive to the dictates and demands of the organizational hierarchy in a rational or 'organized' line of authority and control. Our approach has been to view the precinct as a distinctive and distinct social system, contrived by a particular occupational culture, responsive to sociocultural change and organized and controlled through its own set of rules and procedures.

Early in September 1976 we decided to undertake a long-term field study of police precincts as social systems with a grant from the National Institute of Law Enforcement and Criminal Justice. We were allowed access to two New York City police precincts and spent approximately twelve months in one and six months in the other precinct. Our theoretical orientation for this study centered on the assumption that organized social groups that persist over time are social systems with the character and permanence of social institutions. Our usage of the term social institution deviates somewhat from the usual view, which is excessively static and structural. Institutions, thus, are not fixed, monolithic structures, nor are they transmitted across generations as structures. Institutions are the behavioral patterns learned or first established by people seeking to maximize shared values. What becomes institutionalized in this process is not a structure in the usual sense – a box containing action – but a code of rules governing social action and defining a pattern of behaviors that are productively efficient in maximizing social or individual gains.

Our primary research strategy was to gather data on social organization and behavior by using such traditional anthropological techniques as participant observation over a continuous and extensive period of time, event analysis, and network analysis. Our contacts and the fieldwork took place in the natural work setting of the precinct, where we worked tours similar to the police officers, including observation of all operational units working inside and out of the precinct (that is, radio patrol, anticrime, conditions, detective squad, warrants) as well as clerical and support units.

What we saw and heard over hundreds of hours of contact with officers and precinct personnel and operations leads us to advance a theory that police organization in New York City is characterized by two competing and increasingly conflicting cultures. A pervasive conception of the 'good old days' of policing is the organizing ethos for what we came to call the 'street cop culture', which orients individual officers and precinct social networks in a social system that defines the day-to-day practices of policing. In the good old days, the public valued and respected a cop, fellow officers could be counted on, and superior officers or 'bosses' were an integral part of the police family. Being a cop meant more than public respect and the sense of security that came from being a part of a cohesive, interdependent organization. Cops were treated as professionals who knew their job and how to get it done. A grateful public and understanding City Hall seldom asked questions about how it did get done.

This nostalgic sense of what the good old days were like may or may not be an accurate interpretation of the past, but it represents the way street cops believe police work should be organized and carried out today. The values of this culture, operationalized in a series of maxims guiding day-to-day behavior and performance, form the group reference for precinct-based officers. Interviews as well as observations of collective behavior in the two precincts indicate a widespread belief among officers that a number of social and political forces have weakened the character, performance, and effectiveness of police work and that as a result the policing function is under strong attack. Calumny and contempt rather than respect and obedience are daily experiences in the community and in the media, according to officers with whom we spoke. Frequent charges of brutality and corruption have led to distrust and suspicion within the ranks, and it is these concerns rather than the mutuality of the old days that relates lower ranks to their superiors. These same bosses and their political allies at City Hall, say the cops, tie the hands of the street cop, not only reducing his effectiveness but making it increasingly difficult and dangerous for him on the job. All of these forces combine, says the street cops, to produce a new headquarters-level 'management cop culture' that is bureaucratically and valuationally juxtaposed to the precinct street cop culture. What was once a family is now a factory. Not only the values, say these cops, but the real loyalties of the bosses are no longer to the men but to the social and political networks that make up this management cop culture. While there is some uneasy accommodation between these two cultures, they are increasingly in conflict, and this conflict serves to isolate the precinct from attitudes and activities at headquarters. The result is disaffection, strong stress reaction, increasing attrition, and growing problems with integrity, which reinforces the resistance of the street cop culture to attempts by management to introduce organizational change. Instead, the social organization of the precinct becomes the major reference structure for the men.

## Two cultures of policing: an organizational dilemma

Early in the twentieth century, Max Weber analyzed the characteristics of bureaucracy with such precision that his formulations have influenced all theory and empirical investigation of the topic ever since. Weber approached bureaucracy as one form of institutionalizing authority relations, which he contrasted to traditional authority and charismatic authority. He noted that the bureaucratic form of organization was becoming increasingly dominant in industrialized societies. The counterpart of Weber's theory of bureaucracy can be found in the work of Emile Durkheim, who emphasized an organic model for explaining and analyzing social organization. Durkheim and his followers saw society as being analogous to a biological cell, which has differentiated, albeit interrelated, parts. This model is much more similar to that of the family than to the factory. Emphasis is on the complex interrelationships rather than on division and specialization.

Both models are not really opposing or even competing bodies of theory. Weber recognizes the existence of traditional authority and Durkheim's model recognizes the differentiation functions, although it emphasizes the interrelationships. Both schools address themselves to the distinction between bureaucratic and organic forms of organization. In our study of the police precincts, we recognized the importance of each model to the understanding of behavior, and through an examination of discrete episodes of behavior, we attempted to disentangle the aspects of behavior that were attributable to bureaucratic influences and those attributable to organic relations as well as the impact of those influences on behavior.

One way in which the difference between the bureaucratic and organic models can be expressed in organizational theory is in the disputes between the scientific management and human relations school. It should be noted that the writers of these two schools were not strictly social analysts but were trying to provide prescriptions for better practice. Therefore, the difference between the language of scientific management and the language of human relations is a difference in policy as much as it is a difference in conception.

There also exists a more analytically posed opposition in organizational theory between bureaucratic and organic forms of organization. This is frequently expressed as the difference between formal and informal organization. The formal organization is usually contained in the organizational charts specifying the relations of position and role in the organization; informal organization consists of personal relationships that are not necessarily ordered through a hierarchical system of role and position. A number of organization theorists recommend beginning from the organizational chart and proceeding deductively in the analysis of organizational behavior to determine patterns of informal structures in the organization. In our research, we proceeded in a different fashion, looking at informal structures first. In so doing, we found that the formal bureaucratic structure that emanates from headquarters coexists with rather than contains the local precinct street culture.

From what we were told, this separation of structure was not always characteristic of the New York City Police Department. Most of the cops we talked with were convinced that 'before the Knapp Commission',[2] or 'in the good old days', the department was a cohesive organizational home for a commonly shared ethos, which we have characterized as the 'street cop culture'. This ethos unified the department at all levels through a 'code' of shared understandings and conventions of behavior that were mutually binding on all officers from the top down to the newest recruits. As a result, the department was well integrated with and accommodated to a political organization that valued them and the ethos. Because of their solidarity and their integration into the political system, the department was by and large left to run its own affairs. The results were predictable from what we know about organizational climate in general and political structures in particular. The mutuality and interdependence cloaked by the secrecy that develops in such closed-system organizations produced both organizationally positive and socially negative results. The mutual dependence provided a level of morale and *esprit de corps*; this same mutuality and the secrecy it produced contributed to the institutionalization of wide spread organized graft and corruption in the department.

While even the police emphasize the role of the Knapp Commission's activities in bringing an end to the organic pattern of relationships that this shared ethos provided for the department, there were other equally important pressures for its demise from inside and outside the department. Externally, a changing political system characterized by increasing attention to the rights of disenfranchised minorities and a heightened concern with financial and social accountability from City Hall led to increasing scrutiny of a number of factors in the management of the department that would eventually have produced the same results. Also, as mobility resulting from higher salaries allowed officers to purchase property and homes outside of the city, social bonds were increasingly restricted to work time and were diminished in extra-work settings. The educational level of officers in the department rose along with that of the general population but also as the result of special governmental programs intended to improve police performance through higher education. An unanticipated result was to make available alternative job possibilities and careers outside of the department. This reduced further the need for solidarity, since one's entire career wasn't necessarily tied up with the job or with the importance of establishing strong bonds among fellow officers. In the good old days of the single culture ethos, the department was by and large sexually and racially homogeneous. While there were a few women and some minority officers, their number and their token acceptance for the most part kept them outside the social bonds that organized the rest of the department. Pressures for minority recruitment and redress of past discrimination led to new criteria for promotional advancement, which further eroded the sense of solidarity supported by similar socioeconomic, cultural, religious, or ethnic background.

Yet, this street cop culture still exists, and it is this culture that currently gives salience and meaning to the social organization of the precinct. A competing ethos, however, has developed more recently that is concentrated at the management level of operations, finds its operational ethos not in the traditions of the job but in theories and practice of scientific management and public administration. This management cop culture seeks to maximize those bureaucratic benefits that come from efficient organization, rational decision-making, cost-effective procedures, and objective accountability at all levels of policing. As is true in all classical bureaucracies, the model proposed by this ethos would do away with the organic and therefore nonrational bonds among people as the basis for organization and management. There should be a 'consistent system of abstract rules', and departmental operations should consist of the application of these rules to particular cases. The departmental structure should be hierarchically organized so that each lower office is under the control and supervision of a higher one, with authority and consequent power distributed in the same fashion. Employment and advancement should be based on merit and not on personal characteristics, relationships, or favor exchanges. It is the individual's office or role in the organizational chart rather than personal relationships and informal networks that should define what the job expects of the individual and what the individual can contribute to the organization. Since the management cop culture origins were in the business and industrial sector, it is not surprising that what has resulted is the gradual emergence of a departmental structure that now has an almost classical manager/worker structure. What is even more important is that each of these functionally defined groupings has its own distinctive culture and, while there are mediating points between the two, they are increasingly coming into competition and conflict.

Both cultures share the mission goal of the organization, to combat crime and ensure a safe and secure city. Where they differ is on the definitions of these concepts and in the more concrete operational aspects of the means by which such goals can be achieved. The street cop culture sees local response and flexibility as more important than preplanned and 'packaged' solutions to problems that may or may not ever come up in the day-to-day work of policing. The street cop's standard for performance is the concept of the 'professional' cop. In this context professionalism refers to on-the-job experience and a street sense that permits him to recognize people and situations that are 'dirty'. While planning is not eschewed, it is the 'gut-level' ability to recognize, identify, and respond in the field rather than the internalization of some standardized set of rules and procedures that characterizes 'good' police work. Decision-making thus takes place on a personal and immediate level. Relationships among officers are structured in such a way that they are mutually supportive, and their common interests bind them into a cohesive brotherhood that personalizes task performance as well as social relationships. Precinct relationships are formed in the same way, and the individual's loyalty to his working peers and immediate supervisors is part of the same social bond that incorporates him and his organizational unit into larger organizational structures. Since our study concentrated on the precinct level, we did not systematically trace the social networks upon which the study is based beyond that level. From what we did hear and see within the precincts, however, it seems that the street cop's identification and sense of social integration does not go beyond that level, except when such outside forces intervene in his or her immediate work-group functioning.

Management cop culture, on the other hand, is concerned with the problem of crime on a systemwide or citywide rather than localized level. It is not that management cops are unconcerned with crime at the local level but rather that their sense of territoriality encompasses all of the city. They are placed in the position of having to allocate resources throughout the system based on some set of priorities. These priorities must be weighed and established within a set of political, social, and economic constraints and must be justified within each of these contexts as well as within the policing context. Thus, for example, enforcement of marijuana laws or protection of property must be considered within these various contexts as part of the decision-making process. Here law enforcement is not the immediate day-to-day interaction with individuals in which the police officer is engaged but is intended as a carefully planned, well-designed, and efficiently implemented program in which the individual officer and the unit that is his immediate reference group are impersonal variables to be managed.

Herbert Simon, whose organizational theory has been influential in the development of management concepts, maintains that decisions are made on either valuative or factual premises. Given values and information, he claims that individuals will more likely reach decisions based on values. Whether he is in the street cop or the management cop culture, the individual's identification with groups or task units focuses decision-making on particular goals and behaviors. His group identification requires that he select only such alternatives nominally open to him that will also fit with the behaviors he expects from other members of his group. In addition, however, there are organizationwide values that are meant to influence decisions. The congruency of group (by which we mean precinct) and organizational (by which we mean headquarters) influences is especially pertinent in looking at precinct level versus headquarters level influences on behavior. While either may influence the individual through his set of values or through his information, our observations convinced us that at this point in time, it is the precinct level or street cop culture values that determine the style and practice of policing. Since these values underwrite and inform the social organization of the precinct, they act as a determinant for behavior and for the dispositions and attitudes of its members.

We have characterized the style of relationship between the two cultures as gaming not to trivialize it, since we feel that the future character of urban policing depends on who if anyone wins, but because so much of the precinct level response is to test in what way they can manoeuver around, outwit, or nullify the moves of headquarters decision-makers.

## Social organization and control mechanisms

While street cop culture provides the values and so the ends toward which officers individually and in task groups strive, the generalized meaning of that culture must operate through some specific structures. In formal organizational analysis, an organizational chart describes graphically the hierarchical arrangement of roles and relationships as well as the prescribed channels of communication for information flow throughout the organization. There are no standardized graphics for presenting the informal social organization with the same degree of symbolic, if not actual, clarity. Kinship charts, which look very much like organizational charts, are the closest approximation, but they not only are restricted in use to kinship relationships, they also tend to describe formal patterns of relationship and cannot describe the more social relationships among kin. One reason for the absence of any accepted schematic for organic social organization is that there has been little attempt to describe those structures through which social relationships are organized. In a number of earlier studies, we developed a tentative model for describing social organization (those patterns of behavior through which individuals relate in an organizational context), which we have further refined in looking at the police precinct organization. In this model, the major functions that structure social relations in the precinct are organized into four major structural domains. Each of these structures organizes a distinctive area of enculturation (learning the system) and socialization (learning the rules of the game) for both the formal and informal rules that guide individual and collective behavior.

1.  The socialization structure organizes the system through which an officer learns from others in the precinct what the job is all about in that command. He learns, for example, what the various supervisors are like and how to work with them. He learns what is acceptable and what is not acceptable behavior. In addition to learning the values of the culture and methods for getting the job done, he is at the same time being socialized to prefer modes of behavior in the process that is generally called 'learning the system'. He also learns how to evaluate his fellow officers within the definitions established by those values. He is learning, in effect, what there is to know. The traditional use of a senior, more experienced officer at the precinct, the field training specialist, as the guide to the new rookie ensures the continuity of the informal rules in spite of any 'upgrading' of the academy curriculum.

2.  The authority/power structure organizes the authority and power of various administrative levels from headquarters and intervening levels through the chain of command into and throughout the precinct. An important element here is the difference between the power or authority derived from rank or the authority structure of the system and the power or authority that an individual may hold (regardless of rank) as a result of 'being in the right place at the right time' or 'being connected'. Operationally, this means that there are several, frequently competing, authority/power systems or networks that can be called into operation in decision-making, controlling, and accountability.

3.  The peer group structure concerns the enculturation of culturally sanctioned and socially acceptable maxims or rules for peer-mediated behavior found in different task groups or units within the precinct. Thus, while the values and behaviors particular to street cop culture are shared to some extent by all police officers (including some management cops), they may differ among and between ranks or subunits.

4.  Cross-group structure includes the enculturation of behavior codes for interaction between the precinct and other departmental levels, which includes definitions of mediator roles and communication styles (including the importance of the grapevine as an information collection and dissemination network). Socialization within this area defines how supervisors relate to the men and how the men in turn relate to several levels of supervisory authority as well as the relative rights and responsibilities of each. A very important control dimension involves the role of sergeant as a firstline supervisor. Of considerable importance but often ignored is the process of mediation between the two networks. Mediator roles can be quite formal, as in the case of the police union representative and officials, personnel officers, or official departmental grievance channels. Many unformalized roles, however, emerge in the pattern of relationships established in the precinct. The 'rabbi' or 'hook', for example, can relate a high-ranking officer at headquarters with a street cop who might have been partners at one time. Critical here is the system of exchange of favors and owing someone for a previous favor.

While these structures organize or contain varieties of social action, they are most visible in the major processes that operationalize the structures in the social organization of the day-to-day life of the precinct and adjust the structures to changing demographic, political, social, and economic conditions. These processes appeared with such regularity and persistence in our research that we believe them to be basic for organizing social interaction within and across each of the four major structures in the precinct. The first of these is sorting, in which individuals classify themselves and each other according to a set of culturally defined labels. While the specific labels may differ somewhat from precinct to precinct, the process of sorting is fundamental throughout precincts in defining the patterns of social and work relationships. Police officers sort each other and are sorted by supervisors and other administrators. The fact that there seems to be a discrepancy between the sorting carried out in street cop culture and that which is part of management cop culture is at the heart of some of the tensions and conflicts between these two cultures. The street cop who 'takes care of his own business' on department time may be viewed as 'getting back at the system' by his precinct peers, but he is in violation of departmental rules and regulations according to management. Similarly, the precinct CO who informally accepts such behavior from men who 'deliver when there is a job to be done' may be considered a good boss by his men but a poor supervisor by his superiors. Changes in the sorting process over time usually indicate positive or negative interpretations of the authority/power, the peer group, or the cross-group structures because they modify the pattern of social contact within a particular precinct. In organizational terms, sorting establishes for each officer categories of generalized 'others' based on what can be expected from them and how they will interact within given situations. Thus, a street cop can depend on an officer in the same squad under most circumstances and usually more than an officer from another precinct and can depend on officers in general more than a boss or a civilian.

The second process, territoriality, includes the formal and informal relationship between environment and behavior within the precinct and between the precinct and other organizational environments. There are obvious relationships between space and behavior within the precinct, such as the difference in behavior observable in the locker room, in the vicinity of the front desk, in the radio car, or on the street. Similarly, the characteristics of a precinct community may distinguish a range of individual and collective behaviors. What is more important, however, is that we know from contingency theory about the relationship between organizational behavior and environment.[3] Organizations are affected by their environment in many ways but possibly most importantly in the characteristic way in which effective decision-making depends on the level in the organization at which decisions are made. The most effective level is dependent on the fit between the environment and the decision. This suggests that in diverse and rapidly changing environments, a condition that characterizes such 'discretionary' occupational cultures as policing, it is necessary for many decisions to be made at relatively low administrative or command levels because of the need for immediate response. Different kinds of decisions are appropriate to different levels. Policy decisions involving police organization and control, for example, need to be made fairly high up. In day-to-day policing, however, responsiveness to the immediate territorial and behavioral environment and situation is more crucial, demanding more flexible parameters, and so decisions are more appropriately made at lower levels.

Within the department and even within the precinct, territoriality may also be seen to affect the attitudes and actions of different subunits within the organization. Thus, subunit specialization may be required to deal with the varying demands and requirements of the organization's environment. This same specialization, however, means that each unit and level may have different attitudes or different motives in regard to issues that arise. It is important to keep in mind that this is not only a matter of subgroup loyalties, although these are important as we pointed out earlier. It is also a matter of the kind of environment that the different subunits are in the habit of responding to and the information that they have about the relationship of their portion of the organization to the whole.

Applying these concepts of organization and environment to the distinctions we have pointed out between street cop culture and management cop culture adds some further details to the factors that define the tensions and problems of department organization and management. There are a number of pragmatic and historical reasons for conflicts between the two cultures. Under the old system, idealized in street cop culture, precinct policing was a localized and relatively autonomous process with considerable command discretion by the CO, rather like the local school with a principal in charge. The precinct dealt with local people, and as long as there were no major disturbances that attracted attention to precinct police, they were left pretty much to themselves. Certainly they had obligations to headquarters and presumably through headquarters to the political system, but generally they were well integrated into their territory. Since there was much less mobility from precinct to precinct, this sense of ownership of turf increased over time. Under the new system, the management cop culture centralized much of the decision-making power of the department and consequently, at least in the view of the street cop, took away much of the discretionary decision-making power at the interface between the precinct and its community. In addition, the number of formal activities for which both the individual officer and the precinct were responsible was increased through the establishment of standardized reporting and accountability systems. An increase in responsibility, however, did not include an increase in authority at the local level. Under the assumption that 'familiarity breeds corruption', assignments of commanding officers to precincts were frequently changed and men were also transferred with greater frequency. The new management cop culture thus represented a loss of local autonomy because it imposed tighter external supervision over more areas of activity.

The process of rule making and rule breaking serves as another means of organizing behavior within and between the four major structures. In the precinct, there is a continual proliferation of rules and procedures. There is also, however, differential enforcement of rules. The difference may lie across categories, such as supervisors or men, between different individual enforcers and offenders, over time, and in different places. All of the component factors that cause rules to be made in particular situations and to be variously enforced depending on personnel or circumstances, provide indicators of the social organization of the precinct.

Collectively, processes that mold and channel behavior within the four structures are expressed in the form of behavioral expectations and conventions that set the limits for approved behavior in the precinct. We call this loose connection of understandings the 'cop's code'. By this code we mean a charter for action, a set of shared understandings that, while not written or codified, is understood by all members of the precinct and limits the degrees of variability of behavior permissible for individuals. Such limitations are the price one pays for group membership. It is the charter that provides the formal component in what is usually considered the informal system of social organization in the precinct. A senior officer, for example, will allow certain degrees of freedom for a more junior partner's behavior on patrol before invoking the charter to describe (and sanction) the expected behavior in either the socialization structure or the authority/power structure or both. Similarly, a boss will allow variability in a police officer's behavior until the variation exceeds the limits established by the code's definition of officer behavior or before he invokes the code's sanctions. Invocation, by the way, is used just as frequently (possibly more frequently) by a lower person or group to a higher person or group as a means of redressing some perceived wrong that exceeds the limits established by the code. This is a critical element in relations between officers and sergeants. Our research experience confirms the cop's belief that supervisors are usually reluctant to make decisions on absolute rules that might set a fixed pattern of enforcement. This reluctance to invoke fixed rules and regulations means that much of the daily life of the precinct proceeds from the shared understandings of the code rather than from specific rules. The process of invocation of the code comes to represent the major social control mechanism within the precinct.

The 'cop's code',[4] which is usually described in the literature as informal, is also formal in that while it isn't written, it is understood by everyone. Similarly, the behavioral guides that are part of it are often as closely linked to the formal structure of the department as they are to the informal social system of the cop's code. What the cop's code does is link the formal and informal structures by allowing degrees of freedom within which officers have discretion. In this sense the formal aspect of the code ties back in through the authority/power structure to the management cop culture, since breaking a formal departmental rule means 'they can get you'. But the cop's code also contains conventions and shared understandings of acceptable behavior. Violating one of these rules, which reach through the peer group structure into the street cop culture, will mean social criticism and peer-imposed sanctions because 'you're not behaving like one of us'.

The cop's code is the principal social control mechanism within the precinct social organization, not only shaping behavior but distinguishing or sorting the 'good cop' from the 'bad cop'. Controls within this social system begin with values but ultimately become internalized as maxims that invoke sanctions when they are not followed. We extracted a set of maxims or injunctions from our observations and interviewing in both precincts that form such a code. Once we had developed our version of the cop's code, we repeated it to cops in both precincts and elsewhere in the department to see if our list was recognizable to them. Through this process we discovered that there are really two sets of maxims that make up the cop's code. One regulates relationships in the peer group and relates street cops to each other. The other set of maxims, which is becoming increasingly apparent as a result of the tensions between the two cultures, relates street cops to bosses or supervisors.

## The cop's code

We found that the cop's code, which responds to street cop culture in defining relationships with other cops, contains twelve maxims.

*Watch out for your partner first and then the rest of the guys working that tour* is fundamental and expresses both the strong sense of dependency and mutuality and the sorting that takes place even among peers. 'Watching out' means looking out for the interests of as well as the physical safety of the other guy.

*Don't give up another cop* is an injunction to secrecy that is based on social bonding and might better include 'and then he won't give you up'. It applies across the board, regardless of the seriousness or illegality of the situation. Here again we see the importance of sorting, since there are situations in which being a cop doesn't necessarily mean 'being one of us'.

*Show balls* enjoins the individual to be a man and not to back down, particularly in front of civilians. Once you've gotten yourself into a 'situation', take control and see it through. This also reflects the feeling that the impression conveyed through the actions of any cop will reflect on all other cops.

*Be aggressive when you have to, but don't be too eager* is related to the previous maxim but has a somewhat different connotation. Oldtimers will tell new men that when a 'situation' develops, get on it but don't be too eager or go looking for trouble. If you get a radio run on a 'crime in progress', for example, it will probably end up as a 'past' crime if you don't rush to get there. Experience has shown that most of these calls are unfounded anyway.

*Don't get involved in anything in another guy's sector* is an outgrowth of territoriality that implies that you shouldn't interfere in another man's work space because he is accountable and must live with the consequences. In the 'old' days, we were told, this meant don't muscle in on someone else's action or turf.

*Hold up your end of the work* communicates to a cop that if he slacks off unreasonably or too frequently, someone else has to take up that slack. It also calls attention to everyone.

*If you get caught off base, don't implicate anybody else* is an extension of both the 'don't give up another cop' and 'show balls' maxims. Getting caught off base, which can range from being out of your sector to more serious or even illegal activities, is likely to bring attention to and therefore trouble on the entire group. Anyone who is caught should take his punishment and not implicate others.

*Make sure the other guys know if another cop is dangerous or 'crazy'* means that while you wouldn't give up such a cop to the bosses, you should let other cops who might be working with and depending or dependent on him know what to expect.

*Don't trust a new guy until you've checked him out.* Because the social bonds are so strong and because of the increasing suspicion about field associates,[5] it is necessary to use the grapevine to find out who and what a newcomer is and how far he can be trusted.

*Don't tell anybody else more than they have to know, it could be bad for them* generally means not to volunteer information because you may involve someone else when they don't want to be involved. This is also symptomatic of the general breakdown in mutual trust and reliability.

*Don't talk too much or too little* means that following the norm is important. Someone who talks too much is known as a 'big mouth' and may be covering up, and someone who talks too little may be afraid to implicate himself or may be looking to catch someone else on something; both extremes are suspicious.

*Don't leave work for the next tour* covers a number of possibilities: leaving the car without gas, not making out a complaint report, or anything else that means the next tour has to clean up after you.

There are other less pervasive maxims, such as 'always try and take the same vacation days as your partner' because if you don't, he might get stuck working with someone who no one else wants to work with. There are also job- or situation-specific maxims, but the twelve listed were found operative in both precincts.

There is also a cop's code which contains the maxims concerning relationships with management cop culture through the authority/power structure.

*Protect your ass.* An implicit assumption here is that 'if they want to get you, they will', and so the prudent officer makes certain that he is covered. This injunction is indicative of the individualism and isolation felt by street cops, but the attitude and its behavioral consequences are just as pervasive among headquarters cops. Traditionally, we were told, when one culture unified the department, the system protected the individual. Now it's every man for himself.

*Don't make waves.* Here again, the maxim advises that the officer not be a 'troublemaker' in the bosses' eyes, but it also says 'don't mess with the system'. Being a troublemaker means that supervisors pay more attention to an officer, and consequently the officer brings unnecessary attention to what his peers might be doing as well. Asking too many questions about procedures or making too many suggestions about how the system might be improved also brings too much attention from the bosses.

*Don't give them too much activity.* If an officer is too eager and increases his productivity in a given month, cautions this maxim, he will bring unnecessary pressure and attention not only to himself but to his peers. Next month they will expect him to do even better than he did this month. They will also want to know why his peers aren't giving them as much as he is producing. In the 'old' days, increased productivity could mean favorable attention, which might lead to a detective shield or at least to a few days off from your CO. Now the feeling is that there is no advantage gained personally, so why make the effort?

*Keep out of the way of any boss from outside your command.* In the day-to-day life and work of the precinct, the officer comes to an accommodation with the precinct bosses about what they expect and what they will tolerate. He knows the limits placed on his behavior. Any boss from outside the precinct is an unknown authority who might turn an officer in to a command level outside your precinct. This removes control from the organic relationships (accommodations) within the precinct to the unknown control of the department authority structure and its formal rules and procedures.

*Don't seek favors just for yourself.* Here again, the solidarity of street cop culture tells the officer to look out for his peers in relating to bosses. This is most frequently expressed in terms of not 'sucking up to the old man' (the CO) or to the administrative lieutenant, whose roles in the precinct are more directly related to the individual officer rather than supervisory to him as a member of a work group. The desk lieutenant and patrol sergeants, however, are directly related to on-going work conditions, and keeping them happy hopefully will keep them 'off everybody's back' during that tour.

*Don't take on the patrol sergeant by yourself.* Since the patrol sergeant is in direct supervisory control of the officer and his peers in the task group, the immediacy of the relationship means that his working relationship with the men sets the tone for that tour. Applying pressures against a patrol sergeant in retaliation for a real or perceived wrong will only work if all of an officer's peers cooperate.

*Know your bosses.* One of the first questions an officer asks when he turns out on a tour of duty is, 'who's working, or who has the desk?' He is asking what bosses are around on that tour and specifically what supervisor has ultimate responsibility for actions taken during that tour. Knowing the bosses means that an officer can adjust his expectations for the tour to what he knows about their expectations.

*Don't do a boss's job for him.* In operational terms, this means that if an officer knows that a peer is shirking his duty or involved in some misconduct, it isn't his responsibility to tell a boss about it. While mutual protection is one source for this attitude, it is sometimes expressed as 'that's what the boss gets paid for, why should I do his job?'

*Don't trust a boss to look out for your interest.* This maxim represents the street cop's view of life at the top. The management cop, it is assumed, finds it just as necessary or expedient to 'protect his ass' from his superiors as the cop does. If he has to choose between you and his career, 'he's going to make the same decision you would now'. A number of officers attributed this to the fact that once an officer climbs up the ladder, he holds on for dear life, particularly at ranks above captain, which are appointive. It is interesting also that these cops felt that in the private sector a manager will simply leave and find another job if there is some disagreement with his superior. This option is not as easily available in the department, it is explained, because 'he's stuck in this job just like we are'.

## The organizational implications of two cultures

What we have described as the two separate cultures of the New York City Police Department is not unique to policing or even to large urban police departments. Rather it is a situation that might be expected in any organization in which authority and responsibility are dispersed and a tradition of operation and procedure is being forced to respond to internal and external pressures for change. In the case of the New York City Police Department, the transition from the old to the new 'game' is yet to be completed, so what we have seen is a side-by-side overlap of the old and the newly developing organization and system. Now there are two cultures that confront each other in the department: a street cop culture of the 'good old days', working class in origin and temperament, whose members see themselves as cops for the rest of their careers, and a management cop culture, more middle class, whose education and mobility have made them eligible for alternate careers outside of policing, which makes them less dependent on and less loyal to the street cop culture. In a sense, the management cop culture represents those police who have decided that the old way of running a police department is through (for a variety of external reasons, such as social pressures, economic realities, increased visibility, minority recruit-ment, and growth in size that cannot be managed easily in the informal fashion of the 'old' days), and they are going to get in on the ground floor of something new. They don't, like the street cops, regard community relations, for example, as 'Mickey Mouse bullshit' but as something that must be done for politically expedient reasons, if not for policing ones. The management cop is sensitive to politics and public opinion, and so will not, for example, support a cop whose maverick behavior makes him unpredictable and thus a source of potential embarrassment to the department. The street cops who are still into the old ways of doing things are confused and often enraged at the apparent change in the 'rules' of the system. So they fight back in the only way they have at their disposal: foot dragging, absenteeism, and a host of similar coping mechanisms and self-defending techniques. Nor is all of this likely to change soon; the old and new will coexist for some time because attitudes and values have not changed along with changes in formal departmental policies and procedures, and so behaviour won't change.

The two cultures no longer share a common vocabulary, a common set of work experiences and increasingly have different objectives. The unifying ethic that promised that 'the department takes care of its own', which was the moral for so many of the stories that we heard about the 'good old days', is now reinterpreted as 'the bosses take care of themselves'. As a result, important changes in the pattern of social and organizational relationships have developed in the precinct street cop culture. On the one hand, cops at the precinct seem increasingly to emphasize individual over organizational or even reference group ends. Similarly, they are saying that given this new job attitude, their only responsibility is to themselves and their families.

One of the major results of the loss of a unifying culture in the department is the increasing evidence of organizational stress affecting individual behavior. Police work has always been considered a high stress occupation, with factors such as danger, violence, and idiosyncratic working hours causing serious problems for mental and physical health. The old ethos demanded that the major symptoms of stress, drinking, and marital problems be kept inside the depart-ment and the officer be protected by giving him some nonactive assignment until he straightened himself out or retired. Today, say the cops, those jobs are held by civilians, and the management culture is more interested in early identification and weeding out potentially troublesome officers, than protecting one of their own.

As the unifying culture dissolves and the two cultures are increasingly in conflict, there are also organizational control and role pressures that add to that stress load, often at an unconscious level for both the individual and the organization. Today, the NYCPD has many of the organizational stress characteristics of any large city agency in a time of financial crisis, but there are some that are peculiar to the police function. Organizations provide a behavioral home for the people who work in them, shaping their self-image, career goals and aspirations, their work and how it is organized, and other factors that affect the constructive or destructive results of stress. Organizations can also become stress-provoking when some significant segment feels manipulated by forces beyond their control or by contradictory goals or when they think that their work role or status is demeaning or has been demeaned by others. Organizationally generated stress is increased when groups feel that they are pitted against each other or that some members of the organization are 'against' them.

Finally, there is the problem of the management of stress. Frequently, people in any kind of work that requires face-to-face contact with troublesome or irate clients have difficulty managing their own hostility. Policemen have this frequent provocation to anger and aggression, which is complicated by the added stress of continuous exposure to real and perceived danger as a constant aspect of the job. All of this is made more complex by the policemen's discretionary authority to use force. It is this latter threat that is most disturbing to police management, and the recent escalation of interest in stress in police work by the department is largely oriented toward identifying and eliminating potentially violent officers who might become dangerous to others when under stress. Here again, the precinct cop sees a self-serving management culture, more interested in avoiding public and political repercussions of an incident than they are in organizing police work to reduce dysfunctional organizational stress.

We noted earlier that there is the quality of a game in the present relationship between street cop culture and management cop culture. Thus, headquarters managers can mandate new planning models or procedures, but they cannot make street cops treat these new programs seriously or honestly. The street cops, on the other hand, can and do fight back with the traditional weapons of alienated employees – foot dragging, sabotage, and stealing department time. If the managers do not have the power to require serious acceptance of new policies and practices, then the workers do not have the power to outwit what the managers want altogether. One senses, however, that while street cops know they cannot possibly win the game, they still want to seek some small victory on the way down.

The existence of these two cultures is of more than passing academic interest. Their incongruent value systems and the difference in their expectations are major factors in the growing alienation of the street cop. This displacement of quasi-familial relationships, in which loyalties and commitments took precedence over the rule book, by the more impersonal ideology of modern management is visible in other public service sectors, such as education or social service. Teachers and social workers, for example, increasingly see their administrators as managers rather than fellow professionals. Wherever this shift occurs, it produces conflict that sooner or later must affect the way a client public experiences policies and services. In many urban centers, the growing cynicism of the police is seen by citizens and supervisors alike as little different from worker dissatisfaction in other sectors of the economy. To the street cop, at least to those with whom we worked and spoke, this alienation results from the inconsistencies among the variety of jobs they are expected to do, the resources they are given to do those jobs, and the compromises they must make with themselves, the public, and their job. Whether or not these rationalizations reflect the present relationship between the individual policeman and the structure of urban policing accurately, the critical first step in examining the disparity between policy and performance in urban policing is understanding how and why this differentiation into two cultures has occurred.

The implications of a precinct social organization model containing street cop culture, translated empirically into the cop's code illustrates what can happen in organizations when management attempts to provoke change rather than negotiate it. First of all, well-intentioned but overeager police managers have sought to intervene in police work through replacement rather than adaptation. The replacement method attempts to replace inefficient or outmoded techniques with new, more efficient ones. Adaptation is more gradual and involves re-defining or modifying existing practices. Certainly, there are technological advances that can replace outmoded approaches to policing, but the major changes needed to produce more effective police work require attitudinal and behavioral changes both in precinct personnel and administrators. If relatively permanent (structural) changes are brought about, police officer perspectives on policing must also be changed to introduce appropriate change in attitude as well as behavior and to maintain support for the changes once they are introduced. Often we speak of the need to achieve a certain 'climate' of sentiment and opinion in order to produce change. Such changes in attitudes are essential, but they will not be sustained unless the new ideas or techniques are in-corporated in the value system of the department or become items on the agenda of both precinct and headquarters personnel.

*From Elizabeth Reuss-Ianni and Francis A.J. Ianni, 'Street cops and management cops: the two cultures of policing, in M. Munch (ed.),* Control in the Police Organization *(Cambridge, MA: MIT Press), 1983, pp 251–74.*

## Notes

1　For example, Manning (1977); Punch (1979); Rubinstein (1973); and Westley (1970).
2　The Knapp Commission (1972) was set up under the chairmanship of Whitman Knapp to investigate allegations of police corruption in the New York City Police Department. As a result of the investigation and subsequent charges, many police officers were found guilty of graft and were dismissed from the force. The department instituted many procedural and structural changes throughout the organization in response to findings of this commission.
3　Lawrence and Lorsch (1967).
4　A number of researchers have described specific aspects of the informal cop's code of conduct. Westley (1970), for example, indicates that the code forbids police from informing against fellow officers. This code of secrecy is also described by Stoddard (1968), Reiss (1971), and Savitz

(1970). Skolnick (1966) suggests that danger, and the requirement that officers use authority against civilians, contributes to a sense of solidarity that makes them isolated and dependent on each other. This interdependence provides the basis for a code that is characterized by suspiciousness, clannishness, and secrecy. Manning (1977) points out that because of discretion, the code is made up of rules that are site-specific. He sees a general cynicism about rules that come from superiors and notes the 'cover your ass' perspective as particularly important.

5    In an attempt to respond to some of the areas of real or perceived police corruption pointed out by the Knapp Commission findings, the department instituted an Internal Affairs program whereby officers (field associates) were assigned undercover to precincts as though they were regular officers. In reality their job was to detect and report instances of misconduct or illegality on the part of officers at that precinct. The precinct commanding officers were not informed as to which officer really worked for the Internal Affairs unit.

## References

Knapp, W. *et al* (1972) *Report of the Commission to Investigate Alleged Police Corruption*. New York: George Braziller.

Lawrence, P.R. and Lorsch, J.W. (1967) *Organization and Environment*. Boston: Harvard University Graduate School of Business Administration.

Manning, P.K. (1977) *Police Work*. Cambridge, Mass.: MIT Press.

Punch, M. (1979) *Policing the Inner City*. London: Macmillan.

Reiss, A.J., Jr. (1971) *The Police and the Public*. New Haven, Conn.: Yale University Press.

Rubinstein, J. (1973) *City Police*. New York: Farrar, Straus and Giroux.

Savitz, Leonard (1970) 'The Dimensions of Police Loyalty', in Harlan Hahn (ed.) *Police in Urban Society*. Beverly Hills, Calif.: Sage Publications.

Skolnick, J. (1966) *Justice without Trial*. New York: John Wiley and Sons.

Stoddard, Ellwyn R. (1968) 'The Informal Code of Police Deviancy: A Group Approach to Blue-Coat Crime'. *Journal of Criminal Law, Criminology, and Police Science*, **59** (2).

Westley, W. (1970) *Violence and the Police*. Cambridge, Mass.: MIT Press.

# 20. Culture as figurative action

*Clifford Shearing and Richard Ericson*

The conventional sociological vision of the link between culture and action is that rules guide or direct action.[1] The theoretical hegemony of this rule-based framework does not arise from the strength of the empirical evidence supporting it. Rather the conventional view persuades both because of an absence of conceptual contenders that can compete with the analytic power of rules in providing a solution to the problem of social order,[2] and because action is frequently presented as rule-following by those who produce and observe it.[3]

In accounting for social order theorists set themselves the task of explaining regularities that cannot be explained biologically. This starting point has led them to aspire to a model of motivation that accomplishes at the cultural level what biologists have achieved at the level of the organism. This has prompted the argument that there must be some culturally located program that human beings follow that explains the patterned nature of their conduct. Thus they have sought to 'provide a template or blueprint for the organization of social and psychological processes, much as genetic systems provide a template for the organization of organic processes'.[4,5] Rules, as instructions for action, appear to fit this bill perfectly, and to provide an analytically elegant solution to the problem of social order (see Parsons (1935), Chomsky (1968), Shimanoff (1980), Edgerton (1985); see also Wilson (1970) and (1971), Wieder (1974), and Hilbert (1981) for a discussion of this model[6]).

This solution has a devastating weakness. When one looks for evidence of these rules independent of the actions that they are said to explain, for example, as instructions that people look to in constructing their actions, it is very difficult to find. People simply do not walk around with rules in their heads that they apply to situations, in the midst of action, to decide what to do[7] because, as Wittgenstein has shown, rules simply cannot be used to generate or predict action.[8]

The absence of empirically locatable rules that generate action has led scholars, working within the rule-based paradigm, to posit 'implicit rules'[9,10] that provide 'implicit guidance'[11] to people. To produce these implicit rules theorists formulate rules that 'fit' the activity. These observer-generated rules are then conceived of as implanted in people, via some process of internalization, so that they become 'need dispositions'[12] that generate the activity from which the rules were derived in the first place (see Bourdieu (1977) who traces this process[13]).

In seeking to avoid this tautological reasoning, which 'forces' on people a 'repertoire of rules' that reconstitutes action in terms that are unrecognizable to them,[14] interpretative theorists have re-conceptualized the nature of the cultural 'steering function'[15] rules are used to model. Two central themes have emerged from this work. First, they have criticized the cultural determinism that follows from the genetic parallel and the fact that because the observer typically arrives *'post festum* he cannot be in any uncertainty as to what may happen'.[16,17] In response they have proposed more open-ended conceptions, such as 'strategy', as a way of introducing agency into the conception of action.[18] Second, in seeking to identify how people produce activity that is uncertain and improvisational interpretative theorists have argued that culture affects action through a process of 'analogous reasoning'[19] that provides for the 'analogous transfer of schemes permitting the solution of similarly shaped problems',[20] and not through the atomistic, reductive reasoning so central to the rule-based model (cf. Cassirer[21]; Burke[22] and Shimanoff[23]). However, despite some suggestive concepts and analyses, these developments have remained fuzzy[25] when it comes to demonstrating, in terms of a general model, how it is that culture repertoires and analogous reasoning provide people with the ability to produce and structure action. Faced with a choice between an elegant but deterministic and tautological model that requires the invention of implicit rules that are forced on people, and one that is sensitive to the experience of agents but has an ephemeral and cloud like quality to it, sociologists have, by and large, chosen flawed elegance.[26]

We seek to advance the development of an alternative model through a substantive focus on the everyday practices of police officers. In doing so we draw upon the suggestive analyses and concepts we have just noted to develop an analysis of how it is that culture makes available a process of 'mythological thinking'[27] 'mythmaking'[28] or poetic logic'[29] that allows action to be both orderly and improvisational.

## The conventional view of police culture

The problems encountered with a rule-based conception of action and the difficulty in moving beyond it is nicely illustrated in research on the everyday activity of police officers. As in most other areas of sociological enquiry, research on the police has taken place within a rule-based framework in which rules have been viewed as the source of the action.[30]

In studying policing, sociologists have examined the fit between legal rules, viewed as instructions, and police decisions. Typically they report that police officers deviate from these legal instructions (e.g. Hagan and Morden[31]). Instead of using these findings to question the assumptions of the rule-based paradigm, however, they have accepted as axiomatic the belief that all action is rule-generated and concluded that there must be some other set of rules that is generating police action. The most obvious candidate has been departmental orders and regulations (e.g. Manning[32]). However, as these rules are seldom congruent with police action either, these theorists have been compelled to seek still other rules. This has led them to posit implicit sub-cultural rules; these rules fit the contours of police action perfectly, as the evidence for these rules is the activity they are supposed to explain (cf. Reuss-Ianni and Ianni[33]; for reviews of this literature see Wexler[34] and Manning).

A few sensitive observers have persistently expressed dissatisfaction with this rule-constrained approach to police conduct. Manning,[36] for example, suggests that police culture is 'sort of' rule guided by referring to the directions of the police culture as 'rules of thumb' and, in a reference to Schutz, as constituting a 'recipe knowledge'. Chatterton has gone a step further in describing the relevance of police culture to police practice in terms of a 'concept of style' which 'draws attention to certain fundamental orientations of a police officer, that is, [to] his working philosophy'.[37] However, Chatterton seems unable to unpack 'style', or the associated notion of 'competence', in ways that would permit the development of an alternative conception of how it is that culture shapes action. What we find is a tantalizingly evocative analysis that takes us to the brink of an alternative but not further.

## The ethnomethodological critique

Significant progress has been made by ethnomethodologists in providing an alternative to the rule-based conception. As we plan to build upon, and move beyond, their analysis in our consideration of police culture and its use by police officers it is necessary to consider their position and its relation to the argument we are developing.

Ethnomethodologists argue, following Garfinkel,[38] that the rule-based model captures an important truth about society, namely that the social world presents itself as a Durkheimian reality (that is, as external, obdurate, independent, and normative) and that it does so because people often *present* their own, and others, activity as rule-generated.[39] This is done by constructing intersubjectivities (that is, publically available subjective realms) in which rules are the motivational mainsprings of action.[40] In this analysis rules are identified as an important cultural resource used by people to do the work of accomplishing the sense that activity is ordered.[41] In developing a rule-based model of action, ethnomethodologists argue, conventional social scientists *participate* in this activity of reality construction[42] by using rules, just as lay persons do, to *exhibit* the 'fact' that action is 'typical, regular, orderly, coherent, motivated out of considerations of normative constraint, and the like'[43] instead of examining this process of constitution as a fundamental social phenomenon.[44]

In examining this phenomenon ethnomethodologists have explored how rules are constructed and used to see activity as ordered. People, they argue, use rules to accomplish a sense of order and, as part of this process, instruct each other on how rules are to be used for *doing*, 'seeing' activity as an ordered Durkheimian reality[45] (see Garfinkel and Sacks'[46] discussion of the 'prefix "doing"'). Wieder, for instance, shows how members of a halfway house learned to read their own and each other's activity as normatively constrained by 'the convict code'.

> In conversations which occurred between residents and staff, between residents and researchers, between staff and researchers, the various parties in effect, instructed one another on how to 'see' the behavior of

317

residents by citing the relevance of the convict code to any resident's circumstances and by noting the ways the behavior under question was motivated by it ... Through interactions with me and staff, residents made it happen that their activity would be seen as regular, repetitive, uniform, standardized, independent of their particular doing, and done as a matter of normative requirement ... Thus, the fact that the conduct of residents had an orderly, coherent appearance was the ongoing, practical accomplishment of residents who interactionally provided staff and researchers with 'embedded instructions' for seeing the environment of the halfway house from 'the standpoint of the residents by telling the code' ...[47]

In this analysis culture is not reified as a force that determines order. Rather agency is located directly with people who not only actively instruct one another on how cultural tools are to be used to 'do' a way of seeing but use these instructions to accomplish the particular 'doings' that create the sense of a reified determining culture. Wieder[48] describes this accomplishment, that Garfinkel[49] terms 'documentary interpretation',[50] as one in which people *actively* search for a way in which talk can be heard as evidence of cultural rules, which in turn can be used to order activity by creating rule-driven intersubjectivities.

Clearly ethnomethodologists have moved towards a conception of action that captures the sense of culture as a tool-kit used in the production of order and that provides a conceptual place for rules without falling foul of the problem of tautology noted above. In this chapter we develop this advance by identifying the role that figurative forms play in the accomplishment of a sense of an 'objective' social world. In addition, however, we return to the issue that the rule-based conception sought to address, namely, the ability that people have to produce activity,[51] that is how people 'go on' from one space-time moment to the next. This question, however, can no longer be conceived as a 'problem of order' as it is for the rule-based theorists[52] for order in this sense has been revealed as the accomplishment of methods that reflexively make that activity available as normative, obdurate and so on. While, as we will note in a moment, this is not a question that ethnomethodologists have neglected entirely, their concern with making the process of documentary interpretation a topic of enquiry rather than simply an analytic resource has unfortunately shifted enquiry away from 'the actions of the participants to the way the interpretive process is used by them so as to produce for them the sense of a shared orderly social world'[53] (see also Garfinkel and Sacks'[54] discussion of the 'policy' of 'ethnomethodological indifference').

For the purpose of studying interpretive processes as such, the investigator suspends interest in what actions the actors are performing and why they are doing so, although the actors themselves are of course vitally concerned with these questions. Instead, attention is directed to the 'methods' by which the actors assemble, communicate, and justify accounts to themselves and each other of what they are doing and why they are doing it. Of particular importance is the manner in which the participants produce and sustain through their accounts on a given occasion their sense that their interaction is embedded in an objectively existing world ...[55]

To the extent that they have considered the question of the production of activity, ethnomethodologists have adopted two principal tacks. The first draws upon the insights of the interpretive theorists who argued that 'action is forged by the actor out of what he perceives, interprets, and judges'.[56] In developing this idea ethnomethodologists have explored, often indirectly and incidentally, how a way of seeing, by constructing what people perceive, is a form of power that constrains and shapes action.[57] Thus, for example, Wieder,[58] while concerned primarily with the task set out by Wilson, shows how a reference to the convict code that instructed people on how to constitute a rule-guided subjectivity for participants in the half-way house was also

> a consequential move in the very 'game' that it formulated. As a move in that field of action which it formulated, it pointed to the contingencies in that field as they were altered by this move [for more recent examples see *Social Problems*, 35(4), 1988].

This analysis of documentary interpretation as a mechanism of power fore-shadows contemporary interest in a way of seeing as a form of embedded power.[59] However, it still leaves unanswered the critical question of how people forge a course of action, in light of what they see, that allows them to go on from one space–time moment to the next,[60] to enact activity that will be ordered, in an 'indefinitely revisable'[61] way so that it both constitutes the game being played and is available as a move in that game; that is, the question of how the games people constitute through a way of seeing are played.[62] Thus, Wieder leaves us more or less where Turner[63] and Blumer[64] left us. We know that people `make' rather than 'take' 'roles' and the action is 'built' not 'propelled' this sort of analyses ultimately leaves unanswered the question of just how people go about making and building particular courses of action from moment to moment.

The question to be addressed is how to deal with this issue while avoiding the difficulties endemic to the rule-based model. Difficulties include the problem of 'literal descriptions' given the 'indexical' feature of events,[65] the logical impossibility of rules ever being able to predict activity raised by Wittgenstein,[66] the problems related to the formulation of implicit rules, the problems associated with accepting the subjectivities constituted by people in ordering events as the generating mechanism of action[67] and the empirical problems with respect to the way people actually use rules noted above.

To the extent that the ethnomethodologists have tackled the issue of the production of activity directly, despite the refocussing noted above, they have done so primarily with reference to the production of utterances in conversation, for instance, people's ability to go on in a conversation from speaking turn to speaking turn. Thus, for example, Schegloff analyzes the way in which con-versationalists actually do sequencing as a way of searching for the rules or formulae (see Giddens' (1984)[68] discussion of formulae) they use as methods for 'generating a conversational interaction'.[69] In Utilizing Chomsky's notion of a generative grammar, however, this work, while it does not naively use the sub-jectivities people use as a resource in the way the rule-based theorists do, does not avoid the logical problems that Wittgenstein and the ethnomethodologists have noted about the use of rules to explain and generate activity.

In what follows we take up the suggestions referred to earlier to provide a conception of the production of activity that avoids the problems we have reviewed. In doing so we treat the *doing* of activity as a 'practical', 'skilled', 'artful' accomplishment in the same way that ethnomethodologists regard doing describing, doing formulating, doing accounting and so on as an accomplishment.[70] However, as we have already suggested we do not conceive of this accomplishment as produced by a technical mechanism or 'machinery'[71] of Chomsky-like 'rules, techniques, procedures, methods, maxims that can be used to generate the orderly features we find in conversations' (Sacks, 1984: 413),[72] but rather by a figurative logic that constitutes a way of being in the world.

## The craft of policing

A central problem of policing is knowing how to 'go on' from one time–space moment to the next. This is not a problem peculiar to police work but it is essential to it. Police activity always takes place in a context of action that could have been, but was not, taken. Imagine the following. A police officer sees a vehicle being driven along a road and does not attend to it further. What else could she have done She could have: followed the car to check the speed; run a computerized vehicle check; stopped the car and questioned the driver; searched the car; searched the driver; checked the driver's documents; run a computerized information check on the driver; given the driver a breath test; asked the driver for information about the activities of fellow citizens, and so on.

Decisions taken by those engaged in the 'craft of policing'[73] develop on a moment-to-moment basis, often without, a moment's reflection. Somehow competent officers know what to do. Somehow they see the world in a way that enables them to get to the essentials of a situation immediately. Somehow they move easily and quickly from what is happening to knowing what to do about it; from seeing to doing. How do police do this What is this craft?

When asked if they accomplish their craft by applying rules the police response is unerringly the same. They state emphatically, and categorically, that competent police work is not done by following a book of rules. Police work, they insist, 'is not done by the book'.

> Policing it is argued, cannot be learned scientifically, in the sense that if A is done in Y situation and B is done in X situation, then Z will result. The life police officers confront is too diverse and complicated to be reduced to simple principles.[74,75]

When asked how police work is done officers are unequivocal, they cite experience. When asked to elaborate they respond to researchers in exactly the same way as they do to novice officers who ask the same question; they tell stories and cite aphorisms[76] that 'lovingly describe'[77] ways of being, seeing and, most importantly, acting as a police officer. 'Police conversation' as Bayley and Bittner[78] accurately observe, 'is thick with stratagems.' Police officers respond, as master chess players do to those who seek to perfect the craft of chess playing, with 'case studies' of successful (and failed) gambits firmly located within concrete exemplars of their use.

From within the rule-based perspective, however, police references to 'experience' as the source of their knowledge, and their persistent story-telling, appear as glosses that arise from their inability to identify and articulate the rules that generate their action. Thus, for example, Bayley and Bittner,[79] when faced with police stories in response to their inquiries about the 'craft of policing', write that 'officers cannot readily state the principles that they use to simplify the situational complexities they faced. The best they can do is tell anecdotes'. Accordingly, they dismiss these anecdotes because they are so obviously apocryphal that they cannot possibly be regarded as accurate descriptions of what it is that police officers in fact do. Police stories they conclude

> are so common among officers that they should probably be taken with a grain of salt. The same stories crop up too often, suggesting that they have become part of the mythology of policing passed on uncritically from officer to officer.[80]

The absence of a principled account of the police craft. Bayley and Bittner argue,[81] has left police officers with no option but to 'fall back on the lore that experience generates' instead of a more explicit account that science, with its rule-based approach, can provide (see also Fielding[82]). Once policing is rendered scientific, the 'generalizable procedures'[83] officers are unable to locate, as they peer darkly through the glass of their limited awareness, will be revealed. Then the stories they tell will be replaced by the formulae that program their actions and they will be able, with the help of science, to understand what it is they really do.

But what if, instead of dismissing police officers' stories and their references to experience as flawed conceptions because they do not fit with the assumptions of the rule-based conception, we were to regard them as instructions for seeing the world and acting in it? That is, what if we were to heed Frye's[84] admonition and stopped depreciating this 'mythological thinking' as `very bad conceptual thinking', and stopped trying to replace it with 'scientific conceptions'? What if we took police stories seriously *as stories*? What if we were to treat police officers not merely as persons who know how to *perform* their craft but as insightful persons who know how their craft works and know how to communicate this to others? What if we were to accept Lyotard's view that 'narration is the quintessential form of customary knowledge'?[85] In short, what if we were to see police stories as a key to understanding the practical knowledge police officers use to produce action?

What this would mean is accepting police culture not as a book of rules, albeit informal cookbook rules, but as a story book. It would mean examining police stories as stories, police myths as myths and police anecdotes as anecdotes, that is, as figurative forms with their own logic. If we did this we would then be in a position to ask how it is that this logic forms the basis for the police craft and do so in a way that does not assume that this craft produces pre-ordered activity in the Durkheimian sense. We would then be able to re-think the idea of a 'generative program', take up the hints and suggestions that the rule-based paradigm has stifled, and give more specificity to concepts like 'style' and 'strategy'. Finally, we might be able to discover something more of what is meant by 'analogous reasoning' and how it might provide the key to understanding how people produce activity through the knowledge that 'classic metaphysicians' called 'the domain of practical reason'.[86]

## Police stories

Police stories are told in a variety of settings. Sometimes they are told out of the flow of action when quiet reflection is possible. At other times they are told during action as a 'show and tell' commentary on what is taking place at the time.[87] At times whole stories are told as 'informative' or 'representative anecdotes'[88] that select and highlight reality, like Weber's[89] 'ideal types', to provide cautionary or exemplary messages. At other times stories are condensed into fragments, aphorisms that capture the essence of longer stories by concentrating their meaning into a single figurative phrase 'in much the same way that poems act as condensed prose'.[90]

Similarly, police stories apply to a variety of settings. Along with only a few other occupations, including social science and journalism, the police have all of society, all aspects of organized life, as their potential sphere of operation. This means that it is especially important for the police to develop *general* sense-makers that can be used in myriad settings they face. Police stories function as a search-light rather than a spot-light, ensuring that they experience reality as a fluid and not a solid.

When these stories reflect on activity, they work to accomplish precisely the ordering ethnomethodology has revealed as a fundamental sociological topic.[91] This accomplishment, however, is 'multi-formative',[92] for in providing a retrospective reading that provides an account that constitutes a social world it establishes a way of seeing that makes available future 'interactional possibilities'[93] and as we will see in a moment helps shape a subjectivity out of which action will flow.

Stories, by recounting 'positive or negative apprenticeships', identify 'criteria of competence'.[94] They instruct officers on how to 'read', via a ' "poetic" apprehension' the layers of meaning contained in a situation so that they are able to move beyond the 'obvious' to the 'obtuse' meanings.[95] Sacks[96] illustrates this process as follows:

> As he walks through his beat with a mature officer, persons who to [the novice] appear legit are cast in the light of illicit activities in which the latter knows they are engaged. The novice is shown that he ought to see persons passing him in terms of the activities in which they are engaged. And the activities in which they are engaged are more prurient than he might suppose. The lovely young lady alighting from a cab is now observable as a call-girl arriving for a session. The novice is shown how to see the street as, so to speak, scenes from pornographic films.

As this passage suggests, while stories are often expressed entirely through words, sometimes the parables are played out in living narratives – the 'experience' cited by police officers. In such cases a novice is placed in a situation in which she will be exposed to certain experiences or be permitted to watch a more experienced colleague act in a situation. In both cases the experiences may be accompanied by an ongoing commentary that interprets the significance of the events and experiences being attended to so that the novice learns how to see and experience the world of policing. This may happen as officers ply their beat together or even more spectacularly in living dramas like police funerals[97] that tell a story of police authority, legitimation and danger.

Whatever form these stories take, whether they are lived out or told, they provide officers with a way of seeing by constructing what might be called, following Mills,[98] a 'vocabulary of precedents'.[99,100] Again Sacks[101] is instructive:

> For the police, objects and places having routine uses are conceived in terms of favorite misuses. Garbage cans are places in which dead babies are thrown, schoolyards are places where mobsters hang out, stores are places where shoplifters go, etc.

At the same time that stories construct a way of seeing they also construct a subjectivity that is appropriate to this world: not a public intersubjectivity that makes activity accountable, and hence ordered in the ethnomethodological sense, but an experiential subjectivity, or sensibility. Every meaning has implicit in it a reference to a subjective position that is appropriate to it.[102]

Together a way of seeing and a way of being enable officers to respond to the situations that confront them and produce activities that share a style, what Wittgenstein[103] calls a 'family resemblance', yet allow for innovation, uncertainty, improvisation and the like. This conception of style must be distinguished from a proto-ordering in the rule-based sense. Sudnow[104] makes this distinction when he writes that '[i]n both music-making and talking there is a social world, an organization of ways of doing such [bodily] movements, and an organization of ways of regarding them'. Like biblical parables and legends police stories provide directions for *being* a police officer, guidance as to how officers should experience the world if they are to act as police officers within it.[105] Stories constitute a consciousness, a sensibility, a way of being out of which action will flow, *'point blank, as it were'*, without recourse to specific instructions, 'just as people might casually go about recognizing the color green without the aid of rules to guide them on their course'.[106] Stories employed in this prospective mode do not address action directly but rather constitute a sensibility out of which action flows; they permit an officer to respond appropriately in the heat of action by making the split second choices that will allow her to go on from moment-to-moment.

Some stories only have a very fleeting life, for example, when a police officer points out some feature of the police world quickly and casually as she passes by. Other stories have a well-honed mythical character that arises from being told and retold. This character sets them apart from mere descriptions of the world and establishes them as carefully crafted poetic pieces that capture the insights and wisdom of countless officers who have, through their telling of it, embellished and polished the story. For these stories, which together comprise the story book of police culture, it is precisely their apocryphal character, that discredits them as descriptions of the world,[107] that gives them their power and potency as vehicles for generating the experiential subjectivity appropriate to police action.

In telling such stories police officers are not acting as witnesses in a court who swear to tell the truth, speak plainly and avoid figurative language. Instead, as carriers and formulators of their culture, they are playing an entirely different language game (Wittgensteins's 'Sprachspiel') in which 'truth' refers to the story's ability to uncover and reveal the essential features of the police world and the stance they should take towards it so as to prepare themselves for the task of policing.[108] In their street talk police officers use stories to represent to each other the way things are, not as statements of fact but as cognitive devices used to gain practical insight into how to do the job of policing. For them the appropriate criteria for evaluating stories is not their truth value in a scientific sense but rather whether the knowledge they capture 'works'. Such stories, be they told in words or in action or via spectacles, capture the sedimented residue of generations of police experience and convey it in a form that police officers can capture and use to construct their actions on an ongoing basis. Through a narrative form sensitive to the 'rhythm' and 'beating' of time,[109] police officers learn the 'intuitive' wisdom[110] that is the basis of their craft. Theirs is a 'knowledge of particulars', 'about particular choices' that permits 'the direct apprehension of singular things' and 'the capacity to judge  rightly about concrete problems of choice'.[111]

How do they do this? What is this 'intuition ... the direct apprehension of singular things, or practical wisdom [this] capacity to judge rightly about concrete problems of choice' that police officers insist, along with Unger, 'resists translation into more general precepts'?[112] How do police officers use narrative and poetic forms in this way? How do stories provide the sensibilities that permit police officers to respond to new situations each one of which they insist is unique?[113] How do stories prepare police officers to 'go on'?

We want to suggest three answers to these questions. The first is that stories employ tropes as a vehicle for analogous thinking that permits a transfer of knowledge from one situation and context to another; second that stories provide a library of gambits, vocabulary of precedents; and third, that stories use silences to establish a worldview that provides a way of seeing and experiencing a world.

## Tropes and the generation of activity

Three story fragments cited by Bayley and Bittner[114] illustrate how  police stories use analogous reasoning to suggest and portray a subjectivity, a sensibility, appropriate to policing.

> [O]fficers develop an instinctive wariness, what one officer called 'well-planned lay-back'.
>
> [Police] learn to act with a margin of force just beyond what their would-be opponents might use. One officer likened it to taking a five-foot jump over a four-foot ditch.
>
> Police say repeatedly that it is essential to be nonprovocative in contacts with the public – to adopt a demeanor that pacifies, placates, and mollifies. 'Always act,' said an experienced officer, 'as if you were on vacation.'

In each of these aphorisms knowledge is shared via what Unger calls the 'master device' of analogy, 'we compare issues about which we have the greatest certainty with those that baffle us more'.[115] In each case a different metaphor is used to invite police officers to bring to policing a particular sensibility. Thus, for example, the last aphorism says to the listener: 'you know how *you* feel on vacation, you know the feeling of being on holiday, well allow yourself to feel that way when you are on duty and then act out of that subjectivity.' That is, one learns to act as a police officer by knowing how to act as a vacationer and applying this knowledge to the situation of police work. The second fragment acts in much the same way. It says: 'you know what it would be like to take a five-foot jump over a four-foot ditch, now create the sensibility that implies and then you will know how to do policing.' The first fragment juxtaposes two ideas that are normally thought of as unrelated and says: 'imagine putting these two ideas together and creating a sensibility out of them, well that is the sensibility that you need to be a competent police officer.'

In each case a trope[116] is used to identify an experiential subjectivity and then invites the officer to construct it for herself. Each aphorism seeks to capture a consciousness regarded as essential to policing and provide the officer with a vehicle for grasping and then constructing it. In none of these fragments is the officer offered a rule for action of the if X do Y sort. Rather the officer is offered a sensibility that applies to a whole range of situations, situations which may in fact be quite novel, that will enable her to produce a style of conduct appropriate to policing in a particular department. What the officer is told is not how to act but rather the sensibility out of which she ought to act. Particular actions are not prescribed, rather a whole range of actions consistent with a particular sensibility are made possible. It is this sensibility that gives unity to action. Within this unity the officer is encouraged to improvise and to be creative, to develop a unique set of actions that arise out of a single sensibility. It explains, to put the matter in interactionist terms, how it is that people are able to meet 'a flow of situations in which they have to act' through a process in which 'action is built on the basis of what they note, how they assess and interpret what they note' without positing 'need-dispositions, role requirements, social expectations or social rules.[117]

While the above examples focus directly on a way of being a police officer, other stories, as the passages above from Sacks for example indicate, focus on how the world should be seen if the appropriate terrain in which the sensibility is to operate is to be available. Schön, in a discussion of stories in a very different setting, provides an analysis of how tropes provide a way of seeing that constitutes the 'game' within which 'play' will take place. Schön analyses how a metaphor was used by a team of researchers trying to develop a nylon bristled paintbrush. The researchers were having difficulty getting their product to perform as well as a natural bristled brush when, in the midst of their troubles, they were at a loss as to how to 'go on' with research, someone observed,

> *'You know a paintbrush is a kind of pump!'* He pointed out that when a paintbrush is pressed against a surface, paint is forced through the *spaces between bristles* onto the surface. The paint is made to flow through the 'channels' formed by the bristles when the channels are deformed by the bending of the brush.[118]

In inviting them not only to see the paintbrush as a pump but to act towards it as if it were a pump this metaphor transformed the situation for the researchers, and presented a whole set of options for acting that they had not previously considered.

In the 'show and tell' context of police culture, officers engage in just such a process. They introduce a novice to the craft of policing by showing her, via the poetic logic of tropes, how to see her new world, and then pointing out to her the features that have been highlighted for her.[119] Further, just as seeing a paintbrush as a pump structured action for the researchers by directing them to change and manipulate the spaces between the bristles rather then the bristles themselves, so does the way of seeing presented by police officers. Once Sacks' pretty young woman is seen as a prostitute she becomes the object of a completely different kind of attention.

Tropes create a world by permitting it to be seen and experienced in new ways which, once brought to life persist. They act as 'cognitive instruments for connections that once perceived, are *then* truly present'[120] as features of this world. By considering one thing from the perspective of another tropes generate a way of seeing by identifying what situational features are to be highlighted as foreground and by permitting the rest to fade into an unacknowledged background. The metaphor, Paivio[121] writes, 'is a solar eclipse. It hides the object of study and at the same time reveals some of its most salient and interesting characteristics when viewed through the right telescope'. Tropes, as Davidson[122] writes so poetically, do 'the dreamwork of language'.

Seeing police stories as tropological suggests that they should be 'read' as a text as the literary product they so obviously are, rather than dismissed as simply obscuring the implicit rules that 'must' generate action. As Geertz[123] notes:

> If one takes the [Balinese] cockfight, or any other collective sustained symbolic structure, as a means of 'saying something of something else' (to invoke a famous Aristotelian tag), then one is faced with a problem not in social mechanics but social semantics ... the question is, what does one learn about such principles from examining culture as an assemblage of texts?

One learns culture is a figurative resource used to constitute the sensibilities out of which action flows as well as the world of opportunities within which this action will take place.

We are not proposing an alternative to rules to fill the conceptual space left vacant by the critique of the rule-based model. Our critique is much more fundamental. It goes behind rules to the assumptions that give rise to the quest for recipes. Tropes, such as the 'on vacation' metaphor, are useless as rule-equivalents because they simply do not provide recipe-like instructions. Anyone who tried to use this metaphor as a followable instruction in this way would have no sense whatsoever of how to act. Analogic directions simply do not, and cannot, fill this conceptual space. They require and exist in a different conceptual domain.

We need to re-think the notion of 'directions for action'. The production of action should be thought of as stage directions, as akin to the theatrical director who seeks to promote a particular style of performance and who uses a series of tropes to evoke a sensibility out of which the appropriate action will flow. These directions, unlike recipes, do not seek to promote any particular course of action but simply activity that is evoked by the sensibility. When this is recognized as happening the directions will have 'worked'. Neither the actor nor the director would know what her actions will look like ahead of time (as would be the case if the directions had followed the formal logic of rules) any more than a jazz musician knows what her improvisation will sound like ahead of time. No one, least of all the actor, would know what the action would be before it happened. Yet the director would recognize it after it had happened as either competent or incompetent.

Such action has all the surprise Mead insisted was characteristic of the 'I'. Such action is point blank in exactly the sense that music produced in a jazz jam session is point blank. In such sessions nothing is known in advance except that not just any old thing will count as competent. This is the art and the craft of the jazz musician just as police activity is the art and the craft of the police officer.

Because our argument requires a reconception of the generation of activity it requires a relocation of activity in relation to social order. We accept the ethno-methodological insight that social order, the way the world is recognized, is constituted. We accept moreover that stories, be they ones that reference rules or ones that reference tropes, are actions that are reflexively employed to constitute the meaning of the actions of which they are a part. We accept too that this is always retrospective, as Mead's conception of the 'Me' suggests; that there is no pre-storied identity, no meaning outside of the methods people use to reflexively accomplish the sense of activity as action. We are not attempting to move back from this to a pre-ethnomethodological conception of meaning as somehow given and not ongoingly accomplished. Our concern is not with the 'Me' but with the 'I'. Thus, our task has been to advance Bittner's[124] quest for the craft, the 'practical skill', that provides police officers with ways of seeing and being that allows them to do what jazz musicians do, improvise.

Sudnow[125] conceives this skill that the 'I' knows and practices out of a prospective consciousness as located in the 'body', in the `improvisatory hand' of the jazz musician. This formulation analytically separates the retrospectively constituted mind from the spontaneous, surprising Meadian 'I'. This skill cannot, we have argued, be understood in terms of a formal, linear logic as the quest for recipes tries to do. This logic is the rationality of the retrospectively constituted 'mind', of the 'Me', it is not the logic of the 'body', of the 'I'.

## Stories as precedents

The process of analogous, non-algerbraic reasoning made possible by tropes is also made possible by other features of the narrative form. One way in which police stories accomplish this, as we have already alluded, is by using carefully chosen examples to create a vocabulary of precedents, that operate much like chess gambits to structure and prompt the generation of police action. Bayley and Bittner[126] cite several stories that illustrate this.

> Demonstrating the importance of obtaining control without physical injury in the hierarchy of operating values, patrol officers have a great fund of stories about how violent situations were defused through cunning verbal ploys. For example, an officer who was a born-again Christian spotted religious decor in the home of a couple who had a violent argument. He asked them what they thought the Lord would want them to do and ten minutes later they were reconciled. One tactic is to divert the attention of disputants thus allowing emotions to cool. Noting what appears to be hand-made furniture, an officer may say, 'Do you make furniture? So do I'. Others ask if they may use the bathroom obliging the residents to point it out, or inquire what the score is of the baseball game on TV, or request a cup of coffee or a soft drink. One officer gained control in a domestic dispute by sitting down indifferently in front of the television set and calmly taking off his hat. The husband and wife were so non-plussed at this lack of concern for their fight that shortly they, too, lost interest.

The following exemplary anecdote demonstrates how gambit elaboration can be used in conjunction with metaphoric reasoning.

> An officer is called to a domestic dispute and is unable to get the husband and wife to stop arguing long enough to enable him to talk to them. So, he blows his whistle, throws his white handkerchief in the air and calls out, 'Time out and a fifteen yard penalty for fighting', which had the effect of stopping the fighting and got everyone laughing.[127]

As analysts we have presented the message of the stories and aphorisms we have cited in a discursive form, but this is not done by police officers themselves. This knowledge, as Giddens[128] observes is 'practical rather than theoretical in character'. The point of the story is not stated in so many words, it is not 'easily summarized'.[129] Anecdotes are vehicles for the transmission of a 'practical consciousness', a 'knowledgeability',[130] that constitutes a practical, not a discursive, consciousness. They express the lessons concentrated in aphorisms through concrete images that provide for a poetic apprehension of the way of seeing and sensibility required for the practice of police work without ever presenting this knowledge in discursive form in the way rules do. Stories express and share practical knowledge *qua* practical knowledge. The knowledgeability they provide that permits people to engage in the 'production and reproduction of social practices'[131] is tacitly rather than explicitly communicated and grasped. Analogous reasoning is a tacit, poetic reasoning that operates at a non-discursive level. Stories about concrete situations provide lessons that encourage officers to constitute for themselves the 'generalized capacity' they require 'to respond to and influence an indeterminate range of social circumstance'.[132]

Giddens adopts a notion of rule, drawn from Wittgenstein, as a formula or 'generalizable procedure' that provides for the capacity to 'go on'. This leads to a conception of structure as the site of this 'generalized capacity' of formulae and associated resources (both material and symbolic) that produce activities. This conception of structure as a formula for going on is, as Giddens[133] makes clear, very similar to ethnomethodologists' conception of a generative grammar that provides for turn-taking in conversations or interaction that we have already criticized. What we have been suggesting is an alternative way of conceiving of knowledgeability in terms of figurative forms that work through a poetic logic to promote a way of being in the world that produces a style of activity.

In each of the stories cited above a sensibility is both assumed and reinforced by directing officers' attention to concrete situations of action. What these stories say to police officers is

> Here are some examples of the sort of actions that the sensibility appropriate to police work has produced. Consider these both as gambits you might wish to try yourself and use them to get a better understanding of the sort of sensibility we have been talking about and that you will have to construct if you are to act appropriately as a police officer.

As precedents such stories operate as 'representative or informative anecdotes'[134] that together provide a library of gambits.

## Cognitive sensibilities

We have suggested throughout that communicating a culture is an active process in which the work of the listener (reader) is as vital as that of the teller. Thus, for example, the metaphor of the vacation invites officers to transfer the sensibility appropriate to one environment of action to another. The process of active reading is one that White[135] considers explicitly as he shows how legend acts to construct a worldview, a cognitive sensibility, out of the 'silences' that are intrinsic to great stories. While the police do not have single stories that compare with the great tales of legend together their stories constitute a sizable story book with both explicit content and silences (see for example, Wambaugh, McClure and Gadd,[136] for a review see Reiner[137]).

White considers how stories communicate the resources of a culture in his analysis of Homer's *Iliad*. He shows how legend locates the listener in the concrete world of action, rather than the abstract world of theory, and how this operates to create a 'theoretical' worldview, or 'root paradigm',[138] out of which action arises. He demonstrates how the *Iliad* is both a statement about the world and a set of silences, that engages the listener in actively exploring and appropriating the resources of the culture the story is revealing.

> In the poem itself the world of the *Iliad* is presented not in theoretical summary or outline, as I have done, but in the form in which the real world is experienced, as a sequence of events taking place against an assumed background, as a narrative in a living world … As this story unfolds, the reader is naturally full of questions. Who are the actors in the world? What, for example, does it mean to be a warrior, a priest, or a god? We are invited by the poem itself to ask what resources the culture offers for the definition of character, for social action, for reasoning and persuasion, and for claims of meaning. We are invited to ask, in short, what life would be like lived in such a world as this, and it is part of the work of the poem to offer us a response.[139, 140]

So too police stories reveal a tool kit of cultural resources, each embedded in a concrete occasion of use, and invite the listener to actively participate in understanding and using them. Each story demonstrates that culture

> is not a scheme or a structure but a way of living, and, to be understood, it must be seen as offering a set of resources for speech and conduct: a set of things that it is possible on certain occasions to say – by way for example of appeal, command, claim, or argument; a set of things that it is possible to do, a set of moves with force and shape and meaning of their own …[141]

There is, however, more to each story than the work specific to it. Each story refers implicitly to a larger whole that is expressed through the story but is never fully revealed by it in the same way that each two dimensional view of a three dimensional object refers outside of itself, as Husserl[142] has argued, to other possible views. As a result each story functions as a metonony that invites the listener to construct, out of the specifics of the story, the worldview that makes sense of the story. Police stories operate together to construct a worldview that is grasped in, and through, the concrete accounts which give it expression without ever making this theoretical enterprise a topic in its own right.[143] Thus, the stories cited above about domestic disputes imply a theoretical conception of conflicts as situationally driven without ever making this point abstractly in theoretical terms. Similarly, as Shearing[144] (see also Manning[145]) demonstrates, the ongoing commentary and story telling that police officers engage in as they go about their work of receiving calls from the public for police service imply a general conception of citizens as helpless, stupid, demanding and exploitative without saying so in so many words.

White spells out the 'reflexive', 'indexical' character of this process of constitution when he considers how the clarity of a story's details creates an unstated, but implied, worldview that must be constructed out of the detail in order to make sense of it.

> The special quality that the epic language gives to the world it creates is thus a sense of clarity bounded by silence, of extraordinary certainty placed against the wholly unknown … This silence – the strange reticence of the poet who seems to tell us everything about the universe he presents with such uninterrupted surfaces, but who withdraws from what he has made, leaving us to make of it what we can – is one source of the magnificent life of this poem. For in leaving to us the task of making sense of what is before us, this silence forces our continuous and attentive engagement with the poem itself. Every detail, every shift, may matter.[146]

So too with the poets of the police culture who spin the tales of police work and through the detail of concrete exemplars create a worldview that emerges as much from the silences that surround the stories as they do from the narratives themselves.

This worldview, as a way of seeing, implies a way of being that invites a doing. The stories of the police culture, in structuring the opportunities for action that people see as available to them, and in providing a consciousness out of which action emerges serve to embed power.[147] Thus, stories are revealed as a hegemonic device,[148] or counter-hegemonic device,[149] for producing a way of seeing and being in the world.

## Conclusion

Stories, and the tropes that drive them, provide a very different sort of 'generative program' from that envisioned when such 'programs' are conceived of on the basis of a genetic metaphor *à la* Dawkins – as rule-guided. This conception does not conceive of people as 'cultural dopes'[150] blindly following internalized cultural rules but rather acknowledges them as active participants in the construction of action. The guidance stories provided have an open-ended character. They instruct people on how they should go about constructing action not on what precisely they should do. They invite them to consider particular sorts of gambits and strategies to use in constructing action, and show how this has been done on particular occasions in the past in precisely the same way that books of chess playing instruct players. As Black[151] observes, 'there can be no rules for "creatively" violating rules. And that is why there can be no *dictionary* (though there may be a thesaurus) of metaphors'.

This analysis of police stories suggests that culture should be conceived of as a poetic system that enables action through a trope and precedent based logic. This logic transfers knowledge from one to another via a process of analogous reasoning that invites activity by encouraging the construction of a particular subjectivity. This conception responds to the weaknesses of the rule-based version of action, and the fuzziness of the interpretive alternative from within an ethnomethodological informed context that insists the generation of action not be conceived as a 'problem of social order'. It permits us to understand how it is that action can be both guided and improvisational because it recognizes that any process for enabling human action must have an open-ended character that fosters the sensitivity and openness required for creative choices.[152] It accepts that while people's activity is directed, in the sense in which a theatrical performance is directed, they none the less often 'muddle through, improvise, and make things up as they go along'.[153] It recognizes that police stories provide officers with tools they can use to get them through the business of police work without minimizing the fact that this still requires individual initiative and daring. It also recognizes that officers differ in their competence in using this cultural tool-kit, just as cabinet-markers and surgeons differ in their skills as they use their respective tool-kits. Finally, it recognizes that what they do will be constituted as ordered via the reflexive methods that are part of this doing.

In recognizing all this our model allows for differences between people in responding to situations; for unexpected opportunities to shape responses; for unplanned and unintended consequences; for ambiguity and uncertainty; for the fact that people improvise, take things as they come, go one step at a time, and play it by ear.

*From Clifford Shearing and Richard Ericson, 'Culture as figurative action', British Journal of Sociology, Vol. 42, 4, 1991, pp 481–506.*

## Notes

1  See D.L. Wieder, *Language and Social Reality: The Case of Telling the Convict Code*, The Hague: Mouton, 1974, p.29; R.A. Hilbert, 'Towards an improved understanding of "role"', *Theory and Society*, 10 (2), 1981, pp. 207–25.

2  See T. Parsons, 'The place of ultimate values in sociological theory', *International Journal of Ethics*, 45, 1935, pp. 282–316, where he attempts to construct a voluntaristic theory of action that becomes instead the foundation for a thoroughgoing normative determinism demonstrating the analytic attractiveness of a rule-based framework. See also C.D. Shearing, 'Towards a phenomenological sociology or towards a solution to the Parsonian puzzle', *Catalyst*, 7 (Winter) 1973, pp. 9–14.

3  See H. Garfinkel, *Studies in Ethnomethodology*, Englewood Cliffs, New Jersey: Prentice-Hall, 1967.

4  See C. Geertz, *The Interpretation of Cultures: Selected Essays*, New York: Basic Books, 1973, p.216; A. Giddens, *The Constitution of Society: Outline of the Theory of Structuration*, Cambridge: Polity Press, 1984, pp. 17–21.

5  See R. Dawkins, *The Selfish Game*, New York: Oxford University Press, 1976, pp. 206–7 for an example of a genetic template and a discussion of what an equivalent cultural mechanism would look like.

6  Parsons, 1935, *op. cit.*, p. 191; N. Chomsky, *Language and Mind*, New York: Harcourt, Brace and World, 1968; S.B. Shimanoff, *Communication Rules: Theory and Research.* (Sage Library of Social Research) Beverly Hills: Sage, 1980; R.B. Edgerton, *Rules, Expectations, and Social Order*, Berkeley: University of California Press, 1985; T.P. Wilson, 'Conceptions of interaction and forms of sociological explanation', *American Sociological Review*, 33 (4), 1970, pp. 697–710; T.P. Wilson, 'Normative and interpretive paradigms in sociology', in Jack D. Douglas (ed.), *Understanding Everyday Life*, New York: Aldine, 1971, pp. 29–39; Wieder, 1974, *op.cit.*; and Hilbert, 1981, *op. cit.*, pp. 207–11.

7  See L. Wittgenstein, *Philosophical Investigations* (Trans. G.E.M. Anscombe), Oxford: Basil Blackwell and Matt, 1972, pp. 38–9; A.W. Imershein and R.L. Simons, 'Rules and exemplars in lay and professional psychiatry: an ethnomethodological critique of the Scheff-Gove controversy' (Comment on Scheff, *ASR*, April, 1974 and Gove, *ASR*, April, 1975) *American Sociological Review*, 41 (3), 1976, pp. 559–63; P. Bourdieu, *Outline of a Theory of Practice,*

Cambridge: Cambridge University Press, 1977, pp. 1–22; R. Rosaldo, 'While making other plans'. *Southern California Law Review*, 58, 1985, pp. 19–28.

8   Hilbert, 1981, *op.cit.*, pp. 213–16.

9   See Shimanoff, 1980, *op. cit.* and Edgerton, 1985, *op. cit.*

10  See also Chomsky's (1968, *op. cit.*) 'generative grammar'; E.A. Schegloff, 'Sequencing in conversational openings', *American Anthropologist* (New Series) 70, 1968, pp. 1075–95, for rules for conversational sequencing; and Giddens' (1984, *op. cit.*, pp. 21–2), use and development of Wittgenstein's 'formula'.

11  W.V. Quine, 'Methodological reflections on current linguistic theory', in D. Harman and G. Davidson (eds) *Semantics of Natural Language*, Dordrecht: Reidel, 1972, pp. 442–54.

12  T.P. Parsons, *The Social System*, New York: Free Press, 1951, pp. 38, 42.

13  Bourdieu, 1977, *op. cit.*, pp. 1–2, pp. 29–30.

14  *Ibid.*, p. 2.

15  V. Turner, *Dramas, Fields, and Metaphors: Symbolic Action in Human Society*, Ithaca: Cornell University Press, 1974, p. 36.

16  Bourdieu, 1977, *op. cit.*, p. 9.

17  In developing this argument Bourdieu, *ibid.*, p. 9, argues that 'retrospective necessity becomes prospective necessity' so that the 'whole logic of practice is transformed'; rules eliminate the uncertain, improvisational and opportunistic character of actual practice (Rosaldo, 1985, *op. cit.*). Also cf. J.F. Lyotard, *The Postmodern Condition: A Report on Knowledge* (Trans. from French by Geoff Bennington and Brian Mossumi; Foreword by Frederic Jameson). *Theory and History of Literature: Volume 10*, Manchester: Manchester University Press [1979], 1984, p. 81 and M. Moran, *The Politics of Banking. The Strange Case of Competition and Credit Control*, London: Macmillan Press, 1984. Earlier sociological criticisms have underscored the tendency of the rule-based paradigm to shift attention from the Meadian 'I' to an almost exclusive focus on the 'Me'. See D.H. Wrong, 'The oversocialized conception of man in modern society', *American Sociological Review*, 26, 1961, pp. 183–93 and G.C. Homans, 'Bringing men back in', *American Sociological Review*, 29 (5 December), 1964, pp. 809–18.

18  See Geertz, 1973, *op. cit.*; Rosaldo, 1985, *op. cit.*, A. Swidler, 'Culture in action: symbols and strategies', *American Sociological Review*, 51 (April), 1986, pp. 273–86, and R.J. Coombe, 'Room for manoeuver: toward a theory of practice in critical legal studies', *Law & Social Inquiry*, 14 (1, Winter), 1989, pp. 60–121.

19  See Imershein and Simons, 1976, *op. cit.*, p. 560; R.M. Unger, *Knowledge and Politics*, New York: The Free Press, 1975, p. 259; and Lyotard, 1984, *op. cit.*, p. 19.

20  Bourdieu, 1977, *op. cit.*, p. 83.

21  E. Cassirer, *Language and Myth*, New York: Dover, 1946, pp. 89–92.

22  K. Burke, *A Grammar of Motives*, Berkeley and Los Angeles: University of California Press, 1969, pp. 505–6.

23  Shimanoff, 1980, *op. cit.*

24  For example, Geertz's 1973, *op.cit.*, 'thick description' and 'deep play', Turner's 1974, *op. cit.*, 'social dramas', Bourdieu's 1977, *op. cit.*, 'habitus' and Swidler's 1986, *op. cit.*, p. 275 'tool kit' of strategies made up of 'symbols, stories, rituals, and world views, which people may use in varying configurations to solve different kinds of problems'.

25  Unger, 1975, *op. cit.*, pp. 254–5, notes that our understanding of the practical capacity people have to proceed 'by analogizing particulars directly to each other without relying on abstract principles … remains in a primitive state' despite the fact that its practice is a pervasive feature of social life. This remains true even though one can locate brilliant analyses, of particular events, that operate outside of a rule-based frame (cf. Bourdieu's, 1977, *op. cit.*, analysis of parallel cousin marriages).

26  T. Kuhn, *The Structure of Scientific Revolutions*, Chicago: University of Chicago Press, 1967, and Shearing, 1973, *op. cit.*

27  N. Frye, *The Great Code: The Bible and Literature*, New York: Harcourt Brace Jovonovich, 1982, p. 38.

28  R. Barthes, *Mythologies*, Glasgow: Paladin. [1957], 1973.

29  See Burke, 1969, *op. cit.*, p. 33, and H. White, *Tropics of Discourse: Essays in Cultural Criticism*, Baltimore: Johns Hopkins University Press, 1978, p. 7.

30  This makes intuitive sense as policing takes place within an explicit legal regime of rules that define what is, and what is not, legitimate police conduct.

31  J. Hagan and P.C. Morden, 'The police decision to detain: a study of legal labelling and police deviance', in Clifford D. Shearing (ed.), *Organizational Police Deviance*, Toronto: Butterworths, 1981, pp. 9–28.

32  P.K. Manning, *Police Work: The Social Organization of Policing*, Cambridge Mass.: The MIT Press, 1977.

33  E. Reuss-Ianni and F.A.J. Ianni, 'Street cops and management cops: the two cultures of policing', in Maurice Punch (ed.), *Control in the Police Organization*, Cambridge, Mass.: The MIT Press, 1988, pp. 251–74.

34  M.N. Wexler, 'Police culture: a response to ambiguous employment', in C.L. Boydell, C.F. Grindstaff and P.C. Whitehead (eds), *The Administration of Criminal Justice in Canada*, Toronto: Holt, Rinehart and Winston, 1974, pp. 126–51.

35  P.K. Manning, 'The police occupational culture in Anglo-American societies', in L. Hoover and J. Dowling (eds) *Encyclopedia of Police Science*, New York: Garland, 1989.

36  *Ibid.*

37  M.R. Chatterton, 'Police work and assault charges', in Maurice Punch (ed.), *Control in the Police Organization*, Cambridge, Mass.: The MIT Press, 1983, pp. 194–221, esp. p. 196.

38  Garfinkel, 1967, *op. cit.*

39  Wieder, 1974, *op. cit.*

40  Wilson, 1970, *op. cit.*, pp. 700–1. See also R. Turner, 'Role-taking: process versus conformity', in A.M. Rose (ed.), *Human Behavior and Social Process: An Interactionist Approach*, Boston: Houghton Mifflin, 1962, pp. 20–40, esp. p. 28.

41  Wieder, 1974, *op. cit.*, pp. 30–1.

42  D.H. Zimmerman and M. Pollner, 'The everyday world as a phenomenon', in Jack D. Douglas (ed.), *Understanding Everyday Life*. Chicago: Aldine, 1970, pp. 80–103.

43  Wieder, 1974, *op. cit.*, p. 224.

44  Garfinkel, 1967, *op. cit.*, p. vii.

45  Wilson, 1970, *op. cit.*

46  H. Garfinkel and H. Sacks, 'On formal structures of practical actions', in John C. McKinney and Edward A. Tiryakian, *Theoretical Sociology: Perspectives and Developments*, New York: Appleton-Century-Crofts, 1970, pp. 337–67.

47  Wieder, 1974, *op. cit.*, pp. 219, 220.

48  *Ibid.*, p. 220–1.

49  Garfinkel. 1967, *op. cit.*

50  Wilson, 1970, *op. cit.*, pp. 700–1.

51  See Giddens, 1984, *op. cit.* and D. Sudnow, *Ways of the Hand: The Organization of Improvised Conduct*, Cambridge: Harvard University Press, 1978 and D. Sudnow, *Talk's Body: A Meditation between Two Keyboards*, New York: Knopf, 1979.

52  Parsons, 1935, *op. cit.*

53  Wilson, 1970, *op. cit.*, p. 707.

54  Garfinkel and Sacks, 1970, *op. cit.*, pp. 345–7.

55  Wilson, 1970, *op. cit.*, p. 707.

56  *Ibid.*, p. 701.

57  See J.R. Gusfield, *The Culture of Public Problems: Drinking-Driving and the Symbolic Order*, Chicago: University of Chicago Press, 1981, and R. Wagner-Pacifici, *The Moro Morality Play: Terrorism as Social Drama*, Chicago: University of Chicago Press, 1986, for recent, ethnomethodologically informed, considerations of this issue; see also Barthes, 1973, *op. cit.*, pp. 43–6 for a similar analysis from within a different theoretical tradition.

58  Wieder, *op. cit.*, p. 169.

59  Q. Hoare and G. Nowell Smith (eds), *Selections from the Prison Notebooks of Antonio Gramsci*, New York: International Publishers, 1971; M. Foucault, *Discipline and Punish: The Birth of the Prison*, New York: Vantage Books, 1979. M.J. Edelman, *Constructing the Political Spectacle*, Chicago: University of Chicago Press, 1989a; M.J. Edelman, 'Skeptical studies of language, the media, and mass culture', *American Political Science Review*, 82 (4, December) 1988b, pp. 1333–9.

60  See Giddens, 1984, *op. cit.*, pp. 21–3.

61  Wilson, 1970, *op. cit.*, p. 704.

62  E. Bittner, 'The police on skid row: a study of peace keeping', *American Sociological Review*, 32 (5, October), 1966, pp. 699–715.

63  Turner, 1962, *op. cit.*

64  H. Blumer, *Symbolic Interactionism: Perspective and Method*, Englewood Cliffs, New Jersey: Prentice-Hall, 1969.

65  Wilson, 1970, *op. cit.*, p. 704.

66  See Hilbert, 1981, *op. cit.*, pp. 213–16 and Giddens, 1984, *op. cit.*, p. 21.

67  Wilson, 1970, *op. cit.*, pp. 705–6.

68  Giddens, 1984, *op. cit.*, pp. 20–1.

69  Schegloff, 1968, p. 1091.

70  Garfinkel and Sacks, 1970, *op. cit.*

71  *Ibid.*, p.355.

72  H. Sacks, 'On doing "being ordinary"', in J. Maxwell Atkinson and John Heritage (eds), *Structures of Social Action: Studies in Conversation Analysis*, Cambridge: Cambridge University Press, 1984, pp. 413–29.

73  D. Bayley and E. Bittner, 'Learning the skills of policing', *Law and Contemporary Problems*, 47 (4, Fall) 1984, pp. 35–59 and Bittner, 1967, *op. cit.*

74  See Bayley and Bittner, 1984, *op. cit.*, p. 35 and Bittner, 1967, *op. cit.*

75  Sudnow (1978 *op. cit.*, p. 25) references this insistence in relation to his experience with jazz lessons. In seeking to learn how to improvise he would push his teacher to provide him with a recipe for doing improvisation but could not get him to provide him with the required principles. I would ask 'what was that?' He would say 'what was what?' I said 'that little thing you just did over the G minor chord there'. Now a characteristic 'trouble' occurred …[H]e would have a hard time finding what he had 'just done'. He would at times frankly say, 'I'm not following rules so I don't really know what I just did' (and on other occasions admit, 'I just improvise, I really cannot tell you how, you have to have a feel for it').

76  See N. Fielding, *Joining Forces: Police Training, Socialization and Occupational Competence*, London: Routledge, 1988, and J. Van Maanen, *Tales of the Field: On Writing Ethnography*, Chicago: University of Chicago Press, 1988.

77  Bayley and Bittner, 1984, *op. cit.*, p. 47.

78  *Ibid*, p. 41.

79  *Ibid*, p. 49.

80  *Ibid.*, p. 46.

81  *Ibid*, p. 47.

82  N. Fielding, 'Police socialization and police competence', *British Journal of Sociology*, 35 (4, December), 1984, pp. 568–90.

83  Giddens, 1984, *op. cit.*, p. 21.

84  See Frye, 1982, *op. cit.*, p. 38. See also D. Schön, 'Generative metaphor: a perspective on problem-setting in social policy', in Andrew Ortony, *Metaphor and Thought*, Cambridge: Cambridge University Press, 1979, pp. 254–83.

85  Lyotard, 1984, *op. cit.*, p. 19.

86  Under, 1975, *op. cit.*, p. 144.

87  H. Sacks, 'Notes on police assessment of moral character', in David Sudnow (ed.) *Studies in Social Interaction*. New York: Free Press, 1972, pp. 280–93.

88  Burke, 1969, *op. cit.*, p. 59.

89  M. Weber, *The Theory of Social and Economic Organization* (Trans. By A.M. Henderson and Talcott Parsons), New York: The Free Press, [1947], 1964, pp. 88–90.

90  Wagner-Pacific, 1986, *op. cit.*, pp. 167–68, and Cassier, 1946, *op. cit.*, pp. 90–91.

91  Wieder, 1974, *op. cit.*; see J.B. White, *When Words Lose their Meaning: Constitutions and Reconstitutions of Language, Character and Community*, Chicago: University of Chicago Press, 1984 and J.B. White, *Heracles' Bow: Essays on the Rhetoric of Poetics Law*. Madison: University of Wisconsin Press, 1985. See his conception of 'reading' for a remarkably similar analysis to Wieder's but one that comes out of an entirely different tradition.

92  Wieder, 1974, *op. cit.*, p. 1969.

93  See Bittner, 1967, *op. cit.*, p. 705.

94  See Lyotard, 1984, *op. cit.*, pp. 19–20.

95  R. Barthes, 'The third meaning: research notes on several Eisenstein stills', [1970] in R. Barthes, *The Responsibility of Forums: Critical Essays on Music, Art and Representation* (Trans. Richard Howard), New York, and Wong, 1985, pp. 41–62, esp. pp. 43–4.

96  Sacks, 1972, *op. cit.*, p. 285.

97  See Manning, 1977, *op. cit.*

98  C. Wright Mills, 'Situtated actions and vocabularies of motives', *American Sociological Review*, 5 (October), 1940, pp. 904–13.

99  R.V. Ericson, P.M. Baranek and J.B.L. Chan, *Visualizing Deviance: A Study of New Organization*, Toronto: University of Toronto Press, 1987.

100  Sudnow (1978, *op. cit.*, p. 28) indicates how in learning jazz piano playing the novice learns to stock pile a host of gambits and precedents as possible places and routes for the hand to go.

101  Sacks, 1972, *op. cit.*, p. 292.

102  D.E. Smith, *The Everyday World as Problematic A Feminist Sociology*, Toronto: University of Toronto Press, 1987, pp. 69–78.

103  Wittgenstein, 1972, *op. cit.*, p. 32.

104  Sudnow, 1979, *op. cit.*, p. 4.

105  Frye, 1982, *op. cit.*, p. 49 and White, 1984, *op. cit.*

106  See Hilbert, 1981, *op. cit.*, p. 214.

107  Bayley and Bittner, 1984, *op. cit.*, p. 46.

108  See Bittner, 1967, *op. cit.*, p. 705 and M. Black, 'More about metaphor', in Andrew Ortony (ed.) *Metaphor and Thought*, Cambridge: Cambridge University Press, 1979, pp. 19–43, esp. pp. 40–1.
109  Lyotard, 1984, *op. cit.*, p. 22.
110  See Bayley and Bittner, 1984, *op. cit.*, p. 35 and Unger, 1975, *op. cit.*, p. 254.
111  *Ibid.*, p. 254.
112  *Ibid.*, pp. 254–5.
113  Bayley and Bittner, 1984, *op. cit.*, p. 35.
114  *Ibid.*, pp. 42, 50.
115  Unger, 1975, *op. cit.*, p. 258.
116  There are four principal tropes. Syndoche invites a seeing of the whole in terms of the part or the part in terms of the whole, the metonymy communicates the abstract through the concrete, while in irony meaning is conveyed through a reference to its antithesis. The metaphor, often considered the master trope (see U. Eco, *Semiotics and the Philosophy of Language*, Bloomington, Indiana: Indiana University Press, 1984, p. 87), analogizes one situation with another; it invites the hearer to see and experience one thing as she would another.
117  Blumer, 1969, *op. cit.*, p. 16.
118  Schön, 1979, *op. cit.*, p. 257.
119  Blumer, 1969, *op. cit.*, pp. 10–12; 15–20.
120  Black, 1979, *op. cit.*, p. 39.
121  A. Paivio, 'Psychological processes in the comprehension of metaphor', in Andrew Ortony (ed.) *Metaphor and Thought*, Cambridge: Cambridge University Press, 1979, pp. 150–171, esp. p. 150.
122  D. Davidson, 'What metaphors mean', in Mark Johnson (ed.), *Philosophical Perspectives on Metaphor*, Minneapolis: University of Minneapolis Press, 1981, pp. 200–1, esp. p. 200.
123  Geertz, 1973, *op. cit.*, p. 449.
124  Bittner, 1967, *op. cit.*
125  Sudnow, 1979, *op. cit.*
126  Bayley and Bittner, 1984, *op. cit.*, p. 46.
127  Personal communication with David Bayley in response to an earlier draft of this paper.
128  Giddens, 1984, *op. cit.*, pp. 21–3.
129  Bittner, 1967, *op. cit.*, p. 705.
130  Giddens, 1984, *op. cit.*, p. 21.
131  *Ibid.*
132  *Ibid.*
133  *Ibid.*
134  Burke, 1969, *op. cit.*, p. 60.
135  White, 1984, *op. cit.*
136  J. Wambaugh, *The Onion Field*, New York: Delacorte Press, 1973; J. McClure, *Cop World*, London: Pan Books, 1984; R. Gadd, *Our Cops – Their Stories*, Aliston, Ontario: Bulldog Press, 1986.
137  R. Reiner, *The Politics of the Police*, Brighton, Sussex: Wheatsheaf Books, 1985.
138  Wagner-Pacifici, 1986, *op. cit.*, pp. 164–8.
139  White, 1984, *op. cit.*, p. 28.
140  This view of culture as constructed in a process that involves both those who tell and those who listen to narratives is succinctly expressed by Van Maanen 1988, *op. cit.*, p. 7. Culture is not strictly speaking a scientific object, but is created, as is the reader's view of it, by the active construction of a text.
141  White, 1984, *op. cit.*, p. 28.
142  E. Husserl, *The Crisis of European Sciences and Transcendental Phenomenology: An Introduction to Phenomenological Philosophy* (Translation and Introduction by David Carr), Evanston: Northwestern University Press, 1970. See also, A. Gurwitsch, 'Intentionality, constitution, and intentional analysis', in Joseph J. Kockelmans (ed.), *Phenomenology: The Philosophy of Edmund Husserl and its Interpretations*, Garden City, New York: Anchor Books, 1967, pp. 118–37, and J.J. Kockelmans, *First Introduction to Husserl's Phenomenology*, USA: Duquesne University Press, 1967, pp. 197, 200.
143  This idea is developed by S.R. Levin, *Metaphoric Worlds: Conceptions of a Romantic Nature*, New Haven: Yale University Press, 1988, pp. x–xi, with reference to Wordsworth as follows: Thus the world view that I attributed to Wordsworth is a conception in the sense of a general schematization; such as, it constitutes a fundamental component of Wordsworth's epistemological outlook. On the one hand, in his employment of individual metaphors ... Wordsworth expresses conceptions of a particular kind; these conceptions are local, constituting individual and specific intentional acts, acts in which Wordsworth responds in a characteristic way to features and events in his personal environment. It is by abstracting from

the particular and characteristic conceptions that Wordsworth expresses in his metaphors that we arrive at his general conception of how the world is ordered.

144   C. Shearing, 'Cops don't see it that way', in T. Fleming and L. Visano (eds), *Deviant Designations; Crime, Law and Deviance in Canada*, Toronto: Butterworths, 1983, pp. 375–88.
145   P.K. Manning, *Symbolic Communication*, Cambridge: MIT Press, 1988.
146   White, 1984, *op. cit.*, p. 27.
147   See Foucault, 1979, *op. cit.*, C.D. Shearing and P.C. Stenning, 'From the panopticon to Disney World: the development of discipline', in A.N. Doob and E.L. Greenspan (eds), *Perspectives in Criminal Law: Essays in Honour of John Ll. J. Edwards*, Toronto: Canada Law Book, 1984, pp. 335–49; and F. Lentricchia, *Ariel and the Police: Michel Foucault, William James, Wallace Stevens*, Madison: The University of Wisconsin Press, 1988, pp. 38–9.
148   See Gusfield, *op. cit.*, p. 174; R. Bocock, *Hegemony*, New York: Tavistock Publications, 1986, p. 8; and Wagner-Pacifici, 1986, *op. cit.*, p. 189.
149   A. Boal, *Theatre of the Oppressed*, New York: Urizen Books, 1979.
150   Garfinkel, 1967, *op. cit.*
151   Black, 1979, *op. cit.*, p. 25.
152   K.E. Weick, *The Social Psychology of Organizing*, Don Mills, Ontario: Addison Wesley, 1979.
153   Rosaldo, 1985, *op. cit.*, p. 20.

# 21. Changing police culture

*Janet Chan*

In 1992 a television documentary *Cop It Sweet* made national headlines and drew public outcries against police racism in Australia. The documentary depicted the harsh reality of police work in Redfern, one of the most socially disadvantaged areas of inner Sydney with a high concentration of Aboriginal population. Compared with the weekly diet of action-oriented police dramas on television, *Cop It Sweet* was unexceptional viewing. As a real-life *exposé* of police deviance it paled against the brutal beating of Rodney King. What shocked the audience, however, was not so much the crude and uncompromising message. It was true that the officers depicted were racist, sexist, ignorant, insensitive, and hypocritical, but what was most disturbing of all, in the words of a viewer, was that the police were 'on their best behaviour for the cameras' (*Sydney Morning Herald*, Letters, 7 March, 1992). This gave the impression that what was presented was 'business as usual'.[1]

The irony of this public disgrace of the New South Wales Police is that it came at a time when the force had been undergoing major organizational and cultural reforms for some years. In 1984 a new Police Board was created and John Avery, a dedicated reformer, was appointed Commissioner. Avery's mission was to rid the force of institutionalized corruption and open the door to a new police culture in which service to the community is a major motivation for police work. Many sweeping changes were introduced, including a complete reorganization of the command structure, the implementation of new recruitment criteria and training programmes, and the adoption of community-based policing as the principal operational strategy. Some initiatives were specifically aimed at improving police/minority relations; others were simply blanket reforms for building a more professional, accountable, and open police force. *Cop It Sweet*, then, not only raised questions about the force's policy direction, the quality of training, and the effectiveness of supervision, it cast serious doubts on the entire programme of police reform. Critics were quick to point out that 'nothing's changed' after eight years of reform.

What happened in New South Wales offers an excellent opportunity for a detailed examination of the problems and vagaries of police reform. The pressing question for researchers and practitioners alike is: why is it so difficult to change police practice? Conspiracy theory aside, the most powerful and currently popular explanation for the recalcitrance of police organizations against change is to postulate the existence of a 'police culture'. Police culture has become a convenient label for a range of negative values, attitudes, and practice norms among police officers. It is suggested that because police officers at the rank-and-file level exercise enormous discretion in their work, their informal working rules can subvert or obstruct policing reforms initiated at the top, or law reforms imposed externally (Reiner, 1992: 231–2). In the Queensland Police Inquiry, for example, police culture was identified as being responsible for police misconduct and a major obstacle to the success of reform (Fitzgerald Report, 1989: 200–12).

In this chapter, the utility of police culture as an explanatory concept is critically reviewed. It is argued that the concept has been poorly defined and is of little analytic value. A new framework for understanding police culture is suggested which recognizes the interpretive and creative aspects of culture, allows for the existence of multiple cultures, and takes into account the political context and cognitive structures of police work. The model draws on Bourdieu's concepts of 'field' and 'habitus' and adopts the framework on cultural knowledge in organizations developed by Sackmann (1991). Thus, police cultural practice results from the interaction between the socio-political context of police work and various dimensions of police organizational knowledge. The utility and implications of this framework for understanding the impact of policing reforms are discussed in relation to a study (Chan, 1992) that examined the implementation of initiatives to improve police/minorities relations in New South Wales.

[...]

## Police culture: a critique of existing theories

The concept of police culture originally emerged from ethnographic studies of routine police work, which uncover a layer of informal occupational norms and values operating under the apparently rigid hierarchical structure of police organizations (Cain, 1973; Manning, 1977, 1989; Holdaway, 1983). Interest in police culture has grown in recent years out of a concern that it is seen as one of the main obstacles in the way of police reform. Coincidentally, the concept of organizational culture gained prominence in the last two decades among organizational theorists as a result of the apparent failure of traditional Western corporate managerial strategies (Ouchi and Wilkins, 1985). It is believed by some analysts that corporate culture is a determinant of corporate performance (see Czarniawsk-Joerges, 1992). Thus managers, including police managers, want to know how organizational culture can be managed to improve organizational performance.

The concept of police culture in the criminological literature is loosely defined. Manning (1977: 143) refers to the 'core skills, cognitions, and affect' that define 'good police work'. It includes 'accepted practices, rules, and principles of conduct that are situationally applied, and generalized rationales and beliefs' (Manning, 1989: 360). Reiner (1992) equates it with the 'values, norms, perspectives and craft rules' that inform police conduct. Skolnick (1966) speaks of the 'working personality' of a police officer – a response to the danger of police work, the authority of the police constable, and the pressure to be 'productive' and 'efficient' in police work. Reiner (1992: 111–29) isolates certain features of police culture that are related to this 'working personality', including a cynical view of the world, a machismo and racist attitude, a strong sense of solidarity with other officers, and a conservative political outlook.

Police culture is not, however, primarily negative. It is seen to be functional to the survival of police officers in an occupation considered to be dangerous, unpredictable, and alienating. The bond of solidarity between officers 'offers its members reassurance that the other officers will "pull their weight" in police work, that they will defend, back up and assist their colleagues when confronted by external threats, and that they will maintain secrecy in the face of external investigations' (Goldsmith, 1990: 93–4). The development, transmission, and maintenance of this culture are assumed to be also related to the demands of police work (Reiner, 1992: 109).

Four major criticisms of the way police culture has been conceptualized will be presented. In spite of Reiner's acknowledgment that the 'cop culture' is not `monolithic, universal nor unchanging' (Reiner, 1992: 109), police culture is often described as though it is. Indeed, the first criticism concerns the failure of existing definitions of police culture to account for internal differentiation and jurisdictional differences. What is often being described as the police occupational culture in fact refers to the 'street cop culture', rather than the 'management cop culture' (Reuss-Ianni and Ianni, 1983). Manning (1993) has recently suggested that there are 'three subcultures of policing': command, middle management, and lower participants. My research in New South Wales supports this: officers in middle management positions held a distinctively negative view of the organization. Differences were also detected between officers holding different functional responsibilities (Chan, 1992). Thus, a theory of police culture should account for the existence of multiple cultures within a police force and variation in cultures among police forces.

The second criticism relates to the implicit passivity of police officers in the acculturation process. Reiner (1992: 109) has suggested that officers are not 'passive or manipulated learners', but did not elaborate on the nature of the 'socialization' process. Fielding's research in Britain has demonstrated that the individual officer is the 'final arbiter or mediator' of the structural and cultural influences of the occupation (Fielding, 1988: 10). While the culture may be powerful, it is nevertheless up to individuals to accommodate or resist its influence:

> One cannot read the recruit as a cipher for the occupational culture. The occupational culture has to make its pitch for support, just as the agencies of the formal organization exert their influence through control of resources. The stock stories of the occupational culture may be effective as a means of ordering perception which maximizes desirable outcomes. If they contradict the recruit's gathering experience they are likely to be dismissed (Fielding, 1988: 135).

Similarly, the salience of work demands and occupational pressures is mediated by individual experiences. For example, a focus on risk and uncertainty is part of the enacted environment (Weick, 1969) of police work, since the perception of danger 'is constructed and sustained by officers in the course of their routine work' (Holdaway, 1983: 19; also see Manning, 1989; Fielding, 1988). Thus, a sound theory of police culture should recognize the interpretive and active role of officers in structuring their understanding of the organization and its environment.

The third criticism of police culture as currently formulated is its apparent insularity from the social, political, legal, and organizational context of policing. Some have argued that police corruption and misconduct could not exist without the tacit approval of the community: 'for the police force to be willing to do the job of "shovelling shit", they had to be allowed to sleep on the job, be rude, harass defendants, and extort bribes' (Sparrow *et al.*, 1990: 133–4). There is evidence that the secrecy and solidarity of the culture sometimes break down under the strain of external investigations. Punch (1985) has documented the internal conflict and divisions caused by a corruption scandal in a Dutch police force, although he was pessimistic about its eventual impact on corrupt practices. Research in New South Wales shows that top police management was not insulated from public scandals but was constantly in 'damage control' mode (Chan, 1995). A theory of police culture must, therefore, situate culture in the political and social context of policing.

The final criticism is related to the first three: an all-powerful, homogeneous and deterministic conception of the police culture insulated from the external environment leaves little scope for a cultural change. As Manning (1993) suggests, 'the tensions apparent in the occupational culture generally and between the organization and the environment are the dialectic source of change in policing'. A satisfactory formulation of police culture should allow for the possibility of change as well as resistance to change.

In the following sections, I will outline an alternative theoretical framework for understanding police culture. The framework will have to address the criticisms raised in this section: it must account for the existence of multiple cultures, recognize the interpretive and creative aspects of culture, situate cultural practice in the political context of policing, and provide a theory of change.

## A reconceptualization

Several useful ways of theorizing about culture can be found in the literature. In particular, Sackmann's cognitive perspective of culture provides for the existence of multiple cultures within a police organization. Shearing and Ericson's phenomenological treatment of culture recognizes the active and creative role played by members of the police force. Finally, Bourdieu's relational theory, which explains cultural practice as the result of interaction between cultural dispositions (habitus) and structural positions (field), situates culture in the social and political context of police work.

All three perspectives provide for some theorizing of change. Each of these perspectives will be discussed in turn.

*Culture as knowledge*

Sackmann describes the essence of culture as 'the collective construction of social reality'. Her cognitive model encompasses all forms of shared organized knowledge: 'the form of things that people have in their minds; their models for perceiving, integrating, and interpreting them; the ideas or theories that they use collectively to make sense of their social and physical reality' (Sackmann, 1991: 21). She classifies cultural knowledge in organization into four dimensions: (1) *dictionary knowledge*, which provides definitions and labels of things and events within an organization; (2) *directory knowledge*, which contains descriptions about 'how things are done' generally in the organization; (3) *recipe knowledge*, which prescribes what should or should not be done in specific situations; and (4) *axiomatic knowledge*, which represents the fundamental assumptions about 'why things are done the way they are' in an organization. Axiomatic knowledge, often held by top management, constitutes the foundation for the shape and future of the organization. These may be adjusted or revised from time to time as a result of critical evaluations or growing experience.

Sackmann sees cultural cognitions as being held by groups rather than individuals. These cognitions are socially constructed, and may be changed or perpetuated by organizational processes through repeated applications. In time, these cognitions are imbued with emotions and acquire degrees of importance; they also become 'habits' of thoughts that translate into habitual actions.

The significance of Sackmann's formulation lies in its ability to account for multiple cultures. While top management may have imposed or negotiated a consensus about the rationale of the organization (axiomatic knowledge), there is no reason to assume that the other dimensions of knowledge are invariant throughout the organization. Sackmann's own case study found that both dictionary and recipe knowledge varied according to members' responsibilities and positions in the hierarchy.

Sackmann's formulation, however, leaves a number of questions unanswered. For example, how does knowledge lead to action, and under what conditions does it happen? Sackmann postulates that axiomatic knowledge is held by top management who may initiate change as a result of internal or external threats. However, it is possible that lower level members of the organization may hold rather different views about 'why things are done the way they are'. Punch (1983) has suggested that police culture has its primary allegiance not to the organization but to the job and the peer groups. If axiomatic knowledge is not shared between top management and the lower-ranking members, what, then, would be the implications for the other dimensions of knowledge? There is also little discussion in Sackmann about how the various dimensions of knowledge are related to the power relations external to the organization, and those between organizational members and the environment.

*Culture as construction*

Not all formulations of police culture treat officers as passive objects moulded by the almighty culture. Using the ethnomethodological critique of a rule-based conception of culture, Shearing and Ericson (1991) have argued that rather than being socialized into, and guided by, the police culture in their work activities, police officers are active in constructing and making references to the culture as guiding their actions. For police officers, the police culture is a 'tool-kit' used in the production of a sense of order, and the constant 'telling' of the culture accomplishes for the officers a 'factual' or 'objective' existence of this culture. The transmission of this culture is not by a process of socialization and internalization of rules, but through a collection of stories and aphorisms which instruct officers on how to see the world and act in it. Stories prepare officers for police work by providing a 'vehicle for analogous thinking', creating a 'vocabulary of precedents' (Ericson *et al.*, 1987) and create a way of seeing and being through the narratives and the silences that surround the stories.

This way of interpreting police culture removes the deterministic framework of a rule-based theory of action and provides for variations in the application of police cultural knowledge:

> It recognizes that police stories provide officers with tools they can use to get them through the business of police work without minimizing the fact that this still requires individual initiative and daring. It also recognizes that officers differ in their competence in using this cultural tool-kit ... Finally, it recognizes that what they do will be retrospectively constituted as ordered via the reflexive methods that are part of this doing. (Shearing and Ericson, 1991)

Thus, cultural knowledge in the form of police stories presents officers with ready-made schemas and scripts that assist individual officers in particular situations to limit their search for information, organize information in terms of established categories, constitute a sensibility out of which a range of actions can flow, and provide officers with a repertoire of reasonable accounts to legitimate their actions. This model of police culture, however, is silent about the social and political context of police work, even though police stories undoubtedly contain implicit or explicit expressions of power relations within police organizations.

### Culture as relations

Instead of viewing culture as informal influences which seek to undermine or subvert the formal goals or rules of organizations, researchers are increasingly looking to sources of irrationality in the formal structure itself (see Powell and DiMaggio, 1991: 13). Ericson (1981), for example, found that departures from due process protections of the accused were not 'extra-legal' rules at all, they were decisions legitimated by the criminal law itself. The question remains: how do formal structures influence cultural practice?

A useful approach to understanding the formation of cultural practice is found in the social theory of Pierre Bourdieu. Two key concepts of relevance here are those of the *field* and the *habitus*:

> A field consists of a set of objective, historical relations between positions anchored in certain forms of power (or capital), while habitus consists of a set of historical relations 'deposited' within individual bodies in the form of mental and corporeal schemata of perception, appreciation and action. (Wacquant, 1992: 16)

For Bourdieu, society is constituted by an ensemble of relatively autonomous fields. A field is a social space of conflict and competition, where participants struggle to establish control over specific power and authority, and, in the course of the struggle, modify the structure of the field itself. Thus a field 'presents itself as a structure of probabilities – of rewards, gains, profits, or sanctions – but always implies a measure of indeterminacy' (Wacquant, 1992: 18). In terms of police work on the streets, for example, the field may consist of the historical relations between certain social groups and the police, anchored in the legal powers and discretion police are authorized to exercise and the distribution of power and material resources within the community.

Habitus, on the other hand, is closer to what has earlier been described as cultural knowledge. It is a system of 'dispositions', which integrate past experience and enable individuals to cope with a diversity of unforeseen situations (Wacquant, 1992: 18). Instead of seeing culture as a 'thing', e.g. a set of values, rules, or an informal structure operating on actors in an organization, Bourdieu argues for the primacy of *relations*, so that habitus and field function fully only in relation to each other. Habitus generates strategies which are coherent and systematic, but they are also 'ad hoc because they are "triggered" by the encounter with a particular field' (*ibid.*, 19). Like the police stories discussed earlier, habitus allows for creation and innovation within the field of police work. It is a 'feel for the game'; it enables an infinite number of 'moves' to be made in an infinite number of situations. It embodies what police officers often refer to as 'commonsense' (see Manning, 1977) and what are commonly known as 'policing skills' (see Brogden *et al.*, 1988).

Police practices have the appearance of rationality but the 'cop code' is more the result of 'codification' by researchers and police officers than a set of rules which generate practice. Bourdieu has argued that rationality rarely plays a part in practical action:

> The conditions of rational calculation are practically never given in practice: time is limited, information is restricted, *etc.* And yet agents *do* do, much more often than if they were behaving randomly, 'the only thing to do'. This is because, following the intuitions of a 'logic of practice' which is the product of a lasting exposure to conditions similar to those in which they are placed, they anticipate the necessity immanent in the way of the world. (Bourdieu, 1990: 11)

Thus, Bourdieu's theory recognizes the interpretive and active role played by police officers in relating policing skills to the social and political context of policing. It also allows for the existence of multiple cultures since officers in different organizational positions operate under different sets of field and habitus.

*Cultural change*

The three perspectives outlined all allow some scope for cultural change. Shearing and Ericson have the least to say about change but their model provides for human action that is both 'guided and improvisational' (Shearing and Ericson, 1991). With Bourdieu, cultural change is possible through changes in the field or in the habitus, although no explicit theory of change is outlined. Sackmann's work, on the other hand, offers the most theorizing about the processes of change. Cultural knowledge is postulated as a link between strategy and organizational processes. Thus changes in organizational culture first occur at the top in terms of axiomatic knowledge, which in turn sets off other changes [...]:

> ... existing cultural knowledge, strategy and organizational processes began to be questioned when the top management group perceived threats in the internal and external environments of the firm. As a first step they debated and negotiated axiomatic knowledge. Once in place this axiomatic knowledge defined the firm's purpose, its strategic intention, its design, and characteristics of preferred members ... In the process of negotiating axiomatic knowledge, existing dictionary and directory knowledge was altered. This knowledge then guided the thoughts, attention, and actions of organizational members both in terms of organizational processes and in terms of strategic concerns and their implementation. Their actions, and the outcomes of their actions, in turn, maintained, reinforced, and further adjusted directory, dictionary and axiomatic knowledge ... (Sackmann, 1991: 156)

In summary, it has been argued in this section that Bourdieu's concepts of field and habitus provide a useful framework for conceptualizing police culture. In addition, Sackmann's dimensions of organizational knowledge can be a fruitful way of filling out the habitus of police work. This way of thinking about police culture overcomes most of the weaknesses in existing theories. In the following sections, the relevance of this framework will be discussed in relation to the situation in New South Wales.

## The field and habitus of policing

I will begin by describing elements of the 'field' and the 'habitus' which constitute the culture of policing in New South Wales. The description of the field is based mainly on a study of reforms to improve police/minorities relations in New South Wales (Chan, 1992), while the discussion of the habitus draws on a range of findings from the literature.

### The field

Bourdieu's definition of the field emphasizes the historical, structural relations between positions of power. To understand the relations between the police and visible minorities communities in New South Wales, it is important to provide a brief overview of three elements of the field: the social and political status of visible minorities, discretionary powers of the police and legal protection against police abuse.

### Social and political status of minorities

Historically, the relations between police and Australia's indigenous people have been conflictual and tense. White settlement in Australia in 1788 led to a dramatic decline in the number of Aboriginal people –from nearly one million to around 80,000 by the 1930s – through 'disease, conflict and the disintegration of traditional society' (Human Rights and Equal Opportunity Commission [HREOC] 1991: 59). It has been estimated that 20,000 Aborigines were killed In frontier conflict – randomly shot, massacred, and even poisoned by white settlers for many years. Aborigines were deprived of the possession of their own land (Reynolds, 1987: 1–5). The concept of native title has only recently been recognized by the federal government. For many years Aborigines were segregated and detained in reserves and Aboriginal children removed from their families and placed in institutions. Aborigines were not recognized as Australian citizens with full voting rights until 1967. In New South Wales, police were used for many years to enforce the Aborigines Protection Act 1909, which until 1969 turned the police into a state agency responsible for issuing rations, removing 'neglected' children from parents, controlling people's movement on Aboriginal reserves, as well as more traditional policing functions such as maintaining order (Foley, 1984). A National Inquiry into Racist Violence found widespread racist violence against Aborigines and Torres Strait Islanders across Australia, with the conduct of police officers being a major problem (HREOC, 1991: 69–122).

The Australian record in relation to other ethnic minorities was not a great deal better. The White Australia Policy which was in force until the 1970s discriminated against the immigration of non-Europeans, while British immigrants were encouraged via a system of assisted passage. The result was that by the late 1940s, almost 90 per cent of Australia's population was of British descent. The relaxation of immigration restrictions and a shift to a policy of multiculturalism in the 1970s have led to a steady increase in immigrants from non-English speaking backgrounds (HREOC, 1991: 47–54). By the late 1980s, about 25 per cent of the population were from non Anglo-Celtic origins. From 1976 to 1986 there was a doubling in the percentage of overseas-born population from Asia (HREOC, 1991: 60–1). During the 1980s, the volume and composition of immigrants have become a matter of public concern through the so-called 'immigration debate'. The pace of Asian immigration, in particular, was seen to be detrimental to the interest of 'national cohesion' by some commentators. The National Inquiry into Racist Violence found that among reported cases of victimization, Asian and Arab Australians were more likely to be subjected to intimidation, harassment, and violence (HREOC, 1991: 172–5). Consultations with ethnic youth confirmed that Asians, particularly the Vietnamese, were increasingly the targets of racist comments and discrimination in the school and in the workplace (Cahill and Ewen, 1987; Office of Multicultural Affairs, 1990).

*Discretionary powers of the police*
Police have wide discretionary powers to stop, question, and arrest suspects. The most problematic aspect of police practices in this regard is what is perceived by the minority communities as the unfair targetting and harassment of certain groups (Youth Justice Coalition, 1990: 232; NSW Ethnic Affairs Commission, 1992; HREOC, 1991: 94–5). Both the *degree* of police intervention, e.g. the use of specialist police task force, and the *nature* of that intervention, e.g. the discriminatory use of public order offences, against Aborigines have been a serious cause for concern (HREOC, 1991: 90–1).

The use of 135 police officers including members of the Tactical Response Group (TRG) in a pre-dawn raid on Redfern in 1990 was a high-profile example in New South Wales of the heavy-handed method of policing against an Aboriginal community. 'Operation Sue' involved the entry and search of ten dwellings in Redfern. The justification of the raid was in terms of an abnormal increase in crime and the prevalence of a drug culture in the Aboriginal community (Landa Report, 1991: s. 2.1). The use of TRG was, according to the findings of the Ombudsman, 'not called for' for the majority of the targets. The Aboriginal Legal Service saw Operation Sue as an 'intimidatory offensive against the Redfern Aboriginal community' and 'a racist operation'. Although police denied this intention, the Ombudsman observed that 'there was so little attention paid to the detail of the operation and the intelligence on which individuals were targeted … that the evidence supports a strong inference that the police intention was to have a general impact' (Landa Report, 1991: s. 8.22).

*Legal protection against police abuse*
The Racist Violence Inquiry reported numerous incidents of police abuse of their powers in their dealings with Aboriginal communities, including spotlighting, entering Aboriginal homes at night without a warrant to conduct searches and inquiries about alleged offences, and discriminatory and intimidating policing practices in relation to Aborigines in public places and private functions (HREOC, 1991: 82–8). Most disturbing, however, was the 'overwhelming' evidence presented to the Inquiry by Aboriginal and Islander people in relation to police violence: the use of excessive force while making arrests, actual or threat of physical violence in custody, and the 'rough handling' of women by male officers (HREOC, 1991: 80). There were allegations of rape while in custody, sexual threats and abuse, in addition to verbal (sexist and racist) abuse and physical violence (HREOC, 1991: 88–9). Similar treatment of juveniles was reported in a number of states. Cunneen's (1990) survey of 171 Aboriginal and Islander juveniles in state detention centres in Queensland, New South Wales, and Western Australia found an alarming level of alleged police violence: 85 per cent reported that they had been hit, punched, kicked or slapped, and 63 per cent hit with *objects, including* police batons, telephone books, torches, and other objects. With adult Aborigines in custody, practices such as brutal assault, hosing

down detainees, denial of medical treatment, forcing detainees to drink water from toilet bowls, and other forms of abuse were reported to the Inquiry (HREOC, 1991: 105). Perhaps the most reprehensible of all was the evidence that police officers made suggestions of suicide or threatened to hang Aborigines when they were taken into custody (HREOC, 1991: 98).

A survey of community organizations conducted by the NSW Ethnic Affairs Commission also reveals concerns about 'occasional physical abuse by police, victimisation by police through the selective use of police powers, police brutality whilst youth are being detained or questioned by police' (NSWEAC, 1992). Community workers consulted in the course of the New South Wales project (Chan, 1992) raised similar concerns about unfair targetting of young people from certain ethnic groups, verbal or physical abuse during police interrogation or in police custody, and active or passive condoning of racial conflicts by the police. Community workers cited incidents of harassment and brutality against young people. At least one of these cases went before the Ombudsman but others were not formally dealt with.

The ineffectiveness of existing anti-discrimination laws and police instructions and guidelines to control police malpractice has been commented on by the Racist Violence Inquiry (HREOC, 1991: 27–9; 319). The Inquiry also raised doubts about the adequacy of the present system of police accountability:

> The perception that police are not accountable for their actions and that racist violence perpetrated by them goes either unnoticed or unpunished was widespread. When asked how they had responded to alleged racist violence by police most Aboriginal people told the inquiry that they had either done nothing or complained but with no effect … (HREOC, 1991: 211)

The Inquiry was told that most people did nothing because they believed that it would be a waste of time. The fact that complaints were to be lodged with police and investigated by police was a deterrent to people.

A survey conducted by the Commonwealth Ombudsman in 1992 found that 43 per cent of people of non-English speaking background and only 30 per cent of Aborigines had heard of the office of the Ombudsman, compared with over 60 per cent of the respondents from Australia or other English-speaking countries. Among those who were aware of the Ombudsman there was a generally poor level of understanding of the process and a fair degree of distrust of the system. The NSW Ombudsman explains the low level of complaints from Aborigines as follows:

> The lack of complaints may also reflect … the perception that the system is structured against them. Complaints have to be in writing and provide enough detail on which to pursue inquiries. Where literacy is not an insurmountable problem, letters often relate a litany of grievances against many authorities and the police role is bound up with more general matters. The scope of the Ombudsman's jurisdiction is often difficult to explain. Aboriginal Legal Services tend to advise against complaining

because they have little confidence in the system and they fear the possibility of a complaint compromising their position in any related criminal charges. (NSW Ombudsman, 1992: 44)

Again the issue of police investigating themselves and a fear of future harassment were raised as real concerns among Aborigines.

### The habitus

Many of the complaints raised by minority groups against the police can be linked to aspects of the police occupational culture: the regular use of racist language, stereotyping of ethnic communities, unfair targetting and harassment of minorities, and in some instances the abuse of police powers or excessive use of force against suspects. These practices can be analysed in terms of the relation between the field and habitus of police work. The following discussion of habitus makes use of what the research literature has informed us about the four dimensions of cultural knowledge in street-level police work: dictionary knowledge (which sets up categories about people police come into contact with), directory knowledge (which informs officers on how to go about getting their work done), recipe knowledge (which prescribes the menu of acceptable and unacceptable practices in specific situations), and axiomatic knowledge (which constitutes the basic rationale of policing).

*Dictionary knowledge: the rough and the respectable*
Research has shown that police make a clear distinction among the public between 'the rough and respectable elements, those who challenge or those who accept the middle-class values of decency which most police revere' (Reiner, 1992; 117–18). The nature of patrol work is such that officers develop indices of respectability for different categories of people in the community, as a Canadian study of a suburban police force shows:

> This identification with middle-class respectability makes some officers react negatively to any groups whom they cannot place within it. Thus, in discussion among themselves, there is derision of certain racial and ethnic minorities, as well as citizens at the bottom end of society's 'scheme of things' who do not appear to be seeking upward mobility in a way that would indicate an identification with the values of middle-class respectability. Indeed in this latter group are persons identified by patrol officers as 'Coasters' (people from the Maritime region of Canada) and 'pukers' (apparently hedonistic young people whose activity, dress, and demeanour indicate a departure from middle-class respectability). There is constant talk about these types being 'the scum of the earth', 'the source of all police problems', and so on. (Ericson, 1982: 66–7)

Ethnic stereotyping works to reinforce police perception of respectability. Even though criminologists have had difficulties sorting out whether immigrants commit more or less crime than Australian-born people (Francis, 1981; Hazlehurst, 1987; Geis and Jesilow, 1988), police have often been accused of forming stereotypical opinions about the criminality of certain ethnic groups (Australian Law Reform Commission, 1992: 201; NSWEAC, 1992: s. 2B4). Aborigines were regularly considered to be a 'problem' and Aborigines were blamed for various forms of social disorder (Cuneen and Robb, 1987). Most police officers, however, would deny that their assumptions about Aborigines and certain minority groups were the result of racial prejudice; rather, they were typifications formed through police work among these minority groups. The problem is that it becomes a vicious circle: critics of the police have argued that over-policing was partly responsible for the gross over-representation of Aborigines in the criminal justice system (Cuneen and Robb, 1987) while the statistical over-representation of Aborigines in police statistics justified increased surveillance and harassment.

*Directory knowledge: look for the unusual and take shortcuts*
This dimension of cultural knowledge informs police officers about the way police work is normally carried out. For example, in proactive work, officers look for signs of the 'unusual':

> Patrol officers themselves develop their own criteria for deciding what is worthy of proactive activity. Most of these are developed collectively as 'shared-recipe' knowledge about whom to stop for what purpose in particular circumstances. In general, patrol officers develop and use cues concerning (1) individuals out of place, (2) individuals in particular places, (3) individuals of particular types regardless of place, and (4) unusual circumstances regarding property. (Ericson, 1982: 86)

Following these 'cues' may be routine police work, but the effect may be serious for minorities:

> What is important to realise is that measuring people against their surrounding is an essential part of police activity. A policeman [*sic*] is chronically suspicious and he [*sic*] is forced, by the nature of the duty with which he is entrusted, to make snap decisions about the appropriateness of what people are doing. Since he is looking for the unusual, his decisions are environment-specific; what action he takes depends upon what is perceived to be common for that area. The fact that policemen are alert for incongruity probably does not militate against minority persons. (Bayley and Mendelsoh, 1969: 93)

In Redfern, Sydney, for example, an individual 'out of place' is an Aborigine driving a red Laser (as mentioned in the television documentary *Cop It Sweet*). Young people congregating in parks, shopping malls, pinball parlours, *etc.*, are obvious targets for proactive stops.

Westley's study of an American police force found that the use of violence was not seen to be illegitimate by almost 40 per cent of the 74 policemen surveyed if the purpose was to maintain respect for the police (Westley, 1970: 122). A Canadian researcher has commented on the use of physical force as a means of taking charge of situations:

Taking charge efficiently may seem to call for minor and sometimes major shortcuts in legal niceties. The *officer may* bluff or bully, mislead or lie, verbally abuse or physically 'rough up' the alleged offender. Senior officers are not concerned to eliminate such short-cuts, but merely to manage them, so as to keep citizens' complaints ... at a minimum while getting the day's work done. The most important learning required of the rookie in his first six months is the ability to keep his/her mouth shut about the deviance from law and police regulations which veteran officers consider necessary if the police are not to be 'hamstrung' in their control of social order ... The rookie who survives on the force learns to look at the world through the needs of his/her occupation ... (Lee, 1981: 51)

Baldwin and Kinsey (1982: 50) found in their study in Britain that police would often use the threat of violence to obtain information or confession ('if you don't tell us the truth you're going to get bounced all over the station'), but reserve actual violence to those who 'cut up rough'. ('The only deterrent is to hit him back fucking harder than he hit you and to let him know that it's not just one – there's two and a half thousand of us that'll keep on hitting him.')

The use of violence by police is in fact very much part of the repertoire of police strategies to maintain authority, to control suspects and to obtain information. Thus, Cunneen (1991) acknowledges that his research did not suggest that alleged police violence was more common among Aboriginal youth than among non-Aboriginal youth, but that there appeared to be widespread perception among young people that police violence was 'normal'.

### Recipe knowledge: cover yourself and don't rat on others

Recipe knowledge about how things should or should not be done in specific situations is crucial to police work. Manning (1977: 185–6) cited Van Maanen's example which suggested the pervasiveness of the motto 'cover your ass' in a police organization. Consequently, written records of events were frequently manipulated by police officers to protect themselves against supervisors (Manning, 1977: 191). One aspect of recipe knowledge that most concerns critics is the apparent 'code' of silence and solidarity among police officers when faced with allegations of misconduct. The shield of secrecy and solidarity among police officers has often been remarked upon by researchers. Westley's (1970: 112–13) study, for example, found that if faced with a partner's misconduct, 11 of the 16 police officers to whom he posed the question would not be willing to report this misconduct, but ten of them would be prepared to perjure themselves in court to protect their partner. Reiner sees solidarity as a response to the working conditions of policing:

Internal solidarity is a product not only of isolation, but also of the need to be able to rely on colleagues in a tight spot, and a protective armour shielding the force as a whole from public knowledge of infractions ... The offences which colleagues shield are not necessarily major infractions to be protected from external eyes. Rank-and-file solidarity is often aimed at concealing minor violations ... from the attention of supervisory officers. (Reiner, 1992: 116)

One documented case in New South Wales shows the hazards faced by whistle blowers within the force. When a relatively inexperienced police officer reported that his supervising sergeant assaulted a person in custody, he was given the 'cold shoulder treatment' by senior officers and others who sided with the sergeant. The same sergeant was seen by a probationary constable two months later assaulting another offender. The probationary constable reported the matter to his senior officers. The sergeant was subsequently recommended for dismissal by the Police Tribunal. Both constables who had complained against the sergeant had since resigned from the Police Service. The lack of support from senior officers during the investigation and court proceedings was considered the main reason for the first officer's decision to resign (NSW Ombudsman, 1991: 130–2).

*Axiomatic knowledge: the war against crime*
The basic assumptions about 'why things are done the way they are' in police work are encapsulated in what police see as their mandate to wage the war against crime, to maintain order, and to protect people's lives and property. Reiner points out that police officers regard their work with a sense of mission, which is 'reflected in their sense of themselves as "the thin blue line", performing an essential role in safeguarding social order, which would lead to disastrous consequences if their authority was threatened' (Reiner, 1992: 112). This means that occasionally dubious, aggressive or even illegal tactics may need to be used and civil rights and due process may have to be sacrificed, especially if the accused person is believed to be guilty (Holdaway, 1983).

By relating these aspects of habitus with the field of policing, we can see how police practices of the kind being complained about by ethnic minorities can result. Thus, stereotyping, harassment, abuse of power, violence and apparent lack of accountability occur regularly in a policing field characterized by the lack of power among minorities, the wide discretion accorded the police, and the inadequacy of legal protection against abuse. In the following section, I will describe the range of reforms that took place in New South Wales and discuss how these reforms have affected police practices.

## Change strategies and outcomes

Before 1984, the image of the NSW Police Force was that of an inefficient and ineffective force (Lusher Report, 1981), with dark clouds of corruption allegations hanging over many of its senior officers. In the years that followed his appointment until his retirement in 1991, Commissioner Avery was responsible for introducing some significant and fundamental changes to the concept of policing in New South Wales. In his first two years in office, Avery was relentless in his campaign against institutionalized corruption within the force, but his vision of community-based policing proved to be an even more radical policy, questioning the very basis of police work. In 1986, the force adopted a set of corporate objectives which emphasized crime prevention, community involvement, and the minimization of corruption (NSW Police Department, 1986: 16).

## Change strategies

### Organizational restructuring

In 1987, the government adopted community-based policing as the principal operation strategy of the NSW Police Force and this was implemented through a massive restructuring of the organization through regionalization. The main thrust of regionalization was to replace functional division by geographical division. There followed a progressive devolution of centralized areas such as the Criminal Investigation Branch and the Traffic Branch, to regional command. The restructuring was said to have reduced the chain of command from 14 to seven levels and brought 'senior Police decision makers closer to citizens and their problems' (NSWPD, 1987: 24–5). Hand in hand with organizational restructuring was another major change: the shift from a seniority-based to a merit-based promotion system for police officers. Even this initiative was very much related to Avery's campaign against police corruption, since professional integrity was considered a crucial dimension of merit. The move also facilitated younger officers who were not resistant to change to move up to positions where they could exert an influence.

### Changes to recruitment and training

Substantial changes were also introduced in the area of recruitment and training. In 1986 a new set of recruitment criteria was introduced. Height restrictions were abandoned, whereas educational and physical requirements were updated. Job-related agility tests and aptitude tests were also introduced (NSWPD, 1987: 103). By 1988 a set of recruitment objectives was developed, with a stated commitment to recruit more women and ethnic minorities (NSWPS, 1988a: 59).

In 1990 the Police Service introduced a new battery of job-related aptitude tests for screening applicants. These include: observation skills, verbal comprehension, drawing conclusions, reasoning skills, and decision making (NSWPS, 1990). Applicants with linguistic or other 'multicultural skills' were given an advantage in recruitment (NSWPS, 1988a: 29). To encourage Aboriginal people to join the police, a Tertiary Preparation Course was introduced in 1991 to provide a 'bridging' programme for Aborigines who need to acquire the necessary educational prerequisites to enter the Police Service.

The Police Academy adopted a totally new educational philosophy, a redesigned recruit training curriculum, and a different policy in relation to the staffing and administration of the Academy. The new approach 'called for police training and education to be built upon progressive adult education principles including experiential learning, case study, educational contextual studies and the importance of practicum' (NSWPS, 1991: 11).

Police recruits receive their first training in multicultural issues and cross-cultural awareness in the core course *Policing and Society* in the Police Recruit Education Program (PREP). The course gives students an introduction to the historical and contemporary social context of policing. The section on 'Multiculturalism and Policing' aims to provide students with knowledge and an appreciation of 'the variety of cultures in Australian society ... and the threat posed to good policing by stereotyping, prejudice, discrimination and racism' (NSWPREP, 1991).

*Development of community-based programmes*
In terms of community programmes directed at minority ethnic communities, a number of important initiatives have been implemented:

(a) The development of an Ethnic Affairs Policy Statement (EAPS) and an Aboriginal Affairs Policy Statement (AAPS)[2] which commit the organization to provide accessible, ethical, and appropriate services to all members of minority groups.
(b) The appointment of an Ethnic Client Consultant and an Aboriginal Client Consultant, whose primary responsibilities include liaison and mediation between the police and the minority communities, providing advice to the police executive on Aboriginal and ethnic issues and developing policy and programmes to improve police/minority relations.
(c) The appointment of civilian Ethnic Community Liaison Officers and Aboriginal Community Liaison Officers in selected patrols to establish a dialogue and facilitate understanding between police and minority communities.
(d) The establishment of Community Consultative Committees (CCC) 'to bring Police closer to the community they serve and to deal with the issues which are of most concern to the community' (NSWPD, 1987: 78).
(e) The introduction of beat policing. As part of their community organizing function, beat officers meet regularly with residents and business people in their beat area. Beat officers are encouraged to help organize and motivate the community to develop strategies for problem solving within the community. They are usually involved with programmes such as Neighbourhood Watch, Business Watch, Community Consultative Committees, Safety House programmes, and so on.

*Outcomes*

The scope and pace of change in the New South Wales police organization over the last few years were unprecedented in the history of the force. It may well be too early to try to assess the extent to which the reforms have made any difference to police/minority relations. The following is a brief summary of the findings[3] of my research (see Chan, 1992 for details).

*(a) Awareness of policy*
The Ethnic Affairs Policy Statement[4] was not widely known or understood throughout the organization, even among officers working in patrols with sizeable proportions of non-English speaking background people. Less than half (45 per cent) of the respondents in the survey were able to mention the *general idea* of the policy. The results suggest that the EAPS had not filtered through to the rank-and-file officers, and even at the level of 'paying lip service' to the policy, officers in the survey showed a remarkable lack of concern regarding ethnic affairs.

*(b) Awareness of programmes*
Respondents in the survey were asked to report what has been done at a Patrol,

District, Region and State Executive level in the Police Service about police/minority problems. The responses indicate either a serious lack of awareness of the initiatives taken, a basic apathy, or a lack of support for these activities. It would appear that respondents were most aware of what was happening at the Patrol level. The percentages of 'do not know', negative, or blank responses increase as the question progresses to each higher level of management.

### (c) Acceptance of policy

Even though many respondents were not aware of the official policy towards ethnic minorities, an overwhelming majority (97 per cent) agreed with the principle that people from different cultural groups should have equal access to police services: In terms of attitudes towards community policing, respondents in the survey were almost equally split between agreeing with and disagreeing with the statement 'Real police work is about arresting criminals'. These results indicate that the organization was still very divided regarding the objectives of 'real police work'. Probationers and senior officers were less likely to consider real police work as essentially about arresting criminals. When analysed by duty, detectives were the most likely to agree with the statement, compared with general duty officers, beat police, and others.

### (d) Participation in programmes

Results of the survey indicate that there was a fair degree of participation in community programmes directed at visible minorities.

### (e) Degree of implementation

Since regionalization the responsibility for implementing programmes no longer rests with any central body, but with individual patrols. Apart from Beat Policing, there appeared to be no centralized data collection or monitoring system to determine the extent of implementation and the degree of success. A recent report noted 'severe gaps in the collection of data for planning and evaluation purposes' in the area of ethnic affairs (Ingram, 1991: 28).

The police officers' survey provides some indication of the extent to which various initiatives and community-based policing programmes have been implemented. However, some of the results were plainly inaccurate, casting doubt on the general validity of the responses. Given the low level of awareness of programmes implemented, such results were perhaps not surprising. Nevertheless, the items most frequently reported to have been implemented were: on-the-job training, training in the Academy, introduction of Beat Policing, recruitment of officers from ethnic groups, and provision of cards showing different languages. The results indicated that each of the programmes/initiatives mentioned had been implemented in the patrols of over half of the respondents.

### (f) Achievement of outcomes

The 1988 EAPS laid out strategies and target dates for various strategies to be implemented but did not specify any concrete outcomes or indicators of performance against which outcomes can be measured. The quantitative indicators being used generally to measure police performance in the NSW Police Service have been: crime statistics, road safety statistics, personnel statistics such as attrition, sick leave and overtime, as well as complaints statistics. None of these statistics can be disaggregated for analysis of performance in relation to ethnic or Aboriginal communities. Since 1988, community surveys have been conducted at six-monthly intervals. These surveys canvass specific aspects of people's opinions of the NSW Police Service, their support for community policing programmes, and their fears and concerns about crime. Some of the results pertain to 'ethnic groups', based on whether the respondent speaks a language other than English at home. The 'ethnic' sample is usually quite small (183 out of 1,300 in the October 1991 to March 1992 sample) and although some interesting trends are found, it is impossible to link these results with any specific programmes undertaken.

In the absence of systematic data on outcome indicators, assessments of the NSW Police's performance in the ethnic and Aboriginal affairs policy areas have tended to take the form of complaints and criticisms raised by external bodies or individuals (e.g. NSWEAC, 1992; HREOC, 1991; complaints by youth workers in Cabramatta), or high-profile cases of police 'failure', followed by desperate attempts by the Police Service to control the damage by stressing the positive achievements of community-based policing.

The interview programme conducted in Chan (1992) provides some impressionistic information on the outcomes of these reforms. Many of the officers interviewed were chosen because they had played some part in the reorganization and transformation of the police organization in recent years. Others were chosen because they had direct contact or responsibility for the servicing of visible minorities. These officers' assessments of the outcomes of the organizational changes and the initiatives brought about as part of community-based policing were generally positive and optimistic, although not uniformly so. These views, of course, were not representative of everyone within the organization, perhaps not even the majority. As the results of the survey show, a wide range of views did exist within the organization. Officers who took part in the interviews were not asked to assess the success of individual police programmes or initiatives. Rather, they were asked to give a general assessment of the outcomes of reform. There appeared to be a consensus that, as a result of all the organizational and structural changes, institutionalized corruption had virtually disappeared, community-based policing was changing police practices and police culture, regionalization was improving police accountability to local communities, recruitment and training programmes were producing more professional police officers, and police were gradually gaining the support and confidence of the community. Many problems, however, remained to be solved. These include: a general lack of understanding of the language and process of 'corporate planning', the failure of some patrols to implement policies decided by headquarters, the lack of quality control of police work at all levels of the organization, the speed and zeal of change, which left many officers feeling dislocated and sometimes resentful, the tendency of police managers to be defensive and dismissive when faced with criticisms, the lack of management skills among police supervisors, the gap between police training and police work, a 'belt' of resistance to change among middle-ranking officers, and a high degree of misunderstanding about the meaning of community policing throughout the police organization.

## Interpretation of results

While senior police and the majority of rank-and-file officers seemed fairly positive about the performance of the Police Service, and community surveys appeared to indicate a high degree of general satisfaction with police service, the public image of the NSW Police Service has been marred in recent years by some high-profile cases of blundering, incompetence, or unprofessional activities. Notable cases which were the subject of major inquiries include the killing of David Gundy in 1989 during a raid by the Special Weapons and Operations Squad (Wootten Report, 1991); the arrest, charging, and subsequent withdrawal of charges against a retired policeman Harold Blackburn in 1989 (Lee Report, 1990); Operation Sue, the raid of Redfern by the Tactical Response Group in February 1990 (Landa Report, 1991), and the shooting of Darren Brennan in June 1990 during a search by the police and the Tactical Response Group (Staunton Report, 1991). Other damaging publicity includes the National Inquiry into Racist Violence report, the findings of which have already been highlighted; the television documentary *Cop It Sweet*; and a home video broadcast on ABC television news showing two police officers with their faces blackened and nooses around their necks mocking two Aborigines, the death of whom had been the subject of the Royal Commission into Aboriginal Deaths in Custody. In addition to these high-profile cases, a number of complaints have been raised in relation to the treatment of Indo-Chinese youths in Cabramatta (SMH, 20 April 1992) and the charging and subsequent cautioning of a number of Asian youths in the North Shore (SMH, 10 February 1992).

There appeared to be, therefore, two images of police – one being upheld by the organization, mainly top management, which tended to be positive and optimistic, and one being constituted by its environment, mainly the media and minority groups, which tended to be negative and critical. These contradictory images can be explained by analysing the reform process in terms of the changing of cultural knowledge in the organization.

### Shift in basic assumptions and beliefs (axiomatic knowledge)

Following Avery's appointment, the NSW Police adopted a shift in the basic assumptions about the force's functions and objectives. The new objectives gave priority to crime prevention, services that are responsive to the needs and feelings of the community, citizens' involvement in policing, and the minimization of corruption. This defines what Sackmann refers to as the axiomatic knowledge of the organization. Once in place these assumptions guided strategies and processes of reform. Thus, within a short time, community-based policing was adopted by the police force as the principal operational strategy. The implementation of this strategy was achieved through regionalization, merit-based promotion; changes in recruitment policy, a radical redesign of the training and education programme, and the development of a variety of community-based programmes, including the appointment of client consultants, liaison officers, the introduction of beat policing, and other community crime prevention programmes. According to Sackmann's model, the implementation and realization of these strategies would influence the dictionary knowledge of police officers. At the same time, the change in organizational objectives led to the enactment of certain organizational processes. For example, the processes of community consultation were designed to help accomplish these objectives. Similarly, the development of performance indicators, the conducting of quality audits and more recently the establishment of customer councils were internal processes which were supposed to ensure that corporate objectives were realized. The EAPS process was also designed to set in motion strategic planning which involves the participation of operational police [...].

### Changes in definition (dictionary knowledge)

The adoption of community-based policing strategies and the implementation of the various changes based on those strategies should inevitably lead to some redefinitions of the situations in which officers find themselves. For example, regionalization forced patrol commanders to get to know the social, cultural, and demographic characteristics of their geographical communities; they were required to allocate resources and plan policing strategies to meet the needs of these communities. Community-based programmes were designed to encourage police officers to consult with and be in constant contact with the communities they police, so that they saw them as real people, not stereotypes. Community consultation was also meant to cover all members of the community, not simply the respectable types who support the police. In general, the extent to which changes in dictionary knowledge followed the changes in organizational objectives and strategies depends on the degree to which implementation of these objectives and strategies had been successful. My research suggests that community-based policing was interpreted in a superficial way and was mainly seen as a public relations exercise. Apart from the predominance of middle-class, respectable citizens in community consultative committees, there was some concern about the tokenistic use of minority community 'leaders' as representing the interests of minority groups, the exclusion of operational issues as appropriate for community consultation, and the tendency to see the setting up of committees as an achievement in itself. Similarly, changes in recruitment and training were only partly successful in changing definitions, since there was a lack of reinforcement once officers came into contact with 'real' police work. Consequently, many of the old definitions still prevailed, and ethnic stereotyping, for example, was still seen as a useful way of categorizing citizens at the street level of police work.

### Changes in practice methods (directory knowledge)

Where strategies were partially implemented and processes had not taken the intended directions, existing ways of accomplishing organizational tasks were not replaced by new ones. Since members found that they could get away with the way things were done in the old days, real changes to police practices were difficult to achieve. Where strategies and processes matched the new axiomatic knowledge, for example, in Avery's relentless fight against institutionalized corruption, changes did occur and these changes led to modifications of members' directory knowledge (i.e. corruption is not tolerated). Changes in directory knowledge in turn affected what officers considered as 'the way things should or should not be done', i.e. recipe knowledge. Such changes would serve to reinforce and maintain the implementation of reform strategies. Conversely, where existing directory knowledge was left unchallenged, reform strategies and processes could be undermined.

### Changes in practice norms (recipe knowledge)

Changes to what officers perceived as the way things should or should not be done in particular situations followed changes in the other dimensions of knowledge. Given that many of the strategies and processes outlined earlier had not been adequately implemented, and dictionary knowledge as well as directory knowledge had not been radically altered, it is therefore not surprising that recipe knowledge was substantially unchanged.

### Changing the field

The key to understanding why these apparently dramatic changes to the New South Wales Police have not led to a substantial improvement in relations between police and minority groups may be that many of the changes were directed at the habitus but not the field. Minority communities are still in relatively powerless positions in society, and Aboriginal communities have been socially disadvantaged for centuries. Police still possess wide discretionary powers, while existing legislative mechanisms have been ineffective for changing discriminatory police practices (HREOC, 1991: 269). Complaints against the police still involve an onerous and uncertain process for the complainants. Even the implementation of reforms have not been subject to any serious monitoring or evaluation.

Members of the organization who were interviewed appeared to see a great deal of success in Avery's attempt to minimize police corruption.[5] An examination of how anti-corruption strategies were implemented and what organizational processes were activated could give some guidance to the secret of success. The relative success of Avery's anti-corruption campaign may be due to the fact that the campaign did not simply involve an attempt to change the habitus, it was accompanied by a change in the field. In other words, there was genuine and widespread community and political concern about police corruption in New South Wales at the time, and the police administration was prepared to make use of all the available legal and disciplinary tools to pursue the goal of fighting corruption. There has not been the same type of campaign against police racism or police abuse of power.

This analysis suggests that researchers who emphasize the importance of police occupational culture considerably underestimate the power of the field, i.e. the social, economic, legal, and political sites in which policing takes place. Changing police culture requires changes in the field at both management and street level decisions. These may include the restoration of land rights to

Aboriginal communities in recognition of the injustices done in the past, a stronger commitment to the monitoring of 'access and equity' issues in policing by the government, a more adequate allocation of resources for community assistance, the enactment of statutory right to interpreters, the establishment of a more accessible and efficient complaints procedure, and increased internal and external auditing of police practices.

## Conclusion

In their review of the police literature Brogden *et al.*, (1988) distinguish between two major approaches to police reform: the first advocates *rule-tightening* as a means of controlling police discretion, while the second believes in *changing the informal culture* of police organizations. In a recently published evaluation of the British law reforms in the 1980s, McConville *et al.*, seriously question the utility of law reform as a method of changing police practice, since the occupational subculture of the police 'appears resistant to change' (McConville *et al.*, 1991: 193). The authors suggest that to change police practice, an 'attack upon police occupational culture' would be necessary. This is to be achieved by redefining the police mandate and instituting new forms of accountability. Similarly, Reiner notes the uneven impact of law reform on police practice and concludes that legal regulation alone is of limited effectiveness for changing police practice: 'the key changes must be in the informal culture of the police, their practical working rules' (Reiner, 1992: 232). Brogden *et al.*, however, do not see the crucial question as whether formal rules should be tightened *or* the cop culture co-opted, but the *relationship* between formal rules and subcultural values. In fact, they argue for a position opposite to Reiner's: the key is to tighten the formal rules, since it is the 'permissiveness' of the formal rules that 'creates the *space* for occupational culture to flourish' (Brogden *et al.*, 1988: 167, 170).

This chapter sheds new light on this debate. I have tried to demonstrate that police culture should not be understood as some internalized rules or values independent of the conditions of policing. Bourdieu's conceptions of field and habitus assist our understanding of the relationship between the formal structural context of policing and police cultural practice. Changes in the field (e.g, in the formal rules governing policing) inevitably alter the way the game is played, since habitus interacts with the field, but the resulting practice may or may not be substantially or even discernibly changed. Once again the analogy of sports may be useful here. If the rules of a game or the physical markings on the field have been changed, an experienced player may be able to adjust quickly to the new rules and hence shows no sign of changing his/her performance. Conversely, changes to habitus (e.g. in the objectives of policing) also affect practice, but unless the field is changed in a way that reinforces the new habitus, habitus itself may revert to its old dispositions. It is therefore unproductive to debate whether rule-tightening or changing culture was more important. It may be that tightening the law is easier to achieve than changing police culture, but the results of both can be unpredictable. Moreover, changing the field can be just as difficult as changing habitus when the distribution of power and resources is the target of change.

Sackmann's four dimensions of cultural knowledge, when used as a way of elaborating on Bourdieu's habitus, contribute to our understanding of the processes of change. They are particularly useful for suggesting ways in which cultural change can be initiated and maintained. The police literature has tended to lump values, beliefs, attitudes, informal rules, practices, *etc.* together under the label of police culture. Sackmann's model provides a way of distinguishing the dimension of cultural knowledge that can be changed by management, i.e. axiomatic knowledge, from those dimensions which can only be changed and reinforced by the successful implementation of strategies and enactment of processes that are supportive of the direction of change. By integrating Bourdieu's conception of field and habitus with Sackmann's dimensions of cultural knowledge, I have presented a model of police cultural change that emphasizes the relationship between the social, legal, and organizational context of policing and the schemas as, classifications, and vocabulary of precedents central to the craft of policing.

*From Janet Chan, 'Changing police culture', British* Journal of Criminology, *Vol. 36, no 1, 1996, pp 109–34.*

## Notes

1   Even the documentary maker expressed surprise that the officers were more concerned about whether they were wearing their hats when the cameras were rolling than about the racist slurs and disparaging comments they routinely made about Aborigines (Brockie, 1994: 178).

2   The nature and historical context of the two policy statements are in fact very different. The EAPS was a governmental requirement – all departments had to submit an EAPS and report annually to the Ethnic Affairs Commission regarding the progress of implementing EAPS. The AAPS was developed by the police in the wake of the furore following the broadcasting of *Cop It Sweet* to improve police/Aborigines relations.

3   This assessment is based on 42 face-to-face interviews with selected police staff, including managerial and operational officers, a questionnaire-based survey of police officers (332 respondents) and an examination of a variety of documents. The questionnaire survey was conducted on a random sample of officers in 56 patrols with at least 15 per cent ethnic population. The sample was stratified by rank (one out of eight officers below the rank of senior sergeant and one out of two officers at or above the rank of sergeant). The response rate was 56 per cent. The sample characteristics were as follows: *sex* – male (87 per cent); *age* – under 25 years of age (37 per cent), 25 to 29 (21 per cent), 30 to 39 (18 per cent), 40 and over (25 per cent); *experience* – five years of service or less (53 per cent), six to 10 years (12 per cent), 11 to 20 years (12 per cent), over 20 years (24 per cent); *rank* – probationary constables (14 per cent), constables – various classes (59 per cent), sergeant (12 per cent), senior sergeant (11 per cent), inspector or above (5 per cent). The profile of respondents was similar to that of the population of officers in 1991, with younger, less experienced officers somewhat over-represented in the sample.

4   At the time of the survey, the Aboriginal Affairs Policy Statement had not yet been developed. It was subsequently launched in December 1992.

5   Police corruption has again become a major issue in New South Wales, with a Royal Commission due to report its findings at the end of 1996.

## References

Australian Law Reform Commission (ALRC) (1992), *Multiculturalism and the Law*, Report   57. Commonwealth of Australia.

Baldwin, R., and  Kinsey, R. (1982), *Police Powers and Politics*. London: Quartet Books.

Bayley, D. H., and Mendelsohn, H. (1969), *Minorities and the Police: Confrontation in America*. New York: The Free Press.

Bourdieu, P. (1990), *In Other Words: Essay towards a Reflexive Sociology*. Cambridge: Polity Press.

Bourdieu, P., and Wacquant, L.J.D. (1992), *An Invitation to Reflexive Sociology*. Cambridge: Polity Press.

Brockie, J. (1994), 'Police and Minority Groups', in D. Moore and R. Wettenhall, eds., *Keeping the Peace: Police Accountability and Oversight*. Canberra: University of Canberra and the Royal Institute of Public Administration Australia.

Brogden, M., Jefferson, T., and Walklate, S. (1988), *Introducing Policework*. London: Unwin Hyman.

Cahill, D., and Ewan, J. (1987), *Ethnic Youth: Their Assets and Aspirations*, Report of the Department of Prime Minister and Cabinet. Canberra: AGPS (quoted in FECCA, 1991).

Cain, M. (1973), *Society and the Policeman's Role*. London: Routledge and Kegan Paul.

Chan, J. (1992), *Policing in a Multicultural Society: A Study of the New South Wales Police*. Final Report to the New South Wales Police Service.

Chan, J. (1995), 'Damage Control: Media Representation and Responses to Police Deviance', *Law/Text/Culture*, 2.

Cunneen, C. (1991), 'Aboriginal Juveniles in Custody', *Current Issues in Criminal Justice*, 3/2: 204–18.

Cunneen, C., and Robb, T. (1987), *Criminal Justice in North-East New South Wales*. Sydney: Bureau of Crime Statistics and Research.

Czarniawski-Joerges, B. (1992), *Exploring Complex Organizations: A Cultural Perspective*. Newbury Park, CA: Sage.

Ericson, R. (1981), 'Rules For Police Deviance', in C. Shearing, ed., *Organizational Police Deviance: Its Structure and Control*. Toronto: Butterworths.

Ericson, R. (1982), *Reproducing Order: A Study of Police Patrol*. Toronto: University of Toronto Press.

Ericson, R., Baranek, P. and Chan, J. (1987), *Visualizing Deviance: A Study of News Organization*. Toronto: University of Toronto Press.

Federation of Ethnic Communities Council of Australia (FECCA) (1991), *Background Paper on Ethnic Youth Prepared for FECCA's Multicultural Youth Conference*. Sydney: FECCA.

Fielding, N. (1988), *Joining Forces: Police Training, Socialization, and Occupational Competence*. London and New York: Routledge.

Fitzgerald Report (1989), *Report of a Commission of Inquiry Pursuant to Orders in Council*. Brisbane: Commission of Inquiry into Possible Illegal Activities and Associated Police Misconduct.

Foley, M. (1984), 'Aborigines and the Police', in P. Hanks and B. Keon-Cohen, eds., *Aborigines and the Law*. Sydney: Allen and Unwin.

Francis, R. (1981), *Migrant Crime in Australia*. St Lucia: University of Queensland Press.

Geis, G., and Jesilow, P. (1988), 'Australian Immigrants and Crime: A Review Essay', *ANZJ of Criminology*, 21/3: 179–85.

Goldsmith, A. (1990), 'Taking Police Culture Seriously: Police Discretion and the Limits of Law', *Policing and Society*, 1: 91–114.

Hazelhurst, K. (1987), *Migration, Ethnicity, and Crime in Australian Society*. Canberra: Australian Institute of Criminology.

Holdaway, S. (1983), *Inside British Police: A Force at Work*. Oxford: Basil Blackwell.

Human Rights and Equal Opportunity Commission (HREOC) (1991), *Racist Violence*, Report of the National Inquiry into Racist violence in Australia. Canberra: AGPS.

Ingram, E. (1991), NSW Police Service: Evaluation Framework and Performance Indicators for Ethnic Client Group Program, unpublished paper.

Landa Report (1991), *Operation Sue*, report under section 26 of the Ombudsman Act.

Lee Report (1990), *Report of the Royal Commission of Inquiry into the Arrest, Charging and Withdrawal of Charges against Harold James Blackburn and Matters Associated therewith*.

Lee, J.A. (1981), 'Some Structural Aspects of Police Deviance in Relations with Minority Groups', in C. Shearing, ed., *Organizational Police Deviance*, 49–82. Toronto: Butterworths.

Lusher Report (1981), *Report of the Commission of Inquiry into New South Wales Police Administration*.

Manning, P. (1977), *Police Work*. Cambridge, MA: MIT Press.

Manning, P. (1989), 'Occupational Culture', in W.G. Bailey, ed., *The Encyclopedia of Police Science*. New York and London: Garland.

Manning, P. (1993), 'Toward a Theory of Police Organization: Polarities and Change', paper given to the International Conference on Social Change in Policing, 3–5 August 1993, Taipei.

McConville, M., Sanders, A., and Leng, R. (1991), *The Case for the Prosecution: Police Suspects and the Construction of Criminality*. London: Routledge.

New South Wales Ethnic Affairs Commission (NSWEAC) (1992), Policing and Ethnicity in NSW, unpublished report.

New South Wales Ombudsman (1991), *Annual Report*. Sydney: Office of the Ombudsman.

New South Wales Ombudsman (1992), *Annual Report*. Sydney: Office of the Ombudsman.

New South Wales Police Recruit Education Programme (NSWPD) (1985–6), *Annual Reports*.

New South Wales Police Recruit Education Programme (NSWPREP) (1991), *Course Documentation*.

New South Wales Police Service (NSWPS), (1988–91), *Annual Reports*.

New South Wales Police Service (1988a), *Ethnic Affairs Policy Statement*.

Office of Multicultural Affairs (1990), *Youth and Multiculturalism*, Research Report (quoted in FECCA, 1991).

Ouchi, W.G., and Wilkins, A.L. (1985), 'Organizational Culture', *Annual Review of Sociology*, 11: 457–83.

Powell, W.W., and DiMaggio, P.J., eds. (1991), *The New Institutionalism in Organizational Analysis*. Chicago: University of Chicago Press.

Punch, M. (1985), *Conduct Unbecoming: The Social Construction of Police Deviance and Control*. London: Tavistock.

Punch, M. (1983), 'Officers and Men: Occupational Culture, Inter-Rank Antagonism, and the Investigation of Corruption, in M. Punch, ed., *Control in the Police Organization*. Cambridge, MA: MIT Press.

Reiner, R. (1992), *The Politics of the Police*, 2nd edn. Hemel Hempstead: Harvester Wheatsheaf.

Reuss-Ianni, E., and Ianni, F. (1983), 'Street Cops and Management Cops: The Two Cultures of Policing', in M. Punch, ed., *Control in the Police Organization*. Cambridge, MA: MIT Press.

Reynolds, (1987), *The Law of the Land*. London: Penguin.

Sackmann, S. (1991), *Cultural Knowledge in Organizations*. Newbury Park, CA: Sage.

Shearing, D.D., and Ericson, R.V. (1991), 'Culture as Figurative Action', *British Journal of Sociology*, 42: 481–506.

Skolnick, J. (1966), *Justice without Trial*. New York: John Wiley and Sons.

Sparrow, M.K., Moore, M.H., and Kennedy, D.M. (1990), *Beyond 911: A New Era for Policing*. New York: Basic Books.

Staunton Report (1991), *Report of the Police Tribunal of New South Wales to the Minister for Police and Emergency Services Pursuant to an Inquiry under Section 45 of the Police Regulation (Allegations of Misconduct) Act 1978 into Certain Matters Relating to Discipline in the Police Force ('Brennan TRG Inquiry')*.

Wacquant, L.J.D. (1992), 'Toward a Social Praxeology: The Structure and Logic of Bourdieu's Sociology', in P. Bourdieu and L. Wacquant, *An Invitation to Reflexive Sociology*. Cambridge: Polity Press.

Weick, K. (1969), *The Social Psychology of Organizing*. Reading, MA: Addison-Wesley.

Westley, W. (1970), *Violence and the Police*. Cambridge, MA: MIT Press.

Wootten Report (1991), *Report of the Inquiry into the Death of David John Gundy*, Royal Commission into Aboriginal Deaths in Custody.

Youth Justice Coalition (NSW) (1990), *Kids in Justice: A Blueprint for the 90s*. Sydney: Youth justice coalition.

# 22. Police (canteen) sub-culture: an appreciation

*P.A.J. Waddington*

The notion that the police possess a distinctive occupational sub-culture lies at the centre of much research and theorizing about policing and police work. It derives from the discovery that police work is rarely guided by legal precepts, but that police officers exercise extensive discretion in how they enforce the law. That discretion and many other routine police practices are thought to rely upon the taken for granted beliefs and values shared by the police generally, but particularly by the lower ranks who are most likely to encounter members of the public in conditions of 'low visibility' (Goldstein, 1960). However, these beliefs and values are widely regarded as having a malign influence upon criminal justice, being responsible for many of the routine injustices that are perpetrated against vulnerable people and also mobilizing the lower ranks to resist enlightened change. Thus, the notion of the sub-culture of the lower ranks is frequently invoked by academic researchers and commentators to explain and condemn a broad spectrum of policing practice.

In this chapter, I seek to review the now voluminous literature on the police subculture in order to offer an alternative conception of it: one that is 'appreciative', rather than condemnatory.

## Talk and action

The core referents of 'police sub-culture' are clear enough: its sense of mission; the desire for action and excitement, especially the glorification of violence; an 'Us/Them' division of the social world with its in-group isolation and solidarity on the one hand, and racist components on the other; its authoritarian conservatism; and its suspicion and cynicism, especially towards the law and legal procedures (Reiner, 1992). It should be noted immediately, that this list represents a *de facto* operationalization of a much broader theoretical construct, an operational definition that is both narrower and concerned with only certain cultural expressions. In common with general sociological and anthropological definitions of culture, the police sub-culture refers to what Peter Manning calls the 'accepted practices, rules and principles of conduct that are situationally applied and generalized rationales and beliefs' (Manning, 1989: 360). *In fact,* what researchers focus upon is what the police *say*, that is, the *oral* culture. As Fielding (1994) quite correctly – but only implicitly – acknowledges, 'police sub-culture' is operationally reduced to the 'canteen culture'.

This is more than simply an operational convenience, facilitating reliance on data collection through interviews and attitude scales, but a theoretical necessity; for canteen talk becomes the explanation of police action. As Reiner puts it:

> An understanding of how police officers see the social world and their role in it – 'cop culture' – is crucial to an analysis of what they *do and* their broad political function. (1985: 85, emphasis added)

Talk and action are related in either of two ways: on the one hand, 'police sub-culture' might be conceived narrowly as attitudinal variables that seek to explain police behaviour. Alternatively, 'police sub-culture' might be conceptualized as a hypothetical construct that lends coherence and continuity to the broad spectrum of police thought and practice. Either way, the concept seeks to bridge what officers say and do in one context, usually the privacy of the police station or police car, with what they do elsewhere, most notably in encounters with members of the public. Thus, if police act in a racist fashion when performing their duties, this can be readily attributed to racist motives produced and sustained by racist canteen banter.

However, this conceptual bridge looks decidedly rickety as it spans the obvious and frequently acknowledged chasm between what officers say and what they do. Observational studies of police behaviour on the street have overwhelmingly concluded that the principal explanatory variables are contextual. The pioneering research by Black and Reiss discovered that despite the undoubted racism expressed by officers in the privacy of the car and canteen, they could not detect any racial discrimination in the way those same officers dealt with incidents (Black, 1970, 1971). Even Friedrich's reanalysis of the Black and Reiss data, showing that more prejudiced officers used more force than their less prejudiced colleagues, still concludes that the only variables to make a significant explanatory contribution are contextual (Friedrich, 1980; see also Coates and Miller, 1974; Locke, 1996; Smith *et al.* 1984). Sherman's (1980) secondary analysis of the observational data available before 1980 likewise concludes that the seriousness of the offence is massively the most significant determinant of whether police decide to arrest or not. Since then research published by Sykes and Brent (1983), Rubin and Cruse (1973) and Worden (1996, 1989) have all testified to the importance of contextual variables and relative insignificance of attitudinal and related factors. Equally, ethnographers have often deliberately abstained from suggesting that talk and action are consonant. Most notably, the Policy Studies Institute researchers frankly admitted that they were surprised at the discrepancy between canteen racism and actual treatment of black people, especially victims (Smith and Gray, 1983). I too found a gap between the identification of certain protest groups as 'the opposition' and the extensive steps routinely taken to facilitate their holding peaceful protests. Equally, the widespread republicanism amongst senior Metropolitan Police officers was not evident in their excessive responsiveness to royal sensibilities (Waddington, 1994, 1994b, 1993). Holdaway (1983) draws attention to the exaggeration that often accompanies the telling of stories, suggesting a gap between canteen chatter and the reality it purports to depict. Finally, evidence for the gap between canteen talk and action on the street is to be found issuing from the mouths of police officers who dismiss most of what they are called upon to do as 'rubbish'. Routine policing is *not* experienced as the expression of police values, but as its negation. In sum, if there is little relationship between the privately expressed views of police officers and their actual behaviour on the streets, it appears that the concept of a police sub-culture contributes little to the explanation of policing.

This is much less surprising than it first appears, for it represents little more than a specific manifestation of the divorce between talk and action that has preoccupied social psychology for over 50 years. In the 1930s LaPiere (1934) tested whether hoteliers, restaurateurs and others would act on their professed prejudice against people of oriental origin by confronting them with a Chinese couple requiring service in their respective establishments – they did not refuse service as they claimed they would. Since then those social psychologists who have sought to emphasize the causal role of subjective states – personality traits, attitudes, beliefs – have been obliged to retreat in the face of mounting evidence. Obvious, and for our purposes pertinent, examples are Milgram's (1974) well-known experiments on obedience to authority and Haney *et al.'s* (1973) simulated prison. In Milgram's case experimental subjects were selected who displayed no overtly authoritarian attitudes, but this did not prevent them inflicting distressing, injurious and possibly fatal electric shocks on what, they were led to believe was a hapless fellow subject. Likewise, student subjects were selected randomly to occupy positions of guards and inmates in Haney *et al.'s* simulated prison, yet the behaviour of the 'guards' was so authoritarian that the experiment was concluded prematurely on ethical grounds. Nor are these particular experiments unusual, indeed the literature on social psychological experimentation *per se* repeatedly reaffirms that it is the circumstances in which subjects find themselves that dictate their behaviour, not the attitudes and beliefs that they bring with them into the experiment. Even those social psychologists who challenge the experimental method, do so on the grounds that people act – as they do on any other 'social occasion' – according to the 'demand character-istics' presented to them (Orne, 1962). If we turn our gaze from the experimental laboratory to social history that conclusion is reinforced: societies have periodically conducted their own 'experiments' in which thousands of people – mainly men – find themselves confronting circumstances that demand extra-ordinary behaviour. In wartime, armies of conscripts have willingly slaughtered fellow human beings and faced almost certain death themselves for no better reason than it was demanded of them.

Police are not unusual in saying one thing and doing another, indeed they might well be typical. If so, then the talk that constitutes much of what passes for police sub-culture provides little explanation of police behaviour.

### If at first you don't succeed ... complicate!

Analysts of police sub-cultures are aware of this gap between talk and action and its implications. They have sought to salvage the concept by suggesting that police sub-cultures are more complex and have a more subtle relationship to action than is allowed by a simple causal model. However, neither amendment succeeds in overcoming the inherent flaws in the concept.

## The case of the disappearing sub-culture

Aware of the gap between talk and action, it has become a commonplace of police research that the police sub-culture is neither homogeneous nor monolithic. Individual police organizations are accused of developing their own distinctive culture. For example, in the wake of the Rodney King beating, it has been suggested that the Los Angeles Police Department had acquired an aggressive law enforcement ethos tolerant of excessive force (Skolnick and Fyfe, 1993; Christopher, 1991; Chevigny, 1995). Others have drawn a more general distinction between urban and rural police, suggesting that the former are more detached from the public they serve and inward looking (Cain, 1973; Websdale and Johnson, 1997). Several writers have drawn attention to the hierarchical divisions within the police sub-culture, between 'management cops' and 'street cops' (Holdaway, 1983; Reuss-Ianni and Ianni, 1983; Punch, 1983). Chan quotes Manning as claiming that the police contains a threefold hierarchical division of command, middle management and lower echelons (Chan, 1997: 66). Fielding (1995) argues that amongst the lower ranks there are distinct sub-cultures amongst officers engaged in routine patrol, on the one hand, and 'community constables', on the other. Jefferson (1990) hints that 'paramilitary' units, like the Special Patrol Group, have a particular and aggressive variant of the police sub-culture (see also Kraska and Paulsen, 1997). According to Hobbs (1988) and Young (1991) detectives too have their distinctive sub-culture that reflects regional characteristics of the wider society. Analogously, one might expect there to be divisions between traffic officers, dog handlers arid others engaged in various specialist tasks. Divisions also emerge between officers of different sexes (Fielding, 1994; Martin, 1979) and races (Holdaway, 1996, 1997) and even combinations of both (Martin, 1995). Indeed, in his research on the socialization of police recruits, Fielding (1988) suggests that individual officers select from amongst the various aspects of the sub-culture those elements they find acceptable. However, faced with all this diversity, it seems that sub-culture – as a set of *shared* artefacts – almost disappears entirely.

### Needless complexity

Not only does sub-culture disappear into a near-infinity of multiple sub-cultures, the static causal model is replaced by a much more dynamic process in which action and culture are imagined to influence each other. Hence Holdaway (1996, 1997) has recently argued that the racism of police culture is embedded in routine practices such as joking and banter and shared pastimes like off-duty drinking, that are not intrinsically racist, but which succeed in excluding ethnic minority officers and reinforcing racial stereotypes. It is through such processes that the police sub-culture 'lives'. This approach finds some support in Fielding and Fielding's (1991) research on police attitudes to law and order issues which found that recruits' initially strongly conservative views became increasingly subtle and equivocal in the face of experience. However, it is difficult to reconcile the equivocation of such a process with the robust rejection of liberalism with which police sub-culture is often credited.

Perhaps the most conceptually sophisticated version of this processual argument is to be found in Shearing and Ericson's (1991) analysis. Taking issue with rule-based models of cultural influence generally, they argue that culture is conveyed metaphorically through stories, myths and anecdotes that do not dictate any particular course of action in any given situation, but enable, none the less, officers to act in ways that are intelligible to their peers as competent. Whilst this approach elevates the study of police sub-culture above the normal diet of macho, racist, sexist thugs, it retains the assumption that the police sub-culture is the principal guide to action. This assumption can be challenged on several grounds: first, that even if their general model of 'culture as figurative action' is accurate, it does not follow that the *police sub-culture is* the exclusive or even prime source of cultural influence. Officers might be influenced far more by the stories, myths and anecdotes of their wider culture, for example, 'urban legends'. Secondly, even if police action is generated by an internal culture, this does not establish that canteen banter has any influence. It is perfectly possible that police culture is bifurcated and consists of a canteen culture that generates behaviour in that context and an *operational* culture that guides action on the streets. Certainly, those who have analysed operational policing depict practices of much greater complexity and sophistication than could be extrapolated from canteen chatter (see most notably Bittner, 1967a, 1967b). Thirdly, they accept uncritically the notion that policing is a craft containing subtlety and insight, whereas most routine police patrol is conducted by young, inexperienced officers who lack subtlety. Finally, whilst the processes of which Shearing and Ericson write *may* produce the actions of officers it is difficult to imagine how this could be ascertained, for the processes are elusive. Before submitting to such analytical extravagance, perhaps simpler alternatives should first be exhausted.

## Interpretative over-reach

The value of 'culture' as a sociological construct is that it relates a broad spectrum of thoughts and actions into a coherent whole. What is also implied is that that set of cultural artefacts is *distinctive* to the group. Mission, cynicism, solidarity and so forth are aspects of *police* sub-culture because these are defining attributes of police officers when compared to others, whereas the use of the English language is a cultural attribute shared with native English speakers far beyond the confines of the police occupation. However, there is the danger that just because a group like the police exhibits a *common* trait, that is too readily interpreted as a *distinctive* characteristic attributable to their culture, especially when the focus is exclusively on the group in isolation. For example, the widespread sexism found amongst police officers is often assumed to be an expression of their peculiarly 'macho' sub-culture (Martin, 1979; Brown and Campbell, 1991; Brown et al., 1992; Brown, 1995). Yet, it seems clear that sexism is not restricted to the police by any means (see, for example, Bucke, 1994) and that in this regard the police are probably influenced mainly by patriarchal beliefs embedded in the wider culture and shared by many occupations. This is not to excuse police sexism, but merely to point out that what police share in common with much of the population cannot be explained by social forms – police sub-culture – that are purportedly distinctive to them.

The temptation to attribute common, but not necessarily distinctive, traits to the police sub-culture is exacerbated by the methodological difficulties of conducting *comparative* ethnography. When an ethnographer describes the police sub-culture as, say, racist, against what comparison standard is such a conclusion reached? On the one hand, it might be an ideal standard of zero racism, but that would be singularly uninformative, if not misleading, for against such an ideal virtually every other occupational sub-culture might be equally racist and the implicit distinctiveness of the *police* sub-culture attributed erroneously. Alternatively, the comparison might be drawn with occupational sub-cultures familiar to researchers, but this too is obviously misleading since researchers are likely to be most familiar with a very peculiar cultural milieu – academia. Indeed, there is the distinct possibility that the literature on police sub-culture tells us more about the peculiarities of academic life than it does about the distinctiveness of the police.

It is in this connection, of course, that quantitative methods possess the advantage over their more qualitative alternatives, for police can be compared with other occupations and general population norms. When they are, so the portrayal of police officers as conservative, racist, cynical authoritarians has become more difficult to sustain. Bayley and Mendelsohn (1969) found few differences between Denver police officers and their white peers; Belson (1975) discovered that his sample of police officers in London were not distinctly cynical, a conclusion endorsed by research on American police that found them not distinctively dogmatic or racist either (Lefkowitz, 1973). Some researchers actually discover that police are *less* racist and *more* tolerant than other groups in the population: Rafky found with one exception, 'Lake City' officers 'when compared to Whites in general … are either more sympathetic or as sympathetic in their recognition of civil rights' (Rafky, 1973: 75). Brodsky and Williamson (cited in Lester, 1996) found that when they presented police and fire officers with scenarios in which police used excessive force, police were more censorious than their fire service counterparts. Nor does it seem that increased exposure to the police sub-culture ingrains particular attitudes ever more firmly. Genz and Lester (1976) found no increase in authoritarianism amongst officers with greater experience, but did find statistically significant differences between state and municipal police. Similarly, Scripture (1997) recently found few differences in the social and political attitudes of experienced officers and recently recruited trainees. Comparisons between police officers with only modest educational attainment and those with college degrees have failed to find the expected higher levels of liberalism and tolerance in the latter (Miller and Fry, 1976; Roberg, 1978; Dalley, 1975). Even when researchers trawl through a battery of possible psychological traits that might be influenced by education, the best they come up with are modest correlations (Cascio, 1977). Perhaps most surprising of all is that when compared to social workers – normally thought of as representing the opposite psychological profile to the police – the police officer emerges as 'slightly lower than the social worker on the Move Against Aggressors scale, indicating that he was no more likely than the average individual in the norm group to counter-attack when someone acted toward him in a belligerent or aggressive manner' (Trojanowicz, 1971: 558–9). Even where researchers have discovered statistically significant differences between police officers and other groups, there is usually, if not invariantly, considerable overlap between police and others. Thus, it is far from the case that the police are a repository for authoritarianism, racism and conservatism within a liberal population brimming over with the milk of human kindness. Their culture might be less 'sub' than is often supposed and instead be the expression of *common* values, beliefs and attitudes within a police context.

**Redundant explanation**

There are perfectly straightforward explanations at both macro and micro levels for police actions that do not rely on police sub-culture. For example, the notion of a police sub-culture adds little to the argument that the police routinely 'build a case' against nominated suspects (McConville *et al.*, 1991). Their structural position as servants of the prosecution in an adversary system surely provides the principal incentive for the practices that that research has revealed. Variations in styles of policing from one society to another are perfectly explicable in terms of the structures and traditions of those societies. Although it did possess curious sub-cultural elements, the sub-culture of the South African Police did not explain its brutally oppressive actions. These were dictated by the nature of the apartheid state that it served (Brewer, 1994; Brogden, 1989; Brogden and Shearing, 1993; Cawthra, 1993). The divergent evolution of policing in Ireland and England had everything to do with the colonial structure of the former as opposed to the liberal traditions of the latter (Palmer, 1988) and almost nothing to do with the canteen banter of either. At the other end of the scale, the disproportionate shootings of ethnic minority suspects by American cops – initially and erroneously, thought to be an unthinking application of racist cultural values (Goldkamp, 1982; Meyer, 1982; Takagi, 1982; Kohler, 1975*a*, 1975*b*) – turned out, on further examination, to be perfectly explicable in terms of factors such as departmental policies, the racial composition of the area and its crime mix and the propensity of black suspects to commit more serious armed crime (Fyfe, 1982*a, b, c*; Sherman, 1983; Reiss, 1980; Fyfe, 1981; Locke, 1996; Tennenbaum, 1994). Equally, the likelihood of arrest is explained perfectly well by such events as the arrested person breaching an 'adjacency pair' (for example, by replying to an officer's question with a question of their own – 'What's going on here?', 'Who wants to know?' (Sykes and Brent, 1983). Nor does this conclusion rest only on behaviouristic analyses: ethnographic studies of policing on the streets suggests that officers are guided by context-specific strategies (Muir, 1977; Norris, 1989; Chatterton, 1979, 1983; Kemp *et al.*, 1992).

## Condemning police behaviour

If the concept of 'police sub-culture' explains so little, why do police researchers adhere so tenaciously to the concept of the police sub-culture? Janet Chan recently remarked that 'Police culture has become a convenient label for a range of negative values, attitudes and practice norms among police officers' (Chan, 1996: 110), which raises the issue, 'convenient' for what purpose? Clearly, it is not a convenient *explanation*, because precious little is actually explained. Its 'convenience' lies in its condemnatory potential: the police are *to blame* for the injustices perpetrated in the name of the criminal justice system. Such a normative overtone can clearly be discerned in many, if not most, accounts of the police sub-culture and to be sure much of what is described is utterly contemptible. For example, Holdaway (1983) clearly and explicitly (and no doubt rightly) repudiates the sub-culture of his former colleagues that he so carefully documents, as does Young (1991). Outside observers clearly find the police sub-culture disagreeable, or worse. The Policy Studies Institute researchers make no attempt to disguise their distaste for the sub-culture of the London Metropolitan Police, captured, for instance, in such brief asides as their likening it to a rugby club (Smith and Gray, 1983: 90) – which left me wondering who should be more offended: the police or the thousands of rugby players and supporters! McConville and Shepherd (1992) attribute many of the problems of policing inner-city areas to the malign influence of the police sub-culture that encourages aggressive confrontation. These normative overtones license even such sophisticated and sensitive observers of the police subculture as Nigel Fielding (1994) to indulge in wholly speculative suggestions that the 'macho' sub-culture is in some way responsible for the various high-profile miscarriages of justice that have occurred.

Nor is this terribly surprising given the 'original impulse' of such research, which, as Reiner reminds us, 'was a civil libertarian concern about the extent and sources of police deviation from due process of law' (Reiner, 1985: 85). The purpose of research has not been merely to describe and analyse, but to reform – as Holdaway makes clear:

> If I desire anything for this book, it is that it may make a small contribution to our search for a more loving and just society and therefore a more loving and just police. (Holdaway, 1983: vi)

It is this reformist orientation that justifies the inclusion of some elements of the sub-culture as 'core' and the exclusion of others. As Chan notes in the citation above, it is the *negativity* of the 'values, attitudes and practice norms' to which the concept of a police subculture draws attention. For example, apart from its negativity there seems to be little empirical or analytical rationale for privileging, say, the 'cult of masculinity' as a *core* element compared to the preoccupation that officers seem to have with avoiding 'trouble' (Chatterton, 1979, 1983; Norris, 1989; Waddington, 1994*b*).

## Appreciating the police sub-culture

The great contribution of criminology and sociology generally to our understanding of deviancy has been to look beyond normative condemnation and seek to appreciate even the most offensive behaviour. The canteen chatter of police officers *is* offensive to liberal values, but that poses the intellectual challenge of seeking to *understand* why officers express such views. Merely to condemn and dismiss such behaviour is to retreat from the explanatory task. As Matza (1969) insisted, a generation ago, even deviant sub-cultures require *appreciative* analysis.

What needs appreciative understanding is not the supposed influence that canteen chatter has on police behaviour (for it seems to be little), but the chatter itself. In other words, if talk does not inform practice why do police officers invest so much effort in talking about their work? If policing is mundane and boring, why do police officers expend so much time trying to convince each other and themselves that it is action-packed? If women officers perform their police role indistinguishably from their male colleagues, why do those male colleagues insist that they do not? In what follows I attempt such an appreciation that follows in the steps of criminologists who have sought to understand other deviant sub-cultures as a *response* to the structural contingencies that delinquents face (Downes, 1966).

### Sub-culture as rhetoric

In her attempted reconceptualization of police sub-culture, Chan (1996, 1997) employs Bourdieu's distinction between 'habitus' and 'field' to emphasize that culture does not exist in a vacuum. This is a welcome reminder that no culture is free-standing: police sub-culture does not just exist, but exists for a purpose. What is that purpose if it is not to guide action? I suggest that it is simple and straightforward: it is a rhetoric that gives meaning to experience and sustains occupational self-esteem. As Harré and Secord (1972) have argued, human behaviour is *principally* expressive: people spend an enormous amount of time and energy constructing accounts of routine events in order to maintain the integrity of their cognitive world. Eiser (1986) has also argued that attitudes are not causal agents, but cognitive constructs that give meaning and coherence to actions and events. This perspective is particularly germane to the police, who act largely in conditions of organizational invisibility (Goldstein, 1960). Moreover, as Bittner has observed, those actions are context-specific (Bittner, 1967*a,b*), which implies that they must be 'situationally justified' (Manning and Van Maanen, 1977). Amongst the audience to which such justification must be offered are one's peers and the arena for this display of what Fielding (1984) calls 'competence' is the canteen. Because the canteen is a 'backstage' area it does not mean that officers are not staging performances. On the contrary, the canteen offers one of the rare opportunities for officers, whose actions on the street are normally 'invisible', to engage in displays before their colleagues. Here officers retail versions of events that affirm their worldview: the canteen is the 'repair shop' of policing and jokes, banter and anecdotes the tools.

Essentially, therefore, police sub-culture operates mainly as a palliative, rather than as a guide to future action. An example of this is Brewer's (1990b) analysis of how police in Northern Ireland cope with the ever-present threat of violence. In this account, the cavalier fatalism, routine accommodation and emphasis on one's skilful avoidance of danger that police officers voice are recognized as functional coping strategies. For example, adherence to fatalism does not mean that officers neglect to check beneath their cars or keep a close watch on their rear-view mirrors to ensure they are not being followed. Like medical staff and fire-fighters, when police officers adopt a fatalistic attitude they do so as a means of coping with a fearful reality that might otherwise overwhelm them (Menzies, 1960; Ivlanksch, 1963; Simpson, 1967; Clisby, 1990). It is clear why officers should invest so much in negating fear and anxiety, but why do they also invest time and effort in affirming other aspects of their sub-culture? What is their investment in being 'macho' and why denigrate ethnic minorities?

### The universality and tenacity of police subculture

In contradistinction to the intellectual fashion that seeks to erode and relativize police sub-cultures, I maintain that there is indeed *a* police sub-culture whose core elements are to be found across a remarkably broad spectrum of police talk in a wide variety of jurisdictions. Throughout the United States, which contains many significant internal divisions between jurisdictions and law enforcement agencies, the core elements of the police sub-culture remain recognizably the same. Those elements are shared throughout the various jurisdictions that constitute the United Kingdom, including Scotland and even Northern Ireland (with its very particular historical and contemporary differences from Great Britain (Brewer, 1990a). Throughout the former British Empire, with its distinctive history of colonial policing, the police sub-culture remains recognizable in Canada (Ericson, 1982), Australia (Chan, 1996; White and Alder, 1994; Finnane, 1987, 1990; Stevens *et al.*, 1995; Bryett and Harrison, 1993) and even in India with its very distinctive social structure and traditions (Bayley, 1969). Nor are these similarities restricted to the Anglo-Saxon tradition of policing (Bayley, 1982), but extend to continental Europe (of which we admittedly know less). When Punch (1979a) describes the policing of inner-city Amsterdam, he might just as easily be describing a British, American or Australian city. Even in a country as socially, politically and culturally distinct as Japan, patrol officers share many of the same prejudices as their counterparts elsewhere (Ames, 1981; Bayley, 1976,1991) whilst detectives act much like they do in other jurisdictions (Miyazawa, 1992). True, there are also substantial differences to be observed, such as the curious religiosity that infected the culture of the South African police under the apartheid regime captured so brilliantly by Brogden and Shearing (1993). Yet, even here police officers subscribe to many values that are found elsewhere. Whilst differences between police operating in varying social, political, economic and legal contexts are hardly surprising, it is their common subscription to mission, macho, 'Us/Them' and cynicism that deserves attention.

Moreover, police sub-cultures within societies show remarkable tenacity. Holdaway (1983) notes how, despite the enormous reorganization of patrol work that intervened between his own research and that of Cain and Chatterton that preceded it, the similarities are more apparent than the differences. The subsequent publication of the Policy Studies Institute report on the London Metropolitan Police served merely to reinforce his contention (Smith and Gray, 1983). Recent oral histories of policing further reinforce the suggestion that there is remarkable continuity in police sub-culture (Brogden, 1991; Weinberger, 1995).

Significant features of the police sub-culture are not only to be found across jurisdictions and over time, but they are also endorsed by groups who are thought to suffer adversely from them, most notably ethnic minorities and women. There has been relatively little comparative research on black and white police, or male and female officers, with regard to their beliefs and values. However, what little evidence there is suggests that they conform to much the same pattern as their white male counterparts. For example, female officers seem to value the same aspects of policing as their male counterparts. In one of the few comparisons of men and women Jones (1986) examined the tasks that each sex most valued and there was a remarkably high correlation between them, most notably with respect to the high value given to law enforcement. Heidensohn cites a typical response from one of her American sample of women officers: 'One shooting, two stabbings. Hauling bums. I love it' (Heidensohn, 1992: 176), sentiments that would sit as easily on the lips of a male colleague. When women officers complain about sex discrimination, it usually refers to being prevented from doing 'real police work', that is all those things that male officers value and try to keep for themselves (Bryant et al., 1985).

Taken together this suggests that the source of sub-cultural talk lies deep within the fundamentals of policing itself. Fundamentals that are relatively unaffected by the jurisdictional differences at least throughout the Western liberal democracies. Skolnick's (1966) pioneering study of police in a Californian city usefully attributes the 'working personality' of the police officer to the twin essentials of his role – authority and danger. Since this widely endorsed couplet was postulated most attention has been focused on 'danger', probably because Skolnick links it, through the notion of 'symbolic assailants', to race. However, in so far as police officers confront danger as an essential feature of their work it is because they exercise authority. Moreover, the authority that the police exercise is founded ultimately upon coercion. In Bitmer's (1970, 1974) felicitous phrase the police are 'monopolists of force in civil society' a definition now widely accepted by academic researchers and commentators. I would quibble with this precise formulation of the police role, but it will serve the purpose of this article well enough.

### Telling it like it is

Many elements of the police sub-culture reflect the reality of their authority position more or less directly. The most obvious, of course, is their authoritarianism, indeed a psychological scale purporting to measure this trait and on which the police did not score highly would be of questionable validity. The same applies to the conservatism of most police officers, for the maintenance of order is an inherently con-servative function. Thus when officers advocate strong 'law and order' politics, they are affirming the value of what they routinely do: policing is an authoritative and conservative vocation and it is no surprise that officers regard it as a necessary one.

Likewise, Holdaway's (1983) observation of how police regard themselves as having rights of ownership over 'the ground' and developing a more or less detailed topography of trouble, danger and work, is a direct reflection of their omnibus responsibilities. For the duration of their tour of duty the area they police is theirs, for they are, as he concedes, custodians of state authority on the street and anything that threatens, challenges or disturbs that authority must be sub-ordinated or else authority itself is negated. Hence, their awareness of locations associated with trouble and danger.

### Talking a good fight

The analysis of the police sub-culture would be simple if it only reflected the realities of the occupation, but other aspects of the police sub-culture reflect less directly the fundamental realities of the police role. A notable illustration is the glorification of action and excitement, for routine police work is nothing if not boring and few encounters involve the use of force (Southgate and Ekblom, 1986, 1984; Skogan, 1994; Southgate and Crisp, 1993; Sykes and Brent, 1983). Yet, it remains the case that police intervention in the lives of others is invariably *authoritative* – an authority that is ultimately backed by force. So, when police tell exaggerated 'war stories' that appear to 'glorify violence' they are doing what those in other occupations do – celebrating what they and most observers recognize as the 'real job' (Manning, 1980). Displaying courage in the face of threat is something that is widely valued and it is no surprise that officers dwell upon those events when their essential purpose is most clearly manifested. Police celebrate other skills and attributes, but the core of the police's oral tradition lies in the glorification of violence over which they hold the legitimate monopoly. However, as Uildriks and Mastrigt (1991) point out, it is more important that officers 'act tough' rather than 'be tough' and the stage on which to *act* is the canteen and the personnel carrier.

Nor is it surprising that this celebration is generalized to a 'cult of masculinity', for the exercise of coercive authority is not something that just anybody can do. It is traditionally the preserve of 'real men' who are willing and able to fight. Confronting physical threat is widely regarded as 'tough' work and such work is traditionally associated with masculinity. Indeed, it is instructive that Bern's (1974) Sex Role Inventory lists as typically (and exclusively) masculine traits: 'aggressive', 'assertive', 'forceful', 'willing to take a stand' and 'willing to take risks' – all of which seem intuitively compatible with the exercise of coercive authority. It has already been noted that the attitudes of female police officers do not challenge the essentially masculine aspects of the police role, however if policing was to be thoroughly feminized, it would, as Walklate suggests, fundamentally challenge 'what counts as policework' (Walklate, 1995: 203) . In which case the female officer *does* represent a profound threat to the very notion of policing. The mere presence of women officers, especially if they are as effective as their male counterparts, symbolically undermines traditional notions of policing and it is pre-dictable that male officers resist such a threat (Fielding and Fielding, 1992).

### Citizenship and isolation

Whilst the notion that police exercise coercive authority is widely accepted, those to whom that force, or the threat of it, is directed have received much less attention. I do not mean here the individual members of the public who happen to come into some adversarial confrontation with particular police officers, but the general relationship between the police and the remainder of the population. Instituting a police force entails the general population licensing a specific occupational group to exercise authority over them – to intrude into their privacy, interfere in their conduct and ultimately to use force against them (Klockars, 1985). Moreover, the police institution was created at the same time as the civil element of citizenship began to take hold in the early nineteenth century (Marshall, 1976). Indeed, I would contend that, paradoxically enough, the installation of a police force was itself an expression of that development of citizenship, since it separated the state's monopoly of force into civil and military realms (Waddington, 1999).

The crucial distinction between the police and the military is that the former do not confront an 'enemy', but fellow *citizens* and that makes their position acutely marginal, for they must exercise coercive authority whilst retaining at least the grudging acquiescence of those over whom such authority is wielded. It is a marginality of which ordinary police officers are acutely, albeit inarticulately, aware. It is why the police are everywhere (throughout the liberal democracies at least) so insular: they find social encounters with non-police friends, acquaintances, neighbours and others fraught with difficulty (McNamara, 1967; see also Cain, 1973). They feel more relaxed with fellow officers who share the same 'backstage' aspects of the role and with whom it is, therefore, unnecessary to maintain appearances. Despite the liberal democratic mythology of the police as 'citizens in uniform', the reality is that they are set apart by the authority that they wield.

### 'Dirty work'

Policing is a species of 'dirty work' (Hughes, 1962) for police routinely violate the normal rules of conduct. In routinely exercising coercive authority the police act in ways that would otherwise be exceptional, exceptionable or illegal. Few of us would feel entitled to approach a fellow citizen in a public place and demand, however politely, an account of themselves; but this is something that police officers frequently do. Young officers intervening in a violent domestic quarrel may find themselves exercising authority over adults old enough to be their parents. Even when officers provide a service, like searching for a missing child, they violate the privacy of those whom they serve, for they will demand to know whether, for example, a family quarrel has prompted the disappearance. Most crucially of all, the use of force is, as Bittner (1970) observed, *tainting*: to overcome *resistance by* the threat or use of violence is a fundamental breach of liberal values (Waddington, 1991). Of routine policing, Ericson has rightly observed:

> If he [the patrol officer] decided to initiate encounters, these were very often directed at the dirty work of 'street cleaning' 'pukers', 'bikers' and

other 'marginal types'. Whilst this work may serve to order the population, it hardly brings personal dignity to anyone involved. (Ericson, 1982: 206)

Like all 'dirty workers' police devoted considerable attention to *normalising*, indeed dignifying, it – hence their profound sense of mission. Apart from celebrating the essential quality of the police role, glorifying violence and the general 'cult of masculinity' is a means through which the exceptional and exceptionable is made heroic. The vision of a 'thin blue line' not only places the police in the position of valiant protectors of society, but also of those who are knowledgeable of the dark side of society and, therefore, in a uniquely privileged position to apprehend the danger that threatens. In their own eyes, the police are the cognoscenti, whereas the remainder of the population are 'know nothings' and naïve 'civvies' who cannot possibly understand the (under)world and, therefore, cannot legitimately evaluate the contribution of the police. Thus, not only is heroism secured, but also cynicism engendered, for the police *know* that the order that 'civvies' take for granted is always precariously teetering on the brink of chaos (Holloway, 1983).

### Telling it like it ain't: crime-fighting

There is little doubt that the occupational self-image of the police is that of 'crime-fighters' and this is not just a distortion of what they do, it is virtually a collective *delusion*. A mountain of research has indicated that police have little impact on crime rates, are responsible for discovering few crimes and detecting fewer offenders, do not spend much duty-time on crime-related tasks and so forth (for a review of this literature see Morris and Heal, 1981). Indeed, it would be as accurate, if not more so, to associate policing with the provision of help and assistance (Cumming *et al.*, 1965; Punch and Naylor, 1973; Punch, 1979b), but this is an aspect of policing invariably dismissed by officers as 'rubbish', a distraction from the 'real job'. Why does this delusion reign supreme in so many jurisdictions?

Scholars have long been aware that the image of the police as 'crime-fighters' serves to legitimate the police to external audiences (Manning, 1977). What has received little recognition is the role of this mythology for sustaining the occupational self-esteem of the police themselves, who believe it most avidly. The very fact that police devote so much rhetorical effort to affirming what their daily experience denies should alert us to its ideological importance. The exercise of coercive authority over fellow citizens poses an obvious and acute challenge to the legitimacy of the police. Policing has historically been transformed from a potential threat to fellow citizens into their protection by ideologically identifying the police with crime-fighting. Criminals lie beyond the moral community of society, the suppression of whom 'serves and protects' (as the legend on many an American police car reminds its) the remainder of the respectable citizenry. It is yet a further affirmation that policing is heroic: coercive authority is exercised in the service of the highest ideals of *the law*.

## The rhetoric of exclusion

Distinguishing criminals from citizens is part of a wider strategy that excludes certain groups from citizenship, for once this is achieved the exercise of coercive authority can be conducted almost without restraint. This can be clearly seen in colonial forms of policing where the civil populations throughout the British Empire were universally regarded as potentially rebellious subjects upon whom state authority had to be *imposed* – a perception that licensed significant and arbitrary use of force (Anderson and Killingray, 1991, 1992; Ahire, 1991). This was not merely racist oppression of native peoples, to which the oppressive policing of South African Boers (Grundlingh, 1991; Brogden, 1989; Brogden and Shearing, 1993; Brewer, 1994), gold prospectors in the Yukon (Morrison, 1991) and, most notoriously perhaps, Irish Catholics (Townshend, 1992, 1993) all testify.

Domestically, the situation is more problematic, at least in notionally liberal democratic societies in which citizenship is virtually universal. However, whilst Marshall rightly pointed out there is much more to citizenship than its 'civil element' (Marshall, 1976), it is equally true that for some sections of the population notional citizenship is severely circumscribed in practice. Criminals exclude themselves from full citizenship, but criminality is too individualistic and conditional to serve as a basis for the routine exercise of coercive authority. To be rendered manageable, policing requires that those over whom authority can be exerted be identified in advance. In class divided societies police have historically exploited the division between the 'roughs' and the 'respectable', as Brogden explains:

> The expansion of police powers at the end of the 1860s narrowly focused on a specific group, a focus which in Liverpool, as elsewhere, seems to have had the assent of both working-class and bourgeoisie. Organizational factors within the police institution contributed to an easier relation with the respectable working-class and to the institutionalized exclusion of the lower classes. The antagonistic milieu of the street for patrolling police officers resulted in practical compromises. If police officers as individuals wished to survive and if the police institution as a corporate body aimed to gain a measure of consent, tolerance was necessary. Discretionary law enforcement led to a truce with one class at the cost of joint *criminalization of the lower orders*. (Brogden, 1982: 190–1, emphasis added)

The identification of the 'dangerous classes' not only focused police repression, but simultaneously reassured the 'respectable classes' that they would not suffer the same fate and enhanced the self-esteem of the police as protectors of 'ordinary decent people'.

In societies characterized more by racial and ethnic divisions the distinction between 'citizens' and others is ready-made for exploitation by the police. Even in Britain, groups such as Irish 'navvies' were identified as a sub-citizenry of 'police property'. As black immigration grew after the second world war there was created a distinct section of the population who, as 'outsiders', were by definition 'police property – a situation replicated in Holland with the

Surinamers (Punch, 1979*a*) and in Japan in relation to Koreans (Awes, 1981). In the United States ethnic and racial divisions have always predominated and that is reflected in police practice, as it is in Australia with regard to aboriginal peoples.

Holdaway (1996, 1997) has recently argued that police racism has its origins in the occupational need for the police to draw distinctions speedily and authoritatively between people they encounter. But there is more to it than this, for police not only identify their 'property', they *despise* them: terms such as 'toe-rag', 'scumbag', 'scrote' and 'puker' do not describe, they denigrate. An obvious explanation for this denigration is that police routinely come into conflict with the most marginal groups in society and, like antagonists generally, they demean their opponents. One can only be struck at the facility with which soldiers invent or resurrect abusive descriptions of adversaries. For instance, no sooner had the task force set sail for the Falkland Islands in 1982 than the troops had dredged from obscurity the term 'spics' to apply to Argentinean forces and as the Coalition forces gathered in the Gulf British soldiers quickly devised the notion of 'ragheads' to demean Iraqi troops. Whilst this undoubtedly plays a part, there is more to it than conflict alone. Some observers have complained about how the police sub-culture facilitates deviancy by offering techniques of neutralization akin to those employed by delinquent gangs (Fielding, 1994; Sykes and Matza, 1957; Kappeler *et al.*, 1994) . What these observers fail to appreciate is that the techniques of neutralization to which they draw attention are not restricted to obviously deviant actions, but serve to neutralize the taint that would otherwise accompany the exercise of coercive authority over fellow citizens *per se* (Bittner, 1970). If the police can persuade themselves that those against whom coercive authority is exercised are contemptible, no moral dilemmas are experienced – the policed section of the population 'deserve it'.

*Defensive solidarity*

Policing is more than psychologically precarious; exercising coercive authority over fellow citizens may be injurious to the individual officer. Of course, there is always the unpredictable possibility of an adversary inflicting injury or death, but policing is not a distinctively dangerous occupation. The truly ever-present danger lies in taking action that is judged improper. Policing is a 'punishment-centred bureaucracy' in which officers are rarely praised for good practice, often because it is invisible to the organization, but face draconian penalties if they are deemed to have behaved improperly. This is not some wilful imposition of police management, but a consequence of policing citizens, for police may lawfully take action against citizens that would otherwise be illegal or at least an abuse of authority. Therefore, if the lawfulness of the action can successfully be challenged, the actions of the officer would be transformed from the proper to the improper. Whether or not behaviour was improper might not become apparent until long after it took place. The use of force is a good illustration of this: in Britain, the police are entitled to use 'as much force as is reasonable in the circumstances' to effect a lawful purpose, but what is 'reasonable in the circumstances' can only be ascertained after-the-fact. This is not a curiosity of British law as the Rodney King beating illustrates: for the officers most involved in that incident were *acquitted of* the assault, but then *convicted* of denying King his civil rights (Cheh, 1996; Perez and Muir, 1996; Klockars, 1996). Police officers are acutely aware of this, hence the observed preoccupation with avoiding and minimizing 'in the job trouble' (Chatterton, 1979, 1983; Norris, 1989; Waddington, 1994*b*; see also Bayley and Bittner, 1984). It gives rise to the defensive solidarity of the lower ranks who perceive every action they take to be fraught with danger and hence adopt the cynical posture of 'lay low and don't make waves' (van Maanen, 1973, 1974, 1975).

## Conclusion: whither agency?

The normative orientation to the police sub-culture tells us little about why the police in so many jurisdictions express the beliefs and values they do. Identifying the defining characteristic of policing as the exercise of coercive authority and also the central problematic with which police must come to terms enables an empathetic understanding of even the most disagreeable features of the police sub-culture. The 'cult of masculinity' is the celebration of the core aspect of the role – the willingness and ability to use force; the sense of a crime-fighting mission provides ideological justification for the authority that is exercised against fellow citizens; the abusive, and often racist, denigration of 'police property' is the means through which moral dilemmas are routinely neutralized; and the defensive solidarity of the lower ranks is the frank recognition of the precariousness of their position. What this analysis of the police sub-culture incidentally exposes is the essential *fragility* of what appears at first sight to be a robustly powerful social institution. Police work so hard at affirming what their experience denies because they occupy a *marginal* position in any society that has pretensions to liberal democracy.

If the rhetoric of the canteen is divorced from action on the streets, how is the latter explained? Does this approach consign officers to being the playthings of situational constraints, lacking agency? Not at all: it does mean that what officers do in one arena (the canteen) is not necessarily, or even substantially, carried over into quite a different arena. Agency is forged on the street, encountering members of the public and dealing with incidents employing often unarticulated practices (in contrast to the excessive articulation *of* canteen banter). It is motivated by goals such as the avoidance of 'trouble' (Chatterton, 1979, 1983; Norris, 1989; Waddington, 1994), which go almost entirely unacknowledged within the arena *of* the canteen. If we wish to *explain* (and not just condemn) police behaviour on the streets, then we should look not in the remote recesses of what officers say in the canteen or privately to researchers, but in the circumstances in which they act.

*From P.A.J. Waddington, 'Police (canteen) sub-culture: an appreciation'*, British Journal of Criminology, *Vol. 39, no 2, 1999, pp 287–309.*

# References

Ahire, P.T. (1991), *New Directions in Criminology. Imperial Policing: The Emergence and Role of the Police in Colonial Nigeria 1860–1960*. Buckingham: Open University Press.

Ames, W. (1981), *Police and Community in Japan*. Berkeley: University of California Press.

Anderson, D.M. and Killingray, D., eds (1991), *Policing the Empire: Government, Authority and Control, 1830–1940*. Manchester: Manchester University Press.

Anderson, D.M. and Killingray, D., eds (1992), *Policing and Decolonisation: Politics, Nationalism and the Police, 1917–65*. Manchester: Manchester University Press.

Bayley, D.H. (1969), *The Police and Political Development in India*. Princeton: Princeton University Press.

Bayley, D.H. (1976), *Forces of Order: Police Behaviour in Japan and the United States*. Berkeley: University of California Press.

Bayley, D.H. (1982), 'A World Perspective on the Role of the Police in Social Control', in R. Donelan, ed., *Maintenance of Order in Society*. Ottowa: Canadian Police College.

Bayley, D.H. (1991), *Forces of Order: Police Behaviour in Japan and the United States*, 2nd edn. Berkeley: University of California Press.

Bayley, D.H. and Bittner, E. (1984), 'Learning the Skills of Policing', *Journal of Law and Contemporary Social Problems*, 47/4: 35–59.

Bayley, D.H. and Mendelsohn, H. (1969), *Minorities and the Police*, New York: Free Press.

Belson, W.A. (1975), *The Public and the Police*. London: Harper and Row.

Bem, S.L. (1974), 'The Measurement of Psychological Androgyny', *Journal of Consulting and Clinical Psychology*, 42/2: 155–62.

Bittner, E. (1967), 'Police Discretion in Emergency Apprehension of Mentally ill Persons', *Social Problems*, 14: 279–92.

Bittner, E. (1967b), 'The Police on Skid-Row: A Study of Peace Keeping', *American Sociological Review*, 32/5: 699–715.

Bittner, E. (1970), *The Functions of the Police in a Modern Society*. Washington, DC: US Government Printing Office.

Bittner, E. (1974), 'Florence Nightingale in Pursuit of Willie Sutton: A Theory of the Police', in H. Jacob, ed., *Potential for Reform of Criminal Justice*. Beverly Hills: Sage.

Black, D.J. (1970), 'The Production of Crime Rates', *American Sociological Review*, 35: 733–48.

Black, D.J. (1971), 'The Social Organization of Arrest', *Stanford Law Review*, 23: 1087–111.

Brewer, J.D. (1990a), *Inside the RUC*. Oxford: Clarendon.

Brewer, J.D. (1990b), 'Talking about Danger: The RUC and the Paramilitary Threat', *Sociology*, 24/4: 657–74.

Brewer, J.D. (1994), *Black and Blue: Policing in South Africa*. Oxford: Clarendon.

Brogden, M. (1982), *The Police: Autonomy and Consent*. London: Academic.

Brogden, M. (1991), *On the Mersey Beat*. Oxford: Oxford University Press.

Brogden, M.E. (1989), 'The Origins of the South African Police – Institutional versus Structural Approaches', in W. Scharf, ed., *Acta Juridica*. Cape Town: Faculty of Law, University of Cape Town.

Brogden, M. and Shearing, C. (1993), *Policing for a New South Africa*. London: Routledge.

Brown, J. (1995), 'European Policewomen: A Comparative Research Perspective', paper presented to the Political Studies Association of the United Kingdom, Politics of Law and Order Group Seminar: The Politics and Policy of Law and Order; European Perspectives, 28 October.

Brown, J. and Campbell, E. (1991), 'Less than Equal', *Policing*, 7/1: 324–33.

Brown, J., Maidment, A. and Bull, R. (1992), 'Appropriate Skill-Task Matching or Gender Bias in Deployment of Male and Female Police Officers', *Policing and Society*, 2: 1–15.

Bryant, L., Dunkerley, D. and Kelland, G. (1985), 'One of the Boys', *Policing*, 1/4: 236–44.

Bryett, K. and Harrison, A. (1993), *An Introduction to Policing: Policing in the Community*, vol. 4, Sydney: Butterworth.

Bucke, T. (1994), *Equal Opportunities and the Fire Service*, Home Office Research and Statistics Department, Research Findings No. 13. September.

Cain, M. (1973), *Society and the Policeman's Role*. London: Routledge and Kegan Paul.

Cascio, W.F. (1977), 'Formal Education and Police Officer Performance', *Journal of Police Science and Administration*, 5: 89–96.

Cawthra, G. (1993), *Policing South Africa*. London: Zed Books.

Chan, J. (1996), 'Changing Police Culture', *British Journal of Criminology*, 36/1: 109–34.

Chan, J.B.L. (1997), *Changing Police Culture: Policing in a Multicultural Society*. Cambridge: Cambridge University Press.

Chatterton, M.R. (1979), 'The Supervision of Patrol Work under the Fixed Points System', in S. Holdaway, ed., *The British Police*. London: Edward Arnold.

Chatterton, M.R. (1983), 'Police Work and Assault Charges', in M. Punch, ed., *Control in the Police Organization*. Cambridge, MA: MIT Press.

Cheh, M.M. (1996), 'Are Lawsuits an Answer to Police Brutality?', in W.A. Geller and H. Toch, eds, *Police Violence: Understanding and Controlling Police Abuse of Force*. New Haven, CT: Yale University Press.

Chevigny, P. (1995), *Edge of the Knife: Police Violence in the Americas*. New York: New Press.

Christopher, W. (1991), Report of the Independent Commission on the Los Angeles Police Department, Chairman, Warren Christopher. Los Angeles.

Clisby, D. (1990), 'Assistant Division Officer Dick Clisby', in R. Dinnage, ed., *The Ruffian on the Stair: Reflections on Death*. London: Viking.

Coates, R.B. and Miller, A.D. (1974), 'Patrolmen and Addicts: A Study of Police Perception and Police Perception and Police–Citizen Interaction', *Journal of Police Science and Administration*, 2/3: 308–21.

Cruse, D. and Rubin, J. (1973), 'Police Behaviour: Part 1', *Journal of Psychiatry and Law*, 1: 18–19.

Cumming, E., Cumming, I. and Edel, L. (1965), 'Policeman as Philosopher, Guide and Friend', *Social Problems*, 17: 276–86.

Dalley, A.F. (1975), 'University and Non-University Graduated Policemen: A Study of Police Attitudes', *Journal of Police Science and Administration*, 3: 458–68.

Downes, D. (1966), *The Delinquent Solution*. London: Routledge.

Eiser, J.R. (1986), *Social Psychology: Attitudes, Cognitions and Social Behaviour*. Cambridge: Cambridge University Press.

Ericson, R.V. (1982), *Reproducing Order*. Toronto: University of Toronto Press.

Fielding, N. (1984), 'Police Socialization and Police Competence', *British Journal of Sociology*, 35/4: 568–90.

Fielding, N. (1994), 'Cop Canteen Culture', in T. Newburn and E. Stanko, eds, *Just Boys Doing Business: Men, Masculinity and Crime*. London: Routledge.

Fielding, N.G. (1988), *Joining Forces: Police Training, Socialization and Occupational Competence*. London: Routledge.

Fielding, N.G. (1995), *Community Policing*. Oxford: Clarendon.

Fielding, N. and Fielding, J. (1991), 'Police Attitudes to Crime and Punishment: Certainties and Dilemmas', *British Journal of Criminology*, 31/1: 39–53.

Fielding, N. and Fielding, J. (1992), 'A Comparative Minority: Female Recruits to a British Constabulary Force', *Policing and Society*, 2: 205–18.

Finnane, M. (1987), *Policing in Australia: Historical Perspectives*. Kensington, NSW: New South Wales University Press.

Finnane, M. (1990), 'Police Corruption and Police Reform: The Fitzgerald Inquiry in Queensland, Australia', *Policing and Society*, 1/2: 159–71.

Friedrich, R.J. (1980), 'Police Use of Force: Individuals, Situations and Organizations', *Annals of the American Academy of Political and Social Science*, 452: 82–97.

Fyfe, J.J. (1981), 'Who Shoots? A Look at Officer Race and Police Shootings', *Journal of Police Science and Administration*, 9/4: 367–82.

Fyfe, J.J. (1982a), 'Administrative Intervention on Police Shooting Discretion: An Empirical Examination', in J.J. Fyfe, ed., *Readings on Police Use of Deadly Force*. Washington, DC: Police Foundation.

Fyfe, J.J. (1982b), 'Blind Justice: Police Shootings in Memphis', *Journal of Criminal Law and Criminology*, 73: 707–20.

Fyfe, J.J. (1982c), 'Race and Extreme Police–Citizen Violence', in J.J. Fyfe, ed., *Readings on Police Use of Deadly Force*. Washington: Police Foundation.

Genz, J.L. and Lester, D. (1976), 'Authoritarianism in Policemen as a Function of Experience', *Journal of Police Science and Administration*, 4/1: 9–13.

Goldkamp, J.S. (1982), 'Minorities as Victims of Police Shootings: Interpretations of Racial Disproportionality and Police Use of Deadly Force', in J.J. Fyfe, ed., *Readings on Police Use of Deadly Force*. Washington, DC: Police Foundation.

Goldstein, J. (1960), 'Police Discretion Not to Invoke the Criminal Process. Low Visibility Decisions in the Administration of Justice', *Yale Law Journal*, 69/4: 543–94.

Grundlingh, A. (1991), ' "Protectors and Friends of the People"? The South African Constabulary in the Transvaal and the Orange River Colony, 1900–08', in D.M. Anderson and D. Killingray, eds, *Policing the Empire: Government, Authority and Control, 1830–1940*. Manchester: Manchester University Press.

Haney, C., Banks, C. and Zimbardo, P. (1973/1984), 'A Study of Prisoners and Guards in a Simulated Prison', *Naval Research Reviews*, September. Reprinted in E. Aronson, ed., *Readings About the Social Animal*, 4th edn. New York: W.H. Freeman.

Harré, R. and Secord, P. (1972), *The Explanation of Social Behaviour*. Oxford: Blackwell.

Heidensohn, F. (1992), *Women in Control: The Role of Women in Law Enforcement*. Oxford: Oxford University Press.

Hobbs, D. (1988), *Doing the Business: Entrepreneurship, the Working Class and Detectives in the East End of London*. Oxford: Clarendon.

Holdaway, S. (1983), *Inside the British Police*. Oxford: Blackwell.

Holdaway, S. (1996), *The Racialisation of British Policing*. Basingstoke: Macmillan.

Holdaway, S. (1997), 'Constructing and Sustaining "Race" within the Police Workforce', *British Journal of Sociology*, 48/1: 18–34.

Hughes, E.C. (1962), 'Good People and Dirty Work', *Social Problems*, 10/1: 3–11.

Jefferson, T. (1990), *The Case against Paramilitary Policing*, Buckingham: Open University.

Jones, S. (1986), *Policemen and Equality: Formal police v Informal Practice*/ London: Macmillan.

Kappeler, V.E., Sluder, R.D. and Alpert, G.P. (1994), *Forces of Deviance: Understanding the Dark Side of Policing*. Prospect Heights, IL: Waveland.

Kemp, C., Norris, C. and Fielding, N.G. (1992), *Negotiating Nothing: Police Decision-Making in Disputes*. Aldershot: Avebury.

Klockars, C.B. (1985), *The Idea of Police*. Beverly Hills: Sage.

Klockars, C.B. (1996), 'A Theory of Excessive Force and its Control', in W.A. Geller and H. Toch, eds, *Police Violence: Understanding and Controlling Police Abuse of Force*. New Haven, CT: Yale University Press.

Kobler, A.L. (1975a), 'Figures (and Perhaps Some Facts) on Police Killings of Civilians in the United States, 1965–1969,' *Journal of Social Issues*, 31/1: 185–91.

Kobler, A.L. (1975b), 'Police Homicide in a Democracy', *Journal of Social Issues*, 31/1: 163–84.

Kraska, P.B. and Paulsen, D.J. (1997), 'Grounded Research into US Paramilitary Policing: Forging the Iron Fist inside the Velvet Glove', *Policing and Society*, 7/4: 253–70.

La Piere, R.T. (1934), 'Attitudes *vs* Actions', *Social Forces*, 13: 230–7.

Lefkowitz, J. (1973), 'Attitudes of Police towards their Job', in J.R. Snibbe and H.M. Snibbe, eds., *The Urban Policeman in Transition*. Springfield, IL: Charles Thomas.

Lester, D. (1996), 'Officer Attitudes toward Police Use of Force', in W.A. Geller and H. Toch, eds, *Police Violence: Understanding and Controlling Police Abuse of Force*. New Haven, CT: Yale University Press.

Locke, H.G. (1996), 'The Color of Law and the Issue of Color: Race and the Abuse of Police Power', in W.A. Geller and H. Toch, eds, *Police Violence: Understanding and Controlling Police Abuse of Force*. New Haven, CT: Yale University Press.

Manksch, H. (1963), 'Becoming a Nurse: A Selective View', *Annals of the American Academy of Political and Social Science*, 346: 88–98.

Manning, P.K. (1977), *Police Work*. Cambridge, MA: MIT Press.

Manning, P.K. (1980), 'Violence and the Police Role', *Annals of the American Academy of Political and Social Science*, 452: 135–44.

Manning, P.K. (1989), 'Occupational Culture', in *Encyclopedia of Police Science*. New York: Garland.

Manning, P.K. and Van Maanen, J. (1977), 'Rules, Colleagues and Situationally Justified Actions', in P.K. Manning, ed., *Policing: A View from the Street*. New York: Random House.

Marshall, T.H. (1976), *Class, Citizenship and Social Development*. Westport, CT: Greenwood Press.

Martin, S.E. (1979), 'POLICEwomen and PoliceWOMEN: Occupational Role Dilemmas and Choices of Female Officers', *Journal of Police Science and Administration*, 2/3: 314–23.

Martin, S.E. (1995), 'The Interactive Effects of Race and Sex on Women Police Officers', in B.R. Price and N.J. Sokoloff, eds, *The Criminal Justice System and Women: Offenders, Victims and Workers*, 2nd edn. New York: McGraw-Hill.

Matza, D. (1969), *Becoming Deviant*. Englewood Cliffs, NJ: Prentice-Hall.

McConville, M., Sanders, A. and Leng, R. (1991), *The Case for the Prosecution*. London: Routledge.

McConville, M. and Shepherd, D. (1992), *Watching Police, Watching Communities*. London: Routledge.

McNamara, J.H. (1967), 'Uncertainties in Police Work: The Relevance of Police Recruits' Background and Training', in D. Bordua, ed., *The Police: Six Sociological Essays*. New York: John Wiley and Sons.

Menzies, I. (1960), 'A Case Study in the Functioning of Social Systems as a Defense against Anxiety', *Human Relations*, 13: 95–121.

Meyer, M.W. (1982), 'Police Shootings at Minorities: The Case of Los Angeles', in J.J. Fyfe, ed., *Readings on Police Use of Deadly Force*. Washington, DC: Police Foundation.

Milgram, S. (1974), *Obedience to Authority*. London: Tavistock.

Miller, J. and Fry, L. (1976), 'Reexamining Assumption about Education and Professionalism in Law Enforcement', *Journal of Police Science and Administration*, 4: 187–98.

Miyazawa, S. (1992), *Policing in Japan: A Study on Making Crime*, trans. Frank G. Bennett, Jr with John O. Haley. Albany: State University of New York Press.

Morris, P. and Heal, K. (1981), *Crime Control and the Police: A Review of Research*, Home Office Research Study No. 67. London: Home Office.

Morrison, W.R. (1991), 'Imposing the British Way: The Canadian Mounted Police and the Klondike Gold Rush', in D.M. Anderson and D. Killingray, eds, *Policing the Empire: Government, Authority and Control, 1830–1940*. Manchester: Manchester University Press.

Muir, W.K. (1977), *Police: Streetcorner Politicians*. Chicago: Chicago University Press.

Norris, C. (1989), 'Avoiding Trouble: The Patrol Officer's Perception of Encounters with the Public', in M. Weatheritt, ed., *Police Research: Some Future Prospects*. Aldershot: Avebury.

Orne, M.T. (1962), 'On the Social Psychology of the Psychologist Experiment: With Particular Reference to Demand Characteristics and their Implications', *American Psychologist*, 17: 776–83.

Palmer, S.H. (1988), *Police and Protest in England and Ireland, 1780–1850*. Cambridge: Cambridge University Press.

Perez, D.W. and Muir, W.K. (1996), 'Administrative Review of Alleged Police Brutality', in W.A. Geller and H. Toch, eds, *Police Violence: Understanding and Controlling Police Abuse of Force*. New Haven, CT: Yale University Press.

Punch, M. (1979a), *Policing the Inner City*. London: Macmillan.

Punch, M. (1979b), 'The Secret Social Service', in S. Holdaway, ed., *The British Police*. London; Edward Arnold.

Punch, M. (1983), 'Officers and Men: Occupational Culture, Inter-Rank Antagonism and the Investigation of Corruption', ed., *Control in the Police Organization*. Cambridge, MA: MIT Press.

Punch, M. and Naylor, T. (1973), 'The Police: A Social Service', *New Society*, 24/554: 358–61.

Rafky, D.M. (1973), 'Police Race Attitudes and Labelling', *Journal of Police Science and Administration*, 1/1: 65–86.

Reiner, R. (1985), *Politics of the Police*. Hemel Hempstead: Wheatsheaf.

Reiner, R. (1992), *Politics of the Police*, 2nd edn. Hemel Hempstead: Wheatsheaf.

Reiss, A.J. (1980), 'Controlling Police Use of Deadly Force', *Annals of the American Academy of Political and Social Science*, 452: 122–34.

Reuss-Ianni, E. and Ianni, F.A. (1983), 'Street Cops and Management Cops: The Two Cultures of Policing', in M. Punch, ed., *Control in the Police Organization*. Cambridge, MA: MIT Press.

Roberg, R.R. (1978), 'An Analysis of the Relationships among Higher Education, Belief Systems and Job Performance of Patrol Officers', *Journal of Police Science and Administration*, 6: 336–44.

Scripture, A.E. (1997), 'The Sources of Police Culture: Demographic or Environmental Variables?' *Policing and Society*, 7/3: 163–76.

Shearing, C.D. and Ericson, R.V. (1991), 'Culture as Figurative Action', *British Journal of Sociology*, 42/4: 481–506.

Sherman, L.W. (1980), 'Causes of Police Behaviour: The Current State of Quantitative Research', *Journal of Research in Crime and Delinquency*, 17: 69–99.

Sherman, L.W. (1983), 'Reducing Police Gun Use: Critical Events, Administrative Police and Organizational Change', in M. Punch, ed., *Control in the Police Organization*. Cambridge, MA: MIT Press.

Simpson, I.H. (1967), 'Patterns of Socialization into Professions: The Case of the Student Nurse', *Sociological Inquiry*, 37: 47–54.

Skogan, W.G. (1994), *Contacts between Police and Public: Findings from the 1992 British Crime Survey*, Home Office Research Study No. 134. London: HMSO.

Skolnick, J.H. (1966), *Justice without Trial*. New York: John Wiley and Sons.

Skolnick, J.H. and Fyfe, J.J. 1993), *Above the Law: Police and the Excessive Use of Force*. New York: Free Press.

Smith, D.J. and Gray, J. (1983), *Police and People in London*, Vol. 4, *The Police in Action*. London: Policy Studies Institute.

Smith, D., Visher, C.A. and Davidson, L.A. (1984), 'Equity and Discretionary Justice: The Influence of Race on Police Arrest Decisions', *Journal Criminal Law and Criminology*, 75/1: 234–49.

Southgate, P. and Crisp, D. (1993), *Public Satisfaction with Police Services*, Research and Planning Unit Papers No. 72. London: HMSO.

Southgate, P. and Ekblom, P. (1984), *Contacts between Police and Public: Findings from the British Crime Survey*, Home Office Research Study No. 77. London: HMSO.

Southgate, P. and Ekblom, P. (1986), *Police–Public Encounters*. Home Office Research Study No. 90. London: HMSO.

Stevens, A., Ostini, R., Dance, P., Burns, M., Crawford, D.A. and Bammer, G. (1995), 'Police Opinions of a Proposal for Controlled Availability of Heroin in Australia', *Policing and Society*, 5/4: 303–12.

Sykes, G.M. and Matza, D. (1957), 'Techniques of Neutralization', *American Sociological Review*, 22: 664–70.

Sykes, R.E. and Brent, E.E. (1983), *Policing: A Social Behaviourist Perspective*. New Brunswick, NJ: Rutgers University Press.

Takagi, P. (1982), 'A Garrison State in a "Democratic Society" ', in J.J. Fyfe, ed., *Readings on Police use of Deadly Force*. Washington: Police Foundation.

Tennenbaum, A. (1994), 'The Influence of the Garner Decision on Police Use of Deadly Force', *Journal of Criminal Law and Criminology*, 85/1: 241–60.

Townshend, C. (1992), 'Policing Insurgency in Ireland, 1914–23', in D.M. Anderson and D. Killingray, eds, *Policing and Decolonisation: Politics, Nationalism and the Police, 1917–65*. Manchester: Manchester University Press.

Townshend, C. (1993), *Making the Peace: Public Order and Public Security in Modern Britain*. Oxford: Oxford University Press.

Trojanowicz, R.C. (1971), 'The Policeman's Occupational Personality', *Journal of Criminal Law, Criminology and Police Science*, 52/4: 551–9.

Uildriks, N. and van Mastrigt, H. (1991), *Policing Police Violence*. Aberdeen: Aberdeen University Press.

Van Maanen, J. (1973), 'Observations on the Making of Policemen', *Human Organization*, 32/4: 407–18.

Van Maanen, J. (1974), 'Working the Street: A Developmental View of Police Behaviour', in H. Jacob, ed., *The Potential for Reform of Criminal Justice*. Beverly Hills, CA: Sage.

Van Maanen, J. (1975), 'Police Socialization: A Longitudinal Examination of Job Attitudes in an Urban Police Department', *Administrative Science Quarterly*, 20: 207–22.

Waddington, P.A.J. (1991), *The Strong Arm of the Law*. Oxford: Clarendon.

Waddington, P.A.J. (1993), 'Dying in a Ditch: The Use of Police Powers in Public Order', *International Journal of Sociology*, 21/4: 335–53.

Waddington, P.A.J. (1994a) 'Coercion and Accommodation: Policing Public Order after the Public Order Act', *British Journal of Sociology*, 45/3: 367–85.

Waddington, P.A.J. (1994b), *Liberty and Order: Policing Public Order in a Capital City*. London: UCL Press.

Waddington, P.A.J. (1999), *Policing Citizens*. London: UCL Press.

Walklate, S. (1995), 'Equal Opportunities and the Future of Policing', in F. Leishman, B. Loveday and S.P. Savage, eds, *Core Issues in Policing*. London: Longman.

Webdale, N. and Johnson, B. (1997), 'The Policing of Domestic Violence in Rural and Urban Areas: The Voices of Battered Women in Kentucky', *Policing and Society*, 6/4: 297–317.

Weinberger, B. (1995), *The Best Police in the World: An Oral History of English Policing from the 1930s to the 1960s*. Aldershot: Scolar.

White, R. and Alder, C., eds (1994), *The Police and Young People in Australia*. Cambridge: Cambridge University Press.

Worden, R.E. (1989), 'Situational and Attitudinal Explanations of Police Behaviour. A Theoretical Reappraisal and Empirical Reassessment', *Law and Society*, 23/4: 667–711.

Worden, R.E. (1996), 'The Causes of Police Brutality: Theory and Evidence on Police use of Force', in W.A. Geller and H. Toch, eds, *Police Violence: Understanding and Controlling Police Abuse of Force*. New Haven, CT: Yale University Press.

Young, M. (1991), *An Inside Job*. Oxford: Clarendon Press.

# Part D

# Policing strategies

## Introduction

As Chapter 7 by Kelling and Moore noted in Part A, policing in the last quarter of the twentieth century began slowly to move in the direction of problem-solving as a central strategy. Arguably no one was more influential in this process than Herman Goldstein (**23**, 392) whose work on problem-oriented policing has not only influenced practical policing worldwide in the last 30 years but has spawned a variety of cognate policing models during that time. Reflecting on the 'reform era' Goldstein notes that whilst the aim of professionalizing and streamlining the police organization may have been an important and necessary goal, once achieved the reform effort tended not to continue on from the means to the ends of policing – with the impact that a professionalized police department or service might have. The police, he wrote, 'seem to have reached a plateau at which the highest objective to which they aspire is administrative competence'. However, a number of important pressures forced police managers and others to question this attitude, including: a growing financial 'crisis' or, at least, tendency to scrutinize police finances; research findings that questioned the efficacy of certain police tactics; growing consumerism; and resistance to change from within police organizations.

Goldstein's response to these pressures was to suggest that policing needed to develop a greater commitment to systematic analysis of the problems confronting it. This it should do, he argued, by taking much greater care in the process of defining problems (and providing a detailed breakdown of them), by researching the problem – its nature and magnitude – in much greater detail, by exploring alternatives to current approaches to the problem identified (physically, technically, organizationally and in terms of the provision of information, skills and community resources) and greater attention to implementation. Such a focus on problems, he argues, as well as being a logical approach to improving police work, has the added 'political' advantage of being attractive to both citizens and police officers – for the latter not least because it avoids some of the more worrisome challenges to the prevailing police value system – though readers familiar with the literature in Part C of this volume may raise a query as to whether this isn't something of an underestimate of the conservatism of much police culture.

John Eck and William Spelman (**24**, 412) pick up on Goldstein's theme of problem-solving. In illustrating the potential of such an approach they offer two neighbourhood case studies and two non-neighbourhood case studies. Of the neighbourhood problems, one involved a problem of street robbery, the other the virtual abandonment of a local park because of fears of rowdy and sometimes drunken youths who occupied one part of the park. In both cases Eck and Spelman explore the ways in which some elementary research identified – with a greater degree of specificity than previously had appeared possible – the actual source of the problem (poor maintenance and structural conditions leading to considerable fear among elderly, especially female residents, in the former and a shed – the 'treehouse' – where some local youth met to drink and socialize, in the latter). The non-neighbourhood problems ranged from thefts of vehicles from near a shipyard to domestic violence. Their aim is both to demonstrate that problem-solving is a crucial strategy in successful policing and that as a technique it is not confined to local or specific neighbourhood problems. Should such a strategy become standard practice, they argue that it will lead to three other sets of related changes to police departments: the decentralization of decision-making; the reconsideration of the police officer's role and, in particular, much closer working with local communities; and, finally, the realization that such work involves not only greater gains but also increased risks.

In recent times, talk of problem-oriented policing has largely been superceded by the idea of 'community policing'. As is often the case, with such terms, however, it is easy for them to mask as much as they reveal. What precisely is community policing and how should we assess it? Two of the most thoughtful writers on community policing, Wes Skogan and Susan Hartnett, take up this theme (**25**, 428). As they warn, 'community policing is an organizational strategy that redefines the goals of policing, but leaves the means of achieving them to practitioners in the field. It is a process rather than a product'. They suggest that community policing has four general principles. First, organizational decentralization and reoriented patrol work based on police–community dialogue. Secondly, it requires a commitment to problem orientation. Thirdly, it demands that police be responsive to public demands in setting priorities and determining tactics. Finally, it implies a commitment to helping communities solve their own problems. But does it work? The evidence from the Chicago CAPS programme in the 1990s showed some important improvements (though uneven) in citizen involvement and officer 'buy-in'. More positively still the Chicago community policing experiment did appear to have a positive impact on crime problems, on neighbourhood conditions and on police responsiveness – though it appeared not to succeed in involving the local Hispanic community – and Skogan and Hartnett, though noting the difficulty of sustaining such initiatives, are generally positive about the potential of community policing.

Carl Klockars (**26**, 442), by contrast, takes a more critical line arguing that 'the modern movement toward what is currently called "community policing" is best understood as the latest in a fairly long tradition of circumlocutions whose purpose is to conceal, mystify, and legitimate police distribution of non-negotiably coercive force'. Klockars' argument, at heart, is that the community policing movement uses a series of rhetorical devices – 'community', 'decentralization', 'reorientation of patrol', 'civilianizaton' – to produce a romanticized and unrealistic picture of the nature and likely impact of policing. Like militarization, legalization and professionalization before it, community policing, Klockars argues, is a story 'about some very good things we might gladly wish, but which, sadly, cannot be'.

Klockars' chapter is followed by what is by now probably the most famous piece of criminological writing on the policing of neighbourhood problems. Published originally in *The Atlantic Monthly*, James Q. Wilson and George Kelling's 'Broken Windows' (**27**, 460) begins from a conundrum identified in the Newark foot patrol study, namely, that although increased foot patrol didn't appear to reduce crime it did appear to increase local citizens' sense of security. Moving from this, Wilson and Kelling argue that local citizens assign a high value to the importance of public order and that at the community level disorder and crime are inextricably linked. Untended disorder (the unmended broken window) breeds crime: 'serious street crime flourishes in areas in which disorderly behaviour goes unchecked.' The police are key, they argue, to order maintenance. Though local communities may have an important role to play, they cannot do it by themselves. Wilson and Kelling's concluding rallying cry is to suggest that 'above all, we must return to our long-abandoned view that police ought to protect communities as well as individuals'.

'Broken windows' has not only become hugely well known but has also exerted a considerable influence in recent times. This was perhaps most obviously the case in the early to mid-1990s in New York City when Rudy Giuliani was Mayor and his first Commissioner of Police, Bill Bratton, was in post. The policing style adopted by the NYPD at that time, variously and often misleadingly referred to as either 'zero-tolerance policing' or 'quality of life policing' drew on elements of the 'Broken Windows' argument. Bratton's (**28**, 472) description of New York at the time he was appointed is straight out of the Wilson and Kelling manual:

> graffiti, burned out cars and trash seemed to be everywhere ... then as you entered Manhattan you met the unofficial greeter for the City of New York, the Squeegee pest ... Proceeding down Fifth avenue ... unlicensed street peddlers and beggars were everywhere ... This was a city that had stopped caring about itself.

Bratton describes a programme of policing activity covering the hiring of many additional officers, the restructuring of the organization and the introduction of greater authority for, and accountability of, commanding officers, particularly via what became known as Compstat. The result, record declines in crime. Why? The title of his chapter provides the answer: blame the police.

Needless to say, this is a far from an uncontested version of the history of crime and policing in New York in the 1990s. Numerous authors have analysed the crime drop and policing tactics and drawn somewhat different conclusions (Blumstein and Wallman, 2001). Nevertheless, the idea of 'zero-tolerance policing' became one of the most successful criminological commodities of the late twentieth century, finding disciples across Europe, in South America and in Australia. David Dixon (**29**, 483), reviewing the 'New York miracle', casts significant doubt on its relevance to Australian policing, pointing to the very different criminological, cultural and political circumstances in the different jurisdictions. Critical both of much of the approach wrapped up in so-called 'zero tolerance' and of the broken windows philosophy that underpins it, Dixon argues for a 'new policing' to replace old styles and rhetorics – however grandly repackaged.

However contentious the history of so-called zero-tolerance policing, one of the innovations introduced by the NYPD in the 1990s, Compstat, appears to have had a significant impact on policing well beyond New York City. Weisburd and colleagues (**30**, 508) describe the spread of Compstat and seek to assess its impact. They describe Compstat as a 'strategic control system' designed to collect and disseminate information about crime in New York and to help manage the police department's efforts to reduce crime. Local crime data, updated weekly, were used both as a means of designing local solutions and strategies and, via a public meeting, as a means of interrogating precinct commanders and holding them to account. Weisburd *et al.* identify six core characteristics of the NYPD's approach to strategic problem-solving: mission clarification; internal accountability; geographic organization of operational command; organizational flexibility; data-driven problem identification and assessment; and innovative problem-solving tactics. Compstat's association with successful policing strategies in New York has led to spectacular diffusion through the USA with between one fifth of police departments (in the North Central region) to two fifths (in the South) having taken it up within five years of its inception in the NYPD.

Why has Compstat spread so swiftly? Weisburd *et al.* suggest that it is the ability to increase management control over field operations that will have an impact on serious crime that has most attracted police departments. In a critical response to Weisburd *et al.*'s work, Mark Moore (**31**, 530) takes a slightly different view. First, he is more sceptical of the notion that Compstat is at heart a strategic tool. Rather than reorienting the mission and goals of the police organization, he suggests that Compstat reinforces the crime-fighting function and image of policing. Indeed, he argues that Compstat took one element of recent thinking about problem-solving community policing – 'the strand that focused on the relationship among disorder, fear and crime' – and privileged aggressive preventive patrol as the solution to the difficulties identified. The rapid spread of Compstat, he suggests, rests partly on the fact that it fits comfortably with existing policing culture and structures and enables police leaders to be seen to be keeping up with latest developments (irrespective of their efficacy). Not only does Compstat lead to an overemphasis on preventive patrol, he argues, but it 'gives very little attention to what I take to be an important goal of policing, namely, doing justice as well as reducing crime'. The danger, Moore argues, is that in the long run this may lead to less effective policing.

What links problem-oriented policing, community policing and the more recent changes to policing associated with, and in part facilitated by, Compstat? The link is information, and the assumption that the management and utilization of information is at the core of effective modern policing. In this vein, and influenced by contemporary social theory, Ericson and Haggerty (**32**, 550) describe the police as 'first and foremost knowledge workers who think and act within the risk communication systems of other institutions'. This is a very different perspective on knowledge work from that implied in accounts of Compstat. Rather than performing some internal function, Ericson and Haggerty argue that the police are merely a link – and potentially far from the most important link – in a vast communication network. Indeed, in this view 'much of the knowledge about crime is produced for institutions other than criminal justice'. Using Jonathon Simon's notion of 'governing through crime' (Simon, 1997), Ericson and Haggerty outline a picture of policing in which fear and insecurity are utilized as the basis for increased surveillance, further commodification of security technologies and the trade in information about risks.

As such they offer a corrective to what they see as scholarship that unrealistically privileges criminal law enforcement as a core police function and views police work as low in visibility. 'To the contrary', they argue, 'in the context of demands from external institutions, the police engage in numerous kinds of institutionalized publicity that make their work an exercise in high visibility.'

## References

Blumstein, A. and Wallman, J. (2001). 'The recent rise and fall of American Violence', in Blumstein and Wallman (eds) *The Crime Drop in America*. New York: Cambridge University Press.

Simon, J. (1997). 'Governing Through Crime' in G. Fisher and L. Friedman (eds) *The Crime Conundrum*. Boulder, CO: Westview.

# 23. Improving policing: a problem-oriented approach

*Herman Goldstein*

Complaints from passengers wishing to use the Bagnall to Greenfields bus service that 'the drivers were speeding past queues of up to 30 people with a smile and a wave of a hand' have been met by a statement pointing out that 'it is impossible for the drivers to keep their timetable if they have to stop for passengers'.[1]

All bureaucracies risk becoming so preoccupied with running their organizations and getting so involved in their methods of operating that they lose sight of the primary purposes for which they were created. The police seem unusually susceptible to this phenomenon.

One of the most popular new developments in policing is the use of officers as decoys to apprehend offenders in high-crime areas. A speaker at a recent conference for police administrators, when asked to summarize new developments in the field, reported on a sixteen-week experiment in his agency with the use of decoys, aimed at reducing street robberies.

One major value of the project, the speaker claimed, was its contribution to the police department's public image. Apparently, the public was intrigued by the clever, seductive character of the project, especially by the widely publicized demonstrations of the makeup artists' ability to disguise burly officers. The speaker also claimed that the project greatly increased the morale of the personnel working in the unit. The officers found the assignment exciting and challenging, a welcome change from the tedious routine that characterizes so much of regular police work, and they developed a high *esprit de corps*.

The effect on robberies, however, was much less clear. The methodology used and the problems in measuring crime apparently prevented the project staff from reaching any firm conclusions. But it was reported that, of the 216 persons arrested by the unit for robbery during the experiment, more than half would not have committed a robbery, in the judgment of the unit members, if they had not been tempted by the situation presented by the police decoys. Thus, while the total impact of the project remains unclear, it can be said with certainty that the experiment actually increased the number of robberies by over 100 in the sixteen weeks of the experiment.

The account of this particular decoy project (others have claimed greater success) is an especially poignant reminder of just how serious an imbalance there is within the police field between the interest in organizational and procedural matters and the concern for the substance of policing. The assumption, of course, is that the two are related, that improvements in internal management will eventually increase the capacity of the police to meet the objectives for which police agencies are created. But the relationship is not that clear and direct and is increasingly being questioned.

Perhaps the best example of such questioning relates to response time. Tremendous resources were invested during the past decade in personnel, vehicles, communications equipment, and new procedures in order to increase the speed with which the police respond to calls for assistance. Much less attention was given in this same period to what the officer does in handling the variety of problems he confronts on arriving, albeit fast, where he is summoned. Now, ironically, even the value of a quick response is being questioned.[2]

This chapter summarizes the nature of the 'means over ends' syndrome in policing and explores ways of focusing greater attention on the results of policing – on the effect that police efforts have on the problems that the police are expected to handle.

### The 'means over ends' syndrome

Until the late 1960s, efforts to improve policing in this country concentrated almost exclusively on internal management: streamlining the organization, upgrading personnel, modernizing equipment, and establishing more business-like operating procedures. All of the major commentators on the police since the beginning of the century – Leonhard F. Fuld (1909), Raymond B Fosdick (1915), August Vollmer (1936), Bruce Smith (1940), and O.W. Wilson (1950) – stressed the need to improve the organization and management of police agencies. Indeed, the emphasis on internal management was so strong that professional policing was defined primarily as the application of modern management concepts to the running of a police department.

The sharp increase in the demands made on the police in the late 1960s (increased crime, civil rights demonstrations, and political protest).[3] The published findings contained some criticism of the professional model of police organization, primarily because of its impersonal character and failure to respond to legitimate pressures from within the community.[4] Many recommendations were made for introducing a greater concern for the human factors in policing, but the vast majority of the recommendations that emerged from the reassessments demonstrated a continuing belief that the way to improve the police was to improve the organization. Higher recruitment standards, college education for police personnel, reassignment and reallocation of personnel, additional training, and greater mobility were proposed. Thus the management-dominated concept of police reform spread and gained greater stature.

The emphasis on secondary goals – on improving the organization – continues to this day, reflected in the prevailing interests of police administrators, in the factors considered in the selection of police chiefs and the promotion of subordinates, in the subject matter of police periodicals and texts, in the content of recently developed educational programs for the police, and even in the focus of major research projects.

At one time this emphasis was appropriate. When Vollmer, Smith, and Wilson formulated their prescriptions for improved policing, the state of the vast majority of police agencies was chaotic: Personnel were disorganized, poorly equipped, poorly trained, inefficient, lacking accountability, and often corrupt. The first priority was putting the police house in order. Otherwise, the endless crises that are produced by an organization out of control would be totally consuming. Without a minimum level of order and accountability, an agency cannot be redirected – however committed its administrators may be to addressing more substantive matters.

What is troubling is that administrators of those agencies that have succeeded in developing a high level of operating efficiency have not gone on to concern themselves with the end results of their efforts – with the actual impact that their streamlined organizations have on the problems the police are called upon to handle.

The police seem to have reached a plateau at which the highest objective to which they aspire is administrative competence. And, with some scattered exceptions, they seem reluctant to move beyond this plateau – toward creating a more systematic concern for the end product of their efforts. But strong pressures generated by several new developments may now force them to do so.

### 1. The financial crisis

The growing cost of police services and the financial plight of most city governments, especially those under threat of Proposition 13 movements, are making municipal officials increasingly reluctant to appropriate still more money for police service without greater assurance that their investment will have an impact on the problems that the police are expected to handle. Those cities that are already reducing their budgets are being forced to make some of the hard choices that must be made in weighing the impact of such cuts on the nature of the service rendered to the public.

### 2. Research findings

Recently completed research questions the value of two major aspects of police operations – preventive patrol and investigations conducted by detectives.[5] Some police administrators have challenged the findings[6]; others are awaiting the results of replication.[7] But those who concur with the results have begun to search for alternatives, aware of the need to measure the effectiveness of a new response before making a substantial investment in it.

### 3. Growth of a consumer orientation

Policing has not yet felt the full impact of consumer advocacy. As citizens press for improvement in police service, improvement will increasingly be measured in terms of results. Those concerned about battered wives, for example, could not care less whether the police who respond to such calls operate with one or two officers in a car, whether the officers are short or tall, or whether they have a college education. Their attention is on what the police do for the battered wife.

## 4. Questioning the effectiveness of the best-managed agencies

A number of police departments have carried out most, if not all, of the numerous recommendations for strengthening a police organization and enjoy a national reputation for their efficiency, their high standards of personnel selection and training, and their application of modern technology to their operations. Nevertheless, their communities apparently continue to have the same problems as do others with less advanced police agencies.[8]

## 5. Increased resistance to organizational change

Intended improvements that are primarily in the form of organizational change, such as team policing, almost invariably run into resistance from rank-and-file personnel. Stronger and more militant unions have engaged some police administrators in bitter and prolonged fights over such changes.[9] Because the new costs in terms of disruption and discontent are so great, police administrators initiating change will be under increasing pressure to demonstrate in advance that the results of their efforts will make the struggle worthwhile.

Against this background, the exceptions to the dominant concern with the police organization and its personnel take on greater significance. Although scattered and quite modest, a number of projects and training programs carried out in recent years have focused on a single problem that the public expects the police to handle, such as child abuse, sexual assault, arson, or the drunk driver.[10] These projects and programs, by their very nature, subordinate the customary priorities of police reform, such as staffing, management, and equipment, to a concern about a specific problem and the police response to it.

Some of the earliest support for this type of effort was reflected in the crime-specific projects funded by the Law Enforcement Assistance Administration.[11] Communities – not just the police – were encouraged to direct their attention to a specific type of crime and to make those changes in existing operations that were deemed necessary to reduce its incidence. The widespread move to fashion a more effective police response to domestic disturbances is probably the best example of a major reform that has, as its principal objective, improvement in the quality of service delivered, and that calls for changes in organization, staffing, and training only as these are necessary to achieve the primary goal.

Are these scattered efforts a harbinger of things to come? Are they a natural development in the steadily evolving search for ways to improve police operations? Or are they, like the programs dealing with sexual assault and child abuse, simply the result of the sudden availability of funds because of intensified citizen concern about a specific problem? Whatever their origin, those projects that do subordinate administrative considerations to the task of improving police effectiveness in dealing with a specific problem have a refreshing quality to them.

## What is the end product of policing?

To urge a more direct focus on the primary objectives of a police agency requires spelling out these objectives more clearly. But this is no easy task, given the conglomeration of unrelated, ill-defined, and often inseparable jobs that the police are expected to handle.

The task is complicated further because so many people believe that the job of the police is, first and foremost, to enforce the law: to regulate conduct by applying the criminal law of the jurisdiction. One commentator on the police recently claimed: 'We do not say to the police: "Here is the problem. Deal with it." We say: "Here is a detailed code. Enforce it."'[12] In reality, the police job is perhaps most accurately described as dealing with problems.[13] Moreover, enforcing the criminal code is itself only a means to an end – one of several that the police employ in getting their job done.[14] The emphasis on law enforcement, therefore, is nothing more than a continuing preoccupation with means.

Considerable effort has been invested in recent years in attempting to define the police function: inventorying the wide range of police responsibilities, categorizing various aspects of policing, and identifying some of the characteristics common to all police tasks.[15] This work will be of great value in refocusing attention on the end product of policing, but the fact that it is still going on is not cause to delay giving greater attention to substantive matters. It is sufficient, for our purposes here, simply to acknowledge that the police job requires that they deal with a wide range of behavioural and social problems that arise in a community – that the end product of policing consists of dealing with these problems.

By problems, I mean the incredibly broad range of troublesome situations that prompt citizens to turn to the police, such as street robberies, residential burglaries, battered wives, vandalism, speeding cars, runaway children, accidents, acts of terrorism, even fear. These and other similar problems are the essence of police work. They are the reason for having a police agency.

Problems of this nature are to be distinguished from those that frequently occupy police administrators, such as lack of manpower, inadequate supervision, inadequate training, or strained relations with police unions. They differ from these most often identified by operating personnel, such as lack of adequate equipment, frustrations in the prosecution of criminal cases, or inequities in working conditions. And they differ, too, from the problems that have occupied those advocating police reform, such as the multiplicity of police agencies, the lack of lateral entry, and the absence of effective controls over police conduct.

Many of the problems coming to the attention of the police become their responsibility because no other means has been found to solve them. They are the residual problems of society. It follows that expecting the police to solve or eliminate them is expecting too much. It is more realistic to aim at reducing their volume, preventing repetition, alleviating suffering, and minimizing the other adverse effects they produce.

## Developing the overall process

To address the substantive problems of the police requires developing a commitment to a more systematic process for inquiring into these problems. Initially, this calls for identifying in precise terms the problems that citizens look to the police to handle. Once identified, each problem must be explored in great detail. What do we know about the problem? Has it been researched? If so, with what results? What more should we know? Is it a proper concern of government? What authority and resources are available for dealing with it? What is the current police response? In the broadest-ranging search for solutions, what would constitute the most intelligent response? What factors should be considered in choosing from among alternatives? If a new response is adopted, how does one go about evaluating its effectiveness? And finally, what changes, if any, does implementation of a more effective response require in the police organization?

This type of inquiry is not foreign to the police. Many departments conduct rigorous studies of administrative and operational problems. A police agency may undertake a detailed study of the relative merits of adopting one of several different types of uniforms. And it may regularly develop military-like plans for handling special events that require the assignment of large numbers of personnel.[16] However, systematic analysis and planning have rarely been applied to the specific behavioral and social problems that constitute the agency's routine business. The situation is somewhat like that of a private industry that studies the speed of its assembly line, the productivity of its employees, and that nature of its public relations program, but does not examine the quality of its product.

Perhaps the closest police agencies have come to developing a system for addressing substantive problems has been their work in crime analysis. Police routinely analyze information on reported crimes to identify patterns of criminal conduct, with the goal of enabling operating personnel to apprehend specific offenders or develop strategies to prevent similar offenses from occurring. Some police departments have, through the use of computers, developed sophisticated programs to analyze reported crimes.[17] Unfortunately, these analyses are almost always put to very limited use – to apprehend a professional car thief or to deter a well-known cat burglar – rather than serving as a basis for rethinking the overall police response to the problem of car theft or cat burglaries. Nevertheless, the practice of planning operational responses based on an analysis of hard data, now a familiar concept to the police, is a helpful point of reference in advocating development of more broadly based research and planning.

The most significant effort to use a problem orientation for improving police responses was embodied in the crime-specific concept initiated in California in 1971[18] and later promoted with LEAA funds throughout the country. The concept was made an integral part of the anticrime program launched in eight cities in January 1972, aimed at bringing about reductions in five crime categories: murder, rape, assault, robbery, and burglary.[19] This would have provided an excellent opportunity to develop and test the concept, were it not for the commitment that this politically motivated program carried to achieving fast and dramatic results: a 5 percent reduction in each category in two years and a 20 percent reduction in five years. These rather naïve, unrealistic goals and the emphasis on quantifying the results placed a heavy shadow over the program from the outset. With the eventual abandonment of the projects, the crime-specific concept seems to have lost ground as well. However, the national evaluation of the program makes it clear that progress was made, despite the various pressures, in planning a community's approach to the five general crime categories. The 'crime-oriented planning, implementation and evaluation' process employed in all eight cities had many of the elements one would want to include in a problem-oriented approach to improving police service.[20]

## Defining problems with greater specificity

The importance of defining problems more precisely becomes apparent when one reflects on the long-standing practice of using overly broad categories to describe police business. Attacking police problems under a categorical heading – 'crime' or 'disorder', 'delinquency', or even 'violence' – is bound to be futile. While police business is often further subdivided by means of the labels tied to the criminal code, such as robbery, burglary, and theft, these are not adequate, for several reasons.

First, they frequently mark diverse forms of behavior. Thus, for example, incidents classified under 'arson' might include fires set by teenagers as a form of vandalism, fires set by persons suffering severe psychological problems, fires set for the purpose of destroying evidence of a crime, fires set by persons (or their hired agents) to collect insurance, and fires set by organized criminal interests to intimidate. Each type of incident poses a radically different problem for the police.

Second, if police depend heavily on categories of criminal offenses to define problems of concern to them, others may be misled to believe that, if a given form of behaviour is not criminal, it is of no concern to the police. This is perhaps best reflected in the proposals for decriminalizing prostitution, gambling, narcotic use, vagrancy, and public intoxication. The argument, made over and over again, is that removing the criminal label will reduce the magnitude and complexity of the police function, freeing personnel to work on more serious matters and ridding the police of some of the negative side effects, such as corruption, that these problems produce. But decriminalization does not relieve the police of responsibility. The public expects drunks to be picked up if only because they find their presence on the street annoying or because they feel that the government has an obligation to care for persons who cannot care for themselves. The public expects prostitutes who solicit openly on the streets to be stopped, because such conduct is offensive to innocent passersby, blocks pedestrian or motor traffic, and contributes to the deterioration of a neighbourhood. The problem is a problem for the police whether or not it is defined as a criminal offense.

Finally, use of offense categories as descriptive of police problems implies that the police role is restricted to arresting and prosecuting offenders. In fact, the police job is much broader, extending, in the case of burglary, to encouraging citizens to lock their premises more securely, to eliminating some of the conditions that might attract potential burglars, to counselling burglary victims on ways they can avoid similar attacks in the future, and to recovering and returning burglarized property.

Until recently, the police role in regard to the crime of rape was perceived primarily as responding quickly when a report of a rape was received, determining whether a rape had really occurred (given current legal definitions), and then attempting to identify and apprehend the perpetrator. Today, the police role has been radically redefined to include teaching women how to avoid attack, organizing transit programs to provide safe movement in areas where there is a high risk of attack, dealing with the full range of sexual assault not previously covered by the narrowly drawn rape statutes, and – perhaps most important – providing needed care and support to the rape victim to minimize the physical and mental damage resulting from such an attack. Police are now concerned with sexual assault not simply because they have a direct role in the arrest and prosecution of violators, but also because sexual assault is a community problem which the police and others can affect in a variety of ways.

It seems desirable, at least initially in the development of a problem-solving approach to improved policing, to press for as detailed a breakdown of problems as possible. In addition to distinguishing different forms of behavior and the apparent motivation, as in the case of incidents commonly grouped under the heading of 'arson', it is helpful to be much more precise regarding locale and time of day, the type of people involved, and the type of people victimized. Different combinations of these variables may present different problems, posing different policy questions and calling for radically different solutions.[21]

For example, most police agencies already separate the problem of purse snatching in which force is used from the various other forms of conduct commonly grouped under robbery. But an agency is likely to find it much more helpful to go further – to pinpoint, for example, the problem of teenagers snatching the purses of elderly women waiting for buses in the downtown section of the city during the hours of early darkness. Likewise, a police agency might find it helpful to isolate the robberies of grocery stores that are open all night and are typically staffed by a lone attendant; or the theft of vehicles by a highly organized group engaged in the business of transporting them for sale in another jurisdiction; or the problem posed by teenagers who gather around hamburger stands each evening to the annoyance of neighbors, customers, and management. Eventually, similar problems calling for similar responses may be grouped together, but one cannot be certain that they are similar until they have been analyzed.

In the analysis of a given problem, one may find, for example, that the concern of the citizenry is primarily fear of attack, but the fear is not warranted, given the pattern of actual offenses. Where this situation becomes apparent, the police have two quite different problems: to deal more effectively with the actual incidents where they occur, and to respond to the groundless fears. Each calls for a different response.

The importance of subdividing problems was dramatically illustrated by the recent experience of the New York City Police Department in its effort to deal more constructively with domestic disturbances. An experimental program, in which police were trained to use mediation techniques, was undertaken with obvious public support. But, in applying the mediation techniques, the department apparently failed to distinguish sufficiently those cases in which wives were repeatedly subject to physical abuse. The aggravated nature of the latter cases resulted in a suit against the department in which the plaintiffs argued that the police are mandated to enforce the law when *any* violation comes to their attention. In the settlement, the department agreed that its personnel would not attempt to reconcile the parties or to mediate when a felony was committed.[22] However, the net effect of the suit is likely to be more far reaching. The vulnerability of the department to criticism for not having dealt more aggressively with the aggravated cases has dampened support – in New York and elsewhere – for the use of alternatives to arrest in less serious cases, even though alternatives still appear to represent the more intelligent response.

One of the major values in subdividing police business is that it gives visibility to some problems which have traditionally been given short shrift, but which warrant more careful attention. The seemingly minor problem of noise, for example, is typically buried in the mass of police business lumped together under such headings as 'complaints', 'miscellaneous', 'noncriminal incidents', or 'disturbances'. Both police officers and unaffected citizens would most likely be inclined to rank it at the bottom in any list of problems. Yet the number of complaints about noise is high in many communities – in fact, noise is probably among the most common problems brought by the public to the police.[23] While some of those complaining may be petty or unreasonable, many are seriously aggrieved and justified in their appeal for relief: Sleep is lost, schedules are disrupted, mental and emotional problems are aggravated. Apartments may become uninhabitable. The elderly woman living alone, whose life has been made miserable by inconsiderate neighbors, is not easily convinced that the daily intrusion into her life of their noise is any less serious than other forms of intrusion. For this person, and for many like her, improved policing would mean a more effective response to the problem of the noise created by her neighbors.

### Researching the problem

Without a tradition for viewing in sufficiently discrete terms the various problems, making up the police job, gathering even the most basic information about a specific problem – such as complaints about noise – can be extremely difficult.

First, the magnitude of the problem and the various forms in which it surfaces must be established. One is inclined to turn initially to police reports for such information. But overgeneralization in categorizing incidents, the impossibility of separating some problems, variations in the reporting practices of the community, and inadequacies in report writing seriously limit their value for purposes of obtaining a full picture of the problem. However, if used cautiously, some of the information in police files may be helpful. Police agencies routinely collect and store large amounts of data, even though they may not use them to evaluate the effectiveness of their responses. Moreover, if needed information is available, often it can be collected expeditiously in a well-managed department, owing to the high degree of centralized control of field operations.

How does one discover the nature of the current police response? Administrators and their immediate subordinates are not a good source. Quite naturally, they have a desire to provide an answer that reflects well on the agency, is consistent with legal requirements, and meets the formal expectations of both the public and other agencies that might have a responsibility relating to the problem. But even if these concerns did not color their answers, top administrators are often so far removed from street operations, in both distance and time, that they would have great difficulty describing current responses accurately.

Inquiry, then, must focus on the operating level. But mere questioning of line officers is not likely to be any more productive. We know from the various efforts to document police activity in the field that there is often tremendous variation in the way in which different officers respond to the same type of incident.[24] Yet the high value placed on uniformity and on adhering to formal requirements and the pressures from peers inhibit officers from candidly discussing the manner in which they respond to the multitude of problems they handle – especially if the inquiry comes from outside the agency. But one cannot afford to give up at this point, for the individualized practices of police officers and the vast amount of knowledge they acquire about the situations they handle, taken together, are an extremely rich resource that is too often overlooked by those concerned about improving the quality of police services. Serious research into the problems police handle requires observing police officers over a period of time. This means accompanying them as they perform their regular assignments and cultivating the kind of relationship that enables them to talk candidly about the way in which they handle specific aspects of their job.

The differences in the way in which police respond, even in dealing with relatively simple matters, may be significant. When a runaway child is reported, one officer may limit himself to obtaining the basic facts. Another officer, sensing as much of a responsibility for dealing with the parents' fears as for finding the child and looking out for the child's interests, may endeavor to relieve the parents' anxiety by providing information about the runaway problem and about what they might expect. From the standpoint of the consumers – in this case, the parents – the response of the second officer is vastly superior to that of the first.

In handling more complicated matters, the need to improvise has prompted some officers to develop what appear to be unusually effective ways of dealing with specific problems. Many officers develop a unique understanding of problems that frequently come to their attention, learning to make important distinctions among different forms of the same problem and becoming familiar with the many complicating factors that are often present. And they develop a feel for what, under the circumstances, constitute the most effective responses. After careful evaluation, these types of responses might profitably be adopted as standard for an entire police agency. If the knowledge of officers at the operating level were more readily available, it might be useful to those responsible for drafting crime-related legislation. Many of the difficulties in implementing recent changes in statutes relating to sexual assault, public drunkenness, drunk driving, and child abuse could have been avoided had police expertise been tapped.

By way of example, if a police agency were to decide to explore the problem of noise, the following questions might be asked. What is the magnitude of the problem as reflected by the number of complaints received? What is the source of the complaints: industry, traffic, groups of people gathered outdoors, or neighbors? How do noise complaints from residents break down between private dwellings and apartment houses? How often are the police summoned to the same location? How often are other forms of misconduct, such as fights, attributable to conflicts over noise? What is the responsibility of a landlord or an apartment house manager regarding noise complaints? What do the police now do in responding to such complaints? How much of the police procedure has been thought through and formalized? What is the authority of the police in such situations? Is it directly applicable or must they lean on somewhat nebulous authority, such as threatening to arrest for disorderly conduct or for failure to obey a lawful order, if the parties fail to quiet down? What works in police practice and what does not work? Are specific officers recognized as more capable of handling such complaints? If so, what makes them more effective? Do factors outside the control of a police agency influence the frequency with which complaints are received? Are noise complaints from apartment dwellers related to the manner in which the buildings are constructed? And what influence, if any, does the relative effectiveness of the police in handling noise complaints have on the complaining citizen's willingness to cooperate with the police in dealing with other problems, including criminal conduct traditionally defined as much more serious?

Considerable knowledge about some of the problems with which the police struggle has been generated outside police agencies by criminologists, sociologists, psychologists, and psychiatrists. But as has been pointed out frequently, relatively few of these findings have influenced the formal policies and operating decisions of practitioners.[25] Admittedly, the quality of many such studies is poor. Often the practitioner finds it difficult to draw out from the research its significance for his operations. But most important, the police have not needed to employ these studies because they have not been expected to address specific problems in a systematic manner. If the police were pressured to examine in great detail the problems they are expected to handle, a review of the literature would become routine. If convinced that research findings had practical value, police administrators would develop into more sophisticated users of such research; their responsible criticism could, in turn, contribute to upgrading the quality and usefulness of future research efforts.

## Exploring alternatives

After the information assembled about a specific problem is analyzed, a fresh, uninhibited search should be made for alternative responses that might be an improvement over what is currently being done. The nature of such a search will differ from past efforts in that, presumably, the problem itself will be better defined and understood, the commitment to past approaches (such as focusing primarily on the identification and prosecution of offenders) will be shelved temporarily, and the search will be much broader, extending well beyond the present or future potential of just the police.

But caution is in order. Those intent on improving the operations of the criminal justice system (by divesting it of some of its current burdens) and those who are principally occupied with improving the operating efficiency of police agencies frequently recommend that the problem simply be shifted to some other agency of government or to the private sector. Such recommendations often glibly imply that a health department or a social work agency, for example, is better equipped to handle the problem. Experience over the past decade, however, shows that this is rarely the case.[26] Merely shifting responsibility for the problem, without some assurance that more adequate provisions have been made for dealing with it, achieves nothing.

Police in many jurisdictions, in a commendable effort to employ alternatives to the criminal justice system, have arranged to make referrals to various social, health, and legal agencies. By tying into the services provided by the whole range of other helping agencies in the community, the police in these cities have taken a giant step toward improving the quality of their response. But there is a great danger that referral will come to be an end in itself, that the police and others advocating the use of such a system will not concern themselves adequately with the consequences of referral. If referral does not lead to reducing the citizens' problem, nothing will have been gained by this change. It may even cause harm: Expectations that are raised and not fulfilled may lead to further frustration; the original problem may, as a consequence, be compounded; and the resulting bitterness about government services may feed the tensions that develop in urban areas.

The search for alternatives obviously need not start from scratch. There is much to build on. Crime prevention efforts of some police agencies and experiments with developing alternatives to the criminal justice system and with diverting cases from the system should be reassessed for their impact on specific problems; those that appear to have the greatest potential should be developed and promoted.[27] Several alternatives should be explored for each problem.

### 1. Physical and technical changes

Can the problem be reduced or eliminated through physical or technical changes? Some refer to this as part of 'reducing opportunities' or 'target hardening'. Extensive effort has already gone into reducing, through urban design, factors that contribute to behavior requiring police attention.[28] Improved locks on homes and cars, the requirement of exact fares on buses,[29] and the provision for mailing social security checks directly to the recipients' banks exemplify recent efforts to control crime through this alternative.

What additional physical or technical changes might be made that would have an effect on the problem? Should such changes be mandatory, or can they be voluntary? What incentives might be offered to encourage their implementation?

### 2. Changes in the provision of government services

Can the problem be alleviated by changes in other government services? Some of the most petty but annoying problems the police must handle originate in the policies, operating practices, and inadequacies of other public agencies: the scattering of garbage because of delays in collection, poor housing conditions because of lax code enforcement, the interference with traffic by children playing because they have not been provided with adequate playground facilities, the uncapping of hydrants on hot summer nights because available pools are closed. Most police agencies long ago developed procedures for relat-ing reports on such conditions to the appropriate government service. But relatively few police agencies see their role as pressing for changes in policies and operations that would eliminate the recurrence of the same problems. Yet the police are the only people who see and who must become responsible for the collective negative consequences of current policies.

### 3. Conveying reliable information

What many people want, when they turn to the police with their problems, is simply reliable information.[30] The tenant who is locked out by his landlord for failure to pay the rent wants to know his rights to his property. The car owner whose license plates are lost or stolen wants to know what reporting obligations he has, how he goes about replacing the plates, and whether he can drive his car in the meantime. The person who suspects his neighbors of abusing their child wants to know whether he is warranted in reporting the matter to the police. And the person who receives a series of obscene telephone calls wants to know what can be done about them. Even if citizens do not ask specific questions, the best response the police can make to many requests for help is to provide accurate, concise information.

### 4. Developing new skills among police officers

The greatest potential for improvement in the handling of some problems is in providing police officers with new forms of specialized training. This is illustrated by several recent developments. For example, the major component in the family-crisis intervention projects launched all over the country is instruction of police officers in the peculiar skills required to de-escalate highly emotional family quarrels. First aid training for police is being expanded, consistent with the current trend toward greater use of paramedics. One unpleasant task faced by the police, seldom noted by outsiders, it notifying families of the death of a family member. Often, this problem is handled poorly. In 1976, a film was made specifically to demonstrate how police should carry out this responsibility.[31] Against this background of recent developments, one should ask whether specialized training can bring about needed improvement in the handling of each specific problem.

## 5.  New forms of authority

Do the police need a specific, limited form of authority which they do not now have? If the most intelligent response to a problem, such as a person causing a disturbance in a bar, is to order the person to leave, should the police be authorized to issue such an order, or should they be compelled to arrest the individual in order to stop the disturbance? The same question can be asked about the estranged husband who has returned to his wife's apartment or about the group of teenagers annoying passersby at a street corner. Police are called upon to resolve these common problems, but their authority is questionable unless the behavior constitutes a criminal offense. And even then, it may not be desirable to prosecute the offender. Another type of problem is presented by the intoxicated person who is not sufficiently incapacitated to warrant being taken into protective custody, but who apparently intends to drive his car. Should a police officer have the authority to prevent the person from driving by temporarily confiscating the car keys or, as a last resort, by taking him into protective custody? Or must the officer wait for the individual to get behind the wheel and actually attempt to drive and then make an arrest? Limited specific authority may enable the police to deal more directly and intelligently with a number of comparable situations.

## 6.  Developing new community resources

Analysis of a problem may lead to the conclusion that assistance is needed from another government agency. But often the problem is not clearly within the province of an existing agency, or the agency may be unaware of the problem or, if aware, without the resources to do anything about it. In such cases, since the problem is likely to be of little concern to the community as a whole, it will probably remain the responsibility of the police, unless they themselves take the initiative, as a sort of community ombudsman, in getting others to address it.

A substantial percentage of all police business involves dealing with persons suffering mental illness. In the most acute cases, where the individual may cause immediate harm to himself or others, the police are usually authorized to initiate an emergency commitment. Many other cases that do not warrant hospitalization nevertheless require some form of attention. The number of these situations has increased dramatically as the mental health system has begun treating more and more of its patients in the community. If the conduct of these persons, who are being taught to cope with the world around them, creates problems for others or exceeds community tolerance, should they be referred back to a mental health agency? Or, because they are being encouraged to adjust to the reality of the community, should they be arrested if their behavior constitutes a criminal offense? How are the police to distinguish between those who have never received any assistance, and who should therefore be referred to a mental health agency, and those who are in community treatment? Should a community agency establish services for these persons comparable to the crisis-intervention services now offered by specially organized units operating in some communities?

Such crisis-intervention units are among a number of new resources that have been established in the past few years for dealing with several long-neglected problems; detoxification centers for those incapacitated by alcohol, shelters and counseling for runaways, shelters for battered wives, and support services for the victims of sexual assault. Programs are now being designed to provide a better response to citizen disputes and grievances, another long-neglected problem. Variously labeled, these programs set up quasi-judicial forums that are intended to be inexpensive, easily accessible, and geared to the specific needs of their neighborhoods. LEAA has recently funded three such experimental programs, which they call Neighborhood Justice Centers.[32] These centers will receive many of their cases from the police.

Thus, the pattern of creating new services that bear a relationship with police operations is now well established, and one would expect that problem-oriented policing will lead to more services in greater variety.

### 7. Increased regulation

Can the problem be handled through a tightening of regulatory codes? Where easy access to private premises is a factor, should city building codes be amended to require improved lock systems? To reduce the noise problem, should more soundproofing be required in construction? The incidence of shoplifting is determined, in part, by the number of salespeople employed, the manner in which merchandize is displayed, and the use made of various anti-shoplifting devices. Should the police be expected to combat shoplifting without regard to the merchandizing practices by a given merchant, or should merchants be required by a 'merchandizing code' to meet some minimum standards before they can turn to the police for assistance?

### 8. Increased use of city ordinances

Does the problem call for some community sanction less drastic than a criminal sanction? Many small communities process through their local courts, as ordinance violations, as many cases of minor misconduct as possible. Of course, this requires that the community have written ordinances, usually patterned after the state statutes, that define such misconduct. Several factors make this form of processing desirable for certain offenses: It is less formal than criminal action; physical detention is not necessary; cases may be disposed of without a court appearance; the judge may select from a wide range of alternative penalties; and the offender is spared the burden of a criminal record. Some jurisdictions now use a system of civil forfeitures in proceeding against persons found to be in possession of marijuana, though the legal status of the procedure is unclear in those statutes define possession as criminal and call for a more severe fine or for imprisonment.

### 9. Use of zoning

Much policing involves resolving disputes between those who have competing interests in the use made of a given sidewalk, street, park, or neighborhood. Bigger and more basic conflicts in land use were resolved long ago by zoning, a concept that is now firmly established. Recently, zoning has been used by a number of cities to limit the pornography stores and adult movie houses in a given area. And at least one city has experimented with the opposite approach, creating an adult entertainment zone with the hope of curtailing the spread of such establishments and simplifying the management of attendant problems. Much more experimentation is needed before any judgment can be made as to the value of zoning in such situations.

## Implementing the process

A fully developed process for systematically addressing the problems that make up police business would call for more than the three steps just explored – defining the problem, researching it, and exploring alternatives. I have focused on these three because describing them may be the most effective way of communicating the nature of a problem-oriented approach to improving police service. A number of intervening steps are required to fill out the processes: methods for evaluating the effectiveness of current responses, procedures for choosing from among available alternatives, means of involving the community in the decision-making, procedures for obtaining the approval of the municipal officials to whom the police are formally accountable, methods for obtaining any additional funding that may be necessary, adjustments in the organization and staffing of the agency that may be required to implement an agreed-upon change, and methods for evaluating the effectiveness of the change.

How does a police agency make the shift to problem-oriented policing? Ideally, the initiative will come from police administrators. What is needed is not a single decision implementing a specific program or a single memorandum announcing a unique way of running the organization. The concept represents a new way of looking at the process of improving police functioning. It is a way of thinking about the police and their function that, carried out over an extended period, would be reflected in all that the administrator does: in the relationship with personnel, in the priorities he sets in his own work schedule, in what he focuses on in addressing community groups, in the choice of training curriculums, and in the questions raised with local and state legislators. Once introduced, this orientation would affect subordinates, gradually filter through the rest of the organization, and reach other administrators and agencies as well.

An administrator's success will depend heavily, in particular, on the use made of planning staff, for systematic analysis of substantive problems requires developing a capacity within the organization to collect and analyze data and to conduct evaluations of the effectiveness of police operations. Police planners (now employed in significant numbers) will have to move beyond their traditional concern with operating procedures into what might best be characterized as 'product research'.

The police administrator who focuses on the substance of policing should be able to count on support from others in key positions in the police field. Colleges with programs especially designed for police personnel may exert considerable leadership through their choice of offerings and through the subject matter of individual courses. In an occupation in which so much deference is paid to the value of a college education, if college instructors reinforce the impression that purely administrative matters are the most important issues in policing, police personnel understandably will not develop their interests beyond this concern.

Likewise, the LEAA, its state and local offspring, and other grant-making organizations have a unique opportunity to draw the attention of operating personnel to the importance of addressing substantive problems. The manner in which these organizations invest their funds sends a strong message to the police about what is thought to be worthwhile.

## Effect on the organization

In the context of this reordering of police priorities, efforts to improve the staffing, management, and procedures of police agencies must continue.

Those who have been strongly committed to improving policing through better administration and organization may be disturbed by any move to subordinate their interests to a broader concern with the end product of policing. However, a problem-oriented approach to police improvement may actually contribute in several important ways to achieving their objectives.

The approach calls for the police to take greater initiative in attempting to deal with problems rather than resign themselves to living with them. It calls for tapping police expertise. It calls for the police to be more aggressive partners with other public agencies. These changes, which would place the police in a much more positive light in the community, would also contribute significantly to improving the working environment within a police agency – an environment that suffers much from the tendency of the police to assume responsibility for problems which are insolvable or ignored by others. And an improved working environment increases, in turn, the potential for recruiting and keeping qualified personnel and for bringing about needed organizational change.

Focusing on problems, because it is a practical and concrete approach, is attractive to both citizens and the police. By contrast, some of the most frequent proposals for improving police operations, because they do not produce immediate and specifically identifiable results, have no such attraction. A problem-oriented approach, with its greater appeal, has the potential for becoming a vehicle through which long-sought organizational change might be more effectively and more rapidly achieved.

Administrative rule-making, for example, has gained considerable support from policy makers and some police administrators as a way of structuring police discretion, with the expectation that applying the concept would improve the quality of the decisions made by the police in the field. Yet many police administrators regard administrative rule-making as an idea without practical significance. By contrast, police administrators are usually enthusiastic if invited to explore the problem of car theft or vandalism. And within such exploration, there is the opportunity to demonstrate the value of structuring police discretion in responding to reports of vandalism and car theft. Approached from this practical point of view, the concept of administrative rule-making is more likely to be implemented.

Long-advocated changes in the structure and operations of police agencies have been achieved because of a concentrated concern with a given problem: The focus on the domestic disturbance, originally in New York and now elsewhere, introduced the generalist–specialist concept that has enabled many police agencies to make more effective use of their personnel; the problem in controlling narcotics and the high mobility of drug sellers motivated police agencies in many metropolitan areas to pool their resources in special investigative units, thereby achieving in a limited way one of the objectives of those who have urged consolidation of police agencies; and the recent interest in the crime of rape has resulted in widespread backing for the establishment of victim-support programs. Probably the support for any of these changes could not have been generated without the problem-oriented context in which they have been advocated.

An important factor contributing to their successes is that a problem-oriented approach to improvement is less likely to be seen as a direct challenge to the police establishment and the prevailing police value system. As a consequence, rank-and-file personnel do not resist and subvert the resulting changes. Traditional programs to improve the police – labeled as efforts to 'change', 'upgrade' or 'reform' the police or to 'achieve minimum standards' – require that police officers openly acknowledge their own deficiencies. Rank-and-file officers are much more likely to support an innovation that is cast in the form of a new response to an old problem – a problem with which they have struggled for many years and which they would like to see handled more effectively. It may be that addressing the quality of the police product will turn out to be the most effective way of achieving the objectives that have for so long been the goal of police reform.

*From Herman Goldstein, 'Improving policing: a problem-oriented approach', in* Crime and Delinquents, *Vol. 25, April 1979, pp 236–58.*

## Notes

1   Newspaper report from the Midlands of England, cited in Patrick Ryan, 'Get Rid of the People, and the System Runs Fine', *Smithsonian*, September 1977, p. 140.
2   The recent study in Kansas City found that the effect of response time on the capacity of the police to deal with crime was negligible, primarily because delays by citizens in reporting crimes make the minutes saved by the police insignificant. See Kansas City, Missouri, Police Department, *Response Time Analysis*, Executive Summary (Kansas City, 1977).
3   See President's Commission on Law Enforcement and Administration of Justice, *The Challenge of Crime in a Free Society* (Washington, D.C.: Govt. Printing Office, 1967); National Advisory Commission on Civil Disorders, *Report of the National Advisory Commission on Civil Disorders* (Washington, D.C.: Govt. Printing Office, 1968); National Commission on the Causes and Prevention of Violence. *To Establish Justice, to Insure Domestic Tranquility*, Final Report (Washington, D.C.: Govt. Printing Office, 1969); President's Commission on Campus Unrest, *Report of the President's Commission on Campus Unrest* (Washington, D.C.: Govt. Printing Office, 1970); and National Advisory Commission on Criminal Justice Standards and Goals, *Police* (Washington, D.C.: Govt. Printing Office, 1973).
4   See, for example, National Advisory Commission on Civil Disorders, *Report*, p. 158.
5   George L. Kelling *et al.*, *The Kansas City Preventive Patrol Experiment: A Summary Report* (Washington, D.C.: Police Foundation, 1974); and Peter W. Greenwood *et al.*, *The Criminal Investigation Process*; 3 vols. (Santa Monica, Calif.: Rand Corporation, 1976).

6 For questioning by a police administrator of the findings of the Kansas City Preventive Patrol Project, see Edward M. Davis and Lyle Knowles, 'A Critique of the Report: An Evaluation of the Kansas City Preventive Patrol Equipment', *Police Chief*, June 1975, pp. 22–7. For a review of the Rand Study on detectives, see Daryl F. Gates and Lyle Knowles, 'An Evaluation of the Rand Corporation's Analysis of the Criminal Investigation Process', *Police Chief*, July 1976, p. 20. Each of the two papers is followed by a response from the authors of the original studies. In addition, for the position of the International Association of Chiefs of Police on the results of the Kansas City project, see 'IACP Position Paper on the Kansas City Preventive Patrol Experiment', *Police Chief*, September 1975, p. 16.

7 The National Institute of Law Enforcement and Criminal Justice is sponsoring a replication of the Kansas City Preventive Patrol Experiment and is supporting further explorations of the criminal investigation process. See National Institute of Law Enforcement and Criminal Justice, *Program Plan, Fiscal Year 1978* (Washington, D.C.: Govt. Printing Office, 1977), p. 12.

8 Admittedly, precise appraisals and comparisons are difficult. For [...] an examination by the press of one department that has enjoyed a reputation for good management, see 'The LAPD: how Good is it?' *Los Angeles Times*, Dec. 18, 1977.

9 Examples of cities in which police unions recently have fought vigorously to oppose innovations introduced by police administrators are Boston, Massachusetts, and Troy, New York.

10 These programs are reflected in the training opportunities routinely listed in such publications as *Police Chief*, *Criminal Law Reporter*, *Law Enforcement News*, and *Crime Control Digest*, and by the abstracting service of the National Criminal Justice Reference Center.

11 See, for example, National Institute of Law Enforcement and Criminal Justice, Law Enforcement Assistance Administration, 'Planning Guidelines and Program to Reduce Crime', mimeographed (Washington, D.C., 1972), pp. vi–xii. For a discussion of the concept, see Paul K. Wormeli and Steve E. Kolodney, 'The Crime-Specific Model: A New Criminal Justice Perspective', *Journal of Research in Crime and Delinquency*, January 1972, pp. 54–65.

12 Ronald J. Allen, 'The Police and Substantive Rulemaking Reconciling Principle and Expediency', *University of Pennsylvania Law Review*, November 1976, p. 97.

13 Egon Bittner comes close to this point of view when he describes police functioning as applying immediate solutions to an endless array of problems. See Egon Bittner, 'Florence Nightingale in Pursuit of Willie Sutton', in *The Potential for Reform of Criminal Justice*, Herbert Jacob, ed. (Beverly Hills, Calif.: Sage, 1974), p. 30. James Q. Wilson, *Varieties of Police Behavior: The Management of Law and Order in Eight Communities* (Cambridge, Mass.: Harvard University Press, 1968), p. 31.

14 I develop this point in an earlier work. See Herman Goldstein, *Policing a Free Society* (Cambridge, Mass.: Ballinger, 1977), pp. 30, 34–5.

15 In the 1977 book I presented a brief summary of these studies. Ibid., pp. 26–8.

16 For a [...] description of the concept of planning and research as it has evolved in police agencies, see O.W. Wilson and Roy C. McLaren, *Police Administration*, 4th ed. (New York: McGraw-Hill, 1977), pp. 157–81.

17 For examples, see National Institute of Law Enforcement and Criminal Justice, *Police Crime Analysis Unit Handbook* (Washington, D.C.: Govt. Printing Office, 1973), pp. 90–2, 113–21.

18 For a brief description, see Joanne W. Rockwell, 'Crime Specific ... an Answer?' *Police Chief*, September 1972, p. 38.

19 The program is described in Eleanor Chelimsky, *High Impact Anti-Crime Program*, Final Report, vol. 2 (Washington, D.C.: Govt. Printing Office, 1976), pp. 19–38.

20 Ibid., pp. 145–50, 418–21.

21 For an excellent example of what is needed, see the typology of vandalism developed by the British sociologist, Stanley Cohen, quoted in Albert M. Williams, Jr., 'Vandalism', *Management Information Service Report* (Washington, D.C.: International City Management Association, May 1976), pp. 1–2. Another excellent example of an effort to break down a problem of concern to the police – in this case, heroin – is found in Mark Harrison Moore, *Buy and Bust: The Effective Regulation of an Illicit Market in Heroin* (Lexington Books, 1977), p. 83.

22 See Bruno *v.* Codd, 90 Misc. 2d 1047, 396 N.Y.S.2d 974 (1977), finding a cause of action against the New York City Police Department for failing to protect battered wives. On June 26, 1978, the city agreed to a settlement with the plaintiffs in which it committed the police to arrest in all cases in which 'there is reasonable cause to believe that a husband has committed a felony against his wife and/or has violated an Order of Protection or Temporary Order of Protection'. See Consent Decree, Bruno against McGuire, New York State Supreme Court, index #21946/76. (Recognizing the consent decree, the New York Appellate Court, First Department, in July of 1978 [#3020] dismissed an appeal in the case as moot in so far as it involved the police department. From a reading of the court's reversal as to the other parts of the case, however, it

appears that it would also have reversed the decision of the lower court in sustaining the action against the police department if there had not been a consent decree.)

23 It was reported that, on a recent three-day holiday weekend in Madison, Wisconsin, police handled slightly more than 1,000 calls, of which 118 were for loud parties and other types of noise disturbances. See 'Over 1,000 Calls Made to Police on Weekend', *Wisconsin State Journal* (Madison, Wisc.: June 1, 1978).

24 See, for example, the detailed accounts of police functioning in Minneapolis, in Joseph M. Livermore, 'Policing', *Minnesota Law Review*, March 1971, pp. 649–729. Among the works describing the police officers' varying styles in responding to similar situations are Wilson, *Varieties of Police Behavior*; Albert J. Reiss, Jr., *The Police and the Public* (New Haven, Conn.: Yale University Press, 1971); Jerome H. Skolnick, *Justice without Trials: Law Enforcement in Democratic Society* (New York: John Wiley, 1966); and Egon Bittner, *The Functions of the Police in Modern Society: A Review of Background Factors, Current Practices, and Possible Role Models* (Washington, D.C.: Govt. Printing Office, 1970).

25 See, for example, the comments of Marvin Wolfgang in a Congressionally sponsored discussion of federal support for criminal justice research, reported in the U.S. House, Committee on the Judiciary, Subcommittee on Crime, *New Directions for Federal Involvement in Crime Control* (Washington, D.C.: Govt. Printing Office, 1977). Wolfgang claims that research in criminology and criminal justice has had little impact on the administration of justice or on major decision makers.

26 For further discussion of this point, see American Bar Association, *The Urban Police Function*, Approved Draft (Chicago: American Bar Association, 1973), pp. 41–2.

27 Many of these programs are summarized in David E. Aaronson *et al.*, *The New Justice: Alternatives to Conventional Criminal Adjudication* (Washington, D.C.: Govt. Printing Office, 1977); and David E. Aaronson *et al.*, *Alternatives to Conventional Criminal Adjudication: Guidebook for Planners and Practitioners*, Caroline S. Cooper, ed. (Washington, D.C.: Govt. Printing Office, 1977).

28 The leading work on the subject is Oscar Newman, *Defensible Space: Crime Prevention through Urban Design* (New York: Macmillan, 1972). See also Westinghouse National Issues Center, *Crime Prevention through Environmental Design – A Special Report* (Washington, D.C.: National League of Cities, 1977).

29 For a summary of a survey designed to assess the effect of this change, see Russell Grindle and Thomas Aceituno, 'Innovations in Robbery Control', in *The Prevention and Control of Robbery*, vol. 1, Floyd Feeney and Adrianne Weir, eds (Davis, Calif.: University of California, 1973), pp. 315–20.

30 In one of […] a growing number of studies of how police spend their time, it was reported that, of the 18,012 calls made to the police serving a community of 24,000 people in a four-month period, 59.98 percent were requests for information. Police responded to 65 percent of the calls they received by providing information by telephone. See J. Robert Lilly, 'What are the Police Now Doing?' *Journal of Police Science and Administration*, January 1978, p. 56.

31 *Death Notification* (New York: Harper and Row, 1976).

32 The concept is described in Daniel McGillis and Joan Mullen, *Neighborhood Justice Centers: An Analysis of Potential Models* (Washington, D.C.: Govt. Printing Office, 1977). See also R.F. Conner and R. Suretta, *The Citizen Dispute Settlement Program: Resolving Disputes outside the Courts – Orlando, Florida* (Washington, D.C.: American Bar Association, 1977).

# 24. Who ya gonna call? The police as problem-busters

*John E. Eck and William Spelman*

Charlie Bedford couldn't sleep. Most nights, his residential Newport News street was quiet, marred only by the low rumble of an occasional truck on Jefferson Avenue two blocks away. But lately, Friday and Saturday nights had been different: groups of a dozen or more rowdy teenagers kept him awake, with their loud music and their horseplay. There had been no violence. But there had been some vandalism, and the kids seemed unpredictable. More disturbing, the kids came from another section of town, miles away. One sleepless Friday night it became too much. Charlie Bedford called the cops.[1]

Problems like Mr. Bedford's plague many urban neighborhoods. Disorderly behavior and other incivilities make life difficult for residents while creating fears of more serious harm. Wilson and Kelling (1982) have suggested that without intervention, citizens' fear may spark disinvestment in neighborhoods, leading to decay, more crime, and more fear. Because of concerns like these, incivilities have become a focus of researcher interest and police action.[2]

The increased interest in social order, fear, and community policing is the latest development of a continuing discussion about the role of the police in the community. The last two decades have seen a variety of proposals to bring the police closer to the community – community relations units, team policing, neighborhood watch, and foot patrol, among others. At the same time there has been equal interest in police operational effectiveness, especially with regard to crime control; directed patrol, case screening, crime analysis, and differential response were but a few of the ideas proposed and tested. For the most part, these two lines of thinking have developed independently. But we can help the Charlie Bedfords of our communities by combining the two areas. To see why, let us take a closer look at what might be called 'community policing' and 'crime control policing'.

### Community policing

Largely as a result of the riots of the 1960s, police began to examine their ties to the communities they served. Black and Hispanic communities were concerned largely with controlling police use of force. The police were concerned with defusing the dissension, creating a more favorable image for themselves. Perhaps because these aims were so politically charged, these first attempts were formal, involving new bureaucratic structures such as community relation units and civilian review boards. Both were limited: community relations units had little effect on the behaviour of street officers; line officers objected so strenuously to civilian review boards that most were dismantled or rendered impotent shortly after they were implemented (Goldstein, 1977).

Dissatisfied, some police administrators began efforts aimed at bringing police closer to people. The most ambitious of these efforts, team policing, typically involved a radical restructuring of the police bureaucracy. The hierarchical structure of policing was to be abandoned; decision making was to be decentralized; police officers were to be well-rounded generalists, rather than specialized technicians. These operational changes were to put police decision making closer to the communities served. In practice, team policing proved too hard to implement, and few efforts survive today. But three team policing strategies survived: storefront police stations, foot patrol, and community crime watch.

Storefront police stations put police officers in the community at all times, forcing them to deal with the public constantly. And, presumably, members of the public would be more willing to walk into a station located in an unpretentious setting in their own neighborhood if they wished to provide information or make a complaint. Storefronts were often well accepted by the communities they served, and increased the amount of communication between police and citizens. There were indications that they helped to reduce fear of crime, too. But officers who did not staff the storefronts often regarded these jobs as 'public relations', far removed from 'real police work'.[3]

Foot patrols cast police in the most traditional of roles. Because they are in direct contact with the public at almost all times, foot officers become informal authority figures, wielding the (usually) discreet threat of force to get results (Kelling, 1987). The bulwark of policing at the turn of the century, foot patrols were enjoying a comeback as early as the mid-1960s. The trend has become more pronounced in the last few years. Evaluations of foot patrol programs conflict over whether they reduce serious crime (Trojanowicz, n.d.; Police Foundation, 1981; Williams and Pate, 1987). However, they agree that foot patrols lead to increased contact between police and citizens, often leaving the citizens feeling safer and more satisfied with their police services. Perhaps more important, foot patrol officers learned more about the neighborhood's problems; the best foot patrol officers tried to solve them.

Finally, community crime watches emerged as an important means of police–citizen communication in the 1970s. At first, police just provided citizens with crime prevention information. Later, police grew more ambitious, and tried to organize communities. Organized communities were supposed to exert more control over rowdy youths and wayward adults, thus reducing illegal and threatening behavior. Despite some initial successes (for example, Cirel et al., 1977), crime watch programs have led to few sustained crime reductions nor do they seem to make people feel much safer. Indeed, there are indications that the organizing tactics usually used by police leave people more afraid than before (Lavrakas, 1985; Rosenbaum, 1987).

Most evidence suggests that storefronts, foot patrols, and crime watches do little to control crime. But they are all successful in increasing communication between the police and the public, and sometimes they have made people feel safer. Surely this is a gain, particularly in light of research that suggests that citizens may be more harmed by fear of crime than by victimization itself (Taub, Taylor, and Dunham, 1984; Greenberg, Rohe, and Williams, 1984)? To the degree that fear of crime is a vague and somewhat irrational sense of unease, sighting an officer on foot, in a local station, or standing before a neighborhood meeting can help to reduced it. But most research indicates that fear of crime is quite rational, grounded in reasonable perceptions of vulnerability (Skogan, 1987; Fowler and Mangione, 1974). To the degree that fear of crime is rational, we can expect that fear will return to its prior levels, so long as the conditions that cause it do not change. Indeed, there are indications that fear-reduction strategies based on increased police–public communication are only effective in the short run (Fowler and Mangione, 1983).

The community policing projects also showed the disparity between the problems people face and the problems police attack. Most citizens' concerns are not directly related to crime. Trash on the streets, noise, abandoned and ill-maintained buildings, barking dogs, and the like form the bulk of calls for police service. In many areas, residents judge these problems to be more serious than street crime (Spelman, 1983). Still, police are oriented to crime control. Given the attention police have paid to crime over the years, one would expect that they would have learned to control it. In fact, the opposite is true.

## Crime control policing

Also as a result of the riots of the 1960s, researchers began to examine the ability of the police to control crime. Over the next two decades, researchers steadily undermined five basic premises of police crime control practice.

First, the Kansas City Preventive Patrol Experiment questioned the usefulness of random patrol in cars (Kelling *et al.*, 1974). Second, studies of response time undermined the premise that the police must rapidly send officers to all calls (Kansas City Police Department, 1980; Spelman and Brown, 1984). Third, research suggested, and experiments confirmed, that the public does not always expect fast response by police to nonemergency calls (Farmer, 1981; McEwen, Connors, and Cohen, 1984). Fourth, studies showed that officers and detectives are limited in their abilities to successfully investigate crimes (Greenwood, Petersilia, and Chaiken, 1977; Eck, 1982). And fifth, research showed that detectives need not follow up every reported unsolved crime (Greenberg, Yu, and Lang, 1973; Eck, 1979). In short, most serious crimes were unaffected by the standard police actions designed to control them. Further, the public did not notice reductions in patrol, response speed to nonemergencies, or lack of follow-up investigations.

Random, unmanaged patrol operations did not seem to work. Special units, although occasionally successful, were expensive and could not be used routinely. But, police administrators reasoned, perhaps the problem was not that patrol and investigation tactics did not work. Perhaps they just needed to be managed better.

Research was showing that patrol officers and detectives had time available that could be better used (Gay, Schell and Schack, 1977; Greenwood, Petersilia and Chaiken, 1977). And additional time could be created, since citizens did not notice changes in patrol or detective operations. To free up patrol officer time, differential police response strategies were developed. Citizen calls that could be handled over the phone, through the mail, or by the caller appearing at a police station were diverted from patrol officers to civilians. Nonemergency calls requiring an officer received a scheduled response instead of an immediate dispatch (Farmer, 1981; McEwen, Connors and Cohen, 1984). To free up detective time, crimes that had no leads, short of murder or rape, were no longer investigated once a patrol officer had completed the initial investigation. Managers would direct investigative efforts so that the free time could be used effectively in the fight against crime (Eck, 1982). To direct these efforts, information about crime and criminals was needed. Crime analysis seemed to be the answer.

Crime analysis units used police records describing initial and follow-up investigations, arrests of offenders, and police encounters with suspicious persons to analyze the nature of crime and criminals (Reiner, Greenlee and Gibbens, 1976). The crimes that analysts reviewed were usually burglaries, robberies, and, in a few agencies, rapes and auto thefts. Crime analysts looked for patterns. They plotted the locations and times of burglaries to direct patrol officers to the most likely targets. They mapped robberies to deploy stakeouts by patrol officers and detectives. They collated offender descriptions to identify suspects for detectives. In some agencies, crime analysts even gave information about crime patterns to neighbourhood watch groups.

These efforts showed that collecting and analyzing information about crimes may improve police operations. But it is doubtful whether they reduce crime (Gay, Beall and Bowers, 1984). Crime analysis units have too many limitations to have more than a marginal influence on crime, or any other problem. One limitation is particularly critical: crime analysis is an attempt to find out where to apply established police responses. The responses are set before problems are understood, the same responses are used on widely differing problems. Instead, the aim should be to understand a problem, and then determine what is needed to solve it.

Street operations do need more and better management. In order to manage, police managers need better information about local problems. But they must understand the problem before designing a solution. They must look for solutions to such problems as vandalism, rowdy behavior, drug use, drunkenness, and noise.

Community policing has used the same responses – foot patrol, storefront stations, and neighborhood watch – to address a wide variety of community concerns. Crime control policing has applied another standard set of procedures

– patrol, investigations, surveillance, and stakeouts – to a wide variety of crime problems. In neither form of policing has there been a systematic attempt to tailor the responses to the characteristics of each particular problem.

> Sergeant Hogan was on duty when Mr. Bedford called. He assigned the problem to Officer Paul Summerfield. Summerfield suspected that the source of the problem might be a roller skating rink. The rink had been trying to increase business by offering reduced rates and transportation on Friday and Saturday nights. At two in the morning, as he drove north along Jefferson Avenue to the rink, Summerfield saw several large groups of youths walking south. Other kids were hanging around at the rink. Summerfield talked to several of them and found that they were waiting for a bus. The other kids, he was told, had become impatient and begun the three-mile walk home. Summerfield talked to the rink owner. The owner had leased the bus to pick up and drop off kids who lived far from the rink. But there were always more kids needing rides at the end of the night than the bus had picked up earlier.
>
> Officer Summerfield returned to the skating rink early the next evening. He saw fifty or so youngsters get out of the bus rented by the skating rink. But he saw others get out of the public transit buses that stopped running at midnight. And he saw parents in pajamas drop their kids off, then turn around and go home. Clearly the rink's bus would be unable to take home all the kids who would be stranded at closing time. Summerfield left, perplexed.

## Problem-oriented policing

How could Officer Summerfield solve this problem? Herman Goldstein [...] has described an approach that could help (Goldstein, 1979). According to Goldstein, police have lost sight of their objectives in their efforts to improve management. They must begin focusing on problems the public expects them to solve. Problems are 'the incredibly broad range of troublesome situations that prompt citizens to turn to the police'. Management improvements, though important, are only a means for improving police capacities to solve problems. Goldstein described three key elements of this problem-oriented approach.

First, problems must be defined more specifically. Broad legal definitions, such as burglary or robbery, should be replaced by descriptions that include such characteristics as location, time, participants' behaviors and motivation, and so on.

Second, information about problems must be collected from sources outside the police agency and not just from internal sources. The officers who have to deal with problems are a good source of information that is seldom exploited. But businesses, other government agencies, and private citizens can often provide data needed to understand problems fully.

Third, police agencies must engage in a broad search for solutions, including alternatives to the criminal justice process. The best solutions often involve public and private individuals and organizations who have a stake in seeing the problem resolved.

The Baltimore County Police Department and the Newport News Police Department have begun to implement problem-oriented policing. Let us look at how these agencies diagnose problems and try to resolve them.

*Baltimore County*

Two sensational murders within a week brought fear of violent crime among Baltimore County residents to a head in August, 1981. The incidents were unrelated and unlikely to be repeated, and the murderers were soon caught and eventually imprisoned for their acts. Still, the public's concern did not subside. In response, the Baltimore County Council provided its police department with 45 new officers.

Realizing that these officers would be spread very thin in a 1,700-officer department, Chief Cornelius Behan and his command staff decided to concentrate them into a special, 45-officer unit to combat fear of crime –the Citizen-Oriented Police Enforcement unit (COPE).

In 1981, no one knew much about fighting fear of crime. As a result, COPE officers confined their activities in target neighborhoods to directed patrol, motorcycle patrol, and community crime prevention. Despite some modest successes, COPE managers were dissatisfied with their efforts. Chief Behan had given them a charge to be innovative; so far, they had done little that had not been done many times before.

Gary Hayes, the late Executive Director of the Police Executive Research Forum and a friend of Chief Behan's was asked to help. Hayes arranged for Herman Goldstein to train COPE supervisors in the theory and practice of problem solving. Almost immediately, COPE began to take on a sense of direction it had lacked in its first year of operation.

COPE's approach to problem solving relies heavily on a unique combination of creativity and standard procedures. A problem is usually referred to COPE by another unit of the police department, or by another county agency. An initial assessment of the nature of the problem is made, and one officer is assigned to lead the solution effort. COPE officers then conduct a door-to-door survey of residents and businesses in the problem neighbourhood. The officers also solicit other opinions: patrol officers, detectives, and officials from other agencies are often important sources of information. The results are used to define the problem more specifically, and to identify aspects of the problem the police never see.

The COPE officers assigned to solve the problem then meet to consider the data they have collected, and to brainstorm possible solutions. Next they design an action plan, which details the solutions to be attempted and a timetable for implementing them. Once the solutions are in place, COPE officers often conduct a second survey, to see whether they have been successful.

Three years after its inception, these procedures have become the COPE unit's primary approach to reducing fear. But this is not the only method of solving problems; in Newport News, a complementary approach was designed.

*Newport News*

In 1984 the National Institute of Justice funded the Police Executive Research Forum to develop and test a new approach to crime analysis. Darrel Stephens, then Chief of the Newport News, Virginia, Police Department, was particularly interested in this approach and he invited the Forum to test it in his agency. Like the COPE unit, this project relies heavily on Goldstein's problem-oriented approach, and Goldstein consulted with the project staff and officials of the Newport News Police.

There are several differences between the Newport News Police Department's project and the Baltimore County COPE project. First, problem-oriented policing is an agencywide strategy in Newport News. All department members, including supervisors, are responsible for identifying, analysing, and solving problems. Second, any type of problem is fair game, whether it is crime, fear, or another disorder. Third, less emphasis is placed on procedures in Newport News. Instead, a department task force under the guidance of Chief Stephens developed a 'problem analysis model', a set of guidelines for data collection and thinking.

But the Newport News approach has many similarities with Baltimore Country's. Both departments emphasize careful definition and analysis of problems prior to developing solutions. Evaluating solutions is also stressed. In both departments, supervisors encourage officers analyzing problems to look beyond the police department for information. This means talking to residents, businesspeople, offenders, city agency personnel, and anyone else who could know something about the problem. Similarly, supervisors encourage officers to work with people and organizations outside policing to develop solutions. Criminal justice responses, although not discouraged, are seen as only one option among many.

## Problem-oriented policing at work

Let us look at how these two agencies have handled several common problems. Much attention has been devoted to crime and fear in residential neighborhoods, so we will first look at two problems of this type. Problems occur in non-residential areas, as well; we next describe an effort to solve a problem occurring in a downtown area with few residents and little commercial activity. Finally, some problems are not confined to a small geographic area, but affect people everywhere. As our last case study shows, the problem-oriented approach can be applied equally well to problems like these.

*Neighbourhood problems*

*Loch Raven Apartments (Baltimore County)*
Residents of the Loch Raven Apartments were shocked and frightened when beset by a spate of street robberies in 1984. While patrol officers and detectives tried to solve the crimes, COPE was called in to deal with the problem of fear. Officer Wayne Lloyd was assigned to lead the effort.

Officer Lloyd first coordinated a door-to-door survey of Loch Raven residents. He found that most of the residents were elderly women who felt particularly vulnerable to street attacks. Most were unwilling to leave their apartments after dark. Their feelings were exacerbated by the conditions of the complex: many street and building lights were broken; unkempt trees and shrubs created many hiding places; rats, stray dogs, and unrepaired structural damage all contributed to the feeling – widespread among residents – that they were trapped.

Reasoning that many solutions were needed for so complex a problem, Lloyd and his colleagues found a way to get almost everyone involved. Representatives of two local neighborhood associations agreed to help Loch Raven Apartments residents form their own association. The police convinced a variety of organizations to assist the new neighborhood group: a local printer produced crime prevention information, free of charge; a local church donated its meeting facilities; a local baker contributed free donuts. Other agencies helped in other ways. Alerted to the poor lighting situation, Baltimore Gas and Electric repaired its street lights and installed new ones. The walkways and hallways of Loch Raven Apartments were visited by representatives of numerous local agencies, including the Animal Control, Health, Fire, and Housing Departments. The apartment manager bowed to the accumulated pressures, and began to refurbish the buildings.

Perhaps because of the deterrent effect of patrolling dog catchers, building inspectors, and the like, the string of robberies stopped completely. Burglaries in the complex, running at a rate of six per month prior to the COPE unit's intervention, dropped to one every two months; it has remained at that level ever since. Perhaps most important, COPE provided the residents with better living conditions and a new Community Association that can help them obtain further improvements.

As the Loch Raven case illustrates, the police can draw upon the resources of many other public and private agencies in their problem-solving efforts. These 'hidden allies' may only need guidance as to where they can be most effective. In this case, a variety of agencies respected the COPE unit's opinion that Loch Raven was a trouble spot that deserved their attention.

### The Belmont Treehouse (Baltimore County)
No one ever seemed to use the Belmont Community Park. Casual passersby would rarely see a child in its playground, or a jogger on one of the park's tree-shaded walks. Had they looked closely, they might have seen the reason: rowdy youths frequented one corner of the park. They used drugs and drank, and resisted all attempts by patrol officers to remove them. Neighborhood residents kept their children – and themselves – far away, fearing intimidation and exposure to alcohol and drugs. Residents had complained to various local government agencies for years with no response. Finally, one of the residents read about COPE in his community newspaper and called the unit.

COPE Officers Sam Hannigan and James Chaconas were assigned to handle the Belmont problem. Their survey of neighborhood residents revealed that the problem did not focus on the park, after all; instead, it centered on a shed, dubbed the 'treehouse', that older youths had constructed in the vacant, wooded lot next door. The treehouse was often used as a crash pad and drinking place by a few local teenagers.

Hannigan and Chaconas felt that the public nature of the drinking and drug abuse was mostly responsible for the residents' fears. So, at the suggestion of several neighborhood residents, they decided to make the drinking and drug abuse less visible by removing the treehouse.

Their first efforts went nowhere. The County Roads Department agreed that the treehouse posed a hazard and was in violation of city codes. They refused to take the problem seriously, however, since no one lived there. The Health and Fire Departments felt the same way. Even if they had been willing to condemn the shack, the formal process would have taken months.

Instead, the officers decided to work with the owner. They searched through tax records to find the owner of the vacant lot. When interviewed at his home, the owner readily admitted that the treehouse was a nuisance and a hazard, and that he had no use for it whatever. Still, he feared retaliation from the kids who had constructed it, and was unable to pay the costs of demolishing the building.

Hannigan and Chaconas discussed the situation with Central COPE Lieutenant Veto Mentzell. They agreed that the two officers should demolish the treehouse themselves. Two employees of the County Roads Commission agreed to help out. Next Saturday morning, the four, armed with saws and sledge-hammers, quickly reduced the treehouse to rubble. Then they carted the pieces to a waiting county truck and took them to the dump.

The kids still drink and use drugs, and most of them have stayed in the neighborhood. They now meet in private places, however, where they are not visible to their neighbors. Most important, residents are no longer subject to their unpredictable, loud, and threatening behaviour. The Belmont Neighborhood Association reports that residents are less fearful. One tangible result of the fear reduction is that, for the first time in years, the park is filled with children.

The Belmont case shows that an apparently intractable problem – here, fear created by teenage drinking and drug abuse – can be ameliorated with a little analysis, and through some simple actions. The Treehouse case took two weeks from start to finish. The key was to accept the neighborhood's definition of the problem (threatening public behavior) rather than the usual police definition (illegal drinking and drug abuse).

### A non-neighborhood problem

Not all problems occur in areas used by people who have common concerns. Some parts of cities have no real community of interests. Our next example shows how the problem-oriented approach can be applied in this sort of area.

### Thefts from vehicles (Newport News)

For years, thefts from vehicles parked near the Newport News Shipyard have constituted around 10% of all index crime reported in Newport News. In 1984, 738 such thefts were reported; dollar losses from the thefts – not including damage to the vehicles – totaled nearly $180,000. Patrol Officer Paul Swartz was assigned to analyze the issues involved and to recommend solutions. He reviewed offense and arrest reports for the parking lot area going back three years and began tracking current cases. Because of these efforts, he was able to identify several parking areas where large numbers of thefts had taken place. These theft-prone areas became the focus of patrol officers' efforts. Swartz also interviewed patrol officers and detectives familiar with the area and talked to members of the Shipyard's security force. As a result, Swartz identified a couple of brothers who stole from vehicles in the northern lots, and a few individual offenders who stole in the southern lots.

Swartz gave the descriptions of the known offenders to the officers patrolling the lots. These officers began to stop and talk to suspects when they were seen in the area. Meanwhile, Swartz interviewed several thieves already convicted and sentenced for breaking into vehicles in these parking lots. He promised the offenders that nothing said in the interviews would be used against them. Swartz learned that drugs were a prime target of the northern thieves, but stereo equipment and auto parts were also targets. They especially looked for 'muscle' cars, cars with bumper stickers advertising local rock and roll stations, or cars with other evidence that the owner might be a marijuana smoker or cocaine user (for example, a roach clip or a feather hanging from the rearview mirror). The southern thieves did not focus on drugs, but instead concentrated on car stereo equipment and auto parts. Swartz also learned the names, descriptions, and addresses of other thieves; he confirmed that a few were particularly frequent offenders. This information was passed on to other street officers, who made several in-progress arrests. The detectives and the prosecutor worked to ensure that the most frequent offenders were convicted and sentenced to several months in jail.

As of this writing, the department is still developing a long-term solution to this problem. It will probably include working with the Shipyard and its workers to develop a theft prevention strategy. In the interim, there has been a 55% decrease in the number of these thefts since April, 1985 (from 51 per month to 23 per month), when the field interrogations and arrests of the repeat offenders began.

This is an example of using previously untapped information. Some street officers had knowledge of who was involved in the thefts, but this information was never put to use until Swartz began his analysis. Offenders were another source of information that had not been used before. As with the community problems described above, collecting information about nonneighborhood problems gives the police the ability to design a response that has a good chance of solving the problems. In this case, the solution involved standard police practices, but they were the practices that fitted the need.

### A jurisdictionwide problem

In addition to problems occurring in small geographic areas, police must deal with problems that affect their entire jurisdictions. Among these problems are some of the most troublesome issues confronting the police: juvenile runaways, drunk driving, and spouse abuse, for example. The last example describes how an officer dealt with a jurisdictionwide problem.

*Domestic violence (Newport News)*

Marvin Evans was a Newport News homicide detective. He was also a member of the task force that designed the department's approach to problem-oriented policing. Frustrated with investigating murders after they had been committed, Evans decided to find a way to prevent them. His analysis of homicide data indicated that most occurred in the southern part of the city; but, more important, half were the direct result of domestic violence, and half of these cases involved couples who had come to police attention previously. When Evans reviewed national research on domestic violence he found that his findings were typical. This encouraged him to look into the handling of these cases locally. So he began interviewing counselors at the local women's shelter, assistant state's attorneys, judges, ministers, and anyone else who had an interest in the problem.

Since his fellow officers had an important role in dealing with this issue he sought their views. Evans used a survey to determine how officers handled domestic cases and their knowledge of the available options. He found that officers were unaware of the fact that they could file a complaint that could result in a warrant, even if the victim refused. He found that officers did not like handling domestic violence cases because those officers who did handle these cases spent many frustrating hours processing them.

So Evans decided to bring together a group of interested people who could design a better way of handling these cases. This group included representatives of the local women's shelter, the State's Attorney's Office, the Circuit Court, churches, the local newspaper, the Army, and other organizations, as well as the police.

The result of their efforts was a comprehensive plan for handling family violence in the city. The objective was to keep families together while showing both the abuser and the victim how to handle stressful situations without resorting to violence. Although a mandatory arrest policy was adopted for specific types of circumstances (incidents involving injuries, the presence of a weapon, or a prior history of violence, for example), arrest was not seen as an end in itself, but as a means to provide treatment that could preserve the valuable aspects of the families involved. To support this strategy, the State's Attorney's Office and the Court agreed that they would not drop charges if the victim refused to prosecute. Instead they would use the threat of legal sanctions to get both parties into counseling.

The program was pretested in the Fall of 1985 and officers were instructed as to its operation. In January the program was officially begun, and in February the local newspaper published a 20-page special section on domestic violence. Virtually all aspects were covered, from the causes of domestic violence as seen by victims, offenders, and researchers, to the responses to domestic violence by the police, courts, and counselors.

This example shows that line officers can identify problems, conduct an analysis, and organize a communitywide response. In this case the solution included the entire city. In addition to mobilizing many private and public organizations to help reduce domestic killings and assaults, Evans was able to convince the local newspaper to show the public what they could do to curb domestic violence.

## Summary

As these cases illustrate, the problem-oriented approach can be applied to a wide variety of problems. Problem-solving can assist in the resolution of neighbourhood problems, but it is equally applicable to problems that affect areas with no residential population, or to citywide problems. Problem-oriented policing relies on and supports community policing, but it is not synonymous with community policing.

Moreover, the experience of Baltimore County and Newport News shows that police officers have the skill and interest needed to conduct through studies of problems, and to develop creative solutions. Training and management direction can improve officers' problem diagnosis and analysis skills. And officers involved in problem-solving seem to enjoy improving the quality of life of the citizens whom they serve. For many, problem-solving is more satisfying than traditional police work, because they can see the results of their work more clearly (Cordner, 1985).

The case studies also demonstrate that police have the time available to handle their current workload, and to solve problems as well. Differential patrol response, investigative case screening, and similar practices can free up time for non-traditional activities.

The additional free time can be structured in a variety of ways. Baltimore County adopted one approach – it created a special unit. Newport News adopted a different approach – it had all department members solve problems, part of the time. In Newport News, problem-solving time was structured in two ways. For a few problems, an officer was temporarily assigned to attack the problem full time. (For example, Officer Swartz was assigned full time to the parking lots problem.) For most others, an officer was assigned to handle the problem in addition to his or her other duties. (Detective Evans created a domestic violence program while investigating homicides, for instance.) Each of the three methods offers its own set of costs and benefits, and it is too soon to tell which methods are best. Most likely different methods will work better for different problems and police agencies.

Finally, the case studies make it clear that problem-oriented policing is a state of mind, and not a program, technique, or procedure. The keys are clear-headed analysis of the problem and an uninhibited search for solutions. These can be achieved by applying standard operating procedures (as is typically the case in Baltimore Country) or a looser analytic model (as in Newport News). There probably is no single best method for developing this state of mind. The best method for any given agency will depend on the characteristics of the agency.

### Long-run considerations

As problem-oriented policing becomes standard practice in more and more departments, we can expect to see three other fundamental changes in the way police do business. The problem-oriented police department will probably have to change its internal management structure. The role of the police will change, and with it their relationship with the community and other parts of the city bureaucracy. Finally, although problem-solving creates the opportunity for greatly increased benefits, it also brings with it the potential for increased risks. Let us consider these long-run considerations in more detail.

### Management structure

As we have emphasized, the point of problem-solving is to tailor the police response to the unique circumstances of each problem. Inevitably, this means that decision-making authority must be decentralized; the discretion of line officers and their supervisors – those members of the department who know most about each problem – must increase. As a result, we can expect that mid- and upper-level managers will need to develop new methods of structuring this increased discretion.

Decentralizing authority will affect all levels of the hierarchy, but it will probably affect line supervisors – sergeants – the most. As a result, agencies adopting a problem-oriented approach will have to provide much more extensive policy guidance and training to their sergeants. Problem solving puts a dual burden on these officials. On the one hand, they must make many of the tough, operational decisions. Line supervisors – those members of the department who know most about each of their officers, set priorities among different problems, facilitate work with other divisions of the police department and outside agencies, and make sure their officers solve the problems they are assigned. On the other hand, the sergeants must also provide leadership, encouraging creative analysis and response. So a first-line supervisor under problem-solving might come to resemble the editor of a newspaper, or the manager of an R&D unit, more than an army sergeant.[4] Indeed, in Baltimore County there are indications that these changes are beginning to happen (Taft, 1986).

### Police role

It is almost certain that problem-solving will influence the police officers who undertake it to reconsider their role in society. As we have described above, identifying, studying, and solving problems requires that officers make more contacts with people and organizations outside the police agency. As they do this, they will become exposed to a wider variety of interests and perspectives. Many officers will discover that they can accomplish more by working with these individuals and groups. As a consequence, they will begin to take a broader, more informed view of the problems they must handle.

This is all to the good, but few improvements are without complications. A police agency taking on a complex problem may find itself in the midst of a contentious community power struggle. This could undermine the authority of the agency in other, less controversial area. As a result, police agencies may avoid important but controversial problems. On the other hand, the problem-oriented police agency may find that it must get involved in controversial problems to avoid favoring one side over another.

Political problems will probably not be limited to police–community relations. Solving problems will require police agencies to work closely with a host of other public agencies, as well. This raises the issue of 'turf'. Other public agencies may view a problem-solving endeavor as encroachment, rather than collaboration.

This is especially likely when the problem is largely due to the failure of another agency to do its job. Even if police are successful in avoiding conflict with other agencies and with the public, problem-solving will almost certainly increase the political complexity of managing a police agency.

### Increased risks and benefits

The case studies described above suggest that police agencies who take on a broader, problem-solving role can be more effective than before, either through inadvertent mistakes or through outright abuses of authority.

Even creative responses based on careful analysis will sometimes fail. Some responses may even make matters worse. This has always been true of police work, or the work of any government agency. Currently, however, failures to handle calls adequately seldom result in difficulties for the public at large. Few people are involved in each incident, and the scope of police intervention is usually very limited. The consequences of a failure to solve a problem may be much more serious: problems involve many people; ill-advised responses may have far-reaching social implications.

Abuse of authority presents an even thornier issue. The police will be actively intervening in situations they had previously left alone, presenting more opportunities for abuse.

At the same time, however, the problem-oriented approach encourages police to analyze problems in detail and solicit the cooperation of outside organizations and individuals before responding. This will help to reduce the likelihood of both errors and abuses. In addition, because problem-oriented policing emphasizes noncoercive responses, inappropriate use of force and sanctions should become less likely. Mistakes and abuses will persist, of course; whether they are more or less benign than present mistakes and abuses remains to be seen.

In any case, it is clear that the limits of police authority will become more and more an issue as problem-solving becomes standard practice. Who will set these limits? The short answer is, some combination of the same actors who already set and enforce police standards: informal pressure from private citizens in their contacts with individual officers; elected officials; the staff of other public and private agencies; and the police themselves. What limits will be established is an open question, considered at greater length elsewhere (Goldstein, 1987). One thing is certain: Problem solving will require a new consensus on the role, authority, and limitations of the police in each jurisdiction that tries it.

Full implementation of problem-solving will be a slow and sometimes difficult process. No agency will be able to 'adopt' problem-solving simply by making a few changes in standard operating procedures, or just by telling officers to go to it. If it becomes a fad – if police managers try to implement it too quickly, without doing the necessary spadework – problem-oriented policing will fail. As Charlie Bedford's case shows, however, careful planning can yield great benefits for an agency that works to solve its community's problems.

> Officer Summerfield consulted Sergeant Hogan. They agreed that the skating rink owner should be asked to bus the kids home. Summerfield returned to the rink and spoke with the owner. The owner agreed to lease

more buses. By the next weekend, the buses were in use and Summerfield and Hogan saw no kids disturbing Mr. Bedford's neighborhood.

Sergeant Hogan summed it up: 'Look, we can have the best of both worlds. People here can get their sleep and the kids can still have fun. But we can't do it by tying up officers and chasing kids every Friday and Saturday night. There has to be a way of getting rid of the problem once and for all.'

*From John E. Eck and William Spelman, 'Who ya gonna call? The police as problem-busters',* in Crime and Delinquency, *Vol. 33, January 1988, pp 31–52.*

## Notes

1 This case study and those that follow are true. Names of citizens have been changed, but names of police officials and places have not been. The information on which these case studies are based came from two projects being conducted by the authors [...]
2 See, for example, Skogan and Maxfield (1981); Skogan (1987); Police Foundation (1981); Williams and Pate (1987); Brown and Wycoff (1987).
3 For descriptions and evaluations of the effectiveness of storefronts in Detroit and Houston, see Holland (1985); and Brown and Wycoff (1987).
4 For examples of supervision in an R&D unit and a high-tech firm, see Kidder (1981) and Auletta (1984). For a broader discussion of this management style, see Drucker (1985) and Peters and Waterman (1982).

## References

Auletta, Ken. 1984. *The Art of Corporate Success: The Story of Schlumberger.* New York: Penguin.

Brown, Lee, and Mary Ann Wycoff. 1987. 'Policing Houston: Reducing Fear and Improving Service.' *Crime & Delinquency, 33,* 1.

Cirel, Paul, Patricia Evans, Daniel McGillis, and Debra Witcomb. 1977. *Community Crime Prevention Program, Seattle, Washington: An Exemplary Project.* Washington, DC: Department of Justice, National Institute of Justice.

Cordner, Gary W. 1985. *The Baltimore County Citizen Oriented Police Enforcement (COPE) Project: Final Evaluation.* Final Report to the Florence V. Burden Foundation. Baltimore: Criminal Justice Department, University of Baltimore.

Drucker, Peter F. 1985. *Innovation and Entrepreneurship: Practice and Principles.* New York: Harper and Row.

Eck, John E. 1979. *Managing Case Assignments: The Burglary Investigation Decision Model Replication.* Washington, DC: Police Executive Research Forum.

Eck, John E. 1982. *Solving Crimes: The Investigation of Burglary and Robbery.* Washington, DC: Police Executive Research Forum.

Farmer, Michael, ed. 1981. *Differential Police Response Strategies.* Washington, DC: Police Executive Research Forum.

Fowler, Floyd J. Jr., and Thomas W. Mangione. 1974. 'The Nature of Fear.' Center for Survey Research Working Paper. Boston: Center for Survey Research, University of Massachusetts and Joint Center for Urban Studies, Massachusetts Institute of Technology and Harvard University.

Fowler, Floyd J. Jr., and Thomas W. Mangione. 1983. *Neighborhood Crime, Fear and Social Control: A Second Look at the Hartford Program.* Washington, DC: Government Printing Office.

Gay, William G., Thomas M. Beall, and Robert A. Bowers. *A Four-Site Assessment of the Integrated Criminal Apprehension Program.* Washington, DC: University of City Science Center.

Gay, William G., Theodore H. Schell, and Stephen Schack. 1977. *Prescriptive Package: Improving Patrol Productivity, Volume 1, Routine Patrol,* Washington, DC: Government Printing Office.

Goldstein, Herman. 1977. *Policing a Free Society.* Cambridge, MA: Ballinger.

Goldstein, Herman. 1979. 'Improving Policing: A Problem-Oriented Approach.' *Crime & Delinquency* 25: 236–58.

Goldstein, Herman. 1987. 'Toward Community-Oriented Policing: Potential Basic Requirements and Threshold Questions.' *Crime & Delinquency*, 33, 1.

Greenberg, Bernard, Oliver S. Yu, and Karen Lang. 1973. *Enhancement of the Investigative Function, Volume I, Analysis and Conclusions*. Final Report, Phase I. Springfield, VA: National Technical Information Service.

Greenberg, Stephanie W., William M. Rohe, and Jay R. Williams. 1984. *Safe and Secure Neighborhoods: Physical Characteristics and Informal Territorial Control in High and Low Crime Neighborhoods*. Washington, DC: Government Printing Office.

Greenwood, Peter, Joan Petersilia, and Jan Chaiken. 1977. *The Criminal Investigation Process*. Lexington, MA: D.C. Heath.

Holland, Lawrence H. 1985. 'Police and the Community: The Detroit Ministation Experience.' *FBI Law Enforcement Bulletin* 54 (February): 1–6.

Kansas City Police Department, 1980. *Response Time Analysis: Volume II – Part I Crime Analysis*. Washington, DC: Government Printing Office.

Kelling, George L. 1987. 'Acquiring a Taste for Order: The Community and Police.' *Crime & Delinquency*, 33, 1.

Kelling, George L., Tony Pate, Duane Dieckman, and Charles E. Brown. 1974. *The Kansas City Preventive Patrol Experiment: A Technical Report*. Washington, DC: Police Foundation.

Kidder, Tracy. 1981. *Soul of a New Machine*. New York: Avon.

Lavrakas, Paul J. 1985. 'Citizen Self-Help and Neighborhood Crime Prevention Policy.' In *American Violence and Public Policy*, edited by Lynn A. Curtis. New Haven: Yale University Press.

McEwen, J. Thomas, Edward F. Connors, and Marcia I. Cohen. 1984. *Evaluation of the Differential Police Response Field Test*. Alexandria, VA: Research Management Associates.

Peters, Thomas J., and Robert H. Waterman. 1982. *In Search of Excellence: Lessons from America's Best-Run Companies*. New York: Warner.

Police Foundation. 1981. *The Newark Foot Patrol Experiment*. Washington, DC: Author.

Reiner, G. Hobart, M.R. Greenlee, and M.H. Gibbens. 1976. *Crime Analysis in Support of Patrol*. National Evaluation Program: Phase I Report. Washington DC: Government Printing Office.

Rosenbaum, Dennis P. 1987. 'The Theory and Research behind Neighborhood Watch: Is it a Sound Fear and Crime Reduction Strategy?' *Crime & Delinquency*, 33, 1.

Skogan, Wesley G. 1987. 'The impact of Victimization on Fear.' *Crimes & Delinquency*, 33, 1.

Skogan, Wesley G. and Michael G. Maxfield. 1981. *Coping with Crime: Individuals and Neighborhood Reactions*. Beverly Hills, CA: Sage.

Spelman, William. 1983. *Reactions to Crime in Atlanta and Chicago: A Policy-Oriented Reanalysis*. Final report to the National Institute of Justice. Cambridge: Harvard Law School.

Spelman, William and Dale K. Brown. 1984. *Calling the Police: Citizen Reporting of Serious Crime*. Washington, DC: Government Printing Office.

Taft, Philip B. Jr. 1986. *Fighting Fear: The Baltimore County C.O.P.E. Project*. Washington, DC: Police Executive Research Forum.

Taub, Richard, D. Garth Taylor, and Jan Dunham. 1984. *Patterns of Neighborhood Change: Race and Crime in Urban America*. Chicago: University of Chicago Press.

Trojanowicz, Robert C. n.d. *An Evaluation of the Neighborhood Foot Patrol Program in Flint, Michigan*. East Lansing: Neighborhood Foot Patrol Center, Michigan State University.

Williams, Hubert, and Antony M. Pate. 1987. 'Returning to First Principles: Reducing the Fear of Crime in Newark.' *Crime & Delinquency*, 33, 1.

Wilson, James Q., and George L. Kelling. 1982. 'Broken Windows: The Police and Neighborhood Safety.' *The Atlantic Monthly* (March): 29–38.

# 25. Community policing in Chicago

*Wes Skogan and Susan Hartnett*

### What is community policing?

In a definitional sense, community policing is not something one can easily characterize. It involves reforming decision-making processes and creating new cultures within police departments; it is not a packet of specific tactical plans. It is an organizational strategy that redefines the goals of policing, but leaves the means of achieving them to practitioners in the field. It is a process rather than a product. Efforts to do it share some general features, however. Community policing relies upon organizational decentralization and a reorientation of patrol in order to facilitate two-way communication between police and the public. It assumes a commitment to broadly focused, problem-oriented policing and requires that police be responsive to citizens' demands when they decide what local problems are and set their priorities. It also implies a commitment to helping neighborhoods solve crime problems on their own, through community organizations and crime-prevention programs.

These principles underlie a host of specific programs and policing tactics. Under the rubric of community policing, departments are opening small neighborhood substations, conducting surveys to measure community satisfaction, organizing meetings and crime-prevention seminars, publishing newsletters, forming neighborhood watch groups, establishing advisory panels, organizing youth activities, conducting drug-education projects and media campaigns, patrolling on horses and bicycles, and working with municipal agencies to enforce health and safety regulations. These activities are often backed up by organizational goals that are spelled out in 'mission statements'; and departments all over the country are rewriting their missions to conform to new ideas about the values that should guide policing and the relationship between the police and the community.

There are four general principles. First, community policing relies on organizational decentralization and a reorientation of patrol in order to facilitate communication between police and the public.

Traditionally, police departments were organized on the assumption that policies and practices were determined at the top and flowed down in the form of rules and orders. The job of supervisors was to see to it that these rules and orders were carried out. Of course, this organizational chart did not reflect the reality of policing, which is that operational decision making is radically decentralized and highly discretionary, and that most police work takes place outside the direct control of supervisors. But departments maintained an elaborate para-military structure anyway, for it helped sustain the illusion that police were under control. Police were also amazingly successful at maintaining proprietary information about themselves and crime; they released what was useful and were secretive about the rest.

The community-policing model is more in accord with the way in which departments actually work. It involves formally granting neighborhood officers the decision-making authority they need to function effectively. Line officers are expected to work more autonomously at investigating situations, resolving problems, and educating the public. They are being asked to discover and set their own goals, and, sometimes, to manage their work schedules. Decentralization facilitates the development of local solutions to local problems and discourages the automatic application of central-office policies. The police are not independent of the rest of society, where large organizations have learned that decentralization often allows flexibility in decision making at the customer-contact level. To increase responsiveness, police are also emulating the general trend in large organizations toward shedding layers of bureaucracy; most departments that adopt a serious community policing stance strip a layer or two from their rank structures to shorten lines of communication within the agency. Police are also reorganizing to provide opportunities for citizens to come into contact with them under circumstances that encourage an information exchange, the development of mutual trust, and an opportunity for joint or coordinated action. An improvement in relationships between police and the community is a central goal of these programs.

The second principle of community policing is that it assumes a commitment to broadly focused, problem-oriented policing. On its own, problem-oriented policing represents a minor revolution in police work. It signifies a reversal of the long-standing disdain that police held for tasks that were not, in their view, 'real police work'. It represents a shift away from the crime-fighting orientation that police departments have professed since the 1920s. Adopting that stance was useful at that time. It provided a rationale for disconnecting police from politicians and insulating police management from narrow political concerns. Rigid discipline was imposed to combat internal corruption, and officers were shifted rapidly from one assignment to another, so that they would not get too close to the communities, they served. Controlling their work from downtown, via centralized radio dispatching, was a way to ensure that they stuck to the organization's agenda. Later, when big-city riots threatened, focusing on 'serious' crime at the expense of maintaining order, and adopting a detached professional manner were ways to keep out of trouble. 'Just the facts, ma'am,' was all they wanted.

But police departments now are experiencing the liabilities of having disconnected themselves from any close attachment to the communities they serve. Problem-oriented policing encourages officers to respond creatively to problems they encounter, or to refer them to public and private agencies that can help. More important, it stresses discovering the situations that produce calls for police assistance; identifying the causes which lie behind them; and designing tactics to deal with these causes. This involves training officers in methods of identifying and analyzing problems. Police work traditionally consisted of responding sequentially to individual events, while problem-solving calls for recognizing patterns of incidents that help identify their causes and suggest how to deal with them. Police facilitate this with computer analyses of 'hot spots' that have concentrated volumes of complaints and calls for service (Sherman, 1992). Problem-oriented policing also recognizes that dealing with such incident patterns may involve other agencies and may not, in fact, be police work; in traditional departments, this would be cause for ignoring these problems.

Third, community policing requires that police respond to the public when they set priorities and develop their tactics. Indeed, effective community policing requires responsiveness to citizen input concerning both the needs of the community and the best ways in which the police can help meet these needs. It takes seriously the public's definition of its own problems. This is one reason why community policing is an organizational strategy but not a set of specific programs – how it looks in practice *should* vary considerably from place, to place, in response to unique local situations and circumstances.

Listening closely to the community can produce different policing priorities. In our experience, officers involved in neighborhood policing learn quickly that many residents are deeply concerned about problems that previously did not come to the department's attention. The public often focuses on threatening and fear-provoking *conditions*, rather than on discrete and legally defined *incidents*. Residents are often concerned about casual social disorder and the physical decay of their community, rather than traditionally defined 'serious' crimes, but the police are organized to respond to the latter. Residents are unsure that they could (or even should) rely on the police to help them deal with these problems. These concerns thus do not generate complaints or calls for service, and as a result, the police know surprisingly little about them. The routines of traditional police work ensure that officers will largely interact with citizens who are dis-tressed because they have just been victimized, or with suspects and troublemakers. Accordingly, community policing requires that departments de-velop new channels for learning about neighborhood problems.

An important corollary of this commitment to responsiveness is that police need to find ways to evaluate their ability to satisfy the concerns expressed by the public. This is a 'customer satisfaction' criterion for assessing the quality of policing. Some police departments use questionnaires to evaluate their programs on a continuing basis. Most mail them to people who have called for assistance, which is a very inexpensive process. Others conduct telephone interviews with residents to assess the visibility and quality of police service.

The fourth principle is that community policing implies a commitment to helping neighborhoods solve crime problems on their own, through community organizations and crime-prevention programs. The idea that the police and the public are 'coproducers' of safety predates the current rhetoric of community policing. In fact, the community crime-prevention movement of the 1970s was an important precursor to community policing. It promulgated widely the idea that crime was not solely the responsibility of the police. The police were quick to endorse the claim that they could not solve crime problems without the community's support and assistance (it helped share the blame for rising crime rates); and now they find that they are expected to be the catalyst for this effort. They are being called on to take the lead in mobilizing individuals and organizations around crime prevention. These efforts include neighbor-hood-watch programs, citizen patrols, and education programs that stress household target hardening and the rapid reporting of crime to the police.

## Why community policing, and why now?

Why is this happening? What lies behind this sudden burst of innovation? Some of the factors that explain it are unique to policing, but community policing did not emerge in a vacuum. Parallel and supportive changes are taking place in society.

In many cities, the most important factor underlying the acceptance of community policing is politics. Groups that too frequently have hostile relations with the police, including African-Americans and Hispanics, are a potent political force in big cities and many smaller ones. While they are certainly con-cerned about crime, they also have an interest in curbing police abuse, and their leaders profit from promoting a style of policing that serves their constituents, rather than targeting them for enforcement. Political leaders of all backgrounds also share an interest in preventing the kind of collective violence that arose following the televised beating of Rodney King in Los Angeles in 1991. Since the mid-1960s, riots in American cities have frequently been sparked by conflicts between African-Americans and the police. In fact, studies of riots in the 1960s found that half were sparked by abusive incidents, and that tensions between the police and African-Americans were high in the months preceding the violence in every riot city (Kerner, 1967). The threat persists, as evidenced by riots during the 1990s in Los Angeles, Miami, and other cities. When developing departmental policies and choosing police administrators, politicians pay careful attention to how their actions will be received by racial and ethnic minorities. The rhetoric of community policing is favorably received in this political environment.

As a result, being involved in community policing is a way for police officers who aspire to high position to develop their careers. Cities that search for progressive and innovative police chiefs – who will be sensitive to racial tension – find that a commitment to community policing is an attractive credential. A long list of police chiefs gained their reputations as senior commanders of community-policing projects in Houston, Philadelphia, Los Angeles, and other cities. Upwardly mobile police commanders who are looking to attain visibility in other cities are therefore well advised to become involved in community-policing projects.

Interest in community policing has also been encouraged by the emergence of a cadre of well-educated and sophisticated administrators at the top of prominent police departments. Armed with university degrees in management, law, operations research, and the social sciences, they can be receptive to outside pressures for change. They have been impressed by two decades of research on policing, which has highlighted some of the limitations of the way in which it traditionally has been organized. This research has challenged the effectiveness of routine patrol and of rapid responses to most telephone complaints; detectives' investigation practices; the sufficiency of occasional crackdowns on outdoor drug markets; and the manner in which police handle domestic-violence cases. The efficacy of many of the alternatives to these traditional practices remains unproven, but their weaknesses have been exposed, and the confidence that practitioners and informed outsiders have in many traditional policing practices has been undermined. This all comes at a time of concern about the cost and the effectiveness of the police. The fiscal crisis in American cities challenges police to work within existing financial constraints – there will not be much more of the same in the form of more hiring of officers to conduct policing in the traditional style. Both police and their political masters are looking for ways to get more out of less.

The work of policing intellectuals like Herman Goldstein, John Alderson, James Q. Wilson, and George Kelling also laid the groundwork for the appearance of community policing on the policy agenda. Early innovative projects, like the one in San Diego (Boydstun and Sherry, 1975) that encouraged problem identification and problem-solving by beat officers, introduced both a community orientation to policing and the idea that experiments should be systematically evaluated. Later, the concept spread because of aggressive marketing by federal agencies and Washington, D.C. think tanks. Their target is not just police chiefs, but also the professional managers that run a majority of American cities. Cities are also encouraged to share ideas, due to the need to write grant proposals in order to secure federal funds; these proposals typically demand reviews of similar programs in other cities and summaries of what research suggests about the effectiveness of proposed programs. Proposals to experiment with new programs are more likely to be funded, because the results will be more visible. The spread of community policing throughout the country has been supported by the development of nationwide networks of police managers, who communicate with each other and with government policy-makers, consultants, professional police planners, and policing intellectuals. They communicate their ideas through conferences, magazine articles, research reports, and professional newsletters. Police officials are now more frequent visitors to other cities, sometimes touring progressive departments to see, firsthand, new forms of policing in action. They know what is going on around the country, and where the policing field seems to be moving.

Lying behind all of these factors are long-run shifts in societal organization that have facilitated the adopting of community policing. These include a general trend toward the decentralization of large-scale organizations into smaller, more flexible and responsive units; a flattening of them, to cut the number of management layers between top management and those who meet the customers; and a widespread impetus to privatize the delivery of public services, coupled with an increasing reliance on markets or marketlike mechanisms, to secure a customer orientation in government agencies. Technology is another powerful force that is driving change in organizations of all kinds. Even policing – traditionally among the least-capital-intensive functions – is being affected. We are now feeling the impact of a mobile-communications revolution that may rival the effect of the first linking of the public to the police via radio dispatch in the 1930s. In some cities, technology is being used to directly connect patrol officers to community residents through cell phones, beepers, and voice mail. In many areas, foot patrol officers carry electronic paging devices that enable residents of the area to contact them directly while they are in the field. As more citizens and police carry portable communications devices, the immediacy of their messages will increase. As the ability of citizens to directly communicate with individual officers increases, the role of centralized dispatching will diminish, along with the illusion of control over officers' performance that this gave to the top brass downtown.

Finally, community policing is popular because it seems as American as apple pie. Community policing is characterized by 'Officer O'Leary' strolling down the avenue, holding an apple in one hand and twirling a nightstick, in the other, shooing away pesky street urchins as he warmly greets passersby. It's the quintessential village constable or the night watchman, who lives in the same community that he serves. At a mythic level, community policing reminds us of a world we think we once had, but have now lost. Of course, it only seems that way. Police during that bygone era were often more brutal, lazy, and corrupt than they are today, probably by a wide margin. But these myths have a power that derives not from their accuracy, but from the cultural understandings that they represent (Crank, 1994).

[ ... ]

## Chicago accomplishments

Chicago's first accomplishment was that something happened: Major alterations were made in the way police went about their business. In a world where programs often do not progress further than the press releases that announce them, this was significant. Entire districts were drafted for the effort, and we have noted that they were big and diverse places. Furthermore, CAPS [Chicago Alternative Policing Strategy] was built on the districts' original complement of officers, not on volunteers or special-duty officers showered with overtime pay. The personnel in their management structures also were used (except for captains, who had to go), and we judged that two of the five original district commanders did not care for the idea of community policing at all. Officers' jobs were restructured, so that when they went to work every day, they did different things than they had done in the past. Teams of officers were assigned to beats for at least a year, and the dis-patching system was changed so that the volume and character of their workload was different. They had more time to engage in community-oriented work; they responded mostly to calls from their beat; and they were sent to many calls that were relevant to their turf orientation. Other calls were picked up by free-ranging rapid-response officers, and they could handle the load because more police were assigned to the districts, on the basis of the consulting firm's calculations.

Not everything got done during the first 16 months of prototyping. For one thing, CAPS was based in the uniformed-patrol division and did not really involve the rest of the department. Chicago was committed for the long term to involving all elements of the organization in community policing – including detectives and other special units – However, little progress was made toward integrating them into the program in the prototype districts. The city's plan also included computerized crime analysis, which was to provide the department's knowledge base for problem identification. R&D staff members devised an extremely useful computer program that could have done the job. However, bureaucratic snafus kept the department from acquiring the right equipment on a timely basis; nobody could set the computers up or train users; and the hardware's electrical-power demands threatened to black out some of the older district stations. Beat profiles were another problem-solving tool that did not see the light of day. Notebooks (beat planners) maintained by beat officers were supposed to record the results of a systematic canvas of each beat's problems, resources, institutions, and contact people. These were to be the basis for drawing up profiles of beat problems and identifying potential solutions to them. However, the beat planners got tangled up in legal problems; decades earlier, the city had signed a consent decree agreeing not to maintain illegal intelligence files (this had been the task of the department's Red Squad), and the city's attorney feared that beat planners fell into this category. Districts that did experiment with the planners found it difficult to get officers interested in filling out new forms, and little progress was made on beat profiling during our evaluation period.

### Citizen involvement

Structural changes were also made to facilitate the involvement of neighborhood residents in CAPS. Some are surprised that this has proven to be a stumbling block in many cities. Participation in, and even sympathy for, community policing has been at low levels in neighborhoods that need it most. Perhaps the most unique feature of Chicago's program was the beat meeting. During the prototyping period 15,000 people assembled to meet with police who were serving their area. The meetings were held on a regular basis and in prominent neighborhood locations. We found that, to a certain extent, Chicago avoided the middle-class bias that has plagued volunteer-based crime-prevention efforts (Skogan, 1988, 1989). Attendance indeed proved to be higher in higher-crime and poorer beats, and rates of attendance were highest in areas heavily populated by African-Americans (albeit due in part to low participation rates among Hispanics). The bad news was that attendance in black and poor areas was principally driven by crime problems.

What happened at the meetings had mixed results. Too many were dominated by neighborhood-relations specialists or did not involve a productive dialog between police and residents. Residents identified many local problems, but police dominated the solution side of the equation, and they clung to traditional enforcement-oriented approaches to resolving issues. The districts' success rate ranged from 10 to 60 percent in terms of how effectively the meetings were conducted, and from 7 to 38 percent, on the basis of how much problem-solving went on. Everyone knew that they had become more productive, and, to tackle this issue, a training program for residents was begun in 1995.

When the CAPS program was first announced, organizations all over the city were enthusiastic about bringing the program to their communities. We found that many groups in the selected prototype districts invested heavily in support of CAPS. Depending on the area, up to 90 percent of groups sent representatives to beat meetings; over 80 percent encouraged people to attend the meetings, worked with beat officers, and identified service needs; as many as two-thirds distributed newsletters or flyers about CAPS; and up to half held their own anticrime meetings. This was important, because CAPS depended on community activists to get people to turn out for beat meetings; to get involved in activities sponsored by the district advisory committees; and to play a role in problem-solving.

However, our study of these organizations, and our case studies of problem-solving efforts, highlighted some very real difficulties in sustaining citizen involvement in community policing. Organizations serving white and home-owning constituencies got involved quickly, because it fit their volunteer-based, block-oriented, neighborhood orientation. Organizations serving the poor and African-Americans were heavily skewed toward providing them with individualized services, and they were staffed by paid employees rather than volunteers. Community policing did not help them much. Organizations serving Hispanics fit this profile; in addition, they pursued cultural, legal, and family-oriented goals that also did not fit well with CAPS's beat orientation. This was important, because our case studies suggested that unorganized individuals found it difficult to sustain even simple problem-solving efforts. *Ad hoc* groups emerged in reaction to specific threats, but even with some police support, the people who got involved did not stick with the effort.

### Officer buy-in

We identified a number of strategies for encouraging officer commitment to community policing, and during the first 16 months, the department tried most of them. As noted [earlier] all manner of policing reforms – community policing among them – have foundered on the rocks of police culture and resistance to change, so this was of great concern. Officers (and many of their bosses) were concerned about the potential loss of police autonomy, the diversion of resources from the traditional core functions of policing, the imposition of unrealistic programs by civilians and the out-of-touch brass downtown, and any demeaning of their status as tough-minded enforcers of the law. To counter this threat, CAPS's managers restructured officers' jobs, tackled the department's very traditional management style, avoided conflict with the union and the social-work label, and made a very significant commitment to training.

There was evidence of modest success on this front. Figure [25.1] summarizes many of the changes that we detected in officers' attitudes. Unlike our analysis of the impact of CAPS on the public, there was no comparison group of officers without any involvement in the program. By the time we interviewed them again in 1995, all of the officers questioned in 1993 had been through roll-call training and had at least a little actual experience with community policing. And, of course, the department had been buzzing about the program for years. We anticipated that there would be more changes among officers serving in the prototypes, since they had more training and actual experience with the program. This turned out to be the case.

Figure [25.1] presents changes in the summary officer-attitude scores described [earlier] – separately for prototype-district officers and for those serving in other districts. Each pair of scores describes their views in 1993 and 1995. The dividing line for the scores is the neutral-attitude position. Those below the zero line describe opinions that were negative; for example, the opinion that, on average, they disagreed that the department was a good place to work. Those above the zero line describe opinions that were, on the whole, positive. Officer-satisfaction views regarding the department as a place to work, and their views about the impact of CAPS on police autonomy, were fairly negative even after almost two years of CAPS; prototype-district officers became very slightly less negative over time, while those serving in other areas grew more negative. At the other end, both prototype-district and other officers were more positive about CAPS in the spring of 1995 than they were in early 1993. They were more optimistic about the impact of CAPS on traditional policing and on the community; about their personal capacity to engage in problem solving; and about the viability of community-oriented policing activities.

However, the department did not succeed in finding a way to link an officer's aptitude for community policing to any of the organization's performance measures, nor to their pay or chances for promotion. This is a generic problem, not just Chicago's, and it is one that will continue to plague policing. There is a need for rewards for doing a good job, especially in organizations in which civil service regulations and union contracts constrain the ability of managers to

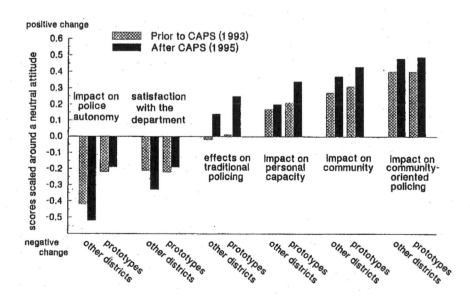

**Figure [25.1]**   Changes in officer optimism in prototype and other districts

decide who will work for them, or to match people to positions. During the evaluation period, there was also an obvious disjunction between the official new mission of the department and the views of key members of the senior command staff. Officers who were looking for a rationale for withholding a commitment to the program could point to these views as evidence that the organization was not completely committed to its new course of action.

### Integrating service delivery

Another distinguishing feature of Chicago's program was its effective integration of city services into the structure of community policing. CAPS inevitably involved an expansion of the traditional police mandate, so finding a way to deliver on the promise of neighborhood problem-solving was high on the mayor's agenda as well as on the agenda at police headquarters. The mayor used his clout with city-agency executives, while at the street level, his office monitored the responsiveness of the bureaucracies to special service needs that were identified and prioritized by district officers. The districts varied in terms of how effectively they used this process, and our surveys found evidence of declines in specific problems in the districts that focused their attention on them. Overall, physical decay (including combined reports of abandoned cars and buildings, trash and junk, and graffiti) went down significantly in two districts but not in their comparison areas, and in another district decay declined in tandem with the comparison area. Morgan Park was aggressive about pursuing selected services, but its decay problems were so small that they could not go down much further, while Rogers Park simply did not make effective use of the CAPS service-delivery system.

The real challenge will be to make this process work when the program expands to encompass the entire city. The prototypes were special places that got special treatment, but after CAPS becomes a citywide program, every district cannot be singled out. In principle, CAPS could make the existing service capacity of the city more effective because it helps target the most significant problems, and it could make them more responsive because street officers, beat-meeting participants, and community activists have a say in how services are prioritized. Behind the scenes, the mayor and his advisors anticipate that the resource targeting and computerized monitoring that his office conducts, regarding how long it takes agencies to fix problems, will also enhance their general efficiency, a spin-off benefit of community policing for his hard-pressed budget.

### Program impact

To judge the impact of CAPS, we compared changes in the five prototypes to trends in their matched comparison areas. We used this approach to examine residents' assessments of the quality of police service, and to gauge the impact of community policing on the quality of life in the city's neighborhoods.

While our surveys did not find any evidence of growing awareness of the CAPS program, residents of the prototype districts did spot changes in the frequency and character of policing in their communities. They saw officers more frequently, and in four of the five prototypes, they saw them doing informal and community-oriented work more often. There was no evidence that they noticed a decline in the frequency of motorized patrol or enforcement activity – a potential trade-off that in other cities has ignited a political backlash against community policing. In four districts, residents reported significant improvements in police responsiveness to neighborhood concerns. These changes were general ones: Whites, African-Americans, renters, and homeowners living in the prototypes grew more positive about the police; only Hispanics appeared to be unaffected by the program. An analysis of the impact of CAPS on perceptions of police misconduct found that the views of African-Americans grew more positive. Whites (who were already very positive) and Hispanics (who were even more negative than blacks) did not change their opinions.

We also found evidence that CAPS improved neighborhood conditions. There was at least one positive change in every district. Victimization went down in Morgan Park and Rogers Park. Street crime dropped in Rogers Park and in Austin, according to several measures. Drug and gang problems declined in Englewood and in Austin, and graffiti went down in Marquette. Problems with abandoned buildings and trash-filled vacant lots declined in Englewood, which made the most extensive use of the city agencies responsible for these problems. To summarize all of this, figure [25.2] describes the impact of the program on the three clusters of neighborhood problems and presents the summary of perceived police performance that we examined in detail [earlier]. It presents 'net' scores that deduct changes in the comparison areas from the 'gross', or over-time changes in the program areas. Where the values drop below zero, problems went down more in the prototypes than in the comparison areas; the bars go up when police responsiveness improved more in the prototypes. Figure [25.2] also indicates which of the changes were statistically significant. The fewest changes took place in Morgan Park, where problems were of considerably smaller magnitude than in the other districts.

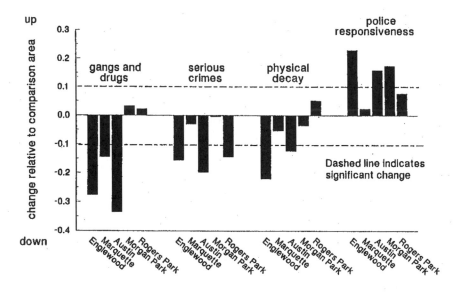

**Figure [25.2]** Changes in problems and police responsiveness

By these measures, Chicago's success rate was close to that of other cities that have conducted carefully evaluated community-policing programs. A review of 11 community-policing projects found that they had a success rate of just over 50 percent (Skogan, 1994). These projects targeted victimization, fear of crime, casual social disorder (like loitering, panhandling, public drinking, and street harassment), drug availability, and the perceived quality of police service. They were carried out in experimental neighborhoods in Houston, Newark, Oakland, Birmingham, Madison, and Baltimore. Each was evaluated using roughly the same approach that we employed in Chicago: matched comparison areas; two waves of resident surveys; and the collection of census, crime, and other official data. To give an example of the findings, fear of crime was a target of all 11 projects, and it went down probably as a result of the program in 6 of them. Overall, compared to what happened in the comparison areas, changes like the one related to fear occurred in 27 of the 51 outcomes that were monitored – a success rate of 53 percent.

Because we evaluated the impact of the program in two different ways, we calculated two success rates, but they turned out to be almost identical. Our first approach was to monitor the fate of the four biggest problems in each of the five districts, as identified by the people who lived there. There was evidence of program impact on 9 of these 20 problems, for a success rate of about 45 percent. Our second approach to assessing the impact of CAPS on the neighborhoods was to examine over-time changes in four clusters of problems: drugs and gangs, serious crimes, physical decay, and police responsiveness. The results of this analysis are summarized in figure [25.2]. Of the 20 outcome changes summarized, there was evidence of significant program effects in 10 instances, for a success rate of 50 percent.

In other words, Chicago seems to be about at the national mark. It fielded somewhat different community-policing efforts, of varying quality, in five experimental districts; the programs we cited previously also varied considerably from city to city. In every city, some projects were well conceived and well executed, while others did not get very far. In the aggregate, they all succeeded about half the time.

But one important difference to keep in mind is that in every other city considered here, the evaluators were looking at small pilot projects. They all focused on very small areas; they typically involved no more than a dozen volunteer officers; and they often were run directly out of the chief's office. In contrast, Chicago's prototype districts were large and diverse, and the project was staffed by regular units and not-always-sympathetic managers. The scale of the city's prototyping experiment exceeded the change effort that would be involved in totally remaking policing in many of the nation's largest cities.

One of the biggest challenges to community policing in Chicago will be to find ways to involve the Hispanic community in it. Recall that our analysis of the roots of the program stressed the importance of Hispanics in the balance of political power in the city – the political winner needs to keep them in the fold. However, they were more unhappy even than African-Americans about the quality of police service in their neighborhoods, and they faced serious crime problems. While rates of crime in Hispanic neighborhoods were somewhat lower than those in black areas, crime counts there were still two-to-four times the rate for white Chicago.

But at almost every point, we found that Hispanics were left out of CAPS. Heavily Hispanic beats had the lowest rate of attendance at beat meetings; in a multivariate statistical analysis, we found this was the strongest factor working against participation. Our observations of who came to meetings indicated that they did not turn out in large proportions unless the beat was at least 75 percent Hispanic. And organizations serving Hispanics were the least likely to be involved in supporting beat meetings. The prototype district where most of the Hispanics were concentrated did not have very effective top-level leadership during the early months of the project. The district advisory committee there was deeply divided by race and spent a great deal of its energy on resolving internal matters. We even found that rank-and-file Hispanic police officers tended to share the skepticism of white officers, rather than the enthusiasm about community policing that was expressed more often by black officers.

Perhaps as a result, our surveys found that Hispanics knew the least about the program, and that their lives were not much touched by it. The most heavily Hispanic district was the only one in which there was no discernible improvement in ratings of police responsiveness, and the views of police expressed by Hispanics living in all the prototypes did not change over time. Except for a reduction in graffiti problems, they did not observe any benefits of the program for their neighborhoods.

### Implications for community policing

What are the implications of Chicago's experience for the country? We think there are two: It is hard to get community policing off the ground, but it can be made to work.

The first challenge to police and municipal executives is to get something concrete to happen on the street. The obstacles to reinventing policing, involving municipal agencies, and engaging the public in a meaningful way, [are subject to debate]. For mayors or the attentive public to demand that the police 'go do it' is inadequate. Community policing has to be the community's program, representing a commitment by the city's political leaders and taxpayers. It still can easily fail, for a dozen reasons, so it will require adroit leadership as well as broad support. Learning from the successes and failures of other cities should be part of the process.

A related problem is *sustaining* commitment to the enterprise. The six cities already mentioned in this chapter are instructive in this regard. Of the 11 experimental projects that were carried out in these cities, only one survived: Madison kept its experimental district station open and expanded its beat-officer program. All of the other projects closed down – victims of lapsed federal funding, pressure to respond to surging 911 calls, opposition from officers and midlevel managers, and city politics (Skogan, 1994). Chicago's capacity to stay the course has not yet been demonstrated, although the signs of it are favorable. If community policing gets off the ground, it can be made to work. While there is an ample supply of failed experiments and of cities where the concept has gone awry, there is evidence in Chicago and elsewhere that it can succeed at tackling tough issues. Evaluations find that a public hungry for attention has a great deal to tell police, and it is grateful for the opportunity to do so. When people see more police on foot or working out of a local substation, they feel less fearful. Officers have become committed to making community policing work, and where they have developed sustained cooperation with com-munity groups and fostered self-help programs, they have witnessed declining levels of crime, social disorder, and physical decay. However, the making-it-work stage primarily requires something that many cities have too little of – patience. One of Chicago's biggest lessons for other cities is that they may have to stick with the effort for many years. If their success rate is also only 50 percent, it means that they too will have to engage in an iterative, make-it-work development process in order to get it right in future attempts.

*From Wesley G. Skogan and Susan Hartnett*, Community Policing, Chicago Style *(New York: Oxford University Press, 1998, pp 5–12, 237–246.*

## References

Boydstun, John and Michael Sherry. 1975. *San Diego Community Profile: Final Report*. Washington, D.C.: Police Foundation.

Crank, John P. 1994. 'Watchman and Community: Myth and Institutionalization in Policing.' *Law and Society Review* **28**, 325–51.

Kerner, Otto. 1967. *Report of the National Advisory Committee on Civil Disorders*. Washington, D.C.: U.S. Government Printing Office.

Sherman, Lawrence W. 1992. 'Attacking Crime: Policing and Crime Control.' In Michael Tonry and Norval Morris (eds.), *Modern Policing*, 159–230. Chicago: University of Chicago Press.

Skogan, Wesley G. 1988. 'Community Organizations and Crime.' In Michael Tonry and Norval Morris (eds), *Crime and Justice: A Review of Research*, vol. 8. 39–78. Chicago: University of Chicago Press.

Skogan, Wesley G. 1989. 'Communities, Crime and Neighborhood Organization.' *Crime and Delinquency* **35**, 437–57.

# 26. The rhetoric of community policing

*Carl B. Klockars*

The police are a mechanism for the distribution of non-negotiably coercive force employed in accord with an intuitive grasp of situational exigencies.

The proposed definition of the role of the police entails a difficult moral problem. How can we arrive at a favourable or even accepting judgment about an activity which is, in its very conception, opposed to the ethos of the polity that authorizes it? Is it not well nigh inevitable that this mandate be concealed in circumlocution? (Egon Bittner, 1970).

In *The Functions of Police in Modern Society*, Egon Bittner (1970) posed the problem of the relationship between police and the people they police in an extremely general but remarkably provocative form. Bittner advanced the argument that for nearly two centuries the core cultural goal of Western society has been the establishment of peace, both international and domestic, as a condition to every-day life. Our failures to achieve peace between nations are no secret, but each one of these failures, be it either of two world wars, Korea, or Vietnam, seems to have strengthened both our cultural commitments to the virtue of peace, as well as our resolve that such destructive failures to secure it should not occur again. While diplomacy, treaties, trade, and aid are pursued as alternatives to forceful conflict on the international level, bureaucracy, democracy, education, and a host of social services are promoted as the proper, noncoercive terms of the relation-ship between the state and citizens domestically. In both domestic and international relations, it is not merely that peace has become a nearly universal cultural goal, but that it is believed to be a goal that can *only* be successfully secured through the development and application of peaceful means to its achievement.

In ways wholly consistent with this aspiration to achieve peace through peaceful means as a condition of everyday domestic life, Western societies have sought to circumscribe to the greatest degree possible the legitimacy of the use of force by its citizens. Save for occasions of self-defense from criminal attack and intrafamily discipline of children by their parents, Western states have all but eliminated the rights of its citizens to use coercive force. The historical trade-off for this elimination of citizen rights to employ coercive force is, of course, the allocation of an exclusive right to it to police. After repeated failures of attempts to do so otherwise, a major component in the move toward the elimination of violence as a condition of everyday domestic life in every modern Western society has been to seek to extend a virtual monopoly on the legitimate right to use coercive force to police.

While no one whom it would be safe to have home to dinner argues that modern society could be without police, this situation places police in a most uneasy relationship with both the society and the state that authorize it. In their aspiration to eliminate violence as an acceptable means of conducting human affairs, both are forced to accept the creation of a core institution whose special competence and defining characteristic is its monopoly on a general right to use coercive force. Understood in this light, the police are not only fundamentally and irreconcilably offensive in their means to the core cultural aspiration of modern society, but an ever present reminder that all of these noble institutions, which should make it possible for citizens to live in non-violent relations with one another and with the state, often come up very short.

It is this truth that Bittner argues must be 'concealed in circumlocution'. That is, in order to reconcile itself with an institution whose means are irreconcilably offensive to it, society must wrap that institution in signs, symbols, and images that effectively conceal, mystify, and legitimate police actions. In *Functions*, Bittner attends to three of these circumlocutions, the legalization, the militarization, and the professionalization of police inconsiderable detail.

The thesis of this [reading] is that the modern movement toward what is currently called 'community policing' is best understood as the latest in a fairly long tradition of circumlocutions whose purpose it to conceal, mystify, and legitimate police distribution of nonnegotiably coercive force. However, before we look directly at the cluster of circumlocutions that constitute the community policing movement, it will be helpful to follow some of Bittner's leads in analysis of legalization, militarization, and professionalization.

### Legalization

> As late as 1900 when Chicago's police department numbered 3,225 men, there was no organized training. New policemen heard a brief speech from a high ranking officer, received a hickory stick, a whistle, and a key to the call box, and were sent out to work with an experienced officer. Not only were policemen untrained in law, but they operated within a criminal justice system that generally placed little emphasis on legal procedure. Most of those arrested by police were tried before local justices who rarely had legal training. Those arrested seldom had attorneys so that no legal defense was made. Thus, there were few mechanisms for introducing legal norms into street experience and crime control activities of police (Haller, 1976: 303).

Although the quote above from Mark Haller's 'Historical Roots of Police Behavior, Chicago, 1890–1925' describes Chicago police at the turn of the century, the situation was not very different in any major U.S. city at that time. At

443

the turn of the century, the newly formed U.S. police were under no illusions that they were a 'law enforcement' agency nor that their mandate or principal activity was to enforce law. While there is no question but what they understood that they were engaged in law enforcement in some formal sense, 'the law' for U.S. police in their early years was but one of many tools they might be called upon to use in their work. By no means was it as crucial to that work as their whistle, call box key, or hickory stick.

Things are, of course, very different today, and Haller's observations on big-city policing at the turn of the century provide an ideal vantage point from which to lay a perspective on those changes. Although, in fact, contemporary police may not mobilize the law with any greater frequency than their turn-of-the-century predecessors, modern police view themselves, at least publicly, as 'law enforcement agencies' and are widely understood to be fairly closely governed in their work by the courts through the procedural and evidentiary requirements of the criminal law. Historically, this process of the progressive legalization of the enterprise of policing is widely appreciated to have begun at the federal level in 1914 with the *Weeks* decision, a decision whose exclusionary rule principles were extended to all jurisdictions in 1961 by *Mapp*. Since *Mapp*, literally dozens of fourth, fifth, eighth, and fourteenth amendment decisions have promoted this view of the intimate and binding relationship between the police, the courts, and the law.

In light of these and other developments in laws that bear upon police behavior, it is probably fair to say that no other police anywhere in the world are as thoroughly 'legalized' as the U.S. police. How then can we, following Bittner, speak of their 'legalization' as a 'circumlocution'? To do so requires the appreciation of three major points, one of which is analytical and the other two of which are empirical. The analytical point is offered by Bittner (1970: 25): 'Our courts have no control over police work, never claimed to have such control, and it is exceedingly unlikely that they will claim such powers in the foreseeable future, all things being equal.' Bittner's point hinges on the meaning of 'control'. He argues that the relationship between the courts, the law, and police is rather like that between independent consumers and suppliers of services. What the courts offer to police is the opportunity, if they wish to take advantage of it, to seek the state's capacity to punish. In effect, the courts say to the police that if they wish to make use of that capacity, they must demonstrate to the courts that they have followed certain procedures in order to do so. Thus it is Bittner's point that only on those occasions that the police wish to employ the state's capacity to punish do the two institutions have any relationship of any kind. Despite the enormous growth in police law in the past quarter century, the courts have no more 'control' over the police than local supermarkets have over the diets of those who shop there.

Even that analogy, however, may give more substance to the relationship between the police and the courts than is actually warranted in fact. Empirically, it is probably the case that the cost and kind of products supermarkets offer do influence the diets of the people who shop there. It is likewise the case with police that it is almost inevitable that they will seek to secure the state's capacities to punish in certain instances. For example, in cases of reported homicides, police behave on the assumption that the case may well end up in court. On these occasions, procedural requirements certainly influence how police behave (and what they choose to report to the courts on their behavior).

Empirically, however, we know two major things about the terms of this relationship between the police, the law, and the courts. The first is that the felony arrest rate for patrol officers is very, very low even in areas in which felony offense rates are very high. For example, a recent study by Walsh (1986) found that 40 percent of the 156 patrol officers assigned to a very high crime area in New York City did not make a single felony arrest during the entire year under study, and that 68.6 percent of these officers made no more than three felony arrests.

The second empirical fact we know about police behavior has to do with the frequency with which police choose not to arrest when they have every legal right and all the evidence necessary to do so, or, alternatively, choose to make arrests when they have no legal grounds to do so whatsoever. For example, in his well-known study of 299 cases of dispute settlements by police, Black (1980: 183) found that in 52 cases in which there was ample evidence that a violent felony had occurred, police made arrests in only 27 percent of those cases. In cases of violent misdemeanor offenses, the arrest rate dropped to 17 percent. Black also found that in 78 cases in which police had no grounds for legal action of any kind, they nevertheless made arrests in 17 percent of those cases as well. Similar results are reported in many other studies. Collectively, they constitute the major empirical discovery of police research of the past two decades: the discovery of selective enforcement and the enormous influence on police discretion of such things as suspect demeanor, complainant preference, and a host of other factors that have nothing to do with 'the law'.

## Militarization

While legalization is probably the most powerful circumlocution currently mystifying the institution and functions of police in modern society, the militarization of police runs a close and complicating second. Begun as a reform movement in the history of U.S. police, an effort to establish discipline within police ranks and to extricate police from the stink of municipal machine politics, militarization drew upon a powerful and abiding analogy (Fogelson, 1977, especially Ch. 2, 'The Military Analogy': 40–67). The analogy held that police were, in effect, a domestic army engaged in a 'war' on crime.

The analogy drew upon three compelling themes. First, by associating police with the heroes and victories of the military rather than the back rooms of city politics, the military analogy sought to confer some honor and respect on the occupation of policing. Second, the idea of a war on crime struck a note of emergency that gave the movement to militarize the U.S. police a moral urgency and a rhetorical tone that was difficult to resist. To fail to support the police in their war on crime, to stand in their way, or to be stingy with the resources they would need to fight it was siding with the enemy and metaphorically tanta-mount to treason. Third and finally, the military analogy sought to establish a relationship between local politicians and police chiefs that was analogous to the relationship between elected executives at the national level and the general of the U.S. military. The politicians would, of course, retain the right to decide whether or not a given war ought to fought, but the conduct of the battles and the day-to-day discipline and management of the troops was to be left to the control of the generals. At bottom then, the military analogy was a way of talking about police that sought to wrest from the hands of local politicians and place into the hands of police chiefs the administrative tools – hiring, firing, promotion, demotion, assignment, and discipline – that those chiefs needed to manage the organizations they headed.

To a degree that no turn-of-the century police chief could have imagined, the military analogy proved a smashing success. The popularity of police and the size of police budgets have grown enormously. While no one would argue that the police are free of political control or influences (and no thoughtful person in a democratic society can argue that they should be), the political 'autonomy' of police makes them a major, independent political force in many U.S. cities. The real problem in policing today is more often to find ways of putting politics into policing than it is to find ways of taking it out.

While extricating police from the shabby sides of urban politics and establishing discipline within the ranks were no small achievements in the history of the U.S. police, the military metaphor that made those achievements possible brought with it some mighty long-term costs. Administratively, it left U.S. police with a quasi-military administrative structure that is wholly inappropriate as a device for managing the highly discretionary activity of police work. Almost wholly punitive in its approach to controlling employee behavior, it stifles innovation, imagination, experimentation, and creativity. It is no accident that the CYA (cover-your-ass) syndrome is endemic in U.S. police agencies, supported as it is by the absolute organizational truth that the department administration is preoccupied with punishment.

Equally important as a long-term cost of the militarization of the U.S. police is the dramatization of the police role in fighting crime that the military metaphor required. The fact is that the 'war on crime' is a war police not only cannot win, but cannot in any real sense fight. They cannot win it because it is simply not within their power to change those things – such as unemployment, the age distribution of the population, moral education, freedom, civil liberties, ambitions, and the social and economic opportunities to realize them – that influence the amount of crime in any society. Moreover, any kind of real war on crime is something no democratic society would be prepared to let its police fight. We would simply be unwilling to tolerate the kind of abuses to the civil liberties of innocent citizens – to us – that fighting any kind of a real war on crime would inevitably involve.

These absolute limitations on the police capacity to influence crime notwithstanding, the expectation that police should be able to do so remain and are routinely reinforced by police themselves. Police take credit for drops and blames for rises in the crime rate. So strong is the crime-fighting image of the U.S. police, that for the past 50 years virtually every purchase of equipment, every request for additional personnel, and every change in operating procedure has had to be promoted or defended in terms of its role in fighting crime.

The impassioned, crime-fighting rhetoric of militarization is often juxtaposed to the supposedly restraining metaphor of legalization. For example, we find that motif magnified in images suggesting that the courts are 'handcuffing' the police. However, in two important ways, both of which mystify police activity and shield it from scrutiny, the rhetorics of militarization and legalization are profoundly complementary. First, both focus exclusively on crime. While the military analogy holds that fighting crime is the *raison d'etre* of police, the circumlocution of legalization holds that police are controlled by the courts because they must show compliance with certain procedures on occasions when they petition the courts to punish.

Second, both legalization and militarization tend to discourage police accountability to political authorities. Legalization does so by sponsoring the impression that the courts oversee and control police practice. Insofar as the police can be understood as simply 'law enforcement' and the consequences of law enforcement governed by the judgments of the courts, there is apparently very little room or need for legitimate political accountability of police. The metaphor of militarization makes essentially the same point, only more strongly. It holds that in the war against crime, political involvement is suspect. Only someone interested in aiding the enemy would have reason to interfere with police.

**Professionalization**

Like militarization and legalization, the circumlocution that police administrators were to call 'professionalization' also sought to distance police from the influence of the political process. And, like militarization, it did so by drawing upon an analogy. The professional analogy held that, like doctors, lawyers, engineers, and other professionals, police possessed a body of special skills and knowledge that were necessary both to do and to understand their work. Hence it would be no more appropriate for a politician to instruct a police officer on how to do his or her work than it would be for a politician to instruct a doctor on how to remove an appendix, or an engineer on how to build a bridge. It followed from this analogy that to do the work of professional policing, police administrators would require not only the highly sophisticated technological tools of professional policing, but also officers of intelligence and education to employ them. Only in a police agency equipped and staffed in this way, and working in an environment free from political interference, could truly professional policing flourish.

Although the professional analogy was effective in getting improved personnel and technical resources for police, in encouraging police research, and in in-creasing the political autonomy of police, the analogy was not without its difficulties. Even on its own metaphorical terms, it was defective. While it is true that no politician should have a hand on a surgeon's scalpel during an appendectomy or calculate weight displacement factors for an engineer's bridge, political involvement in medicine, engineering, and numerous other professions is thoroughgoing and, by most accounts, needs to be. While politicians do not dictate the depth of a surgeon's cut, they do influence where hospitals are built, what kinds of health insurance programmes may be offered in a state, how and in what form health care will be provided for indigent patients, and to what extent the government will support specialized clinics, medical certification, education, and specialization. On a still broader political scale, state agencies review petitions for experimental surgical procedures and supervise in minute detail the development of all new medications. On balance and despite the intended political thrust of the professional analogy, it is probably fair to say that the state plays a much larger and more systematically influential role in the practice of medicine that it does in influencing the practice of policing.

The professional analogy also concealed a second major circumlocution. The fact is that the 'professional' police officer, as conceived by the professional police model, was understood to be a very special kind of professional, a kind of professional that taxes the very meaning of the idea. The distinctive characteristic of the work of professionals is the range of discretion accorded them in the performance of their work. By contrast, the police view of professionalism was exactly the opposite. It emphasized centralized control and policy, tight command structure, extensive departmental regulation, strict discipline, and careful overview. While the professional model wanted intelligent and educated police officers and the technological appearance of modern professionals, it did not want police officers who were granted broad, professional discretion. It wanted obedient bureaucrats.

Of course, it never really got them. The reason it did not is that the shape and variety of tasks and situations police encountered in their day-to-day work were too complex to be covered by the crude provisions of general bureaucratic regulations. Understanding this, the professional model focused its regulatory apparatus not on what police do with citizens, but on the behaviour of police within the department bureaucracy. If one looks at the manuals that most modern police departments publish, some of which are hundreds and even thousands of pages long, one finds that virtually all the rules within them govern how the officer is supposed to behave within the department. With the exception, perhaps, of a policy on when to use deadly force, they are silent on the question of how they should treat the people they police.

It is against this backdrop of the three major circumlocutions in the history of the U.S. police that the emerging circumlocution of community policing must be considered. Although the mystiques of legalization, militarization, and professionalization have been largely demystified in the scholarly literature, they remain a part of the popular consciousness and continue to influence police conceptions of themselves. While they are assuredly myths about policework, they are not myths that can be dismissed. They have hardened into beliefs that govern police management and officer self-conceptions. They are driven deeply into the organizational structure and administrative apparatus of police agencies. Community policing thus must face the twin problems of dealing with the long-term consequences of those circumstances, and of replacing those circumlocutions with others powerful and compelling enough to permit a societal reconciliation with an 'activity which is, in its very conception, opposed to the ethos of the polity that authorizes it' (Bittner, 1970).

## The circumlocutions of community policing

There are many notions of what community policing is, what it means, and what it can mean (Kelling, 1985; Wilson and Kelling, 1982; Sykes, 1986; Klockars, 1985). Perhaps the most comprehensive attempt to identify the critical elements of the movement is to be found in Jerome Skolnick and David Bayley's *The New Blue Line* (1986). The chief virtue of that book from our perspective is that it is uniformly cheerful about the movement and wholly without critical reservations as to its capacities and limits. Conceding that a more measured advocacy of community policing might provoke a less-revealing analysis of the rhetoric of community policing, we will, nevertheless, focus on what Skolnick and Bayley identify as the four elements of community policing that make it the 'wave of the future' (p. 212): (1) police–community reciprocity, (2) areal decentralization of command, (3) reorientation of patrol, and (4) civilianization.

### Police–community reciprocity

The first and most distinctive element of the community policing movement is what Skolnick and Bayley term 'police–community reciprocity'. The term as Skolnick and Bayley employ it embodies practical, attitudinal, and organizational dimensions. Practically, it implies that 'the police must involve the community ... in the police mission'. Attitudinally, police–community reciprocity 'means that police must genuinely feel, and genuinely communicate a feeling that the public they serve has something to contribute to the enterprise of policing' (p. 211). Organizationally, police–community reciprocity implies that 'the police and the public are co-producers of crime prevention. If the old professional leaned toward, perhaps exemplified, a 'legalistic' style of policing ... the new professionalism implies that the police serve, learn from, and are accountable to the community' (p. 212).

Two central circumlocutions mark this vision of the relationship between police and the people they police. They are: (1) the mystification of the concept of community, and (2) the mixed metaphors of reduced crime. Although the two circumlocutions are heavily intertwined, let us begin by considering each of them separately.

### The mystification of the concept of community

Sociologically, the concept of community implies a group of people with a common history, common beliefs and understandings, a sense of themselves as 'us' and outsiders as 'them', and often, but not always, a shared territory. Relationships of community are different from relationships of society. Community relationships are based upon status not contract, manners not morals, norms not laws, understandings not regulations. Nothing, in fact, is more different from community than those relationships that characterize most of modern urban life. The idea of police, an institution of state and societal relations, is itself foreign to relations of community. The modern police are, in a sense, a sign that community norms and controls are unable to manage relations within or between communities, or that communities themselves have become offensive to society. The bottom line of these observations is that genuine

449

communities are probably very rare in modern cities, and where they do exist, have little interest in cultivating relationship of any kind with police. University communities, for example, have often behaved indthis way, developed their own security forces and judicial systems, and used them to shield students (and faculty) from the scrutiny of police.

The fact that genuine communities do not exist or are very rare and are largely self-policing entities in modern society raises the question of just why it is that the community policing movement has chosen to police in their name. An hypothesis suggests itself. It is that nonexistent and uninterested communities make perfect partners for police in what Skolnick and Bayley have termed the 'co-production of crime prevention'. What makes them perfect partners is that while they lend their moral and political authority as communities to what police do in their name, they have no interest in and do not object to anything that might be done.

The flaw in this thesis is that it asks police to behave like good sociologists and use their concepts carefully. Of course, police do not behave in this way and it is probably unfair to ask them to do so. If we admit this flaw and excuse police for using the concept of 'community' in far too casual a sense, we are obliged to ask 'what 'police–community reciprocity' implies if it is not policing 'communities'. One answer is 'neighborhoods', 'districts', and 'precincts', each of which can often be spoken of as having legitimately identifiable characters and character-istics that police rightly and routinely take into account when working there.

There are, however, two major difficulties with substituting real entities like neighborhoods, districts, or interest groups for the concept of community. The first is that doing so misrepresents what working police officers in those places do. Those officers who actually work in those areas see themselves policing people and incidents, perhaps even 'corners', 'houses', 'parks', 'streets', or even a 'beat'. But the concept of a patrol officer policing an entire neighborhood, district, or precinct extends the notion of a police officer's sense of territorial responsibility beyond any reasonable limits.

The only persons in police departments who can be said to police entities as large as entire neighborhoods, districts, or precincts are police administrators. It is police administrators who can be pressured by representatives of groups or associations from those areas. In policing such areas, police captains, inspectors, and police chiefs have rather limited resources and a rather limited range of real things they can do for or offer to such groups. By and large, police administrators at captain rank or above, the only persons in police agencies who can be said to police areas of the size of communities, police those areas with words. Thus the idea of police–community reciprocity becomes a rhetorical device for high-command-rank police officers to speak to organizations or groups in areas that are at once, geographically, too large to be policed and, politically, too large to be ignored.

The second major difficulty with substituting a concept like neighborhood for the too casual police use of community is that such a term tends to belie the character of the entities with which police leaders interact. In speaking to traditional neighborhood groups, police community relations officers have always had their 'community-is-the-eyes-and-ears-of-the-police' speeches. But what is distinctive about the community policing movement is that it places the burden of bringing those groups into being and giving them an institutional or organizational reality on police. The typical strategy involves creating some form or organization that can act as a public forum for information exchange. In Santa Ana, California, the model community policing agency in Skolnick and Bayley's study, the department's organizational efforts are described as follows:

> Each of the four community areas has 150–250 block captains who may be responsible for thirty or forty neighbors … Block captains are actively involved as liaisons, communicating with the Police Department. The result is quite extraordinary. The Police Department has not only responded to the community it has, in effect, *created* a community – citywide – where formerly none existed. Neighbors who were strangers now know each other. A sociologist who wants to consider the 'positive functions' of the fear of crime need only look at the Santa Ana team policing experience. Consider that up to 10,000 residents annually participate in a 'Menudo cook-off and dance' organized by participants in community-oriented policing programs. This sort of community support is obviously important for social adhesion. It is equally significant for the Police Department. Community support is not simply an abstraction. It is also a grassroots political base, assuring the department a generous portion of the city budget (of which in 1983 it received 30.7 percent) (pp. 28–9).

The city-wide community the Santa Ana police have created is, of course, not in any meaningful sense of the word a community at all. Nor is it a neighborhood, precinct, district, or any other form of indigenous, area-based entity. It is, rather, a grassroots political action organization, brought into being, given focus, and sustained by the Santa Ana police.

As such, it is a very new form of political organization and one that our review of the history of circumlocutions in U.S. policing has prepared us to understand. Historically, each of those circumlocutions has served to increase the autonomy and independence of police, making them not only less receptive to demands from indigenous neighborhood action and interest groups, but also less tractable to control by elected political leaders. Progressively, these movements eventually left a void in municipal government. For while they increased the autonomy of police, they robbed them of both their popular and political support.

From the police point of view, the type of organization Skolnick and Bayley describe in Santa Ana as a model for community-oriented policing fills the void perfectly. It does so because it creates a political base for police that not only is independent of other municipal political organizations – indeed it deems itself 'apolitical' in the case of the Santa Ana organization – but is totally dependent upon, organized by, and controlled by police themselves.

### The mixed metaphors of reduced crime

Despite the fact that for the past 50 years the police have been promoting themselves as crime fighters, devoting enormous resources to the effort, taking credit for drops in the crime rate and criticism for rises in it, the best evidence to date is that no matter what they do they can make only marginal differences in it.

The reason is that all of the major factors influencing how much crime there is or is not are factors over which police have no control whatsoever. Police can do nothing about the age, sex, racial, or ethnic distribution of the population. They cannot control economic conditions; poverty; inequality; occupational opportunity; moral, religious, family, or secular education; or dramatic social, cultural, or political change. These are the 'big ticket' items in determining the amount and distribution of crime. Compared to them what police do or do not do matters very little.

While all of this is true for police, it is equally true of the kind of political entities the community policing movement calls communities. This reality is not lost on Skolnick and Bayley. Unlike some authors in the community policing movement (Kelling, 1985; Wilson and Kelling, 1982; and Sykes, 1986) and some community action groups, Skolnick and Bayley have chosen poses with respect to the prospect of controlling crime that leave the community policing movement some important outs and may even have diversified sufficiently to withstand the depression that is inevitable when it is realized that they have failed once again.

The Skolnick and Bayley construction of the relationship of community-oriented policing to crime control appears to consist of three images. The first is the image of the police and the people working side by side as coproducers of crime prevention. Describing community-oriented policing as the 'new professionalism', Skolnick and Bayley (pp. 212–13) write: 'The new professionalism implies that the police serve, learn from, and are accountable to the community. Behind the new professionalism is a governing notion: that the police and the public are coproducers of crime prevention.' If ordinary citizens are actually to become crime prevention coproducers, reciprocity is a necessity. Communities cannot be mobilized for crime prevention from the top down. Members of the community have to become motivated to work with and alongside professional law enforcement agents.

*Prevention.* Historically, the most significant semantic shift in the relationship between police and crime is the shift from promises to reduce it to promises to prevent it. The difference is important because, practically speaking, failures of crime reduction are measurable while failures of crime prevention are not. It is possible, though difficult, to test promises of crime reduction by determining whether there is more or less crime today than last year or the year before. By contrast, the success of crime pre-vention can only be evaluated against a prediction of what would have happened had the crime prevention effort not been made. Given that such predictions are presently impossible and that prevention efforts of any kind are able to produce at least some anecdotal evidence of occasional successes, the promise of successful prevention is virtually irrefutable. Skolnick and Bayley (p. 48) write of Santa Ana:

> Measures of police department effectiveness continue to baffle those inside departments as well as those who try to write about them. One measure is the crime rate. Santa Ana Police Department statistics show crime rising less than had been projected between 1970 and 1982. It is possible, however, that the overall rise in reported crime rates is attributable to citizen

willingness to report having been victimized. Another [sic!] indicator of Santa Ana success is the willingness of banks to provide loans to residents where they would not have been so willing a decade earlier.

Skolnick and Bayley do not report how the 12-year predicted rise in crime rates was arrived at, what the actual rise in crime rates was, nor how they arrived at measures of the 'not so' willingness of banks to provide loans a decade ago, or of their alleged willingness to do so today.

*Coproduction.* Even though prevention efforts will invariably be judged successful, a second rhetorical line of defense should prevention somehow be found to be slightly less successful than was hoped is provided by the contention that it is the product of the police and community coproduction. As this co-production cannot be imposed from the top down, shortcomings in preventive efforts will be attributable to a lack of genuine community support. Although police may then step up their community organizing efforts, the blame for shortcomings will fall on the community.

*The virtue of crime.* Skolnick and Bayley lay atop the notions of prevention and coproduction a third theme to guard against the possibility that community-oriented policing might be judged a failure against some crime control standard. Even though controlling crime is the manifest justification for coproductive prevention efforts. Skolnick and Bayley suggest a line of argument that, if taken seriously, leads to the conclusion that even if such efforts failed completely, coproductive prevention efforts would in and of themselves be sufficient evidence of community-oriented policing's success (1986: 214):

> We have spoken freely about 'neighborhoods' and 'communities'. In actuality, these forms of social organization – implying face-to-face interaction and a sense of communal identity may be weak ... [T]he police may find they have to activate neighborhood and community associations. In our often anomic urban society, the transcendent identity of many city dwellers is that of crime victim. Their neighbors may be the very people they fear. In such circumstances, police departments can facilitate, even create, a sense of community where one did not previously exist or was faintly imprinted ...
>
> Could it be that crime, like war and other disasters, might turn out to be America's best antidote to anomie in the United States?

It is with this third theme that Skolnick and Bayley's circumlocution of the idea of community-oriented policing comes full circle. Community-oriented policing is brought into being with the expectation that it will reduce crime. Political action groups are organized by police under that assumption. The assumption itself is converted into an untestable and irrefutable promise of prevention, coupled with an escape clause under which failure to achieve prevention becomes the fault of the 'community'. Finally, in the face of their failure to reduce crime, the organizations police created for the manifest purpose of reducing it become ends in themselves – success as antidotes to the problems of urban anomie. Indeed, such success would appear to be much like the success of war and often disasters.

## Areal decentralization of command

After police–community reciprocity, understood as we have outlined it above, the second theme Skolnick and Bayley identify as crucial to community-oriented policing is 'areal decentralization of command'. It refers to the creation of ministations, substations, storefront stations, and the multiplication of precincts, each of which is given considerable autonomy in deciding how to police the area in which it is located. 'The purpose behind all of them,' explain Skolnick and Bayley (p. 214), 'is to create the possibility of more intensive police–community interaction and heightened identification by police officers with particular areas.'

As a symbolic gesture of police focus on a particular area, the ministation concept has considerable surface appeal. But as Skolnick and Bayley themselves admit, such decentralization does not automatically lead to the kind of community-oriented policing they advocate. They merely create conditions under which police assigned to these substations might engage in that type of behaviour if they were motivated to do so. For example, Detroit had over 100 ministations before 1980, which were considered a joke by local residents, an administrative nightmare by police administrators, and a rubber-gun assignment by police officers.

The Skolnick and Bayley position on ministations, which is that unless they are genuinely committed to and motivated to do neighborhood organization, they will not promote community-oriented policing, conceals an administrative paradox. The paradox is that the more latitude and autonomy one gives to ministations to decide what is best for their local area, the less capacity one has to ensure that those decisions are made in the genuine interest of that local area. Under such conditions, one simply has to trust that ministation crews embrace the community-oriented policing philosophy to a degree that will prevent them from perverting their autonomy for their own ends.

Perhaps the greatest danger in a police administrative structure in which command is radically decentralized to hundreds of ministations is corruption. Skolnick and Bayley (p. 215) are well aware of this problem and in acknowledgment of it they write:

> [T]here is a significant potential problem with the delegation of command to relatively small areas. Where a department has an unfortunate history of corruption, decentralization could prove to be a disaster, creating the exact conditions that facilitate further corruption. Where corruption prevails, however, it is unlikely that one would find much genuine interest in the sort of community crime prevention philosophy we have described here.

Their words are not, to say the least, very assuring. Their argument is that only a department with an 'unfortunate history' of corruption would be subject to the danger of corruption in their ministations. The fact is that such decentralization of command invites new corruption to develop as surely as it invites old corruption to spread. Their further argument that departments in which corruption prevails would not have much 'genuine' interest in developing an operating philosophy that creates the 'exact conditions that facilitate further corruption' is even less comforting.

*Reorientation of patrol*

The third rhetorical pillar in Skolnick and Bayley's construction of the idea of community policing is what they term the 'reorientation of patrol'. Practically speaking, the term means two things: increased use of foot patrol, and a reduction in police response to telephone calls for emergency service. Skolnick and Bayley offer four claims in favor of foot patrol, all of which they report are supported by their observations and other studies. According to Skolnick and Bayley, foot patrol: (1) prevents crime, (2) makes possible 'order maintenance' in ways motor patrol does not, (3) generates neighborhood goodwill, and (4) raises officer morale.

While it is not possible to refute Skolnick and Bayley's observational claims for these meritorious effects of foot patrol – except perhaps to say that they were made by observers who were categorically convinced of its virtues before they began their observations – at least some of those observations run directly counter to systematic, empirical evaluations of the effects of foot patrol. It is generally conceded that foot patrol can have some effect in reducing citizen fear of crime and in affecting positively citizen evaluations of the delivery of police service. It is also accepted that in certain very high-density urban areas foot patrol officers can engage in certain types of order maintenance policing that motor patrol officers cannot easily do. However, there is no evidence whatsoever that foot patrol can reduce or prevent crime (Police Foundation, 1981).

Moreover, it is of utmost importance to add to these observations on the effects of foot patrol that all of them are the product not of foot patrol alone, but of foot patrols added to areas already patrolled at normal levels by motor patrol. This fact is especially bothersome in light of the second theme in Skolnick and Bayley's idea of 'reorientation of patrol'. In *The New Blue Line* (pp. 216–17), they write:

> Police departments are also trying in various ways, though they don't like to admit it, to unplug the 911 emergency dispatch system selectively for patrol officers. By doing so, they free themselves for community development and crime prevention activities of their own devising. In many cities, the 911 system with its promise of emergency response has become a tyrannical burden ... The pressure of 911 calls has become so great that few officers are available for proactive community development. Moreover, patrol personnel can exhaust themselves speeding from one call to another, using up the time needed for understanding the human situations into which they are injected.
>
> ... So, cautiously, [community-oriented police departments] are experimenting with measures that have the effect of reducing 911 pressure. Some departments are directing officers to park patrol cars periodically and patrol on foot; ... others encourage patrol officers to take themselves 'out of service' and simply stop and talk to people; and still others help them to prepare individualized plans for meeting local crime problems, even if it means not responding to calls or going under cover.

We are obliged to point out that not one of the measures Skolnick and Bayley identified above has, as they claim, 'the effect of reducing 911 pressure'. The pressure remains constant. Only the level of police response to its changes when patrol officers take themselves out of service or otherwise make themselves unavailable to respond.

### Civilianization

The fourth and final rhetorical dimension Skolnick and Bayley fashion into the circumlocution of community policing is 'civilianization' – the employment of nonsworn employees to do jobs that were formerly done by police officers. 'Where civilianization does not prevail – and it does not in most police departments – it is difficult to offer much more than lip service to crime prevention' (p. 219).

Of all the arguments in *The New Blue Line*, the argument linking civilianization to community policing may be the most puzzling. There is, of course, a simple, powerful, and straightforward argument in favor of civilianization. It is that it can be significantly cheaper to have civilian employees do certain types of tasks than to have full-fledged, sworn officers do them. This argument is well accepted in police agencies in the United States, virtually all of which are concerned with finding ways to save money. In fact, it is probably difficult to find a U.S. police department that has not already civilianized at least a portion of its traffic control, motor pool, maintenance, clerical, and communication functions. At present, about 20 percent of the employees of the typical U.S. police agency are civilians. Moreover, it is quite likely that as the costs of police officers' salaries and benefits increase, police agencies will continue to civilianize certain routine tasks and duties that are unlikely to require the use of coercive force.

It is obvious that this economic argument in favor of civilianization is totally silent on the question of community-oriented policing. Its only premise is that police agencies have some interest in saving money and its only promise is that through civilianization they may do so. However, while Skolnick and Bayley accept this economic argument, they find that civilianization leads almost directly to the creation of successful community organization and crime prevention programs. '[O]ur investigations have persuaded us,' say Skolnick and Bayley, 'that the more a department is civilianized, the greater the likelihood that it will successfully introduce and carry out programs and policies directed toward crime prevention' (p. 219).

Skolnick and Bayley attempt to link the economic argument for civilianization to successful community crime prevention via two different but parallel arguments. The first argument holds that once some portion of their present duties are civilianized, police officers can be made available for crime prevention and community liaison activities. The second argument holds that by civilianizing the community liaison or crime prevention activities in a police officer's role, the officer can be freed to attend to genuine emergency situations.

Both arguments rest upon four highly questionable assumptions. The first assumption is that civilianization will be achieved by adding civilian employees to an agency's payroll rather than replacing sworn employees with civilians. No one is freed for any new forms of work if a department merely replaces retired police officer clerks, evidence technicians, or dispatchers with less costly civilian employees.

The second assumption is that new civilian employees performing tasks formerly assigned to police officers are not hired in lieu of needed additional police officers. If, for example, an agency concludes that it needs ten new police officers in its patrol division, but obtains them by hiring ten civilian employees who, in turn, free ten officers already employed for patrol duty, no one, neither sworn officer nor civilian, is freed for any new form of work.

The third assumption linking the economic argument for civilianization with the conclusion that it leads to community-oriented policing is the belief that any additional funds or personnel resources, police or civilian, gained by civilianization will be devoted to crime prevention and community organization. Needless to say, such additional funds and resources must compete with every other need for funds and resources in a modern police agency and there is no reason to believe that crime prevention will gain or merit first priority.

Fourth and finally, Skolnick and Bayley link civilianization with community-oriented policing with the assumption that civilian employees will be more sensitive, receptive, and responsive to community needs and values than sworn police officers. 'If civilians are drawn from within the inner-city communities that are being policed, they are likely to possess special linguistic skills and cultural understandings … [which can] further contribute to strengthening mobilization efforts to prevent crime' (p. 219). This assumption pales quickly when one begins to examine its credibility in numerous other municipal government agencies. Consider it in light of urban education, transportation, social welfare, public housing, and sanitation, none of which are much appreciated for their sensitivity, receptivity, or responsiveness to the communities they serve, even though all of them are 100 percent civilianized.

## Whither the circumlocution of community policing?

This [reading] attempts to point out the errors, in fact, logic, and judgment, that mark the modern movement that goes by the name of community policing. Whatever the merit of the arguments and observations advanced here, they will undoubtedly strike some readers as misdirected and perhaps even mean spirited. Its difficulties, exaggerations, misrepresentations, and shortcomings notwithstanding, some will find it offensive to be critical of a movement that aspires to diminish urban anomie, to prevent crime by enlisting local support for police, and to make police agencies more sensitive to the cultural complexities of the areas they police. This reaction is to be anticipated and its appearance is central to the core argument of the [reading].

The only reason to maintain police in modern society is to make available a group of persons with a virtually unrestricted right to use violent and, when necessary, lethal means to bring certain types of situations under control. That fact is as fundamentally offensive to core values of modern society as it is unchangeable. To reconcile itself to its police, modern society must wrap it in concealments and circumlocutions that sponsor the appearance that the police either are something other than what they are or are principally engaged in doing something else. Historically, the three major reform movements in the history of the U.S. police, their militarization, legalization, and professionalization, were circumlocutions of this type and all sought to accomplish just such concealments. To the extent that these circumlocutions worked, they worked by wrapping police in aspirations and values that are extremely powerful and unquestionably good.

The movement called community policing is precisely this type of concealment and circumlocution. It wraps police in the powerful and unquestionably good images of community, cooperation, and crime prevention. Because it is this type of circumlocution, one cannot take issue with its extremely powerful and unquestionably good aspirations. Who could be against community, cooperation, and crime prevention? To do so would not only be misdirected and mean spirited, it would be perverse.

This [reading] is not against any of these aspirations. What it does oppose is the creation of immodest and romantic aspirations that cannot, in fact, be realized in anything but *ersatz* terms. Police can no more create communities or solve the problems of urban anomie than they can be legalized into agents of the courts or depoliticized into pure professionals. There is no more reason to expect that they can prevent crime than to expect that they can fight or win a war against it.

Be that as it may, the circumlocution of community policing, like the circumlocutions of militarization, legalization, and professionalization before, enjoys a peculiar form of rhetorical immunity that it is likely to sustain in the face of even the most damaging criticism. At the International Conference on Community Policing at which an early draft of this [reading] was first presented, Chris Murphy of the Office of Canadian Solicitor General captured the sense of this immunity elegantly by observing that criticizing community policing was 'like criticizing the tune selection of the singing dog'. It is not that the police dog is singing well that is so remarkable, but that he is in fact singing.

What this [reading] attempts to show is that it is not all remarkable that we should find the new song of community policing being sung by or about police. We have heard the songs of militarization, legalization, and professionalization in the past and we will no doubt continue to hear the tunes of community policing in the future. An echo of the songs that preceded it, this tune also is about some very good things we might gladly wish, but which, sadly, cannot be.

*From Carl B. Klockars 'The rhetoric of community policing' in J.R. Greene and S.D. Mastrofski (eds),* Community Policing: rhetoric or reality *(New York: Praeger) 1988, pp 239–58.*

## References

Bittner, E. 1970. *The Functions of Police in Modern Society*. Washington, D.C.: National Institute of Mental Health.

Black, D.J. 1980. *Manners and Customs of Police*. New York: Academic Press.

Fogelson, R.M. 1977. *Big-City Police*. Cambridge, Mass.: Harvard University Press.

Haller, M.H. 1976. 'Historical Roots of Police Behavior: Chicago, 1890–1925.' *Law and Society Review* 10(2): 303–323.

Kelling, G.L. 1985. 'Order Maintenance, the Quality of Urban Life, and Police: A Line of Argument.' In W.A. Geller (ed.), *Police Leadership in America Crisis and Opportunity*. New York: Praeger, pp. 296–308.

Klockars, C.B. 1985. 'Order and Maintenance, the Quality of Urban Life, and Police; a Different Line of Argument.' In W.A. Geller (ed.), *Police Leadership in America: Crisis and Opportunity*. New York: Praeger, pp. 309–21.

Skolnick, J.H., and D.H. Bayley. 1986. *The New Blue Line: Police Innovation in Six American Cities*. New York: The Free Press.

Sykes, G. 1986. 'Street Justice: A Moral Defense of Order Maintenance.' *Justice Quarterly* 3(4).

Walsh, W.F. 1986. 'Patrol Officer Arrest Rates: A Study of the Social Organization of Police Work.' *Justice Quarterly* 2(3); 271–90.

Wilson, J.Q., and G.L. Kelling. 1982. 'The Police and Neighborhood Safety: Broken Windows.' *Atlantic Monthly* 127(March): 29–38.

# 27. Broken windows: the police and neighborhood safety

*James Q. Wilson and George L. Kelling*

In the mid-1970s the State of New Jersey announced a 'Safe and Clean Neighborhoods Program', designed to improve the quality of community life in twenty-eight cities. As part of that program, the state provided money to help cities take police officers out of their patrol cars and assign them to walking beats. The governor and other state officials were enthusiastic about using foot patrol as a way of cutting crime, but many police chiefs were skeptical. Foot patrol, in their eyes, had been pretty much discredited. It reduced the mobility of the police, who thus had difficulty responding to citizen calls for service, and it weakened headquarters control over patrol officers.

Many police officers also disliked foot patrol, but for different reasons: it was hard work, it kept them outside on cold, rainy nights, and it reduced their chances for making a 'good pinch'. In some departments, assigning officers to foot patrol had been used as a form of punishment. And academic experts on policing doubted that foot patrol would have any impact on crime rates; it was, in the opinion of most, little more than a sop to public opinion. But since the state was paying for it, the local authorities were willing to go along.

Five years after the program started, the Police Foundation, in Washington, D.C., published an evaluation of the foot-patrol project. Based on its analysis of a carefully controlled experiment carried out chiefly in Newark, the foundation concluded, to the surprise of hardly anyone, that foot patrol had not reduced crime rates. But residents of the foot patrolled neighborhoods seemed to feel more secure than persons in other areas, tended to believe that crime had been reduced, and seemed to take fewer steps to protect themselves from crime (staying at home with the doors locked, for example). Moreover, citizens in the foot-patrol areas had a more favorable opinion of the police than did those living elsewhere. And officers walking beats had higher morale, greater job satisfaction, and a more favorable attitude toward citizens in their neighborhoods than did officers assigned to patrol cars.

These findings may be taken as evidence that the skeptics were right – foot patrol has no effect on crime; it merely fools the citizens into thinking that they are safer. But in our view, and in the view of the authors of the Police Foundation study (of whom Kelling was one), the citizens of Newark were not fooled at all. They knew what the foot-patrol officers were doing, they knew it was different from what motorized officers do, and they knew that having officers walk beats did in fact make their neighborhoods safer.

But how can a neighborhood be 'safer' when the crime rate has not gone down – in fact, may have gone up? Finding the answer requires first that we understand what most often frightens people in public places. Many citizens, of course, are primarily frightened by crime, especially crime involving a sudden, violent attack by a stranger. This risk is very real, in Newark as in many large cities. But we tend to overlook another source of fear –the fear of being bothered by disorderly people. Not violent people, nor, necessarily, criminals, but disreputable or obstreperous or unpredictable people: panhandlers, drunks, addicts, rowdy teenagers, prostitutes, loiterers, the mentally disturbed.

What foot-patrol officers did was to elevate, to the extent they could, the level of public order in these neighborhoods. Though the neighborhoods were predominantly black and the foot patrolmen were mostly white, this 'order-maintenance' function of the police was performed to the general satisfaction of both parties.

One of us (Kelling) spent many hours walking with Newark foot-patrol officers to see how they defined 'order' and what they did to maintain it. One beat was typical: a busy but dilapidated area in the heart of Newark, with many abandoned buildings, marginal shops (several of which prominently displayed knives and straight-edged razors in their windows), one large department store, and, most important, a train station and several major bus stops. Though the area was run-down, its streets were filled with people, because it was a major transportation center. The good order of this area was important not only to those who lived and worked there but also to many others, who had to move through it on their way home, to supermarkets, or to factories.

The people on the street were primarily black; the officer who walked the street was white. The people were made up, of 'regulars' and 'strangers'. Regulars included both 'decent folk' and some drunks and derelicts who were always there but who 'knew their place'. Strangers were, well, strangers, and viewed, suspiciously, sometimes apprehensively. The officer – call him Kelly – knew who the regulars were, and they knew him. As he saw his job, he was to keep an eye on strangers, and make certain that the disreputable regulars observed some informal but widely understood rules. Drunks and addicts could sit on the stoops, but could not lie down. People could drink on side streets, but not at the main intersection. Bottles had to be in paper bags. Talking to, bothering, or begging from people waiting at the bus stop was strictly forbidden. If a dispute erupted between a businessman and a customer, the businessman was assumed to be right, especially if the customer was a stranger. If a stranger loitered, Kelly would ask him if he had any means of support and what his business was; if he gave unsatisfactory answers, he was sent on his way. Persons who broke the informal rules, especially those who bothered people waiting at bus stops, were arrested for vagrancy. Noisy teenagers were told to keep quiet.

These rules were defined and enforced in collaboration with the 'regulars' on the street. Another neighborhood might have different rules, but these, everybody understood, were the rules for *this* neighborhood. If someone violated them, the regulars not only turned to Kelly for help but also ridiculed the violator. Sometimes what Kelly did could be described as 'enforcing the law', but just as often it involved taking informal or extralegal steps to help protect what the neighborhood had decided was the appropriate level of public order. Some of the things he did probably would not withstand a legal challenge.

A determined skeptic might acknowledge that a skilled foot-patrol officer can maintain order but still insist that this sort of 'order' has little to do with the real sources of community fear – that is, with violent crime. To a degree, that is true. But two things must be borne in mind. First, outside observers should not assume that they know how much of the anxiety now endemic in many big-city neighborhoods stems from a fear of 'real' crime and how much from a sense that the street is disorderly, a source of distasteful, worrisome encounters. The people of Newark, to judge from their behavior and their remarks to interviewers, apparently assign a high value to public order, and feel relieved and reassured when the police help them maintain that order.

Second, at the community level, disorder and crime are usually inextricably linked, in a kind of developmental sequence. Social psychologists and police officers tend to agree that if a window in a building is broken and is left un-repaired, all the rest of the windows will soon be broken. This is as true in nice neighborhoods as in rundown ones. Window-breaking does not necessarily occur on a large scale because some areas are inhabited by determined window-breakers whereas others are populated by window-lovers; rather, one unrepaired broken window is a signal that no one cares, and so breaking more windows costs nothing. (It has always been fun.)

Philip Zimbardo, a Stanford psychologist, reported in 1969 on some experiments testing the broken-window theory. He arranged to have an automobile without license plates parked with its hood up on a street in the Bronx and a comparable automobile on a street in Palo Alto, California. The car in the Bronx was attacked by 'vandals' within ten minutes of its 'abandonment'. The first to arrive were a family – father, mother, and young son – who removed the radiator and battery. Within twenty-four hours, virtually everything of value had been removed. Then random destruction began – windows were smashed, parts torn off, upholstery ripped. Children began to use the car as a playground. Most of the adult 'vandals' were well- dressed, apparently clean-cut whites. The car in Palo Alto sat untouched for more than a week. Then Zimbardo smashed part of it with a sledgehammer. Soon, passersby were joining in. Within a few hours, the car had been turned upside down and utterly destroyed. Again, the 'vandals' appeared to be primarily respectable whites.

Untended property becomes fair game for people out for fun or plunder and even for people who ordinarily would not dream of doing such things and who probably consider themselves law-abiding. Because of the nature of community life in the Bronx – its anonymity, the frequency with which cars are abandoned and things are stolen or broken, the past experience of 'no one caring' – vandalism begins much more quickly than it does in staid Palo Alto, where people have come to believe that private possessions are cared for, and that mischievous behavior is costly. But vandalism can occur anywhere once communal barriers – the sense of mutual regard and the obligations of civility – are lowered by actions that seem to signal that 'no one cares'.

We suggest that 'untended' behavior also leads to the breakdown of community controls. A stable neighborhood of families who care for their homes, mind each other's children, and confidently frown on unwanted intruders can change, in a few years or even a few months, to an inhospitable and frightening jungle. A piece of property is abandoned, weeds grow up, a window is smashed. Adults stop scolding rowdy children; the children, emboldened, become more rowdy. Families move out, unattached adults move in. Teenagers gather in front of the corner store. The merchant asks them to move; they refuse. Fights occur. Litter accumulates. People start drinking in front of the grocery; in time, an inebriate slumps to the sidewalk and is allowed to sleep it off. Pedestrians are approached by panhandlers.

At this point it is not inevitable that serious crime will flourish or violent attacks on strangers will occur. But many residents will think that crime, especially violent crime, is on the rise, and they will modify their behavior accordingly. They will use the streets less often, and when on the streets will stay apart from their fellows, moving with averted eyes, silent lips, and hurried steps. 'Don't get involved.' For some residents, this growing atomization will matter little, because the neighborhood is not their 'home' but 'the place where they live'. Their interests are elsewhere; they are cosmopolitans. But it will matter greatly to other people, whose lives derive meaning and satisfaction from local attachments rather than worldly involvement; for them, the neighborhood will cease to exist except for a few reliable friends whom they arrange to meet.

Such an area is vulnerable to criminal invasion. Though it is not inevitable, it is more likely that here, rather than in places where people are confident they can regulate public behavior by informal controls, drugs will change hands, prostitutes will solicit, and cars will be stripped. That the drunks will be robbed by boys who do it as a lark, and the prostitutes' customers will be robbed by men who do it purposefully and perhaps violently. That muggings will occur.

Among those who often find it difficult to move away from this are the elderly. Surveys of citizens suggest that the elderly are much less likely to be the victims of crime than younger persons, and some have inferred from this that the well-known fear of crime voiced by the elderly is an exaggeration: perhaps we ought not to design special programs to protect older persons; perhaps we should even try to talk them out of their mistaken fears. This argument misses the point. The prospect of a confrontation with an obstreperous teenager or a drunken panhandler can be as fear-inducing for defenseless persons as the prospect of meeting an actual robber; indeed, to a defenseless person, the two kinds of confrontation are often indistinguishable. Moreover, the lower rate at which the elderly are victimized is a measure of the steps they have already taken – chiefly, staying behind locked doors – to minimize the risks they face. Young men are more frequently attacked than older women, not because they are easier or more lucrative targets but because they are on the streets more.

Nor is the connection between disorderliness and fear made only by the elderly. Susan Estrich, of the Harvard Law School, has recently gathered together a number of surveys on the sources of public fear. One, done in Portland, Oregon, indicated that three fourths of the adults interviewed cross to the other side of a street when they see a gang of teenagers; another survey, in Baltimore, discovered that nearly half would cross the street to avoid even a single strange youth. When an interviewer asked people in a housing project where the most dangerous spot was, they mentioned a place where young persons gathered to drink and play music, despite the fact that not a single crime had occurred there. In Boston public housing projects, the greatest fear was expressed by persons living in the buildings where disorderliness and incivility, not crime, were the greatest. Knowing this helps one understand the significance of such otherwise harmless displays as subway graffiti. As Nathan Glazer has written, 'the proliferation of graffiti, even when not obscene, confronts the subway rider with the inescapable knowledge that the environment he must endure for an hour or more a day is uncontrolled and uncontrollable, and that anyone can invade it to do whatever damage and mischief the mind suggests'.

In response to fear people avoid one another, weakening controls. Sometimes they call the police. Patrol cars arrive, an occasional arrest occurs but crime continues and disorder is not abated. Citizens complain to the police chief, but he explains that his department is low on personnel and that the courts do not punish petty or first-time offenders. To the residents, the police who arrive in squad cars are either ineffective or uncaring: to the police, the residents are animals who deserve each other. The citizens may soon stop calling the police, because 'they can't do anything'.

The process we call urban decay has occurred for centuries in every city. But what is happening today is different in at least two important respects. First in the period before, say, World War II, city dwellers – because of money costs, transportation difficulties, familial and church connections – could rarely move away from neighborhood problems. When movement did occur, it tended to be along public-transit routes. Now mobility has become exceptionally easy for all but the poorest or those who are blocked by racial prejudice. Earlier crime waves had a kind of built-in self-correcting mechanism: the determination of a neighborhood or community to reassert control over its turf. Areas in Chicago, New York, and Boston would experience crime and gang wars, and then normalcy would return, as the families for whom no alternative residences were possible reclaimed their authority over the streets.

Second, the police in this earlier period assisted in that reassertion of authority by acting, sometimes violently, on behalf of the community. Young toughs were roughed up, people were arrested 'on suspicion' or for vagrancy, and prostitutes and petty thieves were routed. 'Rights' were something enjoyed by decent folk, and perhaps also by the serious professional criminal, who avoided violence and could afford a lawyer.

This pattern of policing was not an aberration or the result of occasional excess. From the earliest days of the nation, the police function was seen primarily as that of a night watchman: to maintain order against the chief threats to order – fire, wild animals, and disreputable behavior. Solving crimes was viewed not as a police responsibility but as a private one. In the March, 1969, *Atlantic*, one of us (Wilson) wrote a brief account of how the police role had slowly changed from maintaining order to fighting crimes. The change began with the creation of private detectives (often ex-criminals), who worked on a contingency-fee basis for individuals who had suffered losses. In time, the detectives were absorbed in municipal agencies and paid a regular salary simultaneously, the responsibility for prosecuting thieves was shifted from the aggrieved private citizen to the professional prosecutor. This process was not complete in most places until the twentieth century.

In the 1960s, when urban riots were a major problem, social scientists began to explore carefully the order maintenance function of the police, and to suggest ways of improving it – not to make streets safer (its original function) but to reduce the incidence of mass violence. Order maintenance became, to a degree, coterminous with 'community relations'. But, as the crime wave that began in the early 1960s continued without abatement throughout the decade and into the 1970s, attention shifted to the role of the police as crime-fighters. Studies of police behavior ceased, by and large, to be accounts of the order-maintenance function and became, instead, efforts to propose and test ways whereby the police could solve more crimes, make more arrests, and gather better evidence. If these things could be done, social scientists assumed, citizens would be less fearful.

A great deal was accomplished during this transition, as both police chiefs and outside experts emphasized the crime-fighting function in their plans, in the allocation of resources, and in deployment of personnel. The police may well have become better crime-fighters as a result. And doubtless they remained aware of their responsibility for order. But the link between order-maintenance and crime-prevention, so obvious to earlier generations, was forgotten.

That link is similar to the process whereby one broken window becomes many. The citizen who fears the ill-smelling drunk, the rowdy teenager, or the importuning beggar is not merely expressing his distaste for unseemly behavior; he is also giving voice to a bit of folk wisdom that happens to be a correct generalization – namely, that serious street crime flourishes in areas in which disorderly behavior goes unchecked. The unchecked panhandler is, in effect, the first broken window. Muggers and robbers, whether opportunistic or professional, believe they reduce their chances of being caught or even identified if they operate on streets where potential victims are already intimidated by prevailing conditions. If the neighborhood cannot keep a bothersome panhandler from annoying passersby, the thief may reason, it is even less likely to call the police to identify a potential mugger or to interfere if the mugging actually takes place.

Some police administrators concede that this process occurs, but argue that motorized-patrol officers can deal with it as effectively as foot patrol officers. We are not so sure. In theory, an officer in a squad car can observe as much as an officer on foot; in theory, the former can talk to as many people as the latter. But the reality of police–citizen encounters is powerfully altered by the automobile. An officer on foot cannot separate himself from the street people; if he is approached, only his uniform and his personality can help him manage whatever is about to happen. And he can never be certain what that will be – a request for directions, a plea for help, an angry denunciation, a teasing remark, a confused babble, a threatening gesture.

In a car, an officer is more likely to deal with street people by rolling down the window and looking at them. The door and the window exclude the approaching citizen; they are a barrier. Some officers take advantage of this barrier, perhaps unconsciously, by acting differently if in the car than they would on foot. We have seen this countless times. The police car pulls up to a corner where teenagers are gathered. The window is rolled down. The officer stares at the youths. They stare back. The officer says to one, 'C'mere'. He saunters over, conveying to his friends by his elaborately casual style the idea that he is not intimidated by authority. 'What's your name?' 'Chuck.' 'Chuck who?' 'Chuck Jones.' 'What'ya doing, Chuck?' 'Nothin'.' 'Got a P.O. [parole officer]?' 'Nah.' 'Sure?' 'Yeah.' 'Stay out of trouble, Chuckie.' Meanwhile, the other boys laugh and exchange comments among themselves, probably at the officer's expense. The officer stares harder. He cannot be certain what is being said, nor can he join in and, by displaying his own skill at street banter, prove that he cannot be 'put down'. In the process, the officer has learned almost nothing, and the boys have decided the officer is an alien force who can safely be disregarded, even mocked.

Our experience is that most citizens like to talk to a police officer. Such exchanges give them a sense of importance, provide them with the basis for gossip, and allow them to explain to the authorities what is worrying them (whereby they gain a modest but significant sense of having 'done something' about the problem). You approach a person on foot more easily, and talk to him more readily, than you do a person in a car. Moreover, you can more easily retain some anonymity if you draw an officer aside for a private chat. Suppose you want to pass on a tip about who is stealing handbags, or who offered to sell you a stolen TV. In the inner city, the culprit, in all likelihood, lives nearby. To walk up to a marked patrol car and lean in the window is to convey a visible signal that you are a 'fink'.

The essence of the police role in maintaining order is to reinforce the informal control mechanisms of the community itself. The police cannot, without committing extraordinary resources, provide a substitute for that informal control. On the other hand, to reinforce those natural forces the police must accommodate them. And therein lies the problem.

Should police activity on the street be shaped, in important ways, by the standards of the neighborhood rather than by the rules of the state? Over the past two decades, the shift of police from order-maintenance to law enforcement has brought them increasingly under the influence of legal restrictions, provoked by media complaints and enforced by court decisions and departmental orders. As a consequence, the order maintenance functions of the police are now governed by rules developed to control police relations with suspected criminals. This is, we think, an entirely new development. For centuries, the role of the police as watchmen was judged primarily not in terms of its compliance with appropriate procedures but rather in terms of its attaining a desired objective. The objective was order, an inherently ambiguous term but a condition that people in a given community recognized when they saw it. The means were the same as those the community itself would employ, if its members were sufficiently determined, courageous, and authoritative. Detecting and apprehending criminals, by contrast, was a means to an end, not an end in itself; a judicial determination of guilt or innocence was the hoped-for result of the law-enforcement mode. From the first, the police were expected to follow rules defining that process, though states differed in how stringent the rules should be. The criminal-apprehension process was always understood to involve individual rights, the violation of which was unacceptable because it meant that the violating officer would be acting as a judge and jury – and that was not his job. Guilt or innocence was to be determined by universal standards under special procedures.

Ordinarily, no judge or jury ever sees the persons caught up in a dispute over the appropriate level of neighborhood order. That is true not only because most cases are handled informally on the street but also because no universal standards are available to settle arguments over disorder, and thus a judge may not be any wiser or more effective than a police officer. Until quite recently in many states, and even today in some places, the police made arrests on such charges as 'suspicious person' or 'vagrancy' or 'public drunkenness'– charges with scarcely any legal meaning. These charges exist not because society wants judges to punish vagrants or drunks but because it wants an officer to have the legal tools to remove undesirable persons from a neighborhood when informal efforts to preserve order in the streets have failed.

Once we begin to think of all aspects of police work as involving the application of universal rules under special procedures, we inevitably ask what constitutes an 'undesirable person' and why we should 'criminalize' vagrancy or drunkenness. A strong and commendable desire to see that people are treated fairly makes us worry about allowing the police to rout persons who are undesirable by some vague or parochial standard. A growing and not-so-commendable utilitarianism leads us to doubt that any behavior that does not 'hurt' another person should be made illegal. And thus many of us who watch over the police are reluctant to allow them to perform, in the only way they can, a function that every neighborhood desperately wants them to perform.

This wish to 'decriminalize' disreputable behavior that harms no one.' – and thus remove the ultimate sanction the police can employ to maintain neighborhood order – is, we think, a mistake. Arresting a single drunk or a single vagrant who has harmed no identifiable person seems unjust, and in a sense it is. But failing to do anything about a score of drunks or a hundred vagrants may destroy an entire community. A particular rule that seems to make sense in the individual case makes no sense when it is made a universal rule and applied to all cases. It makes no sense because it fails to take into account the connection between one broken window left untended and a thousand broken windows. Of course, agencies other than the police could attend to the problems posed by drunks or the mentally ill, but in most communities especially where the 'deinstitutionalization' movement has been strong – they do not.

The concern about equity is more serious. We might agree that certain behavior makes one person more undesirable than another but how do we ensure that age or skin color or national origin or harmless mannerisms will not also become the basis for distinguishing the undesirable from the desirable? How do we ensure, in short, that the police do not become the agents of neighborhood bigotry?

We can offer no wholly satisfactory answer to this important question. We are not confident that there is a satisfactory answer except to hope that by their selection, training, and supervision, the police will be inculcated with a clear sense of the outer limit of their discretionary authority. That limit, roughly, is this

– the police exist to help regulate behavior, not to maintain the racial or ethnic purity of a neighborhood.

Consider the case of the Robert Taylor Homes in Chicago, one of the largest public-housing projects in the country. It is home for nearly 20,000 people, all black, and extends over ninety-two acres along South State Street. It was named after a distinguished black who had been, during the 1940s, chairman of the Chicago Housing Authority. Not long after it opened, in 1962, relations between project residents and the police deteriorated badly. The citizens felt that the police were insensitive or brutal; the police, in turn, complained of unprovoked attacks on them. Some Chicago officers tell of times when they were afraid to enter the Homes. Crime rates soared.

Today, the atmosphere has changed. Police–citizen relations have improved – apparently, both sides learned something from the earlier experience. Recently, a boy stole a purse and ran off. Several young persons who saw the theft voluntarily passed along to the police information on the identity and residence of the thief, and they did this publicly, with friends and neighbors looking on. But problems persist, chief among them the presence of youth gangs that terrorize residents and recruit members in the project. The people expect the police to 'do something' about this, and the police are determined to do just that.

But do what? Though the police can obviously make arrests whenever a gang member breaks the law, a gang can form, recruit, and congregate without breaking the law. And only a tiny fraction of gang-related crimes can be solved by an arrest; thus, if an arrest is the only recourse for the police, the residents' fears will go unassuaged. The police will soon feel helpless, and the residents will again believe that the police 'do nothing'. What the police in fact do is to chase known gang members out of the project. In the words of one officer, 'We kick ass'. Project residents both know and approve of this. The tacit police–citizen alliance in the project is reinforced by the police view that the cops and the gangs are the two rival sources of power in the area, and that the gangs are not going to win.

None of this is easily reconciled with any conception of due process or fair treatment. Since both residents and gang members are black, race is not a factor. But it could be. Suppose a white project confronted a black gang, or vice versa. We would be apprehensive about the police taking sides. But the substantive problem remains the same: how can the police strengthen the informal social-control mechanisms of natural communities in order to minimize fear in public places? Law enforcement, *per se*, is no answer: a gang can weaken or destroy a community by standing about in a menacing fashion and speaking rudely to a passersby without breaking the law.

We have difficulty thinking about such matters, not simply because the ethical and legal issues are so complex but because we have become accustomed to thinking of the law in essentially individualistic terms. The law defines *my* rights, punishes *his* behavior and is applied by *that* officer because of *this* harm. We assume, in thinking this way, that what is good for the individual will be good for the community and what doesn't matter when it happens to one person won't matter if it happens to many. Ordinarily, those are plausible assumptions. But in cases where behavior that is tolerable to one person is intolerable to many others, the reactions of the others – fear, withdrawal, flight – may ultimately make matters worse for everyone, including the individual who first professed his indifference.

It may be their greater sensitivity to communal as opposed to individual needs that helps explain why the residents of small communities are more satisfied with their police than are the residents of similar neighborhoods in big cities. Elinor Ostrom and her co-workers at Indiana University compared the perception of police services in two poor, all-black Illinois towns – Phoenix and East Chicago Heights with those of three comparable all-black neighborhoods in Chicago. The level of criminal victimization and the quality of police–community relations appeared to be about the same in the towns and the Chicago neighborhoods. But the citizens living in their own villages were much more likely than those living in the Chicago neighborhoods to say that they do not stay at home for fear of crime, to agree that the local police have 'the right to take any action necessary' to deal with problems, and to agree that the police 'look out for the needs of the average citizen'. It is possible that the residents and the police of the small towns saw themselves as engaged in a collaborative effort to maintain a certain standard of communal life, whereas those of the big city felt themselves to be simply requesting and supplying particular services on an individual basis.

If this is true, how should a wise police chief deploy his meager forces? The first answer is that nobody knows for certain, and the most prudent course of action would be to try further variations on the Newark experiment, to see more precisely what works in what kinds of neighborhoods. The second answer is also a hedge – many aspects of order maintenance in neighborhoods can probably best be handled in ways that involve the police minimally if at all. A busy bustling shopping center and a quiet, well-tended suburb may need almost no visible police presence. In both cases, the ratio of respectable to disreputable people is ordinarily so high as to make informal social control effective.

Even in areas that are in jeopardy from disorderly elements, citizen action without substantial police involvement may be sufficient. Meetings between teenagers who like to hang out on a particular corner and adults who want to use that corner might well lead to an amicable agreement on a set of rules about how many people can be allowed to congregate, where, and when.

Where no understanding is possible – or if possible, not observed – citizen patrols may be a sufficient response. There are two traditions of communal involvement in maintaining order: One, that of the 'community watchmen', is as old as the first settlement of the New World. Until well into the nineteenth century, volunteer watchmen, not policemen, patrolled their communities to keep order. They did so, by and large, without taking the law into their own hands – without, that is, punishing persons or using force. Their presence deterred disorder or alerted the community to disorder that could not be deterred. There are hundreds of such efforts today in communities all across the nation. Perhaps the best known is that of the Guardian Angels, a group of unarmed young persons in distinctive berets and T-shirts, who first came to public attention when they began patrolling the New York City subways but who claim now to have chapters in more than thirty American cities.

Unfortunately, we have little information about the effect of these groups on crime. It is possible, however, that whatever their effect on crime, citizens find their presence reassuring, and that they thus contribute to maintaining a sense of order and civility.

The second tradition is that of the 'vigilante'. Rarely a feature of the settled communities of the East, it was primarily to be found in those frontier towns that grew up in advance of the reach of government. More than 350 vigilante groups are known to have existed; their distinctive feature was that their members did take the law into their own hands, by acting as judge, jury, and often executioner as well as policeman. Today, the vigilante movement is conspicuous by its rarity, despite the great fear expressed by citizens that the older cities are becoming 'urban frontiers'. But some community-watchmen groups have skirted the line, and others may cross it in the future. An ambiguous case, reported in *The Wall Street Journal* involved a citizens' patrol in the Silver Lake area of Belleville, New Jersey. A leader told the reporter, 'We look for outsiders'. If a few teenagers from outside the neighborhood enter it, 'we ask them their business,' he said. 'If they say they're going down the street to see Mrs. Jones, fine, we let them pass. But then we follow them down the block to make sure they're really going to see Mrs. Jones.'

Though citizens can do a great deal, the police are plainly the key to order maintenance. For one thing, many communities, such as the Robert Taylor Homes, cannot do the job by themselves. For another, no citizen in a neighborhood, even an organized one, is likely to feel the sense of responsibility that wearing a badge confers. Psychologists have done many studies on why people fail to go to the aid of persons being attacked or seeking help, and they have learned that the cause is not 'apathy' or 'selfishness' but the absence of some plausible grounds for feeling that one must personally accept responsibility. Ironically, avoiding responsibility is easier when a lot of people are standing about. On streets and in public places, where order is so important, many people are likely to be 'around', a fact that reduces the chance of any one person acting as the agent of the community. The police officer's uniform singles him out as a person who must accept responsibility if asked. In addition, officers, more easily than their fellow citizens, can be expected to distinguish between what is necessary to protect the safety of the street and what merely protects its ethnic purity.

But the police forces of America are losing, not gaining, members. Some cities have suffered substantial cuts in the number of officers available for duty. These cuts are not likely to be reversed in the near future. Therefore, each department must assign its existing officers with great care. Some neighborhoods are so demoralized and crime-ridden as to make foot patrol useless; the best the police can do with limited resources is respond to the enormous number of calls for service. Other neighborhoods are so stable and serene as to make foot patrol unnecessary. The key is to identify neighborhoods at the tipping point – where the public order is deteriorating but not unreclaimable, where the streets are used frequently but by apprehensive people, where a window is likely to be broken at any time, and must quickly be fixed if all are not to be shattered.

Most police departments do not have ways of systematically identifying such areas and assigning officers to them. Officers are assigned on the basis of crime rates (meaning that marginally threatened areas are often stripped so that police can investigate crimes in areas where the situation is hopeless) or on the basis of calls for service (despite the fact that most citizens do not call the police when they are merely frightened or annoyed). To allocate patrol wisely, the department must look at the neighborhoods and decide, from first-hand evidence, where an additional officer will make the greatest difference in promoting a sense of safety.

One way to stretch limited police resources is being tried in some public housing projects. Tenant organizations hire off-duty police officers for patrol work in their buildings. The costs are not high (at least not per resident), the officer likes the additional income, and the residents feel safer. Such arrangements are probably more successful than hiring private watchmen, and the Newark experiment helps us understand why. A private security guard may deter crime or misconduct by his presence, and he may go to the aid of persons needing help, but he may well not intervene – that is, control or drive away – someone challenging community standards. Being a sworn officer – a 'real cop' – seems to give one the confidence, the sense of duty, and the aura of authority necessary to perform this difficult task.

Patrol officers might be encouraged to go to and from duty stations on public transportation and, while on the bus or subway car, enforce rules about smoking, drinking, disorderly conduct, and the like. The enforcement need involve nothing more than ejecting the offender (the offense, after all, is not one with which a booking officer or a judge wishes to be bothered). Perhaps the random but relentless maintenance of standards on buses would lead to conditions on buses that approximate the level of civility we now take for granted on airplanes.

But the most important requirement is to think that to maintain order in precarious situations is a vital job. The police know this is one of their functions, and they also believe, correctly, that it cannot be done to the exclusion of criminal investigation and responding to calls. We may have encouraged them to suppose, however, on the basis of our oft-repeated concerns about serious, violent crime, that they will be judged exclusively on their capacity as crime-fighters. To the extent that this is the case, police administrators will continue to concentrate police personnel in the highest-crime areas (though not necessarily in the areas most vulnerable to criminal invasion) emphasize their training in the law and criminal apprehension (and not their training in managing street life), and join too quickly in campaigns to decriminalize 'harmless' behavior (though public drunkenness, street prostitution, and pornographic displays can destroy a community more quickly than any team of professional burglars).

Above all, we must return to our long-abandoned view that the police ought to protect communities as well as individuals. Our crime statistics and victimization surveys measure individual losses, but they do not measure communal losses. Just as physicians now recognize the importance of fostering health rather than simply treating illness, so the police – and the rest of us – ought to recognize the importance of maintaining, intact, communities without broken windows.

*From James Q. Wilson and George L. Kelling, 'Broken windows'* Atlantic Monthly, *Vol. 249, no 3, pp 29–42.*

# 28. Crime is down in New York City: blame the police

*William J. Bratton*

New York City, a city that only three years ago had a reputation as 'the crime capital of the world' is now being lauded as one of the safest big cities in the world. How did this quick turnaround happen? Blame it on the police. The men and women who make up the New York City Police Department (NYPD) are principally responsible for the dramatic crime decline that continues today in New York City. Over the past three years, the City's crime rate has dropped by 37 per cent. The homicide rate alone has plummeted over 50 per cent.

To truly appreciate the significance of the dramatic crime decline in New York City, it is important to take a walk back through time to understand how New York City gained its reputation as the 'crime capital of the world' in the first place. It is also important to understand how American policing has changed over the past quarter century to effect the decline in the crime rate presently being experienced in cities across the nation.

## The professional era

During the 26 years I have been involved in American law enforcement, there have been several very significant changes in policing throughout the United States. I entered policing during the 1970s, a time in America when the Vietnam War was still raging. Huge demonstrations were occurring. We had just come through the race riots and resultant civil rights era of the sixties and were fast becoming a much more permissive society. Coupled with this was the nationwide phenomenon of deinstitutionalization of our mental institutions, many of whose former patients became the 'homeless' populations of our inner cities. Simultaneously, American society and its cities' streets were becoming more disorderly and fear-inducing. American policing was also moving into a new era called 'The Professional Era', which ironically reduced police presence and control of the streets simultaneously with the new social disorder problems that would provide so much fear and crime in the 1980s and 1990s.

The Professional Era of policing is best defined as the time police relied on what I call the 3 Rs: Rapid Response, Random Patrol and Reactive investigation. As we began to take advantage of emerging technologies like the 9-1-1 system[1] and computer-aided dispatch, police also began to reply upon motorized patrol, replacing the foot patrol officer in most American cities. The ever expanding number of 9-1-1 calls required us to take police off walking posts and put them into cars so officers could rapidly respond to the growing number of calls the system was creating. When not on call, these cars would randomly patrol, hopefully preventing and deterring crime. And as they had always done, once something did happen, police reacted and investigated.

There was an old television show called *Dragnet* that best epitomised the Professional Era of Policing. *Dragnet*'s main character, Sergeant Jack Webb, was famous for his style of questioning a witness or taking a citizen complaint. He was best known for one famous line: 'Just the facts Ma'am, just the facts.' This line was typical during the Professional Era which called for no personal touch and required little personality. The almost computer-generated voice which the fictitious Sergeant Webb used ironically fitted this period's environment characterized by an increasing use of computers throughout the policing profession. The policing style of the 1970s was going to be the end-all policing methodology; objective, detached and impersonal. During the Professional Era, by focusing on process and not results, police were going to finally be able to successfully control crime using modern technology, rapid response and better management systems.

What happened, however, was quite different. This new type of modern-day policing was ill-prepared for the large volume of calls that were generated by the 9-1-1 system. Most major American cities were overwhelmed. As other city services were declining, the police became the catchall. Dial 9-1-1 and they would come. Police had more and more calls and less time to investigate, less clearance and solving of crime. And perhaps most importantly, the police had less time to interact in a positive way with members of the community.

And then came the 1980s, a time characterised in the United States by the growing phenomenon of drugs. Drugs, particularly cocaine and the emerging crack cocaine, came into vogue in the mid-1980s. With the drugs came guns, increasingly more powerful weapons such as semi-automatics with fifteen and seventeen rounds instead of the old thirty-eight with five or six rounds of ammunition. Drug-related gun violence, especially among youth, became a mean reality. In what we once thought were safe areas of our cities arose random violent crime. When New York City experienced this in the late 1980s and early 1990s, it began to scare everybody. The problems and violence of the ghettos suddenly seemed to be everywhere. Nobody seemed safe. As noted by George Kelling, co-author of the broken windows article, we had effectually de-policed the streets of our cities.[2]

## The evolution of community policing

The late 1980s saw some police researchers and police leaders beginning to realize that some of the basic assumptions behind the Professional Era were flawed. The effects of rapidly responding to crimes were muted because research showed it took people almost 10 minutes to decide to call the police in the first place. And police riding in air-conditioned squad cars, rapidly going from call to call, did not make people feel safer. In fact, it further separated the police from the public, the consumers of police services.

Fortunately, the researchers and practitioners did not stop their work at finding what was not working, but began to look at how to think differently about crime and disorder and develop strategies that would work. From this evolved the concept of community policing. It began all over the country in little bits and pieces culminating in a process at Harvard University's John F. Kennedy School of Criminal Justice where, through a federal grant over a period of several years, police leaders, academics, community leaders, media and politicians came together to talk about policing and the development of community policing. The primary focus was prevention. Policing had come full circle, returning to the concept of being a part of the community, not apart from it, with an emphasis on preventing crime, not just responding to it.

Community policing is a concept that you hear a great deal about. There is a continuing debate as to whether community policing is a philosophy, style of policing or programme and whether it is tough or soft on crime. However, I have always discussed community policing in simpler terms. Just as the three Rs best described the Professional Era, community policing is defined by three Ps: Partnership, Problem-Solving, Prevention. Remember in the 1970s and 1980s police said: 'If you give us additional personnel, equipment and resources we'll take care of your problems and control crime.' This didn't happen because there was no partnership with the community to jointly identify those problems. By working in partnership with the community, other institutions of government and the criminal justice system, police can have a significant impact on crime and disorder. This is the basic premise behind community policing and, when properly applied, it is tougher on crime than anything else we've ever tried. New York City's experience is proof positive of this.

Chasing after those thousands of 9-1-1 calls meant putting bandages on the symptoms of the problems generating the calls. We were not taking effective action to solve the problem that generated the call in the first place. Repeat calls brought police back to the same street corner time and time again to kick the same group of rowdy kids off the corner or address the same domestic violence problem. During the Professional Policing Era, police managers had focused more on measuring response time and time spent on calls. Efforts were focused more on process versus the results of preventing and reducing crime and disorder. Police needed to work harder and more strategically at solving the problem. Community policing enabled police to refocus resources on the most basic reason for our being. The primary reason that London Metropolitan Police force was created by Sir Robert Peel in 1829 was to *prevent* crime from occurring in the first place.

Interestingly, policing's shift from the Professional Era to community policing did not involve a complete changeover. It was more a melding of ideas and strategies. The three Rs still have their place for certain crime situations, but not all and not as an overall crime control methodology. Blending the benefits of rapid response and random patrol as well as top notch investigative work with the development of strong community partnerships to solve problems that lead to crime reduction and prevention describes the foundation of policing in America in the 1990s and in New York City in particular.

## Policing in New York City in the 1990s

The cover of *Time* magazine calling New York City the Rotten Apple and the 'Do Something Dave' headline in the *New York Post*, begging then Mayor David Dinkins to take action against rising crime and disorder, characterize the state of frustration in New York City in 1990.

How did New York City get such a negative image? How did it become a city so seemingly out of control? In New York City over the previous twenty years, as a result of police corruption scandals in the 1970s, the City consciously opted to remove its police from dealing with anything with the potential for corruption. Police were precluded from entering licensed premises and from giving citations or summonses on many disorder-related street conditions for fear of corruption. The direct result of these restrictions as well as the impact of the Professional Policing model were that the NYPD seemed to withdraw from controlling behaviour on the streets of New York and conditions worsened. Graffiti and other signs of disorder abounded. In the 1970s and most of the 1980s, there was not a subway car in the City that was not completely covered with what some inappropriately described as an urban art form, graffiti. Subway stations became shantytowns for the homeless and aggressive begging increased, exacerbating a climate of fear, compounded by a significant and notorious decline in the quality of life as a whole.

When I first came to New York City from Boston in 1990 as the new Chief of Police for the City's Transit Police Department, I remember driving from LaGuardia Airport down the highway into Manhattan. Graffiti, burned out cars and trash seemed to be everywhere. It looked like something out of a futuristic movie. Then as you entered Manhattan, you met the unofficial greeter for the City of New York, the squeegee pest. Welcome to New York City. This guy had a dirty rag or squeegee and would wash your window with some dirty liquid and ask for or demand money. Proceeding down Fifth Avenue, the mile of designer stores and famous buildings, unlicensed street peddlers and beggars were everywhere. Then down into the subway where everyday over 200,000 fare evaders jumped over or under turnstyles while shakedown artists vandalized turnstyles and demanded that paying passengers hand over their tokens to them. Beggars were on every train. Every platform seemed to have a cardboard city where the homeless had taken up residence. This was a city that had stopped caring about itself. There was a sense of a permissive society allowing certain things that would not have been permitted many years ago. The City had lost control. It was the epitome of what Senator Daniel Moynihan had described as a process of 'defining social deviancy down' – explaining away bad behaviour instead of correcting it.

## The beginning: hiring additional police officers

In 1990, Mayor David Dinkins and the City Council realized something had to be done and, with public support, enacted legislation to hire an additional 7,000 police. This hiring was designed to support the community policing programme that was being implemented in the New York City Police Department (NYPD).

475

However, then Police Commissioner Lee Brown wanted to dedicate these 7,000 new young police officers to 1,500 beats throughout the City. The average kid joining the NYPD at that time was a 22-year-old, with only a high school (12 years) education.

- Many of the new hires had never held a job until they applied to the NYPD.
- Many had never even driven a car.
- Many lived outside the City and had never interacted with a minority person.
- Many were under 21 and not even old enough to legally drink.

And these were the 7,000 young police officers who were supposed to solve the problems of New York City, one of the most complex cities in the world, after only six months of police academy training. They were simply not equipped to deal with the city's problems of race, crime and disorder.

Although legislating the hiring of 7,000 additional police officers in the early 1990s was a start and crime began to go down slowly, more was needed. When I became Police Commissioner in January 1994, aware of this deficiency in the previous administration's approach, I undertook a strategic re-engineering of the NYPD that significantly contributed to the dramatic crime reduction and quality-of-life improvement that continues in New York City today.

### Re-engineering the organization

Like many private corporations that have chosen to re-engineer, the NYPD was an organization that wasn't living up to its potential. The process of re-engineering requires the setting of clear-cut goals, the restructuring of the organization to meet those goals and priorities and maximum involvement of Department personnel and outside expertise. Instead of being satisfied with incremental declines in crime, we set ourselves the mission of dramatically reducing crime, disorder and fear. We re-engineered the NYPD into an organization capable of supporting these goals. We created 12 re-engineering teams covering areas crucial to achieving short- and long-term crime reduction goals such as training, equipment and technology re-engineering teams. We tapped expertise from inside and outside the Department to work on goals and implementation strategies to meet these goals.

### Decentralization

In 1994, precinct commanders had very little authority to do anything unless headquarters demanded it. We cut through the 'wedding cake' of centralized hierarchical bureaucracy and put the focus of crime prevention and disorder reduction back on the police in the precincts. In other words, we decentralized policing in New York City.

We pushed responsibility and accountability down, but not to the new, inexperienced beat cop, as the previous administration had done, but rather to the precinct commander level, so that we really had 76 miniature police departments. In view of the complexity of many of New York City's problems the earlier policy had been setting those newly-hired young men and women up for failure by putting them in charge of problem-solving efforts. We changed the focus from that young officer to a more mature (by fifteen years on average) college-educated, veteran police commander who knew how to police the city.

We demanded that precinct commanders place dual emphasis on quality-of-life or signs of crime as well as on serious crime. New York City government had not paid attention to the quality-of-life drinking and minor street crime that citizens had experienced every day for over 25 years. As a result the police had stopped enforcing many of the City ordinances which were intended to prevent these violations. I set the macro-level goal of crime reduction and enhancing quality-of-life, but then let precinct commanding officers manage at the precinct or micro-level by determining how best to do this. In addition to decreasing felony crime, this led to a successful city-wide effort to reduce and prevent graffiti as well as an ongoing elimination of those infamous squeegee pests.

Essential to police enforcing quality-of-life laws for the first time in 25 years was public and political support. New York fortunately had this. In 1994 the newly elected Mayor Rudolph Giuliani had campaigned on the issue of crime and disorder. Upon his election, unlike his predecessors, he authorized the police and their new Police Commissioner to develop and implement strategies to deal with identified problems. As Mayor, he then co-ordinated the activities of other city agencies to support these crime control strategies.

### Strategic crime fighting

Over a two-year period, the police developed eight crime control strategies to address drugs, guns, youth crime, auto theft, corruption, traffic, domestic violence and quality-of-life crime throughout the City. We developed a geographically-based strategic drug reduction initiative that has been implemented in two areas of New York City with successful preliminary results. We created an innovative system to measure the success of the crime control goals called the Compstat Process. Compstat stands for Comprehensive Computer Statistics. It incorporates four basic premises: timely accurate Intelligence data; rapid response of resources; effective tactics and relentless follow-up. In the NYPD, at twice-weekly Compstat meetings, the Department's top executives meet. Each command presents the results of their efforts in the previous month compared to their plan for the same period of time.

### Changes at the precinct level

Before I became Police Commissioner, the emphasis on community policing had resulted in police being assigned to beats in the neighbourhood with the responsibility to solve all crime problems. New police officers, many no more than 20 or 21 years old, were expected to use problem-solving methodologies associated with community policing to address any crime problem, from youths loitering on street corners to rampant drug dealing on their beats. This approach was not working. Some neighbourhoods were so crime-ridden that these young officers could not cope with such complex problems and issues.

Precinct commanding officers had little control over these officers who were assigned via a strictly enforced community policing deployment formula from Police Headquarters. Moreover, resources were more difficult to allocate appropriately under a rigid plan that placed authority and accountability at multifunctional and poorly co-ordinated higher levels. To correct this situation, as previously mentioned, I decided to focus accountability and authority at the precinct commander level. This meant that precinct commanders could decide how many and how best to use beat officers. They were charged with developing problem-solving initiatives because precinct commanding officers had the experience and knowledge to solve complex crime issues. Working within the framework of the Department's eight strategies and Compstat process, they developed problem-solving tactics and deployed officers according to a strategy they developed specifically to work on problems in their precinct.

## Commanding officer authority and accountability

Beat officers were just one example of commanding officers' lack of authority over the men and women who worked in their precinct. Specialized units, such as detectives, narcotic units and anti-crime units, were also controlled by other police managers at headquarters. Precinct commanders did not have authority or influence over the assignment and management of these officers. Their hands were tied under a one-dimensional, function-orientated hierarchical police structure. Precinct commanders had been denied greater authority and accountability because it was feared that there was a risk of corruption if headquarter's overview could no longer be achieved through specialized service provided to the precincts, particularly in traditionally corruption-prone areas.

I ensured that commanding officers were put in charge of their personnel and their assignments. They were given the authority to put together a co-ordinated and focused plan to attack crime in their precinct. They were able to identify crime 'hot spots' and assign necessary patrol officers, detectives, undercover and narcotics officers to these problems. I gave precinct commanding officers the authority and made them accountable. Precinct commanders could bring sufficient deterrents to bear on difficult crime areas, resources could be re-allocated from one 'hot spot' to another within the precinct, results could be measured with greater consistency and reliability, and the precinct was a large enough unit to support its own specialized forces.

## The Compstat meeting

As precinct commanders became the focal point for carrying out their own and the Department's crime-reduction strategies, the Compstat meetings and associated activities became the engine for the effort. They were a product of the favourite four-step philosophy for action of Jack Maple, Deputy Commissioner for Crime Control Strategies and Operations. This philosophy has become a mantra in the Department: (1) accurate timely information, (2) rapid, focused deployment, (3) effective tactics, (4) relentless follow-up and assessment. Twice-weekly Compstat meetings require precinct commanders to be ready to review their up-to-date computer-generated crime statistics and relate what they are going to be doing to achieve crime reduction. These meetings are held at Headquarters in the Department 'War Room' which contains large computer-fed screens and other devices for displaying statistics. One reporter sitting in a Compstat meeting described it as follows:

> Maple called the precinct commanders to the front of the room in turn, questioning, prodding, cajoling and occasionally teasing information out of them. They discussed on-going investigations, special operations and any unusual criminal activity. When the men and women from the 81st Precinct got their call, the precinct commanding officer and his staff were asked to explain a recent spate of shootings.
>
> What's going on, Maple wanted to know. Why are these shootings happening? Is it a turf war? No? Well, somebody's not happy. Maybe they're cranky 'cause it's hot outside, but something's happening. When the shooting locations were put up on the huge map projected on the wall, along with those of drug complaints in the precinct, there was a clear overlap. Maple asked what was being done about the drug spots, and one of the narcotics officers said it was a tough area because the business was done inside and there were lots of lookouts. That's fine, Maple said. That's why we're detectives. Tell me what tactics we can employ to penetrate these locations. The detectives said they would try some buy-and-bust operations and maybe get a couple of guys behind the Plexiglas to rat when an arrest was hanging over their heads. Maple wasn't satisfied. I want you back here next week with a plan, he said to the Precinct Captain. Normally each precinct comes in once every four to five weeks.[3]

In order to respond to the kinds of questions posed at Compstat meetings, precinct commanders began bringing with them representatives from other bureaux, such as detectives who were assigned to their precincts. Compstat meetings thus encouraged inter-bureau functional co-ordination.

## Making drug arrests

We also changed the Department's position against police officers making drug arrests. In the past, it was deemed too risky for street officers to make drug arrests. Since there was a great deal of cash involved in drug transactions, it was thought that the risk of corruption was too great. Heavily supervised special squads had primary responsibility for enforcing drug laws. We changed this policy and even encouraged officers to seek out drug arrests during peak drug dealing times.

## Internal affairs investigations

Similarly, I changed the way Internal Affairs were conducted in the NYPD. Prior to my tenure, the Head of the Internal Affairs Bureau and the Police Commissioner were sometimes the only two people who had overall knowledge about corruption investigations in the Department. I changed this policy as well, noting that you have to have confidence and be able to trust the integrity of the command staff and precinct commanders. NYPD's 76 precinct commanders in essence ran 76 mini-police departments. Not trusting them with on-going investigations occurring or involving members of their precincts weakened their authority as well as sending a negative message about their trustworthiness. Inclusion became a very strong team builder and motivation tool.

## Computer access for detectives

Before my tenure, detectives were not allowed to use a number of computer systems because it was thought they would jeopardize the integrity of other investigations. In other words, they were not trusted. These systems included such basic investigatory tools as the computer-assisted robbery system, narcotics databases and on-line warrant system. I gave the detectives access to these computer systems. Integrity was not jeopardized and the NYPD continues to experience some of the steepest crime declines in the country. During my tenure, violent crime has been reduced by 38 per cent and the murder rate has declined by 51 per cent.

## Give the police the credit

However, even as the crime numbers continue to decline today at unprecedented rates across the entire city, there are other sceptics. Some are criminal justice researchers, others are political pundits. They cite theory after theory as to why crime is falling except the one that is of the most significance in New York City: better, smarter and more assertive policing in partnership with the criminal justice system and the community we serve – community policing.

To these critics I unequivocally can say the crime rate did not fall because of the weather. It did not drop due to changing socio-demographic trends. Crime is not down as a result of changes in the economy. The declines may have been affected somewhat by higher prisoner incarceration rates, but the drop in crime in the City has been so precipitous over such a short period of time that the traditional causes of crime, or what we believed to have been the principle causes of crime increases or reductions, just don't apply.

In January 1994, all the young kids in the city did not suddenly become old. All criminals did not suddenly march into jail. 1995 was one of the mildest winters in New York City history: 1994 was one of the worst. Crime went down dramatically in both years, so the weather did not have a significant impact on crime. Murder is not a crime that can be covered up or over-reported. The murder rate has declined by over 50 per cent in New York City because we found a better way of policing. We are results-focused. We are decentralized. We are co-ordinated. We have enough cops and we are using them more effectively. We have partners. We have shown in New York City that police can change behaviour, can control behaviour and, most importantly, can prevent crime by their actions – independently of other factors. We have, in summary, to again quote George Kelling, 're-policed our city streets'.

In response to the criticism that this new policing is too assertive and that citizens are being abused in significantly greater numbers, I am comfortable in saying there is no sustainable evidence to support these assertions. In response, I point to the 166,737 fewer victims of violent crime in the three-year period 1994–96 under our new policing strategies, with our emphasis on prevention rather than reaction, and in public order maintenance as a way of changing behaviour to reduce crime. Did complaints against police increase? Yes they did, but it should be noted that there are over 38,000 police officers making over 300,000 arrests and issuing millions of summonses each year. Compare that activity to the approximately 9,000 citizen complaints that were filed in 1996.

New Yorkers are reporting that they are feeling safer. Residential and commercial real estate markets are booming. The economy has stabilized. Tourism is skyrocketing. New York City is slowly revitalizing itself. There are still serious crime problems in New York City that will require additional strategizing and resources. However, as illustrated by the initial success of the newly-implemented geographically-based rather than functionally-based drug reduction strategies in the Brooklyn North and the upper Manhattan areas of the City, the police can have an impact on even long-standing crime problems. The NYPD, or for that matter any successful policing organization, cannot solve all problems or all crime. However, they should be recognized for what they can do and how well they are doing it today. Fair is fair. We shouldered most of the blame when crime went up. Give us some of the credit when it goes down – and stays down as I confidently predict it will in New York City. And the good news is, 'if you can make it in New York you can make it anywhere'.

## And finally ... a word about 'zero tolerance'

Many police, policy and political leaders have adopted the phrase 'zero tolerance' to characterise the model of policing I initiated in New York City – a phrase used in the title of this book. While the phrase is used more widely in Britain than in the United States, it has gained some currency there as well. The phrase is troublesome.

Throughout my career as a police officer and police administrator, I have been impressed by the complexity of, first, the problems police face and, second, police responses to problems. This was not always apparent in American policing where, within my memory, it was believed that patrol officers handled 'simple' incidents with rote responses – riding in cars, responding rapidly to calls for service, and arresting offenders. My own experience as a young police officer in Boston, especially with early variations of community policing – called neighbourhood team policing during the late 1970s – confirmed for me what a generation of police research has shown: there is nothing rote about police work, it is incredibly complex.

Phrases such as 'zero tolerance' send powerful messages. That is why they catch on so quickly. Clearly, zero tolerance conveys a forceful message about the importance of civility and order in complex societies and about the need for police to restore and maintain order. But it sends other messages as well, and this is what worries me about the equation of 'New York-style' policing with zero tolerance.

First, the phrase smacks of over-zealousness – a real danger when communicating expectations about policing. No one familiar with the business of order maintenance really believes that complex problems such as prostitution, aggressive begging, drug dealing, teen drinking, and others are going to be eradicated in society. They can be managed: that is, they can be reduced and their social costs lessened, but such problems have been, and always will be with us. Second, it is not a credible policy: it communicates to political leaders and the general public an unrealistic view of what police can accomplish. Moreover, it is not credible to trouble-makers. Many know the limitations of police power and authority. For too long, police and other criminal justice agents have sent 'tough' messages to offenders and miscreants and then have not been able to deliver, either because of limitations on their power (limitations that are given in democracies) or because of lack of recourses and facilities. Third, and finally, zero tolerance as a slogan belies the complexity of police work. The idea, which some unthinking police administrators have put forward, that 'Tomorrow we will adopt a zero tolerance or "broken windows" philosophy' and follow it up with a few general orders, dooms order maintenance. Reviving order maintenance as an integral aspect of policing requires leadership, planning, training, guidance and ongoing managerial direction. Given its potential for crime prevention and the improvement of the quality of urban life, it is well worth the effort. Improperly and unthinkingly done, however, order maintenance has considerable potential for trouble, especially in the form of improper, discriminatory, or abusive policing.

Consequently, zero tolerance is neither a phrase that I use nor one that captures the meaning of what happened in New York City, either in the subways or on the streets.

*From Willian J. Bratton, 'Crime is down: blame the police, in Norman Dennis (ed.)* Zero Tolerance: policing a free society *(London: IEA), 2nd edition, 1998, pp 29–42.*

## Notes

1    The US equivalent of the 999 emergency services telephone number.
2    Wilson, J.Q. and Kelling, G.L., 'Broken Windows', *Atlantic Monthly,* March 1982, pp. 29–38.
3    Harvard Business School Case Study #N9-396-293, 11 April 1996, pp. 8–9.

# 29. Beyond zero tolerance

*David Dixon*

## Introduction

'Zero tolerance policing' has several meanings and references.[1] Firstly, those who claim to support it are often merely using a fashionable slogan which condenses and expresses a range of commitments to harshness in criminal justice with no particular reference to specific policing strategies or tactics. Senior police officers often distance themselves from it.[2] It could be objected that, in this form, 'zero tolerance' is not worthy of our attention. None the less, there is something important here, both criminologically and politically. In the degenerate context of law and order politics, it is not possible to dismiss zero tolerance as inconsequential.[3] The political power of tabloid newspapers and talk-back radio should not be underestimated. Unfortunately, many politicians treat policing as a realm where populist common-sense prevails, rather than as an important and complex area of public administration in which policy development should draw on extensive research-based knowledge (Sherman, forthcoming).

Secondly, and literally, 'zero tolerance' would mean that police should fully enforce the criminal law and that discretion would be eliminated from policing. Far from being anything new, this expresses an approach to the law-policing relationship which has long been discredited. For many years, the true nature of American policing was disguised by legal duties of full enforcement – the myth that police could and did enforce the law to the letter without the mediation of discretionary decision-making. Non-enforcement was equated with corruption or inefficiency. This legalistic myth could not survive the emergence of academic research on policing practice which 'discovered' that policing was highly discretionary and that most of it did not involve law enforcement (Dixon, 1997: ch. 1).

It is trite to observe that police have to exercise discretion simply because it is physically impossible to do otherwise. The point was made well by that fine commentator on policing (and ex-police officer) C.H. Rolph in 1959, when he noted that 'The truth is (luckily for us) that there's too much law to be enforced' (1985: 68) and listed 38 offences which he noticed during a brief walk. These were only the tip of an iceberg of 'other things too numerous to mention', such as littering and parking offences. If an officer dealt with one, 'all the rest would have got away ... But it has to be faced that the great majority of policemen (*sic*) would have chosen none of them (1985: 69).

More importantly, 'zero tolerance' suggests that 'zero' is an objectively attainable goal. This is totally to misunderstand the role of law in policing public order. Ironically, it is J.Q. Wilson who provides a classic explanation:

> Most criminal laws define acts ... (P)eople may disagree as to whether the act should be illegal ... but there is little disagreement as to what the behavior consists of. Laws regarding disorderly conduct and the like assert, usually by implication, that there is a condition ('public order') that can be diminished by various actions. The difficulty, of course, is that public order is nowhere defined and can never be unambiguously defined because what constitutes order is a matter of opinion and convention, not a state of nature (1968. 22–3).

Police do not just choose which public order offences to prioritize: they constitute the offence by choosing to intervene. There is no 'offensive language' until an officer decides to define speech as such. The law does not direct police intervention, but rather provides a resource used to categorize, justify, and account (Dixon, 1997). From this perspective, zero tolerance is fundamentally flawed because it is based upon an erroneous conception of law's relationship to policing. A great attraction of zero tolerance is that it purports to eliminate police discretion about what (and who) is to be targeted for attention. Once the impossibility of this is acknowledged, we return to more difficult questions of what should be the priorities of policing, and whose voices should be heard in setting them.

It is the third application of 'zero tolerance' policing which deserves our closer attention. Here, it is shorthand for a group of three related policing strategies. First, police focus on disorder and street offences in attempts to improve 'quality of life' in local areas. Second, police maintain the same focus, but with the expecta-tion that doing so will reduce serious crime – the 'broken windows' thesis. Third, police engage in proactive, intensive operations directed at people, places, and property identified by risk assessment techniques. Clearly, 'zero tolerance' is used very loosely in relation to the last of these.[4] Indeed, my argument is that we need to shift the focus of debate from the misleadingly simple concept of zero tolerance to more complex and significant developments in policing.

This chapter has two objectives. First, it presents a critique of the commonplace argument that the 'broken windows' thesis has been proven to be correct by experience in New York and that Australian police could emulate this success by adopting similar tactics Particular attention is devoted to a critique of Kelling and Coles' *Fixing Broken Windows* (1996). Secondly, it comments on the focus and priorities of current developments in policing. It will be argued that there is great potential in the new strategies for crime control. However, it will also be suggested that criteria of success are inadequately formulated and, specifically, that the need for police legitimacy is both underemphasized and misunderstood. Sources include several related empirical studies of policing Cabramatta,

Australia's leading heroin market (Dixon and Maher, 1998; Maher and Dixon, 1999; Maher *et al.*, 1997, 1998).

## Lessons from America

According to the widely publicized account, the idea of zero tolerance policing came from an article in the *Atlantic Monthly* in which J.Q Wilson and George Kelling hypothesized (without empirical basis[5]) that serious crime could be reduced by clamping down on minor incivilities and disorder.[6] The argument was based on the metaphor of 'broken windows'. Wilson and Kelling claimed that if a broken window in a building is not repaired, others will be broken. The rest of the building, then the street, then the neighbourhood, will deteriorate. The human equivalent of a broken window is 'the ill-smelling drunk, the rowdy teenager, or the importuning beggar … The unchecked panhandler is, in effect, the first broken window' (Wilson and Kelling, 1982: 34).[7] If human 'broken windows' are not fixed, disorder will turn into serious crime because 'serious street crime flourishes in areas in which disorderly behavior goes unchecked' (Wilson and Kelling, 1982: 34). The theory is based on a kernel of common sense or 'folk wisdom' (Wilson and Kelling, 1982: 34): little problems lead to big problems. It also relies on popular but inaccurate accounts of social decline resulting from moral and social indiscipline (the fall of the Roman Empire thesis). Indeed, it is arguable that zero tolerance and 'broken windows' are fundamentally 'not about crime at all, but a vision of social order disintegrating under glassy-eyed liberal neglect' (Shapiro, 1998: 5).

Its supporters claim that the 'broken windows' thesis was proved to be correct[8] in New York in the mid-1990s, when the potent combination of Mayor Rudolph Giuliani and Police Commissioner William Bratton claimed credit for 'the New York miracle' – spectacular falls in recorded crime rates. Felony crime rates halved, while homicides plummeted from 2,245 in 1990 to 767 in 1997. Not surprisingly, this has attracted great interest from police officers, politicians, and media from around the world. All too often, those dispatched on 'study tours' to New York return with a simplistic message courtesy of City Hall's and the NYPD's publicity management: New York has discovered the philosopher's stone which enables police to reduce crime significantly. Bratton confidently asserts 'the good news … "if you can make it in New York, you can make it anywhere"' (1997: 42). Symptomatically, Shane Stone (then Chief Minister of Australia's Northern Territory) announced on his return from New York that 'whether you're talking about New York, Darwin, Melbourne, the lessons are the same'.[9]

## Doubting the miracle

My evaluation of the argument that Australia should seek to emulate the 'New York miracle' suggests that claims about police responsibility for the reduction in crime are exaggerated, that any police effect was not due solely to zero tolerance policing, that any such effect in New York is largely irrelevant to Australia, and that account needs to be taken of the costs of such strategies.

### i. 'Crime is down in New York City: blame the police'

William Bratton (1997; 1998: 289–90) claims not just that the NYPD contributed to the fall in crime, but were solely responsible for it. Against this must be set the fact that significant declines in crime rates in the mid-1990s were recorded in 17 of the 25 largest American cities and in 12 of the 17 advanced industrial countries (Travis, 1998; Young, 1998: 2–4). We do not know why this happened, although it seems likely that key factors are long-term economic revivals and demographic shifts (particularly a declining youth population). But we do know that zero tolerance policing was not responsible, because crime rates dropped in places across the U.S. where very different police strategies were implemented (Pollard, 1997: 43).

In New York, economic, social and demographic changes have to be taken into account, despite Bratton's response to critics that 'We lined up their alternate (*sic*) reasons like ducks in a row and shot them all down' (1998: 290). These are complex matters, open to varying statistical interpretations.[10] Most importantly, there is a significant connection between the falling homicide rate and the decline of the crack cocaine epidemic. Crack was highly conducive to violence both because of its physiological effects and the market competition which its low price encouraged (Goldstein *et al.*, 1989). As the crack epidemic peaked in the late 1980s (Maher, 1997: 21), so the appalling violence which characterized it abated. Bratton claims that the percentage of arrestees who tested positive for cocaine did not decline (1998: 290). It is of course true that cocaine (whether in the form of crack or otherwise) did not simply disappear. However, Bratton ignores the crucial point which is that fewer people initiated crack use: the rate of cocaine use among younger arrestees 'went from 70 percent in 1988 down to 31 percent in 1991 ... Then it declined even further to 22 percent in 1996'.[11] In order to make sense of the extraordinary reduction in homicide in New York City, one has to pay close attention to changes in the illegal drug market (Zimring and Hawkins, 1997: ch. 9). By contrast, smaller cities which are now belatedly experiencing crack epidemics 'are defying the national downward trend in crime rates' (Harcourt, 1998: 337).

### ii. Changes in policing other than 'zero tolerance'

It would be foolish to mirror Bratton's absolutism and claim that the NYPD had no effect on crime. It seems plausible that they did, not least because crime rates declined further in New York City than elsewhere. It should be noted however that even the dramatic fall in homicide was not confined to New York and that Jacksonville, Florida, not New York, had the greatest decline in homicide in the early 1990s (Travis, 1998: 3).

Zero tolerance street policing was merely the most-publicized feature of wide-ranging changes in policing in New York during this period. More policing was also done: police numbers grew significantly during the 1990s.[12] The NYPD also adopted intelligence-led policing, in which traditional reactive tactics are secondary to computer assisted identification of places and people at risk.[13] While this new, technologically-driven policing may be harder to sell to a public fearful of crime than a catchy slogan like zero tolerance, its impact may well be more significant. Computer mapping was a tool of significant managerial changes, in which close supervision and scrutiny of police performance were introduced, notably via the Compstat process, in which local commanders were called to account to the Comissioner and his staff for their performance (Safir nd; Kelling and Coles, 1996: 146–8).[14]

It is claimed that before Bratton's arrival officers were reluctant to focus on street activities because of (a) fears of corruption allegations in relation to drug, vice and gambling enforcement; (b) constitutional challenges to prohibitions on activities such as begging and vagrancy on the basis of rights to free speech and requirements of legal certainty; (c) inadequate supervision and demoralization. More research is needed on changing patterns in the NYPD's work, but this image of a police department which had abandoned street policing prior to zero tolerance is exaggerated. The claim that the NYPD 'has finally wiped the smirk off the faces of millions of streetwise guys who had grown up thinking the police were a joke, rendered nearly impotent by a string of Supreme Court decisions' merely indicates ignorance of policing in New York.[15] Certainly, people whose neighbourhoods were occupied by the NYPD's Tactical Narcotics Teams would have been surprised by suggestions that police had given up street policing in the late 1980s and early 1990s (Maher, 1997: 25; Sviridoff, Sadd, Curtis and Grinc, 1992). The Mollen Commission hardly painted a picture of a department immobilized by legal restriction. However, it did report serious problems in supervision, culture, and morale (Mollen, 1994). The legacy of bitterness and cynicism among the 5000 officers laid off between 1975 and 1978 was significant (McAlary, 1994: 33–8). If a police service is reformed after years of institutional corruption, laziness, and incompetence in some quarters (Pollard, 1997: 50), it should not be not surprising that its efficiency and effectiveness improves.

### iii.  The (ir)relevance of the New York experience

It seems reasonable to accept, within the limits outlined above, that zero tolerance policing may have had some effect on crime in New York. However, the assumption that what 'worked' there will work here is fundamentally misguided. There are major differences between Australia and New York which sharing a common language may obscure.

First, patterns of crime are very different. In New York, the relationship between minor offences and serious crime may have had some validity in the early 1990s. The police were dealing with a highly criminalized, heavily armed population. If an officer stopped and searched a male suspect or arrested him for, say, public drunkenness, there was a good chance that he would be found in possession of an illegal firearm or that he would be the subject of a warrant or on parole for a serious offence. Zero tolerance policing allowed police to deal with serious crime both preventively (deterring carrying unlicensed guns) and directly (taking unlicensed guns off the street and locking up those subject to criminal justice controls). In Australia, the situation is quite different. When police do intensive street operations, they may find people with outstanding warrants, but these are more likely to be for the kind of minor offences which facilitated the intervention than for serious matters. In Australia, people still do not routinely carry guns, as was the case in sections of New York. These points are related to fundamental differences in patterns of violent crime. First, the New York miracle' was essentially about tackling a homicide rate which towers above that in Australia (Zimring and Hawkins, 1997; Fagan *et al.*, 1998; Langan and Farrington, 1998). Secondly, it is almost a cliché to point out that the most problematic form of violence in Australia is private rather than public, and that homicides in Australia overwhelmingly occur between people who are intimates or acquaintances. Our homicide and serious violence rates are unlikely to be affected significantly by zero tolerance policing.

It may, as Don Weatherburn has argued, be worth finding out what kind of offences come to light if warrant checks are done on drunk drivers or fare evaders.[16] Even if, as argued above, doing so is unlikely to affect the homicide or serious violence rate, it might have an impact on offences such as break and enter. But such an experiment would not be an expression of zero tolerance policing: it would merely involve police doing more rigorous checks on people who are already in custody. This has to be distinguished from proactive intervention for the purpose of facilitating a warrant check, e.g. stopping and searching a person when the criterion of reasonable suspicion is not satisfied or enforcing subjective street offences such as offensive language or behaviour.

Secondly, the place of law in Australian life and culture is different in crucial respects from the legalistic, rights-oriented US. As noted above, one of the constraints on NYPD activities in the 1980s and early 1990s was legal: indeed, a substantial part of Kelling and Coles' manifesto for 'broken windows' (1996) strategies is devoted to the extensive constitutional and other legal limits on street policing (see also Ellickson, 1996; Livingston, 1997). Police in Australia have suffered no such constraint, despite what is often said in a remarkably ill-informed public debate about police powers. For example, in NSW, the unqualified power to arrest for any offence, (recently extended) powers to stop and search in the Crimes, Summary Offences, and Drug Misuse and Trafficking Acts, powers to demand name and address and to move on, and the reservoir of power provided by widely-drawn offences such as goods in custody, offensive behaviour, and offensive language provide NSW police officers with an extensive resource of legal authority (Dixon, 1997: ch. 2). While there have been controversies over the particular wording of offensive language and offensive behaviour offences, the legality of such statutes is beyond challenge in Australia. Such offences have not just existed on the statute book: they have been the bread and butter of Australian policing. Far from abandoning public order, our police have always had street offences as their daily fare.

Furthermore, the letter of the law and policing practice are different matters. Anyone who has any knowledge or experience of how street policing actually operates, or has bothered to read the Report of the Royal Commission into the NSW Police Service (Wood, 1997), would be puzzled by assertions that our police work with their hands tied by legal restrictions. Research indicates that street policing in NSW is constrained little by the law (Dixon, 1997: ch. 2, 5). 'Reasonable suspicion' in stop and search can be minimal because it is ineffectively regulated (despite the provision of a new code of practice) and is rarely tested by supervision, whether from superior officers or by the courts. In any case, the need for legal power can be routinely obviated by obtaining 'consent'. The police officer who 'asks' a young person to turn out his or her pockets on the street has no more need of a legal power than the shop attendants or airline security personnel who check your bag: an explicit or implied consent (which in practice may be no more than acquiescence) is all that is needed (Dixon, 1997: ch. 3). Pointing out that policing in NSW is comparatively unregulated in practice by law is not, in itself, a criticism: legalistic policing may be poor, while good policing may be determined by factors other than the law. My objection here is to the quite misleading account of policing in NSW whose accuracy is so often taken for granted.

Fundamental differences in politics and state organization between Australia and the United States need also to be acknowledged. Zero tolerance is a policy designed for a society which regards criminal justice and punishment as its primary tools of social policy. Zero tolerance is a policy for a society divided by chasms of class and particularly race, in which the fear of 'the underclass' permeates. In a highly influential text, J.Q. Wilson writes 'we are terrified by the prospect of innocent people being gunned down at random, without warning and almost without motive, by youngsters who afterwards show us the blank, unremorseful face of a seemingly feral presocial being' (1995: 492). Wilson is too politically adroit to specify the race of these 'youngsters' and disingenuously distances himself from judgment ('seemingly'), but we – and his influential U.S. audience –know what he means. In contrast, Australian society retains (despite growing challenges) a commitment to a broader state capacity in welfare and public health and to inclusive policies of multiculturalism and reconciliation. Indeed, comparison with the US makes resistance to current challenges to fundamental aspects of Australian society particularly pressing.

### iv. Costs of zero tolerance

Despite what has been suggested above, it may still be argued that zero tolerance should be tried because it will have some effect on serious crime. Alternatively, the emphasis may shift away from serious crime: it may be argued that zero tolerance should be used because of its direct effects on minor offences and other disorder. Improvement of the 'quality of life' in an area may be presented as a more appropriate objective. In both respects, it is necessary to take account of the potentially counterproductive effects of zero tolerance policing. What is gained may not be worth the cost.

First, there is a documented history of intensive, proactive street policing leading to serious social disorder (Pollard, 1997: 60). Indeed, I remember reading 'Broken windows' when it appeared in 1982 and being struck by its irrelevance because of the authors' apparent ignorance of this. I was then in England, where the policing debate was dominated by the 1980–81 riots. Attention focused principally on the Brixton riots which were set off by intensive stop and search operations carried out by the Metropolitan Police. Lord Scarman's report on Brixton eloquently dismissed the argument that police actions were justified by a duty to enforce the law. According to Scarman, maintenance of public order is the primary mandate and the law has to be exercised with the discretion which 'lies at the heart of the policing function' (1981: para. 4.58). Scarman went on to argue that discretion could only be properly used by police who had good relations with the local community, consulted, them, and were (in this limited sense) accountable to them (1981: paras. 4.60, 5.56–58). He was reflecting the knowledge learnt from the experience of the riots in US cities in the 1960s: the counterproductive failure of intensive policing had led to the search for new policing strategies, such as community and problem-oriented policing. Today's police may be less concerned than before about public disorder: they are much better prepared both in tactics and equipment to respond. However, the inability of the Los Angeles Police Department – the epitome of modern police paramilitarism – to contain the riots following the trial of Rodney King's assailants should lead even the hardest head to question the desirability of relying on superior force (Cannon, 1997).

To point out that overpolicing may spark disorder is familiar. Less so, but equally important, is the argument that underpolicing may do the same. Wilson and Kelling's 'Broken windows' argued that policing should target neighbourhoods in decline. (However, it should be pointed out that complaints about disorder often come most loudly from upwardly mobile areas, in which new residents are discomforted by the presence of unrespectable neighbours and street people: inner Sydney provides several such examples.) What of places which have already 'declined'? Wilson and Kelling suggested that some neighbourhoods are so 'demoralized and crime-ridden' that proactive policing is impossible (1982: 38).[17] Irvine Welsh's 'Detective Sergeant Bruce Robertson' puts it more bluntly: 'Zero tolerance of crime in the city centre; total *laissez faire* in the schemie hinterlands. That's the way forward for policing in the twenty-first century' (1998: 273). The consequence of police withdrawing from areas except in response to emergency calls was seen in the riots in the sump public housing estates of Northern England in the early 1990s. This time, it was under-, not over-policing that was crucial. 'Communities' whose structures had been eaten away by mass unemployment and the accompanying social, economic, and political marginalization turned upon themselves (Campbell, 1993).

Secondly, even if serious disorder is not instigated, zero tolerance is likely to worsen relations between police and the communities whose activities are no longer tolerated. It represents a serious threat to a conception of community policing as founded on close, cooperative relations between police and people. Those targeted by police have to be marginalized as 'not part of the community'. The persistent attempt to explain away the British riots of the 1980s and early 1990s as the work of 'outsiders' always faltered before the evidence that most of those rioting were *part* of the community. A local example is provided by our research in Cabramatta: police mistreatment of young Indo-Chinese heroin users has implications for relations not just with that group, but with the broader Indo-Chinese community (Maher, Dixon, Swift and Nguyen, 1997). As even Bratton acknowledges (1998: 291–2), the increase in complaints of police brutality in New York in the mid-1990s was a clear indicator of the cost of encouraging police aggression.[18] The danger is that, however fancy the packaging of zero tolerance, operational officers receive it as coded order to do the 'dirty work' (Kelling and Coles, 1996: 121), a mandate to get tough on the streets, just to return to 'how policing used to be'.[19] The NYPD officers who, while sexually assaulting and beating Abner Louima, declared 'This is Giuliani time'[20] were not, as J.Q. Wilson claims (1997), merely bad apples: their actions have to be understood in the context of zero tolerance policing. This applies *a fortiori* to the shooting of Amadou Diallo by the Street Crimes Unit (Kolbert, 1999).

A third cost of zero tolerance (combined with sentencing policies providing mandatory sentences for accumulated lesser offences) may be expansion of the prison population. New York State has more than three times as many people in gaol now as it did in 1980 (Massing, 1998: 8)[21] This cost may be acceptable: indeed, some, like Giuliani, regard the growth of imprisonment as one of his administration's achievements. In criminal justice, we may be certain of little: but one thing we surely do know is that imprisonment should be minimized because of its counterproductive effects. Indeed, if one *wanted* to make minor crime lead to major crime, sending to jail those who commit the former would be an excellent way of doing so. (On the criminogenic effects of zero tolerance tactics, see Sherman, 1997: 18.) In addition, those concerned about crime, disorder and victimization should recognize their existence *inside* prisons: mass warehousing of offenders creates criminogenic and often very dangerous conditions.

A fourth example of counterproductive effects is provided by the experience in Australia of applying tactics influenced by the New York experience to the policing of drug markets (Dixon and Maher, 1998). Cabramatta has been the subject of intensive policing for some time, but in the period since July 1997 intensive deployment of uniformed officers in Operation Puccini has attempted to drive heroin use and sales out of the CBD. In this programme of saturation policing, between mid-1997 and mid-1998 'more than 16000 ... had their details checked by police' (Cassidy, 1998: 4). Influenced by zero tolerance policies, police have used minor offences as a way of deterring drug users and of facilitating searches and warrant checks: for example, 4,286 railway infringement notices were issued (Cassidy, 1998: 4). If the objective was to improve the quality of (some people's) life in central Cabramatta, it has had some (but certainly not total) success. But such success has been bought at considerable public health costs (encouraging unsafe practices in storing and transferring illegal drugs and in using and disposing of injecting equipment), social, geographical and substance displacement, and hardening of the target by encouraging drug market participants to become more organized (Dixon and Maher, 1998; Maher and Dixon, 1999; Maher et al., 1998). The amount of heroin sold and bought in South West Sydney does not appear to have been reduced: the market is affected only to the extent that some heroin is being sold in different ways, by different people, in different places. Meanwhile, the price of heroin has declined significantly and a market for injectable cocaine has become established.[22]

## The criminal justice cringe

A disappointing characteristic of debates on policing in Australia is the criminal justice cringe – the assumption that we should copy what has been done in the

United States. It is encouraged by some American academics and officials who are apparently oblivious to the irony of presenting U.S. society and its criminal justice system as an exemplar. As suggested above, zero tolerance is a policy for a society very different from Australia. Of course, it would be equally foolish to suggest that there is nothing to be learned from the U.S. Specifically, the New York experience provides important lessons about crime management, proactive policing, and the use of new technologies. The NSW Police Service is developing programmes drawing on some aspects of this experience.

However, another feature of the criminal justice cringe is inadequate recognition of superior elements within our own institutions and policies. In significant respects, zero tolerance is archaic. New York-style policing involves using enforcement of the criminal law as the primary tool in dealing with the disorderly behaviour of people who are intoxicated, homeless or mentally ill (Travis, 1997). For us, this would mean reverting to methods of dealing with social problems which have long been discredited. It beggars belief that zero tolerance should be promoted to deal with alcohol abuse in the Northern Territory's Aboriginal communities.[23] In that case, zero tolerance is a policy whose time has come and gone: that time was between 1943 and 1970, when arrests for public drunkenness accounted for between 32% and 54% of all non-traffic arrests in NSW (Brown *et al.*, 1996: 922). As a method of dealing with the social, economic and health problems of Aboriginal communities, we know that zero tolerance was an abject, shameful failure: the Royal Commission into Aboriginal Deaths in Custody should surely have brought that message home. Politicians and others who ignore this are culpably irresponsible (Cunneen, 1999).

New York-style policing means fighting a war on drugs although Australian police leaders recognize the futility of such an approach and support harm minimization. Australia has a considerable international reputation for our bipartisan commitment to harm minimization as the foundation of its national drug strategy. Our priority here should be translating harm minimization into policing practice (Maher and Dixon, 1999), rather than indulging in 'bizarre American fantasies of "zero tolerance"' (Pearson, 1992: 18). Once again, zero tolerance is not new, and we know what it produces: the U.S. commitment to zero tolerance of illegal drugs has been a recipe for harm maximization (Drucker, 1998; Wodak and Lurie, 1996).

Similarly, zero tolerance may involve the criminalization of prostitution or the use of street offences and powers to disrupt strolls. The costs of inevitably un-successful attempts to prohibit prostitution are well-recognized in Australia and the priority is to develop modes of regulation which allow prostitution to be conducted in ways which minimize prostitution-related harms by seeking to ensure the safety and protect legitimate interests of both prostitutes and residents. In addition, as noted above, New York-style policing will greatly expand the prison population a time when it is widely accepted in Australia that the sensible policy is to minimize the use of imprisonment because of its cost and its counterproductive effects.

Finally, there is a tendency to undervalue the potential contribution of Australian researchers, some of whom are producing work of international quality. We underestimate our own policies, resources and institutions when we slavishly look to the United States for guidance. In many of the matters involved here, we have as much to teach New York as to learn from it.

## Zero tolerance and community policing

Some police and commentators distance themselves from 'zero tolerance' but accept key elements of it in more acceptable neologisms such as 'confident', 'in your face', 'firm but fair' or 'back to basics' policing. These are indicators of a troubling trend in contemporary policing which is best illustrated by the work of Kelling and Coles (1996). They present their major work, *Fixing Broken Windows*,[24] as if it conforms with the paradigms of community policing and community crime prevention. They provide an excellent critique of 'professional policing' (1996: ch. 3) and present their work as advocating the 'new paradigm of community-based policing' (1996: 7). This, however, is disingenuous, because the programme advocates an approach which would subvert community policing. This is not the place for a definition, but by this I do not merely mean neighbourhood watch, beat patrols, consultative committees, and inter-agency cooperation, but a philosophical abandonment of the claims to autonomy and expertise which were characteristic of 'professional' policing. 'Broken windows' and its offspring, zero tolerance, amount to an attempt to colonize community policing and community crime prevention and to turn them into tools of professional crimefighting in a way that would threaten the significant progress in policing over the last quarter of this century.

For some thirty years, those who prefer to see (and do) policing as the work of autonomous, hierarchical law enforcers and crime fighters have been threatened by advocates of community policing (in all its many guises) who have argued that reactive crime-fighting is inefficient and marginal to key policing tasks. Broken windows and zero tolerance square the circle, promising that law enforcement will reduce crime and restore public order, allowing aggressive law enforcement to be done in the name of community policing (cf Johnston, 1997; Pollard, 1997: 49). If *Fixing Broken Windows* was simply advocating a problem-oriented, 'whole of government' approach (as Kelling and Coles insist), then it says nothing new: indeed, it fails to take account of the most interesting conceptual and empirical work in the field (e.g. Crawford, 1994, 1995, 1997; Hope and Shaw eds 1988; Liddle and Gelsthorpe, 1995; Pearson *et al.*,1992). They merely offer old clichés: for example, they insist that police–community partnerships 'must be fully inclusive of all racial, ethnic, religious, and economic groups' (1996: 234), but they say nothing about the practicalities and problems of achieving this. What is new (and problematic) is the role to be played by law enforcement. Their commitment to inter-agency problem-solving is skin-deep. They promote the police as the lead agency, with law enforcement as the primary strategy of problem-solving, and show no recognition of the problems which this assumption of leadership causes in inter-agency partnerships (Crawford, 1997; Liddle and Gelsthorpe, 1994).

Kelling displays a lamentably narrow knowledge of the criminological literature. He speaks of the left's axioms: To deal with crime one must deal with the social 'causes' of crime – poverty, racism and social injustice; minor offences like prostitution and aggressive panhandling are victimless crime; police order-maintenance activities constitute a 'war against the poor and minorities'; behaviours called disorderly are really expressions of cultural diversity that challenge middle-class mores; and finally, individual rights eclipse community interests ... (1997b: 5).

It may be true that some expressions of this peculiar blend of vulgar marxism, simplistic labelling theory, and civil libertarianism can still be found in the deep backwoods of U.S. criminology. But to identify it with contemporary critical criminology is either dishonest or ignorant. Left realism began to emerge twenty-four years ago (Young, 1975) and has constituted a major new paradigm in criminology for the last decade. The key studies were by English criminologists.[25] While the parochialism of criminology in the U.S. may explain Kelling's myopia, one might expect him to be aware of such developments via the work of writers such as Elliott Currie (e.g. Currie, 1985, 1998).

In *Fixing Broken Windows*, Kelling and Coles try desperately to claim the centre ground, flaunting their commitment to community policing and insisting that policing must be moral and legal. This position is deeply flawed. Their commitment to community policing is rhetorical. Their claims about police commitments to community policing can be undermined by going to the horse's mouth: William Bratton's self-aggrandizing[26] autobiography makes quite clear that what happened in New York in the mid-1990s was not community policing, but the application of new strategy, tactics, and technology by a police leadership which was committed to very traditional conceptions of police autonomy, social order, and crime.[27] Bratton's book may be 'full of anodyne prose about the importance of cooperation between the cops and the community', but the 'idea of cooperation ... doesn't remotely describe what happened in New York under Bratton ... Indeed the police under Bratton were determined not to work with the community' (Massing, 1998: 4). John Timoney (a key member of Bratton's inner circle and now chief of police in Philadelphia) 'contemptuously dismissed the idea that the police should enlist neighbourhood residents in fighting crime ... "It's the cops' job to fight crime. Community policing" said the cops "can't do it alone." Our answer was, "Yes, they can"' (Massing, 1998: 7).

Their insistence that policing must be legal has an obvious superficial attraction. However, it expresses a legalistic belief that police illegality is the key problem and that law provides solutions. This ignores the crucial work in the sociology of policing which has shown how law has facilitated abuse, and that the significant distinction is not between law and practice, but between legal ideology and law's substance (McBarnet, 1983; Dixon, 1997: 28–40).

Perhaps most problematically, there is their use of the term 'community'. It is a cliché to point out that this has been a problematic term in the community policing literature. Nevertheless, for most it has denoted a political (liberal/social democratic) aspiration towards inclusion and consultation: 'community' means as much of society as possible. In Kelling, Coles, and Wilson's writing, there is a politics of exclusion which operates through dichotomies: 'decent folk' versus 'drunks and derelicts' (Wilson and Kelling, 1982: 30); a 'stable neighborhood of families' versus one populated by 'unattached adults' (Wilson and Kelling, 1982: 31, 32); 'the public' versus 'aggressive panhandlers, dishevelled vagrants, and rude teenagers' (Kelling and Coles, 1996: xiv); 'good citizens' versus 'the homeless' (Kelling and Coles, 1996: 218); 'prostitutes harassing husbands in front of their wives and kids, panhandlers sticking cups under peoples' (sic) noses'; 'citizens ... trying to protect their own territory' threatened by 'predators'. Wilson and Kelling's list of human 'broken windows' could be a quotation from Tom Robinson's 'Power in the Darkness' – 'disreputable or obstreperous or unpredictable people: panhandlers, drunks, addicts, rowdy teenagers, prostitutes, loiterers, the mentally disturbed' (1982: 3). According to Kelling and Coles, 'ordinary citizens' are those 'who travel daily along streets and by public transportation to work, to school, to shop, in pursuit of all the ordinary activities of everyday life' (1996: 108). Ranged against them (or, rather, 'us', for 'we experience the problem': 1996: xiv – this is a conspiracy of inclusion as well as of exclusion) are 'the unruly and predators', 'those who behave in outrageous ways, and who prey on the weak and the vulnerable (1996:9).[28]

Of course, the function of dichotomies such as these is to express the superiority of one side over the other. The way in which Kelling and Coles construct their dichotomies has a peculiarly legalistic character. In their argument that the courts have ill-advisedly interfered with police attempts to control disorder, they claim that this has involved privileging 'the rights of these individuals' over 'the interests of the community' (Coles, 1997). The disorderly are individualized and isolated from the groups which their proponents seek to protect:

> Many people think that trying to regulate disorder means jumping on the homeless and pitting the rights of the rich against those of the poor. That sort of thinking is a definite obstacle. What we need to focus on is dealing with *acts by people* and regulating troublesome unlawful behaviour. (Coles, 1997, original emphasis)

> The *act* of pan-handling, the *act* of public drinking, are disorderly behaviors of concern here – not being poor ... The issue is behavior (Kelling and Coles, 1996: 40).

This approach is strengthened by undermining the claims to status by those who use the law in order to challenge police actions: notably, people are said to be not really homeless, but to have chosen to live on the street when other arrangements were available. Predictably, they introduce a new version of the hoary distinction between the deserving and the undeserving poor. They adopt Scheidegger's classification of the 'have-nots', who are 'the genuinely poor'; the 'can-nots', who are 'the seriously mentally ill and addicted'; and the 'will-nots', who are 'those for whom living on the streets and hustling, including criminality, has become a life style ... (T)he have-nots are not generally the problem; repeated and continuous antisocial behavior by the can-nots and will-nots is' (1996: 68).

Yet they are inconsistent: here they insist on the individual focus, but in rejecting court-imposed limitations, they argue that judges looked at 'acts by people' rather than their 'agglomeration' effect. Coles criticizes courts for looking 'at individual cases apart from the broader context within which they take place ... Judges are asked to make decisions about the lawfulness and the impact of individual acts. This is problematic' (Coles, 1997; cf Wilson and Kelling, 1982: 9). Having discredited one group status – homeless, poor – Kelling and Coles inscribe another – disorderly, criminal – which excludes people from the category of 'citizen'. As such, it is a notable example of how 'social exclusion' is constructed and mobilized (Finer and Nellis, eds 1998; Jordan, 1996).

They individualize litigants and reduce their rights to personal claims: a concept of rights as *part of* a communal interest is alien to this philosophy. In counterpoising 'the legitimate rights of individuals' and 'the interests of neighborhoods and communities' (1996: 5), Kelling and Coles express a conventional conservative resistance to the expansion of rights which reflects the schlock jurisprudence of their mentor, who asserts that 'Courts are institutions whose special competence lies in the discernment and application of rights. This means that to the extent courts decide matters, the drift of policy will be toward liberty and away from community' (J.Q.Wilson, in Kelling and Coles, 1996: xiv).

Their work expresses a fundamental misunderstanding of 'community'. These neat dichotomies of 'us' and 'them' misrepresent a reality in which criminals and the disorderly are part of, not alien predators on, communities. Drug markets are particularly significant examples of this, as a *New York Times* reporter explained:

> ... while many people on the block say they hate the sight of dealers and users on the streets where their children play, many also concede that these soldiers of the drug trade are less invaders than part of the community's tangled web of blood ties and friendships (quoted in Maher, 1997: 24).

Our research in Cabramatta found not dichotomy but complexity: street-level user-dealers are people's sons, daughters, brothers, sisters, grandchildren. Their families would like the drug trade to stop. But when police mistreat their young people in the ways which usually accompany crackdowns, they resent it and police–public relations are harmed.

This misunderstanding of community in the work of Kelling and Coles stems at least in part from their methods. They see the world (literally as well as figuratively) from a police perspective (ironically echoing familiar elements of police culture) and have no contact with 'the other' except when protected by a police officer's presence (see 1996: 236–7). Kelling stares at four Afro-American boys, 'something he would not have done had the officer not accompanied him' (1996: 236). They are dehumanized in his description: they sit with their 'shoulders slouched over, vulture like' (1996: 236). Kelling's fears are confirmed by a report that, soon afterwards, the four mugged someone. Some thirty years ago, sociologists of deviance showed that to explain, we have to understand, and to understand, we have to do research which involves contact with 'the other'.

Only work of this kind (e.g. Maher, 1997) allows real and inclusive under-standing of community.

Ever concerned to anticipate accusations of illiberalism and to wrap themselves in defensive consensus, Kelling and Coles insist that they 'have the same concerns about homelessness, poverty, and social injustice as do the vast majority of the population' (1996: 64; see also Kelling, 1997b). None the less, the politics of their account is an unmistakably conservative lament about social decline. The behaviours of disorderly individuals are the product of 'individualism', their synonym for permissiveness.

> The primacy of the 'self' and the right to be 'different'; a corresponding emphasis on individual needs and rights, and the belief that such rights were absolute; a rejection, or at least serious questioning of middle-class morality; the notion that stigmatizing individuals as criminals or deviants turned them into criminals or deviants; and the positing of solutions such as mental hospitals, therapies, and other interventions as more insidious than the problems they were designed to address ... The increase in urban disorder that has occurred in the past thirty years, in many senses is rooted in these very changes ... (1996: 41–2).

Here is a very familiar social conservative account which traces the roots of contemporary problems to the challenges to authority and slackening of discipline supposedly characteristic of the 1960s. As Margaret Thatcher told us, 'We are reaping what was sown in the Sixties. The fashionable theories and permissive claptrap set the scene for a society in which the old virtues of discipline and self-restraint were denigrated'.[29] William Bratton's view is similar: he 'disliked everything about the sixties' (1998: 35), while he saw the late 1970s as 'an anything-goes era' in which 'society was becoming increasingly tolerant of aberrant behavior' and its standards declined in consequence (1998: 87).

In summary, beneath Kelling and Coles' patina of consensus, there lies a series of political standpoints on policing, crime, and community which are, to those who do not share their brand of social conservatism, highly problematic.

## Policing and crime control

### i. From zero tolerance to the new policing

Far from being an insignificant slogan, zero tolerance is but part of a new paradigm in policing. Its emergence may presage as significant a shift as that which occurred when community policing challenged law enforcement policing. Zero tolerance is to be understood in the context of broader changes in criminal justice practices and rhetorics. Clearly there are dangers of overstating their unity and novelty, and ignoring the differences between what is said and done. Nevertheless, there is a shape here in which a variety of trends are articulated, not in a formal programme, but in a significant tendency. This is indicated by the shift in conceptual foundations from

*certainty/individual/guilt/rights/reactive response*
to
*flexibility/group/risk/safety/proactive intervention.*

It is not possible to develop this argument here: the significant point for present purposes is to insist that the broader political and social implications of broken windows and zero tolerance policing deserve serious attention. There is considerable danger that we may complacently dismiss zero tolerance, while allowing ourselves to shuffle crab fashion into something much more significant. Such change in the criminal justice process is driven by deeper social, political and economic changes: returning to older conceptions of policing is simply not an option. The significant choices involve attempts to direct, rather than reverse, the course of change.

There are elements of the new policing which are desirable. Greater managerial involvement in and supervision of policing strategies may be beneficial: the NSW Police's Operations and Crime Review process shows how lessons can be taken from Compstat. Technologies such as risk assessment, crime mapping and proactive strategies which involve the deployment of resources where they are most needed are potentially valuable in responding to problems of crime and disorder which a realist criminology must recognize as more than law and order rhetoric. There are some interesting projects of this kind in NSW.[30] While critical of some aspects of Operation Puccini, I would argue that drug policing by means of law enforcement may, if carefully deployed, make a significant contribution to a harm minimization strategy (Pearson, 1992). Such policing must be proactive, targeted, information-led and intensive – all features of the new policing. The issue is not whether such strategies are appropriate, but how they are used, how their targets are identified, whose opinions count, and how their benefits and costs are calculated.

### ii. Can police control crime?

A foundation stone of modern policing studies and policy is the body of research on police activity which has found that conventional policing – random patrol and reactive investigation – cannot substantially reduce crime (Reiner, 1992: 147–9). The classic example here is the Kansas City Preventive Patrol Experiment (Kelling *et al.*, 1974), in which comparative deployment of various styles of policing was found to have no significant effect on crime, on fear of crime, or on attitudes towards the police. Indeed, it appears that the variation was hardly noticed by many residents. Most criminal activity is unaffected by police either because it is not reported or is, to all intents and purposes, undetectable (Bayley, 1994: ch. 1). An illustrative example is provided by our recent study of the illicit drug market, which shows that the risks of arrest per street-level heroin transaction in Australia are relatively low. Using data from the Australian Bureau of Criminal Intelligence on the total number of heroin arrests in Australia for 1996–7, we calculate the risk of arrest per transaction as being between one in 2,600 and one in 10,900 (Maher, Dixon, Lynskey and Hall, 1998).

Within levels of resources and powers which can realistically be provided, it is unlikely that conventional policing can significantly reduce general crime rates.[31]

Such research findings were sometimes misinterpreted as a part of a simplistic claim that 'nothing works'. For example, Gottfredson and Hirschi concluded: 'no evidence exists that augmentation of police forces or equipment, differential patrol strategies, or differential intensities of surveillance have an effect on crime rates' (1990: 270, quoted in Sherman, 1992: 167). The flaws in this position are apparent. If it is accepted that police have *some* effect in controlling crime,[32] then there is no reason to believe that the extent of this effect is determined and unchangeable. The significant issue is how that effect can be altered. The continuing importance of studies such as the Kansas City project is that they demonstrate that changes in policing of the kind that are conventionally demanded will be ineffective: 'Hiring more police to provide rapid 911 responses, unfocused random patrol, and reactive arrests does not prevent serious crime' (Sherman, 1997: 1).

Such studies do not show that 'nothing works'. As Sherman demonstrates, careful analysis of the extensive research literature shows that some things have worked: there is research evidence that certain strategies and tactics can reduce crime in particular contexts. I say 'have worked' rather than 'do work' to emphasize a point that Sherman makes: the studies show that certain strategies and tactics have worked in reducing or preventing crime at particular times in particular places. There is no guarantee that they will work elsewhere, particularly when 'elsewhere' is another country (Sherman, 1998: 26). The cautionary tale of Sherman's own work on mandatory arrest policies to counter domestic violence illustrate the point best. One study appeared to demonstrate that arrest was the most effective police action. Police forces in many jurisdictions consequently advised or instructed officers to arrest suspects in domestic violence cases. However, subsequent research has shown that, in some areas, the same beneficial arrests have not been produced, while in others arrest increases subsequent violence. According to Sherman's interpretation of these data, the effect of arrest depends upon the suspect's socio-economic status (1992: 203–12).

The first lesson to take from this is that great care should be taken in adopting new strategies because their success cannot be guaranteed and, to the contrary, they may actually increase rather than control crime (other counterproductive effects are considered below). Secondly, they need to be specific: 'crime' is far too imprecise a target. Everything we know to date suggests that claims that police activity has significantly reduced 'crime' should be treated sceptically. The worthwhile questions are more specific: how can particular police tactics affect particular patterns of crime in particular places and what lessons can be learnt about the applicability of such tactics elsewhere? Thirdly, we need much more high-quality research on Australian policing. Some excellent work has been (and is being) done, but compared to the vast U.S. Literature, there is much more to do.

A recent review by Ross Homel emphasizes that successful crime control necessitates moving well beyond conventional policing strategies: policing can affect particular types of crime, 'but usually only in cooperation with other agencies and only if they adopt strategies which are in stark contrast to those dictated by the "professional law enforcement" model' (Homel, 1994: 32; cf

Sherman, 1997). There is a real danger that the coincidence of conventional policing strategies (notably crackdowns) and crime reductions wholly or largely the result of factors outside police control may lead to misplaced confidence in the efficacy of such strategies.

### iii. Assessing crime control strategies

As Sherman puts it 'it is not necessary to like punishment or devalue due process to value the development and testing of police crime-control strategies' (1992: 17). However, it is necessary to add some qualifications to claims about the success of certain policing strategies.

First, there is a tendency to rely on easily quantifiable measures of police performance. Rates of stop/search, move on, and arrest have their uses, but also dangers. Focusing too closely on what can be counted is not always the best way to identify good policing, or good police officers. It is notable that the NSW Audit Office's first study of policing (1998) focused on response times, despite extensive research showing that reducing response times does not reduce crime (Bayley, 1994: 6; Sherman, 1997: 7–9). Criticism of the impact of the Audit Commission's work on policing policy and practice are relevant to developments in NSW (Leishman *et al.*, eds, 1996; Power, 1997). Audit-accountability is limited by its dependence on what can be counted. Politicians and policy-makers might do better to consult the research literature and to educate themselves and the public about what is significant in policing.

A related point is obvious, but still significant: real temptation is put before police officers whose performance is assessed according to statistics that they themselves provide (Pollard, 1997: 52–3). Manipulation of statistics was an entrenched practice in New South Wales until its exposure by Philip Arantz (Arantz, 1997). In 1998, the *New Times* reported 'charges of falsely reporting crime statistics in Philadelphia, New York, Atlanta and Boca Raton, Fla., resulting in the resignation or demotion of high-ranking police commanders'. The New York subway, site of Kelling and Bratton's first triumph, was involved: the 'head of the police department's transportation bureau was forced to resign ... over allegations of a scheme to reclassify incidents on the subway as street crimes ... (M)anipulation had gone on for many years and had underestimated crime in the subways by about 2 percent'.[33]

Secondly, 'success' should not be judged purely in terms of effects on crime: policing strategies may have significant effects other than those on which police usually focus. For example, Operation Puccini, a series of intensive crackdowns on the Cabramatta heroin market, is presented by the NSW Police Service as an 'outstanding success' (Cassidy, 1998). However, as noted above, our research reports that such success has been bought at a significant price in terms of displacement, public health, and damage to police–community relations (Dixon and Maher, 1998; Maher and Dixon, 1999; Maher *et al.*, 1997, 1998). Such outcomes have not been adequately considered as potential consequences of intensive policing operations.

It may be that, if they were, the strategies would still be considered a success. More significantly, there is room for legitimate disagreement about criteria for defining success. In other words, defining success is not exclusively a matter of science, but also one of policy and politics. The issue of displacement provides a particularly important example here. Displacement was an *intended* effect of Operation Puccini. Those responsible for the strategy regard it as desirable, arguing that a dispersed drug market is both more controllable and more equitable: the key analogy is to aircraft noise (Dixon and Maher, 1998). While I consider this to be a serious misunderstanding of the nature and effects of displacement in the context of drug markets,[34] the significant point for present purposes is simply that there is room for legitimate disagreement about such issues.

This specific example illustrates a crucial general point. The choices made in the new policing are not matters of autonomous professional judgment, just police business. They involve the exercise of significant political discretion. Targeting and setting priorities involves as a corollary that some policing tasks are allocated less resources and lower priority. This is not an argument for reviving the call for 'democratic control' of the police. Rather, it requires us to look forward to new modes of governance which provide effective, just and accountable policing. In this respect, the discussion and recommendations by the Royal Commission into the NSW Police Service were particularly disappointing (Dixon, 1999). Its discussion of parliamentary accountability relied on a division between policy and operational matters which had not only been discredited in the academic literature, but the inadequacies of which were clearly illustrated by the Report's treatment of the dispute over replacing the Special Branch. As regards broader 'community' accountability, the Royal Commission provided an accurate critique of consultative committees in England and Wales, then inexplicably went on to recommend something very similar for New South Wales. These were to be complemented by higher level committees to advise the Police Commissioner. It may be useful for the Commissioner to have such resources, but they have little to do with accountability or meaningful consultation when the consultation is on the terms set by and with whom he chooses to appoint. It is hard to see how they could, as was expected, connect with local level committees.

The key issue is political in a broader sense. Policing is, to use an old but useful cliche, too important to be left to the police. Most of their key concerns are not just police issues: they are social, economic, and health issues. Drug policing provides the obvious example. An effective public policy response must be one in which interdisciplinary, multi-agency approaches are translated from rhetoric into real commitment. The problems resulting from police operations in Cabramatta which our research has demonstrated are strong examples of how the new policing will be problematic unless it learns what should be some old lessons about the limitations of a form of policing which is defined by the police.

### v. *Legitimacy and efficiency*

The harm which some police strategies and tactics can do to police–public public relations has been noted above. It is worth emphasizing the instrumental significance of police legitimacy: the point is that legitimate policing is not just more popular, but is also more efficient. It is in this context that the need for legitimacy receives appropriate and welcome recognition in Sherman's survey of what works in policing for crime prevention:

> the less respectful police are towards suspects and citizens generally, the less people will comply with the law. Changing police 'style' may thus be as important as focusing police 'substance'. Making both the style and substance of police practices more 'legitimate' in the eyes of the public ... may be one of the most effective long-term police strategies for crime prevention (1997: 1).

He cites significant research (notably Tyler, 1990) which reports a 'strong correlation ... between perceived legitimacy of police and willingness to obey the law' (1997: 22). While Sherman argues that zero tolerance tactics such as intensive field interrogations can be used 'in a polite manner that fosters rather than hinders police legitimacy', he acknowledges that this has often not been the case and that they 'have often been a flash point of poor police–community relations' (1997:18).

In NSW, it appears that this relationship between legitimacy and efficiency is sometimes inadequately appreciated and, in traditional fashion, it is expected that legitimacy will be a by-product of efficiency. It seems unfortunate, for example, that consideration of complaints and other indicators of police–community relations was not built into the Operations and Crime Review process from the start. There is a commitment to consider complaints, but its implementation will come when the tone and priorities of OCRs has been established. At times, the reform process is presented as a distraction from the key task of fighting crime: officers are encouraged to put the Royal Commission behind them and to get back to fighting crime. Indeed, the Commission is sometimes presented as a diversion which criminals exploited as 'the Police Service had "taken its eye off the ball" while it cleaned up corruption within the force and that was the cause of the State's high crime rate'.[35]

> The arrest rates have gone down ... that's why crime is going up ... What I have to do is say to the cops: 'Never mind this reform business this is what it will mean to you over time and we'll get there. But for now concentrate on ... getting crime down'.[36]

The attractions of such rhetoric are clear enough; however, its dangers should also be recognized. Far from putting the Commission behind them, officers should be reminded of it every day. If policing in New South Wales is to be fundamentally refashioned (as Wood showed it needs to be), then the active involvement of every officer in the process will be needed. A commitment to fighting crime is not enough (Dixon, 1999).

The counterpoising of legitimacy and efficiency is related to other common dichotomies such as crime control versus due process and police powers versus suspects' rights. As I have argued elsewhere (Dixon, 1997), such dichotomies have consistently obstructed constructive discussion and policy development in criminal justice. Recent legislation in NSW such as the Young Offenders Act and the Detention After Arrest Act provide important examples of changes in criminal justice which cannot be simplistically slotted into one or other side of these dichotomies. A more mature approach to criminal justice would appreciate that legitimacy and efficiency (like due process/crime control and police powers/ suspects' rights) are not necessarily counterpoised.

## Conclusion

I have argued in this chapter that great care needs to be taken in taking lessons from policing in New York (or, indeed, anywhere else). Rhetoric about the effectiveness of zero tolerance obscures important and complex questions of evaluation, policy, and principle. What we need is a new policing, not the old 'professionalism' dressed up with tactics, technology, and rhetoric.

*From David Dixon, 'Beyond zero tolerance' in 'Mapping the boundaries of Australia's criminal justice system', Proceedings of the Australian Institute of Criminology's, Third National Outlook Symposium on Crime in Australia, Canberra, 22–23 March 1999* (http://www.aic.gov.au/conferences/outlook99/dixon.html).

## Notes

1   Zero tolerance also has other, related applications outside policing, e.g. in drug policy.
2   An exception is in Cleveland (England), although even here an alternative neologism, 'confident policing', is offered (Dennis and Mallon, 1997; Romeanes, 1998).
3   On Australia, see Hogg and Brown, 1998. In Britain, 'New' Labour has enthusiastically associated itself with zero tolerance (Morgan and Newburn, 1997; Palmer, 1997). The Crime and Disorder Act 1998 is a legislative expression of the tensions in New Labour's criminal justice policies: 'anti-social behaviour orders' sit alongside requirements for inter-agency cooperation.
4   Both Police Minister and Police Commissioner have described intensive operations against NSW drug markets as adaptations of zero tolerance policing.
5   This much-reprinted article is often treated as if it reports research: it does not, *contra* e.g. Adam Graycar, have 'findings' (Graycar, 1998: 2).
6   It should be noted that while zero tolerance usually prioritises law enforcement, 'Broken windows' suggested a broader order maintenance strategy, not least because some of the targeted behaviour was not illegal and because some of the police methods advocated to deal with disorder were unlawful.
7   While usually a metaphor, 'broken windows' is sometimes used literally, in claims that environmental decay leads to social disorder, and then to more serious crime: see e.g. Wilson's foreword to Kelling and Coles, 1996: xv.
8   Skogan had attempted to prove that disorder was significantly related to serious crime in his *Disorder and Decline* (1990). Kelling and Coles make much of Skogan's findings (1996: 22–7). However, Harcourt's rigorous reexamination of Skogan's data concludes that they do not show that disorder leads to crime and, consequently, 'do not support the broken windows hypothesis' (1998: 296).
9   *ABC Lateline*, 4 June 1998.
10  See e.g. Fagan *et al.*'s discussion (1998) of the effects of demographic change on homicide: apart from analysing at-risk groups separately from the general population, researchers have to take account of nonlinear effects, such as thresholds after which trends increase or decrease.
11  Travis, 1998: 5. For details, see Golub and Johnson, 1994; Johnson *et al.*, 1998a; 1998b. For an important argument that the decline of crack was due not to external, official action but to changes by and within marginalized communities, see Curtis, 1998.

12 Even this apparently straightforward matter is disputed: compare Harcourt, 1998: 333–4 and Bratton, 1998: 290. The effects of attrition and the merging into the NYPD of Transit and Housing Authority officers into the NYPD cause the difficulty.

13 What is novel is the capability provided by new technology and the strategic deployment of risk assessment (Ericson and Haggerty, 1997; Johnson, 1998). As Sherman suggests, identification of 'high-risk locations, victims and offenders' as a policing tactic goes back at least as far as Fielding's and Colquhoun's foundational policing in the eighteenth century (1992: 162).

14 The NSW Police Operations and Crime Review process draws heavily on Compstat, providing a good example of what can usefully be learnt from the NYPD's experience.

15 R. Basham, quoted in 'Combating crime' NSW Police News, August 1998 at 43.

16 Interview on the ABC Law Report 25 August 1998; transcript at: http://www.abc.net.au/rn/talks/8.30/lawrpt/lstories/1r980825.htm

17 But contrast Kelling and Coles' suggestion that 'Even those neighborhoods struggling with significant levels of predatory behavior ... can benefit from taking the first steps toward attempting to restore order' (1996: 242).

18 Force allegations peaked in 1995, but declined in the following three years before beginning to rise again. For analyses of official statistics, see Brereton, 1999; Harcourt, 1998: 377–80; Shapiro, 1998. For a more controversial analysis, see Amnesty International (1996). As significant as complaint statistics is the expression of public concern associated with causes célèbres such as Louima and Diallo: see e.g. Kolbert, 1999 and 'Thousands gather again to protest police shooting,' New York Times, 10 February 1999.

19 Mike Bennett's letter to the Police Review (20 September 1996) expresses this well: 'As I enter my thirty-sixth year of service, I realise that I am considered a dinosaur but I have policed the streets in the style that Bratton used in New York and it does work. It ... would need the total commitment from chief constables who appear to want to involve themselves with the social conditions instead of upholding the law as they were sworn to do.'

20 'Zero tolerance policy questioned after assault', Washington Post, 20 August 1997, A03.

21 Assessment is complicated by the countervailing trend of declining crime rates (Brereton, 1999) and the use of the 'process as the punishment' in zero tolerance arrests, so that charges are not pursued after offenders have been detained for a few hours by police.

22 See 'Illicit drug reporting system', Drugs Trends Bulletin, October 1998.

23 'Drunks to get zero tolerance,' The Australian, 13 May 1998.

24 Despite the title, their main concern is not the link between disorder and serious crime. They believe that it exists, but are more concerned about tackling disorder per se than doing so a mode of serious crime prevention. They criticize the 'policy bias toward serious crime' (1996: 5), arguing that it diverts attention from significant problems of disorder and does so by promoting counterproductive 'solutions' such as 3 strikes and capital punishment. More generally, Kelling and Coles soften the message of the original 'Broken windows', ignoring for example the original essay's apparent approval of extra-legal police violence. For his response to such criticism, see Kelling, 1997b.

25 For a summary, see Young, 1997; n.b. also the Australian adaptation and development e.g. Hogg and Brown, 1998.

26 n.b. his book's subtitle.

27 Kelling and Coles felt some discomfort from Bratton's 'tough talk' and acknowledged that 'in its emphasis on aggressive order maintenance, the NYPD appears to some to have moved outside the pale of community policing and to be involved in a revival of reform-model policing (1996: 161).

28 See Harcourt (1998: 297–8, 303–5) for a perceptive discussion of the use and meaning of dichotomies in the 'broken windows' literature.

29 Quoted in The Observer, 28 March 1982.

30 For example, the NSW Police Waratah area reports good results from the targeting of recidivist offenders and hotspots in Operation Digos: see Police Service Weekly, 31 August 1998, pp. 4–5.

31 This assumes that the police in question work with reasonable efficiency. If a department is institutionally corrupt, with substantial numbers of lazy and incompetent officers, one could expect even reform along traditional professional policing lines to improve effectiveness.

32 If this really needs to be demonstrated, studies of what happens when police strike are available: see Sherman, 1997: 6–7.

33 'Pressure to manipulate crime data worries police', New York Times, 3 August 1998. For discussion of related problems, see Coleman and Moynihan, 1996: 32–6.

34 In addition, it was informed by research analysis which was weak and ill-informed: see Dixon and Maher, 1998. 'Smart policing' needs a better research and analysis basis than it currently has. Another example of inadequacy with damaging consequences is analysis of 'Asian crime and culture' upon which NSW Police have drawn: for a critique, see Dixon, 1998.

35 'Stay out of politics Ryan told' *Daily Telegraph*, 25 September 1997; see also 'Crime is soaring says Ryan' *Sun-Herald*, 21 September 1997.
36 Quoted, 'Get back on the beat' *Sun-Herald*, 21 September 1997.

## References

Amnesty International (1996) *Police Brutality and Excessive Force in the New York City Police Department*, Report AMR 51/36/96 (New York: Amnesty International).

Arantz, P. (1997) *A Collusion of Powers* (Sydney: P.Arantz).

Audit Office (1998) *Police Response to Calls for Assistance* (Sydney: Audit Office).

Bayley, D. (1994) *Police for the Future* (New York: Oxford University Press.

Bratton, J. (1997) 'Crime is down in New York City: blame the police', in N. Dennis, ed. *Zero Tolerance: Policing a Free Society* (London: Institute of Economic Affairs) 29–42.

Bratton, W. (1998) *Turnaround: How America's Top Cop Reversed the Crime Epidemic* (New York: Random House).

Brereton, D. (1999) 'Zero tolerance and the NYPD', paper presented to the Australian Institute of Criminology Conference 'Mapping the Boundaries of Australia's Criminal Justice System', Canberra, March 1999.

Brown, D., Farrier, D. and Weisbrot, D. (1996) *Criminal Laws* (Sydney: Federation).

Campbell, B. (1993) *Goliath. Britain's Dangerous Places* (London Methuen).

Cannon, L. (1997) *Official Negligence: How Rodney King and the Riots Changed Los Angeles and the LAPD* (New York: Random House).

Cassidy, B. 1998) 'Outstanding success of Operation Puccini', *Police Service Weekly*, 1 June 1998, pp. 4–5.

Coleman, C.A. and Moynihan, J. (1996) *Understanding Crime Data* (Buckingham: Open University Press).

Coles, C.M. (1997) 'The promise of public order', http://www.theatlantic.com/unbound/bookauth/broken/broke.htm

Crawford, A. (1994) 'The partnership approach: corporatism at the local level?' *Social & Legal Studies* 3: 497–519.

Crawford, A. (1995) 'Appeals to community and crime prevention', *Crime, Law & Social Change* 22: 97–126.

Crawford, A. (1997) *The Local Governance of Crime* (Oxford: Clarendon Press).

Cunneen, C. (1999) 'Zero tolerance policing: implications for indigenous people', paper prepared for the Aboriginal and Torres Strait Islander Commission (Sydney: Institute of Criminology).

Currie, E. (1985) *Confronting Crime* (New York: Pantheon).

Curtis, R. (1998) 'The improbable transformation of inner-city neighborhoods: crime, violence, drugs and youth in the 1990s', *Journal of Criminal Law and Criminology* 88 (4).

Currie, E. (1998) *Crime and Punishment in America* (New York: Henry Holt).

Dennis, N. and Mallon, R. (1997) 'Confident policing in Hartlepool', in N. Dennis, ed. *Zero Tolerance* (London: Institute of Economic Affairs) 61–86.

Dixon, D. (1997) *Law in Policing: Legal Regulation and Police Practices* (Oxford: Clarendon Press).

Dixon, D. (1999) 'Changing police? Reform, regression and the Royal Commission into the NSW Police Service, in D. Dixon ed. A *Culture of Corruption: Changing an Australian Police Service* (Sydney: Hawkins Press).

Dixon, D. and Maher, L. (1998) 'The policing of drug offences', in J. Chan, D. Dixon, L. Maher and J. Stubbs *Policing in Cabramatta*, unpublished report for the NSW Police Service.

Dixon, D. and Maher, L. (1999) 'Walls of silence', in G. Hage and R. Couch, eds *The Future of Australian Multiculturalism*, (Sydney, Research Institute for Humanities and Social Sciences).

Drucker, E. (1998) 'Drug prohibition and public health', http://www.of-course.com/drugrealities/acrobat.htm

Ellickson, R.C. (1996) 'Controlling chronic misconduct in city spaces,' *Yale Law Journal* 105: 1165–248.

Ericson, R. and Haggerty, K.D. (1997) *Policing the Risk Society* (Oxford: Clarendon Press).

Fagan, J., Zimring, F. and Kim, J. (1998) 'Declining homicide in New York City,' *Journal of Criminal Law and Criminology* 88 (4).

Finer, C.J. and Nellis, M. eds (1998) *Crime and Social Exclusion* (London: Blackwell).

Goldstein, P.J. *et al.* (1989) 'Crack and homicide in New York City,' *Contemporary Drug Problems* 16:651–82.

Golub, A. and Johnson, B.D. (1994) 'A recent decline in cocaine use among youthful arrestees in Manhattan', *American Journal of Public Health* 84: 1250–4.

Gottfredson, M.R. and Hirschi, T. (1990) *A General Theory of Crime* (Stanford: Stanford University Press).

Graycar, A. (1998) 'Incivility and crime in Australia', paper to conference on Partnerships in Crime Prevention, Australian Institute of Criminology, Hobart, February.

Greene, J.A. (1999) 'Zero tolerance: a case study of police policies and practices in New York City', *Crime and Delinquency* 45:171–87.

Harcourt, B.E. (1998) 'Reflecting on the subject: a critique of the social influence conception of deterrence, the broken windows theory, and order-maintenance policing New York style', *Michigan Law Review* 291–389.

Hogg, R. and Brown, D. (1998) *Rethinking Law and Order* (Sydney: Pluto).

Homel, R. (1994) 'Can police prevent crime?', in K. Bryett and C. Lewis eds *Unpeeling Tradition* (Brisbane: Centre for Australian Public Centre Management) 7–34.

Hope, T. and Shaw, M. eds. (1988) *Communities and Crime Reduction* (London: HMSO).

Johnson, B.D., Thomas, G. and Golub, A. (1998a) 'Trends in heroin use among Manhattan arrestees from the heroin and crack eras', in J.A. Inciardi and L.D. Harrison eds *Heroin in the Age of Crack Cocaine* (Beverly Hills: Sage).

Johnson, B.D., Dunlap, E. and Associates (1998b) *Natural History of Crack Distribution/Abuse*, Final Report to the National Institute on Drug Abuse, unpublished (New York: NDRI).

Johnston, L. (1997) 'Zero tolerance policing: a civilising mission', paper presented at the British Criminology Conference, Belfast, July 1997.

Johnston, L. (1998) 'Policing communities of risk', in P. Francis, P. Davies and V. Jupp eds *Policing Futures* (London: Macmillan) 186–207.

Jordan, B. (1996) *A Theory of Poverty and Social Exclusion* (Cambridge: Polity).

Kelling, G.L. (1997a) 'The promise of public order' http://www.theatlantic.com/unbound/bookauth/broken/broke.htm

Kelling, G.L. (1997b) 'Crime control, the police, and culture wars: broken windows and cultural pluralism', lecture to the National Institute of Justice, 2 December 1997.

Kelling, G.L. and Coles, C.M. (1996) *Fixing Broken Windows* (New York: Free Press).

Kelling, G., Pate, T., Dickerman, D., and Brown, C. (1974) *The Kansas City Preventive Patrol Experiment* (Washington DC: Police Foundation).

Kolbert, E. (1999) 'The perils of safety', *The New Yorker* 22 March 1999, 50–5.

Langan, P.A. and Farrington, D.P. (1998) *Crime and Justice in the United States and in England and Wales, 1981–96* (Washington: National Institute of Justice).

Lardner, J. (1997) 'Can you believe the New York miracle?' *New York Review of Books* 14 August 1997, 54–8.

Leishman, F., Loveday, B., and Savage, S.P. eds (1996) *Core Issues in Policing* (London: Longman).

Liddle, A.M. and Gelsthorpe, L. (1994) *Inter-Agency Crime Prevention* (London: HMSO).

Livingston, D. (1997) 'Police discretion and the quality of life in public places: courts, communities and the new policing', *Columbia Law Review* 97: 551–672.

McAlary, M. (1996) *Good Cop, Bad Cop* (New York: Pocket Star).

McBarnet, D. (1983) *Conviction* 2nd ed. (London: Macmillan).

Maher, L. (1997) *Sexed Work: Gender, Race and Resistance in Brooklyn Drug Market* (Oxford:Clarendon.

Maher, L. and Dixon, D. (1999, in press) 'Policing and public health: law enforcement and harm minimization in a street-level drug market', *British Journal of Criminology*.

Maher, L., Dixon, D., Swift, W., and Nguyen, T. (1997) *Anh Hai: Young Indo-Chinese People's Perceptions and Experiences of Policing*, UNSW Law Faculty Research Monograph (Kensington: UNSW Law Faculty).

Maher, L., Dixon, D., Lynskey, M. and Hall, W. (1998) *Running the Risks: Heroin, Health, and Harm in South West Sydney*, NDARC Monograph no. 38 (Sydney: National Drug and Alcohol Research Centre).

Marlow, A. and Pitts, J. (1998) 'Law and order, crime control and community safety', in A. Marlow and J. Pitts eds *Planning Safer Communities* (Lyme Regis: Russell House) 1–10.

Massing, M. (1997) 'The blue revolution', *New York Review of Books* 19 November 1998 (references to version on http//www.nybooks.com).

Mollen, M. (1994) *Report of the Commission to Investigate Allegations of Police Corruption and the Anti-Corruption Procedures of the Police Department* (New York: Mollen Commission).

Mogan, R. and Newburn, T. (1997) 'Tomorrow's world', *Policing Today*, June, 42–5.

Palmer, D. (1997) 'When tolerance is zero', *Alternative Law Journal* 22: 232–6.

Pearson, G. (1992) 'Drugs and criminal justice', in P.A O'Hare *et al.* eds *The Reduction of Drug-Related Harm* (London: Routledge) 15–29.

Pearson, G., Blagg, H., Smith, D., Sampson, A., and Stubbs, J. (1992) 'Crime, community and conflict: the multi-agency approach', in D. Downes ed. *Unravelling Criminal Justice* (London: Macmillan).

Pollard, C. (1997) 'Zero tolerance: short term fix, long-term liability?' in N. Dennis, ed. *Zero Tolerance: Policing a Free Society* (London: Institute of Economic Affairs) 43–60.

Power, M. (1997) *The Audit Society* (Oxford: Clarendon).

Reiner, R. (1992) *The Politics of the Police* (Hemel Hempstead: Harvester/Wheatsheaf).

Rolph, C.H.(1985) 'Police discretion', in C.H. Rolph, *As I was Saying* (London: Police Review Publications) 68–71 (reprinted from *New Statesman* 11 October 1959).

Romeanes, T. (1998) 'A question of confidence', in R.H. Burke ed. *Zero Tolerance Policing* (Leicester: Perpetuity Press) 39–48.

Safir, H. (nd) *The Compstat Process* (New York: NYPD).

Scarman, L. (1981) *The Brixton Disorders* (London: HMSO).

Shapiro, B. (1998) 'Zero-tolerance gospel' http://oneworld/issue497

Sherman, L. (1993) 'Why crime control is not reactionary', *Police Innovation and Control of the Police* (New York: Springer-Verlag) 171–89.

Sherman, L.W. (1997) 'Policing for crime prevention', in L.W. Sherman, D.C. Gottfredson, D.L. MacKenzie, J. Eck, P. Reuter and S.D. Bushway, *Preventing Crime: What Works, What Doesn't, What's Promising* (Washington: National Institute of Justice), references to http://www.ncjrs.org/works/chapter8.html

Sherman, L.W. (1998) Paper to conference on 'Crime Prevention through Social Support', Conference Proceedings, Standing Committee on Law and Justice, NSW Parliament Legislative Council, Report #11.

Sherman, L.W. (forthcoming) 'Evidence-based policing', in E. Waring and D. Weisburd eds *Crime and Social Organization*.

Silverman, E. (1998) 'Below zero tolerance: the New York experience', in R.H. Burke ed. *Zero Tolerance Policing* (Leicester: Perpetuity Press) 49–56.

Skogan, W. (1990) *Disorder and Decline* (New York: Fress Press).

Sviridoff, M., Sadd, S., Curtis, R., and Grinc, R. (1992) *The Neighborhood Effects of Street-Level Drug Enforcement* (New York: Vera Institute of Justice).

Travis, J. (1997) 'The mentally ill offender', speech to the National Association of State Forensic Mental Health Directors, 3 September.

Travis, J. (1998) 'Declining crime and our national research agenda', inaugural lecture, John Jay College, 9 March.

Tyler, T. (1990) *Why People Obey the Law* (New Haven: Yale University Press).

Walker, S. (1984) ' "Broken windows" and fractured history', *Justice Quarterly* 1: 75–90.

Welsh, I. (1998) *Filth* (London: Jonathan Cape).

Wilson, J.Q. (1968) *Varieties of Police Behaviour* (Cambridge: Harvard University Press).

Wilson, J.Q. (1995) 'Crime and public policy', in J.Q. Wilson and J. Petersilia eds *Crime* (San Francisco: ICS Press) 489–507.

Wilson, J.Q. (1997) 'Policing: zero tolerance and the broken windows theory', workshop presentation, Centre for Independent Studies, Sydney, 16 October.

Wilson, J.Q. and Kelling, G.L. (1982) 'Broken windows', *The Atlantic Monthly* (March) 29–38.

Wodak, A. and Lurie, P. (1996) 'A tale of two countries: attempts to control HIV among injecting drug users in Australia and the US', *Journal of Drug Issues* 27: 117–34.

Young, J. (1975) 'Working class criminology', in I. Taylor, P. Walton and J. Young eds *Critical Criminology* (London: Routledge and Kegan Paul).

Young, J. (1997) 'Left realist criminology', in M. Maguire, R. Morgan and R. Reiner eds *The Oxford Handbook of Criminology*, 2nd edition (Oxford: Clarendon) 473–98.

Young, J. (1998) *The Criminology of Intolerance* (Middlesex: Centre for Criminology).

Zimring, F.E. and Hawkins, G. (1997) *Crime is not the Problem: Lethal Violence in America* (New York: Oxford University Press).

# 30. Reforming to preserve: Compstat and strategic problem solving in American policing

David Weisburd, Stephen D. Mastrofski, Ann Marie McNally, Rosann Greenspan and James J. Willis

Reform, that you may preserve – Lord Macaulay, 1831.

If we want everything to remain the same, then everything is going to have to change – Giuseppe di Lampedusa, 1958.

Introduced as recently as 1994 by then Commissioner William Bratton of the New York City police department, Compstat has already been recognized as a major innovation in American policing. In the few years since its appearance, it has been reported that police departments around the country have begun to adopt Compstat or variations of it (Law Enforcement News, 1997; Maas, 1998; McDonald, 2001). In turn, the program has received national publicity (including awards from Harvard University and former Vice President Al Gore) and has been credited by its originators and proponents with impressive reductions in crime and improvements in neighborhood quality of life in New York City. Other cities, such as violence-plagued New Orleans, have reported success with their versions of Compstat (Gurwitt, 1998; Remnick, 1997), and agencies from around the nation and the world are flocking to New York City to learn more about the program (Maas, 1998).

The attention shown this reform indicates it may become the twenty-first century ideal of what it means to be a progressively managed department, much as Theodore Roosevelt's 'good government' approach to policing did a century ago (Berman, 1987). As with Roosevelt's reforms, Compstat did not emerge full-blown and unprecedented in New York City. Commissioner Bratton and his staff drew heavily on management principles that had already received acclaim as state-of-the-art and forward-looking (Bratton, 1998; Micklethwait and Wooldridge, 1996; Simons, 1995). These principles included developing a management commitment and capacity to ((1) clarify the agency's mission by focusing on its basic values and embodying them in tangible objectives, (2) give priority to operational objectives over administrative ones, (3) simplify managerial accountability for achieving those objectives, (4) become more adept at scanning the organization's environment to identify problems early and develop strategies to respond (e.g., being 'data-driven'), (5) increase organizational flexibility to implement the most promising strategies, and (6) learn about what works and what does not by following through with empirical assessment of what happened. These among other features of management style, have come to be characterized as 'strategic leadership' and 'strategic choice' (Beer, 1980: 45; Finkelstein and Hambrick, 1996).

Elements of strategic leadership date back to Philip Selznick (1957), but they received tremendous attention in the United States in the 1980s, when organizational development leaders made them bywords of progressive management in the private sector (Micklethwait and Wooldridge, 1996). Since then, elements of this approach have been introduced to government agencies in general (Osborne and Gaebler, 1992), and to the police in particular under the rubric of problem-oriented policing (Goldstein, 1990). Compstat brings many of these management prescriptions together in a single program customized for police organizations. We characterize this approach more generically as 'strategic problem solving'. 'Strategic' is an apropos descriptive because it highlights the thrust of this reform to establish a big-picture approach to police management's need to deal with an uncertain and unstable environment.

This chapter provides the first national description of Compstat programs, considered in the framework of strategic problem solving. Relying on a survey of American police departments conducted by the Police Foundation, we examine the diffusion of Compstat programs and the nature of Compstat models throughout the United States. We also assess the penetration of models of strategic problem solving more generally into American policing. Our findings document a process of 'diffusion of innovation' (see Rogers, 1995) of Compstat-like programs in larger police agencies that follows a rapid pace. At the same time, our data suggest that many elements of strategic problem solving had begun to be implemented more widely across American police agencies before the emergence of Compstat as a programmatic entity, and that such elements have been adopted broadly even by departments that have not formally adopted a Compstat program.

To understand the rapid diffusion of Compstat-like programs in large police agencies in the United States, we will argue that this innovation should be seen less as a revolution in American policing than as an evolution of principles that have been developing on the American police scene over the last two decades. However, the fact that many of the components of Compstat were being implemented in police agencies as part of a more general trend toward strategic problem solving is not enough in our view to explain the rapid adoption of Compstat programs that we document in our chapter. Nor is the much touted, although largely undocumented promise of Compstat as a crime-prevention tool (Bouza, 1997; Eck and Maguire, 2000; Witkin, 1998) sufficient as an explanation for its extraordinarily rapid diffusion among contemporary police organizations in the United States (Crank and Langworthy, 1992; Manning, 1997; Mastrofski, 1998). We show in our chapter that specific components of this innovation that reinforce traditional hierarchical structures of police organization have taken a predominant role in the implementation of Compstat-like programs nationally. This leads us 'to question whether the rapid rise of Compstat in American police agencies can be interpreted more as an effort to maintain and reinforce the 'bureaucratic' or 'paramilitary' model of police organization (see Bithier, 1980; Goldstein, 1977; Punch, 1983) that has been under attack by scholars for most of the last two decades (Goldstein, 1990; Greene and Mastrofski, 1988; Mastrofski, 1998; Skolnick and Bayley, 1986; Weisburd *et al.*, 1988) than as an attempt to truly reform models of American policing.

We begin our chapter by describing the emergence of Compstat in New York City and defining core elements of the Compstat model. We then describe our study and findings and conclude with a discussion of their implications.

## Compstat and organizational change: history and core elements

The Compstat idea emerged as a new administration took office in New York City, promising to control crime and disorder. Viewed in a broader context, the shape of organizational reform derived from several sources. First are the failures, both perceived and documented of 'traditional' policing (Fogelson, 1977; Goldstein, 1990; Kelling and Moore, 1988; Weisburd and Braga, 2003): entrenched bureaucracies that focused more on administration than real performance, rising crime rates, increasing fear of crime, studies showing that traditional reactive enforcement approaches had no effect on crime, and competition from the private sector in the form of corporation-provided security services. In this context as Mark Moore has written, 'Commissioner Bratton's bold statement – reacceptance of responsibility for controlling crime – was a very important moment in leadership of the criminal justice system' (1997: 67). Second is the ambiguity of setting priorities under community policing programs, and especially the challenge of finding ways to harness the diffuse forces that pressure a police agency once it commits to decentralizing decision making, increasing the participation of the rank-and-file, and encouraging community input in setting priorities and partnership strategies with the police (Mastrofski, 1998).

On the positive side, four rapidly growing and interrelated trends made strategic problem solving in the context of Compstat both appealing to police leaders and feasible to implement. First among these is problem-oriented policing (Goldstein, 1990), an approach that, above all, stresses the importance of data-driven decision making about what to do. A second trend is the growth in knowledge about crime and effective responses to crime (Braga, 2001; Sherman, 1990; Sherman and Weisburd, 1995; Sheet, man *et al.*, 1997). A third trend is the ready availability of rapidly growing technology in computers, data management and analysis, geographic information systems, and communications – all of which make it possible to process large amounts of information and disseminate it to diverse users on a timely basis (Anselin *et al.*, 2000; Weisburd and McEwen, 1997). Finally, police leaders have become increasingly open to the prescriptions of progressive management, communicated to them by consultants, trainers, and contractors outside policing who apply the most recent terms, methods, and approaches to strategic management developed for corporations in the private sector (Klockars and Harver, 1993; Micklethwait and Wooldridge, 1996). These positive and negative trends have attracted and driven police leaders toward an increasingly accepting view of strategic problem solving.

A review of the emergence of Compstat in New York helps us understand what Compstat is and why it emerged there. The particulars of Compstat's origins have been described in considerable detail elsewhere (Bratton, 1998; Kelling and Coles, 1996; Maple, 1999; McDonald *et al.*, 2001; Silverman, 1999). The impetus behind Compstat was Commissioner Bratton's intention to make a huge organization, legendary for its resistance to change (Sayre and Kaufman, 1960), responsive to his leadership, a leadership that had clearly staked out crime reduction and improving the quality of life in the neighborhoods of New York City as its top priorities (Bratton, 1999). Based on his belief in principles of strategic leadership and his own experiences with the Boston Police Department and the New York City Transit Police, Bratton and his lieutenants set out to disprove skeptics who claimed that the police can do little about crime and disorder.

At the outset, Bratton and his administration's analysis of NYPD's problems revealed several deficiencies that have long been identified as forms of bureaucratic dysfunction (Merton, 1940). First, the organization lacked a sense of the importance of its fundamental crime control mission. Second, NYPD was not setting high enough expectations about what its officers could do and accomplish; consequently, a lot less was getting done than was possible. Third, too many police managers had become moribund, content to continue doing things the way they had always been done, rather than searching for better ways to accomplish results. The police were not taking advantage of new theories and studies that highlighted promising strategies to reduce crime and improve the quality of life in neighborhoods. Fourth, the department was beset with archaic, unproductive organizational structures that did more to promote red tape and turf battles than to facilitate teamwork to use scarce resources effectively; operational commanders were 'handcuffed' by headquarters, lacking authority to customize crime control to their precinct's needs. Finally, the department was 'flying blind'; it lacked timely, accurate information about crime and public safety problems as they were emerging; it had little capacity to identify crime patterns; and it had difficulty tracking how its own resources were being used. And middle managers were not in the habit of monitoring these phenomena, thus serving as a weak link in the chain of internal accountability between top brass and street-level police employees.

Bratton used a 'textbook' approach to deal with these problems, following the major prescriptions offered by organizational development experts to accomplish organizational change (Beer, 1980). He brought in outsiders to obtain a candid diagnosis of the organization's strengths and weaknesses. He incorporated both top-down and bottom-up processes to implement change (Silverman, 1996). He sought and obtained early indicators of the success of the change efforts, and he sought ways to reinforce the individual efforts of his precinct commanders and the rank-and-file, by using both incentives and disincentives (Bratton, 1996).

Strictly speaking, Compstat refers to a 'strategic control system' developed to gather and disseminate information on NYPD's crime problems and track efforts to deal with them. As such, it addresses the problem of inadequate information described above, and in this sense, it is a structure intended to serve the implementation of NYPD's Crime Control and Quality of Life Strategies (Office of Management Analysis and Planning, undated: 1). But it has become shorthand for the full range of strategic problem solving in the department. These elements of NYPD's Compstat approach are most visibly displayed in the twice-weekly Compstat 'Crime Control Strategy Meetings', during which precinct commanders appear before several of the department's top brass to report on crime problems in their precincts and what they are doing about them.

This occurs in a data-saturated environment in which Compstat reports play a central role. Precinct crime statistics and other information about the precinct and its problems are projected onto overhead screens, and commanders respond to queries about what they are doing to deal with those problems. Crime data that were once three to six months late are now available to precinct commanders on a weekly basis *for the past week*. The report includes weekly, monthly, and annual tallies of crime complaints, arrests, summonses, shooting incidents, and victims, organized by precinct, borough, and citywide. In addition, electronic pin maps are generated to show how crimes and police activities cluster geographically. Hour-of-the day analyses and 'crime spike' analyses are also carried out. In addition, the precinct commander's background is profiled, as well as other features of the precinct under his or her command (e.g., demographic data, workload data, and various activities).

Compstat reports serve as the database for commanders to demonstrate their understanding of the crime problems in their areas and discuss future strategies with the top brass and other commanders present. Cross-unit coordination is planned, if necessary, and all of the plans are thoroughly documented. When the precinct is reselected for participation in a Compstat meeting, the commander must demonstrate that he or she has followed up on these strategies. Sometimes commanders bring subordinates with them so that they can report on their efforts and receive recognition. The Press and other outside agencies are sometimes invited to attend these sessions, with as many as 200 people in attendance, thus providing 'great theater' and developing in the public a greater awareness of how the department is being managed (Bratton, 1998: 296).

But there is far more to Compstat than this (Giuliani and Safir, 1998; Gurwitt, 1998). Drawing from what those who developed Compstat have written (see Bratton, 1996, 1998, 1999; Maple, 1999) as well as what those who have studied Compstat have observed (see Kelling and Coles, 1996; McDonald *et al.*, 2001; Silverman, 1999), we identify six key elements that have emerged as central to the development of strategic problem solving in Compstat programs: mission clarification, internal accountability, geographic organization of command, organizational flexibility, data-driven problem identification and assessment, and innovative problem solving. Together they form a comprehensive approach for mobilizing police agencies to identify, analyze, and solve public safety problems.

### Mission clarification

Compstat assumes that police agencies, like military organizations, must have a clearly defined organizational mission in order to function effectively. Top management is responsible for clarifying and exalting the core features of the department's mission that serve as the overarching reason for the organization's existence. Mission clarification includes a demonstration of management's commitment to specific goals for which the organization and its leaders can be held accountable, such as reducing crime by 10% in a year (Bratton, 1998).

### Internal accountability

Internal accountability must be established so that people in the organization are held directly responsible for carrying out organizational goals. Compstat meetings in which operational commanders are held accountable for knowing their commands, being well acquainted with the problems in the command, and accomplishing measurable results in reducing those problems, or at least demonstrating a diligent effort to learn from the experience, form the most visible component of this accountability system. However, such meetings are part of a more general approach in which police managers are held accountable and can expect consequences if they are not knowledgeable about or have not responded to problems that fit within the mission of the department. 'Nobody ever got in trouble because crime numbers on their watch went up. I designed the process knowing that an organization as large as the NYPD never gets to Nirvana. Trouble arose only if the commanders didn't know why the numbers were up or didn't have a plan to address the problems' (Maple, 1999: 33). Internal accountability in Compstat establishes middle managers as the central actors in carrying out the organizational mission, and it holds them accountable for the actions of their subordinates.

### Geographic organization of operational command

Although Compstat holds police managers to a high level of accountability, it also gives commanders the authority to carry out the agency's mission. Organizational power is shifted to the commanders of geographic units. Operational command is focused on the policing of territories, so central decision-making authority on police operations is delegated to commanders with territorial responsibility (e.g., precincts). Functionally differentiated units and specialists (e.g., patrol, community police officers, detectives, narcotics, vice, juvenile, traffic, *etc.*) are placed under the command of the precinct commander, or arrangements are made to facilitate their responsiveness to the commander's needs. Silverman notes that in New York, 'Rather than allow headquarters to determine staffing and deployment on a citywide basis, it was decided that reducing crime, fear of crime, and disorder would flow from patrol borough and precinct coordination of selected enforcement efforts' (1999: 85).

### Organizational flexibility

Middle managers are not only empowered with the authority to make decisions in responding to problems, but they are also provided with the resources necessary to be successful in their efforts. Compstat requires that the organization develop the capacity and the habit of changing established routines to mobilize resources when and where they are needed for strategic application. For example, in New York City, 'Commanding officers (COs) were authorized to allow their anticrime units to perform decoy operations, a function that had previously been left to the Citywide Street Crime Unit. Precinct personnel were permitted to execute felony arrests warrants, and COs could use plainclothes officers for vice enforcement activities. Patrol cops were encouraged to make drug arrests and to enforce quality-of-life laws' (Silverman, 1999: 5).

### Data-driven problem identification and assessment

Compstat requires that data are made available to identify and analyze problems and to track and assess the department's response. Data are made available to all relevant personnel on a timely basis and in a readily usable format. According to Maple, 'We needed to gather crime numbers for every precinct daily, not once every six months, to spot problems early. We needed to map the crimes daily too, so we could identify hot spots, patterns, and trends and analyze their underlying causes' (Maple, 1999: 32).

### Innovative problem-solving tactics

In our discussion of strategic problem solving, we identified the importance of problem-solving models in the development of Compstat. Middle managers are expected to select responses because they offer the best prospects of success, not because they are 'what we have always done'. Innovation and experimentation are encouraged; use of 'best available knowledge' about practices is expected. In this context, police are expected to look beyond their own experiences by drawing on knowledge gained in other departments and from innovations in theory and research about crime prevention.

These six key elements constitute the core of organization development prescriptions associated with Compstat. Although there is much anecdotal evidence of the adoption of Compstat models by American police agencies outside New York, there has been little systematic examination of whether and to what extent departments are implementing the various elements of Compstat. It is also unclear whether the adoption of Compstat truly represents a radical departure from models of policing that are carried out in departments that have not adopted the Compstat model. Our study seeks to address these core concerns in understanding the diffusion and implementation of Compstat programs.

## The diffusion of Compstat-like programs

Our data are drawn from a survey of a stratified sample of American police agencies with municipal policing responsibilities conducted by the Police Foundation (see Weisburd et al., 2001). The mail survey was sent to all such police agencies with over 100 sworn police officers and to a random sample of 100 agencies with 50 to 99 sworn officers. We surveyed the universe of larger departments because Compstat programs were seen to be more relevant to and feasible in such agencies, but we also drew a random sample of smaller departments in order to identify whether Compstat programs were an appreciable factor for them.

The sample was drawn from the most complete listing of American police agencies in 1999, the 1996 Directory Survey of Law Enforcement Agencies conducted by the Bureau of Justice Statistics (BJS) and the Census Bureau (Bureau of Justice Statistics, 1998). There were 515 agencies with 100 or more sworn officers, and 698 agencies with 50 to 99 officers. Surveys were mailed in August 1999, and the last completed survey was received in January 2000. Overall, 86% of the departments we selected sent responses back to the Police Foundation.[1] The characteristics of our survey sample follow closely national characteristics of departments in terms of geographic distribution and size (see Weisburd et al., 2001). In this chapter, we report primarily on the survey findings, but we also draw on observations made during 15 two- to three-day site visits to Compstat programs, and three on-site observations of model Compstat programs, each taking several months (see Greenspan et al., 2003; Willis et al., 2003).

### Self-reported adoption of Compstat programs

The survey presented police agencies with a listing of 'features that have been associated with Compstat and similar programs'.[2] We then asked whether their department had already implemented or was planning to implement a 'Compstat-like program'. A third of the departments in the sample of agencies with 100 or more sworn officers reported that they had implemented a 'Compstat-like program'.[3] An additional quarter of these departments claimed to be planning such a program. Although not evenly distributed across the nation's regions, there was sufficient distribution among large departments to say that Compstat enjoys widespread interest across the country (42% of departments in the South, 32% in the West, 27% in the Northeast, and 22% in the North Central regions). As expected, departments in the small agency sample were much less likely to report having adopted a Compstat model. Although about 30% of these departments claimed to be planning to implement a Compstat-like program, only 9 (11%) had already done so at the time of the survey. Because the number of adoptors here is very small, we focus our statistical analyses and discussion below only on responses from the survey of police agencies with 100 or more sworn officers.

We also asked departments when their Compstat or Compstat-like program was implemented. [The] large growth in implementation of Compstat programs in larger police agencies occurred a few years after New York's program had begun to gain wide-scale publicity, between 1997 and 1998. [A] downward trend in 1999 is likely an artifact of the timing of the survey, which was sent to respondents in August 1999 and thus generally provided data on imple- mentation for less than the complete year.

Eighteen departments in our large agency sample report implementation before 1994 – the year NYPD introduced Compstat. This suggests that a few police agencies in our survey thought that they had fully implemented the key elements of strategic problem solving before New York had coined the term Compstat. Moreover, 'many other departments reported that they had implemented specific elements of Compstat before New York City's model had become prominent [...]. For example, about a quarter of departments with 100 or more sworn officers claimed to have 'set specific objectives in terms that can be precisely measured' or to have held 'regularly scheduled meetings with district commanders to review progress toward objectives' at least six years before the survey, a time that predates the creation of Compstat in New York City.

Whether or not police agencies around the nation anticipated the emergence of Compstat, New York has clearly led the way in promoting its dissemination. Seventy-two departments reported visiting New York to observe Compstat, whereas the next three most frequently visited departments mentioned had 12, 9, and 2 visitors, respectively. Virtually all departments with more than 500 sworn that had implemented Compstat also reported that they were 'very or somewhat familiar' with NYPD's version, and 90% of those that had not implemented Compstat reported the same. Among the agencies in the 100 to 299 officer range, 73% of the Compstat implementers said they were very or somewhat familiar with NYPD's Compstat, aid fully 55% of the non-implementers reported the same.

Our survey shows that larger American police agencies claim to have adopted Compstat at a high rate and very rapidly. How does this compare with the adoption of other social or technological innovations? In recent years, there has been growing interest in the analysis of innovation, which has been found to have a fairly consistent form, called the 's' curve of innovation (Rogers, 1995). The s curve is developed by measuring the cumulative adoption of an innovation over time. [...]

Can we argue [...] that the diffusion of Compstat-like programs suggests a rapid rate of innovation? Arnulf Grübler (1991) provides a yardstick. He analyzes two samples of technologies, including such areas as energy, transport, communication, agriculture, military technologies, as well as some social changes such as literacy, in the United States for which data on diffusion of innovation were available. He constructs a measure, delta $t$, which is the time period it takes for an innovation to go from 10% to 90% of its saturation or highest level of adoption. He finds that between 13% and 25% of different types of technology progress from 10% to 90% of their saturation level within 15 years. Another 25% to 30% of his samples reached this saturation level in 30 years.

It is not possible to calculate delta $t$ precisely for the adoption of Compstat-like programs before the saturation process is complete. However, we can estimate the cumulative adoption curve using the data available from our survey. Rogers notes that the adoption of an innovation generally 'follows a normal bell-shaped curve' when plotted over time as a frequency distribution (Rogers, 1995: 257). [We developed] a cumulative adoption curve based on this assumption extrapolating from our observed data.[4] Based on this distribution and allowing saturation to include all police departments in our sample, we estimate a 90% saturation level between 2006 and 2007. As 10% saturation using the observed data was defined as occurring between 1996 and 1997, our estimate of delta $t$ is about 10 years. Accordingly, if the adoption of Compstat-like programs was to follow the growth patterns observed in our data, Compstat would rank among the most quickly diffused forms of innovation.

### Motivations behind the adoption of Compstat

What are the principal motivations for adopting Compstat, and how do these differ from those of agencies that do not intend to adopt Compstat? The survey affords an opportunity to observe patterns in priorities from which we might infer such motivations. Respondents were asked to rank the top five goals that the chief executive pursued in the previous 12 months, selecting from a list of 19.[5] We assigned a score of 5 to the top priority goal identified by each respondent, a 4 to the second ranking goal, and so on, giving all unranked goals a score of 0. Because we wanted to examine priorities of departments close to when they implemented a Compstat program, we excluded all departments that had implemented Compstat before 1998. We compare these departments with those that stated in the survey that they had not implemented a Compstat-like program and they were not planning to do so.

The average ranking for the 19 goals was 0.78 for the large department sample. Only four of the 19 items showed a statistically significant difference ($p < 0.05$) between the two groups of departments. Accordingly, there is a good deal of consensus in these police agencies regarding the priority goals for policing. However, departments that had recently implemented Compstat tended to rank the reduction of serious crime and increasing management control over field operations substantially higher than did departments that were not planning implementation of Compstat. Departments that were not planning to implement a Compstat-like program tended to score much higher than did departments that claimed to recently have adopted Compstat on the ranks they assigned to improving officer policing skills and employee morale.

Departments that had recently implemented Compstat gave the reduction of serious crime a priority ranking 1.5 (3.32/2.26) times that of departments not planning to implement Compstat and increasing management control a ranking of 2.1 (.91/.44) times that of such departments. Similarly, although in reverse, departments not planning to implement Compstat gave priority rankings to improving police officer skills that were on average 2.1 (.96/.46) times those of agencies that claimed to have recently implemented a Compstat like program, and priority rankings for improving employee morale that were on average 2.4 (.68/.28) times those of such agencies. This pattern is consistent with the interpretation that the dominant motivations for implementing Compstat are to secure management control over field operations that will reduce serious crime. At the same time, focus on improving skills and morale of street level officers, which for example have been high priorities in many community-policing programs, are relatively lower priorities for recently implemented Compstat departments.

## Implementation of key elements of Compstat in Compstat versus non-Compstat departments

Clearly, many larger police agencies claim to have adopted a Compstat program. But do these agencies report having implemented the specific components we have defined as core elements of Compstat? Moreover, given our description of the emergence of strategic problem solving more generally in American policing, are there significant differences in claimed adoption of these elements of Compstat between departments that report having a Compstat or Compstat-like program and those that do not? Perhaps American police agencies have moved in the basic direction of strategic problem solving irrespective of the existence of

Compstat. To analyze these issues, we identify specific practices that are associated with the six core elements of Compstat identified earlier. We asked a series of targeted questions meant to gauge the extent of a department's reported implementation of each of these components of the Compstat model.

### Mission clarification

Two items measure the degree of mission clarification in Compstat departments, one about the specificity of the goal and the other about the simplicity versus multiplicity of the goal structure. [The] degree of implementation of Compstat appears uneven, although a substantial proportion of these departments still meet these standards for mission clarification. Less than half of the departments that claim to have implemented a Compstat-like program had announced a goal of reducing crime or some other problem by a specific number, and almost a third of these departments have focused on 'many different goals', reducing the clarity of the mission message. Nonetheless, we find statistically significant differences when we compare Compstat and non-Compstat departments. Compstat departments were more than twice as likely to set a public goal of reducing crime or other problems by a specific number. Although Compstat departments were significantly less likely to set many different goals, the absolute difference between Compstat and non-Compstat departments is only 11%.

### Internal accountability

Punishing middle managers who fail to meet the standards of Compstat accountability or rewarding those who do is a key element of internal accountability in the New York model (Bratton, 1998). Many Compstat departments take this element of Compstat seriously, and they are significantly more likely to report upholding accountability structures than are non-Compstat departments […] Almost seven in ten agencies claiming to have implemented a Compstat-like program say that district commanders would be somewhat or very likely to be replaced if they do not know about the crime patterns in their district. This was true for less than half of the non-Compstat departments. In turn, Compstat departments were twice as likely as non-Compstat departments to report that a district commander would be replaced simply if crime continued to rise in a district. Although the use of 'punishment' to maintain accountability is apparent in Compstat departments, we find that they are much less likely to use reward in ensuring internal accountability […]. If crime in a district declines, fewer than a quarter of Compstat departments report that it is very or somewhat likely that the district commander will be rewarded with a promotion or desired job assignment. Nonetheless, this is still about twice as many as report rewarding district commanders in non-Compstat departments.

The one area of internal accountability where there are not statistically significant differences between Compstat and non-Compstat departments is that related to special units. Both Compstat and non-Compstat departments claim that special unit commanders are likely to be replaced if they frequently fail to 'fulfill requests for cooperation from district commanders'. In turn, about 37% of both Compstat and non-Compstat departments report special unit commanders are likely to be rewarded if they routinely fulfill requests for assistance from district commanders.

### Geographic organization of operational command

When we ask whether departments give authority to middle managers to select problem-solving strategies for low-level problems we find strong support for the Compstat emphasis on geographic organization of command […]. Ninety percent of departments claiming to have implemented a Compstat-like program report giving district commanders, line supervisors, or specialized unit commanders such authority. However, this was also true for 86% of non-Compstat departments. In the case of high visibility problems, there is somewhat less support for allowing commanders at that level the authority to choose problem-solving strategies, and in this case, there is significant difference between Compstat and non-Compstat departments. This was the case for 70% of Compstat departments and 54% of non-Compstat departments.

When we examine the extent to which departments are willing to give middle managers greater responsibility for determining beat boundaries or staffing levels, we find less support for the idea of geographic organization of command. Only four in ten departments that claim to have implemented a Compstat-like model give district commanders, line supervisors, or specialized unit commanders the authority to determine routine staffing levels for patrol shifts, and this is not significantly different from the proportion of non-Compstat departments. Moreover, only 19% of Compstat departments and 14% of non-Compstat departments claim to give such commanders the authority to determine beat boundaries.

### Organizational flexibility

We examined organizational flexibility in two ways. First, we asked departments whether middle managers had general authority to approve requests for flexible hours or to mobilize SWAT units to support specific operations […]. Although these two items also reflect the commitment of the department to geographic organization of command, they do focus directly on whether there is flexibility in the allocation of departmental resources. Three-quarters of Compstat departments responded that they allow district commanders, line supervisors, or specialized unit commanders to decide on flexible hour requests, and 65% allow them to mobilize SWAT units. Importantly, however, the difference in the proportions of Compstat and non-Compstat departments that evidenced these indicators of organizational flexibility is small and not statistically significant.

We also examined how much organizational flexibility departments reported in dealing with 'the crime/disorder problem that used more of the department's effort than any other problem in the last 12 months' […]. Again, departments that claim to have implemented a Compstat-like program do appear to allow a good deal of organizational flexibility. Eighty-four percent of these departments had reassigned patrol officers to new units, areas, or work shifts to address this problem. And on this measure, Compstat departments were significantly different from non-Compstat departments in which only 69% claimed such reassignments. Eighty percent of the departments had used overtime to provide personnel to deal with the problem, although this proportion is close to that in non-Compstat departments. Although few of the departments allowed reassignment of civilian employees, reflecting perhaps contract or other restrictions, about six in ten Compstat departments had reassigned criminal investigators (as compared with 51% of non-Compstat departments) and 66% other sworn specialists (as compared to 53% in non-Compstat departments) to new units, areas, or work shifts.

### Data-driven problem identification and assessment

Compstat departments claim to have the capability to manage and analyze crime data in sophisticated ways, and they are significantly more likely to claim this than non-Compstat departments [...]. Over 90% of these departments claim to conduct 'crime trend identification and analysis' (as contrasted with 72% of non-Compstat departments), and almost 90% claim to use 'database or statistical analysis software for crime analysis' (as contrasted with 76% of non-Compstat departments). In turn, we find meaningful differences between Compstat and non-Compstat departments in the claimed availability of analysis tools. The largest differences are found in regard to crime mapping, reflecting the centrality of crime mapping to Compstat programs. But even here many departments that have not implemented a Compstat-like program are using crime mapping. For example, there is a 32% gap between Compstat and non-Compstat departments in use of mapping software. Nonetheless, more than half of the non-Compstat departments report that they are using mapping software for crime analysis.

Departments that claim to have implemented a Compstat-like program are clearly sophisticated in their ability to use data, but are those data available in a timely fashion? Again, Compstat departments appear very much to follow the emphasis placed on timely data in the Compstat model [...]. But here we find little difference between those departments that claim to have implemented a Compstat-like model and others. About three-quarters of all the departments report that calls for service information are immediately available or available the same day. Arrest data are also very timely, with more than half the departments reporting that such data are available immediately or on the same day.

### Innovative problem-solving tactics

We considered two ways in which problem solving might be innovative: how problems are analyzed and selected and whether the solutions selected were a break from traditional law-enforcement methods. Police have long collected data and compiled statistics, but those data were rarely used to make important decisions about how to solve problems (Mastrofski and Wadman, 1991). Compstat is intended to harness problem-solving decisions to data analysis. When asked specifically whether statistical analysis software is used for problem solving, about 70% of the Compstat departments answer yes [...]. Sixty-seven percent say that crime-mapping software is used for problem-solving efforts. In this case, Compstat departments are significantly more likely to claim to use such technologies for problem solving than are non-Compstat departments. Nonetheless, a majority of non-Compstat departments claim to use data base or statistical analysis software for problem solving, and more than a third claim to use mapping software for problem solving.

Both compstat and non-Compstat departments use crime-mapping and other innovative data analysis approaches for problem solving, but this does not necessarily mean that such efforts have significant depth. One element often mentioned by those advocating innovation in problem solving is that departments look beyond their own experiences in identifying innovative strategies to solve problems. This does not seem to be the case very often in Compstat or non-Compstat departments. When we asked departments how they decided on a problem-solving strategy to address 'the one crime/disorder problem that used more of the department's efforts than any other problem in the last 12 months', they were most likely to tell us that they relied on the department's previous success with that approach [...]. Very few of the departments stated that they draw significantly from outside experts. Nonetheless, reflecting the growing openness of police agencies to research, they were more likely to tell us that 'research evidence' was very important in deciding a strategy. About four in ten Compstat departments and three in ten non-Compstat departments reported this, and this difference was statistically significant. About a third of the departments overall reported that they had drawn from experiences of other departments.

When we look at specific tactics used to address the priority crime/disorder problem identified by sample departments in the last 12 months, we also find a good deal of similarity between Compstat and non-Compstat departments. The most common strategies used by both Compstat and non-Compstat departments relied on traditional police-enforcement strategies. For example, the first ranked strategy for both types of departments was 'saturation of an area with police', noted by 79% of Compstat Departments and 76% of non-Compstat departments. Many of the departments said that they had used such innovative tactics as nuisance abatement or altering the physical environment. Tactics that sought to involve the community in crime control efforts also ranked high, for example, in 'educating the public' and 'mobilizing community groups'. In only 5 of the 23 tactics examined were differences between Compstat and non-Compstat departments found to be statistically significant [...]. Compstat departments were significantly more likely to increase arrests for targeted offenders, and target repeat offenders, use checkpoints, increase gun seizures, or improve victim services.

### Discussion: Compstat and traditional police organizational culture

One of the clearest findings of our study is that Compstat has spread widely and quickly across larger American police agencies. In our survey, conducted just five years after the New York City police department had coined the term Compstat, a third of departments with 100 or more sworn officers reported that they had implemented a 'Compstat-like program', and an additional quarter of these departments claimed to be planning such a program. This speed of diffusion of innovation places Compstat among those social and technological innovations that are adopted most quickly. We suspect, although we do not have comparative data on American police innovations, that this speed of adoption is also unusual for innovations in American policing. Compstat as a cohesive program debuted only in 1994. Moreover, unlike community policing, the federal government has not provided direct financial incentives for its implementation (Roth *et al.*, 2000).[6] It is fair to say that Compstat as a recognized programmatic model has literally burst on to the American police scene.

Why has Compstat diffused so quickly and widely? One reason is the promise of Compstat in controlling crime. Although it is generally recognized that technical success of programs is not a sufficient explanation for their adoption in police agencies (Crank and Langworthy, 1992; Manning, 1997; Mastrofski, 1998), police departments that have implemented a Compstat-like program often point to the promise of Compstat as a crime-prevention tool. In turn, although there is significant debate in academic circles regarding the effectiveness of Compstat (e.g., see Eck and Maguire, 2000; Kelling and Sousa, 2001), there has been much less reticence among those who created the program and the media in touting its success. The program was widely discussed in the popular and professional news outlets, even leading to William Bratton being featured on the cover of *Time Magazine* in January 1996. In turn, the agency that created this program was the most visible local police agency in the nation and did a great deal to publicize it and show other agencies how it operates. As other big cities began to adopt their own Compstat programs, this too increased the 'buzz' in the Press and among police agencies, helping to make it the 'hot' program for local law enforcement leaders.

Our study illustrates a second reason why Compstat has spread so quickly: A number of American police agencies had already adopted many of its features before the term Compstat was coined and marketed. At the outset of our chapter, we described a wider movement toward strategic problem solving in American policing. Our survey shows that many elements of strategic problem solving had begun to be implemented more widely across American police agencies before the emergence of Compstat, and have been adopted broadly even by departments that have not formally adopted a Compstat program. Some even claimed to have been engaged in all of the elements of Compstat before 1994. So, the New York City Police Department's contribution appears to be its leadership in bringing all of these elements together into a single program, giving it a clear, coherent role and providing a highly publicized set of claims that link it to performance – the decline of crime and disorder in the nation's most visible city.

However, our study suggests that Compstat's origins in a highly visible police agency, the attractiveness of its crime control promises, and the fact that many of its components were already being implemented in other departments before its emergence as a formal programmatic entity provide only part of the story behind the rapid adoption of Compstat-like programs in larger American police agencies. Compstat is appealing precisely because it holds out the promise of innovation in police organization, strategies, and tactics but does not demand a revolution in the organizational structure of American policing. Rather, it preserves – indeed, claims to reinvigorate – the traditional hierarchical structure of the military model of policing, a structure that has been attacked by a powerful reform wave over the last two decades.

Many scholars have used the terms 'bureaucratic' or 'para-military' to describe the form of traditional police organization (e.g., see Bittner, 1980; Davis, 1981; Goldstein, 1977; Melnicoe and Menig, 1978; Punch, 1983; Weisburd *et al.*, 1988). Police departments have traditionally relied on a highly articulated set of rules defining what officers should and should not do in various situations to ensure internal control. This supervisory system is strongly hierarchical and essentially negative, relying primarily on sanctions for noncompliance with police rules and regulations. Importantly, this bureaucratic, military model of organization increasingly came under attack as scholars sought to understand and respond to a growing body of research that suggested the police were ineffective in controlling crime and responding to community problems (Bayley, 1994; Goldstein, 1990; Greene and Mastrofski, 1988; Mastrofski, 1998; Skolnick and Bayley, 1986). As Weisburd *et al.* (1988: 31–32) note:

> Whatever the historical achievements of the bureaucratic, military model of organization, its shortcomings are increasingly evident to scholars and police administrators who argue that the demands of contemporary urban society undermine the assumptions upon which traditional police structures were built. While the military model depends on predictability, many of the situations to which officers are asked to respond cannot be anticipated. Though the norms that define appropriate responses may reduce the vulnerability of officers to criticism, they often do not provide useful guides for developing effective solutions to the problems encountered. Finally deployment patterns which treat patrol officers as if they were interchangeable parts (as well as highly centralized structures of authority and decision-making) prevent police officers from learning and responding to distinctive problems, needs and resources of the neighborhoods they serve.

The challenge to the military model of American police organization was most clearly articulated by advocates of community policing. Community policing emerged on the scene in the 1980s and quickly became the most important police reform of the decade (Bayley, 1988; Greene and Mastrofski; 1988). At a time when many scholars had literally given up on the possibility that the police could increase the safety of American communities (Bayley, 1994; Gottfredson and Hirschi, 1990), community policing offered the promise of an American policing that would not only allow Americans to feel safer but that would actually make them safer. Although community policing is most commonly associated with a movement toward greater police recognition of the role of the community in the police mission, it included a strong current of dissatisfaction with traditional bureaucratic, top-down command-and-control management (Mastrofski, 1998; Weisburd *et al.*, 1988). Community policing, at least as articulated by some of its most visible advocates (Brown, 1989; Goldstein,1990; Skolnick and Bayley, 1986; Trojanowicz and Bucqueroux, 1990), promotes the true professionalization of the rank-and-file, who, equipped with the necessary training, education, and motivation to solve problems, are supposed to use their best judgment to make important decisions about how to serve the neighborhoods to which they are assigned. Some scholars have called this a movement toward 'decentralization of command' or 'debureaucratization' (Mastrofski, 1998; Skolnick and Bayley, 1987). In turn, resistance of police organizations to the challenge of decentralization has been noted as an important impediment to the implementation of community policing (Weisburd et al., 2002).

Compstat presents an alternative model for police organization that also holds promise for improving American policing. It replaces the bubble-up professionalism proposed by many community policing advocates with a revitalized cadre of middle managers (especially district commanders), who are given general objectives by top management and given the authority and resources to get things done. But they are at the same time held accountable for at least making the effort to achieve management's goals and are required to be well informed about the consequences, even if the desired results are not always forthcoming. Compstat seeks to empower police organization by harnessing the hierarchy to achieve top management's objectives.

But if Compstat preserves, or perhaps enhances, the relevance of the hierarchy for controlling the organization, it still deserves to be called innovative, at least in principle. Rather than the sort of constant surveillance thought effective in running organizations that require standardization (e.g., assembly lines), a model once blessed by police reformers, but realized only chimerically, the Compstat model requires striking a delicate balance between empowerment and control (Simons, 1995). The question is, what sort of balance have America's Compstat police agencies actually struck? Our survey data, although certainly not the last word on this issue, suggest that most Compstat agencies have in fact opted for a model much heavier on control than on empowerment.

When we compared department goals of recent innovators with those who were not intending to develop a Compstat program, we found that the most significant differences were in the areas of crime control, increased control of managers over field operations, improving rank-and-file policing skills, and improving police morale. Importantly, departments that had claimed to have recently adopted Compstat were more concerned with reducing crime and increasing internal accountability than were departments that reported neither to have nor to be planning to develop a Compstat-like program. In contrast, they ranked much lower on items that emphasized rank-and-file professionalism and *esprit*. These findings are certainly consistent with a view that sees Compstat programs as reinforcing the traditional control elements of the military model of police organization.

In turn, although fairly strong on mission clarification, internal accountability, and use of data, in our survey, Compstat agencies were largely indistinguishable from non-Compstat agencies on measures that gauged geographic organization of command, organizational flexibility, the timely availability of data, and the selection and implementation of innovative strategies and tactics. More generally, our data present a picture of departments that have embraced control of middle managers (tending to rely more heavily on punitive than on positive consequences) and adopting advances in information technology. At the same time, we find that Compstat departments are more reluctant to relinquish power that would decentralize some key elements of decision making geographically (letting precinct commanders determine beat boundaries and staffing levels), enhance flexibility, and risk going outside of the standard tool kit of police tactics and strategies. The combined effect overall, whether or not intended, is to reinforce a traditional bureaucratic model of command and control.

But does Compstat empower police organization more generally through its emphasis on the accountability of police managers? In theory, the original developers of Compstat did not dispute the community policing view that giving 'cops more individual power to make decisions is a good idea' (Bratton, 1998: 198). However, they believed that in the real world of police organization, street-level police officers 'were never going to be empowered to follow through' (Bratton, 1998: 199). Compstat was seen as offering a solution to this problem. It did not necessarily lead to a de-emphasis on the training and *esprit* of street-level police officers, but it did place the burden on empowering police organization in the hands of middle managers.

Our survey of police agencies cannot demonstrate it, but our observations in Compstat departments suggest that the rank-and-file remain largely oblivious to Compstat and that it intrudes little, if at all, into their daily work (Willis *et al.*, 2003). As one patrol officer put it when asked about Compstat, 'if you don't go [to Compstat meetings], you don't know'. In that department, in contrast to almost the entire command staff, only two or three patrol officers are present at any given Compstat meeting. They may answer a question or two, and they may give a brief presentation, but they play a peripheral role. A high-ranking officer we interviewed remarked that 'patrol officers can hide in the meeting and get away without saying anything'. Whereas members of the command staff in Compstat departments we observed, in particular, the sector captains, are expected to respond to the Chief's questions, line officers are rarely called on to explain a particular decision. It is true that a sector captain who has been 'roasted' in Compstat for an inadequate strategy may return to his sector and rebuke his line officers, but the force of the message is considerably weakened for three reasons: (1) Compstat ultimately holds middle managers, not line officers, accountable; (2) the message is not being delivered by the highest ranking official in the police department; and (3) it does not result in public censure on the same scale.

Our field observations suggest that in Compstat agencies the problem-solving processes are principally the work of precinct commanders, their administrative assistant, and crime analysis staff (sometimes available at the precinct level, as well as at headquarters). The pressures on these people can be quite profound. One precinct commander noted, 'We're under constant pressure. It's the toughest job in this department. We're held a little closer to the fire ... I'll go home at night after ten hours at work and keep working – 50–60 hours per week on average'. His lieutenant reinforced this. 'A precinct commander has no life [outside Compstat].' Although this level of intense accountability was commonly expressed by middle managers in Compstat departments, we found nothing remotely resembling that at lower levels in the organization, except on the rare occasion when a rank-and-file officer was required to make a substantial presentation at a department Compstat meeting. A few agencies we visited did routinely conduct precinct-level Compstat meetings, and here there appeared to be greater involvement by a large number of first-line supervisors and some of their subordinates. Kelling and Sousa (2001) argue that this is what is happening in New York City, where they observed numerous instances of creative precinct-level problem solving. Just how widespread such a practice becomes among the precincts of Compstat departments around the nation remains to be seen.

## Conclusions

In introducing our chapter, we presented two very different views of the role of innovation in preserving organizations. The first is that of the great Whig orator, Lord Macaulay, who recognized that change was sometimes necessary to preserve institutions. He told his colleagues in Parliament: 'Reform, that you may preserve.' The second is drawn from di Lampedusa's novel *The Leopard* describing the conflicts that surrounded the reunification of the Italian peninsula in the nineteenth century. Here reform is seen as more illusory: 'If we want everything to remain the same, then everything is going to have to change.'

Our chapter documents a process of 'diffusion of innovation' (see Rogers, 1995) of Compstat-like programs in larger police agencies that follows a surprisingly rapid pace. At the same time, our data suggest that many elements of strategic problem solving had begun to be implemented more widely across American police agencies before the emergence of Compstat as a programmatic entity, and they had been adopted broadly even by departments that had not formally adopted a Compstat program. In many ways, the rapid ascendance of Compstat can be seen as evidence of Lord Macaulay's prescription. In order to reinvigorate and preserve police organization, police managers have adopted a model of strategic problem solving (Compstat) that in theory allows police agencies to utilize innovative technologies and problem-solving techniques while empowering traditional police organizational structures. However, our analysis suggests that at this stage, what most characterizes Compstat departments and distinguishes them from others is the development of the control element of reform. This of course raises the question of whether American police agencies have adopted Compstat enthusiastically more because of its promise of reinforcing the traditional hierarchical model of police organization than for its efforts to empower problem solving in police agencies. In this context, we may wonder whether in practice, although not necessarily with intent, police agencies have followed an approach that is more consistent with that described by di Lampedusa than by Lord Macaulay.

*From David Weisburd, Stephen D. Mastrofski, Ann Marie McNally, Rosann Greenspan and James J. Willis 'Reforming to preserve: Compstat and strategic problem solving in American policing,* Criminology and Public Policy, *Vol. 2, 3, 2003, pp 421–456.*

## Notes

1 Response rates were similar for the survey of large departments (86%) and the small department sample (85%).
2 For each 'feature', we also asked if and for how long 'the department has been doing this'.

3 One reviewer of our paper suggested that the claimed implementation of a Compstat-like program was likely to be overstated in our survey because police executives and ranking police managers – those who were most likely to fill out this part of the survey – would want their agency to be seen as cutting edge. (In more than half of the surveys, the chief executive of the police organization claimed to answer this series of questions, whereas in the bulk of the remaining cases, another high-ranking police executive or an assistant to the chief executive responded.) As we promised complete confidentiality for the departments in our survey, we suspect that the motivation to make the departments look good would likely not have been an important factor. Moreover, in each of the 15 cases where we conducted site visits, survey responses were generally consistent with our observations.

4 In estimating the normal frequency distribution on which the s curve is based, we relied upon the observed data between 1995 and 1998. We excluded the 1999 year because of the timing of the survey, which likely underrepresented the number of adoptions. We also excluded years before 1995, because the number of cases were relatively small and likely to lead to unstable estimates. In developing an estimated value for the standard deviation unit of the normal curve, we compared each year's frequency between 1995 and 1998 and then took the average estimate gained. After defining the normal frequency distribution, we then converted the estimates to a cumulative distribution curve.

5 The 19 goals in the order listed were: reduce serious crime, reduce quality of life offenses, reduce fear of crime, reduce calls for service, increase citizen satisfaction with the police, increase service to citizens living in high-crime areas, increase efficiency of service (reduce cost per unit of service), reduce conflict among different segments of the community, increase citizen participation in police programs, increase citizens' ability to make their own neighborhoods better places to live, give citizen groups more influence over police policy and practice, improve coordination with other public and private organizations, reduce complaints about police misbehavior, increase police managers' control over actual field operations, improve officers' policing skills, improve employee morale, be more responsive to the priorities of individual neighborhoods, provide better service to crime victims, improve the physical appearance of neighborhoods.

6 However, federal 'community policing' grants have supported some key elements of Compstat, such as the promotion of problem solving and the acquisition of computers and other information technology to support crime analysis.

## References

Anselin, Luc, Jacqueline Cohen, David Cook, Wilpen Gorr, and George Tita (2000) Spatial analyses of crime. In David Duffee, David McDowall, Brian Ostrom, Robert D. Crutchfield, Stephen D. Mastrofski, and Lorraine Green Mazerolle (eds), *Measurement and Analysis of Crime and Justice*. Washington, D.C.: National Institute of Justice.
Bayley, David (1988) Community policing: a report from the Devil's advocate. In Jack R. Greene and Stephen D. Mastrofski (eds), *Community Policing: Rhetoric or Reality*. New York: Praeger.
Bayley, David (1994) *Police for the Future*. New York: Oxford University Press.
Beer, Michael (1980) *Organization Change and Development: A Systems View*. Santa Monica, Calif.: Goodyear Publishing Company.
Berman, Jesse (1987) *Police Administration and Progressive Reform*. New York: Greenwood.
Bittner, Egon (1980) *The Functions of the Police in Modern Society*. Cambridge, Mass.: Oelgeschlager, Gunn and Hain.
Bouza, Tony (1997) NYPD blues – good, lucky, or both? *Law Enforcement News* (January 31): 8, 10.
Braga, Anthony (2001) The effects of hot spots policing on crime. *Annals of the American Academy of Political and Social Sciences* 578: 104–25.
Bratton, William (1996) Cutting crime and restoring order: what America can learn from New York's finest. Heritage Foundation Lectures and Educational Programs, Heritage Lecture #573. Available at www.nationalsecurity.org/heritage/library/categories/crimelaw/lect573.html.
Bratton, William (1998) *Turnaround: How America's Top Cop Reversed the Crime Epidemic*. New York: Random House.
Bratton, William (1999) Great expectations: how higher expectations for police departments can lead to a decrease in crime. In Robert H. Langworthy (ed.), *Measuring What Matters: Proceedings from the Policing Research Institute Meetings*. Washington, D.C.: National Institute of Justice.

Brown, Lee P. (1989) *Community Policing: A Practical Guide for Police Officials*. Washington, D.C.: National Institute of Justice.

Bureau of Justice Statistics (1998) *Census of State and Local Law Enforcement Agencies, 1996*. Washington, D.C.: U.S. Department of Justice, Bureau of Justice Statistics.

Crank, John P. and Robert Langworthy (1992) An institutional perspective of policing. *Journal of Criminal Law and Criminology* 83: 338–63.

Davis, E.M. (1981) Professional police principles. In H.W. More, Jr. (ed.), *Critical Issues in Policing*. Cincinatti, Ohio: Anderson Publishing Company.

Eck, John E. and Edward R. Maguire (2000) Have changes in policing reduced violent crime? An assessment of the evidence. In Alfred Blumstein and Joel Wallman, (eds), *The Crime Drop in America*. Cambridge, U.K.: Cambridge University Press.

Finkelstein, Sydney and Donald C. Hambrick (1996) *Strategic Leadership: Top Executives and their Effects on Organizations*. St. Paul, Minn.: West Publishing Co.

Fogelson, Robert F. (1977) *Big City Police*. Cambridge, Mass.: Harvard University Press.

Giuliani, Rudolph W. and Howard Safir (1998) *Compstat: Leadership in Action*. New York City: New York City Police Department.

Goldstein, Herman (1977) *Policing a Free Society*. Cambridge, Mass.: Ballinger Publishing Company.

Goldstein, Herman (1990) *Problem-Oriented Policing*. New York: McGraw-Hill.

Gottfredson, Michael R. and Travis Hirschi (1990) *General Theory of Crime*. Stanford, Calif.: Stanford University Press.

Greene, Jack R. and Stephen D. Mastrofski (1988) *Community Policing: Rhetoric or Reality*. New York: Praeger.

Greenspan, Rosann, Stephen D. Mastrofski, and David Weisburd (2003) *Compstat and Organizational Change: Short Site Visits Report*. Washington, D.C.: Police Foundation.

Grübler, Arnulf (1991) Diffusion and long-term patterns and discontinuities. *Technological Forecasting and Social Change* 39: 159–80.

Gurwitt, Rob (1998) The comeback of the cops. *Governing* (January): 14–19.

Kelling, George L. and Catherine M. Coles (1996) *Fixing Broken Windows: Restoring Order and Reducing Crime in our Communities*. New York: Free Press.

Kelling, George L. and Mark H. Moore (1988) From political to reform to community: the evolving strategy of police. In Jack R. Greene and Stephen D. Mastrofski (eds), *Community Policing: Rhetoric or Reality*. New York: Praeger.

Kelling, George L. and William H. Sousa, Jr. (2001) *Do Police Matter? An Analysis of the Impact of New York City's Police Reforms*. New York: Center for Civic Innovation at the Manhattan Institute.

Klockars, Carl B. and William E. Harver (1993) *The Production and Consumption of Research in Police Agencies in the United States*. Report to the National Institute of Justice. Newark: University of Delaware.

*Law Enforcement News* (1997) NYC's Compstat continues to win admirers. (October 13): 5.

Maas, Peter (1998) What we're learning from New York City. *Parade* (May 10) 4–6.

Manning, Peter K. (1997) *Police Work: The Social Organization of Policing*, 2d ed. Prospect Heights, Ill.: Waveland Press.

Maple, Jack (1999) *The Crime Fighter: Putting the Bad Guys out of Business*. New York: Doubleday.

Mastrofski, Stephen D. (1998) Community policing and police organization structure. In Jean-Paul Brodeur (ed.), *How to Recognize Good Policing: Problems and Issues*. Thousand Oaks, Calif.: Sage.

Mastrofski, Stephen D. and Robert C. Wadman (1991) Personnel and agency performance measurement. In William A. Geller (ed.), *Local Government Police Management*, 3d ed. Washington, D.C.: International City Management Association.

McDonald, Phyllis Parshall, Shelden Greenberg, and William Bratton (2001) *Managing Police Operations: Implementing the NYPD Crime Control Model Using COMPSTAT*. Belmont, CA: Wadsworth Publishing.

Melnicoe, William and Jan Minnig (1978) *Elements of Police Supervision*. Encino, Calif.: Glencoe Publishing Co.

Merton, Robert K. (1940) Bureaucratic structure and personality. *Social Forces* 18: 560–8.

Micklethwait, John and Adrian Wooldridge (1996) *The Witch Doctors: Making Sense of the Management Gurus*. New York: Random House.

Moore, Mark H. (1997) The legitimation of criminal justice policies and practices. In *National Institute of Justice, Perspectives on Crime and Justice: 1996–1997 Lecture Series*. Washington, D.C.: U.S. Department of Justice.

Office of Management Analysis and Planning (undated) *The Compstat Process*. New York: New York City Police Department.

Osborne, D. and T. Graebler (1992) *Reinventing Government*. Reading, Mass.: Addison-Wesley.

Punch, Maurice (1983) Management, supervision and control. In Maurice Punch (ed.), *Control in the Police Organization*. Cambridge, Mass.: The MIT Press.

Remnick, David (1997) The crime buster. *The New Yorker* (February 24 and March 3): 94–109.

Rogers, Everett M. (1995) *Diffusion of Innovations*. New York: Free Press.

Roth, Jeffrey, Joseph F. Ryan, Stephen J. Gaffigan, Christopher S. Koper, Mark H. Moore, Janice A. Roehl, Calvin C. Johnson, Gretchen E. Moore, Ruth M. White, Michael E. Buerger, Elizabeth A. Langston, and David Thatcher (2000) *National Evaluation of the COPS Program – Title I of the 1994 Crime Act*. Washington, D.C.: National Institute of Justice.

Sayre, Wallace Stanley and Herbert Kaufman (1960) *Governing New York City: Politics in the Metropolis*. New York: Russell Sage Foundation.

Selznick, Philip (1957) *Leadership and Administration*. New York: HarperCollins.

Sherman, Lawrence W. (1990) Police crackdowns: initial and residual deterrence. In Michael H. Tonry and Norval Morris (eds), *Crime and Justice: A Review of Research*. Chicago: University of Chicago Press.

Sherman, Lawrence W. and David Weisburd (1995) General deterrent effects of police patrol in Crime 'hot spots': a randomized controlled trial. *Justice Quarterly* 12: 625–48.

Sherman, Lawrence W., Denise Gottfredson, Doris MacKenzie, John Eck, Peter Reuter and Shawn Bushway (1997) *Preventing Crime: What Works, What Doesn't, What's Promising?* Washington, D.C.: U.S. Department of Justice, National Institute of Justice.

Silverman, Eli B. (1996) Mapping change: how the New York City Police Department reengineered itself to drive down crime. *Law Enforcement News* (December).

Silverman, Eli B. (1999) *NYPD Battles Crime: Innovative Strategies in Policing*. Boston, Mass.: Northeastern University Press.

Simons, Robert (1995) Control in an age of empowerment. *Harvard Business Review* 73: 1–7.

Skolnick, Jerome H. and David H. Bayley (1986) *The New Blue Line: Police Innovations in Six American Cities*. New York: Free Press.

Trojanowicz, Robert and Bonnie Bucqueroux (1990) *Community Policing: A Contemporary perspective*. Cincinnati, Ohio: Anderson Publishing Company.

Weisburd, David and Anthony Braga (2003) Hot spots policing. In H. Kury and J. Obergfell-Fuchs (eds), *Crime Prevention: New Approaches*. Manz: Weisser Ring.

Weisburd, David and Thomas J. McEwen (eds) (1997) *Crime Mapping and Crime Prevention*. Munsey: Criminal Justice Press.

Weisburd, David, Jerome McElroy, and Patricia Hardyman (1988) Challenges to supervision in community policing: observations on a pilot project. *American Journal of Police* 7: 29–50.

Weisburd, David, Orit Shalev, and Menachem Amir (2002) Community policing in Israel: resistance and change. *Policing: An International Journal of Police Strategies and Management* 25: 80–109.

Weisburd, David, Stephen Mastrofski, Ann Marie McNally, and Rosann Greenspan (2001) *Compstat and Organizational Change: Findings from a National Survey*. Washington, D.C.: The Police Foundation.

Willis, James, Stephen D. Mastrofski, David Weisburd, and Rosann Greenspan (2003) *Compstat and Organizational Change: Intensive Site Visits Report*. Washington, D.C.: Police Foundation.

Witkin, Gordon (1998) The crime bust. *U.S. News and World Report* (May 25): 28–36.

# 31. Sizing up COMPSTAT: an important administrative innovation in policing

*Mark H. Moore*

Weisburd *et al.*, have provided quantitative evidence documenting what seems to be an important trend in policing, namely, the widespread adoption of what they characterize as COMPSTAT-like management systems in American police departments. They have also done a thoughtful job of trying to say just what COMPSTAT is, and what parts of it are old and which parts are new. And they have begun the process of evaluating COMPSTAT by trying to locate it in a wider set of trends in the way that police departments are structured and managed to produce particular results. All of this is exceptionally helpful to interested citizens, police managers and leaders, and police researchers as they try to take the measure of this important innovation in police management.

[...]

My comments will focus on what I take to be the important lessons of COMPSTAT. More specifically, I would like to take up the following issues raised by their chapter, and by the commentators:

1   What exactly is COMPSTAT?
2   How new is it?
3   How 'strategic' is it?
4   Why did it disseminate so quickly?
5   What gives COMPSTAT its behavioral power inside police department?
6   Does it tend to support or suppress innovation and learning in a police department?
7   Does it increase the capacity of the police to reduce crime?
8   Is reducing crime necessarily the same as increasing the 'public value' of a police department?

## What is COMPSTAT?

The Kennedy School of Government has for many years run a program with the Ford Foundation that seeks to find and celebrate important 'innovations' in government. As Weisburd *et al.*, note, COMPSTAT won a coveted innovation award in this national competition. This suggests that we must have known what the innovation was. In fact, however, one of the most interesting things about the Innovation Awards process is how difficult it turns out to be to specify the particular innovation that is being celebrated. Views about the exact nature of the innovation are almost as numerous as those who examine it closely.

Viewed from the narrowest perspective, COMPSTAT can be seen as a technical system that collects a particular set of statistics providing quantitative measures of demands for police services and levels of police activity. This information can be disaggregated to the precinct level, and it is published on a virtually real-time basis (e.g., within a week of being collected).

Viewed from a slightly broader perspective, COMPSTAT could be viewed as a *combined* technical and managerial system that embeds the technical system for the collection and distribution of performance information in a broader managerial system designed to focus the organization as a whole, and a subset of managers who are relied on to exercise leadership in meeting the organization's objectives, on the task that the organization faces. It becomes a powerful managerial system in part because the technical capacity of the system allows it to produce accurate information on important dimensions of performance at a level that coincides with a particular manager's domain of responsibility. This has the effect of not only measuring performance, but also pinpointing responsibility for action to improve performance. COMPSTAT also becomes a powerful managerial system because of the alignment of the measures with the cultural values of the organization, and the way that the information is used in the organization's managerial processes. The fact that the information collected by the system aligns very closely with what the organization understands its purposes to be helps to give the technical system its behavioral power. The fact that top management uses the information to discuss the performance of the mid-level managers, and to give them a chance to request help from other parts of the organization in dealing with the problems they face, also helps to give the technical information behavioral weight in the organization. The information becomes both the basis for evaluating managerial performance and the occasion for mid-level managers to get help from others if they need it.

Viewed from a still broader perspective, COMPSTAT can be viewed as a managerial system that tends to reinforce the 'old' *management style* in a police department that emphasized central control over individual initiative, and compliance with policies and procedures over imaginative efforts focused on solving the substantive problems the police were supposed to handle; or it can be viewed as part of a 'new' style of police management that encourages a focus on substantive performance, and an emphasis on experimentation and learning.

Viewed from a still broader perspective, COMPSTAT can be viewed as a managerial system that tends to reinforce an 'old' strategy of policing that viewed reducing crime as the only important objective of policing, and viewed actions taken by the police as the best way of reducing crime, or as one that supports a 'new' strategy of policing that views the goals of policing as including but not limited to controlling crime, and that views the community as an important partner in seeking to control crime, fear, and disorder.

For the purposes of analysis, I think it is best to think of COMPSTAT at the second level – as a combined technical and managerial system that seeks to develop a certain kind of focused internal accountability in a police department.

The reason is that we should leave the important question of whether the particular form of accountability created by COMPSTAT and its variants tends to change working relationships within the department, to support imaginative problem solving and learning, and changes the basic strategy of a police department to be *investigated* rather than assumed at the outset. In short, I think we should look at COMPSTAT as a particular kind of administrative innovation in a police department, treat that innovation as an independent variable, and then examine the effects that this innovation has on how a police department does its work, both organizationally and substantively.

I have the sense that Weisburd *et al.*, want to skip the important step of defining COMPSTAT as a particular kind of managerial system that has predictable effects on the way the police department operates, and move more directly to the evaluation of how COMPSTAT can be seen to fit into the ongoing discussion about what purposes police departments should pursue, and how they can best be managed to pursue those purposes. I have that sense as a result of two features of their discussion. First, from the very beginning of the chapter, they want to focus attention on whether COMPSTAT is a *stabilizing* innovation that allows the police to carry on as they have in the past in somewhat new circumstances, or whether it is a *destabilizing* innovation that moves the police to a new range of possibilities. (This is importantly related to the question of what is old and what is new about COMPSTAT.) Second, they suggest that COMPSTAT is the police version of a new kind of public management approach that could be called 'strategic problem-solving'. The very name suggests a view that COMPSTAT is, in fact, 'strategic', and that it supports imaginative 'problem-solving'. But they offer little in the form of either argumentation or evidence to support this particular claim. It seems that they want to appropriate COMPSTAT (whatever it is) for the cause of supporting a kind of police reform that emphasizes the new strategy and tactics of 'problem-solving' over either the old strategy of 'reactive policing' or another new strategy that could be called 'community policing' (that has a close but not perfect relationship to the idea of 'problem-solving policing').

Weisburd *et al.*, make an effort to characterize the 'core elements' of COMPSTAT as a managerial system, namely, mission clarification, internal accountability, geographic organization of command; organizational flexibility; data-driven problem identification and assessment; and innovative problem solving. But to treat all of these things as core elements of COMPSTAT is to piggy-back a wide range of managerial innovations onto what is, in the end, primarily a performance measurement system. It may be that the NYPD clarified their mission under Bratton's leadership to focus on reducing crime. But one could also reasonably say that the mission was clarified in the first instance by Giuliani's political commitments to this cause, and Bratton's embrace of that objective. The important work was the political work of defining the mission; all COMPSTAT contributed was an administrative means for measuring performance and spreading accountability for achieving the mission. The political and cultural commitment had to come before or alongside the creation of COMPSTAT to give COMPSTAT its behavioral power.

It may also be that COMPSTAT helped to create a strong sense of internal accountability by collecting and publishing information about the performance of precinct-level managers in ways that permitted easy comparisons both with their prior performance and with the performance of their peers. But it was also important that Bratton used the information in personnel decisions. He replaced over one-third of the precinct commanders that he inherited within a year of taking office.

What Weisburd *et al.*, characterize as the geographic organization of command and organizational flexibility, I would characterize as an important cultural change in the location of responsibility and status in the organization. The shift in responsibility and status was *from* those who led special functional units *to* those who led the geographically defined, patrol-dominated precincts. Precinct commanders became the individuals the organization was relying on to achieve its goals. In an important change, the rest of the organization was subordinated to their interests and demands.

Of much greater interest, however, is the claim that COMPSTAT was used to support 'data-driven problem identification and assessment' and 'innovative problem-solving tactics'. I hope that is true. But there is little evidence in their chapter that supports the claim that this was the effect of COMPSTAT, and some things that suggest this is not true. For example, in the standard works on problem solving, the police are urged to engage in an 'uninhibited search for information about what the causes of a problem might be, and how it might be successfully addressed'. By definition, this involves searching for information that lies outside the reach of standardized information systems held within an existing police information system. The managerial process of COMPSTAT may encourage police managers to offer novel diagnoses of the problems that face them, and to propose innovative solutions. But it is hard to see how the information provided by the standardized technical information systems of COMPSTAT would routinely generate the information that could be used for detailed problem diagnosis and innovative solutions.

Similarly, if some of the data that might be important to use in defining a problem and gauging its importance is the collection of community views about these matters, there was nothing in the early versions of COMPSTAT that supported the community side of problem identification, prioritization, and assistance in solving the problems that were nominated. So, it may be that COMPSTAT does in fact support data-driven problem identification and assessment and innovative problem-solving tactics, but is might be better to offer evidence of this and to explain how the system works to produce that result rather than use it as a definition of a core element of COMPSTAT.

## How new is COMPSTAT?

If we think of COMPSTAT as a technology-supported performance measurement system embedded in a particular managerial system that organizes the use of that information for purposes of creating internal accountability and organizational learning, it becomes possible to talk about what parts of COMPSTAT are new and which are old, and to consider what the new bits add to the old.

As […] Weisburd *et al.*, […] observe, there is much about COMPSTAT that is old and traditional in police organizations. The idea that precinct commanders were accountable to the Chief for crime that occurred in geographically defined commands is not new. Nor is the idea that the precinct commanders should be held accountable for knowing about the patterns of crime in their precincts and having a plan for dealing with crimes that were occurring. Indeed, in many ways, COMPSTAT does not seem all that far removed from the days in which precincts had pin maps posted on their walls that showed recent crime patterns, and in which precinct commanders got calls from the Chief asking them to report on what had happened in their precincts on the previous day, and what they were doing to deal with the problems. This seems entirely consistent with an operationally oriented, para-military organization. And it is these features that suggest to Weisburd *et al.*, that COMPSTAT is really just an innovation that allows the police to look modern while doing what they have always done.

But there are some things that seem new in COMPSTAT that are worth pondering. The first is the degree to which computer-generated information has replaced pin maps. This may only be a difference in degree. There may be more recent information about more things in the computer-based system than in the pin maps. It may be much easier to manipulate the information than in pin maps. And so on. But it is quite possible that these differences in degree are so great that they really add up to a dramatically improved capacity to figure out what is happening in a precinct, and what might be done about it. I think the only way to know this would be to look in detail at a series of COMPSTAT meetings and see whether and how the diagnosis of situations was enriched, and imaginative problem-solving enabled. If all that happens is that we see a crime spike in time or at a particular geographic location (a hot spot), and get some cops over there to head it off, it is not clear that much new has occurred.

In examining the use of the increased volume of information, that computers made possible, I would be particularly interested in tracking two quite different uses. On one hand, the increased volume of information would allow top managers in the police department to investigate *more separate dimensions of precinct commander performance*. They could look not only at how the commander was handling various crime spikes, but also what the commander's average performance had been on crime in general, how afraid the community seemed to be, how much disorder was occurring in the community, how aggressive the police were in confronting people on the street, what forms of self-defense the community was relying on, whether citizens were satisfied with the level of service they were getting, and so on (assuming, for the moment, that data collection systems existed that could generate this information at the precinct level). This information is important to have because it identifies a particular dimension of performance that might be used to evaluate how well the police are performing their various roles, and at what cost in terms of both money and legitimacy.

On the other hand, the increased volume of information could help police managers understand what was causing them to succeed or fail in producing the results they wanted. It could help them diagnose the causes of the problems they sought to resolve. This *diagnostic* use of information is different from the *evaluative* use of information. And diagnostic information is often different and less easily systematized than the information we use for evaluation. It is also the kind of information that is crucial to imaginative and effective problem solving. If all the police know about a crime or disorder or fear problem is when it occurs and where it is located, their imagination about how to deal with it will be limited to a kind of directed patrol operation that gets the cops to the place at the time when the problem is occurring. If the police have some sense about the people, the relationships, and the circumstances that lie behind the crime, disorder, and fear problems, a much wider range of interventions becomes imaginable, including many that will be lower cost, more effective; more preventive, and more acceptable to the community than some form of aggressive preventive patrol.

The second notable new feature of COMPSTAT is how public and theatrical the proceedings are. In the old versions of command accountability, the chief talked directly and privately to the precinct commanders, or talked to them in the context of some regular staff meetings attended by the command staff. Typically, all commanders made a brief and somewhat superficial report on conditions. In COMPSTAT, in contrast, the discussion is held in front of much of the department and members of the public, and one commander remains the focus of attention for a long period of time. No doubt, this feature increases the overall voltage of the measurement system, and puts increased pressure on the individual commanders. It is one thing to report superficially in private, quite another to report in depth, and then face skeptical questions in public. But the public nature of this grilling has some additional features that are worth noting.

For one thing, it helps create the conditions under which the organization as a whole can learn from the experience of one commander. They learn not only about this new procedure and what it demands of managers, but also something about the nature of the substantive problems the department is confronting, and the variety of ways the commanders have thought to deal with them. In short, the sessions can become a kind of operational seminar on dealing with crime problems, and everyone can have immediate access to the discussion.

In addition, by treating the precinct commander as the focus of attention, and treating the commander's problems as the ones that the organization as a whole is supposed to try to solve, an important change is created in the status and working relationships in a police department. More specifically, as Weisburd *et al.*, […] observe, the precinct commander (usually a patrol commander) becomes more important than the functional specialists. The functional specialists are cast not in the role of units with special responsibilities whose priorities are set by their own commanders, but instead as resources to be made available to precinct commanders who are seen as the front line managers of the police department as a whole. This allows the police to mount multifunctional approaches to crime problems that have been observed and become significant at the precinct rather than at the city wide level.

Finally, the fact that the meetings are held in public creates an interesting opportunity to engage the members of local communities in the prioritization, analysis, and solution of the crime, fear, and disorder problems that they face. It is not clear that this opportunity has been much exploited. Indeed, one could argue that this potentially valuable feature of COMPSTAT has been suppressed by holding the meetings downtown at One Police Plaza rather than out in the communities where the policing happens. This tends to emphasize the centralized command and control aspects of the process rather than the opportunities for community consultation. And the parts of the community that tend to show up will be citywide reps and academics rather than locals. So, the local voices will not necessarily be heard in the particular kind of public process associated with this version of COMPSTAT. But there is no reason why one could not change the paradigm by holding the COMPSTAT meetings in the local communities that were the focus of the discussion. That would make COMPSTAT genuinely new, but principally because it would help establish a different working relationship between the police and citizens.

## How strategic is COMPSTAT?

In a paper I wrote on police innovation several years ago, I made a distinction among four different types of police innovation. Programmatic innovations constituted changes in the ways that police used their resources to deal with particular problems, or accomplish particular goals. Examples included such things as making arrests mandatory in domestic violence cases, relying on decoys to suppress muggers, introducing location-oriented directed patrols to control certain kinds of street crime, or using police officers to lecture elementary school students on the dangers of drug use. These are the sorts of innovations that are typically the focus of program evaluations. They are also the sorts of things that are often the focus of what has come to be called evidence-based policing. They are also the sorts of things that are developed through problem-solving efforts.

Administrative innovations, in contrast, are changes in the ways the police manage themselves. Important examples here include the methods the police use to recruit and train officers; the way in which the police organize themselves along geographic and functional lines; the degree to which a police department decentralizes operational initiative; the methods the police rely on to evaluate the performance of individual officers, of subordinate commands within the department, or of the department as a whole; the structures and processes the police establish for consulting with citizens and communities; the methods they use to deal with corruption and excessive use of force, and so on. These things may well have an important impact on operations, but they differ from programmatic innovations insofar as they represent changes in how a police department manages itself rather than in how it operates programmatically. They create the organization-wide conditions under which operations are carried out, guided, and reported on rather than new substantive and operational methods for reducing crime, disorder, and fear.

Technological innovations I defined as changes that involved new pieces of technical equipment and capacity rather than new methods of using police labor. Note that technological innovations can be used to support either operational or administrative activities in a police department. For example, technological innovations that support operations include the development of DNA testing systems, or nonlethal weapons. Technological innovations that support administrative activities include such things as the 'shoot, don't shoot' simulations that improve the training of officers in the use of deadly force. Among the most important technological innovations shaping policing, of course, are those rooted in enhanced electronic communication and data processing. These sorts of innovations turn out to be particularly important because they affect not only operations, but also administrative systems. By linking officers to information they could not previously obtain in real time, they transform what officers do on the street (a programmatic innovation). By making officer conduct more transparent to higher level managers (both in real time and through the creation of durable records), the new information systems change the structure of working relationships in the department (an administrative innovation).

A strategic innovation, I argued, was an innovation that changed the overall purposes of the police, the principal means they relied on to accomplish their objectives, or the important internal and external working relationships in the organization. I also argued that strategic innovations usually both required and came about as a result of a series of smaller programmatic, administrative, and technological innovations that accumulated (more or less self-consciously directed) into a strategic change.

This simple framework offers us a way of sizing up COMPSTAT as an innovation in policing, and in particular to talk about how strategic this innovation turns out to be. Based on this framework, I would characterize COMPSTAT primarily as an administrative innovation. It is an administrative innovation primarily because it changes the working relationships inside the department, and because it changes the basis on which a particular group of mid-level managers are being held accountable and evaluated. This administrative innovation may change the way the organization operates programmatically. If Weisburd *et al.*, are correct about the way in which the system encourages problem diagnosis and the development of imaginative interventions, it may turn the police department into an organization that is continuously innovating with respect to operational programs. But the point is that it is not in itself a new programmatic idea about how best to deal with the myriad of crime, fear, and disorder problems that a police department faces; it mainly changes the conditions under which such ideas may be invented and tried out.

Viewed from this perspective, however, COMPSTAT does not really seem to be all that strategic. It does not either broaden or change the mission and goals of the police department. Indeed, it hardens the image of a police department as a crime-fighting organization. It does not necessarily transform the principal operational methods the police rely on to achieve their objectives. Indeed, insofar as it emphasizes disorder arrests as a method of dealing with crime and the fear of crime, and insofar as it emphasizes directed patrol operations in response to crime spikes of various kinds, it tends to encourage a style of policing we once characterized as 'aggressive preventive patrol' – a rather old style of policing, and one that got police departments into a great deal of trouble at the end of the Sixties.

And, it does not seem to do much to change the basic internal and external working relationships that characterize a police department. It may be that the internal working relationship between precinct commanders and speciality units changes in a way that gives the precinct commanders a bit more influence over the work of the specialty units, and that might well turn out to be strategically important. It may also be that the system does have the effect of shifting initiative and responsibility for controlling crime from the chief to precinct commanders, and that, too, might turn out to be very important. But there is nothing very radical about these changes compared with traditional practices. The specialty units have not been disbanded and had their officers redistributed to precinct commands. The principal responsibility for imagining an effective response to crime has not been shifted all the way down to individual officers who could be invited to nominate problem-solving efforts to deal with problems they confront on their beats. And, most importantly of all, even though COMPSTAT has become good public theater, it has not been used as a forum for restructuring the relationship between the police and the local communities that have to live with the problems that the police fail to notice or help to create by the way that they police. So, even though Weisburd *et al.*, want to see COMPSTAT as 'strategic', I do not see it that way. COMPSTAT may have the potential to drive toward a strategic change in policing by widening the goals, transforming the methods, and altering the key internal and external working relationships in policing, but it is by no means clear that this has actually occurred.

### Why did it disseminate so fast?

I have less to add to the discussion of why this innovation disseminated so quickly. Indeed, I have only three observations to offer. First, as criminologists begin focusing their attention of the processes that lead to the diffusion of innovations, I think it would be particularly important for them to look at the work of Paul DiMaggio and Woody Powell on what they call 'institutional mimesis'. The idea here is that all organizations in a particular industry come to resemble one another rather closely. One reason for that could be that competition among the organizations forces them all to adopt the most efficient form, and it is that process that produces the similarity. But they point to other mechanisms that could produce this same effect, including, in particular, the organization's desire to court legitimacy by embracing the most modern ideas (regardless of whether they work!). My experience tells me that the police world is much like other professions in which organizations want to have good reputations in their profession, and where they acquire those reputations by embracing new 'best practices' even if those best practices have not been fully understood or tested.

Second, it is important to remember that another innovation that disseminated very quickly was the DARE program – a program that seemed to do very little to reduce drug abuse in the community, but did a great deal to enhance the legitimacy of the police with local communities.

Third, as Klinger observes, ideas that disseminate quickly are often those that fit very comfortably within an existing organizational culture. Given that there are many aspects of COMPSTAT that fit quite comfortably within police traditions (e.g., focus on crime control as the primary if not exclusive objective of policing, use of crime statistics as the basis for evaluating organizational performance, use of the command structure as the basic system of accountability), it should not be surprising that it disseminated rather broadly. Indeed, I would venture a further speculation, namely, that it was these particular pieces of COMPSTAT and not the more challenging ideas associated with community problem-solving policing that disseminated most widely and most quickly. Ideas that deeply challenge institutions typically do not disseminate very quickly or very widely without some significant outside crisis.

## What gives COMPSTAT its behavioral power?

A basic principle of management is that measures of performance can animate and guide organizational behavior. But given that we have all seen measurement systems constructed for organizations that seem to have no impact on how the organization behaves, it is clear that a measurement system alone is insufficient to change organizational behavior. Measurement may be useful, but there is also something in the way that the system is used, and something in what the system measures that gives some measurement systems behavioral power and others not.

By all accounts, COMPSTAT (understood at the first level as simply an organizational performance measurement system) had an important impact on how the NYPD behaved. (The exact evidence for this claim remains elusive, except perhaps in the fact that the NYPD made many more misdemeanor arrests after COMPSTAT than it did before.) Assuming this is so, it is interesting to consider what it was about COMPSTAT other than its existence as a measurement system that gave it its behavioral power. What was it about COMPSTAT that gave it its unusual voltage in animating the actions of the NYPD? Let me list several possibilities.

The first, already noted above, is that both the organizational goals embedded in the system (reducing crime), and the basic tactics encouraged by the system (aggressive order maintenance policing), had strong support from a newly elected mayor and a newly appointed police chief. There was more general political support for a shift away from the 'soft' approach taken by Dinkins, Brown, and Kelly, and, increasingly, professional ideological support for the 'broken windows' approach to dealing with crime. In short, a strong political constituency had been created behind the ideas that came to be embodied in a more concrete form in the COMPSTAT managerial system.

Second, the general political ideas that supported 'broken windows' policing, and the particular tactics encouraged by COMPSTAT, were also closely aligned with the culture of the NYPD. No one was asking the police to seek a goal that they did not think was important. No one was asking the police to occupy a position that threatened their professional status and autonomy. The police were being asked to do what they long wanted to do – reassert their control over the streets. Moreover, they were being asked to do this without worrying too much about financial resources, about limitations on the use of force and authority, or about the importance of consulting with local communities about the way the communities wished to be policed. When people are asked by a performance measurement system to do what they are already committed to doing, the system operates to give focus and meaning to their work rather than to inhibit or frustrate the efforts.

Third, the system was designed technically so that it would be aligned with a particular structure of delegation and accountability in the police department. The leadership of the NYPD primarily through the geographically defined patrol structure, more specifically, through the work of precinct commanders. Given that the precinct commanders (rather than the higher level borough commands, or the off-to-the-side functional commands) were seen as the focus of the Department's efforts to reduce crime, it became important to have a measurement system that could pinpoint the degree to which managers in these particular positions were producing the desired results. Thus, it was crucially important to be able to collect and display all information used in the COMPSTAT at the precinct level. The information about performance had to be precisely linked to the managerial responsibilities of specific individuals.

Fourth, the managers whose behavior was being monitored had to believe that the information would be used in evaluating their performance and in making consequential decisions about their futures. In the NYPD, it was not possible to produce significant variations in pay based on performance as it would be possible to do in the private sector. But it was possible to make continuation in the job and the prospects of future promotion (with subsequent implications for pension benefits) contingent on performance. Thus, it was behaviorally significant that more than one-third of the precinct commanders whom Bratton inherited were replaced over the first year or two of his administration, and that it was believed that these changes were linked to their performance as it was revealed in the COMPSTAT process. This is the way in which a (weak) measurement system becomes a (powerful) incentive system.

Sixth, the public aspects of the performance reviews tended to increase the pressure in the system. In principle, all the information collected by COMPSTAT could have been held at the command level, and used by top management in private conversations with individual managers. That is often the practice in private sector firms. Alternatively, the information could have been published widely throughout the organization, but not formally discussed in public forums. But the NYPD opted for the maximum degree of exposure of this information. The NYPD not only collected the information, reviewed it at top management levels, and published the information throughout the department, but they also required the managers to discuss this information in a public forum that included not only their bureaucratic peers, superiors and subordinates, but also members of the public. The fact that one's successes and failures were highly visible – that there was no place to hide – increased the pressure of the system.

Seventh, because the information was being collected both across precincts and within a precinct over time, it was possible to make comparative judgments about performance. The Department's top management could look at one precinct commander relative to another at a given point in time, and they could look at one precinct commander's performance at one point in time relative to the same commander's performance at a different point in time. The fact that these benchmarks for performance existed gave a certain kind of rough legitimacy to the comparative evaluations. Fewer excuses of the form that the implied standards were unreasonable could be offered and taken seriously.

It is obvious, I think, that all of these factors contributed to the power of COMPSTAT to animate and guide the organization's behavior. The political context, and the commitment of the top leadership of the organization, gave the system weight. So did the fact that it was asking the NYPD to do something and behave in ways it wanted to behave anyway. And finally, some of the particular technical features of the system (the way it was aligned with organizational responsibility, the fact that it was used for consequential personnel decisions, the fact that the evaluations came soon and often, the public nature of the evaluation process, etc.) all tended to give the system unusual power. Indeed, one way to think analytically about the design of performance measurement systems like COMPSTAT is to view each of the factors identified above as a kind of design variable, and to imagine that one could set these variables at different levels, and get quite different degrees of tension running through the system. Thus, if the measurement system was less aligned with the culture of the organization, one would expect it to have less motivational power, and even to be resisted or ignored. If the system was not aligned with any particular jobs, or was not used to evaluate the performance of the people in the jobs, it would have less power than COMPSTAT actually had. In short, one can think of these as knobs one can turn to elevate or reduce the voltage that runs through the system.

An important question not only about COMPSTAT but also in the design of its progeny is how much voltage is it desirable to run through an organization. At the outset, one might be inclined to say 'the more, the better'. This seems particularly true if the principal problem one thinks one has with the performance of an organization is a lack of motivation and accountability. Then, a system that is designed to get officers 'off their backsides' and 'out of the doughnut shops' might be the one that is necessary to improve the output and performance of the organization.

On the other hand, one can imagine situations where turning the voltage way up would have negative effects on the performance of the organization. One effect of increasing the voltage might be to put pressure on the integrity of the measurement system. If a great deal depends on measurements, incentives to manipulate the measures as well as to improve performance indicated by the measures are created. One can keep that in check by more carefully auditing the information included in the system. But that kind of checking is both expensive and dispiriting. One can also imagine a situation where parts of the organization or the entire organization was already working very hard, and the increased voltage was experienced as nothing more than a 'speed up' that burned out and sacrificed some of the organization's best performers.

Most damaging of all, however, would be a system that had significant amount of voltage, but that seemed to deliver its shocks in a way that seemed random to those who were subjected to its evaluations. Psychologists have done experiments with rats in which they can produce a state they describe as 'learned helplessness'. They produce this state by first running an electrical current through a grid that serves as the floor of a rat cage. The rats do not like to be shocked, and they scurry around trying to find some behavior that will stop the current running. At the outset, they are quite animated in this search, and the experimenters give them a way out: They give them a lever to push that will stop the current from flowing. The rats find this lever quickly and learn to push it to relieve their discomfort. Then, the experimenters alter the relationship between pushing the lever and removing the source of discomfort. Sometimes when the rats push the lever, it gets worse. Eventually, when the rats figure out that there is nothing they can do to adjust the current in the cages, they simply give up. They hunker down and take it. The voltage has lost the capacity to motivate them to act or to experiment. They are simply too discouraged to keep trying.

It is not hard to imagine a system coming to have similar effects on human beings. Incentives (in the form of both rewards and penalties tied to bits of behavior) can motivate people to perform in particular ways. If, however, the connection between the behavior and the incentive is broken – if the subjects of the control system can no longer figure out how the system is behaving and what it wants them to do – they can simply become demoralized and give up altogether. This can happen presumably if those who administer the system keep changing their mind about what they want, or if they want what is impossible to provide. So, whether a system works well to motivate people over a long period of time depends a great deal on whether those subject to the system believe it is asking them to do something they think is both valuable and possible for them to do.

### Does COMPSTAT tend to support or suppress?

These observations about the conditions under which a performance measurement system will work have an important connection to the issue of whether the system will actually cause the organization to learn better about how to deal with crime. Viewed from one perspective, the COMPSTAT system held precinct captains of the NYPD accountable for reducing (reported) crime in their geographically defined domains. Changes in levels and types of reported crime were always Exhibit 1 – the beginning of the conversation, the facts that set the tone for the subsequent discussion. It is this simple fact that gives COMPSTAT much of its focusing power. Thus, one might say that it made learning how to deal with crime a very important objective for every precinct commander in the force.

The worry, however, is that although this became the concern of every commander in the force, it does not necessarily follow that the system will produce new ideas about how to deal with crime. As noted above, if precinct commanders do not really think they can do much to control crime, they will not necessarily be motivated to act in any new way to accomplish this goal. They might come to view their performance as measured by COMPSTAT as the result of random forces in their environment that had little to do with them. They can hope that the numbers will be good, but not see any way to *make* them good. To the extent this was true, the organization would not necessarily learn very much about how to control crime.

Alternatively, the commanders, fearful of their evaluations, might decide that the best thing they can do to protect themselves against a negative evaluation would be to fall back on the conventional responses that a police department makes to particular crime problems; e.g., directed patrol operations designed to threaten or make arrests of people committing crimes at particular locations and times, or simply aggressive preventive patrol efforts. They might even try to find out in advance what the organizationally preferred ideas are about how to deal with the crime problems, and do those things rather than think on their own. (Indeed, we used to think that a good police department was one in which precinct captains ensured that the troops followed established policies and procedures in dealing with specific crimes situations!) In both these cases, COMPSTAT would not necessarily drive organizational learning. It would instead increase pressures for organizational conformity and compliance with established policies and procedures – precisely the place we were at before the advent of COMPSTAT.

These observations make one somewhat obscure feature of COMPSTAT particularly worth noting. It is this: Although it is true that COMPSTAT made reducing crime the single most important goal in the NYPD and made precinct commanders liable for producing that result, the system did not operate as a system that imposed strict liability on managers for performance; it gave them an 'out' by giving them credit for having some kind of thoughtful plan for addressing a crime problem even if that plan had not yet borne fruit in terms of improved performance. By a strict liability system, I mean a system in which the precinct commanders were held strictly accountable for their performance with respect to reducing crime: where crime reductions were the only things that mattered, and where the statistics alone told the tale – a system in which no excuses or explanations could be offered, where no credit was given for effort, only for results. Now, there is much about COMPSTAT that makes it look like a strict liability system. The measures are there and used for comparative purposes. Individuals are sanctioned for poor performance measured on these statistics. The humiliation is public.

Yet, it is very important that those who ran COMPSTAT always said that although success in reducing crime was the most important thing, it was also important that managers *had a reasonable plan for responding to a crime problem that they had not yet succeeded in solving*. The reason this is important is that one could, apparently, get credit in this system (at least in the short run), by recognizing a problem, having an idea about how to deal with it, and/or reaching out for advice and help in dealing with the problem as well as dealing with it oneself.

This little chink in the strict liability system is potentially important because it reduces the chance that the managers will succumb to the kind of learned helplessness described above. Even if they have their doubts about their ability to reduce crime, they are encouraged by the system to keep thinking and acting as though they could. They are rewarded for thoughtful ideas as well as for demonstrated results. As a result, their minds and imaginations are engaged in the task of reducing crime. And the setting in which they have and discuss these ideas about how to respond to crime problems is a wide public forum in which many are invited to contribute ideas and even operational assistance to help deal with the problem that the precinct commander faces.

How the opportunity created by the interest of the system in generating new ideas about how to deal with crime problems is used will have a decisive effect on whether COMPSTAT tends to encourage or suppress organizational learning about the control of crime. If the system operates as a strict liability system, never pays much attention to what the managers are trying to do to deal with crime, or rewards them only when they do the conventional things to deal with particular crime problems, then the system will not do much to encourage organizational learning. It will remain ignorant of the connection between the organization's ideas and actions on one hand, and its results on the other. Or it will remain locked in to following pre-existing procedures it has always relied on to deal with crime. If, on the other hand, the system is interested in how managers are thinking about dealing with particular crime problems, and exposes that issue in collaborative discussions about what could be tried to reverse a problematic crime trend, then COMPSTAT can very well serve as a device for increasing the innovativeness and learning of the organization in dealing with selected crime issues.

It is also worth noting that shifting from a strict liability system that holds precinct commanders accountable only for their results in reducing crime to one that holds managers accountable not only for their accomplishments, but also for their efforts to deal with problems tends to change assumptions that structure the working relationships between top-level managers and mid-level managers. In a strict liability system, the assumption is that everyone knows what to do, and the only question is whether someone is personally motivated enough to want to get the job done. Failure is treated as a matter of character and not trying hard enough rather than as a consequence of facing a really hard problem. In contrast, in a system that holds individuals accountable for conscientious and imaginative efforts as well as for results, the assumption is that everyone is trying hard, and the principal difficulty is that it is not always clear what one can do to deal with the problem at hand. The challenge is for the organization as a whole not just to increase pressure on the person to perform, but for it to work with the manager to find a way to succeed through the development of improved methods.

It may well be that one of the nice balances struck by COMPSTAT [...] is the nice balance that is struck between holding managers accountable for results, and for conscientious and imaginative effort in trying to achieve this result. It would be bad to have a system that did not attend to the degree to which managers achieved desired results. But it would also be bad to have a system that failed to notice when managers were facing hard problems that they were making conscientious efforts to solve. This system uses the imaginations of managers as well as their focused effort. The more we imagine that the police face novel rather than standard situations, the more we will need the imagination of the managers as well as their commitments and professional expertise.

Note that so far I have been talking about the impact that COMPSTAT has on a certain kind of learning, namely, the ability of the police department to reduce crime. This is the kind of organizational learning that Chris Argyris would describe as 'single loop learning'. What he means by single loop learning is that the organization is learning how to get better in the doing of its current tasks. He distinguishes this kind of learning from a different kind of learning that he calls 'double loop learning'. In his terms, this is a different, deeper kind of learning in which an organization learns to reconsider some of its basic assumptions about it purposes and means in what might be a profoundly altered external environment. For Argyris, double looped learning is a much more important and more difficult kind of learning for organizations to do.

In a police context, double looped learning might involve a reconsideration of whether the best way to think about the ultimate goal of a police department is to reduce crime without worrying too much about the cost in terms of money or legitimacy it enjoys with elements of the community. It might also involve a reconsideration of whether the best way to deal with crime is through threatening and actually arresting those who commit crimes rather than trying to find other more preventive modes of intervening in the large and small social circumstances that tend to create offenders or the situations that produce offenders. Or, it might involve a rethinking about how the police understand the contributions that citizens make to their own self-defense, and what the police can do to help citizens both reduce crime and deal with their own fears in ways that strengthen rather than weaken community bonds. These kinds of questions that require double looped learning are the kinds of questions we identified above as strategic questions, namely, those that transform understandings about the most valuable purposes, the most important means, and the most important internal and external working relationships that allow the police to make their highest value contribution to the communities that support and rely on them.

Viewed from this perspective, it is not at all clear that COMPSTAT does much to encourage double looped learning in the organization. Indeed, this seems to be the heart of Weisburd *et al.*,'s concerns about COMPSTAT. They do not seem to worry too much about the fact that COMPSTAT focuses obsessively on reducing crime without worrying too much about how much money and public legitimacy is chewed up in the process of achieving these results. Nor do they seem to worry too much about the fact that opportunities for engaging communities in the diagnosis, prioritization, and solution of crime problems is not much emphasized in COMPSTAT. But they do worry a bit that COMPSTAT tends to enshrine old internal working relationships in police departments – particularly those that emphasize top-down accountability and tend to limit the discretion and suppress the initiative of street-level police officers. There was an important kind of double loop learning that was associated with problem-solving policing that emphasized the importance of front line police officers identifying and responding to problems at the beat level rather than precinct level. The idea that community problems could include but were not necessarily limited to crime problems; the idea that these problems came in sizes that were smaller than those that could be seen in precinct-wide crime statistics, and that they could be dealt with by the initiative and action of smaller units than precincts; were both paradigm-changing ideas in policing associated with the general idea of problem-solving. Those ideas are, to some degree at least, at risk in a COMPSTAT system that limits a focus to precinct-sized crime problems, and depends on precinct-level initiatives to deal with these.

I confess that my worries about COMPSTAT go well beyond these particular lost opportunities for double looped learning. I think that the general idea of community problem-solving policing challenged traditional ideas about policing at many levels – in terms of the ends of policing, the means, and the key external and internal working relationships. Somehow, COMPSTAT took one strand of all that interesting thinking (the strand that focused on the relationship among disorder, fear, and crime) and found a solution in an old form of policing that could be described as aggressive, preventive patrol. It then elevated that single, very traditional strand of thought to a prominent position as though this idea was the only, or the most important, or the most operationally useful of all the ideas that had emerged from a very productive period of police innovation. One cannot help but be excited as Weisburd *et al.* […] are about the potential of COMPSTAT to help the police get better at controlling crime. But one also cannot help but be concerned that a great deal of potentially valuable improvements in police operations went by the board when much of the reform energy got sucked into replicating COMPSTAT throughout the country.

### Does COMPSTAT increase the capacity of the police to reduce crime?

By far the most important claim made about COMPSTAT is that it helped the police recover their focus on controlling crime and, with that, their ability to do so. Arguably, this would make COMPSTAT valuable to the world even if some of the criticisms listed above were also true. So, it becomes very important to those who are taking the measure of COMPSTAT to be able to say whether they think COMPSTAT helped to reduce crime and, if so, through what particular means.

With respect to the first question of whether COMPSTAT succeeded in reducing crime, there is still much to be debated. We have the evidence that crime fell in NYC following the introduction of COMPSTAT. We also have a theory as well as some other corroborating evidence that links the kind of policing that COMPSTAT apparently generated in NYC to success in controlling crime. And these two things together have been taken by many reasonable people as a basis to celebrate COMPSTAT and urge its widespread adoption.

But the fact of the matter is that we remain uncertain about whether the police, stimulated to operate in particular ways by the COMPSTAT system, was the active ingredient in producing the reduction in crime. We have evidence that the crime rate was beginning to fall in NYC prior to the introduction of COMPSTAT, and that these declines were linked to increases in the overall size of the police force as well as to the methods of policing that had been initiated under Dinkins, Brown, and Kelly. We have evidence that crime decreased in other cities that did not rely either on COMPSTAT as a management system, or on the tactics of aggressive preventive patrol that COMPSTAT seemed to encourage in NYC. We also have some other plausible explanations for why crime might have decreased in NYC, including the observation that a large fraction of the offending population had been incapacitated in prison as a result of significant changes in sentencing practices.

What makes the link between COMPSTAT on one hand and observed levels of crime on the other particularly difficult to establish is not only that we cannot rule out other explanations for what caused crime to fall in New York, but also that we cannot connect all the links that connect the introduction of COMPSTAT to a reduction in crime. Uncertainty appears at each step along the logic model that connects COMPSTAT to reduced crime. At the outset, as noted above, we cannot say with precision what COMPSTAT is. Is it the technical system of performance measures? Is it that plus the particular ways in which management decided to use the performance measures? If so, are there some parts of the managerial system that are more important than others in producing a particular response? Next, we cannot say for sure exactly how the technical/managerial system actually worked, nor what impact it had on the thoughts of precinct commanders and on the operations that were carried out within their precincts. We cannot get from the management system to observed changes in the operational behavior of the police department. Finally, we cannot get from changes in the operational behavior of the police department to changes in levels of reported crime with a reasonable ability to attribute observed changes to changes in the behavior of the police alone.

So, it remains a bit uncertain about whether COMPSTAT really does cause a police department to behave in ways that reduce crime. We cannot be sure what impact COMPSTAT has on the behavior of police departments. Nor can we be sure what impact the changed behavior has on levels of crime.

### Is reducing crime necessarily the same as increasing the 'public value' of a police department?

Uncertainty about the effects of COMPSTAT on levels of crime alone is not enough reason to lose all our enthusiasm for COMPSTAT as an important administrative innovation in policing. After all, at a scientific level, we have always been uncertain about the relationship between the actions of police departments and the levels of reported crime. We have lived with this uncertainty at least in part because we find it hard to believe at the common-sense level that a kind of policing that succeeds in threatening criminal offenders with arrests and prosecution would not have some impact on crime through the mechanisms of deterrence and incapacitation.

But we also live with our uncertainty about the relationship between what the police do and the levels of crime because we have a different justification for policing than its practical effectiveness in controlling crime. We think that policing is justified at least in part because we think citizens ought to be entitled to having a public organization that can come to their aid when they have been victimized by a crime. We like the idea that we can provide to citizens some kind of response to victimization other than encouraging them to respond in kind. We also think it is just and appropriate that those who commit crimes should be called to account for their crimes. We believe in calling offenders to account partly because we think that reduces the likelihood that they or others like them will offend in the future. But we also believe in calling offenders to account because we think it is just to do so. In short, in policing, we want to protect and realize just relationships among citizens, victims, offenders, and the state as well as to achieve practical results like reducing crime and fear. We can see that these goals are being accomplished when the police solve particular crimes, and not worry particularly about whether the police are also successful in reducing aggregate levels of crime.

Once we remember that one of the purposes of a police department is to produce justice, however, and once we remember that we can think about justice both as an objective condition we associate with the procedural rectitude of the police and a subjective feeling that citizens who are being policed have about the legitimacy of the police and their operations, we come to a more fundamental critique of COMPSTAT than our uncertainty about its practical effect on levels of crime. That concern focuses on the question of whether reducing crime really constitutes the right 'bottom line' for policing. In introducing COMPSTAT to the world, Bratton said that it did: He said that 'reduced crime was the same as profit in a private corporation'.

Now, Commissioner Bratton is a very good police leader and manager, but he is not a very good accountant. The profit earned by a private business is calculated as the revenues earned by selling products and services *minus the costs of producing those goods and services*. If one was to carry this equation into the world of policing, one would say that reduced crime is not really the equivalent of the profit – it is the equivalent of the *revenues earned by the organization's sale of goods and service*, that is, of the value attributed to the organization's output by those who purchased it. The profit earned by a police department would be the value of the crime reduction produced *minus the costs of producing that result*. What Bratton misses in his conception is the cost of producing the result of reducing crime. (He may also miss the fact that the police produce much that is valuable beyond reducing crime, but we will let that one go for now.) The net value of a police department cannot be gauged without looking at costs any more than the net value of a private company could be gauged by looking only at the revenues it earned. We have to look at costs as well as at value and revenues produced.

But what costs do a police generate as they go about their important work of reducing crime? One obvious answer is that they spend our money. This is obvious. And it is not hard to account for the amount of our money that public police departments spend. Less obvious, however, is that the police spend our freedom and liberty. As the Philadelphia Police Study Task Force once wrote:

> The police are entrusted with important public resources. The most obvious is money: $230 million a year flows through the Philadelphia Police Department. Far more important, the public grants the police another resource – the use of force and authority. These are deployed when a citizen is arrested or handcuffed, when an officer fires his weapon at a citizen, and when an officer claims exclusive use of the streets with his siren.

An important question we have to address in identifying the value produced by a police department, thus, is not only how much money was spent, but also how much authority. Now, authority is an odd kind of resource. It is not necessarily finite. When one spends authority, one doesn't necessarily deplete it. Indeed, if the authority is used justly and fairly, the amount of authority an organization has might well go up. We say that its legitimacy and credibility has increased. Conversely, if the organization uses its authority recklessly and inappropriately, we will be inclined to take some of its authority away by limiting its discretion, or subjecting it to increased oversight. We say that the organization has lost its credibility and legitimacy. That is dangerous in general to the extent that authority is valuable in doing its operational work. It is even more dangerous if the organization depends on private citizens to help it with its work. If a police organization needs citizen's contributions to make it effective, and if it has lost the confidence of the citizens it needs, then its performance will inevitably deteriorate. We have been through this process relatively recently in our history when the legitimacy of the police in some cities was so low that they could not keep the citizens from rioting, but had to restore order by calling in the superior force of the National Guard. In the difference between police officers lightly patrolling and soldiers marching the streets is the measure of the degree to which the police have legitimacy.

Given these observations, what I find particularly troubling about COMPSTAT is the fact that it gives very little attention to what I take to be an important goal of policing, namely, doing justice as well as reducing crime. I also find it troubling that COMPSTAT (at least at the outset) included little concern for recognizing or noticing how the force and authority of the police was being used. To the extent that it focused on this, it tended to view arrests (a significant use of authority in pursuit of either crime control or justice or some combination of the two) as a good in itself. The idea that the police might be able to produce less crime and more justice through preventive measures of various kinds that made less extensive (and less belated) use of state authority was therefore suppressed.

Finally and most importantly, the fact that COMPSTAT made no attempt to monitor the legitimacy of the police with those who were policed left the NYPD open to the simplest and worst error that can be made with a performance measurement system. By failing to monitor the use of an asset that the organization needs to be able to succeed, it allows the organization to overuse that asset in the pursuit of the goals that are measured. By failing to monitor the legitimacy of the police with all the citizens of New York, the police set the stage for using up their legitimacy in the pursuit of goals and through the use of means that the police department deemed important, but were less important to the citizens. Over the long run, that may make them a less effective police department not only with respect to the narrow goals of controlling crime, but also to the broader goals of producing safe and just communities.

From Mark H. Moore, 'Sizing up Compstat: an important administrative innovation in policing, Criminology and Public Policy, Vol. 2, no 3, 2003, pp 469–494.

# 32. The policing of risk

*Richard V. Erickson and Kevin D. Haggerty*

### Risk communication

Risk refers to such external dangers as a natural disaster, technological catastrophe, and threatening behavior by human beings. The system for communicating risks – its people, rules, formats, and technologies – is a part of the social meaning of risk. That is, threats and dangers are recognized, responded to, and made real through the human invention and use of risk classifications and technologies.

Risk-communication systems are not simply conduits through which knowledge of risk is transferred. Rather, they have their own logics and autonomous processes. They are themselves the producers of new risks, because it is through them that risks are recognized, subject to calculation, and acted upon. They govern institutional relations, and they affect what individuals and organizations are able to accomplish.

Risk society is comprised of institutions that organize on the basis of knowledge of risk. These institutions expend a significant proportion of their resources on the production and distribution of knowledge of risk. This knowledge is used to manage populations, provide security, and take risks.

[…]

The police are at the fulcrum of risk communication among institutions. They are first and foremost knowledge workers who think and act within the risk-communication systems of other institutions.

[…]

### The police as risk communicators

Whether dealing with crime, vehicle collisions, regulatory matters, social service, or public order, the police operate as a center of calculation (Latour, 1987) for the risk-communication systems of myriad institutions. As such, police mobilization is not only a matter of intervention in the lives of individual citizens, but is also reactive to institutional demands for knowledge of risk. They are required to intersect with, and broker knowledge to and from, a full range of institutions in the risk-communication network.

In large police organizations there is a coterie of specialists who manage the vast and complex systems of risk communication. For example, the [Royal Canadian Mounted Police] RCMP Informatics division with six hundred full-time personnel has a highly specialized division of labor to manage its risk-communication systems. There are telecommunications engineers, information technology specialists, and information system auditors. These risk-communication operators work within the framework of rules compiled in four thick manuals that total sixteen hundred pages. A lot of attention is focused on authorizing acceptable forms. This includes detection and elimination of 'bootleg forms' developed by individual officers to meet their pragmatic needs but that do not fit the system's needs. It also includes policing the classifications used and narratives produced.

At each station level there are editorial control systems in place to patrol the facts. These systems detect any interpretive leakage that has occurred in spite of the use of closed formats. We observed a station-level operation in which patrol officers' reports were initially reviewed by their supervisor for completeness and accuracy. The supervisor would also assign a 'diary date', usually set for two weeks after the initial review, for reviewing the file again. At the time of the second review the supervisor could keep the file open by assigning a new diary date, or close it. When a file was closed, the supervisor 'scored' it in terms of fixed-choice classifications that satisfied various users within the police organization and in external institutions. An internal report on patrol supervisors' responsibilities estimated that 70–80 percent of their time was spent checking reports.

Once a supervisor completed the scoring, the file was passed on to a 'reader' for further editorial scrutiny. The reader was a full-time police officer whose sole function was to review the files once again to ensure that everything was filled out completely and accurately, and that the scoring was correct. The reader functioned only as a data checker and could not, for example, reject a file and ask for further investigation. From the reader a file would go to a data entry clerk, who would again check the completeness of the file and competence of the scoring and seek clarification of any slippage.

In selected cases there was further cleansing of the data. For example, all sexual assault, domestic violence, and major crime files were sent to the second-in-command at the station for additional scrutiny. This officer also conducted random checks on other files. A police officer described this task as one that was 'concerned with how the files are taken care of. He [the second-in-command] is also concerned on the administrative side with how the file is scored because if it is not scored properly then it is going to reflect back on him at audit time'.

Some of the reports reviewed by the second-in-command had to be reviewed further by form managers at the division level. In such cases a form was filled out to flag the fact that a file needed further review and data cleansing. This was designed to ensure the appearance of uniform reporting across the police organization, especially in high-profile cases. A police officer observed that in such instances, '[y]our supervisor reads your work, the sergeant checks his work, staff sergeant looks after him, the commanding officer inspects all of it. Now it goes to another group of people and they inspect it. If they find anything they send it back. You have so many people checking up on what I do on the street it makes it kind of repetitive all of the time'.

In addition to this complex system for case-by-case editing and data cleansing, this police organization had various communication format auditors. There were, for example, division-level auditing teams that spent a week in each station reviewing the quality of data entry. A division-level officer involved in this process said that the main task was a random audit of files 'to make sure they have all the necessary information fields they're supposed to have, compared to the computer printout'; a 5 percent margin of error was allowed. The division also had file auditors in its field-support information unit, who on a three-year cycle audited every recordkeeper in every station. They served, in effect, as supervisors of station-level coders with respect to the reliability and validity of the coders' data collection.

Of course there are still murmurings among the police that information work as the means has become an end in itself, interfering with 'crime fighting' as the 'real' end of police work. But in the vast majority of cases information work is all there is to it. It is both the means and the end of police work, and the reason why there is such an obsession with the production of clean data.

## Police mobilization and knowledge production

The police think and act in relation to the communication formats of external institutions that demand knowledge of risk. As a result, they are mobilized not in terms of consensual order, as criminal law theory would suggest, but rather in terms of the different risk logics of the institutions with which they communicate. In this respect, something only becomes actionable as police work if it fits in the risk-knowledge requirements of external institutions.

This view of police-knowledge work differs sharply from existing research on police organizations that emphasizes how the police produce knowledge for their own *internal* management purposes. Researchers have focused on how line officers do their paperwork with an eye toward 'covering ass' in their dealings with their supervisors (Manning, 1980; Ericson, 1982, 1993; Chatterton, 1991). When studies go beyond the immediate gatekeeping aspects of street-level decisionmaking, they still remain within the police institution and examine only the internal flow of knowledge (Manning, 1988; Chatterton, 1989; Southgate and Mirless-Black, 1991). Knowledge is rarely seen as moving beyond the police institution, only into it, across it, and up it. In this police-centered vision of knowledge work, the possibility of a communication environment outside the police institution is not even imagined. Chatterton even makes the extraordinary claim that the police 'have not been information driven. On the contrary they have made information police property. They have interpreted it in accordance with their own interests and within their own cultural assumptions and typifications. Information has been used to achieve rather than to set objectives' (1991: 8).

The focus on police mobilization as a response to external institutional demands for knowledge of risk is also contrary to the view that police work is of 'low visibility'. Because of their police-centric vision and their emphasis on knowledge reproduction and distribution for internal management purposes, researchers have emphasized secrecy and low visibility in police work. Following Goldstein's (1960) seminal formulation, researchers continue to contend that 'most police decisions are virtually invisible or of low visibility' and that '[s]ecrecy is emphasized ... information is rarely shared' (Manning, 1992: 357, 370; see also Geller and Morris 1992; Chatterton, 1983; Reiss, 1982: 146). To the contrary, in the context of demands from external institutions, the police engage in numerous kinds of institutionalized *publicity* that make their work an exercise in high visibility.

As risk communicators to various institutional audiences, the police not only distribute knowledge widely but also make their own actions highly visible in producing that knowledge. High visibility is augmented by auditing; computer terminals in police cars; surveillance cameras in patrol cars, police stations and mass private property sites; and electronic filing of occurrence reports. Every new technology for the surveillance of populations is also a technology for the surveillance of the population of police. As in other knowledge-based occupations, the police worker, in the very act of producing and distributing the knowledge needed to get the job done, also produces and distributes knowledge about his or her work (Ericson and Shearing, 1986; Poster, 1990, 1995).

### Institutions beyond criminal justice

The risk-communication view of policing we are advancing here obviously de-centers the criminal law and criminal justice aspects of police work. Much of the demand from other institutions is for knowledge of risk that does not relate to crime (for example, vehicle collisions, missing person, unwell person, safety education in schools). Moreover, much of the knowledge about crime is produced for institutions other than criminal justice (for example, insurance, health, education, welfare). [The] vast majority of cases are diverted away from the criminal justice institution, even when prosecution is possible. These cases are left to be handled by other institutions within their own risk-management systems, albeit with the aid of risk knowledge communicated by the police.

At the same time the criminal justice institution itself has moved in the direction of actuarial justice (Feeley and Simon, 1994). There has been a pro-liferation of risk-assessment technologies to decide who to select for surveillance, arrest, bail, special prosecution, penal regimes, jury duty, victims programs, and so on (Royal Commission on Criminal justice, 1993; Ericson, 1994b; Ericson and Haggerty, 1997; Garland, 1996, 1997; O'Malley, 1998). The focus in criminal justice becomes the efficient production and distribution of risk knowledge for the management of populations of victims, informants, suspects, accused, and offenders.

In this context, the law of criminal procedure can be reread as providing the coercion necessary to meet the actuarial justice system's needs for knowledge of risk. The substantial erosion of rights of suspects in recent years (Royal Commission on Criminal justice, 1993; McConville and Bridges, 1994), for example, can be understood as part of the wider decline of innocence (Ericson, 1994a) in risk society, whereby the surveillance system's right to knowledge gains legal as well as pragmatic preference over individual due process rights that force the system to gather evidence unaided. Compulsory DNA testing, erosion of the right to silence, and reduction in accused rights to trial election options all signify the new emphasis on risk-knowledge production and control by policing authorities in risk society.

## Compliance law enforcement within private policing systems

External institutions have their own private policing systems that are based on preventative security arrangements and administrative compliance. These systems for policing risk are much more elaborate; and have greater technological and personnel resources, than the public police (Shearing and Stenning, 1983; Shearing, 1992; Johnston, 1992, 1997; Loader, 1999). A brief consideration of the private policing systems of retail stores and of insurance companies illustrates the policing of risk in conjunction with, and beyond, the public police (Haggerty and Ericson, 1999, 2000).

In the city of Oxford, England, all downtown retail stores have full-time security officers. The security officers in each store are linked to their counterparts in other stores through a radio communication system that also is connected to the local police station. These security officers spend a good part of each day watching customers on surveillance cameras, and they use the video evidence from these cameras to proceed against shoplifters. In many cases the store goods are electronically tagged to trigger an alarm at the store entrance should a shoplifter proceed that far. The private security operatives and their surveillance cameras extend to the public streets outside their stores, so that they also police the downtown public space during the hours of store opening. They do all the work of preventative security, public order policing, detection, apprehension, arrest, rights cautioning, production of evidence, and statement taking. The police only enter the picture when called upon to do so, and then only to refine the information on the offender and offense for brokerage to other institutions.

As introduced earlier, private insurance companies are a key institution of preventative security as they discipline property holders into being self-policing agents. There is no doubt that the retail security arrangements in Oxford described above are heavily influenced by insurance contract stipulations. Property insurance companies often undertake security inspections, making every potential property crime victim also a *suspect*, that is, suspected of not doing enough to reduce the risk of loss. Moreover, every actual property crime victim is also treated as an insurance *offender*. As an offender, she or he is likely to suffer one or more costly penalties on an escalating scale: higher premiums, higher deductible levers, more exclusion clauses, lower insurance limits, cancellation of the policy, and 'redlining' as a bad risk to the point where no insurer can be found (Squires, 1997).

Insurance fraud is typically dealt with by external compliance systems and very rarely dealt with by criminal prosecution (Ericson, Barry and Doyle, 2000). There are many reasons why an insurance adjuster or investigator must tread lightly even when a fraudulent claim is suspected. First, there is often a great deal of ambiguity regarding the evidence for what is claimed. Exaggeration or soft fraud is easy to visualize but difficult to investigate and take action against. Second, in an industry where the operating philosophy is moral utilitarianism and therefore the supreme value is efficiency, it is often judged more expedient to make 'nuisance payments' to claimants rather than investigate their suspected fraudulent claims. Furthermore, the loss can be absorbed in future higher premiums to the claimant and across the pool of insured persons. Third, and pervading the above considerations, is public relations. The claims process is also part of the sales process, since 'all that an insurance company has to sell is its promise to pay' (Baker, 1994: 1401). Indeed, an insurance company may want to keep its dishonest customers because they continue to pay premiums that the company needs to invest and make profits. It is sometimes easier not to bite the hand that feeds, even if one's own hand is nibbled at from time to time.

There is an obvious tension, if not contradiction, in the compliance-oriented private policing of insurance relationships. On the one hand, as we have seen, anyone with a stake in a private property insurance relationship is contractually induced into participating in loss reduction, and penalized for failures. On the other hand a great deal of fraud and other loss through moral hazard is tolerated and even fostered in insurance relationships. As Garland (1997) observes, part of the responsibility of being *homo prudens* in risk society is to recognize which losses are not only inevitable but necessary for the smooth flow of social and economic life. Surveillance for preventive security has limits, as does law enforcement. 'Precisely because crime occurs in the course of routine social and economic transactions, crime reducing intervention must seek to preserve "normal life" and "business as usual". The characteristic modes of intervening involve the implantation of non-intrusive controls in the situation, or else attempts to modify the interests of the actors involved' (Garland, 1997: 87).

In compliance-oriented systems of risk management, such as insurance, the police are relegated to a secondary role as front-end suppliers of risk knowledge. They give insurance investigators routine and full access to police files, a legislated requirement in some insurance fields in Canada. They produce data on loss situations, and on people who create opportunities for loss, via occurrence and vehicle collision reports. Increasingly police involvement in this regard is minimized through self-reporting systems (for example, victim voice entry; self-report forms for minor vehicle collisions), or reports taken only by police clerical staff (for example, for thefts). In one large urban police organization we studied, one-quarter of complaints are recorded without even dispatching a patrol officer. As an officer from this organization explained, 'People will call in the theft of an item. They know there isn't a hope in hell of finding it and they really don't have an interest in reporting it to the police, but they know they can't get their insurance claim until they do report it to the police. It's a paper exercise'.

### Governing through crime

While the police can do little to control crime directly, and are primarily brokers of knowledge about crime and other risks to external institutions, they are nevertheless a central agency of government (Rose, 1999). Indeed, their participation in the risk-communication systems of external institutions has made them part of those institutions and their modes of governance. Crime risk, and fear of it, has become the basis for police involvement in governance well beyond crime control itself. In addition to the governing of crime, there is governing through crime (Simon, 1997). Crime risk, and fear of it, is the basis for proliferating surveillance systems in those public spaces and social institutions that the police still have jurisdiction over. Police involvement in public contact surveillance systems, public schools, watch programs, and missing persons registries are illustrative.

#### Census taking

The 'contact card' is the most pervasive device for police governance of populations. It is used to report police observations of people suspected of being out of place or associating with undesirables. Patrol officers are required to satisfy quotas for the submission of contact cards. The cards are sent to analysts who computerize the data and prepare and distribute profiles of suspect populations and their proper places.

Computer terminals in police vehicles permit the electronic entry of street-check information, This technological innovation has, along with increased quota expectations, encouraged greater numbers of random checks. In the eyes of police officers who have computer terminals, it has created the potential for more pervasive and systematic inspection of populations that appear out of place. As one patrol officer said:

> You can program into this machine a street check ... whereas before I wouldn't have bothered filling out a form ... because they were time consuming, a pain in the ass and nobody ever bothered to do anything with them ... What we are doing is a proactive patrol ... go out in residential areas ... and just write down anything suspicious. Vehicles, young fellow walking down the road at two o'clock in the morning ... [Computers] increase our street checks something like 700 percent ... [Previously] there was no way we could keep track of who was on the go. Now you do your street check, stop a specific car in a neighborhood at four o'clock in the morning and someone may find out that that night there was a specific break [burglary] or car broken into. You can go back and check this person and maybe they are responsible. The more people you know who are moving or who are on the go then the more people you are keeping track of ... We do the subdivision areas late at night and just kind of sneak around and park on the side of the road to see who is moving and do spot checks [on] who is driving or walking.

Another contact card system provides a means of tracing populations that reside in targeted residential areas. Inquiry forms are used to record systematic data on householders interviewed in connection with a crime or other risk in an area. In one police jurisdiction we studied, the attending officer was required to complete a form for each person in the household aged fourteen or older, which had spaces for, among other things, name, marital status, vehicle ownership, occupation and employer, name and address of ex-spouse, and number of persons living in adjacent houses (adult males, adult females, and children). The form included an admonition to the officer to 'Be alert for spontaneous response'. In light of the very low clearance rate in residential burglaries, police officers viewed this brand of police census taking as a tracking device for possible future use, rather than as a means of solving the crime that initiated the inquiry. As one interviewee remarked, 'You have to check with neighbors on the left side and on the right and across the street. To some people that seems like a pain in the ass and you are not going to find anything, but we have found very often that you may be looking for the guy who is across the street down the road. And all of a sudden you have that in your computer'.

*Watch programs*

Police-fostered watch programs have proliferated in myriad school, business, residential, and other public settings. These programs mobilize the inhabitants of local territories to become reflexive with respect to risks. Reflexivity is not only intended to prevent crime and capture criminals but also to help inhabitants confront their emotional responses to risk and to become responsible for governing their own territories. This sensibility is exemplified in a Block Watch brochure that says the program is designed to help people deal with their fears, as well as with crime, through intensive territorial surveillance that includes self-policing: '[Block Watch is] to deter *fear* and incidence of crime ... through saturation ... increase the identification and reporting of suspicious activities ... [and] provide neighborhood cohesiveness ... [G]etting to know your neighbors ... works best in low transient population communities ... [Block Watch requires] an observant eye for any unusual activity and common sense precautions ... Crime prevention is not a series of lectures but a part of daily life.'

One large urban police organization we studied ensured that crime prevention, among other governmental tasks, was made part of daily life by introducing a computerized version of Block Watch. Known as the Personal Computer Community Organization Prevention System, or PCCOPS, this program is based on a computerized telephone dialing system that automatically sends out prerecorded messages to member residents. In a jurisdiction we studied, eight divisional police stations had acquired the system. In one division there were approximately thirteen thousand residents and fifteen hundred businesses in the contact databases. The program was 'mapped' onto neighborhood units of about three hundred telephone numbers in each unit. The system operated four lines, each capable of making four calls at once, which allowed up to 320 three-minute calls to go out each hour.

People who sign up for the program receive messages that begin, 'It's the City Police – Neighborhood Watch Computer – Dialed Alert Calling'. They receive 'alert calls' regarding risks such as recent criminal acts, threats posed by rabid animals, and lost children. They also receive 'information calls' reminding them of their responsibility for managing their own risks. Other functions include informing people about upcoming Neighborhood Watch meetings and in some cases about inconveniences such as public works programs.

PCCOPS exemplifies community policing as risk-communications policing. A police officer told us that even though there were some cases in which the program had led to the capture of criminal suspects, that function was not central to it: 'You can't evaluate its effectiveness [in crime prevention and detection] … It's provided us a means of communicating with the community on a regular basis without having to go and knock on the door to do the town crier bit. We don't have the manpower to do the town crier.' A local government official who had become involved in developing the program said that it was, despite appearances, 'still policing … police and community policing community'. He observed that crime prevention was the best message to initially put forward in selling the program, but that in the long term the program could be used for governance more broadly: 'So I thought the best way of keeping people informed is through a computer link-up. Rather than have the police force or myself whatever, these constant meetings, constant dropping off of pamphlets, letters, it really is a waste of time and money and resources are limited … So you sort of involve yourself in community building, at the same time as crime prevention.'

The police viewed PCCOPS as a convenient tool for making some of their routine tasks easier. When involved in direct, face-to-face relations with the police, people can make annoying demands that are tangential or irrelevant to the task at hand. It is far better, the police think, to avoid face-to-face contact by relying on computer-assisted dialing systems such as PCCOPS:

> [When you go door to door] and you tell them that little Johnny or Mary from next door is missing, they're concerned but they're going to say, 'Are you going to my neighbor?' And you say 'Yes'. [They reply] 'When you tell them could you also mention that their dog is awfully noisy at night?' This happens. So you go five minutes at every house because you get twelve houses on one side of the street and you've used up an hour of your time … I can record a message on the dialer and call sixty to eighty houses in that hour because they're not expecting to tell that machine about the barking dog next door, and it cascades … I can't be rude. I'm there as a professional so [when] it's a two-way conversation … I have to because it's face to face, listen to whatever you're going to say to me.

### Missing persons

As suggested by the use of PCCOPS to trace the whereabouts of 'little Johnny or Mary', risk society hopes to keep track of everyone. People who go missing even temporarily are registered, and the fact that they cannot be traced is in turn communicated to a variety of institutions. The police are at the fulcrum of the missing-persons knowledge system, once again serving as key brokers of risk knowledge to other institutions, including knowledge of how to provide for one's own personal security well beyond crime control *per se*.

Because the vast majority of missing persons are young people, many police organizations coordinate their missing-persons systems through their youth services division. An urban police organization we looked at received approximately thirty-two hundred missing-persons reports each year, almost 85 percent of which concerned young people. It had a full-time missing-persons coordinator who, according to his supervisor, 'doesn't actually go out and search for people – he coordinates the files'. Indeed, apart from the rare occasion when foul play was suspected, or there was a request for information from the voluntary organization Child Find, the unit did not actually investigate disappearances. If the initial missing-person report mentions that the person might be at a certain location, the police will on occasion check it out. Otherwise, all that happens is that a form is completed and filed. There is such a large volume of missing-person cases from social service agencies and group homes for youths that their workers are bound by an agreement with the police not to report a missing-person case until eight hours have elapsed since the disappearance. An officer involved in administering the system said that this arrangement 'saves some paper headaches for us'. If the missing person has a record of disappearances, the responsibility for finding and dealing with the person is returned to the reporting agency. The officer also raised another point – police reluctance in some cases to simply return missing youths to the relatives or friends who report their disappearance: 'We have one very vocal parent who would like us to drag his daughter back by her toenails, but I guess my fear is that she's being sexually abused at home. And here, we, the police, dragging them back to that situation. What we'll do is recommend that social services get involved, you know, crisis unit.'

In missing-persons cases the police are almost exclusively risk-knowledge brokers. They enter missing-persons data into the CPIC system; check other institutional data systems to which they have access, such as those maintained by hospitals; notify school and welfare organizations and volunteer agencies such as Child Find; and, in some cases, distribute photographs of and notices about missing persons. Impelled by a risk-management sensibility, the goal of police knowledge workers in the missing persons field is to have no more than three percent of the year's missing persons still missing at the end of the year. This national standard is set by the RCMP.

The RCMP maintains a Missing Children's Registry staffed by police officers, a research analyst, and statistical analysts. The heavy reliance on statistical expertise emphasizes the fact that the registry's primary tasks are indeed registration and the associated risk profiling of youths who, however temporarily, cannot be accounted for.

[The] vast majority (74 percent) of unaccounted for young people were runaways. Abduction by strangers was very rare indeed. Only 78 of 59,135, or 0.1 percent, of recorded cases in 1991 were a result of 'stranger abduction'. And it must be noted, too, that the definition of 'stranger' used by the registry included close relatives (such as grandparents, aunts, and uncles) and friends who did not have legal custody of the child! The available data do not indicate how many of the seventy-eight stranger abductions were in fact abductions by relatives or friends, but it is reasonable to assume that most fell into that category. Clearly, stranger abductions were not a substantial problem for the authorities, although they have great symbolic importance in our society (Best, 1990).

The police help foster this symbolic importance because it enables them to govern through crime. For example, in addition to routinely supplying news releases to the media, the registry cooperated with the producers of *Missing Treasures*, a 'child find' version of police reality television (Fishman and Cavendar, 1998). This show featured reenactments of high-profile, missing-child cases and solicited public assistance in supplying knowledge relevant to those cases. A police officer involved, talking after the termination of the show, commented:

> It's been a success in that it's brought forward the information to the public. I don't know of any particular case we can point to that we found the child because of that ... [but it helps people to] realize that things like this happen and they have to have some protection for their children ... tips for parents ... keep the problem of missing children there in the forefront to the public so they don't forget about it.

At the symbolic level the police unite with other institutions in promoting the education of parents, who are expected to educate their children about the problem of stranger abductions. Thus, despite its own evidence, the 1991 *Annual Report on Canada's Missing Children* stresses the need to be eternally vigilant about the risk of stranger abductions:

> [B]ecause such high profile is given to any stranger abduction, the public's perception is that this phenomenon is common in Canada. This in fact is not the case. However, it is still prudent for parents to teach their children to be 'street smart' and to be aware of the dangers of our society. Street proofing of children is essential to preventing such tragedies. Many of Canada's police are actively involved in preventative policing and are able to provide tips on personal safety. It is important to remember that the legal definition of 'stranger' is anyone who does not have custody of the child. Therefore, children who are taken by a grandparent, aunt, uncle, or friend of the family would be entered into CPIC under the category of stranger abduction.

Eternal vigilance is fostered by asking parents to include their children in special registration systems. One police organization we studied ran an 'Operation Child Identification Program' in which detailed written descriptions, photographs, and fingerprints were placed on file. A brochure produced by a provincial solicitor general's office and distributed by police throughout the province urged parents to maintain their own home-based knowledge system for mapping and training their children: 'Build a home information centre, which includes a map of your neighborhood and its play areas, and have your child identify where he will be at all times, and when he will return ... Maintain up-to-date records which include a recent photograph of your child, his height and weight, medical and dental histories, and if you wish, a video tape and fingerprint record.' Parents are now also being encouraged to maintain a sample of their child's DNA for potential identification purposes.

A police officer we interviewed saw such urgings as part of the 'continual reinforcement' needed to persuade parents to maintain good records. In her view, these records would be important in the event of an apparent missing-child case, because parents are usually in an 'emotional state' at such times, which interferes with rational, efficient police work. In other words, families are to be like other institutions, providing data that are properly formatted and readily accessible: 'They have that information just there, they can hand it to the officer, it saves a hell of a lot of time in the police officer trying to calm them down enough to ask questions so they can get the information from them – details and description. The person wants the policeman to get out right now and go out and find their kid.'

Parents are not only to keep detailed records of their childrens' identities, they are also to remain perpetually reflexive with respect to risks. The aforementioned brochure stressed that the safety tips it offered 'will not completely protect your child, however they will increase the level of awareness'. Indeed, parents were made aware by the brochure of imagined negative consequences that lurked behind the most mundane aspects of a child's everyday life: 'Avoid clothing and toys which personally display your child's name, because children are less likely to fear a stranger who knows their name ... know all of your children's friends, their families and their phone numbers; insist that your child ask for permission to visit his friends ... accompany your child on door-to-door activities, such as Halloween or school fund-raising.'

As is suggested by the instruction to avoid labeling a child's property with his or her name lest it give dangerous strangers a way of becoming friendly with the child, many of the lessons in the brochure focused on communication. In the brochure, community policing as risk-communications policing extended into the home- and family-based education of the young. For example, children were expected to manipulate appearance and even lie in the interests of risk reduction. 'When children are home alone, [they are] to tell phone callers that you are there, but you are busy and cannot come to the phone, and that the caller should call back later.' Like electronic home-security alarm systems, children were to be given a code that would help signal who were trusted insiders and who were to be excluded from contact: '[U]se a pre-selected code word with your child and those whom you may ask to give your child a ride; where necessary, change the code word with your child after it has been used for a period of time.' No mention was made of the confusion that might ensue for mother trying to remember the codes of the six children being picked up in her station wagon on the way to their Saturday morning hockey game. The parent was to know everything about the child's communications with other adults. In communications between children and adults who were not close family members, confidentiality was to be breached: 'Some secrets – like surprise birthday presents – are fun, but a secret that another adult says only the two of you can know is not right – come and tell me.'

The fear of child abduction has recently been extended literally to the cradle. An electronic ankle bracelet for infants, trademarked 'Hugs', is being marketed to hospitals as a fully supervised and tamper-resistant protection system that automatically activates once secured around an infant's ankle or wrist. Staff is immediately alerted at a computer console of the newly activated tag, and can enter pertinent information such as names and medical conditions. Password authorization is needed to move infants out of the designated protection area and – if an infant is not readmitted within a predetermined time limit – an alarm will sound. An alarm also sounds if an infant with a Hugs tag is brought near an open door at the perimeter of the protected area without a password being entered. The display console will then show the identification of the infant and the exit door on a facility map. Alternatively, doors may also be fitted with magnetic locks that are automatically activated. As well, Hugs can be configured to monitor the progress and direction of the abduction within the hospital. Weighing just 1/3 of an ounce, each ergonomically designed infant tag offers a number of other innovative features, including low-battery warning, the ability to easily interface with other devices such as CCTV cameras and paging systems and time and date stamping. (*Canadian Security* 1998)

## Governing through fear

All of these systems for governing through crime are based on governing through fear. Risk society is characterized by the marketing of (in)security. 'In' or trendy security products are sold in the same way as other consumer products (Slater, 1997; Loader, 1999). The selling is facilitated by the reflexive awareness of insecurity that accompanies the probabilistic thinking of risk knowledge. And the more security products that are available, the more the signs of insecurity and the greater the fear. Fear ends up proving itself (Beck, 1992). It is therefore understandable why some police organizations, such as the Thames Valley Police in England, now include a motto on the side of their vehicle that states their dedication to 'Reducing Crime, Disorder and Fear'.

*From Richard V. Ericson and Kevin D. Haggerty, 'The policing of risk' in T. Baker and J. Simon (eds),* Embracing Risk *(Chicago: University of Chicago Press), 2002, pp 238, 251–8, 262–72.*

## References

Ashworth, Andrew. 2001. 'The Decline of English Sentencing, and Other Stories.' In *Punishment and Penal Systems in Western Countries*, ed. M. Tonry and R. Frase. New York: Oxford University Press.

Baker, Tom. 1994. 'Constructing the Insurance Relationship: Sales Stories, Claims Stories, and Insurance Contract Damages.' *Texas Law Review* 75: 1395–434.

Barclay, Gordon, Cynthia Tavaras, and Andrew Prout. 1995. *Information on the Criminal Justice System in England and Wales*. London: Home Office Research and Statistics Department.

Beck, Ulrich. 1992. *Risk Society: Toward a New Modernity*. London: Sage.

Best, Joel. 1990. *Threatened Children: Rhetoric and Concern about Child-Victims*. Chicago: University of Chicago Press.

*Canadian Security.* 1998. 'The Importance of Hugs.' November/December.

Chatterton, Michael. 1983. 'Police Work and Assault Charges. In *Control in the Police Organization*, ed. M. Punch. Cambridge: MIT Press.

Chatterton, Michael. 1989. 'Managing Paperwork.' In *Police Research: Some Future Prospects*, ed. M. Weatheritt. Aldershot: Gower.

Chatterton, Michael 1991. 'Organizational Constraints on the Uses of Information Technology in Problem-Focused Area Policing.' Paper read at the British Criminology Conference, July. York, England.

Clarke, Ronald, and Michael Hough. 1984. *The Effectiveness of the Police.* Home Office Research Unit. London: HMSO.

Comrie, M., and E. Kings. 1975. 'Study of Urban Workloads: Final Report.' London: Home Office Police Research Services Unit.

Cumming, E., I. Cumming, and L. Edell. 1965. 'Policeman as Philosopher, Guide and Friend.' *Social Problems* 12: 276–86.

Draper, Hilary. 1978. *Private Police.* Harmondsworth: Penguin.

Ericson, Richard. 1982. *Reproducing Order: A Study of Police Patrol Work.* Toronto: University of Toronto Press.

Ericson, Richard. 1993. *Making Crime: A Study of Detective Work.* 2d ed. Toronto: University of Toronto Press.

Ericson, Richard. 1994a. 'The Division of Expert Knowledge in Policing and Security.' *British Journal of Sociology* 45: 149–75.

Ericson, Richard. 1994b. 'The Royal Commission on Criminal Justice System Surveillance.' In *Criminal Justice in Crisis*, ed. M. McConville and L. Bridges. Aldershot: Edward Elgar.

Ericson, Richard, and Kevin Haggerty. 1997. *Policing the Risk Society.* Toronto: University of Toronto Press; Oxford: Oxford University Press.

Ericson, Richard, and Clifford Shearing. 1986. 'The Scientification of Police Work.' In *The Knowledge Society The Growing Impact of Scientific Knowledge on Social Relations*, ed. G. Böhme and N. Stehr. Dordrecht: Reidel.

Ericson, Richard, Dean Barry, and Aaron Doyle. 2000. 'The Moral Hazards of Neo-Liberalism: Lessons from the Private Insurance Industry.' *Economy and Society* 29: 532–58.

Feeley, Malcolm, and Jonathan Simon. 1994. 'Actuarial Justice: The Emerging New Criminal Law.' In *The Futures of Criminology*, ed. D: Nelken. London: Sage.

Fishman, Mark, and Gray Cavendar, eds., 1998. *Entertaining Crime: Television Reality Programs.* New York: Aldine de Gruyter.

Garland, David 1996. 'The Limits of the Sovereign State: Strategies of Crime Control in Contemporary Society.' *British Journal of Criminology* 36: 445–71.

Garland, David. '"Governmentality" and the Problem of Crime: Foucault, Criminology, Sociology.' *Theoretical* Criminology 1: 173–214.

Geller, William, and Norval Morris. 1992. 'Relations between Federal and Local Police.' In *Modern Policing*, ed. M. Tonry and N. Morris. Chicago: University of Chicago Press.

Goldstein, Joseph. 1960. 'Police Discretion Not to Invoke the Criminal Process: Low Visibility Decisions in the Administration of Justice.' *Yale Law Journal* 69: 543–94.

Haggerty, Kevin, and Richard Ericson. 1999. 'The Militarization of Policing in the Information Age.' *Journal of Political and Military Sociology* 27: 233–45.

Haggerty, Kevin, and Richard Ericson. 2000. 'The Surveillant Assemblage.' *British Journal of Sociology* 51: 605–22.

Johnston, Les. 1992. *The Rebirth of Private Policing.* London: Routledge.

Johnston, Les. 1997. 'Policing Communities of Risk.' In *Policing Futures: The Police, Law Enforcement and the Twenty-First Century*, ed. P. Francis, P. Davies, and V. Jupp. Basingstoke: Macmillan.

Jorgensen, Birthe. 1981. 'Transferring Trouble: The Initiation of Reactive Policing.' *Canadian Journal of Criminology* 23: 257–78.

Latour, Bruno, 1987. *Science in Action.* Cambridge: Harvard University Press.

Loader, Ian. 1999. 'Consumer Culture and the Commodification of Policing and Security.' *Sociology* 33: 373–92.

Manning, Peter. 1980. *The Narc's Game: Organizational and Informational Limits on Drug Law Enforcement.* Cambridge: MIT Press.

Manning, Peter. 1988. *Symbolic Communication: Signifying Calls and the Police Response.* Cambridge: MIT Press.

Manning, Peter. 1992. 'Information Technology and the Police.' In *Modern Policing*, ed. M. Tonry and N. Morris. Chicago: University of Chicago Press.

McConville, Michael. 1993. 'An Error of Judgement.' *Legal Action* [September].

McConville, Michael, and Lee Bridges, eds. 1994. *Criminal Justice in Crisis.* Aldershot: Edward Elgar.

McMahon, Maeve. 1992. *The Persistent Prison? Rethinking Decarceration and Penal Reform*. Toronto: University of Toronto Press.

Meehan, Albert. 1993. 'Internal Police Records and the Control of Juveniles: Politics and Policing in a Suburban Town.' *British Journal of Criminology* 33: 504–24.

Moyniban, Daniel. 1993. 'Defining Deviance Down.' *The American Scholar* 62: 17–30.

O'Malley, Pat. 1991. 'Legal Networks and Domestic Security.' *Studies in Law, Politics and Society* 11: 171–90.

O'Malley, Pat. ed. 1998. *Crime and the Risk Society*. Aldershot: Dartmouth.

Poster, Mark. 1990. *The Mode of Information: Poststructuralism and Social Context*. Cambridge: Polity Press.

Poster, Mark. 1995. *The Second Media Age*. Cambridge: Polity Press.

Reiss, Albert. 1982. 'Forecasting the Role of the Police and the Role of the Police in Social Forecasting.' In *The Maintenance of Order in Society*, ed. R. Donelan. Ottawa: Supply and Services Canada.

Reiss, Albert.1987. 'The Legitimacy of Intrusion into Private Spaces.' In *Private Policing*, ed. C. Shearing and P. Stenning. Beverly Hills: Sage.

Rose, Nikolas. 1999. *Powers of Freedom*. Cambridge: Cambridge University Press.

Royal Canadian Mounted Police. 1991. *Annual Report on Canada's Missing Children*. Ottawa: Royal Canadian Mounted Police.

Royal Commission on Criminal Justice. 1993. *Report*. Cmnd. 2263. London: HMSO.

Shearing, Clifford. 1992. 'The Relationship between Public and Private Policing.' In *Modern Policing*, ed. M. Tonry and N. Morris. Chicago: University of Chicago Press.

Shearing, Clifford, and Philip Stenning. 1983. 'Private Security: Implications for Social Control.' *Social Problems* 30: 493–506.

Simon, Jonathan. 1997. 'Governing through Crime.' In *The Crime Conundrum: Essays on Criminal Justice*, ed. G. Fisher and L. Friedman. Boulder: Westview.

Skogan, Wesley. 1990. *The Police and the Public in England and Wales: A British Crime Survey Report*. Home Office Research Study No. 117. London: HMSO.

Slater, Donald. 1997. *Consumer Culture and Modernity*. Cambridge: Polity Press.

Southgate, P., and C. Mirless-Black. 1991. *Traffic Policing in Changing Times*. London: HMSO.

Squires, Gregory, ed. 1997. *Insurance Redlining: Disinvestment, Reinvestment, and the Evolving Role of Financial Institutions*. Washington, D.C.: Urban Institute Press.

Stinchcombe, Arthur. 1963. 'Institutions of Privacy in the Determination of Police Administrative Practice.' *American Journal of Sociology* 69:150–60.

Walsh, W. 1986. 'Patrol Officer Arrest Rates: A Study of the Social Organization of Police Work.' *Justice Quarterly* 2: 271–90.

# Deviance, ethics and control

## Introduction

As we noted earlier in the volume, considerable attention in the literature on policing has been paid to the negative and more problematic areas of police conduct. This section incorporates five chapters which look at police misconduct, how it is to be understood and, potentially, how police behaviour is controlled. The opening chapter by Jerome Skolnick and James Fyfe (**33**, 568) looks at the extraordinary case of Rodney King. Extraordinary, not because of the violence experienced by King at the hands of police officers, but extraordinary because it was all captured on video. Despite the extent of the violence meted out to King – he received 56 truncheon blows, was repeatedly kicked and hit twice by TASER guns – the incident was not as exceptional as one might suppose but 'simply the most visible in a lengthy series of police atrocities involving a police agency that had itself become aberrational'. A series of investigations ensued, and the four officers who beat King were charged with a series of felonies, but were later acquitted. President Bush said he found 'it hard to understand how the verdict could possibly square with the video'. Skolnick and Fyfe ask why the officers involved weren't sickened by the beating. Their answer, they say, is to be found in the culture of aggressive policing that had dominated the LAPD for the majority of its history since the Second World War: 'in this respect, police brutality is like police corruption – there may be some rotten apples, but usually the barrel itself is rotten.'

It might be thought that Clint Eastwood and the sociology of the police had little connection. In perhaps the most famous of all articles tackling the subject of police misconduct – and certainly my personal favourite – Carl Klockars (**34**, 581) demonstrates that this couldn't be further from the truth. Picking up on the dilemma faced by Inspector 'Dirty Harry' Callahan in the eponymous film, Klockars asks the question, 'when and to what extent does the morally good end warrant or justify an ethically, politically, or legally dangerous means for its achievement?' This, as he notes, is a genuine moral dilemma. In looking for solutions, he looks back to the works of the reform police administrators like August Vollmer and O.W. Wilson, to ask whether their vision of 'snappy bureaucrats' responding to rules and procedures offers a way out of the Dirty Harry dilemma. He then revisits the writings of Egon Bittner – on the core task of maintaining order – and Jerome Skolnick – on the craft of policing (both reproduced earlier in the volume; Chapters 12 and 17, respectively) to ask the same question. His answer is that dirty means are always dirty, however just the ends, and punishment of the officers that employ them is therefore necessary – albeit that it creates in its turn a Dirty Harry problem for us (the punishment of those attempting to 'do good'). This teaches us, Klockars argues, 'that the danger in Dirty Harry problems is never in their resolution, but in thinking that one has found a resolution with which one can truly live in peace'.

Picking up the theme of moral dilemmas and moral boundaries, John Kleinig (**34**, 581) explores the edges of corruption and, in particular, the problem of gratuities. Gratuities are different from bribes, he argues, as the latter are offered and accepted with the aim of corrupting authority. At most this is a contingent feature of the offer of gratuities – such an offer may be an entirely genuine token of appreciation. Where should the line be drawn? Was O.W. Wilson right to argue that 'a police officer should not be allowed to accept any gratuity, not even a free cup of coffee'? Kleinig surveys both the sociological literature on corruption and recent police history in this area, and argues in favour of a position that recognises that police officers can, or should be thought to be able to, distinguish between minor perks and bribes. Failure by police chiefs to take this into account may lead to loss of respect and loss of professionalism. It is likely to be more realistic and prudent, he argues, not to assume that a free cup of coffee is inevitably corrupting and that it is possible for an officer to accept such a gratuity. However, in turn, this does not make the acceptance of the cup of coffee right in every circumstance. The conclusion he leads us to, therefore, is that explicit consideration of ethics should be a fundamental aspect of all police training.

How should the broader police organization be held to account? What should the relationship be between local policing and local politics? In an article written in the 1970s, looking back on the issues that gave rise to the establishment of a Royal Commission on the Police in Britain more than a decade previously, the constitutional scholar Geoffrey Marshall identifies two styles of accountability (**36**, 624). These he calls 'subordinate and obedient' and 'explanatory and co-operative'. The former, akin to a relationship in which orders are issued and followed, has largely been replaced by the latter, based on the capacity to require information and explanations for actions and decisions. His conclusion to his review of the territory, that 'law-enforcement policy is made by the exercise of executive discretion but it requires a special style of accountability which our institutions have not as yet fully succeeded in providing', is as true now as it was in 1978.

From the relationship of policing to politics we move to the relationship between the police and law. David Dixon (**37**, 636) explores the meaning and application of the idea of the 'rule of law' to policing and argues forcefully that such a culturally constructed notion should draw our attention to the varying ways in which it may find expression in different jurisdictions. There are a number of core issues in the legal regulation of policing that we forget at our peril. One is that it is not that the activities of police officers should be legally authorized that is crucial, but what kind of rules, and 'what principles, contexts, and objectives inform their production'. A second concerns the limits of legal regulation, and Dixon outlines in some detail the ways in which traditional legalism tends to overstate the potential for constraining officers' discretion through legal regulation. Echoing Kleinig's work discussed earlier, Dixon argues that the 'police should be encouraged to accept responsibility for ensuring that their activities are legal and ethical'. In this model, legal rules are a necessary but not a sufficient condition for the regulation of policing. They are one of many tools of government, and the relationship between law and policing in practice depends on the nature of the law, the nature of policing and the sociopolitical context in which both are deployed.

# 33. The beating of Rodney King

*Jerome Skolnick and James Fyfe*

In many, but not all, Southern communities, Negroes complain indignantly about police brutality. It is part of the policeman's philosophy that Negro criminals or suspects, or any Negro who shows signs of insubordination, should be punished bodily, and that this is a device for keeping the 'Negro in his place' generally. (Gunnar Myrdal, *An American Dilemma*, 1941)

I'm glad you asked that question [about allegations of police brutality toward minorities], but before I get into it, I might point out that in a study I once made of the factors that militate against public understanding of the police service I said that two of the factors were the criticism of the police by certain minority groups in order to distract attention from the high incidence of criminal activity within those groups and the practice of the press in magnifying police failures and in minimizing their successes or accomplishments. (William H. Parker, Los Angeles Police Chief, interviewed by Donald McDonald, 1962)

It all started when George Holliday brought home a camcorder, a Sony CCD-F77, on Valentine's Day, 1991. The thirty-three-year-old, recently married former rugby player, general manager of a local office of Rescue Rooter, a national plumbing company, hadn't had time to load it until March 2, the day before one of his employees was scheduled to run in the Los Angeles marathon. After setting his alarm for 6 am so as to arrive in time for the race, Holliday went to bed early and was awakened at 12:50 am by a blast of siren noise and screeching rubber. The racket was coming from Foothill Boulevard, the main thoroughfare of a middle-class, ethnically mixed Los Angeles exurb with a population about 60 percent Latino, 10 percent black, and the rest Asian and white. When Holliday, who is white, pulled the window shade aside, he could scarcely believe what he saw. The powerful spotlight of a police helicopter was shining on a white Hyundai surrounded by a half-dozen police cars. His first thought was, 'Hey, let's get the camera!'[1]

The videotape Holliday shot showed a large black man down on hands and knees, struggling on the ground, twice impaled with wires from an electronic TASER gun, rising and falling while being repeatedly beaten, blow after blow after blow – dozens of blows, fifty-six in all, about the head, neck, back, kidneys, ankles, legs, feet – by two police officers wielding their 2-foot black metal truncheons like baseball bats. Also visible was a third officer, who was stomping King, and about ten police officers watching the beating along with a number of Holliday's neighbors.

Actually, twenty-three LAPD officers responded to the scene (an interesting number in light of the later claim that the Department is severely understaffed to respond to emergencies). Four officers were directly involved in the use of force; two hovered overhead in a helicopter; ten were on the ground and witnessed some portion of the beating; seven others checked out the scene and left. Four uniformed officers from two other law enforcement agencies – the Highway Patrol and the Los Angeles Unified School District – were also there.

Both Holliday and Paul King, Rodney's brother, tried to report the police abuse. Neither succeeded. When, on Monday morning, Paul King went to the Foothill station to report that his brother had been beaten, the officer at the front desk told him to wait. After waiting and growing impatient, Paul King returned to the desk. Finally, a sergeant came out of the back of the station and proceeded to give Paul King a bureaucratic hard time. The sergeant then left the room for about thirty minutes while Paul King, who had asked about procedures for making a complaint and had told the sergeant about the possibility of a videotape, waited impatiently.

When the sergeant returned, instead of addressing Paul's complaint, he asked whether Paul had ever been in trouble. He told Paul that an investigation was ongoing, and that Rodney was in 'big trouble', since he had been caught in a high-speed chase and had put someone's life in danger, possibly a police officer's. The sergeant told Paul King to try to find the video, but at no time did the sergeant fill out a personnel complaint form. Paul King testified to the Christopher Commission that when he left Foothill Station 'knew I hadn't made a complaint'.

Holliday was busy on Sunday, the day he videotaped the beating. As he had planned, he took his videocam to the LA marathon, then to a wedding. On Monday, March 4, he telephoned the Foothill station, intending to offer his videotape to the police. He told the desk officer that he had witnessed the beating of a motorist by LAPD officers and asked about the motorist's condition. The desk officer told him that 'we [the LAPD] do not release information like that'. He neither asked questions about what Holliday had seen nor recorded a personnel complaint form as a result of Holliday's call. The officer seemed so uninterested in Holliday's information that Holliday decided to try another tack and called Channel 5 (KTLA) in Los Angeles. The station made arrangements with Holliday to bring the tape in, and it was broadcast Monday evening. CNN gave it national and international exposure, playing it repeatedly until it was seen everywhere in the world, from Tokyo to London to Zaïre. The beating of Rodney King became the lead story for several days on the major networks as well, the most explicit and shocking news footage of police brutality ever to be seen on television.[2]

In the ninety-second tape, viewers saw with their own eyes how a group of Los Angeles police officers could act out their anger, frustration, fears, and prejudices on the body of a black man who had led them on a high-speed chase. Like films of the police dogs in Selma or the clubs and tear gas of the 1968 Chicago Democratic Convention, the dramatic videotape gave new credibility to allegations of a sort that many people – including police officers – formerly dismissed as unbelievable. The tape was instantly etched in the memory of every American police chief who watched it and who knew that he or she could scarcely disregard its implications.

Shortly after the King beating occurred, Los Angeles Police Chief Daryl Gates condemned it as an 'aberration'. Actually, the King incident was simply the most visible in a lengthy series of police atrocities involving a police agency that had itself become aberrational. Between 1987 and 1990, 4,400 misconduct complaints were filed against the LAPD. Of these, 41 percent were filed by blacks, who make up only 13 percent of the population. In 1989 Los Angeles paid out $9.1 million to settle lawsuits alleging police misconduct. In 1990 that figure had risen to $11.3 million for suits alleging excessive force, wrongful deaths, false arrests, negligence, misconduct, and civil rights violations. The Christopher Commission found that a significant number of LAPD officers 'repetitively use excessive force against the public and persistently ignore the written guidelines of the Department regarding force' and that 'the failure to control these officers is a management issue that is at the heart of the problem'.[3] What made the King beating different from those earlier events was not the conduct of the police, but the presence of George Holliday's video camera.

Most of those who lived in the south central sections of Los Angeles, in places like Watts, Inglewood, and Compton, knew this. Although the damage and the looting following the verdict could scarcely be justified by horrified viewers, many of whom were black, the origins of the riots could be traced to the history of tension and trouble between the police and black and Hispanic residents. ('For many', *New York Times* reporter Seth Mydans wrote, 'the riot was a simple message to the authorities and larger society. Treat us right. We've been pushed too close to the edge.' Ervin Mitchell, a design engineer interviewed by Mr. Mydans, explained: 'Young blacks and Hispanics have been persecuted, beaten and pulled out of cars because of stereotypes. We're tired of being treated like garbage. We're tired of living in a society that denies us the right to be considered as a human being.'[4]

No one felt this oppression more powerfully than Jessie Larez and his family. Their name may be unfamiliar to those who focused on the King verdict and its aftermath, but their experience perfectly illustrates why so many south central residents bore such hostility to the authorities.

In 1986 Los Angeles police obtained a warrant that authorized them to search the Larez home for a gun. The judge who issued the warrant had not included in it a 'no-knock' authorization that would have allowed the police to make an unannounced forcible entry. Instead, the Larez warrant required the police to knock and announce their presence and, presumably, prohibited them from forcing their way in unless they were denied admission or waited fruitlessly at the door for a response of any kind. According to a unanimous panel of the United States Court of Appeals for the Ninth Circuit, however, officers from the LAPD's appropriately named 'CRASH unit[5] conducted a "crisis entry" which involved breaking the back windows of the house to create a diversion ostensibly aimed at making a front entry safer'.[6] The police did this at 7:00 am on June 13, 1986, while Larez, his wife, and their seven children and grandchildren slept, some in beds and cribs directly beneath those windows. Once inside, according to the Court of Appeals' September 27, 1991 opinion, CRASH officers

… hurled Jessie across the room, grabbed him by the hair, forced him to lie down on the floor with his knee on Jessie's neck and handcuffed him. Police kicked him and smashed his face into the floor. The officers laughed and sneered: they told him they had him where they wanted him. At one point Officer Holcomb pointed his service revolver at Jessie's head and said to him, 'I could blow your fucking head off right here and nobody can prove you did not try to do something'. Officer Keller told Jessie, 'we finally got you, motherfucker'. Jessie sustained a broken nose during the incident. His knees required arthroscopic surgery, and neck surgery was recommended to alleviate the headaches which have persisted since the incident.

Police yelled to [Larez's daughter] Diane to 'get up here with that fucking baby'. Upon approaching, she was seized by her waist-long hair and arm and thrown face first to the floor where she, too, was handcuffed. Upon lifting her head to instruct a family member to take her baby away, Officer Keller grabbed Diane's hair and banged her head to the floor, demanding that she 'put [her] fucking face on the floor'.

[Larez's son] Katsumi, who was sleeping to his room attached to the garage at the time of the search, was awoken [*sic*] when his door was kicked in by police. An officer pointed his gun at Katsumi and shouted, 'I'll blow your fucking head off'. He was taken to the living room where he and his brother Frank, like Jessie and Diane, were also proned out on the floor and handcuffed. Katsumi was kicked in the head and side by Officer Holcomb.

The police left the Larez home 'turned upside down'. Pots, pans, and dishes had been taken from their cabinets and thrown to the floor, and various objects kept on the bar, as well as the VCR, had been thrown on the TV room floor. Katsumi's room looked as if a 'hurricane [had] whipped through it'. [Son] Albertdee saw beds turned over, clothing in heaps on the floor, broken crockery in the kitchen, and broken windows. His bedroom posters had been ripped from the walls, his punching bag had been cut open, and his plants had been dislodged from their pots. Jessie's prized Japanese albums, obtained while he was stationed in Japan [more than thirty years before], were broken by the [police]. Other broken items included a pitcher, a crockpot, a figurine, a dish, a vase, a music box, a lamp, a rice cooker, a coffee pot, wall paneling, a clock, a sliding glass door, picture frames, and a camera lens.

Despite the rigor of their search, the CRASH officers found no gun in the Larez home. No member of the family was charged with any offense related to the gun CRASH allegedly believed was in the house. Still, the police did not leave empty-handed: Jessie was arrested for battery on a police officer, a charge that was dismissed after trial. The police arrest report notes that Jessie, a fifty-five-year-old disabled veteran, was wearing 'no shs, blu pajamas', and that he 'received M.T. [medical treatment] at Jail Division for a small cut on the bridge of his nose and on the corner of his rt eyebrow, no stitches required'.[7] The report includes no mention of other injuries or damage. Jessie's son Eddie also was arrested on unspecified grounds for violating the terms of his parole. According to the Ninth Circuit:

> Jessie lodged a complaint with the LAPD. The department's Internal Affairs division assigned a CRASH detective not involved in the Larez search to investigate the complaint. In a letter signed by Chief Gates, Jessie ultimately was notified that none of the many allegations in his complaint could be sustained.

Outraged, Larez then filed suit against the six CRASH officers, the LAPD, and Chief Gates. When his case came to trial in 1988, one of us gave expert testimony on Larez's behalf. The LAPD investigation of Jessie Larez's complaint, Fyfe testified, was riddled with 'a lot of holes', as were two years' worth of citizens' complaint investigations reviewed in connection with an earlier civil rights suit against LAPD. In these LAPD cases, Fyfe said on the witness stand, whitewashes were so frequent that, regardless of the seriousness or nature of complainants' injuries, 'something has to be done on film for the department to buy the citizen's story'.

The King incident was, of course, electronically memorialized by the amateur cameraman George Holliday and precipitated a national investigation by the Department of Justice and by the U.S. Congress of complaints against police. Within the city of Los Angeles, at least three major investigations were initiated – an internal investigation by the Los Angeles Police Department, another by the Police Commission, and a third by an independent commission formed by the merger of two groups appointed by the mayor and the police chiefs. This last, headed by a Los Angeles attorney and former State Department official, Warren Christopher, wrote of the difference made by the taping of the King incident:

> Our Commission owes its existence to the George Holliday videotape of the Rodney King incident. Whether there even would have been a Los Angeles Police Department investigation without the video is doubtful, since the efforts of King's brother, Paul, to file a complaint were frustrated, and the report of the involved officers was falsified. Even if there had been an investigation, our case-by-case review of the handling of 700 complaints indicates that without the Holliday videotape the complaint might have been adjudged to be 'not sustained' because the officers' version conflicted with the account by King and his two passengers, who typically would have been viewed as not 'independent'.[8]

As information accumulated about the Rodney King episode, testimony about what happened became wildly contradictory. Both the Christopher Report and portions of a 314-page LAPD Internal Affairs report show wide differences of opinion about how King acted during the pursuit and after he stepped out of his car. The California Highway Patrol officers who first attempted to stop King for a traffic violation reported that King fled from them at '110 to 115 m.p.h'. The

Christopher Commission and others have suggested, however that such speeds are about 20 miles per hour faster than can be squeezed out of a Hyundai like King's.[9]

Some of the officers said that King, who suffered multiple injuries and bone fractures after repeated blows, displayed 'superhuman strength' and resisted arrest when he first got out of the car. Sergeant Koon said that King had not responded to a torrential number of blows, leading Koon to fear that he would have to shoot or choke King. That was when he instructed his officers: 'Hit his joints, hit his wrists, hit his elbows, hit his knees, hit his ankles,' and, Koon told investigators, 'that's what they did do, they did exactly as I told them to do and exactly as they're trained.' Several of the officers reported that they had undergone baton training that night before going out on patrol. One of them, rookie officer Timothy Wind, according to Officer Rick Distefano, 'demonstrated excellent technique and made contact in all the right places on the practice board'.

Yet at least two of the bystanding officers saw no need for the vicious beating. Officer Melanie Singer of the California Highway Patrol, for instance, said she believed King was trying to comply with the officer's commands when he was beaten. 'King did not aggressively kick or punch the officers,' she said. 'He was merely trying to get away from the officers.'[10] Similarly, Officer Ingrid Larson, who had been out of the Police Academy only five days, said that 'King did not appear to be combative, but merely used his arms to block the baton strikes'. Paramedics who arrived on the scene also testified that King appeared to be coherent and was not acting violently.

On May 12, 1991, a guest editorial in the *Los Angeles Times* called for the resignation of Chief Daryl Gates. Published more than two months after the incident, this was not the first op-ed piece to call on Gates to resign. What was surprising was the identity of its author, the same Sergeant Stacey C. Koon who had been in charge at the Rodney King beating. Indicted and suspended without pay, Koon said he wrote the commentary to protest Chief Daryl Gates's handling of the incident, in particular his firing of rookie officer Timothy Wind, one of the indicted four. The editorial suggests that the Chief let the officers down, that he felt 'justified to abuse the foundations of the organization to save the organization'. Koon's essay became national news. Patrick Thistle, an attorney for one of the indicted officers, was asked by *CBS Evening News* (May 12, 1991) to comment on Koon's call for Gates's dismissal. 'The LAPD has always stressed that they are a loving, caring family,' said Thistle. 'I think these officers believe that the family has treated them like they are not a member of the group.'

The cops on the scene were responding to a code they believed in and considered to be moral. The code decrees that cops protect other cops, no matter what, and that cops of higher rank back up working street cops – no matter what. From the perspective of the indicted cops, Daryl Gates betrayed the code. Sergeant Koon was, in effect, alleging that Chief Gates was changing the unwritten rules, and consequently undermining the tradition of the organization.

Police department traditions and the norms police live by are sustained by street incidents. When cops brutally beat prisoners and others who challenge their authority, they must have learned from their fellow officers that such conduct is acceptable and will be protected from the top down; when they do so in public, they must understand that their immunity is virtually ironclad.

Mike Rothmiller, a former LAPD detective, recently told the story of his life in the department to writer Ivan G. Goldman. He describes a department where racism and spying were accepted and often even encouraged. So was lying on police reports:

> Again and again Rothmiller watched cops decide for themselves who was guilty, and then weave a spell over the arrest report to make it match their perceptions. Most of the arrest reports he encountered were doctored in some way – facts deleted or invented. It wasn't exactly the frontier justice of a lynch mob, but it wasn't justice either. It was just the way things worked.[11]

Police chiefs know about these unwritten messages. Brutality is an occupational risk of a profession that rides with danger and is trained and authorized to use force, even deadly force. Chiefs know this, and they know they cannot absolutely control their officers' behavior. Yet the best chiefs avoid any signal that excessive force is excusable or that any group of people is a legitimate target.

When brutality is alleged, good chiefs investigate thoroughly and objectively. When brutality is found, examples are made of those who committed it, those who failed to stop it, and those who covered it up. When brutality remains undiscovered in a well-run police department, it is because a few officers have managed to keep the incident a deep, dark secret. But there is no secretiveness in the Rodney G. King videotape. Officers and citizens alike could and did watch the beating Officers – including a supervisor and, apparently, a watch commander – could joke about it in computer conversations they knew were being recorded. For these officers, the threat of review and censure by higher authority was nonexistent: after all, their comments memorialized their actions only on their department's electronic records, rather than on a citizen's videotape. In Los Angeles, the indictments and suspensions came as a shock to the involved officers. They expected the Chief to back them up, as he doubtless had done in the past. But the tape made that impossible, and they were grievously disappointed.

The four Los Angeles cops who beat King were indicted by a grand jury on serious felony charges, and appeared to face a bleak future of imprisonment until they were acquitted by a Simi Valley jury. Yet a total of twenty-seven law enforcement officers were at the scene that night, including twenty-three Los Angeles Police Department officers. Although all or most were disciplined by their departments, those who watched and did nothing to interfere with the beating were not charged by Los Angeles District Attorney Ira Reiner. 'However morally wrong their failure to intercede, in California law there is no criminal statute under which these officers can be indicted,' Reiner said at a press conference on May 10, 1991. 'No matter how reprehensible their action, or their inaction, no person can be charged with a crime unless they have violated a statute.' But the officers were not entirely free of criminal liability. Reiner went on to say that he has referred the case to the U.S. Attorney's office to look into possible violations of federal civil rights statutes. The federal action was not activated until the Simi Valley acquittal, when the President himself expressed astonishment at the verdict and ordered the Justice Department to 'proceed apace'.

Many activists had demanded that the onlookers be charged and were dissatisfied when they weren't. They expressed reactions ranging from concern to outrage. Ramona Ripston, director of the Southern California chapter of the American Civil Liberties Union, argued that Reiner's announcement was a message to Los Angeles area law enforcement personnel that it is acceptable for police simply to stand by when they see other cops abusing people. 'If citizens stand by and see a crime being committed, they are expected to report it,' she said. 'How can we expect less of our police officers?' John Mack, president of the Los Angeles Urban League, said he was deeply disappointed with Reiner's announced conclusion and commented, 'It's a sad day in the history of Los Angeles that some seventeen police officers are going to be able to get away with being accessories to a crime'.[12]

Daryl Gates and his Los Angeles Police Department had few defenders after the beating of Rodney King. One notable exception was Paul Walters, who succeeded Raymond Davis, a major innovator of community-oriented policing, as Chief of the nearby Santa Ana Police Department. In a March 11 guest editorial for the *Los Angeles Times*, Walters, who had been a protégé of Davis, wrote in an editorial that surprised Davis and others who had followed Walters's previous career:

> The task of leading the Los Angeles Police Department is formidable, but Chief Daryl Gates has been outstanding in the performance of his duties. The department, under Gates, has set for itself a high standard of excellence and is one of the few large police departments not tainted by major corruption. The chief has repeatedly sought to conduct his operations according to the letter of the law.[13]

## Police and force

Long before the riot probes and trials and the political conflicts within the city of Los Angeles are ended, police chiefs all over the country, however complacent they may have been about such abuses in the past, will have warned their rank and file that such conduct will not be tolerated. After the King beating, New York's Police Commissioner Lee P. Brown, then also President of the International Association of Chiefs of Police, in concert with a dozen other police chiefs, called on the federal government to develop a system for gathering information on the use of excessive police force. 'The problem of excessive force in American policing is real,' Commissioner Brown said. 'It is, in part, related to the nature of the difficult challenges faced by the police in our urban centers. Regardless of its cause, it cannot be condoned and must be actively countered by concerned professionals.'[14]

Clearly, more and deeper questions need to be raised about the nature of police violence, its centrality to the role of the police, and its prevalence.

Obviously, it is nothing new. Part of the paradox of policing is that police are supposed to use necessary force. As anybody who has ever called a cop knows, police intervention is grounded in a round-the-clock capacity to take decisive action in handling all kinds of emergencies and to employ force where it is needed.

One leading police scholar, Egon Bittner, has even proposed that it makes sense to think of the police 'as a mechanism for the distribution of non-negotiably coercive force employed in accordance with the dictates of an intuitive grasp of situational exigencies'.[15] The question remains, however, as to how much force is justified and in what situations. Certainly, force is sometimes appropriate – that's why cops carry batons and guns. Police should not be labeled 'brutal' simply because they employ forceful measures. Taken alone, a charge of brutality should not be regarded as evidence of guilt. After the Los Angeles riots, such a false charge was made by an ex-convict in Berkeley. The officer who was charged could prove that he was issuing a traffic violation ticket in another part of the city at the time the purported 'victim' claimed to have been beaten. Yet the charge set off a protest march by indignant citizens who believed the allegations without hearing all the evidence.

Still, well-founded allegations of brutality following police vehicle pursuits are all too familiar. Florida's terrible Liberty City riot in 1980 had its roots in a fatal police beating at the end of a police chase and subsequent cover-up attempt. Indeed, long before the King incident, one veteran Los Angeles officer told Fyfe that he had never seen a police chase that did not end with at least a black eye delivered to the subject of the chase. What is it about these events that seems to generate such police rage?

Both authors have had long experience with police. During our years in police cars, we have been at the cop's end of more than thirty high-speed chases. Younger cops, hotshot cops, aggressive cops, relish the exhilaration of these pursuits. People who haven't ridden in patrol cars for a full shift cannot appreciate how tedious policing can be even in the world's most crime-ridden cities. Patrol policing, like military combat and the lives of cowboys, consists mostly of periods of boredom, broken up by interludes of excitement and even of terror. For police, a chase is among the most exciting of all work experiences: the sudden start of a chase is a jolt not unlike that experienced by the dozing fisherman who finds suddenly that he has a big and dangerous fish on the other end of his line.

More than representing excitement, the high-speed chase dramatizes two crucial elements of the policing enterprise: capturing daring criminals and meeting challenges to police authority. Anyone who speeds on a highway or, even worse, on city streets imperils other drivers and pedestrians. Those who speed with the intention of eluding police are, by definition, audacious and dangerous. The escaping driver is often believed to be a felon and – on rare occasions – may turn out to be a person who either has a cache of drugs in his car or has committed a serious crime. When the driver has passengers, as Rodney King had, he is thought to be even more dangerous. Such a driver, when captured, is rarely treated with consideration. He may be pushed, shoved, verbally assaulted, and tightly cuffed.

By now, however, police have learned from both experience and scholarly studies that most motorists who flee from them are not, in fact, threatening offenders. Instead, like King, fleeing motorists typically are troubled young men with bad driving records whose ability to reason has been altered by drugs or alcohol. But regardless of how relatively minor the violations that lead to their flight, fleeing motorists commit a cardinal sin against the police: instead of submitting immediately, they challenge the police and attempt to escape their pursuer's authority. In so doing, in the eyes of police officers accustomed to motorists and other citizens who not only submit immediately to police authority but even check their speedometers in the mere presence of police cars, fleeing motorists become prime candidates for painful lessons at the ends of police nightsticks.

Still, taking all that into account, everyone who watched the LA cops beat and kick Rodney King knew (intuitively, one might say) that the force used was not justified even as a reflexive striking out, that it went far beyond this. As the classical sociologist Emile Durkheim taught, we live in a society of shared moral norms, and we are presumed to know their boundaries. Two officers are seen beating a downed suspect with their nightsticks, even though he has already been hit with an electronic stun gun, has been subdued, and is no longer dangerous. Another officer joins in to kick the fallen man.

Los Angeles Mayor Tom Bradley, a former police officer, said he found the beating 'shocking and outrageous'. Chief Daryl Gates reviewed the videotape and said that he was 'sickened' when he saw it. So did the President of the United States.

After the Simi Valley verdict of acquittal, in a prime-time speech to the nation on May 2, 1992, President Bush said, 'What you saw and I saw on the TV video [of the King beating] was revolting. I felt anger. I felt pain. I thought, "How can I explain this to my grandchildren?"'

'Viewed from the outside,' he continued, 'it is hard to understand how the verdict could possibly square with the video.' In a USA Today poll, 86 percent of white Americans and 100 percent of black Americans answered that the King verdict was 'wrong'. Decidedly few voices were raised praising the. conduct of the LA police in the King incident – in contrast to some of the responses to the flagrantly violent Chicago police conduct during the 1968 Democratic Convention, where the police conduct was said by some to have been provoked.

## 'The LAPD Mentality'

But if the brutality of Rodney King's beating was self-evident to everyone who watched it, why weren't the cops who beat and kicked him sickened? Were they as individuals beyond the pale of the moral understandings expressed by the Mayor, by the President, eventually by Chief Gates himself, and by virtually everyone else who saw the incident? Had they gone berserk? How about the cops who watched? Did they have defective personalities? Hardly. Two or three cops can go berserk. Maybe the cops who administered the beating were especially aggressive and insensitive. But when twenty-three others are watching and not interfering, the incident cannot be considered 'aberrant', as Chief Gates initially suggested.

The incident and its cover-up must be seen in light of the overall philosophy of aggressive policing that began to dominate the LAPD when William Parker became its chief more than forty years earlier. In testimony before the Christopher Commission, Assistant Chief David Dotson said that LAPD clung to a 1950s version of tough policing:

> We reward our people – our field people, the people that got us here to this [Commission] meeting – we reward them for what we call hardnosed, proactive police work. We want them to go out and identify criminal activity and stop it, either before it occurs, or certainly, after it occurs, we want to go out and determine who the criminals were who perpetrated this particular act and get them into jail.
>
> … We expect people to go out and aggressively identify people, and investigate them, and that puts these police officers in the middle between what we evaluate them on and what they are able to do legally.[16]

The dominance of this philosophy – in Chief Gates's terms, 'the LAPD mentality'[17] – suggests that King's beating could scarcely have been an isolated incident. More than twenty LAPD officers witnessed King's beating, which continued for nearly two minutes. Those who administered it assumed that their fellow officers would not report the misconduct and were prepared to lie on their behalf. In this respect, police brutality is like police corruption – there may be some rotten apples, but usually the barrel itself is rotten. Two cops can go berserk, but twenty cops embody a subculture of policing.

The written rule is clear: cops are to use no more force than is necessary to subdue a suspect. Where a departmental subculture condoning brutality prevails, the unwritten rule is: 'Teach them a lesson.' Santa Ana's former police chief, Raymond Davis, who, unlike his successor Paul Walters, was appalled by the King beating, told us that he had once visited the Ramparts Station of the Los Angeles Police Department and saw a sign on the wall that read: 'Burglars Beware! Make Sure Your I.D. is Valid So We Will Know Where to Notify Your Next of Kin.' Such expressions of cop humor, he said, send a transparent message about a police department's values, especially to rookie cops.

The King videotape confirms how these values play out on the street. More important than the beating was the passive witnessing by the other cops and the semi-jocular conversations on the police computer network. Sergeant Stacey C. Koon, who was the supervising officer on the scene of the King beating, reported by computer to the commander of his watch that 'U (patrol unit) just had a big time use of force … tased and beat the suspect of CHP pursuit, Big Time'. The response from the police station was, 'Oh well … I'm sure the lizard didn't deserve it … HAHA I'll let them know OK'.[18] All the officers involved – those who beat, those who watched, and those who talked afterward – had to be confident that their colleagues would remain silent or lie about what really happened and, further, that the Department would believe the officers and reject any citizen's description.

Four days after the incident, Daryl Gates held a press conference in a stuffy, overheated conference room jammed with seventeen television cameras and more than seventy members of the news media. It was here that he began his defense of his department and his record as chief by announcing that four other officers would face criminal charges, and that the others who watched and did nothing could face administrative punishment.

'I preach – I mean I really preach – to every single person who graduates from the Police Academy about the law and their need for a reverence for the law,' Gates said. 'What they should have done, if they really loved their brother officers [was to] have stepped in and grabbed them and hauled them back and said, "Knock it off!" That's what the sergeant should have done [and] that's what every officer there should have done.'[19]

The news conference was contentious. Many of those present indicated by their questions that they did not believe Gates. Over the years he had made a number of highly publicized remarks, famous among Los Angeles reporters, suggestive of racial insensitivity, if not bias. A few months after Gates became police chief in 1978, he had offended Latinos by saying that some Latino officers were not promoted because they were 'lazy'. About two years later he drew complaints from women after he described a local television anchor woman as an 'Aryan broad'. Many Jews were angered when, in 1982, the press obtained an in-house report suggesting that the Soviets were sending criminals disguised as Jewish immigrants to disrupt the 1984 Olympics. Gates again angered Latinos by referring to the killer of a policewoman as a 'drunken Salvadoran'.[20] Nine years earlier, in his most widely publicized intemperate remark, he had said that 'some blacks' may be more susceptible than 'normal people' to police officers' use of a potentially fatal chokehold (which has since been banned). For this remark, the Police Commission publicly reprimanded Gates, and *Esquire* magazine honored him with one of its 'Annual Dubious Achievement' Awards. In 1991 he won a second Dubious Achievement Award for appointing a panel to study reinstituting the chokehold in the wake of criticism about the use of batons and the TASER in the King incident. After the King beating, Gates declared that, 'in spite of the fact that he's on parole and a convicted robber, I'd be glad to apologize'.[21]

*From Jerome Skolnick and James Fyfe,* Above the Law *(New York: Free Press) 1993, pp 1–14.*

## Notes

1   Mike Sager, 'Damn! They Gonna Lynch Us,' *Gentlemen's Quarterly*, October 1991. Sager offers a vivid, detailed description of the events preceding, during, and following the beating of Rodney King.
2   Further details are contained in Warren Christopher *et al.*, *Report of the Independent Commission on the Los Angeles Police Department*, July 9, 1991 (Christopher Report), pp 9–12.
3   *Ibid.*, 'Foreword,' pp. iii–v.
4   Seth Mydans, 'Decades of Rage Created Crucible of Violence,' *New York Times*, May 3, 1992.
5   'CRASH' is an acronym for Community Resources Against Street Hoodlums.
6   *Larez, et al.* v. *City of Los Angeles*, Ninth Circuit Nos. 89-55541, 89-55801, p. 13603, September 27, 1991.

7    Compare this to the arrest report in the King incident: 'Def't. was MT'd for abrasions and contusions on his face, arms, legs and torso areas'; also to Sergeant Koon's official description of Rodney King's injuries: 'Several facial cuts due to contact with asphalt. Of a minor nature. A split inner lip. Suspect oblivious to pain.' Christopher Report, p. 9.

8    *Ibid.*, p, ii.

9    *Ibid.*, p. 4.

10   Officer Singer and her partner – who also is her husband – began the King pursuit when they saw King commit traffic violations. According to the Christopher Report, both she and her husband (who apparently did not confirm her interpretation of the beating) received written reprimands from the California Highway Patrol for 'failing to report the excessive use of force in sufficient detail.' *Ibid.*, p. 13.

11   Mike Rothmiller and Ivan G. Goldman, *L.A. Secret Police: Inside the LAPD Spy Network* (New York: Pocket Books, 1992), p. 33.

12   The quotes from Reiner, Ripston, and Mack are from the *Los Angeles Times*, May 11, 1991.

13   Paul M. Walters, 'A Formidable Task, Well Done,' *Los Angeles Times*, March 11, 1991.

14   *New York Times*, March 8, 1991.

15   Egon Bittner, *The Functions of the Police in Modern Society* (Rockville, MD: National Institute of Mental Health, 1970), p. 46.

16   Christopher Report, pp. 98–9.

17   Gates expounded on the 'LAPD mentality' in Daryl F. Gates, *Chief: My Life in the LAPD* (New York: Bantam Books, 1992), pp. 174–77.

18   Christopher Report, p. 14.

19   *Los Angeles Times*, March 8, 1991.

20   *Ibid.*

21   See, e.g., Michael Kramer, 'Gates: The Buck Doesn't Stop Here,' *Newsweek*, April 1, 1991, p. 25; Frederick Dannen, 'Gates's Hell,' *Vanity Fair*, August 1991, pp. 102–8, 168–73; 'Dubious Achievement Awards of 1981!,' *Esquire*, January 1982; and 'Dubious Achievement Awards of 1991!,' *Esquire*, January 1992.

# 34. The Dirty Harry problem

*Carl B. Klockars*

When and to what extent does the morally good end warrant or justify an ethically, politically, or legally dangerous means for its achievement? This is a very old question for philosophers. Although it has received extensive consideration in policelike occupations. and is at the dramatic core of police fiction and detective novels, I know of not a single contribution to the criminological or sociological literature on policing which raises it explicitly and examines its implications.[1] This is the case in spite of the fact that there is considerable evidence to suggest that it is not only an ineluctable part of police work, but a moral problem with which police themselves are quite familiar. There are, I believe, a number of good reasons why social scientists have avoided or neglected what I like to call the Dirty Harry problem in policing, not the least of which is that it is insoluble. However, a great deal can be learned about police work by examining some failed solutions, three of which I consider in the following pages. First, though, it is necessary to explain what a Dirty Harry problem is and what it is about it that makes it so problematic.

## The Dirty Harry problem

The Dirty Harry problem draws its name from the 1971 Warner Brothers film *Dirty Harry* and its chief protagonist, antihero Inspector Harry 'Dirty Harry' Callahan. The film features a number of events which dramatize the Dirty Harry problem in different ways, but the one which does so most explicitly and most completely places Harry in the following situation. A 14-year-old girl has been kidnapped and is being held captive by a psychopathic killer. The killer, 'Scorpio' who has already struck twice, demands $200,000 ransom to release the girl, who is buried with just enough oxygen to keep her alive for a few hours. Harry gets the job of delivering the ransom and, after enormous exertion, finally meets Scorpio. At their meeting Scorpio decides to renege on his bargain, let the girl die, and kill Harry. Harry manages to stab Scorpio in the leg before he does so, but not before Scorpio seriously wounds Harry's partner, an inexperienced, idealistic, slightly ethnic, former sociology major.

Scorpio escapes, but Harry manages to track him down through the clinic where he was treated for his wounded leg. After learning that Scorpio lives on the grounds of a nearby football stadium, Harry breaks into his apartment, finds guns and other evidence of his guilt, and finally confronts Scorpio on the 50-yard line, where Harry shoots him in the leg as he is trying to escape. Standing over Scorpio, Harry demands to know where the girl is buried. Scorpio refuses to disclose her location, demanding his rights to a lawyer. As the camera draws back from the scene Harry stands on Scorpio's bullet-mangled leg to torture a confession of the girl's location from him.

As it turns out, the girl is already dead and Scorpio must be set free. Neither the gun found in the illegal search, nor the confession Harry extorted, nor any of its fruits – including the girl's body – would be admissible in court.

The preceding scene, the heart of Dirty Harry, raises a number of issues of far-reaching significance for the sociology of the police, the first of which will now be discussed.

## The Dirty Harry problem I: the end of innocence

As we have phrased it previously, the Dirty Harry problem asks when and to what extent does the morally good end warrant or justify an ethically, politically, or legally dangerous means to its achievement? In itself, this question assumes the possibility of a genuine moral dilemma and posits its existence in a means–ends arrangement which may be expressed schematically as [in Figure 34.1].

It is important to specify clearly the terms of the Dirty Harry problem not only to show that it must involve the juxtaposition of good ends and dirty means, but also to show what must be proven to demonstrate that a Dirty Harry problem exists. If one could show, for example, that box B is always empirically empty or

**MEANS**

|  | | Morally good (+) | Morally dirty (–) |
|---|---|---|---|
| **ENDS** | Morally good (+) | A<br>+ + | B<br>– +<br>The Dirty Harry Problem |
| | Morally dirty (–) | C<br>+ – | D<br>– – |

**[Figure 34.1]**

that in any given case the terms of the situation are better read in some other means–ends arrangement, Dirty Harry problems vanish. At this first level, however, I suspect that no one could exclude the core scene of *Dirty Harry* from the class of Dirty Harry problems. There is no question that saving the life of an innocent victim of kidnapping is a 'good' thing nor that grinding the bullet-mangled leg of Scorpio to extort a confession from him is 'dirty'.[2]

There is, in addition, a second level of criteria of an empirical and epistemological nature that must be met before a Dirty Harry problem actually comes into being. They involve the connection between the dirty act and the good end. Principally, what must be known and, importantly, known before the dirty act is committed, is that it will result in the achievement of the good end. In any absolute sense this is, of course, impossible to know, in that no acts are ever completely certain in their consequences. Thus the question is always a matter of probabilities. But it is helpful to break those probabilities into classes which attach to various subcategories of the overall question. In the given case, this level of problem would seem to require that three questions be satisfied, though not all with the same level of certainty.

In *Dirty Harry*, the first question is, Is Scorpio able to provide the information Dirty Harry seeks? It is an epistemological question about which, in *Dirty Harry*, we are absolutely certain. Harry met Scorpio at the time of the ransom exchange. Not only did he admit the kidnapping at that time, but when he made the ransom demand, Scorpio sent one of the, girl's teeth and a description of her clothing and underwear to leave no doubt about the existence of his victim.

Second, we must know there are means, dirty means and nothing other than dirty means, which are likely to achieve the good end. One can, of course, never be sure that one is aware of or has considered all possible alternatives, but in *Dirty Harry* there would appear to be no reason for Scorpio in his rational self-interest to confess to the girl's location without being coerced to do so.

The third question which must be satisfied at this empirical and epistemological level concedes that dirty means are the only method which will be effective, but asks whether or not, in the end, they will be in vain. We know in *Dirty Harry* that they were, and Harry himself, at the time of the ransom demand, admits he believes that the girl is already dead. Does not this possibility or likelihood that the girl is dead destroy the justification for Harry's dirty act? Although it surely would if Harry knew for certain that the girl was dead, I do not think it does insofar as even a small probability of her being saved exists. The reason is that the good to be achieved is so unquestionably good and so passionately felt that even a small possibility of its achievement demands that it be tried. For example, were we to ask, If it were your daughter would you want Harry to do what he did? It would be this passionate sense of unquestionable good that we are trying to dramatize. It is for this reason that in philosophical circles the Dirty Hands problem has been largely restricted to questions of national security, revolutionary terrorism, and international war. It is also why the Dirty Harry problem in detective fiction almost always involves murder.

Once we have satisfied ourselves that a Dirty Harry problem is conceptually possible and that, in fact, we can specify one set of concrete circumstances in which it exists, one might think that the most difficult question of all is, What ought to be done? I do not think it is. I suspect that there are very few people who would not want Harry to do something dirty in the situation specified. I know I would want him to do what he did, and what is more, I would want anyone who policed for me to be prepared to do so as well. Put differently, I want to have as police officers men and women of moral courage and sensitivity.

But to those who would want exactly that, the Dirty Harry problem poses its most irksome conclusion. Namely, that one cannot, at least in the specific case at hand, have a policeman who is both just and innocent. The troublesome issue in the Dirty Harry problem is not whether under some utilitarian calculus a right choice can be made, but that the choice must always be between at least two wrongs. And in choosing to do either wrong, the policeman inevitably taints or tarnishes himself.

It was this conclusion on the part of Dashiell Hammett, Raymond Chandler, Raoul Whitfield, Horace McCoy, James M. Cain, Lester Dent, and dozens of other tough-guy writers of hard-boiled detective stories that distinguished these writers from what has come to be called the 'classical school' of detective fiction. What these men could not stomach about Sherlock Holmes (Conan Doyle), Inspector French (Freeman Wills Crofts), and Father Brown (Chesterton), to name a few of the best, was not that they were virtuous, but that their virtue was unsullied. Their objection was that the classical detective's occupation, how he worked, and the jobs he was called upon to do left him morally immaculate. Even the most brilliant defender of the classical detective story, W.H. Auden, was forced to confess that that conclusion gave the stories 'magical function', but rendered them impossible as art.[3]

If popular conceptions of police work have relevance for its actual practice – as Egon Bittner and a host of others have argued that they do[4] – the Dirty Harry problem, found in one version or another in countless detective novels and reflected in paler imitations on countless television screens, for example, 'Parental Discretion is Advised', is not an unimportant contributor to police work's 'tainted' quality. But we must remember also that the revolution of the tough-guy writers, so these writers said, was not predicated on some mere artificial, aesthetic objection. With few exceptions, their claim was that their works were art. That is, at all meaningful levels, the stories were true. It is this claim I should next like to examine in the real-life context of the Dirty Harry problem.

## The Dirty Harry Problem II: dirty men and dirty work

Dirty Harry problems arise quite often. For policemen, real everyday policemen, Dirty Harry problems are part of their job and thus considerably more than rare or artificial dramatic exceptions. To make this point, I will translate some rather familiar police practices, street stops and searches and victim and witness interrogation, into Dirty Harry problems.

### Good ends and dirty means

The first question our analysis of street cops and searches and victim and witness interrogation must satisfy is, for policemen, do these activities present the cognitive opportunity for the juxtaposition of good ends and dirty means to their achievement? Although the 'goodness' question will be considered in some detail later, suffice it to say here that police find the prevention of crime and the punishment of wrongful or criminal behavior a good thing to achieve. Likewise, they, perhaps more than any other group in society, are intimately aware of the varieties of dirty means available for the achievement of those good ends. In the case of street stops and searches, these dirty alternatives range from falsifying probable cause for a stop, to manufacturing a false arrest to legitimate an illegal search, to simply searching without the fraudulent covering devices of either. In the case of victim or witness interrogations, dirty means range from dramaturgically 'chilling' a *Miranda* warning by an edited or unemphatic reading to Harry's grinding a man's bullet-shattered leg to extort a confession from him.

While all these practices may be 'dirty' enough to satisfy certain people of especially refined sensitivities does not a special case have to be made, not for the public's perception of the 'dirtiness' of certain illegal, deceptive, or *sub-rosa* acts, but for the police's perception of their dirtiness? Are not the police hard-boiled, less sensitive to such things than are most of us? I think there is no question that they are, and our contention about the prevalence of Dirty Harry problems in policing suggests that they are likely to be. How does this 'tough-minded' attitude toward dirty means affect our argument? At least at this stage it seems to strengthen it. That is, the failure of police to regard dirty means with the same hesitation that most citizens do seems to suggest that they juxtapose them to the achievement of good ends more quickly and more readily than most of us.

### The dirty means must work

In phrasing the second standard for the Dirty Harry problem as 'The dirty means must work', we gloss over a whole range of qualifying conditions some of which we have already considered. The most critical, implied in *Dirty Harry*, is that the person on whom dirty means are to be used must be guilty. It should be pointed out, however, that this standard is far higher than any student of the Dirty Hands problem in politics has ever been willing to admit. In fact, the moral dilemma of Dirty Hands is often dramatized by the fact that dirty means must be visited on quite innocent victims. It is the blood of such innocents, for example, whom the Communist leader Hoerderer in Sartre's *Dirty Hands* refers to when he says, 'I have dirty hands. Right up to the elbows. I've plunged them in filth and blood. But what do you hope? Do you think you can govern innocently?'[5]

But even if cases in which innocent victims suffer dirty means commonly qualify as Dirty Harry problems, and by extension innocent victims would be allowable in Dirty Harry problems, there are a number of factors in the nature and context of policing which suggest that police themselves are inclined toward the higher 'guilty victim' standard. Although there may be others, the following are probably the most salient.

1   *The Operative Assumption of Guilt.* In street stops and searches as well as interrogations, it is in the nature of the police task that guilt is assumed as a

working premise. That is, in order for a policeman to do his job, he must, unless he clearly knows otherwise, assume that the person he sees is guilty and the behavior he is witnessing is evidence of some concealed or hidden offense. If a driver looks at him 'too long' or not at all or if a witness or suspect talks too little or too much, it is only his operative assumption of guilt that makes those actions meaningful. Moreover, the policeman is often not in a position to suspend his working assumption until he has taken action, sometimes dirty action, to disconfirm it.

2   *The Worst of all Possible Guilt.* The matter of the operative assumption of guilt is complicated further because the policeman is obliged to make a still higher-order assumption of guilt, namely, that the person is not only guilty, but dangerously so. In the case of street stops and searches, for instance, although the probability of coming upon a dangerous felon is extremely low, policemen quite reasonably take the possibility of doing so as a working assumption on the understandable premise that once is enough. Likewise the premise that the one who has the most to hide will try hardest to hide it is a reasonable assumption for interrogation.

3   *The Great Guilty Place Assumption.* The frequency with which policemen confront the worst of people, places, and occasions creates an epistemological problem of serious psychological proportions. As a consequence of his job, the policeman is constantly exposed to highly selective samples of his environment. That he comes to read a clump of bushes as a place to hide, a roadside rest as a homosexual 'tearoom', a sweet old lady as a robbery looking for a place to happen, or a poor young black as someone willing to oblige her is not a question of a perverse, pessimistic, or racist personality, but of a person whose job requires that he strive to see race, age, sex, and even nature in an ecology of guilt, which can include him if he fails to see it so.[6]

4   *The Not Guilty (This Time) Assumption.* With considerable sociological research and conventional wisdom to support him, the policeman knows that most people in the great guilty place in which he works have committed numerous crimes for which they have never been caught. Thus when a stop proves unwarranted, a search comes up 'dry', or an interrogation fails, despite the dirty means, the policeman is not at all obliged to conclude that the person victimized by them is innocent, only that, and even this need not always be conceded, he is innocent this time.

### Dirty means as ends in themselves

How do these features of police work, all of which seem to incline police to accept a standard of a guilty victim for their dirty means, bear upon the Dirty Harry problem from which they derive? The most dangerous reading suggests that if police are inclined, and often quite rightly inclined, to believe they are dealing with factually, if not legally, guilty subjects, they become likely to see their dirty acts, not as means to the achievement of good ends, but as ends in themselves – punishment of guilty people whom the police believe deserve to be punished.

If this line of argument is true, it has the effect, in terms of police perceptions of moving Dirty Harry problems completely outside of the fourfold table of means–ends combinations created in order to define it. Importantly as well, in terms of our perceptions, Dirty Harry problems of this type can no longer be read as cases of dirty means employed to the achievement of good ends. For unless we are willing to admit in a democratic society a police which arrogates to itself the task of punishing those who they think are guilty, we are forced to conclude that Dirty Harry problems represent cases of employing dirty means to dirty ends, in which case, nobody, not the police and certainly not us, is left with any kind of moral dilemma.

The possibility is quite real and quite fearsome, but it is mediated by certain features of police work, some of which inhere in the nature of the work itself and others, imposed from outside, which have a quite explicit impact on it. The most important of the 'naturalistic' features of policing which belie the preceding argument is that the assumption of guilt and all the configurations in the policeman's world which serve to support it often turn out wrong. It is precisely because the operative assumption of guilt can be forced on everything and everyone that the policeman who must use it constantly comes to find it leads him astray more often than it confirms his suspicions.

Similarly, a great many of the things policemen do, some of which we have already conceded appear to police as less dirty than they appear *to us* – faked probable cause for a street stop, manipulated *Miranda* warnings, and so forth – are simply impossible to read as punishments. This is so particularly if we grant a hard-boiled character to our cops.

Of course, neither of these naturalistic restrictions on the obliteration of the means–ends schema is or should be terribly comforting. To the extent that the first is helpful at all assumes a certain skill and capacity of mind that we may not wish to award to all policemen. The willingness to engage in the constant refutation of one's working worldview presumes a certain intellectual integrity which can certainly go awry. Likewise, the second merely admits that on occasion policemen do some things which reveal they appreciate that the state's capacity to punish is sometimes greater than theirs.

To both these 'natural' restrictions on the obliteration of the means–ends character of Dirty Harry problems, we can add the exclusionary rule. Although the exclusionary rule is the manifest target of *Dirty Harry*, it, more than anything else, makes Dirty Harry problems a reality in everyday policing. It is the great virtue of exclusionary rules – applying in various forms to stops, searches, seizures, and interrogations – that they hit directly upon the intolerable, though often, I think, moral desire of police to punish. These rules make the very simple point to police that the more they wish to see a felon punished, the more they are advised to be scrupulous in their treatment of him. Put differently, the best thing Harry could have done *for* Scorpio was to step on his leg, extort his confession, and break into his apartment.

If certain natural features of policing and particularly exclusionary rules combine to maintain the possibility of Dirty Harry problems in a context in which a real danger appears to be their disappearance, it does not follow that police cannot or do not collapse the dirty means–good ends division on some occasions and become punishers. I only hold that on many other occasions, collapse does not occur and Dirty Harry problems, as defined, are still widely possible. What must be remembered next, on the way to making their possibility real, is that policemen know, or think they know, before they employ a dirty means that a dirty means and only a dirty means will work.

### Only a dirty means will work

The moral standard that a policeman knows in advance of resorting to a dirty means that a dirty means and only a dirty means will work, rests heavily on two technical dimensions: (1) the professional competence of the policeman and (2) the range of legitimate working options available to him. Both are intimately connected, though the distinction to be preserved between them is that the first is a matter of the policeman's individual competence and the second of the competence of the institutions for which (his department) and with which (the law) the policeman works

In any concrete case, the relations between these moral and technical dimensions of the Dirty Harry problem are extremely complicated. But *a priori* it follows that the more competent a policeman is at the use of legal means, the less he will be obliged to resort to dirty alternatives. Likewise, the department that trains its policemen well and supplies them with the resources – knowledge and material – to do their work will find that the policemen who work for them will not resort to dirty means 'unnecessarily', meaning only those occasions when an acceptable means will work as well as a dirty one.

While these two premises flow *a priori* from raising the Dirty Harry problem, questions involving the moral and technical roles of laws governing police means invite a very dangerous type of *a priori* reasoning:

> Combating distrust [of the police] requires getting across the rather complicated message that granting the police specific forms of new authority may be the most effective means for reducing abuse of authority which is now theirs; that it is the absence of properly proscribed forms of authority that often impels the police to engage in questionable or outright illegal conduct. Before state legislatures enacted statutes giving limited authority to the police to stop and question persons suspected of criminal involvement, police nevertheless stopped and questioned people. It is inconceivable how any police agency could be expected to operate without doing so. But since the basis for their actions was unclear, the police – if they thought a challenge likely – would use the guise of arresting the individual on a minor charge (often without clear evidence) to provide a semblance of legality. Enactment of stopping and questioning statutes eliminated the need for this sham.[7]

Herman Goldstein's preceding argument and observations are undoubtedly true, but the danger in them is that they can be extended to apply to any dirty means, not only illegal arrests to legitimate necessary street stops, but dirty means to accomplish subsequent searches and seizures all the way to beating confessions out of suspects when no other means will work. But, of course, Goldstein does not intend his argument to be extended in these ways.

Nevertheless, his *a priori* argument, dangerous though it may be, points to the fact that Dirty Harry problems can arise wherever restrictions are placed on police methods and are particularly likely to do so when police themselves perceive that those restrictions are undesirable, unreasonable, or unfair. His argument succeeds in doing what police who face Dirty Harry problems constantly do: rendering the law problematic. But while Goldstein, one of the most distinguished legal scholars in America, can follow his finding with books, articles, and lectures which urge change, it is left to the policeman to take upon himself the moral responsibility of subverting it with dirty and hidden means.

### Compelling and unquestionable ends

If Dirty Harry problems can be shown to exist in their technical dimensions – as genuine means–ends problems where only dirty means will work – the question of the magnitude and urgency of the ends that the dirty means may be employed to achieve must still be confronted. Specifically, it must be shown that the ends of dirty means are so desirable that the failure to achieve them would cast the person who is in a position to do so in moral disrepute.

The two most widely acknowledged ends of policing are peace keeping and law enforcement. It would follow, of course, that if both these ends were held to be unworthy, Dirty Harry problems would disappear. There are arguments challenging both ends. For instance, certain radical critiques of policing attempt to reduce the peace-keeping and law-enforcing functions of the police in the United States to nothing more than acts of capitalist oppression. From such a position flows not only the denial of the legitimacy of any talk of Dirty Harry problems, but also the denial of the legitimacy of the entire police function.[8]

Regardless of the merits of such critiques, it will suffice for the purpose of this analysis to maintain that there is a large 'clientele', to use Albert Reiss's term, for both types of police function.[9] And it should come as no surprise to anyone that the police themselves accept the legitimacy of their own peace-keeping and law-enforcing ends. Some comment is needed, though on how large that clientele for those functions is and how compelling and unquestionable the ends of peace keeping and law enforcement are for them.

There is no more popular, compelling, urgent nor more broadly appealing idea than peace. In international relations, it is potent enough to legitimate the stockpiling of enough nuclear weapons to exterminate every living thing on earth a dozen times over. In domestic affairs, it gives legitimacy to the idea of the state, and the aspirations to it have succeeded in granting to the state an absolute monopoly on the right to legitimate the use of force and a near monopoly on its actual, legitimate use: the police. That peace has managed to legitimate these highly dangerous means to its achievement in virtually every advanced nation in the world is adequate testimony to the fact that it qualifies, if any end does, as a good end so unquestionable and so compelling that it can legitimate risking the most dangerous and dirtiest of means.

The fact is, though, that most American policemen prefer to define their work as law enforcement rather than peace keeping, even though they may, in fact, do more of the latter. It is a distinction that should not be allowed to slip away in assuming, for instance, that the policeman's purpose in enforcing the law is to keep the peace. Likewise, though it is a possibility, it will not do to assume that police simply enforce the law as an end in itself, without meaning and without purpose or end. The widely discretionary behavior of working policemen and the enormous underenforcement of the law which characterizes most police agencies simply belie that possibility.

An interpretation of law enforcement which is compatible with empirical studies of police behavior – as peace keeping is – and police talk in America – which peace keeping generally is not – is an understanding of the ends of law enforcement as punishment. There are, of course, many theories of punishment, but the police seem inclined toward the simplest: the belief that certain people who have committed certain acts deserve to be punished for them. What can one say of the compelling and unquestionable character of this retributive ambition as an end of policing and policemen?

Both historically and sociologically there is ample evidence that punishment is almost as unquestionable and compelling an end as peace. Historically, we have a long and painful history of punishment, a history longer in fact than the history of the end of peace. Sociologically, the application of what may well be the only culturally universal norm, the norm of reciprocity, implies the direct and natural relations between wrongful acts and their punishments.[10] Possibly the best evidence for the strength and urgency of the desire to push in modern society is the extraordinary complex of rules and procedures democratic states have assembled which prevents legitimate punishment from being administered wrongfully or frivolously.

If we can conclude that peace and punishment are ends unquestionable and compelling enough to satisfy the demands of Dirty Harry problems, we are led to one final question on which we may draw from some sociological theories of the police for assistance. If the Dirty Harry problem is at the core of the police role, or at least near to it, how is it that police can or do come to reconcile their use of – or their failure to use – dirty means to achieve unquestionably good and compelling ends?

### Public policy and police morality: Three defective resolutions of the Dirty Harry problem

The contemporary literature on policing appears to contain three quite different types of solution or resolution. But because the Dirty Harry problem is a genuine moral dilemma, that is, a situation which will admit no real solution or resolution, each is necessarily defective. Also, understandably, each solution or resolution presents itself as an answer to a somewhat different problem. In matters of public policy, such concealments are often necessary and probably wise, although they have a way of coming around to haunt their architects sooner or later. In discovering that each is flawed and in disclosing the concealments which allow the appearance of resolution, we do not urge that it be held against sociologists that they are not philosophers nor do we argue that they should succeed where philosophers before them have failed. Rather, we only wish to make clear what is risked by each concealment and to face candidly the inevitably unfortunate ramifications which must proceed from it.

### Snappy bureaucrats

In the works of August Vollmer, Bruce Smith, O.W. Wilson, and those progressive police administrators who still follow their lead, a vision of the perfect police agency and the perfect policeman has gained considerable ground. Labeled 'the professional model' in police circles – though entirely different from any classical sense of profession or professional – it envisions a highly trained, technologically sophisticated police department operating free from political interference with a corps of well-educated police responding obediently to the policies, orders, and directives of a central administrative command. It is a vision of police officers, to use Bittner's phrasing, as 'snappy bureaucrats',[11] cogs in a quasi-military machine who do what they are told out of a mix of fear, loyalty, routine, and detailed specification of duties.

The professional model, unlike other solutions to be considered, is based on the assumption that the policeman's motives for working can be made to locate within his department. He will, if told, work vice or traffic, juvenile or homicide, patrol passively or aggressively, and produce one, two, four, or six arrests, pedestrian stops, or reports per hour, day, or week as his department sees fit. In this way the assumption and vision of the professional model in policing is little different from that of any bureaucracy which seeks by specifying tasks and setting expectations for levels of production – work quotas – to coordinate a regular, predictable, and efficient service for its clientele.

The problem with this vision of *sine ira et studio* service by obedient operatives is that when the product to be delivered is some form of human service – education, welfare, health, and police bureaucracies are similar in this way – the vision seems always to fall short of expectations. On the one hand the would-be bureaucratic operatives – teachers, social workers, nurses, and policemen – resent being treated as mere bureaucrats, and resist the translation of their work into quotas, directives, rules, regulations, or other abstract specifications. On the other hand, to the extent that the vision of an efficient and obedient human service bureaucracy is realized, the clientele of such institutions typically come away with the impression that no one in the institution truly *cares* about their problems. And, of course, in that the aim of bureaucratization is to locate employees' motives for work within the bureaucracy, they are absolutely correct in their feelings.

To the extent that the professional model succeeds in making the ends of policing locate within the agency as opposed to moral demands of the tasks which policemen are asked by their clients to do, it appears to solve the Dirty Harry problem. When it succeeds, it does so by replacing the morally compelling ends of punishment and peace with the less human, though by no means uncompelling, ends of bureaucratic performance. However, this resolution certainly does not imply that dirty means will disappear, only that the motives for their use will be career advancement and promotion. Likewise, on those occasions when a morally sensitive policeman would be compelled by the demands of the situational exigencies before him to use a dirty means, the bureaucratic operative envisioned by the professional model will merely do his job. Ambitious bureaucrats and obedient timeservers fail at being the type of morally sensitive souls we want to be policemen. The professional model's bureaucratic resolution of the Dirty Harry problem fails in policing for the same reason it fails in every other human service agency: it is quite simply an impossibility to create a bureaucrat who cares for anything but his bureaucracy.

The idealized image of the professional model, which has been responded to with an ideal critique, is probably unrealizable. Reality intervenes as the ideal type is approached. The bureaucracy seems to take on weight as it approaches the pole, is slowed, and may even collapse in approaching.

### Bittner's peace

A second effort in the literature of contemporary policing also attempts to address the Dirty Harry problem by substituting an alternative to the presently prevailing police ends of punishment. Where the professional model sought to substitute bureaucratic rewards and sanctions for the moral end of punishment, the elegant polemics by Egon Bittner in *The Functions of Police in Modern Society* and 'Florence Nightingale in Pursuit of Willie Sutton: A Theory of the Police' seek to substitute the end of peace. In beautifully chosen words, examples, and phrasing, Bittner leads his readers to conclude that peace is historically, empirically, intellectually, and morally the most compelling, unquestionable, and humane end of policing. Bittner is, I fear, absolutely right.

It is the end of peace which legitimates the extension of police responsibilities into a wide variety of civil matters – neighborhood disputes, loud parties, corner lounging, lovers' quarrels, political rallies, disobedient children, bicycle registration, pet control, and a hundred other types of tasks which a modern 'service' style police department regularly is called upon to perform. With these responsibilities, which most 'good' police agencies now accept willingly and officially, also comes the need for an extension of police powers. Arrest is, after all, too crude a tool to be used in all the various situations in which our peace-keeping policemen are routinely asked to be of help. 'Why should,' asks Herman Goldstein, in a manner in which Bittner would approve, 'a police officer arrest and charge a disorderly tavern patron if ordering him to leave the tavern will suffice? Must he arrest and charge one of the parties in a lovers' quarrel if assistance in forcing a separation is all that is desired?'[12] There is no question that both those situations could be handled more peacefully if police were granted new powers which would allow them to handle those situations in the way Goldstein rhetorically asks if they should. That such extensions of police powers will be asked for by our most enlightened police departments in the interests of keeping the peace is absolutely certain. If the success of the decriminalization of police arrests for public intoxication, vagrancy, mental illness, and the virtually unrestricted two-hour right of detention made possible by the Uniform Law of Arrest are any indication of the likelihood of extensions being received favorably, the end of peace and its superiority over punishment in legitimating the extension of police powers seem exceedingly likely to prevail further.

The problem with peace is that it is not the only end of policing so compelling, unquestionable, and in the end, humane. Amid the good work toward the end of peace that we increasingly want our police to do, it is certain that individuals or groups will arise who the police, in all their peace-keeping benevolence, will conclude, on moral if not political or institutional grounds, have 'got it coming'. And all the once dirty means which were bleached in the brilliant light of peace will return to their true colors.

### Skolnick's craftsman

The third and final attempt to resolve the Dirty Harry problem is offered by Jerome Skolnick, who in *Justice without Trial* comes extremely close to stating the Dirty Harry problem openly when he writes:

> ... He (the policeman) sees himself as a craftsman, at his best, a master of his trade ... [he] draws a moral distinction between criminal law and criminal procedure. The distinction is drawn somewhat as follows: The substantive law of crimes is intended to control the behavior of people who wilfully injure persons or property, or who engage in behaviors having such a consequence, such as the use of narcotics. Criminal procedure, by contrast, is intended to control authorities, not criminals. As such, it does not fall into the same *moral* class of constraint as substantive criminal law. If a policeman were himself to use narcotics, or to steal, or to assault, *outside the line of duty*, much the same standards would be applied to him by other policemen as to the ordinary citizen. When, however, the issue concerns the policeman's freedom to carry out his *duties*, another moral realm is entered.[13]

What is more, Skolnick's craftsman finds support from his peers, department, his community, and the law for the moral rightness of his calling. He cares about his work and finds it just.

What troubles Skolnick about his craftsman is his craft. The craftsman refuses to see, as Skolnick thinks he ought to, that the dirty means he sometimes uses to achieve his good ends stand in the same moral class of wrongs as those he is employed to fight. Skolnick's craftsman reaches this conclusion by understanding that his unquestionably good and compelling ends, on certain occasions, justify his employment of dirty means to their achievement. Skolnick's craftsman, as Skolnick understands him, resolves the Dirty Harry problem by denying the dirtiness of his means.

Skolnick's craftsman's resolution is, speaking precisely, Machiavellian. It should come as no surprise to find the representative of one of the classic attempts to resolve the problem of Dirty Hands to be a front runner in response to Dirty Harry. What is worrisome about such a resolution? What does it conceal that makes our genuine dilemma disappear? The problem is not that the craftsman will sometimes choose to use dirty means. If he is morally sensitive to its demands, every policeman's work will sometimes require as much. What is worrisome about Skolnick's craftsman is that he does not regard his means as dirty and, as Skolnick tells us, does not suffer from their use. The craftsman, if Skolnick's portrait of him is correct, will resort to dirty means too readily and too easily. He lacks the restraint that can come only from struggling to justify them and from taking seriously the hazards involved.

In 1966, when *Justice without Trial* first appeared, Skolnick regarded the prospects of creating a more morally sensitive craftsman exceedingly dim. He could not imagine that the craftsman's community, employer, peers, or the courts could come to reward him more for his legal compliance than for the achievements of the ends of his craft. However, in phrasing the prospects in terms of a Dirty Harry problem, one can not only agree with Skolnick that denying the goodness of unquestionably good ends is a practical and political impossibility, but can also uncover another alternative, one which Skolnick does not pursue.

The alternative the Dirty Harry problem leads us to is ensuring that the craftsman regards his dirty means as dirty by applying the same retributive principles of punishment to his wrongful acts that he is quite willing to apply to others'. It is, in fact, only when his wrongful acts are punished that he will come to see them as wrongful and will appreciate the genuine moral – rather than technical or occupational – choice he makes in resorting to them. The prospects for punishment of such acts are by no means dim, and considerable strides in this area have been made. It requires far fewer resources to punish than to reward. Secondly, the likelihood that juries in civil suits will find dirty means dirtier than police do is confirmed by police claims that outsiders cannot appreciate the same moral and technical distinctions that they do. Finally, severe financial losses to police agencies as well as to their officers eventually communicate to both that vigorously policing themselves is cheaper and more pleasing than having to pay so heavily if they do not. If under such conditions our craftsman police officer is still willing to risk the employment of dirty means to achieve what he understands to be unquestionably good ends, he will not only know that he has behaved justly, but that in doing so he must run the risk of becoming genuinely guilty as well.

## A final note

In urging the punishment of policemen who resort to dirty means to achieve some unquestionably good and morally compelling end, we recognize that we create a Dirty Harry problem for ourselves and for those we urge to effect such punishments. It is a fitting end, one which teaches once again that the danger in Dirty Harry problems is never in their resolution, but in thinking that one has found a resolution with which one can truly live in peace.

*From Carl B. Klockars, 'The Dirty Harry problem', in* The Annals of the American Academy of Political and Social Science, *Vol. 452, 1980, pp 33–47.*

## Notes

1  In the contemporary philosophical literature, particularly when raised for the vocation of politics, the question is commonly referred to as the Dirty Hands problem after J.P. Sartre's

treatment of it in *Dirty Hands* (*Les Mains Sales*, 1948) and in *No Exit and Three Other Plays* (New York: Modern Library, 1950). Despite its modern name, the problem is very old and has been taken up by Machiavelli in *The Prince* (1513) and *The Discourses* (1519) (New York: Modern Library, 1950); by Max Weber, 'Politics as a Vocation', (1919) in *Max Weber: Essays in Sociology*, eds. and trans. H. Gerth and C.W. Wills (New York: Oxford University Press, 1946); and by Albert Camus, 'The Just Assassins' (1949) in *Caligula and Three Other Plays* (New York: Alfred A. Knopf, 1958). See Michael Walzer's brilliant critique of these contributions, 'Political Action: The Problem of Dirty Hands,' *Philosophy and Public Affairs*, 2 (2) (Winter 1972). Likewise the Dirty Hands/Dirty Harry problem is implicitly or explicitly raised in virtually every work of Raymond Chandler, Dashiell Hammett, James Cain, and other *Tough Guy Writers of the Thirties*, ed. David Madden (Carbondale: Southern Illinois University Press, 1968), as they are in all of the best work of Joseph Wambaugh, particularly *The Blue Knight*, *The New Centurions*, and *The Choirboys*.

2   'Dirty' here means both 'repugnant' in that it offends widely shared standards of human decency and dignity and 'dangerous' in that it breaks commonly shared and supported norms, rules, or laws for conduct. To 'dirty' acts there must be both a deontologically based face validity of immorality and a consequentialist threat to the prevailing rules for social order.

3   W.H. Auden, 'The Guilty Vicarage,' in *The Dyer's Hand and Other Essays* (New York: Alfred A. Knopf, 1956), 146–58.

4   Egon Bittner, *The Functions of Police in Modern Society* (New York: Jason Aronson, 1975) and 'Florence Nightingale in Pursuit of Willie Sutton,' in *The Potential for Reform of the Criminal Justice System*, vol. 3, ed. H. Jacob (Beverly Hills: Sage Publications, 1974), 11–44.

5   Sartre, *Dirty Hands*, p. 224.

6   One of Wambaugh's characters in *The Choirboys* makes this final point most dramatically when he fails to notice that a young boy's buttocks are flatter than they should be and reads the child's large stomach as a sign of adequate nutrition. When the child dies through his mother's neglect and abuse, the officer rightly includes himself in his ecology of guilt.

7   Herman Goldstein, *Policing a Free Society* (Cambridge, MA: Ballinger Publishing, 1977), 72.

8   See, for example, John F. Galliher, 'Explanations of Police Behavior: A Critical Review and Analysis,' *The Sociological Quarterly*, 12 (Summer 1971), 308–18; Richard Quinney, *Class, State, and Crime* (New York: David McKay, 1977).

9   Albert J. Reiss, Jr., *The Police and the Public* (New Haven: Yale University Press, 1971), 122.

10   These two assertions are drawn from Graeme Newman's *The Punishment Response* (Philadelphia: J.B. Lippincott Co., 1978).

11   Bittner, p. 53.

12   *Ibid.*, p. 72.

13   Jerome Skolnick, *Justice without Trial*, 2nd ed. (New York: John Wiley and Sons, 1975), 182.

# 35. Gratuities and corruption

*John Kleinig*

Surely shoveling society's shit is worth something? (Police officer)[1]

Don't take a dim view of criminals. *Remember, society's shit is your bread and butter.* (Nicholas Ross)[2]

Corruption in police work has been a *pervasive* and *continuing* problem. Almost every serious history of policing and even of particular police departments has had to confront the issue of police corruptibility. Only the smallest and most vigilant departments have escaped its wasting effects. Corruption has been more virulent, visible and deeprooted at some times and in some jurisdictions than at other times and in other jurisdictions. Large urban departments are more prone to corruption than most, though even in small communities police may be just as deeply corrupted. When, from time to time, police corruption has been uncovered, police spokespeople have usually been quick to speak of the rotten apple in every barrel. But it is clear that the corruption has often been much more extensive, claiming not simply lower-ranked officers, or officers on patrol, but involving officers of almost every rank in a network of intrigue, or at least disregard. Indeed, corruption is as much a top-down as a bottom-up problem.

Corruption is also a *serious* problem in police work. This is not only because it violates the ethical norms governing that work, but also because it impairs the ability of police to carry out their work successfully. Corruption is damaging to credibility, and police work, to be effective, needs the confidence and co-operation of the citizenry. It is not only external credibility that is damaged. The internal ethos of the organization is affected: 'The officer who routinely profits by exploiting narcotics addicts and peddlers is not likely to take seriously a request to act with greater respect for minority interests and individual rights'.[3] And as Frank Serpico noted, some of the corrupt officers with whom he was associated were first-class investigators, and would have been highly effective as law enforcement officers had they not spent much of their time pursuing graft.[4]

Although corruption is by no means exclusive to police work, and the extent of police corruption is to some degree an index of wider civic corruption, there are, nevertheless, several factors that have made police work particularly vulnerable to corrupt practices:

1 In their law enforcement role, police are brought into contact with lawbreakers who have an interest in police not doing what they have a duty to do. As possessors of considerable discretionary authority, authority that is not closely supervised, police have significant opportunities to succumb to temptation and pressures. Since those most interested in corrupting police may be people who have little to lose and much to gain from bribery and illegality, and may also be people who have access to substantial benefits and influence, the temptations and pressures may be considerable.

2 Police officers are regularly brought into contact with a side of life that inclines them to moral cynicism. Not only the obviously disreputable, but also many reputable citizens are seen to be corrupt – and corrupting. Police management too may be seen to be, if not corrupt, at least hypocritical. Corruption can come to be seen as a game in which everyone is out to get a larger share. To a certain extent, line officers may even be encouraged to participate. Why should we then expect them to be different? This may be reinforced by what are seen as the unpleasant features of the job. As this chapter's epigraphs suggest, minor corruption can be seen as compensation or even reward for some of 'the Job's' more unpleasant, social sanitation dimensions.

3 Many kinds of minor corruption are tacitly encouraged by the wider community. Commercial establishments often have an interest in maximizing police presence or optimizing police service and so inducements will be offered in the hope that they will be beneficiaries.[5] Many private individuals may also have interests that conduce to corruption. As frequent violators of traffic or parking laws, they will desire to be treated more leniently than would be justified by the facts of the case. They are likely to want a certain degree of openness to deviation.[6] In such cases there will generally be no complainant.

4 Police have frequently been unwilling to admit to significant corruption within their ranks. This has disabled them from confronting it openly and dealing with it head-on. Much corruption has gone undeclared and un-investigated, because people have taken the view that reporting it will get you nowhere. Many have little faith in internal inquiries. As far as large-scale corruption is concerned, it has not usually been until the media have made an issue of it that it has been exposed. Even police management have not wanted to reveal known corruption, lest the media sensationalize it and create problems for the department's image.

## Characterizing corruption

What is involved in corruption? The question is not a simple one. Not only is there disagreement about the nature of corruption, but there is also disagreement about the corruptness or otherwise of particular police practices. What one police officer sees as corrupt, another may consider legitimate. So, while there may be obvious cases of police corruption, from which we can distill a rough sense of its character, the fine-tuning process is made problematic by disagreements about the status of particular practices.

How might we define 'corruption' as it pertains to police work? The following three accounts are fairly representative. According to McMullan's widely-quoted definition:

> A public official is corrupt if he accepts money or money's worth for doing something he is under a duty to do anyway, that he is under a duty not to do, or to exercise a legitimate discretion for improper reasons[7]

Howard Cohen and Michael Feldberg suggest the following:

> Corruption involves accepting goods or services for performing or failing to perform duties which are a normal part of one's job. What makes a gift a gratuity is the reason it is given; what makes it corruption is the reason it is taken.[8]

And Herman Goldstein understands by 'police corruption'

> the misuse of authority by a police officer in a manner designed to produce personal gain for the officer or for others.[9]

Despite their differences, none of these accounts equates police corruption with all forms of police misconduct or deviance. Various types of misconduct, such as use of the third degree to elicit a confession, informal punishments and brutality, perjury to secure a conviction, and petty theft or burglary where an exercise of authority is not involved, lie outside these characterizations. So too do deviations from occupational expectations, such as drinking, sleeping, or having sex while on duty. All three accounts of corruption are concerned with the exercise of police authority animated by the expectation of some form, usually, of material reward or gain. Yet there are significant differences between the three accounts.

In some respects the first two accounts are broader than the third. Goldstein's account focuses on two elements – a particular means (the misuse of authority) *and* a particular end (personal gain for self or others). But, as the other two accounts recognize, corruption need not involve any clear 'misuse' of authority – not if it is understood as a deviation from doing what it is one's duty to *do*. Money or goods may be sought or accepted as a guarantee of 'efficient' service. Behavior is not made less corrupt by the mere fact that officers do what they should be doing *because of* the inducements sought or accepted. Motivation is central to an understanding of corruption.

But on the other side, the first two definitions operate with a somewhat narrower understanding of personal gain than the third. Benefits for which the use of authority may be traded include not only tangibles such as money, goods, and services, but also less tangible items such as status, influence, prestige or future support. Indeed, it is only when we allow corruption to include the latter that we can understand how it is as much an issue for 'white-collar' as for 'blue-collar' policing.

There is a further dimension to Goldstein's account that is not acknowledged by the others. The gain need not be strictly or narrowly personal. The benefit might go to an officer's family or to the department. Officers who used to sell tickets to 'the policeman's ball' were not exclusive beneficiaries of their solicitations. Nor would an officer who accepted help in regard to a relative's employment in return for a 'break' or better service be doing it for narrow personal gain. However, it has to be allowed that, in this latter case, it is only because of the officer's 'identification' with the direct beneficiary that the behavior constitutes corruption. An officer who agreed not to enforce the law if the violator made a sizable donation to charity would probably be acting improperly, but not corruptly.[10]

It may not be possible to give a neat overall characterization of corruption. Each of the definitions quoted above captures a good deal but not all of what would be considered corruption. Nevertheless, I offer the following as a general account of police corruption:

> Police officers act corruptly when, in exercising or failing to exercise their authority, they act with the primary intention of furthering private or departmental/divisional advantage.

In some respects, this is a very radical definition, since it covers many acts and practices that may never *show* themselves as corrupt – for example, doing what one is duty-bound to do solely for personal advancement (say, overtime collars or ignoring small jobs for the large, 'visible' ones). Yet such practices are motivated by the *spirit* of corruption, and belong in the same moral category as corruption that is more visibly deleterious. The mistake involved in most discussions of corruption is to focus almost exclusively on kinds of acts, whereas corruption is primarily a problem of motivation. True, it is the kind of motivation that often manifests itself in deviant acts, but it need not do so.

In this sense corruption is an *ethical* problem before it is a *legal* or *administrative* problem. It becomes a legally and administratively significant problem only because it often expresses itself in deviant acts.

It is because corruption is to be conceived, at its heart, as a *motivational* transgression that the various catalogues and typologies of corruption common to sociological studies of corruption need to be qualified. It is not the deviant activities themselves that are corrupt. The deviance constitutes corruption only because it is animated by some desire for personal or departmental or divisional gain. An officer may fix a ticket for a friend without any thought of 'gaining' from it, or shake down a drug dealer with a view to burning his money, or drop an investigation out of sheer laziness. These represent forms of misconduct, but not of corruption, though they are usually catalogued as forms of corruption. What may be true to say is that there are certain forms of deviant police conduct that are usually motivated by some benefit that will accrue to the officer or those with whom he or she identifies.

There are two further observation to be made about many of the standard catalogues of corrupt activities.[11] First, they focus for the most part on police–citizen interactions, and second, they are oriented to forms of corruption that are more likely to be found at lower levels of the police organization. Police corruption may be internal as well as external There are personal or private gains that may be sought from personnel within a department as well as those that may come from those outside it. The desire for promotion benefits, pay increases, special rosters, convenient vacation arrangements, and so on, may all corrupt the exercise of authority. As well, equipment and funds may be used, and political assistance may be provided, for corrupt purposes. Indeed, there is some reason to think that the level of internal corruption may not be significantly lower than the level of external corruption. Much of the cynicism that develops in police circles and that contributes to external corruption has as one of its sources a cynicism about the integrity of the police organization [ … ].

### Typologies of corruption

Several typologies of police corruption have been developed, most thoroughly by Thomas Barker and his associates.[12] The purpose of such typologies has been to bring a certain explanatory and normative order and coherence into the multitude of acts that are usually denominated corrupt. Although, for reasons I have just outlined, I believe that such typologies focus on the wrong end of corruption – on the corrupted conduct rather than the corrupting motivation – they nevertheless provide us with a sense of the different public interests that may be corruptly subverted and therefore of the different levels of seriousness that may attach to different kinds of corrupt behavior.

Three features of the account that follows should be noted at the outset. First, the typology was initially constructed in response to the New York Police Department scandal of the early 1970s. However, the forms taken by police corruption are limited only by the imagination and opportunities that police have. Second, the authors see corruption as a group phenomenon, and not simply as an individual one. It arises, they believe, because of the character of an organization, and not just as the expression of an individual ego. Police corruption, as a phenomenon that attracts study, arises because departments are characterized by conflicting norms, the relative absence of external controls, impossible external demands, secretiveness, and bonds of loyalty that make 'squealing' exceedingly difficult. Internal linguistic distinctions, such as those between clean and dirty money, help to sustain corrupt practices.[13] And third, the authors see their typology as hierarchical, manifesting 'a progressive process in dynamics, accretion, and gravity, a process that might be checked at any one or more levels of progression by the tolerance limits of the police organization or the community'.[14] I believe, however, that there is more contingency to this progression than the authors acknowledge.

### Corruption of authority

Under this heading Barker gathers those unauthorized and unearned material benefits given an officer solely because he/she is a police officer. They include 'free meals, booze, sex, services, free entertainment admissions, police discounts on merchandise, or other material inducements'.[15] To what extent, if at all, the acceptance of these should be considered corruptions of authority we will discuss a little later in this chapter (Section 9.2). Less ambiguously, they include various 'rewards' for extra services rendered – 'payments by businessmen for property protection extending beyond routine patrol duties; secret payments by property owners to police for arresting robbers and burglars at their establishments; payments by bondsmen acting as bounty hunters to police for the arrest and notification of bond jumpers'[16]

Barker points out that in some of these cases, when the givers are 'respectable citizens', there has been departmental condonation or acceptance, and a veiled rationalization of the 'gratitude' that such gifts are intended to express.

### Kickbacks

Included here are the goods, services, or money that police officers may receive for 'referring business to towing companies, ambulances, garages, lawyers, doctors, bondsmen, undertakers, taxicab drivers, service stations, moving companies, and others who are anxious to sell services or goods to persons with whom the police interact during their routine patrol'.[17] Like gratuities, kickbacks have sometimes been tacitly condoned, as long as the businesses concerned are legitimate and the rewards modest (cash rewards tend to be frowned upon): No laws are broken, and it is rationalized that the businesspersons are simply being 'enterprising'.

### Opportunistic theft

As we reach this level, we cross the line of what has at times been seen as 'ignorable' corruption. It takes a variety of forms: 'Rolled arrestees, traffic accident victims, violent crime victims, and unconscious or dead citizens are generally unaware of the act. Officers investigating burglaries may take merchandise or money left behind by the original thief. Officers may also take items from unprotected property sites discovered during routine patrol; e.g., merchandise or money from unlocked businesses, building materials from construction locations, unguarded items from business or industrial establishments. Finally, policemen may keep a portion of the confiscated evidence they discover during vice raids, e.g., money, booze, narcotics, and property.'[18]

### Shakedowns

Although a shakedown is often seen as officer initiated, Barker understands it to include the opportunistic acceptance of payments for refraining from making an arrest (or issuing a summons) when it would otherwise have been called for. He therefore sees this as a sphere in which the 'clean'/'dirty' graft distinction may operate. This is particularly the case where so-called victimless crimes (crimes without complainants) are involved. Although shakedowns connected with drug pushing, burglary, and other felonies may be 'protected' by a code of silence, if found out they usually attract severe departmental condemnation.

### Protection of illegal activities

It is important to those who engage in illegal enterprises that they operate with a minimum of official harassment. These operators have a strong reason for seeking to induce the police to turn a blind eye to their activities, or at least to go easy in constraining them. In the case of crimes without complainants, which are difficult enough to enforce and about which police may feel ambivalent anyway, there may even be a fair measure of public support for police leniency, albeit not for payments that police might accept or exact. Barker notes the great variety of forms of 'protection' that police may provide: 'Some cab companies and individual cab drivers pay police for illegal permission to operate outside pre-scribed routes and areas, to pick up and discharge fares at unauthorized sites, to operate cabs that do not meet safety and cleanliness standards, to operate without proper licensing procedures. Trucking firms pay for the privilege of hauling overloaded cargoes and driving off prescribed truck routes … Legitimate businesses may also pay police to avoid Sunday "blue" laws … Con-struction companies may pay police to overlook violations of city regulations, e.g., trucks blocking traffic, violating pollution guidelines (burning trash, creating dust, etc.), destroying city property, blocking sidewalks'.[19]

The fact that some of these illegal activities – those without complainants – are difficult to prosecute, effectively functions, according to Barker, 'to drive many honest and dedicated police officers to resignation, ritualism, inaction, or corruption. Moreover, community approval of "protected" illegal goods and services militates for a thoroughly deviant and criminal police organization'.[20] He also suggests that if such protection is to be effective, it requires a fair measure of internal organization.[21]

We might also include within this category, though it does not appear in Barker's catalogue, the selling of confidential police information. Sometimes it might be to criminals, at other times to lawyers or employers who may wish to have it for more legitimate purposes.

### The traffic fix

This involves the 'taking up' or disposing of traffic citations for money or some other benefit. Apparently, this form of corruption was at one time so prevalent that one police agency proudly announced that it had succeeded in producing a 'no-fix' ticket.[22]

### The misdemeanor fix

In this case, the officer acts to quash misdemeanor court proceedings. This may take a number of forms: refraining from requesting prosecution, tampering with the existing evidence, or giving perjured testimony.

### The felony fix

More seriously, but by some of the same means, an officer may act to ensure that a felony action is not proceeded with or will not result in a conviction.

### Direct criminal activities

These occur when officers engage in burglary, robbery, larceny, and so on, for personal gain. Often it is solo, but sometimes a small ring operates. Generally such activities have little departmental sympathy or support, and officers who are involved generally shield their activities from others in the precinct.

### Internal payoffs

Finally, Barker details various forms of internal corruption: 'Internal payoffs regulate a market where police officers' prerogatives may be bought, bartered, or sold. Actors are exclusively police officers. Prerogatives negotiated encompass work assignments, off-days, holidays, vacation periods, control of evidence, and promotions. Officers who administer the distribution of assignments and personnel may collect fees for assigning officers to certain divisions, precincts, units, details, shifts, and beats; for insuring that selected personnel are retained in, transferred from, or excluded from certain work assignments. In departments taking protection money from vice operations, officers may contact command personnel and bid for 'good' (lucrative) assignments'.[23]

As I noted earlier, Barker believes that these different forms of police corruption are progressively more serious. The order, however, is colored by his belief that the factors affecting corruption are to be construed in social rather than individual/psychological terms. It is for this reason that the various 'internal payoffs', though apparently much less serious than some of the other acts of corruption that occur, nevertheless bespeak a much more deeply seated and serious corruption problem than those where criminals induce officers to go easy on them or in which officers opportunistically steal from premises that have already been burgled. A department that allows significant internal corruption is certain to be a department that has little control over the various forms of external corruption.

Like Lawrence Sherman, to whose views in 'Becoming Bent' I shall soon turn, Barker sees something of a slide from one form of corruption to another. Those who engage in one of the less serious forms of corruption are likely to experience less difficulty in engaging in a more serious form of corruption than those who do not engage in any form of corruption. The slide is not inexorable, or the gradient even, but the slope is there.

The so-called slippery slope of police corruption is a persistent theme in both theoretical and biographical discussions of police corruption. It is so pervasive that most departments promulgate rules regarding what Barker sees as the least serious forms – particularly the acceptance of gratuities – and punish infractions with what seems to be a disproportionate ferocity. It is as though everything must be done to keep people off the 'slope', because once on it, it is very difficult to reclaim the high ground. And so it is to that allegedly least serious form, the acceptance of gratuities, and the problem of a slippery slope that I shall now turn.

## Gratuities: the problem

Can we really say, that the acceptance of gratuities discounts, annual presents, and other 'benefits' that police officers might be offered, qualifies as corruption – that is, involves exercises of authority for the sake of private (or sectional) advantage.

There is nothing about a gratuity *per se* to imply that any (anticipated or actual) exercise of authority that has led to the gratuity being offered has been contingent on its being offered. Even if an officer performs an official service *in the expectation of receiving a gratuity,* it does not strictly follow that the service was provided with the intention of receiving the gratuity or that without the expectation of a gratuity the service would not have been provided or provided as efficiently.

In this respect, bribes differ significantly from gratuities. Bribes are offered and accepted in order to corrupt authority. At best this is a contingent feature of gratuities; indeed, many gratuities are offered as unsolicited and voluntary rewards for the proper, and even supererogatory, exercise of police authority. Gratuities also tend to involve smaller benefits than bribes. Because a bribe is offered or sought to deflect an officer from doing his duty, the inducement will need to be large enough to make the corruption of duty 'worth it'. A gratuity, on the other hand, is often just a token, a gesture of appreciation. When police management talk about gratuities, they tend to have in mind free cups of coffee and doughnuts no less than larger gifts; when they talk about bribes, the exchanges are almost always much larger.

Police officers are themselves strongly divided on the propriety or otherwise of gratuities and other gifts. At one end, there are those who see these as 'perks' of the job, or as tokens of appreciation from a generally unappreciative citizenry, harmless benefits that make a somewhat humdrum existence more pleasant, or as rewards, perhaps, for doing some of society's dirty work. At the other end are those who see the acceptance of such benefits as corrupting, if not corrupt. O.W. Wilson is memorably quoted as saying that 'a police officer should not be allowed to accept any gratuity, not even a free cup of coffee'.[24]

Those who hold the first view are challenged to say where they would draw the line – at a free meal (at an expensive restaurant?[25]), $20, a TV? Those who hold the second are said to take their opposition to corruption to unrealistic and absurd lengths. Where does the truth lie?[26] In some ways, though the stakes are rather different, the debate parallels that which occurs in the case of abortion, each side seeking by means of structurally similar arguments to force the other into accepting the untenability of its position. So-called pro-lifers challenge pro-choicers to 'draw a morally significant line' between an early and late abortion or even infanticide, pro-choicers suggest that it is patently absurd to accord to a 'blob of jelly' the kind of regard we normally reserve for a person.

The major contentions of those who would tolerate the acceptance of gratuities and similar benefits are as follows:

1   It is very natural to show appreciation to those who benefit us in some way, even if it is their job to do so. When they do their job particularly well or when we are particularly grateful, a mere 'thank you' does not sufficiently express our gratitude. Something more is called for. Since police often attend us at critical times, we may have reason to be particularly grateful to them, and it is only natural that we express that gratitude by means of a gratuity. It would, moreover, be insulting were they not willing to accept it, since it would cast doubt on the spirit in which it was offered.[27]

2   The usual complaint against the offering and receiving of gratuities is that the practice will buy or cultivate favor. But those who believe that officers ought to be permitted to exercise discretion in the matter argue that most gratuities are not significant enough to be corrupting. Taking advantage of the offer of a half-priced Big Mac[28] or free cup of coffee is no big deal. It is too small to make a police officer beholden to the giver. No officer is going to put his job on the line for something so small.

3   In some cases, where the benefit (say, the half-priced Big Mac) is official company policy, there is nothing about the arrangement or individual transaction that would create a 'personal' sense of obligation. For the company concerned, the arrangement is one way in which it can directly express its gratitude for a public service, increase its patronage, and in addition benefit from a police presence on its premises. These are all morally permissible goals. Since everything is 'up front' there is no attempt or intention to deflect the officer from his/her duty.

4   Police on the beat depend for their effectiveness on establishing good relations with local businesspeople. That way they find out what is going on, who is believed to have done what, what might be in the air, and generally keep open the conduit between police and community. The acceptance of a free cup of coffee or piece of fruit is an integral part of the social give-and-take that is constitutive of effective street policing. An officer who knocks back such small gestures will be looked at as 'unfriendly and will not be confided in or shared with.[29]

5   The 'free cup of coffee' is so deeply entrenched that attempts to root it out will be ineffective and will lead to alienation within and between the ranks. By line officers its prohibition is seen as expressing a 'killjoy' attitude, and its enforcement is viewed as a waste of scarce departmental sources.[30] Cynicism will result.

6   Directives that forbid the acceptance of free cups of coffee treat police officers as fools who cannot distinguish between a friendly gesture or mark of appreciation and a bribe, as moral infants who cannot accept a token of respect and friendship without succumbing to favoritism, or as knaves or moochers who take every opportunity to exploit their position for personal advantage. On the contrary, it is argued, police are generally well aware of why gratuities are being offered. They are capable of exercising a proper discretion in accepting or refusing to accept them. And even if a cup of coffee is offered for the wrong reason, the reason for accepting it need not complement that for offering it.

The major contentions of those who oppose the acceptance of gratuities and similar benefits are:

1   Even the smallest gift, particularly if it becomes regularized, creates a sense of obligation. Or, if it does not create anything as strong as a sense of obligation, it gives at least a rose tint to the relationship. An officer who has previously accepted free cups of coffee will find it harder to take an impartial stand later if he/she is asked to do a 'favor'. Even if a stand is taken, it may be colored by the bond that has been cultivated: A warning might be given where otherwise a ticket would have been issued.

2   Those who accept gratuities find themselves on a slippery slope of corruption on which it becomes progressively more difficult to stop. There is the old saying: 'Sow a thought and you reap an act; sow an act and you reap a habit; sow a habit and you reap a character; sow a character and you reap a destiny'.[31] By accepting a gratuity, the officer is said to abandon a relationship with others that is motivated and directed solely by public duty

to one in which private dealings and personal sentiment begin to play a part. The ground becomes softer, and the officer will find that little by little his/ her actions come to be determined by personal, 'self-interested' factors.

3    Although some, perhaps most, police are able to practice discernment with regard to the acceptance of gratuities, some are not able to do so. They will find that the free cup of coffee sets them on a path of accepting and then expecting gratuities that, because of the opportunities provided by police work, will eventually have few bounds. For the sake of these 'weak', or 'inexperienced' officers, inevitable in any organization, and because of the high trust that is placed in police officers, it is better for policing generally that the 'strong' and 'experienced' forgo what for them would be only a small and harmless benefit.[32]

4    Businesses that offer free cups of coffee, doughnuts, sandwiches, and meals to police officers do so with a partial view to attracting their presence. Naturally police officers are likely to spend more of their time in the vicinity of such businesses than elsewhere. While this may be beneficial to the businesses concerned, it leads to an unfair distribution of the police presence. It is 'antidemocratic'.[33]

### The slippery slope argument

Most of the foregoing arguments lend themselves to further elaboration and defense, and some of them will be pursued a little later. For the moment, however, I want to focus on just one line of argument, that relating to the so-called slippery slope of corruption although there are many theories about the sources of police corruption – some relating to preexisting criminal tendencies and the attractions that police work may present to such people, and others to various aspects of police culture or to the dynamic of external and internal demands on police – it is still very common to find woven into these theories the suggestion that actual corruption starts off in a small way, and then becomes increasingly addictive. The acceptance of gratuities is seen as a major 'small' thing that triggers the decline. And so, whether or not their acceptance is in itself corrupting, it is argued that a bright line needs to be drawn that excludes the acceptance of gratuities.

One thing, it is said, leads to another. And that, in essence, is the slippery slope argument, the general name for a cluster of related arguments, sometimes referred to as the 'wedge', the 'foot-in-the-door', or the 'camel's-nose' *argument* by those who endorse it and as *fallacy* by those who oppose its use, the latter also frequently dubbing (a version of) it the 'bald man' or 'black-and-white' fallacy.[34] In this lamer form it is related to what ancient logicians sometimes spoke of as the 'sorites (heap) paradox'. In the present context, it is claimed that the acceptance of small gratuities such as free cups of coffee by police officers will increase the likelihood of, or lead by degrees to, or is not significantly different from, corruption of the worst kind.

But not only does the slippery slope argument have a number of names, it also has a number of guises. And this sometimes makes it difficult to pin down. It will be useful to start off with James Rachels's distinction between 'logical ' and 'psychological' versions of the argument:[35]

*Logical*

Although Rachels does not draw attention to the fact, there are at least two forms of the logical version of the slippery slope argument.[36] The first version states that once a certain practice is accepted, then, from a logical point of view, we are also committed to accepting certain other practices, since acceptance of the first practice removes any reason there might be for not going on to accept the additional practices. The additional practices, however, are patently and increasingly intolerable. Therefore, it is claimed, the first practice ought not to be permitted.

The argument is applied to police corruption in the following way. Although the acceptance of a free cup of coffee is not seriously wrong, and not in itself the sort of wrongdoing to make an issue of, it is, nevertheless, wrong. And since its implicit rationale – the compromise of impartiality for the sake of some personal benefit – is essentially the same as that involved in more serious forms of corruption, differing from them only in degree, the person who accepts a free cup of coffee has effectively undermined any moral ground he has for refusing to engage in corruption of a more serious kind.[37] The practical conclusion that is drawn from the 'logical' version of the argument is that, in order to distance oneself morally from serious corruption, it is important not to engage in any corruption, albeit corruption of an apparently 'trivial' kind.

According to the second version of the argument, although there appears to be a significant difference between one practice and some other, say $p$ and $z$, where $z$ is patently unacceptable,[38] closer inspection reveals that there is only an insignificant difference between $p$ and $q$, an insignificant difference between $q$ and $r$, an insignificant difference between $r$ and $s$, …and between $y$ and $z$. Therefore, the difference between $q$ and $z$ is more apparent than real, and any distinction between them must be arbitrary. Therefore $p$ ought not to be permitted.

Applied to police corruption, the argument goes somewhat as follows: Although there appears to be a big difference between taking a free cup of coffee and, say, shaking down drug dealers and selling their drugs, that difference can be shown to be an arbitrary one. For there is only a slight difference between a cup of coffee and a cup of coffee and doughnut, and there is only a slight difference between a cup of coffee and doughnut and a free meal, and there is only a slight difference between a free meal and a gift, and … a shakedown. Since there is no precise, natural line to be drawn between the acceptance of a free cup of coffee and engaging in a shakedown, any distinction between them will be arbitrary. Therefore, the acceptance of free cups of coffee ought to be forbidden.

This second form of the logical version of the argument is almost certainly invalid. It is in this form that it has come to be known as an instantiation of the 'bald man' or 'black-and-white' fallacy, or, as Govier dubs it, 'The Fallacy of Slippery Assimilation'. The fallacy resides in refusing to recognize that there is a *cumulative* significance to the individually insignificant differences. This holds true and makes the difference between $p$ and $z$ significant, *even if* we cannot tell with any precision at what point what we want to say about $z$ (say, that it is unacceptable and ought to be prohibited) applies also to a successor of $p$. The person who has 10,000 hairs on his head may not differ significantly from the person who has 9,999 hairs, and the person who has 9,999 hairs may not differ significantly from the person who has 9,998… and the, person who has no hair, but the cumulative effect of those differences makes for a very significant difference between a hairy person (with 10,000 hairs) and a bald one, even though we may not be able to state with any precision where we would draw the line.

### Psychological

The 'psychological' version of the slippery slope argument relies on an empirical connection between the acts or practices at the beginning of the slope and those at the bottom. It states that once a certain practice is accepted, people *are likely* to go on to accept other practices that are increasingly unacceptable. Unlike the previous version, which focuses on a logical or conceptual connection between the 'trivial' and 'serious' wrongdoing (since they can both be included under the same moral or conceptual maxim or label), this version focuses on a contingent but causal connection between the initial practice and the practices to which it is said its acceptance will lead.

One of the interesting features of this version is the ability of those who propound it to concede that the practice at the top of the slope (accepting a free cup of coffee) is not in itself 'unacceptable' or morally troublesome. What they argue is that the practice of accepting a free cup of coffee is 'empirically linked' to other (future) practices that will be morally unacceptable. One leads, if not inevitably, then 'naturally' or easily, to the other. So, in contrast to the logical version of the argument, in which the case allegedly at the top of the slope is morally 'of-a-piece' (at least in the sense of being immoral) with the case at the bottom of the slope, in the psychological version the case allegedly at the top of the slope is morally distinguishable from the case at the bottom of the slope. The difference is one of kind and not merely one of degree.

Those who employ the slippery slope argument may focus on one or both, though usually both, of two features of the metaphor. Some concentrate on the slope itself, how steep and slippery it is; others focus on the 'abyss' or disaster that awaits at the bottom. Those who employ one of the logical versions generally focus on the gradient; those who resort to the psychological version generally focus on the result.[39]

Although both logical and psychological versions of the slippery slope argument are prevalent in the literature, it is the psychological version that gains most attention. Its status is also less easily determinable. Proponents claim that a transition from what we might call the 'plateau' position (no free cups of coffee) to the 'abyss' position is *much* harder to make than the transition from the 'lip' opposition (free cups of coffee) to the 'abyss' position (shakedowns, narcotics, graft, and so on). Better, then, to stay on the plateau. The argument usually trades very heavily on the disaster that awaits those who get onto the slope. But in order to give the spectre of that abyss some realism, its proponents need to show why those who get onto the slope will find themselves faced with disaster. Or, to put it another way, they need to show that the metaphor of a *slope* – and a slippery one at that – is appropriate.

Proponents of the psychological version point to several factors that might be adduced to support their contention of a slope. One factor might be a certain linguistic or conceptual 'fuzziness' in the distinction between the lip and abyss practices. For one thing, the edges of corruption may be very fuzzy. If, for example, there is considerable public controversy over whether and, if so, how the acceptance of gratuities such as free cups of coffee is to be distinguished from the engagement in corruption (albeit minor), or confusion over the distinction between a gift, a gratuity, and a bribe, there will be a less clear distinction between the acceptance of free cups of coffee and the , acceptance of bribes than between the nonacceptance of free cups of coffee its and the acceptance of bribes. This is not the same as the logical argument. The point is not whether there is a significant moral distinction, but whether there is *controversy* about it. The 'environment' in which the various practices take place encourages a certain blurring of boundaries.

The fuzziness may also be produced or exacerbated by the fact that the world does not come to us neatly packaged. Human activities form something of a continuum, and even if our conceptual distinctions are clear, it is not always clear how they are to be applied in particular cases. It is this feature of our experience that forms the centerpiece of the second form of the logical version of the argument. Here, however, the point is not to engage in some form of conceptual assimilation, but simply to note the *practical* difficulty of making the distinction.

A rather different source for the slide can be the 'slippage' that naturally tends to occur in transfers between one person and another. If *a* understands a practice in a certain way, it is unlikely that if the practice is then explained to *b* it will be understood by *b* in exactly the same way. Some of the nuances for *a* may be lost in transit. So, while one police officer may be able to grasp the acceptance of a free cup of coffee in a way that keeps it firmly on the 'lip', another to whom he teaches the practice may understand his engagement in it in a way that will begin the slide toward the 'abyss' of corruption below. This transferential slippage may work with either a general account of 'human finitude and limitedness' or a distinction between the 'strong' and the 'weak'.

Perhaps this helps to explain why, very often, those who present the argument (say, police administrators) will claim that while *they* could engage in the practice at the top of the slope without sliding down, *others* will not be able to do so. A police chief may believe himself/herself able to resist the slide, but also think that (some) officers on the beat will not be capable of resisting it. Or the proponent may wish to claim that while he could *now* engage in the practice at the top of the slope without sliding down, nevertheless he might not be able to do so at some *future* time. Or maybe he will argue that because *he* would not be able to resist the slide, neither will others be able to. Clearly, there are problems about making such differentiations. If one is able to resist oneself, why not credit others with the same capacity? If one is able to resist now, why shouldn't one be able to resist later? If one is not able to resist now, why should one attribute a similar weakness to others? The reactions of such proponents need not reflect moral insensitivity, but the questions raised need to be addressed.

Is the psychological version of the argument valid? The question cannot be answered generally. It depends. It depends on the empirical plausibility of the transition from one point to another on the alleged slope. Each transition needs to be supported by arguments that will show why it is *likely* (and not merely possible) that a person who engages in practice *p* will then engage in practice *q* and then in practice *r* ... and so on to practice. Unfortunately, many who use the argument focus on the horrors of the abyss to deflect attention from the sparse support for the transitional stages. Where, then, does this leave the free cup of coffee? In 'Becoming Bent: Moral Careers of Corrupt Policemen', Lawrence Sherman argues that there is a relatively smooth descent ('a continuum of graft stages'[40]) from the acceptance of minor 'perks', through accepting bribes in relation to bar closing hours, to taking graft or regulative crimes, gambling, prostitution, and ultimately involvement with narcotics. What prompts police officers to get onto this slope, and why, once on it, is it so difficult to stop? Sherman focuses on two factors: *affiliation* – the social considerations that bind police, both corrupt and noncorrupt, together; and *signification* – on the way in which police represent their behavior to themselves to link the various stages of corruption.

As Sherman sees it, early in his career, the young recruit learns that being a police officer binds him to one social group and alienates him from another. Membership of the former includes peer pressure to accept minor 'perks'. Their acceptance has the effect of altering the rookie's self-image in a way that makes him vulnerable to slightly more substantial 'graft': The young recruit who has accepted a free cup of coffee 'has a different image of himself to contend with when a bar owner operating after closing hours offers him a drink'.[41] The slide, though not inexorable, is made smoother by the relatively small moral gap between successive stages of the descent. One solution to the problem, Sherman suggests, is to make the grade on the slope steeper (and hence more daunting) by removing from the books those activities ('vice') that most easily tempt police into accepting graft and that then lead them easily on to more serious corruption.

Even if Sherman's solution to the problem is controversial, his analysis of the transition has a great deal of anecdotal support from corrupt police officers who have subsequently written about their decline.[42] It is not, however, universally shared, and, indeed, many line officers strongly resist its logic. That resistance is encapsulated in Michael Feldberg's rejection of Sherman's position. Most police, Feldberg claims, *are* able to make a firm distinction between minor 'perks' and bribes intended to deflect them from their responsibilities, and invoking the slippery slope argument is 'unrealistic, somewhat hypocritical and insulting to a police officer's intelligence'. A ban on taking such perks will appear (and, in many cases, be) petty, because 'what makes a gift a gratuity is the reason it is given; what makes it corruption is the reason it is taken'.[44] There are many reasons why a police officer might accept a cup of coffee, and only a few of them will express a corrupt intent or tendency. Not that Feldberg is himself comfortable with the police acceptance of minor gratuities; but his unease does not lie in slippery slope considerations Rather, their acceptance detracts from 'the democratic ethos of policing': 'Gratuities are simply an inducement to a police officer to distribute the benefit of his presence disproportionately to some taxpayers and not others'.[45]

The dispute between Sherman and Feldberg is more subtle than appears at first reading. The point is not that one sees a slope where the other does not, but that they have a different understanding of its slipperiness. And they have a different understanding of its slipperiness mainly because they appeal (at least sometimes) to different versions of the argument.

Sherman believes that the police officer who accepts a free cup of coffee *ipso facto* compromises himself morally. His image of himself is changed, and the only issue now is how venal he is willing to be. Feldberg, on the other hand, does not see anything inherently wrong with accepting a free cup of coffee, though he is aware that there are certain risks involved. The issue of moral compromise need not be a pressing one at that stage (even though there may be different, distributional questions).

Sherman sees only a difference in degree between the officer who accepts a free cup of coffee and the officer who gets involved in drug trafficking Moral compromise is already involved. The officer who accepts a free cup of coffee has already tarnished his self-image. Sherman, in other words, adopts what I referred to earlier as the 'logical' version of the slippery slope argument. And the slope, not surprisingly, is much slipperier than Feldberg's. Feldberg, insofar as he sees the risk of a slide, has in mind the 'psychological' version of the argument. There is a risk that the officer who accepts, gratuities will lose a sense of where the line is to be drawn, but a conscientious officer will know when things are going too far, and at the free-cup-of coffee stage, he/she will probably be well short of corruption. As has often been pointed out, experienced and/or cautious skiers are capable of stopping on quite steep slopes.

Let us note, however, that even though Sherman's slope is likely to be slipperier than Feldberg's, it is not perfectly smooth.[46] There may be plateaus on which it is fairly easy to stop. The person who is prepared to tell lies, is not *ipso facto* prepared to steal, to assault, and to murder. And even the person who is prepared to lie (inexcusably) about some things may not be prepared to lie about other things. All of us, even the not-so-virtuous among us tend to draw lines beyond which we will not go. No doubt that was one of the functions of the grass-eater/meat-eater distinction drawn by New York City police in the 1960s.[47] The person who accepts free cups of coffee and sees this as wrong may nevertheless not be prepared to accept a free meal or a kickback. This is not to deny that it will be harder to refuse a free meal or kickback if a free cup of coffee is accepted (especially if they are believed to be wrong for the same reason), but it may not be too difficult And where the acts or practices are believed to be wrong for different reasons, it will probably be much easier to draw the line.

Who is right? If corruption is thought of as an exercise of authority in which a person acts to further some private or sectional end, then the acceptance of a free cup of coffee may be too unimportant in itself to constitute a corrupt (or even corrupting) benefit. People commonly offer each other cups of coffee – whether as friends, business associates, clients, or benefactors – as a gesture of hospitality, friendship, gratitude, and so on. It is a small gesture, enough to express a measure of attentive recognition, but not really enough to create anything like a significant sense of obligation. To the extent that that is Feldberg's position, I think he is probably right.

But the free cup of coffee may not mean only that. Its symbolism may stretch further. It may be intended as a subtle lure, an attempt to create a rapport that can be drawn upon (exploited) at some future time. And if given regularly, it may give the officer who accepts it a slightly too generous view of the giver. Even though taking it will not be corrupting in itself, it may nevertheless pave the way for corrupting conduct in the future. And then, once that compromise has been made, other and larger compromises will more easily (though not inevitably) follow.

Even so, I think Feldberg has a better grasp of the moral relativities than Sherman. Police chiefs who make too big a deal of free cups of coffee and treat their acceptance as a serious compromise or even only as a significant step in the direction of moral compromise, are likely to be seen as going overboard, and they risk losing the respect and confidence of their officers. Like parents who paint lurid pictures of the evils of pot and sex, only to find that their overdramatization has led to a loss of respect (their children experiment and find out that they are anything but dreadful), so police chiefs who make too much of a noise about free cups of coffee may find their authority undermined. And then, of course, like children who have lost respect for their parents and have thrown caution to the wind, only to discover the bedrock of truth in their parents' warnings, those officers who start ignoring warnings may find them coming true in unexpected ways.

It may be more prudent, as well as more realistic, if police chiefs do not pretend that there is something either inherently or inevitably (or even easily) corrupting about the acceptance of a free cup of coffee. That does not mean that it is all right to accept a free cup of coffee. Even if only a few officers succumb to the temptations involved, the serious public consequences may make for better policy if police do not accept gratuities. But beyond that there is Feldberg's argument that a no-gratuity policy assists in the more equitable distribution of police service.[48] If some establishments offer police free cups of coffee, police will be tempted to frequent them more often. Such is often the intention of those who run small businesses. The police presence helps to ensure their freedom from hoodlums, holdups, and may even help to secure a faster response in an emergency. The free cup of coffee is like a very cheap supplemental insurance premium. But it is achieved by getting for those establishments a disproportionate police presence, out of keeping with the equal protection and impartial service that it is the police's public role to provide. In a situation in which police resources are scarce anyway, it may breed competition and unfairly divert police attention.[49] Police, as beneficiaries of the public purse, and not fee-for-service providers, are responsible for the fair deployment of their re-sources, based on need rather than reward.

There is another reason for not overdoing the slippery slope potential of the free cup of coffee. If police chiefs insist on the corrupt and corrupting character of accepting free cups of coffee, then for that reason some officers who accept them may come to see themselves as having been compromised or at least as having something to hide. And insofar as they come to believe that, they may feel themselves on the logical slippery slope of which they have been warned. Believing themselves already compromised, they might then find it easier to make more significant compromises. This would not occur had they been told that the reason for not accepting gratuities was the 'democratic' need to avoid a situation in which the police presence would become unfairly distributed.

For those who feel and thus find themselves on the slippery slope, the issue may now be to find a 'branch' to cling to, such as the distinction between clean and dirty graft, or between active and passive graft. But some of these branches may not be very strong, the distinctions concerned having only secondary moral relevance.

## Whistleblowing

What should officers do when they become aware of corrupt or illegal practices or other forms of misconduct on the part of their fellow officers? Consider the following scenarios:

A. A police officer becomes aware that one of his colleagues has a tendency to mistreat arrestees, particularly those from lower socioeconomic groups. He's told: 'It's the only language they understand.'
B. A police officer is transferred to a precinct in which there operates a fairly elaborate and extensive network of graft; even ranking officers are participants. He is under some pressure to join.
C. A police officer is involved in the investigation of a horrific child abuse/ murder case that, if it goes to trial, will show gross dereliction by the Bureau of Child Welfare. High-ranking Bureau officials have intervened to arrange a plea bargain in which the parents get off very lightly.
D. A police officer is promoted into a specialist unit, known for its effectiveness. He discovers that this effectiveness is made possible because its members engage in various illegal activities – unauthorized wiretapping, withholding of confiscated drugs so that informants can be supplied, and so on. The officer becomes caught up in such activities until an internal investigation traps him. He is told that if he 'cooperates' with the investigating officers – wears a wire, informs on his colleagues, and so on – his own position may be helped.

In each of these cases, the officer knows of and/or is involved in unethical conduct, whether engaged in by a colleague, a department, or an associated agency. What should the officer do?

In practice, there might be several broad options available to the officer He/ she might: (1) join in or actively assist in the unethical conduct; (2) turn a blind eye to it; (3) seek to dissuade those involved; (4) ask for a transfer away from the source of the unacceptable conduct; (5) report the conduct to superiors; (6) go public (by contacting the media or some authority outside the agency); (7) resign (and then go public?); and, if implicated himself/herself, (8) tough it out, or (9) cooperate with the investigating officers. Not all these options are exclusive: for example, (3) might be followed by (4) and/or (5) and/or (6).

There may be no general 'best solution'; it might depend on the kind of unethical conduct involved, the officer's own situation, and the prevailing conditions within a particular precinct, department, or even society. But whichever option is chosen, it will have its problems. It will have its problems because it brings into conflict two strong commitments: on the one hand, the professional (and personal) commitment to integrity; and on the other hand, the institutional or fraternal commitment to loyalty. Both of these may be felt as moral requirements.

Option (1) is of course no ethical 'solution'; it is a sellout, an expedient rather than a principled response. It is most likely to arise where a police officer becomes aware of the unethical conduct by being asked to participate in it. Here, for whatever reason, personal integrity, or at least a basic obligation, is sacrificed – perhaps to the bonds of fraternity, but more likely to weakness of will, to moral cowardice, or, sometimes, to plain greed. Unless rationalized – and cynicism sometimes makes this possible – this option's psychological cost in guilt feelings may be very high.[50]

Option (2) may be the easiest to manage psychologically. Here the officer attempts (with questionable success) to keep a certain 'moral distance' from the unethical conduct, without jeopardizing the bonds of loyalty. Of all such bonds, the police 'code of silence' is one of the strongest, and corrupt police officers have sometimes persisted openly in their corruption in the confidence that even their disapproving colleagues will not 'rat' on them.[51] It is not, however, a morally acceptable option. Turning a blind eye is culpable blindness.

Option (3) may be harder to pursue: In an individualistic culture, it could smack of busybodiness or sanctimoniousness and place considerable strain on fraternal bounds. Of all the advice we give to others, moral advice often seems to be the most intrusive and presumptuous, the least wanted. Unless the intervention is morally effective, trust may be lost, and the officer may find himself/herself suspect and isolated. The ability of an officer to be 'morally effective' in this kind of situation may depend on skills, personality traits, and a preexisting relationship that few will possess.

Option (4) offers genuine distance, and probably will not be taken as betrayal. Of course, it may be costly to the officer if the transfer is unsatisfactory in other ways, and it may require that the officer lie about his or her reasons for seeking a transfer. However, this option may also be seen as cowardly, particularly if, as we presume, the transgressions of the other officer(s) are quite serious.

Option (5) may be a bit easier to accomplish psychologically, but it will usually be viewed as a betrayal, even though the complaint will be to another police officer. In police work, the prime loyalties are generally (albeit problematically) seen as horizontal, not vertical.[52] And the after-costs of perceived betrayal may be very great.[53]

But sometimes internal reporting may seem inadequate. Where systemic and serious corruption is involved, it may be very difficult to find any departmental responsiveness. And option (6) may be chosen. It is this option that generally constitutes 'whistleblowing', though some writers would also include options (5), (7), and (8) under that head.[54] Whistleblowing is often seen by fellow officers as an unforgivable breach of loyalty, even if it has its basis in the officer's sense of integrity.[55] This reaction, based on our deep-seated aversion to 'tattletales', is not confined to police work, but is found in almost any institution, both private and public.

The loyalty evident in option (8) looks admirable, since it is likely to be purchased at considerable personal cost (even though that cost might be said to be deserved). It is, nevertheless, arguable that a public responsibility is being passed over for what appears to be a blind, and misguided, loyalty.

On the other hand, if option (9) is taken, it will usually be argued that the whistleblowing lacks moral worth. Its roots will lie in the selfish desire to save one's skin rather than in any commitment to integrity. This may not be an argument for refusing to cooperate – an overriding public good may be accomplished; but such cooperation will not necessarily redound to the moral credit of the whistleblower.

Is whistleblowing justified, and if so, under what circumstances?

### Whistleblowing defined

Whistleblowers, as the metaphorical characterization suggests, draw public attention to wrongdoing by blowing a whistle. Attempts to define whistleblowing more formally usually generate problems. Compare, for example, Norman Bowie's account with that of Frederick Elliston. According to Norman Bowie:

> A whistle blower is an employee or officer of any institution, profit or nonprofit, private or public, who believes either that he/she has been ordered to perform some act[s] or he/she has obtained knowledge that the institution is engaged in activities which (a) are believed to cause unnecessary harm to third parties, (b) are in violation of human rights or (c) run counter to the defined purpose of the institution and who inform(s) the public of this fact.[56]

Elliston, on the other hand, writes that an act of whistleblowing occurs when:

1 an individual performs an action or series of actions intended to make information public;
2 the information is made a matter of public record;
3 the information is about possible or actual, nontrivial wrongdoing in an organization;
4 the individual who performs the action is a member or former member of the organization.[57]

There are several ways in which the two accounts differ. Elliston's appears to be the more embracing one. It includes former members of an organization as well as those currently employed by it. It allows that any 'nontrivial wrongdoing' may provide an occasion for whistleblowing. However, Bowie's account gives us a better sense of why whistleblowing is seen as morally ambiguous, for it adverts to the tension between organizational and public responsibility. Elliston's account leaves it unclear why the 'public' should be involved. Although it accommodates the reporting of conduct that lacks institutional connivance, its focus on 'going public' makes it unclear why wrongdoing that lacks connivance should be made 'public'.

In the context of policing, both accounts would probably be seen as too restrictive. Within police departments whistleblowing is often understood to involve any reporting outside the immediate circle of officers. Reporting to a high-ranking officer or to internal affairs is often treated as equivalent to whistleblowing in the more restrictive sense.[58] Nevertheless, there is a 'soft' moral basis for restricting whistleblowing to cases in which someone 'goes public'. For the most part, whistleblowing occurs when public interests are being compromised: There is then a public interest in a wider public knowing about and ensuring discontinuance of the activity in question.

Although the foregoing accounts provide a reasonably useful informal account of whistleblowing, there are several issues that remain unclarified. The grounds for whistleblowing remain unclear. Elliston's reference to 'nontrivial wrongdoing' cries out for greater specification; and Bowie's references to 'unnecessary harm to third parties' and to activities that 'run counter to the defined purposes of the institution' also lend themselves to seemingly endless extensions: It may be difficult to see why the *public* should have any interest in some of the violations that would fall under these categories. It is also unclear whether the relevant violations must be ongoing or imminent, or whether they might include past wrongs. In addition, it remains unclear what 'going public' involves – going outside the organization? going to an appropriate external (public?) authority? going to the media? But perhaps this vagueness is as it should be. Unless we propose to define 'whistleblowing' so narrowly that it necessarily refers to a justifiable activity, there is no strong reason to define it so that only those forms of justifiable going public will be included. Nevertheless, there is some reason for giving the practice enough structure to make it responsive to a reasonably unified justificatory argument. That we do when we see the major moral players to be organizational loyalty and the public interest.

### Occasions for whistleblowing

The term 'whistleblower' was coined about twenty-five years ago to provide a more neutral, if not actually positive, characterization of someone for whom there already existed a rich collection of derogatory terms – tattletale, whistler, snitch, rat, weasel, fink, squealer, sneak, and so on. It developed in response to a growing recognition that, on the one hand, the public has become increasingly vulnerable to the doings of large institutions and organizations and, on the other, that many of those institutions and organizations foster and demand a loyalty that can come into conflict with the public trust they seek to have and/or maintain.

Many organizations possess internal mechanisms for rectifying threats to the public interest, but some do not, and sometimes those that do have mechanisms that have become or have been rendered ineffective. A public-minded employee may believe that only if what is perceived to be a wrong within the organization is addressed from the outside will it be rectified. And so what is regarded within the organization as 'confidential' or 'restricted' will be disclosed to a person or persons outside. Such disclosure may have a very serious impact on the organization – on its profitability, its public standing, on the morale of its employees. The public interest that is served thereby may be minor compared to the disruption that is caused, and it may even turn out that what is perceived to be an unrectified wrong was not as it appeared to be. Furthermore, it may turn out the motivation of the whistleblower is suspect, reflective of a desire to 'get ahead' or 'pay back.'

And so it becomes important to establish conditions under which whistleblowing may constitute a justifiable activity. Norman Bowie suggests that whistleblowing may be morally justifiable if the following set of conditions can be satisfied:

1   It is done from the appropriate moral motive, namely, as provided in the definition of whistle blowing.
2   The whistle blower, except in special circumstances, has exhausted all internal channels for dissent before informing the public.
3   The whistle blower has made certain that his or her belief that inappropriate actions are ordered or have occurred is based on evidence that would persuade a reasonable person.
4   The whistle blower has acted after a careful analysis of the danger: (a) how serious is the moral violation, (b) how immediate is the moral violation, (c) is the moral violation one that can be specified?
5   The whistle blower's action is commensurate with one's responsibility for avoiding and/or exposing moral violations.
6   It has come chance of success.[59]

As can be seen from this fairly stringent set of conditions, organizational loyalty is here presumed to be a serious obligation, and the potentially detrimental impact of a public disclosure of wrongdoing is given full consideration. The first condition is designed to exclude revenge, personal advancement, and other self-interested reasons from the range of appropriate motivating considerations. Whistleblowing will be morally praiseworthy only if prompted by some other-regarding concern like the public interest. Although essential to the moral creditworthiness of whistleblowing, the reference to an appropriate motive may not figure quite as centrally in the development of whistleblowing policy. If the exposed threat is serious enough, protection against retaliation might be offered to whistleblowers *even though* their motives are suspect.

Condition 2 shows an awareness of the damage that whistleblowing may cause, and requires that other, less dramatic, alternative means of rectification be explored before the issue is taken to the public. It reflects the fact that the public interest is often best served if organizations possess their own mechanisms for ensuring that the public interest is secured. The damage that can be done by whistleblowing also informs the 'sincerity is not enough' Condition 3. There will, obviously, be disputes about whether a subjective or objective criterion of reasonableness should be adopted. Public policy may favor an objective criterion, though a moral assessment of particular acts may be more amenable to one that is subjective. We may at least regard a misguided act of whistleblowing as morally excusable if it was based on subjectively reasonable grounds. Condition 4 links with Condition 2 in that it focuses on the necessity of going public. If the organizational or personal damage will exceed the public good, or if the danger is not so imminent that it can be averted only by blowing a whistle, or if the supposed danger does not have sufficient specificity, then alternative means of rectification should be pursued or created. Condition 5 is intended to accommodate a situation in which there may be differential responsibilities for dealing with wrongdoing or violations of different kinds. Its role is essentially a subsidiary one; those with specific responsibilities for dealing with violations are likely to be better placed to make decisions about the relevant factual and normative issues. Clearly, however, such organizational differentiation may break down, and any member of the organization who becomes aware of some imminent grave threat to the public interest will be justified in taking appropriate action, including blowing the whistle. Condition 6 acknowledges the essentially consequentialist purposes of whistleblowing: serving the public interest. If blowing the whistle is unlikely to accomplish any significant change for the better, then it will lack any justificatory point. Condition 6 also places a burden on the whistleblower to 'go public' in a constructive and not merely retaliatory manner.

All of the foregoing considerations are relevant to police officers who become aware of various forms of corruption, misconduct, waste, and inefficiency within their departments. Not all such deviations will be serious enough or imminent enough to justify whistleblowing, and any act of whistleblowing – because it is indicative of a failure of the department to look after its own affairs – should be seen only as a last resort. Within most police departments, the 'code of silence' will probably be sufficiently powerful to cast aspersions on the motives of any who would dare to blow the whistle. Yet it should be remembered that *even if* an officer's motives in going public do not reflect creditably on him, it may not follow that the whistleblowing was unjustified. Those failures warrant exposure whatever the motives of those who make them known. Too often police have attempted to deflect attention from the failures of their departments by casting aspersions on the motives of those who have exposed systemic corruption and complicity in corruption.

### Anonymous and implicated whistleblowing

Whistleblowers have often paid a heavy price for their efforts.[60] They have been dismissed, demoted, discriminated against, ostracized, even assaulted. The organizations and institutions involved have often taken the view that that is as it should be. Whistleblowers have violated one of the central canons of organizational solidarity and confidentiality and, like civil disobedients, should be willing to accept the cost of their convictions.[61] What is more, exposing the whistleblower to the possibility of untoward consequences will provide a test of conviction and be a deterrent to self-interested exposures.

Yet, though we may wish to deter wrongly motivated and half-cocked or misguided whistleblowing, stories about the long-term consequences suffered by conscientious and public-spirited whistleblowers whose efforts to protect the public interest have often gone beyond the bounds of any moral duty they might have had make it inappropriate that the consequences be left to happenstance. Some protection should be offered. One option is to allow whistleblowers to hide under a cloak of anonymity. Another is to legislate to secure them against harassment, discrimination, and worse. The former option is often thought to play into the hands of unworthily motivated whistleblowers. But the latter option has often been ineffective. Harassment is often difficult to prove, and even if it can be proved, the whistleblower may have had to suffer considerably in the meantime. It is for that reason that some provisions for anonymity may be necessary. In general, it is probably better to encourage openness in complaint, so that those who are accused may, like those in court, be able to face their accusers. But just because the power and interests of those who have violated the public interest are often so great, disproportionate costs will be imposed on whistleblowers. Just as there are 'witness protection programs' to shield those who testify in court, so there should be similar provisions for protecting whistleblowers in cases where vengeful reprisals are likely to occur and be difficult to monitor.

One of the things that has often excited the retaliatory anger of those who have had the whistle blown against them has been the fact that the whistleblower has been motivated by self-serving ends. This has been particularly true in the case of implicated whistleblowers. They have been 'intercepted' in corrupt activities, and then been offered immunity or the opportunity to lighten their criminal burden in exchange for information that will assist in the conviction of others. It is understandable that others should feel aggrieved and betrayed by such conduct. Even if those involved cannot complain about their penalization, they might reasonably think that the whistleblower has been traitorous and should not be rewarded. In some cases that may be so – the trade-offs are themselves unseemly. But even where the trade-offs seem proportionate, it needs to be remembered that, even though little or no moral credit attaches to the person who blew the whistle, it may have been a good thing that the whistle was blown.[62]

*From John Kleinig*, The Ethics of Policing *(New York: Cambridge University Press), 1996, pp 163–181 and 308–12.*

## Notes

1  This remark was relayed to me by Mark H. Moore.
2  Nicholas Ross, *The Policeman's Bible: Or the Art of Taking a Bribe* (Chicago: Henry Regnery, 1976), p. 4.
3  Herman Goldstein, *Policing a Free Society* (Cambridge, MA: Ballinger, 1977), p. 191.
4  Peter Maas, *Serpico* (New York: Viking Press, 1973), p. 169.
5  It may not be the inducements that are corrupting, but the hypocrisy involved. Gratuities given to increase the police presence are 'advertised' as gestures of appreciation for the civic services provided by police and other uniformed personnel.
6  For a tongue-in-cheek discussion of corruption in this context, see Ross, *The Policeman's Bible*, ch. 3.
7  M. McMullan, 'A Theory of Corruption,' *Sociological Review* 9 (1961), pp. 183–4.
8  Howard Cohen and Michael Feldberg, *Ethics for Law Enforcement Officers* (Boston: Wasserman Associates, 1983), p. 31, quoted in Feldberg, 'Gratuities, Corruption, and the Democratic Ethos of Policing: The Case of the Free Cup of Coffee,' in Frederick A. Elliston and Michael Feldberg (eds), *Moral Issues in Police Work* (Totowa, NJ: Rowman and Allanheld, 1985), pp. 267–8.
9  Goldstein, *Policing in a Free Society*, p. 188.
10  A police chief who, against his better judgment, redeploys personnel to satisfy the political priorities of a mayor who makes it clear that the department's budget will thereby be enhanced does not act corruptly, though his behavior is in certain respects similar to that of the officer who massages his court testimony to secure a conviction. The situation is complicated, however, by the fact that the mayor, as an elected official, may have certain prerogatives so far as the determination of the 'public interest' is concerned.
11  Herman Goldstein, for example, provides the following listing:

   (1) Failing to arrest and prosecute those the officer knows have violated the law. Examples are motorists parked overtime or illegally; traffic violators, including drunk drivers;

gamblers, prostitutes, narcotics users, homosexuals; violators of minor regulatory ordinances, such as those regulating business hours; violators of the conditions of a license administered by the police agency; juvenile offenders; and more serious offenders, such as burglars and persons engaged in organized crime. (2) Agreeing to drop an investigation prematurely by not pursuing leads which would produce evidence supporting a criminal charge. (3) Agreeing not to inspect locations or premises where violations are known to occur and where an officer's presence might curtail the illegal activity – such as taverns in which prostitution or gambling flourishes and probably contributes to the volume of business. (4) Refraining from making arrests on licensed premises where an arrest results in license review that could lead to revocation. This includes taverns, night clubs, dance halls, and motion picture theaters. (5) Reducing the seriousness of a charge against an offender. (6) Agreeing to alter testimony at trial or to provide less than the full amount of evidence available. (7) Providing more police protection or presence than is required by standard operating procedures. Examples are: more frequent and intensive checks of the security of private premises; more frequent presence in a store or other commercial establishment, such as a hotel, club, or restaurant where the officer's presence benefits the owner by keeping out 'undesirables'; observation of parked cars while owners attend a social gathering or meeting in an area where cars are commonly stolen or damaged; and escorting businessmen making bank deposits. (8) Influencing departmental recommendations regarding the granting of licenses, for example, by recommending for or against continuance of a liquor or amusement license by either giving or suppressing derogatory information. (9) Arranging access to confidential departmental records or agreeing to alter such records. (10) Referring individuals caught in a new and stressful situation to persons who can assist them and who stand to profit from the referral. Police can get paid for making referrals to bondsmen or defense attorneys; placing accident victims in contact with physicians or attorneys specializing in the filing of personal injury claims; arranging for delivery of bodies to a funeral home; and selecting the ambulance or tow truck summoned to the scene of an accident or an illegally parked car. (11) Appropriating for personal use or disposal items of value acquired on the job, such as jewelry and goods from the scene of a burglary; narcotics confiscated from users or peddlers; funds used in gambling; items found at the scene of a fire; private property of a drunk or a deceased person; and confiscated weapons (Goldstein, *Policing in a Free Society*, pp. 194–5).

Apart from being somewhat dated, this list provides only a small window into the variety of ways in which police may be corrupted. As Goldstein comments: 'One of the amazing things about police graft is the endless variety of schemes that come to light. Opportunities for personal profit in a corrupt agency seem to be limited only by the imagination and aggressiveness of those intent on realizing private gain' (p. 194).

12  See, for example, Thomas Barker and Julian B. Roebuck, *An Empirical Typology of Police Corruption* (Springfield, IL: Thomas, 1974); Julian B. Roebuck and Thomas Barker, 'A Typology of Police Corruption,' *Social Problems* 21, 3 (1974), pp. 423–37; Thomas Barker, 'Social Definitions of Police Corruption: The Case of South City,' *Criminal Justice Review* 2, 2, (177), pp. 101–10; Tom Barker and Robert O. Wells, 'Police Administrators' Attitudes toward the Definition and Control of Police Deviance,' *FBI Law Enforcement Bulletin* 51, 3 (March, 1982), pp. 8–16; T. Barker and D.L. Carter, *Police Deviance* (Cincinnati, OH: Anderson Publishing Co., 1986).

13  The Knapp Commission Report referred to an almost equivalent distinction between 'grass-eaters' and 'meat-eaters', and noted: 'One relatively strong impetus encouraging grass-eaters to continue to accept relatively petty graft is, ironically, their feeling of loyalty to their fellow officers. Accepting payoff money is one way for an officer to prove that he is one of the boys and that he can be trusted' (New York City Commission to Investigate Allegations of Police Corruption and the City's Anti-Corruption Procedures, *Commission Report* [Whitman Knapp, Chairman], [New York: Bar Press, 1972], p. 65). Such distinctions possess considerable normative power. Compare the distinction more generally made between 'souveniring' and 'stealing'.

14  Roebuck and Barker, 'A Typology of Police Corruption,' p. 435.

15  *Ibid.*, p. 428.

16  *Ibid.*, p. 429. I understand that the bondsmen scam has been cleaned up since their article was written.

17  *Ibid.*

18  *Ibid.*, p. 430.

19  *Ibid.*, p. 431.

20  *Ibid.*, p. 432.

21   *Ibid*. See also Maas, *Serpico*.
22   See Michael Banton, *The Policeman in the Community* (New York: Basic, 1964), p. 195. However, as one former law enforcement officer drily commented: 'It's nice you did it fellows, but it is nothing to shout about' (Jack E. Whitehouse, 'Thou halt Not Be a Moocher' [typescript, n.d.], p. 5).
23   Roebuck and Barker, 'A Typology of Police Corruption,' p. 434.
24   Quoted in Feldberg, 'Gratuities, Corruption, and the Democratic Ethos of Policing,' p. 267. Cf . Patrick V. Murphy: 'Except for your paycheck, there's no such thing as a clean buck', quoted in 'Police Aides Told to Rid Commands of All Dishonesty,' *New York Times*, 29 October 1970, p. A1.
25   In police argot, a 'good' restaurant is not one that is expensive or provides good-quality food, but one that offers good discounts or free meals.
26   My talk here of 'the truth' assumes that I am focusing on a fairly clearly defined phenomenon. And to some extent I am. However, the actual practices are much more varied than those I will focus on. My discussion will not consider discounts that might be available to police via their membership in a police union. These seem to me to have a rather different character from that of free cups of coffee. For one thing, such discounts are probably available to, and negotiated by, a number of other unions, and are seen as inducements to buy rather than – say – corrupt inducements to give favored treatment.
27   For a discussion of the moral etiquette of gratitude, and why saying 'thank you' may not be enough, see Terrance McConnell, *Gratitude* (Philadelphia: Temple University Press, 1993).
28   In Australia, it is McDonald's policy to offer police officers and others in uniform half-price hamburgers. Ostensibly this is a public-spirited gesture intended to show appreciation for the good work that police and others do. More realistically, it is an investment in police presence.
29   This argument is developed in detail in Richard R.E. Kania, 'Should we Tell the Police to Say "Yes" to Gratuities?' *Criminal Justice Ethics* 7, 2 (Summer/ Fall 1988), pp. 37–49.
30   Consider the contempt for management that followed reassignment of a police officer who accepted a double scoop of ice cream for the price of one. What angered many police officers was not simply the lack of understanding shown and the trivial character of the breach, but the fact that after the officer was reported, the ice cream shop was staked out no fewer than eighteen times over the next several months. See Bill Reel, 'Corruption: Here's the Scoop,' *Daily News* (21 February 1988), p. 49; 'Never on Sundae,' *Law Enforcement News* 14, 268 (15 April 1988), p. 4.
31   Quoted in Samuel Smiles, *Life and Labour; or Characteristics of Men of Industry, Culture & Genius* (London: John Murray, 1887), p. 9.
32   Cf. the 'weaker brother' argument used in some religious contexts: I Cor. 8.
33   See Feldberg, 'Gratuities, Corruption, and the Democratic Ethos of Policing'.
34   There is, in fact more than one kind of argument here. Trudy Govier, who rejects most slippery slope reasoning, distinguishes what she calls 'the fallacy of slippery assimilation' (Where do you draw the line?) from 'the fallacy of slippery precedent' (How do you stop?). See *A Practical Study of Argument*, 3rd ed. (Belmont, CA: Wadsworth, 1992), pp. 296–301. For a comprehensive review of slippery slope arguments, see Douglas N. Walton, *Slippery Slope Arguments* (Oxford: Oxford University Press [Clarendon Press], 1992).
35   James Rachels, *The End of Life* (New York: Oxford University Press, 1985), pp. 172–80.
36   The distinction is made, however, in Wibren van der Burg, 'The Slippery Slope Argument,' *Ethics* 102, 1 (October 1991), pp. 44–5.
37   There are two ways of construing the 'logical' connection. One is to see the various practices on the slope connected by virtue of being wrong *for the same reason*. The other is to see them connected by virtue of their wrongness (though not necessarily wrong for the same reason). In the former case, the person, having accepted a particular maxim by virtue of engaging in one practice, is thereby committed to other practices in which the same maxim is operative. In the latter case, the person, having compromised his/her integrity in one instance, now no longer has an integrity to be compromised. This way of construing the connection is something of an amalgam of the logical and psychological versions.
38   I am assuming that z would be horrible. In the case of police corruption that may not be contentious. But we need to remember that what one person sees as 'horrific' another may see as desirable. Cf. the slippery slope argument that starts with abortion and finishes up with euthanasia and infanticide. Not everyone would see those as unacceptable consequences. Cf. also the argument used twenty-five years ago that if motorcyclists were forced to wear safety helmets the time would come when the rest of us would be forced to wear seat belts! (*American Motorcycle Association* v. *Davids*, 158 NW 2d 72 [1968]).
39   See also Bernard Williams, 'Which Slopes are Slippery?' in Michael Lockwood (ed.), *Moral Dilemmas in Modern Medicine* (New York: Oxford University Press, 1985), pp. 126–7.
40   Lawrence Sherman, 'Becoming Bent: Moral Careers of Corrupt Policemen,' in Elliston and Feldberg (eds), *Moral Issues in Police Work*, p. 259.

41   *Ibid.*
42   For example, Robert Leuci, of *Prince of the City* fame, has given two different accounts of his decline, each of which focuses on a slippery slope. See Myron Glazer, 'Ten Whistleblowers and how they Fared,' *Hastings Center Report* 13, 6 (December 1983), p. 33; Robert Leuci, 'The Process of Erosion,' in Dennis Jay Kenney (ed.), *Police and Policing: Contemporary Issues* (New York: Praeger, 1989), pp. 181–7.
43   Feldberg, 'Gratuities, Corruption, and the Democratic Ethos of Policing,' p. 268.
44   *Ibid.*, pp. 267–8.
45   *Ibid.*, p. 274.
46   Sherman himself recognizes this in 'Becoming Bent,' pp. 259–60.
47   Apparently the terms were coined – or at least made public – by the NYPD's Assistant Chief Inspector, Sydney Cooper, during the Knapp Commission hearings. See *The Knapp Commission Report on Police Corruption* (New York: George Braziller, 1972), p. 4.
48   A very similar position is developed in Howard Cohen, 'Exploiting Police Authority,' *Criminal Justice Ethics* 5, 2 (Summer/Fall 1986), pp. 23–31; and also David Hansen, *Police Ethics* (Springfield, IL: Thomas, 1973), chs. 1, 3.
49   And it may also turn police into moochers. The moocher is unseemly rather than corrupt. See Whitehouse, 'Thou Shalt not be a Moocher'.
50   See Michael Daley, 'The Crack in the Shield: The Fall of the Seven-Seven,' *New York* (8 December 1986), pp. 50–9.
51   This, no doubt, is one of the reasons for internal investigative mechanisms such as the NYPD 'field associates' program. See Kevin Krajick, 'Police *vs* Police,' *Police Magazine*, May 1980, pp. 7–20; Vincent Henry, 'Lifting the "Blue Curtain": Some Controversial Strategies to Control Police Corruption,' *National Police Research Unit Review* 6 (1990), pp. 48–55; and Gary T. Marx, 'When the Guards Guard Themselves: Undercover Tactics Turned Inward,' *Policing and Society* 2 (April 1992), pp. 158–72.
52   Cf. Carsten Stroud:

> In every masculine community there are three trials by which each male member will be judged and disposition carried out on his soul, and at none of these trials will a single word be spoken in open court ... [T]he third test is a trial of loyalty. Can this man be loyal, and if so, to whom is his loyalty given? If it's given to the Commissioner, the borough bosses, and the administration, then he fails. If it's placed on the anvil, between the Book and the Street, if he can step back and leave it there, at the mercy of the caprices of cop fate, knowing that there is no way to do a cop's job in the way the city truly calls for it to be done without placing his reputation and career and sometimes his freedom at risk – if he can leave his loyalty on that anvil, then he passes *(Close Pursuit: A Week in the Life of an NYPD Homicide* Cop [New York: Bantam, 1987, p.111).

The primarily horizontal character of police loyalty helps to explain the vehement dislike of internal investigators. Stroud's cop 'hero' reacts: 'Field Associate! What a name! Spy, snitch, stoolie, fink, rat, weasel – they were closer to the mark' (p. 117). The complexities of loyalty in police work are alluded to, but not grappled with in David A. Hansen's seminal *Police Ethics:*

> Loyalty is . . . a coin with more than one side. An officer must be loyal to his calling and to his department. Administrative loyalty comes into play here and unfortunately is the area in which loyalty sometimes dies. Loyalty flows upward and downward. When one flow ceases, so does the other. The chief and the department must be loyal to the officer, his desires, and his needs, and the officer needs to be loyal upward in turn. 'Lateral loyalty' is sometimes a problem. The loyalty of the officer to his department is often strained as a result of competition between patrol and detective divisions, for example. This competition, when carried to extremes, is insidious. Of course the officer 'should be loyal to his primary unit, as with patrol, for example. Misplaced loyalty to the unit, however, can result in noncooperation, disloyalty *vis-à-vis* the department as an entity, or *vis-à-vis* some of the other components and divisions of the department (p. 73).

For more detailed studies of the vertical–horizontal loyalty problem, see Maurice Punch, 'Officers and Men: Occupational Culture, Inter-Rank Antagonism, and the Investigation of Corruption', and Elizabeth Reuss-Ianni and Francis A.J. Ianni, 'Street Cops and Management Cops: The Two Cultures of Policing,' both in Maurice Punch (ed.), *Control in the Police Organization* (Cambridge, MA: MIT Press, 1983), pp. 227–50, 251–74.
53   See Maas, *Serpico;* Myron Glazer, 'Ten Whistleblowers and how they Fared,' pp. 33–41.
54   This seems to be the case with Thomas Wren in 'Whistle-Blowing and Loyalty to One's Friends,' in William C. Heffernan and Timothy Stroup (eds), *Police Ethics: Hard Choices in Law*

*Enforcement* (New York: John Jay Press, 1985), pp. 25–43. Where, as in police work, the primary loyalty tends to be fraternal rather than institutional, reporting unethical activity to superiors may come to have many of the same overtones as 'going public'.

55   See Peter Maas, *Serpico*. Although Frank Serpico is now admired by many, for a long time there was thought to be a police 'contract' on him, and Serpico spent some years in Switzerland. As we shall later see, defenders of 'loyalty' frequently cast doubt on the genuineness of the 'integrity' of whistleblowers. It is sometimes believed that only if option (7) is followed can the whistleblower's motives be trusted.

56   Norman Bowie, *Business Ethics* (Englewood Cliffs, NJ: Prentice-Hall, 1982), p. 142.

57   Frederick Elliston, John Keenan, Paula Lockhart and Jane van Schaick, *Whistleblowing Research: Methodological and Moral Issues* (New York: Praeger, 1985), p. 15.

58   See Wren, 'Whistleblowing and Loyalty to one's Friend'.

59   Bowie, *Business Ethics*, p. 143.

60   See Myron P. Glazer and Penina M. Glazer, *The Whistleblowers: Exposing Corruption in Government and Industry* (New York: Basic, 1989).

61   See further, Frederick Elliston, 'Civil Disobedience and Whistleblowing: A Comparative Appraisal of Two Forms of Dissent,' *Journal of Business Ethics* 1 (Spring 1982), pp. 23–8.

62   As part of the social shoring up that occurs after the whistle is blown, rumors about the motives of the whistleblower will almost inevitably begin to circulate. It is as though one could blow the whistle only for self-serving ends.

# 36. Police accountability revisited

*Geoffrey Marshall*

Fifteen years after the Report of the Royal Commission on the Police seems an opportune occasion to review one of the central issues about the police role debated with some fervour between 1959 and 1964 and as yet unresolved. In what way and to whom should the police be accountable for their activities? The machinery of law enforcement, it is clear, presents special and confusing problems for any theory of democratic accountability. If we divide the functions of government into legislative, executive and judicial, how should we classify the police and especially the prosecutorial function. If it is an executive function those who exercise it ought in principle to be answerable to some elected body. But elected bodies are political bodies and our instincts suggest that partisan influences should be kept at a distance from law enforcement and that the decisions involved should be in some sense taken impartially. Could the function then be considered a judicial one? The judicial function certainly provides a model for impartial decision-making, since we do not suppose that judges should be answerable to elected representatives. But prosecuting is plainly not judicial function and calling it a 'quasi-judicial function' is unhelpful since 'quasi' is simply a label for indecision. (When lawyers and administrators use the word 'quasi' it simply means 'not exactly' or 'after a fashion'.) So perhaps we are faced here with a function that is *sui generis*, or a fourth element in terms of the traditional political scientist's categorisation of governmental functions – one that calls both for a measure of accountability and a measure of independence. The dilemma was aptly described in the Hunt Report on the Police Northern Ireland in 1969.[1] The Police Commissioner, it was said, 'should not be subjected to political pressures' but on the other hand there 'should be some body representative of the community as a whole to which he can be accountable'. The problem, it may be noted, is a general one that is not confined to any particular system of police organisation. It arises as between a national police force and a national legislature and executive as much as it raises an issue for a local or regional body with its police committee on the one hand and its police force on the other. The question can be posed, moreover, both as a legal question and as an issue of constitutional and administrative morality.

## The controversy of 1959–64

Surprisingly enough, no concerted debate on police accountability seems to have arisen before the late 1950s, although in the latter years of the nineteenth century control over police operations in London had raised the issue of the Metropolitan Commissioner's responsibility to the Home Secretary (as police authority for the metropolitan force). Outside London disagreements between county and borough police authorities and their chief officers had been rare. In 1959, however, a brief contest of wills in Nottingham brought to the surface two contrasting views about the independence of chief police officers *vis-à-vis* the county and borough police authorities. The issue in Nottingham turned upon a refusal by the Chief Constable to report to the Watch Committee on certain inquiries being made into the activities of council members and officers. The Town Clerk and Watch Committee considered the inquiries to have manifested a lack of impartiality on the Chief Constable's part and in view of his refusal to comply with their instructions suspended him from duty in exercise of their powers under the Municipal Corporations Act of 1882 – legislation which authorized watch committees to suspend or dismiss any constable whom they considered negligent or otherwise unfit for his duty. At this point the Home Secretary intervened and informed the Watch Committee that he did not consider the suspension justified and that in enforcing the criminal law a chief officer of police should not be subject to control or interference by the police authority. This was an explicit assertion by the Home Office of the view that a chief constable, like any constable, held an independent position as an officer of the Crown. The point had been successfully put by an earlier Home Secretary, Sir John Anderson. 'The policeman', he wrote, 'is nobody's servant ... he executes a public office under the Law and it is the Law ... which is the policeman's master.'[2] Legal support for this view was drawn from the absence of any master and servant relationship between police officers and police authorities. In 1930 in *Fisher* v. *Oldham Corporation*[3] it had been held that the Watch Committee could not be made liable for the wrongful actions of constables in carrying out their law enforcement duties as (to use the words of Mr Justice McCardie) 'servants of the state' and 'officers of the Crown or central power'.

The implications of this thesis did not commend themselves to the local authority associations, and when the Willink Commission began taking evidence in 1961 the Municipal Corporations Association and a number of other witnesses argued strongly that the supervisory powers of watch committees were not as narrow as had been implied; that the Oldham and Nottingham cases were in many ways special cases, and that they could not be used as foundations for a general theory of police independence in all matters of law enforcement. In 1960 the doubts of many who were involved in local government were voiced by the editor of *Public Administration*, Norman Chester.[4] Most people who spoke of law enforcement, he wrote, were thinking of particular cases, and no councillor or watch committee would claim to interfere in individual cases relating to the charging of offenders or would seek to instruct a chief constable not to enforce certain branches of the law; but since they had a duty to ensure that their area was efficiently policed might they not have a general concern with seeing that the law was adequately and properly enforced? Suppose that a chief constable were making no attempt to put down widespread public disorder, or the police were reacting in an over-violent way to political demonstrations, or were ignoring traffic offences, would the watch committee be helpless and could they not in such circumstances properly issue instructions to secure the proper enforcement of the law? Since the law itself gave no precise guidance as to general policies of enforcement what could it mean to say that the chief constable was 'answerable to the law alone'? If a chief constable were entirely independent, in what sense could police be said to be a local authority function?[5]

One other sceptic who gave evidence to the Commission was Professor E.C.S. Wade, editor of Dicey's *Law of the Constitution* and Downing Professor of the Laws of England at Cambridge University. Professor Wade suggested that the prosecuting discretion of a chief constable was not peculiar to him 'since anyone can normally start a prosecution on his own initiative and therefore there is nothing exceptional in a local police authority requiring the police to carry out this duty since each has an equal responsibility for it'.[6] The police authority, he added, could not be absolved from responsibility for enforcement of the law. The maintenance of public order was an executive function not requiring the freedom from interference attaching to judicial functions. In relation to some questions of law enforcement policy (such, conceivably, as the excessive use of force in maintaining order) it would not be *ultra vires* for the watch committee to issue instructions to the chief constable.

These views were not accepted by the police or by the Government in so far as they thought about the issue. The Royal Commission certainly thought about it, but what exactly their thoughts were never became clear. Two different questions arose and neither was clearly resolved by the Commission. First, what did statute and common law have to say, if anything, about the legal relationships of police and police authorities? Did it establish the independence of chief officers in all matters of law enforcement and the impropriety of all instructions even on matters of general policy? Secondly, what, irrespective of the legal position, ought sound administrative practice or constitutional morality to suggest as a proper relationship between police and an elected supervisory authority? Two further questions now need to be put. One is whether the 1964 police legislation that followed the Royal Commission, or any subsequent development, has changed the law. The other is whether anything has happened since 1964 that might affect views about sound or prudent administrative practice. In 1965 in a work entitled *Police and Government* 'the present writer, perhaps rashly, asserted that both the legal and political arguments for police independence were historically unsound and had been formulated in an exaggerated way. The conclusions that seemed appropriate at that time were set out as follows:

1    The legal independence of constables implies that supervisory bodies could not issue instructions that would amount to interferences with the course of justice or that would involve a chief officer who obeyed them in any breach of a duty clearly imposed upon him by statute or common law. An order to release an arrested felon (an example given in *Fisher* v. *Oldham*) or partisan interference in routine prosecution matters would obviously constitute illegal interference.

2    In matters of prosecution policy, whilst any intervention by a police committee would as a matter of strong convention and sound administrative practice normally be by way of advice, question or exhortation, no legal principle ruled out the possibility of an instruction framed in general terms (the position being in principle the same in the provinces as in the metropolitan relationship between the Home Secretary and the Metropolitan Police).

3    In matters other than prosecution, involving the disposition of police forces and law enforcement generally, an effective intervention by way of police authority directions was not unlawful and might in some cases be desirable if there were to be effective accountability for the exercise of executive discretion by the police.

But a question which cannot now be avoided is whether in 1977 all or any of these conclusions can still stand in the light of developments in the past decade. It may be advisable to approach the issue first from the standpoint of legal development and secondly from the standpoint of constitutional and administrative morality.

## The independence of constables: the legal issue

The argument about the misreading of *Fisher*'s case in assessing the degree of independence enjoyed by chief officers in the exercise of their constabulary functions need not be recapitulated in detail.[7] It amounted to saying that the thesis propounded in recent years on the basis of civil liability cases in England and in Commonwealth jurisdictions[8] was ill-founded and novel. The doctrine of constabulary independence in all law-enforcement matters was not, in fact, a well-established constitutional principle, but, on the contrary, one of which it is difficult to find any trace at all in the nineteenth and early twentieth centuries either in the metropolis or in the provinces. The metropolitan relationship is particularly significant since it has figured prominently in the only recent case about the exercise of police discretion, *R. v. Metropolitan Police Commissioner ex parte Blackburn.*[9] Though the exact chronology is unclear there had obviously been a change in the Home Office view of the Secretary of State's powers in relation to operational matters arising in the metropolitan area. In the nineteenth century there was never any doubt about the Home Secretary's right to issue instructions in matters of law enforcement. Home Secretaries such as Sir William Harcourt and Henry Matthews insisted upon and gave effect to the doctrine that it was for the Secretary of State to decide how far he should go in exercising his responsibility for what Matthews called the 'general policy of the police in the discharge of their duty'.[10] Many pertinent examples of intervention in police operations could be given. In 1880 the Home Secretary directed that no action should be taken to suppress advertisements for Irish lotteries. In 1881 Harcourt said that he had instructed that *agents provocateurs* were not to be used without his authority and in 1888 he insisted that whether public meetings were to be allowed or prohibited in the metropolis was 'a question of policy for the Home

Secretary to decide'. In 1913 the Home Office told the Commissioner that proceedings were not to be instituted against whist drives except where there was evidence of serious gambling or profiteering.[11] In fact it could reasonably be concluded that 'the authority of the Home Secretary over the Metropolitan Police was regarded as unlimited, subject of course to the normal principle that public officers cannot be ordered to act unlawfully'.[12] No one supposed that any conflict arose between lawful instructions relating to law enforcement or prosecution policy and the original independent common law status of constables in the metropolis.

One fact is perhaps worth noting about the examples of intervention here cited, namely that they involved for the most part either public order, or cases where the law was unclear or the morality of its enforcement a matter of dispute. Such cases are of course precisely those where advocates of greater accountability might want to argue that the exercise of discretion should be subject to challenge through some mechanism of accountability. By the 1930s, however, the Home Office seems to have begun to disclaim responsibility. Conceivably, they had by then breathed in the spirit of *Fisher* v. *Oldham*. Possibly also they were motivated by a desire to ward off Parliamentary questions directed to the Home Secretary. When the Home Office came to give evidence to the Willink Commission in 1960 they went as far as to say that the Home Secretary 'could not be questioned ... about the discharge by individual police officers of the duties of law enforcement'. Any glance at the index to *Hansard* would reveal that there is something amiss with this statement. In fact the 1929 and 1963 Royal Commissions on Police were both set up as the result of persistent parliamentary questioning of Home Secretaries about the discharge by individual police officers of their duties of law enforcement,[13] as also were the special inquiries into actions undertaken by the Thurso Police in 1959,[14] the Sheffield Police in 1963[15] and the Challenor case in the Metropolitan force in 1965.[16]

Outside the metropolitan area a parallel development took place. In the nineteenth century, borough watch committees frequently treated themselves as being competent to issue general instructions on matters of policing. A good example is the action of the Liverpool Watch Committee in 1890 which issued orders to the Head Constable, Sir William Nott-Bower, 'to proceed against all brothels at present known to the police without any undue delay and such proceedings shall be by way of prosecution'. Sir William saw nothing improper in this. In a public speech he remarked that the police 'were not responsible for Policy or for Results. Policy was made for them, not by them'. The police, he added, 'should be judged by the simple test of whether they carried out their duties in a fair and honest manner in accordance with the policy laid down for them by superior authority, which authority alone must take the responsibility both for it and for its results'.[17] Can it have been *Fisher*'s case alone that brought about a change of heart on the part of the police and the Home Office (though not on the part of the local authority associations)? All that *Fisher*'s case essentially decided was that no action in tort for a constable's wrongful acts would lie against anybody but him. Since no vicarious liability could be fixed upon those who appointed him he could not be in a master–servant relationship for civil liability purposes. Since there was almost a complete absence of any decided cases directly bearing on the constitutional status of the police, it may have been natural enough for the decision in *Fisher*'s case (to the effect that the police were not 'servants' for purposes of vicarious liability) to be picked out by textbook writers and others and given a wider significance than it deserved.

Since 1964 the police have in effect become for civil liability purposes 'servants' beyond a doubt since responsibility for their wrongful acts is now borne by the Chief Constable. S.48 of the 1964 Police Act provides that the chief officer of police for any police area

> shall be liable in respect of torts committed by constables under his direction and control in the performance or purported performance of their functions in like manner as a master is liable in respect of torts committed by his servants in the course of their employment.

The imposition of this 'servitude' upon constables as an incident of the law of tort is, however, as much or as little relevant to the constitutional status of constables as was its denial in *Fisher*'s case. If *Fisher*'s case had really been the foundation of the constable's autonomy then the Act of 1964 must have enslaved him again. In fact, neither the one nor the other helps to delimit the scope of the lawful orders or the degree of constitutional subordination to which constables are subject. It is clear, of course, that constables cannot be given orders to do what it would be unlawful for anyone to do or what would amount to an obstruction of the course of justice if done by them. A police constable is a person who, although not a Crown servant, holds an office under Her Majesty.[18] The oath that he takes on assuming the office is to serve in the office of constable without favour or affection, to cause the peace to be kept and to discharge all his duties according to law. What acts he may lawfully be required to do depends upon the statutes and regulations that govern police organization and upon the powers conferred on police authorities and chief constables.

### Has the law changed?

Could it be argued that any change in the constitutional position was effected by the 1964 Police Act? The answer would seem to be that it left the law in this respect unchanged. The legislation was based, with some exceptions, on the recommendations of the Willink Commission. The Commission's report, though not a model of clarity, certainly suggests that they did not accept all the implications drawn by the Home Office and the police from the *Fisher* case. Indeed one section of the report is even given the title 'Subordination of Chief Constables to Democratic Supervision'. The supervision the Commission had in mind was related to what they called 'police policies in matters affecting the public interest' – the regulation for example of traffic, political demonstrations, strikes, processions and public order generally. The Commission argued that such policies, though involving the enforcement of the law, 'do not require the immunity from external influences that is generally thought necessary in regard to the enforcement of the law in particular cases'.[19] Various provisions were made in the 1964 Act to increase accountability to local police authorities and to the Home Secretary. Both were given formal powers to request reports from Chief Constables, but there was no obvious alteration in the police authorities' direct powers in the field of law enforcement as they existed before the Act. The Act provided that police forces should be under the direction and control of the chief officer, but since chief constables had always exercised the immediate operational direction and control of their forces these words do not seem intended to alter the pre-existing situation. It is noticeable that nothing was enacted directly about the *exclusive* control of the chief constable or the nature of his powers *vis-à-vis* the police authority. What really happened was that the Government avoided this direct issue, in view of the inherent difficulty of framing any precise prescription, and relied upon the Home Secretary's powers to act as a potential buffer and arbitrator between police authorities and chief constables.

Perhaps the most significant legal development touching on to the exercise of police powers since 1964 has been the decision of the Court of Appeal in *Ex parte Blackburn*.[20] The questions at issue here were whether the courts could control the exercise of police discretion in prosecuting and whether the police owed a duty to the public to enforce the law. Surprisingly, an affirmative answer was given to both questions. It was held that a policy instruction by the Metropolitan Police Commissioner not to enforce the provisions of the Betting and Gaming legislation could, had it not been withdrawn, have been controlled by the issue of *mandamus*. It was not asserted that a breach of the duty to enforce the law could be inferred from the mere existence of a policy of non-prosecution (as for example when prosecutions were not brought in relation to attempted suicide or juvenile sexual offences).[21] But some policies, it was suggested, would be improper (for example an instruction not to prosecute any person for stealing goods worth less than £100). In the course of the decision, however, both Lord Denning and Lord Justice Salmon made remarks about the status of the Metropolitan Police Commissioner *vis-à-vis* the Metropolitan Police authority, suggesting amongst other things that he was not subject to the orders of the Home Secretary. 'No minister of the Crown,' Lord Denning remarked, 'can tell him that he must or must not keep observation on this place or that; or that he must or must not prosecute this man or that one, nor can any police authority tell him so.' Like every Chief Constable, 'he is not the servant of anyone save of the law itself. The responsibility for law enforcement lies on him. He is answerable to the law and to the law alone'.[22]

Can any weight be placed on these remarks? Both Salmon LJ and Lord Denning said clearly that it would be impermissible for the Secretary of State to issue any order to the police in respect of law enforcement.[23] But it was by no means clear on what this view was based except the insistence on the responsibility of the Commissioner to the law. This runs together questions about interferences in individual prosecution matters and questions about law enforcement policies and the deployment of forces generally. It is fairly plain that these categorical suggestions were merely repetitions of the orthodox and arguably mistaken inferences from *Fisher*'s case. In any event the points were not in issue. It was unnecessary to decide what the relations of the Home Secretary and the Commissioner were or what the relations of chief constables to police authorities were. The question for decision was simply how far the admitted obligation to enforce the law was subject to judicial control. That in a proper case it would be was the *ratio decidendi* of the decision and it seems justifiable to treat the tangential views of Lord Denning and Lord Justice Salmon on the powers of police authorities and the Secretary of State as being *obiter*.

One other episode since 1964 deserves mention since it reinforces the traditional thesis that the initiation of prosecutions in England is in some sense an act of the private citizen. In 1974 a police constable (P.C. Joy) successfully pursued a private prosecution of a Member of Parliament which his superior officers were unwilling to authorize and in consequence of which it was reported that he might be made subject to disciplinary action. No action was taken, but it need not be the case that such action would necessarily have been legally improper. No one could have prevented Mr Joy as a private person from starting his prosecution. But it does not follow from that that his freedom so to act as a member of a disciplined force subject to a statutory scheme of organization and regulation could not properly be curtailed by his superiors under powers given in the police legislation. So although Joy's case perhaps illustrates the wisdom of the English (as against the American and Scottish) system in not permitting the state to monopolize the prosecution function, it adds nothing to the argument about the relative powers of constables and police authorities, especially in law-enforcement matters other than prosecution.

It seems fair to conclude that neither the 1964 Act nor any subsequent development has changed the law on this subject or given the police any legal immunity from control which they did not enjoy before 1964. If that is so the legal argument for autonomy so frequently based upon *Fisher*'s case remains as defective and unreliable as it always was. Perhaps, however, that is not the most significant feature of the situation that now faces us.

## Accountability and independence in practice

Frequently there is in the British system a difference between the law and the constitution. The law may say one thing, but the political and moral rules followed in practice may differ. Even if it is the case that the issuing of instructions by police committees in matters affecting law enforcement is not un-lawful we still need to ask whether it would be a defensible or desirable administrative practice. And in asking that question in 1977 it may be necessary to take heed of some considerations that were not present twenty years earlier. In 1959 anyone who believed in the value of local control of administration and in democratic accountability could well believe in the need for greater control of police discretion. Situations could even be conceived where, in the interests of more effective or uniform or equitable law enforcement, even positive instruc-tions might be justified. Few would have believed that instructions relating to the institution or withdrawal of particular prosecutions could ever be justified. But general policies related to prosecution and matters of public importance outside the field of prosecution affecting police operations and the disposal of police forces and resources could be conceived as potential areas in which police authorities might properly exercise influence and in the last resort exert control.

All such feelings are, however, contingent upon a number of assumptions about the processes of politics and administration at a particular time. One especially important unspoken premise is that the executive officers and elected persons through whom democratic control is exerted can be assumed to be by and large uncorrupt. But our experience in the last decade raises a serious question as to whether that pristine assumption can still be made. Nothing in British politics and administra-tion is quite what it was in 1959 or ever will be. Suppose it to be the case that we cannot automatically assume that elected politicians will respect the rule of law, or reject bribes or refrain from exploiting their positions for self-interested or party-political, or even corrupt and unlaw-ful, ends. Suppose that Watergates, Poulsons and Clay Crosses are not unique and unrepeatable phenomena. Nobody's faith in councillors or Congressmen or Members of Parliament can now be as firmly held as it was fifteen years ago.

What is the moral? Perhaps that democratic theory no longer gives a simple or straightforward answer here any more than it does in other fields. In many areas such as financial and economic regulation (including such issues as control of the money supply and health and safety requirements) there may be a tension between technical judgment and political preference or necessity. The long-run interests and rights of citizens may well be furthered by the construction of buttresses against some kinds of overt political pressures, even when exerted honestly and in the name of democratic majorities. The occasional frustration of such majority pressures may be required by the need to protect civil liberties and secure the impartial treatment of individuals. Bills of Rights are a standing acknowledgement of this. If therefore in the field of law enforcement we have to give a calculated and unprejudiced answer in 1977 to the question whether civil liberties and impartial justice are more to be expected from chief constables than from elected politicians (whether on police committees or in the House of Commons or in ministerial departments) many liberal democrats would feel justified in placing more trust in the former than in the latter. If that is so then whether or not the theory of police independence as traditionally set out has any sound legal foundation (and it almost certainly has not) it may be possible to defend it as a constitutional and administrative convention.

Such a convention would suggest that direct orders; whether of a positive or negative kind, whether related to prosecution or other law-enforcement measures, and whether related to individual cases or to general policies, ought to be avoided by police authorities even when they involve what the Royal Commission called 'police policies in matters which vitally concern the public interest'.

## Two styles of accountability

Where would such a formula leave the notion of police accountability and what would be its corollaries? Like all conventions it is of course vague at its edges.

Questions can be asked, for example, about the borderline between the enforcement of law and order and the logistical issues involved in the management of police resources that are legitimate matters for political concern and financial control.

In the area of law enforcement itself the implication of independence from direct control is that accountability must take a different form. Other areas of British administration besides policing have shown a need for a form of accountability that differs from the familiar type of ministerial and political responsibility that might be dubbed the 'subordinate and obedient' mode in which the supervisor's responsibility is typically accompanied by administrative control and the ability to direct and veto. In contrast a style of accountability that might be called the 'explanatory and co-operative' mode has emerged in some areas such as the relationships between independent commercial or regulatory bodies on one hand and Ministers and the House of Commons on the other. Something like this style of accountability to Parliament is written into the 1964 Police Act provisions for parliamentary questioning. The Home Secretary's responsibility to Parliament for policing throughout the country is one that rests not on an ability to issue orders but on the capacity to require information, answers and reasons that can then be analysed and debated in Parliament and in the press.

The corollary of a conventional constabulary immunity from mandatory instructions ought to be that explanatory accountability is not confined within any particular bounds. There may be occasions on which it should extend even in prosecution matters to particular cases of prosecution or non-prosecution as well as general policies.

If we examine the central and local machinery that was set up in 1964 and subsequently modified by police reorganization we cannot conclude that it is ideally adapted to the exercise of explanatory accountability. In some degree this is perhaps more the fault of elected members than of the legislative machinery. The Police Act provisions for requesting and debating reports from chief constables on the policing of their areas have not been extensively used either in the House of Commons or in local councils.[24] In the new district councils to which many of the former cities and boroughs have been reduced by local government reorganization these powers cannot be used at all. Nor does there appear to have been much significant debate at the local level of either annual police estimates or of the decisions or activities of police committees. This was a particular difficulty of the combined police area where police committees were composed of representatives drawn from a number of constituent councils.[25] It ought in principle to be less difficult since 1974 with more police committees drawn from a single elected body.[26] As to police committees it is difficult to believe that in the past ten years they have been effective instruments for carrying out the duties (for example those related to complaints against the police) that were placed upon them by the 1964 Act.

The Police Act 1976 and the various regulations made under it have now introduced into the machinery of police accountability a new entity, the Police Complaints Board. Its purpose, however, is to provide a mechanism for the independent review of existing disciplinary procedures related to the activities of individual constables. Whether it succeeds in this task or not, it is not a body which provides a forum for complaints against collective activities or force policies of the kind that were mentioned in the Royal Commission Report as being subject to potential challenge. It may be that a gap remains to be filled by some body that would act in a manner analogous to that of the Press Council, the BBC Complaints Panel or the parliamentary and local government Complaints Commissioners. These provide a clear example of explanatory accountability in that without any power to bind or reverse executive decisions they provide an avenue for challenge, for the requiring of reasoned explanation and for advice and recommendation. The subjection of professional judgment and administrative discretion to this form of challenge and publicity is a relatively novel experiment in British administration, and it seems a mode of accountability well adapted to the area of law enforcement. When the Ombudsman system was introduced at the national level in 1967 there was a deliberate decision to exclude from it the operations of the independent public corporations, the Health Services, local government and the police. Almost all these omissions have now been made good but the police exception remains. The Police Complaints Panel as now constituted does not provide what is needed to round off the machinery of public accountability for executive action. Law-enforcement policy is made by the exercise of executive discretion but it requires a special style of accountability which our institutions have not as yet fully succeeded in providing.

*From Geoffrey Marshall, 'Police accountability revisited', in D. Butler and A.H. Halsey (eds),* Policy and Politics *(London: Macmillan Press) 1978, pp 51–65.*

## Notes and references

1   Cmnd 535 (1969).
2   'The Police', *Public Administration* 7 *(1929) p. 192.*
3   (1930) 2 KB 364.
4   *Public Administration* 38 (1960) pp. 11–15. For similar views see the Minutes of Evidence in the *Report of the Royal Commission on the Police*, Cmnd 1728 (1962), Days 11–12, pp. 630–1 and 668–72.
5   See *Public Administration* 38 (1960), 'The Independence of Chief Constables' by Bryan Keith-Lucas, p. 1; and 'Some Questions' by D.N. Chester, p. 11.
6   Cmnd 1728, Minutes of Evidence, Appendix 11, pp. 33–4. The right of private prosecution is of course a right exercised in England and Wales. Scotland, like the United States, gives a practical monopoly to what are in effect public or state prosecutors. How far this fact modifies the conclusions drawn in England and Wales about the position of the police perhaps requires more discussion than it has had. The rights of private prosecutors, including the police, are now circumscribed in England and Wales by a considerable number of statutes requiring leave to be given by the Attorney-General or the Director of Public Prosecutions. For a complete list of statutes containing such restrictions see *Hansard*, 14 Mar 1977. Cf. J. Ll. Edwards, *The Law Officers of the Crown* (1964) pp. 237–46 and 396–401; and Bernard M. Dickens, 'The Prosecuting Roles of the Attorney-General and Director of Public Prosecutions', *Public Law*, spring 1974, pp. 50–73.
7   See G. Marshall, *Police and Government* (1965) ch. 3, and 'Police Responsibility', *Public Administration* 38 (1960) pp. 213–26.
8   Other cases such as *A.G for N.S. Wales* v. *Perpetual Trustee Co.* (1952) 85 CLR 237; (1955) AC 457 indicate that constables are not servants in that their employers cannot recover against third parties for loss of their 'services'. But 'servant', 'serve' and 'service' are many-coloured terms

and it is hazardous to draw any direct implications about subjection to lawful superior orders from the use of these terms in different contexts. Compare for example the situations of civil servants, judges and soldiers, all of whom 'serve' the Crown in some sense, though not the same sense.

9   (1968) 2 QB 118.

10  330 *Parl. Deb.*, 3rd ser., col. 1174. See G. Marshall, *Police and Government,* ch. 2, pp 29–32 and 53–4. Cf. Sir Frank Newsam, *The Home Office* (1925) p. 104.

11  See R. Plehwe, 'Police and Government: The Commissioner of Police for the Metropolis', *Public Law*, winter 1974, pp. 316–35.

12  Plehwe, p. 332.

13  For the episodes leading to the 1929 Commission see Cmnd 3147, 1928 *(Inquiry in Regard to the Interrogation by the Police of Miss Savidge).*

14  *Report of the Tribunal Appointed to Inquire into the Allegation of Assault on John Waters* (Cmnd 718, 1959).

15  *Sheffield Police Appeal Inquiry* (Cmnd 2176, 1963).

16  *Report of Inquiry by Mr A.E. James, QC* (Cmnd 2735, 1965).

17  Sir William Nott-Bower, *Fifty Two Years a Policeman* (1926) p. 145.

18  *Lewis* v. *Cattle* (1938) 2 KB 454, 457.

19  *Report of the Royal Commission on the Police,* para. 91.

20  *R.* v. *Metropolitan Police Commissioner, ex parte Blackburn* (1968) 2 QB 118. On the issues raised by Blackburn's case see D.G.T. Williams, 'The Police and Law Enforcement', *Criminal Law Review* 58 (July 1968) pp. 351–62; and 'Prosecution, Discretion and the Accountability of the Police' in *Crime, Criminology and Public Policy* (ed. Roger Hood, 1974).

21  For a number of similar examples and of the uses of prosecutionary discretion generally see *The Decision to Prosecute* (1972) by A.E. Wilcox (a former Chief Constable of Hertfordshire); also Glanville Williams, 'Discretion in Prosecution', *Criminal Law Review* 3 (1956) pp. 222–31.

22  (1968) 2 QB 118 at 135–6.

23  For Salmon LJ's view see (1968) 2 QB at 138.

24  There is no easily available information on the use made by local police authorities and councils of their police powers. In Oxford City Council, for example, between 1964 and 1974 only one request was made for a report from the Chief Constable under 5.12 of the 1964 Police Act. This may not be untypical.

25  On the effects of amalgamation on police committees cf. G. Marshall, 'The Government of the Police since 1964', in J.C. Alderson and P.T. Stead, *The Police We Deserve* (1973) pp. 59–60.

26  Some police comment has detected signs of more significant party organisation and party caucussing on county police committees drawn from a single local authority. This has even served to commend regional police forces. ('The prospect of regionalisation presents the service with the opportunity of getting rid of some of its present ills, not least the growing influence of local politics': *Police Review*, 7 Jan 1977.) There may be the beginning here of a reversal of the traditional arguments against a national police force. In the past many have assumed that it was local police forces that preserved England from political interference in law enforcement.

# 37. The legal regulation of policing

*David Dixon*

This [extract] will discuss the relationship between policing and the 'rule of law', some implications of contemporary public law scholarship for the control of policing, and the prospects for the legal regulation of police practices.

## (a)  Policing and the rule of law

In discussions of the regulation of state agencies, the 'rule of law' has been a persistently problematic concept. As a rhetorical device, its plasticity has sometimes allowed it to act as a synonym for 'law and order'. Indeed, it can be argued that it 'has become meaningless thanks to ideological abuse and general over-use'.[1] In legal debates, the conventional beginning of discussions on the rule of law is Dicey's formulation in his *Introduction to the Study of the Law of the Constitution* (1927), a book which has had an enduring influence on English public law.[2] Dicey's 'unfortunate outburst of Anglo-Saxon parochialism' (Shklar, 1987: 16) has caused much confusion and misunderstanding, not least because of its unsatisfactory resolution of the relationship between law and politics. Useful discussion of the rule of law requires concrete analysis and specification of concepts. In an attempt to assess the rule of law in the context of policing, Sanders and Young focus on 'two elements of the concept which seem most relevant to police powers: equality under the law, and the control of state officials' (1994b: 127). Their analysis provides a useful introduction to considering how the 'rule of law' relates to the legal regulation of policing.

### (i)  Equality and balance

As regards equality, Dicey insisted that the 'ordinary law of the realm' should apply to state officials. By this he meant that state officials should be accountable to courts rather than to specialized tribunals: any such tribunals which existed merely added to, rather than replaced, 'the duties of an ordinary citizen' which were enforced by the courts (1927: 190). The inadequacy of his account has long been apparent. Profoundly affected by his opposition to the rise of 'collectivism', he misinterpreted contemporary developments. As Harlow and Rawlings suggest, his interpretation was 'inspired by an ardent belief in individualism,

636

in *laissez-faire* economic policy and in the rectitude of lawyerly values' (1984: 19).[3]

Characteristically, Dicey was primarily concerned with remedies in this discussion of legal equality.[4] However, he is often interpreted as meaning that state officials should not have powers which set them apart from ordinary citizens (Sanders and Young, 1994b: 127). Diceyan analysis was particularly misleading in the case of the police.[5] It clearly informed the Royal Commission on Police Powers and Procedure of 1928–9 which reported influentially that police were merely 'citizens in Uniform' whose powers were essentially those of an ordinary member of the public (RCPPP, 1929: 6; [...]). This attempt to minimize the significance of the 'special powers' held by the police was a product of the Commission's insistence that policing depended fundamentally upon 'the goodwill of the public ... A proper and mutual understanding between the Police and the public is essential for the maintenance of law and order' (1929: 7). This approach can only properly be understood in its historical context: the Royal Commission was appointed at the end of a decade of popular scepticism towards and official concern about lack of confidence in the police (Dixon, 1991: 241–8, 256–61). For present purposes, the Royal Commission's remarks are significant as having formed a central plank in the ideological presentation (and self-delusion) of the English police: the theme of 'citizens in uniform' was to inform and strengthen subsequent arguments for independence from political accountability in the later part of the century.[6] It was, of course, misleading in its failure to appreciate either the extent of police powers at the time or the trend towards their accumulation [...]

Discussion of equality raises the disjuncture between the formal and the substantive in its most familiar form: substantive inequality undermines the law's formal equality. (The classic reference is, of course, to France, 1927: 106.) Sanders and Young are able to draw on overwhelming research evidence showing that police powers are applied 'unequally'. They argue convincingly that this is the product of the police mandate in an increasingly divided society and that this inevitably affects the impact of legal regulation (1994b; see also Brogden *et al.*, 1988: ch. 6). A good example is the inefficacy of the (purported) attempt to inject substantive equality by legal regulation of stop and search: as argued elsewhere, [the Police and Criminal Evidence Act 1984] PACE Code C's provisions on stereotyping have been of largely presentational effect (Dixon *et al.*, 1989). Whether legal regulation will inevitably skim over (or consolidate) substantive inequality is an empirical question, and will depend on contexts, methods, and subjects. It is suggested, for example, that the regulation of police use of firearms in the United States substantially reduced the racial imbalance in deaths resulting from police shootings (Walker, 1993a: 26).

More complex issues are raised by other examples of attempts to equalize relations between state and citizen by balancing powers and rights: notably, the power to detain for investigative purposes is 'balanced' in England and Wales by the right to legal advice which (in a notable concession to the need to take account of substantive matters) is backed by legal aid and duty-solicitor services. The example shows the problems of attempts to 'balance'. Research evidence emphasizes the deficiencies of legal advice in police stations (McConville *et al.*, 1994; Dixon *et al.*, 1990a). Despite this, arguments are made that the balance has 'swung too far the other way' leading, notably, to the restriction of the right to silence (Jackson, 1990; [...]). As Sanders and Young (1994a: 460) suggest ironically, justifying crime control 'by reference to bits and pieces of due process' provides a new application for McBarnet's claim (1979: 39; [...]) that 'due process is for crime control'.

As Ashworth argues, the 'balance' metaphor has been the 'scourge of many debates about criminal justice policy' (1994: 292; cf. Jackson, 1990). Despite repeated exposures of its deficiencies, the balance is usually said to be between the civil liberties of suspects and society's right to protect 'itself' by providing police powers. In cruder references, 'suspects' are replaced with offenders or criminals: by leaping to the conclusion which the justice process is intended to decide upon, this ends any useful discussion. In more sophisticated formulations, it may be acknowledged that there is a communal and not just an individual interest in the protection of rights. This is not merely a matter of principle – i.e. that a democratic society deserving the name should treat its citizens in a certain way. There is also the instrumental interest, which is a glaring but often ignored lesson of the miscarriage cases. If failure to provide suspects with substantial rights leads to a wrongful conviction, then those really guilty escape justice (usually forever, because the investigation has been misdirected for so long).[7] This failure to appreciate 'the double-sided nature of miscarriages of justice ... serves to perpetuate a ... misleading dichotomy between "soft" and "tough" measures, between effective crime control and civil liberties' (Hogg, 1995: 314). It is necessary to see rights as expressing organizational and social, as well as individual, interests. In addition, as Braithwaite points out, empirical evidence belies claims that there is an inevitable 'trade-off between crime control arid respect for civil liberties' and this should challenge the 'conceptualization of some sort of hydraulic relationship' between them (1989: 158–9). More specifically, the example of PACE shows that the complex relationship between police powers and suspects' rights is distorted by a simple metaphor of balance.

This discussion suggests that, seductive as it may be, the concept of balance is inherently problematic. Certainly, experience suggests that it provides an often irresistible temptation to degenerate into crude and unhelpful formulations. Its superficial utilitarianism trivializes important interests and inappropriately treats them as if they can be weighed off against each other. The inability to shift from metaphor to reality is exposed in the tendency of the Royal Commission on Criminal Justice to refer to 'the "balance" favouring one solution rather than another as if this were some ineffable mystery that requires no supporting explanation about how the conclusion was reached' (Ashworth, 1994: 294). Ashworth calls for a fundamental reconsideration of the principles and fundamental purposes of criminal justice, a 'rights-based' approach (1994: 292–6; 1996; cf. Jackson, 1990). But the concept of balance re-emerges in his own account. Arguing that this is an inevitable consequence of an internal perspective, Norrie suggests that it can only be avoided by starting

> not from the internal values and practices of the system, but from the sociological context within which the system operates. Rather than the circular  and ultimately unprofitable approach of applying the values within the system to it, we might get a better picture if we asked: (1) what

are the social and historical conditions that make a criminal system of the kind we have possible?; and (2) what are the structural limits on, and historical dynamics of, change within such a system? (1995: 344).

### (ii) Control

The most important directive of the 'rule of law' is that the activities of state officials should be legally authorized. The legal regulation of policing is not, if interpreted minimally, a particularly difficult or worthwhile objective. It is a jurisprudential cliché that the most tyrannical regime may operate legally by providing legal authority for its actions (for a recent example, see Brogden and Shearing, 1993: 27–32, 60–7). Similarly, parliamentary supremacy can (in constitutional theory) authorize anything (Craig, 1990: 36–9). The issue is what kind of rules are used to regulate policing, and what principles, contexts, and objectives inform their production: if procedural safeguards 'do function to protect citizens against state interventions of various kinds this is not because of their abstract, formal, universal nature ... Rather it depends on certain conditions – social, economic, institutional, etc. – governing the actual processes of justice in question and the context of their application' (Hogg, 1991a: 23).

Sanders and Young have argued strongly that PACE provided a structure of rules, but did not control policing:

> Police officers are rarely inhibited by 'due process' from doing what they want to do. They are not ruled by law even though their behaviour can usually be classified as lawful. This situation arises because either:
>
> – the law is a product of state agencies (the police in particular); or
> – the law is sufficiently flexible to accommodate what the police want to do ...
>
> The police are only governed by the rule of law to the extent that PACE requires them to follow certain routines. The content of those routines, and which routines are adopted, are becoming more and more a matter for the police alone. By this means the police conform to law without being controlled by it (19946: 128–9, 131).

This account relies upon the foundation laid by *The Case for the Prosecution* (McConville *et al.*, 1991a), in which it is argued that the nature of case construction is set by the police role in an adversarial system, that '[l]egal "reform" is very often nothing more than the legitimation of police practice' (1991a: 177), and that managerial and supervisory controls will inevitably be rendered ineffective by police culture and the nature of the police organization. [Earlier ... I] suggested some need for qualification in the presentation of the law's flexibility, in the determinant role ascribed to police culture, and in the distinction between procedure and substance. Rather than rehearse the debate over interpretation of the research evidence on PACE, it is more useful here to consider some conceptual and broader issues raised, directly or indirectly, by their analysis.

First, police influence over legislation is clearly an important issue. Of course, such influence varies over time and place. Some Australian police forces (and police unions) have enjoyed remarkable influence over law-making (Finnane,

1994: 34–7, 48–51; Haldane, 1995: 290–2). The NSW Detention After Arrest Bill of 1994 [...] had it passed, would have been almost a caricature of such laws. In England and Wales, police leaders have become increasingly active and more sophisticated since the 1960s in their attempts to influence public policy (Reiner, 1992a: 91–6). Notably, Metropolitan Police Commissioners Mark and McNee argued that the law should be changed to authorize practices which their officers had unlawfully adopted, having determined that they were necessary for crime control. As Baxter and Koffman suggested it was 'indicative of the prestige and power of the police that an admission of such unconstitutional and lawless behaviour should be accepted with equanimity in a liberal democratic society' (1985: 1).

The complaisance of the Home Secretary of the day has been crucial to the success of police lobbying. The restriction of the right to silence in 1994 was [...] a notable and regrettable example of the police getting what they wanted from Government. In both England and Wales and Australia, police seem devoted to the old cliché that attack is the best form of defence. While exposed to criticism for their contributions to, respectively, miscarriages of justice and corruption, there has been a brazenness in police calls for expansion of their powers and criticism of other sectors of the justice system which is sometimes hard to credit.[8] However, it would be wrong to treat PACE as an unproblematic capitulation to police demands. While police got most of the powers which they had requested (McNee, 1983: 182–3), those powers were accompanied by safeguards and suspects' rights. It is this, of course, which accounts for the critical reception which PACE received from police and civil libertarians alike: both criticized aspects of the legislation which they disliked, while understating those which favoured their interests.

Secondly, Sanders and Young argue that cases of malpractice like the Cardiff Three are rare 'not because the police are usually reined in by the law. It is because they rarely have to go beyond the law to achieve their objective' (1994b: 152). When police stay within the law, it is because it suits them. This argument is flawed by its very uncontrovertibility: it defines out the possibility of police being 'reined in' by law. They argue that we 'need an explanation for patterns of conformity and breach if we are to assess the current effect of legal changes' (1994b: 129) and criticize the limitations of most of the research carried out for the Philips and Runciman Commissions which 'measured the extent of compliance with rules rather than the reasons for compliance and deviance' (Sanders and Young, 1994b: 154). However, they assume that we already know these reasons, that compliance and deviance are unproblematic. On the contrary, I would suggest that these are complex matters of which our understanding is still limited.

Finally, there is an assumption that courts (with all their limitations [...] are central to legal regulation: the 'rule of law is necessarily legalistic. In other words it seeks to control behaviour by setting standards for specific encounters and establishing accountability in court settings for breach of those standards' (Sanders and Young, 1994b: 131). [Judicial] control of police powers has a significant history. Exponents of the rule of law tend to evoke that history while paying less attention to more recent shifts in judicial attitudes or to the practical inaccessibility of judicial remedies.[9] The histories of custodial interrogation [...] did not find much evidence of modern judges enthusiastically protecting individual rights. On the contrary, the record in England and Australia has generally been of complicity with the informal growth of police powers. When there is some significant judicial activism (as in applications of PACE, sections 76 and 78, or in the High Court's rulings on confessions), interventions tend to be unsystematic, episodic, and inconsistent (Dixon, 1991d). However, there may be more to the rule of law than the rule of courts. As the discussion in section (e) will suggest, public law scholarship has substantially shifted attention away from courts in considering the legal regulation of state activity.

While these points suggest some qualification of Sanders and Young's approach, their central question deserves attention: does policing conform to the liberal conception of the rule of law? Specifically, does law protect freedom from arbitrary power in the way it provides police with legal authority? An excessive statutory delegation of discretion is, from a Diceyan perspective, as offensive as arbitrary power (Dicey, 1927; Baxter, 1985: 42). If discretion is limited by boundaries which are too wide and safeguards which are ineffective, then the requirements of the rule of law are not satisfied. From this perspective, the particular reason for failure is not important. For example, a power may be excessively broad because its use is not supervised or regulated (e.g. the power to stop and search under the NSW Crimes Act 1900, section 357E), or because it is closely but ineffectively regulated (stop and search under PACE, section 1), or because it is constructed out of legal loopholes and judicial connivance (detention for questioning in NSW), or because of a variety of legal and other factors (reception into custody under PACE, section 37). Police powers of these kinds offend the rule of law.

Further, [...] police powers may be effectively (if not formally) extended by changes in substantive criminal law, as in broadening of public-order offences. The courts' usual stance has been to refuse to look beyond the alleged offence: they (and Dicey) treat the discretionary decision to proceed against a particular individual as irrelevant. This stance must be set in the context of judicial priorities which Glanville Williams stated bluntly: 'in criminal cases, the courts are anxious to facilitate the conviction of villains and they interpret the law whenever possible to secure this' (quoted Smith, 1985: 610).

Can powers of the kind discussed here be brought within the rule of law? It is certainly the case that legal change can have some substantial effects: legal regulation of custodial interrogation in NSW could bring policing nearer to the rule of law. As regards offences, the decriminalization of some (Lacey, 1995) and the reduction in available maximum penalties for others would be beneficial.[10] But the limits of legal regulation and change have to be acknowledged. [Legal] regulation usually assumes that police powers are used for law enforcement. The reality (notably in the policing of public-order offences and use of stop/search powers) is that officers have other objectives which are at least as significant: pre-eminent among these are maintaining order and imposing authority. It is simply naïve to expect a traditional conception of the rule of law – closely defined legal authority supervised by the courts – to have sufficient purchase. The deficiencies of the rule of law are easy enough to point out: it is important but more difficult to go beyond the traditional conception to appreciate broader conceptions of the rule of law and to consider more active uses of legal regulation in combination with other methods of control.

## (b)    The rule of law: substance and ideology

This section is concerned with possible development of the 'rule of law' beyond its liberal attachments, and some broader issues which its consideration suggests. As noted above, a rule of law which merely provides freedom from interference by others or which is mere legal formalism is of little value or interest. The rule of law must have some positive ambition, such as provision of what Braithwaite and Pettit term 'dominion' (1990: 63, see also Cotterrell, 1996: 466). Rules must not simply be made in the constitutionally prescribed manner, but must meet some standard, in the sense that they must be consistent with certain values and principles. It is this qualitative aspect which has tied the rule of law to the liberal and democratic political traditions.[11] However, to treat the rule of law as having relevance only within liberal-democratic theory would be a mistake.

The rule of law must provide rules which are substantial in their effect (New Zealand Law Commission, 1992: 2). Such an effect may well depend upon factors external to a specific rule. This developed notion of the rule of law was expressed by the Delhi Conference of the International Commission of jurists which declared the rule of law to be a dynamic concept 'which should be employed not only to safeguard and advance the civil and political rights of the individual in a free society, but also to establish social, economic, educational and cultural conditions under which his [*sic*] legitimate aspirations and dignity may be realised' (quoted, Allan, 1985; contrast Raz, 1979: 210–11). In the context of policing, the need for rules to be made substantial by external action is exemplified by the right to legal advice: suspects may have such a 'right', but if no legal aid or duty solicitors are provided, the right is chimerical (Sanders and Young, 1994b: 141). Appreciation of this was the spur to the US Supreme Court's decision in *Miranda* v. *Arizona*.[12] Defining the rule of law as including the action needed to make it substantial may be problematic. It can encourage legal imperialism, and it may dissipate the concept's force (Raz, 1979: 211). However, positivist objections of this sort are unable to appreciate the qualitative dimension of the rule of law which historical and cultural studies can illuminate.

As well as material substance, the rule of law requires ideological substance: the concept that governmental action must be both legal and legitimate must have some meaning for both officials and citizens. There must be 'a widespread assumption within the society that law *matters* and should matter' (Krygier, 1990: 646, original emphasis). If this is the case, 'public discussions and expectations of what is appropriate in public life' are quite different 'from a system where the very idea of subjecting the powerful to the law does not exist – either in principle or as a realistic possibility' (Krygier, 1990: 643). The key text for analysis of this dimension of the rule of law remains Thompson's comments in *Whigs and Hunters*:

> The essential precondition for the effectiveness of law, in its function as ideology, is that it shall display an independence from manipulation and shall seem to be just. It cannot seem to be so without upholding its own logic and criteria of equity; indeed, on occasion, by actually *being* just. And

furthermore it is not often the case that a ruling ideology can be dismissed as mere hypocrisy; even rulers find a need to legitimize their power, to moralize their functions, to feel themselves to be useful and just (1977: 263, original emphasis; cf. Trubeck, 1977: 558).

The rulers of eighteenth-century England were:

> the prisoners of their own rhetoric; they played the games of power according to rules which suited them, but they could not break those rules or the whole game would be thrown away. And … so far from the ruled shrugging off this rhetoric as a hypocrisy, some part of it at least was taken over as part of the rhetoric of the plebeian crowd, of the 'free-born Englishman' with his inviolable privacy, his *habeas corpus*, his equality before the law (1977: 263–4).

The deficiencies of Thompson's argument have been exposed in a number of valuable critiques (e.g. Horwitz, 1977; Fine, 1994). However, its continuing value lies in its insistence that the rule of law must be seen in terms of its reproduction of a mode of discourse in the process of historical friction and transmission between dominant and subordinate ideologies. The rule of law cannot be understood purely at the level of theories of ideology: it must be understood in the historical context of cultural construction in which symbols discourse and rhetoric can play active, constitutive forces.[13] Unger made the point well:

> In societies with a heavy commitment to the rule of law, people often act on the belief that the legal system does possess a relative generality and autonomy. To treat their understandings and values as mere shams is to assume that social relations can be described and explained without regard to the meanings the men [*sic*] who participate in those relations attribute to them. This … would be to blind oneself to what is specifically social about the subject matter and to violate a cardinal principle of method in social theory (1976: 56–7).

The promise of government limited by laws of a certain kind was one which affected popular cultures in complex and unexpected ways. The rule of law's power is well illustrated by Neal's study (1991) of the unlikely emergence and effect of claims based on it in the early convict settlement of New South Wales.

The relevance of this to understanding of law in policing is that attention must be paid to the discursive and ideological, as well as the instrumental, aspects of police law. Account must be taken of the desires, demands, and expectations which the legal form creates among both officials and citizens (Tyler, 1990; Allen, 1996). The United States provides a useful comparison: while the 'due process revolution' may not have the instrumental effects on police practices which were anticipated or feared, Walker argues that there has been a significant effect on both police and popular attitudes to the justice system. The 'landmark Supreme Court cases of the 1960s … focused public attention on police decision making and its impact on individual liberty. This raised the level of public awareness of the constitutional aspects of police work to an extraordinarily high level' (1993a:

51; cf. Leo, 1996a: 259). Even if information was communicated by means of antagonistic fictional representations such as *Dirty Harry* (Smith, 1993: 90–107), public opinion and popular culture were influenced. The result was a 'climate of legality', a rising 'expectation of justice', and a 'shared awareness of the potential for redress' which affected police–public relations (Walker, 1988: 20–2). Walker does not claim that his account is more than a sketch; but as this, it is of real interest. Taking it further in comparative studies would require cultural and geographical specification: Walker relates his thesis to the peculiarly legalistic nature of American society (1988: 3). He suggests the crucial ideological dialectic between public expectation and police culture. Specific instrumental changes stimulated by the Supreme Court such as 'wide-ranging reforms in the education, training, and supervision of police officers' have to be linked to a broader alteration in

> the context of the working environment of policing. The principle of accountability – that there are limits on police powers, that those limits can be set down in writing (whether by a court decision or a departmental rule), and that officers should be routinely expected to answer for whether they comply with those rules has been established, at least as an ideal. This principle is an established fact of life for a new generation of police officers (1993a: 51).

Walker's aside – 'at least as, an ideal' – suggests a weakness in his rather enthusiastic account: the difference between ideal and practice is crucial, and the latter is rarely the direct subject of the studies on which he relies. In addition, [...] (police adherence to legality may be primarily instrumental rather than ideological, and may encourage new investigative tactics which raise new problems of morality and efficacy (Leo, 1994; 1996a). A process by which legal change leads, not to unproblematic compliance, but to adaptation in which some elements are subverted while others are normalized is what should be expected in a more sophisticated account of reform processes (Brown, 1987).

As Baxter suggests, 'if the policeman [*sic*] knows that he will not be able to rely on the passive ignorance of his suspect, then there is an improved chance that the policing function will operate in an atmosphere of mutual respect; where the citizen knows his rights, and where the policeman recognises the limits of his powers' (1985: 48). It is important here that Baxter stresses the need for change in the police: without this, educating young people about their rights would simply be to invite their characterization as 'smart-arses' or challengers to authority. [... There] is some evidence of new values and new attitudes to police work which are collectively described as a 'new professionalism'. Similarly, there may be change in suspects' attitudes, as demonstrated by the steady increase in rates of requests for legal advice (Brown, 1997; Phillips and Brown, 1997).

So it would be too easy to say that there is no practical difference between the systems of custodial interrogation in England and Australia [...]. Differences must be appreciated not just at an instrumental level, but also in terms of ideology and of cultural attitudes to law and rights. Legal regulation is different from (not necessarily better than) a system which relies on consent, legal loopholes, and judicial complicity.

As noted above, Thompson's recuperation of the rule of law provoked vigorous criticism. His most significant critics emphasized the need to appreciate the contradictory nature of the rule of law as an ideological force. 'It undoubtedly restrains power, but it also prevents power's benevolent exercise. It creates formal equality – a not inconsiderable virtue – but it *promotes* substantive inequality by creating a consciousness that radically separates law from politics, means from ends, processes from outcomes' (Horwitz, 1977: 566, original emphasis). Focusing on the inhibition of power distracts attention from law's other functions 'as instrument of domination, means of exchange, measure of right, source of punishment, framework of state, and so on' (Fine, 1994: 205) and from the limitations of the legal form, particularly its individualism and its traditional reliance on judicial decision-making. As McConville *et al.* noted in their critique of McBarnet […] the fundamental principles of criminal justice are constituted from crime control as well as due-process ideologies. The difficult but necessary task is to appreciate these multiple aspects of law without over-emphasizing one.

Another significant objection to Thompson's approach to the rule of law could be that it, ironically, fails to take account of historical change. It can be argued that we no longer live in 'societies with a heavy commitment to the rule of law'.[14] As Gatrell suggests, changing relations between class, property, and the state in the nineteenth century produced a new conception of rights as concessions provided by the state, rather than as the property of citizens who have conceded power to the state (1990: 254–5). While there is obviously a danger here of slipping into rose-tinted nostalgia, notions of legality and justice seem to have lost strength in popular cultures. In England, account must be taken of both the shifts in popular attitudes to authority over the last century (in which the social effects of the World Wars and the rise and decline of corporatist social democracy were crucial). The process has accelerated since 1979, with the neo-conservative reshaping of culture and society. In societies deeply divided by race, gender, and class, it becomes increasingly hard to identify common cultural understandings of citizens' rights and officials' responsibilities. The slackening of communal sensibility, the socio-political and economic marginalization of sections of the working class, and the decline of liberal and democratic commitment are aspects of late-modern societies which directly affect the relationship between policing and law. Perceptive commentators suggest that fundamental changes are under way in the nature of criminal justice processes which threaten to make redundant traditional conceptions of rights and limits on authority (Ericson, 1994a; Feeley and Simon, 1994; Reiner, 1992c).

If, as suggested above, the rule of law is a cultural construct, it should be expected that its English and Australian expressions will vary. In Australia, dominant cultural attitudes to law and authority, have a distinctively dichotomized inflection. On one hand, there is a cynical, distrusting wariness of authority. However, against what is often the preferred self-image must be set a deep social conservatism (McQueen, 1976). Attitudes to crime often present a stone-age lay criminology in which 'criminals' are distinguishable from respect-able society, and the justice system should not be subject to pettifogging, legal restraints in dealing with them. Cynicism has its place here too in acceptance that officials may give ends priority over means. For example, this element of popular culture has constituted a serious obstacle to the reform process in Queensland in the very material shape of juries and magistrates refusing to convict police officers of palpable offences.[15] At the time of writing, New South Wales is being exposed to the consequences of such cynicism, as a Royal Commission demonstrates the pervasion of corruption through the police service. A related form of cynicism is politicians' shameless exploitation of the fear of crime. Fatuous mandatory life sentencing legislation and an unprincipled statute authorizing the detention of a named 'dangerous' individual without the necessity of criminal conviction exemplify a view of criminal justice, not as an important and complex area of public policy, but simply as the administration of a criminal class to be exploited in the scrabble for government.[16]

## (c) Irony and contradiction in policing

Rather than ending in unmitigated post-modernist gloom, this discussion suggests a need to appreciate the complexity of modern policing, particularly the contradictions and irony which run through so many of its aspects. Irony pervades policing. Peter Manning's work traced this brilliantly in his analysis of sacred and profane aspects of police work (1977: 147 and *passim*). Relations between police and 'public' are profoundly ironic: officers serve and protect a social order about which they are cynical and resentful. They venerate 'the law', but deride laws, lawyers and courts [...]

It is wrong to focus only on the 'negative' aspects of police powers as increasing power. The provision of powers may also be positive in defining what police may and may not do: law 'has the great virtue of limiting what it grants'.[17] The combination of empowering and restricting is a characteristic ambivalence of liberal governance (Barry *et al.*, (eds.) 1996; McNay, 1994: ch. 3). As Finnane suggests, regulation 'of any kind is a two-fold process: it not only constrains but opens up a field of action' (1994: 90). If a police practice is recognized by legal authorization, there may also be recognition that rights of those subjected to powers need to be recognized and given substance. For example, if it is acknowledged that police detain suspects for questioning, then specified limits on detention and correlative rights (e.g. to legal advice) become significant issues. Whether the extension of powers is accompanied by positive rights in any particular instance is an empirical matter. The point for present purposes is that it is usually misleading to see power as working in a purely negative way: it may also have positive and unpredictable effects. The corollary also operates: reforms to criminal justice have characteristically 'enhanced rather than diminished the power of legal authorities' (Garland, 1991: 13). This analysis is, of course, consistent with the reconceptualization of power in Foucault's work (e.g. 1975). From a very different perspective, it also fits with developments in public law which are discussed in subsection (d) below.

Another characteristically Foucauldian observation is that power is not monopolized by the state. An example from the PACE project indicates this, but also makes clear that it is not simply spread evenly across society. At 9.35 on a Friday night, I was discussing stop and search with a patrolling officer. On an industrial street, we passed a man carrying a canvas bag. The officer remarked that, if it were later at night, he would routinely stop and search a man walking with a bag in such an area. But at this time, a man carrying a bag is still not incongruous, and therefore not suspicious: he is probably going home from work. The officer knew that, if he stopped and attempted to search the man, strong objection would be likely. The construction and activation of his suspicion had to be understood as taking place in the context of relations and negotiations of power. The man would not have regarded himself as 'fair game' to be stopped and searched: the officer would have been acting out of order if he had done so. Of course, the perception that the police action is unjustified is not enough: the power of being a white, male, 'respectable' worker was necessary. The point was illustrated by the fact that, only a few minutes later, the officer did stop and question some 'suspects' – young people whose presence in that area at that time required explanation, particularly when they identified themselves as being from a 'notorious' council estate some distance away. More generally, young black people's experience of stop and search is, *inter alia*, that of a group without acknowledged resources of legitimate power (Singh, 1994).

A pervasive characteristic of the criminal process is irony, expressed in contradiction and unintended consequences. Many examples could be provided. At a general level, in England and Wales 'many experienced police officers … feel somewhat frustrated at the paradox that public trust in them is at its lowest ebb precisely when professional standards are at an all-time high' (Reiner, 1992c: 773). Without accepting this valuation of modern 'professionalism', there is considerable irony in the fact that the violence and malpractice of policing in the 1950s should be glorified as a 'golden age'.[18] Meanwhile, just as the New South Wales Police Service attracted attention as a leading example of the 'new policing' (Sparrow *et al.*, 1990: 72–7), it was plunged into unprecedented scandals about corruption and misconduct. In the United States, Los Angeles provides an example of a police department apparently winning its fight against corruption, but at the cost of entrenching an authoritarian and militaristic police culture which brought its own problems: 'the accomplishments of police reform through the 1950s set the stage for the police–community-relations crisis of the 1960s' (Walker, 1980: 212).

More specifically, PACE provides numerous examples of counterproductive measures. For example, the attempt to encourage due process by insisting that evidentially useful interrogation must be carried out in police stations has had the effect of subverting due process in arrest and detention practices: the policy of minimizing use of detention power has been gutted by the effect of limiting external questioning. A further irony is that restricting interrogation to stations has not had the desired effect: in-station regulation of questioning is weak; legal advice is often poor, even counter-productive from the suspect's viewpoint; and questioning in cells, in interview rooms when tapes are not turned on, and outside stations continues (Dixon *et al.*, 1990a; McConville *et al.*, 1994; Sanders and Young, 19946: 150).

Examples of technological change suggest that effects may not only be unforeseen, but also may have to be evaluated subjectively. Electronic recording of interviews may be interpreted as serving the interests of both suspect and police, even in the same case: research on video-recording in NSW suggests that quite incompatible interpretations of images may be made (Dixon and Travis,

1997). In respect of other technology, experience in NSW has shown how surveillance and money-tracing technologies developed by police can be used in the detection of corrupt police.[19] As Matza suggests, 'a key element of irony is latency – inherent qualities of phenomena that ... culminate in outcomes that mock the expected result ... Latency occurs in overlap too, which stresses the good that may be obscured in evil, and the vice that lurks in virtue' (1969: 70). These types of irony and contradiction are consistent with the discontinuities and inconsistencies which I have argued characterize the impact of PACE ([...] Dixon, 1992; 1995a). It is easy to caricature an approach such as this as lacking 'any theoretical position except indeterminacy' and implying that 'several factors jostle together with no sense of priority', thereby 'giving up the search for underlying explanations' (McConville and Sanders, 1995: 202, 197). My argument is that contradiction and irony are fundamental features of social life. Relegating them to second-order phenomena misses the vital and often most interesting aspects. In seeking to generalize by looking for patterns, it is vital to appreciate that discontinuities and inconsistencies may be the pattern, and not to obscure that pattern by overlaying a neater, simpler, but less accurate representation.

This does not entail abandoning any concept of determination: patterns may be discontinuous and inconsistent without being random. Rather, it means taking seriously the complexity of 'patterning' or determination once concepts of culture and ideology are treated as being not mere theoretical devices, but as constructed and constructing features of a society's history and structure (Williams, 1977: pt. 2). The resources for this project are unashamedly diffuse: use needs to be made of, for example, the sense of irony in the sociology of deviance, the understanding of culture and ideology in writers such as Williams and Thompson, and the sensitivity to complexity and contradiction in some post-structuralism. For me, reading social histories has been particularly important: the best of them require an attention to agency and contingency, to culture and discourse *as well as* to structure. Both empirical studies (e.g. Gatrell, 1990; Hill, 1954; Thompson, 1977) and theoretical debates and controversies (contrast Dean, 1994; Palmer, 1990) provide a rich resource.

## (d)  Limits of regulation

An abiding problem in references to the 'rule of law' is the implicit Whiggish distrust of the state: the rule of law should protect freedom by insisting on the minimization of state intervention. In this respect, Dicey's rule of law fitted only a liberal ideal of a minimal state. If it is to have relevance for a society characterized by powerful and active institutions (e.g. in which the public police have wide powers and private police have an increasing role), the rule of law has to be developed to provide for the facilitation and regulation (and not merely the disapproval) of activity both by the state and by 'private' bodies carrying out 'public' functions.[20] Indeed, in this context, unspecific references to the 'rule of law' can obscure more than they illuminate.

English public law has been dominated by the Diceyan tradition, despite the evident incoherence resulting from attempts to maintain it in the face of massive changes in state activity (e.g. Wade, 1988). There has been a long-standing 'dissenting' tradition which spawned significant challenges to the dominant tradition in the 1980s (Loughlin, 1992). The contrast between dominant and subordinate traditions in public law is captured well by Loughlin's counter-position of two ideal types, 'normativism' and 'functionalism':

> The normativist style in public law is rooted in a belief in the ideal of the separation of powers and in the need to subordinate government to law. This style highlights law's adjudicative and control functions and therefore its rule orientation and its conceptual nature. Normativism essentially reflects an ideal of the autonomy of law. The functionalist style in public law, by contrast, views law as part of the apparatus of government. Its focus is upon law's regulatory and facilitative functions and therefore adopts an instrumentalist social policy approach. Functionalism reflects an ideal of progressive evolutionary change ... For the normativist liberty might be identified with an absence of legal controls, whereas for the functionalist greater legal controls might mean more liberty (1992: 60, 61).

Similarly, Harlow and Rawlings (1984: chs. 1 and 2) contrast red-light theories (negatively centred on retrospective, judicial control of power in order to maximize individual freedom) and green-light theories (positively centred on prospective, internal control of power in order to encourage its best use in the communal interest).[21]

The relevance to policing of the new public law which has positive state regulation as its central project would seem to be clear. However, in England and Australia, there has been surprisingly little 'cross-over' between public-law and criminal justice: Lustgarten's *The Governance of Police* (1986) was a rare example of a discussion of policing from a public-law perspective. As Lacey suggests, many policing issues 'simply cannot be fitted (or distorted) into the conceptual straitjacket of trial-type process even by generous analogy', and have consequently been neglected in legal analysis (1992: 376). By contrast, in the United States, there has been a considerable body of work which exploits 'the promising potentialities of the simple idea that administrative law thinking can profitably be applied to criminal administration' (Davis, 1974: 703; cf. Davis, 1975: ch. 5). It is not appropriate to provide a full account here: attention will focus on merely the most prominent issue in the field, the use of rules.

If the American Bar Foundation study 'discovered' discretion in criminal justice (see Goldstein, 1960; Ohlin and Remington (eds.), 1993; Walker, 1992 [...] ), it was K.C. Davis who set the terms of the debate about control (Walker, 1993b: 41). In *Discretionary Justice* (1971), a key text of the 'new' public law, Davis argued that discretion was inevitable and, in its proper place, beneficial,[22] that uncontrolled discretion was a major problem, and discretion should be controlled by confining, structuring, and checking. The primary tool was administrative rules, underlain by a broader commitment to open government (Davis, 1971: 98). Davis was concerned with public administration in general; however, policing was a particular interest (Davis, 1974; 1975) and provided many of the examples in *Discretionary Justice* (1971). He insisted that the police should be seen not just as an administrative agency, but as by far the largest; most active, and least regulated administrative agency in the modern state (1971: 222–3; 1974: 703). For Davis, police discretion implies the making of policy about law enforcement and order maintenance. The need for the development of rules to control discretion was widely accepted.[23] His work had widespread influence in the United States, while in England and Wales (and to a lesser extent Australia), it became a standard academic point of reference in public law.

Davis conveniently summarized his 'objectives of a good programme for reform of police practices':

> (1) to educate the public in the reality that the police make vital policy, (2) to induce legislative bodies to redefine crimes so that the statutory law will be practically enforceable, (3) to rewrite statutes to make clear what powers are granted to the police and what powers are withheld, and then to keep the police within the granted powers, (4) to close the gap between the pretences of the police manuals and the actualities of police behaviour, (5) to transfer most of the policy-making power from patrolmen [sic] to the better qualified heads of departments, acting on the advice of appropriate specialists, (6) to bring policy-making out into the open for all to see, except where special need exists for confidentiality; (7) to improve the quality of police policies by inviting suggestions and criticism from interested parties, (8) to bring the procedures for policy determination into harmony with the democratic principle, instead of running counter to that principle, (9) to replace the present police policies based on guess-work with policies based on appropriate investigations and studies made by qualified personnel, and (10) to promote equal justice by moving from a system of *ad hoc* determination of policy by individual officers in particular cases to a system of central policy determination (1971: 90–1).

This list makes clear that Davis's ambition was a wholesale reform of policing and its legal context, rather than the (comparatively) narrow legal regulation of discretionary practices. This makes his insistence on the potential of administrative rule-making more surprising: he thought that '[a]ll ten objectives can be furthered and some can be fully accomplished through rule-making procedure, except that the second and third call for legislation' (1971: 91).[24] There is much to question in Davis's programme: for example, his assumptions about bureaucratic organization and efficiency, about the nature of policy and policy-making (contrast Grimshaw and Jefferson, 1987), and about the commitment and quality of senior officers can all be challenged. He displays many of the characteristics of the legalistic-bureaucratic approach [...]. As Walker comments, Davis had an 'almost uncritical' enthusiasm for administrative rule-making (Walker, 1993a: 17). In his distrust of discretion (other than that exercised by judges), he shared more than he acknowledged with Dicey.

Most important is Davis's belief in the potency of legal regulation. More recent scholarship in public law and criminal justice has often been sceptical of enthusiasm for rules, and Davis's work is now more likely to find itself the subject of critique than praise.[25] This reaction chimes with the critique of rule-focused regulatory regimes by socio-legal scholars, as well as with more general theoretical challenges to legalism from the critical legal studies movement and elsewhere (Braithwaite and Braithwaite, 1995: 336). Indeed, the critique of legal regulation has become widely accepted contemporary wisdom. Across a range of institutions, similar analyses are made and similar remedies are proposed. The force of the critiques will be acknowledged below. Thereafter, it is necessary to return to see what remains of value in regulation by rules and, in particular, to see how rules and other regulatory strategies can, indeed must, be combined.

Davis generally displays problematic characteristic of legalism: individualizing justice, exaggerating the success of rules, seeing decision-making as an event rather than a process, ignoring the patterning of behaviour by non-legal norms, favouring procedure over substance, and assuming that decision-makers are bureaucrats rather than professionals (Baldwin, 1995: 19–33). Individualism is particularly problematic in criminal justice: as Reiss points out, Davis's concentration on individual applications of discretion blinds him to its patterning by race and class (1970: 790). Legalism breaks the subject-matter into legally digestible form – paradigmatically as decisions. The object of study or action is 'a discrete event or mental act which can be isolated, whereas "discretion" might often be thought to inhere in role-related conduct (such as the manner with which an official receives enquiries) and even in processes and situations (such as organizational structure), which cannot be analysed in those terms' (Lacey, 1992: 380). This focus on decisions is the defining feature of the 'criminal justice paradigm' which has dominated understanding of the field since the 1950s (Walker, 1992). It is only gradually being challenged by more sociological paradigms which focus on process rather than decisions and on structure rather than system.

In the case of policing, an excellent example of the limits of legalism is provided by the failure of the legal regulation of stop/search which was largely due to misunderstanding of the processual and contextual nature of street policing (Dixon *et al.*, 1989). Take a very common instance: an officer stops and searches someone who is walking in a residential area late at night. A legalistic interpretation of PACE Code A would suggest that general suspicion would have to be supplemented by an additional factor, 'such as that a burglary has recently been committed in the area' (Stone, 1986: 56). But what if the officer does not know about a specific burglary, but rather his or her experience instills belief that one or more burglaries will, almost certainly, be or have been committed in that area during his or her shift? Such cultural 'knowledge' based on patterns of crime may be valuable and, it can be argued, is enough legally to justify a stop/ search (Leigh, 1985: 162). But it is very different from the individually focused suspicion around which legal discussion usually takes place. A similar analysis could be made of arrest: as Lacey suggests, 'the project of subjecting this kind of discretion to the confining or structuring by standards which Davis advocated seems both unrealistic and misplaced' (1992: 385). Crucially, the potential for confining patrol officers' discretion is overstated: despite his interest in police research, he misunderstood the discretionary nature of policing.[26]

Rules can encourage an instrumentalism in which the unlikelihood of sanctions being applied overwhelms consideration of the rule's purpose. For instance, Davis himself provides excellent examples of the weak purchase of exclusionary rules: police officers who harassed a drug dealer in familiar displays of authority and order maintenance were not interested in trying to secure a conviction, and so were unconcerned about the unlawfulness of their actions (1975: 1620). If procedural rules are seen as just being about what must be followed to get a conviction, policing practices which have other objectives are likely to be dominated by other determinants.

Attempts to regulate by precise rules may find that the innumerability of potential situations exhaust rule-making capacity. Unsuccessful attempts to control by rules encourage pragmatism and instrumentalism: '[d]etailed laws can provide a set of signposts to navigate around.' Some are more able to navigate (or hire navigators) than others: unequal distribution of wealth and power colours the effects of rules (Braithwaite and Braithwaite, 1995: 3360. Some 'regulatees' become particularly adept at soaking up rules without being constrained by them. Some police officers express this with bravado, as in this detective's comment on the PACE requirement to record interrogations: 'I don't give a toss. I'll get round it ... Any rules they want me to work with, I work to find a way round them' (quoted, Dixon *et al.*, 1990a: 133). It would be wrong to take this as evidence of some iron law of police deviance: whatever the law says, officers will try to get around it. More interesting is the pragmatism of those who would probably identify themselves as 'new professionals', who have learnt that their work can be done within the rules, and who, specifically, have accepted the need to change questioning practices. They have no particular devotion to 'due process'. Rather, the key value is efficiency: the new professionals' critique of the 'dinosaurs' has been fuelled by a long series of prosecutions which have failed because officers have refused (or been unable) to change their investigative practices. It might be desirable to have police officers who enthusiastically accepted due process, but the nature of policing makes this improbable (Smith, 1995). 'New professionalism' is probably the best that can realistically be expected in present circumstances: enough has been said above to signal my limited favour for it. However, the impact of such a change should not be underestimated: as new working practices are established, so cultural shifts will occur. As will be discussed in more detail below, Samuel Walker argues strongly that this is one of the significant and under-appreciated effects of the 'due process' revolution in the United States (1988: 120).

A good example of the type of reform which Davis sought to encourage is provided by Wilson and Alprin's report (1974) on administrative rule-making by the Metropolitan Police Department of Washington DC. This programme attempted to structure police decision-making by communicating effectively to officers the ratio of judicial decisions and the priorities of departmental policy. Examples were given relating to suspect identification procedures, vehicle searches, and the use of deadly force. Guidelines were supervised by creating administrative arrangements to review cases when prosecution decided not to proceed with a charge and incidents when a police officer's weapon was fired. Records were maintained of officer and unit performance so that 'patterns, of misconduct or procedural error can be observed and corrected' (1974: 54). It was argued that these methods of control were much more effective than 'the traditional reliance on the exclusionary rule or disciplinary procedures.[28]

What has been the impact of such programmes? An important attempt to assess this is made by Samuel Walker; who follows Davis's 'preliminary inquiry' by providing 'an interim report on what works' in the legal regulation of discretion in the United States (1993a: 18). His 'focus is broad, including other sectors of criminal justice process as well as the police. His general conclusion is 'a moderately optimistic one. The control of discretion is possible. But ... it is possible only as long as expectations are modest and the reforms carefully tailored and implemented' (1993a: 16). His major example of change in policing effected by rules is police shootings: the 'control of deadly force is arguably the great success story in the long effort to control police discretion' (1993a: 25; see *ibid.* 25–33; 1986: 363–4). Between the early 1970s and the late 1980s, the 'number of people shot and killed by the police was reduced by at least thirty per cent ... At the same time, the disparity between black and white citizens shot and killed was cut in half' (1993a: 26). He argues that internal rules and policies were responsible for this.[29]

Walker recognizes the problems of using police shootings as an example (although he is perhaps undercritical of the studies on which he relies). Use of a firearm is likely to be a discrete, public, critical event, and the combination of these characteristics makes it unlike other activities and practices (1986: 375–8; 1993b). Apart from this major but atypical case study, there are few examples of concerted attempts to control police discretion by rules which have been reliably assessed. The lack of research on such matters in the United States is surprising.[30] What comes in its place in the literature all too often is assertion and rhetoric: for example, the confident optimism of Wilson and Alprin about the malleability of discretion (see immediately above) is dismissed by Brown as 'myopic and unrealistic', a classic example of the legalistic–bureaucratic tendency to assume that changing rules will unproblematically change organizational practices, and which is likely to produce 'illusory controls' in the form of presentational rules (1988: 293). By contrast, Walker carefully picks the direct lessons and, more often, implications of the available research literature.[31] His conclusions are sensible and often of wider relevance. He argues that effective legal regulation is possible if the right targets and tools are chosen, and if 'techniques for monitoring compliance' are developed (1986: 372). He concludes that

> First, it is not true that 'nothing works'. Reforms do not necessarily backfire and produce undesirable consequences. Nor are they always negated by covert resistance. Second, controls do not necessarily degenerate into empty formalism ... Third, discretion is not always displaced upstream or downstream ... Fourth, controls do not necessarily induce lying or other forms of improper evasion ... In short, some things work (1993a: 150).

While (perhaps partly because) Walker's evidence of effective rule change is so limited, he insists on the need to look at the indirect effects of rule changes and reform activity. Notably, the research evidence is clear that the heroic Supreme Court cases such as *Mapp, Miranda*, and *Escobedo* had relatively little direct effect on police practices (Leo, 1996a: 287; Leo, 1996c; Walker, 1993a: 44–6). However, Walker and Leo argue, the indirect effects (which are still working through) have been significant.[32] The cases led police organizations to improve their training, supervisory practices, and general professionalism (Walker, 1980: 229–32).[33] They encouraged a cultural shift towards the acceptance of accountability and legality:

the significance of this was discussed in section ii, above. Skolnick writes of a 'legal archipelago … sets of islands of legal values … distributed throughout the broad experience of policing' (1993: 196). Unfortunately, the lack of research evidence is again a problem. Walker relies heavily on Orfield's report on Chicago narcotics officers[34] which found that the exclusionary rule 'had an enormous impact: educating officers about the law and legal principles, deterring misconduct, and stimulating long-term reforms' (Walker, 1988: 19; see also 1993a: 49). While Orfield's work is valuable, the methodological limitations of relying on structured, questionnaire-based interviews have to be acknowledged. Apart from two limited studies in the 1960s (Wald *et al.*, 1967; Milner, 1971), the only observational research on interrogation in the United States is Leo's reports of his observations in 'Laconia',[35] supplemented by his analysis of videorecorded interrogations by two other police departments.[36] Leo argues that '*Miranda* has had a profound impact in at least four different ways: first, [it] has exercised a civilising influence on police interrogation behavior, and in so doing has professionalized police practices; second, [it] has transformed the culture and discourse of police detecting; third, [it] has increased popular awareness of constitutional rights; and fourth, [it] has inspired police to develop more specialized, more sophisticated and seemingly more effective interrogation techniques' (1996c: 668). Such developments (particularly the shift in interrogation from coercion to persuasion, manipulation, and deception) cannot be simplistically categorized as progress. Rather they must be seen as part of a more general reconstitution of techniques of power and processes of control (Leo, 1994: 94–6; 1996a: 285; cf. Marx, 1992).

Studies of regulation to this and other fields confirm the trite observation that the best discipline is that which is internalized: the objective should be compliance rather than obedience (McGowan, 1972: 672; Baldwin, 1995: 302). It is commonplace to indicate the irony that criminologists who have accepted the limits of deterrence in controlling deviance should adopt it as the basis of police regulation (Reiner, 1992a: 214). As Kagan argues 'the attempt to control regulatory enforcement primarily by external legal requirements is deeply troublesome in so far as it induces in both inspectors and the regulated an attitude of legal defensiveness, a concern for adequate documentation rather than substantive achievement, and a degree of rule-bound rigidity' (1984: 58). Regulatory strategies must aim to foster responsibility and competence, not mere rule-following.

How can this be achieved? The literature on regulation is too large and complex for detailed analysis here,[37] but some crucial lessons can be suggested, particularly from the work of John Braithwaite and his colleagues, which is distinguished not least by its positive and constructive emphasis. Sophisticated studies of business regulation have transcended the 'intellectual stalemate' produced by dogmatic dichotomies between co-operative and punitive regulatory strategies (Ayres and Braithwaite, 1992: 3; cf. Fisse and Braithwaite, 1993). Punishment and persuasion, coercion, and compliance are not exclusionary alternatives: 'compliance is optimized by regulation that is contingently cooperative, tough and forgiving' (Ayres and Braithwaite, 1992: 51; cf. Braithwaite, 1995: 55). The 'trick of successful regulation' is their 'synergy' (Ayres and Braithwaite, 1992: 25; […]; Ogus, 1994: 97). In achieving this, understanding of specific structures and cultures of the subject of regulation is vital. But we should not assume too easily that 'we can pick which are the right cases for medicine and which for poison' (Braithwaite, 1995: 55). Persuasion should be adopted first: thereafter, regulatory strategies must be adaptive, responding to the subject's mode of compliance or evasion (Ayres and Braithwaite, 1992; Braithwaite, 1995; Hawkins and Thomas (eds), 1984).

There seems no good reason not to apply such insights to policing (Braithwaite, 1992a; cf. Brogden and Shearing, 1993). This should not be taken to suggest any complacency about the state of the police: this would be particularly peculiar in a critical observer of NSW policing in the mid-1990s. Rather, the driving-force is the need for change by effective police reform. Officers through-out police organizations should be consulted about the standards which they are expected to maintain, both procedural and ethical.[38] This approach is not 'soft': it would emphasize making disciplinary sanctions more effective: if other strategies fail or are inappropriate, punishment must be available in credible form. When police abuse their powers and position, the costs for individual citizens and groups can be high, and this must be reflected in public intolerance of police misconduct and official willingness to act decisively against it. Police disciplinary systems are deeply flawed all too often ignoring procedural breaches,[39] while earning officers' disrespect for severely but unpredictably punishing less significant misconduct. However, such measures should go beyond individual or group punishment: the police organization should also, in appropriate circumstances, bear responsibility. This process could range from judges ensuring that notice is taken of particular cases […] to a programme of 'enforced self-investigation' and externally supervised reform (Braithwaite, 1992a: 3; Fisse and Braithwaite, 1993).

At another level, police should be encouraged to accept responsibility for ensuring that their activities are legal and ethical. The hostility amongst some British commentators (e.g. McConville *et al.*, 1991a) to police self-regulation might be moderated by more familiarity with the literature on regulation outside criminal justice.[40] The policing literature provides no grounds to believe that externally controlled, punishment-oriented regimes are effective. As Walker suggests, 'one of the keys to long-term police reform is the development of the capacity for self-governance by law enforcement agencies' (1986: 384). This does not, of course, mean granting complete autonomy: self-governance must be developed along with procedures for external accountability (see subsect. (e) below). Confirmation of the potential for doing so can be found in the literature on regulatory strategies for dealing with corruption and handling complaints: a 'double-track strategy' combining internal and external elements seems clearly desirable (Mollen, 1994: 152; see also Dixon, 1995a; Goldsmith, 1991).

Nor does it mean simply that we must 'trust the police': trust is to be distinguished from the blind faith which has so often encouraged police misconduct. Rather, it means a police service must be constructed in which we can trust, and that trusting (i.e. requiring the acceptance of responsibility) will be an important part of that process. This provides insight into the crucial distinction between presentational, inhibitory, and working rules (Smith and Gray, 1985: 440–2; […]) and, most significantly for the study of law in policing, how rules can be more or less effective. As Braithwaite and Makkai suggest:

>  When we are trusted to do the right thing and then choose to do it, we
>  convince ourselves that we did it because we believed it to be right; we
>  internalize the conception of right that we are trusted to have. On the other
>  hand, when we comply to secure extrinsic rewards or avoid the punish-
>  ments of distrustful regulators, we convince ourselves that we did it for
>  those extrinsic reasons rather than for the intrinsic virtue of doing right ...
>  When, therefore our distrustful guardians cannot be around to put those
>  rewards and punishments in our path, we do not bother with the
>  extrinsically motivated behavior (1994: 2).

Just as 'knavery is returned in full measure' to police who treat people as knaves
(Braithwaite, 1995: 54), so treating police as knaves will be counter-productive:
'the trouble with institutions that assume that people will not be virtuous is that
they destroy virtue' (Braithwaite, 1995: 54). In contrast to the view that trust is
inevitably abused and even inherently criminogenic, Braithwaite and Makkai
insist that 'trust *nurtures* compliance' and 'engenders trustworthiness' (1994: 1, 2
original emphasis).

This resonates with another theme in Braithwaite's work: the uses and abuses
of shame (Braithwaite, 1989; Braithwaite and Mugford, 1994). Police organizations react defensively to criticism, particularly if it comes in the adversarial
context of a court case or judicial inquiry: they are left feeling 'more angry and
scapegoated than sorry' (Braithwaite, 1992a: 4). This is exemplified by the
response of many New South Wales police officers to the Royal Commission into
the NSW Police Service: complaints abound of low morale and victimization,
while the integrity of the vast majority is stressed. An effective reform process
requires organizations to accept responsibility, through a positive shaming
process, both for problems and for their rectification. This might include
attempts to develop 'restorative' justice which would reintegrate rather than
ignore or exclude minor offenders. The reintegration must, of course, not be into
traditional police cultures and practices. These must be reformed not just by legal
regulation, but also by involving police officers in establishing and maintaining
their own ethical standards.[41] It has been possible here only to indicate the
potential relevance of the literature on regulation and associated fields, not to
explore it or its limitations in depth. Enough has been said to suggest that there is
much of relevance to policing.

### (e) Reforming and regulating

This analysis suggests that the question 'can law control policing?' must not be
reduced to the traditional question 'can rules control discretion?' Rules may
provide a 'framework and focus' (Braithwaite and Braithwaite, 1995: 330); but
are not enough. They are just one of the 'tools of government' (Baldwin, 1995:
292, 304, citing Hood, 1983). Rules are likely to have their place in any
governmental strategy, but they must be used in thoughtful and original ways.
Their objective must be clear, they must be designed and chosen carefully, they
must be appropriate to the specific subject matter, their potential relationship
with existing regulation by other normative systems (such as police cultures)

must be appreciated, and supplements and alternatives to rules should be considered. Other methods of regulation – both legal and non-legal – must be considered: '[j]udging when to employ rules within government involves complex questions of design and strategy' (Baldwin, 1995: 15; cf. Daintith, 1994; Ayres and Braithwaite, 1994: 101; Jewell, 1975: 12–25). As Loughlin suggests, public law 'should adopt as its principal focus the examination of the manner in which the normative structures of law can contribute to the tasks of guidance, control, and evaluation in government' (1992: 264). In this context, the 'traditional rule of law ideal' is of marginal relevance, as 'continuities between the legal, the political and the social' are increasingly recognized (Lacey, 1992: 386).

The need to consider alternatives to rules is emphasized further in Lacey's critique of legal pretensions and particularly the 'intellectual and practical imperialism in which lawyers merely incorporate ever more inappropriate areas of activity into their own analytic and political framework' (Lacey, 1992: 363). The crucial but difficult task is to use legal techniques and principles without slipping into a legal imperialism which denotes everything as 'legal', with all its implications of lawyers' claims to hegemony and its ignorance or dismissal of other disciplines. For example, if Davis's 'program for reform' is freed from its reliance on administrative rule-making, its potential grows: public education about policing, revision of substantive criminal law, clarification and definition of police powers, rewriting of police rule books, open policy-making, public consultation, and democratic accountability, and reliance on reliable research rather than 'common sense' are all desirable (Dixon, 1995b). The relevance of open government for policing deserves emphasis: openness was a key theme of Davis's work, has featured strongly in the programmes of the new public law, and also is stressed (as 'transparency') in Brogden and Shearing's agenda for police reform (1993: 127–9).

The potential for development of legal remedies is a matter of controversy: strong arguments both for and against judicial review can be found among leading public lawyers (Richardson and Germ (eds), 1994). This debate needs to be broadened beyond the public lawyers' circle. For example, D.J. Smith constructively suggested using the law more actively and creatively by legislatively encouraging the courts to subject policing policies to principles of fairness and justice by developing judicial review (1988: 440). Civil actions, so long dismissed as insignificant, are now to be taken seriously despite their acknowledged limitations (Clayton and Tomlinson, 1992: 15). They might be taken more seriously if costs, rather than being absorbed by central funds, were (at least in part) allocated to the 'budget unit' responsible. Similarly, the other tools of public law – complaints procedures, ombudsmen, rights of consultation and participation, freedom of information – are all attracting renewed interest in England and Wales (particularly under the influence of the European Union: see Walker, 1996a) and all have potentially great relevance to the control of policing.

Baldwin's and Lacey's work indicates the need to look beyond traditional legal regulation as a means of dealing with perceived problems in policing: this would include considering 'institutions of political accountability ...; the structure and organization of areas in which discretionary power is exercised (encompassing questions about personnel, powers, and the relations between them); and substantive questions as to the institutional goals and assumptions of particular areas of administration' (Lacey, 1992: 379). Of course, it is hardly original to argue for political accountability of police. For much of the later 1970s and 1980s, it became almost a cliché in English academic debate about policing. Its unreality was brought home with the abolition of the Greater London and metropolitan councils and subsequently the reformation of police authorities.[42] (Its parochialism is indicated by the disbelief in contemporary New South Wales which meets suggestions that local government should or could control policing.) In the mid-1990s, police accountability has attracted more politically astute and theoretically sophisticated attention (e.g. Jones *et al.*, 1994; 1996; Loader, 1996; Reiner and Spencer (eds), 1993).

The experience of the 1980s in England also suggests the limits of proactive legal regulation. A good example is the Scarman-inspired attempt to structure police policy and discretion by legally requiring public consultation. The Police and Criminal Evidence Act, section 106, requires that '[a]rrangements shall be made in each police area for obtaining the views of people in that area about matters concerning the policing of that area and for obtaining their co-operation with the police in preventing crime in the area'. Researchers have been damning in their assessments of the resulting consultative committees: they have 'come to serve as little more than a forum for consensual impression management' (Weatheritt, 1988: 172; see also Morgan, 1992). Committees are unbalanced in their representation of the 'consumers' of police services: while local business will be represented, young black working-class males will almost certainly not be. Committees have been dependent on police for information and consequently reflect police definitions of problems and possible strategies. Police do not allow committees a significant role in policy formulation. Rather, influence is exerted by middle-management officers on committee members and, via them, on police authorities and senior management (Morgan, 1992: 181). Such outcomes were predictable enough: unwillingness to transfer power routinely makes such consultative procedures frustrating and ineffective. It is an example of trying to make the system work in a different way without understanding the structural reasons for its current mode of operation (Hall, 1982). This is a recurrent dilemma for attempts to use legal regulation positively.

It is necessary to emphasize the limits of legal regulation. Policing is conducted in a complex relationship with law, but is not consumed by it. For example, the general duties officer who comes across a sick drug user about to inject has to choose, *inter alia*, between arresting the person, ignoring the incident, and destroying the drugs. Her or his choice involves moral and ethical considerations, as well as, *inter alia*, profane matters such as departmental and local policies, and (official and personal) willingness to commit time to arresting and processing the user.

[P]olicing is for the most part *extralegal*, for while officers (often) work within the constraints of the law, they seldom invoke the law in performing police work; informal action, with or without coercive action, is commonplace, and hence the dimensions of police discretion are not delineated by officers' authority to apply legal sanctions (Worden, 1989: 668).

There are four major dimensions of non-legal policing. First, policing may be conducted within the law, but be substantially unaffected by it: the arguments by Sanders and Young (1994b) were considered above. Secondly, [...], 'policing by consent' is a crucial way of doing police work. Thirdly, while legal regulation focuses on controlling law enforcement, it is commonplace to point out that much police work includes social service and order maintenance as well as or rather than law enforcement. Fourthly, even when officers are dealings with suspected crime, legal influence may be compromised by other pervasive objectives [...]. In achieving these, officers may use extra-legal or illegal means. Alternatively, they may use legal powers tactically, for example arresting and detaining suspects, even though there is no realistic prospect of bringing charges to court.[43] Finally, if, for one of the numerous reasons which produce guilty pleas, officers can be confident that a suspect will not contest the charge, legal supervision of law enforcement is likely to be minimal.

However, scepticism about rules must not be excessive, and must address not the simplicities of the legalistic-bureaucratic model [...], but a more sophisticated account in which both the limits and the possibilities of normative regulation are appreciated (Dixon, 19956). As Goldstein suggests, intelligent rule-making involves alerting 'officers to the alternatives available for dealing with a given situation, to the factors that should be considered in choosing from among available alternatives, and to the relative weight that should attach to each factor'.[44] Insistence on the need for structured discretion within new pro-grammes of community- or problem-oriented policing (Moore, 1992), are particularly important when a critique of legal regulation has been part of arguments that effective crime control, notably the 'war on drugs' (Skolnick, 1994), requires that police should be allowed to slip the leash of legal restraint. In this context, the case for a 'new policing' based on professional use of discretion rather than rules [...] can be a stalking-horse for most undesirable developments in policing (Weisburd et al., 1993; Skolnick, 1993).

Here as elsewhere, 'community' is Janus-faced: it excludes as it includes. The exclusion of those not defined as being of 'the community' is (particularly problematic in its re-articulation of distinctions drawn by police cultures between the respectable and the unrespectable; between those who count, and those who do not (Matza, 1969: 189; Reiner, 1992a: 117–21). A NSW officer expressed the operational consequences: 'you treat good people as good and you treat shit as shit.' The brush is broad: another officer referred to 'the lower working class, the hoodlum element, the housing commission sort of families out west[45] who are brought up to hate coppers'. In acting and thinking in this way, police reproduce social divisions (Finnane, 1994: 103). Ironically, 'good people' sometimes do not appreciate what the police do for them: the outcome is police cynicism. The dichotomies are particularly problematic for legal regulation if rights and safeguards are seen by police as being for 'decent people'.[46] In NSW, a history of cultural distinctions between 'criminals' and 'the community' creates particular difficulties in according full legal citizenship to the former. Such problems are exacerbated in Australia and elsewhere by deepening social and economic divisions, by racism, and by drug-related crime. A fundamental task of police reform must be to help police (and 'the community') to see, e.g., the Vietnamese heroin user, the westie 'hoodlum', or the Aboriginal suspect as part of, not an alien threat to, 'the community'. Another […] is to take the 'ownership' of policing away from the police (Brogden and Shearing, 1993: 170). Finally […] the political significance of policing needs to be understood by its practitioners: as Skolnick argued, their 'professionalism must rest on a set of values conveying the idea that police are as much an institution dedicated to the achievement of legality in society as they are an official social organization designed to control misconduct through the invocation of punitive sanctions. What must occur is a significant alteration in the ideology of police so that police "professionalization" rests on the values of a democratic legal order, rather than on technological proficiency' (1975: 238–9).

It should be clear that legal regulation must be combined with other processes and strategies if police reform is to be effected (Smith, 1986: 94). Emerging as a key issue in considering the future of policing is the provision of positive direction to police officers (Krantz et al., 1979: 53). At one level, there is the need for 'reflection and public debate on the normative political issues of what the role of the police should be in a democratic society' (Lacey, 1992: 385). An important contribution to this process has been made by John Braithwaite's identification of what a 'good police service' would look like (Braithwaite, 1992b). Whether or not Braithwaite's republican theory is accepted, his work shows the benefits of connecting the study and practice of policing with broad social and political theory.

As Norris and Norris demonstrate, defining good policing is a complex matter (1993; see also Bright, 1995; Krantz et al., 1979: 55–6). Officers have to learn to recognize their own success other than in terms of traditional 'performance indicators' such as arrests. For example, as Homel suggests, police contributed to the remarkable effect of random breath-testing in reducing fatal car crashes in New South Wales. Yet 'it is astonishing how many constables in NSW are still not aware of the impact of RBT and their critical role in its ongoing success' (1994: 25). Police organizations must become as adept at identifying good practice and rewarding officers for carrying it out as they are at creating disciplinary rules and punishing officers for breaking them: 'a programme of "positive discipline" stressing and rewarding integrity is crucial' (Punch, 1985: 196). This must involve both individual rewards and organizational recognition, e.g. by the communication of information about successes (Homel, 1994: 25). Police organizations notoriously rely on negative discipline.[47] It is conventional to include them in Gouldner's category of 'punishment centred bureaucracies'. However, it is less often appreciated that the punishment in such bureaucracies is not just applied by management to workers, but also by workers to management (Gouldner, 1954: chs. 11 and 12). Such 'punishment' was described by Punch in his study of corruption and reform efforts in Holland: 'informal resistance within the Amsterdam police was powerful enough to deflect investigations and to impede change' (1985: 199; see also Sherman, 1974: 270). The difficulty of change should not be underestimated: Krantz et al. found that 'many of the problems associated with the use of negative sanctions also hampers the application of positive incentives' (1979: 61). To break away from this model, police organizations need to undergo fundamental cultural and normative change (Dixon, 19956).

Discussing the potential for change involves looking at the nature of policing, at the structural limits and possibilities of change, and the broader social, economic, and political forces which define those limits. The experience of police reformers has been that police organizations are as manœuvrable as oiltankers. This is not just because of the bureaucratic problems which attract attention, such as staff unwillingness to change working practices, difficulties in communicating new policies, inadequate training, and poor human resources. Difficulties in achieving reform and legal regulation of policing are neither fortuitous nor haphazard. Rather they are products of fundamental elements in the practices and mandates of policing. But this should not justify slipping back into an excessively pessimistic determinism: police departments can be changed, have changed, and will continue to change.[49] The challenge is to identify the limits and possibilities of change, and the potential for legal regulation to facilitate, encourage, and contribute to such change (cf. Chan, 1997).

In conclusion, it is appropriate to reflect on some of the themes of this study. Complaints about our lack of knowledge of how law affects policing [...] may now be seen in a rather different light. The now substantial literature (particularly on the impact of PACE) suggests that the issue is not lack of knowledge, but rather theoretical and political differences in its interpretation. This should, of course, surprise nobody except the straw empiricist. I have suggested my interpretation, one which stresses contingency: law's relationship with policing depends upon the nature of the law, the type of policing, and the social and political contexts. This is unfortunately, but again unsurprisingly, unhelpful to anyone seeking a formulaic resolution to the question of whether law can change policing.

From this perspective, law should be seen, not as having some fixed essence, but as an adaptable set of practices, discourses, techniques, and modes of regulation. It can provide both broad, discretionary, pragmatic adaptability and a clear rule-based regime. Its great strength as an ideology and as a mode of domination and accomplishment is that it can do both and can switch between them. Such an approach emphasizes the need for theoretically-based empirical work which explores the conjunctural circumstances in which law appears in particular forms.

Policing is similarly resistant to neat definition. It involves a wide range of practices, institutions, and cultures. Law's impact is modulated by various and varying combinations of these elements. Simple examples are provided by the contrast between activities on the street and in the station and by regional and national variations. Whatever its essential commonalities (Bittner, 1990), policing in England and Australia is crucially different because of its cultural and political contexts: it is for this reason that [...] legal regulation of policing has diverged so markedly in these jurisdictions. [... Law] does not subsume policing as a mode of governance: policing by consent provides a distinct but closely articulated mode. In addition, as noted above, the objectives of policing cannot be reduced to those of the legal process, charge, and conviction. As for studies of policing, the imperative must be breadth of vision, looking outwards to policing in other places and times and to theoretical work across the social sciences: the theoretical sophistication of a new generation of police research[50] suggests grounds for optimism about such developments.

*From David Dixon, 'The legal regulation of policing' in* Law in Policing *(Oxford: Oxford University Press), 1997, pp 280–318.*

## Notes

1  Shklar (1987: 1) suggests, but dissociates herself from, this rejection.
2  While attacks on Dicey may have been 'completely devastating', Davis was wrong to suggest that, in the English context, 'his ideas were brushed aside' (1971: 31–2). They had a major influence which has been recognized in assessments of Dicey's work (e.g. Harlow and Rawlings, 1984: ch. 1; Zellick (ed.) 1985: 583–723; McAuslan and McEldowney (eds.) 1985; Loughlin, 1992: ch. 7). For a significant defence of Dicey, see Allan, 1993.
3  As W.A. Robson pointed out in 1928, a misunderstanding of French administrative law seems to have been responsible for Dicey's view here (Jowell, 1994: 59). Davis (1971: 28–33) groups the Franks Committee, John Dickinson, and F.A. Hayek with Dicey as exponents of this 'extravagant version' of the rule of law.
4  While 'Dicey's obsession with remedies made him oblivious to the importance of rights' (Barendt, 1985: 607), this does not imply that remedies (or their absence) are not of great significance: see Bradley, 1989: 188; Sanders and Young, 1994a: 456–8.
5  See [...] *Malone* v. *Metropolitan Police Commissioner* ([1979] Ch. 344) [...].
6  For example, this analysis of the place of law in policing and police–public relations was endorsed by the Royal Commission on the Police of 1960–2 (RCP 1962: 10–11).
7  It bears emphasizing that cases like the Birmingham Six and the Hilton bombing [...] were miscarriages of justice not only for those who wrongfully spent years in jail, but also for the victims of appalling crimes, and for their families and society generally because of the failure to identify and punish the guilty. This is an aspect of victims' rights too often overlooked in attempts by law-and-order lobbyists to claim victims as their own. Public resistance to this by some victims' families was a notable feature of the 1995 NSW State election. Of course, in some miscarriage cases, there is no 'really guilty' person because there has been no crime: see e.g. the cases of the Ananda Marga (Carrington *et al.* (eds.) 1991) and Errol Madden (details of the latter are in *R.* v. *Police Complaints Board, ex p. Madden* [1983] 2 All ER 353 at 365).
8  See, e.g., Metropolitan Police Commissioner Condon's comments, reported in *Police Review* 17 Mar. 1995, 6
9  e.g. Allan, 1985. While he argues that 'a substantive role for the rule of law' is suggested by analysis of 'the collaborative and integral nature of the enactment of legislation and its subsequent application' (1985: 143), ironically, his analysis is flawed as a result of its narrow legalistic focus.
10  Reiner (1992a: 213) argues that imprisonment is an inappropriate and counterproductive sentence for some offences. A good example is the removal in 1993 of imprisonment as a potential sentence for offensive language under the Summary Offences Act 1988 in NSW. Such amendments have to be supplemented by further action to ensure that those convicted do not go to jail nevertheless for non-payment of fines or non-completion of community service orders.
11  This is not to ignore earlier formulations of the rule of law, but to insist on the distinctiveness of the modern conception: see Loughlin, 1992: 149–50. For discussion of how contemporary liberal jurisprudence on the nature of law relates to the rule of law, see Radin, 1989.
12  384 US 458 (1996).
13  The classic study of such processes is Christopher Hill's essay on the potent myth of rights lost under the 'Norman yoke' (Hill, 1954; see also *id.*, 1996). For an invaluable collection of materials, see Hampton (ed.) 1984. For an account which situates Thompson's comments on the rule of law in the context of his broader historical and political work, see Palmer, 1981.
14  Of course, Unger's central theme was the challenge of 'bureaucratic-administrative' law to legal order.
15  See, e.g., 'Jury Acquits Detective on Drug Charge', *Courier Mail*, 15 Apr. 1994; 'Police Cleared of Abducting Black Children', *The Australian*, 25–6 Feb. 1995. For analysis of the context, see Bolen, 1997.
16  See Community Protection Act 1994 (NSW); Crimes Amendment (Mandatory Life Sentences) Act 1996 (NSW). In *Kable* v. *DPP*, unreported, 12 Sept. 1996, the High Court declared the latter to be constitutionally invalid.

17  James Boyd White, quoted Krygier, 1990: 640. Self-evidently, this depends on the breadth of those limits.

18  The shifts and uncertainty in Reiner's discussion of the golden age – was it real or a myth? – illustrate some of the issues here (1992a: ch. 2, 1994: 753; cf. Loade, 1995).

19  A notable feature of the Royal Commission into the NSW Police Service established in 1994 was the use of sophisticated surveillance technology, followed by skilful use of resulting records in negotiations with informants and suspects.

20  [The] deconstruction of the public–private divide is a key issue in contemporary public law: see, e.g., the replacement of a formal by a functionalist approach in *R. v. Panel on Take-overs and Mergers ex p. Datafin PLC* [1987] QB 815.

21  As both Loughlin and Harlow and Rawlings make clear, these are ideal types. They have long ancestries: as W.A. Robson pointed out, the opposition between what he termed the 'model of law' and the 'model of government' derives from the political conflicts of the seventeenth century (quoted, Harlow and Rawlings, 1984: 35).

22  While making this concession, Davis generally displayed a legalistic distrust of and lack of enthusiasm for discretion.

23  See Goldstein, 1993: 214–18; R.J. Allen provided significant dissent, emphasizing the structural, functional, and political differences between police and administrative agencies to which rule-making could apply (1976; 1977; contrast Davis, 1977).

24  Some subsequent American writers have argued for legislative rather than administrative rules: see e.g. Berger, 1990; Bradley, 1990.

25  Problems of legal regulation in plea-bargaining, sentencing, and parole were influential here (Ohlin, 1993). For a discussion of the relationship between contemporary criminal justice and the role of law, see Allen, 1996.

26  This should not be overstated: Davis appreciated that 'discretion is the essence of police work and is indispensable' (1975: 139). However, he was over-optimistic about the potential for its control by rules.

27  This is the response to rules which McBarnet terms 'creative compliance': [...] Baldwin, 1995: 185–9.

28  See also Krantz *et al.*, 1979 and, for a strong argument in favour of rule making, Caplan, 1974.

29  According to Walker, the Supreme Court's ruling in *Tennessee v. Garner* 471 US 1 (1984) 'merely ratified (and then only inadequately) a national consensus that had already developed' (1993: 33).

30  A rare example is Krantz *et al.*'s (1979) assessment of police policy- and rule-making in Boston, which reported limited success. Despite the extensive literature on mandatory arrest for domestic violence, there are no studies of the long-term effects of such policies in non-experimental settings (Walker, 1993a: 33–9; Manning, 1993).

31  See, e.g., his useful analysis of the comparative potential for regulation of police shootings, pursuits, and domestic violence interventions (1993a: ch. 2).

32  As Leo complains, 'virtually all scholarship on American police interrogation is relegated to doctrinal analysis' (1996a: 262). The lack of empirical studies of the long-term response to *Miranda* has been surprising (Walker, 1993a: 46). However, the decision's 30th anniversary saw publication of Cassell's important study which 'contends that the conventional academic wisdom about *Miranda*'s effects is simply wrong. As common sense suggests *Miranda* has significantly harmed law enforcement efforts' (1996a: 390; see also Cassell, 1996b; Cassell and Hayman, 1996). Cassell's account is challenged by Schulhofer (1996). Thomas argues that the evidence is inconclusive (1996a; 1996b). For the most sophisticated and empirically informed assessment, see Leo, 1996c.

33  Walker (1989: 280) stresses the way in which legal change paved the way for such reforms: this is an important counter to the usual presentations of legal and other reforms as alternatives.

34  Orfield, 1987. Walker describes this as the only 'detailed study of how the exclusionary rule affects day-to-day detective work' (1993: 49). Also now available is Leo's research: see below.

35  'Laconia' is Leo's pseudonym for the large, urban Californian police department in which his main research was carried out: see Leo, 1995.

36  See Leo, 1992; 1994; 1996a; 1996b; 1996c. While Leo's work is valuable and perceptive, it is not clear how representative are the departments and interrogations studied. At least in comparison with English and Australian officers, Leo's interrogators are unusually skilful and committed (cf. Baldwin, 1993a).

37  For useful overviews, see Horwitz, 1980: ch. 2; Ogus, 1994.

38  This has been argued in various ways by e.g. Goldsmith, 1991; Kleinig, 1996; Mastrofski and Greene, 1993: 82–3; Walker, 1993b: 47; Wright and Burke, 1995.

39  The Royal Commission on Criminal Justice reported that 'there are hardly any formal disciplinary hearings for breaches of PACE' (RCCJ, 1993: 48).

40  If not, an argument for the exceptional nature of criminal justice needs to be made cogently. The disregard seems mutual: studies of regulation routinely overlook criminal justice. Indeed, Ogus defines it out of consideration, insisting that regulation is 'fundamentally a politico-economic concept and, as such, can best be understood by reference to different systems of economic organisation and the legal forms which maintain them' (1994: 1). This focus on economic activity unfortunately restricts discussion of issues such as regulatory failure and compliance (*ibid.*, ch. 16).

41  See Dixon, 1995b, Kleinig, 1996, and, e.g. Neil Brewer's current research, 'Development of Ethical Behaviour in Junior Police Officers: A Test of Peer Modelling Effects' (NSW Police Advisory Council, 1996).

42  For a useful review of these developments in the context of the history of police accountability in England and Wales, see Marshall and Loveday, 1994.

43  See, e.g., McConville *et al.*'s finding that no further action was taken against a quarter of their sample of arrested suspects (1991a: 104).

44  1977: 111–12; cf. Davis's preference for rules as 'guides, not inexorable commands' (1977: 1171). Please note, however, Goldstein's later comments on the problem of getting police to treat written directions in this way (1993: 55).

45  i.e. Sydney's western suburbs: see Powell, 1993.

46  [...] Cf. Matza's argument that the 'dilemma of law and order' identified by Skolnick (1975) may be met by providing 'law' to one population and 'order' to another (1969: 188–95). The latter is not *necessarily* repressive: see, e.g., the police role in negotiating gambling law enforcement (Dixon, 1991c: 266).

47  For a scathing critique of the negativity of Australian police forces, see McConkey *et al.*, 1996: 51.

48  Cf. the extensive critiques of community policing: e.g. McConville and Shepherd, 1992; Klockars, 1988.

49  Their resistance should not be exaggerated: judges provide an example of other sectors of criminal justice which are even more resistant to change (Walker, 1993a: 152).

50  [...] For a review, see Dixon, 1997.

# References

Allan, T.R.S. (1985), 'Parliamentary Supremacy and the Rule of Law', *Cambridge Law Journal* 44: 111–43.

Allan, T.R.S. (1993), *Law, Liberty, and Justice* (Oxford: Clarendon Press).

Allen, F.A. (1996), *The Habits of Legality: Criminal Justice and the Rule of Law* (New York: Oxford University Press).

Allen, R.J. (1976), 'The Police and Substantive Rulemaking', *University of Pennsylvania Law Review* 125: 62–118.

Ashworth, A. (1994), *The Criminal Process* (Oxford: Clarendon Press).

Ayres, I., and Braithwaite, J. (1992), *Responsive Regulation: Transcending the Deregulation Debate* (New York: Oxford University Press).

Baldwin, J. (1993a), 'Police Interview Techniques', *British Journal of Criminology* 33: 325–53.

Baldwin, R. (1995), *Rules and Government* (Oxford: Clarendon Press).

Barendt, E. (1985), 'Dicey and Civil Liberties' [1985] *Public Law* 596–608.

Barry, A., Osborne, T., and Rose, N. (eds) (1996), *Foucault and Political Reason* (London; ECL Press).

Baxter, J. (1985), 'Policing and the Rule of Law', in Baxter and Koffman (eds), 38–61.

Baxter, J. and Koffman, L. (1985), 'Introduction', in Baxter and Koffman (eds), 1–4.

Baxter, J. and Koffman, L. (eds) (1985), *Police: The Constitution and the Community* (Abingdon: Professional Books).

Berger, M. (1990), 'Legislating Confession Law in Great Britain', *University of Michigan Journal of Law Reform* 24: 1–64.

Bittner, E. (1990), *Aspects of Police Work* (Boston, Mass.: Northeastern University Press).

Bolen, J. (1997), *The Whitrod Era in Queensland Policing: A Successful Strategy for Reform?* (Sydney: Institute of Criminology).

Bradley, C. (1989), 'Enforcing the Rules of Criminal Procedure', *Federal Law Review* 18: 188–211.

Bradley, C. (1990), 'Criminal Procedure in the "Land of Oz": Lessons for America', *Journal of Criminal Law and Criminology* 81: 99–135.

Braithwaite, J. (1989), *Crime, Shame and Reintegration* (Cambridge: Cambridge University Press).

Braithwaite, J. (1992a), 'Los Angeles and the Pathologies of Criminal Justice?', *Criminology Australia* (April/May), 2–5.

Braithwaite, J. (1992b), 'Good and Bad Police Services and How to Pick Them', in P. Moir and H. Eijkman (eds), *Policing Australia* (South Melbourne: Macmillan), 11–39.

Braithwaite, J. (1995), 'Corporate Crime and Republican Criminological Praxis', in F. Pearce and I. Snider (eds), *Corporate Crime* (Toronto: University of Toronto Press), 48–71.

Braithwaite, J. and Braithwaite, V. (1995), 'The Politics of Legalism', *Social and Legal Studies* 4: 307–41.

Braithwaite, J. and Makkai, T. (1994), 'Trust and Compliance', *Policing and Society* 4: 1–12.

Braithwaite, J. and Mugford, S. (1994), 'Conditions of Successful Reintegration Ceremonies', *British Journal of Criminology* 34: 139–71.

Braithwaite, J. and Pettit, P. (1990), *Not Just Deserts* (Oxford: Oxford University Press).

Bright, B. (1995), 'Good Practice Constables', *Policing* 11: 221–46.

Brogden, M., Jefferson, T., and Walklate, S. (1988), *Introducing Policework* (London: Unwin Hyman).

Brogden, M. and Shearing, C. (1993), *Policing for a New South Africa* (London: Routledge).

Brown, D. (1997), *PACE Ten Years On: A Review of the Research* (London: HMSO).

Brown, D.B. (1987), 'The Politics of Reform', in G. Zdenkowski, C. Ronalds, and M. Richardson (eds), *The Criminal Injustice System* (Sydney: Pluto), 254–81.

Brown, D.B., Barrier, D., and Weisbrot, D. (1996), *Criminal Laws* (Annandale, NSW: Federation Press).

Caplan, G.M. (1974), 'The Case for Rulemaking by Law Enforcement Agencies', in Weistart (ed.), 56–70.

Carrington, K., Dyer, M., Hogg, R., Bargen, J., and Lohrey, A. (eds) (1991), *Travesty: Miscarriages of Justice* (Sydney: Pluto).

Cassell, P.G. (1996a), '*Miranda*'s Social Costs: An Empirical Reassessment', *Northwestern University Law Review* 90: 387–499.

Cassell, P.G. (1996b), 'All Benefits, No Costs: The Grand Illusion of *Miranda*'s Defenders', *Northwestern University Law Review* 90: 1084–124.

Cassell, P.G. and Hayman, B.S. (1996), 'Police Interrogation in the 1990s: An Empirical Study of the Effects of *Miranda*', *University of California Law Review* 43: 839–931.

Chan, J. (1997), *Changing Police Culture* (Melbourne: Cambridge University Press).

Clayton, H., and Tomlinson, C. (1992), *Civil Actions against the Police* (London: Sweet and Maxwell).

Cotterell, R. (1996) '*The Rule of Law in Transition*', *Social and Legal Studies* 5: 451–70.

Craig, P.P. (1990), *Public Law and Democracy in the UK and the USA* (Oxford: Clarendon Press).

Daintith, T. (1994), 'The Techniques of Government', in Jowell and Oliver (eds), 209–36.

Davis, G. (1992), Review of McConville *et al*. (1991a), *Policing and Society* 2: 322–4.

Davis, K.C. (1971), *Discretionary Justice* (2nd edn., Urbana, Ill.: University of Illinois Press).

Davis, K.C. (1974), 'An Approach to Legal Control of Police', *Texas Law Review* 52: 703–25.

Davis, K.C. (1975), *Police Discretion* (St. Paul, Minn.: West Publishing).

Davis, K.C. (1977), 'Police Rulemaking on Selective Enforcement: A Reply', *University of Pennsylvania Law Review* 125: 1167–71.

Dean, M. (1994), *Critical and Effective Histories* (London: Routledge).

Dicey, A.V. (1929), *The Law of the Constitution* (1st edn., 1885 London: Macmillan).

Dixon, D. (1991a), 'Common Sense, Legal Advice and the Right of Silence', *Public Law* 233–54.

Dixon, D. (1991b), 'Politics, Research and Symbolism in Criminal Justice', *Anglo-American Law Review* 20: 27–50.

Dixon, D. (1991c), *From Prohibition to Regulation* (Oxford: Clarendon Press).

Dixon, D. (1991d), 'Interrogation, Corroboration, and the Limits of Judicial Activism', *Legal Service Bulletin* 16: 103–6.

Dixon, D. (1992), 'Legal Regulation and Policing Practice', *Social and Legal Studies* 1: 515–41.

Dixon, D. (1995a), *Issues in the Legal Regulation of Policing* (Sydney: Royal Commission into the NSW Police Service, unpublished).

Dixon, D. (1995b), *The Normative Structure of Policing* (Sydney: Royal Commission into the NSW Police Service, unpublished).

Dixon, D. (1997), 'Criminal Law and Policing in Sociological Perspective', in R. Tomasic (ed.), *The Sociology of Law* (London: Sage).

Dixon, D., Bottomley, A.K., Coleman, C.A., Gill, M., and Wall, D. (1989), 'Reality and Rules in the Construction and Regulation of Police Suspicion', *International Journal of the Sociology of Law* 17: 185–206.

Dixon, D., Bottomley, A.K., Coleman, C.A., Gill, M., and Wall, D. (1990a), 'Safeguarding the Rights of Suspects in Police Custody', *Policing and Society* 1: 115–40.

Dixon, D., and Travis, G. (1997), *The Impact of Electronic Recording of Police Questioning of Suspects on Criminal Justice in New South Wales*, Report to the Australian Research Council (Sydney: Faculty of Law, University of New South Wales, unpublished).

Downes, D. (ed.) (1992), *Unravelling Criminal Justice* (London: Macmillan).

Erickson, R. (1994a), 'The Royal Commission on Criminal Justice System Surveillance', in McConville and Bridges (eds), 113–40.

Feeley, M., and Simon, J. (1994), 'Acturial Justice', in D. Nelken (ed.) *The Futures of Criminology* (London: Sage), 173–201.

Fine, R. (1994), 'The Rule of Law and Muggletonian Marxism', *Journal of Law and Society* 21: 193–213.

Finnane, M. (1994), *Police and Government* (Melbourne: Oxford University Press).

Fisse, B., and Braithwaite, J. (1993), *Corporations, Crime and Accountability* (Cambridge: Cambridge University Press).

Foucault, M. (1975), *Discipline and Punish* (Harmondsworth: Peregrine).

France, A. (1927), 'Le lys route', in id. *Œuvres Complètes* (1st edn., 1894), (Paris: Calmann-Levy, 1–390), ix.

Garland, D. (1991), 'Designing Criminal Policy', *London Review of Books*, 10 Oct. 13–14.

Gatrell, V.A.C. (1990), 'Crime, Authority and the Policeman-State', Thompson (ed.), 243–310.

Goldsmith, A. (1991), 'External Review and Self-regulation', in A.J. Goldsmith (ed.), *Complaints Against Police: The Trend to External Review* (Oxford: Clarendon Press), 13–61.

Goldstein, H. (1977), *Policing a Free Society* (Cambridge: Ballinger).

Goldstein, H. (1993), 'Confronting the Complexity of the Policing Function', in Ohlin and Remington (eds), 23–71.

Goldstein, J. (1960), 'Police Discretion not to Invoke the Criminal Process', *Yale Law Journal* 69: 543–94.

Gouldner, A.V. (1954), *Patterns of Industrial Bureaucracy* (New York: Free Press).

Greene, J.R., and Mastrofski, S.D. (eds) (1988), *Community Policing: Rhetoric or Reality* (New York: Praeger).

Grimshaw, R., and Jefferson, T. (1987), *Interpreting Policework* (London: Allen and Unwin).

Haldane, R. (1995), *The People's Force: A History of the Victoria Police* (2nd edn., Carlton South: Melbourne University Press).

Hall, S. (1982), 'The Lessons of Lord Scarman', *Critical Social Policy* 2 (2): 66–72.

Hampton, C. (ed.) (1984), *A Radical Reader: The Struggle for Change in England 1381–1914* (Harmondsworth: Penguin).

Harlow, C., and Rawlings, R. (1984), *Law and Administration* (London: Weidenfeld and Nicolson).

Hawkins, K., and Thomas, J.M. (eds) (1984), *Enforcing Regulation* (Dordrecht: Kluwer).

Hill, C. (1954), 'The Norman Yoke', in J. Saville (ed.), *Democracy and the Labour Movement* (London: Lawrence and Wishart).

Hill, C. (1996), *Liberty Against the Law* (London: Allen Lane).

Hogg, R. (1991a), 'Policing and Penality', *Journal of Social Justice Studies* 4: 1–26.

Hogg, R. (1995), 'Law and Order and the Fallibility of the Justice System', in Brown *et al.* 1996: 309–15.

Homel, R. (1994), 'Can Police Prevent Crime?', in K. Bryett and C. Lewis (eds), *Un-Peeling Tradition: Contemporary Policing* (Brisbane: Centre for Australian Public Sector Management), 7–34.

Horwitz, M.J. (1977), 'The Rule or Law: An Unqualified Human Good?', *Yale Law Journal* 86: 561–6.

Horwitz, R.B. (1989), *The Irony of Regulatory Reform* (New York: Oxford University Press).

Jackson, J.D. (1990), 'Getting Criminal Justice out of Balance', in S. Livingstone and J. Morison (eds), *Law, Society and Change* (Aldershot: Dartmouth), 114–33.

Jones, T., Newburn, T., and Smith, D.J. (1994), *Democracy and Policing* (London: Policy Studies Institute).

Jones, T., Newburn, T., and Smith, D.J. (1996), 'Policing and the Idea of Democracy', *British Journal of Criminology* 36: 182–98.

Jowell, J. (1975), *Law and Bureaucracy: Administrative Discretion and the Limits of Legal Action* (New York: Denellen).

Jowell, J. (1994), 'The Rule of Law Today', in Jowell and Oliver (eds), 57–78.

Jowell, J. and Oliver, D. (eds) (1994), *The Changing Constitution* (3rd edn., Oxford: Clarendon Press).

Kagan, R.A. (1984), 'On Regulatory Inspectorates and Police', in Hawkins and Thomas (eds), 37–64.

Kleinig, J. (1996), *The Ethics of Policing* (Cambridge: Cambridge University Press).

Klockars, C.B. (1988), 'The Rhetoric of Community Policing', in Greene and Mastrofski (eds), 239–58.

Krantz, S., Gilman, B., Benda, C., Hallstrom, C.R., and Nadworny, E.J. (1979), *Police Policymaking: The Boston Experience* (Lexington, Mass.: Lexington Books).

Krygier, M. (1990), 'Marxism and the Rule of Law: Reflections after the Fall of Communism', *Law and Social Inquiry* 15: 633–63.

Lacey, N. (1992), 'The Jurisprudence of Discretion: Escaping the Legal Paradigm', in Hawkins (ed.), 361–88.

Lacey, N. (1995), 'Contingency and Criminalisation', in I. Loveland (ed.), *Frontiers of Criminality* (London: Sweet and Maxwell), 1–27.

Leigh, L.H. (1985), *Police Powers in England and Wales* (2nd edn., London: Butterworths).

Leo, R. (1992), 'From Coercion to Deception: The Changing Nature of Police Interrogation in America, *Crime, Law and Social Change* 18: 35–59.

Leo, R. (1994), 'From Coercion to Deception: The Changing Nature of Police Interrogation in America', *Crime, Law and Social Change* 18: 35–59.

Leo, R. (1994), 'Police Interrogation and Social Control', *Social and Legal Studies* 3: 93–120.

Leo, R. (1995), 'Trials and Tribulations: Courts, Ethnography, and the Need for an Evidentiary Privilege for Academic Researchers', *The American Sociologist* 26: 113–34.

Leo, R. (1996a), '*Miranda*'s Revenge: Police Interrogation as a Confidence Game', *Law and Society Review* 30: 259–88.

Leo, R. (1996b), 'Inside the Interrogation Room', *Journal of Criminal Law and Criminology* 86: 266–303.

Leo, R. (1996c), 'The Impact of *Miranda* Revisited', *Journal of Criminal Law and Criminology* 86: 621–92.

Loader, I. (1995), 'Policing and the Social: Questions of Symbolic Power', paper presented to the British Criminology Conference, Loughborough.

Loader, I. (1996), *Youth, Policing and Democracy* (Basingstoke: Macmillan).

Loughlin, M. (1992), *Public Law and Political Theory* (Oxford: Clarendon Press).

Lustgarten, L. (1986). *The Governance of Police* (London: Sweet and Maxwell).

Maguire, M., Morgan, R., and Reiner, R. (eds) (1994), *The Oxford Handbook of Criminology* (Oxford: Clarendon Press).

Manning, P. (1977), *Police Work* (Cambridge, Mass.: MIT Press).

Manning, P. (1993), 'The Preventive conceit', *American Behavioral Scientist* 36: 639–50.

Marshall, G. and Loveday, B. (1994), 'The Police: Independence and Accountability', in Jowell and Oliver (eds), 295–322.

Marx, G. (1981), 'Ironies of Social Control', *Social Problems* 28: 221–46.

Marx, G. (1992), 'Commentary', *Crime, Law and Social Change* 18: 3–34.

Mastrofski, S.D., and Greene, J.R. (1993), 'Community Policing and the Rule of Law', in Weisburd *et al.* (eds), 80–102.

Matza, D. (1969), *Becoming Deviant* (Englewood Cliffs, NJ: Prentice-Hall).

McAuslan, P., and McEldowney, J.F. (eds) (1985), *Law, Legitimacy and the Constitution* (London: Sweet and Maxwell).

McBarnet, D.J. (1979), 'Arrest: The Legal Context of policing', in S. Holdaway (ed.), *The British Police* (London: Edward Arnold), 24–40.

McConkey, K.M., Huon, G.F., and Frank, M.G. (1996), *Practical Ethics in the Police Service* (Payneham, South Australia: National Police Research Unit).

McConville, M., and Bridges, L. (eds) (1994), *Criminal Justice in Crisis* (Aldershot: Edward Elgar).

McConville, M., Hodgson, J., Bridges, L., and Pavlovic, A. (1994), *Standing Accused* (Oxford: Clarendon Press).

McConville, M., and Sanders, A. (1995), 'The Case for the Prosecution and Administrative Criminology', in Noaks *et al.* (eds), 191–205.

McConville, M., Sanders, A., and Leng, R. (1991a), *The Case for the Prosecution: Police Suspects and the Construction of Criminality* (London: Routledge).

McConville, M., and Shepherd, D. (1992), *Watching Police, Watching Communities* (London: Routledge).

McGowan, C. (1972), 'Rule-making and the Police', *Michigan Law Review* 70: 659–94.

McNay, L. (1994), *Foucault* (Cambridge: Polity Press).

McQueen, H. (1976), *A New Britannia* (revised edn., Ringwood: Penguin).

Milner, N.A. (1971), *The Court and Local Law Enforcement* (Newbury Park, Cal.: Sage).

Mollen, M. (1994), *Report of the Commission to Investigate Allegations of Police Corruption and the Anti-Corruption Procedures of the Police Department* (New York: Mollen Commission).

Moore, M.H. (1992), 'Problem-solving and Community Policing', in Tonry and Morris (eds), 99–158.

Morgan, R. (1992), 'Talking about Policing', in Downes (ed.) 165–83.

Neal, D. (1991), *The Rule of Law in a Penal Colony* (Cambridge: Cambridge University Press).

New Zealand Law Commission (1992), *Criminal Evidence: Police Questioning*, Preliminary Paper #21 (Wellington: Law Commission).

Noaks. L., Maguire, M., and Levi, M. (eds) (1995), *Contemporary Issues in Criminology* (Cardiff: University of Wales Press).

Norrie, A. (1995), Review of Ashworth: *The Criminal Process* [1995] *Public Law* 342–4.

Norris, C., and Norris, N. (1993), 'Defining Good Policing', *Policing and Society* 3: 205–21.

Ogus, A. (1994), *Regulation: Legal Form and Economic Theory* (Oxford: Clarendon Press).

Ohlin, L.E. (1993), 'Surveying Discretion by Criminal Justice Decision Makers', in Ohlin and Remington (eds), 1–22.

Ohlin, L.E., and Remington, F.J. (eds) (1993), *Discretion in Criminal Justice* (Albany, NY: State University of New York Press).

Orfield, M. (1987), 'The Exclusionary Rule and Deterrence: An Empirical Study of Chicago Narcotics Officers', *University of Chicago Law Review* 54: 1016–55.

Palmer, B.D. (1981), *The Making of E.P. Thompson* (Toronto: New Hogtown Press).

Palmer, B.D. (1990), *Descent into Discourse* (Philadelphia, Penn.: Temple University Press).

Phillips, C., and Brown, D. (1997), *Entry into the Criminal Justice System* (London: HMSO).

Powell, D. (1993), *Out West: Perceptions of Sydney's Western Suburbs* (St. Leonards: Allen Unwin).

Punch, M. (1985), *Conduct Unbecoming: The Social Construction of Police Deviance and Control* (London: Tavistock).

Radin, M.J. (1989), 'Reconsidering the Rule of Law', *Boston University Law Review* 69: 781–819.

Raz, J. (1979) *The Authority of Law* (Oxford: Clarendon Press).

RCCJ (1993), *Report of the Royal Commission on Criminal Justice*, Cm. 2263 (London: HMSO).

RCP (1962), *Report of the Royal Commission on the Police*, Cmnd. 1728 (London: HMSO).

RCPPP (1929), *Report of the Royal Commission on Police Powers and Procedure*, Cmd. 3297 (London: HMSO).

Reiner, R. (1992a), *The Politics of the Police* (Hemel Hempstead: Harvester Wheatsheaf).

Reiner, R. (1992c), 'Policing a Postmodern Society', *Modern Law Review* 55: 761–81.

Reiner, R. (1994), 'Policing and the Police', in Maguire, Morgan, and Reiner (eds), 705–72.

Reiner, R. and Spencer, S. (eds) (1993), *Accountable Policing* (London: Institute for Public Policy Research).

Reiss, A.J. (1970), Review of Davis: 1971, *Michigan Law Review* 68: 789–96.

Richardson, G., and Genn, H. (eds) (1994), *Administrative Law and Government Action* (Oxford: Clarendon Press).

Sanders, A., and Young, R. (1994a), *Criminal Justice* (London: Butterworths).

Sanders, A., and Young, R. (1994b), 'The Rule of Law, Due Process and Pre-trial Criminal Justice', *Current Legal Problems* 47 (2): 125–56.

Schulhofer, S.J. (1996, '*Miranda*'s Practical Effect: Substantial Benefits and Vanishly Small Social Costs', *Northwestern University Law Review* 90: 500–63.

Sherman, L.W. (1974), 'Explanation and Policy Recommendations', in L.W. Sherman (ed.), *Policing Corruption: A Sociological Perspective* (New York: Anchor Books), 268–76.

Singh, S. (1994), 'Understanding the Long-term Relationship between Police and Policed', in McConville and Bridges (eds), 162–72.

Shklar, J.N. (1987), 'Political Theory and the Rule of Law', in A.C. Hutchinson and P. Monaghan (eds), *The Rule of Law* (Toronto: Carswell), 1–16.

Skolnick, J.H. (1975), *Justice without Trial* (2nd edn., New York: John Wiley and Sons).

Skolnick, J.H. (1993), 'Justice without Trial Revisited', in Weisburd *et al.* (eds), 190–205.

Skolnick. J.H. (1994), 'The Challenge of Crime in the 1990s', in *id. Justice without Trial* (3rd edn., New York: Macmillan).

Smith, A.T.H. (1985), 'Comment I' [1985] *Public Law* 608–11.

Smith, D.J. (1986), 'The Framework of Law and Policing Practice', in J. Benyon and C. Bourne (eds), *The Police* (Oxford: Pergamon Press), 85–94.

Smith, D.J. (1988), 'Mr Lustgarten and the Case of the Honest Copper', *Oxford Journal of Legal Studies* 8 434–41.

Smith, D.J. (1995), 'Case Construction and the Goals of Criminal Process', paper presented to the British Criminology Conference, Loughborough, July.

Smith, D.J. and Gray, J. (1985), *Police and People in London* (London: Policy Studies Institute).

Smith, P. 91993), *Clint Eastwood: A Cultural Production* (Minneapolis, Minn.: University of Minnesota Press).

Sparrow, M.K., Moore, M.H., and Kennedy, D.M. (1990), *Beyond 911: A New Era for Policing* (New York: Basic Books).

Thomas, G.C. (1996a), 'Is *Miranda* a Real-world Failure?', *University of California Law Review* 43: 821–37.

Thomas, G.C. (1996b), 'Plain Talk about the *Miranda* Empirical Debate', *University of California Law Review* 43: 933–59.

Thompson, E.P. (1977), *Whigs and Hunters* (Harmondsworth: Peregrine).

Thompson, F.M.L. (ed.) (1990), *The Cambridge Social History of Britain 1750–1950* (Cambridge: Cambridge University Press).

Tonry, M., and Morris, N. (eds) (1992), *Modern Policing* (Chicago, Ill.: University of Chicago Press).

Truebeck, D.M. (1977), 'Complexity and Contradiction in the Legal Order', *Law and Society Review* 11: 529–69.

Tyler, T.R. (1990), *Why People Obey the Law* (New Haven, Conn.: Yale University Press).

Unger, R.M. (1976), *Law in Modern Society* (New York: The Free Press).

Wade, H.W. R. (1988), *Administrative Law* (Oxford: Clarendon Press).

Wald, M.R., Ayres, D., Hess, D.W., Schantz, M., and Whitebread, C.H. (1967), 'Interrogations in New Haven', *Yale Law Journal* 76: 1519–1648.

Walker, N. (1996a), 'Defining Core Police Tasks: The Neglect of the Symbolic Dimension?', *Policing and Society* 6: 53–71.

Walker, S. (1980), *Popular Justice: A History of American Criminal Justice* (New York: Oxford University Press).

Walker, S. (1986), 'Controlling the Cops: A Legislative Approach to Police Rulemaking', *University of Detroit Law Review* 63: 361–91.

Walker, S. (1988), *The Rule Revolution: Reflections on the Transformation of American Criminal Justice, 1950–1988* (Madison, Wisc.: Institute for Legal Studies).

Walker, S. (1989), 'Conclusion: Paths to Police Reform – Reflections on 25 Years of Change', in D.J. Kenney (ed.), *Police and Policing* (New York: Praeger), 271–84.

Walker, S. (1992), 'Origins of the Contemporary Criminal Justice Paradigm: The American Bar Foundation Survey, 1953–1969', *Justice Quarterly* 9: 47–76.

Walker, S. (1993a), *Taming the System: The Control of Discretion in Criminal Justice 1950–1990* (New York: Oxford University Press).

Walker, S. (1993b), 'Historical Roots of the Legal Control of Police Behaviour', in Weisburd *et al.* (eds), 32–55.

Weatheritt, M. (1988), 'Community Policing: Rhetoric or Reality', in Mastrofski and Greene (eds), 153–75.

Weisburd, D., and Uchida, C., with Green, L. (1993), 'Raising Questions of Law and Order', in Weisburd *et al.* (eds), 3–9.

Weisburd, D., and Uchida, C., with Green, L. (eds) (1993), *Police Innovation and Control of the Police* (New York: Springer-Verlag).

Weistart, J.C. (ed.) (1974), *Police Practices* (Dobbs Ferry, NY: Oceana Publications).

Williams, R. (1977), *Marxism and Literature* (Oxford: Oxford University Press).

Wilson, J.V., and Alprin, G.M. (1974), 'Controlling Police Conduct: Alternatives to the Exclusionary Rule', in Weistart (ed.), 44–55.

Worden, R.E. (1989), 'Situational and Attitudinal Explanations of Police Behaviour', *Law and Society Review* 23: 668–711.

Wright, A., and Burke, M. (1995), 'The Greater Manchester Blue Book', *Policing* 4: 331–41

Zellick, G.J. (ed.) (1985), 'All Souls – *Public Law* Seminar: Dicey and the Constitution' [1985] *Public Law* 583–723.

# Part F

# The emerging pattern of policing

## Introduction

This, the final part in the volume, looks at contemporary trends in policing and, by implication at least, where this may be taking us in the future. Clearly recent times have seen some significant changes in the image and substance of policing. Why this might be so is Robert Reiner's (**38**, 675) central question. His answer is that the police are like 'social litmus paper' reflecting in a subtle and mediated manner the changes affecting modern societies. Put crudely, the changes that collectively have shifted the advanced economies from a modern to a 'postmodern' state have in turn transformed the nature of policing. Indeed, the very idea of the police as a single professional force, employing legitimate violence on behalf of the state was, Reiner argues, 'a paradigm of the modern'. As modern social formations have been fundamentally altered by the pluralizing and fragmenting forces of postmodernity so this original conception of the police has become increasingly anachronistic: 'in short policing now reflects the processes of pluralism and fragmentation which have been the hallmarks of the postmodern.'

Pat O'Malley (**39**, 698) picks up where Reiner's arguments end and questions the links between the characteristics of postmodernity and the more specific processes of public police reform. O'Malley's view is that the 'postmodernity thesis', as it relates to policing, is based on some questionable assumptions. First, whether the changes generally associated together in accounts of postmodernity – for example, moral diversification, globalization and consumerism – can really be taken as 'symptomatic or expressive of the rise of an overarching shift into a new order'. Secondly, he questions whether it is really plausible to describe the police as quintessentially 'modern', pointing to what he argues has been their almost premodern, guild-like systems of recruitment, promotion and internal working culture. Finally, he asks whether the fact that many of the changes identified in policing appear to mirror broader social and cultural changes is sufficient as the basis for an explanation of those changes. As one possible, and more particular alternative to the general rubric of postmodernity, O'Malley adopts the lenses of neoliberal political rationalities and the social technologies of managerialism. These, he argues, allow both for a more grounded, less abstract, level of explanation and provide 'a far more politically deployable knowledge'.

In the 'debate' between Reiner and O'Malley there is little dispute over the nature of the changes occurring in policing, merely a different take on how best this might be explained. This is slightly less true in relation to the next two chapters, and another debate over how contemporary policing is to be characterized. In a very widely cited article, David Bayley and Clifford Shearing (**40**, 715) make the provocative statement that 'Modern democratic countries like the United States, Britain and Canada have reached a watershed in the evolution of their systems of crime control and law enforcement. Future generations will look back on our era as a time when one system of policing ended and another took its place'. This epochal change is characterized, they argue, by two developments: the pluralizing of policing – or as they put it 'the end of a monopoly' by the public police; and the search for identity by the public police. The first element of Bayley and Shearing's argument is that recent decades have seen the breaking of the state's monopoly on policing, primarily through the creation of a host of private and community-based agencies involved in crime prevention and detection. Linked with this has been something of a crisis of identity for public policing agencies that have come increasingly to question - and have questioned – their effectiveness in guarding the public from crime. This has led to the gradual acceptance of the limits of the patrol function, the emergence of new strategies such as community policing and the increasing visibility of the police in the marketplace. As a consequence they argue that not only has government's monopoly on policing been broken in the late twentieth century, but the police monopoly on expertise within its own sphere of activity has ended. Policing, they argue, now belongs to everyone.

Bayley and Shearing's argument is directly challenged by Trevor Jones and Tim Newburn (**41**, 733) who take issue with the suggestion that current developments are best understood as representing a major qualitative break with the past. They take issue, first, with Bayley and Shearing's characterization of the recent past in policing and, in particular, the argument that recent times have witnessed and 'end of the monopoly' of the public police. Whilst accepting that growing pluralization of provision is an undoubted and important feature of the contemporary policing landscape, Jones and Newbum argue that the very notion of a public police monopoly radically overstates the degree to which state police dominated policing in the postwar years. The idea of public police monopoly is, rather, an ideological creation reflecting the extent to which police attempts to secure ever-increasing legitimacy had been successful. The second line of criticism concerns the largely North American focus of the Bayley and Shearing thesis. Jones and Newbum argue that a broader focus would illustrate the variety of trajectories and transitions between nation-states that are in evidence and, at least, serve to temper claims that 'modern democratic countries' are experiencing parallel changes. Jones and Newbum's final argument seeks to place the discussion of the transformation of policing into a broader context. They detail the decline in what they term 'secondary social control occupations over the past 50 years' and argue that, rather than a 'pluralization of policing', the trends that they and Bayley and Shearing focus upon are best conceptualized as part of a long-term process of the 'formalisation of secondary social control activities'.

The bulk of the discussion so far has been gender neutral or, more likely, implicitly masculinist. Yet women are now increasingly visible in policing - both public and private. This increasing visibility in policing in the twentieth century was both an expansionist and protectionist move, Heidensohn (**42**, 751) argues; frustrated with the lack of political and legal power, women sought out new areas and avenues in a variety of control agencies. The presence of women in control agencies such as the police should, she argues, lead us to question some of our representations of social control and social order – not least 'the male ownership of social order'. Heidensohn concludes with a series of propositions about social control. First, that gender divisions are central to an understanding of social control and indeed 'perhaps its most integral and abiding features'. In parallel, then, with Reiner's argument earlier about other social transformations, Heidensohn argues that changes in gender roles have consequences in turn for control agencies. However, women, though now comparatively freer and with greater economic and political power, are not in control. 'They might,' she says, 'begin to ask men why.'

As Ericson and Haggerty noted (in Part D, **32**, 550), powerful new information technologies are having a very significant impact on the shape and nature of contemporary policing. As Gary T. Marx (**43**, 760) argues, the new technologies of surveillance are rendering the previously invisible or meaningless, visible and meaningful. Reviewing developments in the use of human informants, visual and audio surveillance, electronic leashes and personal truth technologies, Marx raises the spectre of the 'maximum surveillance society'. This is a society, he argues, in which the boundaries of public and private are 'obliterated', where surveillance is Orwellian in its scope and penetration, and society is akin to a Goffmanesque total institution: there is no longer any 'backstage'. Though guarding against accusations of technological determinism, one can almost hear the pessimism in Marx's voice when he says, 'the fact that technology can be misused does not necessarily mean it will be'. Little has happened in the decade or more since this article was written that would make author or reader more optimistic. A democratic society, Marx quite rightly argues, must guard against such abuse just as it must guard against more obvious physical coercion.

Although the title of this volume includes the word 'policing' much of the focus of the readings, as critics will no doubt note, has been upon the police. Even in this final section, though every contribution recognizes the growing complexity of the policing 'division of labour', there is little direct consideration of private or commercial policing operations. Another development which has long been overlooked in the policing literature is the growing visibility of the military in domestic policing arrangements. Rather like private policing arrangements, of course, the involvement of military in policing has a long history. The creation of state police forces, and the process by which they sought to increase and reinforce their legitimacy, involved the placement of significant limits to military involvement in domestic order maintenance. Recent times have seen some significant changes however. Focusing on the USA, Colonel Charles Dunlap (**44**, 786) illustrates how with the advent of the 'war on drugs' in the 1980s increased military activity has led to a situation in which the case for augmenting local policing efforts – not least in anti-terrorist activity – with military capability has become difficult to resist. 'In important ways,' Dunlap argues, 'we are witnessing a problematic convergence of police and military interests.'

Criminologists, by and large, have tended to neglect the subject of terrorism. The events of September 2001 and, more particularly, the response of the USA and others to those events, has placed terrorism and the 'policing' of terrorism high on the academic agenda. What seems sure is that terrorism will have a major influence on the future shape and direction of international, and much domestic, policing activity. This leads us to another uneasy relationship, that between what Jean-Paul Brodeur refers to as 'cops and spooks'. Following on from his earlier work on 'high and low policing'(1983), Brodeur (**45**, 797) argues that it is time to refocus criminological attention away from its preoccupation with 'low policing'. Doing so, he suggests, will help to draw attention to the fact that one of the most significant challenges to the police 'monopoly' on serious crime inquiries is likely to come not just from the military but also from domestic security services. Taking the Canadian example he argues that if one focuses on policing as surveillance and risk assessment then the security services will 'have a claim in this business'. Though the future is of course uncertain, the authors in this section describe, and foresee, a policing world that is increasingly transnationalized, pluralized and risk focused.

## Reference

Brodeur, J.-P. (1983) 'High and low policing: remarks about the policing of political activities', *Social Problems*, 30 (5): 507–20.

# 38. Policing a postmodern society

*Robert Reiner*

### Introduction: Paradise lost?

Four decades after his first appearance, PC George Dixon, eponymous hero of the long-running TV series *Dixon of Dock Green*, remains for many the embodiment of the ideal British bobby. Dixon, more than any other symbol, conjures up a cosier era when thanks to the wonders of glorious nostalgia vision, life – like TV – was better in black and white.

The Dixon character was unique as a cultural phenomenon, historically and comparatively.[1] In no other country, at no other time, has the ordinary beat-pounding patrol officer been seen as a national hero. If the police were represented as heroic figures at all, it was the glamorous crime-busting detective.[2] The enormous influence and popularity of the Dixon character speaks volumes about the peculiarity of the English veneration of their police in what is often described as the 'Golden Age' of policing.

Public attitudes towards the police in Britain have changed dramatically since the Dixon era. The erosion of the Dixon image is a long process, with roots going back to the late 1950s, the last years of the 'Golden Age' itself, but it has become increasingly precipitous in the last decade of the century. This article will describe and attempt to explain this process of demystification. It will be suggested that underlying the immediate symptoms and causes is a more fundamental transformation of social structure and culture, the advent of what is often described as a 'postmodern' society. The conclusion will assess the ways in which the police have tried to tackle this problem and their chances of success.

The question of why the image and substance of policing in Britain has changed is of fundamental importance to understanding current social change in general. The function of policing is essentially to regulate and protect the social order, using legitimate force if necessary.[3] The dominant theoretical analyses of the state, deriving from Weber, see the hallmark of the modern state as the monopolisation of legitimate force in its territory. The police are the domestic specialists in the exercise of legitimate force. Thus policing is at the heart of the functioning of the state, and central to an understanding of legal and political organisation. The character and style of policing, in particular the extent to which

675

resort has to be made to legitimate force, will be affected by most changes in the social order. The police are like social litmus-paper, reflecting sensitively the unfolding exigencies of a society. Thus understanding policing requires a consideration of the broadest features of social structure and change. Although the almost complete neglect of the police by social science twenty years ago has now been remedied by an explosion of research and comment, almost all of this is narrowly policy-oriented, governed by the immediate practical concerns of the police and police authorities.[4] This is valuable and welcome, but there is also a need for more fundamental social analysis of the determinants, nature and consequences of policing, apart from anything else to make sense of the disparate body of research studies.

This requires a return to the eighteenth-century notion of 'police science', when it was regarded by Adam Smith, Bentham, Colquhoun, and other major social and political thinkers, as a fundamental aspect of political economy. Indeed, Adam Smith referred to it as 'the second general division of jurisprudence ... which properly signified the policy of civil government'.[5] The term 'police' then had a much broader connotation than its contemporary one of large people in blue uniforms, but the eighteenth-century conception of police science as the art of 'governmentality'[6] sensitises us to the mutual interdependence of policing and political economy as a whole. This is obscured by the narrow focus on specific technical aspects of policing which all too often pervades current research and policy. An analysis of the troubled state of policing today, and the sources of the malaise, will have to range much further than the police themselves.

## I Singing the blues: the police in a millennial malaise

The modern British police were established in the 19th century in the face of protracted and widespread opposition.[7] But as new police forces spread out from the Metropolitan heartland established by Sir Robert Peel in 1829 to encompass the whole of England and Wales by the mid-nineteenth century, gradually and unevenly they began to cultivate increasing public consent and support. Painstakingly the police leadership, beginning with Rowan and Mayne, the first two Commissioners of the Metropolitan Police, strove to develop an image of the British bobby as the impartial embodiment of the rule of law and the ethic of public service. This rapidly became the prevailing conception of the police amongst the middle and upper classes, who had little direct personal experience of their stalwart servants in blue. The working class who were far more likely to encounter what contemporaries dubbed 'the plague of the blue locusts',[18] held more negative attitudes towards the new regulators of their social and political activities.

As the working class came gradually to be incorporated into the political, social and economic fabric over the next century, so acceptance of the police spread down throughout the social order. The economically and socially marginal – the 'rough' residuum of the reserve army of labour and indeed young men in general – continued to bear the brunt of the moral street-sweeping which constitutes the core of practical police-work. But the bulk of the settled and respectable working class followed in the footsteps of those higher up the social scale, and began to join in their veneration of the bobby as the very embodiment of the citizenly ideal. This support was brittle, and always fragile at times of industrial conflict. However, in the long social peace of the mid-twentieth century, symbolised successively by the Battle of Britain and the Festival of Britain, the bobbies had their finest hour in terms of popular affection.

Much contemporary evidence apart from the Dixon myth, underlines the status as totems of national pride which the police enjoyed in the 1950s.[9] The most solid evidence is provided by the major survey conducted for the 1962 Royal Commission on the Police Report. This found 'an overwhelming vote of confidence in the police … No less than 83% of those interviewed professed great respect for the police'.

In the three decades since then, there has been a growing questioning of the institution, culminating in recent years in a veritable haemorrhage of public confidence. Optimists could, if pressed, still tell the story another way. The 1988 British Crime Survey (BCS) for instance found that 85 per cent of the public rated the police as very or fairly good in the job they did.[10] Most institutions (including universities and the legal profession) would be delighted with such approval ratings. But there is evidence of continuing erosion of confidence throughout the 1990s. This has now become precipitous in the wake of the great escape of miscarriage of justice skeletons from the Home Office cupboard since the 'Guildford Four' opened the door in 1989.

The regular *British Social Attitudes* surveys conducted by Jowell and his colleagues,[11] as well as the series of national *British Crime Surveys* by the Home Office,[12] show a clear decrease in the standing of the police. One-off surveys conducted since the series of miscarriage of justice scandals came to light, and during the current boom in the crime rate, suggest yet further decline. The *Operational Policing Review* conducted in 1990 for the three police staff associations found that only 18 per cent of a national sample considered that their local police did a 'very good' job.[13]

All these surveys show that opinion of the police is most negative amongst particular groups, those who are routinely at the receiving end of police powers: the young, males, the economically marginal, especially if they are also black and live in the inner-cities. Local surveys in city areas have for many years indicated that amongst these groups, who have been graphically described as 'police property',[14] rejection of the practices of the police (though not the principles of law and order) is the norm.[15]

Most significantly of all for the police, they seem to have become increasingly estranged from the Conservative Government, whose pet public service they were not many years ago. The police fear a 'hidden agenda' in which they are to be made the scapegoats for the failure of the party of law and order to deliver on its election promises, The screws of financial and managerial accountability to the centre have been tightening remorselessly for several years and, much worse from the police point of view is fearfully anticipated.[16]

## II  The deconstruction of Dixon

The declining status of the police is related to a number of changes in organization and policy which have had the unintended effect of undermining legitimacy of the police. These will be considered, prior to analysis of the underlying causes.[17]

### (i)  Recruitment, training and discipline

The first element in the undermining of police legitimacy was the erosion of the image of an efficient, disciplined bureaucracy. Partly this was a question of standards of entry and training which had not kept pace with general educational improvements.

There have been many attempts in the last thirty years to raise police educational and training standards. Since the 1960s, various schemes have been introduced to attract graduates to the service and encourage higher education for serving police officers. However, significant results have only been achieved during the 1990s, when as a result of pay increases (and unemployment outside the service) the intake of graduates has accelerated sharply to about 12 per cent of recruits per annum. There has also been increasing interest from serving officers in specialist criminal justice degrees.[18] Significant changes have occurred in recruit training as well, largely following from the 1981 Scarman Report.[19] Despite the merit of these developments, they have not prevented an erosion of public confidence in police professional standards.

The main way that the image of the police force as a disciplined, rule-bound bureaucracy came to be dented was by the series of corruption scandals which rocked Scotland Yard in the early 1970s. Although there have been no major cases alleging personal corruption since Sir Robert Mark's clean-up of the Yard and the 'Countryman' inquiry in the 1970s, it is undoubtedly true that those scandals damaged severely the image of the police as disciplined law enforcers. While in the 1962 Royal Commission survey 46.9 per cent of the public did not believe bribe-taking occurred, by 1981 the Policy Studies Institute study of Londoners found that only 14 per cent believed that the police 'hardly ever' took bribes.[20] During the 1980s, personal corruption has become less of an issue, and attention has switched to abuses of police powers undermining the rule of law.

### (ii)  The rule of law

The issue of police violations of legal procedures in the course of dealing with offences has become acutely politicised since the 1970s. On the one hand, civil liberties groups have publicised much evidence of police malpractice, while on the other, the police have lobbied for greater powers to aid the 'war against crime'.

The Police and Criminal Evidence Act 1984 (PACE)[21] purported to provide a balanced codification of police powers and safeguards over their exercise synthesising the concerns of the 'law and order' and the civil liberties lobbies. It is highly debatable how far it succeeds.[22] What is certain is that the issue of police abuse of powers has increased rather than abated, especially in the late 1980s and early 1990s. Between 1989 and 1991, public confidence in the police was further shaken by an unprecedented series of scandals revealing serious malpractice. The cases of the 'Guildford Four', the 'Birmingham Six' and Judith Ward are only the most prominent of a large number of miscarriage of justice scandals which have surfaced in the 1990s.

Although these cases profoundly shook public opinion, police representatives often argued that they had occurred before the recent reforms and could not happen under the procedures now in force. This argument was itself weakened by a number of *causes célèbres* which have involved more recent abuses,[23] as well as by the implications of academic research on PACE.

The anxiety produced by these revelations of abuse was enough to make the Home Secretary announce in March 1991 (after the release of the 'Birmingham Six') the establishment of a Royal Commission on Criminal Justice, chaired by Lord Runciman, the first Royal Commission in twelve years.

### (iii)   The strategy of minimal force

The preparedness of the police to cope with public order problems began to be expanded and refined during the 1970s, as political and industrial conflict increased. This militarisation of policing proceeded apace in the 1980s in the wake of yet more serious disorder, beginning with the 1981 urban riots in Brixton and elsewhere.[24]

Without much public debate *de facto* 'third forces' have developed, specifically trained and readily mobilisable to cope with riots. They are coordinated in a crisis by the National Reporting Centre, established in 1972 and located at Scotland Yard. When in operation it is controlled by the current President of the Association of Chief Police Officers (ACPO). Its most controversial and prominent use was during the 1984–85 miners' strike, when a massive, centrally coordinated policy operation was directed by the Centre, amid much criticism of 'police-state' tactics.[25] During the trial of miners on riot charges, it was revealed that in the early 1980s ACPO had produced a secret document, the Tactical Options Manual,[26] setting out the blueprint for a finely graded response to public disorder.

Neither the tougher methods available since the 1981 riots, nor the wider reforms inspired by Lord Scarman's Report, were able to avert the even more serious urban riots of 1985, on the Broadwater Farm estate in Tottenham and elsewhere. Serious public disorder occurred again in an industrial context at Wapping in 1986–87, during picketing outside the News International plant. Many complaints of undue violence were made against the police and the Police Complaints Authority upheld some of these after an investigation.[27] Other controversial uses of public order tactics have occurred in the late 1980s during the policing of hippy convoys converging on Stonehenge.[28] During 1990, anti-poll tax demonstrations were the source of severe public order clashes, especially following a rally in Trafalgar Square on 31 March.

In recent years, however, the greatest public order concerns have not been industrial or political conflicts. A 'moral panic' has developed about disorder occurring in a variety of leisure contexts. In 1988, ACPO raised fears abut growing disorder in rural areas caused by so-called 'lager louts'.[29] In 1989–90, there was great police concern about the spread of 'acid-house' parties. During the summers of 1991 and 1992, serious violence and disorder has broken out on a number of housing estates in different parts of the country, ranging from Bristol to Tyneside, after police attempts to curb 'joy-riding'.[30] The police were subject to criticism, both for under-reacting to the joy-riding and from other quarters, for harassing teenagers suspected of joy-riding. Although the police response to riots remains lower in profile than most foreign forces, there has undoubtedly been a stiffening of strategy and more resort to technology, equipment and weaponry.

Apart from the growing use of riot control hardware, there has been a rapid proliferation of use of firearms by the police. Although still unarmed (apart from the traditional truncheon) on routine patrol, the number of occasions in which firearms are issued to the police has escalated inexorably. Many forces now deploy cars carrying guns in their lockers, which can be used on orders from headquarters. The number of occasions when guns are fired by the police remains small, and the rules are tight. Nonetheless, the traditional unarmed image of the British bobby has faded.

### (iv)   Non-partisanship

The spectacle of James Anderton (Manchester's former Chief Constable) or representatives of the Police Federation preaching at the drop of a helmet about the sinking state of our national moral fibre first became familiar in the 1970s. By 1980 the police, at all levels from Chief Constable down to the rank and file, almost seemed to set the terms of debate on law and order and social policy.

In 1975 the Police Federation launched an unprecedented campaign for 'law and order', which was revived in 1978 specifically to influence the 1979 general election. This proved to be an investment which reaped handsome dividends. The new Conservative government immediately implemented in full the pay increase recommended in 1978 by the Edmund-Davies committee. There ensued a prolonged honeymoon period in which the police were the Conservatives' most favoured public service. This love affair cooled as public expenditure cuts began to bite on the police and a 'hidden agenda' of incipient privatisation, coupled with strict central financial control, began to emerge in the late 1980s.[31]

For its part, Labour has tried hard to repair bridges which had been broken in the early 1980s, following the election of radical local authorities in the metropolitan areas, who adopted policies which were often perceived as 'anti-police'. The high-point of tension between Labour and the police came during the 1984–85 miners' strike.[32]

There is now a tendency to return to cross-party consensus on law and order (accentuated in this and other areas by the replacement of Margaret Thatcher by John Major as Prime Minister in late 1990). The prototype of the outspoken Chief Constable, Sir James Anderton, retired in 1991. He had become ever more controversial in the late 1980s for his supposedly divinely inspired utterances on AIDS and other topics. By then, most other Chief Constables had come to believe overt police interventions in political and social debates were unwise.[33] Nonetheless, the years of partisanship had tarnished, possibly irretrievably, the sacred aura hitherto enjoyed by the British police of being, like the Queen, above party politics.

## (v) The service role

The dominant current of police thinking stresses that, contrary to the popular image of the police as primarily crime-fighters, much if not most of uniformed police work (measured by time or number of incidents dealt with) consists of calls for help, in response to which the police act as a social service more than as law enforcers. The community policing philosophy, which emphasises this, has become influential amongst police chiefs in the UK, the USA and elsewhere.[34] There is evidence, however, that most rank-and-file policemen believe the service aspects of the work should have low or no priority.[35] Since the Scarman Report in 1981 endorsed a kind of community policing philosophy, this has become the orthodox analysis of the police role for all Chief Constables. The evidence of recent decline in public support has led to a redoubling of the effort to define policing in service terms in the Plus Programme of the Metropolitan Police and the ACPO Statement of Common Purpose and Values.[36] The success of these worthy attempts at relegitimation has yet to be seen, but initial research evaluations have not been optimistic.[37]

## (vi) Preventive policing

Peel's original conception of policing emphasised preventive patrol by uniformed constables as fundamental. The notion of the bobby on the beat as the essential bedrock of the force to which all other specialisms are ancillary, remains a philosophy to which most Chief Constables pay homage. But in practice specialist departments have proliferated and foot patrol has been downgraded.[38]

The meaning of prevention shifted away from the scarecrow function of uniform patrol to the development of specialist crime prevention departments, whose function is to provide advice to citizens on methods of minimising the risk of victimisation and alerting them to the dangers of some kinds of offences. At first, crime prevention departments were the Cinderellas of the service, low status, low budget and low key. However, as crime prevention became increasingly central to the Government's law and order policy in the 1980s, so they blossomed into belles of the ball. A proliferation of specialist and plain clothes units, reversing the original Peelite philosophy, has been one consequence of an apparent crisis of police effectiveness in controlling crime.

## (vii) Police effectiveness

Police effectiveness is a notoriously slippery concept to define or measure. But the official statistics routinely produced by police forces and published by the Home Office seem to record an inexorable rise in serious criminal offences and decline in the clear-up rate since the mid-1950s, and especially since the late 1970s. Whereas in the mid-1950s there were less than half a million indictable offences recorded as known to the police in most years, by 1977 this was over 2 million and, by 1991, over 4 million. Before the war, the percentage of crimes recorded as cleared-up was always over 50 per cent. By the late 1950s, it had dropped to about 45 per cent and it is currently around 38 per cent.[39]

The inadequacy of these figures is well known.[40] Many crimes are not reported to the police, so increases in the rate may indicate a greater propensity to report rather than suffer victimisation.[41] The clear-up rate is affected by many other determinants apart from detective effectiveness, including massaging the figures. Nonetheless, it is hard to argue that the recorded trends do not correspond to basic changes in the same direction, and they are certainly associated with a growing public fear of crime and a popular sense that police effectiveness is declining. In addition to the direct effect on public confidence of apparently declining police efficiency, concern about crime has led to the controversial new tactics and law and order campaigns which have already been discussed.

### (viii)   Accountability

All the above concerns have converged on the central issue of accountability: how can the police be brought to book for poor performance? This was the nub of controversy for most of the 1980s. The independence of the British police force from control by any elected governmental institutions has usually been seen as a virtue, although there has also been a long-standing radical critique arguing that it was anomalous in a democracy.[42]

As policing has become more controversial in Britain in the last two decades, so the perception of the mechanisms of accountability has changed. The old mystical substitute of police identification with the public came under strain as the police were seen increasingly as unrepresentative in terms of race gender and culture and alienated from the groups they typically dealt with as offenders and victims.[43]

At the bottom of every specific conflict, critics pinpointed the problem of the police being out of control by any outside bodies and hence unresponsive to the popular will. They have sought to reform the structure of police governance so as to make police policy-making fully accountable to the electoral process. Sophisticated critiques of the existing system by constitutional lawyers appeared[44] and the view that the police were not adequately accountable came to be the orthodoxy of main stream liberal as well as radical analysis of the police. While the police themselves have strongly resisted the full radical package, they have conceded increasingly the legitimacy of some aspects of the critique, especially about the complaints system and the absence of a local police authority for London.[45] For their part, the Conservatives have wanted to maintain the constitutional *status quo*. They have, however, become increasingly concerned to render the police more accountable for their use of powers and, even more crucially, the effective use of resources.

At the same time it is becoming increasingly evident that local accountability to police authorities has atrophied. It is being replaced by a degree of central control amounting to a *de facto* national force.[46] Thus, accountability has been transformed, rather than simply reduced. What is clear is that the perceived lack of adequate local accountability has been a major factor undermining police legitimacy in recent years.

## III   The calculus of consent: social divisions and in desubordination

These eight aspects of police organisation and policy have all been specific, concrete issues of controversy and concern in recent years, symptoms of the erosion of the public standing of the police. Underlying them however, are a combination of deeper social changes which form the social context of the declining legitimacy of the police.

Police activity has always borne most heavily on the economically marginal elements in society, the unemployed (especially if vagrant), and young men, whose lives are lived largely in the street and other public places, 'police property'.[47] Whereas the historical incorporation of the working class modified their resentment of policing, police conflict with the residuum at the base of the social hierarchy remained. Studies of policing in all industrial societies show this to be a constant. The police themselves recognise this and their argot contains a variety of derogatory epithets for their regular clientèle drawn from this stratum. In California they are 'assholes', in Toronto 'pukes', in London 'slag' or 'scum' and on Tyneside 'prigs'.[48] Drawn mostly from the respectable working class, the police are responsive to their moral values and adopt a disdainful scorn for those whose lifestyles deviate from or challenge them. But however conflict-ridden, relations between the police and 'slag' have not usually been politicised. Membership in the marginal strata is temporary (youths mature, the unemployed find jobs) and their internal social relations are atomised, so a sense of group identity is hard to develop.

One important factor which politicised policing in the 1960s and 1970s was the development of social groups with a clear consciousness of antagonism towards (and from) the police. This owes something to the development of more self-conscious, youth cultures, the return of long-term unemployment and the increasing militancy of industrial conflict.

The most crucial change, however, has been the catastrophic deterioration of relations with the black community. There is a long history of police prejudice against blacks and complaints of racial harassment. By the mid-1970s, clear evidence had mounted of blacks (especially black youths) being dis-proportionately involved in arrests for certain offences, largely but not only because of police discrimination.[49] A vicious cycle of interaction developed between police stereotyping and black vulnerability to the situations that attract police attention, resulting from racial discrimination in society generally.

The burden of recent research on police–public relations suggests that while these still remain relatively harmonious with the majority of the population (including most of the working class), they are tense and conflict-ridden with the young, the unemployed, the economically marginal and blacks.[50] What has happened to politicise policing since the 1970s is a growth in the size of these vulnerable groups, primarily due to economic failure and a heightening of their self-consciousness as targets of policing.

This is due to structural changes in the political economy of Western capitalism. Long-term structural unemployment (increasingly never-employment) has re-emerged, leading to the *de-incorporation* of increasing sections of the young working class, especially amongst discriminated against minorities, 'who are being defined out of the edifice of citizenship'.[51] A new underclass has formed which is not simply a result of unemployment, but of its seeming structural inevitability. 'The majority class does not need the un-employed to maintain and even increase its standard of living ... The main point about this category – for lack of a better word we shall call it the "underclass" – is that its destiny is perceived as hopeless.'[32] There is much debate about the now popular concept of an underclass, and its conservative culturalist version has unacceptable connotations of 'blaming the victim'.[53] But the structurally generated formation of a completely marginalised segment of society is a major source of the huge growth recently of crime, disorder and tensions around policing.

Unemployment is certainly not linked to crime or disorder in any straight-forward automatic way, as the Conservatives are ever ready to tell us. But there is now much evidence that in the present period at any rate it is a factor in the emergence of a young underclass which has the motive, the opportunity and the lack of those social controls which are brought by social integration, and thus becomes a key part of the explanation of crime and disorder.[54]

The conflicts between the socially marginal and the police are perennial, although they are now more extensive and structural than during the postwar boom. However, the key to how this is translated into political debate is a long-term cultural change in the articulate opinion-forming middle class.

The police have lost the confidence of certain small but influential sections of the 'chattering classes', what may be described roughly as *The Guardian* or *The Independent* reading circles. This process of a developing gulf with some educated middle-class opinion has a variety of roots, stretching back to the invention of the car. But the most significant are the growth of middle-class political protest since the early 1960s (CND, the anti-Vietnam War demon-strations, the 1960s' student movement and counter-culture) and the politicisation of forms of marginal deviance which involve some middle-class people, notably drug-taking and homosexuality. This conflict with highly articulate and educated sections of the population has been of enormous significance in converting policing into an overt political issue.[55]

Underlying the change in educated middle-class opinion is a broader cultural trend: the decline of traditional patterns of deference and unquestioning acceptance of authority, a process which has been aptly termed 'desubordination'.[56] This is reflected both in the attitudes of those at the receiving end of police powers and the general public audience of policing. Arrests are much less likely to be perceived as the legendary 'fair cop', either by arrestees or by others. The police as symbols of social authority evidently suffer from a culture of desubordination.

The sources of declining public confidence in the police thus lie deeper than any changes in police tactics or policies. We can postulate an equation predicting public consent to policing in which public acceptance is largely a function of the extent of social and cultural consensus. Increasing social divisions and declining deference equal a decline in the public standing of the police. This is because police tactics will move up the menu of coerciveness to deal with the symptoms of division and to overcome the decline of consent. At the same time, controversial tactics, as well as outright abuse, are more likely to be perceived as malpractice by recipients, opinion-formers and policy makers, as well as the general public, due to declining deference.

One possibility this raises is that the obvious response to increasing police scandals and falling public sympathy may be misguided. The conventional assumption across the political spectrum is that standards of police behaviour have declined since the 'Golden Age' of the mid-century. But is this really so?

It is inevitably difficult to assess the extent of police abuse at any particular time, let alone to measure changes over time. Police malpractice, like all deviance, is covert and subterranean. All we know is the amount which comes to light by the uncertain processes of revelation or detection. Criminologists have long stressed this issue when interpreting recorded crime trends, but they have been prepared to accept at face value the apparent increase in deviance amongst the police.

It is clear, however, that there was an enormous amount of hidden police deviance lurking behind the Dixon façade in the middle of this century. This is shown clearly by the evidence of memoirs and oral histories, both from the side of the police and the policed.[57] That most of this police deviance did not come to light was testimony to the more deferential if not authoritarian culture of the policed, as well as the legal establishment.

Whilst there was probably considerable under-reporting of police deviance in the 'good old days', there is reason to believe that today there may actually be less gross malpractice. One reason is that there has been a set of changes which are likely to have diluted, although far from eliminated the 'canteen cop culture' which numerous studies have pinpointed as the engine of abuse.[58] As mentioned above the educational background and training standards of officers have been transformed out of all recognition, although much scope for improvement remains. In addition, whilst they remain grossly under-represented from an equal opportunities standpoint, the proportion of women and ethnic minority officers has risen substantially. So too has the number of part-time volunteers (the 'Specials') and civilian employees. The result is that the backstage areas of police stations now regularly contain people who are far removed from the identikit white macho working-class model of traditional police culture. In addition, a set of legal and policy reforms has tried, with partial success to make police work more 'transparent' in order to secure more effective stewardship by courts and managers of the exercise of police powers.[59] These include the extensive recording requirements (by tape as well as paper records) of the Police and Criminal Evidence Act 1984, the introduction of lay station visiting schemes and the rise in access to legal and social work advisers facilitated by PACE. There have also been relevant advances in forensic science, such as DNA profiling and ESDA testing.

Many of the miscarriages of justice and allegations of malpractice which have been substantiated in recent years have come to light because of these changes. The role of scientific developments in clearing Stefan Kiszko, the Tottenham Three and the Irish cases is well known. The recent conviction of several

Metropolitan Police Constables for a brutal assault was the product of evidence from a woman Special Constable, illustrating the importance of the dilution of cop culture.[60] The crucial change, however, is a general cultural one. There is a greater willingness on the part of those in power, in the media and the legal system, to pursue cases and seek the relevant evidence, and to believe it when it is found. The new Lord Chief Justice, Lord Taylor, revealed as much when he recently admitted that judges had been too ready to believe the police without question in the past, but should and would not be prepared to do so in the future.[61] Several reviews of the case law interpreting PACE have underlined the greater propensity of judges to apply the requirements of its Codes of Practice against the police, rather than the permissive approach which prevailed with respect to breaches of the old Judges' Rules.[62]

These changes all suggest that the apparent wave of police deviance may really be the product of a change in social reaction, not of a real increase in police wrongdoing. This chimes in with the general view of many experienced police officers who believe there is now less flagrant and regularised malpractice than in the not very distant past.[63] They feel somewhat frustrated at the paradox that public trust in them is at its lowest ebb precisely when professional standards are at an all-time high. This may or may not be a more valid view than the conventional one of a rotting of the police institutional framework. What is certain is that the relationship between the extent of police wrongdoing and the revealed amount is as problematic as that between all offending and the official crime rate. There are many mediating processes of perception, labelling, reporting and recording.

The decline in the public standing of the police is thus far from straightforward and due to complex and social changes rather than simply an increase in police malfeasance. The key roles played by increasing social divisions, and declining cultural deference, have already been emphasised. It is in theorising these processes that the concept of postmodern society is helpful.

## IV  Policing a postmodern society

In the last decade, the related clutch of terms 'postmodern', 'postmodernism', 'postmodernity' and 'postmodernisation' have become increasingly fashionable for what is widely seen as a qualitative break in the development of contemporary society. The earliest usage of 'postmodern', in precisely the sense in which it tends to be used today,[64] was by the late C. Wright Mills in a public lecture delivered a at the LSE in 1969.[65] Mills' uncanny prophetic ability to anticipate the shape of things to come gives him a fair claim to be regarded as the H.G. Wells or Jules Verne of social science. Mills declared 'We are at the ending of what is called The Modern Age. Just as Antiquity was followed by several centuries of Oriental ascendancy, which Westerners provincially call the Dark Ages, so now The Modern Age is being succeeded by a postmodern period.'[66]

Mills' characterisation of this 'postmodern period' captures the gist of what contemporary analysts mean by the term: 'Our basic definitions of society and of self are being overtaken by new realities.' This is not, argues Mills, merely because of the pace of change and the struggle to grasp the meaning of it.

Fundamentally, Mills claims, the explanatory and ethical frameworks which we inherited from the Enlightenment and which have dominated the 'modern' age, primarily liberalism and socialism, 'have virtually collapsed as adequate explanations of the world and of ourselves'. Referring to common threads in the work of Bentham, Mill, Freud and Marx, the giant shapers of modern understanding, Mills concludes: 'the ideas of freedom and of reason have become moot ... increased rationality may not be assumed to make for increased freedom.'[67]

The rate at which new volumes bearing the word 'postmodern' in their titles appear on library shelves is alarming, and it is impossible here to deal systematically with all the varying interpretations, diagnoses, periodisations explanations and political reactions in the debate.[68] The basic idea is, of course, that what is now occurring is a qualitative transformation from one kind of social order to another, as Mills' prescient remarks indicate. The use of the term 'postmodern' itself implies that, while it is claimed that there is a break from the 'modern' (itself variously interpreted), the precise contours of the new social formation are hard to pinpoint other than in the negative: they are fundamentally different from the 'modern'.

The key aspect of what is different is usually said to be epitomised by a concept developed by Lyotard.[69] Whereas the hallmark of 'modern' culture was its underpinning by 'grand' or 'meta-narratives', such overarching stories about the direction and meaning of history have lost credibility. In one sense, of course, this claim is evidently self-defeating. For the notion of a breakdown of grand narratives is itself a meta-narrative. But clearly what is meant is the exhaustion of such grand narratives as the ideas of Progress or Enlightenment, the unfolding of Reason or Revolution, which purported to give a positive and unitary meaning to the historical process as a whole.

Claims about the development of postmodernity fall into three distinct yet related thematic clusters. The origin of the recent fashionable use of the term was primarily in aesthetics and art criticism, where commentators like Baudrillard and Lyotard discerned the emergence of a fundamentally new set of styles which they labelled 'postmodernism'.[70] Another line of thought has primarily been philosophical, suggesting an epistemological break in conceptions of knowledge and ethics. This is often referred to generally as 'post-structuralism' or 'post-objectivism'.[71] Finally, analysts from a variety of theoretical and political persuasions have argued that there has occurred a basic transformation in the political economy, culture and social order of contemporary societies. These may be labelled as theories of 'post-industrialism' or 'post-capitalism'.[72] All these theories point to profound changes in knowledge, popular culture and social order, and the relationship between these.

## Knowledge

In a vivid image, Bernstein has characterised the history of modern theories of knowledge as a variety of attempts to cope with 'Cartesian anxiety'. The twin harbingers of the modern – the Renaissance and the Reformation – undermined the absolute framework of understanding provided by Catholicism in the Middle Ages.[73] Descartes provides the prototypical example of a modern philosopher seeking a rational first principle, an Archimedean leverage point for knowledge after the removal of the absolute guarantees of religious revelation. From Descartes' *cogito*[74] to the twentieth-century positivists' falsification principle and logical coherence, modern philosophy has sought some secular substitute for clerical authority. Lurking behind the pursuit of a basis for objectivism was the fear that the only alternative was relativism and cognitive chaos.

MacIntyre tells a similar story about modern moral philosophy in his influential *After Virtue*.[75] The Enlightenment shattered the common language and conceptual framework which allowed meaningful discourse about morality. Although the simulacra of moral discourse remain, words are used with no shared conception of what they refer to. The concept of virtue lacks an agreed underpinning, just as knowledge does. In the postmodern era we have become conscious of what was always implicit in the project of modernity.

To this predicament there are two main responses. It can be celebrated as liberation from authoritarian epistemological or moral shackles. All that counts is what works for particular protagonists in specific contexts, as implied by the pragmatism of philosphers like Rorty.[76] Alternatively, it is only possible to adopt a stoic stance in these new Dark Ages, as recommended by MacIntyre, and shelter in congenial small communities awaiting some new charismatic restorer of the grand tradition of the virtues.[77]

In either optimistic or pessimistic variants, postmodernity is the realisation of the relativist potential implicit in modernity from the beginning. It is the realisation that 'Cartesian anxiety' will not be dispelled by the discovery of some new Archimedean point but has to be lived with. As Bauman, one of the foremost theorists of postmodernity puts it, the role of intellectuals changes from 'legislators', mapping a brave new world, to 'interpreters' of pluralism.[78]

These changes in intellectual culture do not just trickle down into the culture of people in general. However, the abandonment of absolutes is paralleled in popular culture. As Bauman puts it, in postmodern culture the 'pleasure principle' displaces Puritan asceticism and discipline.[79] Consumerism becomes the driving force of social action and the brittle basis of social order.

However, instead of a single dominant conception of the good life post-modernity is characterised by cultural pluralism and ambivalence. A mosaic of different lifestyles is on offer, none able to trump the others in legitimacy. The exclusion of an underclass from participation in the opulent spectacle needs and can have no ideological justification. Religion is no longer the opium of the people, so they will have to make do with opium itself (or its cheaper substitutes).

### Social structure and political economy

The theorists of postmodern society depict it as following a similar path of disorganisation, structural pluralism and decentring. In Giddens' words: 'The postmodern order is split into a multitude of contexts of action and forms of authority … The nation-state declines in importance and the cohesive totality is replaced by a multiplicity of sites of social reproduction.'[80]

Many analysts have offered similar accounts of the dispersion and fragmentation of the concentrated and centralised structure of economic organisation which reached a climax in the corporatist state regulation of the post-Second World War period up to the 1970s. Western societies are now experiencing a transition from 'organised' to 'disorganised' capitalism, in the terminology of Offe.[81]

The influential analysis of 'New Times' by writers associated with *Marxism Today* echoes similar themes.[82] In their account, contemporary capitalism is witnessing the erosion of 'Fordism'. 'Post-Fordism' is consumption not production-led. It involves the disaggregation of the market into specialised sectors, with design as a major selling point, based on the connotation of varying lifestyles rather than simply use-value. This is made possible by the development of information technology to coordinate far-flung and specialist markets and labour processes.[83]

Instead of a mass labour force of mainly semi- or un-skilled workers, a smaller multi-skilled core workforce is required.[84] The peripheral workforce of unskilled workers is low-paid, temporary, often part-time, and increasingly consists of women and ethnic minorities.[85] An underclass of the permanently excluded develops while the core labour force increases its income and freedom, though not security: the so-called 'two-thirds' society.[86] Instead of the primarily bifurcated class structure of competitive or monopoly capitalism, a much more complex system of stratification with cross-cutting lines, such as gender, ethnic identity and region, develops.[87] New forms of oppositional politics emerge, but the position of Conservative parties becomes more secure as the two-thirds of beneficiaries from 'New Times' consistently outvote the one-third who are excluded.[88] The nation-state becomes a less significant locus of power, usurped by a growing internationalization of capital and division of labour on the one hand, whilst the vitality of local identities also increases as the sites of production and reproduction become more scattered and fragmented.[89]

The themes of pluralism, contingency, the undermining of absolutes, ambivalence and disintegration pervade accounts of postmodern society, culture, knowledge and morality. There is much room for argument about the interpretation and significance of all this. What, if any, is the relationship between the material, social and cultural developments? Is there really a 'break' in capitalism, or just an unfolding of its logic to a new stage, as many Marxists argue.[90] Is the project of the Enlightenment unfinished in its emancipatory potential, although threatened by current developments, as Habermas would argue?[91] Or does the present malaise just make explicit the relativist dark side of Enlightenment liberalism, as MacIntyre implies?[92]

Whatever the outcome of such debates, what is clear is that the factors which were outlined earlier as underlying the police fall from grace – deepening social divisions and a less deferential culture – are not temporary aberrations changeable by an election, an upturn in the economy, calls for a return to Victorian values or changes in Government or police policy. They are deeply rooted structural trends, not a passing *fin de siècle* malaise.

## V The prospects of police reform

What are the implications for the prospects of success of current police initiatives to restore their legitimacy? During the late 1970s and 1980s, as the creeping crisis of confidence in the police began to unfold, there emerged a succession of competing agendas for reform. In the late 1970s and early 1980s, debate became increasingly polarised between a conservative 'law and order approach advanced by the police themselves and the Thatcher Government, and a radical rejectionist position, the organisational heart of which was in the Left-wing Labour Metropolitan local authorities elected in 1981.[93] Whilst the Conservatives advocated greater powers for the police, Labour saw the problem as the unfettered autonomy the police enjoyed and sought to reinforce their accountability to elected local authorities. The Scarman Report in 1981 proposed a sophisticated synthesis of these two positions, but with strict law enforcement subordinate in the last analysis to the diplomatic requirements of keeping the peace. This was a policy of back to the future. The ideals of the British police tradition epitomised by Dixon remained intact in principle but had been undermined in practice. Scarman advocated a blend of community consultation and police professionalism, predicated upon an adequately maintained iron fist, to deal with disorder should the velvet glove tactics fail.[94]

Scarmanism rapidly became the orthodox wisdom of government and police policy makers, to which at least lip-service had to be paid. In the hands of such influential police leaders as Sir Kenneth Newman and Sir Peter Imbert, it gave rise to a host of interrelated reforms throughout the 1980s. These were implemented in conjunction with innovations in management style which owed much to the new emphasis on professional management techniques and especially the concern for value for money, which increasingly pervaded the whole public sector. The style of the contemporary police chief correspondingly changed from bobby to bureaucrat.[95]

Opposition to these approaches was rapidly won over, or bludgeoned over. Middle of the road opinion could not resist the *bien pensant* tones of the new philosophy of community policing. The radical end of the spectrum was subject to cruder tactics. The Local Government Act 1985 dealt with the radical critique of policing by abolishing its material base – the Metropolitan local authorities – and replacing them for police purposes with the more manipulable Joint Boards.[96]

The problem with this accumulating avalanche of reforms was that while much changed in the leadership styles and presentational front of policing, the desired end products were not achieved. As discussed above, the end of the 1980s saw all-time record crime increases, renewed public disorder, spectacular scandals involving miscarriages of justice and plummeting public confidence in the police.

The leadership of the service has responded by seeking to model the mission of policing on the service style which their own research suggests is what the majority of the public wants. As described earlier, it has also sought to introduce a variety of managerial changes to monitor and improve the quality of service delivered.[97] The key is seen as changing police culture to incorporate quality of service values. In short, the police elite has turned to the language and style of consumerism – market research, prominently displayed mission statements, codes of ethical service and the like. This chimes in with the general approach to the public sector promulgated by John Major, and is policing designed for the age of the Citizen's Charter.[98]

Like its ideological first cousin, community policing, this consumerist ethos has the great virtue that it is almost impossible to be against it in principle. The issue is whether it fully confronts the realities of policing in the postmodern age. In so far as an emphasis of theorists of postmodern culture is on the centrality of style, design and image rather than use-value, it is clear that the consumerist tack is itself a prime expression of postmodernism.

However, neither this nor any other conceivable strategy will restore the police to the status they enjoyed in Britain in the middle years of this century. This was based on unique social and cultural conditions which are unlikely to re-occur and have certainly never been replicated elsewhere. In all other countries, the police have wielded power rather than authority (in the traditional Weberian distinction). The power of the British police was transmuted into authority primarily because they came to stand for a (largely mythical) national culture of order, harmony and restraint. Their power was legitimated by tradition. In other countries, any legitimation the police have achieved has been rational-legal or charismatic (again using Weber's famous ideal-typical categories).[99] These are more brittle and tenuous sources of legitimacy for the police than the authority of tradition. A first condition for the police to re-attain legitimacy is for them and the public to recognise that the traditional British bobby myth is anachronistic – indeed, it never corresponded to reality.

Beyond this, however, the deeper social changes of postmodemity are transforming the role of the police institution within the whole array of policing processes. The rise of *the* police – a single professional organisation for handling the policing function of regulation an surveillance, with the state's monopoly of legitimate force as its ultimate resource – was itself a paradigm of the modern. It was predicated upon the project of organising society around a central, cohesive notion of order. In Storch's striking phrase, the police were 'domestic missionaries'.[100] The role of the police, especially in Britain, was always more important for its dramaturgical function, symbolising social order, than for any instrumental effects in successfully controlling crime.[101] The changes in social structure and culture which have been labelled postmodernisation render this conception of policing increasingly anachronistic. There can be no effective symbol of a unitary order in a pluralistic and fragmented culture.

Nor can the instrumental functions of the police be straightforward in the 'two-thirds' society. The United States, as the Los Angeles riots of 1992 dramatically showed, indicates the dark end-point of processes which can be seen in less stark form throughout the Western world. The police are confronted with a social order bifurcated between the 'dreadful enclosures' of the underclass (often constructed on racial lines) and the castles of conspicuous consumerism in which the majority live, work and play.[102] The latter are increasingly taking the form of what the Canadian criminologists Shearing and Stenning have called 'mass private property',[103] huge privately owned facilities like shopping centres, leisure parks office or educational campuses, large private residential estates or apartment blocks. The role of the police in regulating the order of these areas is residual at most. A police officer is seldom, if ever, seen in Disneyland or indeed Brent Cross (except as a customer). Instead, control is maintained by architecture, the technology of surveillance and informal social mechanisms, with even the specialist input of private security personnel being vestigial, and primarily concerned with maintaining perimeter security.[104] The role of the police is the rump one of maintaining the order of public spaces, which increasingly are the preserve of the excluded social residuum.[105]

In addition, there remain higher level policing functions which the state must exercise: the control of serious professional and international crime, and the maintenance of state security. But these are increasingly remote from the world of the beat police.

In short, policing now reflects the processes of pluralism, disaggregation and fragmentation which have been seen as the hallmark of the postmodern. Hitherto, the British police have been unique in combining within a single omnibus organisation the disparate functions of patrol, public order, serious criminal investigation, political policing and regulating corporate crime. In most other countries, a variety of specialist organisations cope with these separately. It would seem, indeed, that they call for very different skills and tactics of mobilisation. It is most unlikely that the British police will survive the pressures towards an organisational division of policing labour in the last decade of the millennium. There will probably be a fundamental reorganisation, bifurcated between a variety of high-level units for national and international crime, public order and security functions, with local police forces on the other hand increasingly focused on small-scale crime order and service tasks.[106] The latter will find it increasingly difficult to find a suitable niche in the face of competition from private and environmental security mechanisms. The local police role will increasingly be the Fort Apache syndrome: patrolling the borders between respectable and rough reservations. These processes have been referred to by several commentators as the 'greying' of policing: its diffusion between a variety of institutional processes, with the human element increasingly not clad in blue uniforms.[107] Sadly Dixon is dead. Unlike his first demise in *The Blue Lamp*, we shall wait in vain for a second coming.

### Postscript: postmodern policing

There are three strategies which must be adopted if the police are to achieve what legitimacy is available in the postmodern period. All are already in place as policy of aspirations of the more progressive police leaders. The first is the recognition of the chimerical character of the Dixon ideal and its replacement by more pragmatic conceptions of acceptability. The police are providers of a mundane public service, not sacred totems of national pride.

Second, the personnel of the police must reflect the more diverse and plural demographics of postmodern societies. Specifically, the proportions of women and ethnic minorities must parallel at all levels in the police their numbers in the population policed.[108] Third, local policing must be adjusted to the plural priorities and cultures of a much more diverse social world. Disaggregation downwards of policy making is already the main aspect of leading reforms such as the sector policing experiments in the Metropolitan Police.[109] One vital ingredient which must be taken on board, however, is the integration of elected local authorities into the policy setting process. For London, this means the creation of such a local authority. Opinion polls and market research techniques, on which the police increasingly rely, cannot substitute for the electoral process as a means of registering public opinion.

The above analysis contains much intellectual pessimism. Is there room for optimism of the will?[110] Postmodern culture may have eclipsed the Enlightenment's modern conceptions of social justice, as well as the more ancient prophetic religious ideas of justice which modernism had displaced earlier. But certain harsh realities will not be pushed aside. As Los Angeles, the modern world's dream factory, showed us in May 1992, the backlash of the oppressed can turn complacent reveries into nightmare. To paraphrase Rosa Luxemburg,[111] in the final analysis the only alternatives are social justice or barbarism. Unfortunately, at present, the odds seem strongly to favour barbarism.

*From Robert Reiner, 'Policing a postmodern society', Modern Law Review, Vol. 55, no 6, 1992, pp 761–81.*

## Notes

1 For fuller discussions see Clarke, 'Holding the Blue Lamp: Television and the Police in Britain' (1983) 19 *Crime and Social Justice* 44, and Sparks, *Television and the Drama of Crime* (Buckingham: Open University Press, 1992) pp 25–30.
2 Reiner, *The Politics of the Police* (Hemel Hempstead: Wheatsheaf, 2nd ed, 1992) Ch 5.
3 Bittner, 'Florence Nightingale in Pursuit of Willie Sutton: A theory of the Police' in Jacob (ed), *The Potential for Reform of Criminal Justice* (Beverly Hills: Sage, 1974).
4 Reiner, 'Police Research in the United Kingdom: A Critical Review' in Morris and Tonry (eds), *Modern Policing* (Chicago: Chicago University Press, 1992).
5 Smith, *Lectures on Jurisprudence* (Oxford: Oxford University Press, 1978. Originally published 1763).
6 In Foucault's terminology: cf M. Foucault, 'On Governmentality' (1979) 6 *Ideology and Consciousness* 5.
7 For syntheses of recent research on the origins and development of the British police see Emsley, *The English Police* (Hemel Hempstead: Wheatsheaf, 1991) and Reiner, *op cit* n 2, Chs 1 and 2.
8 Storch, 'The Plague of Blue Locusts: Police Reform and Popular Resistance in Northern England, 1840–57' (1975) 20 *International Review of Social History* 61.
9 Royal Commission on the Police, *Final Report*, Cmnd 1782 (London: HMSO, 1962) pp 102–3. For other contemporary evidence of the high status of the British police in the 1950s, see Gorer, *Exploring English Character* (London: Cresset, 1955) and Almond and Verba, *The Civic Culture* (Princeton: Princeton University Press, 1963).
10 Skogan, *The Police and Public in England and Wales: A British Crime Survey Report* (London: HMSO, 1990).
11 Jowell, Witherspoon and Brook (eds), *British Social Attitudes: The 5th Report* (Aldershot, Gower, 1988) pp 117–18.
12 Skogan, *op cit* n 10, p 1.
13 Joint Consultative Committee of the Police Staff Associations, *Operational Policing Review* (Surbiton, Surrey: The Police Federation, 1990).
14 The term was coined by Cray, *The Enemy in the Streets* (New York: Anchor, 1972). It was developed analytically by Lee, 'Some Structural Aspects of Police Deviance in Relations with Minority Groups' in Shearing (ed), *Organisational Police Deviance* (Toronto: Butterworth, 1981).

15  Smith, Small and Gray, *Police and People in London* (London: Policy Studies Institute, 1983); Kinsey, *The Merseyside Crime Survey* (Liverpool: Merseyside County Council, 1984); Jones, MacLean and Young, *The Islington Crime Survey* (London: Gower, 1986); Crawford, Jones, Woodhouse and Young, *The Second Islington Crime Survey* (Middlesex Polytechnic: Centre for Criminology, 1990); McConville and Shepherd, *Watching Police, Watching Communities* (London: Routledge, 1992).

16  Police concern was accentuated by the fact that the 'Inquiry into Police Responsibilities and Rewards', recently announced by the Home Secretary Kenneth Clarke, consists almost entirely of people from industrial and commercial rather than legal backgrounds, under the chairmanship of Sir Patrick Sheehy of British and American Tobacco. ('Clarke sends for BATman,' *Police*, July 1992, pp 8–9; Loveday, 'A Murky Business,' *Police Review*, 17 July 1992, pp 1318–1319; Butler, 'Paying the Service Charge,' *Police Review*, 24 July 1992, pp 1360–1361.

17  The organisational and policy changes are discussed in more detail in R. Reiner, *op cit* n 2, Ch 2.

18  Brogden and Graham, 'Police Education: The Hidden Curriculum' in Fieldhouse (ed), *The Political Education of Servants of the State* (Manchester: Manchester University Press, 1988); Tierney, 'Graduating in Criminal Justice' (1989) 5 *Policing* 208.

19  Scarman, *The Brixton Disorders*, Cmnd 8427 (London: HMSO, 1981); Fielding, *Joining Forces* (London: Routledge, 1988); Southgate (ed), *New Dimensions in Police Training* (London: HMSO, 1988).

20  Smith *et al*, *op cit* n 15, p 249.

21  PACE was itself the product of a complex political balancing act, unevenly incorporating the major recommendations of the 1981 Report of the Royal Commission on Criminal Procedure. Cf Symposium on the Police and Criminal Evidence Act, *Public Law*, Autumn 1985, pp 388–454, and Leigh, 'Some Observations on the Parliamentary History of the Police and Criminal Evidence Act 1984' in Harlow (ed), *Public Law and Politics* (London: Sweet and Maxwell, 1986).

22  McConville, Sanders and Leng, *The Case for the Prosecution* (London: Routledge, 1991); Reiner, 'Codes, Courts and Constables: Police Powers Since 1984' (1992) 12 *Public Money and Management* 11; Reiner and Leigh, 'Police Power' in Chambers and McCrudden (eds), *Individual Rights in the UK since 1945* (Oxford: Oxford University Press/The Law Society, 1992).

23  Such as the series of cases involving the West Midlands Serious Crimes Squad (disbanded by the then Chief Constable Geoffrey Dear in 1989) and the Court of Appeal decision to uphold the appeals of the 'Tottenham Three', who had been convicted of the murder of PC Keith Blakelock during the 1986 Broadwater Farm riots.

24  For conflicting assessments of the militarization of public order policing, see Jefferson, *The Case against Paramilitary Policing* (Buckingham: Open University Press, 1990) and Waddington, *The Strong Arm of the Law* (Oxford: Oxford University Press, 1991).

25  McCabe, Wallington, Alderson, Gostin and Mason, *The Police, Public Order and Civil Liberties* (London: Routledge, 1988).

26  Northam, *Shooting in the Dark* (London: Faber, 1988).

27  Police Complaints Authority, *Annual Report 1989* (London: HMSO, 1990).

28  Vincent-Jones, 'The Hippy Convoy and Criminal Trespass' (1986) 13 *Journal of Law and Society* 343.

29  Subsequent Home Research has challenged the police view of growing disorder in rural areas, as distinct from towns inside what are formally county force boundaries, of M. Tuck, *Drinking and Disorder: A Study of Non Metropolitan Violence*, Home Office Research and Planning Unit Study 108 (London: HMSO, 1989).

30  cf the reports in *Police Review*, 24 July 1992, pp 1356–7, and 31 July 1992, pp 1404–5.

31  Rawlings, 'Creeping Privatisation? The Police, the Conservative Government and Policing in the Late 1980s' in Reiner and Cross (eds), *Beyond Law and Order: Criminal Justice Policy and Politics into the 1990s* (London: Macmillan, 1991).

32  Reiner, *op cit* n 2, Preface and Ch 7.

33  Reiner, *Chief Constables* (Oxford: Oxford University Press, 1991) pp 210–19.

34  *ibid* Ch 6, and Skolnick and Bayley, *The New Blue Line* (New York: Free Press, 1986) and *Community Policing: Issues and Practices around the World* (Washington DC: National Institute of Justice, 1988).

35  For a recent national survey, see the *Operational Policing Review*, *op cit* n 13, s 6.

36  See the statements by the HM Chief Inspector of Constabulary, Sir John Woodcock, ACPO president Brian Johnson, 1991 and Michael Hirst, Chief Constable of Leicestershire (and one of the main architects of the 'quality of service' initiative) in *Policing*, Autumn 1991.

37  McConville and Shepherd, *op cit* n 15. But for a vigorous defence see Hirst, 'We're Getting it Right,' *Police*, July 1992, pp 40–2.

38  Jones, *Organisational Aspects of Police Behaviour* (Farnborough: Gower, 1989), and McConville and Shepherd, *op cit* n 15.

39  *Report of Her Majesty's Chief Inspector of Constabulary 1991* (London: HMSO).

40  Bottomley and Pease, *Crime and Punishment: Interpreting the Data* (Buckingham: Open University Press, 1986).

41  Hough and Mayhew, *The British Crime Survey* (London: HMSO, 1983); Mayhew, Elliott and Dowds, *The 1988 British Crime Survey* (London: HMSO, 1989).

42  Jefferson and Grimshaw, *Controlling the Constable* (London: Muller, 1984); Lustgarten, *The Governance of the Police* (London: Sweet and Maxwell, 1986) are the seminal discussions.

43  Hanmer, Radford and Stanko (eds), *Women, Policing and Male Violence* (London: Routledge, 1989); Cashmore and McLaughlin (eds), *Out of Order? Policing Black People* (London: Routledge, 1991).

44  Notably L. Lustgarten, *op cit* n 42.

45  Reiner, *Chief Constables*, *op cit* n 33, Ch 11.

46  *ibid.*

47  E. Cray, *op cit*, J. Lee, *op cit.*

48  Skolnick, *Justice without Trial* (New York: Wiley, 1966); Erickson, *Reproducing Order: A Study of Police Patrol Work* (Toronto: University of Toronto Press, 1982); Smith *et al*, *op cit* n 15; Young, *An Inside Job: Policing and Police Culture in Britain* (Oxford: Oxford University Press, 1990).

49  Lea and Young, *What is to Be Done about Law and Order?* (Harmondsworth: Penguin Books, 1984) Ch 4; T. Jefferson, 'Race, Crime and Policing: Empirical, Theoretical and Methodological Issues' (1988) 16 *International Journal of the Sociology of Law* 521; Reiner, 'Race and Criminal Justice' (1989) 16 *New Community* 5.

50  Smith *et al*, *op cit* n 15; Jones *et al*, *op cit*, n 15; Skogan, *op cit* n 10.

51  Dahrendorf, *Law and Order* (London: Sweet and Maxwell, 1985) p 98.

52  *ibid* pp 101–7.

53  Murray, *The Emerging British Underclass* (London: Institute of Economic Affairs, 1989); Field, *Losing Out: The Emergence of Britain's Underclass* (Oxford: Blackwell, 1989).

54  Farrington, Gallagher, Morley, St Ledger and West, 'Unemployment, School-Leaving and Crime' (1986) 26 *British Journal of Criminology* 335. Box, *Recession, Crime and Punishment* (London: Macmillan, 1987); Field, *Trends in Crime and their Interpretation*, Home Office Research Study 119 (London: HMSO, 1990).

55  Waddington, 'Why the "Opinion-Makers" No Longer Support the Police,' *Police*, December 1982.

56  Miliband, 'A State of Desubordination' (1978) 29 *British Journal of Sociology* 399.

57  Mark, *In the Office of Constable* (London: Collins, 1978); Cohen, 'Policing the Working Class City' in Fine *et al* (eds), *Capitalism and the Rule of Law* (London: Hutchinson, 1979); White, *The Worst Street in London* (London: Routledge, 1990); Brogden, *On the Mersey Beat* (Oxford: Oxford University Press, 1991).

58  Holdaway, *Inside the British Police* (Oxford: Blackwell, 1983); Reiner, *op cit* n 2, Ch 3; Young, *op cit* n 48.

59  Morgan, 'Police Accountability: Developing the Local Infrastructure' (1987) 27 *British Journal of Criminology* 87. These measures may, however, have the ultimate function of preserving police autonomy as Morgan has also argued, cf Morgan, 'Policing by Consent: Legitimating the Doctrine' in Morgan and Smith (eds), *Coming to Terms with Policing* (London: Routledge, 1989).

60  See the report in *Police Review*, 10 April 1992, p 662.

61  *The Guardian*, 29 April 1992, p 1.

62  Feldman, 'Regulating Treatment of Suspects in Police Stations: Judicial Interpretations of Detention Provision in the Police and Criminal Evidence Act 1984,' *Criminal Law Review*, July 1990, p 452.

63  It must be emphasized that whilst gross malpractice may have declined, subtle forms no doubt remain rife, as indeed is shown by much of the research evaluating PACE: see for example M. McConville, A. Sanders and R. Leng, *op cit* n 22.

64  The term 'postmodern' itself has been in use for a long time. Arnold Toynbee used it before the Second World War in his *A Study of History*, but to refer to the whole period since the eighteenth century Enlightenment and Industrial Revolutions, ie precisely the heyday of 'modernism' in most current accounts. The *reductio ad absurdum* of attempts to find antecedents for postmodernism was the claim by Kroker and Cooke that the 'postmodern scene … begins in the fourth century … everything since the Augustinian refusal has been nothing but a fantastic and grisly implosion of experience as Western culture itself runs under the signs of passive and suicidal nihilism' (Kroker and Cooke, *The Postmodern Scene*, London:

Macmillan, 1988) p 127. No doubt we shall soon be told that postmodernism began with the Big Bang itself.

65 Published as 'On Reason and Freedom' in Mills, *The Sociological Imagination* (Glencoe: Free Press, 1959) pp 165–76.

66 *ibid*.

67 *ibid*.

68 For some recent general surveys and discussion of the issue, see Bauman, *Legislators and Interpreters: Modernity, Postmodernity and Intellectuals* (Cambridge: Polity Press, 1987); Bauman, *Modernity and the Holocaust* (Cambridge, Polity Press, 1989); Bauman, *Intimations of Postmodernity* (London: Routledge, 1992); Harvey, *The Condition of Postmodernity: An Inquiry into the Origins of Cultural Change* (Oxford: Blackwell, 1989); Turner (ed), *Theories of Modernity and Postmodernity* (London: Sage, 1990); Giddens, *The Consequence of Modernity* (Cambridge: Polity Press, 1990); Rose, *The Post-Modern and the Post-Industrial* (Cambridge: Cambridge University Press, 1991); Rosenau, *Postmodernism and the Social Sciences* (New Jersey: Princeton University Press, 1992); Crook, Pakulski and Waters, *Postmodernisation: Change in Advanced Society* (London: Sage, 1992). An excellent critique is provided by Callinicos, *Against Postmodernism* (Oxford: Blackwell, 1989).

69 Lyotard, *The Postmodern Condition: A Report on Knowledge* (Manchester: Manchester University Press, 1984).

70 *ibid*; Poster (ed), *Jean Baudrillard: Selected Writings* (Cambridge: Polity Press, 1989).

71 Bernstein, *Beyond Objectivism and Relativism* (Oxford: Blackwell, 1983).

72 Bell, *The Coming of Post-Industrial Society* (New York: Basic Books, 1973).

73 This does not mean that all people in medieval times shared a monolitic world view any more than that in modern times there was a single hegemonic dominant ideology, cf Abercrombie, Hill and Turner, *The Dominant Ideology Thesis* (London: Unwin, 1980). But the Church did provide the basic parameters within which disputes and divergences occurred.

74 Hintikka, '*Cogito, Ergo Sum*: Inference or Performance?' in Doney (ed), *Descartes: A Collection of Critical Essays* (New York: Anchor Books, 1967).

75 MacIntyre, *After Virtue: A Study in Moral Theory* (London: Duckworth, 1981).

76 Rorty, *Philosophy and the Mirror of Nature* (Oxford: Blackwell, 1979); *Contingency, Irony and Solidarity* (Cambridge: Cambridge University Press, 1989).

77 MacIntyre, *op cit* n 75.

78 Bauman, *op cit* n 68.

79 *ibid*.

80 Giddens, 'Uprooted Signposts at Century's End,' *The Higher*, 17 January 1992, pp 21–2.

81 Offe, *Disorganised Capitalism* (Cambridge, Polity Press, 1985). See also Lash and Urry, *The End of Organised Capitalism* (Cambridge: Polity Press, 1987).

82 Hall and Jacques (eds), *New Times: The Changing Face of Politics in the 1990s* (London: Lawrence and Wishart, 1989).

83 Murray, 'Fordism and Post-Fordism' and 'Benetton Britain' in Hall and Jacques, *op cit* n 82; Allen, 'Fordism and Modern Industry' in Allen, Braham and Lewis (eds), *Political and Economic Forms of Modernity* (Cambridge: Polity Press, 1992).

84 Braham, 'The Divisions of Labour and Occupational Change' in Allen, Braham and Lewis, *op cit* n 83.

85 *ibid*; McDowell, 'Social Divisions, Income Inequality and Gender Relations in the 1980s' in Cloke (ed), *Policy and Change in Thatcher's Britain* (Oxford: Pergamon, 1992).

86 Dahrendorf, *op cit* n 51, p 103; Therborn, 'The Two-Thirds, One-Third Society' in Hall and Jacques, *op cit* n 82.

87 Bradley, 'Changing Social Divisions: Class, Gender and Race' in Bocock and Thompson (eds), *Social and Cultural Forms of Modernity* (Cambridge: Polity Press, 1992).

88 Galbraith, *The Culture of Contentment* (London: Sinclair-Stevenson, 1992).

89 Held, 'The Decline of the Nation State' in Hall and Jacques, *op cit* n 82.

90 Jameson, *Postmodernism: Or the Cultural Logic of Late Capitalism?* (London: Verso, 1992); Callinicos, *op cit* n 68.

91 Habermas, 'Modernity – An Incomplete Project?' in Foster (ed), *Postmodern Culture* (London: Pluto Press, 1985).

92 MacIntyre, *op cit* n 75.

93 Reiner, *op cit* n 2.

94 Scarman, *op cit*.

95 Reiner, *op cit* n 33.

96 Loveday, 'The New Police Authorities in the Metropolitan Counties' (1991) 1 *Policing and Society* 193.

97 Woodcock, *op cit* n 36; Johnson, *op cit* n 36; Hirst, *op cit* n 36.

98    Barron and Scott, 'The Citizen's Charter Programme' (1992) 55 MLR 526.
99    For a recent general discussion of the Weberian tradition in the analysis of power and legitimacy, see Beetham, *The Legitimation of Power* (London: Macmillan, 1991).
100   Storch, 'The Policeman as Domestic Missionary' (1976) IX *Journal of Social History* 481.
101   Manning, *Police Work* (Cambridge: Mass: MIT Press, 1977) is the most cogent presentation of a dramaturgical analysis of policing.
102   As Davis put it in his account of Los Angeles as prism of the postmodern future (written before the 1992 riots), 'the historical world view and quixotic quest of the postwar LAPD' (Los Angeles Police Department) was 'good citizens, off the streets, enslaved in their high security private consumption spheres; bad citizens, on the streets (and therefore not engaged in legitimate business), caught in the terrible jehovan scrutiny of the LAPD's space programme.' Davis, *City of Quartz* (London: Vintage, 1992) p 253.
103   Shearing and Stenning, 'Private Security: Implications for Social Control' (1983) 30 *Social Problems* 493.
104   As Davis puts it, 'In cities like Los Angeles, on the bad edge of postmodernity, one observes an unprecedented tendency to merge urban design, architecture and the police apparatus into a single, comprehensive security effort ... Los Angeles in its usual prefigurative model offers an especially disquieting catalogue of the emergent liaisons between architecture and the American police state.' Davis, *op cit* n 102.
105   Important accounts of the increasing role of private security in contemporary social control are Shearing and Stenning (eds), *Private Policing* (Beverly Hills: Sage, 1987); South, *Policing for Profit* (London: Sage, 1988); Johnston, *The Rebirth of Private Policing* (London: Routledge, 1992).
106   Anderson, *Policing the World* (Oxford: Oxford University Press, 1989); Dorn, South and Murji, 'Mirroring the Market? Police Reorganisation and Effectiveness against Drug Trafficking' in Reiner and Cross, *op cit* n 31.
107   Hoogenboom, 'Grey Policing: A Theoretical Framework' (1992) 2 *Policing and Society* 17; Johnston, *op cit* n 105.
108   For accounts of the formidable obstacles to achieving this, see Heidensohn, *Women in Control? The Role of Women in Law Enforcement* (Oxford: Oxford University Press, 1992); Holdaway, *Recruiting a Multi-ethnic Police Force* (London: HMSO, 1991).
109   Although this may not be how it is working out in practice. Weeks, 'Sector Policing,' *Police*, July 1992, p 38.
110   In Gramsci's famous formulation, cf Anderson, *Considerations on Western Marxism* (London: New Left Books, 1976) p 89.
110   Luxemburg, *Political Writings* (New York: Monthly Review Press, 1971) p 24.

# 39. Policing, politics and postmodernity

*Pat O'Malley*

Increasingly, observers are locating contemporary shifts in the organization and practice of policing, criminal justice and even criminology in terms of the emergence and development of postmodernity (e.g. Crook et al., Reiner, 1992, 1994; Carriere and Ericson, 1994; Mugford, 1993). With respect to police, the thesis advanced is that national police forces constitute a quintessentially *modern* form of institution and thus predictably are being changed by the impact of postmodernity. Thus for Reiner (1992) the 'rise of *the* police – a single professional organisation for handling the professional policing function of regulation and surveillance with the state's monopoly of legitimate force as its ultimate resource – was itself a paradigm of the modern'. The modernity of (public) police is taken to be manifest especially in its role of enforcing a unitary body of law which is mythically imagined as the consensual expression of the population of the nation-state. The rule of law, in the vision of the modernist state, is understood as a neutral institution expressing a universal truth, as impersonal and impartial, above particularism. The emergence of post-modernity is identified as being corrosive of these and related modernist features of police, through such characteristic influences as the rise of consumerism, the fragmentation of values and moralities, globalization and the disaggregation and hollowing out of the nation-state (Reiner, 1992; Sheptycki, 1995). Each of these arguments may be considered in a little more detail.

## Postmodern police and policing postmodernity

First, the postmodern fragmentation of the modernist project of a unitary truth – itself associated with the assertion of postcolonial, feminist and other voices – is seen to undermine the unitary and neutral vision of law and law enforcement upon which the modern police are founded. Postmodern societies are characterized by diverse and plural demographics and cultural standards, and the idea of a unified national police force policing universal standards thus appears as an anachronism. Public police forces are seen to be disaggregated by the need to retain legitimacy, potency and relevance in this fragmented and localized world (Reiner, 1992). Increasingly police are called to be responsive to local 'communities' – regional and cultural – and this has the potential to undermine both the belief in the impartiality of police and their (national) unity. In postmodernity, the argument goes, police become the regulators of more particularistic moral and local legal concerns, albeit that these may be framed within an overarching but increasingly notional formal legal order 'on the books'.

Second, evidence that this shift is a reflection of postmodernity, and not merely a temporary or isolated phenomenon to be dealt with by specific reforms, is drawn from the fact that the fragmentation of police is paralleled by the fragmentation of the state in general. Increasingly state functions in other areas of government are also being localized, privatized and otherwise dispersed among smaller and more disaggregated units (e.g. Crook et al., 1992, Mugford, 1993). Trends in policing thus are seen as an aspect of the broader process of 'hollowing out' the nation-state that is a feature of the development of postmodernity (Reiner, 1992, Sheptycki, 1995). This hollowing-out process is linked not only to the impact of diversification, localization and privatization but to the impact of globalization. The nation-state is seen to have become an anachronistic form of governance as globalization imposes the transfer of many of its key political and economical functions to transnational entities. Confirmation that changes in policing reflect (or are part of) this postmodernizing of the state is taken from observations that globalizing trends are also registered at the level of state policing; for example, the inadequacy and supersession of national police with respect to policing transnational crime. Overall then, postmodernity's regionalization disaggregates the state and police from below, while its globalization and transnationalism decompose them from above.

Shifts in the character and unity of state policing are also seen to be linked with postmodernity's privileging of commodification and of cultures and institutions of consumption over those of production. For example, as 'the police elite has turned to the language and style of consumerism', so consumer audits, quality of service values, mission statements, charters and the like have come to be a prominent issue for state police in the current age (Reiner, 1992). In the postmodern police thesis, such developments in the commodification of police, as might be expected, are also linked to the shift toward value diversification, as police must provide a service to their (local and diverse) 'customers' rather than enforce an imposed, universal order. Finally, such commodifying tendencies in police work are also taken to be indicative of the impact of postmodernism because the realignment of policing in this way is identified not as dealing with the crucial issues of policing but as purely a matter of form. In turn, 'in sofar as an emphasis of theorists of postmodern culture is on the centrality of style, design and image rather than use-value, it is clear that the consumerist tack is itself a prime expression of postmodernism' (Reiner, 1992).

Such accounts, whether related to police or to changes in any other modernist institution, are quite suggestive, and may provide a much-needed research and theoretical framework for understanding the major shifts that are undeniably occurring in many public police forces. But how far can we take for granted either that police are changing in response to pressures arising from postmodernity or that these pressures are producing the postmodernization of police? As it stands, I would argue that the thesis rests on a series of questionable assumptions.

First is the assumption that a relatively diverse array of social and economic changes – in particular the increased recognition of moral diversification, the emphasis on the local and regional, the impact of globalization and the rise of consumerism – are symptomatic or expressive of the rise of an overarching shift into a new order of postmodernity. In this article, particularly because it is some-what extraneous to the specific questions regarding police, I do not wish to address the question of whether such a thesis is plausible, although clearly this has been raised as a serious problem elsewhere (e.g., Latour, 1994). However, such doubts do provide a background to the substantive case put forward in this study, namely, that many of the changes to which police restructuring are attributed may be linked to processes which do not imply the impact of anything as global in their scope as postmodernity.

Second, it is assumed that police forces take the form of modernist organizations (indeed are 'paradigmatic' of modernist institutions). Yet it may be argued that it is no easier to identify police as modern than it is to argue for their postmodern future. For example, over the course of most of their history police recruitment, entry and training have reflected an apprenticeship model which is guild-like in its operation and form. Members begin as recruits to general policing and normally spend years at this level before (in comparatively limited numbers) becoming specialists of any kind. Promotion substantially has been based on seniority rather than by merit alone. As well as these problematic features of formal organization, the traditionalist and particularistic nature of informal police-working culture, with its intense focus on loyalty to fellow members, has long operated to render police reform almost impotent in its attempts to move toward modern professional forms of organization – often to the frustration of police management (Etter, 1995; Landa and Dillon, 1995). From this point of view, it will be later argued, some of the changes now being attributed to postmodern influences – such as that concerned with commodification of police service – are intelligible not as the impact of postmodernity on modernist organization but more plausibly as the effect of managerially led efforts to turn police into a modern institution. Such problems suggest the interpretive difficulties that arise when we work directly from broad global conceptions such as modernity and postmodernity to such particular institutions as national police forces.

This point leads to a third problem, namely that changes are identified as effects (or aspects) of the postmodern primarily on the basis of an homology between emergent policing forms and the characteristic forms of postmodernity. Generally the *process* whereby homological reflection occurs is not examined: homology by itself is taken to indicate connection. For example, it is assumed that regionalization and consumerization of police reflect or are generated by the postmodern diversification of community values. But there is no evidence presented to demonstrate that 'popular' demands for these changes did cause or even contribute to the transformation of an institution not previously noted for its responsiveness. In addition, the argument discounts evidence of other processes that may be at work. Thus, as noted earlier, Reiner (1992) short-circuits analysis of the impact of police management by arguing that as their reforms will not solve 'crucial' postmodern policing problems, they must reflect post-modernity's emphasis on style rather than content.

Other questions arise when we consider the historical timing of some of the casual connections involved in the postmodern policing thesis. For example, while the consumerist changes in policing attributed to postmodernity – such as the move to customer audits – have become visible only in the last 10 years or so, consumerism has a much longer history. Writers such as Bell (1976) identify the revolutionary effects of consumerism on disciplinarity and the modernist project as having been set in a dominant place by the 1960s. Conversely, other aspects that are attributed to consumerism – such as the privatization of policing – have considerably longer histories than has consumerism itself, and can be attributed to rather different processes. Most notable among these are explanations in terms of the demands of capital for controlling property and labour (e.g. Spitzer and Scull, 1976).

None of this is to say that the accounts linking police changes to post-modernity are necessarily wrong, but the limited value of such a framework becomes clear precisely when commentators have begun to subject such models of postmodern police to systematic analysis. Sheptycki's (1995) insightful work, for example, raises important doubts about the extent to which, with respect to police, there has been a hollowing out of the state and its functions. This research suggests that transnationalization has an uneven effect on national police forces, strengthening and developing some aspects while eroding and weakening others. What emerges is a recognition of the need to pay closer attention to the nature of the changes being implemented, and the ways in which they are linked to their social and governmental contexts. In this chapter, I pursue such an approach by probing more closely into the extent to which the changes to policing attributed to postmodernity may better be understood by examining their nexus with currently ascendant neo-liberal political rationalities and related social technologies of 'new managerialism'.

## Neoliberalism, localization and police consumerism

> We rely on professionals to solve problems, not families and communities. We let the police, the doctors, the teachers, and the social workers have all the control, while the people they are serving have none ... We create programs designed to collect clients rather than to empower communities of citizens. When we do this, we undermine the confidence and competence of our citizens and communities. We create *dependency*. (Osborne and Gaebler, 1993: 51)

By the mid-1970s, the rationalities of collective liberalism appearing under the rubrics of the 'welfare state', the 'interventionist state' and 'Keynesianism', which had been hegemonic for much of the century, were confronting a rising tide of resistance (Gamble, 1988). Rationalities of economic and individualistic liberalism began to find a place in the political forefront within the political credos of neo-liberalism, in more specific forms such as Thatcherism and Reaganism and in such ideological projects as the development of 'Enterprise Culture' (Rose, 1990a, 1990b, 1993; Heelas, 1991; Keat and Abercrombie, 1991). In this context, core elements of neo-liberalism – such as appeals to the efficiency of markets; to the importance of accountability; to the liberty, enterprise, responsibility and independence of individuals; and to the virtues of the non-interventionist state – have become almost the received knowledge of governmental regimes operating under a considerable diversity of party political standards (Keat, 1991: 1).

In many respects, such rationalities revive the modernist political discourses of classical liberalism. But – as the passage from Osborne and Gaebler suggests – this new liberalism differs from its forerunner in that, *inter alia*, it organizes itself around an historically specific rejection of collectivist liberalism and the welfare state. One of its central tenets is that the welfare state created dependent citizens who had to be made active, independent and responsible. Linked to this is the classical liberal idea that markets are the environment most supportive of such subjects. But neo-liberalism applies this traditional liberal principle in a radical fashion, and again in reaction to the welfare state, to require that the state itself should be shaped along market lines and should be forced to compete in the market with respect to many of its activities. Commerical enterprise increasingly has come to be accepted as the paradigmatic form in terms of which the operation and structure of most institutions, and the provision of most goods and services, are to be modelled. This implies also that many areas and services formerly provided by the state should be turned over to private enterprise. As part of this process, the state ceases to be the directive core attracting to itself a monopoly of functions, and instead begins to shed or share many activities and responsibilities. Thus privatization, for example, has begun to sweep across areas such as criminal justice (private prisons, private provision of services within public correctional institutions, privately operated community corrections etc.) in ways that would have been almost unthinkable 20 years ago.

This privileging of market models is quite explicitly a rejection not of what may be identified generally with 'modernity' but specifically of the welfare-state interventionism which had been aimed at scientifically and humanely rationalizing the market (e.g. Thatcher, 1993). It was this technocratic state that neo-liberals regard as having made citizens dependent and unenterprising. The extension of this assumption also has been behind the emphasis on 'consumerizing' the imagery of politics and service delivery, epitomized by the discourse of 'consumers' and 'customers' that has begun to displace the language of 'students', 'patients', 'passengers', 'prisoners', 'clients' and so on. 'Meeting the demands of the "sovereign" consumer becomes the new and overriding institutional imperative' (Keat, 1991: 3). In these discourses, the rhetoric is one in which the consumer leads the way, shaping the nature of services to be provided precisely because this is how neo-liberalism imagines efficiency and effectiveness to be maximized – or to put it another way, how it imagines the market to work most 'competitively' (Abercrombie, 1991; Rose, 1993).

Taken together, these developments imply a *politically driven* decentring of the state. To all appearances, it is not so much that the state is being pulled apart by postmodern pressures from without and, even less, that this is effected by cultural pressures for diversification. Rather it seems that it is being pushed apart by political rationality involving the deployment of very considerable political pressure, often against considerable resistance. Neo-liberals are quite explicit about the need for a strong political state to overcome the resistances of state officials to the carving up and dispersal of their empires; to mobilize a 'dependent' population to act in its own interests; and to expose the torpid 'welfare' citizenry to the invigorating vicissitudes of risk. Most of the initiative and ingenuity that has been applied to these processes (however much one may be dismayed by them) has arisen out of neo-liberal political think-tanks and institutes, party and cabinet meetings and so forth – rather than arising spontaneously 'out of the community'. Indeed (as will be seen later with specific reference to policing), recognition that the community has to be created, empowered, mobilized and made aware of its best interests is one of the hallmarks of neo-liberal politics (O'Malley and Palmer, 1996).

Much of the dynamism of neo-liberal reforms has been centred on the provision of incentives to individuals. The problem with welfarism, in this view, is as much that it failed to reward effort and excellence as it is that it protected the inept and inert. Here the market comes again to the fore, delivering rewards in the form of commodities. In contrast to the self-denying character of classical liberalism, market-based self-gratification is embraced by neo-liberals. In the context of a highly valorized individualism, the variable demands – the 'freedom of choice' – of individual citizens as consumers are given priority. In this context, the political emphasis of contemporary governments on customerization and, in the process, the stress on the accountability of service providers at the local level become intelligible in their own right rather than as symptoms of a global change.

Each of the elements of this shift – the ascendance of consumer discourses, the erosion on individual enterprise and responsibility – is thus linked to a quite specific set of political ideas which emerges as a reaction against state interventionism and collective liberalism. While they overlap with, and incorporate, the ideas associated with postmodernity, the kinds of processes involved appear rather different from those suggested by Reiner and others. The picture that emerges is one inconsistent with the view of a state responding to popular demands created by consumerism, cultural variability and so on – but rather of a political rationality which identifies its mission as changing popular consciousness and activity. Furthermore, many of the processes identified with the postmodern – decentring of the state, consumer focusing, privatizing and the like – are linked to quite explicit and specific doctrines that are driven by conceptions (notably government through responsible and enterprising individuals) which appear to have no current salience in sociological accounts of the postmodern. With respect to policing, consider, by way of initial illustration, the following outline of community policing in the recent strategic plan of the South Australian Chief Commissioner of Police (Hunt, 1995):

Community Policing:

- emphasises the creation of an effective working partnership between the community and the police;
- the success of the police depends not only on the development of their own skills and capabilities but also on the creation of competent communities;
- the role of the community goes beyond merely alerting the police to crimes and other problems, to that of actively helping to keep their own community secure and free from crime; this may or may not involve police;
- police recognise that they work for the community as well as the law;
- police seek wider consultation and more information from the community and community priorities are taken seriously and acted upon;
- the same broad objectives that apply in problem solving policing also apply in community policing, ie crime detection, crime prevention, fear reduction and order maintenance.

In this, and in the mass of similar governmental plans, proposals and accounts, three changes in particular stand out. First has been the development of discourses which focus on localization in determining not simply the site of service delivery but also the nature and content of service delivery. This localization/consumerization, however, not simply is a reflection of the commodity ethic but envisions a quite distinctive model of service and service delivery. These discourses stress that the 'community' needs to apprise its police of the services it requires in its specific locale, and needs to advise 'its' police on what are locally regarded as problems of order and security. They stress a correlative adaptability and accountability of police to local communities (Jensen, 1986; Federal Justice Office, 1992; Loader, 1994). To this end a multitude of Police Community Consultative Committees, Public Audits of Local Policing, Neighbourhood Watch Committees and the like have been established, all (formally at least) with the common aim of increasing the responsiveness of police to local needs and demands (Beyer, 1993).

However, this is not simply a world driven by the spontaneous demands of citizen-consumers seeking policing according to their local values. Rather it is the expression of a political doctrine aimed at responsibilization, so that 'the community must move away from an over-reliance on police and other law-enforcement and regulatory bodies in its attempt to control crime' (Federal Justice Office, 1992). In this version, the community must change in order 'to meet this responsibility' and furthermore 'all sectors of the community must be more involved in crime prevention'. This involves a closely linked focus on the role of individual responsibility both for the prevention of crime and for its commission. There is continual stress on the idea that individuals must henceforward take steps to ensure that they will not become crime victims, that they must provide police with information related to crime. Crime prevention should be based on a model of criminals acting on individual choice, and punishment of offenders should be based on a similar model – implying just deserts and punitivism (O'Malley, 1992). These points, in turn, are linked to police managerial visions for transforming or revitalizing the professionalization of public policing.

## Policing partnerships

Over the past decade, a series of police-originated commentaries began to emerge which made a break from the vision of public 'welfare', client-based dependence on police. In these new visions, models of 'partnership' and 'shared responsibility' began to be promulgated:

> The prevention of crime and the detection and punishment of offenders, the protection of life and property and the preservation of public tranquillity are the direct responsibilities of ordinary citizens. The police are given certain functions to assist the public to do its work but it simply cannot be left to the police. It is destructive both of police and public social health to attempt to pass over to the police the obligations and duties associated with the prevention of crime and the preservation of public tranquillity. These are the obligations and duties of the public, aided by the police and not the police occasionally aided by some public spirited citizens (Avery, 1981: 3).

It is claimed that there has been an erosion of the proper order of things by an increase in public dependency on the state. What is now called for is the return to arrangements believed to have existed before what Avery saw as the 'erosion of the citizen role'. It is clear, however, that rather than a simple 'revitalization' of Peel's principles, a model is developing which promotes elements of police professionalism and integrates them with the political agenda for responsibilization of the public. As argued by the NSW police, 'Police are the professionals who serve as the community's key resource in efforts to deal with the problems of crime, safety and disorder ... (yet) the community must share equally with police the responsibility for developing a safe and orderly environment' (New South Wales Police, 1987). This new policing relationship – of a professionalized police and a responsibilized public – is summed up in the idea of 'the partnership approach' which has been adopted in many jurisdictions (e.g. Home Office, 1990; US Department of Justice, 1992; Crawford, 1994; Vicsafe, nd). In place of the model of police paternalilsm and authoritarianism is the new contractual image of 'Working Together' implying the formation of a *notional contract* (Newman, 1989) or a 'contract of cooperation between police and the public' (Audit Commission, UK, in McLaughlin, 1992).

Yet private individuals (whether seen primarily as customers or partners) are not expected simply to take on their new responsibilities without suitable training or 'empowerment'. The Home Office's *Practical Ways to Crack Crime* (1988) and Australian parallels such as Security and You (Commercial Union Insurance, 1988), and *Creating a Safer Community* (Federal Justice Office, 1992) are typical of the barrage of advice and instruction on how citizens may become active on their own behalf as crime preventers (O'Malley, 1991, 1992). Home owners, women, small-business proprietors, Aboriginal people and many other categories of citizen 'at risk' are provided with both general advice and specific techniques for taking on the task of minimizing their exposure to the risks of crime victimization. In turn, these techniques may be explicitly and closely articulated with private sector-security services and commodities.[1]

The police 'proactive leadership role' in partnership policing is further reflected in a new model of police professionalism. The new role is that of an 'accountable professional practitioner ... a community leader harnessing community resources to tackle the problems which give rise to crime and disorder' (Lauer, 1995). This in itself reflects a key recognition that there is no expectation of a return to the Peelite liberal police. Rather (in distinctively 'new managerialist' prose), 'the police officer of the future must emerge as a responsible professional who is self-regulating in his/her personal conduct, who accepts accountability as an important personal challenge' (Palmer, 1995).

It is in this context that we come again to a 'consumerizing' or more exactly a 'customerization' of policing, for the new professionalism clearly is being recast in this mould. In the case of the police in England and Wales, for example, McLaughlin (1992) has pointed to official policy changes involving 'the reconceptualising of policing as a service and the redesignation of the community as customers' linked with 'the prioritisation of customer needs'.[2] However, we can now recognize the specific place of the 'customerization' of policing in much of the English-speaking world, for while it is obviously linked to commodification, the latter appears in a form shaped crucially by political discourses on the efficiency of markets, the need for enterprising government and the need to mobilize and create responsible, self-governing citizens (Osborne and Gaebler, 1993; Landa and Dillon, 1995; Macdonald, 1995). At the very least, it begins to appear that the relationship between modernist aspects of police forces and the impact of pressures which have been associated with postmodernity are complex, and cannot be reduced to a simple incompatibility between the modern and the postmodern. The movement toward police professionalization, which continues the modernist project of the nineteenth century, is being carried out in close conjunction with a customerization of police work, which in its turn is distinctively marked by a political rationality concerned to overturn not modernism as such, but rather the perceived effects of welfare collectivism.

## Police leaders and professionalizing schemes

I argued at the beginning of this article that police organization has never been quintessentially modern, but in some ways seems more consistent with a medieval craft guild – a characteristic it has shared with such other aspects of the Common Law system as case law and the retention of articled clerkships in the training of lawyers (see Weber, 1954). Recruitment, entry and training reflect an apprenticeship model in which the arts (or 'mysteries') of the craft must be learned through experience under the guidance of practitioners. Until very recently (and in some cases still) all police officers in most forces were recruited into base-grade general policing rather than being inducted at levels appropriate to expertise or qualification. Promotion for most officers is slow, governed as much by length of service as by merit, reinforcing the place of the 'guild mysteries' and their acquisition, and only a comparatively small proportion of members ever more out of the general policing area.

This suggests a reality at odds with the view of police as a *paradigmatically* modern institution, and thus casts some doubts on Reiner's (1992) thesis that it is the incompatibility of the modernist form of police with postmodernism which generates the changes with which he is concerned. This is especially clear when we turn to consider the widespread moves toward police professionalization which have become a characteristic of police managerialism over the past decade and more, for these appear in many ways to indicate efforts to transform late twentieth-century police into a modern organization. Consider, for example, the reforms introduced after 1990 by the Australian Federal Police, themselves modelled on a prior restructuring of the NSW police. These included:

- changes to personnel practices, including: merit promotion; lateral entry; flexible starting salaries; accelerated advancement.
- fixed term appointments (ie performance based contract employment) for all employees, sworn and unsworn;
- the development of a unified workforce with all police and civilians under one employment Act and sharing a common set of corporate values, a common industrial award and a code of conduct. (Johnston, 1991; Etter, 1995)

What is remarkable is that in 1990 the proposals for reform under an avowedly 'new managerial' framework (Etter, 1995; Landa and Dillon, 1995) appear to be dominated by the desire to establish a modernist, unified, merit-based and internally competitive organization. Or again, consider the following points approved by the Australian Police Minister's Council in the same year, as being critical issues concerning the state of Australian policing

- that a critical reform confronting policing was the attainment of full professional status;
- that full professional status would entail national educational standards, formal higher educational qualifications, improved police practice;
- that over the previous decade there had been a fragmented and unco-ordinated development of tertiary courses offered to police and that this *ad hoc* approach should be avoided and efforts be redirected towards establishing uniform national standards;
- that a truly efficient and effective policing would only be achieved when policing developed a professional culture underpinned by superior management practices and a commitment to corporate excellence. (Quoted in Rohl and Barnsley, 1995)

Emerging through the new managerial talk is a clear attempt to develop exactly those features of policing that should have been expected to be characteristic of a modern professionalized institution for many years. But over and above that, in view of arguments about the fragmentation of policing, it is noteworthy that the stress in these instances is on creating national standardization and a degree of unification of police education, training and practice.

It must be accepted that there is a wide gap between such plans and the actual creation of a modern, professional police force – although significant advances have been made, such as in Australia with the establishment of the Australian Graduate School of Police Management and the creation of the Police Agencies National Competency Standards Project. Even so, this takes some reconciling with the vision of a police force which is being fragmented by the forces of post-modernity. Rather, the suggestion is that police have always been fragmented, and while fragmentation persists, and new fragmentations are emerging, other important aspects of policing only now are beginning to move toward unification of sorts – and under the banner of modernist professionalization. At the very least we need to exercise considerable caution in thinking about processes such as the disintegration of police, and to recognize that this is a partial and uneven process shaped in fundamental ways by political rationalities and the social technologies (such as new managerialism) with which they are associated.

## New managerialism and the disintegration of policing

One distinctive feature of current waves of police reform is that not only are routine police practices being reformed, but – more unusually – senior police management is also the *object* of changes. Perhaps, most critically, senior managers are being made more accountable to national and state governments and are being made accountable in new ways. Neo-liberal governments have far more explicit concerns than their predecessors had about whether police are cost-effective and are achieving desired results. They are increasingly requiring new measures of performance (such as audits and cost-benefit analyses) which are not as subject to police expertise for their construction, execution and interpretation. As the Commissioner of the Australian Federal Police notes:

> Police are under pressure to satisfy governments that they are cost effective and achieving the required results. Limited resources have already sub-stantially impacted upon policing as governments apply funding cuts. Police managers have been forced to achieve considerable savings through more stringent and controlled use of finance and other resources. 'Lean and mean' has been the emphasis at management levels in addressing this demand to provide policing services at considerably reduced cost. (Palmer, 1995)

Moreover, the market orientation of these governments means that they are willing to break – and to allow police management to break – the taken-for-granted monopoly of public police where alternative arrangements appear more efficient or effective. A positive move toward new managerialism is being fostered by increasing the autonomy of police managers to act as chief executive officers and to run their forces increasingly along enterprise lines, and there are clear signs that many senior police are relishing the change (e.g. Crawford, 1994; Loader, 1994; Hunt, 1995; McLaughlin and Murji, 1995; Palmer, 1995).[3] Police managers are encouraged, even required, to act increasingly in innovative ways, to be 'change masters' and 'architects of social change' (Normandeau and Leighton, 1990; Etter, 1995). While it is likely that rhetoric will exceed the practical transformation in management, some consequential shifts are already becoming visible.

First, many aspects of routine or 'low policing' are vulnerable to rationalist rethinking in terms of police managers making 'strategic choices as to whether or not certain functions (are) extraneous to the organisation's role, with a view to ceasing or transferring the function elsewhere in government' (Hunt, 1995). Effectively, what this means is the application of new managerial techniques of defining what are to be 'core functions' in terms of the corporate 'mission'. Organizational resources and energies then are to be focused on effective ways of achieving these goals. Both 'ineffective means' and 'extraneous functions' are to be eliminated or hived off to other organizations. In reviewing this process as it has been undertaken by the South Australian Police Department, Hunt (1995) puts forward the interpretation that 'over time a variety of functions and activities which are of marginal relevance to policing, are undertaken as the demand arises. Often in the past, as a service gap in the community is identified, it is the police that are thrown into the breach'. From this viewpoint many functions accumulate to the police role that should not be there, and one of the key criteria used to determine the nature of core policing was whether it was necessary for fully trained, sworn police personnel to carry out these functions. Once activities thus defined as extraneous were located, then 'options to minimize police involvement' were put into effect. Likewise, in Victoria, the neo-liberal state government generated a *Management Improvement Initiative*, typically focusing ideals for good governance on market forms and mechanisms, customer orientation, responsibility, accountability, and minimization of bureaucracy. This required the Victoria Police also to travel down the road of locating its 'key result areas' and 'non-core activities', to exclude or minimize effort and expenditure in non-core areas and to seek productivity improvements in its core functions.

As a result of these and similar exercises in the context of Australian policing, we see emerging many of the features of the 'disintegration' and dispersal of policing that are attributed to postmodernity. In addition to extensive civilianization of police clerical work, substantial areas of police work are already being contracted out to the private sector or to non-police agencies or to both. These include: radar monitoring of speeding traffic, the operation of red-light cameras; administration of random breath-testing; response to security alarms in private (domestic and business) property; transportation of prisoners; serving of summonses for non-payment of fines; assistance in coroners' investigations and the provision of prosecutorial services (e.g. Johnston, 1991; Rawlings, 1991; Hunt, 1995). Similar market pressures brought to bear on state agencies have also been associated with the opening up of aspects of *elite* policing to competitive claims from non-police agencies. In Australia, for example (where state-wide police forces have been virtual monopolizers of public policing), the traditional crime control and surveillance activities of police are under challenge in various areas. Federal police, the National Crime Authority, the Securities Commission and other statutory bodies are engaged in contests over the role of policing drug trafficking, fraud and political corruption. As Moore (1992) comments 'with a number of federally funded organisations competing to provide services in these areas, the opportunities for state police forces to make an effective contribution to High Policing are limited'. Similar processes appear to be underway in the UK where national security services (notably MI5) in search of a role after the collapse of communism, publicly sought a policing role in relation to organized crime, money laundering, the drug trade, computer hacking and even policing animal rights groups (Cohen, 1996). Such changes, while consistent with the generalities of the postmodern policing thesis, are most clearly linked with, and take their character from, specific neo-liberal and new managerial imperatives to apply market and strategic planning principles to police organizations and the delivery of police services.

## Conclusions

It may be argued that this level of analytic magnification locates only the particular avenues and channels through which the pressures of postmodernity are transmitted. Certainly it is possible to point to processes, such as post-Fordism and the restructuring of international markets, that provide accounts for locating the mainsprings of neo-liberalism and new managerialism in something possibly thinkable as postmodernity (e.g. Harvey, 1989). For example, neo-liberalism's emphasis on enterprise and innovation among the citizenry may be linked to the migration of heavy industry to South Asia and the requirement that developed economies now be reinvented in terms of service and tertiary industries.

However, as is revealed by such an attempt to bring the idea of postmodernity to bear, there is an enormous interpretive gap between the hypothesized operation of these global processes and the processes of public police reform. In particular, as postmodernity is identified in terms of a wide array of charac-teristics, there will always be major problems involved in explaining in a non-arbitrary fashion why certain of these characteristics and not others are linked with police changes. Similar problems, as we have seen, involve questions about the timing of changes, how they are to be interpreted as linked to broader conditions of postmodernity, how we explain the forms that they take in particular settings and so on.

In comparison with accounts concerned to connect police reform with postmodernity, the account in terms of the impact of neo-liberal political rationality and its subaltern technology of new managerialism seems almost equally comprehensive, while better able to locate and evidence the *processes* involved in police restructuring, and to account for the particular form taken by the changes. It has also identified a pronounced unevenness and ambiguity in the way in which police reforms are proceeding, such that major changes appear still to be translating some aspects of police organization into forms which, ironically, appear to approximate what may be thought of as modern rather than postmodern.

This throws into doubt not only the extent to which terms such as modernity and postmodernity provide a useful analytic vocabulary for understanding specific institutions such as public police, but further, whether they can contributed to an effective politics of policing. Rather than practices being understood as devised and developed by specific regimes, in line with particular political rationalities and technologies of governance, they appear as the local registering of changes effected at the level of global order. In turn, one danger of this move is that it depoliticizes police reform and/or tends to cast analysis into the kind of pessimism that has become a hallmark of certain brands of postmodern theorizing – an issue which Robert Reiner (1992) also confronts.

More particularly, the key political limitation of the postmodernity thesis is that it is pitched at such an abstract level that it is difficult to see how it can be deployed to generate adequate evaluations of, and responses to, police reforms – let alone to be of use in developing new proposals for policing. Thus in his postscript to 'Policing a Postmodern Society', Robert Reiner (1992) locates 'three strategies which must be adopted if the police are to achieve what legitimacy is available in the postmodern period'. These three are: recognition that police are providers of a mundane service rather than sacred totems of national pride; diversification of police staff to reflect national gender and ethnic demographic distributions; and integration of elected local authorities into the police policy-setting process. But as other work suggests (e.g. Havemann, 1988; Brogden and Shearing, 1994; Shearing, 1995; Bayley and Shearing, 1996) such changes are not likely to effect any transformation in policing sufficient to deal with the issues identified with fragmentation, pluralism, disaggregation and so on. The simple indigenization of policing, for example, may not create any practical change at all, especially insofar as the routine work of policing remains dominated by a closed and defensive police culture, while the gender equalization of staff could imply a strategy of 'just add women and stir'.[4] Or again, localization can lead to vigilantism or to heightened oppression of locally unpopular minorities (notably those – gays, drug users, etc. – who are not visible demographically), while the desacralization of policing may render police less subject to public scrutiny. I would suggest that the inadequacy of such proposals – especially from an insightful scholar such as Reiner – stems from the fact that a focus on postmodernity equips us with a very limited conceptual and political repertory. Again, this would appear to stem from the characteristic analytic 'gap' that opens out between understanding the generalized and vastly inclusive nature of a phenomenon such as 'postmodernity' and the particular institutions and contexts of public policing.

Approaches such as that adopted in this chapter, which have a more modest focus on the rationalities, practices, programmes and techniques of rule, may provide us with a far more politically deployable knowledge.[5] Not only does it provide a theoretical vocabulary which opens up everyday and institutional programmes and practices to critical thinking, it also provides a considerable array of conceptual and empirical work in terms of which interventions can be examined and thought out. For example, the examination of neo-liberal strategies for the *formation* of 'communities' takes us beyond thinking that valorization of such communities is simply the 'structural' effect of postmodernity – and, accordingly, 'democratizing' police at the local and the community level emerges as much more problematic procedure. Such work, in other words, begins to delve critically beneath the often vague conceptual canopy of grander theorizations. At the same time, it generates a framework for a constructive politics. In particular, Shearing and his colleagues (noted earlier) are exploring models for assessing and developing 'community' policing in racialized contexts not simply in terms of broad and vague notions such as commodification, privatization or localization, but in terms of a much closer reading of the mundane practices and potentials of market-based policing. This work includes examining the promise and difficulties associated with many possible models, programmes and techniques of rule, normally blanketed under the broad terminologies of privatized, marketized and voluntarized police. Such models include innovative 'market-like' ways of reallocating public funding for security through voucher systems drawing on state resources, diverse models of making black people 'customers' of security services and so on. As this suggests, such work also leads to possibilities for disaggregating neo-liberal strategies and practices, and rendering their often highly innovative developments available for appropriation and development by a 'progressive' postwelfare politics (Shearing, 1995, cf. also Foucault, 1991; Burchell, 1993).

Whatever the status of the theoretical debates over whether we are in, entering or emerging from a 'late modern', 'postmodern' or 'reflexively modern' age, or whether indeed 'we have never been modern', such concerns neither appear to contribute analytically to our understanding of what is happening to public policing nor to provide politically deployable knowledges in such a context. While the postmodern is understood to be associated with the demise of metanarratives and grand theories, theorization of postmodernity is itself pitched at a grand, even global, level of analysis. The result, I argue, is that the length and complexity of the theoretical and interpretive chain required to link it with changes at institutional levels, such as that of public police reform, means that it will never be more than suggestive of issues – such as those investigated in this chapter – that are better understood in terms of other analytical frameworks.

From Pat O'Malley, 'Politics and postmodernity', Social and Legal Studies, an international journal, *Vol. 6, 1997, no 3, pp 363–81*.

## Notes

[Some] of the material presented in the middle section of the chapter is drawn from O'Malley and Palmer (1996).

1   A close nexus often exists between the police and the insurance industry in which, the industry may fund community police-directed anticrime and domestic-security campaigns and run its own disciplinary programme to train householders in security practices. Police, in turn, may promote the sale of private burglary insurance for domestic property and distribute insurance

industry advertising material which provides hints on how to reduce exposure to crime (O'Malley, 1991).

2   As Lacey (1994) points out, even prisoners are referred to as customers in the new market of criminal justice services.

3   Nicola Lacey (1994) argues that this shift is also characteristic of criminal justice administration in other areas, notably court and prison administration.

4   Brogden and Shearing (1994) discuss the surprising example of African police officers in the South African Police actively adopting racist discourses and practices of enforcement.

5   The post-Foucauldian 'governmentality' work provides such an instance. See, for example, Miller and Rose (1990) and the special numbers of *Economy and Society* (volume 22, number 3 [1993] and volume 25, number 3 [1996]) devoted to the promise and limits of such works.

# References

Abercrombie, N. (1991) 'The Privilege of the Producer', in R. Keat and N. Abercrombie (eds) *Enterprise Culture*. London: Routledge.

Avery, J. (1981) *Police: Force or Service?* Sydney: Butterworths.

Bayley, D. and C. Shearing (1996) 'The Future of Policing', *Law and Society Review* 30: 585–606.

Bell, D. (1976) *The Cultural Contradictions of Capitalism*. New York: Wiley.

Beyer, L. (1993) *Community Policing. Lessons from Victoria*. Canberra: Australian Institute of Criminology.

Brogden, M. and C. Shearing (1994) *Policing the New South Africa*. London: Routledge.

Burchell, G. (1993) 'Liberal Government and Techniques of the Self', *Economy and Society* 22: 267–82.

Carriere, K. and R. Ericson (1994) 'Fragmentary Criminologies', in D. Nelken (ed.) *The Futures of Criminology*. London: Sage.

Cohen, S. (1996) 'Crime and Politics. Spot the Difference', *British Journal of Sociology* 1996: 1–23.

Commercial Union Insurance (1988) *Security and You*. Melbourne: Commercial Union Insurance.

Crawford, A. (1994) 'The Partnership Approach to Community Crime Prevention: Corporatism at the Local Level', *Social & Legal Studies* 3 (4): 497–519.

Crook, S., S. Pakulski and M. Waters (1992) *Postmodernisation and Change in Advanced Society*. London: Sage.

Etter, B. (1995) 'Mastering Innovation and Change in Police Agencies', in B. Etter and M. Palmer (eds) *Police Leadership in Australasia*. Sydney: Federation Press.

Federal Justice Office (1992) *Creating a Safer Community. Crime Prevention and Community Safety into the 21st Century*. Issues Paper. Canberra: AGPS.

Foucault, M. (1991) 'Politics and the Study of Discourse', in G. Burchell, C. Gordon and P. Miller (eds) *The Foucault Effect. Studies in Governmentality*. Chicago, IL: Chicago University Press.

Gamble, A. (1988) *The Free Economy and the Strong State*. London: Macmillan.

Harvey, D. (1989) *The Condition of Postmodernity*. Oxford: Blackwell.

Havemann, P. (1988) 'The Indigenisation of Social Control in Canada', in W. Morse and G. Woodman (eds) *Indigenous Law and the State*. Dordrecht: Foris Publications.

Heelas, P. (1991) 'Reforming the Self', in R. Keat and N. Abercrombie (eds) *Enterprise Culture*. London: Routledge.

Home Office (1988) *Practical Ways to Crack Crime*. London: HMSO.

Home Office (1990) *Crime, Justice and Protecting the Public*. London: HMSO.

Hunt, D. (1995) 'Strategic Management in Policing', in B. Etter and M. Palmer (eds) *Police Leadership in Australia*. Sydney: Federation Press.

Jensen, H. (1986) 'Opening Address', pp. 5–11 in D. Loree and C. Murphy (eds) *Community Policing in the 1980s*. Ottawa: Ministry of the Solicitor General of Canada.

Johnston, L. (1991) 'Privatisation and the Police Function: From the "New Police" to the "New Policing"', in R. Reiner and M. Cross (eds) *Beyond Law and Order. Criminal Justice Policy and Politics into the 1990s*. London: Macmillan.

Keat, R. (1991) 'Introduction: Starship Britain or Universal Enterprise?', in R. Keat and N. Abercrombie (eds) *Enterprise Culture*. London: Routledge.

Keat, R. and N. Abercrombie (eds) (1991) *Enterprise Culture*. London: Routledge.

Lacey, N. (1994) 'Government as Manager, Citizen as Consumer: The Case of the Criminal Justice Act 1991', *Modern Law Review*, 57, 534–54.

Landa, D. and D. Dillon (1995) 'Police Accountability and External Review of Police Conduct', in B. Etter and M. Palmer (eds) *Police Leadership in Australia*. Sydney: Federation Press.

Loader, I. (1994) 'Democracy, Justice and the Limits of Policing: Rethinking Police Accountability', *Social & Legal Studies* 3: 521–44.

Latour, B. (1994) *We Have Never Been Modern.* Hemel Hempstead: Harvester Wheatsheaf.

Lauer, T. (1995) 'Nurturing Innovative Patrol Strategies', in B. Etter and M. Palmer (eds) *Police Leadership in Australia. Sydney: Federation Press.*

Macdonald, R. (1995) 'Skills and Qualities of Police Leaders Required of Police Leaders Now and in the Future', in B. Etter and M. Palmer (eds) *Police Leadership in Australia.* Sydney: Federation Press.

McLaughlin, E. (1992) 'The Democratic Deficit. European Union and the Accountability of the British Police', *British Journal of Criminology* 32: 473–87.

McLaughlin, E. and K. Murji (1995) 'The End of Public Policing?' in L. Noaks, M. Maguire and M. Levi (eds) *Contemporary Issues in Criminology.* Cardiff: University of Wales Press.

Miller, P. and N. Rose (1990). 'Governing Economic Life', *Economy and Society* 19: 1–31.

Moore, D. (1992) 'Police Productivity', in P. Moir and H. Eijkman (eds) *Policing Australia.* Sydney: Macmillan.

Mugford, S. (1993) 'Social Change and the Control of Psychotropic Drugs. Risk Management, Harm Reduction and "Postmodernity"', *Drug and Alcohol Review* 12: 369–75.

New South Wales Police (1987) 'Community Based Policing, Values in Policing', Policy Paper No. 1, *Community Based Policing.* Sydney: New South Wales Government Printer.

Normandeau, A. and B. Leighton (1990) *A Vision of the Future of Policing in Canada.* Ottawa: Solicitor General Canada.

O'Malley, P. (1991) 'Legal Networks and Domestic Security', *Studies in Law, Politics and Society* 11: 181–91.

O'Malley, P. (1992) 'Risk, Power and Crime Prevention', *Economy Society* 21: 252–75.

O'Malley, P. and D. Palmer (1996) 'Post-Keynesian Policing', *Economy and Society* 25: 137–55.

Osborne, D. and T. Gaebler (1993) *Reinventing Government.* New York: Penguin.

Palmer, M. (1995) 'The Likely Environment in the Year 2000 and Beyond', in B. Etter and M. Palmer (eds) *Police Leadership in Australia.* Sydney: Federation Press.

Rawlings, P. (1991) 'Creeping Privatisation? The Police, the Conservative Government and Policing in the Late 1980s', in R. Reiner and M. Cross (eds) *Beyond Law and Order. Criminal Justice Policy and Politics into the 1990s.* London: Macmillan.

Reiner, R. (1992) 'Policing a Postmodern Society', *Modern Law Review* 55: 761–81.

Reiner, R. (1994) *The Politics of the Police,* 2nd edition. Hemel Hempstead: Harvester Wheatsheaf.

Rohl, T. and R. Barnsley (1995) 'The Strategic Transformation of Policing from Occupational to Professional Status', in B. Etter and M. Palmer (eds) *Police Leadership in Australia.* Sydney: Federation Press.

Rose, N. (1990a) 'Governing the Enterprising Self,' P. Heelas and P. Morris (eds) *The Values of the Enterprise Culture.* London: Unwin Hyman.

Rose, N. (1990b) *Governing the Soul. The Shaping of the Private Self.* London: Routledge.

Rose, N. (1993) 'Government, Authority and Expertise in Advanced Liberalism', *Economy and Society* 22: 283–372.

Shearing, C. (1995) 'Reinventing Policing. Policing as Governance', *Interdisziplinäre Studien zu Recht und Staat* 3: 70–87.

Sheptycki, J. (1995) 'Transnational Policing and the Makings of a Postmodern State', *British Journal of Criminology* 35: 613–31.

Spitzer, S. and A. Scull (1976) 'Privatization and Capitalist Development: The Case of Private Police', *Social Problems* 25: 18–29.

Thatcher, M. (1993) *The Downing Street Years.* London: Macmillan.

US Department of Justice (1992) *Community Policing in Seattle: A Model Partnership between Citizens and Police.* Washington, DC: US Department of Justice.

Vicsafe (nd) *Practical Crime Prevention.* Melbourne: Victoria Ministry of Police and Emergency Services.

Weber, M. (1954) *Max Weber on Law and Economy in Society* (ed. M. Reinhart). Cambridge, MA: Harvard University Press.

# 40. The future of policing

*David H. Bayley and Clifford D. Shearing*

Modern democratic countries like the United States, Britain, and Canada have reached a watershed in the evolution of their systems of crime control and law enforcement. Future generations will look back on our era as a time when one system of policing ended and another took its place. Two developments define the change – the pluralizing of policing and the search by the public police for an appropriate role.

First, policing is no longer monopolized by the public police, that is, the police created by government. Policing is now being widely offered by institutions other than the state, most importantly by private companies on a commercial basis and by communities on a volunteer basis. Second, the public police are going through an intense period of self-questioning, indeed, a true identity crisis. No longer confident that they are either effective or efficient in controlling crime, they are anxiously examining every aspect of their performance – objectives, strategies, organization, management, discipline, and accountability. These movements, one inside and the other outside the police, amount to the restructuring of policing in contemporary democratic societies.

The restructuring of policing, which is already well advanced, has profound implications for public life, especially on the level and distribution of public safety, the vitality of civil rights, and the character of democratic government. Yet, despite the fatefulness of these changes, there has been hardly any public debate on the future of policing. If Thomas Jefferson was right that the price of liberty is eternal vigilance, then the current silence about these issues is a source of great risk for democratic societies.

In order to begin a debate that is long overdue, we first describe in greater detail the pluralizing of policing and the changing character of public policing. Second, we examine the impact of these developments on society and government. Third, we predict the likely future of policing by pinpointing the factors shaping each movement. Finally, we specify the policies that are needed to ensure that the current restructuring of policing serves the broad interests of a developed democratic society.

It is very important to be clear about what we mean when we talk about policing. We are not concerned exclusively with 'the police', that is, with people in uniforms who are hired, paid, and directed by government. We are interested in all explicit efforts to create visible agents of crime control, whether by government or by nongovernmental institutions. So we are dealing with policing, not just *police*. At the same time, we say *explicit* attempts to create policing institutions so as not to extend our discussion to all the informal agencies that societies rely on to maintain order, such as parents, churches, employers, spouses, peers, neighbors, professional associations, and so forth. The activities of such people and institutions are undoubtedly critically important in crime control, but they have not been explicitly designed for this purpose. They are rarely objects of explicit crime policy. So the scope of our discussion is bigger than the breadbox of the police but smaller than the elephant of social control. Our focus is on the self-conscious process whereby societies designate and authorize people to create public safety.

## The end of a monopoly

In the past 30 years the state's monopoly on policing has been broken by the creation of a host of private and community-based agencies that prevent crime, deter criminality, catch lawbreakers, investigate offenses, and stop conflict. The police and policing have become increasingly distinct. While the customary police are paid, the new policing agents come in both paid and unpaid forms. The former are referred to as private security; the latter as community crime prevention.

To complicate matters further, private security – the paid part of private policing – comes in two forms: people employed by commercial companies who are hired on contract by others and persons employed directly by companies to work as security specialists. Private police now outnumber the public police in most developed countries. In the United States, for example, there are three times more private security agents than public police officers (Bayley, 1994).[1] There are twice as many private police as public police in Canada and in Britain (Johnston, 1992). In all countries for which there is information, the private security sector is growing faster than the public. This has been true since the early 1960s, when the contemporary rebirth of private security began. Businesses and commercial firms, by the way, are not the only customers for private security. Private guards are now often used to guard many government buildings, including police stations.

The increase in the numbers of private police reflects a remarkable change in their status (Shearing, 1992). Through World War II, private security was looked on as a somewhat unsavory occupation. It had the image of ill-trained bands of thugs hired by private businesses to break strikes, suppress labor, and spy on one another. The police, as well as the public, viewed private security companies as a dangerous and unauthorized intrusion by private interests into a government preserve. Since World War II, however, a more tolerant attitude has developed, with private security seen as a necessary supplement to the overburdened public police. In the past few years especially, governments have gone beyond passive acceptance to active encouragement of commercial private security. There now seems to be a general recognition that crime is too extensive and complex to be dealt with solely by the police and that the profit motive is not to be feared in policing.

In recent years private policing has also expanded under noncommercial auspices as communities have undertaken to provide security using volunteered resources and people. A generation ago community crime prevention was virtually nonexistent. Today it is everywhere – citizen automobile and foot patrols, neighborhood watches, crime-prevention associations and advisory councils, community newsletters, crime-prevention publications and presentations, protective escort services for at-risk populations, and monitors around schools, malls, and public parks. Like commercial private security, the acceptability of volunteer policing has been transformed in less than a generation. While once it was thought of as vigilantism, it is now popular with the public and actively encouraged by the police. Because these activities are uncoordinated, and sometimes ephemeral, it is hard to say how extensive they are. Impressionistically, they seem to be as common as McDonald's golden arches, especially in urban areas.

Policing has become a responsibility explicitly shared between government and its citizens, sometimes mediated through commercial markets, sometimes arising spontaneously. Policing has become pluralized. Police are no longer the primary crime-deterrent presence in society; they have been supplanted by more numerous private providers of security.

**Searching for identity**

During the past decade, police throughout the developed democratic world have increasingly questioned their role, operating strategies, organization, and management. This is attributable to growing doubts about the effectiveness of their traditional strategies in safeguarding the public from crime.

The visible presence of the police seems to be stretched so thin that it fails to deter. Police devote about 60% of their resources to patrolling but complain about running from one emergency call to another, often involving noncriminal matters. The scarecrow has grown tattered in relation to the prevalence of crime. At the same time, regrettably few villains are caught in relation to crimes committed: 21% in the United States, 26% in Britain, and 16% in Canada (1992 statistics).[2] Even fewer receive any sort of punishment through the criminal justice system. Crime pays, as scarcely more than 5% of crimes committed in the United States result in the imprisonment of the criminals involved. Because the police know all this, they are desperately searching for new approaches, responding in part to the competition they face from private security whose strategies overwhelmingly favor prevention over detection and punishment. The central question underlying police soul-searching is whether they can become more effective in truly preventing crime.

One answer to this has been community policing. Its philosophy is straightforward: the police cannot successfully prevent or, investigate crime without the willing participation of the public, therefore police should transform communities from being passive consumers of police protection to active co-producers of public safety. Community policing changes the orientation of the police and represents a sharp break with the past. Community policing transforms police from being an emergency squad in the fight against crime to becoming primary diagnosticians and treatment coordinators.

Although community policing has gotten most of the publicity in recent years, many police believe that law enforcement, their traditional tool in crime fighting, can be made more efficient. This approach might be called crime-oriented policing. It involves developing smarter enforcement tactics so that crime will not pay. Some examples include the setting up of fencing operations to catch habitual thieves and burglars; harassing drug markets so as to raise the cost of doing business; monitoring the activities of career criminals and arresting them for minor infractions of the law; cracking down unpredictably on criminal activity in particular locations; installing video cameras on public streets; and analyzing financial transactions by computer to spot cheating and fraud.

Police are also discussing, and sometimes implementing, a strategy that is a hybrid of community-oriented and crime-oriented policing. It is referred to as order-maintenance policing and involves stopping the disorderly, unruly, and disturbing behavior of people in public places, whether lawful or not. This suppressive activity not only reassures the public, demonstrating the limits for unacceptable behavior but reduces the incidence of more serious crime (Wilson and Kelling, 1982; Skogan, 1990). The New York City Police Department employed this strategy against the 'squeegy men' who extorted money from motorists by washing the windshields of cars stopped at traffic lights and asking for donations. The New York City Transit Police reduced the incidence of robbery on the subways by undertaking an energetic campaign against fare-beaters who vaulted over turnstiles. In both cases, the police reduced menacing activity that frightened law-abiding citizens and warned off criminals who would take advantage of what seemed to be unguarded territory (Kelling and Coles, 1994). Like community policing, order-maintenance policing requires diagnosis and problem solving, but like traditional policing, it emphasizes law enforcement. It might be called community policing with a hard edge.

In addition to rethinking their standard strategies, the police are themselves helping to blur the line between government and nongovernment policing. For example, some police departments now sell the protective services they used to give away. Rather than considering police protection as a public good, free to all citizens, police are increasingly taking the view that people who derive a commercial benefit from police efforts should pay for it. Accordingly, ordinances have been enacted requiring private burglar-alarm companies to be fined or charged a fee if their electronic systems summon police to false alarms more than a specified number of times. Police are also beginning to charge fees for covering rock concerts, professional sporting events, and ethnic festivals. In some cities, businesses have banded together to pay for additional police patrols in order to get the protection they think they need.

In a development that is found across northern America, police not only sell their protective services but allow their own officers to be hired as private security guards – a practice known as 'moonlighting'. Many American police regularly work two jobs, one public, the other private. Indeed, moonlighting is considered a valuable perquisite of police employment. What this means is that the pluralizing of policing is being directly subsidized in the United States by public funds. Private policing uses police that have been recruited, trained, and supported by government. When acting as agents of private entities, police retain their legal authority and powers.

Not only do public police work as private police but civilians – nonpolice people – increasingly share responsibilities within public policing. Special Constables in Great Britain and Cadets, Police Auxiliaries, and Reserves in the United States often work on the street alongside regular police personnel. Though they serve without pay, and often without weapons, they are virtually indistinguishable in appearance from police. Some communities in Britain have hired able-bodied unemployed persons to patrol the streets, and others have deployed partially trained police officers as community liaison officers (Johnston, 1994).

Furthermore, work traditionally performed by uniformed officers has increasingly been given to civilian employees. Usually these are jobs that don't require law enforcement, such as repairing motor vehicles, programming computers, analyzing forensic evidence, and operating radio-dispatch systems. Of all police employees, 27% in the United States are now civilians; 35% in Great Britain; 20% in Canada and Australia; and 12% in Japan (Bayley, 1994). A variation on this is to contract out – privatize – support functions altogether, such as publishing, maintaining criminal records, forensic analysis, auditing and disbursement, and the guarding of police premises. Police departments are also beginning to use senior citizen volunteers to provide specialized expertise as pilots, auditors, chemists, or computer programmers.

Some communities employ special support personnel, often dressed in uniforms similar to those of the police, in frontline functions as well. The most common of these are the now ubiquitous parking-meter patrols. But uniformed civilians also conduct crime-prevention classes, make security inspections of premises, provide follow-up counseling to crime victims, resolve neighborhood disputes, and advise about pending criminal matters (Skolnick and Bayley, 1986).

The innovations that are being made in operational strategies as well as the increasing use of civilians in police work have important implications for the management and organization of the police. For example, police increasingly resent being used by government as an omnibus regulatory agency. So, in an effort to save money and focus on crime prevention, many departments are considering reducing the scope of regulatory activity, such as licensing bars and nightclubs, enforcing parking regulations, maintaining lost and founds, organizing neighborhood watches, conducting crime-prevention seminars, and advising property owners about protective hardware (Johnston, 1994; Bayley, 1985).

Police are also beginning to recognize that the traditional quasi-military management model, based on ranks and a hierarchical chain of command, may not accommodate the requirements of modern policing. Several forces have recently eliminated redundant supervisory ranks, and almost all are talking about the value of participative, collegial management. This involves de-centralizing command and allowing subordinate commanders to determine the character of police operations in their areas. There is also a great deal of talk about treating the public as customers and about measuring performance by surveys of public satisfaction rather than exclusively by the number of crimes and arrests.

Finally, police are being subjected to more intense and rigorous supervision by both government and nongovernment agencies than has ever been true in the past. In Britain, Canada, and Australia civilian review boards have recently been created that can independently investigate instances of police misbehavior, especially those involving allegations of brutality. In the United States, too, 66 major police departments had civilian review by late 1994 and the number was steadily increasing (Walker and Wright, 1994). From the police point of view, the unthinkable is happening: the behavior of individual officers is now subject to civilian overview, including, in some jurisdictions, determining blame and the severity of punishment.

Moreover, great attention is now being given to developing mechanisms for the systematic evaluation of the quality of police service. Checklists of performance indicators have being developed and national data bases assembled to assist the evaluation exercise. Private management consultant firms are now regularly hired to assist local governments in evaluating police. Accrediting organizations have been set up nationally as well as in several American states and Canadian provinces to develop standards of police performance and organization.

Taken together, the pluralizing of policing and the search by the public police for a new role and methodology mean that not only has government's monopoly on policing been broken in the late 20th century, but the police monopoly on expertise within its own sphere of activity has ended. Policing now belongs to everybody – in activity, in responsibility, and in overview.

## What's at stake

Does it matter that policing is being reconstructed? Should we care that policing is pluralizing and that the public police are having an identity crisis? Yes, we should. These developments have fateful consequences for the level of public safety, for access to public security, for human rights, and for accountability. Let us examine restructuring's implications for each of these.

### Safety

Expanding the auspices under which policing is provided increases the number of security agents. If visible policing deters, then communities should be safer if there are private uniformed security guards and designated civilian patrols and watchers to supplement the public police. If the expansion of private policing was occurring at the expense of public police, of course, then safety would not be enhanced. But that does not appear to be happening. Relative to population, there are more police in developed democracies in 1995 than in 1970 despite the growth in private security. It seems reasonable to conclude, therefore, that pluralizing has made communities safer.

Pluralizing the sources of policing affects not only the quantity of policing but its quality as well. Although both public and private police rely on visibility to deter criminality, private police emphasize the logic of security, while public police emphasize the logic of justice. The major purpose of private security is to reduce the risk of crime by taking preventive actions; the major purpose of the public police is to deter crime by catching and punishing criminals.

Arrest is the special competence and preferred tool of the public police. By using it quickly and accurately, they hope to deter criminality. Private police, on the other hand, both commercial and community based, have no greater enforcement powers than property owners and ordinary citizens. Thus, their special competence and preferred tool is anticipatory regulation and amelioration. By analyzing the circumstances that give rise to victimization and financial loss, they recommend courses of action that will reduce the opportunity for crime to occur. These recommendations are followed because they become conditions for employment or participation. For a secretary in an office, locking doors and keeping a purse in a desk drawer is a condition of employment; for a teenager in a shopping mall, wearing shoes and not playing loud music are conditions of access; for a retailer, not selling goods on the sidewalk in front of his store is a condition for acceptance by the local business community; and for airline passengers, passing through a metal detector is a condition of travel. Because such regulations are legitimized by the fiction of being self-imposed, as opposed to being mandated by government, they avoid most constitutional challenge.

There is a closer connection between the end – safety – and the means – policing – with private police, both commercial and volunteer, than with public police. Governments protect communities by providing police and then limiting their authority; private institutions and informal communities protect themselves by determining what circumstances produce crime and then finding people who know how to change them (Shearing, 1996). Private police are more responsive than public police to the 'bottom line' of safety. If safety is not increased, private police can be fired. For public police the bottom line is not safety but clearance rates. But even here failure has few negative consequences. Police are not fired for not achieving this objective.

The public police are beginning to recognize the inherent limitations of their justice-based approach. Through community policing and order-maintenance policing, the public police are developing strategies for reducing disorder and the opportunities for crime that are similar to the practices readily accepted by commercial and informal communities from private police.

Both quantitatively and qualitatively, then, the pluralizing of policing should increase public safety.

The gains in public safety from the soul-searching currently unsettling public policing are less predictable. It depends on which way they go: more of the same, crime-oriented law enforcement, order maintenance, or community policing. Improvements in crime prevention will require commitment to experiment with new approaches and a willingness to subject them to rigorous evaluation. What is required is a shift in the logic of policing from one that conceives of it as remedying past wrongs to one that seeks to promote security.

*Equity*

The pluralizing of policing promises to increase public safety and has already done so in some places. The problem is that pluralizing under market auspices at present does not improve security equally across society. It favors institutions and individuals that are well-to-do. Commercial policing not balanced either by voluntary neighborhood crime prevention or by public policing following a preventive, presumptive logic leads to the inequitable distribution of security along class lines. If public safety is considered a general responsibility of government, perhaps even a human right, then increased reliance on commercial private policing represents a growing injustice.

The effects of pluralization under commercial auspices would be even more harmful if the prosperous sectors of the community who pay most of the taxes were to withdraw resources from the public sector, objecting that they were paying twice for security-once to the government and once again to hired private security. If this were to occur, the government's ability to develop qualitatively improved policing for the poor would be undermined. It might even be difficult to maintain existing levels of police service. Sam Walker (1976) has argued that this has already occurred and explains the chronic underpolicing of lower- and middle-income neighborhoods throughout American history. It may also be happening today in the form of tax revolts, such as Proposition 13 in California. Undoubtedly the people who are most interested in reducing taxes are those who feel relatively secure and spend most of their time in privately protected places.

That people are calculating the cumulative costs of policing would be unambiguously indicated if communities began to ask for vouchers from the government to spend on policing, public or private, as has happened in public education. In such a system, communities could opt out of the public sector, or substitute an alternative public supplier of police services. The contract system of policing in Canada is like this, although communities must choose exclusively among government suppliers. Despite the popularity of the idea of privatization in the public sector, no government we know of has allowed communities to use public money to substitute private for public police. As we will argue shortly this provides one element in a response to the injustice of the growing inequality of access to security.

Some of the efforts the public police are making to restructure themselves may help to solve the equity issue, others will not. If police concentrate on law enforcement, the dualism between rich and poor will be exacerbated. The rich will be increasingly policed preventively by commercial security while the poor will be policed reactively by enforcement-oriented public police. Moreover, since there seems to be a qualitative difference in the efficacy of these approaches – deterrence versus prevention – the poor will also be relatively less secure. There are three ways theoretically to prevent this inequitable dualism from arising, given the unavailability of market mechanisms for poor people.

First, the numbers of traditional police could be increased in poor high-crime areas. Unfortunately, this might be as unpleasant for the poor as the dualism itself, because it would lead to an intensification of traditional law enforcement.

Second, the public police could adopt the community policing model for economically poor high-crime areas. Community and order-maintenance policing incorporates many of the adaptive, consensual, ends-oriented practices of private security. Unfortunately, despite pronouncements to the contrary, police are often reluctant to adopt such policies in high-crime area where they are already feeling hard pressed and where the efficacy of new approaches is unproven. Although community policing in theory is a powerful way to provide preventive policing for the poor, it may be distributed across cities in such a way that it reinforces rather than offsets the growing inequity in public security along class and racial lines.

Third, communities themselves might spontaneously develop their crime-preventing capacities. The chances of community-based pluralizing offsetting the defects of public policing are difficult to predict. Mobilization takes place more easily where people trust one another, possess leadership skills, have a stake in their communities, and are organized politically to achieve it. Although such efforts are growing by leaps and bounds, their efficacy, especially in high-crime areas, is unproven (Rosenbaum and Heath, 1990; Skogan, 1990). The mobilizing activities of the public police through community policing are probably necessary, therefore, to offset the emerging dualism. This alone is likely to be of limited value, however, because experience so far suggests that community policing is harder to introduce in poor than in affluent neighborhoods. The irony may be that community policing compensates for the emerging dualism best where it is least needed and worst where it is most needed.

### Human rights

Because government is deeply distrusted in Anglo-American tradition, the powers of the police are circumscribed; their activities closely monitored. Private commercial policing and community-based private security, on the other hand, are apt to be more intrusive, premonitory, and presumptive than public policing. They impose the more onerous and extensive obligations of custom and public opinion. The pluralizing of policing, therefore, increases the informal regulatory control of crime. This, indeed, is the strength of policing under nonstate auspices: social pressure rather than law ensures discipline.

Seen in these terms, community policing, which is community-based crime prevention under governmental auspices, is a contradiction in terms. It requires the police, who are bound by law, to lead communities in informal surveillance, analysis, and treatment. Community policing is a license for police to intervene in the private life of individuals. It harnesses the coercive power of the state to social amelioration. This represents an expansion of police power, and is much more in keeping with the continental European than with the Anglo-American traditions of policing. Community policing may be an answer to the dualism brought by pluralizing but at the risk of encouraging the 'vigilantism of the majority' (Johnston, 1994).

Community policing, and its cousin community-based crime prevention, are attractive solutions to the problem of security inequity in a society where policing is being pluralized. But both impose costs. Community-based crime prevention, like commercial private policing, imposes social rather than governmental constraints. Community policing, on the other hand, couples social pressure with government direction. The mitigating factor is that community policing, as we note below, can provide for some measure of 'bottom-up' accountability if it is developed in ways that encourage and permit genuine citizen participation.

### Democracy

Democratic principle requires that police be accountable so that they serve the interests of the people. This is surely no less true for policing generically, which, as we have just seen, determines in a practical way the balance between freedom. and order that people experience. At first glance, pluralization would not seem to pose a problem for accountability. Commercial private security is accountable to the market. If customers don't like what their security experts do, they can fire them. This alternative is not available for public police, who can only be fired by revolution. The problem with this view is that the accountability provided by markets accrues to buyers of private security and not to all the people who might be affected by it. Private security inevitably serves employers better than workers, owners better than patrons, and institutions better than individuals. The great advantage of public policing in democratic countries is that it is accountable to every citizen through the mechanisms of representative government.

Furthermore, the pluralizing of security under commercial auspices changes the social basis on which policing is organized. In democratic countries, police have been created to serve the interests of people territorially defined. Public policing is based on geographical communities. Private police, by contrast, serves primarily interest communities, that is, communities united by function rather than geography. It follows that the decentralization of policing that occurs through pluralizing is very different from the decentralization that occurs when government does it. The former is more selective in social terms; the latter includes everyone.

Voluntary community crime prevention, the other way in which pluralizing is occurring, does not suffer from the defect of social selectivity. The social basis for it is the same as under government, namely, people territorially defined. The problem with volunteer private policing, however, is its organizational informality. It may fail to represent the interests of people who are inarticulate, unorganized, and marginalized. The volunteers in private policing are likely to have interests that may differ from those of people who decline to participate. Community crime prevention is policing by the self-appointed, which is what people usually think of as vigilantism.

In sum, commercial private policing provides accountability through the formal mechanism of contracts but on the basis of social interests that may exclude many citizens. Volunteer private security provides accountability through informal mechanisms organized on the basis of citizenship that may or may not include everybody. Public policing provides accountability through formal mechanisms organized on the basis of citizenship that, in principle, cover everyone. Unless new alternatives are developed, it follows that accountability is best achieved through public policing operating according to principles of community policing. Community policing supplements the customary accountability of representative political institutions with grassroots consultation, evaluation, and feedback.

## Trade-offs

What trade-offs among these qualitatively different features – safety, equity, human rights, and accountability – does the current restructuring of policing present?

Broadening the auspices under which policing is organized, especially substituting private for governmental ones, probably raises the level of public safety because it increases the number of security agents and also substitutes a preventive security paradigm for a deterrent one. However, pluralizing increases safety at the cost of equity. This can be offset if community policing is strongly implemented in disorganized poor communities afflicted by crime.

Pluralized policing, however, is less constrained by formal rules and, therefore, puts the rights of the people it polices at risk. Pluralized policing is more security conscious than rights conscious.

Pluralized policing, under both commercial and community auspices, is only fictively consensual and democratic. Although it represents and empowers new groups, it does so on the basis of social interest rather than citizenship, and it provides haphazardly for the representation of all who might be affected by it. Pluralized policing inevitably shifts power away from government, but it does not necessarily distribute it to more people. Community policing, on the other hand, combines the traditional accountability of representative government with the informal accountability of volunteer crime prevention.

The point to underscore is that the changes occurring in policing are more than technical adjustments in the way policing is delivered. They represent the restructuring of government itself and the redistribution of power over one of government's core functions. By shifting policing to new auspices through markets, community action, and police reform, the nature of governance is changing.

## The likely future

Recognizing that fundamental changes are being made in policing that have profound consequences for the quality of civic life, is it possible to predict what the future holds? What balance among the overlapping and competing movements of pluralization and reformation will emerge? Will a new and stable equilibrium be found between state and nonstate policing? Might the state reassert itself, once again dominating policing? Could the public police become increasingly marginalized, confined to the policing of poor inner cities? And what will the character of public policing become – enforcement oriented, community based, or some new combination?

The current restructuring is driven by the public's concern about security. It is hardly an accident that the expansion of private security as well as the development of community policing coincided with rising crime rates throughout the developed world. If the threat to security were to decline significantly, the impetus to restructuring would be largely removed. This is unlikely to happen. Crime, notwithstanding the recent decline in overall rates in some countries, will continue to rise and even perhaps get worse for two reasons. First, crime is disproportionately committed by young males between the ages of 15 and 25. Twenty-nine per cent of serious crime in the United States is committed by people under 19.[3] This group will rise by over 20% in the next decade. In Canada 14% of crime of violence and 25% of crimes against property are committed by people 12 to 17 years old (Statistics Canada, 1993). Second, the violence of crime has been increasing. During the past 10 years the rate at which American teens are murdered has doubled (Blumstein, 1994). The homicide arrest rate for white youths rose by 80% during the past decade, for black youths 125%. This rising lethality can be traced to the increased availability of sophisticated firearms that in turn is related to the penetration of drug markets into poor urban neighborhoods (Butterfield, 1995). Unless circumstances change fundamentally, the violence of crime will continue to be perceived as a serious threat.

Furthermore, whatever happens to crime objectively, the public's fear of crime will certainly not decline. Because crime is fascinating, the media can be counted on to continue to exploit and exaggerate it. Only criminologists and police seem to know that crime is not randomly distributed in society; that it is not a national problem affecting everyone to the same extent. Crime is concentrated in particular localities characterized by unemployment, poverty, poor education, and single-parent homes. Crime has indeed risen and become more deadly during the last generation, but it has only marginally worsened for most of us. Unfortunately, because there seems to be no economic incentive, or political one either, for pointing this out, the public will continue to be terrorized by the exploitation of crime news (Chermak, 1995).

Assuming that crime and the fear of crime are unlikely to decline, can we expect governments to adopt policies that would rectify the underlying conditions, the so-called root causes, that breed crime? If this happened, then the restructuring of policing would be less imperative. This, too, is unlikely for several reasons. The political mood, currently represented by Reagan, Thatcher, Major, and Gingrich, is certainly against large-scale social intervention by government. Rising crime rates are often considered to be evidence that Great Society programs have failed. Ironically, then, the very rise in crime that impels the restructuring of policing may have helped convince people that social programs undertaken by government are a waste of money. Conservative social theorists also argue that government doesn't know how to remedy criminogenic conditions. Social programs are as likely to be counterproductive as they are wasteful (Murray, 1988; Wilson, 1983). The political hostility to amelioration is also fueled by a general perception that taxes are too high. Tax revolt has become a permanent condition, and placating it an enduring political necessity. All governments seem resigned to doing less with less for the foreseeable future.

For demographic, social, and political reasons, then, the threat of crime will intensify. The search for security will not diminish but may grow in desperation.

How, then, will government and the larger community provide for its intense desire for security?

First, government is unlikely to be able to respond effectively through traditional law enforcement programs. It will certainly not be able to do so through simply increasing the number of public police. Most research over the past 30 years has failed to show a connection between variations in the numbers of police and the incidence of crime.[4]

At the same time, the cost of increasing the 'visible presence' of the police, that is, police on the streets, remains dauntingly high. Because of staffing and deployment rules, 10 additional officers must be hired in order to get one extra uniformed police officer on the streets around the clock throughout the year (Bayley, 1985). The incremental cost of a unit of 'visible presence' on American streets is, therefore, about $500,000 – 10 times a patrol officer's average annual salary plus benefits. Few governments are going to be willing to make such investments.

Moreover, the distributional requirements of democratic politics ensure that additional police officers will not be concentrated in high-crime neighborhoods where their marginal utility would be highest, but will parcel them out in dribs and drabs so that every politician can claim to have gotten some police for his or her constituency. The allocations made under the 1994 Crime Control Act in the United States show this clearly. Distributional politics reduces the effectiveness of public expenditures on policing in any democratic society.

Democratic governments are also limited in their ability to respond to crime by political values. In the Anglo-American tradition, government is distrusted. As a result, public pressure to 'get tough' on crime invariably encounters stiff resistance from people concerned about civil liberties. Governments may sometimes enact Draconian policies, but in the long run they swing back and forth between punishment and due process. Deterrence, which will continue to dominate the efforts of modern democratic governments to control crime, clashes with the very precepts on which government has been established. Democratic societies may fear crime, but they fear authoritarianism more.

We believe, therefore, that democratic governments are unlikely to be able to allay the public's desperate need for safety through the criminal justice system. The demand for security is unlikely to be met by governmental action, whether through amelioration or deterrence.

Second, we are unsure but skeptical of the ability of Western societies to respond to the demand for order by spontaneous crime-preventive activities undertaken by communities. Our skepticism arises out of the value Western societies place on individualism. Westerners want to be free not only from government constraint but from social constraint as well. Because people in Western countries, unlike the Japanese, Chinese, and Koreans, place great importance on individual development and freedom, they do not readily submit to the informal discipline of groups (Bayley, 1985, 1991). If they do so, it is for short-term instrumental ends, such as winning a game, obtaining emotional support for a particular problem, making useful contacts, or obtaining particular advantages. The capacity of families, neighborhoods, schools, churches, and employers to discipline their members and to organize against crime and disorder is weak in individualistic societies. Although the vitality of community crime prevention in Western democratic countries currently is impressive and heartening, its staying power and its effectiveness are doubtful. Experience so far indicates that efforts at community organization are difficult to sustain after initial enthusiasm wears off. Moreover, the rigorous research so far done on community crime prevention has failed to show substantial benefits.

Individualistic democratic societies are caught between a rock and a hard place with respect to crime control. On the one hand, they are limited by their political values from authoritarian controls and, on the other, they are limited by their cultural values from the discipline of informal social control.

Third, caught in this bind, it is inevitable that Western democratic societies will continue to resort to the marketplace for security solutions. Free enterprise capitalism is the mechanism the West must rely on to compensate for the deficiencies of governmental control and social cohesion in controlling crime. Market-mediated private security is the natural response of societies like ours, just as privatization generally has been to problems of health, education, research, information dissemination, and income support. Security can hardly not become 'commodified' in individualistic democratic societies. There is no other place to turn.

Commodification of security has been encouraged by the rise of 'mass private property' in the latter half of the 20th century – meaning facilities that are owned privately but to which the public has right of access and use (Shearing and Stenning, 1983). These include shopping malls, educational campuses, residential communities, high-rise condominiums and apartments, banks, commercial facilities, and recreation complexes. The world is no longer divided simply between privately owned space used by its owners and the numerous public streets used by the public. By blurring the distinction between the public and the private, mass private property attenuates and marginalizes government's responsibility for security. It constricts government efforts at preventive policing to clearly public venues. Preventive policing in mass private property has become the responsibility of security specialists bought privately through the market.

If we are right that governments cannot provide satisfactory public safety, that neighborhoods will have only haphazard success in doing so, and that mass private property will continue to dominate urban space, then market-based private security will inevitably increase relative to public policing. It may even begin to cannibalize public policing if affluent people become more reluctant to pay twice for safety. It follows, therefore, that there will be no avoiding the emergence of dualistic policing stratified by race and class. The affluent will be protected by private security agents organized by interest groups and operating according to preventive principles backed up by the requirements of specialized membership or participation; the poor will be protected by a weakened public police operating according to principles of deterrence based on procedurally limited law enforcement. Western democratic societies are moving inexorably, we fear, into a Clockwork Orange world where both the market and the government protect the affluent from the poor – the one by barricading and excluding, the other by repressing and imprisoning – and where civil society for the poor disappears in the face of criminal victimization and governmental repression.

Fourth, there is one more factor that may powerfully influence the security trends outlined here, namely, outbreaks of collective violence, especially in large cities. The United States has already experienced serious but isolated instances of this – the 'Rodney King' riots in Los Angeles, the Thompkins Park and Crown Heights riots in New York City, and the Liberty City riots in Miami. But collective violence is happening in quieter, more pervasive ways that is not so easily recognized. Gang violence in some inner-city neighborhoods has attained the dimensions of an ongoing riot. The former Mayor of Washington, DC, formally requested the deployment of the National Guard in August 1994. And Americans asked why the Army and Marines were sent to Somalia when the United States had its own gang warlords terrorizing inner-city neighborhoods. England now has 'slow riots' in the summer in which unemployed youths from public housing estates regularly burn tires, cars, and sometimes buses 'for fun'.

Collective violence, whether in the form of short, intense riots or persistent, endemic criminality, powerfully reinforces the dualistic tendencies in the current restructuring of policing. Portrayed as unpredictable and random, such violence scares the well-to-do and demonstrates the impotence of the police. This encourages further privatization along class lines. At the same time, collective violence weakens community crime prevention impulses among the disadvantaged by polarizing communities and weakening trust among neighbors and even family members. Furthermore, in the face of collective violence, governments become less willing to allow poor communities to develop self-defense capabilities (Bayley, 1975, 1985). Collective violence is inevitably perceived in political terms. The standard response of governments is, therefore, to centralize policing power rather than allow it to be decentralized among what appear to be unpredictable and politically untrustworthy communities.

Collective violence not only drives a wedge deeper between the rich and the poor; it undercuts the ability of the state to more equitably distribute security among the rich and the poor by undermining the capacity and enthusiasm among the public police for community policing. Persistent collective violence causes the police to centralize decisionmaking, adopt a military style of command, emphasize law enforcement, deploy heavier weaponry, patrol in groups rather than as individuals, take preemptive action, and distrust the public. Collective violence also makes commanders cautious about tying down officers in community-development work. They want to save resources for 'the big event', which weakens their capacity for flexible adaptation and problem solving, both of which are essential elements of community policing. Collective violence is like a bus waiting to broadside the evolution of policing in the late 20th century. If it hits, there may be nothing anyone can do to prevent the emergence of a dualistic system of policing.

### Fateful choices

The fear of crime, the absence of ameliorative social policies, the ineffectiveness of deterrence, the rise of mass private property, and the commodification of security are powerful forces shaping the future of policing. The dualistic tendencies in policing are almost certain to be strengthened, with consequent distortions of equity, human rights, and accountability. In the face of these developments, can modern democratic, individualistic societies provide humane policing equitably for all their members? We believe they can, but only if two policies are adopted.

First, it is necessary to enable poor people to participate in markets for security. For this to happen it will be necessary to develop mechanisms to provide for the reallocation of public funding for security. The objective should be to provide poorer communities with the ability to sustain self-governing initiatives.

One way of achieving this would be through block grants to poor communities so that they can participate in the commercial market for security. Not only does this level up access to security, it vests directive authority in the people most affected. If appropriate mechanisms for community self-government are created, block grants raise the likelihood that policing will be responsive to the wishes of the community. Block grants would encourage poor communities to develop security regimes that fit their problems and mores in the same way that private security adapts to the goals of businesses. In effect, communities would be given security budgets that they could spend on various mixtures of public and private policing. Distributional problems between rich and poor might still arise, of course, particularly if the rich refused to pay. All policies that have any prospect of mitigating the growing class differences in public safety depend on the affluent segments of our societies recognizing that security is indivisible. The well-to-do are paying for crime now; but they have not learned that they will save more by leveling up security than by ghettoizing it.

Second, community policing must become the organizing paradigm of public policing. Through community policing governments can develop the self-disciplining and crime-preventive capacity of poor, high-crime neighborhoods. Community policing incorporates the logic of security by forging partnership between police and public. Since safety is fundamental to the quality of life, co-production between police and public legitimates government, lessening the corrosive alienation that disorganizes communities and triggers collective violence. Community policing is the only way to achieve discriminating law enforcement supported by community consensus in high-crime neighborhoods.

Community policing faces substantial obstacles and will not be easy to achieve. Most police are still not convinced it is needed, and research so far is equivocal about its success. The latter may be attributable more to failures in implementation than defects in the program. Community policing requires substantial revision of organizational priorities within the police and is managerially demanding. It requires new styles of supervision and new methods of evaluating performance. Although community policing sounds appealing, few politicians have the nerve to force community policing on reluctant police departments. They would rather give unrestricted grants to police agencies, thereby earning credit for being tough on crime while not challenging standard operating procedures. Finally, as we have noted, community policing is hardest to achieve in the places that need it most. In terms of resources, it requires government to take the security problems of the poor as seriously as it does the security problems of the rich.

Both of these policies – community block grants and community policing – highlight a fundamental question: does government have the wisdom, even if it has the will, to guide the course of security's restructuring without making it worse? Vouchers and, community policing will work to offset the socially divisive effects of restructuring only to the extent that they empower communities to take responsibility for themselves and, in some cases, to heal themselves. This requires government not only to reform the police but to redistribute political power with respect to one of the core function of government. This is a lot to ask, because faced with shortcomings in public safety, governments will be tempted to enhance directiveness rather than encourage devolution. To avoid this, a radical rethinking of the role of government is required.

Fortunately, while the inclination of government to stipulate rather than facilitate remains strong, there is a widespread and growing movement to challenge this. Just as the past is prologue to the continued restructuring of policing, so, too, there seems to be a growing realization in democratic, individualistic societies that in order to create a more humane, safe, and civil society, government must be reinvented, specifically, that grassroots communities must be made responsible for central aspects of governance. The rethinking of security that our proposals require is consistent with this rethinking of governance. Restructuring is a problem that may contain the seeds of its own solution.

*From David H. Bayley and Clifford D. Shearing, 'The future of policing',* Law and Society Review, *Vol. 30, no 3, 1996, pp 585–606.*

## Notes

1   In the United States there are about 2 million private security people as opposed to about 650,000 sworn police.
2   These calculations are based on clearances for U.S. Index crimes or their near equivalents in Britain and Canada – homicide, rape, aggravated assault, robbery, burglary, larceny, and auto theft. U.S. Bureau of Justice Statistics, 1993; United Kingdom Home Office, 1992; and Statistics Canada, 1993.
3   'After the Respite, Crime Rises,' *Albany Times Union,* 14 Dec. 1994, p. 1.
4   This conclusion has recently been challenged by Stephen Levitt who has demonstrated for the first time that hiring additional police may be cost effective (Levitt, 1994a, 1994b). Levitt's analysis shows that in large American cities each additional officer prevents between 7 and 10 crimes per year, at an annual saving that is $150,000 more than the cost of the officer's hire.

## References

Bayley, David H. (1975) 'The Police and Political Development in Europe,' in Charles Tilly, ed., *The Formation of National States in Western Europe*. Princeton, NJ: Princeton Univ. Press.

Bayley, David H. (1985) *Patterns of Policing: A Comparative International Policing*. New Brunswick, NJ: Rutgers Univ. Press.

Bayley, David H. (1991) *Forces of Order: Policing Modern Japan*. Berkeley: Univ. of California Press.

Bayley, David H. (1994) *Police for the Future*. New York: Oxford Univ. Press.

Blumstein, Alfred (1994) 'Youth Violence, Gangs, and the Illicit-Drug Industry.' Unpub., Carnegie-Mellon Univ., Pittsburgh (July 26).

Brogden, Michael, and Clifford Shearing (1993) *Policing for a New South Africa*. London: Routledge.

Butterfield, Fox (1995) 'Grim Forecast on Rising Crime,' *New York Times*, p. A24 (19 Feb.).

Chermak, Steven M. (1995) *Victims in the New*. Boulder, CO: Westview Press.

Johnston, Les. (1992) *The Rebirth of Private Policing*. London: Routledge.

Johnston, Les. (1994) 'Policing in Late Modern Societies.' Paper for the Workshop on Evaluating Police Service Delivery, Montreal (Nov.).

Kelling, George L., and Catherine M. Coles (1994) 'Disorder and the Court,' *Public Interest*, p. 57 (Summer).

Levitt, Steven D. (1994a) 'Reporting Behavior of Crime Victims and the Size of the Police Force: Implications for Studies of Police Effectiveness Using Reported Crime Data.' Unpub., Harvard Univ. (Aug.).

Levitt, Steven D. (1994b) 'Using Electoral Cycles of Police Hiring to Estimate the Effect of Police on Crime.' Unpub., Harvard Univ. (Nov.).

Murray, Charles (1988) *In Pursuit of Happiness and Good Government*. New York: Simon & Schuster.

Rosenbaum, Dennis P., and Linda Heath (1990) 'The "Psycho-Logic" of Fear-Reduction and Crime-Prevention Programs,' in John Edwards et al., eds., *Social Influence Processes and Prevention*. New York: Plenum Press.

Shearing, Clifford (1992) 'The Relation between Public and Private Policing, in M. Tonry and N. Morris, eds., *Modern Policing*. Chicago: Univ. of Chicago Press.

Shearing, Clifford (1996) 'Reinventing Policing: Policing as Governance,' in O. Marenin, ed., *Policing Change: Changing Police*. New York: Garland Press.

Shearing, C.D., and Philip Stenning (1983) 'Private Security: Implications for Social Control,' 30 *Social Problems* 493.

Skogan, Wesley G. (1990) *Disorder and Decline*. New York: Free Press.

Skolnick, Jerome H., and David H. Bayley (1986) *The New Blue Line*. New York: Free Press.

Statistics Canada (1993) *Canadian Crime Statistics, 1993*. Ottawa: Statistics Canada.

United Kingdom Home Office (1992) *Criminal Statistics: England and Wales, 1992*. London: HMSO.

U.S. Bureau of Justice Statistics (1993) *Sourcebook of Criminal Justice Statistics, 1993*. Washington: Bureau of Justice Statistics.

Walker, Samuel (1976) 'The Urban Police in American History: A Review of the Literature,' *J. of Police Science & Administration*, pp. 252–60 (Sept.).

Walker, Samuel, and Betsey Wright (1994) 'Civilian Review of the Police: A National Survey.' Washington: Police Executive Research Forum.

Wilson, James Q, (1983) *Crime and Public Policy*. San Francisco: ICS Press.

Wilson, James Q., and George L. Kelling (1982) 'Broken Windows: The Police and Neighborhood Safety,' *Atlantic Monthly*, pp. 29–38 (March).

# 41. The transformation of policing? Understanding current trends in policing systems

*Trevor Jones and Tim Newburn*

> Modern democratic countries like the United States, Britain and Canada
> have reached a watershed in the evolution of their systems of crime control
> and law enforcement. Future generations will look back on our era as a time
> when one system of policing ended and another took its place. (Bayley and
> Shearing, 1996: 585).

In recent years, there has been growing consensus that the policing systems of
Western industrial societies are experiencing profound changes. Authors have
highlighted a range of developments, including the expansion of private security
(Shearing and Stenning, 1987; Johnston, 1992; Jones and Newburn, 1998; Loader,
1999), the growing importance of 'transnational' policing organizations and
practices (Anderson *et al.*, 1995; Sheptycki, 1997), changes in the organization
and management of public police forces (Chatterton *et al.*, 1996; Johnston, 1996),
the impact of new technologies upon policing and crime control (Marx, 1988),
and the emergence of new 'risk-based' policing strategies (Feeley and Simon,
1992; Ericson and Haggerty, 1997). Such changes are clearly crucially important
to a deeper understanding of policing systems in Western industrial countries as
we move into the twenty-first century. However, it has further been suggested
that we are currently seeing a transformation in policing of a magnitude at least
as great as occurred with the introduction of the New Police in the early
nineteenth century. This transformation has been variously described as
'post-Keynesian policing' (O'Malley and Palmer, 1996), "pick 'n mix" policing
for a postmodern age' (Reiner, 1997) and, even, the 'End of Public Policing'
(McLaughlin and Murji, 1995).

In this chapter, we aim to address some of the broader issues relating to the
interpretation of current trends, by focusing upon one particular example within
this 'transformation' literature in policing. In 1996, two of the most distinguished
academic criminologists, David Bayley and Clifford Shearing, published an
article entitled 'The Future of Policing' in the journal *Law and Society Review*
(Bayley and Shearing, 1996). In the article they made a series of sweeping claims
about the significant changes they perceived to be taking place in developed
democratic societies. Whilst we must begin by saying that we concur with many
of their observations, there are also some key points at which our respective
views of both the history of policing and, consequently, the future of policing,

diverge. In particular, we question the degree to which current developments in policing should be interpreted as a qualitative break with the past. Here, we begin by setting out the central elements advanced by Bayley and Shearing in their article and then move on to discuss these key points of divergence. We argue that the article, and some of the other writing in the field, whilst identifying some important developments in modern policing, tends to overstate the novelty and the 'epochal' nature of current trends. Furthermore, we feel in general that what we will refer to as the 'transformation thesis' fails to take sufficient account of important differences between the nature and form of policing in North America, and that in other countries such as Britain.[1] Finally, we suggest that rather than seeing current changes as a fragmentation of policing, they are better viewed as an ongoing process of formalization of social control.

## The transformation thesis

Bayley and Shearing open by making clear the radical nature of the focus of their paper. Their concern is with 'the watershed in the evolution' of the systems of crime control and law enforcement in the United States, Britain and Canada. They forcefully argue that that '[future generations will look back on our era as a time when one system of policing ended and another took its place' (1996: 585). This epochal change is characterized by two developments:

- The pluralizing of policing – or as they put it 'the end of a monopoly' by the public police; and
- The search for identity by the public police.

Before exploring each of these in greater detail they make the important point, that the focus of their concerns is with *policing*, not just the *police*. They are interested in 'all explicit efforts to create visible agents of crime control, whether by government or by non-governmental institutions' (1996: 586). The reason for emphasizing explicit efforts is to distinguish the 'elephant of social control' from the `breadbox of policing'.

### The end of a monopoly

The core of Bayley and Shearing's thesis is that 'in the past 30 years the state's monopoly on policing has been broken by the creation of a host of private and community-based agencies that prevent crime, deter criminality, catch law-breakers, investigate offences, and stop conflict' (1996: 586). As a result, they argue, the police and policing have become increasingly distinct. Their conceptualization of the 'pluralization of policing' can be broken down into the following main points:

- There used to be a state monopoly on policing, but this has been fractured during the past 30 years (i.e. since the mid-1960s);

- Evidence for this is to be found in the fact that there are now *three times* as many private as public police in the United States and *twice* as many 'private security agents' than public police officers in the UK; in addition, the private security sector is growing faster than public policing;
- Citizen policing – in the form of car and foot patrols, neighbourhood watches, crime prevention associations, protective escort services, and monitors around schools, malls, and public parks – have been 'transformed in less than a generation' (1996: 587) from something that would have previously been viewed as 'vigilantism' but is now so common that the 'police are no longer the primary crime-deterrent, presence in society'.

*Searching for identity*

Alongside the increasing pluralization of policing, the other major element in the restructuring that is taking place in developed democracies is the increasing questioning of the role of the police – particularly by the service itself. 'This is attributable', Bayley and Shearing (1996: 588) argue, 'to growing doubts about the effectiveness of their traditional strategies in safeguarding the public: from crime'. There are numerous components to this:

- The 'visible deterrent' of patrol has declined as the police have been gradually swamped by the need to respond to emergency calls;
- Clear-up rates remain extremely low;
- There is therefore a search for 'new approaches' – these have included: 'community policing' and 'order maintenance policing' (a hybrid of 'community-oriented and crime-oriented policing');
- The increasing sale by the police of the protective services they used to provide without charge;
- The hiring of police officers as private security guards;
- The increasing civilianization of public policing-including the use of Special Constables or other auxiliaries; and
- The increasingly rigorous supervision of the police by governmental and non-governmental agencies.

Although Bayley and Shearing focus on the search for a new identity, other authors have, in a similar way, highlighted qualitative shifts in the nature of police activity. In particular, although Bayley and Shearing do not mention this specifically, one might include under this point the shifts towards new policing functions identified by writers such as Feeley and Simon (1996) and Ericson (1994). Feeley and Simon argue that the police (and the criminal justice system in general) are increasingly adopting 'actuarial' rather than 'disciplinary' approaches. These techniques are characterized by a pragmatic emphasis on the management of risky populations, rather than aiming to reform, punish or deter individuals. A related point is made by Ericson and Haggerty's (1997) analysis of the transformation of policing functions in developed societies. They argue that the public police role is no longer primarily concerned with law enforcement and peacekeeping, but has moved towards 'information brokering' within a wider patchwork of organizations and individuals concerned with the promotion of security.

Taken together, it is this raft of changes which has been interpreted by some authors as constituting a transformation to a fundamentally new kind of policing system. For example, Bayley and Shearing's (1996: 591) conclusion runs as follows: 'the pluralizing of policing and the search by the public police for a new role and methodology mean that not only has government's monopoly on policing been broken in the late 20th century, but the police monopoly on expertise within its own sphere of activity has ended. Policing now belongs to everybody – in activity, in responsibility, and in oversight'.

As we have already indicated, there is much in these arguments with which we would not argue, particularly in relation to some of the changes taking place in the police organization (see Jones and Newburn, 1997) . However, particularly in relation to what we have elsewhere referred to as the 'policing division of labour' (Jones and Newburn, 1998), it is our view that Bayley and Shearing both overstate the degree of novelty attributable to the changes taking place and posit an 'over-globalized' view of the world. They lose sight of the important continuities in policing systems and, further, fail to make sufficient allowance for the important differences between, for example, North America and the UK. It is to this we turn next.

## How strong is the evidence?

For the purposes of empirical examination, we will consider three distinct elements of what we have termed the 'transformation thesis': the 'end of monopoly', 'the pluralization of policing provision', and 'the changing character of, and the search for a new identity for, the public police'.

### The end of monopoly?

How 'policing' or 'the police' are best characterized has been the subject of considerable academic debate. Most attempts to define or distinguish the police from other policing organizations have focused either on functions or on legal capacities. Neither approach is entirely adequate (see the criticisms contained in Johnston, 1992 and Jones and Newburn, 1998). A functional focus tends to elide the police with policing assuming, implicitly or otherwise, that the two are effectively the same. In response to this, several authors have argued that what distinguishes policing from other activities is the capacity to apply the 'legitimate use of force'. Indeed, the best known of these, Egon Bittner, went further and argued that this was in fact the distinguishing characteristic of *the police* (Bittner, 1974, 1980) . It is this capacity that is often being referred to when the idea of a 'public monopoly' of policing is used.

The term 'monopoly' is defined by economists as the condition that exists when a firm or individual produces and sells the entire output of a commodity or service. The monopolist has total power in the market place to set prices and prevent the entry of new competitors. If all that is meant by 'monopoly' is that the public police were the sole repositories of state-backed coercive power, then the public police monopoly continues today. In Britain at least, it is the public police who retain the legal power to arrest, detain and charge on behalf of the state (backed, if necessary, by the use of *legitimate force*), and there is strong resistance to providing such special legal powers to other bodies, and especially to private security guards.

In relation to policing, however, the term 'monopoly' tends to be used in a broader sense to describe a perceived functional, spatial and above all, symbolic dominance over policing by the public police. In this sense, it is clear that the symbolic monopoly that equated 'policing' with the activities of the public police has fractured in the past 20 years or so. The period most associated with a public police monopoly, especially in Britain, is the two decades immediately following the Second World War. However, although the 1950s still tend to be presented as the 'golden age' of public policing, Reiner (1992b) has persuasively argued that this was as much a matter of image as of substance. Relatively low rates of crime and disorder overall, and high police popularity ratings of the post-war years might be better explained with reference to wider social and economic conditions, than by anything the police were actually doing at the time. Even during the height of the 'golden era', police relationships with certain elements of the population remained difficult and conflictual, and there is no evidence that police malpractice was less common during this period (in fact, there are good reasons to suppose that levels of police deviance may well have been substantially higher than the present day, see Reiner, 1992b). The main point here is that the height of the symbolic 'monopoly' of public policing was an era in which low crime rates and relative social harmony were produced by a wide variety of structural influences which underpinned a more effective network of informal social controls. It is the breakdown of these more effective informal controls that have been a primary contributor to the growing demands upon public policing services, and the increasing soul-searching of state police forces. In an important sense, then, the public 'monopoly' over policing was always a fiction, the idea that sovereign states could guarantee crime control to their subjects always a myth, albeit a powerful one (Garland, 1996) . The crucial change in the current era is that the myth is increasingly explicitly recognized as such, even by those state agencies tasked with dealing with crime.

### The pluralization of policing

We deal with two major elements under this heading: first, *the growth of private security* and second, *the emergence of other policing bodies* (not part of constabularies or the private security sector). Bayley and Shearing argue that private security growth far outstrips public police in both the United States and the UK, is growing faster than the public sector, and that this change dates from the 1960s. They further argue that there has been a growth of *citizen policing* (we return to this below) – automobile and foot patrols, neighbourhood watches, crime prevention associations and so on have been 'transformed in less than a generation' from something that would have previously been viewed as 'vigilantism' into a primary crime-deterrent presence. Other authors (see for example Johnston, 1992, 1996) have highlighted the activities of a range of other policing bodies – including the regulatory and investigatory bodies attached to national and local government – as part of a growing fragmentation of policing provision.

### The growth of private security

In pure numerical terms, and reinforcing our argument above, it is clear that a 'monopoly' in the field of security provision has never really existed. Data from both the US and the UK suggest that, whilst significant changes have certainly taken place in the policing division of labour, the idea of the end of a 'monopoly' is difficult to support. According to Bayley and Shearing, the 'rebirth' of private security occurred sometime around the 1960s. However, the Rand report. (Kakalik and Wildhorn, 1972), which provides the best historical picture of private security in the United States, found that in 1950 there were approximately half as many private security guards as public police staff. This is approximately a decade and a half, *before* the 'rebirth' of private security is alleged to have taken place. Similarly, in Britain, the 1951 census of population estimates about 66,000 private security employees compared with approximately 85,000 police officers.[2] At the very least, therefore, the argument that a public monopoly has been broken in the past 30 years is impossible to sustain. Was there ever a public monopoly? This is also doubtful. In Britain, commercial provision (and other 'private' forms) of policing continued throughout the nineteenth century, despite the introduction and expansion of the New Police, and the early twentieth century contains many examples of private provision, including the development of the guarding industry in the inter-war period (Johnston, 1992). What is clearly true is that the private security industry has become more important since the 1950s, both in absolute terms and relative to public policing. However, we feel that it is important to emphasize that, although the empirical evidence is limited, what there is suggests that the private security industry was relatively well established even during the height of the 'monopoly' era for the public police. In our view, current developments are perhaps therefore better presented as the continuation of a long-term trend extending back several decades rather than a seismic shift occurring in the dying years of the twentieth century. Put another way, there is considerable *continuity* as well as *change*.

Of course, employment estimates alone cannot adequately measure the expanding influence of commercial forms of policing provision. A number of other factors have contributed to the growing visibility of commercial policing. First, there has been a long-term trend within business organizations towards the contracting-out of non-core tasks, such as security. Thus, whereas many of the people working in security and related occupations in the 1950s and 1960s would have been employed in-house, increasingly companies contract in security services from specialist providers (Jones and Newburn, 1998). Second, the functional remit of commercial policing has expanded in recent years, with the private sector undertaking tasks previously viewed as the preserve of state bodies, such as prisoner escort, court guarding, and the patrol of public places. Finally, the spatial remit of commercial policing has arguably grown, with the emergence of private patrols in public spaces (see McManus, 1995; Noaks, 2000), and also the growth of 'mass private property' in the form of large shopping centres, private theme parks etc. However, the available evidence suggests that such changes have been considerably less extensive in Britain than is the case in the USA (Jones and Newburn, 1999a).

### The growth of other forms of policing

Another important aspect of the 'pluralization' of policing (although not an element upon which Bayley and Shearing focus a great deal in their article) concerns the activities of what Johnston (1992) has termed 'hybrid' policing bodies, such as Environmental Health Officers and Health and Safety Inspectors. However, as we have pointed out elsewhere (Jones and Newburn, 1998) it is rather misleading to consider these bodies as though they are part of a relatively recent 'fragmentation' of policing organizations. In the United States, and certainly in Britain, regulatory and investigatory bodies attached to national and local government have been undertaking 'policing' activities for over a century. The fact that criminologists have only recently taken an interest in these perhaps reflects the general assumption, widely held until comparatively recently, that 'policing' can be equated with 'what public constabularies do'.

During the mid to late 1800s in England and Wales, it was local constabularies that delivered services such as inspecting weights and measures, inspections under the Diseases of Animals Act, and inspections of dairies and shops (Critchley, 1967). It was not until the late nineteenth century, beginning with the Local Government Acts of 1888, and the early twentieth century that local government began to undertake these 'policing' functions itself. The post-war expansion of the welfare state introduced new 'policing' functions which were undertaken by public bodies outside of the police (for example, benefit fraud investigation). As Bayley and Shearing correctly point out, many police forces in Britain and North America are currently seeking to divest themselves of what have increasingly been seen as 'ancillary' functions, part of which has involved withdrawal from regulatory activity such as licensing bars, parking regulations and so on. However, in the light of the longer history of the policing of such activities, this is far from a novel development. Rather, it is the latest of a series of functional shifts between different policing bodies. For the large part of the twentieth century, policing functions have been undertaken by this mix of bodies, with the balance shifting between the different elements from time to time. For example, Taylor's (1999) fascinating analysis of policing in England and Wales in the early part of the twentieth century explains a dramatic fall in prosecutions for non-indictable offences such as vandalism and begging by reference to such a functional shift:

> [The Home Office's] argument that society had suddenly civilized to the extent that wife-beating, assaults, truancy, drunkenness, immorality, begging, child cruelty, vandalism and other similar 'minor' offences had really fallen by two-thirds between the first world war and 1931 was unbelievable. Instead, many of these offences must have continued to be committed but, were probably dealt. with by agencies or departments of government other than the police ...

Notwithstanding these functional shifts, over the longer period from the mid-1800s to the mid-1950s it seems that the public police gradually obtained pre-eminence within the complex of policing bodies, in terms of staffing numbers, functions and spatial operation, but particularly in symbolic terms. However, it is clear that they never achieved anything even approaching a total 'monopoly' over the provision of policing services (except possibly – and very briefly – at a symbolic level). This, however, is not to deny the fact that, since this time, the balance has shifted significantly again, and the dominance of the public police has declined. What is less clear is that the current era, rather than any other (for example, the 1890s or the inter-war years) represents a dramatic move into a completely new system of policing.

In fact, taking a longer historical perspective suggests that on one level, policing provision has become less rather than more fragmented. In particular, repeated reorganization over the nineteenth and twentieth centuries has seen a massive decline in the total number of constabularies and bodies of constables. Thus, out of the mixture of formal, semi-formal and informal policing 'bodies' that existed in the eighteenth and nineteenth centuries, there emerged the 'New Police'. Beginning with the Metropolitan Police in 1829 these public policing bodies expanded rapidly in the nineteenth century, to the point where, by 1870, there were over 220 constabularies in England and Wales. From this point until, arguably, the 1960s, a process of centralization and formalization existed – albeit alongside other changes taking place. The number of constabularies was reduced by the Police Act 1946 to 131. Further amalgamations reduced the number of provincial forces to 117 by the early 1960s. In 1966 they were further reduced to 49 and, most recently, the Local Government Act 1972 reduced the number of provincial forces to 41. The Police and Magistrates' Courts Act 1994 gave increased powers to the Home Secretary to amalgamate forces without the need to consult publicly, and such amalgamations may well occur in the future.[3]

### The changing character of the public police

This relates to the view that public policing organizations have somehow fundamentally changed in character as a result of the various pressures under which they have been placed. Bayley and Shearing concentrate on the police drive for improved effectiveness and the application of performance monitoring. As we have suggested, other authors have argued that the basic functions of public policing have now shifted to new actuarial and information-brokering roles. The question for us here is how far such changes represent a trans-formation towards a qualitatively different form of policing? We shall focus on three particular elements that have been linked with the changing character of public policing; the growth of managerialism and quasi-markets, civilianization, and the emergence of citizen-led forms of policing and crime control.

### Managerialism and quasi-markets

The growth of managerialism has undoubtedly been one of the most significant changes in policing of the past 20 years or so. These changes have been widely documented elsewhere, and there is not the space here to analyse these developments in detail. Nevertheless, whilst not doubting their significance, we would argue that these changes, in Britain at least, have not yet been of such a degree as to constitute the transformation to a new policing system. Once again, the work of Howard Taylor (1999) highlights the danger of assuming the novelty of current trends. He has demonstrated how concerns about expenditure on policing, and the promotion of effective use of police resources was a central feature of British policing during the years following the First World War. At this time, centrally-driven management targets were applied to a number of aspects of police work. This is not to deny that the police service in Britain in recent years has again been significantly effected by another, perhaps more vigorous, form of managerialism. As part of the general trend towards 'new public management', the police have been required publish objectives, measure performance against these objectives, charge fees for some services, introduce devolved management structures and link resources to performance (Jones and Newburn, 1997). Clearly, this is a significant development, and one that could fundamentally subvert the nature of policing as a collectively purchased public service, should it be taken to the extreme. However, we would argue that at the present at least, public policing in Britain remains a 'public' service in several crucial ways, and clearly distinguishable from commercial private security. The police remain overwhelmingly (and increasingly) funded by a combination of national and local taxation. The vast majority of their workforce is made up of full-time publicly employed officials. Recent developments have clearly tried to heighten the privatization mentality. For example, section 24 of the Police and Magistrates Courts Act allows local authorities and health authorities to contract with police authorities and pay for extra constables for their areas. To date, however, few developments have been noted. Police forces are increasingly encouraged to charge for services where possible, for example for providing security at rock concerts or at football matches. Although this has grown significantly in recent years, legal provision for this was first made in England and Wales in the 1964 Police Act.

One further difficulty in applying Bayley and Shearing's thesis to, say, the UK, concerns its very particular North American focus (despite their claims to be talking about broader global changes). Thus, they additionally refer to two aspects of the 'privatization mentality' which apply in North America and Canada but which do not apply to Britain. The first involves 'moonlighting' by sworn police officers who may take employment as private security guards. Such activities are forbidden by police regulations in Britain. Second, they refer to the internal market of policing services in Canada, where local authorities may choose between a range of competing public sector providers in a quasi-market. These developments go substantially further than the current situation in Britain. Though the 'transformation thesis' rightly identifies many changes taking place in British policing, it also tends to exaggerate them. It will require the emergence of a significantly more competitive internal market in British policing, for example, before Bayley and Shearing's picture appears an accurate one.

### Civilianization

Another key feature of the fracturing of the public police identity crisis has involved the increasing involvement of civilians within the public police service, both in ancillary roles within the police organization, and in undertaking voluntary duties as 'special' constables or police auxiliaries. We do not currently have data for the US or Canada on these trends. However, the data that are available in Britain do not tend to support the notion of dramatic growth in the involvement of police auxiliaries over the past decade or so. In fact, the available data suggest the opposite, with substantially *fewer* special constables operating in Britain than was the case in the early and mid-twentieth century.

The civilianization of key posts within the police service was an important element of policy encouraged by successive Conservative administrations during the 1980s. Forces were encouraged, by various funding incentives, to replace with civilian employees relatively expensive police officers in posts not directly requiring police powers, training or experience (such as traffic depot managers, force finance officers, administrative functions). Undoubtedly, the main drive to civilianization came after 1980, with up to a third of total police strength in the UK now accounted for by civilian employees. However, as we showed in an earlier study (Jones *et al.*, 1994) the employment of civilians in the police service has a long history dating back to the early years of this century. Although there was a rapid expansion in civilian employment in the police during the 1980s, this expansion has now levelled off.

Turning to the Special Constabulary in Britain there have been various government initiatives aimed at expanding the role (and number) of Special Constables in British police forces, particularly since 1980. Encouragement of the Special Constabulary has been an important priority for governments keen to promote wider public involvement in policing and crime prevention activity. However, taking a longer-term perspective, we can see that despite an expansion of the Special Constabulary over recent decades, total numbers of Specials remain substantially lower than has been the case for the majority of the post-war period. [ ... ]

*The growth of citizen-led policing*
Bayley and Shearing (among numerous others) focus on the significant expansion of citizen involvement in 'policing' activities in the form of neighbourhood watch, citizen patrols and other community-led crime prevention and policing initiatives. It is clear that these are very significant developments. The growth of neighbourhood watch, as an explicit public policy, is a relatively recent phenomenon both in North America and Britain, and is generally agreed to date from the early 1980s. Since the 1980s, governments in most industrial democracies have been engaged in what Garland (1996) calls 'responsibilization strategies' whereby individuals and organizations outside of the state apparatus are encouraged to take responsibility for crime prevention and security. We agree that this is a key aspect of the changes that are currently occurring in policing. However, we are less sure that this can be accurately represented as a part of a shift from public monopoly to mixed economy of policing provision. It is clear that private citizens and organizations are now more involved in organized self-conscious activities aimed at order maintenance, crime prevention and control. However, although much of the current debate focuses upon the growth of private and self-policing mechanisms, purportedly at the expense of an

increasingly beleaguered public police service, we offer here a slightly different interpretation.

Part of the problem for the public police is that citizens in general have been increasingly, rather than decreasingly, taking matters to them for resolution. Calls to the police, reported crime and disorder incidents have grown exponentially across all Western countries (Smith, 1996). Since the demand for formalized policing services has so far outstripped the ability of public police organizations to respond, commercial security and citizen-led approaches have unsurprisingly seen a major growth. But we would suggest that rather than see these developments as a fragmentation of 'policing', with non-state provision benefiting at the expense of public constabularies, what we are seeing is a general trend towards the formalization of social control. In particular, we would argue that the current growth in alternative forms of policing is related to a restructuring in forms of social control not directly connected to formal 'policing', private or public.

We have so far considered some of the changes taking place within public policing together with those occurring in the broader policing division of labour. In thinking through current trends in policing systems this is only part of the picture however. We now want to move on to consider changes in the broader context of policing and social control, changes that we take to have been central to the developments taking place since the Second World War.


## The formalization of policing and changes in social control

A large body of literature has linked current trends in crime control and penal systems to wider structural developments in capitalist societies in the late twentieth and early twenty-first centuries (see for example, Johnston, 1996; Bottoms, 1983; Garland, 2000). There is not the space here to provide a detailed examination of this large body of literature. However, we will highlight just some examples of changes in the nature of wider social control systems that we think may prove helpful to a deeper understanding of what is happening to policing.

As Cohen noted, there is a danger that the term 'social control' can be defined so broadly as to be meaningless, covering 'all social processes to induce conformity, from infant socialization to public execution' (Cohen, 1985: 2). Cohen thus defines social control in terms of 'organized' and 'planned' responses to deviance and socially problematic behaviour 'which are actually conceived of as such'. We have found this to be a helpful definition in beginning the process of thinking about what kinds of activity should come under the rubric of 'policing' (Jones and Newburn, 1998).

Returning to social control, we think it helpful to distinguish three different levels: primary, secondary and tertiary. In this context, *primary social control* we take to refer to crime prevention, peacekeeping, investigatory and related policing activities that are purposively carried out by organizations/individuals that see these activities as a primary defining part of their role. This would include the activities of public constabularies, other policing bodies such as inspectorates or regulatory bodies, and the commercial security sector. Thus, in our terms, primary social control covers those activities that we have previously described as 'policing' (Jones and Newburn, 1998). By contrast, *secondary social controls* may be said to be exerted by functionaries for whom social control activities are not a primary part of their role, but where nevertheless social control is an important secondary aspect of what they do. We would therefore include within this group: teachers, park-keepers, caretakers, railway guards, bus conductors and a range of other similar occupations. What such occupations have in common, in our view, is a very clear social control function, but one that is not a primary defining part of their role. This leaves the third category: *tertiary social control*. This corresponds to Cohen's wider concept of social control and includes the informal social controls exerted by 'intermediate' groups within local communities, including workgroups, churches, trade unions, clubs and societies, and community groups.

Our categorization of social control activities shares some characteristics with Hunter's (1995) work on developments in urban space. There Hunter categorizes three different kinds of 'order': the *public*, the *parochial* and the *private*, each with its particular institutional and spatial domain. The private order is based upon the family and informal 'primary groups' including interpersonal friendship networks and the institutions of kinship. The parochial order arises from the interlocking of these networks and local institutions which service the 'sustenance' needs of local residential community, such as local stores, schools, churches, and community associations. These correspond to the 'intermediate level' institutions outlined above. Finally, the public social order is found mainly in the bureaucratic agencies of the state. The 'public order' related to the state and its monopoly over the legitimate use of force. Hunter argues that growing crime and fear of crime has led to overwhelming demands on the police and criminal justice system. However, we should look to the private and parochial orders for the fundamental sources of this overload. Stronger parochial orders are a prerequisite for more effective social control activities along with the state and the private order. The limitations of the private order in terms of wider social control can be addressed by linking such networks through parochial institutions such as schools, churches and youth clubs.

Several authors have highlighted this apparent decline in informal bases of social control in many Western societies, corresponding roughly to our tertiary level outlined above. For example, Giddens (1990) discussed what he termed 'disembedding', whereby social relations are removed from local contexts due to the increasing mobility of people, of capital and of information. Authors such as Etzioni (1993), Putnam (2000) and Sennett (2000) have highlighted the fact that increasingly, the decline of participation in 'intermediate' level institutions such as community groups, secure employment, trade unions, churches and local societies and organizations, has meant that citizens are more likely to relate to the social world as individuals.

In this connection, we would wish to argue that current trends in policing can be related to the decline of more indirect (and arguably more effective) sources of social control. This is not just in the general sense of a decline of social bonds and indirect (tertiary) controls connected with the parochial sphere, but also with the decline of 'secondary' social control activities. There has been a marked decrease in employment in a range of occupations providing 'natural surveillance' and other low level controls as a corollary to their primary functions. In part, this has been a consequence of the development and spread of new labour-saving technologies such as self-purchasing ticket machines and automatic barriers, CCTV, and automated access control. The spread and impact of such technologies was underpinned and encouraged by neo-liberal public policies which sought to maximize profit, often through reductions in labour costs via 'downsizing'. Much criminological literature has assumed that the 'rise' of private security has been on the back of reductions in (or, at least, restrictions on the growth of) public policing. Whilst there may be a small element of truth in this, in our view it is the decline of 'secondary social control occupations' which is much more significant. In our own local case study of the policing of a London borough, we found commercial security carrying out activities that were previously undertaken not by public police officers, but by caretakers, receptionists, teachers, prefects and park-keepers. Thus, the decline in such occupations as bus conductors, railway station masters, train guards, ticket inspectors, park-keepers etc. has removed an important source of secondary social control (Jones and Newburn, 1998; see also Smith and Clarke, 2000: 177-8). To what extent is it possible to show that this has been a long-term national trend?

[Table 41.1] is derived from Census figures for 1951, 1971 and 1991. The figures should be taken as approximate indicators only, given that in all cases (bar 1951) occupational estimates for the GB are based on a 10 per cent sample only. Furthermore, changes in occupational classifications over the years make comparison over time more difficult. Nonetheless, the figures are reasonably robust and, given the absence of any other reliable longitudinal data, provide the most accurate picture to date of this particular area of occupational change.

As the table indicates there has been a sharp increase in the security and related occupations (i.e. what is often talked of as 'private security') over the past 40 years. In addition to noting that this covers a longer time period than that outlined by Bayley and Shearing, the Census data show that as far back as 1951 the size of this sector was substantial. Indeed, in the first decade after the Second World War the numbers of people employed in the sector represented the equivalent of four fifths of those employed in public constabularies. As we have shown elsewhere, by the early 1960s the sector employed greater numbers than did the public police (Jones and Newburn, 1998). Over the past 50 years there has also been a large increase in the numbers of public police officers, though the extent of the increase has not been as great. The conclusion to draw from this, it

**Table 41.1** Primary and secondary social control occupations in Britain

|  | 1951 | 1971 | 1991 |
| --- | --- | --- | --- |
| Police officers | 84,585 | 115,170 | 149,964 |
| Security guards and related | 66,950 | 129,670 | 159,704 |
| 'Roundsmen/roundswomen' | 98,143 | 48,360 | 49,182 |
| Bus (and tram) conductors | 96,558 | 57,550 | 2,471 |
| Rail ticket inspectors/guards | 35,715 | 46,800 | 15,642 |

Source: Occupational estimates from the 1951, 1971, 1991 Census of Population (GB)

seems to us, is not that the well-documented increase in private security reflects a process of transfer of functions and responsibilities from the public to the private police, though there may be some elements of this. Rather, and more fundamentally, it is better understood as a formalization of 'secondary' social control activities. More particularly, we think it is more accurate to see the declining visibility of occupations with a secondary social control element as being a key contributor to the growth of 'primary' forms of social control – i.e. private *and* public policing. Only a limited number of such occupations can be estimated from Census data, but four key examples are illustrated above. Taking what the Census generally classifies as 'roundsmen/women' – the house-to-house delivery of milk, bread and other goods – there has been a significant decrease in these kinds of occupations since 1951, with numbers approximately halving. Census figures suggest that there has been a very sharp decrease in the number of bus and tram conductors. In 1951, the Census estimated over 96,000 people in such occupations. In stark contrast, the 1991 Census estimated only about 2,500 in Great Britain. There has also been a sharp decrease in Census estimates of the numbers employed as rail ticket inspectors or train guards. This declined from 35,715 in 1951 to 15,642 in 1991. Even though these figures are approximations, they do suggest a quite dramatic fall in some of these occupations with secondary social control effects in public space, whilst policing, both private and public, has expanded.

The decline – and in some cases the almost complete disappearance – of each of these occupations is important in its own right, given the implications they have for both the perception and the reality of safety and security in local neighbourhoods, on buses and trains (and in bus and railway stations), and no doubt in other places too. It is the decline in such occupations that has been explicitly recognized and addressed by new forms of 'municipal' policing such as the employment of uniformed patrollers by some local authorities in Britain (see Johnston, 2000) and similar developments in the Netherlands (see Hauber *et al.*, 1996). Collectively, however, the very rapid transformation in this key set of occupations has, we believe, had an impact wider than simply the formalization of social control – important though that is. Though we have not the space to develop the argument here, it seems plausible to us that the marked decline of 'secondary social control occupations' that has taken place in England and Wales since the war is linked not only to changes in the formal policing division of labour, but is also implicated in the rise in levels of crime during the same period. In explaining the rapid rise in levels of reported crime over the past half century authors have focused on numerous changes in contemporary forms of (particularly urban) life: the unintended consequences of urban renewal (Jacobs, 1992); the dispersal of routine activities (Felson, 1998) , the rise of market society (Currie, 1997; Taylor, 1999) and the 'exclusionary' nature of late modernity (Young, 1999) , to list but a few. Each of these, in different ways, has something important to offer in our attempt to understand post-war social change. Yet each, in our view, would be enhanced if it also contained a focus on the important role played by the decline of secondary social control occupations in the period.

## Conclusion

In short, our argument here has three major elements. First, in our view, much current criminology tends to exaggerate the degree of change, and underplay the extent of continuity, in seeking to explain the transformations taking place in contemporary policing systems. More particularly, we are unsure to what extent it is realistic to present current developments as an 'epochal' change in policing.[4] Some of the changes are undeniably far-reaching. Consequently, it is understandable that commentators should wish to focus on what is novel. It is clearly the case that new institutional forms of policing, outside of nation state boundaries, are developing quickly. Similarly, both the form and content of public policing is changing (though perhaps less radically than some would have us believe), as is the commercial sector. Our concern is that in focusing on such changes, important as they are, it is all too easy to exaggerate their extent, either by failing to recognize the consistencies and continuities that exist, or by misrepresenting what it is supposed used to exist but is now disappearing (e.g. the mythical 'public monopoly' in policing).

Secondly, we are concerned that many current theoretical analyses of policing transformation pay insufficient attention to variation between nation states. Thus, for example, there is a tendency to assume that the changes (believed to be) taking place within North America are, in large part, identical to those affecting other developed economies. Whilst we accept that there are indeed some important commonalities and continuities, nonetheless there are also some extremely important points of departure: the nature, timing and reasons for the growth of the commercial security sector to name but three. To date such differences have remained largely resistant to academic scrutiny. In part, this is due to the relative absence of comparative research. In this regard, it is particularly ironic that we should be critical in this chapter of one of the few scholars in the policing field to have undertaken comparative analyses of policing systems: David Bayley. In such work he has talked persuasively of some of the general lessons that can be learned from policing systems around the world (e.g. Bayley, 1994). As we have suggested, we have no difficulty with Bayley and Shearing's proposition that there are some quite strong common elements to the changes taking place in policing systems in many developed economies. However, it is clearly also the case that not all countries exhibit the same degree of change in their policing systems. More importantly, in our view there is no inevitability about the future direction or degree of change that will affect policing systems in these countries. That is, we should not assume that the policing systems of different countries are all moving in the same direction for the same reasons.

Finally, it is our view that the set of changes taking place 'within' policing can profitably be set within a wider context. It is certainly the case that changes within one part of the 'policing division of labour' can, and do, have effects on other parts – and it is important for us to seek to develop an understanding of such changes. Nonetheless, there is we think a broader social transformation taking place (at least in the UK). It is our view that rather than seeing current changes simply as indicative of a process of fragmentation of policing, rather they are better viewed as part of a long-term process of formalization of social control. In particular, we highlighted in this chapter a shift that appears to have taken place between what we have termed *primary* and *secondary* social control activities. More particularly, there is clear evidence that during the last half century there has been a significant decline in certain key *secondary social control occupations*. It is this set of changes, we argue, at least as much as the changes affecting public policing bodies, that has had a profound impact on the size and visibility of commercial policing (and particularly guarding) sector. Moreover, we think it plausible that these important changes in the labour market have also played an important role in the rise in recorded crime rates since the Second World War.

*From Trevor Jones and Tim Newburn, 'The transformation of policing? Understanding current trends in policing systems*, British Journal of Criminology, *Vol. 42, no 1, 2002, pp 129–146.*

## Notes

1  We have noted a similar problem of ethnocentrism in the literature developments in private security (see Jones and Newburn, 1999).
2  Due to changes in occupational classifications and census estimates, these figures are approximations and should be taken as general indicators rather than exact measurements. However, the estimates for numbers of police officers compare reasonably well with official figures, and it is fair to say that these are currently the best available figures to examine change over time.
3  See, for example, what has happened recently to the probation service in England and Wales.
4  David Wall (1997: 225) notes how the discourse of transformation and 'new age policing' is far from new. It has emerged at various points during the history of policing in Britain, most notably during the early years of the twentieth century when police commentators envisaged the revolutionary impacts that new technologies would have upon the police role.

## References

Anderson, M., Den Boer, M., Cullen, P., Gilmore, W.C., Raab, C.D. and Walker, N. (1995), *Policing the European Union: Theory, Law and Practice.* Oxford: Clarendon Press.
Bayley, D. (1994), *Police for the Future.* Oxford: Oxford University Press.
Bayley, D. and Shearing, C. (1996), 'The Future of Policing', *Law and Society Review*, 30/3: 585–606.
Bittner, E. (1974), 'Florence Nightingale in Pursuit of Willie Sutton: A Theory of the Police', in H. Jacob, ed., *The Potential for Reform of Criminal Justice.* Newbury Park, CA: Sage.
Bittner, E. (1980), *The Function of the Police in Modern Society.* Cambridge, MA: Oelgeschlager, Gunn and Hain.
Bottoms, A.E. (1983), 'Neglected Features of Contemporary Penal Systems', in D. Garland and P. Young, eds., *The Power to Punish: Contemporary Penality and Social Analysis.* Aldershot: Ashgate.
Chatterton, M., Humphrey, C. and Watson, A.J. (1996), *On the Budgetary Beat.* London: Chartered Institute of Management Accountants.
Cohen, S. (1985), *Visions of Social Control.* Cambridge: Polity Press.
Critchley, T.A. (1967), *A History of Police in England anal Wales, 900–1966,* London: Constable.
Currie, E. (1997), 'Market, Crime and Community: Toward a Mid-Range Theory of Post Industrial Society', *Theoretical Criminology*, 1/2: 147–72.
Emsley, C. (1996), *The English Police: A Political and Social History.* Harlow: Longman.
Ericson, R. (1994), 'The Division of Expert Knowledge in Policing and Security', *British Journal of Sociology*, 45: 149–75.

Ericson, R. and Haggerty, K. (1997), *Policing the Risk Society*. Oxford: Clarendon Press.

Etzioni, A. (1993), *The Spirit of Community: Rights, Responsibilities and the Communitarian Agenda*. New York: Simon & Schuster.

Feeley, M. and Simon, J. (1992), 'The New Penology: Notes on the Emerging Strategy of Corrections and its Implications', *Criminology*, 30/4: 452–74.

Feeley, M. and Simon, J. (1996), 'Actuarial Justice: The Emerging New Criminal Law', in D. Nelken, ed., *The Futures of Criminology*. London: Sage.

Felson, M. (1998), *Crime and Everyday Life*. Thousand Oaks, CA: Pine Forge Press.

Garland, D. (1996), 'The Limits of the Sovereign State', *British Journal of Criminology'*, 36/4: 445–71.

Garland, D. (2000), 'The Culture of High Crime Societies: Some Preconditions of Recent "Law and Order" Policies', *British Journal of Criminology*, 40/3: 347–75.

Giddens, A. (1990), *The Consequences of Modernity*. Cambridge: Polity Press.

Hauber, A., Hofstra B., Toornvliet, L. and Zandbergen, A. (1996), 'Some New Forms of Functional Social Control in the Netherlands and their Effects', *British Journal of Criminology* 36/2:199–219.

Hunter, A. (1995), 'Private, Parochial and Public Social Orders: The Problem of Crime and Incivility in Urban Communities', in R. Kasinitz, ed., *Metropolis: Centre and Symbol of our Times*. Basingstoke: Macmillan.

Jacobs, J. (1992), *The Death and Life of Great American Cities*. New York: Vintage.

Johnston, L. (1992) , *The Rebirth of Private Policing*. London: Routledge.

Johnston, L. (1996), 'Policing Diversity: The Impact of the Public-Private Complex in Policing', in F. Leishman, B. Loveday and S. Savage, eds., *Core Issues in Policing*. Harlow: Longman.

Johnston, L. (2000), *Policing Britain: Risk, Security and Governance*. Harlow: Pearson Education.

Jones, T. and Newburn, T. (1997), *Policing after the Act: Police Governance after the Police and Magistrates' Courts Act 1994*. London: PSI.

Jones, T. and Newburn, T. (1998), *Private Security and Public Policing*. Oxford: Clarendon Press.

Jones, T. and Newburn, T. (1999a), 'Policing Public and Private Space in Late Modern Britain', in P. Carlen and R. Morgan, eds., *Crime Unlimited*. Basingstoke: Macmillan.

Jones, T. and Newburn, T. (1999b), 'Urban Change and Policing: Mass Private Property Reconsidered', *European journal on Criminal Policy and Research*, 7: 225–44.

Jones, T., Newburn, T. and Smith, D. (1994), *Democracy and Policing*. London: PSI.

Kakalik, J.S. and Wildhorn, S. (1972), *Private Police in the United States*, Rand Report, 4 vols. Washington: US Department of Justice.

Leon, C. (1991), Special Constables: Air Historical and Contemporary Survey, doctoral thesis. University of Bath School of Humanities and Social Sciences, unpublished.

Loader, I. (1999), 'Consumer Culture and the Commodification of Policing and Security', *Sociology*, 33/2: 373–92.

McLauchlin, E. and Murji, K. (1995), 'The End of Public Policing? Police Reform and the "New Managerialism" ', in L. Noaks, M. Levi and M. Maguire, eds., *Contemporary Issues in Criminology*. Cardiff: Cardiff University Press.

McManus, M. (1995), *From Fate to Choice: Private Bobbies, Public Beats*. Aldershot: Avebury.

Marx, G. (1988), *Undercover: Police Surveillance in America*. Berkeley, CA: University of California Press.

Noaks, L.. (2000), 'Private Cops on the Block: A Review of the Role of Private Security in Residential Communities', *Policing and Society*, 10: 143–61.

O'Malley, P. and Palmer, D. (1996), 'Post-Keynesian Policing', *Economy and Society*, 25/2: 137–55.

Putnam, R. D. (2000), *Bowling Alone: The Collapse and Revival of American Community*. New York: Simon and Schuster.

Reiner, R. (1992a), *The Politics of the Police*, 2nd edn. Hemel Hempstead: Harvester Wheatsheaf.

Reiner, R. (1992b), 'Policing a Postmodern Society', *Modern Law Review*, 55/6: 761–81.

Reiner, R. (1997), 'Policing and the Police', in M. Maguire, R. Morgan and R. Reiner, eds., *The Oxford Handbook of Criminology*. Oxford: Clarendon Press.

Sennett, R. (2000), *The Corrosion of Character: The Personal Consequences of Work in the New Capitalism*. New York: W.W. Norton and Co.

Shearing, C. and Stenning, P. (1987), 'Say Cheese! The Disney Order that is not so Mickey Mouse', in C. Shearing and P. Stenning, eds., Private Policing. Newbury Park, CA: Sage.

Sheptycki, J. (1997), 'Transnational Policing and the Makings of a Postmodern State', *British journal of Criminology*, 35/4: 613–35.

Smith, D.J. (1996), 'Explaining Crime Trends', in W. Saulsbury, J. Mott and T. Newburn, eds., *Themes in Contemporary Policing*. London: PSI.

Smith, M.J. and Clarke, R.V. (2000) 'Crime and public transport', in M. Tonry, (ed.), *Crime and Justice: A Review of Research*, Vol. 20, 169–233. Chicago: University of Chicago Press.

Taylor, H. (1999), 'Forging the Job: A Crisis of "Modernization" or Redundancy for the Police in England and Wales, 1900–39'. *British Journal of Criminology*, 39/1: 113–35.

Taylor, I. (1999), *Crime in Context: A Critical Criminology of Market Societies*. Cambridge: Polity Press.

Wall, D. (1997), 'Policing the Virtual Community: The Internet, Cyberspace and (Cyber–Crime', in P. Francis, P. Davies and V. Jupp, eds., *Policing Futures: The Police, Law Enforcement and the Twenty First Century*. Basingstoke: Macmillan.

Young, J. (1999), *The Exclusive Society*. London: Sage.

# 42. Women in control?

*Frances Heidensohn*

The answer to the question: 'are women now in control?' depends on the phrasing of it. There are women now quite widely employed and less widely deployed in positions of social control. Emphatically, however, they are not in charge of formal control agencies. Not yet anyway.

[...] When posing questions about what Stan Cohen calls 'visions of social control', it is also essential to ask 'whose are the visions?' Cohen seems to suggest that only the powerful seek to establish and maintain order in society. Or rather he, along with a number of other scholars who have explored the history of 'social-control policy' (Cohen, 1985: 15), are vague or coy about who exactly has brought about the historical transformations in the master patterns of deviancy control. There is a distinct lack of a 'sense of agency', of conscious actors and their complex and contradictory decisions (Ignatieff's study is an interesting exception, 1978). There are large sociological and historical issues which can be debated at length here.

As far as this discussion is concerned, I wish only to point out how the history and development of the participation of some women in the control process in two nations can illuminate both the debates and the concept itself. Women's roles have changed and grown. In the nineteenth century, groups of women took part increasingly in a range of activities to do with social control. Notably, they pursued and ran campaigns to change laws, alter public opinion, provide welfare and improve moral standards. They joined and often founded voluntary bodies which dispensed a variety of services as well as inventing an array of organizations and structures to do so. Much of this effort was produced by upper-class and middle-class women and directed at their poorer counterparts among the working class and the destitute. But it is dangerous to over-simplify. Working-class women also took part in missionary and welfare work and while clients could object to their treatment, they also praised what today seems 'maternalism' (Hahn Rafter, 1983).

Women increasingly sought, won, and created wider roles for themselves in informal social control. They also became frustrated at their lack of political and formal powers. Their entry into policing was, initially, one aspect of campaigns to enhance their powers to protect themselves and their own sex. It was at once an expansionist and a protectionist move.

Since that early twentieth-century epoch, only two other steps of significance have been taken. First, women have a wider share and larger stake in the considerable range of control agencies which now exist. Secondly, they have been assimilated into the major institutions of formal control, although in some as a mere token presence. At this stage it remains an open question whether another breakthrough will ever occur. Whether, for instance, women will ever comprise half or more of a large police force, or indeed a government. It is not even clear that these are the goals of any group of women. Where there are groups dedicated to expanding women's role in such ways, they are much more likely to be aiming, still, at what can be called entryism and influence, not supremacy or dominance.

While this theme must remain in doubt there are at least two important conclusions to be drawn in this area. If women have, as I have argued, so long sought to be part of the social-control process, including its most 'masculine' apparatus, then notions about the oppression of women in our society have to be redrawn, or at least modified. Simple notions of patriarchal oppression are already heavily criticized (Scraton, 1990; Sumner, 1990). Even if we conclude that female 'controllers' are ineffective in the face of massed male power, we still need to understand their persistence in seeking such positions and their insistence that they are not ineffective but do in fact find and develop their own strategies and skills.

Such observations have wide implications. There have, for instance, been considerable debates about women in relation to the criminal-justice systems of both the USA and Britain in recent years (Smart, 1977; Heidensohn, 1985, 1986; Morris, 1987; Daly, 1989). These have focused on two main themes: on 'chivalry' and on victimization. The 'chivalry' debate concerns the degree to which the police, courts, and other agencies can be said to 'protect' women from the consequences of their own criminal behaviour. While some contributions (e.g. Eaton, 1986) do consider whether the agent was male or female, many do not. Yet it should obviously be an important aspect of such studies to find out whether sex makes any difference on either side.

As far as victimization is concerned, this too has been over-simplified in some accounts as a matter of gendered oppression. Again this view has been gradually modified as more attention is given to female offenders (Allen, 1986) and especially their use of violence (Heidensohn, 1991b; A. Jones, 1991; McDonald, 1991). What has hardly been considered at all in this context is the *legitimate* use of physical force or even violence by women. Women, as Stanko has tirelessly pointed out (1990a, 1990b), are not merely passive victims of violence. They work out strategies of avoidance and resistance. Sometimes they fight back.

[...] Can [such violence] constitute legitimate self-defence? English law defines 'provocation' in ways which appear to put women at a disadvantage and 'disallows' their strategies. The relevance of this study to such highly-charged topics is to add some information to some of the wider considerations of context. Laws in such situations are very culturally bound. They and their interpretations are based on premises about 'reasonable men' (*sic*). What is lacking from much of the surrounding debate is an awareness that legitimate use of force and violence by women has been extremely constrained and that this may be changing. Men, for instance, may box and wrestle and indulge in contact sports barred to women or socially taboo to them. That police and other women have learnt to handle many kinds of encounters is a dimension which should be added to this debate.

The key image of control in Foucault's work is the carceral archepelago, the remote gulag, cut off from society and the body politic. In Cohen's 'vision' it is more strikingly a net as well as a city. The net tangles and binds, entwining the deviant in its ever-widening meshes. Impressive and seductive as these are as metaphors for worrying features of contemporary problems, I find great difficulties with them [...]. Both seem flawed, even in their own terms, because both describe something more sweeping and oppressive, a true juggernaut, inexorably flattening all before it, a cross between a huge tank and an iron.

[...] Women, often the focus of some of the most oppressive features of society, and nearly always the poorest and least powerful members of it, have sometimes chosen to resist and, occasionally, succeeded. They have also sought to join, change, and share in the agencies concerned. Although they have succeeded in doing all these, it is not clear even now that they are wholly accepted in these roles. Rather, it seems that the current male employees may voice values and beliefs which preclude women's membership, or only on terms set by the former. Most theorists of social control see it as controlled by élite groups for their own ends, almost never by men for theirs. Nor do they generally see the processes of control as the subject of interaction and negotiation. This again is obviously because it makes a great difference if one considers issues about the maintenance of order in terms of sex differences instead, for example, of class differences. It then becomes obvious that some women, at least, have considerable stakes in improving order, or more precisely in curbing the disorder of males. It might be helpful to rethink the problem of what I have called the male ownership of order in the light of this. In other words, what shapes the strong resistance to female police may be a reluctance to share power over order; it may also, and at the same time, be an unwillingness to allow women to police male *disorder*.

## Gender and control

'Gender', as in 'gender studies', 'sociology of gender', is quite often nowadays used instead of women. As Pateman sharply puts it: 'the term gender is now ubiquitous but frequently lies idle, used merely as an often not very apt synonym for women' (1988: 225). In other words, only women are perceived as having, or being, a gender, even though the whole point of the concept is that it expresses a duality; masculinity, and femininity are described in terms of their difference. One is nearly meaningless without the other.

One of the few authors to take such issues seriously and to attempt both an analysis of 'gender order' and to propose strategies for altering it, begins by focusing on power, particularly as demonstrated in both legitimate and illegal forms. 'The main axis of the power structure of gender is the general connection of authority with masculinity,' but, 'the authority of men is not spread in an even blanket across every department of social life.' Specifically, 'there is a "core" in the power structure of gender' and this in advanced capitalist societies consists *inter alia* of 'the hierarchies and work forces of institutionalized violence –

military and paramilitary forces, police, prison systems' (Connell, 1987: 109). Other parts of the 'core' include heavy industry and the state and most crucially 'working class milieux that emphasize physical toughness and men's association with machinery' (Connell, 1987: 109). It is central to Connell's thesis that gender power relations have changed considerably in modern capitalist societies, with traditional domestic patriarchy being displaced 'by masculinities organized much more around technical rationality and calculation' (1987: 131).

While he consistently stresses the importance of history and of the social construction of gender order, Connell does not provide an entirely satisfactory explanation of what he calls 'a central fact', that of 'the control of the means of violence by some men rather than by any women' (1987: 153). He offers a partial answer by insisting that, while state apparatuses can be oppressive of women, as indeed can other institutional forms, nevertheless

> the main objects of physical repression are men … The state both institutionalizes hegemonic masculinity and expends great energy in controlling it. The objects of repression, e.g. criminals, are generally younger men themselves in the practice of violence, with a social profile quite like that of the immediate agents of repression, the police or the soldiers. (1987: 128)

We have, of course, already seen many times that this is a distorted view of policing, albeit one often supported by many police officers and enshrined in the traditional police culture. In this subtle and thoughtful study, Connell does not explore these contradictions fully, but he does extend the debate considerably by stressing the variety and 'historicity' of gender and gender roles. Modern societies are, he argues, more dominated by gender relations than many communities were in the past or than they need to be.

He concludes with proposed strategies for changing gender order, considering both the abolition of gender and 'its reconstitution on new bases'. The second is his preference, even though he acknowledges that 'a great deal of our culture's energy and beauty, as well as its barbarism, has been created through and around gender relations' (1987: 288). Radical alliances will be, he argues, the bases for this restructuring as they have to some extent already become. Connell's is an important study because he does try both to question many assumptions about gender as well as to explain their origins. This approach certainly provides a framework for further exploration but it does not provide some key answers […]. Yet he does provide some key guide-lines, albeit only sketchily, in his presentation of the state and the street as areas of most pronounced masculine dominance of males and hence, presumably, the insistence on excluding women. What Connell does not have scope to explore are the tantalizing questions about why, when women have been incorporated into many activities, their participation has so fiercely been resisted here. These issues must remain, for the present, as addressed but not explained. They await further exploration.

While there have been some attempts, then, to redress this in studying men and masculinity, these have not yet gone very far in areas such as the study of social control. Pieces of a mosaic are already revealed but layers of sand conceal the rest. I think it possible, for example, and timely to advance a series of propositions about gender and control which would be worth testing and exploring.

The first is that gender divisions are central to social control, indeed perhaps their most integral and abiding features. The behaviour most completely learnt, and adhered to is that of sex roles. These are also the most fully underpinned by informal sanctions and support. Take, for instance, the argument that much of the delinquent activity of adolescent males is just 'natural' masculine exuberance.

This is not, of course, to say that gender is rigid and that no one ever deviates from prescribed roles. Neither proposition is true. Indeed, ideas of appropriately masculine and feminine behaviour have altered during the past two centuries. Such alterations do not always occur in a symmetrical fashion. For instance, femininity, it can be argued, has expanded for most of the present century without many comparable shifts in notions of masculinity. Dress codes for women, for instance, now include in western societies almost every possible type of clothing once thought masculine. Hence, [...] the unisex (i.e. men's) uniform worn by all US police officers. Men are still subject to a narrower range of acceptable wear so that male nurses, for example, do not wear 'female' clothing.

As I trust this instance shows, I am *not* arguing that institutionalized sexism is ubiquitous in agencies of the criminal-justice system. (Gelsthorpe (1989) has shown that this is not the case.) Rather, I suggest that gender divisions are universal and that they form part of the processes of control. Their various interactions are complex but profound. Thus all societies regulate sexuality and have rules about gender-appropriate sexual behaviour. While women may face heavier sanctions for breaking some rules – prostitutes are more likely than their clients to be punished – there are exceptions. Male homosexuality has been more rigorously controlled than female in western societies.

If gender is a feature of control, it follows that changes in gender roles have consequences for control agencies. That is clearly what happened in the early twentieth century in our example of women in policing. Women began to use a new freedom in a very conventionally masculine institution. What many of the women really wished to confront was the double standard of morality for men and women upheld by just such agencies. It is hardly surprising that entry proved problematic.

My second proposition is that social control is itself likely to be gendered. By this I mean that the social-control system, or the agencies which form parts of it, may have forms or styles, as well as personnel, which are gendered. I agree with Tamar Pitch, for instance, that social control in a number of post-war western societies has become 'feminized'. This means that certain organizations and issues have operated in less confrontational, less informal, and more negotiated ways. There is an ocean of research on the police which suggests that their culture is overwhelmingly masculine. This is unfortunately kept as a land-locked mass of water. It is not on the whole suggested that the system might change. Indeed much effort has gone into pointing out how functional it is.

While it may be difficult and perhaps even inappropriate to argue against individual agencies, such as the police, being gendered, I suggest that serious issues are raised by the predominance of one or other gender in the system as a whole. Amongst the most important of these are representative bureaucracy, effectiveness, and legitimacy. Any control agency will have difficulties if its staff do not 'represent' the local community. Moreover, if they do not draw on all that community's talents, they will be less effective. This was long seen at its most absurd in the height requirements of Anglo-American policing, which only gave the selectors choice among tall men. Most crucial of all these is legitimacy. Significantly, the police's legitimacy has diminished with some groups in modern times and it is especially clear that women are wary of the criminal-justice system and have lost faith in its ability to protect them from crime and its consequences.

Too often in sociological analysis, gender is equated with sex-role stereotype. Narrow, rigid definitions of gender are assumed to be predominant and even inevitable. But this is not an essential feature of modern society; on the contrary, flexibility and change are possibly and surely desirable. Stereotypes simplify but they can also cause atrophy and fossilization. Gender stereotypes, for example, seem to lie at the heart of some troublesome deviant behaviour, such as domestic violence and football hooliganism. It would seem fairly obvious that such problems can only be touched by the pooling of all kinds of gendered or neutral responses.

Just to give one example. It was policy for quite a long time in Britain to subject young male delinquents to the rigorous penal discipline of a quasi-military kind (Manning, 1985, ed.). It was gradually realized, however, that their treatment was unsuitable and, in this form at least, it ceased. What has hardly happened yet is the full logical continuance of this pattern. If the socialization of girls is apparently so much more successful than that of boys, then surely something might be learned from how they are prepared for the world and life.

## Towards the future

[...]

Some feminists have expressed anxieties about women in positions of control (Enloe, 1988; Cain, 1991). The key to their argument is that power corrupts, or indeed it is already corrupted by its associations and women should have nothing to do with it. Enloe argues this with particular force about the military (1988), but Cain has also suggested it in relation to such people as social workers.

Other writers on such themes have tackled much broader criticisms. Stiehm has, for instance, argued strongly for a larger role for women in the military. She suggests that 'Speculation would be fruitful, too. What if women were given the Air Force and the other three services were left to men?' (1989: 237). Her purpose is both to challenge existing policies on the recruitment and deployment of women in the USA military on rational and democratic grounds and also to challenge feminists who reject women's participation. In doing so she asks a series of provoking questions which are highly relevant to women's role in policing and in other agencies:

Questions asked about women should also be asked about men ... it might be ... valuable to reflect on men's disability – their apparent incapacity to assimilate women or even to accommodate to their presence. I would recommend a shift to the investigation of *men's* limitations and to the study of the military as a male, rather than a human, or national institution. (1989: 239; original emphasis)

Stiehm argues that these are key problems that feminists, as well as military men, must engage with: 'this is intellectual work that *women* must engage in because men are invisible to most men qua men' (1989: 241; original emphasis). Much of what Stiehm has to say about women in the military can be said with even greater force about policing and related activities. Policemen and women are officers of the *peace* by title and convention; in practice their daily routine comprises much that is mundane and peaceable: only occasionally do violence and drama intrude. The relevance of Stiehm's challenging approach is that she accepts nothing as given even in the most unconventional, non-traditional of occupations for women. Following this course in considering gender and control enables us too to consider the unthinkable.

Earlier [In this book] I cited M. Young's suggestion to a group of colleagues that there was no logical reason why the existing male/female ratios could not be reversed (i.e. about 10,000 men and 111,000 women' (1991: 234). Young notes first their 'blank response' and later 'a worried ... "[that] would mean changing not just the police but the whole of the world ..." ' (1991: 234). He concludes that there are still 'substantial barriers' to surmount and, rather disappointingly, goes on to resurrect other very old friends 'the drunks and the disagreeable' (1991: 235) as evidence of female limitations. What would have been much more stimulating would have been Young's own considered response to his point.

After all, [...] there are no rational reasons why men should dominate policing, nor so totally dominate formal social control. They are widely judged not to being doing it very well and to be getting worse. Since they are themselves the sex more likely to be involved in delinquency and crime there are good *a priori* grounds for *not* preferring them.

Now, I am not proposing Young's sex role reversal as a serious future plan. It does, however, provide a valuable vignette to explore some important issues about gender and control. Should one group, men, so dominate policing, and in such a masculine way? What are the consequences to society of their doing so? What would happen if their freehold ceased? The *Guardian* newspaper once suggested that the police should be recruited from among the nation's grand-mothers. This may seem bizarre, but the 'new police' themselves were a peculiar and contested innovation when they first patrolled the streets of London.

Going back to first principles, of primary assumptions at least, in an exercise like this lets us examine just what is central about our notions of control and what is historical accumulation. It is obvious that there is far more of the second than the first. This brings us right back to some aspects of the postmodern condition [...] Ours is a contingent and somewhat arbitrary world in which it is encouraging to find patterns and trends and to do so should always be accompanied by wariness. [...] I have tried to suggest that, within a large-scale masculine-gendered control enterprise, women have established their own activities against all the odds, and sustained them. The question now is: what happens next?

It is possible to reply in two ways. There is a neat list of points to be made about policy and policy changes. [Comparing] British and American experience is highly illuminating on this topic. The American approach is more open to development, more soundly based, and more confident. At its best it is exemplary and shows what can be done with class actions, affirmative action, and conditionally allocated government funds. British experience reveals that one can get quite a long way without most of these, but this also suggests that therefore far more might be achieved with a good mixture of the two.

At the most fundamental and yet highly symbolic level, US experience shows that women and men can wear the same uniforms without a massive breakdown in public order. British experience shows that women officers do not need guns as 'equalizers'. There are, however, much wider issues to face.

Policing, and social control generally, could become much more neutral, or more gender neutral. Police forces of the twenty-first century might not only be more genuinely mixed, they might also be far less macho in culture. There are serious questions to consider here as the policing of more plural and complex societies emerges as a difficult and threatening political conundrum. Should police officers, to reverse an ancient cliché, be recruited so young? Indeed, higher educational requirements in both societies are increasing age at entry already.

A second possible scenario is that control agencies continue along, or are even enforced on, gender-divided lines. A butch police force will still pursue its enquiries along its freemasonic lines. On separate, diverging lines will be other agencies. These will be, like social work, nursing, and education, 'feminine' professions, and they will all have to work on numerous social problems in uneasy multi-agency alliances. They will certainly misunderstand each other often, and co-operation of a few staff will be seen as sell-out by their colleagues. Such a plural solution may be preferable to a more total, corporate, and integrated approach.

A final version of the future might be embodied in gender-segregated institutions for the *clients* of control. Abolition of prisons for women, for instance, has been advocated several times in the late twentieth century (Heidensohn, 1975; Carlen, 1990). While there could hardly be such polarity in other parts of the criminal-justice system, there could certainly be some polarizing in such services. Most pressures to criminalize certain actions will bring more *men* into contact with formal control: such as rape in marriage, wife-beating, child sex abuse, even serious fraud. Male homosexual behaviour might be targeted again as moral panic rises about AIDS and HIV infection. In a dystopian future, this could lead to gender-segregated services in which men man those for the burgeoning numbers of males, or women do so because of their supposed lack of moral taint.

In short, in order to prepare for the future we need to think carefully about what legacies we shall carry forward into it and what we can safely discard. It is an unwise sociologist who tries to foresee the future. Nevertheless; I should like to venture one prediction. […]. As the nineteenth century turned into the twentieth century groups of women took a new place for themselves within the systems of control of two societies. These movements linked and learned from each other.

Much of the motivation which kept them alive over several decades was deep dissatisfaction with the world in which they lived, 'protected' by the stronger, superior sex. They knew all too well the realities of poverty, neglect, abuse, beatings, and double standards. They tried to protect their own sex and to remake society in a more moral fashion,

As another century ends there are clear signs of another era of deep concern among and for women about the moral state of society and how this specifically affects them. It is women who fear crime most. They are the victims of beatings, abuse, and sexual crimes. Men suffer these things too. There is, however, a major difference. Moral symmetry is lacking. Women are beaten and attacked. With relatively few exceptions they do not abuse and attack. Some of the conditions, therefore, for female-led moral protest and protection exist in both Britain and the USA at the end of the twentieth century as they did at its beginning. It might very well not happen. Women are not much more in control at this stage [...]. They are, however, much freer, have greater economic and political power, and are already inside, if not on top of, key control agencies. Women are not in control. They might begin to ask men why.

*From Frances Heidensohn*, Women in Control? The role of women in law enforcement *(Oxford: Oxford University Press), 1992, pp 237–249.*

## References

Allen, H. (1986), *Justice Unbalanced* (Open University Press: Buckingham).

Cain, M. (1991), Paper Delivered to International Feminist Conference on Women, Law, and Social Control (Montreal).

Carlen, P. (1990), *Alternatives to Women's Imprisonment* (Open University Press: Buckingham).

Cohen, S. (1985), *Visions of Social Control* (Polity Press: Oxford).

Cohen, S. and Scull, A. (1983) (eds.), *Social Control and the State* (Blackwell: Oxford).

Connell, R.W. (1987), *Gender and Power* (Polity Press: Cambridge).

Daly, K. (1989), 'Criminal Justice Ideologies and Practices in Different Voices: Some Feminist Questions about Justice', *International Journal of the Sociology of Law*, 17: 1–18.

Eaton, M. (1986), *Justice for Women?* (Open University Press: Buckingham).

Enloe, C. (1988), *Does Khaki Become You?* (Pandora: London).

Gelsthorpe, L. (1989), *Sexism and the Female Offender* (Gower: Aldershot).

Gelsthorpe, L. and Morris, A. (1990) (eds.), *Feminist Perspectives in Criminology* (Open University Press: Buckingham).

Hahn Rafter, N. (1983), 'Chastizing the Unchaste: Social Control Functions of a Women's Reformatory 1894–31', in Cohen and Scull (1983) (eds.).

Heidensohn, F. (1975), 'The Imprisonment of Females', in S. McConville (1975) (ed.), *The Use of Imprisonment* (Routledge: London).

Heidensohn, F. (1985), *Women and Crime* (Macmillan: London).

Heidensohn, F. (1986), 'Models of Justice: Portia or Persephone? Some Thoughts on Equality, Fairness and Gender in the Field of Criminal Justice', *International Journal of the Sociology of Law*, 14.

Heidensohn, F. (1991*b*), 'Sociological Perspectives on Female Violence', paper given at Conference on perspectives on Female Violence, St George's Hospital Medical School, London.

Ignatieff, M. (1978), *A Just Measure of Pain* (Pantheon: New York).

Jones, A. (1991), *Women who Kill* (Gollancz: London).

McDonald, E. (1991), *Shoot the Women First* (Fourth Estate: London).

Manning, N. (1985) (ed.), *Social Problems and Welfare Ideology* (Gower: Aldershot).

Morris, A. (1987), *Women, Crime and Criminal Justice* (Blackwell: Oxford).

Pateman, C. (1988), *The Sexual Contract* (Polity Press: Cambridge).

Scraton, P. (1990), 'Scientific Knowledge or Masculine Discourses? Challenging Patriarchy in Criminology', in Gelsthorpe and Morris (1990) (eds.).

Smart, C. (1977), *Women, Crime and Criminology* (Routledge: London).

Stanko, E. (1990a), *Everyday Violence* (Pandora: London).

Stanko, E. (1990b), 'When Precaution is Normal: A Feminist Critique of Crime Prevention' in Gelsthorpe and Morris (1990) (eds.).

Stiehm, J. (1989), *Arms and the Enlisted Woman* (Temple Univ. Press: Philadelphia).

Sumner, C. (1990), 'Foucault, Gender and the Censure of Deviance', in Gelsthorpe and Morris (1990) (eds.).

Young, M. (1991), *An Inside Job* (Clarendon Press: Oxford).

# 43. The new surveillance

*Gary T. Marx*

> Everywhere the State acquires more and more direct control over the humblest members of the community and a more exclusive power of governing each of them in his smallest concerns. This gradual weakening of the individual in relation to society at large may be traced to a thousand things. (Alexis de Tocqueville, 1835)

> Discovery and invention have made it possible for the government, by means far more effective than stretching upon the rack, to obtain disclosure in court of what is whispered in the closet. (Justice Louis Dembitz Brandeis, 1928)

When I began this research, I was skeptical about the desirability of undercover tactics on specific as well as on general grounds. As applied to the political cases of the 1960s, there was much to be concerned about. Abuses were widespread. Beyond this, the spread of undercover means seemed to represent one more example of the extension of state power feared by Alexis de Tocqueville and later social theorists.

Over the course of the research, my skepticism regarding the tactic itself softened, even as my concern over the general issues raised by Tocqueville increased. It became clear that, given the American context, covert means were sometimes the best means. Furthermore, the recent overall record of such federal agencies as the FBI, BATF, and IRS suggests that (with appropriate preparation and controls) problems could be held to an acceptable level. However, I reached this conclusion reluctantly. At best, in a democratic society, it will never be possible to be too enthusiastic about undercover operations. There is always the risk of becoming overconfident and insensitive to the dangers that literally and figuratively lurk beneath the surface. Something of the caution and respect for danger that characterize professional explorers and adventurers is needed. Once one ceases to doubt the difficulty of the challenge, becomes complacent, and loses any fear, problems are more likely.

The study of undercover police is ultimately about much more than cops and robbers: it is one strand of the new surveillance. Powerful new information-gathering technologies are extending ever deeper into the social fabric and to more features of the environment. Like the discovery of the atom or the unconscious, new control techniques surface bits of reality that were previously hidden or didn't contain informational clues. People are in a sense turned inside out, and what was previously invisible or meaningless is made visible and meaningful. This may involve space-age detection devices that give meaning to physical emanations based on the analysis of heat, light, pressure, motion, odor, chemicals, or physiological process, as well as the new meaning given to visible individual characteristics and behavior when they are judged relative to a predictive profile based on aggregate data.

## Recent developments

### Human informers

Perhaps most clearly related to undercover means, though less costly, is informing. In what amounts to a break with eighteenth- and nineteenth-century American attitudes, informing is now seen as an element of good citizenship, commanding growing institutional and technical support.

Federal cabinet agencies, for example, now provide hotlines for the reporting of instances of 'fraud, abuse, and waste'. Protection for whistle blowers has increased. The Federal Witness Protection Program provides relocation and a new identity to informers.

Programs, such as TIP (Turn In a Pusher), are found in hundreds of communities. Connecticut has a 'turn in a poacher' program, and Seattle encourages motorists to dial 734-HERO to report persons wrongfully driving in expressway lanes reserved for carpools and buses. WeTIP Inc., a private organization that counts large corporations among its clients, offers a nationwide hotline for reporting suspicious activities that employees are hesitant to report locally.

A Texas police sergeant who coordinates a successful crime-reporting program was quoted as saying that 'we get husbands turning in wives, wives turning in husbands – we've even had mothers turn in their sons'. In 1986 the presidential-led war on drugs not only saw parents turning in their children, but children turning in their parents (a drug hotline in Boston averaged twelve such calls a day).[1] There are also more generalized forms of informing: one sheriff's department gives out leaflets that ask, 'Do you know something the sheriff should know?'

### Computers as informers

The scale of human informing is, however, dwarfed by electronic informers and blacklists. The gigantic data banks made possible by computers raise important surveillance questions. Many basic facts are well known. Credit card companies, airlines, hotels, and car rental agencies record what we spend, where we went and how long we stayed. Health records are increasingly computerized, and more than nine out of ten working Americans have individual or group health insurance policies; pharmacies have begun to keep computerized records of patients' drug use and health characteristics; individual financial transactions increasingly involve electronic tellers and electronic check and credit card authorization; electronic funds transfer has become central to banking. Cashless transactions (electronic funds transfer at point of sale) are an increasing percentage of all sales. The size and reach of criminal justice data bases, such as the FBI's National Criminal Justice Information Center, continue to grow.[2] Marketing firms collect demographic, consumption, and life-style data on practically the entire population.

Computers qualitatively alter the nature of surveillance – routinizing, broadening, and deepening it. Organizational memories are extended over time and across space. Rather than focusing on an isolated individual at one point in time and on static demographic data, such as date of birth, surveillance increasingly involves complex transactional analysis, interrelating persons and events (for instance, the timing of phone calls, travel, and bank deposits).[3]

A thriving new computer-based, data-scavenging industry now sells information gleaned from such sources as drivers' licenses, vehicle- and voter-registration lists, birth, marriage, and death certificates, land deeds, telephone and organizational directories, court records, and census-tract records. Bits of scattered information that in the past did not threaten the individual's privacy and anonymity now can be joined.

There is a proliferation of generally unregulated data base services that landlords, doctors, employers, and others can consult (for a fee, of course) to check on prospective renters, patients, and employees, usually without their knowledge. Prospective employers, for example, can check on everything from an individual's political activism to the filing of worker-production claims. Such data bases often contain errors, outdated information, and information that is open to different interpretations. However, our lives are increasingly shaped by them. The chance to obtain basic needs and services such as medical care, insurance, housing, jobs, bank loans, and credit is conditioned by our 'data image' in remote computer files.[4]

It is possible to purchase address lists on a vast array of people presorted into categories such as 'bank credit card holders', 'gay businesses and organizations', 'conch soup buyers', 'antinuclear power contributors/activists', and subscribers to the 'Sex Over Forty Newsletter'.

The government's use of computer matching and profiling has come into increased prominence in the past decade.[5] Matching involves the comparison of information from two or more distinct data sources. In the U.S., hundreds of computer matching programs are routinely carried out by government at state and federal levels. The matching done by private interests is far more extensive. Profiling involves an indirect and inductive logic. Often, clues are sought that will increase the probability of discovering violations. A number of distinct data items are correlated in order to assess how close a person or event comes to a pre-determined model of known violations or violators, or desirable or undesirable applicants. Predictive profiles for letting people into, or out of, systems are increasingly used and rarely subject to public validation or criticism. Decisions are made about persons not as unique individuals or on the basis of their current behavior, but as a result of their membership in a statistical category with a given probability of behaving a certain way in the future.

A common form of matching involves randomly or categorically checking persons and property (such as cars) against various official or unofficial watch and wanted lists, or against more general profiles, such as those believed to be characteristic of drug couriers. An example of such matching is practiced by the large Treasury Enforcement Communication System (TECs), encountered by people leaving or entering the country when their passport information is entered into the computer at the immigration checkpoint. Another example involves the various data bases that make up the National Crime Information Center, most notably its extensive collection of arrest records.

Matching may involve comparing data bases, for example, bank records with welfare records to see if recipients have hidden income. The Selective Service, in addition to making use of drivers' license records in each state, purchased an ice-cream chain's 'birthday club' list and compared this to its list of draft registrants to search for young men who had not registered. In one match that yielded little, boat ownership records in Hawaii were compared against lists of those receiving food stamps.

The IRS generated public controversy when it sought to buy commercially compiled lists that direct-marketing companies use to target customers. The goal was to identify tax violators by correlating their tax returns with income estimates based on such factors as car model owned and census tract characteristics.

Both political and technical developments have encouraged the spread of computer matching. The 1974 Privacy Act passed under the guidance of the late Senator Sam Ervin included a 'routine use' provision for data collected by the federal government. This was intended to prohibit the government from collecting information for one purpose and using it for an unrelated reason. But since 1980 the executive branch has claimed that there is a generalized government interest in any information that happens to be in the federal domain, that is, data collected for a certain purpose may be used for any purpose. The meaning of 'routine use' has been severely stretched.

In addition, the 1984 Budget Deficit Reduction Act now requires states to correlate tax, medical, and social security records in order to receive federal funds for social funds for social welfare programs. This is likely to be extended to any recipient of government benefits, for example, student loans and veteran's benefits. The 1986 tax law requires all children over the age of 5 to obtain a social security number if they are to be claimed as dependents.[6]

Matching also has been facilitated by computer networking. The spread of microcomputers and computer-based communication devices makes record linkage easy to do, but difficult to control. The files to be compared need no longer be on the same computer, and the distinction between physically separate data bases has been blurred. Distributed data processing is making the notion of the single, isolated data bank obsolete.

From the mid-1960s to the early 1970s, Congress – expressing historic American concerns – rejected plans for the creation of a mammoth national data bank. Instead, agencies were to create separate, unrelated files. But recent technical developments have facilitated an end run around the political process. Unique identifiers, such as one's social security number, are not needed to forge links among distinct personal data bases because available software easily permits linking records based on a configuration of common elements, such as the same name, address, and date of birth. There is *de facto* integration of many data bases.

With the low-visibility integration of previously distinct bodies of information, computer matching can centralize authority and eliminate organizational boundaries and checkpoints.

In the near future individuals may become carriers of all their records. A computer chip could be embedded in the skin or, as is currently done in the military, in a tag worn around the neck. A wallet-sized 'smart card' embedded with a chip that can contain up to 800 pages of personal information is now being tested.

### Visual and audio surveillance

The sensing chip for a video camera (unlike the traditional glass lens) requires an opening no bigger than a pinhole. Video cameras can be concealed in walls and other objects, such as picture frames, mannequins, books, and attaché cases. An advertisement promises that, 'When you carry this ordinary-looking briefcase, you're really videotaping everything that occurs … The pinhole lens is virtually invisible, and there's still plenty of room inside the case for papers, etc.' A tiny hand-held video camera the size of a deck of cards is available. The cameras that monitor the interior of many stores are often inside ceiling globes that are capable of complete 360-degree movement. Amber or mirrored surfaces hide where the camera is aimed. A video-scanning device can be placed at roads or bridges to check license plates automatically against those in a data base; at the same time, a picture of a vehicle's occupants can be taken. A video camera exists that can distinguish guards from intruders, and there are efforts to develop one that can identify particular people in a crowd.

'Mini-awacs' that can spot a car or a person from 30,000 feet up have been used for surveillance of drug traffickers. Conversely, a hidden lens can be installed in aircraft as a security device that makes it possible for monitors on the ground to see and hear activity in the plane up to 200 miles away. Satellite photography from 180 miles up (a telescope is aimed back at the earth) has been used for 'domestic coverage' to determine the size and activities of antiwar demonstrations and civil disorders. Computer-enhanced satellite photography can identify vehicles moving in the dark and detect camouflage.

The 'starlight scope' light amplifier developed for the Vietnam War can be used with a variety of film and video cameras or binoculars. It needs only starlight, a partial moon, or a street lamp 500 yards away. When it amplifies light 85,000 times, night turns into day. Unlike earlier infrared devices, it gives off no telltale glow. The light amplifier can be mounted on a tripod or worn as goggles. Attached to a telescopic device, its range is over a mile.

There have been equivalent advances in the detection of sound: lasers and parabolic microphones that, when aimed at a window, permit eavesdropping without the necessity of entering the physical premises; low-level microwaves aimed from outside a building at small cone-shaped metal cavities or steel reinforcing rods hidden in a wall also use sound-wave vibrations for remote eavesdropping; a voice-activated, refrigerator-sized tape machine that can record up to 40 phone conversations at once; and subminiature tape recorders the size of a matchbox. Tiny transmitters can be hidden in clocks, hooks, picture frames, table legs, electric toothbrushes, and umbrellas.

New forms of communication are technically easy to intercept absent special, expensive precautions. The transmission of phone communications in digital form via microwave relays and satellites, cellular automobile and cordless telephones using radio waves for transmissions, and communication between computers offer new possibilities for eavesdropping.[7] Even most conventional telephones are potentially 'hot on the hook'. They can be easily wired so that the microphone in the telephone sends voice signals to a terminal, even when the phone is not in use. Using relatively inexpensive technology the image seen on most unprotected computer screens can be reproduced a mile away without ever gaining access to the premises where the computer is. Even electronic type-writers can be bugged so that a unique electrical signal for each letter typed is transmitted and reproduced elsewhere.

Surveillance of workers on assembly lines, in offices, and in stores has become much more comprehensive with computerized electronic measures.[8] Factory outputs and mistakes can be counted more easily and work pace, to a degree, controlled. Much has been written of the electronic office, where the data-processing machine serves both as a work tool and monitoring device. A bank vice president responsible for workers who code credit card data states, 'I measure everything that moves'.

Software developments permit management to document the activities of anyone using the company computer systems – without the user's knowledge. With a program called CNTRL, managers can observe on their own screen all input entered by the employee and all output from the computer to the user's terminal as it occurs. Subliminal messages can also be sent. One such program called 'The Messenger' can be called up by the VDT operator. Images of mountains and streams are displayed along with subliminal messages, such as 'My world is calm'. More ominous are subliminal programs that the worker may have no knowledge of or control over.[9]

Automatic telephone switching technology can record when, where, to whom, and for how long a call is made, regardless of whether it is long distance or to another extension within the same organization.[10] Phone systems designed as intercoms or paging devices allow managers to listen to conversations in other offices without being detected. Phone and computer monitoring is a condition of work in an increasing number of telecommunications, word processing, pro-gramming, and customer service occupations.

The National Security Agency uses 2,000 staffed interception posts through-out the world, satellites, aircraft, and ships to monitor electronic communication from and to the United States.[11] Its computer system permits simultaneous monitoring of 54,000 telephone calls and cables. Given the secrecy that surrounds this agency, little is known about its efforts involving computer speech recognition. But, to the extent that a machine can instantly pick out particular conversations or voices from thousands that are being monitored, surveillance has taken a quantum step forward.

Video, audio, and other forms of surveillance are often combined. They can be activated by sound, motion, heat, air currents, vibrations, odor, or pressure. Integrated 'management systems' are available that offer visual, audio, and digital information about the behavior of employees and customers. For example, at many convenience stores information may be recorded from cash register entries, voices, motion, standing on a mat with a sensor, or taking an electronically tagged item beyond a given perimeter. Audio and/or visual recordings and alarms may be programmed to respond to a large number of 'triggering devices'. In one system, the camera and voice recorders operate randomly for 15 seconds of every two minutes. They also start running whenever the cash register is open or closed for longer than a specified time, when particular keys on the cash register are hit 'too often' (clear or no sale keys), when more than 50 dollars is in the cash register, or when the last bill is removed (suggesting a robbery). In another system backroom monitors can see on their computer what a cashier rings up, while closed-circuit television shows them what items are actually taken out by the customer. Participants in Behavior Scan, a marketing research endeavor, automatically have their television viewing correlated with records of their consumer purchases.

### Electronic leashes

There are a number of devices that can be attached to a person or an object that permit remote monitoring of location and/or physiological condition. The telemetric devices first used to study the movement of animals are increasingly being applied to humans.

Consider, for example, the electronic 'leashes' marketed for children and convicts. One device consists of a tiny transmitter (complete with animal and balloon decals) that fastens to a child. A monitor gives off an alarm if the child goes beyond a specific distance. An electronic anklet, bracelet, or necklace that signals a central computer via telephone if the device is removed or if the wearer goes more than a short distance from home is being used on probationers. Given prison overcrowding, such devices are likely to be used more extensively.[12] They can be combined with a breathalyzer and video cameras.

The technology, of course, can be used for punishment as well as monitoring. An electrode could be implanted in the body of an offender with 'an automatic shock schedule [that] could be triggered if the offender moved away from the approved probation/parole area'.[13] The severity of the shock could increase as the person moved farther away.

In other systems, where subjects are not restricted to their residence, their whereabouts are continuously known. The radio signal is fed into a modified missile-tracking device that graphs the wearer's location and displays it on a screen. Thus, some police departments have initiated automatic vehicle monitoring (AVM) to help supervisors track patrol cars at all times. Some companies are using satellite technology to pinpoint the location of their trucks on a video screen.

In another system tested in Hong Kong, a small radio receiver in a vehicle picks up low-frequency signals from wire loops set into streets and transmits an identification number, indicating where, when, and how fast a car is driven. Self-contained monitoring devices also can be attached to a vehicle to gather data on the driver's behavior. For example, a computer the size of a paperback book (aptly called the 'Trip-master') can be attached to a truck or car, keeping track of speed, shifting, idling, and when and how long the vehicle is driven.

There also are various hidden beepers that can be attached to vehicles and other objects to trace their movements. A homing device welded to the body of a car has been developed as part of an antitheft system. When a car is reported stolen, a police radio tower broadcasts a signal that causes the transmitting device in the car to emit its own silent pulse, which can be picked up by a police car several miles away. A signal flashes the car's identification number, and a light on a compass-like dial points in the direction of the car.

The use of electronic article surveillance (EAS) systems is constantly being extended, including department and record stores, libraries, hospitals, and even supermarkets. In some supermarkets, a buzzer sounds and lights flash if a customer goes through checkout with a concealed item.

Location also can be tracked through card-security systems. In some work settings, employees are required to carry an ID card with a magnetic stripe and check in and out as they go to various 'stations' (parking lot, main door, a specific office or computer terminal, the bathroom). The computer controls access to each area, making continuous monitoring possible.

There also are nonelectronic leashes, such as chemical tracking agents visible only through ultraviolet light or chemical tests. The Soviet Union's use of an invisible chemical dust to monitor the whereabouts of Americans is an example.

Much more than location can be electronically monitored. A 'nonintrusive appliance load monitor' has been developed at M.I.T. that can generate an 'exact usage history' of all applicances in a home. This can be legally and inexpensively installed on a utility pole, far from the site being monitored and without the consumer's knowledge. As the technology evolves, the seemingly benign, unseen electronic umbilical cords that link us to the outside world will increasingly be drawn on for information about behavior.[14]

### Personal truth technologies

The past decade has seen the increased use of supposedly scientific 'inference' or 'personal truth technology', based on body clues, such as pulse, eye movements, voice, blood, urine, and saliva. The effort to measure physiological responses as indicators of guilt or innocence is part of an unhappy history involving the cruel methods of trial by ordeal, but current efforts seek the mantle of scientific legitimacy. Biological surveillance can be more intrusive than electronic surveillance.

Drug testing has spread as a result of advances in biotechnology with an inexpensive scanning test and confirmatory tests involving gas chromatography and mass spectrometry. An even newer machine scans eye movements and claims to be able to detect the amount and kind of drugs a person has taken. Another technique claims to be able to identify drug use through the analysis of a strand of hair.[15] Another development eliminates the consent required by the traditional breath analyzer. A 'passive electronic sensor' concealed in a flashlight automatically measures alcohol levels in the breath when merely pointed at a person.

The traditional polygraph is increasingly being supplemented by new developments involving the application of laser technology to eye movements and the measurement of stomach flutters and voice tremors. Covert voice stress analysis, for example, electronically analyzes a person's voice for subaudible microtremors, which, it is claimed, occur with stress and deception.[16] Brain waves can be 'read' as clues to certain internal states, such as surprise, concentration, confusion, and fatigue.[17]

A related use of biological indicators is for means of personal identification that go beyond the rather easily faked signature or photo ID. A variety of biometric identification products are available. These are based on the sensing of individual characteristics, such as fingerprints, veins, handwriting, voice, typing rhythms, hand geometry, and retinal patterns. In the last, for example, a person's eyes are photographed through a set of binoculars, and an enlarged print is compared to a previous print on file. Retinal patterns are said to be more individual than even thumbprints. The automated matching of fingerprints and new laser and other techniques for picking up latent prints have significantly increased the precision and usefulness of that technique. More reliable still, although expensive and time consuming, is the DNA matching of blood samples.[18] A computer chip that is read with a scanner has been implanted in cattle for identification and record keeping purposes. Equivalent human applications are likely – perhaps at first for children and those with memory problems.

Different measures can, of course, be combined, for example, a 'hybrid multisensor system' that uses voice, fingerprints, and handwriting. The availability of almost foolproof means of identity fits well with the interests of those who advocate a mandatory national ID system.

## Characteristics of the new technologies

The surveillance devices discussed above differ, of course, from each other, but they are related by being used jointly. Video and audio surveillance often coexist and rely on computer processing. Hotlines generate investigative leads. These, along with night vision devices, beepers, lie detectors, and computer files, are an integral of many sophisticated covert operations. They are also related because they are strands of a broader social trend. The new forms of surveillance tend to share, to varying degrees, ten characteristics that set them apart from most traditional forms of social control.

*The new surveillance transcends distance, darkness, and physical barriers.* As many observers have noted, the historic barriers to the old Leviathan state lay in the sheer physical impossibility of extending the rulers' ideas and control to the outer regions of vast empires; through closed doors; or into the intellectual, emotional, and physical regions of the individual. Technology, however, has gradually made these barriers penetrable. Physical limitations and, to some extent, human inefficiency have lost their usefulness as unplanned protectors of liberty. Sound and video can be transmitted over vast distances; infrared and light-amplifying technology pierce the dark; intrusive technologies can 'see' through doors, suitcases, and fog. Truth-seeking technologies claim to uncover deep, subterranean truths.

*It transcends time; its records can be stored, retrieved, combined, analyzed, and communicated.* Surveillance information can be 'freeze-dried',[19] available many years after the fact in totally different contexts. Abstract and frequently outdated, these records come to have a reality of their own apart from the person or events they purport to describe. Computer records, video and audio tapes and discs, photos, and various other technological 'signatures' have become increasingly standardized and interchangeable. Information can be converted into a form that makes it portable and easily reproduceable and transferable through telecommunications. Data can migrate to faraway places; they can be collected in one place and time and be joined with data collected elsewhere. Data sharing becomes possible on an immense scale.

*It has low visibility or is invisible.* It becomes ever more difficult to ascertain when and whether we are being watched and who is doing the watching. There is a distancing (both socially and geographically) between watchers and watched; miniaturization and remote control increase the difficulty of discovery. Surveillance devices can either be made to appear as something else (one-way mirrors, cameras hidden in a fire extinguisher, undercover agents) or can be virtually invisible (electronic snooping into microwave transmissions or computer files). This contrasts with traditional wiretapping, in which changes in electrical current are clues to the presence of a tap, but, even when wires are used, they may be unrecognizable. There is a special paint that, in conducting electricity, serves the function of a wire from a mike. There is even a bug that literally looks like a bug.[20] Audit trails are even more difficult to establish.

*It is often involuntary.* Information can be gathered without the participation or even awareness of the target.

*Prevention is a major concern.* Anticipatory surveillance strategies seek to reduce risk and uncertainty. Modern management attempts to make control more predictable, reliable, effective, and relatively all-inclusive. As little as possible is left to chance.

*It is capital- rather than labor-intensive,* therefore increasingly economical. Technical developments have dramatically altered the economics of surveillance; it has become much less expensive per unit watched. It becomes economical to monitor persons and situations that were previously ignored. A few individuals can monitor a great many, concurrently or retroactively.

The characteristics that follow are related to the economic changes that facilitate expanded surveillance.

*It involves decentralized self-policing.* As Foucault observes, control is not exercised from afar, as with monarchical power, but is expressed directly from within the social relations and settings to be controlled.[21] Economy is enhanced because persons increasingly participate in their own monitoring. Control, like a pacemaker, is implanted in the very context to be managed. Those watched become (willingly and knowingly or not) active partners in their own monitoring, which is often self-activated and automatic. Beyond hotline reporting, an important aspect of this process is that persons may be motivated to report themselves to government agencies and large organizations or corporations in return for some benefit or to avoid a penalty or to carry a wallet-sized 'smart card' containing vast amounts of personal information, another is the direct triggering of surveillance systems by its subjects when, for instance, a person walks, talks on the telephone, turns on a TV set, checks a book out of the library, and enters or leaves controlled areas; another is the instant feedback on their productivity that pink-collar workers may see on their video display terminals.

*It triggers a shift from targeting a specific suspect to categorical suspicion of everyone* (or at least everyone within a particular category). Between the camera, the tape recorder, the identity card, the metal detector, the tax form, and the computer, everyone becomes a reasonable target. The new forms of control are helping to create a society where everyone is guilty until proven innocent; technologies that permit continuous, rather than intermittent, monitoring encourage this.

*It is more intensive* – probing beneath surfaces, discovering previously inaccessible information. Like drilling technology that can bore ever deeper into the earth, today's surveillance is able to probe ever deeper into physical, social, and psychological areas. It hears whispers, penetrates clouds, and sees through walls and windows. With blood and urine analysis and stomach pumps, it 'sees' into the body, and, with voice stress and polygraph analysis, it attempts to 'see' into the psyche, claiming to go beneath ostensible meanings and appearances to real meanings.

*It is more extensive* – covering not only deeper, but larger, areas. While multiple indicators collect ever more data, unconnected surveillance threads are being woven into gigantic tapestries of information. In sociologist Stan Cohen's imagery, the mesh of the fishing net has not only become finer and more pliable, the net itself is now wider.[22] As the pool of persons watched expands, so does the pool of watchers. The uncertainty over whether or not surveillance is present is an important strategic element. Mass monitoring has become a reality.

## Toward a maximum security society?

The awesome power of the new surveillance lies partly in the paradoxical, never-before-possible combination of decentralized and centralized forms. Surveillance is capable of being laserlike in its focus, as well as absorbent.[23]

The state's traditional monopoly over the means of violence is supplemented by new means of gathering and analyzing information that may even make the former obsolete. Control is better symbolized by manipulation than coercion, by computer chips than prison bars, and by remote and invisible tethers than by handcuffs or straitjackets.

The new surveillance has generally been welcomed by those in business, government, and law enforcement. Examples of its effectiveness are readily available: apprehending criminals, detecting corruption, and preventing crime. It can help verify compliance with arms control and test ban treaties and can monitor health. Americans seem increasingly willing, even eager, to live with intrusive technologies because of their benefits: the ease of obtaining consumer goods with a credit card, the saving of taxpayer dollars because of computer-matching programs, and the comfort of security systems based on video surveillance. Of course, some compliance is voluntary in only the most superficial sense. Advertising may play a role in convincing people they need things that are harmful or destructive. Cooperation with requests for data, or to undergo a lie detector or other tests, is 'voluntary' only at the risk of not obtaining a needed benefit or job.[24]

The new surveillance is justified by positive social goals – the need to combat crime and terrorism, to protect health, or to improve productivity. Extensions occur gradually; it is easy to miss the magnitude of the change and the broader issues its raises. Our notions of privacy, liberty, and the rights of the individual are quietly shifting, with little public awareness or legislative attention.

Observers of the criminal justice system, in focusing on prisoners, have noted how reforms involving diversion, electronic monitoring, halfway houses, and community treatment centers seek to diffuse the surveillance of the prison into the community at large. But what is equally striking is how techniques and an ethos once applied only to suspects or prisoners are applied to the most benign settings.[25]

In a 1791 book, *Panopticon or the Inspection House*, Jeremy Bentham offered a plan for the perfect prison. There was to be constant inspection of both prisoners and keepers; cells were to be constructed with bars (rather than opaque doors) around a central inspection tower. His ideas helped give rise to the maximum-security prison, which today is characterized by perimeter security, thick walls with guard towers, spotlights, and a high degree of electronic surveillance. Many of the kinds of controls found in prison are diffusing into the society at large. It is important to ask if recent developments in technology, culture, and social organization are not pushing us toward becoming a maximum-security society.

The maximum-security society is composed of five interrelated subsocieties:

1 a *dossier society*, in which computerized records play a major role

2 an *actuarial or predictive society*, in which decisions are increasingly made on the basis of predictions about our future behavior as a result of our membership in aggregate categories

3 an *engineered society*, in which our choices are increasingly limited and determined by the physical and social environment

4 a *transparent or porous society*, in which the boundaries that traditionally protected privacy are weakened

5 a *self-monitored society*, in which auto-surveillance plays a prominent role.

In such a society, the line between the public and the private is obliterated; we are under constant observation, everything goes on a permanent record, and much of what we say, do, and even feel may be known and recorded by others we do not know. Data from widely separated geographical areas, organizations, and time periods can be merged and analyzed easily. Control is embedded and preventive; informers, dossiers, and classification are prominent. The society becomes, in Erving Goffman's words, a 'total institution', and there is no longer a backstage.[26]

As the prison ethos diffuses ever more into the society at large, the need for actual prisons may decline. Society becomes the functional alternative to the prison. This, of course, is what the community corrections reform movement has long sought, but it did not envision that the broad population could in a sense become the prisoners, not just those who have been found guilty through a process of adjudication.

The trend in North America and perhaps in other industrial democracies is toward, rather than away from, a maximum-security society. What Ericson and Shearing refer to as the 'scientification of police work' offers not only new ways of doing things, but a new means of legitimizing police power. It is both instrument and ideology.[27]

## Some negative features

We must learn to subvert, sabotage and destroy our enemies by more clever, more sophisticated and more effective methods than those used against us ... It may become necessary that the American people will be made acquainted with, understand and support this fundamentally repugnant philosophy. (The Hoover Commission, 1954)

Experience should teach us to be most on our guard when the government's purposes are beneficent. Men born to freedom are naturally alert to repel invasion of their liberty by evil-minded rulers. The greatest dangers to liberty lurk in insidious encroachment by men of zeal, well-meaning, but without understanding. (Justice Louis Dembitz Brandeis, 1928)

Apprehension over the new surveillance certainly does not mean indifference to pressing issues of national security, crime, drug abuse, productivity, or health. When the goal is important and the proposed means are highly intrusive and/or of questionable reliability, we must consider alternatives. We must be careful not to adopt a cure that is worse than the disease. The morality of the means is as important as that of the ends.

Benjamin Franklin's observation, 'They that can give up essential liberty to obtain a little temporary safety deserve neither liberty nor safety',[28] is too strong for many citizens in today's world. But, where only questionable means are available, it is necessary to think carefully about imposing them. One of the truisms of the last quarter of the twentieth century is that government cannot solve all problems that ideally should be solved. There are some problems it may be better to live with than to solve. With fewer intrusions by government and large organizations, we would no doubt have a less efficient and more disorderly society, but one with increased liberty and privacy.[29]

Without seeking to deny either the positive aspects or complexity of the moral issues, it is worth considering some of the negative features of the new surveillance that generally receive insufficient attention.

There are increasingly fewer places to run or to hide. A citizen's ability to evade surveillance is diminishing. There is not exit from the prying eyes and ears and whirring data-processing machines of government and business. To participate in the consumer society and the welfare state, we must provide personal information. To venture into a shopping mall, a bank, a subway, sometimes even a bathroom, is to perform before an unknown audience. To apply for a job may mean having to face lie-detector questioning or urine analysis. Birth, marriage, and death certificates, driver's licenses, vehicle registrations, voter registration lists, phone directory information, occupational permits, educational and special-interest directories – all present an invitation to more finely attuned manipulative efforts by a new breed of government agents, market researchers, and political campaign planners who use the enormous quantities of data available through computerization.

The new surveillance goes beyond merely invading privacy, as this term has conventionally been understood, to making irrelevant many of the constraints that protected privacy. Beyond the boundaries protected by custom and law, privacy has depended on certain (technically or socially) inviolate physical, spatial, or temporal barriers – varying from distance to darkness to doors to the right to remain silent. An invasion of privacy required crossing these barriers. With much of the new technology, many of them cease to be barriers.

Important American values are increasingly threatened by the permanence and accessibility of computerized records. The idea of 'starting over' or moving to a new frontier is a powerful concept in American culture. The beliefs that once a debt has been paid to society it is forgotten and that people can change are important American traditions. Americans pride themselves on looking at what a person is today rather than what he may have been in past. Devices, such as sealed or destroyed records, prohibitions on certain kinds of record keeping, and consent requirements for the release of information, reflect these concerns.

However, with the mass of easily accessible files, one's past is always present, for erroneous or sabotaged data, as well as for debts that have been paid. This can create a class of permanently stigmatized persons. In the words of sociologist Ken Laudon, computers offer the possibility for 'an automated blacklisting capability thousands of times more powerful, yet considerably more silent than the blacklists of the McCarthy era'. Starting over may be much more difficult. When the search of dossiers is combined with other forms of screening, for example, carriers of AIDS antibodies, and predictive profiles regarding the characteristics of a good worker, it is easy to imagine a work force divided between people thought to be good risks and others. This would create an enormous waste of human resources as people were locked out of jobs for which they were otherwise qualified. Increased crime and demands on the welfare system would be the likely results.

As computerized record-keeping becomes ever more routine, there may be increasing reluctance to seek needed services (as for mental health), to take controversial action (filing a grievance against a landlord), or to take risks for fear of what it will look like 'on the record'. Conformity and uniformity may increase – at the price of diversity, innovation, and vitality.

A related factor is the changing nature and location of the things we wish to keep private. Fifty years ago, our 'private' papers could be kept in a desk drawer or a safe deposit box. Increasingly, personal information is held by such large organizations as banks, credit card and insurance companies, and hospitals. Information as a form of 'private property' is less tangible. It can be seen or sent without a trace, and often without consent. Because the Fourth Amendment was designed for more tangible forms of property and at a time when individuals had much greater physical control over the things they wished to keep private, it does not cover recent incursions. The intrusive nature of the new surveillance is inconsistent with the spirit, if not the letter, of the Bill of Rights. In the face of these developments, it is important to rethink the nature of privacy and to create new protection for it.

Some safeguards, ironically, rely on such technologies as encrypted or scrambled communications and debugging devices. Legislation and heightened public awareness are also important. In the mid-1980s, less than one state in five had laws requiring written standards for the collection, maintenance, and dissemination of personal information.

The new surveillance is relatively one-sided: it is likely to increase the power of large organizations, but not that of small ones or individuals. There is hardly equal access to these means, even if most of them are theoretically available to all and do not remain the exclusive property of the state (as in totalitarian countries).

By offering accessibility (whether legitimately or illegitimately) to data bases, a means of creating alternative communication networks via electronic mail and bulletin boards with links to international telecommunications and a private printing press, the personal computer can break the state's monopoly of information. This is nicely illustrated by the U.S.S.R.'s unwillingness to make personal computers perceived in the U.S. as a symbol of Big Brother and in the U.S.S.R. as a symbol of liberation is partly resolved by separating large, institutionally controlled mainframe computers from small, privately controlled microcomputers.

For those with the resources to employ them, countermeasures may reduce the impact of surveillance, or private citizens or public interest groups may use technology to monitor government and corporate activity. However, the scale is still overwhelmingly tipped toward surveillance by government and large organizations. In spite of the spread of home computers and mail-order snooping (and snooping detection devices), individual consumers, renters, political dissenters, loan applicants, and public interest groups clearly do not have the capabilities of credit card companies, market research firms, landlord associations, police intelligence units, the NSA, banks, or large corporations. As a result, the new surveillance technologies are an important factor in lessening the power of the individual relative to large organizations and government. Privacy and autonomy can be the victims.

Anonymity, involving the right to be left alone and unnoticed, is also diminished. The easy combining and mining of publicly available data bases to generate precise lists, such as for sales pitches and solicitations, can be unsettling. The targeted appeals that become possible through linkage with automatic telephone dialers or word processors can create a sense of invasion and vulnerability that far exceeds one's reaction to junk mail addressed to 'Occupant'. Aside from the annoyance factor, the 'personalized' solicitations make one wonder: 'How do they know this about me? How did they find this out? What else do they know? Who are they?' One need not be a Franz Kafka character to feel uneasy.

The fragmentation and isolation characteristic of totalitarian societies occur at least partly because individuals mistrust each other as much as organizations. To a certain degree, skepticism has always been vital to democracy as well: thus, the system of checks and balances.[30] To question and to not take the world at first

appearances are also important ingredients of wisdom and scientific advancement. However, the new surveillance may be helping to create a degree of
suspiciousness that goes too far. Community, liberty and openness can hardly
thrive in a society of informers or where everyone is treated as a suspect.

Anonymous informing can be conducive to false and malicious accusations; it
encourages distrust.[31] Similarly, trust can be damaged when authorities seek to
create a 'myth of surveillance' by encouraging the perception that any
transaction might be monitored and involve a hidden integrity test, informer,
bug, or camera. A memo entitled 'Responsibilities of Sales Personnel' given to
employees in the large retail firms serviced by a leading private detective agency
perfectly captures this: 'Systematic checkings are made of every employee; you
never know what day or hour you are being checked.'

Deceptive efforts to make people think that surveillance devices are more
powerful than they really are may be undertaken. Many people stand in fear and
trembling of supposedly scientific investigative techniques. Former President
Nixon's remarks on the Watergate tapes are instructive in this regard, 'Listen, I
don't know anything about polygraphs, but I do know that they'll scare the hell
out of people'.[32]

Advocates argue that creating the perception of surveillance is a deterrent to
criminal behavior. It may be. But it may also deter legitimate behavior. Such as
the expression of political positions or obtaining benefits to which persons are
entitled.[33]

When deception is 'sanctioned' through government example, it becomes
both more acceptable to the public and easier to rationalize. Cultural standards
about deception seem to be softening, as the behavior of some investigative
journalists, social scientists, and public relations and marketing specialists
suggests. It does not seem far-fetched to anticipate that husbands or wives or
those considering marriage might someday soon hire attractive members of the
opposite sex to test their partner's fidelity. Beyond commonplace industrial
espionage, businesses might hire undercover agents to involve their competitors
in illegal actions or have saboteurs infiltrate and disrupt their activities. Some
evidence suggests an increased use of undercover means in the private sector.[34]

The proliferation of new techniques may create a lowest-common-
denominator morality. Ironically, in order to protect privacy and autonomy, the
very tactics of those seeking to lessen them may be adopted in self-defense, as the
quotation at the beginning of this section argues. For example, the office of
special prosecutor set up to investigate Watergate had vibration detectors,
closed-circuit television, alarm tapes on windows, venetian blinds closed at all
times, heavy drapes on windows that were drawn whenever sensitive conversations took place, periodic checks for bugs and wiretaps on phones, and 24-
hour security guards.

The technique also may be used offensively, of course. Gathering information
about competitors by using intelligence agency techniques is becoming part of
strategic business planning. It is likely that private citizens will increasingly be
using new electronic forms of surveillance against each other. Through
advertisements in major national periodicals (not simply esoteric security
publications) and mail-order catalogues, a vast array of surveillance and
countersurveillance devices have been brought to mass audiences. In the best

free-market tradition, some firms sell the devices as well as the countermeasures needed to thwart them. One large company offers a 'secret connection briefcase' that includes a 'pocket-sized tape recorder detector that lets you know if someone is secretly recording your conversation', a 'micro-miniature hidden bug detection system which lets you know if you're being bugged', a 'miniature voice stress analyzer which lets you know when someone is lying', a 'built-in scrambler for total telephone privacy', and an 'incredible six-hour tape recorder – so small it fits in a cigarette pack'.

There is a commercially available at-home urinalysis kit with the lovely double-think name of 'U-care', making it possible for parents to mail a child's (or other suspect's) urine sample for analysis. There is a company that will analyze secretly recorded voice tapes for stress and by return mail offer an assessment of truthfulness. The widely sold small unobtrusive transmitters that permit listening at a distance (to a child sleeping or for intruders) can easily be turned to other uses. The secret taping of phone and face-to-face conversations seems to be increasingly common.

Surveillance practices in work settings are also increasing and may produce alienation on the part of employees. Secret testing or monitoring of employees communicates mistrust and may be cynically responded to in kind.

Some other negative aspects can be briefly mentioned. Surveillance may involve 'fishing expeditions' and generalized 'searches' rather than proof of any specific wrongdoing. The spirit of the Fourth Amendment is violated because the burden of proof is shifted from the state to the target of surveillance. These ideas turn the traditional American belief that you are presumed innocent until proven guilty upside down. As one baseball player said, 'I don't take drugs and I don't believe I have to prove I don't'. There is also the danger of presumption of guilt by association or by statistical artifact. Because of the technical and often distant nature of the surveillance, the accused may (at least initially) be unable to face the accuser. It may even be presented as if it were in the individual's self-interest: 'It can offer proof of innocence'; or 'If you have done nothing wrong, you have nothing to hide.' But more than results must be considered. Such arguments ignore the moral component of the means and the fact that the innocent may nonetheless suffer harm from an intrusive investigation. We value envelopes around letters and the confidentiality of spousal communication not to protect illegality, but because liberty is destroyed when such boundaries can be crossed at will.

The focus on prevention can entail the risk of wasting resources on preventing things that would not have occurred or, as is sometimes the case with undercover activities, of actually creating violations through self-fulfilling effects.

Powerful new discovery mechanisms may overload the system. Authorities may discover far more violations than they can act on. There is a certain wisdom to the ignorance of the three 'no evil' monkeys.[35] Having information on an overabundance of violations can lead to the misuse of prosecutorial discretion or demoralization on the part of control agents. Charges of favoritism and corruption may appear when only some offenses can be acted on.

In many science fiction accounts, control is both highly repressive and efficient; there is virtually perfect control over information (whether in the discovery of infractions or in the management of beliefs). As many poignant examples suggest, the new surveillance clearly is less than perfect, and it is subject to manipulation and error.

Computer matching may find valid correlations but can be no better than the original data it deals with, which may be dated or wrong. The data it uses are often rather blunt and acontextual and their meaning unclear. The validity and completeness of criminal record files varies significantly across jurisdictions.[36] Chemical analyses that may correctly identify drugs in a person's system cannot reveal how they got there (thus, THC may appear in the bloodstream because a person smoked marijuana or simply because he was around people who were smoking it). Nor do they reveal current levels of intoxication, because what is measured are the levels of chemical by-products created as the body metabolizes the drug. Evidence of drug use appears some time after the drug has been taken. An intoxicated person can thus score negative, and a person who has not used drugs for several weeks can score positive. Nor does such analysis determine whether a drug was used on or off the job.

There also may be false positives, as a result of the effect of prescription drugs, cold remedies, herbal teas, or the amount of melanin in the skin, or false negatives as a result of switched urine. The electronic transmissions from locational monitors can be blocked by water in a bathtub or waterbed, and the metal in mylar wallpaper, construction beams, and trailers – making it erroneously appear that a person has violated the 'house arrest' requirement of probation. The inquisitor in *1984* tells the frail Winston, 'I am always able to detect a lie'. Such certainty cannot be claimed for the polygraph, a tactic labeled unsatisfactory by the American Psychological Association because it turns up 'an unacceptable number of false positives'.[37]

Machines are not infallible, nor are the humans who administer and interpret the various tests. Fairness and due process require that careful attention be given to issues of reliability and validity. They also require that one be able to confront his or her accuser and know what the evidence is.

Although deterring or discovering some offenders, the routinization of surveillance, ironically, may grant an almost guaranteed means for successful violations and theft to those who gain knowledge of the system and take action to neutralize and exploit it. (The polygraph, for example, can be confounded by biting one's tongue or stepping on a tack in one's shoe, tightening the sphincter muscles, meditation, or drugs.) Over time, many of these systems will disproportionately net the marginal, amateur, occasional, or opportunistic violator rather than the more sophisticated. The systematization of surveillance may grant the latter a license to steal, even while headlines hail the effectiveness of the new techniques.

### Concerns for the future

In focusing on the power of recent surveillance methods, I do not suggest that we are hapless victims of technological determinism who can do little more than bemoan the loss of liberty. The fact that the technology can be misused does not necessarily mean that it will be. To a greater extent than in most countries, the United States has laws and policies in restricting its use.

Even in the unlikely event that no problems occur (or could all be solved), there are still ample grounds for concern. A problem of a different order is seen in the *apocalypse someday* argument. This calls attention to future disasters, rather than current problems.[38] The potential for harm may be so great, should social conditions change, that the creation of certain surveillance systems may not be justified in the first place. Because there has not yet been a catastrophe, this argument is usually not given much credence, but it is essentially the same argument that informs the nuclear debate.

Once the new surveillance systems become institutionalized and taken for granted in a democratic society, they can be used for harmful ends. With a more repressive government and a more intolerant public – perhaps upset over severe economic downturns, large waves of immigration, social dislocations, or foreign policy setbacks – these same devices easily could be used against those with the 'wrong' political beliefs, against racial, ethnic, or religious minorities, and against those with life-styles that offend the majority. A concern with the prevention of disorder could mean a vastly expanded pool of 'suspects'.

In the *Merchant of Venice*, Shakespeare counsels us that 'to do a great right, do a little wrong'. But when intrusive and secret tactics are at hand, more is at stake than the immediate goal. Apart from the principle, there is no guarantee that the ratio would not quickly be reversed – to great wrong yielding little right. At times, the extension of secret police practices may be necessary. They may be exercised with restraint and sensitivity by leaders and agents of high moral character. But, unfortunately, once established, there is no guarantee that, in less demanding times, the practices will be rescinded or that future leaders and agents will be scrupulous, absent the [necessary] legislative controls [...].

Chief Justice Harlan F. Stone argued that, in a free society, the abuses of power associated with secret police 'are not always quickly apprehended or understood'.[39] Each small extension of surveillance can shift the balance between the liberties and rights of individuals and the state and relations among the three branches of government. The impact of such shifts may be incremental, but cumulatively they can change relationships and principles central to our form of government.

If totalitarianism ever came to the United States, it would be more likely to come by accretion than by cataclysmic event. As Sinclair Lewis argued in *It Can't Happen Here*, it would come in traditional American guise, with the gradual erosion of liberties. Voluntary participation, beneficent rationales, and changes in cultural definition of language may hide the onerous and potentially destructive aspects of the new surveillance.[40] Writing about this topic in the mid-1980s, I am forced to recall George Orwell. In a great many areas of domestic affairs, we are far from the distressing society he described, and much current-trend data actually suggest increasing movement in the opposite direction.[41]

The traditional social supports against totalitarianism are strong in the United States: an educated citizenry committed to democratic ideals, a variety of independent channels of mass communication, a plethora of voluntary organizations, and constitutional protections for civil liberties. But to judge the state of freedom and liberty only by traditional standards results in a vision that is too narrow and an optimism that may be unwarranted. There is no reason for concern about the state of privacy, liberty, and autonomy in the Western democracies. Here is a paradox: if the traditional social supports for democracy have become stronger and domestic state violence has declined, what is there to be concerned about?

Orwell's state had both violent and nonviolent forms of social control ('a boot stamping on a human face' and Big Brother watching). In linking these two, Orwell offered only one of several models of totalitarian control. It was a model based on his experiences during the Spanish Civil War and his observations of the U.S.S.R., Germany, and Italy. In contemporary society, violent and nonviolent forms of social control have become uncoupled, and the latter is in the ascendance. Over the past four decades, subtle, seemingly less coercive forms of control have emerged.[42]

Culture as conveyed through the mass media is an important element of nonviolent control. The manipulation of language and symbols may subtly shape behavior. Culture is invisible and usually taken for granted; we are generally unaware that we are accepting its myriad dictates or that a choice has been (implicitly) made for us. In the past, to a much greater extent than today, culture tended to develop more haphazardly from thousands of diverse sources. Today, we are moving closer to the deliberate manufacture and control of culture found in Orwell's society, though private interests are involved to a much greater extent than is the state.

Mass communication is, in some ways, an alternative to the mass surveillance devices considered here.[43] Rather than having the state watch everyone all the time, it is far more efficient to have all eyes riveted on a common mass media stimulus that offers direct and indirect messages of how to behave and morality tales about what happens to those who stray. Mass media persuasion is far more subtle and indirect than a truncheon over the head. In the United States and in democratic industrial societies in general, there has been a relative deemphasis on physical forms of domestic social control. Our psyches are more invaded by the consumer mentality than by any repressive political needs of the state. Psychological theories of management, market research, advertising, and public relations contribute to this. Specialists invent needs, package products (entertainers, politicians, public issues, or breakfast food), and seek to sell them to the public. Their skills are continually improving, though much art and guesswork remain.[44]

An economy and state oriented toward mass consumption has a more benign view of workers and the public than did the nineteenth-century laissez-faire capitalist state. The modern state seeks control partly through the prospect of economic redistribution. The masses are motivated not so much by an ever-increasing scarcity or fear of punishment as by the promise of ever-decreasing abundance. For the affluent, this involves a dazzling array of consumer goods. For the poor, it involves the various direct and indirect supports offered by the welfare state.

Force and direct coercion are increasingly seen as being brutish and anachronistic, as well as less effective. The ideals of universal citizenship and the welfare state are more compatible with other means, but the absence of physical oppression does not guarantee liberty. The existence of new, softer forms of surveillance and control within democratic states certainly does not call for a lessening of vigilance.[45]

I am not suggesting that the pain and suffering caused by the threat or actuality of violence as against deception and manipulation are equivalent, though both involve coercion and seek to counter informed consent and free choice. The end control result may be the same. However, violence may offer a possibility of choice – go along or suffer – which is absent when deception is the means. Forced to choose, the newer forms of control are less unattractive, although to some observers, such as Paul Goodman, the choice between 'the lesser of two evils' is not a choice between half a loaf and a whole one, 'but between a more or less virulent form of rat poison'.

We are far from being a maximum-security society, but the trend is toward – rather than away from – this. What Orwell did not anticipate or develop was the possibility that one could have a society where significant inroads were made on privacy, liberty, and autonomy, even in a relatively nonviolent environment with democratic forms and the presumed bulwarks against totalitarianism in place. The velvet glove is replacing (or at least hiding) the iron fist. Huxley may be a far better guide to the future than Orwell.[46]

My concern [...] has been with domestic law enforcement. Considering matters more broadly, government is hardly the only player. Domestic intrusions by the state pale relative to what may be done internationally by intelligence agencies or by the private sector.[47] With respect to intrusive technologies, there is far less legal accountability in the private sector than in the public sector. The Bill of Rights, for example, applies primarily to the actions of government, not the private sector. Restrictions on government are not a sufficient guarantee of freedom. Taken too far, they may guarantee its opposite, as private interests reign unchecked. For Orwell, the state and the economy were synonymous, and the threat to liberty was only from big government. But, in our age of large and powerful nongovernment organizations, a broader view and new legal and policy protections are required. Ironically, we need protection not only by government, but also from it.[48] The undercover tactic is compelling and controversial partly because it can be a means for both protecting and undermining our most cherished values.

The first task of a society that would have liberty and privacy is to guard against the misuse of physical coercion on the part of the state and private parties. The second task is to guard against 'softer' forms of secret and manipulative control. Because these are often subtle, indirect, invisible, diffuse, deceptive, and shrouded in benign justifications, this is clearly the more difficult task.

In a democratic society, covert police tactics, along with many of the other surveillance techniques, offer us a queasy ethical and moral paradox. The choice between anarchy and repression is not a happy one, wherever the balance is struck. We are caught on the horns of a moral dilemma. In Machiavelli's words: '[Never] let any state ever believe that it can always adopt safe policies ... we never try to escape one difficulty without running into another; but prudence consists in knowing how to recognize the nature of the difficulties and how to choose the least bad as good.' Sometimes undercover tactics will be the least bad. Used with great care, they may be a necessary evil. The challenge is to prevent them from becoming an intolerable one.

*From Gary T. Marx, 'The new surveillance' in* Undercover: Police surveillance in America *(Berkeley: University of California Press), 1988, pp 206–233.*

## Notes

1   E.g., a 13-year-old girl in Tustin, California, turned in her parents for possession of marijuana and cocaine. They were arrested, and she was placed (against her wishes) in a foster home. This well-publicized incident was followed by many other cases – the youngest, a 6-year-old in New Jersey. See G. Marx, '"Yes Sir, That's My Daddy": When Children Turn in Parents,' *Student Lawyer* 15, no. 6 (1986): 8–10.

2   This is the case for absolute numbers, as well as the kinds of information included. In 1981 there were 1.8 million records in the interstate identification index system (arrest data supplied by the state); in 1985, there were 9.5 million. In 1987 a federal advisory committee endorsed a major expansion that would permit federal, state, and local law enforcement agencies to exchange information on 'suspicious persons' who had not been formally charged or tried. A proposal to link the National Crime Information Center with private sector data files was, however, rejected (this time).

3   D. Burnham, *The Rise of the Computer State* (New York: Random House, 1983) offers a useful discussion of this and related themes.

4   K. Laudon, *Dossier Society: Value Choices in the Design of National Information Systems* (New York: Columbia Univ. Press, 1986) develops this concept.

5   For a discussion of computer matching, see. G. Marx and N. Reichman, 'Routinizing the Discovery of Secrets: Computers as Informants,' *American Behavioral Scientist* 3 (March 1984); N. Reichman and G. Marx, 'Generating Organizational Disputes: The Impact of Computerization.' Paper presented at meetings of Law and Society Association, San Diego, 1985; J. Shattuck, 'In the Shadow of 1984: National Identification Systems, Computer-Matching, and Privacy in the United States,' *Hastings Law Journal*, July 1984: 991–1005; *Computer Matching: Assessing its Costs and Benefits* (Washington, D.C.: Government Accounting Office, No. 1986).

6   In Sweden, which is often cited as the prototype for such matters, children are given a number at birth that can never be changed. The average adult is in more than 100 data bases.

7   This is discussed in Office of Technology Assessment, *Federal Government Information Technology: Electronic Surveillance and Civil Liberties* (Washington, D.C.: GPO, 1985). The Electronic Communications Privacy Act of 1986 extends legal protection to these forms of communication, but enforcement is another matter.

8   See, e.g., H. Shaiken, *Work Transformed* (New York: Holt, Rinehart & Winston, 1984); R. Howard, *Brave New Workplace* (New York: Viking, 1985); G. Marx and S. Sherizen, 'How to Protect Property without Destroying Privacy,' *Technology Review*, Nov./Dec. 1986; and U.S. Congress, Office of Technology Assessment, *The Electronic Supervisor: New Technology, New Tensions* (Washington, D.C.: GPO, 1987).

9   One such program entitled 'Subliminal Suggestions and Self-Hypnosis' permits management to send any kind of message – 'Relax', 'Concentrate', or 'Work faster' – unbeknownst to the worker. The messages pass so quickly in front of the watchers' eyes they cannot be consciously detected. See Nine to Five, 'Computer Monitoring and Other Dirty Tricks' (Cleveland, 1986, photocopy). Most office computers do not yet receive information at the speeds such programs require. Messages that can be read, such as, 'You are not working as fast as the person sitting next to you', also can be sent. A different use is found in some department stores, where messages such as 'Honesty pays' are mixed in with music.

10   In a related development, a person whose phone rings now may see a digital display indicating where the call comes from before the phone is picked up. According to some observers, video-telephone communication is likely to be widespread in private homes by the year 2000.

11   J. Bamford, *The Puzzle Palace* (New York: Penguin, 1983).

12   See R. Ball, R. Huff, and R. Lilly, *House Arrest and Correctional Policy: Doing Time at Home* (Beverly Hills, Calif.: Sage, forthcoming); R. Corbett, Jr., and G. Marx, 'When a Man's Castle is his Prison: The Perils of Home Confinement.' Paper delivered at annual meeting of American Society of Criminology, Montreal, 1987; and articles in *Intermediate Punishments: Intensive Supervision, Home Confinement and Electronic Surveillance*, ed. B.R. McCarthy (Monsey, N.Y.: Criminal Justice Press, 1987). A key question is whether it will be used for persons who would otherwise have been sent to prison or be extended to a new class of minor offenders. The

expansive experience with other reforms, e.g., deinstitutionalization and diversion, put forth as ways of reducing demands on the criminal justice system suggests it will be the latter.

13  G. Stephens and W. Tafoya, 'Crime and Justice: Taking a Futuristic Approach,' *The Futurist*, February 1985. The device has obvious health uses, e.g., for victims of Alzheimer's disease. It also can be used to keep persons away from certain persons or locations. Thus, a former spouse under an injunction to stay away from his former wife could wear a device (as could the wife). If the man came to within a given distance of her, an alarm could be triggered, and a message sent to the judge. One can also imagine various chastity devices.

14  G. Hart, 'Computerized Surveillance via Utility Power Flows,' unpublished paper, MIT, 1985.

15  The radio immunoassay method extracts drug residue from the hair. Like rings in a tree, the distance from the root also gives temporal evidence. As one eager advocate put it, the 'beauty of the technique is that it can't be diluted or switched, there are many samples, and it does not demean the suspect, unlike urine testing'. The Yul Brynner look may become very fashionable.

16  One firm offers an 'ultra-miniaturized' hand-held system that 'in business or personal meetings' helps 'determine if your employees are stealing ... if your associates are cheating ... if your friends really are your friends'. The person need not know that they are being tested and 'even your telephone conversations can be analyzed for truth'.

17  E. Donchin, *Psychophysiological Monitoring: Possibilities and Prospects*, report prepared for the Office of Technology Assessment, Washington, D.C., Sept. 1986.

18  Previously, it was only possible to exclude a suspect by showing that blood types did not match; now with DNA analysis there is positive identification. More effective means of identification may reduce the chance of erroneous convictions and increase convictions of the guilty, but it may also lead to broad population screens. The use of genetic markers as criteria in hiring is likely to be much more controversial (e.g., excluding persons from certain jobs because DNA analysis suggests a greater likelihood of developing a particular illness).

19  See the discussion in G. Goodwin and L. Humphreys, 'Freeze-Dried Stigma: Cybernetics and Social Control,' *Humanity and Society* 6 (Nov. 1982).

20  It is fired like a pellet at a window, where it sticks like a squashed fly, picking up sound in the room (*Observer*, Feb. 2, 1986). Another form is embedded in a tiny blob of epoxy that may be hidden in a book binding or stuck under a chair.

21  M. Foucault, *Discipline and Punish* (New York: Pantheon, 1977).

22  S. Cohen, *Visions of Social Control* (Cambridge: Policy Press, 1985). The new surveillance illustrates Foucault's (1977) principle of 'indefinite discipline' (p. 357), where 'never-ending judgments, examinations and observation' emerge as a new mode of control.

23  For a discussion of parallel developments in Norway, see T. Mathiesen, 'The Future of Control Systems' in *The Power to Punish*, ed. D. Garland and P. Young (Atlantic Highlands, N.J.: Humanities Press, 1983). J.P. Brodeur, 'High Policing and Low Policing: Remarks about the Policing of Political Activities,' Social Problems 30, no. 5 (1983) notes a parallel to the historical French tradition of 'high' policing. See also Cohen (1985) for a discussion of master patterns of social control.

24  E.g., an IBM spokesman reports on a policy of testing job applicants for drugs: 'It's any applicant's decision to make – they're not forced to take the test ... but it is required if an applicant wishes to be considered for employment.' When testing is widespread, in an economy where jobs are difficult to find, this is disingenuous. Secretary of State George P. Schultz, who threatened to resign if required to take a polygraph, has career mobility not available to most people. When Exxon subjected 1,000 white-collar workers in Houston to a surprise search by drug-sniffing dogs, employees were required to sign waivers the day of the search. If they refused to sign, they faced the possibility of discipline.

25  For a nice illustration applied to Disneyworld, see C. Shearing and P. Stenning, 'From the Panopticon to Disney World: The Development of Discipline,' *Perspectives in Criminal Law*, 1984.

26  E. Goffman, *Asylums: Essays on the Social Situation of Mental Patients and Other Inmates* (New York: Doubleday, 1964). A related image is the monitoring associated with a hospital intensive care unit.

27  R. Ericson and C. Shearing, 'The Scientification of Police Work,' in G. Bohme and N. Stehr, *The Impact of Scientific Knowledge on Social Structure, Sociology of Science Yearbook*, vol. 10 (Dordrecht: Reidel, 1984).

28  A.H. Smyth, *The Writings of Benjamin Franklin*, 10 vols. (New York, 1905).

29  See the discussions in R. Sennett, *The Uses of Disorder* (New York: Knopf, 1970); J. Rule, '1984 – The Ingredients of Totalitarianism' in *1984: Totalitarianism in our Century*, ed. I. Howe (New York: Harper and Row, 1984).

30  See the discussion in B. Barber, *The Logic and Limits of Trust* (New Brunswick: Rutgers University Press, 1983). Three centuries before the birth of Christ, Demosthenes wrote, 'There is

one safeguard known generally to the wise, which is an advantage and security to all, but especially to democracies as against despots'. 'What is it?' 'Distrust.'

31 In a useful discussion, J. Gross, 'Social Control under Totalitarianism' in *Toward a General Theory of Social Control*, vol. 2, ed. D. Black (New York: Academic Press, 1984) stresses informing as the principal mechanism by which totalitarian states penetrate the private domain: 'The real power of a totalitarian state results ... from its being at the disposal, available for hire at a moment's notice, to every inhabitant.' Informing in such societies differs (in degree) from democratic societies in that the focus is more on political beliefs and loyalty; anonymous informing is strongly encouraged; there are few procedural safeguards; and one's first obligation is to the state rather than to family or friends.

32 Lie detectors (polygraphs) are most effective when persons being tested believe that they work and thus tell the truth. This gives rise to a variety of ruses. In what operators call a 'stim', a trick sometimes used before an interrogation begins to show the subject a monitor with a dial. The subject is then asked to tell a lie and sees the dial go up, supposedly indicating that the lie has been detected. What the subject doesn't know is that the operator causes the dial to move, independent of what the subject has said. With the subject appropriately impressed, the examination begins. Another device is to ask the subject to pick a card from a marked deck or a deck where all the cards are the same. After a series of questions, the examiner then identifies the card.

33 Some persons eligible for benefits may be hurt as well. Thus, many persons withdrew from a food stamp program after publicity about a computer-matching program. Whether all those who withdrew were in fact ineligible and others who were eligible did not apply are important questions. The perception that benefits are difficult to receive and that persons are constantly being checked may mean the underuse of welfare programs. With their focus on fraud or abuse (rather than equity or justice), government computer-matching programs have rarely looked to see if persons are *not* receiving benefits they are entitled to.

34 G. Marx, 'The Independence of Private and Public Police as Illustrated by Undercover Investigations,' *Crime and Justice System Annuals* 21 (1987).

35 On the discovery of violations, see D. Michael, 'Too Much of a Good Thing? Dilemmas of an Information Society,' *Technological Forecasting and Social Change* 25, no. 4 (July 1984). W. Moore and M. Tumin, 'Some Social Functions of Ignorance,' *American Sociological Review* 14 (1949): 787–95, offer a more general consideration of the functions of ignorance.

36 Laudon (1986).

37 The bad news here is not that the tactic is far from perfect (after all what would it be like to live in a society where it was always possible to tell what a person was thinking or when he was telling the truth?). Rather the problem is misplaced confidence in results. On the polygraph's limitations, see, e.g., D. Lykken, 'Detecting Deception in 1984,' *American Behavioral Scientist* 2 (March/April 1984); L. Saxe, D. Dougherty, and T. Cross, 'The Validity of Polygraph Testing,' *American Psychologist* 40 (March 1985): 355–66.

38 See the discussion in J. Rule, D. McAdam, L. Stearns, and D. Uglow, *The Politics of Privacy* (New York: New American Library, 1980).

39 As cited in A. Mason, *Harlan Fiske Stone: Pillar of the Law* (New York: Viking, 1956), p. 153. Similarly in a 1976 letter Justice William O. Douglas wrote, 'As nightfall does not come at once, neither does oppression. In both instances, there is a twilight when everything remains seemingly unchanged, and it is in such twilight that we all must be most aware of change in the air – however slight – lest we become unwitting victims of darkness'. M. Vrofsky, ed., *The Douglas Letters* (Bethesda, Md.: Adler and Adler, 1987).

40 Recall Justice Brandeis's warning that 'experience should teach us to be most on our guard when the government's purposes are beneficent. Men born to freedom are naturally alert to repel invasion of their liberty by evil-minded rulers. The greatest dangers to liberty lurk in insidious encroachment by men of zeal, well-meaning, but without understanding' (*Olmstead* v. *U.S.*, 277 U.S. 438 [1928]).

41 This conclusion is based on other work that reviews a large amount of empirical data that compare American society to the society Orwell described (G. Marx, *Fragmentation and Cohesion in American Society* [Washington, D.C.: Trend Analysis Program, American Council on Life Insurance, 1983]; Marx, 'The Iron Fist and the Velvet Glove,' in The Social Fabric: Dimensions and Issues, ed. J.F. Short, Jr. (Beverly Hills: Sage, 1986). In Orwell's Oceania: (1) the state is all powerful and the citizen has no rights nor input into government; (2) there is no law; (3) mass communication is rigidly controlled by, and restricted to, the state; (4) there are no groups, lodges, clubs, associations, or organizations apart from those directly sponsored and controlled by the state; (5) the society is hierarchically organized, but beyond this there is little differentiation, diversity, or variety – everything possible is standardized and regimented; (6) the political and economic systems are merged; (7) there is little social mobility and a low and declining standard of living where all surplus goes into war preparations rather than

consumption; (8) individuals are isolated from and do not trust each other; (9) private communication is discouraged, and writing instruments such as the pen are prohibited; (10) learning a foreign language and contact with foreigners are prohibited; (11) individuals are increasingly bored, indifferent, and intolerant, and memory of past liberties fades with each year; (12) proper attitudes and feelings are as important as proper behavior or more so.

42  These are found along with increased concern over capital punishment, police use of force, corporal punishment in schools, and family and sexual violence.

43  As Rule (1984) observes, both mass communications and mass surveillance are part of a broader mobilization of the population, wherein the direct ties between central institutions and citizens are intensified. In contrast to the trend of the last century, information about elites now can flow more freely from the center of society to the periphery as well as the reverse. See also E. Shils's important early statement, *Center and Periphery: Essays in Macro-Sociology* (Chicago: Univ. of Chicago Press, 1975).

44  See, e.g., R. Fox and T. Lears, *The Culture of Consumption* (New York: Pantheon, 1983); and M. Schudson, *Advertising, The Uneasy Persuasion* (New York: Basic Books, 1984).

45  R. Nisbet (*Twilight of Authority* [New York: Oxford Univ. Press, 1975]) writes of the 'softening of power'.

46  In a different context, Al Capone correctly observed that you can accomplish more with a kind word and a gun than with a gun alone.

47  Of course, these may be linked with what is first developed for military and intelligence uses later being applied domestically. Public and private police may also be intertwined. Five major forms of interdependence are (1) joint public/private investigations, (2) public agents hiring or delegating authority to private police, (3) private interests hiring public police, (4) new organizational forms in which the distinction between public and private is blurred, and (5) the circulation of personnel between the public and private sectors.

48  James Madison's advice in *The Federalist* (Paper 51) should be updated to read, 'You must first enable the government to control the governed [and large organizations] and in the next place, oblige it to control itself'.

# 44. The thick green line: the growing involvement of military forces in domestic law enforcement

*Colonel Charles J. Dunlap Jr*

On 20 May 1997 a young American shot a Texas high school sophomore to death. Another instance of gang violence? No. In this case the shooter was a U.S. Marine on an antidrug patrol along the Rio Grande, a military operation that was part of a large border surveillance project conducted under the aegis of Joint Task Force 6 (JTF-6).[1] The marine mistook as a threat to his life, and that of the marines with him, the teenager who, though armed with a rifle, was merely tending a herd of goats. Although a subsequent investigation revealed that the shooting was a tragic culmination of mistakes and misperceptions, the incident served to awaken many Americans to the perils of employing the military for domestic security, a function historically the province of civilian law enforcement personnel.[2]

This chapter briefly reviews the background of the use of the armed forces in a police capacity, discusses the growth of that role in the 1980s and 1990s, and forecasts an even greater expansion into that role in the near future due to the emerging threat of 'catastrophic terrorism'. I contend that this increased reliance on military resources for policing is not in the interest of either the armed forces or the public. Finally, I make some observations with a view toward minimizing the dangers of looking to the military to perform law enforcement tasks while ensuring the nation's public safety.

## Background

Americans have traditionally viewed with suspicion the use of the armed forces for any sort of internal security purpose. These misgivings can be traced to an antipathy toward standing armies that is as old as the nation itself.[3] English colonists, cognizant of the excesses of Oliver Cromwell's New Model Army during the English Civil War, were wary of the nefarious potential of a professional military used at home. A further catalyst for this nascent anti-militarism arose when royal troops were employed to suppress the growing independence movement in the American colonies.[4]

Resistance to a law enforcement function for military forces hardly diminished following the American Revolution. Indeed, in framing the

Constitution, one of the main aims was to limit the role of military forces in domestic activities. The final document provides relatively few authorities for employing the military within the nation's borders. Article 1, section 8, for example, allows Congress to provide for 'calling forth the Militia to execute the Laws of the Union [and to] suppress Insurrections'. Additionally, there is the language of article 4, section 4, which requires the federal government to protect the states against invasion and 'on Application of the Legislature, or of the Executive (when the Legislature cannot be convened) against domestic Violence'.

As is suggested above, the framers intended that the needs of national defense would be principally served by reliance not on full-time regulars but on part-time state-based militias. Even though the militia system seldom worked as originally designed, for much of the nation's history relatively small professional forces were augmented in wartime by huge increases in recruitment and conscription. Though this ad hoc approach met with mixed success in fighting the nation's wars, it essentially remained in place until the threat of the Soviet Union in the 1950s necessitated the maintenance of an enormous peacetime military establishment during the Cold War.

Consequently, there actually have been relatively few occasions where troops have functioned as 'policemen' as that term is understood today. A major deviation from this norm took place during the Civil War era. Spurred by the Confederate insurgency, martial law was implemented in various areas of the North.[5] When this exercise of military power extended to the trial of civilians by military commission, the Supreme Court eventually intervened. In the case of *ex parte Milligan*, the court held that conducting such trials where the civil courts remained open was beyond the powers of the armed forces, despite the existence of a civil war.[6]

Nevertheless, federal troops were used extensively to police the South for over twenty years after the Civil War. Again, however, the wisdom of this strategy was questioned, this time by the legislative branch. According to one treatise, 'Reconstruction era abuses, culminating in the use of federal troops to police polling stations in Southern States (some say to influence the outcome of the presidential election of 1876) led to the 1878 Posse Comitatus Act'.[7] That act criminalizes any use of the armed forces to execute the laws except as may be specifically authorized by Congress.

Even though there has never been a prosecution for a violation of the Posse Comitatus Act, for the latter part of the nineteenth and all of the twentieth century, it served to limit the role of the military in anything resembling ordinary police work (except perhaps in the context of constabulary duties in frontier areas).[8] Of course; throughout U.S. history, military forces have been used to enforce civil law against domestic violence, mostly to suppress riots and similar civil disorders; in particular, troops were used on several occasions to counter labor unrest.[9] But such uses were exceptions to the general rule against the regular use of military force for police-like duties.

That paradigm began evolving in the early 1980s with the onset of the drug crisis. Cognizant of the international dimensions of the drug trade, 'convinced that local police forces were being overwhelmed by the problem, and impressed with the efficiency and renewed popularity of the armed forces, Congress passed a number of statutes designed to bring military resources to bear in the 'war' on drugs. These statutes, still in effect today, permit the use of military equipment and expertise in support of civilian law enforcement agencies.[10] However, the law still prohibits a military member from 'direct participation' in most circumstances in the 'search, seizure, arrest, or other similar activity'.[11] Separate legislative authority designates the Department of Defense (DOD) as the lead agency for the 'detection and monitoring of aerial and maritime transit of illegal drugs into the United States'.[12]

These strictures, however, do not necessarily limit the authority of state forces unless and until they are federalized. Included among such state forces is the National Guard, a hybrid organization having both state and federal status. This important legal distinction is often lost on a post-draft era public where fewer and fewer people have any firsthand knowledge of the military. Given that the Guard's uniforms and equipment are virtually identical to that of the regular armed forces, this perception is wholly understandable. The ever more frequent use of Guard personnel for drug operations and other law enforcement functions has the unintended consequence of serving to acclimate the public to the notion of uniformed military personnel performing such duties.

In any event, the end result of almost two decades of statutory change and billions of dollars in budgetary expenditures is the entrenchment of both regular and part-time military personnel in a variety of counterdrug efforts, including Joint Task Force 6.[13] In addition, there have been calls to use troops to augment police forces in high-crime, drug-infested urban areas.[14] More than anything else the drug problem has pushed the armed forces into institutionalized participation in law enforcement matters.

Counterdrug activities and the new statutes supporting them have also stimulated much collaboration between police and military forces. This has contributed to the 'militarization' of police forces as they incorporate a wide range of military equipment into their inventories and turn to the military for advice and training.[15] In important ways we are witnessing a problematic convergence of police and military interests.

## The future

The involvement of the armed forces in what might be considered police or law enforcement activities is poised to increase exponentially in the near future. This is largely because of the growing threat of terrorism. While terrorism has a long history, consciousness of its dangers in the United States has risen markedly in the past few years. Bombings at New York's World Trade Center and Oklahoma City's Murrah Federal Building underlined terrorism's potential. Still, as destructive as those events were, they were efficiently investigated and the perpetrators quickly apprehended by law enforcement agencies with little help from the military.

But an even greater focus on terrorism was generated by the 1995 attack in Tokyo. In that event a religious cult released the deadly gas sarin in a subway, leaving twelve people dead and over twenty-five hundred injured. Such incidents have spawned fear of what is termed 'catastrophic terrorism'.[16] This insidious peril is usefully divided into two forms for purposes of this analysis: (1) that involving weapons of mass destruction (WMD), whether nuclear, biological, or chemical; and (2) that involving threats to microchip-based information and computer systems, so critical to modern societies.

With the new awareness have come new calls to use the armed forces to confront this unprecedented security challenge.[17] In a sense, the use of the military to confront these perils parallels the rationale for its use in the more traditional domestic role of suppression of civil disorders and even its newer role in drug interdiction. Specifically, the threats have the potential to overwhelm police resources, because of the emerging capability of a relatively small number of nonstate actors to use WMD to inflict casualties on a wartime scale.[18]

There has been a variety of DOD responses to the threat of catastrophic terrorism. Today, for example, the armed forces operate the Directorate of Military Support (DOMS) in the Pentagon. This organization serves as a nerve center for military involvement in all kinds of domestic activities ranging from the 'Presidential inaugurations and Olympic Games to terrorist bombings and urban riots'.[19]

In addition, the Pentagon is responsible for the Domestic Preparedness Program, an ambitious effort to train local police, fire, and medical personnel to deal with the dangers posed by biological and chemical devices.[20] Complementing this effort was the formation of several special military units to counter the WMD threat both at home and abroad.[21] In addition, the National Guard is organizing 170 reconnaissance and decontamination teams to respond to domestic WMD attacks.[22]

A related but somewhat different dilemma is presented by the threat to the nation's computer and communications systems. Many experts have long argued that the United States is extremely vulnerable to what has been called 'cyberterrorism' or 'information warfare'.[23] In 1999 President Bill Clinton, following the recommendations of his Critical Infrastructure Protection Commission, sought $1.4 billion for his fiscal year 2000 budget to develop systems to protect the nation's banking, electric, transportation, and other critical industries.[24]

Cyberterrorism is an especially serious problem for the U.S. military, which is heavily dependent on computers for its daily operations and relies on many of the same microchip-based communication and electronic systems used by the general public.[25] Thus, wholly apart from any abstract desire to aid civilian law enforcement agencies, the armed forces have a very great interest in analyzing and defeating this kind of threat. That threat is real: during an exercise in June 1997 it was discovered that DOD computer systems were far more vulnerable than had been previously thought.

As a consequence, the Pentagon recently announced the formation of a Joint Task Force Network Defense. This organization currently has the limited mission of defending DOD computers.[26] However, newly issued Pentagon doctrine suggests that protection of the nation's information infrastructure is properly a responsibility of DOD.[27]

The enormous scope of the threat of catastrophic terrorism has also generated suggestions for new organizations within the armed forces. A plan has been proposed – though scrapped for the moment – to establish a single military commander with authority to oversee domestic defense in the event of terrorist attack. According to press reports, this 'homeland defense commander' would have 'the know-how and authority to quickly dispatch technicians and troops, who could help deal with terrorist attacks that officials fear could inflict thousands of casualties and disrupt whole cities'.[28]

## The emerging issues

What we have seen in the last twenty years is a growing tendency to look to the armed forces to perform tasks that are essentially law enforcement. To many Americans the use of the military for these purposes is of little concern. The armed forces consistently lead public opinion polls as the most trusted institution in American society, topping even organized religion and the Supreme Court. Moreover, as John Hillen, then an analyst for the Heritage Foundation, put it in 1996: 'Why do politicians want to use the military for police duties? To take advantage of one of the few parts of the federal government that actually works.'[29]

Notwithstanding the seeming acquiescence of the public, this growing trend bears further analysis. In truth, there are few instances in modern times where the military effectively conducted a police-like internal security mission consistent with both the maintenance of an authentic combat capability and democratic values. That said, the issues with regard to using the armed forces for law enforcement can usefully be divided into practical problems and philosophical ones.

### The practical problems

One of the principal reasons that many military leaders have long resisted employing their troops as police forces relates to the practical concern that doing so diminishes combat prowess. Despite what the casual observer may think, there are surprisingly few synergies between law enforcement and military missions.

Examining the border shooting incident provides an illustration. There the Marine Corps insisted that the patrol acted in accordance with the 'JTF-6 rules of engagement which include the inherent right of self-defense'.[30] Though resolution of the specific facts of that case is beyond the scope of this chapter, it is easy to see how a dichotomy might arise. Military forces operating in a domestic situation, where the rules of engagement limit the use of force to 'self-defense' situations, might still have an interpretation of the scope of the term that differs from that of local police forces. Under military practice, force may be used in self-defense to 'decisively counter the hostile act or hostile intent and to ensure the continued safety of U.S. forces'. Moreover, under certain conditions, engagement is permitted 'until hostile force no longer presents an imminent threat'.[31]

However, state law, not military doctrine, governs when military forces are acting domestically against civilian suspects outside of a federal enclave.

Accordingly, the legal authority to use deadly force in such situations may be available to any citizen (as opposed to law enforcement officer) in a particular jurisdiction.[32] Thus, state legal requirements that mandate actions such as 'retreat to the wall' before the use of deadly force is permitted are unknown in military practice and unlikely to be well understood by troops in the field.[33]

Indeed, using military forces for tasks that are essentially law enforcement requires a fundamental change in orientation. To put it bluntly, in its most basic iteration, military training is aimed at killing people and breaking things. Consequently, military doctrine has forces moving on a target by fire and maneuver with a view toward destroying that target. Police forces, on the other hand, take an entirely different approach. They have to exercise the studied restraint that a judicial process requires; they gather evidence and arrest 'suspects'. Where the military sees 'enemies' of the United States, a police agency, properly oriented, sees 'citizens' suspected of crimes but innocent until proven guilty in a court of law. These are two different views of the world.

Thus it is difficult for military personnel trained under a regime that emphasizes combat skills to align themselves with the more restrained procedure required for police work in a democratic society. When forced into such situations, military personnel tend to revert to the combat-oriented architecture that they understand and in which they are comfortable operating.

It is therefore not surprising that, for example, marine officers would characterize their deployment during the 1992 Los Angeles riots in the military language of 'domestic peacekeeping'. More troubling, but still comprehensible given their background and training, are reports that some marines 'when faced with violating doctrine or violating federal law ... chose the latter course'.[34]

It is, of course, possible to train military personnel to suppress their previously instilled combat instincts to perform in the more restricted law enforcement environment. Once military personnel are converted into effective policemen, however, the very ethos that makes them succeed in combat has been dangerously eroded. The restraint so necessary for law enforcement could be catastrophic in war. Years before the 1997 JTF-6 incident, a colonel observing marines firing warning shots during a border skirmish with smugglers later argued that 'combat-trained Marines shouldn't be diminishing hard-learned skills by squeezing off warning shots'.[35]

Even when training succeeds in sufficiently purging military personnel of their combat skills, so that they conduct themselves appropriately as law enforcement agents, a significant and costly commitment must be made to retrain them back into war-fighting mind-set once those duties are completed. In an era of fewer and fewer troops and more and more commitments, commanders are understandably reluctant to do anything that saps combat readiness.

Another factor contributing to the reluctance of military commanders to become involved in law enforcement activities is the potential damage to morale and discipline that may result. It is mistaken to assume that individuals who join an all-volunteer force such as the U.S. military are necessarily inclined to perform domestic police duties. Quite obviously, if that were their personal preference they would have joined a police force. Moreover, while military personnel may be mentally well equipped to deal with a vicious battlefield adversary, they are rather less prepared to deal with a sophisticated criminal aiming to corrupt them.[36] Military leaders simply do not wish to expose their troops to this kind of harmful influence.

Additionally, military officers also believe that using military personnel for domestic law enforcement purposes carries great potential to harm civil–military relations. It can bring the military in conflict with civilian society and aggravate what many see as a growing estrangement of the military from the society it serves.[37] The uproar following the shooting in Texas is just one example. This may be one reason why the secretary of defense radically narrowed the circumstances under which such armed patrols might take place.[38]

But it is the emergence of 'catastrophic terrorism' that portends the circumstance with the greatest potential to draw military personnel into domestic security situations. The immensity of threat necessitates military involvement, especially when WMD are involved, as only the armed forces have the infrastructure and training to meet the challenge of mass casualties. Moreover, other, technical aspects of catastrophic terrorism will likely pull military personnel into law enforcement duties more directly, although inadvertently.

Consider the menace of 'cyberattack'. It presents a particular conundrum for military officials because of the technical difficulty of distinguishing between assaults carried out by clever teenagers on a lark and those conducted by cyberterrorists and enemy nation-states bent on inflicting grievous damage to U.S. national security. Given that at the time of a particular assault on a DOD computer system, it may be impossible to know the identity of the attacker, military personnel could find themselves aggressively responding against a fellow citizen in a manner appropriate to a hostile foreign force but inconsistent with what an American rightly expects when merely suspected of a crime.

Conceiving of terrorists as criminals entitled to due process is not intuitive to military personnel or, for that matter, the terrorists themselves. Many terrorists and terrorist organizations like to portray themselves as 'soldiers' engaged in 'wars' against the United States and other mainly Western nations. However, both historical and current, practice in the United States usually characterizes them as common criminals.[39] There are several reasons for this approach, not the least of which is the fact that under international law, lawful combatants in armed conflict are privileged from prosecution for violent acts that are otherwise in compliance with the law of war. In addition, combatants are entitled to POW status if captured.

Terrorists do not ordinarily achieve status as lawful combatants in armed conflict because the international law of war principally governs conflicts between nation-states and certain internationally recognized entities.[40] Though the law of war does apply to certain groups of irregular belligerents, terrorists also ordinarily fail to meet the minimum legal standards applicable to such forces, in that they fail to carry arms openly, wear a distinctive uniform or symbol, and subject themselves to internal military discipline aimed at enforcing the law of war.

In short, though they now may have the capability to inflict cataclysmic damage on the United States, the magnitude of their crimes does not per se transform terrorists into something other than criminals. Thus, perhaps the most formidable threat to U.S. interests in the future is, by its very nature, fundamentally a criminal challenge, albeit of unprecedented dimensions. This presents significant philosophical issues.

### The philosophical issues

To be sure, philosophical reservations about the involvement of military personnel in law enforcement activities did not arise solely with the emergence of the challenge of catastrophic terrorism. Much concern has been expressed over the years about the military's drug control activities, and this uneasiness continues. Former Secretary of the Navy John Lehman wrote recently of the military's role in drug interdiction that 'by accepting that new (and I believe unconstitutional) mission, the services have become *de facto* police. To involve the services in domestic law enforcement is to cross a dangerous line in separation of powers'.[41]

In this connection it is worth remembering that the genius of the traditional American law enforcement system is that most police power is diffused among thousands of communities. Most of these more or less independent police agencies are subject to strict control by elected leaders at the local or state level. The civilian control of the military, however, is centralized in the president and national command authorities in Washington.[42] This system works well when confronting a foreign threat but markedly less well when employed domestically to interact with the citizenry, where force of arms is seldom the appropriate or necessary law enforcement tactic.

The troublesome potential of the enhanced role of the military in counter terrorism is generating the most criticism. Former secretary of defense Caspar Weinberger condemned the proposals by saying that they were 'repugnant to democratic society'.[43] Though there are no current plans to expand military authority into direct law enforcement (e.g., arrest/search authority), it is difficult to see how that could be avoided in a situation that would likely border on mass chaos.

The previously discussed proposal to appoint a single military commander for a 'homeland defense' organization to handle such situations causes one critic to warn about the risk of 'mission creep'. Gregory T. Nojem, legislative counsel on national security for the American Civil Liberties Union, says, 'The danger is in the inevitable expansion of that authority, so the military gets involved in things like arresting people and investigating crimes … It's hard to believe that a soldier with a suspect in the sights is well positioned to protect that person's civil liberties'.[44]

## Concluding observations

Obviously, those concerned with both civil liberties and domestic security are rightly apprehensive about the outcome of the current debates. One important step in setting the right course for the future would be establishing a clear definition of the kinds of threats manifesting a true national security threat, as opposed to those which present a law enforcement problem, recognizing, of course, that overlap can occur from time to time.

In considering this issue, it may be helpful to recall recent experience. As discussed above, during the 1980s and 1990s there was a major effort to transform the national drug issue into a national security threat suitable for the application of military force. Though military intrusion in what was essentially a law enforcement problem did grow, it fell short of full conversion of the armed forces to police work.

Today, we face another peril, that of catastrophic terrorism. This threat, if characterized as a national security risk, carries great potential to force that next step. No one should suffer the illusion that military forces could ever execute the laws with the same sensitivity to civil liberties as regular police forces. To do so is at odds with the central imperatives of military service. Moreover, a successful use of the armed forces for law enforcement may well render it incapable of defeating authentic external military threats.

What does the future hold? Secretary of Defense William Cohen warned in 1997 that 'terrorism is escalating to the point that citizens of the United States may soon have to choose between civil liberties and more intrusive forms of protection'.[45] That may be so, but employing military forces for internal security purposes will surely exacerbate the problem. Confronting terrorism requires, among other things, an intensive intelligence effort and aggressive investigative work. A military organization adept at destroying targets and undermining enemy command and control structures is not necessarily the best organization to do such work in a democracy.

It must be pointed out that in the American experience any call for using the armed forces for police work almost always arises from outside the military establishment. In the case of catastrophic terrorism, the lack of any is immediate alternative complicates short-term solutions. In reporting the proposed terrorism-adapted 'homeland defense' force, the *Washington Post* captured the essence of the dilemma:

> 'Frankly, we are not seeking this job,' said Deputy Secretary of Defense John Hamre. He acknowledged that 'most Americans' are 'apprehensive' about the military getting involved in domestic policing and crisis management. 'But we know we're being asked to be involved because we have the only part of government that has the resources that can be mobilized,' he added.[46]

A recent article in *Foreign Affairs* proposed a program for combating catastrophic terrorism that will require some of the intrusiveness about which Secretary Cohen warns and which Deputy Secretary Hamre recognizes.[47] Still, except for certain aspects of the draft National Terrorism Intelligence Center, it carefully excludes DOD from most activities in the law enforcement realm. (DOD would, however, have a large role in consequence management and preemptive and retaliatory strikes.) Similarly, a Justice Department proposal to take the lead from DOD in counterterrorism preparedness by 2001 appears to be the direction the evolution should take.[48] Although such proposals have real potential, considerable work is required for implementation. As these and other ideas are considered, it is vital that inertia and the penchant for quick fixes not allow responsibility for countering catastrophic terrorism to devolve permanently to the armed forces. The risks of doing so are great, and we should not be seduced by the absence in modern times of significant abuses by the armed forces. The stakes are very high. As Colonel Harry G. Summers, a decorated army veteran and expert on national security affairs, warns: 'Like using fascism as a cure for the Great Depression, the involvement of military forces in civilian law enforcement could prove to be a greater assault on our democracy than any terrorist bombing, for it could destroy that democracy's very foundations.'[49]

*From Col. Charles J. Dunlap Jr, 'The thick green line: the growing involvement of military forces in domestic law enforcement',* in P.B. Kraska (ed.), Militarizing the American Criminal Justice System *(Boston, MA: Northeastern University Press), 2001, pp 29–42.*

## Notes

1 Joint Task Force 6 is a multiservice organization whose mission is to provide surveillance for federal agents in border areas. 'While not allowed to make arrests, they have carried out hundreds of observation sorties along the border, passing on information to the Border Patrol and drug-enforcement agents' (Sam Verhovek, 'In Marine's Killing of Teenager, Town Mourns and Wonders Why,' *New York Times*, 29 June 1997, 1, 12).

2 The marine responsible for the shooting was never prosecuted.

3 Laurie Keliman, 'Domestic Anti-Terror Role for the Military Called Unnecessary,' *Washington Times*, 11 May 1995 6; Richard H. Kohn, *Eagle and Sword: The Federalists and the Creation of the Military Establishment in America, 783–1802* (New York: Free Press, 1975), 3–9.

4 William S. Fields and David Hardy, 'The Militia and the Constitution: A Legal History,' *Military Law Review* 136 (1992): 9–13.

5 Charles Fairman *Martial Law* (Chicago: Callaghan, 1943).

6 71 U.S. 2 (1866); for a discussion of *Milligan* and other cases addressing civil liberties in wartime, see William H. Rehnquist, *All the Laws but One: Civil Liberties in Wartime* (New York: Knopf, 1998).

7 18 U.S.C. §1385; Stephen Dycus, Arthur L. Berney, William C. Banks, and Peter Raven-Hansen, *National Security Law* (Boston: Little Brown, 1990).

8 Following the siege at Wounded Knee South Dakota, in 1973 plaintiffs seeking damages following a stand-off with a group of armed Indians argued that the army and the air force were used in violation of the Posse Comitatus Act. The court concluded that although military personnel did furnish advice and equipment, this did not constitute 'execution' of the laws in violation of the act. *In dicta*, however, the court did observe that uses of the armed forces contrary to the act could result in a finding that evidence thereby obtained was inadmissible. *Rissonette v. Haig*, 776 F.2d 1384, affd, 800 F.2d 812 (8th Cir, 1986) (*en banc*), afd'd, 485 U.S. 264 (1988). Thus litigation involving the act occasionally appears but in the context of using it as an exclusionary rule, not as the basis for a criminal prosecution itself.

9 David E. Engdahl, 'Soldiers, Riots, and Revolution: The Law and History of Military Troops in Civil Disorders,' *Iowa Law Review* 1 (1971): 132–64.

10 See chapter 18 of title 10, U.S. Code.

11 10 U.S.C. §375.

12 10 U.S.C. §124.

13 Jim Garamone, 'DoD Actively Supports Counterdrug Efforts,' American Forces Information Service, November 1998, found at www.defenselink.mil/news/Nov1998/n11301998_9811303.html.

14 Catherine O'Neill, 'Bring in the Army to End the Fear,' *Los Angeles Times*, Washington ed., 29 March 1994, 1.

15 'Police Get Gadgetry Thanks to the Military,' *Washington Post*, 30 November 1998, C4; Christopher M. Loder, 'Cops Turn to West Point for Leadership Skills,' *Newark Star-Ledger*, 28 April 1994, 35.

16 Flora Lewis 'The New Anti-Terrorism is Scary,' *International Herald Tribune*, 29 December 1998, 9.

17 For example, section 324(4) of Public Law 104–32 (cited at 22 U.S.C. §2377 note) states that Congress finds that 'the President should use all necessary means, including covert action and *military force*, to disrupt, dismantle, and destroy international infrastructure used by international terrorists, including overseas training facilities and safe havens' (emphasis added).

18 Fred Bayles, 'U.S. Police III: Prepared for Terror Attack,' *USA Today*, 13 October 1998, 1.

19 Ernest Blazar 'Inside the Ring,' *Washington Times*, 27 August 1998, 12.

20 See 10 U.S.C. §3 82. The effort reportedly has met with mixed success (Bayles, 'U.S. Police III').

21 Bradley Graham, 'U.S. Gearing up against Germ War Threat,' *Washington Post*, 14 December 1997, 1.

22 David Ruppe, 'Guard to Play Major Counter-Terror Role,' *Defense Week*, 19 October 1998, 1.

23 Winn Schwartau, *Information Warfare*, 2d ed. (New York: Thunder Mouth Press, 1996).

24 Heather Harteld, 'Clinton: $1.41B to Fight Cyberterror,' *Federal Computer Week*, 25 January 1999 1.

25 Office of the Under Secretary of Defense for Acquisition and Technology, *Report of the Defense Science Board Task Force on Information Warfare-Defense* (November 1996).

26 Frank Wolfe, 'Joint Task Force to Direct Pentagon's Cyber Defense,' *Defense Daily*, 26 January 1999, 1.

27 Chairman of the Joint Chiefs of Staff, *Joint Doctrine for Information Operations*, Joint Publication 3–13 (9 October 1998).

28 Paul Richter, 'Need for Anti-Terrorism Chief Debated,' *Los Angeles Tines*, 23 January 1999, 3.

29 John Hillen, 'Don't Misuse the Armed Forces,' *Investor's Business Daily*, 28 February 1996, 2.

30 Gary Martin, 'Border Death Probe Branded Inadequate,' *San Antonio Express-News*, 20 June 1998, 1.

31 Chairman of the Joint Chiefs of Staff, *Standing Rules of Engagement for U.S. Forces*, Instruction 3121.01, enclosure A, paragraphs 7 and 8 (1 October 1994).

32 Charles Torcia, ed., *Wharton's Criminal Law*, 14th ed. (Rochester, N.Y.: Lawyer's Co-operative, 1979).

33 See Torcia, *Wharton's Criminal Law*, 126.

34 Thomas E. Ricks, 'On American Soil: The Widening Gap between the U.S. Military and U.S. Society,' in *Project on U.S. Post-Cold War Civil-Military Relations*, Working Paper no. 3, 21–2 (Cambridge, Mass.: John M. Olin Institute for Strategic Studies, Harvard University, May 1996).

35 Bill Torque and Douglas Wallet, 'Warriors without War,' *Newsweek*, 19 March 1990, 18.

36 Indeed, some criminals have succeeded in corrupting military personnel; see, e.g., H. G. Reza, 'A Drug Probe Finds Smugglers in the Military,' *Los Angeles Times*, 13 December 1998, 1.

37 Ricks, 'On American Soil,' 21–2.

38 'Ground Troop Use on Border Curtailed, Officials Say,' *Dallas Morning News*, 30 January 1999, 1.

39 At least one authority contends that some terrorists may also be considered unlawful combatants in an armed conflict; see Lt. Col. Richard J. Erickson, *Legitimate Use of Military Force against State-Sponsored International Terrorism* (Montgomery, Ala.: Air University Press, 1989).

40 This analysis is founded on both conventional (treaty) law and customary international law (*Air Force Pamphlet* 52A, 19 November 1976, 110–31).

41 John Lehman, 'Our Military Condition,' *American Spectator*, October 1998, 24.

42 Steven Wisotsky, 'The War on Drugs and Civil Liberties,' *USA Today Magazine*, July 1993, 17, 19.

43 Keliman, 'Domestic Anti-Terror Role,' 6.

44 William J. Broad and Judith Miller, 'Pentagon Seeks Command for Emergencies in U.S.,' *New York Times*, 28 January 1999, 1.

45 Patrick Pexton, 'Banking on a Revolution,' *Air-Force Times*, 22 September 1997, 3; 'Police Get Gadgetry.'

46 Bradley Graham, 'Pentagon Plans Domestic Terrorism Team,' *Washington Post*, 1 February 1999, 2.

47 Ashton Carter, John Deutch, and Phillip Zelikow, 'Catastrophic Terrorism: Tackling the New Danger,' *Foreign Affairs*, November/December 1998, 80.

48 'Justice Department Poised to Take Pentagon's Counterterrorism Duties,' *Inside the Pentagon*, 8 October 1998, 14.

49 Col. Harry G. Summers, 'Using Military for Civilian Policing Bad Idea,' *Stars and Stripes*, 10 May 1995, 17.

# 45. Cops and spooks: the uneasy partnership

*Jean-Paul Brodeur*

## Introduction

Several authors have argued that the public police forces did not hold anymore a monopoly over policing postmodern societies (Bayley and Shearing, 1996; Johnston, 1992 and 1998; Reiner, 1992 and 1994). In arguing thus, they generally refer to the increasing privatization of policing. With its guards and its elaborate surveillance technology, private security is more of a substitute for police personnel patrolling the streets and other public spaces clad in uniform than to investigators in civilian clothes (the detective units). Although there are many private investigators, they operate in special fields and are not seen as a threat to the public police's hold on the investigation of serious crime.

A challenge to the police's monopoly on inquiries into serious crime may come from other quarters. I will only briefly mention the role of the military in the investigation of crimes against humanity. Bringing the perpetrators of genocide, ethnic cleansing and crimes of war against civilian populations to justice may be an idea whose time has come, but its implementation is only in its incipient stages. The question of who will be responsible for bringing the suspects before international courts has not even begun to be solved.

There is however another type of organization or agency which may eventually compete with the police in the investigation of serious crime on an important scale. It is the security and intelligence services, which have been long involved in the struggle against politically or ideologically motivated violence (terrorism). In my own country – Canada – two federal agencies are supposed to share a partnership in the prevention and repression of terrorism. The first one is the Canadian Security Intelligence Service (CSIS), which is a civilian security service, and the other is the Royal Canadian Mounted Police (RCMP).[1] According both to research and to press reports, these two agencies are acting as much as competitors as partners (Farson, 1990; Cléroux, 1990; Lester, 1998). As we shall see, Canada is not an exception in this regard.

I propose to examine in this chapter the involvement of the security services of different Western countries in the prevention and repression of non-politically or ideologically motivated crime, these functions having been so far the prerogative of traditional police forces. The chapter is divided in three parts. First, I describe major trends in policing and in the evolution of societies and politics, asking how they might warrant the theoretical assertion of a broader implication of the security services in countering criminal activities. Second, I assess the extent of the present involvement of the security services in criminal investigations. Finally, I try to project from the current situation whether the share of the security services in policing will increase or not.

## Part I: trends and theories

Among the many trends which are and may be influential in relation to policing, I will present briefly two, which, for the purposes of this chapter, appear as the most significant. The first one is a sociological trend. Eschewing the jargon of postmodernism, I will simply state what is becoming obvious: we are moving into the 'information age'.[2] This trend impacts on policing, which is increasingly seen as being dependent upon the production of intelligence. In a bold extra-polation, Ericson and Haggerty (1998) went as far as defining police as 'knowledge workers', thus risking to dilute the police's specific function. Indeed, there are a great many different professionals that might be described as knowledge workers, not all of them being police.

The second trend that I want to discuss is no less acknowledged in the literature and the media. Although there was some scepticism in the early 1990s on the end of the Cold War, it is now bygone. An important consequence of the collapse of the Iron Curtain is that security intelligence agencies such as the CIA in the US, the Canadian CSIS, or the British MI5 and MI6 suddenly appeared to be deprived of their core mission – containing the USSR and its allies. Books and reports were published that severely criticized the performance of these agencies (Bissell, 1997; U.S. Congress, 1997); the press[3] and experts on the intelligence community described these agencies as undergoing a profound crisis, some experts even calling for their abolition (Weiner, 1995; Draper, 1997).

These two trends came together in the following reasoning: since there was a growing agreement that policing was to be fuelled by intelligence in the information age, a significant part of the activity of the security intelligence services, which have made the collection and analysis of intelligence their own special trade, should be rechannelled into the struggle against crime. This plea for the reorientation of part of the security services' action was also grounded into the nature of the beast to be fought, *transnational* organized crime being substituted for disintegrating Communism as the new global threat to national security (Sterling, 1990 and 1995; Nicaso and Lamothe, 1995). Having embraced market economy at least in theory, the former Eastern Bloc countries were also willing to fill the void left by the demise of the Cold War by the struggle against the conquering Mafias.

As Naylor (1995) showed, squarely substituting organized crime for the former Cold War as the new threat to national security may be overstating its potential for mischief and, more crucially, its ambition. There is a vast difference between corrupting an official for specific purposes and taking his or her job with all of its duties. For instance, a criminal organization may want to buy police or judicial complacency; however, there is no profitable point for such an organization to replace a whole police department or the judiciary, attempting to discharge all of their duties, regardless of how badly it would do so. Simplistic equations between the former Cold War and the threat of organized crime being put aside, one cannot however dismiss on principle the existence of any significant interfaces between policing, law enforcement and the protection of national security. On first appraisal, the connections between the intelligence services' mandate and criminal investigations would fall, at least in theory, within four categories.[4]

### New forms of terrorism

Countering terrorism is at the core of the mandate of the security services in all countries. According to figures released by the US State Department, incidents of international terrorism have decreased by 54% since 1987.[5] However, the incidents that have recently occurred are among the most spectacular and the most devastating (e.g. the Oklahoma City bombing). International terrorism is generally understood as politically motivated violence. Yet there are new forms of extreme violence, which have the all the hallmarks of terrorism excepting political motivation. Extreme right violence, hate crimes and mass murder perpetrated by the members of religious cults are not viewed by experts on terrorism as being politically motivated, although their motives are certainly different from traditional criminal violence (Kelly and Maghan, 1998). Narco-terrorism and other variants of organized criminal violence fall into an intermediate category. Although motivated by greed, their aim is similar to terrorism, which is to produce mass intimidation of the State apparatus and of the general population.

### Proto-terrorism

I mean by proto-terrorism the acts perpetrated in direct support of terrorism, such as trafficking in firearms, in the components of explosive devices and in dangerous substances, not to mention efforts to smuggle out of the former USSR a nuclear warhead with its delivery system. Dangerous substances are now a special object of concern. They can be divided in three categories: radioactive substances, chemical agents and biological weapons. Radioactive substances include weapons-grade material (uranium-235, plutonium, lithium), other radioactive or dangerous substances (cesium-137, strontium-90 and cobalt-60) and radioactive scrap metal[6] (Joutsen, 1998: 235). Since the end of the Cold War, nuclear reactors and huge arsenals of weapons of mass destruction are not anymore as securely protected as they were, particularly in the Russian Federation. Hence, there is a growing apprehension that actual nuclear weapons or weapons-grade material may become available to terrorist organizations on an illegal market. Chemical agents were developed since the First World War and huge quantities of toxic armament wastes have accumulated in various countries; these include sarin, soman and tabun, which were discovered, produced and stockpiled by Germany prior to the end of World War II (Stock and Lohs, 1998: 25). Biological weapons are living organisms and viruses which may be deliberately used, sometimes in combination with special means of delivery, for hostile purposes to cause disease or death in humans, animals or plants. Closely related are toxin warfare agents, which are poisonous chemical compounds originally used for hostile purposes to cause disease or death (Geissler and Haynes, 1991: 3). The threats posed by all these weapons is quite real, as was shown in March 1995 by the release in the Tokyo subway system of the nerve agent sarin by members of the religious sect Aum Shinrikyo; twelve passengers were killed and more than 5,500 injured by this terrorist act (Cole, 1997: 151–61). Terrorism being the weapon of the weak and of the poor, biological warfare is particularly suited to its purposes. In 1969, a United Nations panel received the following information: 'for a large-scale operation against a civilian population, casualties might cost about $2,000 per square kilometre with conventional weapons, $800 with nuclear weapons, $600 with nerve-gas and $1 with biological weapons' (quoted in Livingstone and Douglas, 1984: 7).

### Espionage and counter-espionage

Both of these activities are also at the core of the operations of security and intelligence agencies. As we shall later see in more details, it may be in this field that the true substitute for the Cold War will be found. Economic competition now approaching the level of economic warfare, secret services are increasingly involved in economic intelligence and counter-intelligence. These activities may not be immediately related to policing, although economic counter-espionage certainly implies the protection of intellectual property, which is police activity in its own right. However, the pursuit of economic intelligence is at least tangentially connected with policing. It is bound to produce at one time or another crucial information on economic crime, such as all forms of contraband, the laundering of illegal profits, the counterfeiting of money, the illegal transfer of technology and political corruption (e.g. an official divulging his country's strategy in trade negotiations in return for money).

### Illegal immigration

The vetting of political refugees and of immigrants is part of the mandate of the security services in many countries. In Canada, our intelligence service is explicitly tasked by the *CSIS Act* to provide advice to the Ministry of Citizenship and Immigration on prospective immigrants, refugees and visitors to Canada (CSIS, 1997: Part IV). The smuggling of illegal aliens has now become a major source of profit for organized crime. In performing their duties in relation to the vetting of immigrants, security services are bound to be involved in gathering intelligence on the criminal networks used to smuggle illegal aliens. The illegal transfer of whole populations is now a major preoccupation of Western-style democracies.

In presenting the preceding interfaces between security intelligence, policing and law enforcement, I have restricted myself to aspects of policing and law enforcement that clearly fell within the ambit of the traditional mandate of the security services (counter-terrorism, espionage and counter-espionage, and the surveillance of aliens on national territory). The overlapping between security and criminal intelligence is potentially much greater, if we take into consideration new forms of crime – e.g. computer crime or, to use the broader designation, digital crime (Barrett, 1997) – against which security and intelligence agencies may be more efficient than police organizations, because of their experience in the storing and processing of information. I shall take up this point in the third part of this chapter.

To conclude, speculating that security and intelligence agencies are or will be claiming a bigger share in the field of policing is not unreasonable in respect to their mandate, as long as we avoid assuming that there *must* be a neat and unique equivalent of the former Cold War. I will now try to assess how much the security and intelligence services of various countries are in effect involved in law enforcement and may cooperate (or compete) with police forces.

## Part II: current involvement of security services in policing

Trying to assess the actual involvement of the security and intelligence services in policing is noticeably difficult. First, these services operate under a thick veil of secrecy, which is not easily lifted. The confidential nature of their operations is protected by stringent legislation such as the various 'Official Secrets Acts' which are in force under one form or another in all countries. One consequence of this obligation to secrecy is that members of these agencies almost never testify in court, in contrast to the police, thus adding to the difficulty of measuring their implication in law enforcement, in the narrow sense of the word. All the open sources that we have to rely on are either indirect or incomplete, the latter case being the rule with the official reports annually tabled by some of these agencies. Second, the so-called end of the Cold War occurred in the early 1990s and is thus a very recent event in terms of history. Even when they are not military or quasi-military organizations, security and intelligence services are conservative organizations that do not quickly adapt to change. Consequently, their involvement in policing is likely to be more programmatic than effective at this stage. Thirdly, there is the methodological difficulty of making general assertions about organizations that may differ considerably from country to country, although they are functionally similar. For instance, there is in France one intelligence agency which is fully integrated into the *Police Nationale*. This agency – the *Renseignements généraux* (General Intelligence) – has always been involved in policing, particularly in relation to the laws that regulate gambling. Despite these reservations, I will review the evidence, which only allows in its present state for qualified conclusions.

[…]

*Economic intelligence and security*

The integration of 'economic well-being' into the definition of national security as one of its major components is a fact that is well documented for all Western democracies and for Japan. In the early 1990s, the French ministry of the Interior created *l'Institut des Hautes Études de la Sécurité Intérieure* (IHESI; the Institute for Higher Learning in Domestic Security). This institute publishes a journal – *Les Cahiers de la Sécurité Intérieure* – which devoted an issue to intelligence (IHESI, 1997). The first section of this issue is comprised of papers emanating from the various French security and intelligence services. Since some these papers are not signed but simply attributed to an official source within an agency, they can be said to represent the position of this agency. These papers – particularly those originating from the two main domestic security agencies – make it abundantly clear that economic security is an important constituent of national security as it is conceived by the French (IHESI, 1997: 21, 24, and 40). The situation is similar in the UK, where 'economic wellbeing' is now an integral part of national security and where 'as regards foreign intelligence', 'espionage' is being supplanted by the protection of 'economic well-being' from external threats by the domestic agencies (Gill, 1998: 8–10). In Canada, CSIS initiated in 1993 the Economic Security and Proliferation Issues (ESPI) programme and created a unit to implement it.

The ramification of economic security into criminal law enforcement is well acknowledged in France, particularly in the field of money laundering (IHESI, 1997: 40; see also Pichot-Duclos, 1993 and Martre, 1994). Likewise, it is an issue in Canada, as shown in a paragraph from the last report of the Security Intelligence Review Committee, where SIRC presents its findings on the operations of CSIS's ESPI unit: 'For example, ESPI investigated several incidents that, we believe, did not have a demonstrable link to a foreign government, including activities that were primarily of a criminal nature' (SIRC, 1997: 13).

Evan Potter, who is one of Canada's foremost experts on economic security also acknowledges the connection between economic counter-intelligence and law enforcement (Potter, 1998: 28).

### Organized crime

The connection between security intelligence work and policing need not pass through the pursuit of economic security. The direct involvement of the security and intelligence services in countering organized crime can be licensed and even compelled by legislation. This is what happened in Germany. In 1994, the German Federal Parliament (*Bundestag*) gave legal authorization to the federal intelligence service to extend its electronic surveillance operations to drug trafficking; in 1995, the German Office of the Protection of the Constitution, an agency that protects German national security, was permitted by the *Land* of Bavaria to target organized crime (Busch, 1997: 279–81). In the UK, despite 1993 denials that there were any plans for MI5 – the domestic security service – to become involved in the investigation of organized crime, Mrs. Stella Rimington, then its director, acknowledged in a 1995 public lecture that the Security Service had positioned themselves to take on an increasing role with respect to organized crime (Gill, 1998: 11; also see UK, 1995 and Urban, 1996: 281–85).

### The former Eastern Bloc countries

The situation in the former Communist countries deserves a special mention. There, the need for the security and intelligence services to find themselves a new mission and a new legitimacy was overwhelming, as they were deeply associated with the most grievous of human rights violations (Rosenberg, 1995). Second, the problem of organized crime is of such magnitude that its solution requires the implications of all available 'forces of order'. In the case of the former Eastern Bloc countries, little argument was needed to justify the *quid pro quo* between organized crime and the Cold War, so pressing was the threat of the former. Nevertheless, the security services have been drastically downsized and some of the disfranchised agents have joined ranks with organized crime. Others went private and are in league with Western consulting firms involved in the provision of economic intelligence, such firms being also staffed with former Western security service employees (Wayne, 1999: 4).

## The United States

I have not yet spoken of the US, although it is at the tip of the evolution that I have been describing. In October 1994, the US Congress chartered a commission to conduct a comprehensive review of US intelligence. Since 'the Cold War had ended', it was 'prudent to reexamine a costly government activity closely tied to that era' (US Congress, 1996: Executive Summary, p. 1). The report of this commission was released in February 1996.

The content of this US report is in dramatic contrast with a similar endeavour undertaken only 6 years before to review the function of the intelligence community in Canada (Canada, House of Commons, 1990). Whereas the Canadian review, shortly conducted before the fall of the Berlin wall, sticks to a past conception of national security, the US report strives to break away from the tradition that dichotomizes the protection of national security and policing. The US commission coined the expression 'global crime' to refer to international terrorism, narcotics trafficking, trafficking in weapons of mass destruction, and international organized crime (US Congress, 1996: Chapter 4, p. 1). More crucially, it recommended:

> that the President create by Executive Order a Global Crime Committee of the National Security Council to direct the U.S. Government's actions against transnational activities that threaten the national security. The Committee should include, at a minimum, the Secretaries of State and Defense, the Attorney General, and the Director of Central Intelligence. The Committee should be chaired by the National Security Advisor (US Congress, 1996: Chapter 4, p. 2).

The commission's position is strongly echoed in the reports from two important nongovernment and not-for-profit organizations based in the US. The first of these reports was commissioned by the Twentieth Century Fund, a foundation well-known for its independence and the excellence of the work that it sponsors (Twentieth Century Fund, 1996). The report contains a series of recommendations devoted to improving the quality of intelligence available to the US government (Twentieth Century Fund, 1996: 15–18). These recommendations are based on a background paper on US intelligence and the world economy commissioned by the Fund (Zelikow, 1996). The report also links the gathering of economic intelligence with the production of information on money laundering, political corruption and organized crime (Twentieth Century Fund, 1996: 16; Goodman, 1996: 33 and 56).

The second report comes from a different kind of organization. The Center for Strategic and International Studies (CSIS/US) is also an independent and not-for-profit organization that sponsors studies in particular fields. It has in this way developed a Global Organized Crime Project. The chairman of this project is William H. Webster, former director of the CIA and of the FBI. Robert Gates, also a CIA former director, Stuart Knight, retired director of the US Secret Service, and William Cohen, the current US Secretary of Defense, are among the members of the project's steering committee. The CSIS/US links with the US government establishment are thus obvious and its report may reflect the thinking of the US government and its intelligence community more closely than the Twentieth Century Fund report. The Global Organized Crime Project commissioned a study on Russian organized crime. The two first key findings of this study are:

> Left unchecked, Russia is in danger of becoming a 'criminal-syndicalist state' under the control of corrupt government bureaucrats, politicians, businessmen, and criminals with which normal relations would be impossible.

> ROC [Russian Organized Crime] constitutes a direct threat to national security interests of the United States by fostering instability in a nuclear-armed major power (CSIS/US, 1997: 10).

Its first recommendation reads as follows:

> ROC should receive public recognition from the president of the United states as a national security threat (CSIS/US, 1997: 12).

Two things are striking with this kind of talk. The first one is how close it is to the language used in the 1996 US Congress commission report that reviewed the function of US intelligence in the post-Cold War era (e.g. the use of the notion of 'global crime'). The second one is its unabashed substitution of Russian organized crime for the Communist threat of the Cold War.

Adding all the preceding evidence, we may conclude that the security and intelligence services are effectively involved in policing and law enforcement. The last public report of the Canadian CSIS sums up our findings, when it categorizes its own operations into 'traditional intelligence activities' on the one hand, and 'economic espionage, information warfare, proliferation and trans-national criminal activity', on the other (CSIS, 1997: Part 111).

This general conclusion must however be qualified in important ways. Not only does this involvement vary significantly from country to country, but in the best of cases it is in its incipient stage, if not wholly programmatic. In Canada, the review committee of CSIS performed 'an operational audit' of the Service's activities. Although it does mention economic espionage, this audit devotes no particular section to operations directed against criminal activity, either domestic or transnational. The greatest impediment to the involvement of the security and intelligence services in policing is that in most Western countries their mandate is enshrined in a legislation that directs their activities mainly against foreign and foreign-sponsored threats. The definition of intelligence proposed by the US Congress commission on American intelligence is particularly telling in this regard, although it is not particularly enlightening:

Although 'intelligence' is defined in law and executive order, neither convey a very clear understanding of the term. The Commission believes it preferable to define 'intelligence' simply and broadly as information about 'things foreign' – people, places, things, and events – needed by the Government for the conduct of its functions (US Congress, 1996: Introduction, p. 4).

With the exception of domestic terrorism, which has all but disappeared since 1973, this quote applies to Canada and, I suspect, to many other Western countries, although they may still experience terrorism. Save for internal terrorism, all articles of CSIS's mandate refer to foreign sponsored activities against Canadian national security.

### Part III: the future of policing revisited

In view of these reservations about the current involvement of the security and intelligence services in crime policing, I will now try to assess what lies in the future. This exercise is, needless to say, speculative, but hopefully it will not be gratuitous. First, I describe some of the current developments in respect to crime and to crime policing strategy and then I examine whether the kind of work performed by the security and intelligence services does not make them uniquely qualified to claim a role in policing.

### Developments in crime

In my preliminary appraisal of the connections between the mandates of the security and intelligence services and criminal investigation, I identified various types of crime that would fall under the sub-headings of this mandate. These crimes share a number of common features.

### Hybridity

The first feature is that these crimes tend to blur the traditional line distinguishing common criminality and national security offenses. It was always acknowledged that acts of terrorism violated the criminal law. For instance, whatever may be its motivation, political assassination is still an act of murder. This acknowledgement first led to the recognition that the police had a role to play in countering terrorism (Farson, 1990). There is now a converse awareness that acts of common criminality have or have had a political dimension and that the security and intelligence services should play an increasing part in law enforcement. Narco-terrorism, as it is practiced in defiance of the State by drug lords in South America and by war lords in South East Asia, is the most frequently quoted example. There are many others. The funding of illegal political activities through the proceedings of common crime is also frequently cited and it generates complex problems for law enforcement. Common criminal violence perpetrated as punishment against persons who do not submit to extortion may have its root in punitive actions originally undertaken by political organizations to fill their war chest; when peace settles in, as is happening in Northern Ireland, the hard core of these organizations cannot give up on the money that terror brought in and splinters into various criminal gangs (Anderson, 1994).

Other kinds of hybrid crimes, such as political corruption, the smuggling of illegal aliens, and the trafficking in dangerous substances have recently come to the foreground, either because of the massive scale on which they are perpetrated or of the extent of havoc that they can create. Organized illegal immigration, which impacts on citizenship, population control, labour policies and fiscality is the prototype of a criminal activity with multiple implications for national security. The most highly mediatized form of hybrid crime is right-wing terrorism and mass violence wreaked by religious cults. Although politically or ideologically motivated, these forms of terrorism were not really considered as threats to national security in Western countries until recently, in great part because they were occurring outside the great confrontation between the US and the USSR and their respective allies. Even with the best of intentions, it was difficult to construe the racist violence of the Ku Klux Klan as part of the global communist conspiracy. With the end of the Cold War, the political or ideological nature of this violence became more apparent and in countries like Canada it was actively targeted by the security service. In one of the most detailed reports to be publicly released on a joint operation by a security service and a police force, the watchdog committee overseeing CSIS described how it joined forces with the Toronto police department to infiltrate several right-wing extremist organizations (SIRC, 1994). Another reason for the increasing realization that right-wing or religiously motivated terrorism poses a national security threat is the number of casualties that can result from an attempt using biological weapons. In the US, abortion clinics have been threatened of being sent mail containing anthrax bacilli. In view of what is filtering out of official investigations, such threats cannot be taken lightly. According to a staff statement released in 1995 by a US Senate subcommittee that investigated the Aum Shinrikyo in the wake of its use of sarin in a Tokyo subway train, Aum representatives went to Zaire during the 1992 breakout of the Ebola virus (Cole, 1997: 3 and 227, note 7). They pretended to be health workers, but, with the benefit of hindsight, it may be asked whether they did not travel to Zaire to obtain virus samples for cultivation and eventual use.

*Complexity*

Regardless of whether it is perpetrated for political or ideological reasons or just for greed, there is one feature of economic and of organized crime which is increasingly salient: it is its sophistication (Brodeur, 1997; Simon and Hagan, 1999). Organized crime may be crude in its activities, but the laundering of its profits is generally a highly sophisticated operation. The most complex form of delinquency yet may well be what is termed 'digital crime' (Barrett, 1997). Digital crime is the use of information networks and computer technology to commit crimes (e.g. using the Internet for laundering money) or the perpetration of crimes against the owners and users of information networks and computer technology (e.g. information vandalism through the infection of databases by malicious computer viruses). With the possible exception of large police organizations committed to expert policing, such as the FBI or the German *Bundeskriminalamt* (BKA), most police forces do not presently have either the human or the technical resources to resolve efficiently the complexity of these crime problems.

### Transnationality

I shall not insist in this feature, which is an indisputable character of most of the forms of crime that I have been discussing. This proliferating aspect of crime contributes in no small way to its complexity.

### Developments in crime policing

There were many significant changes in policing since the early 1980s. The development of the community and of the problem-oriented models of policing was extensively covered in the research literature (Brodeur, 1998). The development of these models was fostered by the growing awareness that there was an urgent need to complement and eventually to supplant reactive policing by crime prevention strategies going beyond rhetoric. There are two implications of the coming of age of crime prevention, which did not receive as much attention as community and problem-oriented policing and which I would like to briefly discuss.

The first one of these implications is the growing emphasis on risk assessment and on risk management. Whether we review the current trends in general sociology (Stehr and Ericson, 1992), in penology (Feeley and Simon, 1992) or in the theory of policing (Ericson and Hagerty, 1997), the notion of risk is superseding the notion of event. There is a crucial difference between risk and event. Even granting that events are shaped by public opinion, the media or historians, they belong to reality rather than to virtuality. Not so with risks, which are actuarial constructs about what might happen. They belong to virtuality and are thus products of knowledge and calculation. A preventive policing strategy which is based on the assessment and management of risk is then basically dependent on knowledge expertise.

The second implication of the emphasis on crime prevention is the importance of surveillance, which is precisely aimed at precluding undesirable events from occurring. Surveillance can be exercised by human personnel, but now relies in great part on the use of electronic technology such as the interception of private communications and video imagery.

Given these developments in crime and in policing, what is to be foreseen with respect to the implication of the security and intelligence services in law enforcement?

### Aspects of security and intelligence work

The answer to this the question may be provided by comparing the preceding traits of crime and of policing with the trade features of security and intelligence in order to see whether there is a match between them.

### Risk assessment

In Canada, as, I believe, in many other countries, the assessment of threats against national security is the core of the mandates of the security and intelligence services. Threats and risks being close neighbours in virtual space, experience in assessing the one can easily be transferred in assessing the other. To the extent that policing will move toward the assessment and management of risk, security and intelligence services do have a claim in this business.

### Resolving complexity

Whatever is needed to solve the increasingly complex issues confronting law enforcement, there is no doubt that the gathering and analysis of intelligence will play a major part in this problem solving process. Following the paper trail left by a money laundering operation requires considerable experience and analytic skills. Providing a precise measure of the level of risk reached in a particular situation actually goes beyond common sense analysis and requires scientific knowledge. Security and intelligence services have been justly criticized for their shortcomings in the analysis of the information that they collected and they try to remedy this deficiency.[7] Even if this attempt is only partly successful, these agencies are generally well ahead of police organizations. In Canada and the US, numerous commissions have shown that the quality of criminal intelligence produced by police organizations was sometimes dismal.[8] If police are to be seen as 'knowledge workers', as was suggested by Ericson and Haggerty (1997), then their colleagues in the security and intelligence services have a solid claim to be involved in policing.

### Technological surveillance

We previously argued that electronic surveillance was an important component of a policing strategy that emphasized crime prevention and risk management. Electronic surveillance can be performed on an *ad hoc* basis as it is presently the case with the police, who request individual legal authorizations to use audio or video technology to monitor the communications or the activities of a person or a group of persons. Most Western countries have an agency similar the US National Security Agency, which uses very powerful technology, including satellites, to sweep communication signals (COMINT/SIGINT) and produce visual images (IMINT).[9] These agencies also harbour units specializing in cryptography. With the advent of the Internet and the multiplication of Intranets, cryptography is already playing a crucial part in countering digital crime. Without claiming that agencies collecting SIGINT and IMINT are ready to turn their considerable panoply of technological means against crime, the possibility that they may be requested to do so – or already have been – should be taken into account.

### Transnational networking

Of all the developments in crime and crime policing that we discussed previously, the spread of global crime and of transnational policing is the most unquestionable. Police have their own formal networks such as Europol and they make use of their informal connections.[10] However, transnational policing is a relatively new invention, if it is compared to the international network binding the security and intelligence community. For instance, as early as 1947, the SIGINT agencies of Australia, Canada, New Zealand, the UK and the US ratified the UKUSA treaty by which they agreed on mutual assistance and cooperation.

Many other instances of mutual help could be quoted. Hence, to the extent that we are being ushered into the age of transnational policing, security and intelligence services can justifiably claim that their extensive transnational networks are a major asset.

The features that we just discussed would appear to qualify the security and intelligence for claiming an increased role in policing. However, there are other features which could be disqualifying, unless remedied. The first one is the traditional reluctance of these services to share information. This reluctance is at its greatest level, when a secret service suspects or even knows that the information shared with the police will be publicly released in the course of a public prosecution of a guilty party. In its report, the US Congress Commission that appraised the American intelligence agencies acknowledged that the potential disclosure in a public prosecution of intelligence originating from a secret service was a serious source of conflict between these services and policing organizations (US Congress, 1996: 2, Chapter 4). There is evidence that the same sort of inter-agency conflict is also experienced in Canada (Bronskill, 1999).

## Conclusion

We have been in the course of this chapter using the words 'law enforcement' in two different senses. Throughout the chapter, these words are taken in their broad sense and are meant to be synonymous with crime policing. There is no need to insist that crime policing is not equivalent with policing as such, the police spending their time in many other ways than crime prevention and crime repression. Furthermore, only a relatively small portion of crime policing actually results in a trial prosecution. A large number of criminal cases are not resolved and when they are, offenders are often not prosecuted. When offenders are criminally charged in North America, they plead guilty in most instances and trial proceedings are avoided. At the end of the chapter, however, we have used the words 'law enforcement' in their narrowest sense – criminal trial proceedings – to highlight an existing source of conflict between police organizations and service and intelligence organizations.

To sum up, we have presented several arguments to the effect that security and intelligence services may in the future be increasingly involved in criminal policing and law enforcement, if the latter words are meant in their broader sense. This assertion becomes stronger when policing is equated with surveillance and risk assessment. Even when law enforcement is more specifically understood as implying criminal prosecution through trial proceedings, there may be ways to resolve the divergence between police organizations and security and intelligence services. It must however be realized that some of these ways could weaken the obligation of fully disclosing the legal evidence against a person charged with criminal offenses. Weakening prosecutorial disclosure may in its turn undermine the transparency of criminal proceedings and violate a suspect's constitutional rights.

Security and intelligence services may be spurred toward involving themselves in policing for yet another reason than the icing of the Cold War. These state agencies are increasingly facing competition on their own turf. As

Potter (1998) makes abundantly clear, the system of economic intelligence is very wide and the security and intelligence community is only one of its components. Furthermore, the number of private firms specializing in security and economic intelligence is on the increase (Gwynne, 1999).[11]

I would not dispute that the preceding conclusions are only tentative and that we have to monitor further developments in policing in order to confirm my assertions. However, this chapter has a theoretical upshot which I claim to be sound and from which I would not back away. In previous work, I argued for a distinction to be made between high and low policing (Brodeur, 1983). High policing is essentially based on the collection and processing of valid information reaching beyond criminal intelligence and into the realms of economics and politics (domestic and international). Low policing refers to the traditional activities of public police departments, such as patrol, order maintenance and the control of street crime. It seems to me that with the advent of the community policing agenda, research on policing has exclusively focused on low policing, at times narrowed down to variations on the theme of foot patrol. I believe that this conception of policing is too reductive and that a successful attempt to understand its nature needs to be grounded in a more systematic and comprehensive approach.

*From Jean-Paul Brodeur, 'Cops and Spooks: the uneasy partnership', Police Practice and Research: an international journal, Vol. 1, no 3, 1999, pp 1–25.*

## Notes

1  All Canadian police forces have to provide support to CSIS in its fight against terrorism. However, Canadian law endows the RCMP with a specific mandate in relation to offenses against the national security of Canada.
2  The most articulate and convincing argument for this transformation was presented by Castells (1996–1998). See particularly Volume I.
3  See, for example, 'Badly Needed Intelligence', *The New York Times*, 8 May 1994, Section 4, Week in Review, p. 16, unsigned editorial.
4  Even if we do not dwell on it in the context of this chapter, we should bear in mind the fact that acts of terrorist violence are prohibited by law in all countries and that any agency engaged in the repression of terrorism is to this extent involved in law enforcement.
5  See Harper's Index, *Harper's*, December 1998, pp. 13 and 77 (for sources).
6  The detonation of a traditional bomb wrapped in radioactive scrap metal would generate a huge panic in the population.
7  In a lecture delivered in the fall of 1998 before the Central Intelligence Retiree's Association, Mr. John Mills, a former agent in the CIA's Direction of Operations and now administrative director of the House Permanent Select Committee on Intelligence, said that the budget for intelligence analysis was not in excess of 1% of the resources allocated to intelligence in the US and that more money was spent on maintaining one surveillance satellite for one year than on all activities of intelligence analysis for the same period of time. See the newsletter *Le Monde du Renseignement*, No. 354, 10 mars 1999, Paris: Indigo Publications, 5.
8  For the latest example, see Québec, 1998: vol. 2, 1132–49; this report was tabled before the Prime minister of Québec on December 29, 1998 and publicly released in January 1999. Its assessment of the intelligence capability of the provincial police of Québec is very severe.
9  Agencies performing the same functions in Canada, France and the UK are respectively called the Communications Security Establishment (CSE), the *Direction du renseignement militaire* (DRM) and the Government Communications Headquarters (GCHQ).
10  Interpol is one of the oldest policing network. However, Interpol never was the object of a formal agreement between states and their respective government and was only struck

between the participating police forces. Assessments of the efficiency of this network show great variation.

11 Many of these firms have now their own site on the Internet. Check, for instance, www.stratfor.com, www.kroll-associates.com, www.ingigo-net.com.

## References

Anderson, Scott (1994). Making a Killing: The High Cost of Peace in Northern Ireland. *Harper's*, February 1994, 45–53.

Barrett, Neil (1997). *Digital Crime: Policing the Cybernation*. London: Kogan Page.

Bayley, David and Shearing, Clifford (1996). The Future of Policing. *Law and Society Review*, 30 (3), 585–606.

Bissell, Richard M., with Jonathan E. Lewis and Frances T. Pudlo (1997). *Reflections of a Cold Warrior: From Yalta to the Bay of Pigs*. New Haven: Yale University Press.

Brodeur, Jean-Paul (1983). High and Low Policing: Remarks about the Policing of Political Activities. *Social Problems*, (30) 5, 507–20.

Brodeur, Jean-Paul (1997). Organized Crime: A Review of the Literature. *Annales Internationales de la criminologie/International Annals of Criminology*, 35 (1/2), 89–129.

Brodeur, Jean-Paul (Ed.) (1998). *How to Recognize Good Policing: Problems and Issues*. Thousand Oaks CA: Sage.

Bronskill, Jim (1999). Disclosure Ruling has Mounties, Spy Agency Feuding. *The Montreal Gazette*, 29 January 1999, 6.

Busch, Heiner (1997). A la recherche de l'ennemi perdu. Une histoire des services secrets ouest-allemands après 1945. *Les Cahiers de la sécurité intérieure*, Le renseignement, No. 30, 269–283.

Canada, House of Commons (1990). *In Flux but not in Crisis. A Report of the House of Commons Special Committee on the Review of the Canadian Security Intelligence Service Act and the Security Offenses Act*. Ottawa: Canadian Government Publishing Center, Supply and Services Canada.

Canadian Security Intelligence Service (CSIS,1997). *1997 Public Report*. Ottawa (www.csisscrs.gc.ca/eng/publicrp/pub 1997e.html#9).

Castells, Manuel (1996). *The Rise of the Network Society. The Information Age: Economy, Society and Culture*. Oxford: Blackwell, Vol. I.

Castells, Manuel (1997). *The Power of Identity. The Information Age: Economy Society and Culture*. Oxford: Blackwell, Vol. II.

Castells, Manuel (1998). *End of Millennium. The Information Age: Economy Society and Culture*. Oxford: Blackwell.

Center for Strategic and International Studies (CSIS/US 1997). *Russian Organized Crime. CSIS Task Force Resort. Global Organized Crime Project*. Washington: The Center for Strategic and International Studies.

Cléroux, Richard (1990). *Official Secrets. The Story behind the Canadian Security Intelligence Service*. Toronto: McGraw-Hill Ryerson.

Cole, Leonard A. (1997). *The Eleventh Plague*. New York: W.H. Freeman and Company.

Draper, Theodore (1997). Is the CIA Necessary? *The New York Review of Books*, 44 (13), 18–22.

Ericson, Richard V. and Haggerty, Kevin D. (1997). *Policing the Risk Society*. Toronto and Buffalo: University of Toronto Press.

Farson, A. Stuart (1990). Criminal Intelligence *vs.* Security Intelligence: A Reevaluation of the Police Role in the Response to Terrorism. In Charters, David S. (Ed.) (1990). *Democratic Responses to International Terrorism*. Ardsley-on-Hudson NY: Transnational Publishers Inc., 191–226.

Feeley, Malcolm and Simon, Jonathan (1992). The New Penology: Notes on the Emerging Strategy of Corrections and its Implications. *Criminology*, 30 (4), 449–79.

Geissler, Ehrard and Haynes, Robert H. (1991). Introduction. In Geissler, Ehrard and Haynes, Robert H. (Eds.). *Prevention of a Biological and Toxin Arms Race and the Responsibility of Scientists*. Berlin: Akademie Verlag, 3–28.

Gill, Peter (1998). *The United Kingdom*. Paper presented at the SIS98 Conference. Security and Intelligence Services: Common Structures, Common Dangers? University of Gothenburg, Sweden.

Goodman, Allen E. (Ed.) (1996). Intelligence in the Post-Cold War Era. Twentieth Century Fund. *In From the Cold: The Report of the Twentieth Century. Fund Task Force on the Future of U.S. Intelligence*. New York: The Twentieth Century Fund Press, 29–95.

Gwynne, Sam C. (1999). Spies Like Us. The Internet is Changing the World's most Dangerous Game. *Time Magazine*, January 25, 1999, 12.

IHESI (1997). Le Renseignement. *Cahiers de la Sécurité Intérieure*, No. 30, 9–51.

Johnston, Les (1992). *The Rebirth of Private Policing*. London: Routledge & Kegan Paul.

Johnston, Les (1998). Late Modernity, Governance and Policing. In Brodeur, Jean-Paul (Ed.). *How to Recognize Good Policing: Problems and Issues*. Thousand Oaks CA: Sage, 193–214.

Joutsen, Matti (1998). The Scope of Transborder Organized Crime around the Baltic. In *Organized Crime in the Baltic Sea Area*, Proceedings, Association Internationale de Droit Pénal, No. 16, Toulouse: Éditions Érès, 227–47.

Kelly, Robert J. and Maghan, Jess (Eds.) (1998). *Hate Crime: The Global Politics of Polarization*. Carbondale and Edwardsville: Southern Illinois University Press.

Lester, Normand (1998). *Enquêtes sur les services secrets*. Montréal: Les Éditions de l'Homme.

Livingstone, Neil C. and Douglas, Joseph D. Jr. (1984). *CBW: The Poor Man's Atomic Bomb*. Cambridge MA: Institute for Foreign Policy Analysis.

Martre, Henri (1994). *Rapport du groupe intelligence économidue et stratégie des entreprises*. Paris: Commissariat général du plan.

Naylor, Robin Thomas (1993). The Insurgent Economy: Black Market Operations of Guerilla Organizations. *Crime, Law and Social Change*, 20, 13–51.

Naylor, Robin Thomas (1995). From Cold War to Crime War: The Search for a New 'National Security' Threat. *Transnational Criminal Organizations*, 1 (4), 37–56.

Nicaso, Antonio and Lee Lamothe (1995). *Global Mafia: The New World Order of Organized Crime*. Toronto: Macmillan Canada.

Pichot-Duclos, Jean (1993). L'intelligence économique: pour un modèle français. *Défense nationale*, 86–87.

Potter, Evan (1998). The System of Economic Intelligence-Gathering in Canada. In Potter, Evan (Ed.). *Economic Intelligence and National Security*. Ottawa: Carleton University Press, 1–77.

Québec (1998), *Rapport de la Commission d'enquête chargée de faire enquête sur la Sûreté du Québec. Pour une police au service de l'intégrité et de la justice*. Sainte-Foy (Québec): Les Publications du Québec.

Reiner, Robert (1994). Policing and the Police. In Maguire, Mike, Morgan, Rod and Reiner, Robert (Eds.). *The Oxford Handbook of Criminology*. Oxford UK: Oxford University Press.

Reiner, Robert (1992). Policing a Postmodern Society. *The Modern Law Review*, 55 (6), 761–81.

Rosenberg, Tina (1995). *The Haunted Land. Facing Europe's Ghosts after Communism*. New York: Random House.

Security Intelligence Review Committee (SIRC, 1997). *An Operational Audit of CSIS Activities* (Annual Report 1996–97). Ottawa: Minister of Supply and Services.

Security Intelligence Review Committee (SIRC, 1994). *The Heritage Front Affair. Report to the Solicitor General*. Ottawa: Security Intelligence Review Committee.

Simon, David R. and Hagan, Frank E. (1999). *White-Collar Deviance*. Boston, Toronto: Allyn and Bacon.

Sterling, Claire (1990). *Octopus: The Long Reach of the International Sicilian Mafia*. New York: Norton.

Stehr, Nico and Ericson, Richard V. (Eds.) (1992). *The Culture and Power of Knowledge*. Berlin and New York: Walter de Gruyter.

Sterling, Claire (1994). *Thieves' World: The Threat of the New Global Network of Organized Crime*. New York: Simon and Schuster.

Stock, Thomas and Lohs, Karlheinz (1997). Characteristics of Chemical Warfare Agents and Toxic Armament Wastes. In Stock, Thomas and Lohs, Karlheinz (Eds.). *The Challenge of Old Chemical Munitions and Toxic Armament Wastes*. New York: Oxford University Press, 15–34.

Twentieth Century Fund (1996). *In From the Cold: The Report of the Twentieth Century Fund Task Force on the Future of U.S. Intelligence*. New York: The Twentieth Century Fund Press.

United Kingdom Intelligence and Security Committee, *Report on Security Service Work Against Organized Crime*. Cm 3065, London: HMSO.

United States Congress (1997). *Report of the Commission on Protecting and Reducing Government Secrecy*. Washington: US Government Printing Office.

United States Congress (1996). *Preparing for the 21st Century. An Appraisal of U.S. Intelligence*. Report of the US Congress Commission on the Review of American Intelligence (Harold Brown, Chairman). Washington: US Government Printing Office. Also available on the Internet: www.access.gpo.gov/int/int002.html.

Urban, Mark (1996). *UK Eyes Alpha. Inside British Intelligence*. London: Faber and Faber.

Wayne, Leslie (1999). Cold War Foes Join as Capitalist Tools. *The New York Times*, 7 February 1999, Section 4, p. 3.

Weiner, Tim (1995). The C.I.A.'s Most Important Mission: Itself. *The New York Times*, 10 December 1995, Section 6 (The New York Times Magazine), 61–105.

Zelikow, Philip (1996). American Intelligence and the World Economy. In Twentieth Century Fund (Ed.). *In From the Cold: The Report of the Twentieth Century Fund Task Force on the Future of U.S. Intelligence*. New York: The Twentieth Century Fund Press, 135–262.

# Index